MARGARET THATCHER

Volume Two

THE IRON LADY

John Campbell

D1349651

JONATHAN CAPE
LONDON

Published by Jonathan Cape 2003

2 4 6 8 10 9 7 5 3

First published in Great Britain in 2003 by
Jonathan Cape
Random House, 20 Vauxhall Bridge Road, London SW1V 2SA

Random House Australia (Pty) Limited
20 Alfred Street, Milsons Point, Sydney,
New South Wales 2061, Australia

Random House New Zealand Limited
18 Poland Road, Glenfield,
Auckland 10, New Zealand

Random House South Africa (Pty) Limited
Endulini, 5A Jubilee Road, Parktown 2193, South Africa

The Random House Group Limited Reg. No. 954009
www.randomhouse.co.uk

A CIP catalogue record for this book is available from the British Library

ISBN 0-224-06156-9

Papers used by Random House are natural,
recyclable products made from wood grown in sustainable forests;
the manufacturing processes conform to the environmental
regulations of the country of origin

Typeset in Bembo by Palimpsest Book Production Limited,
Polmont, Stirlingshire
Printed and bound in Great Britain by
Clays Ltd, St Ives plc

For Alison once again,
and for Robin and Paddy
— two of Thatcher's children

Contents

Illustrations

CREDITS

The author and publishers are grateful to the following sources for permission to reproduce illustrations: Andrew Stawicki/ *Toronto Star* Archives, plate 28; Associated Press, plate 20; Camera Press, plates 1, 7, 13, 18, 21, 22, 24, 26, 31, 34; Churchill Archives Centre, Churchill College, Cambridge, plates 8, 15, 16, 28; HMSO, plate 8 (COI photograph held at the Churchill Archive, part of the Thatcher Papers. © Crown copyright. Reproduced with the permission of the Controller of HMSO and Queen's Printer for Scotland); PA Photos, plates 2, 3, 5, 6, 9, 10, 11, 12, 14, 17, 25, 29, 30, 32; Rex Features, plates 4, 19, 23, 27, 33, 35; Srdja Djukanovic, plates 15, 16, 31.

Acknowledgements

I have accumulated innumerable debts in writing these two volumes on Margaret Thatcher, which I am shocked to realise have taken me more than eight years. Most of the interviewing was done at a fairly early stage of my research, so that some of those who gave me valuable assistance and insights are sadly no longer with us to see the finished book. Others may look in vain for any specific attribution of their help. If it is not explicitly credited, the reason is that I do not tape interviews and so do not generally quote verbatim. But everything they told me fed into my understanding of Mrs Thatcher's personality and methods, so I am grateful to them all. Conversely I hope I have not betrayed any confidences.

Perhaps I should apologise to those with stories to tell whom I did not interview. With a subject as vast as Margaret Thatcher there are probably another thousand people whom I should have talked to; but had I done so I should never have finished the book at all. My general rule has been not to interview those who have written their memoirs or have been extensively interviewed already for television and radio programmes about the 1980s; in my experience they tend – quite understandably – to repeat what they have already said or written. I chose to focus rather on those colleagues, aides and officials who have not had such opportunities to relate their memories.

I should reiterate what I wrote in the first volume, that this is not an 'official' biography, but neither is it exactly 'unauthorised'. Lady Thatcher has not co-operated directly, but she has known from the outset that I was writing it and has not prevented anyone else from helping me, and her office has always been helpful when required. I am grateful to her, and to her publishers HarperCollins, for once again allowing me to quote substantial extracts from her memoirs and other writings. These are mainly short excerpts, but scattered throughout my book they add up to a considerable number of words. When his subject has already written two volumes on her own life, it is impossible for a biographer to ignore them.

I am also grateful to HarperCollins for allowing me to quote from Carol Thatcher's biography of her father; and to Macmillan for allowing me to quote from the three volumes of Woodrow Wyatt's *Journals*, which provide an exceptionally intimate, if partisan, portrait of the last five years of Mrs Thatcher's premiership and the first years of her retirement. Once again I thank Brook Associates for allowing me to quote from the interviews conducted for their television series *The Thatcher Factor*; and I must also thank Pressdram Ltd, the publishers of *Private Eye*, for allowing me to quote the poem 'Ozymaggias'.

I confess that I have not sought permission for every quotation from all the other diaries and memoirs of the period. I take the view that those who write memoirs do so in order to contribute to the historical record and are happy for their words to be so used. If I am wrong in this assumption, I apologise; but I am grateful for the evidence of all these authors.

I am grateful to the United States Government for its admirable policy of allowing access and quotation from the papers of recent Presidents, under the Freedom of Information Act, so much less restrictive than our own; and to the staff of the Carter, Bush and Reagan Presidential Libraries for their helpfulness in guiding me to what I needed to see on a necessarily short visit to the United States in February 2001.

I must also thank Lynn Watson-Powers and Frank Chartrand, who did valuable preliminary spadework for me in the Carter and Reagan Libraries respectively before I got there.

I owe an incalculable debt – as will all future biographers of Mrs Thatcher and historians of the 1980s – to the meticulous scholarship of Chris Collins in compiling the CD-Rom of her complete public statements, published by Oxford University Press in 1997. It is a unique resource, which not only saved me an immense amount of legwork but has made available, at the touch of a key, a wealth of broadcast – and in many cases unbroadcast – material which simply would not have been accessible in the past.

I am grateful to Andrew Riley, archivist of the Thatcher papers at Churchill College, Cambridge, for his help, particularly with pictures. The papers themselves are not yet open, but he was able to point me to other relevant holdings in the Archives Centre which are open, specifically the transcripts of interviews conducted for the British Diplomatic Oral History Programme.

· *Acknowledgements* ·

I should like to thank Professor Lee Estes and his colleagues at Chapman University, Orange County, southern California, for inviting me – with several other British historians and three of Mrs Thatcher's former colleagues – to their Thatcher Symposium in May 2002. It was a most stimulating week from which we all learned a lot, not least from the six Chapman students who were studying various aspects of Mrs Thatcher's government. I wish them all well.

I should also thank Peter Hennessy, Peter Catterall and the other organisers of the witness seminars run by the Institute of Contemporary British History over the past ten years, many of which have provided invaluable insights into the Thatcher period.

I am grateful to the following for giving generously of their time for interviews: Professor John Ashworth; Neville Beale; Sir Kenneth Berrill; Sir Clive Bossom; Lord Brittan; Lord Carlisle of Bucklow; Lord Cockfield; Sir John Coles; Sir Frank Cooper; Lord Crickhowell (Nicholas Edwards); Lord Deedes; Sir Edward du Cann; Sir George Gardiner; Prof. Sir Douglas Hague; Lord Harris of High Cross; Henry James; Lord Jenkin of Roding; Simon Jenkins; Lord Kelvedon (Paul Channon); Lord King of Bridgwater; Lord McAlpine of West Green; Brian MacArthur; Lord MacGregor of Pulham Market; Stuart Maclure; Sir Peter Middleton; Sir Ronald Millar; Lord Moore of Lower Marsh; Sir John Nott; Sir Michael Palliser; Sir Michael Partridge; Chris Patten; Michael Portillo, MP; Lord Powell of Bayswater; Lord Renwick; Raymond Seitz; Julian Seymour; Stephen Sherbourne; Sir Kenneth Stowe; David Tanner; Sir Robert Wade-Gery; Lord Wakeham; Sir Douglas Wass; Lord Whitelaw; Dame Jane Whiteley; John Whittingdale, MP; Mrs Margaret Wickstead; Lord Wyatt of Weeford; Hugo Young; Lady Young of Farnworth; Lord Younger of Leckie.

I am also grateful to the following historians, journalists, politicians and friends with whom I have enjoyed more informal conversations over the years, which have contributed in one way or another to my understanding of Margaret Thatcher: Paul Addison; Rupert Allason; Bruce Arnold; John Barnes; Kathleen Busk; Piers Brendon; Sir Samuel Brittan; John Brown; David Butler; Frank Chartrand; Ian and Joanna Chisholm; Alan Clark; Richard Cockett; Christopher Collins; Liz Cowen; Michael Crick; Sir Robin Day; David Freeman; Mark Garnett; Peter Hennessy; Mark Hollingsworth; Anthony Howard; Lord Howe of Aberavon; Lord Hurd of Westwell; Lord Jenkins of Hillhead; Michael Kinchin-Smith; Lord Lawson of Blaby; Brenda Maddox; Andrew Marr; Lord Parkinson; Madsen Pirie; Alice and Frank Prochaska; John Ramsden; Andrew Riley; Anthony Sampson; Anthony Seldon; Geoffrey Smith; D. J. Taylor; Sir Crispin Tickell; Lord Waldegrave; Lord Weatherill;

David Willetts, MP. If I have forgotten anyone – and I am sure I have
– I ask them to forgive me: it has been a long haul and a lot of conversations.

While I am immensely grateful to all of the above for information
and ideas, I should emphasise that I alone am responsible for any errors
of fact or understanding in the pages that follow. If errors have crept
in, I shall be happy to have them pointed out so that I may correct
them in future editions.

I am enormously grateful to Dan Franklin of Jonathan Cape for
supporting the project throughout and particularly for allowing me to
split it into two volumes when it began to exceed the confines of one;
and also to Mandy Greenfield for her meticulous editing and comments
on the typescript.

I am equally indebted, as always, to my agent, Bruce Hunter of
David Higham Associates, now a friend of very long standing, for
supporting and encouraging me through the years when I thought I
was never going to finish.

I must also thank Liz Jensen for renting me her beautiful house in
France for three and a half months in the autumn of 2002 where, away
from the distractions of London, I was able to bring the book almost
to completion. To her amusement, there is a corner of a foreign field
that is forever Thatcher.

Finally, once again, I owe an inexpressible debt to my long-suffering
wife Alison and to our children, Robin and Paddy, who have grown
to adulthood under the shadow of Margaret Thatcher. To them this
volume, like its predecessor, is dedicated in love and gratitude.

John Campbell
May 2003

1

The Blessed Margaret

'Where there is discord . . .'

MARGARET Thatcher entered Downing Street on 4 May 1979 carrying an extraordinary weight of public expectation, curiosity, hope and apprehension. Her achievement in becoming the first female leader of a major western democracy lent her an unprecedented novelty value, particularly in the eyes of the foreign media which had not, like the British press, had four years to get used to the idea. Even when she led in the polls there had remained a lingering doubt whether the British electorate, when it came to the point in the privacy of the voting booth, would really bring itself to vote for a woman Prime Minister. Conceding defeat, the outgoing James Callaghan made a point of acknowledging that 'for a woman to occupy that office is a tremendous moment in this country's history'.[1] It represented, as a writer in the *Guardian* put it, 'one small step for Margaret Thatcher, one giant stride for womankind'.[2]

Yet Mrs Thatcher determinedly played down the feminist aspect of her victory. When asked on the steps of Downing Street what Mrs Pankhurst would have thought of her triumph, she ignored the question and spoke of her father instead.[3] She always insisted that she did not think of herself as a woman, but simply as a politician with a job to do, the standard-bearer of certain principles, who happened to be female. Though in her thirty-year progress from Grantham via Oxford to Westminster and now Downing Street she had skilfully exploited her femininity for whatever advantages it could bring her, she had rarely presented herself as a pathfinder for her sex and did not intend to start now. It was symptomatic of her uniqueness that the 1979 election saw fewer women returned than at any election since 1951 – just nineteen compared with twenty-seven in the previous Parliament. 'It never occurred to me that I was a woman Prime Minister,' she claimed

I

in her televised memoirs.[4] She preferred to boast of being the first scientist to reach the office.

More important than the novelty of her gender was the widespread sense that she represented a political new dawn and a decisive break with the recent past. 'Goodbye Winter, Hello Spring,' the *Sun* exulted. 'At the exact moment when the grocer's daughter from Grantham became the most important woman in the world, spring sprung. It did. It really did.'[5] Of course no one in 1979 imagined that she would remain Prime Minister for eleven years, stamping her personality and even her name indelibly on the whole of the next decade. But she was unquestionably different. As the High Tory commentator Peregrine Worsthorne recognised in the *Sunday Telegraph*, Mrs Thatcher was 'the first political evangelist to occupy Downing Street' since Labour's postwar landslide in 1945.[6] Her admirers – who included, crucially, many former Labour voters – saw her election as the last chance for a failing country to pull itself out of the spiral of terminal decline. Others – including many in her own party – feared that on the contrary she was a narrow-minded dogmatist whose simple-minded remedies would prove disastrous if she was not restrained by wiser counsel. In between, of course, there were plenty of cynics who were confident that she would in practice turn out no different from any of her recent predecessors whose lofty rhetoric had quickly turned to dust. Nine years earlier Ted Heath had promised 'a change so radical, a revolution so quiet and yet so total, that it will go . . . far beyond this decade and way into the 1980s'.[7] A few years before that Harold Wilson had aspired to forge a new Britain in the 'white heat of the scientific revolution'.[8] With all her brave talk of restoring Britain's 'greatness' – whatever that meant – by reviving the spirit of enterprise, Mrs Thatcher had been remarkably unspecific in opposition about how she was going to do it. Why then should she be expected to succeed where they had failed?

While admitting to feeling 'modified rapture' at her victory, Worsthorne frankly conceded that Mrs Thatcher's 'capitalist cure' might not solve all the nation's ills, yet he called for 'a temporary suspension of disbelief':

> Conceivably it will not work. But since a majority of the British people have chosen to believe that it might . . . let the sceptics and the cynics, at any rate for a time, keep quiet. She deserves a chance. So does the country.[9]

On the same page the *Telegraph*'s cartoonist neatly captured both the optimism and the cynicism of the moment in the form of a lurid film poster showing the new Prime Minister as a female Superman confronting a King Kong-like monster:

> Will Wonder-Maggie arrest the dreaded D. Kline and the Allied Forces of Evil???
> ★ A New Adventure Starting NOW!!
> ★ The Greatest since Supermac![10]

Even the most cynical were curious to see how she would make out.

Mrs Thatcher herself was fiercely determined that her government would indeed be different. She was driven by a burning sense of patriotic mission and historic destiny. 'I can't bear Britain in decline. I just can't,' she insisted during the election;[11] and she had no false modesty about comparing herself with Churchill. 'It will not be given to this generation . . . to create a new empire,' she conceded with perhaps a touch of regret in one of her first speeches after taking office. 'But it is given to us to demand an end to decline, and to make a stand against what Churchill described as "the long dismal drawling tides of drift and surrender, of wrong measurements and feeble impulses."'[12] 'Winston' – as she liked to call him – was not her only inspiration. 'I know that I can save this country and that no one else can,' the Earl of Chatham is supposed to have declared on taking office in the middle of the Seven Years War in 1757. 'It would have been presumptuous of me to have compared myself with Chatham,' Lady Thatcher wrote in her memoirs. 'But if I am honest I must admit that my exhilaration came from a similar inner conviction.'[13]

Of course this was written many years later. But from the moment she walked through the door of Number Ten her officials felt the force of this passionate self-belief. Kenneth Stowe, her first principal private secretary, who had accompanied Callaghan on his last drive to the Palace, then hurried back in time to greet his successor in the hall, recalls that from the first moment she was 'absolutely focused, absolutely committed' and 'very hands-on': she wanted to be briefed about everything and to take charge of everything immediately, even before she sat down to pick her Cabinet. The contrast with the relaxed style of her predecessor could not have been more marked.[14] Mrs Thatcher appeared to need no sleep, nor did she expect anyone else to need it. She was 'clearly hyped up a lot of the time', one member of her new Cabinet recalled;[15] another reported with aristocratic understatement that she was 'proving very dynamic'.[16] All her life, and specifically for the past four years, she had been training herself for this moment. 'I have always had an onerous timetable, but I like it,' she told an interviewer on the first anniversary of her taking office. 'I have a tremendous amount of energy and for the first time in my life it is fully used.'[17]

Yet her missionary impatience was, as always, overlaid with caution. She knew in broad terms what she wanted to achieve. As she told *The Times* in 1984:'I came into office with one deliberate intent: to change Britain from a dependent to a self-reliant society – from a give-it-to-me to a do-it-yourself nation; to a get-up-and-go instead of a sit-back-and-wait-for-it Britain.'[18] She knew there was a tide to seize, a powerful movement of economic thinking in favour of the New Right free-market agenda that she and Keith Joseph had been preaching for the past four years. She was encouraged by the public response to the leaking to *The Economist* of a gloomy dispatch from Sir Nicholas Henderson, the retiring Ambassador to France, which echoed precisely her own diagnosis of Britain's economic failure and international decline since 1945.[19] But at the same time she knew that the opposition of established interests and entrenched assumptions – in Whitehall, in the country and not least in the Tory party – was still very strong, so that she would have to proceed carefully in order to carry the party and the country with her. The election had delivered her an adequate parliamentary majority of forty-three. But the outstanding feature of the result, emphasised by all the press, was the imbalance between the prosperous Tory south of England and the struggling old industrial areas of the north of England, Wales and Scotland, which had still predominantly voted Labour. There was general agreement on that sunny Friday morning that the new Prime Minister's first task would be to unite a divided country. In this light the soothing lines of St Francis of Assisi which her speechwriter Ronald Millar found for her to speak on the steps of Downing Street – 'Where there is discord may we bring harmony . . . Where there is despair may we bring hope' – were thought to strike just the right note. Few commentators noticed the middle lines of the quatrain, which carried a more distinctively Thatcherite message:'Where there is error, may we bring truth; Where there is doubt may we bring faith'. By quoting 'the patron saint of lame ducks', Alan Watkins noted in the *Observer*, Mrs Thatcher had recognised 'the need to proclaim her moderation in all things. She is clearly trying to appear before our wondering eyes as a changed character. Whether she is really changed is another matter.'[20]

She frequently remarked that she would be given only one chance to get it right and she did not intend to blow it. In making her first pronouncements, therefore, in choosing her Cabinet, in taking over the machinery of government and in setting out her initial agenda, she was a great deal more cautious than her rhetoric in opposition had suggested, disappointing her keenest supporters while reassuring those who had feared she might be dangerously headstrong. The heroic picture painted in her memoirs of a radical reformer determined to shake the country from its socialistic torpor is not untrue; but her radicalism was in practice tempered by a shrewd awareness of political reality and a streak of genuine humility. She had no illusions about the scale of the task before her. The second weekend after the election she invited a select group of those who had done most to win it to Chequers for a celebration dinner – Gordon Reece, Tim Bell, Alistair McAlpine and Ronald Millar. But the Prime Minister's mood was far from celebratory. Millar found her 'strangely subdued', feeling thoroughly overwhelmed and insecure in her new surroundings.[21] Such moods did not last long – one of her strengths was a remarkable ability to shrug off setbacks and get on with the job in hand; and she was careful to reveal these moments of weakness only to her closest aides. But, in her early years at least, the sense of insecurity was never far away.

Her long-term ambition, as set out in opposition, was nothing less than the elimination of what she called 'socialism' from British politics, the reversal of the whole collectivising trend of the postwar era and thereby, she believed, the moral reinvigoration of the nation. 'Economics is the method', she declared in 1981. 'The object is to change the soul.'[22] In the short term, however, she was determined to keep her attention firmly on the method. She would not be distracted by foreign affairs; she had no interest in flashy constitutional reform; nor did she have any immediate plans for tackling the welfare state. 'She was adamant,' Nicholas Ridley remembered, 'that she would not start down this sort of road at the beginning.'[23] Even the reform of trade-union law – for which she had an undoubted popular mandate – was not to be rushed. Hence for the leader of a determinedly radical government she had a remarkably thin agenda of specific reforms in May 1979. In opposition since 1975 she had deliberately stuck to general principles and avoided precise commitments. Her fundamental philosophy of anti-socialist economics prescribed a number of broad objectives: the Government should cut public spending, cut taxes, keep tight control of the money supply, refrain from detailed intervention in the economy and generally trust the operation of the free market. But very little of this required legislation. Most of it simply involved not doing things which previous governments of both parties had believed it their function to do.

She had three important factors working in her favour. First, she gained a huge advantage from the timing of the election which had brought her to power. Had the Labour Government fallen at any time in the previous four years, Mrs Thatcher would have been obliged to launch her free-market experiment in far less propitious conditions. But the trade-union-orchestrated chaos of the previous winter had played into her hands. In the ten years since 1969 the unions had destroyed the Wilson, Heath and now the Callaghan Governments. Public tolerance of the assumption that the country could only be governed with the consent of the unions – the conventional wisdom of the past four decades – had finally snapped. There was a powerful mood that it was time for someone to make a stand and face them down; and that someone was Margaret Thatcher. It was not just a question of the Government resisting excessive pay claims, or toughening the law on strikes and picketing, but more fundamentally a realisation that the union culture of protecting traditional jobs by a combination of government subsidy, overmanning and resistance to modernisation had been a drag on the British economy which was damaging international competitiveness and holding back the nation's living standards. By May 1979 there was an unprecedented public acceptance, even among people who still did not think of themselves as Conservatives, that it was time to try a different approach.

At an official level, too, a significant shift had already occurred. Though monetarism – the theory that there was a direct causal relationship between the amount of money in the economy and rising inflation – was still deeply controversial, disputed by many economists and used by politicians as sloppy shorthand for all manner of right-wing extremism, it had in practice been largely accepted and quietly applied by the Labour Government, under the instruction of the International Monetary Fund, for the past two years. Callaghan and his Chancellor, Denis Healey, had kept a tight squeeze on monetary growth on pragmatic, not dogmatic, grounds; the new Conservative Government – or at least the inner group of ministers who would direct its economic policy – believed in controlling the money supply as a matter of principle, even of faith. But the soil had already been prepared for them, and the change of policy within the Treasury was more cosmetic – a matter of presentation – than real. The incoming Government was actually a good deal less innovative in this respect than either the Tories pretended or Labour ex-ministers liked to acknowledge.

The third enormous benefit the new Government enjoyed, which cushioned to some extent the impact of the policies it intended to pursue, was the coming on flow of North Sea oil. It was in June 1980 that Britain became for the first time a net oil exporter. The effect of this fortunate windfall was disguised by the fact that the Government's coming to power coincided with the onset of a major world recession, so that for the first two or three years the economic news appeared to be all bad as unemployment and inflation soared. But the impact of the recession would have been a great deal worse, and maybe politically unsustainable, had it not been for the fortuitous subsidy that Britain's independent oil supply gave to both government revenue and the balance of payments. Mrs Thatcher enjoyed more than her share of luck in her career; but one of her greatest strokes of fortune – as Paul Johnson pointed out in the *Daily Mail* the day after she entered Downing Street – was the 'huge consoling advantage' that, unlike any of her recent predecessors, 'she does not have to get down to work under the debilitating threat of a balance of payments crisis . . . Who was it who said that an oil well (or two) is a girl's best friend?'[24]

Unlike those predecessors, Mrs Thatcher's purpose was not to run the economy from Whitehall, but to teach British industry to survive by its own competitiveness instead of looking to the Government for its salvation. Her immediate priority, therefore, was to take three or four big bold decisions and then have the courage to stick to them. As it happened, this turned out to be more difficult than anticipated as the recession bit, provoking a concerted demand from every shade of the political spectrum that the Government must set aside its ideological preconceptions and act in the national interest in exactly the ways Mrs Thatcher was determined to eschew. It took a strong nerve to resist this chorus of advice. But Mrs Thatcher was morally armoured by her certainty that what she was trying to do was right. Indeed her combative nature positively relished the adversity. The more the apologists of the old consensus insisted that she must change course, the more determined she became not to be deflected, until the importance of being seen not to be deflected became an end in itself, irrespective of the economic arguments. Thus the style of the Thatcher premiership was forged in these first two testing years.

A traditional Tory Cabinet

The formation of the Cabinet reflected this mixture of long-term determination and short-term realism. For all her brave talk in opposition of having a 'conviction Cabinet' with 'no time for internal arguments',[25] Mrs Thatcher had in practice no choice but to confirm in office most of those who had comprised the Shadow Cabinet before the election. Having maintained a broad front of party unity in opposition, she could not suddenly appoint an aggressively Thatcherite

Cabinet in the moment of victory. Had Airey Neave still been there to guide her hand it is possible that she might have risked one or two more daring appointments; but Neave had been assassinated by an Irish bomb at the beginning of the election campaign. As it was, when she sat down, that first evening in Downing Street, with Willie Whitelaw and the outgoing Chief Whip, Humphrey Atkins, to settle the allocation of departments to be announced next day, she let herself be guided to a great extent by Whitelaw. With one major exception, no figure of importance was left out and no new faces were brought in, while several old ones were brought back. Almost all of the new team had served under Heath in 1970–4, and several under Macmillan and Home before 1964. It was in fact a thoroughly traditional Tory Cabinet, containing – as the press did not fail to point out – six Old Etonians, three Wykehamists, only two members (apart from Mrs Thatcher herself) who had not been to public school, only one who had attended a university other than Oxford or Cambridge, six former Guards officers, five barristers, several big landowners, three baronets and two hereditary peers.[26] It did not look like a Cabinet to launch a social revolution. Yet at the same time Mrs Thatcher made sure that the key economic jobs were reserved for those she called 'true believers'.

So far as most commentators were concerned, her trickiest dilemma was whether to include Ted Heath. In fact she never seriously considered it. The former leader had campaigned energetically during the election in what was universally taken to be a late bid for the Foreign Office. He had still been unable to bring himself to mention Mrs Thatcher by name, but he telephoned her at Central Office while she waited to go to the Palace on Friday morning to offer his congratulations on her victory. She pointedly declined to take the call.[27] With an adequate majority and all Heath's senior associates – Whitelaw, Carrington, Pym and Prior – only too anxious to serve her, she had no need of what the *Guardian* called his 'looming presence at the Cabinet table' in order to unite the party.[28] Six months later she frankly explained her decision to one of her first biographers: 'He wouldn't have wanted to sit there as a member of the team. All the time he would be trying to take over.'[29] She sent him by motorbike a brief handwritten letter informing him that, after thinking 'long and deeply about the post of Foreign Secretary', she had 'decided to offer it to Peter Carrington who – as I am sure you will agree – will do the job superbly'.[30] She later added public insult to this perceived injury by offering him the Washington Embassy – a transparent way of trying to get him out of domestic politics – even though he had made clear his determination not to leave the Commons.* For the next eleven years the former Prime Minister's glowering resentment on the front bench below the gangway served as the most effective deterrent to Tory malcontents tempted to criticise the Government.

The price of excluding Heath was that Mrs Thatcher was bound to fill her Cabinet with his former colleagues. Thus Whitelaw – acknowledged but unofficial deputy Prime Minister – became Home Secretary. Francis Pym – another who had hoped for the Foreign Office, having been shadow Foreign Secretary for the last six months in opposition – had to settle for Defence. Carrington asked for and was granted Ian Gilmour as his deputy in the Commons, with a seat in the Cabinet as Lord Privy Seal. James Prior was confirmed as Employment Secretary. Most significantly Peter Walker – the one leading Heathite whom Mrs Thatcher had dropped from the Shadow Cabinet in 1975 – was brought back as Agriculture Secretary. It was widely assumed that she considered Walker (unlike Heath) too dangerous a potential critic to leave on the back benches. In fact she had always regarded him as an effective minister, as she proved by keeping him in a succession of departments for the next ten years. Sending him first to Agriculture was a demotion from the senior jobs he had held under Heath, but she expected him to be a tough negotiator for British interests in Brussels and was not disappointed.

She had much less regard for Michael Heseltine, whom she already distrusted as dangerously ambitious as well as ideologically unsound, but she could not afford to leave him out. In opposition Heseltine had accepted the shadow Environment portfolio only on condition that he would not have to take the same job in government; but after turning down the Department of Energy he reluctantly accepted Environment after all, and then found that it suited him admirably. Patrick Jenkin took on the biggest spending department, Health and Social Security, while Mark Carlisle (Education), Norman St John Stevas (Leader of the House and Arts Minister), George Younger (Scotland, replacing the much more robust Teddy Taylor, who had lost his seat) and Nicholas Edwards (Wales) completed the heavily non-Thatcherite majority in the Cabinet. The vacancy left by the death of Airey Neave was filled by Humphrey Atkins – one of those tall, handsome charmers for whom she always had a soft spot. It did not go

---

*There was a long-standing tradition of Prime Ministers using the Washington Embassy as a way of getting rid of awkward colleagues. Austen Chamberlain was insulted to be offered it by Baldwin in 1923; but Halifax could not very well refuse when appointed by Churchill in 1941.

unnoticed in Belfast that Atkins was the third consecutive Tory Chief Whip to become Secretary for Northern Ireland, with the implication that what Ulster needed was a bit of discipline.

The engine-room of the new Cabinet, however, lay in the economic departments. The relationship between the Prime Minister and Chancellor is central to the success of any Government. Four years earlier Mrs Thatcher had chosen the dogged Geoffrey Howe, rather than her intellectual mentor Keith Joseph, to be her shadow Chancellor. Howe had worked hard in opposition to lay the groundwork of monetarist policies and was said to be 'the only man who can work with Margaret at his shoulder';[31] but she always found his mild manner exasperating and was already inclined to bully him. Rumours persisted that when it came to forming a government she might prefer John Biffen, a former disciple of Enoch Powell whom she honoured as one of the handful of clear-sighted monetarists who had exposed the fallacies of corporatism while she and Joseph were still compromised by serving under Heath. But Biffen's health and stamina were suspect: she felt he had let her down by withdrawing from the Shadow Cabinet for a period in 1976–7. She was to feel let down by him again in the years to come.

Still casting around for a strong Chancellor, however, she actually toyed with the idea of Roy Jenkins, on the strength of his record at cutting public expenditure in 1967–70.[32] This would have been an extraordinary appointment. Apart from the fact that he was barely halfway through his four-year term as President of the European Commission, Jenkins was still at least nominally a member of the Labour party. His appointment would have outraged all sections of the Tory party while sending quite the wrong signals about the Government's intentions. For all these reasons – plus the practical difficulty that it would have required a by-election to get him back into the Commons, presumably as a Conservative – it is difficult to believe that Mrs Thatcher entertained the possibility seriously. But the fact that she considered it at all is a measure of her lack of confidence in Howe.

Howe was joined in the Treasury by Biffen as Chief Secretary (in the Cabinet) and the most brilliant of the younger monetarists, Nigel Lawson, as Financial Secretary (outside the Cabinet), with Peter Rees and Lord Cockfield, both tax experts, as Ministers of State. Keith Joseph went to the Department of Industry – amid accurate predictions that he would prove too compassionate in practice to implement the sort of ruthless withdrawal of subsidies which he advocated in theory;[33] while John Nott got the Department of Trade. (Some had tipped Nott to be Chief Secretary – he would probably have made a tougher one than Biffen – but he had been shadowing Trade in opposition and would have considered it a demotion if he had not got a department of his own.)[34] These five – Howe, Joseph, Biffen, Nott and Lawson – with Mrs Thatcher herself, formed the central group in charge of the Government's economic strategy. In addition David Howell, once an ardent Heathite but now another born-again monetarist who had written a lot of Mrs Thatcher's campaign speeches, was rewarded with the Department of Energy (at the expense of Tom King, who had been shadowing it). The only non-monetarist allowed near an economic job was Jim Prior, whose appointment to the Department of Employment was welcomed by most of Fleet Street – even the Tory papers – as a signal that the new Government did not want an early confrontation with the unions. Prior's job, as the *Guardian* saw it, would be to 'keep the union leaders relatively sweet in the face of the new economic policy'.[35] Mrs Thatcher accepted this analysis. 'There was no doubt in my mind,' she wrote in her memoirs, 'that we needed Jim Prior . . . Jim was the badge of our reasonableness.'[36]

The invitation to Lord Hailsham, now aged seventy-one, to go back to the Woolsack was an act of kindness on Mrs Thatcher's part. She thought he needed cheering up after the recent death of his second wife: she had no intention of keeping him in post for the next eight years.[37] Like Peter Thorneycroft – who continued as party chairman – Hailsham was a father figure whom Mrs Thatcher had known since he came to speak to the Oxford University Conservative Association thirty years before. Particularly after the loss of Airey Neave, she drew reassurance from having a number of such elders around her. More surprising was her resurrection of another grandee from the Macmillan era, Christopher Soames. Since losing his Commons seat in 1966, Soames had served as Ambassador in Paris and then as Britain's first EEC Commissioner; instead of using his European experience, however, Mrs Thatcher made him Lord President of the Council in charge of the Cabinet Office, responsible for the Civil Service, where he was bound to get under her feet. This was a repetition of the mistake she made with Reginard Maudling in 1975 and proved equally short-lived.

She found room for just one veteran right-winger, Angus Maude, who was given responsibility for Government information with the job of Paymaster-General. Thus of twenty-two members of the Cabinet, no more than half a dozen could be counted the Prime Minister's natural allies. Nicholas Ridley thought her failure to appoint more true believers 'inexplicable' and blamed her reliance on Whitelaw. Ridley himself – another old Powellite who, more than anyone, had made the running on privatisation for the past decade or more – was 'bitterly disappointed' to be offered only the non-economic junior job of Minister of State at the Foreign Office. Mrs Thatcher flattered him by telling him she must have one 'sound man' in what she regarded as a hopelessly limp department.[38] In truth she thought Ridley too indiscreet for senior office – not until 1983 did she risk putting him in the Cabinet – though on that argument the Foreign Office was the worst possible place to send him, as soon became disastrously clear.

In general Mrs Thatcher took very little interest in junior appointments, leaving it to Whitelaw and the new Chief Whip, Michael Jopling, to fill most of the positions. Only in one or two cases did she make a point of appointing right-wingers in subordinate positions to stiffen their superiors. She refused to let Jim Prior take Barney Hayhoe with him to the Department of Employment; and when Prior jibbed at Leon Brittan, she insisted that he must have Patrick Mayhew, telling him 'I'm determined to have *someone* with backbone in your department'.[39] Likewise, having dismayed the right by sending Mark Carlisle to Education, she tried to compensate by giving him the former headmaster and prominent opponent of progressive education, Rhodes Boyson, as under-secretary with responsibility for schools. (In fact Carlisle thwarted this intention by switching Boyson to higher education, while Lady Young took over schools.)[40] She also insisted, over Whitelaw's reservations, that Norman Tebbit be found an undersecretaryship in the Department of Trade. His fellow parliamentary Rottweiler, George Gardiner, however, gained no reward for his efforts as a member of the 'Gang of Four': he was left on the back benches for the whole period of Mrs Thatcher's Government. Perhaps her most striking middle-ranking appointment was to reward the former Education Secretary, Reg Prentice, for his defection from Labour by sending him to the Department of Social Security with responsibility for the disabled.

While the right was disappointed, the old guard were correspondingly happy that their majority in Cabinet would give them a veto over policies they regarded as extreme or doctrinaire. Prior complacently dismissed the Treasury team as a bunch of theorists – all barristers and journalists: 'None of them had any experience of running a whelk stall, let alone a decent-sized company'.[41] In fact Howe, Biffen and Lawson were probably the most economically literate Treasury team since Thorneycroft, Powell and Birch in 1957. But Prior thought the balance of the Cabinet as a whole 'better ... than I had dreamt possible'. He reflected later that 'those of us ... who were out of sympathy with Margaret's views grossly underestimated her absolute determination, along with Geoffrey and Keith, to push through the new right-wing policies'.[42] Most press comment likewise found the moderate composition of the Cabinet reassuring and failed to anticipate the way Mrs Thatcher would get around it. Thus the *Daily Mail* applauded the return of Walker and Hailsham, interpreted Maude's inclusion as 'a welcome indication that the real Cabinet is going to be more important than any kitchen cabinet' and saw the heart of the team as the triumvirate of Howe, Joseph and Prior, whom it characterised respectively as 'prudence, passion and pragmatism. Not a bad combination.'[43] In fact, with an instinct for the reality of government which belied her relative inexperience, Mrs Thatcher had calculated better than either her supporters or her opponents that neither the individuals nor the numbers around the Cabinet table mattered. So long as those she came to call the 'wets' had no departmental base from which to develop an alternative economic policy, she and her handful of like-minded colleagues (who naturally became the 'dries') would be able to pursue their strategy without serious hindrance. Budget details are never announced to the Cabinet until a few hours before the Chancellor rises in the House of Commons, and ministers outside the Treasury 'loop' simply do not have the detailed briefing which would enable them to challenge the Prime Minister and Chancellor – as John Nott discovered when he moved to the Ministry of Defence in January 1981, and Prior likewise when he was shifted to Northern Ireland later the same year.[44] Short of resigning – which none of them was keen to do – the 'wets' could only stay and acquiesce in policies they disliked, in the belief that political reality must force a change of direction sooner or later.

From the start, the full Cabinet never discussed economic policy at all. Yet in her early days as Prime Minister Mrs Thatcher operated for the most part quite conventionally through the Cabinet committee structure: economic policy was determined by the 'E' Committee, chaired by herself, on which Prior was in a minority of one. To make absolutely sure, however, she held weekly breakfast meetings with the monetarist inner circle, Howe, Joseph, Biffen and Nott, with just one or two of her own staff in attendance. These Thursday breakfasts remained secret until they were revealed by Hugo Young in the *Sunday Times* in November 1980 – by which time they had achieved most of their purpose and the group was anyway beginning to unravel. On wider matters Mrs Thatcher allowed much freer discussion in the Cabinet than Ted Heath had ever done; partly because she lacked his personal authority among her colleagues (nearly half of whom were older than her and several much more experienced), partly because she always enjoyed a good argument. In the early years she quite often lost the argument; but she never lost control, not only because she had her key allies in the posts that mattered, but also because in a crunch Willie Whitelaw and Peter Carrington would not let her be seriously embarrassed. She never held a vote, so she could not be outvoted. At the same time it was undoubtedly good for her to have powerful opposition within the Cabinet, composed of colleagues of her own age and independent standing who would argue with her, even though she could usually prevail in the end. In later years, when her colleagues were all much younger and owed their positions entirely to her, she lacked that sort of opposition. For this reason her first Cabinet was in some respects her best.

The lynchpin of her authority was Whitelaw. It was many years later that she made the immortal remark that 'Every Prime Minister should have a Willie',[45] but it was in her first term that she needed him most. As the acknowledged leader of the paternalistic old Tories, he could easily have rallied a majority of the Cabinet against her had he chosen to do so. Instead, having stood against her in 1975 and been defeated, he made it a point of honour to serve her with an almost military sense of subordination to his commanding officer. He had strong views of his own on certain matters which he did not hesitate to argue, normally in private. He would warn her when he thought she was getting ahead of the party or public opinion. But he saw his job as defusing tension and ensuring that she got her way. In the last resort he would never set his judgement against hers or countenance any sort of faction against her. Some of his colleagues felt that he thereby abdicated his proper responsibility to act as a traditional Tory counterweight to her more radical instincts; but so long as Willie stood rocklike beside her it was impossible for any other group in the Cabinet successfully to oppose her.

In effect she used him to chair the Cabinet. Contrary to the approved Asquithian model whereby the Prime Minister introduces the discussion, invites contributions from around the table and finally sums up the collective view, Mrs Thatcher's style was to chair from the front. In business terms she acted more like a chief executive than a chairman, concerned not with seeking agreement but with driving decisions forward. She would normally speak first, setting out her own view and challenging anyone with a good enough case to dissent. 'When I was a pupil at the Bar,' she once told the House of Commons, 'my first master-at-law gave me a very sound piece of advice, which I tried to follow. He said: "Always express your conclusion first, so that people do not have to wait for it."' As Prime Minister she made this her regular practice.[46] After a brisk exchange of views, often head-to-head with a single colleague, she would then leave Whitelaw to sum up, which he would do with skilful bonhomie, blandly smoothing away the disagreements while making sure the Prime Minister got her way, or at least was not visibly defeated.

'My style of chairmanship certainly non-plussed some colleagues, who knew their brief a good deal less well than I did,' Lady Thatcher boasted in her memoirs. 'But I adopt this technique because I believe in argument as the best way of getting to the truth – not because I want to suppress argument.'[47]★ 'She certainly was aggressive,' one member of that Cabinet confirms, but 'I never felt that she was dominant . . . On all sorts of issues there was a pretty good ding-dong discussion . . . Nobody kowtowed to Margaret Thatcher.'[49] Yet more often than not she did dominate, not only because she was always thoroughly prepared, but because she had no hesitation in berating ministers in front of their colleagues if she thought they did not know their stuff. 'It's not an error,' she once told Peter Carrington in full Cabinet when he apologised for some trivial inconsistency. 'It's incompetence, and it comes from the top.'[50] Moreover, as Jim Prior wrote, colleagues were given no time to develop an argument at length. 'If a minister tended to be in the slightest bit longwinded, or if she did not agree with his views, Margaret would interrupt.'[51] Veterans of previous Conservative Cabinets – above all Christopher Soames, who had not served with Heath but was used to the old-world courtesy of Macmillan and Alec Douglas-Home – were shocked by her sheer rudeness.

She was the same in smaller meetings, with both ministers and officials. Even Keith Joseph was not spared. Once, leaving his office with one of his juniors for a meeting about British Leyland, the Industry Secretary was asked if he would be needing anything. 'Yes,' he replied. 'Ambulances for two at three o'clock.'[52] That was a joke, but another minister told Patrick Cosgrave: 'I simply could not believe how rude she could be to Keith . . . If she treated him like that, what hope was there for the rest of us?'[53] Peter Thorneycroft fared no better. 'She is a person I prefer not to make too many mistakes in front of,' he told Patricia Murray with a touch of understatement. 'She is always very kind to me but it is preferable not to make too many.'[54]

'What was combativeness to her,' Cecil Parkinson acknowledged, 'was rudeness to a lot of people, particularly relatively junior people

---

★The disadvantage of this style of chairmanship, one senior civil servant commented, was that it effectively closed down discussion at an early stage.[48]

who worked for her.'[55] Undoubtedly some good officials wilted under her assault. Yet others – like Sir Michael Butler, Britain's Permanent Representative in Brussels from 1979 – found her directness stimulating. 'She seemed to me,' he wrote on his retirement in 1986, 'positively to welcome serious argument and to have a high regard for those who argued with her most effectively.'

> Meetings with Mrs Thatcher are not for the faint-hearted or illbriefed. She has normally read all the papers on the subjects under discussion, probably in the middle of the night when her ministers and advisers sleep. She will frequently launch a ferocious attack on a possible weak point in the arguments she is advised to accept. She expects her ministers and officials to defend them with equal vigour if they believe they are right. She will interrupt them if they say something she disagrees with – and yet listen intently if they insist and prove to have an important point to make which she needs to consider. It sometimes seemed to me that she would on occasion tease her advisers by advancing some outrageous proposition in which she did not believe, just to see how they responded to it.[56]

A much more junior Foreign Office official, George Walden, was Lord Carrington's principal private secretary and accompanied him to meetings with the Prime Minister:

> There was absolutely no side to this woman. She treated officials like fully-fledged human beings who (at that stage of her premiership at least) were allowed their say . . . As you talked, the electric blue eyes bored into you, as if probing for insincerities or fuzzy thinking. I liked the way she preferred plain speaking, even when she simplified things outrageously, and admired her 'can-do' style. If you made your point with conviction and could prove you were right, she would take the argument, while avoiding any appearance of doing so.[57]

She was in fact a very good listener when she respected the expertise of the person she was talking to, and really wanted to hear what he had to tell her. To hold her attention, however, it was essential to make your point quickly and then stick to it. 'Waffle was death,' a senior mandarin recalled.[58] Much of her irritation with Geoffrey Howe stemmed from the fact that he never learned to make his point quickly. She had 'instant certainty', which you had to match with equal certainty. 'When she says "Let me finish,"' one of her favourite confidants,

Woodrow Wyatt, wrote in 1984, 'it is essential not to let her until you have made your case. She never resents being talked down. She is exhilaratingly unstuffy and if you cannot keep up with her, that is your weakness, not hers.'[59] She relished argument for its own sake, and would often take a contrary line just to provoke one. It was through argument that she clarified her own mind. 'She would argue vigorously,' the head of her policy unit, John Hoskyns, recalled, 'to satisfy herself that the thinking she was being given was good.'[60] Though she read all the papers, her staff quickly learned that she was never persuaded of anything on paper alone: she had to test the case in argument before she would accept it.[61]

At the same time she was extraordinarily difficult to argue with, because she would never admit to losing an argument, but would become 'unbelievably discursive' and illogical if the point was going against her, abruptly changing the subject in order to retain the upper hand.[62] 'She could on occasions,' Cecil Parkinson has written, 'seize unreasonably on an unimportant secondary point and flog it to death while ignoring much more important and controversial issues.'[63] After 'a wild and whirling interview with her' in October 1979, just before the Dublin European summit, where she was preparing to open her battle to secure a refund on Britain's contribution to the Community budget, Roy Jenkins 'came to the conclusion that her reputation for a well-ordered mind is ill-founded'.[64] 'Don't try persuading me,' she told Jenkins on another occasion. 'You know I find persuasion very counterproductive.'[65] Alan Clark, recording a bout with the Prime Minister some years later, characteristically saw her illogicality as quintessentially feminine: 'no rational sequence, associative lateral thinking, jumping rails the whole time'. Yet he concluded: 'Her sheer energy and the speed with which she moves around the ring makes her a very difficult opponent.'[66] Varying the metaphor only slightly, one of her foreign-policy advisers wrote of her 'unstructured guerrilla style of argument'.[67] What both these accounts emphasise is that she argued not merely to clear her mind, but to *win*.

It was possible to change her mind, but she would never admit to having been wrong. She would furiously resist an argument by every device at her disposal one day, only to produce it unblushingly the next day as her own, with no acknowledgement that she had shifted her ground or that her interlocutor might have had a point.[68] Soon after taking office she subjected the chairman of the British Council, Sir Charles Troughton, to a blistering interrogation from which he emerged shaken and sweating, saying he never wanted to go through that again; but in fact he had persuaded her of his case. The next day he was astonished, and Treasury ministers were correspondingly dismayed, to find that she had reversed her strenuously argued position and now instructed that the Council's grant should not be cut after all.[69] Geoffrey Howe has recounted an even more bruising scene the night before his 1981 autumn statement, when Mrs Thatcher came through from Number Ten to Number Eleven to lend a hand with the drafting and 'proceeded to play to the gallery outrageously':

Anyone who attempted to describe the reformulations on which we had agreed was shouted down. So was I. At one point she exclaimed, 'If this is the best you can do, then I'd better send you to hospital and deliver the Statement myself.'

When the storm eventually blew itself out and the Prime Minister withdrew, Howe's staff quietly got on with finalising their original draft with no substantial alteration. The next day she sent him a honeyed note of congratulation. In all their eleven years of association, Howe reflected, 'I cannot recall Margaret ever coming closer to an apology than this.'[70]

Some colleagues reckoned that this aggressive manner – determined self-assertion sometimes tipping over into outright bullying – was both necessary, at least in the beginning, and effective. Lord Carrington suggests that it was the only way that Mrs Thatcher, as a woman, could have asserted her authority in the circumstances of 1979–81.[71] John Hoskyns likewise believes that she had to be 'impossible, difficult, emotional,' in order to try to bulldoze . . . radical thinking through' against those he termed 'the defeatists' in the Cabinet.[72] Even Geoffrey Howe, the butt of so much of her worst bullying, told Patricia Murray in 1980 of the exhilaration of working with Mrs Thatcher in these early days:

Oh, yes she is *dramatically* exciting! She has an openness, a frankness, an enthusiasm and an unwillingness to be cowed . . . which makes her enormous fun to work with. You can never be quite sure on issues you have never discussed with her what her instinctive reaction will be, but it's bound to be interesting . . . Even on the days when it isn't fun, she thinks it is well worth having a try.[73]

Others, however – particularly those colleagues less resilient than Howe and less robust than Prior – thought her method of government by combat counterproductive and inimical to sensible decision-making. David Howell, a thoughtful politician who had imagined –

perhaps naively – that the Cabinet would function as the forum for an exchange of ideas, was disillusioned to discover that, on the contrary, 'certain slogans were . . . written in tablets of stone and used as the put-down at the end of every argument:

> Of course there is a deterring effect if one knows that one's going . . . not into a discussion where various points of view will be weighed and gradually a view may be achieved, but into a huge argument where tremendous battle lines will be drawn up and everyone who doesn't fall into line will be hit on the head.[74]

'In my experience,' Howell concluded, 'there is too much argument and not enough discussion . . . The argument is of people whose backs are pinned to the wall before they're questioned . . . and that doesn't make for . . . calm discussion.'[75] Another member of the 1979 Cabinet thought it 'an absurd way to run a Government'.[76] To these critics, Mrs Thatcher's inability to delegate and her insistence on interrogating her ministers about the smallest detail of their own departments reflected a deep-seated insecurity, not so much political as psycho-logical: she had to be on top all the time, and keep demonstrating that she was on top. The schoolgirl had not only done her homework, but had to prove that she had done it. On this analysis her aggression was essentially defensive. Several colleagues have echoed Nigel Lawson's exasperation with her 'time-wasting attempts to show off her mastery of detail, at the expense of the main business in hand',[77] while one senior official judged that the Prime Minister herself talked 90 per cent of the time at most meetings. If she had been up all night reading, her colleagues were jolly well going to know it. At the same time she made a practice of asking officials 'detailed, numerical, irrelevant ques-tions', which seemed to be designed to catch them out; or forked questions, which wrongfooted them whichever way they answered. She had an unsettling way of putting them on the defensive all the time.[78]

The negative results of this method were that she exhausted herself and did not get the best out of others. Though she liked to boast that she was never tired so long as there was work to be done – 'it's when you stop that you realise you might be rather tired'[79] – and wrote in her memoirs that there was 'an intensity about the job of Prime Minister which made sleep a luxury'[80] many of those who worked most closely with her insist that this was not true. Undoubtedly her stamina was remarkable. She could go for several days with four hours' sleep a night, and rarely allowed herself more than five or six. But her staff could see that she was exhausted more often than she ever admitted: one sign was that she would talk more unstoppably than ever.[81] Her refusal to acknowledge physical weakness was another way of asserting her dominance. Any minister unwise enough to admit that he needed sleep would find himself written off as a feeble male. 'If you will forgive me, Prime Minister,' Jock Bruce-Gardyne once excused himself as he tried to leave Downing Street after midnight after helping with a speech, 'I must get on with my boxes.' 'And what about *my* boxes?' she demanded. 'Yes, Prime Minister, but you don't seem to need to sleep.'[82]

Alternatively, she would express motherly concern that someone was looking tired; but this, George Walden noted, was another stratagem:

> What she was saying when she commented on how terrible you looked was that you were a man and she was a woman, you were a junior and she was Prime Minister, and yet unlike you she was *never* tired.[83]

In the same way she would insist that other people must have their holidays while refusing to admit that she might need one herself. 'I must govern,' she told a member of her staff in the summer of 1979.[84] Holidays, she frequently implied, were for wimps.[85] But her inability to relax also conveyed the message that she did not trust anyone to deputise for her. She believed that if she stopped for a moment, or let slip her vigilance on everything that moved in Whitehall, the Civil Service would quickly resume its paralysing inertia, her feeble colleagues would backslide and her enemies would combine against her.

By not trusting her ministers to run their own departments, however, Mrs Thatcher diminished them. Michael Edwardes, the dynamic motivator appointed by Callaghan to shake up the perpetually ailing motor manufacturer British Leyland, wrote that from the moment the Conservative Government took over, it was a waste of time dealing with the Department of Industry as he had done under Callaghan:

> Everything of any conceivable consequence was referred to Number 10 – not only the strategic decisions on funding, but even matters such as the chairman's remuneration. Moreover this was no rubber-stamping process. Recommendations . . . were frequently overturned.

'I cannot judge whether she was right to delegate authority so sparingly to her ministers,' Edwardes went on, 'but it certainly tended to undermine their credibility . . . It is not always a good leadership approach, for if you "second-guess" those responsible, you demotivate and sharply reduce effort and commitment.'[86] John Hoskyns, another businessman appalled by the amateurism of government, was equally critical of Mrs Thatcher's neglect of elementary man-management. 'You really have to decide from the outset whether to preside from a position of paranoid and incurable distrust – or to build a happy and united team,' he wrote in January 1981. He had no doubt that she had chosen the former.[87]

Thus from the very beginning Mrs Thatcher's restless interference centralised the business of government, while by concentrating everything on herself, she underused the talents of others. As she grew more dominant, colleagues and officials became increasingly reluctant to tell her things she did not want to hear. The free circulation of information and advice within Whitehall was constrained by the requirement to refer everything upwards to Number Ten; while by battering and badgering, second-guessing and overruling her colleagues she strained their loyalty – ultimately to breaking point.[88] As early as March 1980 her devoted PPS, Ian Gow, was worried that 'Margaret did treat colleagues badly and it would boomerang'.[89]

Unlike Ted Heath's exceptionally harmonious Cabinet half a dozen years before, which had kept its own counsel even when pursuing sensitive and controversial policies, Mrs Thatcher's Cabinet was prone to leaks from the very beginning. The fact that more than half the Cabinet had serious doubts about the economic strategy to which they were committed was well known and widely reported. Mrs Thatcher blamed the so-called 'wets' for trying to subvert by hints and whispers policies they were unable to defeat in Cabinet. 'This cloaked and indirect approach has never been my style,' she declared grandly in her memoirs, 'and I felt contempt for it. I thrive on honest argument . . . I prefer to debate my opponents rather than undermine them with leaks.'[90] This was hokum, though she may have believed it. 'Oh, no, Jim, I never leak,' she assured Prior when he tried to turn the accusation back on her. 'If you tell me that, I must accept it,' he replied. 'But in that case your officials and press people certainly leak for you.' 'Oh, no,' she responded, 'they never know anything, so how could they leak?'[91] The truth was that both sides leaked; this was an inevitable consequence of a fundamentally divided Cabinet. The 'wets' confided their misgivings to journalists because they were denied any opportunity to influence policy from within; while for her part Mrs Thatcher, having been obliged to appoint a Cabinet most of whom she knew were out of sympathy with her objectives, felt justified in bypassing them and appealing, via the press, directly to the public, which she believed understood what she was trying to do. She took a positive pride in presenting herself as more radical than her ministers. Once, early in her first term, she startled the guests at a Downing Street reception by jumping on a sofa and announcing, 'I am the rebel head of an establishment government.'[92]* As time went on she used her press secretary, Bernard Ingham, to convey her private criticism of her colleagues to the press. She was never a good team player, still less a good captain, because she never trusted her team. Even when she had replaced most of her original opponents with younger colleagues more loyal to her − whether from conviction or ambition − the habit of undermining them was too established to be abandoned. She was not loyal to them, she drove an unprecedented number of them to resign, and ultimately in November 1990 the collective loyalty of the survivors cracked.

Inside Number Ten

The wider field over which the new Prime Minister had quickly to assert her authority was Whitehall. From the moment she took office she became responsible for the entire government machine. Yet the British Prime Minister has no department of his or her own through which to co-ordinate this extensive bureaucracy, merely a small private office, based in Number Ten, Downing Street, composed of an anomalous mixture of career officials inherited from the outgoing government, whose job is to provide continuity; a handful of personal staff carried over from the very different world of opposition, more often than not with no experience of government; and a scrum of more or less informal political advisers. Nowhere else in the democratic world does the changeover of power from one government to the next take place so quickly. Some discreet preparations are made at official level for a possible transition; but Mrs Thatcher was always wary of taking anything for granted, so this critical central structure had to be put together over a single weekend, ready to start running the country on Monday morning.

She took office with a deep distrust of the Civil Service based on her limited experience of two relatively low-ranking departments, the Department of Education and Science and the old Ministry of Pensions. She saw what she regarded as the defeatist ethos of Whitehall as one of the causes of Britain's decline, not part of the solution. Over the

---

*She was not the first Prime Minister to have this idea of herself. With much less reason, that great fantasist Harold Wilson had once fancied himself 'the Bolshevik head of a Menshevik government'.[93]

next decade she did indeed revolutionise the service. Yet at the outset – to the despair of some of her supporters who had expected her to be much more radical – her approach to Whitehall was surprisingly conservative. She made few institutional innovations, but broadly accepted the structures and practices of the Whitehall village as she found them; and though she remained suspicious of civil servants as a class, she quickly came to trust the key individuals who served her far more than she did her political colleagues. Having no experience of the Treasury or the Foreign Office, she simply had not realised how good the best officials were. Though in some ways punctilious about observing constitutional niceties, she soon came to operate on a highly personal basis, blurring the categories between officials, colleagues and advisers and dominating the whole government machine by her energy, enthusiasm and example. Professor Anthony King was initially surprised that such an activist Prime Minister did not set up a Prime Minister's department, as Whitehall reformers had been advocating since Harold Wilson's time. In 1985, however, he concluded that Mrs Thatcher did not need a department. 'She was easily her own best advocate and her own chief of staff. She had no need of assistants and intermediaries . . . she wanted to ensure that she was in control.'[94] She was the most restlessly interventionist Prime Minister since Lloyd George.

The two key permanent officials who met her when she walked through the door were her principal private secretary, Kenneth Stowe, and the Cabinet Secretary, Sir John Hunt. Both were due to be replaced before the end of the year, but both played important roles in introducing Mrs Thatcher to her new responsibilities. As head of Callaghan's private office for the past three years (and Wilson's before that) Stowe had already had to deal with the new Prime Minister on a number of sensitive issues where the Leader of the Opposition needed to be kept informed, so she already knew and had come to trust him, and he had learned to handle her. Emollient and self-effacing, he managed the transition from Callaghan to Mrs Thatcher with exemplary smoothness, but stayed in Number Ten for only six weeks – 'six very intensive weeks' as he recalled them – before moving to the Northern Ireland Office and later the Department of Health, which he headed from 1981 to 1987.[95] His replacement, Clive Whitmore, came from the Ministry of Defence. Mrs Thatcher picked him, from a shortlist of four, after he gave her the department's detailed briefing on the nuclear deterrent. Though 'very much the machine man', in the view of one internal critic,[96] Whitmore was instinctively in sympathy with her political objectives and they quickly formed a close working relationship, which lasted for the next three years, after which she sent him back to the MoD as Permanent Secretary at the unusually young age of forty-seven.

Sir John Hunt had been Cabinet Secretary – in effect the Prime Minister's Permanent Secretary – since 1973: Mrs Thatcher was thus his fourth Prime Minister in seven years. He remembered her as Education Secretary under Heath, when it had never occurred to him that she might one day be Prime Minister.[97] Hunt's style was brisk and businesslike: as a newcomer feeling her way, Mrs Thatcher found him a bit managing. She had 'enormous respect for John', one close observer told Peter Hennessy, 'but she thought he tended to push her along when she was not quite ready'.[98] Another characterised their relationship as 'wary'.[99] When Hunt retired at the end of 1979 she was happy to choose as his successor the more obliging, indeed positively Jeeves-like, Robert Armstrong, a classic Eton and Christ Church-educated mandarin who had long been tipped for the top job. His only handicap was that he had been Heath's principal private secretary and was still close to his old chief. There was some expectation that this might rule him out. But he was the model of Civil Service impartiality and selfless professionalism; and the conservative side of Mrs Thatcher's character respected those traditional qualities so long as they were employed to serve and not obstruct her. Though far from Thatcherite by inclination – he was privately horrified by some of her social attitudes – Armstrong served her, rather like Willie Whitelaw, with absolute loyalty and discretion for the next seven years.

Hunt and Stowe – soon replaced by Armstrong and Whitmore – with their various deputies, formed the official core of Mrs Thatcher's Downing Street machine.* On the political side her personal office was still headed, as it had been in opposition, by Richard Ryder, a former journalist who left in 1981 when he was adopted for a safe Tory seat, and the somewhat shadowy David Wolfson, a wealthy businessman from the mail-order firm Great Universal Stores, who was originally brought in to deal with her correspondence. In opposition he had acted as her office manager, and later secretary to the Shadow

---

*Each had four deputies covering different areas of government business, the most senior being responsible for foreign affairs. The deputy Cabinet Secretary handling foreign policy from 1979 to 1982 was Robert Wade-Gery, who had first come to prominence as a member of Heath's 'Think Tank' in the early 1970s and went on to become High Commissioner to India. The foreign-affairs private secretary from 1984 was Charles Powell, who so far gained Mrs Thatcher's confidence that by the end of her premiership he had become more influential than his nominal superiors.

Cabinet; but in government the Civil Service took over those tasks, so it is unclear precisely what his job now was. On taking office Mrs Thatcher grandly announced that 'David is to be my Pug Ismay' – which said more about her own self-identification with Churchill than it did about Wolfson's role, since Ismay was not (as she imagined) Churchill's chief of staff but rather the Chiefs of Staffs' representative in Number Ten.[100] Wolfson had no knowledge of Whitehall, nor did he have sensitive political antennae. In her memoirs Lady Thatcher writes vaguely that he brought 'his charm and business experience [to] the problems of running No. 10'.[101] In fact he seems to have acted as a sort of confidant with whom she could relax and simply gossip. Like Alistair McAlpine, he was rich, agreeable and represented no threat to her. Some of her political colleagues and advisers who fancied their own influence with the Prime Minister were jealous of Wolfson and still tend to play down his importance. Yet John Hoskyns and Norman Strauss in the Policy Unit found him a valuable ally who helped to keep her mind focused on the big strategic issues.[102] 'Tall, elegant, with a languid manner and a rather mocking, teasing humour,' Hoskyns wrote, 'he was clever, numerate, tenacious and prepared to speak very plainly to Mrs Thatcher behind the scenes'.[103] It is often claimed that Mrs Thatcher did not have a kitchen cabinet: but from the beginning she had a court – and Wolfson was at the heart of it.

But Mrs Thatcher's private office also had a strong female component, particularly in the early years, largely because she made so little distinction between work and home. When she titled the first chapter of her memoirs 'Over the Shop' and wrote that living in Number Ten was like going back to her girlhood in Grantham, it was not just a literary flourish, but described exactly how she lived. During her working day she was always popping upstairs to the flat at the top of the building to eat or change or work on a speech before coming down again for a Cabinet committee or to meet a foreign leader: smaller meetings with colleagues and advisers were often held in the flat. Denis, if he was around, sometimes sat in on these informal meetings: late at night it was frequently he who ended them by telling Margaret firmly that it was time for bed. Because she was 'always on the job' – as she once told a delighted television audience[104] – she made no effort to protect her private space from the intrusion of work. Far more than with a male Prime Minister – who might wear the same suit all day and have his hair cut once a month – her clothes, her hair, her make-up were all essential props of her public performance, needing frequent, but very rapid, attention throughout the day. Thus her personal staff was much more mingled with her professional staff than was the case with Jim Callaghan or Ted Heath; secretaries might be pressed into cooking scratch meals at any hour of the day or night.* Though Mrs Thatcher made no secret that she enjoyed being surrounded by subservient men, and in eleven years appointed only one other woman – briefly – to her Cabinet, there was always a distinctly feminine flavour in her immediate entourage. Among the usual Downing Street typists and telephonists, three or four women held positions of real influence.

Caroline Stephens was nominally the Prime Minister's diary secretary, but was in practice an all-purpose personal assistant, working closely with Richard Ryder (whom she married in 1981). More than anyone else she acted as the critical filter on access to Mrs Thatcher, controlling who could get to speak to her behind the backs of her civil servants; personal friends and unofficial 'voices' like John Junor and Woodrow Wyatt, who used to telephone her late at night or over the weekend, found Miss Stephens a valuable backstairs channel of communication. She was a formidable young woman, bred in the public service, whose father had served in Macmillan's private office. Ronald Millar once asked her how she addressed the Prime Minister. 'It depends,' she replied. 'If she's being good I call her Prime Minister. When she annoys me it's Mrs Thatcher.'[106]

Alison Ward, Mrs Thatcher's long-time constituency secretary, also moved into Number Ten and handled much of the practical business of running the household. (It is an extraordinary fact that Downing Street does not have its own live-in cook or housekeeper.) Meanwhile Joy Robilliard, who had been Airey Neave's secretary, took over the constituency role. Miss Ward – another 'wonderfully bossy' girl, who 'could do twenty jobs at once', according to Carol Thatcher – was so much part of the family that Denis used to call her his 'other daughter'.[107] In 1981 she too left to become John Wakeham's secretary, but she still worked for Mrs Thatcher on and off. Later, when she married Wakeham after the death of his first wife in the Brighton bombing, Mrs Thatcher insisted that they hold the reception in Number Ten.

Closest of all was Cynthia Crawford (known as 'Crawfie', like the famous royal nanny). She was originally Wolfson's personal assistant, but somehow transmogrified into Mrs Thatcher's wardrobe mistress,

---

*Mrs Thatcher herself frequently cooked late-night meals too, often insisting on running up a quick supper (lasagne or chicken kiev from the freezer) for aides or MPs helping with a speech. 'Don't stop her cooking,' Denis would tell them. 'It's her form of therapy.'[105]

handling the increasingly complicated business of juggling and co-ordinating the Prime Minister's clothes – often several outfits a day – for every public appearance. By the nature of the job she was the Prime Minister's most intimate confidante: in Carol's biography of her father, 'Crawfie' always seems to be there having a drink at the end of the day or answering the telephone. When President Reagan rang to congratulate Mrs Thatcher when Mark was found after getting himself lost in the Sahara desert, it was 'Crawfie' who answered the phone.[108] Like Joy Robilliard – who took over many of the household tasks from Alison Ward – the faithful 'Crawfie' stayed with Mrs Thatcher throughout her entire premiership and into retirement.

Lady Thatcher was justifiably proud of having created a happy family atmosphere inside Number Ten. However roughly she may have treated her colleagues and advisers, she was always immensely considerate towards her personal staff and towards all those – drivers, telephonists and the like – who kept the wheels of government turning. As John Major somewhat backhandedly told one of his biographers, this was 'her one great virtue':

> He never saw her be unpleasant or rude to people who were serving her in any way. Other politicians, heads of nationalised industries, senior ministers, top members of the armed forces she could be brutally rude and obnoxious to, but never to anyone who was not in a position to answer back.[109]

On the contrary, there are innumerable stories of her kindness to members of staff. On her very first day in Downing Street, when she had been selecting the Cabinet, and the switchboard girls had to stay late while Ken Stowe phoned around making appointments for ministerial hopefuls to come and see her the next day, it was entirely characteristic that she insisted on going upstairs at the end of a long day to thank them all personally.[110] Though she sometimes gave the impression that she did not see why others should need any more sleep than she did, one private secretary who had previously worked for Callaghan told Anthony King that he preferred Mrs Thatcher 'by a wide margin':

> Jim always thought you had absolutely nothing to do in life except work for him. Mrs Thatcher never forgets that you have a wife who may be expecting you home for dinner.[111]

With all her other concerns, she was amazingly good at remembering the names of wives and children and took a close interest in their exams, illnesses and other family worries. When her driver died suddenly in March 1980, she insisted, at the end of a very busy week, on attending the funeral in south London and comforting his widow.[112] Likewise, when Bernard Ingham's wife was involved in an accident in the middle of the Falklands war, she insisted that he must go and look after her: she told him firmly that she did not expect to see him back at work for several days.[113] In his diary Ingham also recorded the Prime Minister's motherly solicitude for one of his press officers who accompanied her on a visit to Salford and Halifax in 1988 when five months pregnant:

> Mrs Thatcher clearly feels we should not now be sending her on arduous regional visits. So she spends the day pampering her, slowing down the visit, making her sit down at every opportunity. And while the rest of the party flies home Colleen travels back to London in the back seat of the Prime Minister's car with instructions to put her feet up across the back seat.[114]

Finally there is the joyfully repeated story of a lunch at Chequers when one of the service personnel waiting at table – a Wren – spilled a plate of hot soup in Geoffrey Howe's lap. The Prime Minister immediately leaped up, full of concern, not for her Foreign Secretary but for the girl. 'There, there,' she comforted her. 'You mustn't be upset. It's the sort of thing that could happen to anyone.' In subsequent versions of the story the soup became a leg of lamb. The contrast between the way Mrs Thatcher fussed over her staff and the cavalier way she treated her colleagues – particularly Howe – was perfectly emblematic. With the benefiit of hindsight, Ronnie Millar (who was actually present) wondered whether she was 'altogether wise to treat Sir Geoffrey any old how'.[115]

Beyond the private office, the next ring of Mrs Thatcher's personal power base was the Number Ten Policy Unit, headed by John Hoskyns. The Policy Unit had originally been established by Harold Wilson in his second administration as a sort of minimal Prime Minister's department under the direction of the Labour academic Bernard Donoughue; but in 1979 it still had no settled existence. Hoskyns – an independent systems analyst with a military background, who had been recruited by Keith Joseph to the Centre for Policy Studies in 1977 – had written (with his partner Norman Strauss) a number of strategy papers for Mrs Thatcher in opposition, notably the highly secret *Stepping Stones*, which had argued the absolute necessity of dealing with the trade unions before the Government could achieve any of its other economic objectives. Not until just before the election, however, did Mrs Thatcher casually tell Hoskyns that she would want him to carry on in some capacity in government if she won. If anyone were to take over Donoughue's role, the press had assumed it would be Adam Ridley from the Conservative Research Department. In fact Mrs Thatcher first proposed that Ridley and Hoskyns should head the unit jointly, until Hoskyns insisted that this would not work; Ridley then went to be Geoffrey Howe's special adviser in the Treasury instead. But the Policy Unit was in the early days a very makeshift operation, comprising just Hoskyns and Strauss, plus Douglas Hague (professor of managerial economics at the Manchester Business School, who had been advising Mrs Thatcher privately in opposition) and one civil servant, Andrew Duguid, seconded from the DTI and described by Hoskyns as 'the most clear-headed, determined and tough-minded young official I met in Whitehall'.[116] Whereas Donoughue had occupied an office next to the Prime Minister's study, that prime position was grabbed in May 1979 by David Wolfson. Hoskyns started with a bare office, a telephone and a kettle in a remote part of the building. It took 'nine months' back-breaking work' to establish his position within Whitehall.[117]

'In those days,' Mrs Thatcher recalled in 1987, 'the No. 10 Policy Unit went into purdah for several months, working out how to get from where we were to where we wanted to be.' Hoskyns, she acknowledged, was 'more prepared than many for the long haul'.[118] Believing that previous governments had failed because they merely tinkered instead of developing a clear strategy to overcome the inertia of Whitehall, he wanted Mrs Thatcher to take on and shake up the whole government machine, indeed the whole political Establishment: he saw himself as the grit in the machine, whose function was to prevent her radicalism being stifled by the bureaucracy. It was 'a major objective' to get Jim Prior moved from the Department of Employment, so that the Government could begin to implement the *Stepping Stones* strategy and start drawing up plans to resist a major strike.[119] Hoskyns was also closely involved in monetary control and public-sector pay, and sat in on meetings of the 'E' Committee. 'Stern-faced,' she reminded him at a dinner after his retirement, 'you stalked the corridors of No. 10 warning against the superficial solutions and the easy compromises'.[120] But Hoskyns was an impatient technocrat, not a politician. Mrs Thatcher did not share his consuming interest in management systems. 'She didn't like his . . . over-numerical, over-analytical, computerised approach to problems.'[121] 'If I asked for a joke for a speech,' she only half-humorously complained, 'I got back twenty pages of strategic analysis.'[122] Hoskyns believed that systems mattered, not speeches. Before taking the job he had tried to stipulate that he would not write speeches; but increasingly that was what he found himself being asked to do. Very soon he felt he was 'knocking his head against a wall'.[123] By the autumn of 1981 he felt that the bureaucracy – specifically Clive Whitmore and Robert Armstrong – had absorbed her. The last straw came at Blackpool in October when Whitmore persuaded her to tone down parts of her conference speech. Hoskyns resigned soon afterwards. Mrs Thatcher was disappointed, but more generous than she was to many who deserted her: she gave him an immediate knighthood and a farewell dinner at which she told him that he had 'brought a whole new dimension to our thinking'.[124] The Policy Unit survived and expanded under a succession of subsequent directors – Ferdinand Mount, John Redwood and finally Brian Griffiths; but it was never so informal or so unconventional again, and eventually it became just another cog in the Whitehall machine, working directly to the Prime Minister and under her personal control.*

Mrs Thatcher did not, as Bernard Ingham states in his memoirs, come to office having given no thought to the appointment of a press officer.[126] On the contrary, she had filled the post several months before the election. Her first choice was actually a tabloid journalist, Tony Shrimsley, the assistant editor of the *Sun*, who would have been a partisan publicist in the manner of Harold Wilson's Joe Haines or Tony Blair's Alastair Campbell. But Shrimsley refused the job. (Later he became Director of Communications at Central Office.) Alternatively she could simply have taken her Tory party press officer, Derek Howe, with her from opposition into government. In fact convention prevailed and she chose – on the recommendation of the parliamentary lobby – Henry James, the former head of the Central Office of Information, recently retired and now working for Vickers. She offered James the job for a whole Parliament; but Vickers would not release him for more than six months, so she settled for that. James had never intended to stay longer; he was therefore upset by reports that his appointment had been prematurely terminated.[127] His relationship with Mrs Thatcher was admittedly difficult at first. She was not sure why she needed a press officer at all; while he, as an old Whitehall hand, found her exas-

---

*Not until 1999 did Hoskyns publish his account of this period. He then described the Policy Unit's role as 'the unending task of clarifying, again and again, as precisely as possible . . . what it was that the Government was trying to accomplish . . . and then checking whether the necessary actions look likely to work in practice'.[125]

peratingly naive, full of preconceived ideas, but very quick to learn. He had to battle for her ear with Derek Howe – now press officer to Angus Maude – who would upset her by showing her all the newspapers. It was James who started the practice (carried on by Ingham) of producing a daily digest for her every morning. His breakthrough came in late July, on the eve of the Commonwealth Conference in Lusaka, when he had to warn Mrs Thatcher that she should expect a rough reception in the Zambian capital; he stayed for two hours drinking whisky and, in his own words, 'fell in love with her'.[128] He was very sorry to leave when his six months were up at the end of October.

His replacement, Bernard Ingham, was another career press officer recruited through normal Civil Service soundings, and initially seen as a disappointingly conventional appointment. He was unusual in being an open and combative Labour supporter, who had previously worked successfully with Barbara Castle in the 1960s and with Tony Benn in the 1970s. Despite this, Mrs Thatcher appointed him on the basis of a two-minute interview. He immediately transferred his loyalty to her and became – like so many converts – one of her most ardent devotees, increasingly straining the limits of Civil Service neutrality by the highly personalised nature of his briefings. Ingham was a Yorkshire bulldog with all the canine virtues: fidelity, pugnacity, protective vigilance and a fearsome bark, which he used to keep the lobby journalists in line. At the same time he was a much more professional, shrewd and subtle operator behind the scenes than his public manner suggested. He stayed with Mrs Thatcher for the rest of her premiership, accompanying her on most of her travels and becoming – more than any previous Prime Minister's press secretary – a controversial personality in his own right. But none of this could have been foreseen in 1979.

Another key figure in Mrs Thatcher's first administration was her Parliamentary Private Secretary, Ian Gow. MP for Eastbourne since February 1974, Gow was a balding, tweedy solicitor who wore waistcoats and a gold watch chain and cultivated a self-consciously old fogeyish manner, though only in his early forties. (He always spoke of Rhodesia, soon to become Zimbabwe, as *Southern* Rhodesia.) He had scarcely met Mrs Thatcher before May 1979, but he was a passionate Ulster Unionist and had acted as Airey Neave's PPS in opposition; this was presumably what brought him to her attention. He was astonished to be invited to become her PPS; but he too immediately fell under her spell. 'Ian loved her,' Alan Clark wrote after Gow's murder in 1990, 'actually loved, I mean, in every sense but the physical.'[129] For the first four years from May 1979 Gow was closer to the Prime Minister than anyone except 'Crawfie' and Denis. He escorted her everywhere, protected her in public and helped her unwind in private with late-night whisky and gossip. At the same time he was the most sensitive link with the back benches that any Prime Minister ever had. 'Known affectionately as "Supergrass",' according to Ronald Millar, 'he had a knack of reporting back to the lady everything she needed to know about the gossip of the bazaars without ever betraying a confidence, a rare feat in the political world.'[130] He was also an old friend of Geoffrey Howe, which helped lubricate the key relationship at the heart of the Government, a relationship that later turned disastrously sour. Gow in fact played a crucial part in Mrs Thatcher's political survival in the dark days of 1981–2 when her premiership hung in the balance. She felt bound to reward him with a ministerial job in 1983; but thereafter she never found a successor with the same qualities. As a result her relationship with her backbenchers steadily deteriorated. Gow was unique and irreplaceable.

Beyond this inner core who comprised her immediate entourage there was also an outer circle of unofficial advisers who were called upon irregularly for specific functions. Chief of these was the playwright Ronald Millar, who continued into government the role he had established in opposition as Mrs Thatcher's most senior and trusted speechwriter. With more speeches than ever to be written, she now had Civil Service help; but she still relied on her favourite 'wordsmiths' to give them her personal imprint. As Prime Minister she continued to devote extraordinary amounts of time to writing important speeches, often far into the night. No one, it was said, wrote speeches for Mrs Thatcher: her wordsmiths wrote speeches *with* her, while she argued, criticised and rejected draft after draft. 'Every written word,' she affirmed in her memoirs, 'goes through the mincing machine of my criticism before it gets into a speech.'[131] This obsessive, interminable and often exasperating process – which frequently came back in the end to something barely distinguishable from the first draft she had rejected hours before – sometimes drove her aides to despair; yet it was her way of ensuring that she was absolutely on top of the facts and thoroughly understood the arguments. Favourite members of her writing team in 1979–82 included John Selwyn Gummer, a still-youthful former student Conservative (he was actually over forty) just re-elected to Parliament after losing his previous seat in 1974, who brought an unfashionably Christian perspective to politics; and the journalist Ferdinand Mount, the Old Etonian heir to a baronetcy, then on the London *Evening Standard* and later political editor of the *Spectator*. Mrs Thatcher so liked Gummer's 'boyish enthusiasm and popular moralising' that she astonished the political world in 1983 by appointing him party chairman.[132] Mount was an equally surprising choice to succeed Hoskyns as head of her Policy Unit; he later found his metier as a novelist and editor of the *Times Literary Supplement*. But Millar was the wordsmith *emeritus* who was always called in to give the final polish, or supply the key phrase, to the most important speeches – above all the annual party confer- ence speech. He was also on big occasions the man who could keep the lady calm: he treated her like an actress before a performance, and she deferred to his suave theatrical professionalism.

Gordon Reece and Tim Bell, her image consultants and publicity gurus in opposition, came to Downing Street when required and were often invited to Chequers at weekends. Mrs Thatcher called them her 'laughing boys' and used them, between elections, for moral support and encouragement as much as actual professional advice. Alistair McAlpine was another courtier whose company she enjoyed as an antidote to her colleagues and officials. He was young – under forty – amusing, and free of the suspicion of place-seeking. In opposition he had been Conservative party treasurer; after the 1979 election Mrs Thatcher made him deputy chairman as well. As Peter Thorneycroft succumbed to 'rising damp' in 1980–1, McAlpine became her most trusted confidant in Central Office. He was not part of the Government or influential in policy terms, but he was one of those whose support kept her going in the difficult times and helped her to feel she was not alone. He was with her at the end in November 1990 as he had been at the beginning.

Alfred Sherman, however, quickly fell from favour. As director of the Centre for Policy Studies(CPS), he had been an important intel- lectual mentor and speechwriter, helping both Keith Joseph and Mrs Thatcher develop their ideas in opposition; but he was an abrasive character who had served his purpose by 1979. 'With his talent for tactless outspokenness,' Richard Cockett has written, 'he could emphati- cally not be a special adviser in government.'[133] Once installed in the Department of Industry, Joseph severed his ties with Sherman completely. Mrs Thatcher thanked him generously for his role in winning the battle of ideas; but – unlike Hoskyns and Strauss – she offered him no role in Number Ten. He continued to bombard her from the outside with memoranda on every subject under the sun and he still contributed material for speeches. But his influence inevitably declined and he became increasingly critical of the Government's performance. His exclusion from the inner circle was sealed when he was forced to resign the directorship of the CPS in 1981 after quar- relling with the new chairman, Hugh Thomas. He was compensated with a knighthood in 1983, but continued to write ever more bitter letters to the press claiming to be the true author of Thatcherism.

Woodrow Wyatt's influence, on the other hand, continued to grow after 1979. Not long after the election Roy Jenkins visited Chequers in his capacity as President of the European Commission, and was surprised to find that the company at dinner consited of just Mrs Thatcher, Denis, himself and Wyatt. 'Woodrow is on very close terms with her,' he noted in his diary, 'talks freely, easily, without self-consciousness, says what he wants to.'[134] A raging snob – wine buff, gourmand, racing enthusiast and ageing lecher – Wyatt was a strange confidant for a puritan Prime Minister, yet he kept his place in Mrs Thatcher's favour for the next ten years. He used to ring her after midnight, or on Sunday morning, with honeyed words of encouragement or sometimes warning. He was a shameless flatterer, but he was also one those licensed favourites – an old socialist turned Thatcherite convert – whose experience of Fleet Street, the Labour party and the trade unions she valued. She may not always have taken his advice, but her ministers got sick of being told what 'Woodrow says' about this or that policy. In fact he was anxious not to be publicly identified as being close to Mrs Thatcher. Much of his usefulness to her – as well as much of his income – derived from writing a weekly column, first in the *Sunday Mirror*, later (after his old friend Rupert Murdoch had acquired them in 1981) in the *News of the World* and, less regularly, *The Times*, which he used in order to fly kites on her behalf. As the supposedly independent 'Voice of Reason', Wyatt tried to keep his relationship with the Prime Minister discreetly veiled: when she sent him to the Lords in 1987, he sat as a crossbencher in order to keep 'some semblance of independence for my articles'.[135] But when Geoffrey Howe wrote in his memoirs that Mrs Thatcher – like Joan of Arc – tended to listen to her private 'voices' in preference to her colleagues and official advisers, it was first and foremost of Wyatt that he was thinking.[136] She rewarded him by several times renewing his comfortable appointment as chairman of the Tote (the Horserace Totalisator Board) even when he was well past retirement age.

There were other 'voices'. Hugh Thomas, the historian of Cuba and the Spanish Civil War, who took over the chairmanship of the CPS from Keith Joseph after the 1979 election, was an important unofficial adviser on foreign affairs; as were Robert Conquest, the historian of Stalin's purges, who had written her 'Iron Lady' speech in 1975, and later Norman Stone, historian of modern Germany and Eastern Europe. There was an American marine general who advised her on defence matters. In fact she had all sorts of surprising contacts drawn from different walks of life, from university professors to her hairdresser, whom she encouraged to give her alternative advice from outside the official government apparatus. This was one way she tried to avoid becoming the prisoner of Whitehall, and one of the reasons she so often had the advantage of her ministers. She was very skilled not only at marshalling all these conflicting voices, but at giving each of them the impression that she particularly valued their advice, while concealing from them who else she had been listening to. By this means she built up an extraordinary network of informers who kept her apprised of where trouble was brewing and how policies were going down in the City, the factories, the services or the schools. The only danger was that her confidants were almost by definition committed Thatcherites, who tended – especially as she became more powerful – to tell her only what she wanted to hear.

One other expert who was actually inside Number Ten but attracted little public notice was the Government's Chief Scientist, John Ashworth. A biochemist who had been seconded to the Cabinet 'think-tank' from his chair at the University of Essex in 1976, Ashworth was young (still only forty-one), iconoclastic and lateral-thinking, and Mrs Thatcher took an immediate shine to him. She was intensely proud of her scientific background and liked to show it off whenever possible, announcing, 'I shall be my own Minister of Science.'[137]* Besides his official function as scientific adviser, she used to call Ashworth in at odd moments to tell her the latest scientific gossip. She liked to give the impression, at least, that she still read the scientific journals; but these sessions were more therapeutic than politically important. Once when he tried to interest her in the coming problem of global warming she was scornful: 'Why are you wasting your time? Are you telling me I should worry about the weather?'[139] 'There is a difference,' he later reflected 'between being a conviction politician and being a rationally guided politician.'[140] Her staff valued Ashworth, however, as one who could exercise a calming influence on the Prime Minister at moments of high tension: Robert Armstrong once asked him to go and see her when she was 'beside herself' over the 1980 steel strike. Until he left in 1981 to become Vice-Chancellor of Salford University (just in time to feel the full force of the Government's higher-education cuts)

---

*A young assistant to the director of the British Steel Corporation (later a Tory MP) who had to brief her in 1982 recalled that 'she seemed to have more genuine interest in the effects of molybdenum and vanadium on the properties of the final product than she did [in] the squabbles between British Steel and the private steel sector'.[138]

Ashworth was one of Mrs Thatcher's favourite sons. He left because he was afraid of becoming a courtier. But then he joined the SDP, and she never spoke to him again.

Finally there was Denis. It was the presence of the Prime Minister's husband, coming and going as he liked amid the press of government business, speechwriting and impromptu meals, that gave Mrs Thatcher's Downing Street much of its special flavour. Denis had officially retired from Burmah Oil in 1975, but he still had a string of non-executive directorships as well as his drinking chums and his golfing companions. He lived his own life, as he and Margaret had always done; but he was continually in and out, and when he was there he often sat in on informal meetings – the Thursday economic breakfasts, late-night sessions with Gow and Wolfson, even her Tuesday and Thursday morning briefings before Prime Minister's Questions – contributing his views without restraint. On business matters where he had real expertise – for instance on British Leyland – she listened seriously to what he had to say. (She once said that she did not need briefing on the oil industry because 'I sleep with the oil industry every night.')[141] On other subjects he served to keep her, and her staff, in touch with what the man in the golf-club bar was thinking. Practically everyone who had anything to do with him – even his daughter Carol – confirms that he talked exactly like the 'Dear Bill' caricature in *Private Eye*, written by John Wells and Richard Ingrams. Bernard Ingham sometimes thought that Denis might almost have dictated it, while Carol felt when she was in Australia that she had only to read *Private Eye* to know what he was thinking. He really did talk of pinkoes, reptiles, 'smellysocks' and the rest.[142] He once quite seriously told the BBC's political editor John Cole, with no offence intended, that 'of course everybody at the BBC's a Trotskyist'.[143] Yet this was at least partly camouflage. Roy Jenkins, after dining at Chequers in 1979, thought Denis 'a caricature of himself in some ways' – talking of his Rolls-Royce as a 'lovely bus', for instance. At the same time he was 'not in the least afraid of her and talks freely. But he does not always talk foolishly . . . Whether he is exactly out of his depth I don't know. He is his own man, I think. He remains a moderately prosperous suburban businessman, who is perfectly self-assured with her.'[144]*

Normally Denis would go to bed long before Margaret, leaving her working. But he was also very protective and she deferred to him.

---

*In every respect bar one Denis was, in his own words, 'an honest-to-God right winger'.[145] The exception was capital punishment which, unlike his wife – perhaps because of his war experience – he consistently opposed.

There are numerous stories of Denis breaking up interminable late-night speechwriting sessions by insisting in his inimitable way that it was time she went to bed ('Woman, bed'); or reminding her, 'Honestly, love, we're not trying to write the Old Testament.'[146] At least at a superficial level he never lost the masculine authority which a husband of his class and generation expected to assert over his wife.* His interventions often came as a relief to her hard-pressed staff. For instance, quite early in her premiership, at the Lusaka Commonwealth Conference in August 1979, Denis realised that she was not taking in something that Henry James thought important. Before going to bed Denis took James aside and told him he would have a private word with her. Next morning she had got the message.[148] Willie Whitelaw was another who frequently found that a quiet word with Denis was the way to get through to her when all else failed.

In fact, living and working above the shop, with neither of them commuting any more, the Thatchers were closer in Downing Street than at any previous time in their marriage. They were both excellent hosts, and Denis was infinitely skilful at supporting and protecting Margaret, talking to those she could not (or did not want to) speak to and deflecting people who tried to monopolise her. He accompanied her on the most important of her overseas trips, and developed his role as the Prime Minister's consort with extraordinary tact and skill. Despite his well-known right-wing views and fruity vocabulary, he contrived to make considerably fewer gaffes than the Duke of Edinburgh. He stuck firmly to his policy of never giving interviews. Almost the only time he embarrassed his wife was when he used Downing Street paper to write an incautious letter to the Welsh Secretary about a planning matter. (He protested that he was writing purely as a private citizen and 10 Downing Street was, after all, his address.) For the rest, the press – particularly the travelling press accompanying the Prime Minister to international summits, who had ample opportunity to witness Denis sounding off over several stiff ones on long flights home – respected his privacy by never quoting him. 'He was off limits, out of bounds,' Bernard Ingham has written. 'Everybody loves him because he is straight and decent and loyal.'[149]

Lady Thatcher has always paid extravagant tribute to Denis' part in

---

*It could work the other way, however. Ronnie Millar recalls one time when she dragged Denis away from a party, telling him, 'If you want me to poach your egg, come *now*.'[147] Right to the end, she made a point of getting back to Downing Street if she possibly could to cook his breakfast in the morning – even though she herself had only an apple and a vitamin pill.

her career. In the early days his contribution was frankly more material than emotional: his money gave her the financial security to pursue her legal and political career. They lived very separate lives, which suited her admirably. But theirs was a rare marriage, which grew deeper the longer it went on: being the Prime Minister's consort gave him the best retirement job imaginable. He had no defined functions, but he played an important humanising role and was always on hand when required, helping to calm her when she was upset or gee her up when she was depressed. At the end of the day, as she told the 1980 party conference, 'there is just Denis and me, and I could not do without him'.[150] After she had been Prime Minister for several years he used to pretend that he wanted nothing more than that she should retire soon; but she took no notice, and it is doubtful that he expected her to. Many of her closest advisers were convinced, however, that the one thing that might have induced her to resign would have been if Denis had ever become seriously ill.

The Prime Minister and Whitehall

Mrs Thatcher hit Whitehall, in Peter Hennessy's words, 'with the force of a tornado.'[151] While many officials actually welcomed the prospect of a dynamic government which knew its own mind, and enjoyed a secure parliamentary majority, after years of drift and hand-to-mouth expediency under Labour, they were not prepared for the degree of positive hostility which the new Prime Minister exuded, and encouraged her ministers to express, towards the Civil Service as an institution. Both from her personal experience of the Department of Education and the Ministry of Pensions, and as a matter of political principle, she came into office convinced that the Civil Service bore much of the blame for Britain's decline over the past thirty-five years: that civil servants as a breed, with some individual exceptions, were not the solution to the nation's ills but a large part of the problem. She considered the public service essentially parasitic, a drag upon national enterprise and wealth-creation: too large, too bureaucratic, self-serving, self-satisfied and self-protective, corporatist by instinct, simultaneously complacent and defeatist. She was determined to cut the bureaucracy down to size, both metaphorically and literally. Word quickly spread through Whitehall that Mrs Thatcher's purpose was to 'deprivilege' the Civil Service.

The phrase was attributed to Hoskyns, but actually originated with Keith Joseph. Either way, it accurately expressed Mrs Thatcher's intention; yet while she shared the diagnosis, she did not fully accept Hoskyns' prescription. While he thought of overcoming official inertia by means of structural reform of the system of government, she had no interest in structures. 'Her job,' she let it be known even before she had won the election, 'was to turn the economy around; she was not going to muck around with the machinery of government'.[152] She was more concerned to encourage a more enterprising spirit in Whitehall by exhortation and personal example. She did not follow the route of many incoming – particularly Labour – governments and flood the departments with special advisers. On the contrary she allowed only ten, three of them in the Treasury. But she took a number of practical steps early on to make it clear that a fresh wind was blowing through the corridors of power.

First, the Civil Service was the softest target for the new government's promised economies in public spending. An immediate freeze was placed on new recruitment – one reason for discouraging special advisers – and pay levels were held down. The resentment that resulted led to an unprecedented strike which in 1981 closed down regional offices, delayed the collection of tax revenues and altogether cost the Government something like £500 million before it was settled. All those directly involved – above all Christopher Soames, the minister somewhat incongruously responsible for the Civil Service – would have liked to compromise earlier; but Mrs Thatcher was determined to make a demonstration of the Government's resolve to control public spending and believed that cutting its own pay bill was the best possible place to start.

Second, she set up an Efficiency Unit in Number Ten, headed by Sir Derek Rayner, managing director of Marks & Spencer, to scrutinise the working of every department, looking for economies. (Rayner was not a newcomer to Whitehall: Heath had used him in a somewhat similar capacity nine years earlier.) By the end of 1982 'Rayner's Raiders', as they were known, had carried out 130 of these departmental scrutinies, saving £170 million a year and 'losing' 16,000 jobs. In the first four years of the Thatcher Government Civil Service numbers were cut by 14 per cent; over the following six years, as the privatisation of nationalised industries removed whole areas of economic activity and administration from the public sector, that figure climbed to 23 per cent, while salaries relative to the private sector fell still further.[153] At the same time the core function of the service was shifted inexorably from policy advice to management: the efficient implementation of policy and the delivery of services. Senior officials who preferred writing elegantly argued memos increasingly found their time taken up by targets, performance indicators and all the other paraphernalia of modern business methods. Paradoxically Mrs Thatcher personally had little time for this sort of systems analysis when it was pressed on her by Hoskyns and Norman Strauss. The leading exponent of business-management systems within Whitehall was actually her least favourite minister, Michael Heseltine, who pioneered a system called MINIS in the Department of the Environment. Nevertheless this was where her insistent emphasis on cost-cutting and efficiency inevitably led. Rayner's Financial Management Initiative (FMI) extended a similar system to all departments in 1982; and his successor, Robin Ibbs, maintained the pressure with the 'Next Steps' programme in 1988, which resulted in the biggest shake-up of Whitehall for a generation.

For two years the Permanent Secretary of the Civil Service Department (CSD), Sir Ian Bancroft, fought 'like a tiger' to protect what he regarded as the integrity of the service. Mrs Thatcher, however, regarded Bancroft as the personification of everything she thought wrong with Whitehall. They were, as his obituarist put it, 'like chalk and cheese'.[154] In 1981 – after she had got rid of Soames – she felt strong enough to abolish the CSD, dividing its functions between the Cabinet Office and the Treasury, while Bancroft was prematurely retired. In a public lecture he charged that the Prime Minister risked destroying in a decade a public-service ethos that had taken more than a century to build.[155] That might have been true, but in identifying the public service with his own department he was defending the wrong target, since the CSD was only created by Harold Wilson in 1968 in the wake of the Fulton Report, to satisfy the empire-building of the then Permanent Secretary of the Treasury, Sir William Armstrong. By scrapping it Mrs Thatcher was merely going back to the traditional arrangement as it had been in the heyday of Sir Norman Brook.

This one piece of surgery apart, Mrs Thatcher showed little interest in structural tinkering. Unlike Wilson and Heath, both of whom had been civil servants themselves before entering politics, she was interested in outcomes, not structures. She did not believe you changed the ethos of an institution just by changing the nameplates on the door. In eleven years in Downing Street, she established only two new departments, and both of those were reversions to an earlier status quo. In 1983 she put the Trade and Industry departments (separated by Wilson in 1974) back together to recreate Heath's DTI – though it was considerably shrunk since Heath's day; and in 1988 she removed Social Security from the DHSS, where Wilson had merged it with Health in 1968, to stand once again on its own. Most important, she did not, as Hoskyns and others urged, create a Prime Minister's department. She simply retained and gradually enlarged the Number Ten

Policy Unit, and appointed special advisers to brief her personally in specific areas.

Nor did she immediately abolish Heath's most famous innovation, the Central Policy Review Staff (CPRS) – popularly known as the 'Think Tank' – though she was strongly predisposed against it. As a matter of principle she did not believe that a 'conviction Prime Minister' like herself needed a group of Whitehall's best brains to tell her what to think. 'Don't tell me what,' she had told her advisers in opposition 'I know what. Tell me how.'[156] 'A government with a firm philosophical direction,' she wrote in her memoirs, 'was inevitably a less comfortable environment for a body with a technocratic outlook.'[157] On the Monday morning after the election she lost no time in summoning the current head of the CPRS, Sir Kenneth Berrill, to justify his existence. She already knew Berrill, who had been chairman of the University Grants Commission when she was Education Secretary, and – unlike most officials she remembered from that time – she retained a favourable view of him. Nevertheless she subjected him to a fierce interrogation – he was astonished that she had already found time to read the brief he had written for her – before he managed to persuade her that it was useful for a Prime Minister to have an alternative brief to set against the departmental view.[158] Though many thought the Think Tank and the Policy Unit rivals for the same patch of turf, Hoskyns' support helped gain Berrill a reprieve. Over the next few weeks the CPRS took up a number of causes which gained Mrs Thatcher's approval: warning against increasing VAT too steeply, for instance, which she came to think was a mistake, and advocating an end to index-linking benefits. The result was that she kept it for four years, under three successive directors, focusing mainly on questions of industrial policy and the nationalised industries, before she felt confident enough to scrap it (provoking a storm of criticism) after the 1983 election.* 'I have to say,' she wrote, 'that I never missed it.'[159]

She spared the CPRS in May 1979 largely because she approved of Berrill; and that was typical of her approach to Whitehall. She was suspicious of the Civil Service as an institution, but was generous in her appreciation of those individuals who won her trust. She even formed a grudging respect for the Permanent Secretary of the Treasury, Sir Douglas Wass, an unrepentant Keynesian who had controversially made public his disbelief in monetarism in a lecture at Cambridge in 1978. Geoffrey Howe and Mrs Thatcher seriously considered replacing

---

*Berrill (1974–80) was followed by Robin Ibbs (1980–2) and John Sparrow (1982–3).

him in May 1979. Wass resisted, on the principle that permanent officials should not be removed on grounds of policy; but a new government could probably have got away with replacing a Permanent
Secretary who was publicly at odds with its central philosophy. In practice Wass was simply marginalised. The new Treasury team took the
advice they wanted from more junior officials, notably Peter Middleton,
then an under-secretary; within six months Terry Burns, a thirty-five-
year-old professor from the London Business School, was parachuted
into the Treasury as Chief Economic Adviser. But Wass prided himself
on his professionalism, and stayed on until 1983 to implement the new
orthodoxy conscientiously. Here again Mrs Thatcher was content to
work through the traditional channels and existing personnel, so long
as they did not actively obstruct her. But when he retired she denied
Wass the peerage that would normally have been his due.

She imposed her will not by structural reform or sacking people
but by sheer force of personality: by showing the Whitehall village
who was boss. One way of doing this was by constant requests for
figures or information at short notice: even quite junior officials felt
the presence of the Prime Minister continually prodding and pressing
their minister for results, never letting an issue go but demanding
'follow-through'.[160] Another way was by personally visiting every
department in turn, something no previous Prime Minister had ever
done, confronting civil servants on their own territory, questioning
their attitudes and challenging their assumptions. This alarming innovation dramatically signalled Mrs Thatcher's determination to make her
presence felt; at the same time it reflected her awareness of her inexperience of departments other than the Department of Education and
Science (DES) and her genuine desire to learn. In fact these visits had
two distinct aspects. On the one hand she was marvellous – as she had
been at the DES – at going round talking to the junior staff, taking
an interest in their work, thanking and encouraging them: something
which most ministers do far too little beyond the immediate circle of
their private office. Her encounters with their superiors, on the other
hand, were often bruising: she lectured more than she listened, and the
exercise tended to confirm rather than modify her preconceptions.

The first department she inspected was, significantly, Employment.
The visit started badly when Jim Prior, coming down in the lift to
meet her, missed her going up in another lift. (This may have been a
deliberate ploy on her part. On another occasion she tried to catch
the Civil Service department napping by arriving early; but they had
seen her coming across Horse Guards' Parade and were ready.) She
then got into an argument with one of the deputy secretaries, Donald

Derx, described by Prior in his memoirs as 'one of the best and most dedicated civil servants I have ever met':

> She insisted on picking an argument without knowing the facts or the legal position on secondary industrial action. Even when Patrick Mayhew intervened in utter frustration she still wouldn't stop. It ended by Donald Derx saying, 'Prime Minister, do you really want to know the facts?'[161]

Derx's career never recovered from this impertinence. When Alan Clark arrived at the department as a junior minister four years later, 'the wretched Donald Derx' was still a deputy secretary but about to take early retirement, 'having "had it conveyed to him" that he will never make Permanent Secretary'. Largely as a result of this episode, Clark found his officials still 'completely terrified' of the Prime Minister – 'and with good reason'.[162]

Clark wrote that Mrs Thatcher had marked Derx's card; and this was literally what she did. When she visited the Department of Trade she sat the Permanent Secretary and his five deputies on one side of the table, with herself, John Nott and his team of ministers on the other side. Cecil Parkinson, one of the junior ministers, noted how she proceeded:

> She asked each of them in turn to give a description of what they and the part of the department they were responsible for did and what its immediate objectives were. After each had spoken I noticed that she was putting three dots under some names and a line under others. I came to the conclusion the line meant good and three dots meant suspect.[163]

As word of these encounters spread it was not surprising that the departments looked forward to these visits with 'fear and trembling' – none more so than the Department of Education, where her former private secretary David Tanner, now the under-secretary in charge of science, was well aware of her reputation for reducing officials to 'blubbering jelly'. To his relief, however, the DES was the department she felt least need to visit. She did not get round to it until 1983, by which time Keith Joseph was Secretary of State; more than most ministers he was able to protect his officials from her inquisition.[164]

Her most bruising confrontation was with all the Permanent Secretaries together at a never-to-be-forgotten dinner in May 1980, just a year after Mrs Thatcher came to power. It was instigated, with the best of intentions, by Willie Whitelaw as an opportunity to mend some of the fences damaged by the impact of her first twelve months. Unfortunately the two sides approached the occasion with very different understandings. The Permanent Secretaries thought it was a chance for them to make some points to the Prime Minister. Mrs Thatcher, on the contrary, seized the opportunity to give the assembled Sir Humphreys a collective wigging. After a short pep talk on the theme of national revival, she invited questions; but the mandarins' courteously phrased concerns seemed to her carping and critical. Sir Ian Bancroft led off and, in the words of one witness, 'absolutely blew it'. He was followed by Sir Peter Baldwin of the Department of Transport, an old Treasury hand who had served in the Cabinet Office under Macmillan; and by Sir James Hamilton of the DES, another of her *bétes noires*. The Prime Minister was hyped up, the only woman among three dozen men whom she identified collectively as the enemy, and consequently at her most aggressive. It happened to be soon after the Special Air Service had stormed the Iranian Embassy to free hostages captured by terrorists. When the Permanent Secretary of the Ministry of Defence, Sir Frank Cooper, left the room to go to the lavatory, Sir Lawrence Airey (Second Permanent Secretary at the Treasury) murmured to his neighbour that he had gone for the SAS to get them all out. Mrs Thatcher heard the remark and was not amused. Airey was soon afterwards packed off to replace her old antagonist Bill Pile as chairman of the Board of Inland Revenue.

Thirteen years later Mrs Thatcher recalled that evening as 'one of the most dismal occasions of my entire time in government'. She was ready for a frank exchange of views; but the Permanent Secretaries served up 'such a menu of complaints and negative attitudes' that she was never tempted to hold such a gathering again.[165] Instead she continued gradually weeding the service of those she considered uncooperative. Over the next decade it was often alleged that she 'politicised' Whitehall by appointing only committed Thatcherites to senior positions. But she was not so crude as that. Mrs Thatcher certainly took a close interest in appointments and intervened more directly than previous Prime Ministers in filling vacancies, not just at Permanent Secretary level but further down the official ladder. She undoubtedly advanced the careers of her favourites, sometimes those who had caught her eye with a single well-judged briefing; conversely she sidetracked or held back those who failed to impress her. Thus the longer she stayed in office, the more she was able to mould the Civil Service to her liking. By 1986 the entire upper echelons of Whitehall were filled by her appointees: in that time she appointed forty-three Permanent

Secretaries and 138 Deputy Secretaries. But her criteria for promotion were more personal than ideological. She favoured energetic, positive characters who shared her belief that problems existed to be solved, ahead of more sceptical temperaments who – in her scornful view – sought only 'the orderly management of decline'.[166] Second, she believed in promoting younger candidates from lower down the hierarchy, often bypassing those whom Whitehall custom considered next in line. Political allegiance, narrowly defined, scarcely came into it.

There was nothing wrong in principle with this approach: quite the contrary. It was natural for a radical Prime Minister to want activist officials who would help, not hinder or obstruct. Most of the more unconventional choices Mrs Thatcher made were excellent appointments, fully merited: among them Peter Middleton, appointed Permanent Secretary to the Treasury at the age of forty-nine, in preference to the internally favoured candidate; Clive Whitmore, aged forty-eight, appointed straight from her private office to head the Ministry of Defence; Michael Quinlan to head the Department of Employment in 1983; Terry Heiser to the Department of the Environment in 1985. But questions did arise about her judgement, particularly lower down the scale: her instant estimates of people – those lines or dots under their names – were not always accurate or fair. Officials often felt that she made up her mind about individuals on first impression (sometimes going back to 1970–4) and then never changed it: Permanent Secretaries became concerned to shield from her wrath excellent public servants whom they feared she might take against. She did not always appreciate that it was sometimes the civil servant's job to raise objections. In her memoirs Lady Thatcher boasted: 'I was never accused of thinking like a civil servant. They had to think like me.'[167] Conversely it was not the official's job to think like a politician. It was only in this sense, however, that she could be accused of 'politicising' the service. Even after ten years, Peter Hennessy wrote, 'the Prime Minister ... would ... find it hard to muster a true believer from the top three grades of the Civil Service.'[168] Really what she did over the next eleven years was to personalise it. Nevertheless there is no doubt that the effect was seriously to demoralise it.

2

Signals of Intent

The economy

The new Parliament met on Wednesday 9 May to re-elect the Speaker, so that Mrs Thatcher's first words in the House as Prime Minister were a purely formal tribute to the 'humanity, warmth . . . and unfailing patient humour' of George Thomas – though she also took the opportunity to pay tribute to Airey Neave.[1] But the House did not meet again for serious business until the State Opening the following Tuesday, with the formal unveiling of the Government's legislative programme in the Queen's Speech.

It comprised a curiously modest assortment of Bills, since the radical thrust of the Government's agenda was not primarily legislative. There was – there had to be, after the events of the previous winter – a measure of trade-union reform; and an undertaking to scale down the interventionist powers of Labour's National Enterprise Board. Legislation was announced to oblige local authorities to sell council houses, and to lift (just as the Heath Government had done in 1970) the obligation on local education authorities to submit schemes for comprehensive schools. Though these were all long-standing Tory policies, they did not herald the start of a counter-revolution. In addition the Government announced tighter immigration controls, the deregulation of inter-city coach services and the establishment of a second commercial television channel.

As usual, however, Mrs Thatcher's language implied a good deal more than the Gracious Speech actually promised. While noting the continuity with Ted Heath's aborted 'Selsdon' agenda, the Labour left-winger Tony Benn thought her speech introducing the Government's programme 'the most rumbustious, rampaging right-wing speech that I've heard from the Government Front Bench in the whole of my

46

life'.[2]★ Contradicting Callaghan, who complacently predicted that the period of Tory rule would be 'a brief interruption' before Labour resumed its forward march, and the Liberal leader David Steel, who reminded her that she had won the lowest share of the poll of any postwar Conservative Government, Mrs Thatcher hailed her victory as 'a watershed election' which marked a decisive rejection of 'the all-powerful corporatist state'. In its place she promised to restore incentives and individual choice, particularly in housing, health and education. Where once she had been sceptical about selling council houses, she now saw the right to buy as one of those things 'so fundamental that they must apply to all citizens regardless of the local authority area in which they live'. The Government was taking power to force reluctant Labour authorities to sell their housing stock because 'we believe that the right to buy council houses should belong to everyone'. She also warned that 'there is no such thing as a free service in the Health Service'.

Significantly, she dealt with the trade-union question under the heading of law and order. Yet she was careful – as she had been throughout the election – not to be provocative. She still went out of her way to stress that 'a strong and responsible trade union movement must play a large part in our economic recovery.'[3] 'I am not confronting anyone,' she declared during her first Prime Minister's Questions a week later. 'I hope that they are not confronting me, either.' Perhaps fearing that she had been too conciliatory, however, she emphasised her personal commitment to action on union reform. 'I am not known for my purposes or policies being unclear,' she assured a backbench questioner. 'I believe that my policies on this are known.' She believed that they were 'overwhelmingly supported by the vast majority of people in this country, who believe that a law must be introduced to deal with certain aspects of the closed shop, picketing and the postal ballot'.[4] To the disappointment of the Tory right, however, Jim Prior's Employment Bill, when it was eventually published at the end of the year, turned out to be a very cautious measure. While she hinted at her sympathy for the hardliners behind Prior's back, Mrs Thatcher had no wish to plunge into battle with the unions before she was ready. All the Government's initial energy was concentrated on setting a new course for the economy. Howe's first budget was fixed for the earliest possible date, 12 June, just five weeks after the election.

★In January 1970 the Conservative Shadow Cabinet had met for a weekend at the Selsdon Park Hotel in Surrey where they were widely (though erroneously) believed to have adopted a programme of radical free-market policies.

The first objective was quite clear. The Prime Minister and her inner group of economic ministers were determined to mount an immediate assault on public spending. But this was a goal easier to proclaim in opposition than to realise in government. On taking office, ministers found their room for major economies seriously constrained – partly by inescapable external factors, but also by their own political choices. On the one hand the value of sterling, already high due to the recent tripling of the price of oil (since sterling was now a petro-currency), was boosted further by the weakness of the dollar and the markets' satisfaction at the Government's election. The high pound sharply increased the cost of British exports, creating unemployment, which swelled the social security budget while reducing revenue. But at the same time ministers had tied their own hands by commitments they had made during the election.

The most avoidable of these was the promise to honour public-sector pay awards made by the pay comparability commission set up by the Labour Government during the 'Winter of Discontent'. Chaired by Professor Hugh Clegg of the University of Warwick, its brief was to ensure comparable remuneration to groups of public-sector workers who lacked the industrial muscle of the train drivers and electricity workers. This ran directly counter to the Tories' intention to abandon any form of incomes policy, as well as their determination to cut the public-sector pay bill. But when Callaghan called the election, Clegg had just started looking at the pay of local authority and university manual workers, NHS ancillary workers, ambulance staff, nurses and midwives. Mrs Thatcher was persuaded by Prior and Peter Thorneycroft that the Tories must undertake to honour whatever pay award he recommended. Years later Howe still maintained that the decision was electorally unavoidable. Had they refused, he believed, 'it would have produced a sense of revulsion so shattering that it would have made progress impossible'.[5] But honouring Clegg turned out much more expensive than they had reckoned – the more so since they kept his commission in being for another year. Pay settlements continued to run well ahead of inflation. Though in principle utterly opposed to any form of pay restraint, statutory or voluntary – 'because I believe that it is far better for people to be faced with the consequences of their own wage claims than to try to save them from them' – Mrs Thatcher nevertheless in her first weeks in office twice refused to rule out a total freeze if it was the only way to cut the public-sector wage bill. Challenged by David Steel to say how she could rule out the one but not the other, she replied crisply: 'Natural caution and good financial instinct'.[6]

Several other expensive commitments, on the other hand, reflected the Prime Minister's deepest convictions. In opposition the Iron Lady had lived up to her reputation by supporting NATO's request for an extra 3 per cent annual spending on defence. Once in office, Howe tried to row back from this pledge, but Mrs Thatcher was immovable: in her book, strong defence took precedence over everything else, even cutting public spending. Likewise she had promised substantial pay rises to the armed forces and the police; and the Tory manifesto also committed the new Government to increase old-age pensions. Finally Patrick Jenkin as Shadow Health Secretary had bounced Howe into promising that spending on the NHS would be protected for at least three years. All these undertakings left very little scope for the sort of big savings the Prime Minister and Chancellor were looking for. As Mrs Thatcher wrote in her memoirs: 'We seemed to be boxed in.'[7]

In fact Howe squeezed £1.5 billion from a variety of soft targets. Civil Service recruitment was frozen and tough limits imposed on local government spending. Prescription charges were raised for the first time in eight years from twenty pence to forty-five pence, foreshadowing virtually annual increases for the next decade. Cuts were announced in the provision of school meals and rural school transport. Most significantly, though the basic old-age pension was increased in the short term, the long-term link between pensions and average earnings was broken – a major saving in the future. Another projected £1 billion was saved by imposing cash limits on departmental budgets; and a further billion by selling shares in public-sector assets, following the lead already set by Labour and condemned by the Conservatives in opposition. This saving of £3.5 billion announced in the June budget was quickly followed by a further £680 million package in October, made up of more Civil Service cuts and steep rises in gas and electricity prices.

These economies were designed to make room for dramatic tax cuts. In the end Howe was able to cut the standard rate of income tax by three pence in the pound, from 33 per cent to 30 per cent, and reduce the top rate from Labour's penal 83 per cent to a more moderate 60 per cent. This was a bold early signal of the new Government's intentions. But it was made possible only by virtually doubling Value Added Tax (VAT). It had always been part of the Tories' strategy to switch a greater proportion of the burden from direct to indirect taxation. But during the election Howe specifically denied that he planned to double VAT. In the event he could not finance the income-tax cuts he was determined on in any other way. Mrs Thatcher was very worried by the drastic impact that such a steep hike would have on prices.

With inflation already rising, she had reason to be worried: however long planned, it was the worst possible moment for such a switch. In his memoirs Howe wryly noted 'the ambivalence which Margaret often showed when the time came to move from the level of high principle and evangelism to practical politics'.[8] Nigel Lawson wrote more bluntly that she was 'fearful' of the political fallout, 'but Geoffrey persuaded her that if we did not grasp this nettle in the first budget it would never be grasped at all'.[9] For her part Lady Thatcher acknowledged that 'Geoffrey stuck to his guns' and overcame her doubts.[10] He kept within the letter of his election disclaimer by setting a new single rate of 15 per cent, where previously there had been two tiers of 8 and 12.5 per cent. But this – the first really unpopular decision the Government had to take, within three weeks of taking office – was not the last time that a cautious Prime Minister had to be hauled over the hurdle by her more resolute colleagues.

Another instance was the abolition of exchange controls. This was arguably the single most important step the Thatcher Government took to give practical effect to its belief in free markets: by doing away with the restrictions on the movement of capital which had been in place since 1939, the Government dared to expose the British economy to the judgement of the global market. It was an act of faith which might have resulted in a catastrophic run on sterling. In the event it had the opposite effect: the markets were impressed by the new Government's show of confidence and the pound, already strong, dipped only momentarily and then went on rising. In her memoirs Lady Thatcher claimed personal credit for this leap of faith, writing scornfully of City experts who were apprehensive: 'Not every capitalist,' she boasted, 'had my confidence in capitalism.'[11] The truth is that while she certainly believed in the principle, she was the last to be persuaded that it was prudent to press ahead so quickly.[12] She acquiesced readily enough to Howe announcing the first stage in his June budget; but she was nervous about going the whole way in October – 'It would be unwise to go too far too fast,' she told the Commons in July[13] – and she contrived to distance herself from the decision in a way that was to become familiar. 'On your own head be it, Geoffrey, if anything goes wrong.' Howe later wrote that the abolition of controls was 'the only economic decision of my life that ever caused me to lose a night's sleep. But it was right.'[14]

In the long run it undoubtedly was; and it was brave to take the decision in the first few months in office. But in the short run it played havoc with the Government's monetary policy. Controlling the money supply was supposed to be the lynchpin of the Government's new monetarist approach. The trouble was that Labour had already been controlling it very effectively before the election. Denis Healey and the Permanent Secretary of the Treasury, Douglas Wass, were not ideological monetarists like Joseph, Howe and Lawson, who had embraced monetarism with quasi-religious certainty: they were 'reluctant monetarists' who had pragmatically concluded – at the prompting of the International Monetary Fund (IMF) – that tight monetary targets were a necessary part of economic policy. In practice, therefore, monetary policy did not change in May 1979 so dramatically as either Labour or the Government liked to pretend. When Healey denounced Tory policies it sometimes suited Mrs Thatcher to remind the House that 'the previous Labour Chancellor was more of a monetarist than he now cares to admit'.[15] Howe's June budget announced a marginal tightening of Labour's target for monetary growth, measured by £M3, from a range of 8–12 per cent to 7–11 per cent per annum.* But the effect of abolishing exchange controls, on top of the unstoppable rise in Government borrowing, soon rendered this target unattainable. Before long Howe's monetary targets were actually higher than Healey's – and the Government was still not meeting them.

Howe's first Budget was a bold statement of political intent, taking a huge gamble on early tax cuts at the risk of inflation. 'Either she succeeds,' the *Daily Mirror* commented, 'or we go bust.'[16] It was 'a dogmatically anti-egalitarian budget', the *Observer* commented, 'a race track without escape roads' which left the Government 'with very little alternative but to go for a Grand Slam in spades on their freemarket, incentives, no rescue of lame ducks philosophy. That was doubtless the corner into which Mrs Thatcher wished to box herself and her colleagues . . . The reserve hope must be that, if the present policy becomes impossible, Mrs Thatcher has colleagues who know how to guide her on the long road back.'[17] It was taken for granted that though Howe held up the dispatch box outside Number Eleven, the political will had come from Number Ten. Though the truth was quite the opposite, Mrs Thatcher was reported to have insisted on a bigger tax cut than the expenditure savings warranted and on a steeper rise in VAT than her Chancellor had wanted. In the Commons, Denis Healey – the roles in his long duel with Howe now reversed – labelled it 'a she-wolf's budget in sheep's clothing'.[18] While Labour's criticism was predictable, Enoch Powell was also unimpressed, accusing the Government of 'trying to have their cake before they have baked it'. He disapproved of the switch from direct to indirect taxation and even

---

*£M3 measures the amount of money in circulation, including bank deposits.

denied one of Mrs Thatcher's central beliefs – that tax cuts were an incentive to work harder: two reminders that Thatcherism was not at all the same as Powellism.[19]

Altogether the impact of Howe's June budget was as damaging as its critics predicted. The virtual doubling of VAT and the cutting of subsidy to the nationalised industries, along with the ending of pay and dividend controls and John Nott's swift abolition of the Price Commission, added 6 per cent to the Retail Price Index almost overnight, leading inevitably to large compensating pay claims, while the income-tax cuts boosted consumption and further fuelled inflation that way. For a Government that had come into office proclaiming the conquest of inflation as its first priority, this was a perverse beginning. Inflation actually doubled from 10.3 per cent to 21.9 per cent in the first year. As industry laid off workers under the impact of the high pound, benefit payments had to keep pace with inflation, while Government revenue fell. Set against these rising commitments, Howe's two packages of spending cuts were insufficient to dent the inexorable rise in Government borrowing. The Government's only other means of curbing the growth of money was raising interest rates. Howe had already raised the minimum lending rate (MLR) from 12 to 14 per cent in June. He warned that it would not fall until the money supply and public-sector borrowing were under control; but this only caused more money to flow into London. Instead of falling, £M3 actually rose by 14 per cent in four months between June and October. In November Howe was obliged to hike the lending rate another three points to 17 per cent – an unprecedented rise to an unprecedented level. Thinking more of the effect on mortgages than of the cost to industry, Mrs Thatcher hated having to do this. 'It bothered me enormously,' she told Patricia Murray. 'It really was devastating.'[20] But monetarism prescribed no other remedy, so she bit the bullet. 'We would not print money,' she insisted at Prime Minister's Questions; therefore 'it was necessary to raise interest rates to conquer inflation'.[21] Thus the Government got the worst of both worlds: its first actions were simultaneously too much and too little, painful enough to raise howls of fury from industry, unions, homeowners, educationists and others, yet ineffective in cutting spending and positively counterproductive with regard to inflation. Mrs Thatcher and her economic team had come into office with a doctrinaire prescription which they proceeded to apply, undeterred by the most unfavourable economic circumstances. After a few months of rising unemployment, rising inflation and record interest rates, the Government's monetarist experiment was already widely dismissed as a dogmatic folly.

This, however, was where the composition of the Cabinet prevented any loss of purpose. The central quintet of Mrs Thatcher, Howe, Joseph, Nott and Biffen was firmly in control of economic policy. Sceptics like Prior, Peter Walker, Ian Gilmour and Michael Heseltine first learned of the abolition of exchange controls when they read it in the newspapers.[22] Prior complacently believed that 'the Treasury team were out of their depth' and took it for granted that the damage being done to British industry would rapidly bring them to their senses.[23] While individual ministers fought more or less successfully to defend their own budgets, it was too soon for any concerted rebellion. The most unflinching doctrinaire was Geoffrey Howe, whom Hoskyns considered 'the best thinker in the Cabinet' and the most interested in pursuing a long-term strategy.[24] It is clear from the memoirs of both Howe and Lawson, and the recollections of Nott and Biffen, that if any one of the central directorate faltered in the early days it was the Prime Minister herself. Not that her sense of purpose faltered. Relentlessly every Tuesday and Thursday in the House of Commons and in radio and television interviews she reiterated the simple message that the country must learn to live within its means, that public expenditure must be cut to a level the wealth-producing taxpayer could support, that the Government must tax and spend less of the national income.[25] Publicly she never weakened; but she was always vividly conscious of the political risks. It was the Chancellor, intellectually stiffened by Lawson, who stubbornly put his head down and got on with what he was determined must be done. The Prime Minister's function, quite properly, was to be the last to be persuaded that each course of action – doubling VAT, abolishing exchange controls, scrapping the Price Commission or raising interest rates – was both necessary and politically practicable. In her memoirs, despite their later differences, she paid due tribute to Howe's tenacity: 'In my view these were his best political years.'[26] In truth she could not have done without him. Though their relationship deteriorated later, for these first two or three years of the Thatcher Government they made a formidable combination, perhaps the most successful Prime Minister–Chancellor partnership of the century.

First steps in foreign policy

It was really after Howe moved to the Foreign Office in June 1983 that their relationship deteriorated. By that time – after the Falklands war and with the assurance of a second term in front of her – Mrs Thatcher's self-confidence in foreign affairs had grown and she was ready to be her own Foreign Secretary. In 1979, by contrast, she was conscious of her relative lack of experience and was content to leave foreign policy largely to Lord Carrington. This was a surprising abdication, since one of her prime ambitions was to restore Britain's 'greatness' in the eyes of the world. As a schoolgirl back in Grantham in the 1930s, following the darkening European crisis under her father's tutelage, it was foreign affairs much more than economics which had first fired her interest in politics. Her hero, then and ever since, was Winston Churchill. Since 1945 Soviet Russia had replaced Nazi Germany as the evil enemy to be stood up to and defeated. But like Churchill she had a clear view of Britain's place as America's foremost ally in the global battle against Communism, and she regarded the Foreign Office as a nest of appeasers, superciliously devoted to promoting their own defeatist view of international affairs instead of advancing Britain's national interest. For her first sixteen years after entering Parliament in 1959 her energies had been almost exclusively diverted to domestic responsibilities: pensions, energy, transport and education. On becoming Leader of the Opposition in 1975, however, she had quickly made up this deficit, marking her arrival on the world stage by launching a series of uncompromising verbal assaults on the Soviet Union. For four years she had avoided appointing a shadow Foreign Secretary with the authority to make the portfolio his own, but travelled tirelessly in parliamentary recesses to educate herself and meet the leaders she hoped to have to deal with in office.

Once elected, however, she recognised that she could not do everything. Her priority was the economy. Moreover she believed that restoring British influence abroad depended essentially on restoring the economy at home. 'A nation in debt,' she told the House soon after becoming party leader, 'has no self-respect and precious little influence.'[27] For all these reasons she told her aides that she did not intend to waste her time on 'all this international stuff'.[28] In appointing Peter Carrington as her first Foreign Secretary, with Ian Gilmour his deputy in the Commons, she made a tacit concordat to leave the detail of foreign policy to them, while Carrington in return suppressed his doubts about her economic policy.

In fact she soon found that there was a crowded calendar of international meetings which she was bound to attend: European councils, G7 summits (attended by the leaders of the seven leading industrial nations) and Commonwealth conferences. That first summer there was one of each, respectively in Strasbourg, Tokyo and Lusaka. She confessed to Patricia Murray in 1980 that she had been 'surprised at the amount of time we actually have to spend on foreign affairs. The amount of summitry we have now is terrific.'[29] At first she was nervous – though she was careful not to show it. Conscious of her inexperience, she felt patronised by senior European leaders like the West German Chancellor Helmut Schmidt – her first foreign visitor in Downing Street just a few days after the election – and the French President, Valéry Giscard d'Estaing, who treated her with patrician disdain which stopped barely short of outright rudeness. She did her homework more anxiously than ever, only to find that they were much less well briefed than she was. Her self-confidence visibly increased as she discovered that with the Rolls-Royce machine of the despised Foreign Office behind her, she was more than a match for any of them.[30]

By chance one of her first meetings was with the Soviet leadership. The Soviet Union was one major country she had not visited in opposition, preferring to denounce the Communist menace from the safety of Kensington Town Hall. But on her way to the Tokyo summit at the end of June her plane made a refuelling stop in Moscow. To her surprise Prime Minister Kosygin, with half the Politburo, came out for an unscheduled dinner in the airport lounge. They were reported to be 'very curious' to meet the famous 'Iron Lady' who wore their intended insult as a badge of pride. 'They were absolutely mesmerised by her,' Lord Carrington recalled, 'because . . . she was very direct with them.'

> She wasn't in the least overawed by Mr Kosygin and all the hier-archy of the Soviet Union . . . She just abruptly told them what she thought, and asked them questions, and said, 'No, I don't agree. I think that's absolutely wrong.' They were mesmerised by this.[31]

She questioned them specifically on the plight of the Vietnamese 'boat people' – refugees from Communist persecution who had taken to the sea in a perilous effort to reach Hong Kong – and was unim-pressed by their answers. This brief stopover confirmed her contempt for the moral and intellectual bankruptcy of the Soviet system, without in the least diminishing her perception of the challenge it posed to the West.

In retirement Lady Thatcher prided herself on her undiplomatic style: 'Certainly diplomacy wasn't my forte,' she boasted on television. 'It was the policy which was right for Britain which was my forte. I spoke with a directness, a truth and a strength to which they [the Foreign Office] were not used.' The Foreign Office, she believed, was all about negotiation and compromise; whereas she was about standing up for Britain's interests.[32] As usual the truth was somewhat less clearcut than her self-serving mythology. Sir Nicholas Henderson – Ambassador to the United States from 1979 to 1982 – noted in 1981 that 'she has acquired enough of the laudatory humbug necessary to keep international wheels turning, however much she likes to criticise the Foreign Office for wetness'.[33] Nevertheless, as Carrington recalled, 'distrust of the FO . . . was never far from the surface, and could erupt in impatient hostility unless ably countered'.[34]

Ably countered it usually was: this was Carrington's great skill. Certainly they had their rows. But better than anyone else in her first Cabinet he knew how to handle the Prime Minister. For all her belief in meritocracy, Mrs Thatcher had a curious weakness for a genuine toff; and the sixth Baron Carrington was the real thing. Though a close colleague of Ted Heath, who personified many of the attitudes of the Establishment she most despised, Carrington's hereditary peerage gave him a special immunity: unlike the other Heathites in the Cabinet he posed no threat to her leadership. At the nadir of her popularity in 1981 there was actually a flurry of speculation that he might renounce his peerage to challenge her; but Carrington firmly quashed the idea.[35] He was delighted to get the Foreign Office and had no greater ambition. Moreover he was effortlessly charming, undeferential and irreverent: he made her laugh. Sometimes when she was inclined to lecture visiting foreign leaders without drawing breath, he would pass her a note saying 'He's come 500 miles, let him say something.' Once, with the Chinese leader, Chairman Hua, the situation was reversed: it was Mrs Thatcher who could not get a word in as Hua talked non-stop for fifty minutes. So Carrington passed her a note saying, 'You are speaking too much, as usual.' 'Luckily,' he recalled, 'she had a handkerchief – she held it in front of her face and didn't laugh too much.'[36] The episode became part of Foreign Office mythology; but none of her subsequent Foreign Secretaries would have dared to tease her in this way. One junior minister saw their relationship as almost flirtatious. Mrs Thatcher matched Carrington's charm with calculated charm of her own, until he would get the giggles and she won the trick.[37]

Whatever her general intentions, there was one central area of foreign policy where Mrs Thatcher was always going to take the lead. She came into office determined to restore Britain's credentials as America's most reliable ally in the war against Soviet expansionism. That central ideological struggle was the global reflection of her mission to turn back socialism at home. Although in practice she was quickly drawn into two major foreign-policy questions in other spheres – the acrimonious quarrel over Britain's contribution to the European Community budget and the long-running saga of Rhodesia – these were to her mind subordinate sideshows to the overarching imperative of the Cold War. Accordingly she was keen to visit Washington as soon as possible to forge a special relationship with President Jimmy Carter.

Mrs Thatcher's premiership overlapped so closely with the presidency of her Republican soulmate Ronald Reagan that it is easily forgotten that Reagan was not elected President until November 1980. For her first twenty months in Downing Street Mrs Thatcher had to deal with his very different Democratic predecessor. She had met Jimmy Carter once, when visiting Washington in 1977; but US Presidents do not have much time for opposition leaders, and Carter and his National Security Adviser Zbigniew Brzezinski had enjoyed particularly good relations with Callaghan. They met again at the G7 summit in Tokyo in June, when Carter was not altogether impressed. 'A tough lady,' he wrote in his diary, 'highly opinionated, strong willed, cannot admit that she doesn't know something.'[38] After this encounter the State Department put Mrs Thatcher off until December. Before she left Carrington privately 'doubted whether Mrs Thatcher would become great buddies with President Carter'.[39] In fact, they got on better than he expected. As she later wrote, 'it was impossible not to like Jimmy Carter'. He was a more serious man than his rather folksy manner suggested – 'a deeply committed Christian and a man of obvious sincerity', with a scientific background and a grasp of detail equal to her own. Though in retrospect she was scathing about his 'poor handle on economics' and what she saw as weakness in the face of Soviet expansionism, he was the leader of the free world and she was determined to get on with him.[40]★

She arrived in Washington six weeks after the seizure of fifty American diplomats in Teheran. It was a measure of her early uncertainty that she initially intended to say nothing about the prolonged hostage crisis, feeling that to do so would be to intrude on a private American agony. Carrington and Frank Cooper had to tell her that the Americans were interested in nothing else at that moment: she must give them unequivocal support. She agreed only reluctantly ('Margaret, you have got to say yes. You have got to,' Carrington urged her). But then, once persuaded, she came out with a 'clarion call' on the White House lawn which instantly confirmed the impact she had made on her first visit to Washington as leader in 1975:

★White House drafts of Carter's speech of welcome suggest that a wry appreciation of her character had gone before her. 'As Charles Dickens said of someone in the *Pickwick Papers*,' the President was due to toast her, 'She knows wot's wot, she does.' Whether he actually said it is not recorded.[41]

At times like these you are entitled to look to your friends for support. We are your friends, we do support you. And we shall support you. Let there be no doubt about that.[42]

'The effect was like a trumpet blast of cheer to a government and people badly in need of reassurance from their allies,' the British Ambassador, Sir Nicholas Henderson, recorded.[43] The rest of her visit was a triumph. On Henderson's advice she was carefully non-polemical in her conversations with Carter; but then, addressing Congress, she threw off all restraint and wowed her audience with a ten-minute 'harangue' on the virtues of the free market and the evil of communism, followed by questions which she handled with an informality and relish the like of which Washington had never seen before from a visiting leader. More than one Congressman invited her to accept the Republican nomination for President. She went on the next day to address an audience of 2,000 at the Foreign Policy Association in New York, where the directness of her message again made a tremendous hit. The Russians, she boasted, had called her the Iron Lady: 'They're quite right – I am.'[44] In that moment – a year before Reagan entered the White House – Margaret Thatcher became a heroine to the American right.

Ten days later the Soviet Union invaded Afghanistan. In her memoirs Lady Thatcher described this action as 'one of those genuine watersheds which are so often predicted, which so rarely occur'. She immediately saw the invasion as bearing out her warnings of worldwide Soviet expansionism, part of a pattern with Cuban and East German intervention in Angola and Namibia, all taking advantage of the West's gullible belief in *détente*. She was determined that the Russians must be 'punished for their aggression and taught, albeit belatedly, that the West would not only talk about freedom but was prepared to make sacrifices to defend it'.[45] On this occasion Carter needed no prompting. When he rang her at Chequers three days after Christmas he likened the Soviet action to their invasion of Czechoslovakia in 1968. 'In effect Moscow had changed a buffer nation into a puppet nation under Soviet direction,' he told her. 'This would have profound strategic consequences for the stability of the entire region . . . He did not think we could let the Soviets get away with this intervention with impunity.' Mrs Thatcher agreed, 'and observed that when something like this occurred it was important to act right at the beginning'.[46] She quickly pledged British support for economic and cultural sanctions to punish the invader. In particular they agreed that the best way to hurt the Russians would be a western boycott of the forthcoming Moscow

Olympics. To her fury, however, she found that this was something she could not deliver. While the United States Olympic Committee did stay away from Moscow the following summer, most British athletes declined to give up their medal hopes at the behest of the Prime Minister. As Enoch Powell pointedly reminded her, Britain was a free country: 'the citizen is perfectly free to do what the law does not forbid.'[47] The junior minister charged with trying to bully them into conformity, Douglas Hurd, later recalled that 'of all the things that I was asked to do as Minister of State that was the only one that struck me at the time and strikes me now as deeply foolish'.[48]

More seriously she discovered that her call for a resolute response to the Soviet action was not supported by the rest of Europe. The invasion of Afghanistan sharply highlighted the gulf between American and European perceptions of the Cold War. The Europeans, particularly the Germans, had always gained more tangible benefits from *détente*, in the form of trade and cross-border co-operation, than the Americans and British, and were anxious not to jeopardise them. They were disinclined to view the Soviet action as part of a strategy of world domination, but rather as an understandable response to Iranian-type Islamic fundamentalism on their southern border. Mrs Thatcher's instincts were strongly with the Americans; but to Washington's disappointment she proved unable to deliver concerted European backing for significant sanctions.*

'The Bloody British Question'

If Mrs Thatcher could not bring her European partners with her on Afghanistan, this was partly because she had already antagonised them over Britain's contribution to the Community budget. This was a matter she could not possibly leave to the Foreign Office, combining as it did her two favourite themes of patriotism and good housekeeping. It was exactly the sort of issue on which she thought the Foreign Office liable to give up vital British interests for the sake of being good Europeans. It offered a wonderful early opportunity to be seen battling for Britain on the international stage, cheered on by the tabloid press, on a simple issue that every voter could understand. At a time when the economy was already proving intractable, Europe offered a much more popular cause in which to display her determination not to

---

*Washington did not always distinguish as clearly as she would have liked between her strength and the reluctance of the rest of Europe. 'Zbig,' Carter scribbled on one memo from his National Security Adviser in January 1980, 'UK and other European reactions to SU/Afghan situation are *very* weak. J.'[49]

compromise, and she seized it with relish. It took five years before she finally achieved a satisfactory settlement. The long battle helped set the style of her premiership. It also got her relationship with the European Community off to a bad start from which it never recovered.

There is no dispute that there was a genuine problem, left over from the original terms of Britain's entry to the Community negotiated by Ted Heath in 1971 and not resolved by Callaghan's essentially cosmetic renegotiation in 1974–5. The fundamental imbalance derived from the fact that Britain continued to import more than other members from outside the Community, so paying more in import levies, while having a much smaller farming sector, and consequently gaining much less benefit from the Common Agricultural Policy (CAP). Over the past decade Britain's growth had fallen behind that of other countries, so the budget contribution fixed in 1971 had become disproportionately high. By 1980 Britain was paying about £1,000 million a year more into the Community than she was getting out.

The existence of an imbalance was recognised in Brussels. Callaghan and his Foreign Secretary, David Owen, had been making efforts to correct it; but Labour was handicapped by its history of hostility to the Community. The election of a Conservative Government with a more positive attitude to Europe was expected to make agreement easier. Callaghan exaggerated when he told the House of Commons: 'We took the shine off the ball, and it is now for her to hit the runs.'[50] But with goodwill it should not have been difficult, by the normal processes of Community bargaining, to achieve an equitable adjustment without a bruising confrontation. The Foreign Office would have considered a rebate of about two-thirds both satisfactory and achievable.[51] It was the heads of government on both sides of the Channel – Mrs Thatcher on one side, but equally Schmidt and Giscard on the other – who played to their domestic galleries and elevated the issue into a trial of political strength.

By chance the first overseas leader to visit London the week after the British election was Helmut Schmidt. Their talks in Downing Street actually went quite well. Though he was supposed to be a socialist, Mrs Thatcher approved of his sound economic views, while Schmidt in turn told the Bundestag (a touch patronisingly) that he was impressed by her 'knowledge, authority and responsibility'.[52] But she left the German Chancellor in no doubt that she regarded Britain's present budget contribution as unacceptable and intended to seek a rebate. That was quite right and proper; but she soon struck a discordant note by talking truculently about getting 'our' money back, as though the Community had stolen it, and declaring that she was not going to be 'a soft touch', as though her European partners were a bunch of con-men.[53] This sort of talk went down badly in Paris, Bonn and Brussels, because it showed a fundamental failure to understand how the Community worked.

First of all, the Community did not recognise the concept of 'her' money; funds contributed by each member country belonged to the Community, to be expended by the Commission for the benefit of the Community as a whole. The idea of each member keeping a profit-and-loss account was strictly *non-communautaire*. Within this broad principle there was certainly a case that Britain was paying more than her fair share; but if Mrs Thatcher was going to be legalistic about it, her partners could argue that Britain had signed up in 1972 and could not now rewrite the contract because it had turned out to be disadvant-ageous. They were particularly unsympathetic since Britain's economic position had now been transformed by North Sea oil, a benefit which no other member enjoyed. Moreover in the wider context of European trade, the sums involved were really very small.

Second, Mrs Thatcher exasperated her partners – and not least the President of the Commission, Roy Jenkins, whose job it was to broker a deal – by insisting that Britain's demand for a budget rebate should be treated as an issue entirely on its own, not settled as part of a wider package, as was the Community's normal way. Schmidt and several of the other leaders were willing to help Britain, but they expected Mrs Thatcher in turn to be flexible and constructive in other difficult areas like lamb, fish, oil and the European Monetary System (EMS). This she adamantly refused. 'We simply cannot do so,' she told the Commons in March 1980.[54] In opposition just twelve months earlier she had repeatedly condemned Labour's counterproductive obstructiveness towards Europe.[55] But now she wanted Britain's grievance settled before she would allow progress on anything else.

The other leaders first realised what they were up against at the European Council at Strasbourg on 21–2 June, where Mrs Thatcher began by trying to get the budget issue placed first on the agenda, which naturally irritated Giscard. When they eventually reached it, Jenkins wrote in his diary, she 'immediately became shrill' and picked an unnecessary quarrel with Schmidt, 'which was silly because he was absolutely crucial to her getting the result that she wanted'.[56] She herself was well pleased with her performance. 'I felt that I had made an impression as someone who meant business.' She was delighted to overhear 'a foreign government official' comment that 'Britain is back' – 'a stray remark that pleased me as much as anything I can remember'.[57]

She deliberately set out to be difficult. But Giscard and Schmidt, the experienced European statesmen, both in office since 1974, should have handled her better. After five years of Wilson and Callaghan, they had every reason to welcome the return of a British Government unambiguously committed to Europe. Giscard particularly welcomed British support for the French nuclear *force de frappe*. They should have set out to disarm her. Instead, at the purely personal level, Giscard as the host at Strasbourg went out of his way to snub her, first by failing to seat her next to himself at either lunch or dinner, and then by insisting on being served first – asserting his precedence as head of state over the normal courtesy due to her sex.[58] French gallantry alone might have dictated an effort to make a fuss of her. She was susceptible to Gallic charm, as François Mitterand later proved. Instead she thought Giscard's behaviour, with reason, 'petulant, vain and rather ill-mannered'.[59] When the French President came back to dinner in Downing Street later that year she got her own back by deliberately seating him opposite full-length portraits of Nelson and Wellington.[60] More seriously, the two European leaders (and Giscard in particular) seem to have decided that the way to deal with the British Prime Minister was to put her down.

'I had the strong feeling,' she wrote in her memoirs, 'that they had decided to test whether I was able and willing to stand up to them. It was quite shameless: they were determined to keep as much of our money as they could.'[61] In fact the money was much less important to Giscard than it was to her; but her impression that they were out to test her was widely shared. Christopher Tugendhat, Britain's second EC Commissioner at this time, remembers a senior French official telling him before the Dublin summit: 'This meeting will show what your Prime Minister is made of.'[62] In part this is a familiar problem faced by successive British Prime Ministers trying to break in on the Franco-German duopoly. But Mrs Thatcher's sex added a new dimension. Another Commissioner confirmed that Schmidt and Giscard were 'very rude, even patronising, in their treatment of her. They made it clear that she, a mere woman, wouldn't be able to stand up to these two experienced and knowledgeable men in hard negotiation.'[63]

They misjudged their woman. Once she had defined the issue as a trial of her strength, she would not – could not – back down. Carrington, caught uncomfortably in the crossfire, thought the Europeans' handling of her was 'pretty stupid . . . enormously short-sighted and selfish'.[64] They would have done much better to have taken her aside right at the outset, before Strasbourg, and offered her a generous out-of-court settlement before the political stakes were raised too high. As it was, Mrs Thatcher spent the interval between Strasbourg and the next European Council at Dublin in November working herself into a position of determined intransigence. 'I have the money,' she told Nicholas Henderson in August, 'and they won't get their hands on it.'[65] Back in Strasbourg in October to deliver a Winston Churchill memorial lecture, she declared the present budget situation to be 'demonstrably unjust' and 'politically indefensible'. 'I cannot play Sister Bountiful to the Community,' she warned, 'while my own electorate are being asked to forgo improvements in the field of health, education, welfare and the rest.'[66] In the House of Commons, pressed both by Labour and by anti-Market Tories, she talked up what she hoped to achieve at Dublin by adopting frankly military language ('What general would reveal his tactics before the battle has even begun?') and promising that she would not settle for 'half a loaf'. What she wanted was 'a broad balance between what we put in and what we get out'.[67]

In fact she was offered a refund of just £350 million for the current year. Instead of taking it as a starting point for bargaining, she rejected it with contempt as 'a third of a loaf'. Roy Jenkins had a ringside view of what followed. 'She kept us all round the dinner table for four interminable hours,' he wrote in his diary,[68] 'for the greater part of which,' he later recalled, she talked without pause, but not without repetition.[69] 'It was obvious to everyone except her that she wasn't making progress and was alienating people.' Analysing her performance, Jenkins thought she had 'only one of the three necessary qualities' of a good advocate. She had 'nerve and determination to win' in abundance. But she did not properly understand the case against her, which meant that 'her constantly reiterated cry of "It's my money I want back"' struck 'an insistently jarring note'. In addition, 'she bored everybody endlessly by only understanding about four of the fourteen or so points on the British side and repeating each of them twenty-seven times'.[70]

What infuriated her was that no one bothered to argue with her. Giscard ostentatiously read a newspaper, while Schmidt pretended to go to sleep. This was perhaps inexcusable, though they for their part felt provoked by her aggressive insensitivity. But it was not only the big players that she antagonised. For good measure she gratuitously 'upbraided . . . the little countries for their pusillanimous attitude' to nuclear weapons.[71] There was only one flash of light relief. In the middle of a tirade about 'my oil' and 'my fish', she exclaimed 'My God', at which someone audibly interjected, 'Oh, not that too!'[72]

Earlier Schmidt had told Jenkins that he wanted to help her if he could, 'but she really had to compromise and think about things much more sensibly, or she would be in great trouble.'[73] Eventually he left the dinner 'shaking with rage', saying, 'I can't stand this any longer . . . I can't deal with someone like that.'[74] By any standards this was a serious failure of diplomacy. The next morning she continued 'banging away' at the same points, still getting nowhere, before Jenkins and Carrington took her aside and persuaded her to agree to a postponement on the basis – 'the words coming out of her with almost physical difficulty' – 'that she would approach the next meeting at Luxembourg in April 'in a spirit of genuine compromise'.[75]

Back in the House of Commons she was mocked by Labour for having failed to bring home the rebate she had promised: derided by Tony Benn as a 'paper tigress', charged by Callaghan with preparing to compromise. As a result she became even more unbending, insisting that she would not be 'palmed off' with £350 million.[76] Hitherto she had always insisted that she would negotiate hard but without recourse to illegality. 'We must obey the law,' she declared before Dublin. 'The law of the United Kingdom is to observe the edicts of the European Court.'[77] She now began to hint that she might – 'in the last resort' – threaten to withhold VAT payments.[78] In her memoirs she admits that 'for practical and legal reasons this always seemed a non-starter'. Nevertheless, 'even the possibility caused satisfactory anxiety in the Commission'.[79] Egged on by Little Englanders behind her as well as in front, she did not disguise her relish for the battle. After the Dublin stand-off she boasted that 'some of my European colleagues were a lot more shaken than I was'; while she dismissed suggestions that she should disrupt the business of the Community by adopting an 'empty chair' strategy. 'I believe that I am more effective by being in my seat than by leaving it empty.'[80]

She was constantly under pressure from Labour and Tory anti-Europeans to leave the Community altogether. But that was an option she refused to countenance. She certainly felt no emotional or visionary commitment to the idea of Europe; and the more she saw of its institutions in practice, the less respect she felt for them. She regarded it as an organisation founded upon compromise and horse-trading, which she despised. Nevertheless she still accepted without question, as she had done since Macmillan's first application in 1961, that Britain's place was in the Community. When pressed, however, she always tended to justify membership in the context of her overriding preoccupation with defence. In his first conversation with her after the election Roy Jenkins was disconcerted to find her 'thinking always a little too much in terms of the EEC and NATO as two bodies which ought to be amalgamated'.[81] Nine months later she was happy to agree with a friendly questioner in the Commons that 'Europe needs to be united, and to stay united as a free Europe against the unfree part of Europe which is bound by bonds of steel around the Soviet Union'.[82] The Cold War set the framework of her thinking.

On this basis she started out moderately pro-European. In her speech to the Tory Party Conference just before Dublin she promised to fight Britain's corner as a committed member of the Community, asserting that it was 'no good joining anything half-heartedly'.[83] She was happy to acknowledge that there were lessons Britain could profitably learn from Europe: 'If we want a German and French standard of living we must have a German and French standard of work.'[84] Or again: 'There are many Continental practices that one would like to assume in this country, including the Continentals' tendency not to spend money that they have not got.'[85] But the budget dispute quickly brought out her instinctive underlying hostility to Europe and an unpleasant streak of contempt for the Europeans. 'They are all a rotten lot,' she told Roy Jenkins just before Dublin, couching her scorn as usual in terms of defence. 'Schmidt and the Americans and we are the only ones who would do any standing up and fighting if necessary.'[86] Her belief in the essential superiority of the British was founded on two ideas. First, her memory of the war, when most of continental Europe had been overrun and occupied and had to be liberated by Britain (and the Americans). 'We,' she once exclaimed, 'who either defeated or rescued half Europe, who kept half Europe free when otherwise it would have been in chains . . .'[87] The idea that the Europeans were not permanently grateful to Britain – as she was to the Americans – never ceased to offend her. Second, she contrived to believe that the sense of justice was an essentially British (or, more specifically, English) characteristic which foreigners did not understand. 'There's not a strand of equity or fairness in Europe,' she declared in her television memoirs. 'They're out to get as much as they can, that's one of those enormous differences.'[88] In *The Downing Street Years* she complained of 'the quintessentially un-English outlook displayed by the Community', and quoted one of her favourite Kipling poems which encapsulated that belief. The Norman baron, she explains, is warning his son about 'our English forefathers':

> The Saxon is not like us Normans. His manners are not so
>   polite.
> But he never means anything serious till he talks about justice
>   and right.
> When he stands like an ox in a furrow with his sullen set eyes
>   on your own,
> And grumbles, 'This isn't fair dealing', my son, leave the Saxon
>   alone.[89]

Oddly for one who claimed to have been collecting Kipling since she was at university, she says she only 'came across' these lines later. But Kipling's stubborn Saxon was clearly the inspiration for Mrs Thatcher's stand on Britain's EC budget contribution. Three days after Dublin she told Alan Clark in the Commons: 'Equity . . . is historically a British concept, but I think it is one that we bring to the Community.'[90] This attitude of moralising condescension towards the benighted continentals did Britain's cause in Europe no good over the next ten years.★

The next European Council met in Luxembourg in April 1980. This time Britain was offered a rebate of £700 million a year, roughly two-thirds of the disputed loaf, which Jenkins regarded as 'a very favourable offer'. 'To almost universal amazement', however, Mrs Thatcher again rejected it.[92] She was 'much quieter, less strident, less abrasive than at Dublin', but still adamant. When Jenkins told her she was making a great mistake, 'she good-humouredly but firmly said "Don't try persuading me, you know I find persuasion very counterproductive."'[93] The French Commissioner, Claude Cheysson, sensed that Mrs Thatcher positively relished her isolation. 'Not only didn't she mind about it,' he recalled, 'but she was pleased with that. She was very anxious that Britain would be Britain, and Britain needed no ally. Britain could stand on its own.'[94] Long before the Falklands she was already striking Churchillian poses.

Faced with another *impasse* at heads of government level, the Commission now dressed up 'approximately the same deal in somewhat different form' – still only a two-thirds refund but extended for the next three years – to present to the council of foreign ministers the next month in Brussels. On their own responsibility Carrington and Gilmour accepted this, and thought they had done well. Carrington, in Jenkins' view, 'showed himself a more skilful and sensible negotiator than his head of government. He knew when to settle. She did not.'[95] The Foreign Secretary and his deputy then flew back to Britain and drove straight to Chequers, feeling pleased with themselves. But if they expected congratulation they were swiftly disillusioned. 'My immediate reaction,' Lady Thatcher wrote in her memoirs, 'was far from favourable.'[96] 'Had we been bailiffs arriving to take possession of the furniture,' Gilmour wrote, 'we would probably have been more cordially received. The Prime Minister was like a firework whose fuse had already been lit; we could almost hear the sizzling.' Without

---

★Her hostility to all things European was already assuming an element of self-parody. In August she teased Hoskyns for daring to like 'all those terrible EEC cheeses like Brie and Camembert'.[91]

even offering them the drink they were dying for, she bombarded them with 'an interminable barrage of irrelevance', accusing them of selling the country down the river, vowing to resign rather than accept it.[97] Eventually they escaped back to London, where Gilmour ignored the Prime Minister's reaction and briefed journalists that they had secured a diplomatic triumph. The next day's papers duly hailed a great victory for her tough tactics. Temporarily outmanoeuvred, Mrs Thatcher was forced to swallow her objections and accept the deal, consoling herself that if not the end of the matter, it represented 'huge progress from the position the Government had inherited'.[98]

'Her objection,' Gilmour believed, 'was to the fact of the agreement, not its terms. That was not because we had succeeded where she had failed. It was because, to her, the grievance was more valuable than its solution.'[99] There is no doubt that the dispute was a godsend to her in her first year, providing what she always needed, an external enemy against whom to vent her aggression and prove her mettle. Greedy foreigners trying to get their hands on Britain's money offered the perfect outlet for patriotic indignation, a priceless distraction as inflation continued to rise and unemployment began to mount alarmingly. The EC budget battle set the style of her premiership and fixed the tabloid image of battling Maggie swinging her handbag and standing up for Britain against the wiles of Brussels. For the moment she was obliged to make the best of the interim settlement Carrington had secured, while still holding out for a permanent solution, which was not finally achieved until the Fontainebleau council of June 1984. Until then the 'Bloody British Question', as it was known in Brussels, continued to paralyse all other progress in the Community and poison Britain's relationship with Europe. Mrs Thatcher remained intensely suspicious that the other members were always looking to do Britain down. Having pinned her long-term hopes of reform on the expectation that her opportunity would come when the Community ran out of money and required unanimity to raise the 1 per cent VAT contribution to increase the budget, she was outraged in May 1982 when the council of agriculture ministers overrode Britain's objection to raising farm prices. 'The idea that we can go ahead with changes in the CAP without changes in the structure of the budget is a breach of faith,' she railed. The use of majority voting in defiance of the hitherto accepted Luxembourg Compromise was 'very serious and could be even more serious if . . . applied to other aspects of Community work'. She still refused to contemplate leaving the Community, but as a full and equal member, she protested, Britain was entitled to fair treatment.[100]

She won in the end when two new leaders, François Mitterand in

France and Helmut Kohl in Germany, realised that they would get no peace till Mrs Thatcher got what she demanded. But her victory was achieved at a considerable cost. First, however much she claimed to be a full and equal member, her exclusive preoccupation with the budget prevented Britain playing a full role in the development of the Community, thus confirming the dismal pattern of critical semi-detachment already set by Labour. Second, Mrs Thatcher's jingoistic rhetoric, gleefully amplified by the *Sun* and the *Daily Mail*, set a tone of popular prejudice, hostile to the Community and all its works, which endured long after the budget problem was resolved. Third, the ultimate success of her uncompromising campaign encouraged Mrs Thatcher's conviction that intransigence was the only language foreigners understood. 'The outcome,' Nigel Lawson observed, 'persuaded her that it always paid to be bloody-minded in dealings with the Community. This was to prove increasingly counterproductive in practice.'[101]

Was it worth it? Judgements differ. On the one hand there is wide agreement that Mrs Thatcher's bloody-mindedness ultimately achieved a better settlement than the Foreign Office would ever have won by more conventional diplomatic methods. 'Margaret's firmness and intransigence were the key factors in getting us a proper settlement,' Carrington admitted in his memoirs.[102] 'It was a bit uncomfortable at times,' he recalled. 'But in the end I think it worked rather well . . . I don't believe that a softer approach would have had the same effect.'[103] 'The way the rules of the game were set up by Schmidt and Giscard d'Estaing,' Tugendhat concurred, 'Mrs Thatcher had no option but to be very tough.'[104] On the other hand, the collateral damage was arguably more costly than the prize. As President of the Commission, Roy Jenkins saw the damage Mrs Thatcher's penny-pinching histrionics did to Britain's potential influence in Europe. By haggling over the budget 'she caused a justified but limited dispute . . . totally to dominate the Community for five years and to run into the sand any hopes of . . . a British leadership role within the Community.'[105] In Jenkins' view she got the issue totally out of proportion. 'The gap around which the argument revolved . . . was tiny in relation to, say, the size of Britain's defence budget. But it was capable of destroying a large part of the influence which that defence budget was designed to foster.'

Furthermore, in order to relieve her feelings and justify her position, Mrs Thatcher built up a groundswell of anti-European and particularly anti-French opinion at home . . . Once the genie was encouraged to come out of its bottle it was difficult to get it back in again.

In this way she began to undermine the Tory commitment to Europe which she had inherited from Macmillan and Heath, leading within ten years to a deep split in the party which would eventually destroy her and bedevil the life of her successors. 'It was a heavy price to pay for 400 million ecus.'[106]

Rhodesia into Zimbabwe

The long-running problem of ending colonial rule in Rhodesia, by contrast, was a subject on which Mrs Thatcher, very soon after taking office, dramatically changed her mind and modified her initial instinct, leading to a settlement which reflected her flexibility and pragmatism. Unlike Europe or the Cold War, Rhodesia was not an issue with which she felt any visceral involvement. Her sympathies were instinctively with the white settlers – 'our kith and kin', as the British press liked to call them. Denis had business connections with Rhodesia, and she could not forget that Ian Smith, the rebel Prime Minister, had served in the RAF during the war. The African leaders, by contrast, she regarded as Communist-sponsored terrorists. Nevertheless Rhodesia was marginal to her central concerns, a tiresome responsibility which she simply wanted to dispose of honourably.

Ten years after Smith's illegal declaration of independence from Britain, it was the collapse of the Portuguese empire in Angola and Mozambique in 1975 which spelled the end of the line for rebel Rhodesia. As the two rival African guerrilla groups, ZIPRA and ZANU, led by Joshua Nkomo and Robert Mugabe, stepped up their military incursions from neighbouring Zambia and Mozambique, South Africa decided it could no longer go on shoring up its northern satellite and began to put pressure on Smith to bow to the inevitable and accept majority rule. In 1977 Smith rejected an Anglo-American peace plan put forward by David Owen and the US Secretary of State, Cyrus Vance, and negotiated his own internal settlement – heavily favourable to the whites – with the more accommodating Bishop Abel Muzorewa. Callaghan and Owen – and Carter – immediately declared it unacceptable and refused to recognise it.

Mrs Thatcher's instinct was to support the Smith/Muzorewa settlement, and this remained her position up to the General Election. In April she sent the former Colonial Secretary Lord Boyd to observe the Rhodesian elections for the Tory party. Bishop Muzorewa won and duly became the country's first black Prime Minister at the head of a power-sharing government. But with Nkomo and Mugabe (now allied as the Patriotic Front) boycotting the elections, most international opinion declared them meaningless. Boyd, however, declared them fair and valid, and Mrs Thatcher accepted his report. In her first speech in the Commons as Prime Minister she warmly welcomed the elections as marking a 'major change' and promised to build on them.[107] Six weeks later, stopping off in Canberra on her way back from the Tokyo summit at the end of June, she again hinted that Britain would recognise Muzorewa, provoking a storm of protest led by the Australian Prime Minister Malcolm Fraser, who warned her that she was isolating herself from the rest of the Commonwealth, and indeed the world. President Carter had already rejected the result of the elections and announced – in defiance of Congress, which voted to lift them – that American sanctions against Rhodesia would be maintained.

On her return to Britain, Carrington persuaded her to change her mind. Recognition of Muzorewa, he argued, would not only split both the Commonwealth and the Atlantic alliance, boost Soviet influence in Africa and damage Britain economically; it was also futile, since the internal settlement would not end the war in Rhodesia, but only widen it, with the Soviet Union backing Nkomo and China backing Mugabe. Britain would be left holding nominal responsibility before the United Nations for an escalating conflict. As Lady Thatcher subsequently wrote in her memoirs: 'Unpleasant realities had to be faced . . . He turned out to be right.'[108]

She also found other grounds to change her mind. She was persuaded that there were legal flaws in Smith's gerrymandered constitution, which was unlike any other that Britain had bequeathed her former colonies. Strict regard for legality was something Mrs Thatcher always took very seriously. In addition, following the failure of the Vance–Owen initiative, she liked the idea of Britain going it alone to achieve a settlement without American help. 'How do we decolonise a colony when there is no problem at all?' she asked her advisers. 'We get all the parties round a table at Lancaster House,' they replied. 'They work out a constitution that suits them all; then they have an election on that constitution and that's goodbye.' Very well, she concluded, 'Let's go down that road and see what happens.'[109]

For all these reasons – though not without a last-minute wobble when she appeared to go cold on the whole idea – Mrs Thatcher had made up her mind before she flew to Lusaka for the Commonwealth Conference in August that the only solution lay in a comprehensive settlement involving all the parties. She actually signalled her shift of view in the House of Commons on 25 July, when the Foreign Office succeeded in writing into her speech a carefully phrased statement that any settlement must be internationally recognised – effectively adding a seventh to the six principles which Harold Wilson had laid down in

1965.[110] But scarcely anyone noticed the significance of her words: it is not certain that she fully recognised it herself.[111] Carrington insists that she had determined what she wanted to achieve before she went to Lusaka. But it was still generally assumed that she would be walking into a lions' den, setting herself against the united view of the rest of the Commonwealth. She was certainly prepared for a hostile reception.

Fears had been raised for the Queen's safety in Lusaka. It was reported that Mrs Thatcher had advised her not to go.[112] In fact she did not believe there was any danger to the Queen, but she did think that she herself was a possible target.[113] On the flight to Zambia, Carrington was mystified to see that she had brought with her a large pair of dark glasses. 'What on earth are those for?' he asked, since they were due to land at night. 'I am absolutely certain,' she replied, 'that when I land at Lusaka they are going to throw acid in my face.' Carrington told her that Africans would never do anything like that: they were more likely to cheer her. 'I don't believe you,' she said. Where she derived this oddly specific fear is not clear; but there is no doubt that she was seriously afraid. Yet when they landed she walked down the aircraft steps quite calmly, without dark glasses, to be warmly greeted by Kenneth Kaunda and cheering crowds. Carrington noted that her apprehension betrayed 'her inexperience and mistrust of Africa'; but he was indelibly impressed by her physical and moral courage.[114] To make matters worse she was suffering from a stomach bug and nearly fainted on arrival. Then she was 'virtually hijacked', separated from her press secretary, Henry James, and whisked off to a difficult press conference.[115] To one hostile observer she appeared 'shaken, fighting tears and distressed';[116] but others thought she displayed extraordinary poise, spontaneity and spirit. The BBC correspondent John Simpson thought it 'a magnificent performance'.[117]

Though Denis had travelled extensively in Africa, Mrs Thatcher had no connection with either the old or the new Commonwealth; nor – unlike Callaghan or Wilson – did she feel any political sympathy with Africa's liberation struggle. On the contrary, like Ted Heath, she found the hypocrisy of the African leaders preaching democracy for others while operating one-party states themselves, reviling Britain one moment while demanding increased aid the next, very hard to swallow. Yet she did not want to see the club break up; and in practice, once exposed to them privately in the relaxed atmosphere of a Commonwealth Conference, she discovered most of the African leaders to be much more agreeable and a good deal less 'Marxist' than she had expected.[118] In particular, as Carrington noted, she 'blossomed in the warmth of Kenneth Kaunda's friendly personality'.[119] At Lusaka she even scored a memorable diplomatic coup by dancing with him: since her Oxford days she had been an excellent dancer, and the resulting photographs did more than any diplomatic communiqué to dissolve tensions.*

Much of the credit for the success of Lusaka has been given to the Queen for helping to create the family atmosphere in which Mrs Thatcher and President Kaunda were able to overcome their mutual suspicion.[121] But at least as much is due to Mrs Thatcher herself, first for allowing Carrington to change her mind on the central issue and then, having changed it, for her determination to hammer out – with Malcolm Fraser, Michael Manley (of Jamaica) and the Commonwealth Secretary-General Sonny Ramphal – the lines of an agreement which could bring Mugabe and Nkomo to Lancaster House. Carrington paid tribute to the skill with which she exploited the element of surprise at her unexpected reversal. Ever-concerned to get the legal framework right, she insisted that Rhodesia must first return to its constitutional status as a colony, with the appointment of a new Governor and all the flummery of British rule. In return she agreed that Britain would send troops to enforce and monitor the ceasefire. This was a risk which Callaghan had not been prepared to take. But Mrs Thatcher accepted that Britain had a responsibility to discharge; she was determined not to have the United Nations involved.[122] More than anything else it was this guarantee of British military commitment which persuaded the Patriotic Front to lay down its arms. By the concerted pressure of South Africa, the neighbouring 'Front Line' states, the rest of the Commonwealth and the United States, all parties to the conflict were cajoled into agreeing to attend peace talks in London in September.

Carrington still had no great hopes of a settlement. But for fifteen weeks he put the whole weight of the Foreign Office into the effort to achieve one, believing that his tenure would not last long if he failed.[123] Having played her part at Lusaka, Mrs Thatcher left her Foreign Secretary to chair the talks with minimum interference. While Kaunda

---

*Some years later Ronald Millar recorded a telling exchange between Mrs Thatcher and Denis, when they were discussing Carrington's achievement as Foreign Secretary:

Margaret:	'Be fair, dear. He was very good over Rhodesia.'
Denis:	'Yes, but he didn't dance with Kaunda.'
Margaret:	'I should hope not.'
Denis:	'You did – and that's what turned the trick.'
Margaret:	'I doubt if that's what history will say.'
Denis:	'History wasn't there. I was.'[120]

flew to London to impress on Nkomo that he must settle, and Samora Machel of Mozambique similarly leaned on Mugabe, Mrs Thatcher's role behind the scenes was to make plain to the whites that they could not look to Britain to bail them out. Setting her private sympathies aside, she told John Junor that while she would have dearly loved to have a private talk with Smith, 'it would be misunderstood by Mr Mugabe and the others. So I daren't.'[124] The negotiations were tense and protracted – a walk-out by one or other party was never far away; but an agreement was eventually signed just before Christmas, providing for elections in the New Year, a ten-year embargo on the transfer of land and British help in forging a united army out of the previously warring forces. Christopher Soames was appointed Governor to oversee the elections and bring the new state of Zimbabwe to independence – a much better use of his formidable pro-consular talents than trying to cut the Civil Service at home.

Mrs Thatcher would frankly have preferred that the Marxist Mugabe had not won the elections. Right up to the last moment, diehard whites still hoped that she would declare the result invalid. But she refused to do so, and firmly quashed any thought that she might recognise a military coup. She was their last hope, and when she spelled out the reality they knew the game was up. 'Her strategic objective was to solve the Rhodesian problem,' Sir Anthony Parsons – Ambassador to the UN, later her foreign policy adviser – summed up. 'Once she had taken that decision, she was pragmatically prepared to accept the chips to fall where they might.'[125] Mugabe's victory was in fact the best possible outcome, since winning power through the ballot box served – at least in the short term – to de-radicalise the Patriotic Front.* Once in power, Mugabe quickly declared Zimbabwe a one-party state; but for the best part of twenty years it seemed a relatively successful one. Only at the end of the century did the issue of the unequal ownership of land – shelved at Lancaster House – erupt in Government-sponsored violence against white farmers as the ageing dictator clung to office, wrecking the country's once-prosperous economy and throwing its multiracial future into doubt.[127]

Mrs Thatcher watched the independence ceremony on television in her room in the House of Commons, with Ian Gow and a number of other Tory MPs. As the Union Jack came down she wept. 'The poor

---

*Even the Americans were happy. President Carter lost no time in congratulating Mugabe and invited him to Washington. He also publicly praised Mrs Thatcher's 'wisdom and courage' and Carrington's 'skill and tenacity' in achieving the result.[126]

Queen,' she said. 'Do you realise the number of colonies that have been handed over from the British Empire since she came to the throne?'[128] Her emotion vividly reveals where her real feelings lay. At heart she still believed in the Empire – not the Commonwealth – as the source of British power and pride: she recognised that it had to go, but she wept for its passing. Meanwhile the imperial assumptions of her adolescence still fundamentally shaped her view of Britain's place in the world.

The contrary pulls of patriotic sentiment and geopolitical realism were to be seen again in relation to other remnants of Britain's imperial history: the Falklands, Grenada and Hong Kong. In the case of Rhodesia, as in Hong Kong, realism prevailed. For fourteen years since 1965 the colony had been a running sore in British politics, the annual vote on the maintenance of sanctions a source of division and embarrassment to the Tory party in particular. All Mrs Thatcher wanted in 1979 was to be honourably rid of it. She was lucky that the circumstances came together to make a solution possible just as she came into office. But she deserves credit for seizing the opportunity, against her initial instinct, and for exerting her influence to secure a tolerable settlement. The outcome gained her a good deal of international credit, not only with black Africa but also in Washington, at a time when the Government's domestic economic record was already looking bleak. After seven difficult months, the Zimbabwe settlement was her Government's first unquestionable success.

The end of the beginning

By the time the Zimbabwe settlement was signed at the end of 1979, the Government's honeymoon, such as it was, was over. The Lancaster House agreement was the one bright spot in an otherwise darkening picture. The novelty of a woman Prime Minister had quickly worn off. Her style was established: brisk, didactic, combative, with a touch of syrup. There was no lingering doubt about her capacity to do the job. She had established her domination of the Cabinet and Government machine, despite the barely concealed scepticism of many of her senior colleagues. By her mastery of detail and clarity of purpose she had asserted her command of the House of Commons despite having to shout over a perpetual hubbub of heckling and interruption.

She had achieved a notable coup in November by her unprecedentedly full disclosure of the facts surrounding the unmasking of the distinguished art historian Sir Anthony Blunt – the Keeper of the Queen's Pictures – as a one-time Soviet spy, the 'fourth man' who had tipped off his friends Guy Burgess and Donald Maclean, enabling them to escape to the Soviet Union in 1951, and then done the same for Kim Philby in 1963. It was a tricky task for a new Prime Minister to reveal that Blunt's treachery had been suspected since 1951 and known to the security services since 1964, but covered up by successive Home Secretaries and Attorneys-General in return for a full confession. But she carried it off with considerable aplomb, raising hopes – not to be fulfilled – that she would inaugurate a more open regime where MI5 and MI6 were concerned. Willie Whitelaw was actually working on a new Protection of Information Bill to replace the catch-all provisions of the 1911 Official Secrets Act; but this was abandoned when Andrew Boyle, the journalist who had exposed Blunt, asserted that he could not have done so under the new provisions. Characteristically the lesson which Mrs Thatcher drew from the Blunt saga was that the Government must keep its guard up:

> It is important not to be so obsessed by yesterday's danger that we fail to detect today's. We know today what happened to a very few of that pre-war generation who had Marxist leanings and betrayed their country. We find it contemptible and repugnant. Our task now is to guard against their counterparts of today . . . The Government's purpose is to do everything possible to improve the morale and efficiency of the Security Service and to do nothing to undermine or weaken it.[129]

It was another ten years before her government returned to the reform of the Official Secrets Act, and then it was to tighten, not loosen, its provisions.

Mrs Thatcher also won considerable admiration for her response to further Irish atrocities. At the end of August the former Viceroy of India, Lord Mountbatten, and two members of his family were blown up while on holiday in the Irish Republic; and the same day eighteen British soldiers were killed at Warrenpoint in County Down. Mrs Thatcher not only condemned the attacks but paid an unannounced visit to Northern Ireland two days later to demonstrate her defiance of the terrorists and her support for the troops. She visited some of the victims of previous IRA bombs in hospital, went on a courageous walkabout in the centre of Belfast protected by just a handful of flak-jacketed policemen, had lunch with army commanders at Portadown and then flew by helicopter to the republican stronghold of Crossmaglen, where she 'enthusiastically donned a combat jacket and a beret of the Ulster Defence Regiment'.[130] This 'nation-rallying trip,' *The Times* wrote at the end of the year, 'was a stroke of genius.'[131] She repeated it just before Christmas and made a point of going at least once a year over the nex decade.

She enjoyed a rapturous victory conference at Blackpool in October, at which she thanked her party for keeping faith during the years of opposition and looked forward boldly to 'the far longer years of Conservative Government that are to come':

> For this Government, it's not the first hundred days that count; it's the first five years and the next five after that. We have to think in terms of several Parliaments. We have to move this country in a new direction . . . to create a wholly new attitude of mind . . . It will take time, and it will not be easy.[132]

In this and other speeches she repeated the Government's determination to tackle the four linked problems of inflation, public spending, taxation and industrial relations. But by the end of 1979, as the commentators looked back on the Government's first six months, it seemed that in every one of those areas its first actions had only made a bad situation worse. Howe's budget had given an apparently wilful hike to inflation, with the result that pay settlements in both the private and public sectors (fuelled by Clegg) were leapfrogging to keep ahead. Unemployment was rising, interest rates were painfully high, output low and falling. Industry was suffering and Tory backbenchers were already expressing alarm. Strikes were mounting, particularly in the engineering industry, with a major confrontation looming at British Steel, while the TUC was gearing up to oppose Prior's Employment Bill.

On the credit side, opinion polls still showed overwhelming public support for action to curb the unions, and the Government was further heartened by votes against strike action by the miners and the British Leyland car workers. 'I believe there are really encouraging signs . . . of economic realism permeating through,' Mrs Thatcher told the Parliamentary Press Gallery in December. The miners' ballot in particular was 'one of the signs that our philosophy and belief strike a chord in the hearts of most people'.[133] Yet despite lurching hard to the left since losing office, Labour was once again ahead in the polls. Looking into the new decade, the *Guardian's* veteran parliamentary correspondent, Norman Shrapnel, saw the ghosts of the 1930s on the march again.[134] Even those who wished the Government well were holding their breath. Fred Emery, political editor of *The Times* – which was returning to publication in November after a year-long dispute – wrote that the dominant reaction to the Prime Minister's first six months was one of awe for the 'marvellous flair' of 'this unflinching woman' who had swept her doubtful party into 'a high-risk policy gamble'. 'The awe reflects Mrs Thatcher's private and public dominance, making our system more presidential than ever.' But many wondered 'whether Mrs Thatcher has quite grasped yet how bad the economy could be'.[135]

The Government was sailing into stormy waters.

3

Heading for the Rocks

The failure of monetarism

The two years 1980 and 1981 were the critical period for the Thatcher Government, when the Prime Minister and her Chancellor, with dwindling support even from former true believers in the Cabinet, confronted by appalling economic indicators and widespread predictions of disaster, set their faces against the storm and stubbornly held – more or less – their predetermined course. Economically, in truth, things did not go according to plan. Some targets were quietly abandoned, others were hit only at huge cost: economists still dispute whether more lasting good or harm was done to the economy by the monetarist experiment. Politically, however, Mrs Thatcher won through without being seen to change course. There was no overt U-turn, such as her critics had confidently predicted. Instead, by the end of 1981 she had purged her Cabinet of the most persistent doubters and laid the basis of the reputation for unwavering resolution which would keep her in Downing Street for another nine years.

By all the normal measures of economic management the Government's performance was dismal during 1980. Inflation, gratuitously boosted by Howe's first budget, went on climbing for several months, reaching 22 per cent in May before finally starting to fall as the doubling of VAT twelve months earlier dropped out of the reckoning. By the end of the year it had fallen to 13 per cent, but that was still higher than it had been when the Conservatives came in. Meanwhile unemployment continued to soar under the impact of high interest rates, the consequent over-valued pound and the Government's spending cuts, reaching 2.8 million by the end of 1980: the sort of level no one had ever expected to see again. The Tories' 1978 poster showing a winding dole queue with the caption 'Labour Isn't Working' was revealed as a cynical mockery.

The worst problem was the pound, which reached \$2.40 in September 1980 (compared with \$2.08 in May 1979). The rise was partly due to the rising oil price, partly to the falling dollar and partly – some economists would say mainly – to the Government's determination to keep interest rates high, which impressed the markets. Whatever the cause, the effect on British manufacturing industry was devastating. Hundreds of small companies went out of business, while even the giants struggled. ICI recorded its first-ever quarterly loss. Industrial leaders queued up to blame the Government. In November the chairman of the CBI (Confederation of British Industry), Sir Terence Beckett, called dramatically for 'a bare-knuckle fight' with the Government.[1] Sir Michael Edwardes of British Leyland said it would be better to leave North Sea oil in the seabed than let it do such damage;[2] while the chairman of ICI asked the Prime Minister privately if she wanted his company to stay in Britain. This last warning momentarily shook her.[3] In principle, however, she was inclined to believe that the high pound was a good thing: first because she always had a simple patriotic belief that the currency was a barometer of national prosperity, and second because she thought it would administer a healthy shock to industry, forcing it to become more competitive to survive. Industrialists faced with closure were not so sanguine. 'It is all very well to talk of industry rising like a phoenix from the ashes,' the chairman of the West Midlands CBI protested, 'but what if all we are left with is the ashes?'[4] 'I am aware that the exchange rate is causing some difficulty for some exporters,' Mrs Thatcher conceded, 'but it is also keeping down the rate of increase in inflation in this country.'[5] 'If our top priority is to squeeze inflation out of the economy, we must inevitably suffer some unemployment in the short term.'[6] The monetarists' real problem, one sceptic told the *Observer*'s William Keegan, 'was that they could not make up their mind whether the squeals from British industry were a good thing or not'.[7]

The critics' case is that by sticking to their predetermined strategy, despite the oil-price increase and deepening world recession, Mrs Thatcher and her Treasury team wilfully exacerbated an already threatening situation. 'Undeterred by the prospect of a world recession ahead,' Ian Gilmour has written, 'they proceeded to create their own far worse recession at home,' permanently destroying in the process much of Britain's manufacturing base.[8] The Thatcherites, by contrast, argued at the time – and still argue – that British industry was overmanned and featherbedded and needed shaking out. A shift from old manufacturing to new service industries – what Mrs Thatcher called 'tomorrow's jobs'[9] – was both inevitable and necessary: the recession of 1980–1 merely accelerated this process which was the precondition for subsequent recovery. To which the Keynesians reply that there was bound to be some recovery eventually from such a deep trough, but that it was only partial, and more delayed than it need have been, while much of manufacturing industry never recovered at all.

Geoffrey Howe's second budget, introduced in March 1980, unveiled what Lady Thatcher later called the 'cornerstone' of her Government's success – the so-called Medium Term Financial Strategy (MTFS).[10] Its purpose was to bring down public spending and monetary growth by announcing fixed targets for several years ahead, instead of just one year at a time. The strategy was the brainchild of Nigel Lawson, Financial Secretary to the Treasury, who successfully sold the idea to Howe with the slogan 'Rules rule, OK'.[11] Lawson was always looking for some self-imposed or external restraint to enforce financial rectitude; it was for the same reason that he was later so keen to join the Exchange Rate Mechanism (ERM) of the EMS. Howe pragmatically agreed: he always insisted that the MTFS was 'commonsense rather than revolutionary'.[12] As so often with ideas she subsequently adopted as her own, however, Mrs Thatcher was initially hostile. Though in theory all in favour of squeezing the money supply, 'she reacted instinctively against what she called "graph-paper economics"', which smacked of socialist planning. Encouraged by Douglas Wass and John Biffen, she disliked closing her options – though this was precisely what the MTFS was designed to do. In the end she was persuaded that fixed targets would both put a ceiling on high-spending ministers and make it possible to reduce interest rates.[13] In fact the targets were not fixed at all. Like George Brown's derided National Plan in 1965–6, the MTFS was no more than a statement of desirable objectives. Its effect – as Mrs Thatcher came to realise – was essentially declaratory. 'The MTFS would only influence expectations in so far as people believed in our determination to stick to it: its credibility depended . . . on the quality of my own commitment, about which I would leave no one in doubt. I would not bow to demands to reflate.'[14] On that basis she was converted, elevating the MTFS into a symbol of her personal resolution – Denis Healey dubbed it 'Mrs Thatcher's Final Solution'[15] – and subsequently blaming Lawson, its author, for abandoning it.

The fact is that monetarism in the strict sense did not work. Paradoxically the importance of controlling the money supply was now almost universally accepted. Although it suited both parties to gloss the fact after 1979, Healey had run a pretty successful monetary regime from 1976. The difficulty Howe and Lawson had was in measuring the growth of money – particularly after they had scrapped exchange controls. As Biffen anticipated, by elevating the control of money into the central totem of policy, the Government made a rod for its own back. At one level it was perfectly correct for the Prime Minister and Chancellor to maintain that monetarism was not some 'minority doctrinal obsession, pursued blindly for its own sake',[16] but 'simple common sense', long accepted in Switzerland and Germany.[17] 'My fellow Heads of Government find our policies not strange, unusual or revolutionary,' Mrs Thatcher told the 1980 party conference, 'but normal, sound and honest.'[18] 'Monetarism,' she insisted in the House of Commons, 'means honest money. It means that money is backed properly by the production of goods and services.'[19] The trouble lay not in the principle but in the practice. Of the various available yard-sticks – M0, M1, M3, M4 – they took as their measure of money in circulation Sterling M3, which included not only notes and coins but bank deposits. They were then made to look ridiculous when £M3 rose during 1980, despite the Government's best efforts to curb it, by 18 per cent against a target of 6–10 per cent – that is, nearly twice as fast as before 1979.

This embarrassing inability to control the very indicator on which the Government had publicly staked its reputation caused serious fric-tion between Downing Street and the Bank of England. Mrs Thatcher took a closer personal interest in the minutiae of monetary control than any previous Prime Minister. Yet she lacked a trained economist's sense of the subject's intrinsic fallibility. Rather she had a scientist's literal belief in money as a finite substance which must be able to be measured. As Lawson somewhat wearily recalled, 'There was no more assiduous seeker for gimmicks which would supposedly give us tight money without high interest rates than Margaret Thatcher.'[20] For a time she was very keen on a system of Monetary Base Control devel-oped by one of her private gurus, a City stockbroker named Gordon Pepper. The Bank was not convinced by this or any of her other gimmicks. The result, as Jock Bruce-Gardyne observed, was 'a conflict of personalities between an exceptionally determined Prime Minister and an exceptionally formidable Governor'.[21] Appointed by Ted Heath in 1973, and now serving his fourth Prime Minister, Gordon Richardson was the most dominant Governor of the Bank of England since Montagu Norman in the 1930s. He objected to being treated like an errant schoolboy who had got his sums wrong. The crunch came in the summer of 1980, when Mrs Thatcher was taking a rare, brief holiday in Switzerland. £M3 rose 5 per cent in July alone and another 5 per cent in August. She furiously consulted various Swiss bankers, then came storming home to charge the Deputy Governor,

Eddie George – Richardson was on holiday – with rank incompetence. When Richardson returned he got 'a bawling-out . . . which left him shaken and furious'. Five weeks later, *The Times* reported, 'it still reverberates around the corridors and salons'. While Downing Street insisted that the Prime Minister was 'not rattled, they admit that she needs some sturdy reassurance'.[22] It was provided by the return from the United States of her favourite monetarist guru Alan Walters, who told her to forget about £M3. 'Bugger £M3!' he is supposed to have said. 'Sterling is obviously far too high. That can only mean that sterling is scarce.'[23] He proposed commissioning an independent report from another monetarist academic, Professor Jurg Niehans of Berne University, who duly supported Walters' diagnosis, giving Howe impeccable authority to loosen the monetary squeeze. 'The appreciation of sterling in the last two years,' he reported, 'is largely a monetary phenomenon' – in other words, it was not due to oil:

> UK monetary policy not only seems to have rejected any concession to 'gradualism' but also refused to allow any allowance for real growth. It thus appears to have been more abrupt than even the most ardent monetarists ever advocated.[24]

The theory was right, but the implementation was wrong, he told Hoskyns. 'If the Government goes on with its present monetary squeeze, you won't just have a recession, you'll have a slump.'[25]★

To the CBI's relief, Minimum Lending Rate was cut by 2 per cent in November, and previous monetary targets were discreetly modified in the 1981 budget. Mrs Thatcher never forgave Richardson for having been right. The irony is that it took a pair of monetarist theorists like Walters and Niehans to moderate the politicians' dogmatism. At the beginning of 1981 Walters formally moved into Downing Street as the Prime Minister's personal economic adviser. Justifying his appointment in the House of Commons, Mrs Thatcher allowed herself to betray a rare touch of uncertainty: 'If the . . . supposition, with which I do not

---

★This was music to Hoskyns' ears. As early as the previous August he had written despairingly that Howe and Mrs Thatcher were wrecking the economy 'out of sheer technical ignorance'.[26] More charitably Samuel Brittan of the *Financial Times* commented some years later: 'I think the incoming Conservative Government made a mistake of so many politicians, they tried to be too clever, too economically literate . . . too concerned to show that they understood what economics was telling them, instead of remembering that most economists are wrong most of the time.'[27]

wholly agree, is that the monetary policy is in ruins, it seems to me
to be very advisable to take on a person who is an expert in putting
it right again.'[28]

Both Howe and Lady Thatcher in their memoirs defend the attempt
to control £M3, though they concede with hindsight that the squeeze
may have been excessively severe. Critics of monetarism, on the other
hand, like Prior and Gilmour, are thankful that the Government failed
to hit its targets. 'If the Government had squeezed the economy as
much as it wanted to,' *The Times* economics editor David Blake wrote
in November 1981, 'the recession would have been even worse.'[29] But
hitting the targets, it turns out, was not really the point. Nigel Lawson
concedes that the MTFS 'was not fulfilled in any literal sense, at least
not on the monetary side . . . Nevertheless, in terms of its fundamental aims, the MTFS succeeded.' It provided a strong framework
for controlling public spending. 'We could not have kept the show
on the road . . . without it.'[30] Professor Patrick Minford likewise argued
in 1989 that while monetarism strictly failed, it actually worked by
lowering inflationary expectations.[31] In other words the MTFS was a
blind – just a fancy smokescreen for an old-fashioned deflation. What
finally got inflation back to single figures by the spring of 1982 was
not the control of money but heavy pressure on public spending,
higher indirect taxation and lower borrowing – 'sado-monetarism' or
'punk monetarism', Denis Healey called it – resulting in nearly three
million unemployed.[32] 'If Keynesianism stood accused of buying
employment at the price of inflation,' Peter Clarke has suggested,
'Thatcherism could plausibly be accused of simply inverting the
process.' The Government came in preaching the painless alchemy of
Milton Friedman but ended up delivering the harsher medicine of
Friedrich Hayek.[33]

Howe's 1980 budget took another £900 million out of planned
public spending for 1980–1, mainly from social services. Sickness and
unemployment benefit were made liable to income tax, child benefit
was raised by less than the rate of inflation, prescription charges were
doubled again – to £1 per item, five times the level of a year before.
Higher education took the heaviest cuts; university funding was severely
(but unequally) reduced, and overseas students were required to pay
the full cost of their tuition. All these measures evoked furious outcry
from those affected. The *Guardian* accused the Government of waging
'war against the poor';[34] the *Observer* worried that 'if past experience
of milder recessions is any guide, the industrially weak will suffer, and
those with muscle will still force their pay rises.'[35] In July the Cabinet
agreed a further package, though several of the biggest spenders –

Patrick Jenkin at the DHSS and above all Francis Pym at Defence – fought successfully to limit the impact on their departments. Pym threatened resignation and deployed the Chiefs of Staff to exercise their right of access to the Prime Minister to defend his budget. The more the Government tried to cut, however, the more the cost of social security kept on rising. In her memoirs Lady Thatcher recalled that cutting public expenditure at this time felt like 'running up the "Down" escalator'.[36] Obliged to make a virtue of failure, she pointed out that spending in 1979–80 was actually slightly up on the year before, 'which should give the lie to those who accuse us of savage cuts'.[37] In October 1980 she admitted that the Government's revised objective was merely to hold spending to its current level; but insisted that since some expenditure was expanding, this inevitably necessitated economies elsewhere.[38]

At least half the Cabinet, however, believed it was wrong to be trying to cut spending at all when unemployment was rising. Not only the established 'wets' – Prior, Walker, Gilmour, Carlisle, Stevas – but even some of those previously counted 'dry' were beginning to shrink from the social consequences – notably John Biffen, who as Chief Secretary was responsible for wielding the Treasury axe, but quickly concluded that no really major cuts were practicable. Conventional wisdom took it for granted that no Government could survive unemployment at two or three million. Less than a decade earlier the Heath Government had been forced to reverse its strategy when unemployment hit one million. The Cabinet 'wets' and most commentators assumed that the Thatcher Government would sooner or later be forced to do the same. Even within her private office, Wolfson told Hoskyns gloomily that 'Prior and Co . . . are simply biding their time for a forced U-Turn, when she will have to resign.'[39] It was not as if the Conservatives had given warning that unemployment would have to rise. On the contrary, they had denounced Labour's record as opportunistically as any opposition, with the specific charge that 'Labour Isn't Working'. Ever since 1975 Labour (and privately many Tories) had warned that monetarism, strictly applied, would inevitably cost jobs: Keith Joseph had on occasion admitted it. Yet it seems that Mrs Thatcher and her economic team had genuinely not expected unemployment to take off as it did as soon as they got into office. They were alarmed by the mounting figures and protested that they were doing everything possible by means of tax cuts and other incentives to encourage the new industries and businesses which would create new jobs. Yet Mrs Thatcher had staked her political reputation on not repeating Heath's U-turn. Whatever the economic arguments which came from every part of the political spectrum, her credibility would have been destroyed if she were seen to reverse her insistence that squeezing inflation must remain the top priority. From political necessity, then, but also with extraordinary nerve (and a good deal of luck), Mrs Thatcher contrived to stand conventional wisdom on its head by making a virtue of her refusal to change tack – almost indeed making a virtue of unemployment itself. The recession was a shock, Lawson admitted, but a beneficial one. 'A shock was needed if attitudes were to change.'[40]

Mrs Thatcher frequently professed her sympathy for the unemployed. 'I couldn't live without work,' she told the *News of the World* in May 1980. 'That's what makes me so sympathetic to these people who are unemployed. I don't know how they live without working.'[41] At the party conference that year she called unemployment 'a human tragedy . . . Human dignity and self-respect are undermined when men and women are condemned to idleness.'[42] But her sympathy always seemed to imply a moral failing on the part of the unemployed themselves:

> I learned from childhood the dignity which comes from work and, by contrast, the affront to self-esteem that comes from enforced idleness. For us, work was the only way of life we knew, and we were brought up to believe that it was not only a necessity but a virtue.[43]

This was small comfort to the victims of industrial change, but it was all she offered. Answering questions from a television audience in the summer of 1981, she acknowledged that unemployment was 'unacceptably high'. 'I feel deeply concerned when I have people who want jobs and can't get them. But I know that I can't conjure them out of thin air . . . I do feel deeply about it. Of course I do. I wouldn't be human if we didn't.'[44] In the House of Commons she faced uproar every month when the latest figure was published: Labour MPs accused her of creating 'an industrial desert' and using unemployment deliberately to cow the unions. She responded with a mixture of angry retaliation and patient lectures on the facts of economic life.

On the one hand she constantly recalled that, for all their handwringing, unemployment had doubled under Labour. 'We all hate unemployment, but we all remember it was the previous Government who increased it so much.'[45] 'We shared his distress at that,' she told Michael Foot in January 1981. 'I hope he will share ours.'[46] 'Unemployment is no part of my policy whatsoever.'[47] On the other hand she repeatedly explained that it was not Government policy or heartlessness which destroyed jobs but the uncompetitiveness of British industry. Over the past five years the country had priced itself out of world markets by paying itself 100 per cent more for producing 2 per cent less. The result was that other countries had the jobs 'and we have a large proportion of the unemployment'.[48] Increased public spending was not, as Labour – and half her own Cabinet – believed, a recipe for more jobs: 'It is a recipe for inflation and even fewer jobs.'[49] She repeatedly recalled Jim Callaghan's speech to the 1976 Labour Party Conference when he acknowledged: 'We used to think we could just spend our way out of a recession . . . I tell you in all candour that that option no longer exists':[50]

> It seems to me that the Opposition has deliberately turned their backs on the lessons of the past quarter of a century. Their proposals are a return to the very policies that led to our problems in the first place.[51]

She insisted that there was no painless remedy. Only by becoming competitive would new jobs in the new industries eventually be created. Cutting public expenditure, far from exacerbating unemployment, was actually the way to reduce it by releasing resources for the private sector, which was the productive sector. 'It is the sector from which the jobs will come.'[52] As the recession endured and deepened, she increasingly accepted an obligation on the Government to 'cushion the harsher effects of change' by promoting enterprise zones, training schemes and new technology;[53] but she also insisted that the unemployed must be willing to move to where the new jobs were – advice classically embodied at the 1981 party conference by Norman Tebbit's story about his father in the 1930s, who just 'got on his bike' and looked for work.[54] Labour continually demanded where the new jobs were, and pointed out that the Government's policy of selling council houses was impeding labour mobility by reducing the availability of rented housing. But finding that she could not prevent the numbers of the jobless rising remorselessly, Mrs Thatcher found a way of turning the pain of unemployment to her advantage. Skilfully seizing on one of the most positive role models peculiarly available to a woman Prime Minister, she portrayed herself as a nurse – or sometimes a doctor – administering nasty medicine to cure the country's self-inflicted illness.

'We have taken all the necessary steps and they will work through,' she assured *The Times* on the first anniversary of her election:

It's like a patient, there's a time when you're still suffering from the disease, and you take the medicine, and there's a time when you are suffering from both the disease and the medicine. That doesn't mean you stop the medicine, you know you have to take the medicine if you are to be cured of the disease.[55]

'After almost any major operation,' she declared in a party television broadcast, 'you feel worse before you convalesce. But you don't refuse the operation when you know that without it you won't survive.'[56] 'Which is the better nurse?' she asked on another occasion:

The one who smothers the patient with sympathy and says 'Never mind, dear, there, there, you just lie back and I'll bring you all your meals . . . I'll look after you.' Or the nurse who says 'Now, come on, shake out of it . . . It's time you put your feet on the ground and took a few steps . . .' Which do you think is the better nurse? . . . The one who says come on, you can do it. That's me.[57]

This was clever presentation, and it worked. After the dismal spiral of inflation, strikes and steadily mounting unemployment through the 1970s, the public was at least half ready to believe that any effective cure for the nation's sickness was bound to be painful, and was masochistically ready to endure it. The figure of the strict Nurse Thatcher struck a chord in the British psyche. Though the Conservatives had not campaigned on any such prospectus, and opinion polls showed the Government's popularity sinking ever lower, Labour was increasingly distracted and marginalised by its bitter internal power struggle, which the left was clearly winning. In November 1980, when Callaghan retired, the party abdicated any claim to be a serious opposition by electing the sentimental old left-winger Michael Foot in preference to the robust and realistic Denis Healey. At a level deeper than opinion polls the electorate seemed to accept that there was indeed, as Geoffrey Howe asserted, 'no alternative'.[58] The phrase was originally the Chancellor's, but the nickname TINA – 'There Is No Alternative' – quickly attached itself to the Prime Minister. 'It is no good dreaming about U-turns,' she declared in a confidence debate just before the House rose in July 1980. 'There aren't any available . . . We are doing what the country elected us to do. The Government will have the guts to see it through.'[59]

Three months later, at the party conference in Brighton, she made her most famous retort to the fainthearts who were calling for a U-turn, supplied as usual by Ronnie Millar. 'You turn if you want to,' she told the delighted representatives, then paused while they laughed, thinking that was the punchline. 'The Lady's not for turning.'[60]★ Privately she had already given the same assurance to her staff. John Hoskyns, Norman Strauss and David Wolfson warned her that if she was going to do a U-turn she had better tell them in good time. 'She made it absolutely clear,' Hoskyns recalled, 'she would really rather be chucked out than do a U-turn. She was in an absolutely sort of burning the boats frame of mind about that.'[64] Whether the policy was economically right or wrong, whether or not it was true that there was no alternative, her resolution conveyed itself to the country and won its grudging admiration. After the Wilson–Heath–Callaghan years of drift and compromise, Mrs Thatcher's sheer defiance was a bravura performance which deflected – or at least suspended – criticism.

Softly, softly

But the heart of Thatcherism was not in monetarism anyway. Monetarism was merely an economic theory which few ministers, let alone commentators or the public, fully understood. Mrs Thatcher herself rarely used the word and scorned the idea that she was in thrall to any academic theory. 'If I could get back to some of the things on which I was brought up,' she told Sue Lawley on *Nationwide*, 'I wouldn't need to have any economic theory.'[65] Rather 'monetarism' was used by her political opponents as a convenient shorthand for the Government's hard-faced policy of cuts in public services. To Mrs Thatcher monetarism offered an appealingly simple formula which promised a foolproof method of controlling inflation, but which turned out to be more problematic than she had been led to believe. It was essentially a tool, not a dogma, to be discarded if it did not work. Her real purpose was much more political: purging what she called socialism from the economy by encouraging enterprise in place of subsidy and regulation, cutting overmanning and restrictive practices, particularly in the public sector, and above all curbing the power of the over-mighty unions.

Union power was the great symbolic dragon which Mrs Thatcher had been elected to slay. It was the unions which had humiliated and

---

★The line derived from the title of Christopher Fry's 1948 verse play, *The Lady's Not for Burning*. (Mrs Thatcher may actually have seen it during her courtship with Denis.) It was really pretty obvious once the nickname 'The Lady' was in common use: *The Times* had already applied the original phrase to the Prime Minister.[61] Millar had expected a laugh on the first part; he never dreamed that the second would make such an impact.[62] But as Hoskyns says: 'The punchline worked perfectly and she delivered it just right.'[63]

ultimately destroyed the last Conservative Government in 1972–4, and union-fostered anarchy which had done more than anything else to bring the Conservatives back to power in 1979, with a clear mandate to bring the bully-boys to heel. In opposition Mrs Thatcher had been obliged to tread a careful line between the conciliatory approach of her shadow Employment Secretary, Jim Prior, and the much more confrontational strategy secretly formulated by John Hoskyns, embodied in the never-published document *Stepping Stones*. The events of the 'Winter of Discontent', however, had weakened Prior's hand and strengthened public and party expectation that the new Government would lose no time in taking firm measures.

In the event this was another area in which Mrs Thatcher proceeded cautiously. Her treatment of trade-union reform, indeed, offers a case-book example of prudence overruling instinct, her head ruling her heart. For one thing she needed Prior in her first Cabinet. In her memoirs she wrote scornfully of Prior as the type of 'false squire' she believed had most damaged the Tory party in her lifetime. 'They have all the outward show of a John Bull – ruddy face, white hair, bluff manner – but inwardly they are political calculators who see the task of Conservatives as one of retreating gracefully before the Left's inevitable advance.'[66] But Prior was a tougher character than this suggests – both the most forthright and the most popular of the wets, a political heavyweight with a down-to-earth appeal not unlike Kenneth Clarke a decade later. He had invested heavily in his consensual approach to industrial relations and enjoyed the support of other old Heathites like Willie Whitelaw and Peter Carrington. Mrs Thatcher had little choice but to confirm him as Employment Secretary in May 1979, and having once appointed him she could not afford to lose him, so she had to go along with his approach, frustrating though it was to her backbench zealots.

At the same time she recognised that Heath and his Employment Secretary Robert Carr had courted disaster in 1971 by trying to reform the whole of industrial relations law in one comprehensive Bill. The political climate was much more propitious now than then. But still there was a shrewd argument for tackling the problem one step at a time, carrying public opinion with the Government and denying the unions a single emotive cause to rally round. Her strategy, therefore, was not to confront the unions but to outflank them by appealing over the heads of the unrepresentative and timewarped leaders to the rank-and-file members who had voted Conservative in unprecedented numbers in May and who – polls showed – overwhelmingly supported reform. Her constant theme was that it was not only the public but ordinary trade unionists who suffered from the abuse of union power. These ordinary members had voted Tory, she believed, because they recognised that 'our policy represents their ambition for their own future and for their families, for a better standard of living and better jobs'.[67] The purpose of the Government's reform was to encourage those ordinary Tory-voting trade unionists to reclaim their unions from the control of the militants.

She further marginalised the union barons by ignoring them. She did agree to meet the TUC General Council, 'at their request', six weeks after taking office. But it was 'a bad meeting', the leader of the Post Office workers, Tom Jackson, recalled. 'There was a coldness . . . which I hadn't seen before when the TUC had gone to Downing Street . . . It was the start of a real divorce between the government and the trade union movement.'[68] The TUC Secretary-General, Len Murray, complained that Mrs Thatcher 'rejected the idea of trade unions as valid institutions within society . . . which, even if you didn't like them, you were stuck with and had to come to some sort of agreement.'[69] For her part, finding 'no willingness on their side to face economic facts or to try to understand the economic strategy we were pursuing', Mrs Thatcher resolved not to invite them again.[70] She was happy to let Prior talk to Murray, even on occasion to mouth conventional pieties herself about the important role that 'a strong and responsible trade union movement' could play in Britain's economic recovery.[71] But in practice she firmly denied them the role they had come to see as their right by eschewing any form of pay policy, refusing to intervene in industrial disputes and letting economic realities and the rising toll of unemployment educate the workforce and emasculate the militants.

Legislation played only a supporting role in this process. Following a consultation document in July, Prior published his Employment Bill in December 1979. Its scope was modest, proposing only what had been promised in the Tory manifesto. Secondary picketing – that is, picketing workplaces not directly involved in a dispute – was outlawed, but not secondary strike action. Employees who refused to join unions were given increased rights of appeal and compensation against the operation of closed shops; but the closed shop itself was not banned (despite Mrs Thatcher repeating that she was 'absolutely against the closed shop in principle').[72] Thirdly, Government money was made available to encourage unions to hold secret ballots. There was no mention in the Bill of any of the more draconian measures demanded by the Tory right: cutting strikers' entitlement to benefits, making union funds liable to action for civil damages, or making members who wished to support the Labour party 'opt in' to paying the political levy,

instead of requiring those who did not to opt out. All these were more
or less explicitly left to further Employment Acts further down the
road.

The Institute of Directors, Aims of Industry and right-wing backbenchers like George Gardiner and Nicholas Winterton – to say nothing
of Hoskyns in the Number Ten Policy Unit and Alfred Sherman in
the CPS – blamed Prior for this craven moderation and urged Mrs
Thatcher publicly and privately to sack him. But the skill of his approach
was demonstrated by the unions' predictably exaggerated response. By
vowing 'total opposition' to what Murray called 'a fundamental attack'
on workers' rights, the TUC only confirmed its reputation as an
unthinking dinosaur.[73] Prior's strategy was perfectly designed to demonstrate that the union leaders were out of touch with their members.
When the TUC tried to revive the memory of its successful campaign
against Heath's Industrial Relations Bill by calling a 'Day of Action' in
May 1980, it failed dismally when no more than a few thousand activists
stayed off work. 'People will have no truck with political strikes,' Mrs
Thatcher asserted in the House of Commons. 'They would rather get
on with the job.'[74] Earlier she hailed the miners' rejection of their
leaders' call for strike action against the National Coal Board's pay offer
as an encouraging sign that moderate members could regain control
of their unions without further legislation.[75]

Up to the end of January 1980, Mrs Thatcher stoutly defended
Prior's 'modest and sensible' Bill as 'a very good start'. Even after the
steel unions began a bitter strike against the British Steel Corporation's
plans to rationalise the industry, she specifically ruled out – 'for the
moment' – action on secondary strikes and strikers' benefits.[76] In
February, however, the situation was transformed. First, the steel dispute
spread, with secondary picketing of private steelmakers leading to
violent scenes reminiscent of the previous winter. At the same moment
the House of Lords' judgement in an important test case, *Express
Newspapers v. McShane*, confirmed the trade unions' legal immunity
from liability for the consequences of their members' actions. These
events increased the pressure on the Government to widen the scope
of Prior's Bill. A hundred Tory MPs signed an Early Day Motion. The
papers built up the issue as the critical first test of the Government's
mettle. 'If you don't act now,' the *Daily Express* warned, 'the writing
will be on the tombstone of the Tory Government.'[77] Geoffrey Howe
– long a hardliner on union immunities – infuriated Prior by calling
his Bill merely 'the first step in a long process of law reform' and promising that further measures would follow 'with all deliberate speed'.[78]

Mrs Thatcher was bound to respond. Not only were the backbench hawks her core supporters, whose instincts she entirely shared, but she could not afford to be outbid from the right by Howe. She accordingly pressed Prior to add a new clause outlawing secondary action. Since that would not have immediate effect on the steel strike, she also wanted to rush forward a single-clause Bill to ban secondary picketing immediately, without waiting for the Employment Bill to go through all its stages. But Prior resisted both proposals, and was supported in Cabinet by a powerful combination of senior ministers including Whitelaw, Carrington, Hailsham, Gilmour and Walker. Hoskyns noted that the Prime Minister, Howe and Joseph were 'almost completely isolated'.[79] Defeated in Cabinet in the morning, however, Mrs Thatcher got her own back the same afternoon by simply announcing at Prime Minister's Questions that plans to cut strikers' benefits were going ahead after all. 'I hope that we shall be in a position to make an announcement soon.'[80] Prior was 'amazed' by her announcement:

It was quite obvious that she'd thought the thing through and she was determined to get it on the record in case, when it came to the crunch, the wets prevailed. And that was quite often her way of doing things. Very effective.[81]

Provision for cutting strikers' benefits was duly included in Howe's budget six weeks later.

Then Mrs Thatcher went on *Panorama* and trailed the idea of banning secondary strikes as something for the next instalment of union legislation. Prior's Bill, she now told Robin Day, went 'some way but not all the way'. If it turned out to be insufficient, there was 'a lot to be said for going further . . . By the time the next election is here we have got to have done it.' In the same interview she took the chance to rap Prior's knuckles for appearing to take sides – the wrong side – in the steel dispute by criticising the management of the BSC. 'I think it was a mistake,' she said in her most schoolmistressy style, 'and Jim Prior was very, very sorry indeed for it . . . but you don't just sack a chap for one mistake.'[82] Perhaps not, but Prior was very publicly on probation.

An attempt was made to introduce a new clause on secondary action while the Bill was going through the Lords in July. Quintin Hailsham and Peter Thorneycroft ensured that it was heavily defeated; but not before Mrs Thatcher had met the rebel peers and left them in no doubt of her sympathy.[83] Meanwhile – before his Bill was even on the Statute Book – Prior was pressured to publish a Green Paper foreshadowing further curbs on the closed shop and other measures. But he still firmly resisted ending the unions' legal immunity. 'Sometimes it requires courage to stand against the stream,' he told the Commons. 'If I am overridden I shall resign.'[84] Mrs Thatcher missed no opportunity to repeat that she intended to go further: 'The Bill is a first step,' she said in July. 'It is not a last step.'[85] But it was clear that the next step would have to await a new Employment Secretary; and she was not yet strong enough to be rid of Prior.

In this way she got the best of both worlds. On the one hand she saw a significant first measure of reform enacted without provoking serious union opposition, and opened the way for another, while gaining credit for moderation and keeping her Cabinet intact. On the other she contrived to preserve her reputation with her core supporters as a radical who would have liked to do more, were she not constrained by her colleagues. Her blatant undermining of Prior on television and in the Commons was an early instance of what became a familiar tactic whereby she distanced herself from her own Government, running with the hare while hunting with the hounds. It was clever politics, but it was essentially two-faced and disloyal to colleagues who never felt they could rely on her support. They were always liable to have the rug pulled from under them, either openly by Mrs Thatcher herself or more insidiously by an unattributable briefing from Number Ten. In the short run this skilful ambiguity helped establish her authority over colleagues, many of whom were not naturally her supporters. But over time it strained the loyalty even of her handful of 'true believers', undermined the cohesion of her Government and ultimately wrought her downfall.

Over the whole decade 1979–90, curbing the power of the unions was perhaps the Thatcher Government's most unarguable achievement, ending a culture of institutionalised abuse which had hobbled enterprise and broken three previous Governments – Labour and Conservative – in the previous ten years. It can be argued that the successive Employment Acts, of which Prior's was the first, were actually less instrumental in emasculating the unions than unemployment. 'In a sense,' Ian Gilmour has written, the legislation 'registered rather than caused the decline of the unions'.[86] It is certainly true that unemployment critically weakened the unions as both their industrial muscle and their membership declined dramatically over the decade. Membership fell from over thirteen million to less than ten million.[87] But in fact the legislative and economic pressures reinforced one another: the Government's legislation was successful just because it was introduced against a background of high unemployment in cumulative instalments which offered the demoralised unions no popular cause on which to make a stand. The result vindicated Prior's gradualism – but also Mrs Thatcher's caution in backing him. In her memoirs she contrasts his 'timid and over-cautious' policy with her own impatience 'to stake out a more determined approach'.[88] In fact she deserves more credit than she gives herself for letting Prior do it his way. With hindsight even John Hoskyns acknowedged that Prior's slow track was vindicated by the result.[89]

The success of that first instalment of trade-union law reform in disarming opposition and opening the way to further instalments in 1982, 1984, 1988 and 1990 illustrates an important truth about the Thatcher Government: that her first administration was in some ways her best. The fact that she did not command a majority of supporters in the Cabinet before 1983 enforced a degree of compromise and consideration for other views which produced better legislation, and better government altogether, than was often the case after 1983 when the Prime Minister's personal dominance was unchallenged and she could usually impose her will with very little opposition.

Joseph on the rack

The second great dragon waiting to be tackled was the nationalised sector of the economy. Here again the Government's first steps disappointed its keenest supporters. Just a few years later, when Mrs Thatcher's second administration was successfully embarked on an ambitious programme of wholesale denationalisation which transferred back to the private sector most of the staple industries and public utilities nationalised by the Attlee Government after 1945, the idea gained currency that privatisation – as it came to be called – was a policy into which the Government had stumbled by accident, driven more by Treasury cost-cutting than ideological conviction. The fact that privatisation on the scale that occurred after 1983 was not foreshadowed in the 1979 manifesto gave rise to a belief that it was not on the Government's agenda when Mrs Thatcher first came to power, but was merely a sort of opportunist afterthought. There is enough truth in this to give the story an ironic piquancy, but it is not the whole truth.

It was always a central part of the vision of an enterprise economy that the nationalised sector, if it could not be wholly eliminated, should at least be substantially reduced. In his alternative 'Morecambe budget' of 1968 Enoch Powell had proposed radical denationalisation as a means of halving income tax. His disciple Nicholas Ridley wrote papers for Heath's Shadow Cabinet in 1968 and again for Mrs Thatcher's a decade later in which he set out a target list and a timetable of nationalised industries which could be sold off. On both occasions his ideas were firmly vetoed by the leadership before they could reach the manifesto. By the standard of what actually occurred after 1983 Ridley's proposals were notably modest: he did not believe, for instance, that it would ever be possible to privatise the monopoly utilities.[90] Mrs Thatcher was instinctively much keener on privatisation than Heath. She believed that the public sector was inherently inefficient and a drag on the wealth-creating enterprise of the private sector, and talked freely in private about the need to reduce it. But up to 1979 her overriding concern was not to alarm the voters by striking attitudes that could be labelled 'extreme'. Nigel Lawson insists that, far from being a 'happy accident', privatisation was 'a central plank in our policy right from the start'; but he adds that 'the enthusiasts for privatisation were Keith Joseph, Geoffrey Howe, David Howell and me, rather than Margaret'. Little detailed work was done in opposition because of 'Margaret's understandable fear of frightening the floating voter'.[91] Howe admitted in 1987 that privatisation was 'an idea whose importance was underestimated when we came into office'.[92] In his memoirs he wrote that 'it was always a conscious objective, but for years it was never quite on the agenda'.[93]

By the time Lady Thatcher came to write *her* memoirs she had convinced herself that privatisation was always central to her purpose:

> Just as nationalisation was at the heart of the collectivist programme by which Labour Governments sought to remodel British society, so privatisation is at the centre of any programme of reclaiming territory for freedom.

Yet on the next page she admitted that in the late 1970s the idea was so revolutionary as to be 'all but unthinkable'.[94] 'Just a few years ago,' she acknowledged in 1985, 'privatisation was thought to be a pipedream. Now it is a reality and a popular one.'[95] There is no question that privatisation did take off unexpectedly after 1983. That is not to say, however, that finding ways of cutting the public sector was not a high priority from the beginning. In her very first speech as Prime Minister, Mrs Thatcher spoke of making a start 'in extending the role of private enterprise by reducing the size of the public sector – adding emphatically: 'It needs reducing';[96] and a few weeks later she promised proposals for 'attempting to have less public sector ownership and more private sector ownership'.[97] Her language constantly suggests that she did not think it would be easy. What she mainly meant in these early days was selling shares in profitable state-owned companies like BP – where Labour had already shown the way – and dismantling the ragbag portfolio of odd companies taken into public ownership by Labour's National Enterprise Board (NEB) (which Joseph hoped to wind up within five years). She was particularly keen to give priority to the workers employed in these firms, so that 'those who work in industry . . . should make great strides towards being real capital owners'.[98] Neither she nor anyone else at this stage envisaged selling whole industries, mainly because their concern was less with ownership than with promoting competition. The Government's early effort was concentrated on selling off profitable ancillary parts of the nationalised industries, like gas and electricity showrooms, British Rail hotels and the cross-Channel hovercraft. They did not see how the core utilities themselves could be sold. 'In those industries,' Mrs Thatcher told the Commons in November 1981, 'we must ensure that the absence of market forces is replaced by other pressures to induce greater efficiency.'[99] While clear about the desirability of the objective, she remained persistently cautious, always talking of 'trying' to denationalise 'wherever possible' and stressing the practical difficulties.[100]

Nevertheless a very substantial start was made in 1979–82. Only by comparison with what came later can it be represented as small beer. Even the manifesto commitment was not so 'exiguous' (Lawson's word) as is sometimes made out. Though limited to reversing Labour's most recent nationalisations – road haulage (1968) and aircraft and shipbuilding (1977) – this was not a negligible programme for the first term. In fact the first Thatcher Government did a good deal more. Norman Fowler, as Transport Secretary, duly sold the National Freight Corporation, but also deregulated long-distance coach travel, creating new private competition with the state-owned railways. Keith Joseph began the process of selling British Aerospace (49 per cent in February 1981). Several large NEB holdings were successfully sold: ICL computers, Fairey (aircraft parts), Ferranti engineering, along with Amersham International, Cable and Wireless and other companies which Governments, both Labour and Conservative, had acquired over the years. As Energy Secretary, David Howell began the process of turning the British National Oil Corporation (BNOC), the North Sea oil exploitation company, into Britoil as a first step to privatising it. (Lawson completed this operation when he moved to Energy in 1981.) The sale of British Airways was also planned, under the dynamic leadership of John King, one of Mrs Thatcher's favourite businessmen, but had to be delayed for commercial reasons. Most significantly, Joseph split up the Post Office, creating a separate telecommunications company

(British Telecom), initially as a way of attracting private money to pay for new technology; he also licensed a private telephone company, Mercury, to inject some competition into the telecommunications business.

By any standard except that of the bonanza years 1983–90, this was a remarkable record. Moreover in November 1981 Lawson announced the principle that 'No industry should remain under State ownership unless there is a positive and overwhelming case for it so doing.'[101] The momentum of privatisation was well under way before the 1983 election. The Tory manifesto for that election targeted British Telecom, British Airways and the profitable parts of British Steel, British Shipbuilders and British Leyland. Yet ministers themselves did not realise the scale of the revolution that was around the corner.

In a sense, however, all this activity was marginal because it did not touch the core of the Government's problem – the great loss-making dinosaurs of the nationalised sector: British Rail, British Steel, the National Coal Board and the permanently struggling car maker, British Leyland. Much as they would have loved to have been rid of them, Mrs Thatcher and Keith Joseph were stuck with these monsters. Their ambition in 1979–81 was limited to trying to cut their costs, to reduce the drain on the Exchequer of their annual losses as part of the drive to cut public borrowing. To this end Joseph imposed tight cash limits on each industry, within which financial discipline they were expected to operate as far as possible like commercial companies – shedding surplus labour, raising productivity, selling off ancillary businesses and resisting unearned pay demands in order to meet their financial targets within a fixed timescale; meanwhile the Government ostentatiously stood back and proclaimed its refusal to print money to buy off strikes or underwrite further losses. In 1981 the CPRS proposed a scheme for groups of outside industrialists to monitor the nationalised industries; and a search was set in hand for a new breed of tough, commercially minded managers from the private sector to replace the old style of corporatist bosses like Sir Peter Parker (British Rail), Sir Charles Villiers (British Steel) and – Mrs Thatcher's particular *bête noire* – Sir Derek Ezra (National Coal Board).

Joseph, however, found the practice of non-intervention much harder than the theory. He arrived at the Department of Industry with a famous reading list of twenty-nine free-market texts which he required his officials to study.[102] As a humane man, however, and as a practical politician, he could not wash his hands while whole industries went to the wall. He could not simply close down British Steel, British Leyland or the Belfast shipbuilders Harland and Wolff, however chronic their losses. So he agonised and, against his principles, ended up – to his subsequent shame – spending more taxpayers' millions: in two years his budget actually increased by 50 per cent, from £2,200 million to £3,300 million per annum.[103] Mrs Thatcher despaired of him. He was both her economic mentor and the man who, more than anyone else, had opened the way for her to become Prime Minister. 'Margaret admired him, treasured him,' Jim Prior wrote, 'looking on him as a mother who cannot refrain from indulging a favourite son, even though she knows it will do him no good.' She still listened to his advice in private; but he was a hopelessly indecisive minister. 'In the end it all became impossible and Keith was moved to Education.'[104]

Joseph's first big test was a major steel strike at the beginning of 1980. The ostensible issue was pay; but behind that lay the British Steel Corporation's plans for drastically restructuring – that is, shrinking – the industry. In the first half of 1979 British Steel lost £145 million; by the end of the year it was losing £7 million a week. Clearly this could not continue. Joseph set the BSC a target to cut its deficit by the end of 1980. At the end of November 1979 the corporation announced the closure of plants at Corby, Shotton, Cleveland and Port Talbot, with the loss of 50,000 jobs – one-third of the workforce. At the same time it offered the remainder a pay rise of just 2 per cent. The two main steel unions called a strike from 2 January; both unions and management then sat back and waited for the Government to come up with more money. But Joseph refused to intervene. The effect of a long steel strike on the rest of industry was potentially devastating. Mrs Thatcher was worried – she personally chaired a special group of ministers and officials to keep close watch on the situation – but she was adamant that the Government would not weaken. When Callaghan told her that she had 'no moral right to sit back while this creeping paralysis creeps across the country' she retorted that it was the strikers themselves who were destroying their own jobs. She rejected his assertion that steel was a 'strategic industry' which the Government had a duty to protect. 'The size of an industry is determined by what it can sell and the quality and delivery dates of its products.'[105] 'I am aware of a sense of desperation,' she told Michael Foot at the beginning of February:

> There is a great sense of desperation when a whole people provide a whole industry with the latest and best equipment so that it may become the best and most efficient steel producer in the world, and those who work in the industry do not take the opportunity to use it but go on strike to demand more from the taxpayer.[106]

She was determined to teach the lesson that steel must stand on its own feet.

The unions stepped up their pressure by spreading the dispute to the private-sector steelmakers, with mass secondary picketing leading to violent scenes at private steelworks. Courageously Joseph went to south Wales himself to explain to the steelworkers that they were pricing themselves out of a shrinking world market. 'I was perhaps arrogantly sure that I was right,' he reflected later, 'that they were in process of committing industrial suicide.'[107] He was jostled and spat at for his pains. The management did increase its offer, first to 6 per cent and then to 10 per cent. Finally the two sides agreed to an old-fashioned inquiry, headed by the former Labour Cabinet Minister, Harold Lever. Mrs Thatcher was deeply suspicious; her doubts were confirmed when Lever predictably split the difference between the BSC's final offer and the union's demand and recommended a settlement around 16 per cent, including productivity deals. (Inflation was then around 20 per cent.) Both sides accepted it and the strike was called off at the beginning of April.

On the face of it this was not much of a victory for the Government. Yet Joseph and Mrs Thatcher had made their point by not intervening, despite great pressure from the rest of industry (and much of the Cabinet), leaving management and unions to make their own deal. The real victory for the Government was that, under cover of the pay rise, BSC's plant closures were accepted. On this basis Joseph agreed to carry on subsidising the corporation for another year. Then, after a long search, the sixty-eight-year-old Scottish-born but Americanised Ian MacGregor − a tough manager with a reputation for defeating strikes − was recruited from Lazard Freres at a huge salary (plus an unusual performance-related compensation package to Lazards for letting him go) to sort the corporation out. 'The terms are unusual,' Mrs Thatcher wrote to Edward Boyle, chairman of the Top Salaries Review Board:

> We have had great difficulty in finding somebody who has both the stature and ability, and is willing to take on the uniquely important job of restoring BSC to enduring profitability. After a number of disappointments over the last nine months I believe that in MacGregor we have secured an exceptionally well-qualified man.[108]

She was right: MacGregor earned his salary. In two years he transformed British Steel from the least efficient to one of the best steelmakers in Europe, bringing it almost into profit − at the cost of losing nearly half the workforce, cut from 166,000 to 85,000. Five years later the slimmed-down corporation was successfully privatised. This was Thatcherite industrial policy as it was meant to work – the long-term reward for the Government standing firm in the early months of 1980.*

Less happy in the short term – indeed a major embarrassment to a government pledged not to support lame ducks – was the necessity to go on funding British Leyland. BL symbolised everything that was wrong with British industry: it was over-manned, under-productive, racked by unofficial strikes, a once-major car manufacturer increasingly unable to compete with European and Japanese rivals. Though not strictly a nationalised industry, it had been repeatedly bailed out by successive governments but was still losing market share – down from 33 per cent to 20 per cent of the UK market between 1974 and 1979 – and money. Here was a prime candidate for the new Government's free-market philosophy: if Joseph was true to his convictions, he would refuse to subsidise BL any further but simply close it down. Nothing the Government could have done in its first year would have sent a clearer message to the rest of industry. But two considerations pulled the other way. First, BL was a big employer in the politically marginal West Midlands, providing 150,000 jobs directly, plus as many again in its component supply industries. The effect of closure would have been devastating. Second, BL had (since November 1977) a dynamic new chairman, the South African-born Michael Edwardes, who was making a real effort to solve the company's labour problems. This was a factor that made a special appeal to Mrs Thatcher. 'I knew that whatever we decided to do about BL would have an impact on the psychology and morale of British managers as a whole,' she wrote in her memoirs, 'and I was determined to send the right signals . . . We had to back Michael Edwardes.'[109]

In December 1979 BL was given an additional £300 million, with a warning that if the latest Corporate Plan was derailed by the militants there would be no more. Yet the company lost another £93 million in the first half of 1980. By the end of the year Edwardes was asking for another £900 million to carry forward his restructuring during 1981–2. The same arguments applied. In Cabinet Committee before Christmas Joseph still favoured paying up; he was supported by Biffen and Prior, with only John Nott ready to pull the plug. Mrs Thatcher was pragmatically clear that, for political not economic

---

*The casualties – apart from the workers who lost their jobs – were ironically the private steelmakers who were forced out of business while BSC was subsidised into profitability.

reasons, 'BL had to be supported.'[110] After agonising over Christmas, however, Joseph changed his mind; he came back to the committee to argue, against his own paper, that the time had come to abandon the company. He was outvoted, probably to his own relief. 'I didn't have the guts to desubsidise Leyland,' Joseph told his biographer. 'I could have said I would desubsidise it and would resign if my colleagues didn't support me. I myself flinched from the recommendations of my own analysis.'[111]

But Joseph's anguished advocacy of the pure free-market case embarrassed Mrs Thatcher, who compensated first by giving him a hard time in Cabinet and then by adding a strong Thatcherite spin to the announcement of the continued subsidy, switching the emphasis – to Edwardes' fury – from another rescue package to preparation for privatisation. She wanted BL to sell off its profitable elements, like Land-Rover and Unipart; Edwardes wanted to keep his company together. On television she graphically presented the decision to keep on funding BL as a matter of timing. With productivity improving and a new model – the Metro – soon to be launched, she explained in one of those surprising phrases which occasionally came to her that this was not the moment to say, 'No, I'm going to chop you off at the stocking tops.'[112]* This was a bravura defence of what might easily have been seen as a U-turn. In fact this rescue too was vindicated in the long run. After a couple of hiccups, BL – its name by then changed to Rover – was finally sold to the already privatised British Aerospace in 1987. By that time Mrs Thatcher was just glad to be rid of it.

Two hard-nosed managers like Michael Edwardes and Ian MacGregor provided cover for the Government continuing to fund British Leyland and British Steel through their difficulties. No such figleaf was available to explain a third reversal, which really did seem to suggest that the Government's resolution was weaker than its rhetoric when it came to implementing its industrial strategy. This third challenge came from the miners – still the vanguard of the union movement, whose two strikes in 1972 and 1974 had humiliated and then destroyed the previous Conservative Government. Of all the beasts in the industrial jungle, the National Union of Mineworkers (NUM) was the one Mrs Thatcher knew she would have to take on and defeat at some point. Detailed planning to withstand a coal strike had begun the moment the Government came into office: an unusual mixed

---

*Was it a memory of the playground, or a film seen long ago in Grantham? Or does it refer to the thrifty mending of old clothes?

committee of ministers and officials, chaired jointly by Willie Whitelaw
and the deputy Cabinet Secretary Robert Wade-Gery, was established
to prepare the Government's position.[113] Yet when the opportunity for
a showdown with the NUM arose in February 1981 it was Mrs Thatcher
who backed down. It was her decision, overriding her Energy Secretary
David Howell, who was preparing to stand firm. (The Cabinet was
not consulted.) Three years later, of course, it was very different. Then
Mrs Thatcher was ready to mobilise the whole resources of the
Government and the police to defeat the quasi-revolutionary challenge
of Arthur Scargill. That epic confrontation in 1984–5 sealed her rout
of the unions. From the perspective of 1985 the earlier retreat could
be understood as merely tactical. But at the time it appeared to show
that Mrs Thatcher had learned from Ted Heath's experience that it was
wiser not to tangle with the miners.

The issue, as in 1984, was the closure of uneconomic pits. On the
question of pay there had been encouraging signs, from the
Government's point of view, that the miners had no wish to revisit
the battles of the early 1970s. In December 1979 they voted – against
the recommendation of their Executive – to accept a settlement of 20
per cent (only just above the level of inflation); and in 1980 they
accepted less than 10 per cent. But the NCB's announcement of plans
to close twenty-three pits with the loss of 13,000 jobs raised more
fundamental fears for the future of the industry. Faced with the threat
of a strike, Mrs Thatcher was initially robust. Asked by Michael Foot
in the Commons if she would reconsider the closures before she was
forced to, she replied defiantly: 'No, Sir . . . I am not forced to do
many things.'[114] Pit closures were a matter for the NCB. 'I am not
directing that industry.'[115] But she was appalled to discover that the
NCB had made no contingency plans to withstand a strike: surplus
coal was piling up at the pithead, but there were only minimal stocks
at the power stations where it was needed. (What had Whitelaw's
committee been doing?) With her instinct for the realities of power
she swiftly concluded that this was a dispute the Government could
not win. 'Defeat in a coal strike would have been disastrous,' she wrote
in her memoirs. 'All we could do was cut our losses and live to fight
another day.'[116]

In fact it was not so much a matter of cutting losses as finding an
additional £300–400 million to keep the threatened pits open. Better
that, however, than fight a losing battle. 'In dealing with the coal
industry,' she later rationalised, 'you must have the mentality of a general
as much as of an accountant. And the generalship must often be Fabian
rather than Napoleonic.'[117] But the NUM's crowing, and her own

supporters' undisguised dismay, must have been hard to bear. Even Bernard Ingham was embarrassed defending the U-turn to the press.[118] The *Observer* gleefully reported that the Government 'did not even wait to see the whites of their eyes before climbing down'.[119] In the Commons she defended the Government's retreat as 'swift, decisive and realistic'. But when Foot satirically told her that 'every time she turns she will get a nice bouquet from me', or even dinner, she could only parry that it was 'a lady's prerogative to say "no"'. 'Not to the miners,' the Labour MP Joe Ashton chortled.[120] The NUM was unwise to gloat, however. In the long war between the miners and the Tories, 1981 was a Pyrrhic victory. Her ignominious retreat only hardened Mrs Thatcher's determination to exact a decisive revenge when the time was ripe.

One group of workers she had no compunction about taking on, however, was the Civil Service. For one thing, civil servants were the Government's own employees, for whose pay and numbers ministers were directly responsible. Any Government intent on cutting public spending was bound to start with its own servants. But more than that, it was Mrs Thatcher's positive intention to 'deprivilege' the Civil Service. Though she admired individual officials, she regarded the bureaucracy as a whole as an obstacle to the culture she was trying to create. One of Geoffrey Howe's first actions in 1979 was to set a target to cut the Civil Service by 100,000 jobs over the next five years. At the beginning of 1981 he announced that the 6 per cent cash limit already set for local authorities would also apply to central government; the independent Civil Service Pay Research Unit was abolished. The nine Civil Service unions promptly rejected an offer of 7 per cent (which, with a little fiddling, could be financed within the 6 per cent limit) and started a highly effective campaign of selective strikes directed at Inland Revenue collection, customs and excise, vehicle licences and other Government agencies – including the secret intelligence monitoring centre at Cheltenham (GCHQ).

This last enraged Mrs Thatcher more than all the others; but after three months the loss of revenue to the Government was becoming serious. The Cabinet Office minister responsible for the Civil Service, Christopher Soames – fresh from his proconsular triumph in Zimbabwe – applied his heavyweight experience to trying to negotiate a settlement. He succeeded, with a very modestly increased offer of 7.5 per cent; but Mrs Thatcher would not have it. 'Margaret firmly and personally refused to sanction a settlement at that figure at that date,' Howe recalled. 'She took the view that it was sloppy thinking of that kind which had already taken the figure up too high . . . and too soon.'[121]

She wanted to make a demonstration of the Government's determination to stick to its cash limit, whatever the cost. Her judgement was also swayed by her dislike of Soames: more even than Prior, he was exactly the type of bluff grandee she most despised. In Cabinet she threatened to resign rather than accept Soames' deal: this was one of those occasions when Willie Whitelaw had to intervene to prevent her being embarrassingly isolated. In fact a few weeks later – at the end of July – she was persuaded to settle at the same figure that she had earlier rejected, plus an inquiry to be chaired by a High Court judge. It was an expensive display of Prime Ministerial stubbornness which was estimated to have cost the Government anything between £350 million and £500 million. Nigel Lawson, still at the Treasury, thought it was worth it; but Geoffrey Howe felt that 'the line on which we were obliged to stand was not well chosen'.[122] In her memoirs, Lady Thatcher consigned the episode to a footnote.[123] As usual she took her revenge. In her Cabinet reshuffle that September Soames was sacked – punished, many of his colleagues felt, for the sin of being right when she was wrong. More than that, the Civil Service Department itself was abolished, its Permanent Secretary prematurely retired and the management of the Civil Service split between the Treasury and the Cabinet Office. This was not only a matter of public spending, but a critical assertion of Mrs Thatcher's subordination of Whitehall.

The 1981 Budget and the routing of the wets

The key turning point in the critical first two-and-a-half years was Geoffrey Howe's third budget in March 1981. This was the make-or-break moment when the increasingly embattled Prime Minister and her dogged Chancellor defied the whole weight of conventional economic wisdom and political punditry to demonstrate beyond doubt their determination to stick to their fundamental strategy. The timing was important. It was just coming up to two years since the Government took office – exactly the point at which so many previous Governments which had started out with high ambitions had run into a brick wall of economic reality – Attlee in 1947, Wilson in 1966, above all Heath in 1972. Everyone at Westminster knew these precedents, particularly the last. Few expected Mrs Thatcher's experience to be any different. The long anticipated U-turn would surely become inevitable in 1981. Despite her defiant declaration at the party conference, there were signs by the end of 1980 that the Thatcher experiment was running out of conviction.

After eighteen months, 'monetarism' was not delivering what it had promised. Public spending was not down but up, largely due to the rocketing cost of unemployment benefit. Inflation was coming down at last, but was not yet back to where the Labour Government had left it. (Moreover the Tories could not blame Labour, even on a monetarist argument, since Howe had controlled the money supply less successfully than Healey.) If the press and public were increasingly critical – the Government's approval rating fell to 29 per cent in December, despite Labour's widening divisions – the Prime Minister's keenest supporters were equally dismayed by her failure to grasp the union nettle or stop subsidising lame ducks. Inside Number Ten, John Hoskyns was becoming disillusioned with her reluctance to tackle the fundamental structure of the welfare state.[124] In September Alfred Sherman – still director of the CPS – wrote contemptuously to Mrs Thatcher that Joseph had once again been swallowed up by his officials, just as he had been in 1970–4: 'History is repeating itself . . . I wonder whether I should continue to lend intellectual respectability to an enterprise which diametrically contravenes our aspirations.'[125] Even the following year the chairman of the Selsdon Group of free-market MPs was still complaining that 'the Government has all the handicaps of appearing . . . to be radical and extreme – but if you look at what it does it is very little different to any other'.[126]

Mrs Thatcher was acutely sensitive to such criticism. 'Unpopularity I could live with,' she wrote in her memoirs. 'But a loss of confidence in our capacity to deliver our economic programme was far more dangerous.' She believed that the Government's radicalism was being continually undermined by leaked whispers of the wets' unhappiness. She prided herself on her own directness. 'This cloaked and indirect approach,' she claimed, 'has never been my style and I felt contempt for it.'[127] But this is disingenuous. First, the wets were deliberately denied any opportunity to oppose the policy directly in Cabinet, so they had no option but to question it indirectly. Second, leaking was a game played by both camps. Bernard Ingham was tireless in feeding Mrs Thatcher's views to the press. When she indignantly denied it, Prior concluded that she simply did not regard Ingham's dissemination of her own views as leaking.[128] Nor did the dissenting Cabinet ministers only voice their reservations off the record. Several of the most prominent did not shrink from making their barely coded criticism public: Gilmour in a speech at Cambridge in February 1980 and another in November, Walker in New York, Pym in his constituency. Over Christmas, therefore, Mrs Thatcher determined on her first reshuffle.

The single victim was Norman St John Stevas – the softest target among the wets. Gilmour's dissent was more serious and more blatant, but he was protected by his boss at the Foreign Office, Peter Carrington. Walker was an effective minister whom she had only just restored to office and did not want to lose so soon. Stevas, by contrast, was expendable. He had proved a popular Leader of the House, but his major innovation – the introduction of select committees with power to call ministers to account – was not one for which Mrs Thatcher had much enthusiasm: had he not seized the chance to push them through in the very first weeks while she was occupied with more urgent matters, she would never have approved them. Moreover his mannered flippancy, which had amused her in opposition, annoyed her in the serious world of government. His irreverent nicknames for her – 'The Leaderene', 'The Blessed Margaret','Attila the Hen' – were increasingly disrespectful. 'Norman,' she told Roy Strong, 'was too much.'[129] Finally, she wanted to move Francis Pym, who had fought too successfully against cuts in his defence budget, embarrassing her by turning her own arguments against her. He was too senior to be easily sacked, but the Leadership of the House was a suitably dignified sideways move, appropriate for a former Chief Whip. So Stevas was the scapegoat. He was devastated. Ever since his time as a junior minister at the Department of Education in 1972–4 he had believed that Mrs Thatcher saw him as a kind of licensed jester. He asked what he had done wrong. Ingham gave it out that it was because he leaked. Stevas vehemently denied it, and actually forced a public retraction from her.[130] But that did not save his job.

With just this one dismissal Mrs Thatcher simultaneously achieved a significant rebalancing of the Cabinet. As well as Pym from Defence, she also moved John Biffen from the Treasury, where he had proved a disappointingly soft touch as Chief Secretary. Biffen was switched to Trade, while John Nott was sent to sort out the Ministry of Defence. 'Both Margaret and I,' Howe wrote, 'saw Nott as a trustie who could be relied upon to get on top of the brass hats.'[131] Nigel Lawson, the principal architect of the Medium Term Financial Strategy, had a strong claim to the Chief Secretaryship. In matters of personnel, however, Mrs Thatcher still let herself be guided by Willie Whitelaw, who distrusted Lawson. He preferred Leon Brittan, another rising star with a formidable intellectual reputation, but a lawyer, not an economist. Lawson was sufficiently upset to protest to the Prime Minister, who promised him the next Cabinet post that came up. (She kept her promise eight months later.) Below the Cabinet she upset Prior by sacking his under-secretary, Jim Lester; but balanced that by appointing Kenneth Baker to a new post in the Department of Industry, in charge of information technology. Overall the effect of the changes represented a slight tilt to the right.

But something more dramatic was required. The first weeks of 1981 saw the British Leyland rescue, and the Government's retreat from confrontation with the NUM. At the end of February Ian Gow warned Mrs Thatcher of 'a serious deterioration in the morale of our back-benchers'.[132] In this atmosphere Howe's forthcoming budget took on huge importance. Its content was already the subject of anxious argument between the Treasury and Number Ten. Which one prevailed over the other was still jealously disputed in the memoirs ten years later. Lady Thatcher, as always, portrays herself as the fearless radical overcoming the hesitations of a more cautious Chancellor. Howe's recollection, substantially supported by Lawson, is rather different. Hoskyns' view on this occasion is closer to Lady Thatcher's than Howe's, but he thought that both of them were initially 'in denial' about the need for 'a really draconian budget'. Not until Alan Walters arrived from America did they really grasp the nettle.[133] But in fact the allocation of credit between the Government's economic inner circle is beside the point; more important is that the rest of the Cabinet was entirely excluded. The Prime Minister with her private advisers – Hoskyns, Strauss and Wolfson, now reinforced by Alan Walters – essentially agreed with Howe and his Treasury team (overriding the Permanent Secretary, Douglas Wass) that the first priority must still be to maintain the pressure on inflation by redoubling the attack on public borrowing. Their argument among themselves was about how, and by how much, the borrowing requirement could be cut. The alternative strategy – the orthodox Keynesian approach, followed by every previous British Government since the war – prescribed on the contrary that at a time of increasing unemployment, public spending must be allowed to rise. This would have been the policy of three-quarters of the Cabinet, had they been consulted. But they were not.

'I doubt if there has ever been a clearer test of two fundamentally different approaches to economic management,' Lady Thatcher subsequently wrote:

> If you believed . . . that increased government borrowing was the way to get out of recession, then our approach was inexplicable. If, on the other hand, you thought, as we did, that the way to get industry moving again was above all to get down interest rates, then you had to reduce government borrowing.[134]

Mrs Thatcher was undoubtedly convinced of the need to keep on cutting borrowing: she had staked her reputation on it, yet so far it had only kept on rising. What she wanted from the budget was above all an emphatic demonstration that the Lady was not for turning. Her version is that when they first met to discuss the budget, she and Walters wanted to cut the public sector borrowing requirement (PSBR) by more than Howe thought politically possible. She was even prepared to increase income tax, if it could not be done by cutting spending.[135] Howe by contrast recalls that 'Margaret . . . endorsed my judgement of what was necessary,' adding that Walters 'played a most useful part in persuading her in that direction'. It was Walters who advocated raising taxes. 'Margaret reacted angrily, exclaiming that she had not been elected to put up taxes.'[136] Howe's instinct was the same as hers: having cut both the basic and higher rates in his first budget two years earlier, he was not keen to put them up again. To do so would be an admission that his earlier action had been premature. The solution was provided by Lord Cockfield – the Tory party's longstanding tax specialist going back to Heath's time, now a Minister of State in the Treasury. By freezing personal allowances, withholding the usual increases in tax thresholds, he suggested, the Chancellor could achieve the same effect without the political odium. For Mrs Thatcher 'This was the turning point. I was glad that Geoffrey had accepted the argument.'[137] Even so, Hoskyns recalls that she was the last to be persuaded. 'It's all very well for you,' she told him. 'You don't have to stand up and sell this in the House.'[138] As so often, she knew what she wanted, but would not commit herself until she was sure it was politically practicable. Once convinced, however, she was resolved.

Having started out in January looking at a PSBR forecast for 1981–2 of around £14 billion, Howe eventually got the figure down to £10.5 billion. Once again spending actually increased; but the borrowing requirement was held down by a combination of tax increases and new taxes totalling nearly £7 billion. In addition to freezing personal allowances (£2 billion), he raised £2.5 billion from the usual duties (alcohol, tobacco, petrol and car tax), £1 billion from increased National Insurance contributions, plus £1 billion from North Sea oil and another £400 million from a special windfall tax on bank profits. At the same time the money-supply target was quietly relaxed and the minimum lending rate cut again to 12 per cent, encouraging the pound to fall. In this respect the 1981 budget actually marked the abandonment of strict monetarism in favour of what has been termed 'fiscalism'.[139] But it delivered a massive deflationary squeeze to an already depressed economy. This was what horrified the wets when the budget was revealed to the Cabinet a few hours before Howe was due to present it in the House of Commons. It was also the objection of the 364 university economists – including five former Chief Economic Advisers to successive governments – who famously wrote to *The Times* to denounce it:

> There is no basis in economic theory or supporting evidence for the Government's belief that by deflating demand they will bring inflation permanently under control and thereby introduce an automatic recovery in output and employment. Present policies will deepen the depression, erode the industrial base of our economy and threaten its social and political stability.[140]

The budget's authors, on the contrary, argued that it was not deflationary at all, merely an unavoidable response to the Government's inability to control public expenditure. If anything it was actually reflationary. Government spending, Lawson admitted in his memoirs, had *risen* from 44 per cent to 47.5 per cent of gross domestic product (GDP). 'It was because of this perverse development . . . that we had to increase the tax burden in flagrant conflict with our longer term objective.'[141] 'Actual public expenditure is not restrictive; it is expansive,' Mrs Thatcher argued in the Commons. 'If I agree to the expenditure I do not flinch from paying the bill.'[142] She knew whom to blame for this unpalatable necessity. The day after the budget she had an engagement to speak at a *Guardian* Young Businessman of the Year lunch; she used the occasion to launch a blistering public attack on half of her own Cabinet. 'What really gets me,' she exploded, 'is this':

> It is very ironic that those who are most critical of the extra tax are those who were most vociferous in demanding the extra expenditure . . . I wish some of them had a bit more guts and courage than they have . . . I tell you what they really mean. They mean 'We don't like the expenditure we have agreed, we are unwilling to raise the tax to pay for it. Let's print the money instead.' The most immoral path of all.[143]

Ian Gilmour, the most cerebral of the wets, rejects this – as he rejects the whole philosophy of Thatcherism – maintaining that the homely analogy of 'housewife' economics is false, since when Government cuts its spending it also cuts its income: it merely balances the books at a lower level of economic activity. This is what happened in 1981. In the short term the budget did further depress the economy – or would have done if the Government had stuck to its monetarist guns. Instead the loosening of personal credit controls in the summer fuelled an expansion of demand which led to the beginnings of a recovery.[144]

The fact is, once again, that the budget was less an act of economic management than of political will. Its economic effect is still disputed. Howe and Lawson insist that it laid the foundations of the recovery, which took off spectacularly after 1983; Gilmour counters that recovery from the Government-exacerbated recession of 1979–81 would have come anyway, and was actually delayed by the budget. Unemployment went on rising for another five years.[145] The monetarist economist Patrick Minford allows that the budget 'badly worsened the supply side and incentives', but thinks it achieved its broader objective by lowering inflationary expectations.[146] Inflation did continue to fall, though more slowly than the Treasury had hoped. It was still 12 per cent at the end of 1981. Sterling also fell, which assisted the recovery; it fell so far, however – to $1.91 – that Howe was forced to raise interest rates in August and again in October, taking them back to 16 per cent – thus more than cancelling what was supposed to have been one of the main benefits of the budget.[147] This is an argument that can never be settled. What is indisputable is that the budget marked a decisive stage in Mrs Thatcher's routing of the wets.

Despite the experience of the previous two years, the wets were taken by surprise by Howe's 1981 budget. Since 1979 they had failed abjectly to make a stand against policies they considered disastrous. There are several explanations of their quiescence. One is complacency: they simply did not believe that any sensible government could hold for long to policies they regarded as half-baked. Prior later admitted that 'those of us in Cabinet who were out of sympathy with Margaret's views grossly underestimated her absolute determination, along with Geoffrey and Keith, to push through the new right-wing policies'.[148] Since they took it for granted that common sense would sooner or later prevail, they felt no need to rock the boat in the meantime.

Second, they were hamstrung by the loyalty of their natural leaders, Willie Whitelaw and Peter Carrington, who had bound themselves to the Prime Minister, abdicating – as Gilmour complained – their own judgement in favour of hers.[149] Ever since 1975 Whitelaw had conceived it his duty to subordinate his views to Mrs Thatcher's. He would argue with her in private – generally about the timing and presentation of policy rather than fundamental objectives; but he would not oppose her directly, and he would allow no hint of factionalism to develop. Carrington likewise, as a peer, with his own sphere of influence as Foreign Secretary, was not in the business of interfering in economic policy. Knowing that whatever happened she could always rely on these two senior colleagues immensely strengthened the Prime Minister's position. Without a lead, or any tacit encouragement, from the 'big beasts' in the Cabinet, the younger and more economically minded wets were both morally and practically inhibited from mounting any sort of co-ordinated challenge.

Third, they were given no opportunity to make common cause. The Cabinet simply did not discuss economic policy, while ministers not on the 'E' Committee did not get the economic briefing that would have enabled them to challenge the Chancellor. 'We won the economic arguments,' Nott recalled, 'because we were in the economic departments, we had the facts . . . They were mainly silent.'[150] Each of them had his own departmental battles to fight – whether like Pym, Carlisle or Walker, to preserve their budgets or, like Prior, Soames and Gilmour, to be allowed to run their own policy in their own way. They all gained their individual victories; the derided 'wets' in Mrs Thatcher's first Cabinet offered a good deal more opposition to her dominance than their successors after 1983. But such is the nature of Cabinet Government that one minister's victory is another's defeat. Mrs Thatcher was instinctively ruthless in her ability to divide and rule.

In the last analysis, however, the real weakness of the wets' position was that – as Mrs Thatcher contemptuously jeered – they had no practical or principled alternative. They knew that they did not like the policy of deflation and high unemployment, and feared the social consequences; they congratulated themselves when the money supply turned out not to be the philosopher's stone the monetarists had pretended. But their criticism amounted to warning that the Government's measures were too harsh in current circumstances. As Conservatives they accepted in principle that public spending took too large a share of GDP and should be reduced: they were simply afraid of the consequences of trying to cut it during a recession. Right or wrong, the Prime Minister and her Chancellor were following a positive strategy which attracted admiration for its sheer conviction; by contrast the wets' anguished mutterings were easily portrayed as feeble. The universal adoption of the term 'wet' damned them to irrelevance.

Prior, Walker and Gilmour met for breakfast on budget day. Howe had given Prior a hint of what was in store the previous evening – so much for Prior's membership of the 'E' Committee, which was supposed to put him on the inside track. This breakfast was their first attempt to mount any form of concerted response; but it was already too late. In retrospect both Prior and Gilmour regretted that they did not resign; but at the time they recognised that it would have made no difference. They were presented with a *fait accompli*. Whitelaw and Carrington were solidly with the Chancellor; Pym was sceptical but reconciled. At the morning Cabinet they registered their dismay; but their dissent was taken for granted and discounted. Their failure to resign only underlined their impotence. The fact that Mrs Thatcher could not merely carry such a budget with no resignations, but could then go to the *Guardian* lunch the next day and publicly charge her colleagues with cowardice and immorality, was the proof that she was not only winning the internal argument: she had already won it. The wets were beaten before they had taken the field.

Much of the press comment was fiercely critical. Even before the 364 economists published their anathema, words like 'disastrous', 'perverse' and 'economically illiterate' were common currency. Even a friendly commentator like Samuel Brittan (brother of the Chief Secretary) thought it 'badly judged'.[151] Francis Cripps and Wynne Godley of the Cambridge University Department of Applied Economics predicted 'a hyper-slump such as Britain has never seen before'.[152] At least one prominent Tory backbencher, Peter Tapsell, not hitherto counted a wet, called for the Chancellor's resignation, while the majority of Tory MPs were said to be 'bewildered and uneasy'.[153] Edward du Cann, chairman of the 1922 Committee and a sensitive barometer of party pressure, joined those calling for expansion. The smack of unpopular measures, however, was just what those who feared that the Government had lost its way were looking for. The *Daily Telegraph* hailed the budget as 'bold, harsh and courageous'; *The Times* rather more hesitantly agreed.[154] 'Almost regardless of the merits of the budget,' John Hoskyns believed, 'it was such a courageous, almost fool-hardy thing to do that it enormously strengthened the moral ascendancy . . . of the Prime Minister and the Chancellor.'[155] 'Her enemies in the Cabinet and elsewhere began to realise that if she and Geoffrey could do what they had done, then they were far tougher and stronger than people had thought.'[156] Speaking to the Conservative Central Council in Cardiff at the end of the month, Mrs Thatcher dramatically reaffirmed, in characteristically personal terms, her determination to hold the moral high ground. 'I do not greatly care what people say about me . . . This is the road I am resolved to follow. This is the path I must go.'[157] She won a standing ovation. Boldness was its own reward.

She had flattened the wets and she could always trounce Michael Foot in the House of Commons, puncturing his windy outrage with reminders of his own record laced with helpful quotations from Callaghan and Healey. Within weeks of the budget, however, two new developments occurred which were harder to deal with. First, at the end of March the Labour party finally split. The pro-European right led by Roy Jenkins (recently returned from Brussels) and three former Cabinet Ministers (Shirley Williams, David Owen and Bill Rodgers) sealed their disillusion with the leftward direction of the party and resigned to form a new Social Democratic Party (SDP), which imme-diately linked up with the Liberals and began to register high levels of support in the opinion polls. In July, at the new party's first elec-toral test, Jenkins came within 2,000 votes of capturing the safe Labour seat of Warrington. The SDP's direct challenge was to Labour; but the huge appeal of the new Alliance sent a warning to worried Tories of the danger of abandoning the middle ground. One Conservative MP crossed the floor to join the SDP, and all summer there were rumours that others might follow.

Second, beginning in April in Brixton, then spreading in July to other rundown areas of Liverpool, Birmingham and other cities, there was a frightening explosion of riots and looting on a scale not seen in Britain since Victorian times. This was precisely the sort of civil disorder that Prior and Gilmour had predicted if the Government was not seen to show more concern about unemployment. The riots seemed to confirm the conventional analysis that a level of 2.5 million unem-ployed was not politically sustainable, and increased the pressure from worried backbenchers for a change of policy.

Mrs Thatcher reacted characteristically to both challenges. She despised the SDP defectors for running away instead of fighting their corner in the Labour party. There was no room in her conviction poli-tics for centre parties. Whereas she told the BBC's political editor John Cole that 'the Labour party will not die; Labour will *never* die',[158] and warmly welcomed those converts from Paul Johnson to Reg Prentice who had seen the light and crossed right over to the Tories, she regarded those who sought a halfway house as merely milk-and-water social-ists who lacked the courage of their convictions. 'They hadn't the plain guts to fight when they were in,' she declared on television, 'and they're the same people now.'

It was they who put us under the thumb of the trade unions . . . It was they who took us to the I.M.F. They are the self-same people, and they haven't changed, they didn't fight then, they went the easy way, and they want the easy way now.[159]

In her memoirs she called them 'retread socialists who . . . only developed second thoughts about socialism when their ministerial salaries stopped in 1979'.[160] There was enough truth in this to make it an effective argument. Though the Alliance undoubtedly represented an unpredictable electoral danger to the Government, tapping a deep well of public distaste for both the 'extremes' of militant Labour and Thatcherite Conservatism, it lacked a clear political identity; while clarity was Mrs Thatcher's principal asset. The SDP was just another gang of wets.

She was shaken by the riots, on two levels. First, she was genuinely shocked at the violence and destruction of property. Her famous exclamation, on seeing the extent of the damage, 'Oh, those poor shopkeepers!', was a heartfelt cry of identification with the victims.[161] She was horrified that such mindless anarchy could erupt in Britain. She felt no sympathy whatever with the rioters, or interest in what might drive a normally quiescent population to rebel. After the first Brixton explosion she insisted that 'Nothing, but nothing, justifies what happened . . . I cannot condemn it too strongly.'[162] She asserted that the Government had 'done everything we can by law' and praised the 'marvellous' police.[163] She was determined to treat the episode as a purely law-and-order matter, though she did allow Whitelaw, as Home Secretary, to appoint a liberal judge, Lord Scarman, to inquire into strained relations between the local black population and the police.

The second wave of disturbances, which started in the Toxteth area of Liverpool on 3 July and spread over the next three weeks to Manchester, Birmingham, Blackburn, Bradford, Leeds, Derby, Leicester and Wolverhampton, involving young whites as well as blacks, was much more serious, since it could be interpreted not simply as an outbreak of local tension but as a political challenge to the Government. Now she was alarmed at a different level. One colleague observed, 'the Prime Minister's nerve seemed momentarily to falter'.[164] Political opponents she could deal with, but widespread civil insurrection might destroy her. On television she looked unusually nervous, and succeeded only in displaying the limitations of her approach. 'Not for the first time,' *The Times* commented, 'she was unable to strike the right note when a broad sense of social understanding was required.'[165] She delivered another homily on the rule of law. 'We all know that violence will destroy everything we value . . . That is why the violence must be stopped. The law must be upheld. People must be protected. Then we can put these terrible events behind us.'[166]★ Two days later she visited Brixton police station and spent the night in the operations room at Scotland Yard to show her support for the police. She returned

---

★She had not wanted to refer to the riots at all, because it would 'look like panic'. She was persuaded by Millar and Hoskyns that she must, but Hoskyns thought her condemnation – written by Gummer – 'hopelessly platitudinous'.[167]

to Downing Street to impress on Willie Whitelaw the urgency of arming them with the latest American anti-riot equipment.

'She was always very firm,' Whitelaw recalled. 'Unemployment was no part of it.'[168] In fact she did admit in the Commons that 'unemployment may well be a factor, but I do not believe it is the principal factor'.[169] 'One is naturally anxious to get closer to the causes,' she conceded on 7 July,[170] but two days later she seized gratefully on a *Daily Mirror* report which declared that the looting was nothing to do with unemployment or bad housing, but simply 'a spree of naked greed'. Much of it, she argued, could have nothing to do with unemployment since it was committed by school-age children. ('Stupid woman,' the Labour left-winger Eric Heffer interjected.)[171] On 13 July she went to Liverpool to see the scene of the trouble for herself. 'Driving through Toxteth,' she wrote in her memoirs, 'I observed that for all that was said about deprivation, the housing there was by no means the worst in the city.' She was told that the young people had nothing to do:

> But you only had to look at the grounds around those houses with the grass untended . . . and the litter, to see that this was a false analysis. They had plenty of constructive things to do if they wanted . . . What was clearly lacking was sense of pride and personal responsibility – something which the state can easily remove but almost never give back.[172]

Back in the Commons she blamed the permissive society – and its godfather, Roy Jenkins. 'A large part of the problem we are having now has come from a weakening of authority in many aspects of life over many, many years. This has to be corrected.'[173] Prompted by a friendly backbencher, she condemned Jenkins' dictum that 'a permissive society is a civilised society' as 'something that most of us would totally reject. Society must have rules if it is to continue to be civilised.'[174]★

Whitelaw 'totally disagreed' with her view that the trouble could simply be condemned as lack of discipline. 'If you were Home Secretary,' he later recalled, 'you were bound to see it slightly differently, because

---

★Back in the 1960s, as an opposition frontbencher, Mrs Thatcher had actually voted for most of the legislation generally regarded as embodying the permissive society. She opposed the liberalisation of divorce law, but voted in favour of both the legalisation of homosexuality and David Steel's Abortion Bill (see *The Grocer's Daughter*, pp. 191–2).

... *you* had to cope with why the ill-discipline was there.'[175] Nevertheless the assertion that there was no connection between crime and social deprivation was stubbornly maintained, in the face of statistical evidence and common sense, by Conservative spokesmen for the next fifteen years. In truth Mrs Thatcher was very lucky. The riots that summer died down as suddenly as they had erupted, dissolved in a warm glow of patriotic sentiment surrounding the 'fairytale' wedding of the Prince of Wales to Lady Diana Spencer on 29 July. There was a further outbreak in September 1985 affecting the Handsworth area of Birmingham, the former docklands of Bristol and the Broadwater Farm estate in east London, where a policeman was brutally murdered. But there was no political violence directed against the Government until the anti-poll tax demonstrations of 1990, which did help to destroy her. In 1981 she contrived to transform a potentially devastating crisis for her Government into a vindication of her own analysis of society. Since the riots mainly occurred in derelict inner cities long ruled by Labour councils, they only reinforced her conviction that social problems would not be solved by socialist policies of endless subsidy, but by the resolute application – to housing, education and welfare – of Thatcherite principles of individual responsibility. But that was an agenda for a second or third term – if she could survive that long.

In the meantime, having recovered her nerve, she successfully spiked Michael Heseltine's attempt to use the riots to promote a more interventionist industrial policy. In the immediate shock of the eruption she was persuaded to appoint Heseltine as 'Minister for Merseyside' with special powers to bring together business, Government agencies and local government to create jobs and improve the environment. 'He made a great impression,' she conceded with uncharacteristic cynicism, 'which was undoubtedly politically helpful to us.'[176] But Heseltine had bigger ambitions. He produced a famous memorandum, entitled 'It Took a Riot', proposing to extend his Liverpool experience to the whole country, and lobbied energetically for it around Whitehall. He took his ideas to the Conservative Party Conference in October and managed to bring the constituency faithful to their feet cheering a visionary programme for the regeneration of the inner cities. Mrs Thatcher was not amused. She made sure that Heseltine's memorandum was submitted to a carefully chosen Cabinet committee which duly stifled it; and moved him from the Department of the Environment at the first opportunity. In her memoirs she poured cold water on his efforts for Liverpool. 'Liverpool has defeated better men than Michael Heseltine.'[177]

Lord Scarman's report into the Brixton troubles was likewise implemented only selectively. He made a number of recommendations to improve relations between the local community and the police, including a programme of positive discrimination to combat racial disadvantage; but it was only his more punitive conclusions which were translated into legislation, notably the restoration of the hated 'sus' law (previously repealed) by which young men could be arbitrarily arrested on the mere suspicion of having committed an offence. At the same time police forces were supplied with the most modern anti-riot technology: shields, truncheons, vehicles, rubber bullets and water cannon. This armoury was to prove as critical as the building up of coal stocks in the Government's confrontation with the miners in 1984–5.

Mrs Thatcher *was* worried that summer. Caroline Stephens was concerned at her 'physical and mental exhaustion';[178] and David Wood in *The Times* suggested that the Iron Lady was 'showing signs of metal fatigue'. He felt she was becoming dangerously isolated from her own Cabinet, so that her credibility might suddenly crack, like Harold Macmillan's in July 1962 or Harold Wilson's in November 1967.[179] Kenneth Baker, as a junior minister in the Department of Industry, often had to sit in when she met MPs worried about factory closures in their constituencies. 'She was very tired and harassed,' he recalled. 'She never doubted that what she was doing was right, but she did feel cornered and that the press was unfairly hostile.'[180] Nicholas Henderson, visiting London from Washington at the beginning of July, found the Prime Minister 'characteristically resilient, though worried by events in Ireland and the falling pound'. The news, he wrote in his diary, was 'unredeemably bad':

> Economic decline, rising unemployment . . . violence in Ulster, riots in many towns in England. I find that the hopes I entertained exactly two years ago that we might be going to turn over a new leaf under Maggie have been dashed. Our plight is worse than two years ago because we appear to have tried something new and it has failed.

Even American Republicans, Henderson reflected, who once looked to Mrs Thatcher as 'a beacon of the true faith' now saw her as an awful warning, 'a spectre that haunts them'. Yet he was still 'impressed by her vitality and will':

> She is more beleaguered now than ever before, but she remains indomitable – and immaculate. There was not a hair out of place. There was no self-pity. I would not say that she was relaxed; that would give too calm an impression of her personality; but there was nothing flustered about her.

Things might yet come right, he concluded. It was bound to take time. 'It is not, therefore, the moment to lose faith in her.'[181]

Some who had hitherto supported her, however, were losing faith, or patience. The shock of the riots rang alarm bells well beyond the ranks of the acknowledged wets, sparking a new wave of calls for a change of direction, a change of rhetoric or even, failing that, a change of leader. With the Conservatives now regularly trailing third in the opinion polls, Tory MPs were getting nervous of an electoral debacle. There were whispers of a leadership challenge in the autumn: Geoffrey Rippon's name was canvassed as a possible standard bearer. These rising tensions found expression just before Parliament broke for the summer recess in significant interventions by Francis Pym, now Leader of the House, and Peter Thorneycroft, chairman of the party – the two men specifically charged with presenting the Government's message. On 30 July Howe rashly announced that the recession was over, since manufacturing output was beginning to grow again. Technically this may have been correct; but with unemployment still rising, the Chancellor's optimism struck a hollow note. The next day Pym, in a speech in Northumberland, and Thorneycroft, in an end-of-session message to Tory MPs followed by a radio interview, bluntly contradicted him, emphasising that there were few signs of an early recovery and calling for 'remedial measures' (Pym) or a 'survival package' (Thorneycroft) to ease the pain.[182] Pym was a longstanding wet, saying nothing that Gilmour, Walker and others had not been saying more or less openly for the past two years. But Thorneycroft was Mrs Thatcher's own appointee, whose reputation as a champion of sound money went back to his resignation from the Treasury in 1958. His admission of 'rising damp' was serious, suggesting that the famous 'men in grey suits', the party grandees, had decided that the moment had come to bring the Prime Minister to heel. Their disloyalty was furiously denounced by Thatcherite backbenchers like William Clark and John Carlisle, but commended by *The Times* – recently acquired by Rupert Murdoch, but initially edited by Harold Evans – which detected wide support for Thorneycroft in the constituency parties:

Faced with soaring unemployment and unused resources, it strikes most people as obvious that a government is not doing its job if it fails to stimulate public works and investment. Not long ago an alternative of honest money, less borrowing and a squeeze on inflation carried at least as much conviction . . . All that is less inspiring now, for obvious reasons, which is why these experienced warhorses of the Tory party expect from the trumpet a new sound.[183]

But Pym and Thorneycroft were only giving public voice to a revolt which had surfaced a few days earlier in the Cabinet. The occasion was unprecedented: a full Cabinet review of public-spending strategy. The one concession the wets had managed to wring from their defeat in March was a promise that the Cabinet should never again have the budget sprung on them without advance warning, but should be allowed to discuss broad economic strategy in advance. Mrs Thatcher agreed reluctantly as a sop to Geoffrey Howe, who felt that Prior and Gilmour had 'some justification' for feeling excluded from 'a secretive monetarist clique'; he believed that, given a more collegiate style, he could persuade them that there really was no alternative to his policy.[184] Howe's faith in his power of advocacy does him credit; but Mrs Thatcher's political sense was more acute. The first test of the new openness demonstrated exactly why she had been right to fear it.

Howe and Leon Brittan produced a paper proposing a further package of spending cuts for 1982–3. They were supported by Keith Joseph but by virtually no one else. Practically the whole of the rest of the Cabinet rebelled. Michael Heseltine, backed by Peter Walker and Christopher Soames, proposed the ultimate heresy in a Thatcher Cabinet, a pay freeze, intended to free resources for investment. Quintin Hailsham was 'apocalyptic in his criticisms'.[185] Most seriously, from Mrs Thatcher's point of view, two of her original handful of 'true believers', John Biffen and John Nott, defected. Nott attacked Howe's 'lousy' paper specifically because it made a political, not an economic case for further cuts; whereas the political judgement of most of the Cabinet was that the cutting had already gone too far. Biffen thought that they were 'trying to achieve too much too quickly against a challenging social background'. 'Although very much committed to the philosophy,' he recalled, 'my guess was that we had to move a little more modestly, whereas I felt the Treasury, and certainly the Prime Minister, was very much devoted to a kind of Prince Rupert cavalry charge to secure the objectives.'[186]

But Biffen, though a monetarist by long conviction, was always sceptical by temperament and had been making damp noises for some time. It was Nott's desertion which most upset the Prime Minister. Hitherto she had seen him as her next Chancellor. But in her memoirs she dismissed him witheringly as 'a mixture of gold, dross and mercury . . . His vice was second thoughts.'[187] In the four months since the budget, Howe thought he had been infected by the 'big-spending culture' of the Ministry of Defence.[188] At any rate the defection of Nott and Biffen left the Prime Minister and Chancellor dangerously isolated. 'All at once,' Lady Thatcher recalled bitterly, 'the whole strategy was at issue':

> It was as if tempers suddenly broke. I too became extremely angry
> . . . I just was not interested in this kind of creative accounting that
> enabled fair-weather monetarists to justify an about-turn.[189]

At this potential crisis of her premiership Willie Whitelaw's position was crucial. As Home Secretary he had borne the full impact of the summer riots; he did not believe they had nothing to do with Government policies. Now if ever was the moment when he might have exerted his influence, without disloyalty, on the side of an easing of policy. In fact he stayed true, vainly urging loyalty on the rest of the Cabinet. With his protection, Mrs Thatcher was able to close the meeting without conceding any ground, promising that the discussion would be resumed in the autumn.

But that Cabinet never met again. The July revolt convinced her that she must assert herself or lose control of the Government. After two years she could legitimately drop some of those she had felt obliged to include in 1979. She may also have been influenced by a 'block-buster' memo she received in August from Hoskyns, Wolfson and Millar, warning her bluntly that she was failing – and would fail – unless she improved her management techniques. (Incidentally Millar's involve-ment gives the lie to his pretence that he was just an apolitical word-smith.) Mrs Thatcher furiously resented such advice. 'I got your letter,' she hissed to Hoskyns. 'No one has ever written a letter like that to a Prime Minister before.' She never mentioned it again.[190] Nevertheless it surely stiffened her conviction that she must be seen to take a grip. So in September – after the summer holidays but before the party conference – she struck. Yet once again she showed caution in her choice of victims, picking off only those of the wets – Gilmour, Soames and Carlisle – who had least following in the party. Gilmour went with the most style, marching out of Downing Street to announce that throwing a few men overboard would not help when the ship was steering 'full steam ahead for the rocks'.[191] Soames' outrage could be heard across Horse Guards' Parade. He told friends he would not dismiss a gamekeeper with so little courtesy as Mrs Thatcher had shown him. In her memoirs she retorted that he had behaved as though he was being 'dismissed by his housemaid'.[192] Mark Carlisle was probably less surprised to be sacked than he had been to be appointed in the first place. He was more annoyed that his departure had been trailed for weeks in advance by Bernard Ingham.[193] In fact he was unlucky.

Though unquestionably wet, he had been inoffensive. But Mrs Thatcher wanted his job for Keith Joseph, who specifically requested Education when he earned his release from the Department of Industry.

Paradoxically the biggest casualty of the reshuffle was Jim Prior, who remained in the Cabinet. He was clearly earmarked for a move, since Mrs Thatcher was determined on another measure of trade-union reform. Over the summer Downing Street let it be known that he was going to be offered Northern Ireland. Prior in turn told the press he would refuse, insisting that he wanted to retain an economic job. (He had his eye on the Department of Industry.) But Mrs Thatcher called his bluff. When it came to the point he could not refuse the poisoned chalice of Northern Ireland without appearing cowardly. As consolation she let him keep his nominal membership of the 'E' Committee. But in a trial of strength it was Prior who blinked. In his memoirs he confessed ruefully that he had been outmanoeuvred. 'That is probably why she was Prime Minister and I was certainly never likely to be.'[194] More than the sacking of Gilmour and Soames, it was her trumping of Prior that showed the surviving wets who was boss.

Meanwhile she used the vacancies she had created to shift the balance of the Cabinet to the right. In a wide-ranging reshuffle, three new entries were significant. Nigel Lawson went to the Department of Energy, to give new impetus to the privatisation of gas and ensure that the Government was ready the next time the miners threatened to strike; Norman Tebbit – one of the sharpest critics of Prior's soft approach to trade-union reform – took over at Employment; and Cecil Parkinson, to general amazement, was plucked from a junior post in the Department of Trade to replace Thorneycroft as party chairman, with the additional job of Paymaster-General and the right to attend Cabinet, though he was not officially a member.*. In addition Patrick Jenkin moved to Industry and Norman Fowler began what turned out to be a six-year stint at the DHSS. David Howell moved from Energy to replace Fowler at Transport, while Humphrey Atkins moved from Northern Ireland to take Gilmour's place at the Foreign Office. Finally – after some delay – Mrs Thatcher picked Janet Young, the only other woman she ever appointed to the Cabinet, to take Soames' place as

---

*Thorneycroft had warned her in July that 'unless she learned to work with her colleagues her own position would be in jeopardy'; he urged her to form an inner Cabinet. Her response was to get rid of Thorneycroft and find herself new colleagues that she could work with.[195] The job of chairman, she told Parkinson, was 'very straightforward: we just have to win the next General Election together, and we know what will happen to us if we do not.'[196]

Leader of the Lords. Below the Cabinet she signalled that there would be no change of direction at the Treasury by moving Nicholas Ridley into Lawson's place and Jock Bruce-Gardyne to be Minister of State (almost immediately promoted to Economic Secretary).

It is an exaggeration to claim, as Lawson does, that with this reshuffle Mrs Thatcher 'at last secured a Cabinet with a Thatcherite majority'.[197] Even if Biffen and Nott are included, she could still count no more than nine or ten 'true believers' in a Cabinet of twenty-two. The arrival of three of her most committed supporters, the departure of Soames and Gilmour and the banishing of Prior undoubtedly gave a different feel to the Cabinet. For the first time she had some of her own protégés around the table. She herself remarked on how much more 'agreeable' meetings of the new Cabinet were.[198] This does not mean, however, that she felt much more secure. 'She doesn't know who to trust,' Denis told John Junor in October – some weeks after the reshuffle. 'Her authority is being eroded . . . There are times when she feels like jacking it in.'[199] On Remembrance Sunday – the day Michael Foot wore a famously unsuitable coat at the Cenotaph – she was still 'pretty close to despair'. 'Willie, Geoffrey, Cecil and Norman I can count on,' she told Junor, 'but the others . . . are in an utter funk about the election.' She felt 'quite boxed in'.[200] She still preferred to deal with her colleagues individually, in carefully chosen committees or in *ad hoc* groups. Though the new Cabinet should on paper have been more amenable, she 'practically never' held another general economic discussion as long as she was Prime Minister.[201]

The autumn actually brought very little respite. The party conference gathered in Blackpool in an atmosphere of crisis, fuelled by the worst opinion-poll ratings of any Government since the war, a stock-market crash, another rise in interest rates (back to 16 per cent) and a powerful intervention by Ted Heath, lending his voice to the chorus calling for a national recovery package to tackle unemployment. Speaking in Manchester a week before the conference opened, he threw off the relative restraint he had observed since 1979, calling for 'a completely fresh assessment of Conservative economic policy', the abandonment of 'dogmatic policies' and 'a return to consensus politics'.[202] Mrs Thatcher was in Australia attending the Commonwealth Conference, but a text of Heath's speech reached her in advance, enabling her to get her response in first. What was consensus? she demanded:

To me consensus seems to be the process of abandoning all beliefs, principles, values and policies in search of something in which no one believes, but to which no one objects . . . [It is] the process of avoiding the very issues that have to be solved, merely because you cannot get agreement on the way ahead. What great cause would have been fought and won under the banner 'I stand for consensus'?[203]

Geoffrey Rippon retorted that 'the alternative to consensus is confrontation. That way lies disaster for us all.'[204] *The Times* backed Heath, as it had previously backed Thorneycroft and Pym. 'This time the Conservative reflex which brands him as disloyal will be struggling with a growing suspicion . . . that he is saying exactly what needs to be said.'[205] In fact nothing more effectively rallied the party behind Mrs Thatcher than Heath attacking her. Edward du Cann, who six months earlier had made a very similar plea himself, now denounced Heath as a splitter, warning that the Tory party 'wants no Teddy Benns'.[206] A group of fourteen of the brightest of the 1979 Tory intake, known as the 'Blue Chips' – including Chris Patten and William Waldegrave – who had published a mildly dissenting programme titled *Changing Gear* just before the conference felt obliged to distance themselves strenuously from the former Prime Minister.[207] At the conference itself, Heath was coolly received when he repeated his criticism and was effectively answered by Howe, who quoted back Heath's own 1970 pledge to put the conquest of inflation first, 'for only then can our broader strategy succeed'. 'If it was true then,' Howe argued, 'when inflation was half as high, it is twice as true today.'[208] Howe won a standing ovation.

Two days later Mrs Thatcher's own speech was unusually conciliatory. She actually scrapped an uncompromising first draft written by Hoskyns and Ronnie Millar in favour of a more moderate version written by John Gummer and Clive Whitmore. *The Times* reported that she had 'lost her nerve'.[209] Millar believed that this was 'the final straw that had a lot to do with Hoskyns leaving Downing Street'.[210] It is true that she offered Heath an olive twig – acknowledging his right of dissent and welcoming his intention to campaign for the party in the forthcoming Croydon by-election. Yet she gave no ground where it mattered. She repeated that she would not print money to buy illusory jobs at the cost of further inflation. 'That is not obstinacy,' she insisted. 'It is sheer common sense. The tough measures that this Government have had to introduce are the very minimum needed for us to win through. I will not change just to court popularity.'[211] If her delivery was gentler than the previous year, she made it plain that the Lady was still not for turning. She too got her usual rapturous reception. Not for the first or last time, the party faithful at conference backed her against the parliamentary doubters.

The same slight softening of tone was detectable when the Commons returned at the end of October. Labour immediately tabled a confidence motion. Mrs Thatcher had no difficulty demolishing Foot's emotional demands for a full-scale Keynesian reflation. 'His recipe is to spend more, borrow more, tax less and turn a blind eye to the consequences. He wants all that,' she mocked, 'and he wants a reduction in interest rates!' But she also met her Tory critics by taking credit, for the first time, for the fact that public spending had not fallen, but was actually some £3 billion higher than the Government's initial plans. They had poured money into youth training schemes – Tebbit announced another large expansion in December – and into industry: she specifically mentioned British Leyland, British Telecom and Harland and Wolff. 'To accuse us of being inflexible is absolute poppycock,' she declared. 'We have increased public spending, but not to profligate levels.' As a result, she concluded, 'I believe that underneath the surface and beginning to break through is a spirit of enterprise which has lain dormant in this country for too long.'[212] Though there had been talk of a revolt, there were no Conservative abstentions in the division.

Still the Government's position in the country remained precarious, as the Alliance bandwagon gathered a heady momentum. First the Liberals won North-West Croydon, the Government's first by-election loss, on a swing of 24 per cent against the Conservatives. Mrs Thatcher brushed this off, saying that she remembered other Liberal triumphs, at Orpington in 1962 and Sutton and Cheam in 1972, which had been reversed at the subsequent General Elections. Then a month later Shirley Williams swept aside a Tory majority of 18,000 to win the well-heeled Lancashire seat of Crosby for the SDP. This was a landslide of a wholly different order, suggesting that no Tory seat was safe. December's Gallup poll gave the Alliance 50 per cent, with Labour and the Conservatives equal on 23 per cent. The Government's approval rating was down to 18 per cent and Mrs Thatcher's to 25 per cent: she was now the most unpopular Prime Minister since polling began. Admittedly Michael Foot was even more unpopular; but with a credible third force for the first time offering a serious alternative to the Labour/Conservative duopoly, it would take more than just a normal swing back to the Government to secure Mrs Thatcher's re-election. 'With fewer reasons than before for the electoral cycle to reassert itself,' wrote the psephologist Professor Ivor Crewe, 'the prospects for a full Conservative recovery now look very slim.'[213]

In fact the end of 1981 was the nadir of Mrs Thatcher's popularity. Despite unemployment hitting three million in January, there were some shoots of economic recovery – output was rising, inflation continued to fall and interest rates fell back again – and the polls responded. 'We are through the worst,' she claimed in an end-of-year message.[214] By the spring the Alliance had slipped back and the three parties were roughly level-pegging at 30–33 per cent each. This is the basis for the claim that the Government was already on the way back before the Falklands war changed everything. Clearly it is true up to a point. Alliance support had hit a peak in December which it could never have sustained; but it gained a fresh boost with Roy Jenkins' stunning victory at Glasgow, Hillhead, in March 1982 – just a week before the Argentine invasion of the Falklands. There is no reason to think that the Alliance was about to fade away. Three-party politics introduced an unpredictability into election forecasting which makes it impossible to say that the Tories, without the Falklands, could not have won a second term. But it is most likely that no party would have won a majority in 1983 or 1984. In expectation of a hung Parliament academics like David Butler and Vernon Bogdanor started writing books with titles like *Governing Without a Majority* and *Multi-party Politics and the Constitution*. Mrs Thatcher's popularity may indeed have touched bottom at the end of 1981. The economy may have been beginning to recover. But her Government was still desperately belea-guered when events in the South Atlantic turned the whole landscape of British politics upside down.

4

Salvation in the South Atlantic

Falklands or Malvinas?

The Argentine invasion of the Falkland Islands on 2 April 1982 was by far the greatest crisis Mrs Thatcher ever faced. After nearly three years of mounting unemployment, a record level of bankruptcies and unprecedented public disorder, she was already the most unpopular Prime Minister in living memory, with a huge mountain to climb if she was to have any hope of being re-elected. If nothing else, however, she had taught the public to see her as the Iron Lady: she presented herself above all as a champion of strong defence, a resolute defender of British interests and British pride. Failure to prevent the seizure of British territory by a tinpot South American *junta* could easily have been the end of her. Instead, over the following ten weeks, she turned potential national humiliation to her advantage and emerged with an improbable military triumph which defined her premiership and set her on a pedestal of electoral invincibility from which she was not toppled for another eight years.

Yet it was a deeply ironic triumph, since it should not have been necessary at all but for serious errors by her own Government in the previous two years. Mrs Thatcher snatched victory out of a disaster caused by her own failure, for which she might easily have been arraigned before Parliament for culpable negligence. Not only that, but the result of her military recovery was to land Britain indefinitely with precisely the expensive and burdensome commitment which successive Governments had quite properly been trying to offload. By any rational calculation of political results the Falklands war was a counterproductive folly. Yet it was a heroic folly, the sort of folly of which myths are made, and instead of finishing her, it was the making of her.

The legal title to the Falkland Islands – *las Malvinas* in Spanish –

has been disputed between Spain, France, Britain and Argentina for centuries and still remains debatable. Following the Argentine invasion, Mrs Thatcher took her stand on the defence of British sovereignty: she was on stronger ground asserting the islanders' right of self-determination. Situated just 300 miles off the coast of Argentina, but 8,000 miles from Britain, the islands were an anomalous legacy of imperial adventurism; it was natural that Argentina should claim them. Generations of young Argentines had been brought up to believe in their patriotic duty to recover them. But the awkward reality was that they had been colonised since 1833 by British emigrants who had built up a British way of life and developed a fierce loyalty to the British flag – as well as total dependence on the British taxpayer.

Successive British Governments had been discreetly trying to give away the sovereignty of the islands since at least 1965, so long as they could guarantee certain safeguards for the population. Since they were militarily indefensible if the Argentines chose to take them by force, the Foreign Office had concluded that the islanders' practical interests would be better served by reaching an accommodation with Argentina than by living in a permanent state of siege. Negotiations had been proceeding perfunctorily on various schemes to protect the islands' way of life, punctuated by bursts of militaristic rhetoric from Argentina. But the islanders stubbornly refused to be persuaded. There were only 1,800 of them, yet they enjoyed an effective veto on any proposals to transfer sovereignty between London and Buenos Aires. Much like the Ulster Unionists in Northern Ireland, they suspected that the Foreign Office was trying to sell them down the river, and were similarly determined to defend their right to remain British.

By the time Mrs Thatcher came into office, the Foreign Office's favoured solution was a 'leaseback' scheme by which Britain would have ceded sovereignty to Argentina in return for a ninety-nine-year lease which should protect the islands' British way of life. Mrs Thatcher instinctively disliked the idea of handing over British subjects to foreign rule, just as she initially resisted bringing Nkomo and Mugabe into the Rhodesian talks. Nevertheless she was persuaded to go along with the scheme if the islanders could be brought to agree. Unfortunately securing a settlement of the Falklands dispute was a lower priority than ending the Rhodesian imbroglio. The Minister of State given the task of persuading the islanders was the chronically undiplomatic Nicholas Ridley. In July 1980 the islanders sent Ridley home with a flea in his ear; they then mobilised their substantial lobby in the House of Commons to savage the scheme when Ridley tried to sell it there.

The opposition ranged across all parties, from Julian Amery, Bernard Braine and Viscount Cranborne on the Tory right through the Liberal Russell Johnston and the Scottish Nationalist leader Donald Stewart to Labour patriots like Peter Shore and Douglas Jay.[1] Already in trouble with her colonialist right wing for selling out Ian Smith, Mrs Thatcher needed no more prompting to scotch the idea; and Peter Carrington saw no need to press it.

In truth some variety of 'leaseback' offered the only sensible solution. British sovereignty could be maintained in the long term only by a willingness to defend the islands by military force. To be taken seriously this would have involved skewing Britain's whole defence posture towards the South Atlantic. But John Nott's 1981 defence review reassessed Britain's defence needs in quite the opposite direction. Sent to the Ministry of Defence specifically to make the sort of economies Pym had resisted, Nott judged – quite rationally – that naval warfare was the least likely form of conflict the country could expect to face in the last decades of the twentieth century. He therefore proposed, with Mrs Thatcher's approval, to scrap one aircraft carrier, *Hermes*, and sell a second, *Invincible*, to Australia (leaving only one, the ageing *Illustrious*). As it happened these two ships provided the core of the task force which retook the Falklands in 1982; had the Argentines waited a few months longer before invading, they would no longer have been available. The number of frigates and destroyers was to be cut from sixty to forty; the assault ships *Fearless* and *Intrepid* – which played a key role in the Falklands landings – were also to be scrapped.

After the war was over Mrs Thatcher proclaimed the victory as a triumph of her strong defence policy. 'By not cutting our defences,' she asserted in a speech in her constituency, 'we were ready.'[2] This was simply not true. The cuts she had made had not yet taken effect. But the announcement of these cuts sent a clear signal to Buenos Aires that Britain had no long-term will to defend the islands. To make the message clearer still, Nott also announced the withdrawal of the ice-patrol ship *Endurance* from the South Atlantic. The red-painted *Endurance* – known as 'the Red Plum' – had little military value (just a few light guns and two helicopters) but she was an important listening post for gathering Argentine intentions; above all she was the symbol of Britain's presence in Falkland waters. Her removal – as Carrington strenuously argued – was practically an invitation to Argentina to invade. In the Commons Jim Callaghan warned of 'an error that could have serious consequences'.[3] But Mrs Thatcher threw her weight behind Nott. At the same time the British Antarctic Survey announced the closure of its station on the uninhabited dependency of South Georgia; and, most bitter of all for the islanders, the new British Nationality Act which passed through Parliament in the summer of 1981 – a measure aimed principally at denying the Hong Kong Chinese the right to come to Britain – casually deprived them of their British citizenship. No one could have guessed that a few months later Mrs Thatcher would be declaring the Falkland islanders as British as the inhabitants of Margate or Manchester.

Negotiations with Argentina continued at the United Nations in New York. But with any discussion of sovereignty off the agenda, the Foreign Office had no cards to play. Reading the signals, the new Argentine *junta* headed by General Leopoldo Galtieri calculated that a swift seizure of the islands in the late summer of 1982 would present Britain and the world with a *fait accompli*. With a reduced navy, in the worst of the South Atlantic winter, there was no way Britain could have recaptured them even if she had wanted to. A few diplomatic protests and perhaps some half-hearted United Nations sanctions would have been the end of the matter. The humiliation might well have forced Mrs Thatcher's resignation, but no successor would have attempted to reverse the coup. The Argentines were actively planning the operation from January onwards. As so often happens, however, the intended timetable was upset by accident. At the beginning of March an Argentine scrap-metal merchant with a legitimate contract to dismantle a disused British whaling station on South Georgia landed without specific authorisation and raised the Argentine flag while his men went about their business. Carrington persuaded Mrs Thatcher that this was exactly the sort of thing *Endurance* existed to prevent; she agreed to send *Endurance* with twenty marines from Port Stanley to South Georgia to throw the intruders off. This in turn provoked the Argentines to accelerate their preparations.

After the war was over the Franks Committee, set up to inquire into its origins, devoted most of its attention to asking whether the Government could or should have anticipated or prevented the Argentine invasion in March 1982. It concluded that it could not have done, since the Argentines themselves took the decision only at a very late date. This was widely dismissed as a whitewash. The report itself exposed serious failures in both gathering and interpreting intelligence. Yet the suggestion that the Government could have forestalled the invasion by sending a task force – or just a submarine, as the Callaghan Government had done at a somewhat similar moment of tension in 1977 – is in reality beside the point. By the time of the South Georgia incident it was already too late to have sent any sort of force to the Falklands in time to do any good. The action the Government did take – sending *Endurance* – had the opposite effect to that intended; and when they dispatched three nuclear-powered submarines on 29 March the Argentines merely took it as the final signal to delay no longer. The Foreign Office was working on the assumption that the Argentines would build up pressure on the islands gradually, by diplomatic demands and commercial sanctions, as they had always done before, rather than rush into military adventure; its concern was not to provoke them into precipitate action by over-reacting to what was assumed to be familiar sabre-rattling. In fact the intelligence was not altogether wrong: it was the South Georgia incident which changed the *junta's* timetable. But the Foreign Office and Ministry of Defence certainly remained complacent for too long after that episode. Mrs Thatcher was sufficiently alarmed to call – in a note scribbled in the margin of an MoD telegram on 3 March – for 'contingency plans' to be drawn up. The Ministry's response stressed the logistical difficulty of operating at such a distance, and none were made.[4] But by that time Britain could have done nothing to forestall an invasion anyway.

The fuse was lit much earlier, by the abandonment of the leaseback option, confirming the islanders' veto on any discussion of transferring sovereignty, combined with the 1981 defence review which scrapped the only means by which British sovereignty could have been permanently maintained. Mrs Thatcher was a great believer in the principle of deterrence; but in this case – for domestic economic reasons – she cut the deterrent against a known threat, while simultaneously refusing to negotiate a pragmatic compromise, as she was willing to do in Rhodesia and later in Hong Kong. The fact was that she did not take the Falklands problem seriously – Carrington failed to persuade her to take it sufficiently seriously – until it was too late. Then, to save her political skin, she was obliged to take it far more seriously than the fate of 1,800 far-flung colonists deserved.

The Saturday debate

Mrs Thatcher was genuinely outraged by the Argentine invasion of the Falklands. First, she had never believed that the Argentines, after all their blustering, would actually resort to anything so crude as military seizure: in the modern world even South American dictators did not do such things. (She had no difficulty believing it of the Soviet Union in Afghanistan, but that was different: that was aggressive Communism; this was mere petty nationalism – and Argentina had longstanding traditional links with Britain.) Second, she was outraged that anyone could seize British territory and think they could get away with it: it was a measure of the decline in Britain's standing in the world – the very decline she had come into office to reverse – that someone like Galtieri should imagine he could twist the lion's tail. Third, her human sympathies were immediately engaged by the thought of the islanders (for whom she had shown little enough concern up to now) subjected to the daily indignity of foreign occupation: it was as though Grantham had been invaded by the Germans. All these reactions expressed themselves over the following weeks in high-principled appeals to the great causes for which Britain was prepared to go to war. It was not just for the 1,800 Falklanders that she was prepared to fight, but for the principles of self-determination and democracy against dictatorship and naked aggression; the restoration not merely of Britain's national honour, but of the rule of international law. With her instinctive ability to draw abstract principles from specific events, she immediately elevated the prospect of war for a cluster of bare rocks in the South Atlantic into a crusade of world-historical importance.

All these emotions – of shock, anger, shame and sympathy – she undoubtedly felt deeply and instinctively. But she was also well aware, from the moment of 29 March when it suddenly became clear that the Argentines were seriously bent on invasion, that the unpreventable loss of the islands posed a desperate threat to her personal position and the survival of her Government. All her fine talk of strength and resolution would be shown to be worthless unless she could meet this crisis with an uncompromising and convincing show of determination to reverse the national humiliation. For two days she was seriously worried: the MoD advice stressed only the difficulties of mounting an effective military response so far from home. Travelling to Brussels for an EC meeting, she and Carrington agreed to send three submarines south immediately; but these would take ten days to reach the islands. They sailed too late to deter; and in fact the news of their sailing – which the Foreign Office minister Richard Luce was unable to deny when pressed in the House of Commons – only encouraged the Argentines to go ahead. In desperation Mrs Thatcher turned to the Americans. First, Carrington asked Secretary of State Alexander Haig; then she herself asked President Reagan – just three months into his presidency – to try to persuade the invader to stay his hand. On 1 April Reagan had a fifty-minute telephone conversation with General Galtieri, but failed to shift him. With ecstatic demonstrators already on the streets of Buenos Aires it was too late for the *junta* to back down. The Argentine flag flew over Port Stanley the next day.

But by then the decision to send a naval task force had already been taken. At a famous meeting in her room in the House of Commons on 31 March Mrs Thatcher was given the advice she wanted to hear – that, given the political will, the navy could recapture the islands. The man who gave this advice should not even have been at the meeting. The Chief of the Defence Staff, Admiral Sir Terence Lewin, was away on a visit to New Zealand. In his absence the Defence Secretary, John Nott, and his Permanent Secretary, Sir Frank Cooper, were closeted with the Prime Minister and Foreign Office ministers and officials, considering the options. (Carrington was also away, visiting Israel – a measure of how unworried he was by the Falklands situation.) The military advice was still gloomy, the Foreign Office was still seeking to lower the temperature, when the First Sea Lord, Sir Henry Leach, arrived with a very different story. Leach had bitterly opposed the proposed shrinking of the navy in Nott's defence review: he regarded Nott as a miserable accountant who was scuttling Britain's great naval tradition. He had lost the battle within the MoD; but the Falklands crisis offered a heaven-sent opportunity to prove his case. He had already been in touch with senior admirals on exercises in mid-Atlantic to warn them of what was in the wind. He now gate-crashed the conclave at the Commons – in full dress uniform – and dramatically swept aside Nott's caution, telling the Prime Minister that, despite the difficulties, a naval task force could be assembled in a matter of days which could recapture the islands if they were indeed seized.

This was the advice Mrs Thatcher needed if she was to survive. There was of course no certainty that the navy could deliver what Leach promised. Sending a task force to retake the islands would be an enormous gamble: the problem, if it really came to fighting, would be assembling adequate air cover to permit an opposed landing. William Waldegrave, then a junior education minister, recalls a routine meeting with university vice-chancellors at Number Ten on 1 April. During the meeting Mrs Thatcher switched her mind totally to the deficiencies of higher education; but the moment it was over she gripped his arm and confided urgently, 'William, the problem is we shall have no proper air cover.'[5] But that was a problem for later. Few of those who agreed to send the task force, politicians or military, believed that it would actually come to an opposed landing: the sending of the force was a declaratory statement designed to strengthen Britain's hand in the diplomatic negotiations which must now resume while the ships steamed slowly south. The essential thing was that Mrs Thatcher had something positive to announce when the House of Commons met

– for the first time on a Saturday since Suez in 1956 – on the morning after the invasion was confirmed.★

The House met in a mood of high jingoistic outrage, but she was equal to it. When even Michael Foot – popularly seen as a sentimental old pacifist – was demanding a military response to wipe away the stain of national humiliation, Mrs Thatcher was not to be outdone.†
She was 'clearly shaken', David Owen noted. 'There was none of the self-confident hectoring we were used to.'⁷ She had actually been booed on the short drive from Downing Street to the House. An instant opinion poll showed that 60 per cent of the public blamed her for allowing the invasion to occur. But it was proper that she should be shaken. What mattered was that she was quietly and convincingly deter-mined to reverse it. The Argentine action, she declared bluntly, 'has not a shred of justification nor a scrap of legality'. The Falklands were 'British sovereign territory . . . No aggression and no invasion can alter that simple fact.' It was the Government's intention to free them from occupation and return them to British administration 'at the earliest possible moment'. Accordingly 'a large task force will sail as soon as preparations are complete'. HMS *Invincible* would be in the lead and would be ready to leave port on Monday.⁸

A task force ready to sail in forty-eight hours was more than the Government's most excited critics could have hoped to hear. The announcement regained Mrs Thatcher the initiative. When Enoch Powell menacingly asserted that the weeks ahead would show of what metal the Iron Lady was really made, she nodded her acceptance of the challenge. She was already on the way to meeting it. Her mixture of moral indignation and uncompromising belligerence perfectly matched the mood of the House. She lost it only briefly when she lapsed into party point-scoring and tried to blame Labour for letting the Argentines occupy the dependency of Southern Thule in 1976.

★The parallel with Suez was in many minds, though it meant little to anyone under forty. The moral difference was clear, but the scope for a military or diplo-matic fiasco seemed appallingly comparable. 'I think all of us who remembered Suez were haunted by Suez,' Willie Whitelaw recalled.⁶ The great unspoken fear was of sending a military expedition and then having to recall it – as in 1956 – with the object humiliatingly unachieved.

†In fact Foot was not a pacifist at all. As an ardent young journalist he had been one of the authors of *Guilty Men*, the famous indictment of the Chamberlain Government's unreadiness for war in 1939, and he still harked back to 1940 as emotionally as any Churchillian. In his very different way he expressed the national mood of outraged patriotism as authentically as Mrs Thatcher herself.

She did better holding onto the moral high ground and embodying the united sense of national resolve, as she did successfully for the rest of the crisis. There was still considerable disquiet and some muttering among Tory dissidents who hoped that the invasion would destroy her. 'The lobbies hummed with the prospect of her departure,' Julian Critchley remembered.[9] John Major, a young and somewhat naive backbencher, was shocked to overhear two Cabinet ministers in the washroom dismiss the sending of the task force as 'ludicrous' and 'a folly'.[10] The loyalist Alan Clark was disgusted by 'the predictable front-men making their coded statements, whose real purpose was to prepare the way for a coup if events should lead to humiliation or disaster'.[11] But overt criticism was silenced as soon as British troops were committed. From the moment the first ships of the task force – eventually comprising a hundred ships and 26,000 men and women – sailed from Portsmouth on 5 April amid scenes of Edwardian enthusiasm, Mrs Thatcher identified herself emotionally with 'our boys' and skilfully rode the wave of jingoism and national unity.

But if the announcement of the task force enabled her to recover the initiative, the House still craved a scapegoat to purge the sense of national disgrace. First, John Nott winding up the debate in the chamber, then Peter Carrington in a committee room upstairs, were savaged by furious backbenchers scenting blood. Carrington, unused to the rough manners of the Commons, determined to resign. Having warned repeatedly against the withdrawal of *Endurance*, his department bore less immediate culpability for the invasion than the MoD – or the Prime Minister. But a mixture of *noblesse oblige* and lordly disdain – the former prompting him that someone should carry the can and the latter that it might as well be him – made up his mind to go. Nott, who had previously felt no inclination to resign, now reasoned that if Carrington went, then so must he. But Mrs Thatcher refused to accept his resignation. She was implicated in his policies (not just towards *Endurance* but the whole 1981 defence review) far more directly than she was in Carrington's. Nott's resignation would have left her dangerously exposed. One scapegoat – or rather three, since two of Carrington's departmental juniors, Humphrey Atkins and Richard Luce, insisted on resigning with him – was enough. Carrington's self-sacrifice was quixotic but it had exactly the desired effect, satisfying the need for someone to be seen to take responsibility so that the Government and the country could unite behind the task force.

Losing Carrington, whom she both liked and trusted – even if she did not always act on his advice – was nevertheless a blow, compounded by the fact that she was obliged to promote one of her least-favoured colleagues in his place. Alan Clark claims that she very nearly appointed Julian Amery, but lost her nerve and accepted the whips' (and doubtless Whitelaw's) advice to go for Francis Pym – thus swapping, as she wrote in her memoirs, 'a gloomy Whig for an amusing one'.[12] Pym's elevation was ironic, not just because she disliked and thoroughly distrusted him, but because it was he who had fought for the defence budget in 1980 when she had been intent on cutting it. Had Pym agreed to the sort of cuts she had wanted a year earlier, the navy might not now have had the ships available to form the task force. Yet she was now the Warrior Queen while he was cast as the voice of inglorious appeasement.

Britannia at war

On finding herself unexpectedly plunged into a possible war for which she had no training or preparation, Mrs Thatcher very sensibly sought advice. She invited Sir Frank Cooper, Permanent Secretary at the MoD, to the upstairs flat at Number Ten for Sunday lunch. 'Carol took lunch out of the fridge,' Cooper recalled, 'a bit of ham and salad. We had a gin and she asked me "How do you actually run a war?"'

> I said 'First you need a small War Cabinet; second it's got to have regular meetings come hell or high water; thirdly, you don't want a lot of bureaucrats hanging around.' Then we talked about its composition.[13]

In her memoirs Lady Thatcher attributes this advice not to Cooper but to Harold Macmillan, who asked to see her two days later. Of her five surviving predecessors, Macmillan was the one with the most relevant experience of military emergencies – not so much from his time in Number Ten as from serving with Churchill and Eden. But it seems that Cooper – with equally long experience of Berlin, Korea, Malaya, Suez and Cuba – got to the Prime Minister first. Acting on their advice she duly formed a small War Cabinet – officially the South Atlantic subcommittee of the Overseas and Defence Committee (ODSA) – to handle both the military and the diplomatic aspects of the crisis. For the next ten weeks it met at Number Ten every morning at 9.30 a.m. and at Chequers at the weekend. Most of its members chose themselves. Pym and Nott, as Foreign and Defence Secretaries, were *ex officio*, and Willie Whitelaw as deputy Prime Minister very nearly so: in any case she would not have wanted to go into her most dangerous test without the one senior colleague on whom she could always rely. Geoffrey Howe, on the other hand, was excluded: there was no role for the Treasury in a cause where money was no object. 'The future of freedom and the reputation of Britain are at stake,' she told the Commons on 8 April. 'We cannot therefore look at it on the basis of precisely how much it will cost. That is what the Contingency Reserve is for.'[14] The fifth place was filled instead by Cecil Parkinson, ostensibly in his capacity as Tory party chairman, in reality for his smooth presentational skill on television and above all as Mrs Thatcher's protégé. (He 'not only shared my political instincts but was brilliantly effective in dealing with public relations'.)[15] It was actually Nott who suggested Parkinson – his former junior at the Department of Trade – to counter an anticipated 'wet' alliance between Pym and Whitelaw. But such an alliance never materialised. If anything Nott himself more often sided with Pym, as the MoD combined with the Foreign Office to warn of the dangers – both military and diplomatic – of launching an amphibious war on the other side of the world. Mrs Thatcher had good reasons of her own for appointing Parkinson to give her a reliable majority on the five-man committee.

In practice the membership of the War Cabinet was normally supplemented by Sir Terence Lewin, Frank Cooper, the Permanent Secretary of the Foreign Office, Sir Anthony Acland, and other relevant officials.* Sir Michael Havers, the Attorney-General, advised on international law. The political direction of the war was concentrated in these few hands. As the conflict escalated, however, Mrs Thatcher was careful to cover her back by securing the endorsement of the full Cabinet for every major decision, starting with the sending of the task force. This was one of the very few occasions when she went round the table counting heads: only John Biffen openly dissented.[17] Throughout the crisis, indeed, Mrs Thatcher showed herself – as Peter Hennessy has written – 'almost Churchillian in the punctilio she showed to Cabinet and Commons'.[18] She even introduced a second weekly meeting, every Tuesday after the meeting of the War Cabinet, to keep the full Cabinet informed of developments.

At the same time a reduced executive, with no role for the service ministers, suited her admirably. The streamlined command structure worked extraordinarily smoothly, mainly because Mrs Thatcher got on

---

*Acland took over as head of the Foreign Office in the very week of the Argentine invasion. But on Macmillan's advice Mrs Thatcher retained his predecessor, Sir Michael Palliser, as her personal adviser for the duration of the war. Palliser had planned to go on holiday when he retired. '*Of course* you must have your holiday,' she agreed – then allowed him three days before she expected him back to Number Ten the following Wednesday.[16]

well with the military top brass, particularly Lewin, a quietly authoritative man of the type she most respected. Before March 1982 she
had had very little to do with the armed forces – though the drama
of the SAS's ending of the Iranian Embassy siege in May 1980 had
given her a brief, exciting taste of what they could do.* But once she
had stopped worrying about their cost, she immensely admired their
dedication and professionalism. She contrasted the navy's decisive
response to the Argentine invasion, assuring her that they could recover
the islands and would be ready to sail in a few days, with the ingrained
defeatism of the Foreign Office, which always emphasised the difficulties. 'Are you sure you can do this?' she would ask Lewin at critical moments. 'Yes, Prime Minister,' he unfailingly assured her.[20] She
trusted the military, and they in turn trusted her not to let them down
halfway through the operation. They too remembered Suez.

Nor was it only the top brass she admired. She established an even
more remarkable rapport with the men who would actually do the
fighting. Just as she identified with the aspirations of suburban homeowners whom she called 'our people', so a part of her reached out,
adopted and idealised the tough young soldiers, sailors and airmen who
became 'our boys'. She had first used the phrase in 1978, referring to
the troops in Northern Ireland, but only took to doing so regularly
and possessively during the Falklands campaign.[21] It could have been
appallingly presumptuous; it is hard to imagine any other Prime
Minister getting away with it. But in fact it worked both ways. The
forces recognised 'Maggie' as a politician with a difference, a fighter
like themselves who actually understood them better than the would-
be peacemakers, who sought a diplomatic settlement to prevent the
loss of life which would be inevitable in retaking the islands by force.
Men like Colonel 'H' Jones, who was killed at Goose Green throwing
himself recklessly at the enemy guns, knew very well the risk they ran;
but they had not been training all their lives to have their one chance

---

*On 30 April 1980 six armed terrorists demanding autonomy for southern Iran
seized the Iranian embassy in Kensington, taking twenty hostages including a
police officer and two BBC journalists. Willie Whitelaw, as Home Secretary, was
in charge of the six-day police operation to end the siege. But Mrs Thatcher took
a close interest, making it clear that there should be no substantial negotiations
and that the terrorists should not be allowed to get away with it. As soon as they
started shooting hostages she approved Whitelaw's decision to send in the SAS
to storm the building – live on television, at teatime on Bank Holiday Monday
– killing five of the hostages and capturing the sixth. Afterwards she and Denis
went in person to congratulate and thank the assault team at their HQ in Regent's
Park.[19]

of action denied them.[22] To the men in the South Atlantic 'Maggie' was not just a civilian Prime Minister playing politics with their lives. She was a leader they were proud to fight for 'with a passion and loyalty', the military historian John Keegan has written, 'that few male generals have ever inspired or commanded'.[23] Her sex inspired all sorts of contradictory loyalties not available to a male leader, both maternal and erotic. She was a warrior queen, a goddess of war; but she was also a mother figure, and a pin-up. 'For the armed forces,' it was reported, 'she is far and away the favourite object of sexual fantasy.'[24] Less intensely, the public at home recognised that she was no longer just another politician: the war transformed her from a bossy nanny into the breast-plated embodiment of Britannia.

Her love affair with her forces suffered just one moment of doubt before it was fully consummated. The very first military operation that Lewin had to report to her was a disaster, when two helicopters crashed in the attempt to retake South Georgia in a howling blizzard on 22 April. In that painful moment he sensed her fear that maybe the navy could not deliver after all.[25] Within a few hours, however, news came through that the crews had survived the crash and had all been brilliantly rescued. Two days later South Georgia was successfully recaptured: a threatened fiasco had been turned into the first tangible victory of the war. This was when Mrs Thatcher exhorted reporters on the pavement outside Downing Street who had asked Nott what was going to happen next: 'Rejoice. Just rejoice at that news, and congratulate our forces, and the marines.'[26] Her repetition of the word 'rejoice' was interpreted – and is still widely remembered – as bloodthirsty triumphalism. It was not; it was sheer relief.

From her teens Mrs Thatcher had idolised Churchill. She often invited ridicule – and infuriated the Churchill family – by suggesting a totally unwarranted familiarity with 'Winston'. Whether standing up to the Soviet Union or defying the wets in her Cabinet, she did not shrink from casting her struggle in Churchillian terms. At the time of the 1981 budget she stiffened her resolve by reading Churchill's wartime speeches and reciting them aloud to her staff.[27] She visited Churchill's underground war rooms beneath Whitehall before they were opened to the public. She could never have dreamed that she would have the chance to play Winston in reality. But the Falklands invasion gave her – on a minor scale – that opportunity. Eagerly, as if she had been in training for this moment all her life, she adopted a Churchillian rhetoric of Britain alone fighting for liberty, Britain standing up to the dictators, everything subordinated to the single aim of victory. 'Failure?' she declared grandly in one television interview, this time quoting

Queen Victoria: 'The possibilities do not exist.'[28] She summoned the spirit of 1940 and, remarkably, by the power of her conviction and the heroism of her sailors and soldiers, she lived up to it.

In fact, on her Lilliputian scale, she was in some ways a better war leader than Churchill because, while on the one hand she gave her commanders the confidence of her absolute political support and embodied Britain's cause brilliantly to the country and the world, she also recognised her own complete ignorance of military matters and the making of war and did not interfere in the conduct of operations. She asked searching questions, as was her way: she wanted to understand everything. But she respected their professionalism, and though she was often impatient for results – particularly when under political pressure to accept a settlement before the job was done – she never overruled their judgement. 'From the military man's point of view,' Lewin recalled, 'she was an ideal Prime Minister . . . One wanted a decision and she gave it.'[29] The only time a commander on the ground was ordered to act against his own judgement – Brigadier Julian Thompson's premature and strategically irrelevant attack on Goose Green – the pressure on Thompson to get on with it came as much from Operation Headquarters in Northwood as it did from Downing Street.

In one way Mrs Thatcher's inexperience of war was a positive advantage. Practically every senior politician, soldier and diplomat involved in the Falklands is convinced that no male Prime Minister, except perhaps Churchill, would have done what she did – ordered the task force to sail and then backed it to reconquer the islands, accepting the certainty of casualties if it came to a shooting war. Most of the men around her had personal experience of war. Whitelaw and Pym both had the Military Cross; even the owlish Nott had served as a professional soldier with the Gurkhas in Malaya. A man, they all believe, would have been more vividly aware of what war involved. 'She had a sort of television view of war,' one adviser recalled.[30] Nicholas Henderson felt that the American Secretary of State, General Alexander Haig, shuttling tirelessly between London and Buenos Aires trying to prevent the outbreak of hostilities, had always in mind the memory of the bodybags in Vietnam.[31] Admiral Lewin warned Mrs Thatcher that there would be casualties. She hated the idea, of course; but she accepted the inevitability so long as the navy and the army judged the risk proportionate to the goal. Fighting, after all, was what the forces were for.

When casualties occurred, however, she probably felt them more deeply than her male colleagues. Several of her closest confidants have described her 'acute distress' at the news of losses. 'She was stricken far more than a man would have been in her position,' Woodrow Wyatt wrote. 'She felt them personally inside herself.'[32] Ronnie Millar was with her when she was told of the sinking of HMS *Sheffield*, just before she spoke to the Conservative Women's Conference on 29 May. She tensed, turned away, clenched her fists, struggled for control and quietly wept; then she composed herself and proceeded to make her speech, calmly and with dignity, but cut to twenty minutes.[33] Michael Havers – whose naval experience during World War Two made him 'a very good hand-holder'[34] in these days – recalled another occasion when Lewin broke bad news:

> She just put her head down and stared at the table . . . I felt that she had really withdrawn herself from the War Cabinet – for about a minute. [Then] she'd sort of mentally shake herself and come right back in again. Tears running down her face.[35]

She made a point of writing personally to the families of all the men who died. She later claimed, without irony, that her own anxiety when Mark was lost in the Sahara earlier that year gave her an insight into what the Falkland mothers were going through. ('I was lucky,' she told Miriam Stoppard in 1985. 'They weren't.')[36] The old hands around her – Whitelaw, Wyatt, Havers and not least Denis, who had served in Italy in 1943–5 – all had to console her at times with the reminder that casualties were inevitable. Lewin actually felt that the loss of the *Sheffield* was 'a bit of a relief when it happened, because it explained to the politicians that you can't fight wars without losing people'.[37] Once the casualties started, however, they only made her more determined to finish the job.

Her sex was really beside the point. What made Mrs Thatcher a successful war leader – apart from the quality of the forces under her command and a large slice of luck – was the clarity of her purpose. She had an unblinking single-mindedness about achieving her objective and an extraordinary simple faith that because her cause was right it would prevail. In war as in economics, it was this moralistic certainty, not her gender, which set her apart from her male colleagues, enabling her to grasp risks they would have baulked at. In the messy trade-offs of domestic politics, her clear-cut sense of righteousness was a mixed attribute – a source of strength up to a point, but also a weakness which narrowed her capacity for human sympathy. In war it was pure strength. It was nevertheless unfair of her, at the time and subsequently, to contrast her resolution with others' doubts. Cecil Parkinson was deeply upset on one occasion when she rounded on him for voicing a note of caution, telling him there was 'no room for faint hearts' in the War Cabinet.[38] It was the job of her colleagues in the War Cabinet to weigh the risks, and specifically the job of Pym as Foreign Secretary to pursue every diplomatic possibility of averting war – if only to keep world opinion on Britain's side. As it happened, she was right to see from an early stage that there was no genuine compromise available. As Max Hastings and Simon Jenkins point out, she understood her enemy: 'Her certainty of Argentine intransigence, fully justified in the event, reflected a remarkable ability to think herself into the junta's mind.'[39] She recognised that General Galtieri could no more back down without winning the sovereignty of *las Malvinas* than she could accept their continued occupation. So she was vindicated in her determination that there was no alternative to war.

Yet the fact remains that she, with all her determination, still could not have retaken the islands if the Chiefs of Staff had not advised her that it was militarily possible, or if they had judged the risk too great. Theirs was the real responsibility, first for putting together a task force in five days when they had no serious idea of what it should do when it reached the Falklands, then for evolving a series of improvisations when their original plans became unfeasible due to the weather, lack of air cover, the unanticipated range of the Argentine air force and the loss of ships and helicopters. Mrs Thatcher's role was to make and sustain the political judgement that if the military said it could be done, then it should be done. By the force of her own conviction she won and kept the backing of her Cabinet for her unswerving line. It is this judgement that colleagues doubt that any other modern Prime Minister, or potential alternative Prime Minister in 1982, would have made. In the event, she won her war and liberated the islands, with relatively little loss of life; and the victory was judged to have been worth the cost. Nevertheless the cost was very high – 255 British lives; six ships sunk and others damaged; the huge cost of defending the islands for an indefinite future – and it could very easily have been much higher. The risk was never properly calculated in advance, and the Argentines should have inflicted much heavier damage than they did. Would public opinion have stood the loss of many more ships? What would have happened if the navy had become unable to support and supply the landing force as the winter closed in? It was in fact a very close-run thing. All the elements of the task force were operating at the extreme limits of their capacity, with virtually no margin for error; some units outside Stanley were down to their last six rounds of ammunition when the Argentine surrender came.[40] The peacemakers were right to explore every possibility of averting Mrs Thatcher's appalling gamble.

The diplomacy of war

As the task force steamed slowly south during April and early May, Mrs Thatcher's position was very delicate, since she had to be seen to be willing to accept a reasonable settlement, if one could be negotiated, even though she was personally determined to agree to nothing less than the full recovery of British sovereignty over the islands. She recognised that she must keep the diplomatic option open in order to retain world and above all American opinion on Britain's side – though she had difficulty understanding how the Americans could fail to support their most faithful ally against what seemed to her a clear-cut case of unprovoked aggression. In fact the first instinct of the Reagan administration, which had taken office in Washington at the beginning of 1981, was to remain neutral. There was a strong lobby, most powerfully represented by the outspoken Ambassador to the United Nations, Jeane Kirkpatrick, which considered the preservation of good relations with Latin America more important than pandering to British imperial nostalgia. President Reagan himself, bemused by the importance Mrs Thatcher attached to what he called 'that little ice-cold bunch of land down there', stated on 6 April that America was friends with both Britain and Argentina.[41] It was on this basis, to Mrs Thatcher's fury, that Secretary of State Al Haig set out to try to broker an even-handed settlement.

It was not, as is often assumed, Mrs Thatcher's special relationship with Ronald Reagan which swung American sentiment in Britain's favour over the next few weeks, but a brilliant exercise in old-fashioned diplomacy by two paladins of the despised Foreign Office – Sir Anthony Parsons, Britain's Ambassador to the United Nations in New York, and Sir Nicholas Henderson, the British Ambassador in Washington. In addition, and crucially, the US Defense Secretary, Caspar Weinberger, accorded Britain on his own initiative vital military co-operation – the use of the US base on Ascension Island, with unlimited fuel and spares, accelerated purchase of Sidewinder missiles and access to American intelligence – long before the White House had officially come off the fence, and despite the fact that the US military viewed the attempt to retake the islands as 'a futile and impossible effort' which could not succeed.[42] For this help beyond the call of duty Weinberger was awarded an honorary knighthood after the war.

Anthony Parsons pulled off an extraordinary coup, just one day after the invasion, by persuading the UN Security Council to pass a resolution (Resolution 502) condemning the Argentine action and calling for the withdrawal of the occupying troops pending a diplomatic solution. To obtain the necessary two-thirds majority – discounting the Communist and Latin nations – he had to twist the arms of Togo, Zaire, Uganda, Guyana and Jordan. He managed the first four, before calling in Mrs Thatcher to make a personal appeal by telephone to King Hussein. She succeeded. The Argentines had never imagined that Britain could mobilise the UN in support of an imperialist quarrel. As in Rhodesia, Mrs Thatcher would much rather have done without the involvement of the UN. But in the eyes of the world, Resolution 502 gave priceless legitimacy to Britain's claim to be standing up for freedom, self-determination and international law. Over the next few days Nico Henderson toured the television studios of Washington projecting Britain's cause to the American public; while – no less important – the FO's men in Brussels persuaded the European Community collectively (and most of the EC countries individually) to impose sanctions on Argentina. Most crucially the French froze the export of Exocet missiles and spare parts for those they already had. Mrs Thatcher was always grateful for President Mitterand's prompt and unconditional support. Within a week of the invasion Galtieri and his *junta* – who had expected no more than token protests – found not only Britain in arms but most of the world arrayed against them.

This gratifying approval, however, was accorded on the assumption that Britain remained ready to negotiate. The six-week hiatus before the task force reached the South Atlantic allowed ample time for a peaceful settlement to be found. Even once he had appreciated the strength of Mrs Thatcher's resolution – 'That's a hell of a tough lady,' he told his aides on returning to his hotel after his first meeting with her[43] – it remained Al Haig's assumption that she would have to compromise. It is plain from his published diary that Henderson – even as he sold her tough line to the American public – was alarmed by her bellicosity.[44] Even after hostilities had started, Reagan never ceased to beg her to accept a ceasefire. In fact Mrs Thatcher played an extraordinary lone hand against the entire foreign-policy establishment of both Britain and America to ensure that all their well-intentioned peacemongering should not forestall the military victory which she was convinced was the only outcome Britain could accept. In her memoirs she gloried in her isolation. 'I was under an almost intolerable pressure to negotiate for the sake of negotiation . . . At such a time almost everyone and everything seems to combine to deflect you from what you know has to be done.'[45] But she recognised that she would forfeit international support if she appeared inflexible. 'We . . . had to stand firm against the pressure to make unacceptable compromises while avoiding the appearance of intransigence.'[46]

Haig's initial proposals provided for Argentine withdrawal from the islands followed by an interim joint administration while a permanent settlement was negotiated. Over the next two months numerous variations were spun on these three central ideas, first by Haig himself, later in the names of the Peruvian President Bellaunde and the UN Secretary-General, Javier Pérez de Cuellar. Through various intermediaries London and Buenos Aires haggled over how far each might be willing to withdraw its forces (if both returned to their home bases, the Argentines would still be 300 miles, Britain 8,000 miles, away); over the composition and character of the interim administration (some sort of tripartite arrangement, with the Americans, the Peruvians or the UN holding the ring; but would it respect the islanders' existing institutions, or could the Argentines swamp them with new immigrants?); and over the right of the islanders to exercise a veto on the eventual outcome. Through all the comings and goings, however, Mrs Thatcher remained adamant on two points: first, that the occupying force must withdraw before anything else could be considered – Carol describes her sitting on the floor in Downing Street, surrounded by peace plans, insisting like a stubborn child, 'I'm not agreeing to anything until they get off';[47] and second, that the wishes of the islanders in any eventual settlement must be 'paramount'. But Galtieri and his colleagues were equally adamant that the islands were Argentine and they would not let go what they had seized without a guarantee of eventual sovereignty. Between these two sticking points there was no compromise. But thanks to Parsons' diplomatic coup Mrs Thatcher had UN authority for her position. Resolution 502 not only called for Argentine withdrawal and guaranteed the right of self-determination; Article 51 of the UN Charter asserted the right of self-defence against aggression. So long as she showed a willingness to compromise on hypothetical details the Charter endorsed her essential demands.

At first she did not have too much difficulty holding her line. On 23 April, to her disgust, Pym bowed to intense American pressure and was persuaded to recommend a package which she described as 'conditional surrender'.[48] 'I could not have stayed as Prime Minister had the War Cabinet accepted Francis Pym's proposals,' she wrote in her memoirs. 'I would have resigned.'[49] She averted that necessity, as she often did before crucial Cabinets, by squaring Willie Whitelaw in advance. As usual he did not let her down. Rather than send Pym back to Haig with a flat rejection, however, Nott proposed that they ask him to put his package to the Argentines first, in the expectation that they would reject it – as they duly did. 'It was the Argentine invasion which started this crisis,' she told the Commons, 'and it is Argentine withdrawal that must put an end to it.'[50] That was relatively easy. Next day came news of the recapture of South Georgia, and a few days later the US Government formally came out on Britain's side, promising material and intelligence support. 'We now have the total support of the United States,' Mrs Thatcher announced, 'which we would expect and which I think we always expected to have.'[51]

The next time round the track was much more difficult. On 2 May the British submarine *Conqueror* sank the Argentine cruiser *General Belgrano*, with the loss of 368 lives; next day, in retaliation, the Argentine air force sank the destroyer *Sheffield*, killing twenty-one of her crew. Suddenly war was a reality. Immediately international pressure on Britain to refrain from escalating the conflict grew more urgent. 'The perception started to reverse itself,' Parsons recalled. 'It began to look as though . . . a horrid NATO country [was] clobbering a poor Third World non-aligned state . . . I could see this happening.'[52] At the same time British enthusiasm was severely dented by the loss of a British warship. In this changed atmosphere the Bellaunde peace plan – though essentially no different from Haig's – demanded to be taken a lot more seriously.

The question of why the War Cabinet agreed to sink the *Belgrano* has generated more controversy than any other aspect of the Falklands war. Britain had declared (on 12 April) a maritime exclusion zone of 200 miles around the islands, inside which it warned that any Argentine ship was liable to be sunk. But the *Belgrano* was outside the zone on 2 May and – it later transpired – steaming away from the islands. To attack her in these circumstances appeared to be an act of unprovoked escalation – even a war crime. In fact there were good military reasons for doing so. The Argentine fleet was at sea, with orders to attack British ships: the previous day it had launched, but aborted, an Exocet attack. The direction in which the *Belgrano*, with her two accompanying Exocet-armed destroyers, was temporarily headed was, in Lewin's view, 'entirely immaterial'.[53] The commander of the task force, Admiral 'Sandy' Woodward, suspected that she was engaged in 'a classic pincer movement' and requested permission to sink her.[54] Lewin backed his request, and the War Cabinet had little hesitation in agreeing. By 2 May the original exclusion zone had been superseded; the Argentines had been warned that from 26 April any ship operating in the area of the task force would be liable to attack. Both Whitelaw and Nott – Pym was absent in New York – felt they had no option but to grant Woodward's request. The *Belgrano*, Mrs Thatcher told the Commons next day, 'posed a very obvious threat to the men in our task force. Had we left it any later it would have been too late and I might have had to come to the House with the news that some of our ships had been sunk.'[55] She has always subsequently maintained that the decision was taken for strictly military reasons to counter 'a clear military threat which we could not responsibly ignore'.[56] Moreover even critics have had to admit that the action was justified by its result, since the Argentine navy never ventured out of port again for the duration of the conflict.[57]

What is surprising is that the War Cabinet did not hesitate longer over the political implications of Woodward's request. Hitherto they had been sensitive to the importance of retaining the moral high ground. They had refused permission to shoot down Argentine civilian aircraft which were being used to shadow the task force; and refused to allow the submarine *Spartan* to sink a minelayer off Port Stanley. They were very anxious not to incur the international odium of inflicting the first casualties while the search for a peaceful settlement was still going on. In this context sinking the *Belgrano* was a huge propaganda risk, which did in fact cause a significant loss of sympathy for Britain both at the UN and in the EC – Ireland joined Italy in moves to end sanctions against Argentina – until it was overtaken by the sinking of the *Sheffield* next day. In fact the decision was not taken lightly. Havers insisted that the implications were 'very carefully discussed . . . She wouldn't move without my legal advice, saying that I thought we were justified' under the UN Charter.[58] To recapture the islands Britain was bound to have to strike the first blow at some stage. What no one anticipated was the heavy loss of life that sinking the *Belgrano* would entail, largely because her supporting destroyers fled back to port as soon as the *Belgrano* was hit, without waiting to pick up survivors. It was the undue scale of casualties which made the *Belgrano* such a *cause célèbre*, compounded by the Government's lack of frankness in the subsequent recriminations, which clouded the issue with contradictory explanations. Nevertheless in the unfolding context of the war the sinking was both defensible and effective. It certainly sent the clearest possible signal to anyone who still doubted that Mrs Thatcher's intentions were serious.

The allegation that the *Belgrano* was sunk deliberately to scupper the Peruvian peace plan does not stand up. On the contrary, the loss of the *Belgrano* and the *Sheffield* did more than anything else to get President Bellaunde's initiative off the ground. Now that both sides had shown the other what they could do, there was growing demand both at home and abroad for a ceasefire before further carnage was unleashed. On 5 May Mrs Thatcher felt obliged to seek the support of the full Cabinet. This time she did not get it. Bellaunde's scheme was essentially the same as Haig's – 'Haig in a poncho'; it was still clear that the Argentines were prepared to discuss interim administrations only on the understanding that sovereignty would eventually be theirs. But now even Willie Whitelaw believed they had no choice but to keep talking.[59] As the Prime Minister went round the table only Michael Heseltine and Quintin Hailsham held to the uncompromising line.[60] The next day Mrs Thatcher was obliged to announce that 'we have made a very constructive response' to the Peruvian proposals. In her memoirs she slides over this meeting very quickly. The Cabinet, she claims, did not like the US/Peruvian proposals any more than she did. 'But we had to make some response.'[61] In the Commons she remained adamant that Britain could not accept a ceasefire while the Argentines were still on the islands:

> That would be a very evident ploy to keep them in possession of their ill-gotten gains and we are right to be very wary of it. The whole of Resolution 502 must be accepted and there can be no ceasefire unless it is accompanied by a withdrawal that is fully and properly supervised.[62]

Once again she was relying on the Argentines rejecting half a cake; and once again Galtieri did not let her down. Nevertheless this was the first time since 2 April that Mrs Thatcher had let herself be committed to accept a compromise settlement, with some form of condominium or UN trusteeship replacing simple British sovereignty. The full Cabinet discussed a range of different options in exhaustive detail; she could no longer get her way by threatening resignation.[63] This was the moment when the *junta* could have achieved a share in the government of the islands, had they had the sense to grasp it. A word from Foreign Minister Costa Mendes to the UN Secretary-General in New York that evening, and Britain could not have defied American and world opinion by pressing on.

Instead the countdown now quickened. On 8 May the task force sailed south from Ascension Island. Nott and others had always felt that this was the critical point after which it would not be possible to recall it with the job half done.[64] The same day the War Cabinet approved Woodward's plan for an amphibious landing on the western side of East Falkland, at San Carlos Bay, to begin on 21 May. On 12 May the requisitioned passenger liner *Queen Elizabeth II* left Southampton carrying another 3,000 men of the 5th Infantry Brigade – Welsh Guards and Scots Guards – to reinforce the Marines and Paras

who would make the initial assault. In the Commons on 13 May Mrs
Thatcher was visibly irritated by further talk of peace. 'May I make it
perfectly clear,' she told a Tory questioner, 'that we are working for a
peaceful solution, not a peaceful sell-out.'[65] Later she practically bit
Reagan's head off when the President rang to urge further negotiations: 'He couldn't get a word in edgeways,' one of his aides recalled.[66]
In a belligerent speech to the Scottish Conservative Conference the
next day she left no doubt that she was impatient to get on with it.
'Of course we will continue to negotiate,' she declared:

> We will go on doing all we humanly can to reach a peaceful settle-
> ment – a settlement in which the Argentines leave the islands they
> now unlawfully occupy.
>
> But I should not be doing my duty if I did not warn you in the
> simplest and clearest terms that . . . a negotiated settlement may
> prove unattainable.
>
> Then we should have to turn to the only course left open to us.[67]

The following day, Sunday 16 May, she held an all-day meeting of
the extended War Cabinet at Chequers to agree the form of words of
Britain's final negotiating stance – in effect an ultimatum. No one
expected it to be accepted: Mrs Thatcher's mind was fixed on the trial
ahead. But Parsons and Henderson were still concerned to frame as
conciliatory a text as possible to demonstrate Britain's willingness to
go to the limit of concessions to avert war. Henderson's diary describes
a torrid day:

> The problem was of course, that the PM veered the whole time
> towards being uncompromising, so that the rest of us, and particu-
> larly the FCO participants, constantly found themselves [*sic*] under
> attack from her for being wet, ready to sell out, unsupportive of
> Britain's interests, etc.

She harried them relentlessly with high-principled talk of democracy,
aggression, self-determination and the Americans' moral obligation to take
Britain's side, insisting on clarity where they favoured diplomatic fudge:

> We heard this speech frequently throughout the day, as we worked
> our way line by line through the text. I was in no doubt that she
> really preferred the idea of a fight than the accusation of compromise.[68]

That word 'accusation' says everything about the state of moral

excitement Mrs Thatcher had worked herself into. In the Commons
three days later she explicitly cleared the decks for war. Blaming the
Argentines' 'obduracy and delay, deception and bad faith' for thwarting
every effort over the past six weeks to negotiate a peaceful settlement,
she announced with ill-concealed relief that the effort was over. While
Britain had offered reasonable proposals, including acceptance of
interim UN administration of the islands, following an Argentine withdrawal and pending long-term negotiations 'without prejudgement of
the outcome', Argentina had 'sought merely to confuse and prolong
the negotiations, while remaining in illegal possession of the islands. I
believe that if we had a dozen more negotiations the tactics and results
would be the same.' Therefore, she announced, the British proposals
were now withdrawn. 'They are no longer on the table.' Pressed by
David Owen to keep the door open, she repeated: 'They have been
rejected. They are no longer on the table.'

> Difficult days lie ahead; but Britain will face them in the convic-
> tion that our cause is just and in the knowledge that we have been
> doing everything reasonable to secure a negotiated settlement . . .
>   Britain has a responsibility towards the islanders to restore their
> democratic way of life. She has a duty towards the whole world to
> show that aggression will not succeed, and to uphold the cause of
> freedom.[69]

Victory and after

Once the order was given, four days later, to launch the counter-invasion,
Mrs Thatcher had little further role to play: like everyone else she could
only wait for news and trust the forces to deliver what Leach and Lewin
had rashly promised seven weeks before. The risk of failure was still very
real. The landing at San Carlos Bay without adequate air cover (the navy
had no airborne early-warning system, and only forty Harriers against
160 Argentine planes) broke all the canons of warfare. American admirals later admitted that they would not have attempted it.[70] Helped by
bad weather, the assault force reached San Carlos Water undetected – the
Argentines had expected a landing nearer to Port Stanley – beachheads
were successfully secured and 4,000 men put ashore on 21 May. But in
the crucial battle for air superiority over the next four days two frigates
(*Ardent* and *Antelope*) and the destroyer *Coventry* were sunk, and several
more ships damaged. The losses would have been worse if several Argentine
bombs had not failed to explode; but they were bad enough to force
Woodward to keep *Hermes* and *Invincible* at a greater distance than
intended, which in turn reduced the combat capacity of the Harriers.

Militarily most serious was the sinking on 25 May of the transport ship *Atlantic Conveyor*, with the loss of three of the task force's four Chinook helicopters, with which it had been planned to lift the Marines and Paras across the island to Port Stanley. Now they had to 'yomp' the whole way on foot, carrying their heavy equipment. Fortunately – and inexplicably – the Argentines failed to bomb the beachheads before the troops were ready to move off. Fortunately the Harriers performed better than could have been predicted, inflicting heavier losses on the Argentine air force than its commanders in Buenos Aires (never very keen on Galtieri's war) were prepared to accept. Fortunately, too, the Argentine submarines stayed in port; while their land forces, though they outnumbered the British by 2–1, turned out to be unwilling conscripts from the warmer climate of northern Argentina, physically and psychologically less suited to the bitter Falklands winter than the Arctic-trained British professionals. Once the Marines and the Paras had begun their advance on Stanley – by way of a diversion to Goose Green – there was little doubt that they would get there; but the casualties could have been much greater had the Argentines put up more determined resistance. As it was, the last big blow to the British forces was the sinking of the troopship *Sir Galahad* at Fitzroy on 8 June, with the loss of fifty-one Welsh Guardsmen. The inadequately protected landing at Fitzroy was one perilous operation that went tragically wrong, giving a chilling glimpse of what might easily have been; but it did not delay the final push towards Stanley. Six days later the tin-roofed settlement was surrounded and the Argentine commander surrendered without need for a final onslaught.

During these climactic three weeks, when the fate of the task force, and of her Government, hung on events 8,000 miles away which were beyond her control, Mrs Thatcher lived on her nerves, barely sleeping, impatient for news, yet obliged to keep up as far as possible a normal round of duties and engagements. On the day of the San Carlos landing she was due to open a warehouse in Finchley: a date she had already cancelled once. 'Of course,' she told Carol, 'all my thoughts were in the South Atlantic. I was desperately worried . . . But if I hadn't gone to the function, people would have thought something was wrong – I had to carry on as normal.'[71] On her way to the constituency, she was told that the operation – just like South Georgia – had started badly: two Gazelle helicopters had been shot down, and three men killed. Her new agent, Andrew Thomson, remembered the visit vividly. Mrs Thatcher arrived, dressed in black and 'wearing a look of great depression', supported almost physically by Denis. As she walked to the warehouse through a crowd of 600 people, the band of the Royal Marines struck up; she froze on the spot until Denis pulled her on. At the ceremony she spoke briefly but emotionally of the men of the task force, whose courage and skill had 'made us realise once again that we are all really one family. For us, geographically distant though we may be, they are but a heartbeat away.'[72] As she left the lunch a *Daily Mirror* cameraman took a picture. 'The photograph would have shown the British Prime Minister crying, her face awash with tears as she climbed into the car.' To the relief of her staff, it was not printed. Back at the constituency office in Ballard's Lane she rested for an hour and a half before another engagement, a retirement party for her former agent, Roy Langstone. 'Her exhaustion was almost complete.' While she was there, however, the news came through that the bridgehead had been established at San Carlos Bay:

> For the second time that day the Prime Minister froze, but there was no Denis with her this time and she stayed motionless for a full thirty seconds. Then her whole body came alive again with a huge jerk, as she said: 'That's it. That's what I've been waiting for all day. Let's go!' The bustling practical Margaret Thatcher was back in action.[73]

Back in Downing Street later that evening she was transformed. 'These are nervous days,' she told the crowd which had by then gathered, 'but we have marvellous fighting forces: everyone is behind them. We are fighting a just cause, and we wish them Godspeed.'[74]

The following days were intensely difficult for her. 'I'm sure she would have preferred to be charging around Goose Green with a gun,' Carol recalled, 'rather than sitting at Number Ten waiting for news. She made a conscious decision not to ring up and ask how it was going. I remember her saying "I wish I knew, I wish I knew", and Denis calmly replying, "This is how it is in war."'[75] In fact she was admirably restrained. She only visited operational HQ at Northwood twice, first during the South Georgia action on 23 April, when her supportiveness and determination made a deep impression, and then at the very end, when she and Nott went to monitor the final hours of the campaign. In the latter stages she was very hyped-up and sometimes, in the words of one member of the War Cabinet, 'dangerously gung-ho': she had to be restrained from ordering an attack on the Argentine aircraft carrier *Veinticinco de Mayo* which at that stage would have been seen as a gratuitous provocation of world opinion, far worse than the *Belgrano*.[76] Her impatience was reinforced by renewed

American and UN pressure for a ceasefire. Once the beachhead at San Carlos had been achieved, still more once Goose Green had been taken, the Americans urged that Britain had made her point: to go on would merely be to inflict humiliation on Argentina. Mrs Thatcher had no problem with that. It would have been 'quite wrong', she wrote in her memoirs 'to snatch diplomatic defeat from the jaws of military victory'.[77] Besides, she could not leave her troops stranded in inhospitable terrain halfway to Stanley. So she was 'dismayed' and 'horrified' when Reagan (prompted by Jeane Kirkpatrick) telephoned her again on 31 May, begging her to follow Churchill's dictum of 'magnanimity in victory'. So far as she was concerned the victory was not yet won. 'There's no possibility whatever in what they are thinking of,' she told Henderson. The idea was 'pure Haigism':

We were prepared to negotiate before, but not now. We have lost a lot of blood, and it's the best blood. Do they not realise that it is an issue of principle?[78]

On 4 June Parsons had to use Britain's veto to block a Security Council resolution calling for a ceasefire (while the Americans performed a humiliating 'flip-flop' and ended up facing both ways at once). Simultaneously at the G7 summit at Versailles Reagan presented new proposals for a UN peace-keeping administration, with US involvement to prevent the Argentines using it to swamp the islands with new immigrants. By now both the Foreign Office and the Ministry of Defence were becoming alarmed at the implications of a military victory which would commit Britain to defending the islands for an indefinite future. On 6 June Henderson even found Mrs Thatcher herself marginally more ready to consider a solution short of the restoration of full colonial rule. 'I can't say that she liked it, but she listened.' Realising that there was a problem, however, she persuaded herself that the answer lay in the economic development of the islands. 'She has the rosiest view of the islands' future and talked much of the development of the fishing industry and the wildlife possibilities,' dropping the name of the naturalist Peter Scott with naive awe. She toyed with the idea of a South Atlantic Federation of British dependencies, including Ascension, St Helena and South Georgia, which would attract Latin American investment, under US protection; but she still resented the need to show flexibility in order to secure American support. '"Flexibility" is almost as odious a word to the Prime Minister as "magnanimity".' She insisted that she would be very reasonable – 'provided I get my way'. Henderson was reminded of Henry V's speech before Agincourt: 'Then lend the eye a terrible aspect.'[79] She was still determined to brook no compromise short of total victory.

She finally got her victory on Monday 14 June. Just seventy-two days after the traumatic Saturday debate on 2 April she was able to tell a cheering House of Commons that white flags were flying over Port Stanley[80] – though the official Argentine surrender did not come until some hours later. She then returned to Downing Street where the crowd sang 'Rule Britannia'. This was the defining moment of her premiership. While careful to share the credit with the commanders who had planned the campaign and with 'our boys' who had executed it so heroically, there was no mistaking her determination to extract the maximum political dividend for herself and her Government. In the flush of victory, recriminations about the responsibility for letting the Argentine invasion happen in the first place were easily brushed aside. A commission of inquiry, chaired by the veteran mandarin Lord Franks, had to be set up, with a carefully balanced team of senior privy councillors and civil servants to look into the course of events leading up to the invasion. But it was inconceivable that its report – delivered the following January – would seriously criticise the victorious Government. From the humiliation of 2 April Mrs Thatcher had plucked a national and personal triumph; she had gambled dangerously but she had hit the political jackpot and no one could take her winnings from her now. She was determined to project the defeat of General Galtieri – and implicitly all those fainthearts at home and abroad who had tried to thwart it – as the vindication, first, of her personal qualities of courage, strength and resolution; and, second, of her patriotic vision of a Britain reborn, a vision as applicable to eradicating socialism at home as it was to sorting out bullies in the South Atlantic. 'A Labour Government,' she told Foot scornfully, 'would never have fired a shot.'[81] Over the weeks and months following the Argentine surrender she had no compunction about exploiting her victory for all it was worth.

Amid all the congratulations, the most gratifying tribute came from Enoch Powell in the Commons on 17 June. Back in April, Powell had warned that the crisis would test the Iron Lady's metal. Now, picking up the same metaphor, he solemnly submitted his report:

It shows that the substance under test consists of ferrous metal of the highest quality. It is of exceptional tensile strength, resistant to wear and tear, and may be used with advantage for all national purposes.

Mrs Thatcher accepted the compliment with no pretence of modesty. 'I agree with every word he says.'[82] The faithful Ian Gow framed Powell's words and presented them to her as a trophy of the war.

Clearly she could not make a habit of exalting her own contribution – she attracted a good deal of criticism when she took the salute at a victory parade through the City of London in October, usurping, many thought, a function that was properly the Queen's – but over the summer she lost no opportunity of beating the patriotic drum. 'We have ceased to be a nation in retreat,' she claimed in a speech at an open-air rally on Cheltenham racecourse on 3 July. 'Britain found herself again in the South Atlantic and will not look back from the victory she has won.'[83] On 21 July she was at Portsmouth for the emotional homecoming of HMS *Hermes*; and a few days later she attended – with the Royal Family and members of the victorious forces – a service of thanksgiving at St Paul's Cathedral. The Tory Party Conference in October was shamelessly turned into another victory rally. Colonel 'H' Jones' widow was given a seat on the platform, while Mrs Thatcher's triumphal entry, preceded by 'Rule Britannia', was greeted by a tumult of Union Jacks recalling the Last Night of the Proms. In her opening words she invoked 'the spirit of the South Atlantic' which was 'the spirit of Britain at her best', but then contradicted her earlier boast by declaring:

It has been said . . . that British patriotism was rediscovered in those spring days. Mr Chairman, it was never really lost.[84]

Of course what she meant was that it had been mislaid under previous Governments, but under her leadership had been recovered. She did not intend that it should be mislaid again.

Margaret Roberts had always been a flag-waving British patriot. From the very start of her career as a young Tory candidate in Dartford in 1949, her speeches were full of the ambition of restoring British 'greatness'. Thirty years later she entered Downing Street passionately committed to reversing the sense of national 'decline'. She had relished fighting Britain's corner against the rest of the EC at Dublin and Strasbourg; she hated lowering the flag on Rhodesia. But nothing gave her such an opportunity to wrap herself in the Union Jack as did the Falklands. The symbolism and language of military leadership gave her patriotism a new resonance. A Prime Minister in war – with a real enemy, troops committed, ships being sunk, lives lost – is a national leader in a way that he or she can never be in peace. Most other contemporary British politicians would have been uncomfortable in the role of war leader: Mrs Thatcher instinctively embraced it, enthusiastically identifying herself with 'our boys' and glorying unashamedly in the combat, the heroism and the sacrifice of war.★ It was from this time that she began to be portrayed, without irony, as Britannia, or Boadicea, or Elizabeth I – the very personification and embodiment of Britishness, at once warlike and female. Victory in war lent her an iconic status as a national emblem matched by none of her predecessors, with the single exception of Churchill.

It also transformed her political prospects. Despite the precedent of Churchill in 1945, it was now practically impossible that she could lose the next election, whenever she should choose to hold it. Only six months earlier she had been the most unpopular Prime Minister in polling memory, her Government divided and her party facing wipeout at the hands of a two-pronged opposition. By March there had been some recovery, but just a week before the invasion of the Falklands Roy Jenkins had won the Hillhead by-election to keep the SDP momentum rolling; the electorate was still divided equally between the Government, Labour and the Alliance. Both opposition parties had had a difficult war – Labour increasingly critical but constrained by Foot's initial support for the task force, the Alliance (despite David Owen's best efforts) looking weak and irrelevant. By July Mrs Thatcher's personal approval rating had doubled (to 52 per cent) and the Conservatives had left the other parties scrapping for a distant second place – which is how the position remained up to June 1983. Mrs Thatcher was not only virtually guaranteed a second term in Downing Street; after three years of battling her own colleagues, her authority within the Tory party was suddenly unassailable. 'She has made the "wets" her footstool,' David Watt wrote in *The Times*. Her position was 'positively monarchical'; the general view was that she could be Prime Minister 'forever'.[87]

The Falklands war was a watershed in domestic politics, leading directly to the unprecedented domination that Mrs Thatcher established over the next eight years. As well as hugely boosting her authority and

---

★'When you have spent half your life dealing with humdrum issues like the environment,' she was reported to have told the Scottish Conservative conference in the middle of the war, 'it is exciting to have a real crisis on your hands.'[85] In fact this was a very rough paraphrase of what she said. But her actual words did express very much the same sentiment. 'What really thrilled me, having spent so much of my life in Parliament and talking about things like inflation, Social Security benefits, housing problems, environmental problems and so on, is that when it really came to the test what thrilled people wasn't those things, what thrilled people was once again being able to serve a great cause, the cause of liberty.'[86]

self-confidence, the experience of war leadership encouraged autocratic tendencies which had hitherto been contained. 'War seemed to release abilities in her that she didn't really know she had,' Simon Jenkins observed, 'and relieved her from many of the obligations of leadership at which she knew she wasn't very good.'[88] In particular the speed and convenience of working through a small War Cabinet led her increasingly to bypass the full Cabinet in favour of decision-making through hand-picked *ad hoc* committees. Several branches of the Establishment had earned her lasting displeasure by their lack of martial spirit. Despite the debt she owed to Anthony Parsons and Nico Henderson, for example, the war thoroughly confirmed her poor opinion of the Foreign Office. Henceforth – saddled with a Foreign Secretary she detested in place of the trusted and skilful Carrington – she ran her own foreign policy. She installed Parsons (later replaced by Sir Percy Cradock) in Number Ten as her private foreign-policy adviser to give her independent advice (just as she had already imported Alan Walters to undercut the Treasury). Meanwhile the conviction that it was only her firmness which had brought victory encouraged her belief that a refusal to compromise was the only language foreigners understood.

Another offender was the BBC. Mrs Thatcher and some Conservative backbenchers had been enraged by what they regarded as the Corporation's excessively even-handed coverage of the war – referring to 'the British' and 'the Argentines' instead of 'our forces' and 'the enemy', as it had done in 1939–45; pursuing the inconsistencies in the Government's account of the sinking of the *Belgrano*; and inviting retired generals to predict on television where the task force might attempt to land.[89] She resolved to bring the broadcasters to heel in her second term. She was likewise infuriated by the Archbishop of Canterbury's language of reconciliation at the thanksgiving service on 26 July, when he had the Christian temerity to remember the Argentine dead as well as the British: the Church of England was marked down in that moment as another nest of fifth columnists needing to be sorted out.

The Falklands gave Mrs Thatcher a unique opportunity to become a truly national leader. Matthew Parris was one Tory MP who hoped that she might now 'emerge as a bigger person; she will acquire mercy; she will find grace'.[90] Unfortunately it had the opposite effect. Victory in the South Atlantic exacerbated her worst characteristics, not her best. After 1982 she used her augmented authority to pursue more self-righteously than before her particular vision of British society, and to trample on those groups, institutions and traditions which did not share it. Having routed the external enemy, she was soon looking for enemies within on whom she could visit the same treatment.

The war undoubtedly enhanced British prestige in the world, though possibly to a lesser extent than Mrs Thatcher wished to believe. It certainly confirmed the high professional reputation of Britain's armed forces: the Americans frankly contrasted the success of the Falklands operation with some of their own forces' bungled efforts in Lebanon and Iran, and British military advisers found themselves in demand around the world to train foreign armies. It also increased Mrs Thatcher's personal visibility on the international stage: her status as a global superstar, mobbed by crowds wherever she went, reflected credit, or at least heightened interest, back on Britain. But the world was as much amazed as it was impressed by the lengths Britain was prepared to go to recapture the Falklands. Mrs Thatcher invoked fine principles of defending democracy and standing up to dictators, investing the war with high global symbolism that went down well in Berlin, Hong Kong, Gibraltar and other threatened enclaves. But to many elsewhere the Falklands seemed a cause too petty to justify the expense of lives and treasure. To send an expedition 8,000 miles to reconquer two tiny islands of no strategic or commercial value and inhabited by fewer than 2,000 souls was indeed a wonderfully British thing to do, but only because it was so eccentric, disproportionate and anachronistic: an example of the famous British sense of humour. It was a Gilbert and Sullivan or a Monty Python war.

Of course it was disproportionate. The final casualty count was astonishingly low – 255 British servicemen killed, 777 wounded (and about one-tenth of those permanently disabled). This was actually fewer than were killed in the first five years of the Northern Ireland troubles; but it was still a high human price, and it could easily have been much higher.[*] The material cost was six ships and twenty aircraft lost. The immediate financial cost has been reckoned anywhere between £350 million and £900 million; the longer-term expense of replacing lost vessels, ordnance and equipment at nearly £2 billion. Another £250 million was spent over the next three years on extending the runway at Port Stanley and improving the islands' defences, quite apart from the expense of keeping a garrison on the Falklands for the foreseeable future. Altogether the cost of the war and its immediate aftermath was around £3 billion.[91] It would have been cheaper to have given every islander £1 million to settle elsewhere. This was an ironic outcome of a crisis whose origins lay in the MoD's plans to cut defence expenditure. Moreover those cuts themselves had to be substantially reversed.

---

[*]In fact it was much higher. It was revealed in 2002 that more Falklands veterans have taken their own lives since the end of the war than were killed during it.

The sale of *Invincible* to Australia was cancelled (and three aircraft carriers retained); *Endurance* and the assault ships *Fearless* and *Intrepid* were reprieved; and the navy's complement of frigates and destroyers was restored to fifty-five. If Sir Henry Leach had an ulterior motive in proposing sending the task force on 31 March he was resoundingly successful. By recovering the Falklands the navy saved itself. But from the global perspective of British strategic defence policy, the war was a disastrous diversion from sanity. Its outcome was to preserve in perpetuity, at vastly increased expense, the anomaly which successive British governments, including Mrs Thatcher's, had been trying to offload.

Having staked her political destiny on the recovery of the islands, Mrs Thatcher could not subsequently admit to any doubts that they were worth it.[92] Not noted for her sense of irony, she had no choice but to elevate the hardy but notoriously unenterprising 'kelpers' into models of British grit and rugged independence. She invested the homely names – Goose Green, Tumbledown, Fitzroy and Mount Kent – with the glamour of Alamein and Agincourt. Towards the end of 1982 John Nott visited the islands and gave the Cabinet on his return a graphic description of how cold, wet and dismal they were, ending, 'You must go there, Prime Minister' – at which everybody laughed.[93] But Mrs Thatcher did not laugh. She wanted to see for herself where her destiny had been decided. So in January 1983, in great secrecy, accompanied by Denis and Bernard Ingham, she made the long uncomfortable flight by VC-10 to Ascension Island, then on by Hercules bomber to Port Stanley to receive the islanders' gratitude in person. It was an emotional but also a comic trip – memorably recorded by her host, the restored Governor Rex Hunt.[94] Mrs Thatcher reverently walked – in most unsuitable shoes – over the hallowed soggy terrain where 'H' Jones and other heroes had fought and died (she refused to wear wellingtons), while Denis memorably characterised the islands as 'miles and miles of bugger all' and sighed for a snifter in the Upland Goose. At one point, being driven over West Falkland, she spotted an abandoned ammunition box. 'What a terrible waste!' she exclaimed. 'For God's sake, woman,' Denis begged, 'don't get out and count them.'[95] The return journey was even more uncomfortable, since their intended Hercules developed engine trouble. The replacement, hurriedly made ready for them, offered light or warmth, but not both. Mrs Thatcher chose light, huddled herself in as many blankets as could be found, and settled down to read the Franks Report into the causes of the war.

The Falklands was a war that should not have happened. Politically and diplomatically it arose from a sequence of miscalculations.

Actuarially it was a nonsense. Yet once diplomatic blunders had created an unstoppable momentum for war, it cannot be denied that it was, in its way, magnificent – in part *because* the cause was so ludicrous. Noël Annan, in his book *Our Age*, quoted the Norwegian captain's answer to Hamlet asking why young Fortinbras was marching to Poland:

> We go to gain a little patch of ground
> That hath in it no profit but the name.
> To pay five ducats, five, I would not farm it.

When Hamlet reasonably concludes: 'Why, then the Polack never will defend it', the captain assures him that there is more to war and peace than actuarial calculation:

> Rightly to be great
> Is not to stir without great argument,
> But greatly to find quarrel in a straw
> When honour's at the stake.[96]

Mrs Thatcher saw recapturing the Falklands as a matter of honour – her honour as well as the nation's honour – which could not be ducked without lasting national shame. Having determined to accept the challenge, the manner in which she and her forces carried it through was an astonishing feat of will, courage, skill and improvisation, a legitimate source of national pride. Generally speaking, Thatcherism was a utilitarian philosophy which subjected every aspect of national life to rigorous accountancy and undervalued what could not be costed. The Falklands war was the one great exception on which money was lavished unstintingly for the sake of an idea, an obligation, a conception of honour. Many would have preferred the coffers to have been opened for some other cause nearer home. But overall the public approved, believing that the war – like landing on the moon – was something which had to be done, without regard to cost, and took pride that it was done supremely well. It was unquestionably Mrs Thatcher's finest hour. She never achieved that moral grandeur again.

5

Falklands Effect

The emergence of Thatcherism

With the successful conclusion of the Falklands war, Mrs Thatcher's position was transformed. She could now look forward to almost certain re-election whenever she chose to go to the country. There was some speculation that she might cash in on the euphoria of victory by calling a quick 'khaki' election in the autumn. But that, she told George Gale in an interview for the *Daily Express*, would be 'basically wrong. The Falklands thing was a matter of national pride and I would not use it for party political purposes.' This was humbug. In fact she had no scruple about claiming the war as a specifically Conservative – indeed Thatcherite – achievement. 'Not don't knows, not consensus, not compromise,' she told Gale, 'but conviction, action, persistence . . . We're grateful that we were in government when it happened.'[1] (She was becoming noticeably fond of that royal 'we'.) She had no hesitation in applying the lessons of the South Atlantic explicitly to problems nearer home, contrasting striking railwaymen who held the public to ransom with the heroic shipyard workers who had got the task force ready to sail in a few days. 'Why does it need a war to bring out our qualities and reassert our pride?' she demanded in her speech at Cheltenham racecourse on 3 July. 'Why do we have to be invaded before we throw away our selfish aims and begin to work together?'

> Just look at the Task Force as an object lesson. Every man had his own task to do and did it superbly . . . By working together each was able to do more than his best. As a team they raised the average to the level of the best and by each doing his utmost together they achieved the impossible. That's an accurate picture of Britain at war – not yet of Britain at peace. But the spirit has stirred and the nation has begun to assert itself. Things are not going to be the same again.[2]

But she realised that to call a snap election would have looked cynically opportunist and might have backfired. Besides, it was unnecessary. Why should she cut short her first term just when she had finally secured her dominance? She could carry on for nearly two more years if she wished, to the spring of 1984. Her preference, she hinted to an end-of-session meeting of the 1922 Committee, was to go on to the autumn of 1983.[3] That gave her another full parliamentary year to reap the political harvest of her enhanced authority, and time to show some clear economic results from the pain of the last three years.

In the meantime something like normal politics resumed, and the Government could still be embarrassed by the unexpected. On 9 July there occurred an incident, trivial as it turned out, that was potentially almost as humiliating as the seizure of the Falklands. An intruder named Michael Fagan not only broke into Buckingham Palace, but found his way into the Queen's bedroom and sat on the end of her bed; fortunately he was unarmed and harmless, and she coolly engaged him in conversation until help arrived. (The Duke of Edinburgh, the public was fascinated to learn, slept in another room.) But the implications were alarming. It turned out that it was not the first time that Fagan had broken into the Palace. If security at the Palace was so poor, was it any better at Downing Street and Chequers? 'I was shocked and upset,' Mrs Thatcher told George Gale. 'Really I was very, very upset . . . Every woman in this country was upset because we all thought, oh lord, what would happen to me?'[4] Willie Whitelaw accepted responsibility as Home Secretary and initially felt he must resign. Having already lost Carrington, however, Mrs Thatcher could not face losing Whitelaw too, and persuaded him to change his mind. The incident was complicated over the following days by the revelations of a homosexual scandal affecting the Queen's personal protection officer, Commander Trestrail. But now Whitelaw's popularity in the House protected him. Trestrail resigned, some police officers were disciplined, security at the Palace was tightened, and the bizarre episode passed off with no lasting political damage.

Yet the economic upturn was slow to materialise. Though Geoffrey Howe declared that the recession had officially ended in the third quarter of 1981, growth during 1982 was still only 0.5 per cent; industrial output was the lowest since 1965. Several times the Department of Employment massaged the basis of calculating the unemployment figure, but still it went on rising. Many analysts reckoned the true figure to be nearer four million than the three million the Government admitted. The CBI remained as critical as the TUC, still regularly calling on the Government to take more positive action to stimulate recovery. From within the Cabinet, too, Jim Prior continued to warn that the present level of unemployment was unsustainable and claimed that it could easily be relieved by 'some additional activity' which need not involve any more Government spending.[5] Howe and Mrs Thatcher rejected such siren voices as firmly as ever. 'When the rulers of old started to debase and clip the coinage,' she asserted, 'they were in difficulty. That's what reflation is and I'll have nothing of it.'[6]

On the other hand inflation – the Government's preferred measure of its success – continued to fall. It was down to 5 per cent by the end of 1982, enabling Howe to reduce interest rates steadily (to 9 per cent by November), which helped raise both living standards and the sense of well-being of those in work. The heavy shedding of manpower eventually produced higher productivity in those parts of the manufacturing economy that had survived, while industry was relieved by a steep fall in sterling – due largely to a fall in the oil price – which eventually forced Howe to raise interest rates again in December. While maintaining a tight spending framework overall (his 1982 budget cut the PSBR yet again, while raising benefits by less than the rate of inflation, provoking a small backbench rebellion), Howe also pursued an imaginative supply-side programme of deregulation and targeted incentives: more free ports, double the number of enterprise zones, loan guarantee schemes, grants to assist in the introduction of computers. For all these reasons, economic activity slowly picked up. Public spending, though still higher as a proportion of GDP than in 1979, was at last coming under control – despite the war, which was indeed paid for out of the contingency reserve, as Mrs Thatcher had promised – so that by the spring of 1983 Howe was in a position to make some modest but timely tax concessions in what was likely to be his election-year budget. He did not actually cut the basic rate again, but he raised personal allowances and thresholds, increased child benefit and restored the previous year's cut in the value of unemployment benefit.

After three years of restraint the Chancellor and Prime Minister provoked general amazement in late 1982 by suddenly urging local authorities and other public bodies to spend more on capital investment. 'I agree that it is vital to maintain the nation's infrastructure,' Mrs Thatcher conceded in the debate on the Queen's Speech in November – 'its roads, its buildings, its water supply and its drains.' She claimed that large sums were earmarked for all these things, yet actual investment fell short of allocation 'by a staggering £1,600 million'.[7] In fact she was not telling local authorities to spend more, but rather to spend more of the money provided on capital projects and less on wages. This was perfectly consistent with her perennial theme that the country – and specifically the public sector – was paying itself more than it earned. Her insistence that the economy was slowly being turned around was balanced by repeated warnings that Britain's productivity still lagged behind that of her principal competitors. Britain's inflation rate, she warned in October, was still twice Germany's.[8]

She was much more confident now in dismissing Labour allegations that she did not care about unemployment. 'I have come to the conclusion,' she retorted, 'that they do not want to get rid of unemployment. They wallow in it.'[9] She took credit for the millions of pounds the Government was spending on training schemes, and insisted that most unemployment was temporary. 'One million are long term unemployed,' she asserted in March 1983. 'The other two million will find jobs. Many, many jobs – something like six million – are found in the year as a whole.'[10] In a changing economy, new jobs came from new industries and small businesses, not from old industries. 'It is no good the Opposition yowling about it. It is a fact.'[11] When Roy Jenkins, now back in Parliament as leader of the SDP, wondered ironically how she could take credit for falling inflation but accept no blame for unemployment, she feigned amazement that he could not see that the Government was directly responsible for controlling the money supply but could not create jobs.[12] 'One gains jobs by gaining customers,' she explained simply. 'There is no other way.'[13]

By the time Mrs Thatcher went to the country in June 1983, the Government could plausibly claim, against all its critics, that its central economic strategy was working: inflation was being squeezed out of the economy and the way was now clear for a soundly based recovery which would soon bring real jobs. Sceptics countered that on the contrary, GDP was still 4 per cent lower, and manufacturing output 17 per cent lower, than it had been in 1979. Britain had suffered a more severe recession than the rest of Europe, while the Government's boasted recovery was shallow and patchy, based disproportionately on finance, property and services, and concentrated in the south of England, leaving the manufacturing regions of Scotland, south Wales and the north of England permanently devastated. Economically this is undeniable; the impact of the Government's policies was cruelly unbalanced. The political fact, however, was that the Government had won the argument. Mrs Thatcher's toughness could be seen to be showing results – not so clear-cut, perhaps, as in the Falklands, but sufficient to lend credence to her repeated claim that what had worked in the South Atlantic was also applicable at home. A level of unemployment hitherto held to be insupportable was discovered to be tolerable after all: there were no more riots. Meanwhile, as the political world adjusted to the probability of a second Thatcher term, a number of distinctively 'Thatcherite' policies were beginning to take shape.

First, Norman Tebbit carried the Government's second instalment of trade-union reform. Tebbit had been appointed Employment Secretary in September 1981 specifically to do what Prior had successfully resisted. The expectation therefore was that the Chingford skinhead would waste no more time in sorting out the unions once and for all. In fact Tebbit displayed a more subtle touch than his aggressive rhetoric suggested; he produced another carefully judged package which was considerably less punitive than the Institute of Directors and right-wing backbenchers had been demanding.

The main thrust of his Employment Bill, introduced in January 1982, was to remove the unions' immunity from civil action arising out of unlawful trade disputes, while narrowing the definition of what constituted lawful action, thus rendering unions liable for damages (up to £250,000) for secondary and sympathetic strikes. Henceforth the law would only recognise disputes over pay, jobs and working conditions between groups of workers and their own employers. This was the crucial step which ended the privileged legal status granted the unions by Campbell-Bannerman's Liberal Government following the Taff Vale judgement in 1906 – the anomaly on which the whole history of the abuse of union power since the 1960s had been founded.

Tebbit's Bill simultaneously tightened restrictions on the operation of closed shops; made it easier for employers to dismiss persistent troublemakers like the notorious 'Red Robbo' at British Leyland; and offered Government funds to finance union ballots. But it still did not require ballots to be held before official strikes. It did not try to outlaw strikes in essential services – something Mrs Thatcher had talked of in opposition and still threatened whenever such disputes arose. Nor did it touch the Tories' oldest grievance, the unions' political levy, which still required members to contribute to the Labour party unless they specifically opted out. In all these areas the Prime Minister's habitual caution still prevailed. In his memoirs Tebbit regretted that mandatory strike ballots were still in 1982 'a bridge too far'.[14] But Mrs Thatcher was committed to the gradualist approach – 'I was convinced that the giant step being taken by Norman on the immunity of trade union funds was sufficient for the moment';[15] while Tebbit himself admits that it was only with her support that he was able to get even that much past a still-doubtful Cabinet. Strike ballots and abolition of the political levy were foreshadowed in another Green Paper in January

1983, but their implementation was left to a third instalment of reform brought in by his successor, Tom King, in 1984.

Once again this was shrewd strategy, which disarmed opposition by its carefully calculated moderation. As usual trade-union and Labour leaders furiously denounced the proposed legislation. The TUC General Secretary Len Murray warned that unions which accepted Government money for ballots risked expulsion from the TUC. Not only Michael Foot, but even Jim Callaghan asserted that the unions had 'a contingent right' to break what they considered bad laws.[16] At the Tory Party Conference Mrs Thatcher pounced on this heresy of her predecessor, 'the last Labour Prime Minister – and I do mean the last,' she added. 'None of us has a right, contingent or otherwise, to uphold the law that suits us and break the one that does not. That way lies anarchy.'[17] Thereafter she never missed an opportunity to quote Callaghan's weaselly dictum as proof of Labour's essential disregard for the rule of law. Polls showed that public opinion overwhelmingly supported Tebbit's Bill; more important, the great majority of ordinary trade unionists supported it. By acting moderately but firmly to curb the abuses of the past fifteen years the Government was seen to be redeeming one of the clearest promises on which it had been elected.

The unions were additionally weakened by the level of unemployment, which severely cut their bargaining power; 1982 saw two long-running public-sector strikes – one on the railways, one by NHS workers – both of which ended in clear defeat for the unions without the Government's new legislation even being called upon. Mrs Thatcher vigorously condemned the strikers, condemned Foot for supporting them, warned that train drivers striking against the introduction of flexible rostering merely drove business off the railways, and resolutely refused to intervene.[18] 'If you want more unemployment and more job losses,' she told them bluntly, 'then keep on striking. Don't blame me.'[19] Meanwhile the miners, content with their humiliation of the Government in 1981, voted no fewer than three times to reject the calls of their new President, the left-wing militant Arthur Scargill, to strike against pit closures. British Leyland workers likewise voted in October to accept a pay offer which their leaders urged them to reject. The TUC called off a threatened 'day of action' in support of the NHS workers, and also refused to back legal action by the train drivers and the printing unions. Tebbit's Bill was really a case of kicking the unions when they were already down. The industrial climate had been transformed since 1979. The unions' power to enforce unproductive overmanning and delay the introduction of new technology was already broken; management was recovering the power to manage. Some major battles still lay ahead; but by 1982 the dinosaur which had humbled Wilson, Heath and Callaghan was already mortally wounded.

The second distinctively Thatcherite policy which began to take clear shape in 1982 was large-scale privatisation. The breakthrough from a limited programme of asset disposals to the selling of whole industries came about quite suddenly as a result of the convergence of a number of factors. First, the arrival of Patrick Jenkin at the Department of Industry and Nigel Lawson at the Department of Energy in the September 1981 reshuffle gave a new impetus to policies which Keith Joseph and David Howell had initiated but failed to carry through. Then the easing of the recession offered a more propitious economic climate. The likelihood of the Government winning a second term on the back of post-Falklands euphoria gave potential investors the confidence to buy shares in privatised companies without fear of a returning Labour Government immediately re-nationalising them. Finally, and perhaps most important, the newly established telephone company British Telecom urgently needed a massive injection of capital to finance the new digital technology.

Keith Joseph had split off BT from the Post Office precisely in order to attract private finance into it. But by the time he left the Department of Industry he had got no further than inviting the public to invest in BT by buying 'Buzby Bonds'. (Buzby was a cartoon bird sitting on a telegraph wire.) The idea of selling the whole company was not in Jenkin's in-tray when he took over, nor did it feature in his speech to the 1981 party conference the following month. It was the recently appointed BT chairman, Sir George Jefferson, who convinced him that the only way to raise the required sums was outright privatisation. Once persuaded, Jenkin had a battle with the Prime Minister, who was sympathetic but still at that stage more concerned with promoting competition than with wider ownership. She did not want to privatise BT as a virtual monopoly – the newly licensed rival, Mercury, offered only token competition – but to break it up. Jenkin told her that this would take years: if she wanted to do it quickly, BT must be sold as a single business. The scale of the operation was formidable. The rest of Whitehall was stunned when Jenkin first circulated his proposal, the City doubted whether it was feasible, and the unions promised total obstruction. But the Treasury was keen to shift the burden of financing the modernisation of BT from the public purse. Once satisfied that it was possible, Mrs Thatcher gave the green light to go ahead.[20]

She also needed some persuasion to privatise Britoil, formerly the British National Oil Corporation (set up in 1976 by Tony Benn). This time her reservations were patriotic, reflecting a widely shared feeling that North Sea oil was a national asset which should remain under national control. Mrs Thatcher's belief in the free market was always in potential conflict with her nationalism. Though she regularly pointed out, as a debating point against Labour, that North Sea oil had been discovered and brought ashore by private enterprise, David Howell's proposal to privatise BNOC as early as 1980 foundered, in Nigel Lawson's view, on 'Margaret's acute sensitivity that privatisation . . . implied that Britain would somehow lose control of part of her oil'.[21] She certainly made no bones about referring to 'my oil' when negotiating in Strasbourg and Brussels. In fact BNOC actually produced only 7 per cent of North Sea oil, though Benn had given it the right to buy and sell a large proportion of the rest. Lawson's solution was to split the production side of the business from the trading side and sell only the former, retaining for the Government a 'golden share' to prevent the company falling into unsuitable (that is, foreign) hands. The first 51 per cent of Britoil shares were put on the market in November 1982. Despite an unexpected drop in the price of oil which left the underwriters with large losses, the sale raised £334 million for the Treasury, making it by far the biggest privatisation to date. The BT privatisation – much bigger again – was not ready to go before the 1983 election and had to be restarted in the next Parliament.

'We are only in our first term,' Mrs Thatcher told the party conference in October 1982. 'But already we have done more to roll back the frontiers of socialism than any previous Conservative Government. In the next Parliament we intend to do a lot more.'[22] In due course the 1983 manifesto earmarked BT, British Airways and 'substantial parts' of British Steel, British Shipbuilders and British Leyland, plus the offshore interests of British Gas, as targets for the second term. As it turned out, building on the unexpected success of the BT sale, the Government went much further than this, privatising the whole of British Gas before moving on to target electricity and water. But already, she admitted in her memoirs, this was a programme 'far more extensive than we had thought would ever be possible when we came into office only four years before'.[23]

Right up to 1983, however, she was reluctant to use the term privatisation. 'It is an ugly word,' Lawson wrote. 'Mrs Thatcher disliked it so much that for a time she refused to use it.'[24] She preferred the familiar 'de-nationalisation'. But the two words reflected different perceptions of the process. 'De-nationalisation' emphasised the macro-economic withdrawal of state intervention. By contrast 'privatisation' – the word was said to have been coined by David Howell – stressed the transfer of assets to individuals who bought the shares. Mrs Thatcher's semantic conservatism mirrors the Government's slow realisation of the potential political bonanza to be gained from encouraging popular share-owning.

The form of popular capitalism she did enthusiastically embrace before 1983 was the sale of council houses. Back in 1975 she had worried that this would be unpopular with existing homeowners ('What will they say on my Wates estates?').[25] Long before 1979, however, she had overcome her doubts on this score, and Michael Heseltine enshrined the 'right to buy' – at a substantial discount – in his 1980 Housing Act. By October 1982, 370,000 families had already taken advantage of the legislation to buy their homes, and Mrs Thatcher was cheekily boasting to the party conference that the Conservative Government had achieved the revolutionary ambition of the Labour left:

> Half a million more people will now live and grow up as free-holders with a real stake in the country and with something to pass on to their children . . .
>
> This is the largest transfer of assets from the state to the family in British history . . . This really will be an irreversible shift of power to the people.

Labour had fought the sale of houses tooth and nail, she went on; but they would not dare to reverse it 'because they know we are right, because they know it is what people want'.[26] While the Government was still feeling its way gingerly towards the privatisation of public utilities, she now knew that with the sale of council houses she was onto an electoral winner. It is probably too simple to suggest that those 370,000 families – it was 500,000 by the time of the election – were turned from Labour to Conservative voters overnight: many of them had already made the crucial switch in 1979. But more than anything else this one simple measure, promised in opposition and spectacularly carried out, both consolidated and came to symbolise Mrs Thatcher's capture of a large swathe of the traditionally Labour-voting working class.

The limits of radicalism

Council-house sales, trade-union reform and the beginnings of privatisation were major initiatives which changed the landscape of British politics. Yet beyond these three areas, some of Mrs Thatcher's keenest supporters were disappointed that her avowedly radical government did not have more to show for its first term. 'See where her writ does not run,' wrote the historian-turned-columnist John Vincent – he wrote in both *The Times* and the *Sun* – in January 1983:

> Local government, the services, the education industry, the nationalised industries, the intelligentsia, the health service: the great fiefdoms remain intact, going their own sweet way, and there is not much she can do about it . . . The long march through the institutions has hardly got anywhere since 1979.

Nor did Vincent think it would be different in the second term. Mrs Thatcher, he suggested, was not really so powerful as post-Falklands euphoria made her appear:

> As children, we see the bossy lady from the WVS as authority incarnate; only later do we understand that she is just a dear old thing doing her job. She looks strong, because at the moment she is not trying to do anything very difficult, and the country finds it hard to see anyone else doing her job. If she tried to do the things she really wants to do, it probably would not work, and she would look a weak Prime Minister.[27]

Radicals like Sherman and Hoskyns were particularly frustrated that the Government had shied away from any serious effort to reform the welfare system. But this reflected the fact that the party had done little serious thinking about welfare while in opposition. David Willetts, who joined the Downing Street Policy Unit in 1984, later recalled that Mrs Thatcher had 'a set of instincts' about the welfare state:

> She had a sense that it cost a lot . . . She suspected, or feared, that quite a lot of it was inefficient. And she did have a feeling that . . . it could rot people's moral fibre . . . But she had no clear programme.[28]

It was partly that she simply did not have time to spare for social policy: at this stage the economy, the trade unions and the nationalised industries were her domestic priorities. In truth she was not really very interested in it: having served her ministerial apprenticeship in social security and education, she was happy to have escaped to wider horizons. But she was also very wary of the political danger in tackling the welfare state – particularly the National Health Service – which for all its emerging inadequacies was rooted in popular affection. On trade unions and council houses Mrs Thatcher was confident that the public shared her instincts; on welfare she was not so sure. 'She feared that the welfare state was Labour territory – that we weren't going to win on it.'[29] The result was curiously negative. In no branch of social provision was there much in the way of positive policy between 1979 and 1983; but health, social security, education and public-sector housing were all squeezed to a greater or lesser degree by spending cuts which gave practical effect – as it were by stealth – to the Prime Minister's instincts.

Overall public spending actually rose from 41 to 44 per cent of GDP – largely because spending commitments grew while growth was stagnant. After defence (up 23 per cent), social security showed the biggest increase (up 21 per cent). But this was mainly due to the huge numbers drawing unemployment benefit: the level of individual benefits was cut. Spending on health, which Patrick Jenkin – with Howe's approval – had specifically promised to protect, also increased by 14 per cent. By contrast education fell by 6 per cent, and housing (by far the biggest casualty) by 55 per cent. Public-spending figures are notoriously open to interpretation. The Government claimed that real health spending was 3 per cent higher in 1983 than when it took office: Mrs Thatcher repeatedly boasted of 6,500 more doctors and 45,000 more nurses since 1979.[30] But *per capita* spending on the health service actually fell, so the public perception of cuts was accurate. To reduce costs Jenkin and then Norman Fowler repeatedly raised prescription charges by one steep hike after another – from twenty pence in 1979 to £1.40 in 1983 – and imposed charges for eye and dental checks. (Certain charges were ruled out, however: Mrs Thatcher had personally committed herself against charges for visits to the doctor or stays in hospital.)[31] Jenkin abolished one tier of the disastrously bureaucratic reorganisation of the NHS introduced by Keith Joseph in 1973; and Fowler, having defeated a long and bitter strike by ancillary workers against the Government's 4 per cent pay ceiling, took steps to force the health authorities to contract out laundry, cleaning and catering services by competitive tendering – another form of privatisation which further weakened the unions. But this was all tinkering, not the radical shake-up that Tory zealots had hoped to see from a Thatcher Government.

The real question concerned the funding of the service. Almost since its inception in 1948, Conservative policymakers had been looking at ways to switch funding at least partly from general taxation to an insurance basis. As Minister of Health under Macmillan in 1960–3, Enoch Powell actually began to move in that direction. But insurance schemes had always been found to be less efficient and more impractical, most recently by a Royal Commission set up by Labour in 1976, which reported in July 1979. Both Howe and Jenkin were still keen to explore the insurance option, however, and in July 1981 Jenkin set up a departmental working party to study alternative funding options. Mrs Thatcher was sympathetic. In her very first Commons speech as Prime Minister she had warned, with a clear echo of Milton Friedman, that 'there is no such thing as a free service in the Health Service'.[32] She never forgot that the cost of universal healthcare fell on the public purse and believed that self-reliant individuals should bear the cost of insuring themselves instead of relying on the state.* She was keen, as a matter of principle as well as of economy, to encourage private health provision, which duly mushroomed after 1979 with an influx of American healthcare companies, a rush of private hospital building and more private beds in NHS hospitals. Kites flown by free-market think-tanks like the Adam Smith Institute and the Social Affairs Unit (an offshoot of the Institute of Economic Affairs, founded in 1980) fuelled the impression – sedulously fostered by Labour – that the Tories were planning to privatise the NHS. But when it came to the point the Government drew back.

In the summer of 1982 the CPRS came up with a review of radical options for deep cuts in public spending, which would become necessary if growth did not pick up. The ideas floated included all the New Right's favourite nostrums – education vouchers, ending the state funding of higher education, freezing benefits, an insurance-based health service; it even considered scrapping the Trident nuclear deterrent. In fact Norman Fowler, on replacing Jenkin, had already kicked health insurance back into the long grass – supported by his robustly pro-NHS Minister of State, Ken Clarke. The other suggestions were all equally non-starters. But Howe unwisely circulated the CPRS report to the Cabinet on 9 September, along with a more circumspect Treasury paper. The result was, in Nigel Lawson's experience, 'the nearest thing to a Cabinet riot in the history of the Thatcher administration'.[34] (Lawson had not been in the Cabinet the previous July.) The wets and the grandees – still the majority – for once combined effectively to condemn the paper. Then someone (believed to have been Peter Walker)

---

*'Margaret thought that anybody who could afford to should pay for their own health,' Ken Clarke – at this time a junior health minister – recalled. 'She could never understand why people, Willie Whitelaw as well as I, used to be rather proud of the fact that we used the National Health Service. She thought we should be ashamed that people like ourselves who could afford to pay for ourselves required the taxpayer to pay such a basic expense for our family.'[33]

leaked it to *The Economist*, where its publication sparked a tremendous furore by seeming to confirm the Government's secret agenda to dismantle 'huge chunks of the welfare state' and the health service in particular.[35]

In her memoirs Lady Thatcher claims that the think-tank report should never have been circulated. 'I was horrified by this paper. As soon as I saw it, I pointed out that it would almost certainly be leaked and give a totally false impression . . . It was all the greatest nonsense.'[36] But there would have been no need for a Cabinet riot had she not initially supported it. Contemporary evidence suggests that she not only backed Howe in putting it to Cabinet on 9 September – it could not have been circulated without her approval – but then 'clung on' to the report for some weeks more 'until, following the *Economist* story, the majority of ministers told her she had made a terrible blunder . . . When the voices were collected she said, in what one minister called a petulant huff, "All right, then, shelve it." '[37]

The result of the CPRS leak was that Mrs Thatcher was compelled not merely to shelve the report but to swear ever more strenuously her devotion to the NHS and deny any intention of privatising or even radically reforming it. At the party conference the next month she boasted of the Government's 'magnificent record' on the health service:

This year we are spending 5 per cent more in real terms on the Health Service than Labour, so under the Conservatives we have more doctors, more nurses, more money. Hardly the behaviour of a Government bent on destroying the Health Service.

'Of course,' she conceded, 'we welcome the growth of private health insurance. It brings in more money; it helps to reduce waiting lists; and it stimulates new treatments and techniques.'

But let me make one thing absolutely clear. The National Health Service is safe with us. As I said in the House of Commons on 1 December last, 'The principle that adequate health care should be provided for all, regardless of ability to pay, must be the foundation of any arrangements for financing the Health Service.' We stand by that.[38]

The quotation was carefully plucked from a parliamentary answer, seven months before the date of the CPRS report, in which she had acknowledged the existence of Jenkin's inquiry into alternative methods of funding the health service.[39] The suspicious also noted that 'adequate' healthcare for all fell some way short of Nye Bevan's vision of the best for all, leaving open the possibility of the NHS becoming a second-class service for those who could not afford private treatment. When speaking off the cuff Mrs Thatcher frequently gave just that impression. For instance in February 1983 she told Betty Boothroyd flatly that 'the Health Service is there', before going on much more enthusiastically to defend the freedom of those who wished to spend their own money on private medicine.[40] In practice, however, she was stuck with her promise that 'the National Health Service is safe with us' or, as it quickly became, 'safe in our hands'. That pledge effectively limited her options in relation to healthcare, not just for her second term but for the third as well.

Social security was less of a sacred cow than health, largely because it was less used by Tory voters. There was no comparable embargo on radical reform; but here too policy proceeded by an accumulation of small cuts rather than a coherent programme. Jenkin and his successors were under no electoral obligation to maintain social-security spending, except on pensions; and even here Howe made a very significant long-term economy by cutting the link with average earnings. Though little noticed at the time – it was disguised by inflation – this led to a steady fall in the relative value of the state pension over the next two decades. All short-term benefits – unemployment benefit, housing benefit, even child benefit – were devalued more rapidly simply by not being up-rated in line with inflation. A persistent handful of Tory backbenchers staged a number of minor rebellions, arguing that the unemployed and their families were unfairly being made to bear the cost of the Government's industrial shake-out. In the case of redundant steelworkers and some other high-profile casualties, Mrs Thatcher occasionally recognised the Government's responsibility to introduce 'generous . . . remedial measures'[41] to 'try to reduce hardship and suffering'.[42] But in practice her view was that the unemployed could be encouraged back to work by cutting benefit. 'We really have got to tackle this problem of people better off out of work,' she once told Jenkin. 'I think we will have to go back to soup kitchens.' 'Soup kitchens, Prime Minister?' he boggled. 'Take that silly grin off your face,' she replied. 'I mean it.'[43]

In public she was more tactful but equally clear: 'We want a bigger gap between income in work and income out of work,' she told the Commons.[44] 'The standard of living of a family must come not from the Government but from the action of the breadwinner.'[45] She was markedly unsympathetic to those struggling to live on benefit. 'They are able to get sufficient for their needs,' she declared in April 1983, several times pointing out – as if it was a great achievement after thirty-five years – that the real value of supplementary benefit was twice the level the Attlee Government had set in 1948.[46] From her experience as a parliamentary secretary in the Ministry of Pensions twenty years before she retained the conviction that the benefit system was a wasteful mechanism for recycling money from the hard-working to the lazy. Then at least it had been her job to face the reality of a lot of individual cases. Now she saw only the huge cost to the Treasury and a disincentive to enterprise and self-reliance. She believed that the prosperity of those in work would – in the American phrase – 'trickle down' to lift the living standards of all. She averted her eyes from the impoverishment of millions of families whose breadwinners were desperate to work if only the jobs had been there. Apart from throwing ever-larger sums at complicated youth-training schemes – money not for the most part well directed – the Government in its first term made no serious attempt to reform the benefit system.

Housing was the area where the Government most clearly favoured the better off at the expense of the poorer. The central plank of its housing policy was the sale of council houses. But while the best houses were sold on generous terms to those more prosperous tenants in secure jobs who could afford to buy them, rents for the rest – usually on the least desirable estates – were steeply increased. New council building almost completely ceased. Local authorities were debarred from using the revenues from council-house sales to renew their housing stock, leading in time to a housing shortage and the very visible phenomenon of homelessness which emerged at the end of the decade.* In the Commons Mrs Thatcher defended the near-doubling of council rents on strictly economic grounds, arguing that in 1979 they covered only 47 per cent of the true cost and represented only 6 per cent of average pay: by 1982 the latter figure was still only 10–11 per cent.[48] Housing was another service Mrs Thatcher did not really believe the state should be providing at all: her Government's purpose was to encourage and reward home ownership. While cutting subsidy to council tenants, therefore, she was determined to protect and even

---

*In his memoirs Michael Heseltine claims that over the whole eighteen years of Tory Government the sale of council houses raised £24 billion for English local authorities, 'much of which was ploughed back into improving the nation's housing stock', and that by breaking up 'the monolithic local authority estates . . . we had begun . . . to create a less polarised society'.[47] The first statement is a travesty of the truth, while the second can most kindly be described as wishful thinking.

extend mortgage-interest tax relief for home buyers – an anomalous middle-class subsidy which the Treasury had long wanted to phase out.

In *The View from No. 11* Nigel Lawson described the conflict of principle between the Treasury's belief that the ideal tax system works by 'eliminating privileges and exemptions of all kinds', and 'Margaret's passionate devotion to the preservation of every last ounce of mortgage interest relief'.[49] As early as July 1979 she spiritedly denied newspaper reports that MIRAS was going to be cut. 'I am delighted to deny it. One's advisers are not always right, and I often tell them so.'[50] Not till his 1983 budget did Howe make a serious effort to reduce it. Again she firmly pre-empted him, telling the Commons that there was no truth in rumours of abolition, 'and there will not be so long as I remain First Lord of the Treasury'.[51] On the contrary, she wanted Howe to raise the ceiling from £25,000 to £35,000. She made no bones about seeing mortgage tax relief as a perk for 'our people'. Howe resisted, but eventually settled for increasing the upper limit to £30,000.[52] In the Commons Mrs Thatcher candidly presented the increase as a reward: 'The extra relief is well deserved.'[53]

As Education Secretary, Mark Carlisle had an unenviable task, with the Treasury demanding heavy cuts in his budget and Mrs Thatcher bullying him to punish her old department. Less than a decade earlier she had been vilified for cutting free milk for primary schoolchildren, yet she finished up as a notably expansionist Education Secretary, having announced ambitious plans particularly for pre-school education, which sadly were aborted by the 1973 oil crisis. As Prime Minister, however, she showed no interest in reviving these plans, only the memory of the Milk Snatcher. Carlisle was compelled to enforce cuts in the provision of school meals and rural school transport – though the latter was partly reversed following a rebellion in the House of Lords led by the heavyweight combination of Rab Butler and the Duke of Norfolk. The axe fell hardest on the universities, which suffered a 13 per cent cut in funding over three years. The University Grants Committee (UGC) responded by dividing its reduced resources unequally, protecting the older and supposedly best institutions at the expense of the newest like Aston and Salford, whose budgets were cut by 20–30 per cent. Mrs Thatcher, with little love for universities and less respect for the great majority of academics, distanced herself from the resulting outcry, maintaining that it was a matter for the UGC how it distributed the available funds.[54] Paradoxically the losers were precisely the more vocational scientific and business-oriented institutions which Mrs Thatcher wanted to encourage. Her chief scientific adviser, John Ashworth, had left to become Vice-Chancellor of Salford just before the cuts were announced: disgusted, he responded by joining the SDP and was dropped like a hot brick.[55] As the universities tried to protect standards by restricting entry, the winners – at least in the short term – were the polytechnics, then still funded by their local authorities and not yet rate-capped, which expanded to meet the demand. This was the beginning of a decade of confusion, demoralisation and falling standards in higher education.

Like Margaret Thatcher before him, Carlisle failed – or did not seriously try – to slow the onward march of comprehensive schools. Of 315 grammar schools remaining in May 1979, another 130 had gone comprehensive by 1982. On the other hand Carlisle did introduce – under the influence of his special adviser, Stuart Sexton – one distinctly Thatcherite initiative, the Assisted Places Scheme, which tried to bridge the widening educational apartheid by enabling a small number of bright pupils from poorer homes to go to independent schools. After Carlisle's removal in September 1981, Keith Joseph went to Education specifically to try to introduce the holy grail of right-wing educationists – education vouchers, which would open the state system to market forces by giving parents the spending power to shop around between the schools of their choice. Mrs Thatcher was in principle keen on the idea (though she preferred to call them 'cheques' or 'credits') but as usual cautious in practice.[56] Joseph's theoretical enthusiasm soon ran into practical difficulties, and vouchers did not make it into the 1983 manifesto.

Another pet project which did not materialise in the first term was the abolition of domestic rates. This was a promise Mrs Thatcher had made as shadow Environment Secretary in October 1974 and had felt herself bound by ever since. For some reason she did not feel equally bound by her more widely publicised pledge in that election to subsidise the mortgage interest rate. But the perceived unfairness of the rates was a long-standing Tory grievance – going right back to her earliest days in politics – which she was determined to correct. The difficulty was finding a practicable alternative. During 1979–81 Michael Heseltine and his Minister of State, Tom King, raked over all the possible options: local income tax, a local sales tax, a property tax or some form of poll tax. Like every previous inquiry since 1971 they found insuperable objections to each one. Mrs Thatcher initially favoured the local sales tax, but was forced to accept that local variations would create impossible anomalies. In November 1981 she still stressed the Government's determination to do something. 'We are all concerned about very high rates,' she announced in the debate on the Queen's Speech. 'The system was never designed to bear the levels of taxation now being placed on it.'[57] If she could not abolish the system she was at least determined to limit the size of rate demands. 'I will not tolerate failure in this area,' she minuted on an early draft of Heseltine's Green Paper.[58] The Green Paper duly rejected all the options, but proposed as an alternative the idea of local referenda to give democratic sanction to rate increases. Rates, she argued in support of this constitutional departure, 'are not exactly a shining example of a democratic tax. Only a minority of electors are ratepayers and many ratepayers have no vote.'[59]

Had the Government persisted with this idea, the chroniclers of the poll tax have written, 'the history of local government in the following decade might have been radically different'.[60] Instead, as Mrs Thatcher wrote in her memoirs, the proposal 'drew howls of protest from local authorities and the Tory backbenchers whom they so easily influenced', and 'had to be withdrawn'.[61] Heseltine went back to trying to curb local spending by cutting the rate support grant, which merely had the effect of driving rates up further. Ministers constantly claimed that local government spending was wildly out of control. In fact – as Heseltine admits in his memoirs – local-authority expenditure actually *fell* between 1980 and 1983, both in real terms and as a proportion of overall public spending: it was central government that was failing to cut its expenditure.[62] Most of the alleged overspending was concentrated in a very few authorities – notably the Greater London Council (GLC), captured in May 1981 by an ostentatiously left-wing regime led by the flamboyant Ken Livingstone, which openly defied Heseltine's spending limits and made a point of giving grants to blacks, gays, prostitutes and provocative minorities, as well as subsidising London Transport. Heseltine believed that taking legal powers to cap the rates would not merely run counter to the Tories' traditional belief in local government, but would actually be unconstitutional. Thwarted in so many other directions, however, Mrs Thatcher determined to impose her will. She took the opportunity of John Nott's resignation from the Government in January 1983 to replace Heseltine with the more malleable Tom King, and insisted that King get on with it, in time to include a promise of legislation in the manifesto. At the same time she determined that the way to deal with Livingstone was to abolish the GLC and six other Labour-controlled metropolitan counties altogether.

These big city councils – Greater Manchester, Merseyside, South Yorkshire, Tyne and Wear, West Midlands and West Yorkshire – had only been created by the Heath Government in 1973. The GLC dated only from 1964, when the previous Conservative Government extended the old London County Council area by bringing in the predominantly

Tory outer suburbs to balance the permanently Labour inner city. Since then control of the expanded council had changed with every swing of the political pendulum: Labour's victory in May 1981 merely reflected the Thatcher Government's unpopularity at that time. But Tory suburbs like Bromley – and Mrs Thatcher's own Finchley – bitterly resented having to pay for what they regarded as Labour's politically inspired extravagance. There was unquestionably a case for reforming the GLC – even perhaps for abolishing it. Arguably it was an unnecessary tier of government with too few real responsibilities and too much power to tax, a propaganda pulpit wide open to abuse by an ambitious self-publicist like Livingstone. Mrs Thatcher was particularly enraged by his displaying the ever-rising total of London's unemployed in huge figures on the roof of County Hall, just across the river from the House of Commons; and by his open support for the objectives – and by implication the methods – of the IRA. Abolition of the GLC had been talked of in London Tory circles for years, but the way a commitment to do so was suddenly thrust into the manifesto at a late stage, with no proper consultation process, made it appear high-handed and politically vindictive.

Victorian values

One reason that Mrs Thatcher seized so eagerly on abolition of the metropolitan councils to ginger up the manifesto was that the Government had given very little thought to the agenda for a second term. Given the enormous problems of trying to promote an enterprise economy against the background of a severe recession, with Heathite sceptics in most of the spending departments and no certainty – indeed little likelihood, up till mid-1982 – of re-election, it is understandable that the Government attempted so little major reform of social institutions before 1983. It is much harder to explain why, after the Falklands victory had transformed the political landscape and her own authority, Mrs Thatcher did not then grasp her opportunity with a radical programme for the next stretch of road that now extended before her. She evidently found it hard to explain herself. In her memoirs she blamed Geoffrey Howe, whom she was persuaded to put in charge of policy formulation to compensate for his exclusion from the Falklands War Cabinet. 'There has never been a more devout believer in the virtues of consultation than Geoffrey.' The implication is that he was too consensual – 'too safe a pair of hands'.[63] But this is unfair. Howe had a much longer record as a radical policy thinker than she had, going right back to his chairmanship of the Bow Group in the 1950s and fully maintained in opposition and in government since

1975. He had been a hawk on trade-union reform, bolder than herself on the abolition of exchange controls and a driving force for privatisation. More important was her surprising choice of Ferdinand Mount to head the Downing Street Policy Unit when Hoskyns resigned at the end of 1981.

Hoskyns had left in disillusion, believing that Mrs Thatcher had allowed herself to become institutionalised by the Civil Service and as a result had failed, like all her predecessors, to launch the sort of root-and-branch assault on the structure and assumptions of government which he believed necessary. He had been frustrated by her caution on trade-union reform and dismayed by the lack of forward thinking on the welfare state. By 1981 he felt the Government had run out of steam. He saw no possibility of another *Stepping Stones* for the second term 'if the "client" was not able to set aside even an afternoon to think about it'.[64] Though his departure was quite amicable – Mrs Thatcher gave him a handsome farewell dinner in Number Ten, plus a knighthood – he left to become Director-General of the Institute of Directors.

Unfortunately his successor was not the man to revive a flagging government. An unconventional Old Etonian and the heir to a baronetcy, Ferdy Mount had worked in the Conservative Research Department during the 1970s, but he had no experience of Whitehall or of business; he was currently the *Spectator*'s political columnist: charming, original but distinctly wet – 'generally thought', as *The Times* put it, 'to belong more among the old soft Tories than the new hard version'.[65] A week before taking up his appointment in May 1982 he bravely called for a ceasefire in the Falklands. It was his ideas on social policy which had caught the Prime Minister's eye. In his book *The Subversive Family*, published in 1982, Mount saw the family not as a mere building block for government policy but as a sphere of individual responsibility, a source of independence from the state. This chimed with Mrs Thatcher's desire to see breadwinners take more responsibility for their own families. On this somewhat narrow basis she appointed him head of her Policy Unit and simultaneously set up an *ad hoc* group of ministers which was supposed to put the family at the heart of social policy. Over the next few months it considered all sorts of bright ideas but failed to develop anything that could be called a programme. Mount's appointment, wrote *The Times* somewhat prematurely, marked 'a final defeat for the radical approach to government which the Prime Minister promised but never dared deliver'.[66] He used his literary skills to advantage as Mrs Thatcher's chief speechwriter – a role Hoskyns had always refused – for the period up to and including the election. His fellow wordsmith Ronnie Millar summed him up: 'A delightful man, Ferdy Mount, but running the Policy Unit was not a literary pursuit and, to everyone's regret, he opted to return to the polished political column for which he was famous.'[67] He subsequently found his niche as editor of the *Times Literary Supplement*.

The truth is that a Government's energy stems from its head, and even Mrs Thatcher confessed to being a little tired by the end of the Falklands summer. Just before the recess she admitted that she intended to take a good holiday 'after this momentous year' – quickly adding, in case anyone should see this as a sign of weakness: 'I do not think I could take more than another ten years such as this has been.'[68] She actually went to Switzerland for ten days before going into hospital – briefly and of course privately – for an operation for varicose veins.★ In her memoirs she suggests, most unusually, that one reason for giving Howe charge of policy formulation was 'reducing the burden on me'.[70] After the high tension of the Falklands she was perhaps mentally unprepared for her sudden breakthrough to popularity and genuinely did not know what to do next. A year earlier she would not have dared talk of another ten years. There is a sense in the autumn of 1982 of Mrs Thatcher – still only fifty-seven years old – pausing for breath, resting on her oars for a moment, until she got used to the idea of going on and on.

Her speech at the party conference in October was very short on signposts to the future. Apart from signalling the privatisation of Britoil and BT, celebrating the sale of council houses and promising not to touch the NHS, she was extraordinarily vague. Using an autocue for the first time – Ronald Reagan's 'sincerity machine' which she had first seen demonstrated by the President when he spoke to MPs in Westminster Hall in June – her peroration was utterly hollow:

> On what moral basis would we be entitled to ask for the nation's support next time? The only way we can achieve great things for

---

★The hour-long operation, under general anaesthetic, was performed by the leading varicose-veins specialist, Stanley Rivlin, at the Fitzroy Nuffield Hospital in Bryanston Square. Exceptionally, Mrs Thatcher was discharged the same day. The press photograph of her leaving the hospital is a very rare picture of her wearing trousers. Her GP, Dr John Henderson, told the press that he was 'overwhelmed . . . with the way this woman has recovered. She is really behaving as though nothing had happened. She simply won't allow herself to be ill.'[69] A week later she visited Scotland, followed almost immediately by a strenuous tour of the Far East.

Britain is by asking great things of Britain. We will not disguise our purpose, nor betray our principles. We will do what must be done. We will tell the people the truth, and the people will be our judge.[71]

Paradoxically, in fact, this most political of Prime Ministers became for a time almost apolitical. As if to soften, or balance, the warrior image she had projected during the Falklands war, she gave a rush of interviews over the summer to women's magazines – *Woman, Woman's Own, Vogue* – all filled with human and domestic detail, followed over the autumn and winter by several more in the women's pages of the *Sunday People*, the *News of the World* and the *Sun*. The interviewers – usually women – were fascinated by how she coped with the practical aspects of being a woman Prime Minister: her clothes, her hair, her health, the secret of her amazing stamina, the strain and agony of a mother required to send other mothers' sons to lose their lives on the other side of the world; and she was happy to tell them. She stressed how important her family had been in supporting her through these times, and continually strove to present her life as much more ordinary than it really was – shopping, cooking, gardening, reading, watching television. She admitted that she did not have time to see a lot of television; but she liked *Yes Minister*, naturally, and claimed to have enjoyed the recent BBC serialisation of Trollope's *Barchester Towers* and 'things like *The Professionals*', as well as Morecambe and Wise and the Two Ronnies. She claimed to read a lot, too – not only history and 'a good deal of philosophy', she told the *Sun*, but light fiction: John le Carré, Frederick Forsyth, Hammond Innes, 'detective stories of any sort . . . All these novels I read, lap them up, to read late at night.'[72]

To the *News of the World* she pretended that she liked nothing so much as 'pottering in the kitchen' or in the garden at Scotney Castle (the weekend flat in Kent that she and Denis still retained, though in fact they more often went to Chequers). 'Really what I like best is to go down there for about five days in the summer and just potter.' No one who knew her would have recognised this picture for a moment. But a little later she admitted that what she meant by pottering was vigorous cleaning and clearing up. 'Again always you turn everything out so that it's perfect . . . so that it's spanking when you leave.'[73] She was too honest to keep up the pretence that she was ever idle for long.

On Remembrance Sunday she appeared on the BBC's religious programme, *Songs of Praise*, talking with heavy emotion about the men who had died in the Falklands and choosing an appropriately military hymn:

O Valiant hearts, who to your glory came
Through dust of conflict and through battle flame . . .[74]

She also chose a favourite prayer to be broadcast on Radio 4's *Today* programme; did a question-and-answer session with an audience of children for Thames TV; and appeared – for the second time – with Jimmy Savile on the popular BBC children's programme, *Jim'll Fix It*.

It was also in this period leading up to the 1983 General Election that Mrs Thatcher began to lay claim to 'Victorian values'. Though she had actually used the phrase once before – in Australia in 1976 – and had frequently in opposition expressed her admiration for the untrammelled individualism that she believed had made Britain great, it was Brian Walden, interviewing her on *Weekend World* in January 1983, who put it to her that she believed in 'what I would call Victorian values'.[75] She agreed enthusiastically, adopted the phrase as her own and repeated it several times over the next few weeks as the basis of her political philosophy.

'Honesty and thrift and reliability and hard work and a sense of responsibility for your fellow men are not simply Victorian values,' she told the Glasgow Chamber of Commerce on 28 January. 'They are part of the enduring principles of the Western world.'[76] 'Self-reliance, personal responsibility, voluntary help, being prepared to lend a hand to others,' she declared during the election, 'those are not Victorian values, they are eternal truths.'[77] In a radio interview she located them specifically in her own childhood:

I was brought up by a Victorian grandmother. You were taught to work jolly hard, you were taught to improve yourself, you were taught self-reliance, you were taught to live within your income, you were taught that cleanliness was next to godliness. You were taught self-respect, you were taught always to give a hand to your neighbour, you were taught tremendous pride in your country, you were taught to be a good member of your community. All these things are Victorian values.

When the interviewer suggested that to most people the word 'Victorian' carried connotations of 'work-houses and shocking conditions in industry, all sorts of deplorable things that were also part of the Victorian scene', she launched into a passionate celebration of voluntary hospitals, church schools and prison reform, insisting that 'in fact you found a tremendous improvement in conditions during Victorian times because people were brought up with a sense of duty.

I was brought up with a tremendous sense of duty . . . There are some values which are eternal.'[78]

One Labour shadow minister complained in January that since the Falklands Mrs Thatcher had raised herself 'above politics'. The coverage of her visit to the islands had been more like the reporting of a royal progress than a political event; while the maverick Tam Dalyell's relentless harrying of her over the *Belgrano* was equated by most of the public with Willie Hamilton sniping at the Queen – harmless if not positively counterproductive. The same shadow minister found that he lost his audience if he attacked Mrs Thatcher personally. 'They don't mind a good swipe at the Government's policies, but they don't want to hear criticism of her.'[79]

The quasi-presidential image she now projected was embodied above all in an independent television portrait entitled *The Woman at Number Ten*, transmitted in March 1983 (though filmed three months earlier), which was designed to demonstrate that she was thoroughly at home in Downing Street and expected to be there for a long time. For the benefit of the cameras she gave one of her favourite gurus, the anthropologist/philosopher Laurens van der Post, a guided tour of the house. 'No one can have shown off an official residence with such proprietorial *chic* since Jacqueline Kennedy,' one critic commented.[80] Exploiting the Falklands for all it was worth, Mrs Thatcher drew attention to the portraits of Nelson and Wellington ('I thought of Wellington very much during the Falklands'), displayed a porcelain statuette of British paratroopers raising the flag at San Carlos Bay ('I think it just portrays everything that is marvellous about the British soldier . . . The dignity, the calm and the kindliness') and sat in the Prime Minister's chair in the Cabinet room ('Where Winston sat'). She drew a different sort of inspiration from another of her predecessors, Robert Walpole. 'It is a great comfort to many of us,' she purred outrageously, 'that he stayed here for twenty-one years.' To further underline the point a little later she remarked that 'the great Lord Salisbury was Prime Minister for thirteen years . . . I often look back to his work.'

She gave a rose-tinted account of her journey from the Grantham grocer's shop to Number Ten, and expounded the Christian basis of her political philosophy. ('The heart of the Christian message is that each person has the right to choose.')[81] In fact the whole programme amounted to 'a lengthy plug for Mrs Thatcher's ideas and values'.[82] Prompted only by van der Post's soft questioning, she was allowed to present herself unchallenged as the natural successor to a line of British heroes and statesmen who embodied the nation's greatness. The twin themes of the broadcast – historical continuity and British military prowess – shamelessly anticipated the central themes of the Conservatives' campaign for re-election just a few weeks later. By all the normal canons of political broadcasting, Michael Foot should have been offered the right of reply. Had he demanded such an opportunity, however, Foot would have had to concede the right of the Alliance for equal treatment. Since Labour's only realistic ambition was to make sure of beating the Alliance in the contest for second place, he did not press the point.

'We are the true peace movement'

With a dearth of new policy proposals to unveil, Central Office was preparing to fight the coming election on the perennial appeal of Tory Governments seeking re-election, classically formulated by Colman, Prentis, Varley for Macmillan in 1959: 'Life's Better under the Conservatives: Don't Let Labour Ruin it'. In 1983 the claim was rather that life was *getting* better under the Conservatives. It was admitted that the country had been through a tough three years, but the rewards were now becoming clear: inflation and interest rates were coming down, economic activity was picking up and unemployment – the Government's Achilles heel – would soon begin to fall as prosperity returned. The warning was the same, however: the return of a Labour Government would throw away all the hard-won gains. Saatchi and Saatchi's variation on the old theme was uninspired but made the point: 'Britain is on the Right Track. Don't Turn Back Now'. The Tories' prospectus for the second term was more of the same, with very little detail about what that might entail.

The manifesto, written by Ferdinand Mount and Adam Ridley from drafts worked up between the Research Department and the Policy Unit under Howe's chairmanship, was described in the Nuffield study of the election as 'a remarkably anodyne document'.[83] Hoskyns called it 'almost content-free, if one is brutal about it'.[84] It did in fact promise more privatisation and further tightening of trade-union law, but this was now taken for granted; the only novelty was the promised abolition of the GLC and the metropolitan councils. Hugo Young in the *Sunday Times* judged it 'smooth, self-congratulatory and unmenacing'; another sceptical commentator, Peter Jenkins, concluded in the *Guardian* that 'Thatcherism is dead – at least for the present'.[85]

With hindsight, Nigel Lawson saw the manifesto's blandness as a positive virtue, since it left the re-elected Government free to pursue its objectives uninhibited by prior commitments. 'The bad manifesto,' in his view, 'was its much less well-written 1987 successor, replete with policy commitments which had not been properly thought through.'[86]

In one respect Lawson was right, since a bland manifesto, giving no hostages to fortune, was all that was needed to win the election. The opposition parties – divided, poorly led and easily dismissed as respectively extreme (Labour) and woolly (the Alliance) – offered no serious challenge to Mrs Thatcher's inevitable return. Yet the failure to put forward a positive programme for its second term, besides being democratically dishonest, left the Government directionless after the election, prey to untoward events for which it tried to compensate, as the next contest approached, with precisely those hasty initiatives – above all the poll tax – which Lawson condemned. The result, from the point of view of developing the Thatcherite project, was that much of the second term was wasted, while the third was blighted by the need to make up for lost time. On this analysis the 1983 manifesto was a missed opportunity which coloured the whole of the rest of Mrs Thatcher's premiership.

The trouble was that Labour offered too easy a target. Even after the defection of the SDP in 1981, the party was still riven by a bitter civil war. The Bennite hard left had seized control of the party's internal arrangements – the mechanism for electing the leader, the selection of candidates and the formation of policy. Yet senior social democrats like Denis Healey, Roy Hattersley and Gerald Kaufman remained in the Shadow Cabinet, visibly unhappy but helpless to arrest the leftward slide. In Michael Foot the party was stuck with an elderly leader, elected in a vain effort to preserve unity, whom the electorate found it impossible to imagine as Prime Minister: his approval rating – rarely over 20 per cent – was consistently the lowest since polling began. Moreover as the election approached, Labour saddled itself with an entire platform of unpopular left-wing policies, any one of which might have rendered the party unelectable: wholesale nationalisation, massive public spending, the restoration of trade-union privileges, withdrawal from Europe and unilateral nuclear disarmament. If the Tories' manifesto was vague, Labour's was appallingly specific: Gerald Kaufman famously dubbed it 'the longest suicide note in history'.[87] Of all its suicidal policies the most crippling handicap was Foot's passionate commitment to unilateral nuclear disarmament.

Not for half a century had the major parties been so far apart on the issue of national defence Ever since 1945 a broad consensus had obtained between the two front benches on the question of nuclear weapons. From the Bevanites to Tony Benn, the Labour left had kept up a more or less constant agitation for unilateral disarmament; but with the partial, ambiguous exception of Harold Wilson in 1963–4 successive Labour leaders had maintained a firm line on the retention of the British independent deterrent. Now, with the election of a life-long unilateralist to the leadership coinciding with a revival of support for the Campaign for Nuclear Disarmament, that consensus was ended. For the first time, nuclear weapons were set to be a major issue at the coming General Election. In the triumphant afterglow of her Falklands victory nothing could have suited Mrs Thatcher better.

Ever since becoming Tory leader in 1975, she had taken a strong line on the need to maintain and modernise NATO's nuclear defences against the Soviet nuclear threat. Her blunt warnings about Soviet expansionism had led the Russian press to christen her 'the Iron Lady', and she wore the intended insult with defiant pride. She was no more diplomatic in office than she had been in opposition. She had no interest in the polite bromides of 'peaceful coexistence' with Communism but believed that the West was engaged in a life-or-death struggle with the Soviet Empire – a struggle which she confidently expected the West to win, though she did not foresee the timescale. As early as May 1980, in a newspaper interview on the first anniversary of her election, she was looking forward to the fall of Communism. 'The major challenge to the Communist creed is coming now,' she told Brian Connell in *The Times*:

> For years they were saying the march of communism and socialism is inevitable. Not now, not now. I would say that in the end the demise of the communist creed is inevitable, because it is not a creed for human beings with spirit who wish to live their own lives under the rule of law.[88]

In the Commons she promised to wage 'the ideological struggle . . . as hard as I can'.[89]

That meant imposing sanctions following the Soviet invasion of Afghanistan, and trying to persuade British athletes to boycott the Moscow Olympics. It meant supporting the struggle of the Polish Solidarity movement, which began in 1981, and keeping up the pressure over Soviet treatment of dissidents in breach of the Helsinki undertakings on human rights. It meant increasing Britain's contribution to NATO military spending by 3 per cent, as she had promised in opposition. Above all it meant firmly rejecting the siren call of nuclear disarmament and matching the Russians' nuclear deployment missile for missile.

When the Conservatives came into office they were faced almost immediately with the need for a decision – which Labour had postponed – on replacing Britain's obsolescent nuclear deterrent, Polaris.

As is the way with nuclear decisions in every government, this one was confined to a small *ad hoc* subcommittee composed of the Prime Minister, her deputy, the Foreign and Defence Secretaries and the Chancellor.[90] They lost no time in opting to buy the American submarine-launched Trident system, at a cost of £5 billion spread over ten years. The problem was that the expenditure could only be afforded by making cuts elsewhere: hence John Nott's 1981 defence review which so nearly left the navy unable to defend the Falklands. Mrs Thatcher, however, had no doubts. She believed passionately in nuclear weapons, both as a positively good thing in themselves, which had kept the peace in Europe for thirty years and would continue to do so as long as the balance of deterrence was preserved, but still more as an emblem of national power, prestige and independence. She never had any truck with the criticism that Britain's 'independent' deterrent was in practice wholly dependent on the Americans for spares and maintenance and would never in any conceivable military circumstances be used without American consent. The decision to buy Trident, she told the Commons in July 1980, 'leaves us master of our own destiny . . . We are resolved to defend our freedom.'[91] At the party conference that year she asserted frankly that it was 'very important for the reputation of Britain abroad that we should keep our independent nuclear deterrent'.[92] In the Commons she insisted that the purchase of Trident was 'extremely good value for money'.[93]*

But then the Americans changed the arithmetic by developing a new, more sophisticated version of Trident. In January 1982 the Government had to decide all over again whether to buy the upgraded D5 model in place of the original C4, at still greater expense. John Nott – sent to the MoD specifically to cut the defence budget – was opposed. Even Mrs Thatcher was worried, but she was still determined that Britain must have the best and latest system, whatever it cost. This time, however, she deployed the full Cabinet to outnumber the doubters; they were treated to a two-hour presentation by the MoD's brightest nuclear expert Michael Quinlan, whose card she had already marked for early promotion. She also drew on her special relationship with President Reagan to persuade him to let Britain buy the D5 on exceptionally favourable terms. Before the decision was even taken she pre-empted it by publicly declaring her own position.

---

*She told Callaghan that the Government had to make 'difficult choices' in deciding how to spend the available money 'in the way best suited to the defence of the people of these islands'.[94] She did not say anything about defending any other islands.

'The expenditure of this money,' she told the Commons – sounding exactly like a housewife in a soap-powder commercial – 'secures a far greater degree of deterrence than expenditure of the same amount of money on ordinary conventional armaments.'[95]★

Mrs Thatcher was also eager to accept the deployment of American cruise missiles at military bases in Britain as part of NATO's response to Soviet SS20s targeted on the West. 'The fact is,' she announced in June 1980, 'that the Soviet Union has the latest nuclear missile – the SS20 – and it is facing Europe. We must have an effective deterrent.'[96] The deployment of cruise in several European countries had first been proposed by the West German Chancellor, Helmut Schmidt, as a way of locking the Americans into the defence of Europe at a time when it was feared they might otherwise walk away. Mrs Thatcher strongly supported it, not only to keep the Americans committed but also to demonstrate Europe's willingness to share the burden of its own defence. She was witheringly scornful when the Germans and other European governments began to weaken in the face of anti-nuclear protests; but at the same time she relished the opportunity to demonstrate once again that Britain was America's only reliable ally. When Britain agreed in September 1979 to station 144 cruise missiles at Greenham Common in Berkshire and RAF Molesworth in Cambridgeshire, the announcement caused little stir. But over the next three years, as the time for deployment approached, the mood changed. Increased tension between the superpowers, the spectre of a new nuclear arms race and the West's rejection of several plausible-sounding Soviet disarmament offers fuelled a Europe-wide revival of the fear of nuclear war, fanned by a widespread perception of Ronald Reagan as a sort of trigger-happy cowboy who might be tempted to use nuclear weapons against what he called (in March 1983) 'the evil empire'.[97] In Britain the Campaign for Nuclear Disarmament (CND), dormant since the great days of the Aldermaston marches in the early 1960s, suddenly sprang back to life, drawing large numbers to marches, rallies and demonstrations. Its membership jumped from 3,000 to 100,000 in three years. Moreover its cause was now backed by the official opposition.

★Trident was costing 12 per cent of the total defence budget by 1986. More fundamental than the question of value for money, however, was what Trident was actually *for*. Its critics argued that it was a far more sophisticated system than Britain would ever need. It tied Britain closely to American technology, yet the only circumstances in which it was conceivable that it would be used would be if the special relationship had broken down. If Britain really needed an independent nuclear deterrent at all it would have made more strategic sense to develop its own system, like the French, tailored to its own needs.

Mrs Thatcher welcomed a fight on the issue, first because she thought defence more fundamental even than economics; second because she believed that unilateral disarmament was absolutely wrong in principle and would make nuclear war more likely, not less; and third because she was confident that the country agreed with her. Opinion polls reflected public anxiety about specific weapons systems – the cost of Trident or the siting of American missiles in Britain – and a clear demand that Britain should possess a 'dual key' to prevent the Americans firing missiles from British soil without British consent, which she insisted was unnecessary. Yet when it came to the point the public overwhelmingly wanted to retain Britain's independent nuclear capacity. Keeping the bomb was at bottom, for the electorate as for Mrs Thatcher, a matter of national pride and identity. She was scornful of the woolly-minded wishful thinking of those who imagined that the USSR would respond in kind if the West tamely dismantled its weapons. 'Any policy of unilateral disarmament,' she told the Commons in June 1980, the day after a huge CND rally in Hyde Park addressed by Michael Foot, 'is a policy of unilateral surrender.'[98] The Warsaw Pact currently possessed a 3–1 superiority over NATO in nuclear weapons in Europe, she pointed out in July. 'Those who seek to have a nuclear-free Europe would do well to address their efforts in the first place to Soviet Russia.'[99] So long as the Soviets enjoyed superiority she scorned Brezhnev's offer of a moratorium. 'We cannot have a reduction that would leave one side very much better off than the other.'[100] She was all for disarmament, she insisted. The so-called 'zero option', whereby all nuclear weapons would eventually be scrapped, was 'absolutely the best' – though she never pretended that she thought it realistic. In the meantime, 'in the absence of the zero option we must have balanced numbers . . . If the SS20s are not taken down, we must start to deploy cruise missiles.'[101]

Her refusal to countenance disarmament except from a starting point of equality, however, often sounded alarmingly aggressive to those worried about the threat of nuclear escalation. Particularly after the Falklands she sometimes seemed to relish military hardware for its own sake. 'We should have every bit as much strategic nuclear weaponry at our disposal as the Soviet Union, every bit as much intermediate nuclear weaponry at our disposal as the Soviet Union,' she told the Commons in November 1982.[102] The next time she spoke in the House about deploying cruise she was greeted with cries of 'Warmonger'.[103] Her response to this allegation was to insist repeatedly that nuclear weapons did not cause war but were actually the surest way to prevent it. She gave her fullest exposition of this argument at that year's party conference, when she devoted a long section of her televised speech to spelling out the ABC of deterrence. 'I want to see nuclear disarmament,' she told the representatives; but she added: 'I want to see conventional disarmament as well.'

I remember the atomic bombs that devastated Hiroshima and Nagasaki. I remember too, the bombs that destroyed Coventry and Dresden. The horrors of war are indivisible. We all want peace, but not at any price . . .

I understand the feelings of the unilateralists. I understand the anxieties of parents with children growing up in the nuclear age. But the fundamental question for all of us is whether unilateral nuclear disarmament would make a war less likely. I have to tell you that it would not. It would make war more likely . . .

Because Russia and the West know that there can be no victory in nuclear war, for thirty-seven years we have kept the peace in Europe . . . That is why we need nuclear weapons, because having them makes peace more secure.[104]

It was at a joint press conference with Helmut Kohl at the end of the Chancellor's visit to London in February 1983 that she found the phrase that encapsulated her paradoxical faith. 'We really are a true peace movement ourselves,' she claimed, 'and we are the true disarmers, in that we stand for all-sided disarmament, but on a basis of balance.'[105] She always loved stealing Labour's slogans for herself. 'We are the true peace movement' became her favourite refrain throughout the General Election and beyond.[106]

Realising that defence, and the nuclear argument in particular, was going to be a key battleground in the coming contest, Mrs Thatcher took the opportunity of John Nott's intention to leave politics by removing him from the Ministry of Defence in January 1983 and replacing him with the much more combative figure of Michael Heseltine. Much as she distrusted Heseltine, she recognised that he had the populist flair to tackle CND head on; she was also happy to get him away from Liverpool. Whatever her motives, this was one of her most successful appointments; Heseltine responded exactly as she had hoped in the months leading up to the election, energetically countering the unilateralists in the television studios and on the radio. His most successful coup was to upstage CND's Easter demonstration, when they had planned to form a human chain around the Greenham Common airbase on Good Friday. Heseltine stole their thunder by visiting Germany the day before and having himself photographed looking over the Berlin Wall, thus dramatising the enemy whom NATO's nuclear weapons were intended to deter. He also provoked controversy by publicising the far-left connections of several prominent CND leaders, suggesting that the bulk of its well-meaning members were the innocent dupes of Soviet foreign policy which sought to lure the West into dismantling its defences without a shot fired. Labour had no answer to this allegation. With all its other doctrinal baggage, unilateralism was the biggest millstone round the Labour party's neck, and Heseltine made the most of it. The contrast with the recapture of the Falklands did not need spelling out.

Landslide: June 1983

If the result of the election was never in much doubt, its timing was a matter of uncertainty up to the last moment. All Mrs Thatcher's instincts inclined her to carry on until October: she was naturally cautious, she had a perfectly adequate majority with another year to run, and she worried that it would seem opportunist to go for a quick advantage.[107] But she was under strong pressure from the party managers to go as soon as possible after the new electoral register came into force in February 1983: the redrawn constituency boundaries were expected to yield the Tories an extra thirty seats. Cecil Parkinson and Central Office wanted to go early, and the temptation was great. Moreover Nigel Lawson believes that she was superstitious: having won in May four years before, she was keen to go again in early summer if she could justify it.[108] During the spring she repeatedly refused to be hustled, but equally declined to rule out the option. She was sensitive to suggestions that she was planning to 'cut and run'. When Denis Healey teased her in the Commons on 19 April she summoned a rare piece of Lincolnshire dialect to taunt him back:

> The right hon. Gentleman is afraid of an election, is he? Afraid? Frightened? Frit? Could not take it? Cannot stand it? If I were going to cut and run I should have gone after the Falklands.[109]

The polls had been showing a solid Tory lead for months; but two by-elections affected the calculation. First, at Bermondsey in February, Labour's divisions were devastatingly exposed by the adoption of the very left-wing – but not at that time openly gay – Peter Tatchell as candidate to replace the old-style right-wing dockers' MP and former Chief Whip, Bob Mellish. Foot first declared Tatchell unacceptable, then was obliged to acquiesce in his selection. The Liberal Simon Hughes took advantage to seize the seat for the Alliance, leading to calls for Foot to be replaced by Healey – which was the last thing the Tories wanted. Much hung on the next by-election, at Darlington in March. But this time a poor SDP candidate allowed Labour to hold the seat, halting the Alliance bandwagon and saving Foot's position as sacrificial victim for the coming slaughter. The Tories breathed a sigh of relief.

The last runes to be read were the local election results on 5 May. Mrs Thatcher called a meeting of her inner circle at Chequers on the following Sunday: just three members of the Cabinet, Whitelaw, Howe and Tebbit, plus Parkinson and his deputy Michael Spicer from Central Office; Michael Jopling, the Chief Whip; Ian Gow, David Wolfson and Ferdinand Mount from her private office; Tim Bell from Saatchi and Saatchi; and Gordon Reece, her personal public-relations adviser, recalled from America for the election. The results were good: the Tories gained 128 council seats in England and Wales. Practically everyone present wanted to press the button. But still Mrs Thatcher was nervous of committing herself.

She sought every excuse for indecision. First she argued that she had promised President Reagan that she would attend the G7 summit at Williamsburg, Virginia, at the end of May: this would entail her being out of the country at a crucial stage of the campaign. She was persuaded that her absence could be turned to electoral advantage, with media coverage underlining her stature as an international stateswoman. Then she worried that the manifesto was not ready. Parkinson told her that it could be made ready in a couple of hours, at which she immediately started rewriting it herself, line by line, until only Parkinson, Jopling and Gow remained. Finally she found another problem: even if she wished to call an election, she objected, the Queen would not be available at such short notice to grant a dissolution. Gow slipped out of the room and returned a few minutes later to say that Her Majesty would see her at noon the next day. 'I am still not sure,' Parkinson wrote, 'that the look she shot at him was one of gratitude.'[110] She went to bed still saying she must sleep on the decision. But the next morning she went to the Palace as arranged. Polling day was set for Thursday 9 June.

However favourable the polls, Mrs Thatcher made a point of never counting her chickens. With characteristic prudence and a touch of pre-emptive superstition she actually spent every spare moment she could find in the next few weeks clearing up the accumulated clutter in Number Ten in case she had to leave hurriedly on 10 June. Visiting Chequers a few weeks earlier, Carol had found her mother in 'somewhat maudlin' mood, speculating on the possibility of never seeing the house again. 'If we lose,' she reflected, 'I've had the best four years of one's life. You do think, perhaps I won't be here again.'[111] (She always veered interchangeably between 'I', 'we', 'you' and 'one'.) When she called the election, however, Carol was in Australia and taken by surprise: she had expected her mother to go on to the autumn. She hurried home, ready to vacate Flood Street, where she had been living, in case her parents needed it back. 'I have no intention of needing Flood Street back,' her mother responded crisply.[112] She had no serious fear of losing.

The Tory campaign was frankly concentrated on Mrs Thatcher, highlighting her strength and resolution, clear convictions and strong leadership. The contrast with Foot was so obvious that it scarcely needed spelling out. Few other Cabinet ministers played much part at all. Each day the Prime Minister herself chaired the morning press conference at Central Office, flanked by two or three colleagues; most of the Cabinet was paraded, but few featured more than once, and their role was clearly subordinate. Mrs Thatcher answered most of the questions. Besides herself only three ministers appeared in the party's television broadcasts; and those three (Parkinson, Tebbit and Heseltine) were not the most senior. It is not surprising that an opinion poll of intending Tory voters found that 46 per cent were influenced by Mrs Thatcher's leadership, 31 per cent by Tory policies and only 11 per cent by her team of ministers.[113]

The campaign closely followed the successful pattern of 1979. After the press conference each morning she set off each day by plane from Gatwick or helicopter from Battersea for whistle-stop visits around the country, meeting up with her campaign coach to inspect shiny new factories or do walkabouts in shopping malls, carefully chosen to provide good pictures for the local media and the national TV news; she went mainly to Tory constituencies, where only the local members were told in advance that she was coming, to ensure that she met an enthusiastic reception and to minimise the risk of hostile demonstrations. Apart from her flying visit to America over the Whitsun bank holiday, she slept only one night out of London – in Inverness on 31 May, when she stayed at the Station Hotel and held her press conference next morning in Elgin. She made only a handful of major speeches – in Cardiff, where she had launched her 1979 campaign, in Harrogate, Edinburgh and Birmingham – and those were delivered to carefully vetted audiences of Tory supporters well supplied with Union Jacks. In addition she gave two interviews to friendly newspapers, the *Mail on Sunday* and the *Daily Express*; did two major radio interviews – one with Jimmy Young at the beginning of the campaign, another near the end answering listeners' questions on the BBC's *Election Call*; and five major TV interviews – two taking audience questions and three with heavyweight interviewers. Altogether the Nuffield study of the election found that she was featured on radio and television news broadcasts 331 times. The next most prominent Tory was Norman Tebbit with eighty-one appearances, followed by Parkinson, Howe and Pym. For Labour, Foot scored 317 mentions, but Healey got 175, followed by Peter Shore, Neil Kinnock and Roy Hattersley.[114]

She was accompanied on her daily sorties by a sizeable entourage normally composed of Ian Gow (or sometimes Michael Spicer), a press officer, various secretaries, researchers and typists, plus Denis, more often than not, doing his Duke of Edinburgh act, and Carol, who was writing a diary of the campaign but made herself useful as a general dogsbody. But this was only the visible part of the Prime Minister's campaigning day. Each evening when she came back to Downing Street she would have a quick supper and then get on with preparing speeches for the following day. The drafts were largely written by Mount, with additional material provided by Wolfson, Gow, Gummer and of course Ronnie Millar; but Mrs Thatcher would rewrite and correct them far into the night. Next morning she would arrive at Central Office at 8.15 for an hour's briefing before the 9.30 press conference. Gordon Reece attended these briefings and also helped rehearse her for her television appearances. But above all in this election she put herself in the hands of Cecil Parkinson, who had the knack of soothing tensions and keeping her calm when things went wrong. She trusted him completely. 'If Cecil says not to do it,' she said after one mix-up on the bus when she had wanted to change plans, 'we won't do it.'[115] When it was all over she was generous in giving him the credit for victory.

Despite the best-laid plans of Central Office, some of her appearances did not go smoothly, however. Carol's diary is a gently cynical record of cock-ups and confusion. There was an early fiasco in a Finchley supermarket on 21 May, with Mrs Thatcher pretending to shop while a mob of photographers stood on frozen-food cabinets to get pictures; when she came to the till with an odd assortment of items that she had managed to reach – ham, pâté, ox tongue, Lymeswold cheese and light bulbs – she had no money and had to wait for Carol to push through the crush to come and pay for her.[116] There was another shambles five days later when the media circus descended on Harry Ramsden's famous fish-and-chip shop near Leeds. Mrs Thatcher served out portions for the benefit of the cameras, and even ate a plateful herself; but she looked out of place and did not win many votes from the locals who had chosen the wrong day for a quiet lunch.[117]

As in 1979, everything was done for the benefit of the cameras. From Harry Ramsden's she moved on to Otley to be photographed in a hard helmet driving a dumper truck, very cautiously.[118] In Norfolk she posed with a Jersey cow; near Bristol she cut a birthday cake for a Falklands war veteran – 1915 vintage. Given the chance, she was an excellent campaigner who relished talking with real voters when they were allowed to get near her; but most of the time she was too hemmed in by the scrum of journalists, photographers and minders. On factory visits, as Frank Johnson noted in *The Times*, she made 'full use of her gift of being piercingly interested in whatever is being explained to her'.[119] She inspected knitwear in Leicester, computer graphics in Newbury, thermostats in Inverness. But she was always inclined to lecture as much as she listened. In Birmingham she toured a Cadbury's confectionery factory and joined women sorting almonds at a conveyor belt. 'Making marzipan from almonds is a brute of a job,' she told them with all the benefit of five minutes' experience.[120] There was nothing she would not try for the sake of a photograph.

Throughout the campaign, even in her big speeches, she offered little that was positive or new, but concentrated on attacking Labour relentlessly on what she called the 'gut issues'.[121] She paid close attention to Labour's manifesto, which she called 'the most chilling and alien manifesto ever put before the British people by a major political party'.[122] (Saatchis made the same point with a poster showing the Labour and Communist manifestos side by side, with the caption 'Like your manifesto, Comrade'.)[123] In her opening speech at Cardiff on 23 May she repeated the gibe that it was 'the longest suicide note ever penned' and asserted that it would be 'a suicide note for Britain, too' if the electorate endorsed it. She excoriated Labour's plans for further nationalisation, claiming that they would 'take your pension contributions and your life assurance premiums' to pay for them. 'The Labour party goes in for nationalisation like other people go in for stamp collecting,' she mocked:

> They want at least one of each – one of the big banks, one of the big pharmaceutical companies, one of the big building firms. Beechams. GEC, Glaxo, Plessey . . . nobody could know who would be next.

'Under a Labour Government,' she warned, 'there's virtually nowhere you could put your savings where they would be safe from the State.'

Put your savings in a bank – and they'll nationalise it. Put your savings in a pension fund or a life assurance company – and a Labour Government would force them to invest the money in their own socialist schemes.

'Put your savings in socks,' she added, departing from her script, 'and they'd nationalise socks.'[124] In this way she kept the issue focused not on the Tory plans for more privatisation, but on the socialist bogey of further nationalisation.

Likewise she said very little about Tory proposals for further trade-union reform, but concentrated her fire on attacking Labour's promised 'new partnership' with the unions. 'It was Labour's old partnership with the unions,' she declared at Harrogate on 27 May, 'that brought this country to its knees. The strikes, the restrictive practices, the over-manning, the political blackmail – all of it endorsed over and over again by Labour leaders – and not least by the present one.'[125] Memories of the Winter of Discontent still provided the best reason for not voting Labour again.

Above all she hammered away at Labour's commitment to 'one-sided disarmament'. On a radio phone-in on 22 May she pulled no punches with a listener who suggested that she had got her priorities wrong in worrying about missiles when millions were out of work. 'James, I must disagree with you,' she purred emphatically:

I could not possibly go along with a policy which says we must abandon our independent nuclear deterrent while we leave colossal numbers, I think two thousand strategic ballistic missiles, in the hands of our sworn enemies, enemies that didn't hesitate to go in and crush Hungary and Czechoslovakia and Afghanistan.[126]

Nuclear weapons, she reiterated time and again, had kept the peace in Europe for forty years. 'We are the true peace movement.'[127]

She covered the Government's weakest flank – unemployment – by counter-attacking Labour's record in the 1970s. 'In the end Labour always runs away,' she jeered in her adoption speech at Finchley on 19 May:

They are running away from the need to defend their country . . . They are fleeing from the long overdue reform of the trade unions . . . They are running out on Europe . . . Above all, Labour is running away from the true challenge of unemployment.

Promising to create millions of jobs, she insisted, was 'no more than an evasion of the real problem'. Real jobs could only be created by gradually building up a competitive economy with profitable industries that could hold their own in world markets. 'We Conservatives believe in working with the grain of human nature, in encouraging people by incentives, not in over-regulating them by too many controls.' 'A quick cure,' she repeated several times in another favourite formulation, 'is a quack cure.'[128]

The Tories' only other weak point was the widespread belief that the Government had a secret agenda to 'privatise' or somehow dismantle the National Health Service. Mrs Thatcher had already declared repeatedly that the NHS was 'safe with us'; but she had to go on repeating it until she finally rebutted it with the strongest disclaimer at her disposal: 'I have no more intention of dismantling the National Health Service,' she declared at Edinburgh, 'than I have of dismantling Britain's defences.'[129] Labour's allegations to the contrary, she told Robin Day on *Panorama*, were 'false, bogus, phoney and calculated to deceive'.[130] 'There is no secret manifesto,' she assured a disbelieving questioner on *World in Action*.[131] These reiterated protestations were probably not necessary in order to win the election; but they had the effect of making it impossible for the Government to give serious attention to the deepening crisis of the health service until after 1987. Moreover Mrs Thatcher tied her hands almost as tightly on social security. A couple of years later, when he came to conduct a major review of benefit policy, Norman Fowler found his options severely limited by the number of pledges the Prime Minister had given during the election that this or that benefit would not be cut.[132]

The Government's lack of any positive programme was most glaringly exposed in her big speech at Birmingham on 4 June, when she offered six reasons for voting Conservative, which were no different from those Ted Heath might have given in 1970:

> Because the Conservatives offer real hope of new jobs.
> Because the Conservatives keep prices down.
> Because the Conservatives reform trade union law.
> Because the Conservatives give council house tenants the
> chance to own their own home.
> Because the Conservatives protect the social services.
> Because the Conservatives ensure that this nation is properly
> defended.[133]

As in 1979, she was going to the country on a thoroughly conservative platform.

The radicalism was all in her personality, which conveyed the impression of an irresistible whirlwind of unspecified reform. Watching her press conferences on television, David Owen – normally a considerable admirer of the Thatcher style – was appalled by the way she dominated whichever of her ministers were lined up to appear with her. 'The way she humiliated, patronised and even bullied grown men at these conferences,' he wrote some years later, 'was all too revealing', giving the public a vivid glimpse of how she ran her government.[134] She twice slapped down Francis Pym, first when he implied that the sovereignty of the Falklands might at some point in the future be negotiable[135], and again when he unwisely suggested on television that landslide majorities tended not to make for good government. She dismissed this as typical Chief Whip's caution, adding witheringly: 'You know there's a club of Chief Whips. They're very unusual people.'[136] (Ted Heath, of course, was a former Chief Whip: she may have momentarily forgotten that Willie Whitelaw was another.) She had no doubt that she wanted the biggest majority possible. 'The Labour party manifesto is the most extreme ever,' she declared on a whistle-stop tour of Norfolk on 25 May, 'and it deserves a very big defeat.'[137] 'As a professional campaigner,' Carol observed, 'she did not think there was such a thing as winning too well.'[138] Mrs Thatcher warned repeatedly against complacency, believing that 'You can lose elections in the last few days by not going flat out to the winning post.'[139] 'We need to have every single vote on polling day.'[140]★

Just as she dominated her colleagues, she also reduced television interviewers to pliant ciphers. Robin Day, Alastair Burnet and Brian Walden were worsted in turn. 'Don't interrupt me now, I'm in full flow,' she told Walden; while Day actually apologised for interrupting her, only to be brushed aside: 'That's all right, I can cope with you.' Day – the original tough interrogator – felt that he had let his viewers down by letting the Prime Minister walk all over him; but in all his long experience he had not been treated like this before. He was used to asking questions which the politicians would then make some attempt to answer: he was unprepared for Mrs Thatcher's new technique

---

★On the other hand Mrs Thatcher personally cancelled a final series of full-page newspaper advertisements which Parkinson, Tim Bell and the Saatchis wanted to run in the last week. She did not believe they were needed and the unnecessary expenditure offended her sense of thrift. One was a blank page, meant to represent the Alliance manifesto. 'People will think that a total waste of paper.'[141]

of ignoring the questions and simply delivering whatever message she wanted to get across.[142] 'In all her set-piece encounters,' Michael Cockerell wrote, 'the top interviewers scarcely succeeded in laying a glove on her. She said what she had come prepared to say and no more.'[143] By comparison both Foot and Jenkins were clumsy, long-winded and old-fashioned.

The only person who rattled her was an ordinary voter, a geography teacher named Diana Gould, who pressed her about the sinking of the *General Belgrano* on BBC TV's *Nationwide*, seizing on the discrepancy in her answers about whether or not the ship was sailing towards or away from the British task force, and refusing to be deflected. 'No professional would have challenged a Prime Minister so bluntly,' wrote Martin Harrison in the Nuffield study, 'and precisely because she was answering an ordinary voter Mrs Thatcher had to bite back her evident anger.'[144] Carol does not mention Diana Gould in her diary. Instead she quotes at length another tetchy exchange about pensions on the same programme; but she calls the whole *Nationwide* episode 'an example of the most crass nastiness and discourtesy shown to a Prime Minister on a television programme', complaining that there were only seven questions in thirty-five minutes and that the programme 'was allowed to ramble on and on in an unattractive and unproductive fashion'.[145] Mrs Thatcher came off the air talking wildly of abolishing the BBC.[146] 'Only the BBC could ask a British Prime Minister why she took action to protect *our* ships against an enemy ship that was a danger to our boys,' she railed, forgetting that it was not the presenter, Sue Lawley, who had asked the question, which in any case was directed at the inconsistency of her explanations, not at her reasons.[147] Mrs Gould rattled her because she could not slap her down the way she could Tam Dalyell in the Commons. At the same time she was entitled to resent armchair strategists who persisted in questioning the sinking of the *Belgrano* long after the event. 'They have the luxury of knowing that we came through all right,' she told Carol. 'I had the anxiety of protecting our people on *Hermes* and *Invincible* and the people on the vessels going down there.'[148]

Recriminations about the Falklands did Mrs Thatcher no harm, however, merely keeping the memory of her triumph before the electorate, without the Tories having to boast about it. Labour knew the war was bad territory for them, and tried to keep off it. But two leading figures could not resist. First Denis Healey, in a speech at Birmingham, talked about Mrs Thatcher wrapping herself in the Union Jack and 'glorying in slaughter'; he was obliged to apologise the next day, explaining that he should have said 'glorying in conflict'. Then

Neil Kinnock – Labour's education spokesman – responded still more crudely on television to a heckler who shouted that at least Mrs Thatcher had guts. 'And it's a pity that people had to leave theirs on Goose Green in order to prove it,' he retorted. Kinnock was publicly unrepentant; but he too was obliged to write to the families of the war dead to apologise.[149] These wild charges only damaged Labour. There was no mileage in trying to denigrate Mrs Thatcher's achievement in the Falklands – particularly since the Opposition was supposed to have supported the war. Such carping merely confirmed her charge that Labour never had the guts to carry anything through.

Unlike most Tory campaigns – certainly unlike 1987 – there were no serious wobbles in 1983. There were no rogue polls: the Tories' rating never dropped below 41 per cent (and was usually much higher), while Labour's increasingly struggled to reach 30 per cent. The only slight worry was the Alliance, which crept up steadily to around 26 per cent.[150] Tory strategy had been to treat the Alliance (like the Liberals of old) as an irrelevance. It was not a party at all, Mrs Thatcher scoffed on 27 May; it had no principles, no cohesion, not even a single leader – it was just 'a miscellany'.[151] But as the third-party bandwagon picked up, Central Office began to worry that it might take enough Tory votes to let Labour steal some crucial seats. ('If they get more votes,' Mrs Thatcher warned on 1 June, 'they in fact would put in a Labour Government.'[152] In fact the Alliance was drawing its vote almost entirely from Labour, making no impression on the Tories' impregnable lead. Roy Jenkins – named as the Alliance's 'Prime Minister-designate' – proved a disappointingly ponderous performer in the age of sound-bites and photo-opportunities; at a crisis 'summit' on 31 May he was obliged to yield a more prominent role to the more quickwitted and telegenic David Steel. It was only after this that the Alliance began to gain ground. By splitting the anti-Conservative vote, however, the would-be mould-breakers only served to inflate Mrs Thatcher's majority.

The one serious mistake of the Tory campaign was a spectacular youth rally staged by Harvey Thomas at Wembley on 5 June, the Sunday before polling day. This featured a line-up of rock bands, sports personalities, soap stars and comedians before an audience of 3,000 ecstatic Young Conservatives wearing 'I Love Maggie' T-shirts and chanting 'Maggie, Maggie, Maggie, In, In, In' – the first time this sort of showbiz event had been tried in British politics. But one of the warm-up acts, the zany comic, Kenny Everett – a risky act to book for a political platform – made two jokes widely felt to be in poor taste. 'Let's kick Michael Foot's stick away,' he chortled; and then, 'Let's bomb Russia.'

Mrs Thatcher would normally have disapproved of this sort of thing. She had earlier vetoed a cruel Saatchi poster featuring a picture of Michael Foot with his stick and dog and the caption 'Under the Conservatives, all pensioners are better off'.[153] But on this occasion she loved it. 'Some of the sourer critics,' she wrote in her memoirs, 'chose to take offence at joke remarks made by the comedian who preceded me on stage. What they really took offence at was the broad social appeal of the new Conservative Party demonstrated both by the unconventional people on stage and in the audience.'[154] 'Could Labour have organised a rally like this?' she exulted. 'In the old days perhaps, but not now. For they are the party of yesterday. And tomorrow is ours.'[155] To many this ringing assertion carried a disturbing echo of the Nazi song in the 1972 film *Cabaret*; and the whole event smacked unpleasantly of Nuremberg. Ronnie Millar was appalled, especially when Mrs Thatcher came straight on from Wembley to record her final broadcast 'on the wrong sort of high, the adrenaline pumping furiously'. Millar had wanted her to do a mood piece. '"No! No!! No!!!" she flew at me . . . "I want facts, not moods."' When Millar dared to tell her he thought the Wembley rally vulgar, she berated him for going 'wobbly' and told Gow to find someone else to write her script. He eventually got Brian Walden to do it – so much for the impartiality of TV interviewers.[156]

She started and finished her campaign, as usual, in Finchley. In marked contrast with her triumphalism two miles down the road, Mrs Thatcher always appeared at her most modest and humble among her own people, still the model constituency Member they had elected in 1959. In all her years as Tory leader and Prime Minister she never missed a constituency function if she could help it. 'In my diary are three dates,' she once declared; 'my annual meeting, Finchley Carnival and the Christmas party down on the Grange Estate – and if President Reagan or Foreign Ministers want to see me they know now they can find me in Finchley.'[157] In fact she was there much more often than that. Except when she was out of the country she still held her regular surgery every Friday evening, usually preceded by meetings with businessmen or a visit to a local school or hospital, and followed by supper with her constituency officers and perhaps a branch meeting. Her insistence on keeping these appointments made for a running battle with Number Ten, which always had more pressing calls on her time. She was deeply possessive about Finchley; she was furious when press reports suggested that she might – quite unnecessarily – seek a safer seat in Gloucestershire. Finchley had been her political base for more than twenty years and she liked everything there to be as it always had been. She might be a revolutionary in Downing Street, her agent wrote, 'but as soon as she crosses the North Circular she becomes in all matters relating to her Conservative Association the original stick-in-the-mud'.[158]

Her personal address delivered through the letterboxes of her own electors was extraordinarily understated, ticking off the Government's achievements on prices, pensions, the health service and home ownership and promising further progress on union ballots, youth training, jobs and limiting rate increases – plus the abolition of the GLC – while maintaining 'traditional liberties' and 'the defence policies which have kept the peace in Europe for 38 years'. The only glancing reference to her own position came in the form of a tribute to her voters:

> Wherever I have travelled on Britain's behalf I have been inspired and refreshed by the friendship and confidence of the people of Finchley and Friern Barnet.
>
> I hope that you will support me on Polling Day, and that I can continue to serve this constituency for another Parliament.[159]

As well as Labour and the Alliance, she faced for the first time a phalanx of fringe candidates – not only the imperishable 'Lord' David Sutch of the Official Monster Raving Loony Party, but a Greenham Common peace campaigner; anti-motorway, anti-licensing and anti-censorship campaigners; and a 'Belgrano Bloodhunger' candidate (who came with just thirteen votes). All these diversions delayed the declaration of her result until 2.30 a.m., long after the Conservatives' national victory was confirmed. When the 326th Tory seat was formally declared, Alastair Burnet on ITN announced that 'Mrs Thatcher is back in Downing Street'. 'No, I'm not!' she shouted furiously at the screen, 'I'm still at Hendon Town Hall.'[160] Eventually she secured a slightly increased majority over Labour, with the Alliance third and the rest nowhere:

Mrs M. Thatcher (C)	19,616
L. Spigel (Lab)	10,302
M. Joachim (Lib/All)	7,763
(Eight others)	736
Majority	9,314[161]

She left almost immediately for Conservative Central Office, where she thanked the party workers and was photographed waving from a first-floor window with the architect of victory, Cecil Parkinson. She had won, on the face of it, an enormous victory. The eventual Conservative majority was 144 over all other parties: they held 397 seats in the new House (compared with 335 in the old) against Labour's 205 and just twenty-three for the Alliance, two Scottish Nationalists, two Plaid Cymru, and seventeen from Northern Ireland. Within that landslide there were several individually pleasing results. Tony Benn – largely due to boundary changes – lost the Bristol seat he had held for thirty years. Both Crosby and Croydon North-West were regained from the Alliance. Fifteen seats were gained from Labour in the north of England, including Darlington; and the Tories held all their twenty-one seats in Scotland, only failing to regain Roy Jenkins' Hillhead. Mrs Thatcher was particularly gratified that the Tory candidate finally captured her own youthful testing ground in Dartford (now renamed Erith and Crayford) – though this was only because the former Labour MP had joined the SDP. On the other hand the Tories lost the formerly safe seat of Yeovil to an energetic Liberal challenger, Paddy Ashdown.

Nationally, however, the scale of her victory owed a great deal to the Alliance. Her hugely swollen majority actually rested on a lower aggregate vote, and a lower share of the vote, than she had won in 1979 – down from 43.9 per cent to 42.4 per cent. Though it was rewarded with pitifully few seats, in terms of votes the Alliance ran Labour very hard for second place, winning 25.4 per cent to Labour's 27.6 per cent – less than 700,000 votes behind. The effect of the Alliance surge, which nearly doubled the Liberal vote of 1979, was not, as the Tories had feared, to let Labour in but, on the contrary, to deliver the Government a majority out of all proportion to its entitlement. In the whole of southern England outside London – south of a line from the Severn to the Wash – Labour won only three seats out of 168. Even in the north, the Alliance helped the Tories gain additional seats on a much smaller swing. Behind the triumphalism, therefore, June 1983 was by no means the massive endorsement of Thatcherism that the Tories claimed. It was 'manifestly less a victory for the Conservatives', the *Annual Register* concluded, 'than a catastrophe for the Labour Party'.[162] Perhaps the most significant statistic to emerge from analysis of the result was that less than 40 per cent of trade-union members voted Labour (31 per cent voted Conservative and 29 per cent Alliance).[163] What Mrs Thatcher had achieved since 1979 – with critical help from the Labour leadership itself, from Tony Benn and the Militant tendency, the SDP defectors, General Galtieri and the distorting electoral system – was to smash the old Labour party, leaving herself without the inconvenience of an effective opposition for as

long as she remained in office. As Francis Pym had anticipated, this
was not an unmixed blessing, either for the cause of good government
or even for Mrs Thatcher herself.

Into the second term

With the second term secured and her personal authority unassailable,
Mrs Thatcher now had an almost unprecedented political opportunity
before her. Her opponents within the Tory party were conclusively
routed. For the first time she was in a position to appoint her own
Cabinet, with no debts to anyone except perhaps Geoffrey Howe, Cecil
Parkinson and the ever-loyal Willie Whitelaw. Yet she made remarkably few changes. The September 1981 reshuffle which brought in
Lawson, Tebbit and Parkinson remained the crucial watershed: June
1983 largely confirmed the team that fought the election. There were
indeed only three casualties. By far the most significant was Francis
Pym. She had never wanted him as Foreign Secretary, but in April
1982 she had had little choice. She could not sack him after the
Falklands either; but his removal was already widely trailed before his
remark about large majorities gave her the excuse she needed. She
called him in the morning after the election and told him bluntly:
'Francis, I want a new Foreign Secretary.'[164] What she really wanted,
as she grew more confident of her capacity to handle foreign policy
herself, was a more amenable Foreign Secretary from her own wing
of the party, preferably one without a traditional Foreign Office background. The man she had in mind was Cecil Parkinson, as his reward
for masterminding the election.

In the very moment of victory, however, at Central Office in the
early hours of Friday morning, Parkinson confessed to her that he had
been conducting a long-standing affair with his former secretary, Sara
Keays – herself an aspiring Tory candidate – who was pregnant with
his child. He told Mrs Thatcher that he had promised to leave his wife
in order to marry Miss Keays. She reluctantly concluded that he could
not become Foreign Secretary with this incipient scandal hanging over
him, but thought he would be less exposed in a less senior job. She
sent him instead to Trade and Industry. With some misgiving she then
gave the Foreign Office to Geoffrey Howe.

She had already decided to move Howe from the Treasury. Four
years is a good stint for a Chancellor and he was ready for a change.
Had Parkinson not been compromised, however, Howe would presumably have had to settle for the Home Office – the other traditional
berth for an ex-Chancellor, sanctioned by the precedent of Jim
Callaghan in 1967 and Roy Jenkins in 1974 – unless he had been

willing to leave the Commons to become Lord Chancellor, which in 1983 he was not. In retrospect the Foreign Office seems the natural progression. In fact Mrs Thatcher had doubts about the appointment, and by the time she came to write her memoirs she had persuaded herself it was a mistake.[165] At the Treasury Howe's quiet determination had been invaluable both in riding the political storms and in stiffening her own resolve. At the Foreign Office, by contrast, his views – particularly towards Europe – increasingly diverged from hers, while his dogged diplomacy and air of patient reasonableness exasperated her as much as Pym's had done. She also became convinced that Howe was ambitious for her job. Nevertheless Howe was a good appointment. For the whole of Mrs Thatcher's second term, at summits and international negotiations, they made an effective combination on the global stage, each complementing the other's qualities, while he put up heroically with being treated as her punchbag.

The hot tip to become the new Chancellor was Patrick Jenkin, who had done well both at the DHSS and at Industry, where he had shown himself a committed privatiser. But Mrs Thatcher now had the self-confidence to choose the more flamboyant Nigel Lawson, overriding Whitelaw's suspicion of him. As she wrote tartly in her memoirs: 'I had by now come to share Nigel's high opinion of himself.'[166] If Howe had been the perfect helmsman for the first term, Lawson's slightly Regency style presented the right image of prosperity and expansion for the calmer waters of the second. This combination too worked well for the next four years, though Lawson was always more independent and self-confident than Howe had been.

Below these two key appointments, the rest of the Cabinet-making was largely a rearrangement of the pack. Jenkin, denied the Treasury, had hoped for the reconstituted DTI, but was given the poisoned chalice of Environment instead, charged with abolishing the GLC and looking again at alternatives to the rates. At his brief interview, Mrs Thatcher flattered him that he was particularly good at getting difficult legislation through the House.[167] Willie Whitelaw left the Commons and the Home Office to become Lord President of the Council and Leader of the House of Lords. This was a position from which he could better exercise his non-departmental role as deputy Prime Minister; but it entailed the displacement of Lady Young, thus ending the short-lived experiment of a second woman in the Thatcher Cabinet. There was never another.

Whitelaw's replacement at the Home Office was one of Mrs Thatcher's least well-judged appointments. She had really wanted to appoint Norman Tebbit, which would have raised a few eyebrows but pleased the party faithful. Whitelaw, however, if he could not block Lawson, still had enough clout to veto Tebbit. So she turned to Leon Brittan, who had done well as Chief Secretary to the Treasury and seemed to be a rising star. But he was at once too junior, too brainy and – it must be said – too Jewish to satisfy the Tory party's expectations of a Home Secretary. Where Whitelaw had needed all his authority to resist the punitive instincts of the party conference, Brittan was always under pressure, from both the party and the Prime Minister, to act tougher than he really was.

Brittan's place at the Treasury was filled by Peter Rees, to the chagrin of Nicholas Ridley, whose hopes Mrs Thatcher continued cruelly to disappoint. The third casualty of the reshuffle was David Howell, who had been lucky to survive his removal from Energy in 1981; his place at Transport was now taken by Tom King (demoted from his brief reign at Environment). One of the most significant sideways moves was Peter Walker from Agriculture to Energy to handle the anticipated showdown with the NUM; Walker was the one unrepentant 'wet' who retained Mrs Thatcher's confidence as an effective minister. Of the rest, Pym was now dispatched to the back benches, where he tried feebly to mount a moderate challenge under the vacuous slogan 'Centre Forward'. Prior remained – for another year – marginalised in Northern Ireland. Michael Heseltine, who had only been at the Ministry of Defence since January, stayed where he was to carry on the rout of CND. So did John Biffen, Keith Joseph (now at Education), Norman Tebbit, Norman Fowler, George Younger and Nicholas Edwards. Lord Hailsham, though now seventy-six, went back to the Woolsack. Lord Cockfield, relieved of the Department of Trade, also stayed in the Cabinet as Chancellor of the Duchy of Lancaster with no clear role except that he was useful in committee and in the Lords. Michael Jopling replaced Walker at Agriculture, while John Wakeham took over as Chief Whip. That was the new team. It was a measure of the change already wrought since 1979 that the Cabinet could no longer be usefully classified into 'wets' and 'dries'. In the medium term the only likely threat to Mrs Thatcher's dominance came from the undisguised ambition of Michael Heseltine.

6

Popular Capitalism

High noon

Two decades on, the second Thatcher Government looks like the zenith of Thatcherism. This, after all, was the period of economic recovery, when the economy – at least in the south of England – finally emerged from the recession of the early 1980s into the heady expansion of what came to be known as the 'Lawson boom'; it was the heroic period of privatisation, with the successful sell-off of whole utilities undreamed of in the first term; it was the time of deregulation in the City of London – the so-called 'Big Bang' – when quick fortunes were suddenly there to be made by young men in red braces known to the press as 'yuppies'; a time of tax cuts, easy credit and rapidly increased spending power for the fortunate majority able to enjoy it, leading to a heady consumer boom which helped float the Government back to office for a third term amid excited talk of a British economic 'miracle'. It was the moment when the hundred-year-old political argument between capitalism and socialism seemed to have been decisively resolved in favour of the former. The moral and practical superiority of the market as an engine of wealth creation and the efficient delivery of public services was incontestably established, its critics reduced to impotent irrelevance, while the Conservative party, under its all-conquering leader, the tireless personification of this liberation of the nation's energy, seemed likely to retain power for as long as she wanted. Her hegemony appeared complete; or in the catchphrase of the day, picked up from graffiti scrawled on a thousand walls, 'Maggie Rules OK'.

Yet it did not feel quite like that at the time. The years 1983–7 were seen by many of the Prime Minister's keenest supporters as a period of drift and wasted opportunity – Nicholas Ridley called them 'the locust years'[1] – when the Government, if not exactly blown off-course, was distracted from pursuing its long-term objectives by a series of bruising political battles and an accumulation of accidents which so sapped its energy and authority that, contrary to the legend of unchallenged dominance, the Tories actually trailed the supposedly unelectable Labour party – and sometimes the Alliance too – in the opinion polls for more than half the period. Margaret Thatcher's hyperactive personality unquestionably dominated the political stage; but her popularity steadily dwindled so that in 1986 her poll rating was barely higher than in the darkest days of 1981. Though in the event she was comfortably re-elected the following year, her ascendancy was never so secure as the triumphalism of her instant myth-makers contrived to suggest.

The second term got off to a bad start with a series of minor embarrassments described by the press as 'banana skins'. Then most of the second year, 1984–5, was overshadowed by a critical confrontation with the Tories' old nemesis, the National Union of Mineworkers, which stirred deep passions on both sides and brought parts of the country close to civil war. The Government eventually prevailed, but it used up a lot of political energy and capital in doing so. At the same time it had picked a harder battle than it expected over the abolition of the Greater London Council, as well as several more tussles with Labour-controlled local authorities around the country over the level of their spending. It faced serious challenges to public order at the Greenham Common air base, where the first American cruise missiles arrived in November 1983; in parts of London, Birmingham and Liverpool, where another wave of riots erupted in September 1985; and in London's docklands, where through much of 1986 the police fought pitched battles with the printing unions who were attempting to defy the Australian magnate Rupert Murdoch's imposition of new technology in the newspaper industry. A series of security controversies – from the high-handed banning of trade-union membership at the Government's satellite listening post at Cheltenham to the unsuccessful prosecution of a Ministry of Defence official, Clive Ponting, who admitted leaking classified information to the opposition but was nevertheless acquitted of breaching the Official Secrets Act – further served to keep the administration on the defensive.

In October 1984 an IRA bomb planted at the Conservative Party Conference hotel in Brighton claimed five lives, seriously injured two members of the Cabinet and only narrowly failed to kill Mrs Thatcher herself. The Government was more seriously destabilised in January 1986 by a major political crisis arising from the future of the Westland helicopter company, which cost two senior ministers their jobs and for a time even threatened the Prime Minister. Between them these events necessitated several hasty reshuffles which disrupted the ministerial team. Nigel Lawson and Geoffrey Howe survived as Chancellor and Foreign Secretary throughout, ensuring an element of continuity at the top. (Both, indeed, endured into the third term too.) But the second Thatcher Government saw two Home Secretaries, two Defence Secretaries, three Environment Secretaries, three Transport Secretaries and no fewer than four Secretaries of State for Trade and Industry. In addition Mrs Thatcher's attention was increasingly diverted from the domestic front by an exceptionally demanding foreign-policy agenda: not only the European Community, but Hong Kong, South Africa, Anglo-Irish negotiations on the future of Northern Ireland, the fallout from American military adventures in Grenada, Lebanon and Libya, and the emergence of a promising new leader in the Soviet Union who held out the possibility of an end to the Cold War – all these helped to ensure that even Mrs Thatcher's phenomenal energies were very fully stretched. There was not much time to chart the way ahead.

Recalling the period after Westland in her television memoirs, Mrs Thatcher herself admitted: 'It became a time when we stumbled over small things and were stopped from doing some of the things which I wanted to do because you couldn't go ahead, the timing just wasn't right.'[2] Harold Macmillan's famous dictum that governments are subject to the pressure of 'events, dear boy' has become a tiresome cliché. But it was more than usually true of Mrs Thatcher's second term.

As a result, she was never quite so dominant as she appeared. Immediately after the 1983 election Michael Foot announced that he was standing down as Labour leader. Though the party's laborious processes took three months to elect his successor, the result was never in much doubt. Neil Kinnock was young (forty-one), inexperienced (he had never held even junior office) and came from the left of the party: he was as emotionally committed as Foot to CND, and not much less hostile to Europe. Nevertheless he was fresh, idealistic and eloquent, if incurably verbose; he had grasped that Labour must change to make itself electable and quickly showed himself ready to jettison most of the left's unpopular ideological baggage. From the moment he took over, Labour's fortunes began to improve. There was, as it turned out, still a long way to go; but in the summer of 1984 the opposition registered its first lead in the polls since the invasion of the Falklands two years earlier.

At the same time Roy Jenkins was replaced as leader of the SDP by the much younger, more dashing and dynamic Dr David Owen. Owen's relationship with the Liberal leader David Steel was never easy; yet under the double-headed leadership of the two Davids the Alliance too quickly recovered its standing and from the end of 1984 maintained a regular presence between 25 and 33 per cent in the polls, winning a string of spectacular by-election victories as it had done in 1981–2. Mrs Thatcher's command of her party was never seriously challenged. Yet a powerful chorus of senior dissidents kept up a steady critique of the Government and its policies. The increasingly open condemnation of Ted Heath, now joined on the back benches by Francis Pym, was discreetly echoed from within the Cabinet by Peter Walker, Jim Prior and even John Biffen, and from the House of Lords by the old playactor himself, Harold Macmillan, now ennobled as the Earl of Stockton. The focus of their dissent was the high and still-rising level of unemployment which was splitting the country more sharply than ever before into Two Nations: the affluent and the jobless, the new service industries and the old manufacturing base, the increasingly prosperous south and the excluded north. From the beginning of the Parliament Mrs Thatcher was claiming that the recovery had begun; by its end Nigel Lawson was boasting of an economic transformation. But the Government's success was always hotly disputed by a wide coalition of critics, and was never in reality more than partial. Contrary to collective memory, the Thatcherite revolution did not carry all before it, even in 1983–7.

Banana skins

The first 'banana skins' began to afflict the Government as soon as the new Parliament met. On the very first day Mrs Thatcher was rebuffed over the choice of a new Speaker. She was sorry to see George Thomas retire, and made the mistake of allowing it to be known that she did not favour his deputy, Bernard Weatherill, to succeed him. She had hoped to use the job as a suitably dignified niche for Francis Pym or, when he declined, one of the other ex-ministers she had put out to grass – Humphrey Atkins, Norman St John Stevas or the former Solicitor-General, Sir Ian Percival. But the House of Commons is jealous of its independence and Tory and Labour backbenchers alike rallied to Weatherill. 'What seems to have clinched his election,' *The Times* commented, 'was the discovery by his fellow MPs that he did not have the Prime Minister's full approval.'[3] Then the Queen's Speech, as the programme of a new Government just re-elected with a massive majority, was generally seen as unimpressive. The only new elements were Bills to establish an independent prosecution service, cable television and a measure of data protection. *The Times* was disappointed that there really was no 'hidden manifesto', as Labour had consistently alleged. 'There is no evidence of a radical edge to the programme.'[4]

Mrs Thatcher showed her hand more clearly with two acts of Prime Ministerial prerogative. First, she finally did what many had expected her to do in 1979 and scrapped the Central Policy Review Staff – the Cabinet 'Think Tank' – explaining in a statement from Downing Street that 'the purposes for which the CPRS was set up are now being met satisfactorily in other ways'.[5] Its fate had been anticipated, but nevertheless shocked Whitehall. 'If an intelligent woman cannot profitably use fifteen of the best and brightest that Whitehall, the City, industry, the universities and the professions can provide,' *The Times* considered, 'there is a gap in her make-up.'[6] The *Guardian* recalled that the Think Tank 'was designed to serve the whole Cabinet and not just the Prime Minister' and saw its abolition as worrying evidence of the centralisation of power in Number Ten.[7] Then in the dissolution honours she refused Michael Foot's request for twenty-seven new Labour life peers to strengthen the opposition's presence in the Upper House, granting him only seven. More provocatively still, she fulfilled her long-trailed promise to resume the creation of hereditary peers, abandoned by Harold Wilson in 1964. Admittedly the first two she named, Willie Whitelaw and George Thomas, had no heirs – Whitelaw had only daughters and Thomas was unmarried – so the provocation was purely academic. But the message appeared to be defiantly anti-democratic.

There quickly followed two more parliamentary rebuffs. On 13 July the Government gave the new House an early opportunity to debate the re-introduction of capital punishment. With a large influx of new Tory Members, supporters of hanging, including the Prime Minister, hoped that this time – having failed in 1979 – they might be able to restore the death penalty, at least for terrorist murders and the killing of policemen. The new Home Secretary, Leon Brittan, reversed his previous opposition and spoke in favour of restoration. In the event capital punishment was still rejected by unexpectedly decisive majorities ranging from eighty-one (for the murder of a policeman) to 175 (for murder in furtherance of theft). The Cabinet was evenly divided, with Mrs Thatcher as always voting for restoration. Jim Prior, sitting beside her on the front bench, suggests that on this occasion she was in fact ambivalent, committed by her lifelong support for hanging yet aware of the practical difficulties for the Government, particularly in Northern Ireland, if it were restored. When the result was declared, however, 'her populist politics got the better of her. She shouted at Gerald Kaufman, Roy Hattersley and Peter Shore across the dispatch box that they didn't know what the people wanted, and that on the council housing estates the Labour leadership would get stick for turning down hanging.'[8]

The second slap in the face was on the question of MPs' pay. The Government threw out a recommendation by the Top Salaries Review Body that would have given Members an increase of 31 per cent. 'We thought that Ministers could not possibly take increases of that magnitude,' Mrs Thatcher explained. 'And we trusted that Members of Parliament would take the same view.'[9] She was too sanguine. The Government's offer of just 4 per cent provoked fury on both sides of the House, with Edward du Cann, the chairman of the 1922 Committee, acting as shop steward for the Tory rebels. In the event John Biffen was able to negotiate a compromise: increases of 5.5 per cent every year for the 1983 Parliament, with a permanent link to a certain grade of the Civil Service in the next. Ministers would take only an additional 1.3 per cent, and Mrs Thatcher herself continued to draw only the same as any other Cabinet minister (about £40,000), voluntarily forgoing an additional £10,000 as she had been doing since 1979. Nevertheless on 20 July seventy Tories supported an amendment to raise the grade with which their pay would be linked, and the Government was defeated by eight votes. This was further evidence that Mrs Thatcher's swollen majority would not always do her bidding, at least where their own interests were involved.

Just before the summer recess Lawson signalled his arrival at the Treasury by announcing a £500 million package of emergency spending cuts designed to reassure the City that there was to be no loosening of monetary policy. The cuts fell most heavily on defence and on the NHS, thus angering both the Tory right and the opposition simultaneously. The health cuts caused particular outrage, coming so soon after an election at which Mrs Thatcher had promised that the NHS was 'safe' with the Tories. In a series of damage-limitation interviews she now insisted that a reduction of less than 1 per cent in NHS staffing was merely prudent housekeeping, not a betrayal of election promises. 'If you see expenditure overrunning your forecast . . . then you obviously have to take action to keep it within your budget . . . And that's very, very good government.'[10] A few days later Patrick Jenkin raised fresh hackles by announcing the Government's intention to take powers to cap the rates of high-spending local councils. Mostly, of course, these would be Labour councils; but many traditionalist Tories were alarmed at this attack on the autonomy of local government and warned of opposition when the legislation came before the House in the autumn.

Finally, in the middle of all these ructions, the Government suffered the embarrassment of very nearly losing Willie Whitelaw's seat in the by-election caused by his elevation to the Lords. The voters of Penrith took a dim view of being asked to turn out a second time in seven weeks, and on a low poll the Alliance candidate cut the Tory majority from over 15,000 to just 552. Less than two months after the triumph of June, the Government reached the summer recess distinctly battered.

For some time Mrs Thatcher had been suffering from a torn retina in her right eye, which was affecting her vision. So at the beginning of August she underwent a laser operation at a private hospital in Windsor. This time she was obliged to stay in for three days – she was said to have done some work on the third day – and emerged wearing tinted glasses. But she resented being forced to admit to any hint of weakness, as an unlucky radio reporter who questioned her as she came out discovered. 'I'm fine,' she insisted, 'but then I always am. It's only just that we had this little bit of trouble . . . I can see clearly . . . I can see everything that's wrong with you.'[11] She went to Chequers for a few days and then to Switzerland for a full two weeks' holiday. Before she left she was reported to have signed 1,200 letters replying to well-wishers.[12]

During September Mrs Thatcher visited first Holland and Germany, then the United States and Canada, returning just in time to face a new headache when *Private Eye* broke the story of Cecil Parkinson's relationship with Sara Keays. Knowingly or not, the magazine actually named another Tory MP as the father of Miss Keays' baby. But the effect was to force Parkinson to issue a statement on 6 October acknowledging the truth, confessing that he had at one point proposed marriage to Miss Keays but had now decided after all to stay with his wife. Mrs Thatcher in turn revealed that she had known about the affair when she had appointed him to the DTI in June and stated firmly that 'the question of resignation does not and will not arise'.[13] Alan Clark – a shameless adulterer himself – was reassured to note that she did not take a moralistic attitude to Parkinson's infidelity but was determined to keep him in the Government.* It soon emerged that it was she who had persuaded Parkinson – as the price of retaining office – to stay with his wife, despite receiving 'stroppy letters' and 'all kinds of threat' from Colonel Keays, Sara's father.[15] Tory MPs admired her loyalty but doubted that she would be able to save him. By no coincidence the scandal had broken just before the party conference,

*On the contrary she was fascinated. Tim Bell told Woodrow Wyatt in 1989 that Mrs Thatcher was 'very interested in the peccadilloes of her entourage. When it was announced that . . . Sara Keays was pregnant she sat there looking very puzzled. She worked it out on her fingers and said, 'It must have been during the election campaign that he did it. I can't think how he found the time.'[14]

which should have been a victory rally with Parkinson the hero of the hour. When he spoke to the conference on Thursday 13 October he was still warmly received. The same day, however, Miss Keays gave an angry statement to *The Times*. She was enraged by editorials suggesting that she should have had the child aborted, while Parkinson had only been guilty of a 'silly blunder'. She revealed that Parkinson had first asked her to marry him as long ago as 1979; reneged in May 1983 when he learned that she was pregnant; changed his mind in June and again proposed marriage, when she accepted; and finally told her in September that he was going to stay with his wife after all.[16] Parkinson was now exposed as feeble as well as faithless, batted back and forth between two formidable women. There was nothing more Mrs Thatcher could do to save him. He resigned at midnight and left Blackpool before *The Times* had even hit the streets.

In her book, *A Question of Judgement*, Sara Keays was bitterly critical of Mrs Thatcher for making Parkinson break his promise to marry her, and for orchestrating a press campaign against her. 'It would appear that she allowed the authority of her office to be used to propagate lies in the media in order to conceal the true facts from the public and to discredit me,' she wrote.[17] There is no doubt that Miss Keays was the victim of some very unpleasant briefing designed to present her as a scorned and vengeful woman bent on inflicting maximum damage on her lover and on the whole Tory party. Mrs Thatcher, on the other hand, was widely praised. 'The only person who comes out of the affair with any credit is the Prime Minister,' Norman St John Stevas wrote in the *Sunday Express*. 'She has been compassionate, concerned, tolerant and Christian.'[18] She was represented as fighting for the sanctity of marriage. In truth she too was fighting for her man. Parkinson was not just a personal favourite, one of those who had been close to her during the Falklands, but her chosen heir, whom she had been grooming for the eventual succession. Even after his resignation she remained keen to have him back as soon as possible. 'He thinks very much the same way as I do and he is a source of great strength,' she told John Junor in 1986.[19] She would have liked to bring him back before the 1987 election; but John Wakeham persuaded her that Parkinson would not be considered to have purged his guilt until he had been re-elected by his constituents.[20] She was obliged to leave him in the sin-bin for four years.

With the sinner departed, the conference gave Mrs Thatcher a rapturous reception on Friday morning. Conscious that the Government had appeared to stumble since June, she struck a strongly upbeat note. She was careful to spread the credit for the achievements of the first term, paying tribute in turn to Howe, Lawson, Tebbit, Whitelaw and even Heseltine, as well as 'the man who so brilliantly organised the campaign' – whom she had no need to name. The Tories had won more than just an election victory on 9 June, she boasted. 'Something remarkable has happened in this country . . . I believe we have altered the whole course of British politics for at least a generation.' Back in 1975 Keith Joseph had set out the ambition not to occupy the centre ground but to create a new 'common ground' on the Conservatives' agenda of enterprise and competition. Less than ten years later she claimed, the Labour and Alliance conferences showed they had achieved it:

> We have created the new common ground, and that is why our opponents have been forced to shift their ground . . . We have entered a new era. The Conservative Party has staked out the common ground, and the other parties are tiptoeing onto it.[21]

Parkinson's downfall necessitated the first unintended Cabinet reshuffle. Norman Tebbit moved to the DTI; Tom King took over the Department of Employment; and Nicholas Ridley finally made it to the Cabinet, taking King's place at Transport. In addition Mrs Thatcher had already taken the precaution, before the conference, of appointing a new party chairman: her surprising choice was the youthful, eager but lightweight John Selwyn Gummer. Her reasoning was that she needed someone young – Gummer was forty-four – to combat Kinnock, Steel and Owen;[22] but Gummer lasted only two years in the job. None of these hasty appointments, in fact, was conspicuously successful; but Ridley's was the most significant. John Major, at the time an assistant whip, remembers being 'astonished' at Ridley's elevation: he had 'an original mind' but was 'wonderfully politically incorrect'.[23] To Mrs Thatcher, however, 'Nick's arrival was a silver lining to the cloud that hung over us following Cecil's departure.'[24] Once arrived, Ridley was to remain one of her most ardent and loyal disciples until one final indiscretion brought him down just before her own fall.

The Cabinet was now supposed to be united, with the old argument between wets and dries resolved; but it did not look much like it in the autumn of 1983. At conference both Prior and Biffen openly opposed Lawson's declared objective of pursuing tax cuts at the expense of public spending; while Peter Walker, in a message to the Tory Reform Group in December, echoed Pym's warnings from the back benches that the country faced social catastrophe if the Government did not make a priority of tackling unemployment.[25] But the worst embarrassment of all was the American invasion of Grenada – a Commonwealth country – to put down a Communist coup, with minimal reference to Britain. Both Geoffrey Howe, who in the Commons just the day before had confidently ruled out any prospect of American action, and Mrs Thatcher herself, whose vaunted special relationship with President Reagan was called into question, were publicly humiliated. At the turn of the year there was general agreement that the Government, when it should have been setting out confidently on its second term, had suffered 'six indifferent months': its handling of a whole range of issues had been 'visibly inept'.[26] 'There are always banana skins,' Mrs Thatcher had told the BBC's John Cole in May, 'but you don't have to tread on them.'[27] Since June she seemed unable to avoid them.

Ronald Butt in *The Times* was one writer who asked himself what had gone wrong. The truth, he suggested, was that Mrs Thatcher was not really a radical at all, but rather a cautious pragmatist who, since the election, was no longer surrounded by the unconventional advisers – John Hoskyns, Alfred Sherman, Alan Walters – who had provided her initial energy. The new head of her Policy Unit, the thirty-two-year-old John Redwood, was clever, 'but his political instinct is said to be chilly'. At the same time she had also lost Ian Gow, who had played a crucial role in the first term. His replacement, Michael Alison, was 'a reserved and rather remote figure, not naturally gregarious, who is not a natural liaison officer'. The result was that relations between the Prime Minister and her parliamentary troops had become 'a little distant . . . There is a feeling . . . that the Government has lost its political drive.' Yet most Tory MPs, Butt concluded, were actually happier with the prospect of a quieter life.[28] If so, their hopes were to be disappointed.

From bust to boom

Amid all the Government's minor embarrassments, however, the central political front was as always the economy: and here there were definite signs of recovery. An OECD (Organisation for Economic Cooperation and Development) report in December showed Britain enjoying the fastest growth in Europe; a CBI survey in January confirmed the trend of rising activity. GDP, Mrs Thatcher told the Commons, was now back to its 1979 level – a somewhat limited success after four and a half years, but one which had been achieved, she pointed out, 'with 1.7 million fewer people in the workforce'.[29] In other words unemployment was up, but so was productivity. She insisted that unemployment would start to fall with the creation of new jobs, and over the next few weeks looked forward variously to the growth of an 'enterprise culture' – the first time she had used the phrase[30] – and 'a go-getter society'[31] to create them. More than 200,000 new jobs had already been created in the service sector, she claimed, in the first nine months of 1983.

In Nigel Lawson she now had a Chancellor who shared her own ability to project a bullish sense of optimism. Her relationship with Lawson was very different from that with Geoffrey Howe. Whereas she was frequently impatient with Howe's pedestrian manner, knowing that he was no more of an economist than she was, she respected Lawson's expertise to the extent that she was slightly in awe of him.* 'Nigel is an outstanding Treasury minister,' she told George Gale a few days after appointing him, 'and has a total command, I should think an almost unrivalled command in everything related to the Treasury.'[33] This was a recipe for trouble in the long run, because she was very insistent on her own prerogative as First Lord of the Treasury, and their instincts – on taxation, on interest rates and on the exchange rate – increasingly diverged. But for the moment she was happy to indulge him. A journalist at heart and a natural gambler, Lawson was mercurial and defiantly ill-disciplined; whereas Howe would have his budget speech virtually drafted by January, Lawson needed the inspiration of a deadline and would leave as much as possible to the last moment. Howe had worked hard at keeping his relationship with Mrs Thatcher as smooth as possible: when Alan Walters was her special adviser in 1981–3, for instance, Howe was careful to keep him fully involved in the Treasury 'loop', so as to minimise friction between Number Ten and Number Eleven. Long before the ructions of 1988–9, Lawson was much more jealous of his independence and played his cards much closer to his chest.[34] He had unbounded confidence in his own judgement and disliked being at the Prime Minister's beck and call. It was 'not pleasant' living next door to Mrs Thatcher, his wife told Woodrow Wyatt in 1986. 'He can be sent for far too easily and she can come through at any time.'[35] The longer he stayed at the Treasury – and he

---

*Not only did Mrs Thatcher never dare to bully Lawson the way she bullied Howe, but he was one of very few colleagues who could silence her when necessary. Once when she kept interrupting Keith Joseph, Lawson 'suddenly leant across the table and snapped, "Shut up, Prime Minister, just occasionally let someone get a word in edgeways." For the first and last time,' Nicholas Edwards recalled, 'I saw Margaret Thatcher blush and then for twenty minutes she was silent . . . I don't remember any other occasion when a Cabinet colleague was quite so blunt.'[32]

was the longest-serving Chancellor since Lloyd George – the more he
felt that managing the economy was his preserve, which she should
leave to him.

Even with hindsight, though she blamed him unambiguously for
'errors' towards the end of her premiership, Mrs Thatcher was much
more forgiving of Lawson than she could ever bring herself to be of
Howe. He was 'a Chancellor of rare technical grasp and constructive
imagination', she wrote in her memoirs. He 'did not generally like to
seek or take advice', and his way of proceeding was 'impossibly secretive', so that she had to plant her own spies in the Treasury who
'furtively filled me in' on what he was up to.[36] But with very talented
people, she recognised on television, 'you have to take the rough with
the smooth'.[37]

Lawson's first budget, in March 1984, delighted her. In their respective memoirs Lawson describes the Prime Minister as 'ecstatic', while
she characterised it as 'Nigel at his brilliant best'.[38] Though no further
cuts in the basic rate were possible just yet, the new Chancellor boldly
signalled his ambitions as a tax reformer. First, he took Howe's switch
from direct to indirect taxation a stage further by raising personal
thresholds, taking 850,000 low earners out of income tax altogether,
compensating by raising excise duties and extending VAT to takeaway
food and building repairs.* More important, he cut corporation tax
over three years from 52 to 35 per cent, as an incentive to investment;
abolished the 15 per cent surcharge on investment income; and
completed Howe's phasing out of the National Insurance surcharge
(the so-called 'tax on jobs'). At the same time, he managed to project
a sharp fall in the PSBR, though in the event this was foiled by the
cost of the miners' strike. One friendly commentator called this 'the
most Thatcherite' budget so far.[39] Somewhat prematurely, Ronald Butt
judged that it established Lawson's credentials to succeed Mrs Thatcher
in due course.[40]

Clever tax changes, however, did nothing – at least in the short term
– to meet the rising clamour for action to tackle unemployment. The
Falklands Factor was now double-edged: if Mrs Thatcher could spend
millions recapturing and now defending some barely inhabited islands
in the South Atlantic, it was asked, why could she not apply some of
the same resolution to conquering the great social evil on her doorstep?

---

*The former was splashed by the tabloids as a tax on fish and chips. But the
latter, by making the repair and restoration of old buildings more expensive than
demolishing them and building anew, had far more serious long-term consequences in cities, towns and villages up and down the country.

She now enjoyed a huge majority; the recession was officially over and the economy was supposed to be recovering; yet unemployment was still rising. She was running out of alibis. In fact the economic prospect was much less sunny than the Government claimed. The balance of payments was sliding into deficit as imports rose but exports did not; sterling was falling, forcing Lawson to raise interest rates to 12 per cent, which risked strangling the recovery in its cradle. At the same time the miners' strike against pit closures was settling into a long and bitter struggle. Twelve months after her almost uncontested re-election, Labour showed that it was back in business by gaining fifteen seats in the European elections in June. The same month Francis Pym voiced the reviving discontent of One Nation Tories in a slim, elegant critique of the Thatcher style entitled *The Politics of Consent*. He applauded some of what the Government had achieved in its first term, but regretted its 'harsh public tone' and called once again for an industrial strategy built on consensus and national investment.[41] Just before the summer recess, Mrs Thatcher was forced to make an unusually defensive reply to Neil Kinnock's first no-confidence motion since becoming Labour leader.

'Creating new jobs is the main challenge of our time,' she acknowledged. But the Government was meeting it by tackling the 'fundamental causes' of unemployment, not just the symptoms. Thanks to the 'prudent financial policies' of Howe and Lawson, she insisted, 'the prize of lower inflation has been won, and we shall not put it in jeopardy now. Stable prices remain our eventual goal.' New jobs would come from new technology, but she accepted an obligation to mitigate the hardship of transition 'by generous redundancy payments, by retraining and by helping to create new businesses'. The number of people in work was actually rising – she claimed that 340,000 were finding jobs every month – but the number seeking work was rising even faster. School leavers had outstripped those entering retirement by over a million since 1978.[42]

This was all true, but it did not cut much ice against the relentlessly rising headline figure of 3.2 million unemployed. In August Mrs Thatcher bowed to pressure to be seen to be doing something by appointing David Young from the Manpower Services Commission (MSC) as an unpaid Minister without Portfolio to head a new 'Enterprise Unit' in the Cabinet Office – or as Bernard Ingham encouraged the press to spin it, 'Minister for Jobs'. Young was an energetic businessman with a special interest in training who had become a director of the Centre for Policy Studies in 1979 and an adviser to Keith Joseph at the Department of Industry, before Norman Tebbit appointed him to the

MSC. He had no background in politics, and was not even a member of the Conservative party, but over the next few years – ennobled as Lord Young of Graffham – he rose by rapid steps to a key position in Mrs Thatcher's court, attracting a good deal of jealousy from colleagues who had struggled up the hard way. His initial appointment inevitably upset the Employment Secretary, Tom King, on whose territory he was set to trespass.[43] But Mrs Thatcher would hear not a word against him. 'Others bring me problems,' she was reported to have said. 'David brings me solutions.'[44] In fact Young caused her more than his share of problems in the next few years; but in her memoirs she still praised him warmly as someone who 'understood how to make things happen'.[45] In 1984 that was a gift she badly needed.

At the party conference at Brighton in October – this was the conference overshadowed by the IRA's bombing of the Grand Hotel – she defied the terrorists and insisted that the Government must and would prevail against the miners; but she had to devote the longest section of her speech to unemployment. 'To suggest . . . that we do not care about it is as deeply wounding as it is utterly false.' Rejecting 'Keynesian' arguments for government stimulation of the economy, she asserted that Keynes' modern followers misrepresented what he actually believed. 'It was all set out in the 1944 White Paper on employment. I bought it then. I have it still . . . I re-read it frequently,' she claimed, though on this occasion she did not actually produce it.* 'On page one it states, "employment cannot be created by Act of Parliament or by Government action alone" . . . It was true then. It is true now.' The White Paper, she said, was full of 'basic truths' about the danger of inflation and the importance of enterprise:

> If I had come out with all this today some people would call it Thatcherite, but in fact it was vintage Maynard Keynes. He had a horror of inflation, a fear of too much State control and a belief in the market.

Having established that Keynes was a good Thatcherite, she once again placed her faith in new technology to create new jobs, blamed the unions for obstructing training schemes, but insisted in characteristically personal style that there was not a bottomless pot of Government money for capital investment:

---

*Two weeks later in the Commons, challenged at Prime Minister's Questions by the young Tony Blair, she did reach into her handbag and bring out her well-marked copy.[46]

If we want more for investment I have to ask my colleagues in Cabinet: 'What are you going to give up? Or you? Or you? Or you?' Or should I perhaps ask them, 'Whose pay claim are you going to cut? The doctors'? The police's? The nurses'? I do not find many takers.

She listed some projects for which the Government had – 'by careful budgeting' – found money: the M25 motorway, the electrification of British Rail ('if it can make it pay'), forty-nine new hospitals since 1979. 'Of course we look at various things like new power stations, and in a year after drought we look at things like more investment in the water supply industry.' But the message was clear: there would be no massive spending programme to create jobs.[47] On the contrary she specifically repeated during the autumn that the road to prosperity lay through tax cuts.

Accordingly the chorus of criticism swelled. Pym, Heath, Walker – the usual dissidents – were joined in December, first by one of the original postwar founders of the One Nation Group, Lord Alport,* who warned that Mrs Thatcher 'will end up destroying the party she leads and will leave behind her . . . a nation divided against itself' unless she changed her policies;[48] and then by the even older Harold Macmillan, making his maiden speech in the House of Lords at the age of ninety, twenty years after leaving the Commons. The alarm of these grandees was magnified by the news that for the first time in modern history the UK was about to record a trading deficit on manufactured goods. This, combined with the strength of the dollar, caused a sharp fall in the value of sterling, leading in January 1985 to a full-scale crisis when the pound – from a value of $1.40 twelve months earlier – practically touched parity with the dollar. The crisis was aggravated by Bernard Ingham blithely telling the press that the Prime Minister was unworried by the falling pound. For once Ingham was out of touch with his mistress's thinking. Though theoretically she believed in letting sterling find its own level on the money markets, in practice, as Nigel Lawson recalled, she was 'schizoid' about exchange rates and 'fixated' on the dollar: the prospect of parity 'put the fear of God into her'.[49] To show that the Government was not prepared to let sterling fall any further, Lawson raised interest rates by 2 per cent and then had to repeat the dose, to 14 per cent, when a second panic

---

*Cuthbert Alport had been the local Tory candidate when Margaret Roberts was a Young Conservative in Colchester in 1948–9 (see *The Grocer's Daughter*, pp.69–71).

followed at the end of the month; while Mrs Thatcher privately persuaded President Reagan to lend American support and publicly went on television to 'talk up' the pound by insisting that its current valuation was too low (and the dollar too high). The medicine worked. By March the pound was back to £1.25, and Lawson was able to start bringing interest rates down again. But it had been a nasty few weeks, which exposed an underlying weakness in the British economy. It was all very well blaming the strong dollar; but the same consideration did not affect other European currencies as it affected sterling. The primary cause of the collapse of sterling, Roy Jenkins wrote in a letter to *The Times*, was that 'the rest of the world cannot see how we are going to pay our way when the oil runs down'.[50]

So the pressure was unrelenting. At Mrs Thatcher's insistence, Lawson was obliged to flag his 1985 budget as 'a budget for jobs'. This was not at all his priority. The previous autumn he had declared that unemployment was a social, not an economic problem, and cheerfully told an American journalist that 'economically and politically, Britain can get along with double-digit unemployment'.[51] His headline priority was sterling, and his real interest was further tax reform. He wanted to finance a further reduction in the basic rate by cutting middle-class tax perks – not only mortgage-interest tax relief but also relief on private pension payments. Lawson believed as a matter of principle in phasing out the accumulated clutter of sticks and carrots in pursuit of a 'neutral' tax system. But Mrs Thatcher would not hear of it. 'Our people won't stand for it,' she told him.[52] Second, Lawson wanted to extend VAT to newspapers and magazines and to children's clothes: the latter was an obvious vote loser, which the Prime Minister was firmly pledged against, while she insisted that it was no time to antagonise the press. All he could do – with patently little enthusiasm – was cut National Insurance contributions, and put another £400 million into the Youth Training Scheme and the Community Programme. After the plaudits for his first budget twelve months earlier, this lacklustre package pleased nobody.

That spring, for the first time since before the Falklands war, there was talk of a leadership challenge in the autumn. In the county-council elections in May the Tories lost a lot of seats, mainly to the Alliance, and control of several traditionally Tory shires, and now trailed third in the opinion polls. Patrick Cormack, a backbencher not previously seen as wet – indeed he had once edited a collection of Thatcherite essays entitled *Right Turn* – voiced widespread frustration with the Government's 'unimaginative laissez-faire attitude to the greatest social problem of our time' and demanded a concerted effort to cut unemployment by at least 500,000 in the next eighteen months.[53] A few days later Francis Pym launched his new Tory dissident group, Centre Forward, asserting in a speech at Cambridge that 'responsible financial management does not itself constitute an economic strategy'.[54] In fact most of the grumblers were still afraid to put their heads above the parapet; apart from a few hardened malcontents – Ian Gilmour, Robert Rhodes James, Julian Critchley – the press found it hard to discover anyone who would admit to belonging: several supposed members quickly backed off, and the group entirely failed to establish an identity. But the evidence of discontent – focused perhaps more effectively in a new all-party pressure group, the Unemployment Institute – was sufficient to force Mrs Thatcher to promise, in a radio interview on 24 May, that the Government would take further action if unemployment did not fall within a year. She denied talk of 'jitters' in the party, rejected Pym's critique and dismissed the polls as the usual mid-term dip. 'There are no jitters,' she protested rather too strenuously. 'Let us get this straight! There are no jitters and it is no earthly good using that word . . . There are no jitters!' She accepted that there was 'unease' about unemployment and high interest rates – 'of course there is' – but insisted that Lawson's measures would take effect in time. 'It will take about a year to work through. Then we will have to have a look and see if that is enough, and if not then we shall have to consider other things.' She stressed how much the Government was spending on roads, hospitals and water supply, and actually suggested that this work was being undertaken to create jobs. 'We hope that it will finish in reducing the numbers of the unemployed. That is why we are doing it.'[55] She could not get much more Keynesian than that.

At the beginning of August the Government lost the previously safe seat of Brecon and Radnor to the Alliance, and the Tories' opinion-poll rating sank to 24 per cent. Just as in the dark days of 1980–1, Mrs Thatcher tried to make a virtue of her refusal to change tack, dismissing calls for flexibility. 'People do not want a government to be so flexible that it becomes invertebrate,' she told the *Sun*. 'I think they want a government with a bit of spine . . . You don't want a government of flexi-toys.'[56] But she was becoming privately 'dejected' that the public was not responding to the evidence of economic recovery.[57] She was irritated by the negativity of the media in harping constantly on the bad news. Once, visiting a factory in Wallsend making drilling equipment for the North Sea, she turned angrily on a TV reporter who suggested that she should meet some of the 20 per cent unemployed in the region. 'Look, I cannot do everything!' she exclaimed. She tried

to highlight the success stories: that was the way to encourage investment and get more jobs to the north-east – 'not always standing there
as moaning minnies. Now stop it!' she told him. 'Cheer up and go
and boost the success and you're much more likely to get more jobs
that way.'⁵⁸ Like Heath and Wilson before her, she was becoming frustrated by British industry's slowness to take advantage of all that she
felt the Government was doing to help it.

The traditional response to party jitters is a Cabinet reshuffle; and
so at the beginning of September Mrs Thatcher rearranged her pack
to bring on some fresh faces – mainly from the Heathite wing of the
party. 'I generally found,' she wrote in her memoirs, 'that the Left
seemed to be best at presentation'.⁵⁹ Better presentation was what the
Government needed at this moment, particularly in three areas. First,
she acknowledged the salience of unemployment by moving David
Young to the Department of Employment, displacing the rather
wooden Tom King, and partnered him with the rumbustious Kenneth
Clarke as Paymaster-General to represent him in the Commons. She
now had two energetic and ambitious ministers visibly responsible for
tackling unemployment.

Second, the Government had been losing the propaganda war over
the abolition of the GLC: Patrick Jenkin at the Department of the
Environment had proved to be no match for the populist skills of Ken
Livingstone, so Mrs Thatcher replaced him with Kenneth Baker, another
former Heathite now working his way back into favour, who was reckoned to be good on television. Though never as close to her as Cecil
Parkinson had been, Baker offered the same smooth presentational
skills, which she always valued and later deployed to good effect in
Central Office.

Third, and most important for the presentation of the Government's
case in the country, she moved Norman Tebbit from the DTI to
replace John Gummer as party chairman. Gummer, she wrote in her
memoirs, 'just did not have the political clout or credibility to rally
the troops. I had appointed him as a sort of nightwatchman: but he
seemed to have gone to sleep on the job.'⁶⁰ Even before his serious
injuries in the Brighton bombing, Tebbit had not proved a great
success at the DTI: he was, she reflected in her memoirs, 'not a first-
class administrator'.⁶¹ He had been – understandably – not the same
man since Brighton, but she hoped he would bring a more robust
approach to Central Office. In another populist touch she appointed
the millionaire novelist (and former Tory MP) Jeffrey Archer to be
deputy chairman to help re-enthuse the faithful in the constituencies.
Mrs Thatcher wisely never trusted Archer very far, but she thought

he could do no serious harm, and might possibly raise morale, as a cheerleader.

Tebbit's replacement at the DTI was Leon Brittan, woundingly removed from the Home Office where he had never looked convincing. Douglas Hurd, a much safer pair of hands, stepped up from Belfast to be the new Home Secretary, while Tom King took over Northern Ireland. (Prior had left the Government the previous year.) One further change saw Peter Rees replaced as Chief Secretary to the Treasury by John McGregor – yet another former political secretary of Ted Heath. The old wets had been severely culled since 1979, and the Thatcherite true believers had begun to take their places in September 1981; but September 1985 marked a third stage in the evolution of the Thatcher Cabinet, with the advance of a new generation who – though happy to serve her – were not instinctive Thatcher supporters.

As it happened, the Westland imbroglio forced yet another reshuffle only four months later, in January 1986. The gaps left by the departure of Michael Heseltine and Leon Brittan were filled by George Younger and Paul Channon respectively, while Malcolm Rifkind – the first of a still younger generation, not yet forty – took Younger's place at the Scottish Office. In May 1986 Keith Joseph's retirement necessitated yet a further round of musical chairs. This time the Prime Minister did manage to do more for the right: Baker moved on to Education, but Nicholas Ridley was promoted from Transport to Environment, John Moore took over Transport, while outside the Cabinet another rising younger Thatcherite, Norman Lamont, became Financial Secretary to the Treasury. The effect of the rapidly changing personnel around her was to focus attention more than ever on Mrs Thatcher herself.

The autumn of 1985 brought no relief. In September and early October another wave of rioting broke out in the Handsworth district of Birmingham and spread to Brixton, Toxteth and, most seriously, Tottenham in north London, where a policeman was brutally murdered. The spark in every case was tension between black youths and the police. Enoch Powell grimly recalled his 1968 prophecy of racial violence; but despair arising from unemployment, not race, was clearly the underlying cause. Soon afterwards a House of Lords select committee – chaired by Ted Heath's old confidant Lord Aldington, but nevertheless regarded as authoritative and well informed – published a report warning of the irreparable loss of industrial capacity since 1979 and challenging the Government's belief that expanding service industries would fill the gap. Services could not bridge the looming balance-of-payments deficit for the simple reason that they were not exportable. As the *Observer*'s William Keegan put it, 'A proliferation of part-time barmaids was not enough.'[62] Again at the party conference Mrs Thatcher insisted that there was 'no problem which occupies more of my thinking' than unemployment. 'Scarce a day passes without the Government looking at new ways of speeding job creation'; and she listed all the schemes David Young was introducing to encourage employment.[63] But still unemployment went on rising. In December the Church of England joined in the chorus of concern with a report on social breakdown and demoralisation in the inner cities, entitled *Faith in the City*. The Government's attempt to dismiss the report as 'Marxist' – a response attributed to an unnamed Cabinet minister – was ridiculed as ludicrously wide of the mark.

'We will not reflate,' Mrs Thatcher promised at Blackpool. 'You cannot choose to have either inflation or unemployment. They are not alternatives . . . You cannot build a secure future on dishonest money.'[64] The conquest of inflation, she declared later in the year, was still the Government's 'paramount objective'.[65] In his Mansion House speech in the City of London in October, Lawson appeared to say the same thing. 'The inflation rate,' he told the assembled bankers and financiers, 'is judge and jury.'[66] Yet behind this outward agreement, a divide was beginning to open between the Prime Minister and her Chancellor. What Lawson was signalling in this speech was his abandonment of formal monetarism. In its pure form, at the time of the Medium Term Financial Strategy, monetary targets – £M3 – had been the judge and jury. Hit those, Lawson had then believed, and low inflation would inevitably follow. Now he had lost faith in £M3. Inflation had fallen since 1982 even though £M3 had far exceeded its target. Seeking a more reliable indicator, he had started targeting the exchange rate instead, believing that a stable pound would keep inflation under control. In declaring that inflation was 'judge and jury' he was covertly substituting pragmatism for fixed targets. The proof of the Government's pudding would be in the eating: the only useful measure of inflation was inflation itself. 'This,' William Keegan comments, 'was breathtaking stuff from the architect of the MTFS.'[67]

It was the traumatic plunge and recovery of sterling at the beginning of 1985 which converted Lawson to the idea that the time had come to join the Exchange Rate Mechanism of the European Monetary System. Initially sceptical of international co-operation, he had become fascinated – Lady Thatcher would later say seduced – at meetings of the G7 finance ministers by the flattering delusion that a handful of wise men could manage the money markets. The first fruit of this international action was the Plaza Agreement – signed in the Plaza Hotel, New York – in September 1985, by which the Americans agreed to try to drive the dollar down by 10 per cent. As part of this process Lawson was ready to recommend to Mrs Thatcher that Britain should sign up to the ERM. He was supported by all his senior officials, by his predecessor Geoffrey Howe, now converted to the Foreign Office line, and by the Governor of the Bank. But Mrs Thatcher was resolutely opposed.

'I knew they were ganging up on me,' she later declared on television.[68] And in her memoirs she wrote scornfully: 'There is nothing more obstinate than a fashionable consensus.'[69] So on 13 November she convened a carefully chosen *ad hoc* meeting of colleagues whom she thought she could count on to support her: Leon Brittan, Norman Tebbit, John Biffen and Willie Whitelaw. Armed with a paper from Alan Walters, she raised every possible practical objection. Contrary to her expectations, however, Brittan and Tebbit both came out in support of Lawson, which persuaded Whitelaw to lend his weight, as usual, to what he thought was the overwhelming consensus. 'If the Chancellor, the Governor and the Foreign Secretary are agreed,' he concluded, 'then that should be decisive. It has certainly decided me.'[70] To have her way, Mrs Thatcher was forced into one of the crudest assertions of Prime Ministerial will of her entire premiership. Faced with the unanimity of her senior colleagues, she told them bluntly: 'I disagree. If you join the EMS you will have to do so without me.'[71] 'There was a deathly silence,' Lawson recalled, 'and then she left the room.'[72] Shattered, Lawson wondered if he should resign; but Whitelaw and Tebbit assured him that if he persisted she would eventually come round, as she did on so many other issues to which she was initially opposed.[73] In fact this was one matter on which she remained immovable right up to October 1990.

Though she framed her objections as matters of timing and judgement, she was actually adamantly opposed on principle – or rather two principles, economic and patriotic. On the one hand she believed, as part of her free-market economic philosophy, that exchange rates could not be fixed and it was folly for governments to try to buck the markets. Though in practice she sometimes wavered, she remembered the Heath Government's inglorious attempt to join the European 'snake' in 1972, which lasted only a few weeks, and she did not intend to suffer the same humiliation. On the other hand, and somewhat contradictorily, she was instinctively opposed to sacrificing any shred of sovereignty over the value of the pound or the British Government's right – illusory as it might be in practice – to set its own interest rates to try to fix it. These two objections, fiercely maintained for the next five years against the growing determination of both Lawson and Howe to join the ERM by the back door if necessary, represented a ticking bomb at the heart of the Government. In their memoirs, Howe and Lawson both argue that the failure to join the ERM in 1985 was a missed opportunity which, had it been seized, would have averted most of the problems of the late 1980s. In hers, conversely, Lady Thatcher blames the return of inflation on Lawson's attempt to join the ERM by stealth. The two positions are irreconcilable and ultimately unprovable. What is certain is that this fundamental disagreement between a determined Prime Minister and an equally stubborn Chancellor ultimately destroyed them both.

It was in 1986 that Lawson's economic management finally began to show results. In February Mrs Thatcher was driven to admit that unemployment would probably not begin to fall before the next election.[74] In fact David Young's training schemes at last began to take effect, and in October the headline figure turned down, for the first time since 1979. At the beginning of the year a sudden drop in the price of oil stymied Lawson's hopes of dramatic cuts in income tax in his budget; but he still contrived to take a penny off the standard rate (bringing it to twenty-nine pence). Battered by the fallout of the Westland crisis, Lawson wrote, 'Margaret was delighted . . . once I had reassured her that the overall Budget arithmetic was prudent.'[75] Characteristically, however, she was nervous when Lawson announced that his goal was a standard rate of twenty-five pence; this seemed to her a hostage to fortune. In fact the sliding oil price proved unexpectedly beneficial: sterling fell against other European currencies, giving British exports over the year the benefit of an effective 16 per cent devaluation, without the political odium that accompanies a formal devaluation. Suddenly the economy entered a 'virtuous circle'.[76] Low inflation and low interest rates combined to promote 3 per cent growth (the fastest in the EC). Faster growth meant falling unemployment and higher tax revenues. Higher revenues, further boosted by increased VAT on soaring consumer spending and the windfall proceeds of privatisation, enabled the Chancellor in his 1987 budget to achieve the elusive hat-trick of higher spending, reduced borrowing and further tax cuts, just in time for a summer election. No wonder that from the autumn of 1986 the polls began to move back in the Government's favour, or that by the spring the Tories were once again ahead.

Lawson once told William Keegan that his ambition was to be 'the British Erhard' – a reference to the West German finance minister, Ludwig Erhard, celebrated as the architect of the German 'economic miracle' of the 1950s.[77] By 1987 he was boasting that he had achieved it. The press hailed him as the most successful Chancellor of modern times; Mrs Thatcher and jubilant Tory backbenchers alike basked in his reflected glory. The key to the apparent success was that most of the population – the twenty-five million in work – had more money to spend and were spending it, stimulating an explosion of small businesses and services: new shops, restaurants and wine bars, electrical consumer goods like videos and microwaves, conservatories and home improvements of every sort. Economic growth was visible, the City of London was booming and there was suddenly a heady whiff of optimism and opportunity in the air – just as the Tories had always promised would flow from deregulation and incentives.

Even as the Lawson boom took off, however, sceptical critics warned that it was not merely partial and unbalanced, but even on its own terms fragile and unsustainable. It was a boom founded on reckless consumer spending, stimulated by pay rises way above the rate of inflation, by easy credit and tax cuts paid for by oil and privatisation revenues, not based on long-term investment or increased domestic production. In fact it blatantly belied all Mrs Thatcher's homilies about good housekeeping. Both individual families and the nation as a whole were living beyond their means. While average incomes rose by 35 per cent between 1983 and 1987, personal indebtedness rose four times as fast in the same period: new bank lending trebled, and the number of mortgages doubled in 1986–7 alone. For the first time ever the average British household was spending more than it earned. On the national scale, increased consumption was sucking in imports at twice their 1979 level, while manufacturing output was only just back to the 1979 figure. The deficit was covered only by the temporary bonus of North Sea oil, which was not being invested for the future. The domestic manufacturing capacity to supply the new demand had been destroyed in 1979–81 and was no longer there to be revived: industrial investment was actually 16 per cent less in 1986 than it had been in 1979. The illusion of an economic miracle since 1983 was a statistical sleight-of-hand achieved by measuring growth only from the trough of the economic cycle in 1981; measured from peak to peak, average growth over the cycle was still only 1.8 per cent – actually lower than in the previous Labour cycle of the late 1970s.[78] In 1987 Britain's GNP fell behind that of Italy – an event gleefully hailed by the Italians as *il surpasso*.

Lawson's boom, in short, contained the seeds of both renewed inflation and the next slump. Having abandoned the excessive restraints of monetarism, he had swung to the opposite extreme and unleashed a headlong pre-election spending spree that was essentially no different from the previous Tory booms of Reggie Maudling (1963–4) and Tony

Barber (1972–3) – except that he had now deprived himself of the traditional tools which previous Chancellors had used to check over-heating: incomes policy, credit controls, exchange controls. Exuding a gambler's confidence, Lawson professed himself blithely unconcerned about the growing trade gap, still insisting that manufacturing no longer mattered.[79] He was likewise unworried by the warning signs of returning inflation, assuring Woodrow Wyatt in December 1986 that a small increase before the election would remind people 'how awful inflation would be if Labour got back'. When Wyatt suggested that he was getting into a dangerous position with wages rising twice as fast as inflation, Lawson replied cheerfully: 'Yes, but it's very good elec-torally.' His priority was frankly to win the election, then make any necessary adjustments afterwards.[80] Like the sorcerer's apprentice, he assumed that he could turn the tap off when he needed to.

Mrs Thatcher was instinctively more prudent: already in the autumn of 1986 she sensed that something was going wrong. At a Chequers seminar on 19 October she voiced her worries about another Barber boom. Lawson dismissed her fears, and claims in his memoirs to have been right to do so, since her facts were wrong. In particular she thought that borrowing was out of control, when the PSBR was one indicator that was actually well below its target, and she worried unnecessarily about the falling pound when she herself had refused to peg it by joining the ERM.[81] In December she refused to let Lawson raise interest rates when hindsight suggests it would have been right to do so. (This was a long-running battle between them, with Mrs Thatcher always sensitive to the effect on mortgages.) Nevertheless her intuition – as Lawson grudgingly concedes – was right. 'Perhaps,' as the former Labour minister Edmund Dell commented, 'if Lawson had paid more atten-tion to her hunches and less to her reasoning, his economic manage-ment might have been better. But that would have been too much to expect from so cerebral a Chancellor.'[82] For her part, Mrs Thatcher failed to act decisively on her hunch. On the one hand she was still in thrall to her Chancellor's greater expertise. On the other she was grateful for the turn-up in the polls and was swept up in the general excitement surrounding what she called 'popular capitalism'.

The phrase is said to have been coined, ironically, by Michael Heseltine, at a Young Conservative conference shortly after he walked out of the Cabinet at the beginning of 1986, though *The Times* report of his speech refers only to 'caring capitalism' – a rather different thing.[83] A year earlier Lawson had hailed the privatisation of British Telecom as marking 'the birth of people's capitalism'.[84] Mrs Thatcher first used the words on *The Jimmy Young Programme* on 26 February

1986, when she declared: 'We've got what I call popular capitalism.'[85] Thereafter she made the phrase her own, trying it out again in an interview for Italian television on 10 March ('And so I often say that what I am trying to do is to have popular capitalism. That means everyone has an opportunity to acquire either some land or savings or goods, or have . . . some savings behind them') and several times more in the next few weeks.[86] She adopted it as the defining slogan of her political project in a speech to the Conservative Central Council, meeting at Felixstowe, on 15 March. This was a critical speech in which Mrs Thatcher tried to put the trauma of Westland behind her and came out fighting for her political life. First she looked back, listing the principal achievements of her Government so far – taming the unions, curbing inflation and beginning to dismantle the public sector:

> Seven years ago, who would have dared forecast such a transformation of Britain? This didn't come about because of consensus. It happened because we said: This we believe, this we will do. It's called leadership.

Then she looked forward, with perhaps her first dangerous touch of hubris:

> There has been the odd report recently that Thatcherism has run its course and is on the way out. As an informed source close to Downing Street, I have to report that those reports are eyewash. We are only just beginning . . .
>   You may feel that the first seven years of Conservative Government have produced some benefits for Britain. And so they have. But the next seven are going to produce more – many more. And the next seven after that, more still.

At a time when the Tories were third in the polls, it took some nerve to set her horizon on the year 2000. But fired up by adversity, Mrs Thatcher expounded her vision. Conservatism, she explained, was 'not some abstract theory [but] a crusade to put power in the hands of ordinary people':

> And a very popular crusade it is proving. Tenants are jumping at the opportunity to buy their own council houses. Workers are jumping at the opportunity to buy shares in their own privatised companies. Trade unionists are jumping at the opportunity . . . to

decide 'who rules' in their union. And the rest of Britain looks on with approval. For popular capitalism is biting deep.

By contrast, she concluded, socialist crusades to go back to the old ways were 'muted nowadays':

For popular capitalism, which is the economic expression of liberty, is proving a much more attractive means for diffusing power in our society.

Socialists cry 'Power to the people', and raise the clenched fist as they say it. We all know what they really mean – power over people, power to the State.

To us Conservatives, popular capitalism means what it says: power through ownership to the man and woman in the street, given confidently with an open hand.[87]

Property-owning democracy

'Popular capitalism' was Thatcherite shorthand for three separate revolutions in British economic life: wider home ownership, wider share ownership and an 'enterprise economy' characterised by more small businesses and more people becoming self-employed. The first revolution was well under way in Mrs Thatcher's first term, with half a million council houses already sold before the 1983 election. But the second and third took off only in the second term. The first was simple and irreversible, a major social change. The second turned out to be rather less significant than was pretended at the time, at least so far as individuals were concerned. The third was economically by far the most important: though stimulated by the Government's supply-side reforms and initially associated with the unsustainable euphoria of the Lawson boom, it represented the British reflection of universal trends – globalisation and computerisation – and an irresistible transformation of economic attitudes and behaviour, which long outlasted Mrs Thatcher and showed little sign of slackening in the early years of the next century.

The sale of council houses was a specifically British social revolution which reflected the British obsession with home ownership. Arguably it did not have very much to do with capitalism – since its effect was to tie up a far greater proportion of the national wealth unproductively in bricks and mortar than was the case in other countries – but it was an aspiration which went to the heart of Mrs Thatcher's personal values. It is difficult to explain why she felt such a deep emotional identification with home ownership as the defining virtue of good citizenship. It was probably important that her parents had owned – with the help of a mortgage – her childhood home above the shop in Grantham. On the other hand she and Denis had been happy to rent their first married flat in Chelsea until the Conservative Government de-controlled the rent and it became better value to buy a house in Kent. In her early political career she strongly endorsed the Tories' commitment – perhaps more rhetorical than real – to the goal of a 'property-owning democracy'. Yet she initially opposed the policy of selling council houses when it was first promoted by Peter Walker and Michael Heseltine in the 1970s. Once she had grasped its potential for identifying and rewarding precisely those people whom she wanted to wean from socialism, however, she elevated the sale of council houses to be the very symbol of her political faith. To promote the ultimate social virtue of home ownership she was prepared to override almost all her other ideological beliefs: distorting the market by subsidising mortgages, encouraging reckless lending and borrowing and thereby refuelling inflation, which eventually hit hardest the very people whom she had encouraged to buy.

By doing everything she could to encourage home ownership Mrs Thatcher personally engineered a huge switch of Government subsidy from the poor to the better-off. Both Geoffrey Howe and Nigel Lawson fought with her for years to be allowed to phase out mortgage-interest tax relief in the interest of a 'neutral' tax regime. Among her closest supporters not only paid-up monetarists like Nicholas Ridley, John Biffen and Jock Bruce-Gardyne, but even populist Thatcherites like Norman Tebbit, believed that MIRAS was an unjustified subsidy which distorted the housing market and pushed up prices, diverting national resources from wealth creation into owner-occupation.[88] The Duke of Edinburgh chaired an inquiry by the National Federation of Housing Associations which called for its replacement by a needs-related housing allowance for all.[89] But Mrs Thatcher would not hear of cutting support for 'her' people, which she saw frankly as both a reward and a bribe. 'These mortgage subsidies,' Simon Jenkins has written, 'were Thatcher's personal bounty . . . the most glaring instance of her belief in the dominance of politics over economics and of social policy over the free play of market forces.'[90]

Over the eleven years of her premiership, the share of the national budget spent on housing increased overall; but the increase went almost entirely to the private sector. The amount of public money spent on subsidising mortgages doubled, while support for public-sector housing was more than halved. Owner-occupation grew from 55 per cent of the population in 1980 to 64 per cent in 1987 and 67 per cent in

1990. This was the object of the exercise, and was immensely popular with those who gained from it. But that still left more than one in five of the population (22 per cent) living in council accommodation (another 11 per cent rented privately), who had no share in Mrs Thatcher's middle-class reward scheme. While subsidies to homeowners were protected, local authorities were forced to raise council rents to a commercial level, driving up the numbers having to claim housing benefit, while the building of new council houses almost completely dried up. Where Heseltine and Howe had allowed local authorities to spend half the proceeds from the sale of council houses on new building to replace their stock, Lawson and Jenkin cut the figure to 20 per cent. As a result, completions of new public housing dwindled from 170,000 units a year under Labour in the mid-1970s to a mere 35,000 in 1990, and most of those were built by housing associations, not by local authorities.[91]

More than most things that happened between 1979 and 1990, this was the Prime Minister's personal policy. From a mixture of prejudice and principle Mrs Thatcher really believed that public-sector housing ought to be abolished. On the one hand she thought that council estates were breeding grounds of socialism, dependency, vandalism and crime. The journalist Simon Jenkins remembered showing her round some London estates when he was on the *Evening Standard* and she was Opposition spokesman on the environment in 1974; when he tried to tell her that there were some good ones, she insisted firmly that there were only bad ones.[92] She had no interest in trying to make them better because she believed on principle that housing was not a commodity which the Government ought to provide, except for special categories like the elderly and disabled. In her memoirs she wrote unambiguously that the state should withdraw from the building and management of housing 'just as far and as fast as possible'.[93] She could not, when in office, act on this principle as decisively as she might have wished; but she certainly did everything she could to shrink the public sector and very little to help those compelled by circumstances to live in it.

In July 1984, for instance, there was a full-scale Cabinet showdown when Patrick Jenkin – supported by his housing minister, Ian Gow – resisted Lawson's demand for a cut of £600 million in the council-house building and maintenance programme. When Gow threatened to resign on the issue, Mrs Thatcher told him he was 'wet': this was not what she had expected when she sent her faithful bag carrier to the Department of the Environment. But Jenkin took his case to Cabinet and found enough support to force the Prime Minister and

Chancellor – following a half-hour adjournment – to back down. 'Patrick won,' Kenneth Baker wrote, 'but I do not think Margaret ever really forgave him.' A year later he was sacked and replaced by Baker (who had clearly got the message); while Gow was moved to the Treasury to teach him the virtue of economy.[94]

Mrs Thatcher thought the sale of council houses an unalloyed good, both social and economic. She made a point of attending the handover of the millionth house to be sold – at Forres in the north of Scotland – in September 1986, and at the Tory conference the following month proclaimed triumphantly: 'Now let's go for the second million.'[95] By the time she fell in 1990, the number sold was up to nearly 1.5 million, and the total proceeds had accrued £28 billion to the Treasury, which counted them – 'duplicitously', in Simon Jenkins' view[96] – against public spending. Spread over eleven years, this was the biggest privatisation of them all, bigger than British Telecom, British Gas and electricity put together. But the blessings were not so unmixed as she believed.

For one thing, some of those families who were persuaded to buy their houses, particularly towards the end of the decade, tempted by the easy mortgages on offer from banks falling over themselves to lend, soon found themselves, when inflation rose and the recession of the early 1990s bit, committed to payments they could not keep up. As prices fell back to more realistic levels, many found that their houses were worth less than their mortgages – the phenomenon of 'negative equity'. Many bright dreams of ownership ended in the nightmare of repossession five years later.

Second, it was naturally the best and most desirable houses that were sold – very few flats – and the more prosperous and upwardly mobile tenants who bought them, leaving the less salubrious high-rise estates to become sinks for the unemployed and problem families. Of course Nye Bevan's dream that council estates should house a broad cross-section of classes and occupations had never been fulfilled; but the effect of Mrs Thatcher's sell-off was to leave the social mix even narrower than before, with a much higher proportion of tenants dependent on benefit. Her belief that there were no good estates was therefore self-fulfilling.

Third, the non-replacement of the houses sold and the consequent decline in the stock of council housing, combined with the late-1980s' explosion in house prices in the private sector, at a time when there were still nearly three million unemployed, left an absolute shortage of affordable housing and led by the end of the decade to the shocking appearance of a tribe of homeless people sleeping on the streets of

London and other major cities. This was the most serious negative consequence of a popular policy to which Mrs Thatcher resolutely closed her eyes.

The family silver

The second 'crusade' of popular capitalism was privatisation. It had of course been under way, from cautious beginnings, since 1979. But it only really took off as a rolling process in Mrs Thatcher's second term, when it quite suddenly became the Government's 'big idea', the central pillar of Thatcherism, both the symbolic embodiment and the practical realisation of the reversal of socialism which she had been talking about since 1975. The privatisations of the first term had been marginal – relatively small companies which had mainly been taken into public ownership by accident, to save them from going bust, and which the Treasury was now keen to unload. Now, starting with British Telecom, the Government moved on to the major state-owned corporations which had supplied the nation's essential services since 1945, services which only a few years earlier no one but a few free-market fanatics had imagined could be run by anyone but the state: the telephone system, gas and electricity, the national airline, the airports, even water supply. The expectation was successfully created that, as Nigel Lawson had asserted in 1981, 'No industry should remain under State ownership unless there is a positive and overwhelming case for doing so.'[97] A momentum was established which led on – after Mrs Thatcher's own fall – even to the two great behemoths of the public sector, coal mining and the railways. This was a huge and unexpected transformation of the economic landscape. Each successive privatisation was fought tooth and nail by both opposition parties, by the unions and most of those who worked in the affected industries, and by the public as a whole, as measured by opinion polls. But each was accepted once it had happened, even by the Labour party, as an irreversible *fait accompli*. More than that, the privatisation process itself, to ministers' amazement, actually generated a wave of popular excitement, fanned by an enthusiastic press. The key was the sale of shares, at knockdown prices, not just in the City but directly to the public.

Mrs Thatcher's role was crucial. Of course she believed that public ownership was inherently a bad thing. But she believed many things were bad which she still felt obliged to put up with. Up to 1983 she was the most cautious among her economic colleagues and advisers in her estimate of what was politically feasible. After 1983, by contrast, she was convinced, and once convinced she led from the front. A significant pointer was the choice of John Redwood, an ardent privatiser, to succeed Ferdinand Mount as head of the Downing Street Policy Unit. Redwood was delighted to find that 'a lot of the caution and the worry had abated. Now the issue was not "will the public buy it?" but "how can we do it technically?"'[98] The problem was no longer public opinion but persuading the City. Lawson remembers a dinner with leading merchant bankers, all of whom – with one exception – 'roundly declared that the privatisation [of BT] was impossible: the capital market simply was not large enough to absorb it'.[99] Redwood claims the credit for persuading Mrs Thatcher that the answer was to bypass the bankers and sell the shares direct to the public by mail order, television and newspaper advertisements. 'She . . . became excited by the possibilities and gave me the backing I needed at the Treasury and in the City.'[100]★

The one bank prepared to make the necessary act of faith was Kleinwort Benson. The unprecedented advertising blitz was undertaken by Dorland, a subsidiary of Saatchis. The response exceeded all expectations: two million people applied for a prospectus, and when the first instalment went on sale in November 1984, the offer was four times over-subscribed. More than a million small investors applied for shares, including 95 per cent of BT employees, defying the advice of their union; most of these had never owned shares before, but the sale was weighted to favour those who applied for the smallest number. The price was kept deliberately low – 130 pence – for political reasons, since from the Government's point of view the sale simply had to succeed. The result was a bonanza for the lucky applicants; the price rose 90 per cent on the opening day, as many buyers sold on immediately. The second instalment in June 1985 was similarly over-subscribed. In the end the sale – of just 51 per cent of the company at this stage, in three instalments over eighteen months – raised nearly £4 billion. The company's profits jumped spectacularly and by the end of 1985 the share price – for those buyers who had retained them – stood at 192 pence.[102]

Immediately the success of the BT sale became clear, Mrs Thatcher was impatient to repeat it.[103] The obvious next candidate was British Gas. This, however, was not plain sailing. Nigel Lawson, backed by his new Financial Secretary John Moore, was determined not simply to privatise the gas industry, replacing a public with a private monopoly, but to break it up, in order to introduce an element of competition. Against him stood the formidable chairman of British Gas, Sir Dennis

---

★As late as 1986, however, she still disliked the word 'privatisation'. In her speech at the Lord Mayor's banquet that year she described it apologetically as 'a dreadful bit of jargon to inflict on the language of Shakespeare'.[101]

Rooke. Whereas it was the chairman of BT, Sir George Jefferson – a Thatcher appointee – who had pressed for privatisation, Rooke was an old-style nationalised industry boss, appointed by the Callaghan Government in 1976 and determined to defend the industry in which he had spent his entire working life. In the middle, the minister responsible was Peter Walker, a surviving and still-defiant 'wet' whose authority had been enhanced by his successful handling of the miners' strike: Walker was not against privatisation, but he was determined to do it his own way and in his own time. He supported Rooke's opposition to breaking up the industry. To Lawson's dismay, Mrs Thatcher – more concerned with speed and the need for another political success – chose to back Walker.

She certainly made another political killing. 'For sheer size, prodigality of advertising, and the opportunity to involve small punters and large investing institutions alike in the calculation of a quick profit,' the *Annual Register* wrote, 'the launch of British Gas in the private sector made history.'[104] With the whole City now keen to get a share of the action, Rothschilds won a 'beauty contest' to handle the sale; the advertising was placed in the hands of Young and Rubicam, who came up with the frankly populist slogan 'Tell Sid'. The campaign cost the taxpayer £159 million; but four and a half million Sids rushed to buy the shares. Once again they were deliberately under-valued and once again they were hugely over-subscribed: on the first day of trading the price leaped by 50 per cent. Labour furiously condemned the Government's cynical under-pricing of a national asset in order to bribe the public with their own money: in his first front-bench job as a Treasury spokesman Tony Blair alleged that the sell-off would cost the taxpayer £20–30 per household.[105] But the Government had achieved its aim of making shareholding popular as never before. There is no question that Sid voted Tory in 1987 – though he had probably already done so in 1983 and 1979.

True devotees of the free market, both inside the Government and outside, regretted Mrs Thatcher's caving in to Rooke and Walker; they continue to believe the privatisation of gas as a single supplier to have been a missed opportunity.[106] Walker, conversely, claims gas as the most successful privatisation: the element of competition, in his view, was provided by the customer's option of choosing other fuels.[107] For her part Mrs Thatcher admitted no regrets, writing in her memoirs that she still thought she was right to back Walker, since 'the privatisation was a resounding success'.[108] Nevertheless she was sufficiently stung by the criticism to determine that electricity, when its time came, should be broken up between competing rivals.

The third high-profile privatisation of the second term – though in revenue terms much smaller than British Telecom and British Gas – was British Airways, which had been successfully brought into profit by one of Mrs Thatcher's favourite businessmen, Sir John King, and was sold off in February 1987. 'The World's Favourite Airline' was now a successful international leader which investors were keen to buy into; this time the shares were eleven times over-subscribed, and the price jumped 82 per cent on the opening day. Just before the election another glamorous name, Rolls-Royce – controversially nationalised by the Heath Government in 1971 – was also returned to the private sector. The only hiccup in this stage of the programme came with Britoil – the former British National Oil Corporation – which was floated in 1985 just when the oil price was falling. Millions of shares were not taken up; but the loss was the underwriters', not the Government's, and the political embarrassment at least did something to counter the charge that the share price of the assets sold was always set too low.

With the success of privatisation Mrs Thatcher had stumbled on an ongoing narrative which gave a central theme to her Government, and she was keen to keep the momentum going. British Steel, drastically slimmed down and restored to profitability by Ian MacGregor, was already well down the road. The 1987 Tory manifesto earmarked electricity and water as the next targets. Both posed special problems: nuclear energy on the one hand, and the public-health implications of commercialised water on the other. Still she was determined to press ahead. At the same time, however, she had not abandoned her habitual caution. She was no ideologue, but a canny politician, and she foresaw only trouble in trying to privatise the railways. Simon Jenkins, appointed a member of the British Rail board by Norman Fowler in 1979 specifically to press the case for privatisation, observed her hesitation at first hand:

> She disliked trains and avoided travelling in them. She regarded them as a dirty and inefficient corner of the public sector, yet one for which the public had a perverse affection. Privatisation would be technically difficult and unpopular. As a result she shut her mind to it.[109]

Nicholas Ridley, Transport Secretary from October 1983 to May 1986, accepted the Prime Minister's veto. But his successors – John Moore (1986–7), Paul Channon (1987–9) and Cecil Parkinson (1989–90) were all keen to grab a share of the privatisation glory. There is no better example of Mrs Thatcher's shrewd political instinct than the fact that she persistently warned them off. She was happy to see British

Rail forced to sell off its profitable assets – hotels, ferries, hovercraft and acres of undeveloped trackside property – which only made privatisation of the rest of the business harder; but she had the good sense not to try to sell the track or the trains.

For somewhat similar reasons she would not touch the Post Office, pleading the Queen's attachment to the Royal Mail as an excuse, or the remaining coalmines that were left after the trauma of the miners' strike. In fact, with her usual mixture of timing and luck, Margaret Thatcher triumphantly rode the first wave of privatisation, accomplishing all the easier sell-offs where public opinion, though initially sceptical, was fairly quickly persuaded of the benefits, while leaving the really hard cases to her successor.

During the 1980s the most effective opposition to the principle of privatisation in fact came not from the Labour party, whose defence of the public sector seemed merely a reflex function of its backward-looking dependence on the trade unions, but from her own side. A single phrase in a characteristically nostalgic speech by Harold Macmillan did more damage to the idea of privatisation than all the outraged anathemas of Neil Kinnock and Roy Hattersley. Speaking to the Tory Reform Group at the Carlton Club in November 1985, the former Prime Minister was said to have likened privatisation to a once-wealthy family fallen on hard times 'selling the family silver'. In fact, as is so often the case with famous phrases, Macmillan never used the words reported. What he actually said was: 'First the Georgian silver goes. And then all that nice furniture that used to be in the saloon. Then the Canalettos go . . .'[110] Despite the remoteness from most voters' experience of the aristocratic world he conjured up, Macmillan's words touched a chord. Quite ordinary families have some inherited 'family silver', little used but which they do not like to sell. The image of ministers, like a lot of dodgy house-strippers, knocking down the nation's heirlooms at a cost well below their true worth subtly undermined Mrs Thatcher's carefully created reputation for thrifty house-keeping. In vain the Government's supporters retorted that the industries being sold off were not assets at all, but liabilities which the Treasury was well rid of. Six days after the original speech Macmillan himself explained in the House of Lords that he was not against the principle of transferring loss-making public utilities to more efficient private ownership. 'I ventured to criticise the fact that these huge sums were used as if they were income.'[111] In other words what he was warning against was not privatisation itself, but the way the proceeds were being spent on consumption, not investment. In this he was voicing a critique that was beginning to be widely shared.

Unquestionably privatisation yielded real benefits, to the consumer and to the Treasury. The level of service to the customer undoubtedly improved. This was most obvious in the case of telephones: where the Post Office had routinely made new subscribers wait weeks to be connected, BT would now install a new line in a few days, with a choice of receivers and a whole range of new services. A greater responsiveness was also apparent in gas and electricity supply and other privatised companies. Arguably this reflected the spread of a more commercial culture generally and the loss of power by the unions, rather than simply the change of ownership. The major efficiency gains in both British Steel and British Airways, for instance, occurred while they were still in the public sector. British Rail and the Post Office also raised their performance while still nationalised. But the privatisers would argue that the crucial factor was the removal of the safety net hitherto provided by the bottomless public purse. As Keith Joseph put it: 'The magic of privatisation is to make activities that were not bankruptable, bankruptable. It's that threat of bankruptability that galvanises management and workers, in the last resort, to serve the consumer.'[112]

The result was that the Treasury, instead of endlessly subsidising losses, now actually drew revenue from the profits. As Mrs Thatcher boasted at the 1989 party conference: 'Five industries that together were losing over £2 million a week in the public sector [are] now making profits of over £100 million a week in the private sector.'[113] Beside this, the argument that the shares had been sold too cheaply paled into irrelevance. Total proceeds from the sale of assets were in the order of £24 billion by 1989.[114] Almost certainly the Government paid too much to the City firms which handled the sales. Once BT had revealed the unexpected scale of the public appetite for low-priced shares, the huge sums paid to Rothschilds and others – described by one commentator as 'the icing on the Big Bang cake'[115] – were far greater than the level of risk they undertook. The City did very well indeed out of privatisation. Nevertheless the Treasury could still be said to have achieved a bargain. The real criticism of Lawson and Mrs Thatcher is that they blew this windfall on a short-term consumer boom, instead of investing it on long-overdue repairs to the crumbling national infrastructure.

The Government's other great boast – that privatisation had created a nation of small capitalists – also turned out to be something of an illusion. On paper the number of individuals who owned shares certainly rocketed, from around three million in 1980 to eleven million in 1990. But few owned very many; and this was anyway a smaller number than appeared to have been lured into the stock market in the heady days of 1984–6. Many of these new investors immediately cashed in their allocation for a quick profit; others proudly retained their original small purchase of BT or British Gas shares but bought no more. The number who went on to build up portfolios of shares in different companies was disappointingly small, so that the proportion of shares owned by private individuals actually fell. By 1991 over 80 per cent were held by big institutional investors, whose interests predominated more than ever: disillusion spilled over at the British Gas AGM in 1994 when small shareholders, angry at the excessive bonuses paid to directors, found themselves systematically outvoted by the big institutions. Popular capitalism in this respect failed to fulfil its promise of democratic empowerment: the small investor was still the pawn of Big Money.

Finally, disappointment with privatisation, particularly among those who had most supported it, focused on the failure to promote real competition in most of the newly privatised industries, and on the fact that prices were still not properly subject to the market but regulated by a succession of unaccountable bodies – Oftel, Ofgas, Ofwat – appointed by the Government and still in practice sensitive to political pressure. The new service providers were no more truly private companies than their nationalised predecessors, but hybrids operating in a grey area somewhere between the two: still clearly in the 'public domain', as Simon Jenkins wrote in his incisive study *Accountable to None*, even though no longer in the public sector. 'The regulators were soon caught between public and consumer pressure to act toughly against monopoly abuse, and no less fierce pressure from industries whose share price . . . the regulator could determine.'[116] The Government today still takes as close an interest as ever in the performance of the privatised services, but the criteria for controlling them are arbitrary and opaque. Lady Thatcher in her memoirs maintains that 'regulation which had, when in the public sector, been covert now had to be overt and specific'.[117] But Jenkins points out that the regulators – in effect a single individual for each industry – are answerable neither to Parliament nor even formally to ministers, who are free to deny responsibility when it suits them. 'Of all the institutions of Thatcherism,' he concludes, 'the utilities regulators were the least coherent or democratic.'[118]

This was perhaps an inevitable function of the way privatisation happened – pragmatically, opportunistically and piecemeal. There was an aspiration, but never a clearly worked-out blueprint – any more than there had been for nationalisation forty years earlier. Nevertheless it turned out (at least in Mrs Thatcher's time) to be an outstanding political success: the problems only revealed themselves over the following decade. Moreover the idea had universal application. In the great global retreat from socialism of which Thatcherism was merely the British reflection, it was Britain which pioneered both the concept and the techniques of moving state-owned industries into the private sector. As early as 1986 Mrs Thatcher was boasting that privatisation was on the agenda in countries as various as Turkey, Malaysia, Japan, Mexico and Canada. 'People are no longer worried about catching the British disease,' she crowed. 'They're queuing up to obtain the new British cure.'[119] British bankers, accountants and consultants, having struck gold from privatisation at home, found a ready market to sell their expertise all round the world. The collapse of Communism in 1989 opened up a huge new field for lucrative exploitation, with a gratifying bonus of missionary kudos. At home Thatcherism had many strands and different connotations; but around the world the word was synonymous with privatisation.

An enterprise society?

Meanwhile there were signs of real cultural change at all levels of the economy, from the City of London to every provincial high street, a tangible liberalisation of all those attitudes and practices which had held back the performance of the British economy for decades. In large part this was the deliberate result of the Government's 'supply-side' strategy of cutting regulation, cutting taxes, increasing incentives, curbing the unions and generally freeing up the labour market. But equally important was the fact that all this coincided with an explosion of new technology, above all communications technology – the so-called 'third industrial revolution' – which was rapidly making the old ways obsolete by promoting small-scale consumer-driven service industries in place of the mass-employment heavy industry of the past. In this respect Thatcherism merely reflected and facilitated the march of global progress. Nevertheless the revolution in British life was palpable.

First, there was the 'Big Bang' which transformed the City in October 1986, sweeping away centuries of tradition by admitting foreign brokers and jobbers and switching to a global standard of regulation in place of the gentlemanly conventions – 'my word is my bond' – on which the square mile had hitherto prided itself. This was an overdue recognition of a technological imperative which was pushed through by Nigel Lawson in alliance with Cecil Parkinson during the latter's brief time at the DTI, in return for calling off a pending prosecution by the Office of Fair Trading following an investigation of restrictive practices in the Stock Exchange. As with the abolition of exchange controls in 1979, of which 'Big Bang' was a natural corollary, Mrs Thatcher was initially cautious, worried that the Government would appear to be intervening to rescue its friends in the City while manufacturing industry went to the wall. But the political flak was short-lived and the outcome was a spectacular success, allowing London to join fully in the emerging computerised global economy by enabling it – just in time – to compete successfully with Tokyo, Frankfurt and New York.

The effect of 'Big Bang', combined with Lawson's tax cuts and the bonanza of privatisation, which offered huge rewards not only to the merchant banks which bore the risk but also to an army of consultants, advertising agencies and public-relations companies which rode the wave of lucrative new business, meant that quite suddenly the City became glamorous. No longer the preserve of middle-aged men in sober suits and the occasional defiantly anachronistic bowler hat, it became almost overnight the playground of classless twenty-three-year olds switching huge sums instantly around the world, working extraordinary hours but earning correspondingly enormous salaries and even bigger bonuses. In the mid-1980s, as never before, it was in finance and related activities, not in industry or the professions, that big money was to be made. The new wealth was manifest in the rise of huge new glass and steel towers, with lofty atria and potted palms, like Richard Rogers' new Lloyd's Building, the NatWest tower, the massive Broadgate development near Liverpool Street station, complete with shops, cafés and an outdoor skating rink; and eventually the new Stock Exchange. But the phenomenon which caught the public imagination was the new class of computerised whizz-kids – dubbed 'yuppies', an acronym for young upwardly mobile professionals – who suddenly materialised to populate these palaces of mammon. In fact they were not, as the media liked to suggest, all former East End barrow boys: many were young public-school boys suddenly earning more in a year than their fathers in similar jobs had earned in a lifetime – not by thrift and hard work, as Mrs Thatcher preached, but by speculating and dealing, buying and selling options at the right moment: purely paper transactions – except that they were no longer done on paper but electronically onscreen. Transformed by the new technology, the business of making money was no longer boring and respectable on the one hand, or shady and vulgar on the other, but fashionable and exciting. This shift in perception was precisely pinpointed in David Lodge's acute satire of the period, *Nice Work* (1988), when Professor Philip Swallow – an academic at the fictional University of Rummidge – reflects: 'Isn't it extraordinary how interesting money has become lately? I've suddenly started reading the business pages of the *Guardian,* after thirty years of skipping straight from the arts pages to the sports pages.'[120] Professor Swallow was not alone.

But it was not only in the City that money was being made. Out in the real economy too, things were changing. Deregulation, the easy availability of credit and the rapid proliferation of personal computers created a climate in which small businesses flourished, helping to create more than three million new jobs (mainly in the service sector) between 1983 and 1990 to make up for those lost in manufacturing at the beginning of the decade. More people than ever before left their employers – often involuntarily but in many cases voluntarily – to strike out on their own in small desktop enterprises which identified a gap in the market and set out to fill it. By 1989 three million people – 11 per cent of the workforce – were self-employed. Enterprise flourished not only in the south of England but in the north as well, irrespective of politics. As one of Scotland's last remaining Tory Members noted in 1989, Glasgow was 'a city which has not got one single Conservative MP, and yet the entrepreneurship has just mushroomed. And the funny thing is it's mushrooming in the 25 to 30 year old category who wouldn't think in a million years of voting Tory. Yet they are the Thatcher children.'[121]

In fact the most prominent heroes of this new culture were children of the 1960s and 1970s who used the expanding opportunities of the 1980s to realise visions nurtured in the pop and fashion industries of their youth: people like Richard Branson (whose empire started with Virgin Records); Alan Sugar (whose Amstrad PCs were practically everyone's first home computer); Sophie Mirman (whose Sock Shop, started with a £45,000 Loan Guarantee Scheme, had sixty-one shops by 1988 and a turnover of £14 million a year); and Anita Roddick (whose Body Shop created a demand for all sorts of pampering unguents that previous generations had not known they needed). All these and more flourished during the Lawson boom. For the new economy was as much about spending money as making it.

Not only yuppies had more to spend than ever before: everyone in work benefited. As income tax fell, average real wages rose by 3 per cent a year between 1981 and 1987 (or more than 20 per cent between 1983 and 1987). At the same time hire-purchase restrictions had been lifted in 1982, and financial deregulation led to an unprecedented credit boom as banks and building societies competed to offer ever easier loans; credit cards and hole-in-the-wall cash dispensers also took off in the middle of the decade, and shops stayed open longer too, so that opportunities to spend multiplied. Higher disposable incomes created demand for every sort of home improvement – central heating, double glazing, stone cladding, designer kitchens – and new types of consumer goods – freezers, video recorders, stereos and home computers; as well as new cars – by 1987 62 per cent of families owned one car and 20 per cent owned two; new leisure opportunities – theme parks, golf courses, shopping malls and fast-food restaurants; and holidays to ever more exotic locations. Above all, big salaries and easy credit fuelled a boom in property. Average household indebtedness rose by 250 per cent between 1982 and 1989, and most of this borrowing went into mortgages. Average house prices more than doubled between 1985 and 1989. While it lasted everyone seemed a winner, and those who had bought their council houses at a discount did best of all. Former tenants who had bought their houses for £10,000 found a few years later that they were worth four times as much. 'I think it was the greatest thing the ordinary working person ever had offered to him,' one grateful couple told the lifestyle guru Peter York. 'We're landowners.'[122]

All this was exactly what Mrs Thatcher and her Chancellors had dreamed of. 'The genius of the tax cut philosophy was that it got the party mood going, it got us all *glowing*,' another grateful voter enthused. 'The tax man shared our dreams – he really did. It made us all feel *good* about getting and spending and not being ashamed any more.'[123] 'The eighties are a long story about fun, greed and money,' a third celebrated, 'when the majority went out and took what the minority had previously thought of as its own. It was a bloodless revolution . . . We expected Big Brother. We got Big Bang.'[124]

But at the same time a lot of people were left out. While the comedian Harry Enfield captured the upside of Mrs Thatcher's booming Britain in the exultant catchphrase 'loadsamoney', the northern playwright Alan Bleasdale graphically portrayed the downside in his television series *The Boys from the Blackstuff*, which followed the lives of a group of unemployed labourers in Liverpool, summed up in the bleak, despairing appeal 'gissajob'. Unemployment went on rising inexorably until January 1986; and even when it began to fall the shadow did not suddenly go away. Not until 1989 did the headline figure drop below two million, and then it promptly started rising again, back to three million in 1993. The blight was heavily concentrated in the old manufacturing regions which were devastated by the loss of the mills, factories, mines and steelworks which had been their livelihood since the nineteenth century. The 1997 film *The Full Monty* – about a group of Sheffield steelworkers driven to stripping to survive – extracted comedy from one enterprising response to the desperation of long-term unemployment, but its defiant humour did not disguise the bitter sense of rejection felt by whole communities while the rest of the country prospered.

In addition to those officially registered as unemployed – and their families – there were many others trapped outside the virtuous circle of success: old people dependent on the shrinking state pension; single parents, mainly unmarried or abandoned mothers, struggling with low-paid part-time jobs to make ends meet; and a growing number of young, rootless dropouts, the victims of unemployment, homelessness, family breakdown, drugs or a self-reinforcing combination of them all: in other words all those dependent on state benefits, whose real value was steadily cut as the cost of living rose. While the average household saw its income rise by 36 per cent over the decade (and the top tenth by 62 per cent), that of the bottom tenth fell by 17 per cent. Around 25 per cent of the population was living on less than half the national average and one survey concluded that a quarter of the nation's children lived in families officially classed as 'poor'.[125] Such figures are always open to dispute, and there were always Government apologists to deny them; but there was no doubt – it was obvious to anyone who walked around any of Britain's city centres at night – that in the midst of rising wealth, poverty was also increasing, creating a new and permanently excluded underclass.

Mrs Thatcher strenuously denied that poverty was growing alongside wealth. She had always argued in principle that everyone would benefit from rising standards, according to the theory known in America as 'trickledown', by which the spending of the rich was supposed to trickle down to benefit the poor; or as she put it in 1977: 'When the tide comes in, all the boats rise.'[126] But she also continued to insist in the face of the evidence that everyone *had* benefited. In one part of her mind she genuinely believed that her purpose was to spread the ownership of wealth more widely so as to create what she called in her memoirs 'a society of "haves", not a class of them', and persuaded herself that council-house sales and wider share ownership were having this effect.[127] But at the same time she also believed that inequality was not just inevitable but necessary, indeed positively beneficial, as a stimulus to enterprise, a reward for success and a penalty for failure or lack of effort. At heart she believed that no one remained poor for long except by their own fault: everyone could make a success if only they worked hard and showed a bit of gumption. Lacking empathy with those born without her abilities, she had little sympathy for those struggling to live on social security. When the Tory MP Matthew Parris bravely tried it for a week for a television programme to demonstrate that it could not be done, she was scornful. 'It's absolutely typical of Matthew Parris,' she scoffed. 'I could have survived on £26 a week.'[128]

The truth was that she had very little understanding of people whose life experience was different from her own. She approved of those she called 'our people', the hard-working, homeowning, taxpaying middle class whom she regarded as the backbone of England – she once asserted confidently that 'every citizen aspired to a conservatory';[129] and correspondingly disapproved of those so lazy, feckless or lacking in self-respect that they were content to live in subsidised housing or on benefits. But this strict moral framework founded on thrift and self-improvement also meant, paradoxically, that she was not comfortable with the culture of unapologetic greed that was popularly associated with Thatcherism in practice. In fact she was extraordinarily ambivalent about the consumerist philosophy which bore her name.

On the one hand she vigorously defended the urge to make and spend money as the essential motor of a prosperous economy. She admired successful entrepreneurs, as 'the wealth creators and job-creators on whom all our social services depend';[130] but she also had what Woodrow Wyatt called 'a weakness for people who make large sums of money quickly' and ascribed it 'to their endeavour and worthwhile enterprise. Often it is not.' Wyatt cited Sir Jack Lyons, one of those convicted of insider trading in the Guinness affair, and a number of other 'raffish characters' – Ralph Halpern, Michael Richardson and Jeffrey Sterling, all knighted during the 1980s – as examples of associations which were 'dangerous for her'.[131] She had no time for those she called 'the middle-class softies who have guilt complexes about earning more than others and crave to be chastised with higher taxes' and was disappointed by the public reaction against Lawson's cutting of the top rate to 40 per cent in 1988, lamenting that 'There's still a lot of envy.'[132] She was irritated when church leaders condemned the Government for encouraging materialism. 'The Church keep saying we must relieve poverty,' she complained, 'and when we do they say we're making everybody materialistic.'[133] She thought much of the condemnation of materialism sheer hypocrisy.

Yet she was personally puritanical about money. Since May 1979 she had voluntarily forgone about a quarter of the salary to which she was entitled as Prime Minister, and she and Denis continued to maintain a fairly frugal lifestyle. Very wisely as it turned out, they declined pressing invitations to become Lloyd's 'Names' – 'She felt there was something vaguely wrong about it' – and she did not really approve of the Stock Exchange, believing at heart that wealth should be earned by making and selling real goods and services, not by gambling and speculation.[134] For the same reason she refused to sanction the introduction of a national lottery, which had to wait until 1992 to get the go-ahead under her successor. She hated being in debt herself and always punctiliously paid off the smallest sums if she was obliged to borrow – as she often was, since she never carried money – and she disapproved of credit cards, even as she presided over an unprecedented credit explosion. 'It's perfectly true that the PM gets very emotional about the plastic cards and she thinks it's all very damaging and dangerous,' Jock Bruce-Gardyne reflected ironically in 1989.* Yet by far the greatest component of national indebtedness was mortgages, which she did approve of:

> Some of us sometimes have suggested to the PM that if she is worried about the scale of . . . debt, then one area where the Government certainly could influence our behaviour is by the withdrawal of mortgage interest relief. And needless to say that meets with an extremely frosty reception . . . There is an obvious contradiction here.[136]

The foundation of her political faith was moralistic, derived from the thrifty precepts of her father and her upbringing in the Finkin Street Methodist church. Asked by Peter Jay in 1985 what she meant by questioning whether colleagues were 'one of us', she replied: 'Are they hard-working, do they believe in personal responsibility, do they believe in endeavour, do they believe in the voluntary spirit? Do they believe fundamentally the same philosophy I believe in?'[137] These were moral, not political criteria. But at the same time she believed that the pursuit of wealth – far from being the root of all evil – was a force for good in the world. Her gloss on the parable of the Good Samaritan was that he was able to help the mugged man only because 'he was a man of substance';[138] and she saw no difficulty about a rich man entering the kingdom of Heaven. 'Because we give people the chance to better themselves,' she told the 1988 party conference, 'they accuse us of encouraging selfishness and greed . . . The truth is that what we are actually encouraging is the best in human nature . . . The fact is that prosperity has created not the selfish society but the generous

---

*Long after her retirement there was an awkward incident when she was campaigning in the 1997 election and tried to do some shopping in Tesco's without a cheque guarantee card. 'It looked as though Lady Thatcher did not know what a cheque guarantee card was,' Matthew Parris wrote in *The Times*. 'Plastic has not entered this baroness's life.'[135]

society.'[139] 'Only by creating wealth,' she insisted, 'can you relieve poverty. It's what you do with your wealth that counts.'[140] She claimed that charitable giving – encouraged by tax relief – had doubled in ten years since 1979. In this way she hoped that the shortfall in public funding of schools, hospitals, universities and libraries would be filled, as in America, by private benefactions. The trouble was that despite her wishful harking back to the Victorians, that culture of philanthropy does not exist on a sufficient scale in Britain; aside from a handful of Sainsburys and Gettys there are still not enough huge corporations and public-spirited millionaires to fill the gap. As a result over the last twenty years Britain has suffered from the worst of both worlds, with public services receiving neither European levels of public spending nor American levels of private finance. The Blair Government has gone further than Mrs Thatcher ever dared in trying to attract private money to build public projects; but the level of public resistance is still high, and the legacy is plain to see. It was accurately described by the American economist J.K. Galbraith nearly half a century ago as 'private affluence and public squalor'.

The central paradox of Thatcherism is that Mrs Thatcher presided over and celebrated a culture of rampant materialism – 'fun, greed and money' – fundamentally at odds with her own values which were essentially conservative, old-fashioned and puritanical. She believed in thrift, yet encouraged record indebtedness. She lauded the family as the essential basis of a stable society, yet created a cut-throat economy and a climate of social fragmentation which tended to break up families, and tax and benefit provisions which positively discriminated against marriage. She disapproved of sexual licence and the public display of offensive material, yet promoted an untrammelled commercialism which unleashed a tide of pornography, both in print and on film, unimaginable a few years earlier.

Above all, she believed passionately in the uniqueness of Britain among the nations. Asked in 1987 to define the distinctive quality of Thatcherism, she acknowledged the centrality of sound money and free enterprise, but she had never claimed that there was anything specifically British about that. Much more than economics, she told Rodney Tyler, Thatcherism was 'about being worthwhile and honourable'; it was about the family, and the legacy of the empire, 'something which is really rather unique and enterprising in the British character – it's about how we built an empire and how we gave sound administration and sound law to large areas of the world'.[141] She still believed that Britain had a mission to teach 'the nations of the world how to live'.[142] Indeed she came close to believing that the individual's duty was not to serve the general good by pursuing his own self-interest – the orthodox Adam Smith view – but rather to serve his country. 'It is not who you are, who your family is, or where you come from that matters,' she told the 1984 party conference. 'It is what you are and what you can do for your country that counts.'[143] 'A man may climb Everest for himself,' she told the same audience four years later, 'but at the top he plants his country's flag.'[144] Yet market forces respect no boundaries. While beating the drum for Britain, Mrs Thatcher presided over an unprecedented extension of internationalism – not only in the European Community, where she did try, in her last three years, to slow the momentum towards further integration, but rather in the explosion of American-led global capitalism, eliminating economic sovereignty and homogenising local identities, in Britain as across the world.

Mrs Thatcher rode this liberalising tide and averted her eyes from consequences which offended her deepest values. She enjoyed huge political success because she released the power of the middle class. Her revolutionary discovery was that the middle class – and those who aspired to be middle-class – formed the majority of the population. Labour had always assumed that the working class, if properly mobilised, was the majority. All previous postwar Tory administrations had likewise taken it for granted that no Government could hope to be re-elected with more than a million unemployed. Mrs Thatcher demonstrated that, on the contrary, she could ignore the unemployed and still win elections, so long as the middle class felt prosperous. On this analysis she was not a true liberal at all, but a class warrior who waged and won the class war on behalf of her own kind by using free-market policies, tempered with blatant bribes like mortgage tax relief and other perks, as a method of social reward, switching the emphasis of society from collective provision to individual gratification. While she denied that individualism was merely a cover for selfish hedonism, she was helpless to dictate how the new middle class should spend its money; still less could she control the amoral power of international capital.

The paradox of Thatcherism is piquantly embodied in the history of her own family. Think back to Alfred Roberts in his Grantham grocery, the small town shopkeeper, patriot and preacher, husbanding the ratepayers' pennies and raising his clever daughter to a life of Christian service, diligence and thrift. Then look forward to the future Sir Mark Thatcher, an international 'businessman' possessed of no visible abilities, qualifications or social conscience, pursued from Britain to Texas to South Africa by lawsuits, tax investigations and a persistently unsavoury reputation. Imagine what Alfred would have thought of Mark. It is well known that Denis – a businessman of an older generation – took a dim view of his son's activities. Yet for Lady Thatcher Mark could do no wrong. The world in which he acquired his mysterious fortune was the world she helped to bring to birth: the values he represents are the values she promoted. Torn between pious invocations of her sainted father and fierce protectiveness towards her playboy son, Margaret Thatcher is the link between two utterly opposed moral systems which reflect not only the ambivalence of her own personality but the story of Britain in the twentieth century: Alfred Roberts to Mark Thatcher in three generations.

7

Iron Lady I:
Special Relationships

Mrs Thatcher and the Foreign Office

By the time she embarked on her second term in June 1983, Mrs Thatcher was far more confident in foreign affairs than she had been in 1979. Then she had been the new girl on the international block, admittedly inexperienced and up against established leaders at the head of all her major allies: Jimmy Carter in Washington, Helmut Schmidt in Bonn and Valéry Giscard d'Estaing in Paris. But already by October 1982 – when Schmidt was replaced by Helmut Kohl – she was boasting in her constituency that she was now the most senior western leader.[1] (She did not count Pierre Trudeau, who had been Prime Minister of Canada on and off since 1968.) The longer she remained in office, the more she was able to exploit what she called in her memoirs the 'huge and cumulative advantage in simply being known both by politicians and by ordinary people around the world'.[2] She had scored a notable diplomatic success in Zimbabwe, partial victory on the European budget issue and above all a stunning military triumph in the Falklands. Before the Paras had even landed in San Carlos Bay she was proclaiming, in refutation of Dean Acheson's famous gibe that Britain had 'lost an empire and not yet found a role': 'I believe Britain *has* now found a role. It is in upholding international law and teaching the nations of the world how to live.'[3] Once the war was won there was no holding her belief that Britain was once again a model to the world.

From now on she travelled extensively and was royally received wherever she went; she milked her global celebrity to the full. But she always travelled with a purpose, to promote her views and British interests, not just to inform herself as she had done in opposition.

Correspondents who accompanied her have described her punishing schedule: up at dawn to lay a wreath at the local war cemetery, every hour filled with engagements, but with no time for cultural visits. 'It was always work,' Julia Langdon recalls. 'She didn't relax . . . She didn't like sight-seeing and she wasn't really interested in culture. She didn't want anyone to think she was . . . enjoying herself – except of course in a political sense.'[4] Visiting Turkey in 1988 she wanted to skip planned visits to Santa Sofia and the Topkapi Palace, until the British Embassy insisted there would be a diplomatic incident if she did not go.[5] Wherever she went she exploited the Falklands triumph as a symbol of Britain's rebirth under her leadership, her resolution in the cause of freedom, and proven military prowess. 'Better than any Prime Minister since Macmillan,' David Reynolds has written, 'she understood that prestige was a form of power.'[6] British ambassadors in foreign capitals suddenly felt their status boosted in the diplomatic pecking order; and ministers and even Tory MPs found themselves welcomed as her representative.[7] Conversely every foreign leader who came to London, however insignificant, wanted to be photographed with Madame Thatcher to boost his prestige back home. She posed with them all in front of the fireplace in the entrance hall of Number Ten, and sent them away with a lecture about the free market or the need to combat Communism.*

Like all long-serving Prime Ministers, she increasingly wished to be her own Foreign Secretary. She quickly replaced Francis Pym with the more amenable Geoffrey Howe, then treated Howe as little more than her bag carrier, entrusted with the tiresome detail of diplomacy while she handled all the important conversations. When she wanted to send Howe on an extended visit to South Africa in 1985, she told him quite seriously that she could look after the Foreign Office in his absence.[9] She liked dealing directly with other heads of government but had no inhibitions about receiving their foreign ministers or lesser emissaries

---

*Raymond Seitz, American Ambassador in London in the mid-1980s, accompanied numerous Senators and Congressmen to see her. She would receive them in the first-floor drawing room at Number Ten, perched 'prim and intent . . . at the edge of a sofa near a fireplace that was never lit. She rarely carried a piece of paper because she knew her message by heart, whatever it happened to be, and her mission was usually to stiffen the spine of whoever sat across from her. The visitor would start the conversation with something such as, "Thank you for seeing me, Madam Prime Minister" . . . to which Mrs Thatcher would respond for about thirty minutes without drawing breath.' She would finish with 'one or two courtesy points about Ronnie' before the visitor emerged dazed into Downing Street repeating, 'What a woman! What a woman!'[8]

and thoroughly enjoyed subjecting them to the same sort of interrogation she gave her own ministers: few of them came up to scratch.
As Charles Powell put it: 'She was ready to go toe-to-toe with any
world leader from Gorbachev to Deng Xiaoping . . . She had the huge
advantage of being unembarrassable.'[10] As a woman she could say things
to foreign leaders – most of whom had little experience of female
politicians – that no male Prime Minister could have got away with.[11]
Richard Perle, the US Assistant Secretary of Defense, was impressed
by her 'extraordinary leadership qualities – the ability to sit down with
a world leader . . . and drill the British point of view into her inter-
locutors'. He found her 'a very powerful personality and a persuasive
one, and always extraordinarily well-briefed'.[12]

The relationship with Howe brought out the bully in her. Howe's
quiet reasonableness, transferred from the economic to the diplomatic
stage, exasperated her and she harried him mercilessly in front of
colleagues and his officials. She would continually interrupt him and
brush aside his carefully argued views with barely disguised contempt.
Once when he was making a long presentation in his dogged monotone, she asked for the windows to be opened, saying: 'We can't have
people falling asleep.'[13] Colleagues were embarrassed for him, but generally kept their heads down. Some felt that Howe himself was something of a masochist who invited this treatment: 'She would handbag
him, and he would cower to receive it – actually cower. She loved to
humiliate him and he loved to receive it.'[14] But Howe was tougher
than this suggests. One official likened him to a battleship steaming
through heavy seas, periodically disappearing from view, then reappearing, ploughing on regardless, where many flashier vessels would
have sunk.[15] And if she denigrated him it was partly because she feared
him as a rival waiting to displace her if she stumbled. Howe had put
down his marker in the 1975 leadership contest, when he won nineteen votes, and she believed that his ambition was nurtured by his wife
Elspeth, whom she frankly loathed. She reassured herself that 'Howe
has not got the calibre to be Prime Minister.'[16] But for most of her
time in Downing Street he was the most likely beneficiary if she had
fallen.

In her memoirs – soured by the events of November 1990 – she
damned him with faint praise, 'Geoffrey was always good at the actual
process of negotiation',[17] and conceded that 'he was a perfect right-
hand man for the European Councils I attended'; but concluded
contemptuously that 'he fell under the spell of the Foreign Office
where compromise and negotiation were ends in themselves . . . In
the end, Geoffrey's vision became finding a form of words.'[18] This is

unfair: Howe and Mrs Thatcher made an excellent partnership precisely because he was the perfect foil to her rampaging style. She positively prided herself on being undiplomatic; but for that very reason she needed him to smooth ruffled feathers and mend broken fences in her wake. In truth she resented the fact that the policies she followed were very often closer to Foreign Office advice than her rhetoric implied. Howe deserves as much of the credit for her foreign policy successes in the second term as he does for holding firm at the Treasury in the first.

Mrs Thatcher's conviction that the Foreign Office – officially the Foreign and Commonwealth office – was a limp institution dedicated to giving away Britain's vital interests had only been reinforced by her experience since 1979. She felt in particular that the FCO had let her down over the Falklands, first by failing to foresee the Argentine invasion and then by continuing to pursue peace options when she had long determined that there was no alternative to war. After the war, she appointed Sir Anthony Parsons, fresh from his brilliant performance at the UN, to be her private foreign-policy adviser in Number Ten. Parsons was a relaxed Arabist who disagreed with her on most subjects but had impressed her during the Falklands crisis by standing up to her. 'I think in her mind she wanted to replicate the American system,' he recalled, '[and] have a kind of competitor to the Foreign Office advice. I made it plain to her that I wouldn't accept the job on those terms.' He would co-operate with the FCO, not compete with it. The FCO was wary but Parsons was one of its own, so it did co-operate with him – unlike the Ministry of Defence, which would have nothing to do with the defence adviser Mrs Thatcher appointed and quickly froze him out. A large part of Parsons' job, as he described it, was to try to anticipate crises, so that she would not be 'caught short again as she had been over the Falklands'.[19] He stayed for only a year, but was replaced by Sir Percy Cradock, a China specialist who initially handled the Hong Kong negotiations but stayed on to become her general foreign-policy adviser right up to 1990, attending all relevant meetings except the Cabinet (which never discussed foreign affairs anyway). 'This did not mean automatic disagreement with the Foreign Secretary,' Cradock has written; 'but it did ensure a second opinion.'[20] He shared her attitude to the Soviet Union, but found it increasingly impossible to advise her on Europe, where her prejudices were fixed and immovable.

She punished the FCO in all sorts of other ways, too. She took the Joint Intelligence Committee (JIC) away from it and put it under the Cabinet Office instead, where it was chaired by Sir Anthony Duff, and

later by Cradock, and reported directly to her.[21] She also hived off the
job of co-ordinating European policy from the FCO to the Policy
Unit, where it was under her own control. Her instinct was to reject
the Office's advice on principle. 'The Foreign Office?' she scoffed when
she was contemplating holding a Chequers seminar to reconsider policy
towards the Soviet Union. 'What do they know about anything?'[22] In
November 1986 she circulated 'a scathing note about the "flabby"
suggestions that had come up from the Foreign Office' on Hong
Kong.[23] And another time, when the FCO had succeeded in persuading
her to withdraw military attachés from South Africa, she presented the
policy as if it had nothing to do with her. 'They've withdrawn military attachés,' she told a visiting African leader scornfully, 'whatever
good that may do.'[24]

Increasingly she travelled with no Foreign Office presence in her
party at all, but was accompanied even on important trips only by her
own private advisers. When she first visited President Reagan in 1981,
for example, she took with her a whole phalanx of senior mandarins
(Robert Armstrong, Michael Palliser, Frank Cooper) and several juniors.
By the time she flew right round the world from Beijing and Hong
Kong to bend the President's ear about his 'Star Wars' programme in
December 1984 she was accompanied only by her two private secretaries, Robin Butler and Charles Powell, plus Bernard Ingham. And
towards the end it was usually just Powell and Ingham.

She continued to seek foreign-policy advice from independent
academic experts outside the Foreign Office – Hugh Thomas, Robert
Conquest and later George Urban, Norman Stone and Timothy
Garton-Ash, all specialists in Eastern Europe. Though to an extent these
tended to tell her what she wanted to hear – or more accurately she
chose advisers who would tell her what she wanted to hear – it is to
her credit that she tried to go beyond the narrow circle of official
advice. Nevertheless both her special advisers, Parsons and Cradock,
were former FCO insiders; and the most influential of all from 1984
onwards – Charles Powell – was ironically a Foreign Office man *par
excellence*.

A career diplomat in his early forties who had served in Helsinki,
Washington, Bonn and Brussels, Powell succeeded John Coles as Mrs
Thatcher's foreign-affairs private secretary in June 1984 and immediately established an exceptional rapport with her. The basis of their
relationship was his skill at drafting: he was brilliant at finding acceptable diplomatic language to express what she wanted to say without
fudging it. Second, he needed as little sleep as she did: he was unflag-
ging and ever-present, never went to bed but seemed to be always at

her side. As time went on he became indispensable to her. In addition, he had a knack of getting things done by informal personal diplomacy of his own: he would go direct to Washington or Paris, behind the back of the official Foreign Office, and fix what she wanted with a word in the right place. Inevitably this caused friction in Whitehall, as Powell far exceeded his nominal role as one of five private secretaries, blurring and frequently overstepping the line between official and political advice, so that he came to be seen as the second most powerful figure in the Government, no longer confined exclusively to foreign affairs but the real deputy Prime Minister, practically her *alter ego*. 'It was sometimes difficult,' Cradock wrote, 'to establish where Mrs Thatcher ended and Charles Powell began.'[25]

After three or four years, by normal Whitehall practice, it would have been time for Powell to move on. But Mrs Thatcher refused to let him go. It was not only Powell himself she could not bear to lose: she was also devoted to his Italian wife, Carla, a vivacious socialite who was one of the few people – rather like Tim Bell – who could make her laugh and genuinely get her to relax. 'A series of desperate conferences' was held between Robin Butler – who succeeded Robert Armstrong as Cabinet Secretary in 1988 – and the Permanent Secretary of the Foreign Office, Sir Patrick Wright, to try to find some way of getting Powell out of Number Ten by appointing him ambassador to Berne, Madrid or even Washington. But still, as Cradock wrote, 'Mrs Thatcher would not let him go.'[26] This might not have mattered if he had been just an indispensable Jeeves. But in fact the longer he stayed the more his views began to influence Mrs Thatcher's. Despite having an Italian wife, Powell's service in Bonn and Brussels had left him profoundly sceptical about the European Community, and Germany in particular. Whereas in the earlier years of her premiership Mrs Thatcher was surrounded by overwhelmingly pro-European advice, from about 1986 Powell's informed and articulate Euroscepticism increasingly encouraged her to follow her own anti-Community and anti-German prejudice – with serious results both for herself and for Britain.

Critics of Mrs Thatcher's diplomatic style – and by the end these included close advisers like Cradock and George Urban – tended to dismiss her as ignorant, narrow-minded, insensitive, one-dimensional, oblivious to other points of view and concerned only with securing Britain's short-term interests. Until she was properly briefed she had only her prejudices, which old Foreign Office hands regarded as embarrassingly crude.[27] Yet when she was authoritatively briefed she did listen. 'Mention of the office in the collective sense brought out the worst in her,' Cradock wrote;[28] but she respected expertise and would listen carefully to quite junior officials if she thought they knew their stuff. It was 'not easy to convince her to change her views', Anthony Parsons recalled, but once she was convinced 'she was perfectly prepared to change her view and act in a different way'.[29] She would argue to the last and then keep on niggling away at the course she had been persuaded to adopt, but the overwhelming pattern of her premiership is that she followed Foreign Office advice far more than she liked to pretend – on Zimbabwe, Hong Kong, Northern Ireland, Eastern Europe and even during her second term on the EC. Though she went to war for the Falklands, she liquidated most of the last vestiges of empire around the world; though famously hostile to Communism, she was persuaded that she could do business with a new generation of Soviet leaders; though an instinctive Unionist, she was likewise persuaded that the only chance of peace in Northern Ireland was with the involvement of Dublin; and against her instinct she took the decisive steps in committing Britain to an integrated Europe.

'Margaret Thatcher's diplomacy,' Charles Powell has written, 'was less concerned with making friends than with winning battles.'[30] Yet she not only won battles but made friends as well. Judged by the objectives she set herself, one popular history of modern Britain concludes, she was 'hugely successful' in foreign affairs.[31] First, she played Ronald Reagan skilfully to revive and maximise the US 'special relationship'; then she spotted and encouraged Gorbachev, and acted successfully as an intermediary between him and Reagan. She finally settled the EC budget row and went on to set the pace in promoting the introduction of a single European market. She achieved as good a settlement as could be hoped for in Hong Kong. She defied the world by pursuing her own route to ending apartheid in South Africa and arguably was vindicated by the result. And despite her strongly expressed views, she managed to maintain good relations with almost everyone, not only the leaders of both superpowers, but on both sides of the Jordan and the Limpopo too. In short, she 'utterly transformed Britain's standing and reputation in the world'.[32]

Ron and Margaret

The unshakeable cornerstone of Mrs Thatcher's foreign policy was the United States. She had no time for subtle formulations which saw Britain as the meeting point of overlapping circles of influence, maintaining a careful equidistance between America on the one hand and Europe on the other, with obligations to the Commonwealth somewhere in the background. She had no doubt whatever that Britain's primary role in the world was as Washington's number-one ally. No Prime Minister since Churchill had believed so unquestioningly in the mission of 'the English-speaking peoples' to lead and save the rest of the world. But she had no illusions about who was the senior partner, nor did she seek to deny the reality of British dependence on the United States. It was the Americans – with British help – who had liberated Europe from the Nazi tyranny in 1944; it was American nuclear protection which had defended Western Europe from Soviet aggression since 1945. 'Had it not been for the magnanimity of the United States, Europe would not be free today,' she reminded the Tory Party Conference in 1981 (and repeated on innumerable other occasions). 'We cannot defend ourselves, either in this island or in Europe, without a close, effective and warm-hearted alliance with the United States.'[33]

Moreover she increasingly believed that it was not just America's military might that underwrote the survival of freedom in the West, but American capitalism, which was the pre-eminent model of that freedom. Nothing made her angrier than the condescension of the British political establishment which viewed America as crude, refreshingly vigorous but sadly naive. She envied the energy and optimism of American society – the unapologetic belief in capitalism and the refusal to look to the state for the solution to every social problem – and wanted Britain to become in every respect (from penal policy to the funding of the arts) more American. She was herself, as one US Ambassador in London shrewdly noted, a very American type of politician: patriotic, evangelical, unafraid of big abstract words, preaching a message of national and even personal salvation quite unlike the usual British (and European) style of ironic scepticism and fatalistic damage limitation.[34] Proud as she was of Britain's glorious past, at the end of the twentieth century a part of her would really rather have been American. Her entourage felt the almost physical charge she got whenever she visited America. 'When she stepped onto American soil she became a new woman,' Ronnie Millar noted. 'The slightest feeling of fatigue . . . was gone in a flash and she looked ten years younger. She loved America . . . and America loved her back. There is nothing like the chemistry of mutual admiration.'[35]

She was distressed and angered by the overt anti-Americanism of British liberals who professed to see little difference between the Americans and the Russians, or nuclear disarmers who painted the United States as a greater threat to peace than the Soviet Union. There was no group she more passionately despised than academics who abused their personal freedom by equating Tyranny and Freedom. Her world view was uncomplicatedly black and white. 'This party is pro-American,' she declared roundly at the 1984 Tory Party Conference.[36] Whatever differences she might have with the Americans on specific issues, she was determined to demonstrate on every occasion Britain's unqualified loyalty to the Atlantic Alliance. 'My view,' she wrote in her memoirs, 'was that ultimately we must support American leadership.'[37] Critics who believed that Britain's interest lay in closer links with Europe condemned her for making herself the poodle of successive American administrations. She did not mind. 'I saw it as Britain's task to put the American case in Europe.'[38] If she could not be the leader of the free world herself, the next best thing was to be his first lieutenant.

Just as she was lucky in her enemies, Mrs Thatcher was extraordinarily fortunate to coincide for most of her eleven years in Downing Street with an American President who allowed her to play a bigger role within the Alliance than any other Prime Minister since the days of Roosevelt and Churchill. During her first year and a half in office she tried hard to cultivate a good relationship with Jimmy Carter. Deeply as she revered his office, however, she enjoyed no rapport with the well-meaning but in her view hopelessly woolly-minded Democrat. The election of Ronald Reagan in November 1980, by contrast, changed everything. It was not just that Reagan was an ideological soulmate, elected on the same sort of conservative programme – tax cuts and strong defence – that had brought her to power in Britain. It is not uncommon – rather it is the norm, reflecting a deep rhythm of the electoral cycle – for Tory Prime Ministers to overlap with Republican Presidents, and Labour Prime Ministers with Democrats: Eisenhower and Churchill, Kennedy and Macmillan; Johnson and Wilson; Nixon and Heath; Carter and Callaghan. Ideological symmetry, however, does not guarantee a good relationship: it is just as likely to make for rivalry. Far more important than the similarity of their ideas was the difference in their political personalities.

Temperamentally Reagan was Mrs Thatcher's opposite, an easy-going, broad-brush politician who made no pretence of mastering the detailed complexities of policy, but was happy to let others – including on occasion Mrs Thatcher – lead and even bully him. The bond of their instinctively shared values was reinforced by sexual chemistry: he had an old-fashioned gallantry towards women, while she had a weakness for tall, charming men (particularly older men) with film-star looks. Out of his depth with most foreign leaders, Reagan knew where he was with Mrs Thatcher, if only because she spoke his language: he understood her, liked her, admired her and therefore trusted her. Unlike with Helmut Schmidt, he did not feel threatened in his 'male pride' by a strong woman: as Americans often remarked, Margaret Thatcher held no terrors for a man who had been married for thirty years to Nancy Davis. For a politician, Reagan was unusually secure in his own skin. Unlike Mrs Thatcher he did not have to win every argument: he knew what he believed, but shrank from confrontation. Once when she was hectoring him down the telephone from London, he held the receiver away from his ear so that everyone in the room could hear her in full flow, beamed broadly and announced: 'Isn't she marvellous?'[39]

Thus was forged what Percy Cradock called an 'unlikely partnership' between, on the one hand, 'the bossy, intrusive Englishwoman, lecturing and hectoring, hyperactive, obsessively concerned with detail', and on the other, 'the lazy, sunny Irish ex-actor, his mind operating mainly in the instinctive mode, happy to delegate and over-delegate, hazy about most of his briefs, but with certain stubbornly-held principles, a natural warmth and an extraordinary ability to communicate with his constituents'.[40] Their contrasting styles served to disguise the disparity in power between Washington and London and for eight years made something approaching reality of the comforting myth of a 'special relationship' between Britain and the United States. The closest parallel in recent years had been the quasi-paternal relationship between Harold Macmillan and John Kennedy in the early 1960s, when the anglophile young President made a show of deferring to the experience and patrician style of the much older Macmillan. But this was of a different order.

Mrs Thatcher exploited her opportunity with great skill – and uncharacteristic tact. Privately she was clear-sighted about the President's limitations. 'If I told you what Mrs Thatcher really thought about President Reagan it would damage Anglo-American relations,' Nicholas Henderson told Tony Benn some years later.[41] 'Not much grey matter, is there?' she once reflected;[42] or, another time, 'There's nothing there.'[43] But she would never hear a word of criticism from others. In Reagan she put up with a bumbling ignorance she would have tolerated in no one else, partly because he was the President and leader of the free world, but also because she realised that his amiable vagueness gave her a chance to influence American policy that no conventionally hands-on President would have allowed her – as was quickly demonstrated when Reagan was succeeded by George Bush.

François Mitterrand was amazed by her exaggerated deference to Reagan. 'Mrs Thatcher, who can be so tough when she talks to her European partners, is like a little girl of eight years old when she talks to the President of the United States. You have to cock your ear to hear her, she's really so touching.'[44] Others, conversely, have commented on the way she mothered him. David Gergan, for instance, Reagan's chief of staff, has described how behind closed doors, Mrs Thatcher would 'talk over issues with him as an equal'.

But just before they went out to see the press she turned motherly:

'Mr President, can I suggest that you say this . . . and then I might say this . . .' And so on. People say she thought Reagan was incompetent, but I never saw a hint of condescension. Like Shultz [Secretary of State from 1982] she was gentle and caring, trying to make sure he navigated safely.[45]

His instinct was likewise to protect her – not that she needed it. At the G7 summit in London in 1984 Pierre Trudeau dared to criticise Mrs Thatcher's chairmanship as high-handed and undemocratic. Afterwards Reagan told her that Trudeau had been 'way out of line', but that she had handled him very well. 'Oh,' she told him, 'women know when men are being childish.'[46]

The basis of their partnership was laid back in 1975, when Mrs Thatcher was a newly elected Leader of the Opposition and the ex-Governor of California was just beginning to be talked of as a Presidential candidate. They had immediately found themselves on the same wavelength, and in due course each was delighted by the other's election. Yet their relationship in office took a little time to develop. By no coincidence Mrs Thatcher was the first major foreign visitor to Washington after Reagan's inauguration.* Before she left she told an American audience in London that she hoped her visit would 'mark the opening of a period of particularly close understanding between the two Governments and a particularly close understanding between the two Heads of Government.'[47] She stated her position unambiguously at the welcoming ceremony on the White House lawn: 'We in Britain stand with you . . . Your problems will be our problems, and when you look for friends we will be there.' Reagan responded in kind. 'In a dangerous world,' he asserted, there was 'one element that goes without question: Britain and America stand side by side.'[48]

But this was the conventional rhetoric of these occasions. At this stage the two leaders were still addressing each other formally on

---

*Contrary to British press reports, she was not quite the first: both the Prime Minister of Jamaica and the President of South Korea had got there before her.

paper as 'Dear Mr President . . . Dear Madame Prime Minister'.[49] Their working partnership really began at the Ottawa G7 in July 1981. This was Reagan's first appearance on the global stage, while she was now relatively experienced: he was grateful for her support, both personal and political. She chaperoned and protected him, and made the case for American policy more effectively than he could, on the one hand for market solutions to the world recession against most of the other leaders who favoured more interventionist measures; and on the other in standing firm in support of the deployment of cruise missiles, from which the Europeans – faced with anti-nuclear demonstrations – were beginning to retreat. At the same time she warned Reagan privately that American criticism of European 'neutralism' risked provoking exactly the reaction it sought to prevent.[50]

Afterwards Reagan wrote to her for the first time as 'Dear Margaret', thanking her for her 'important role in our discussions. We might still be drafting the communiqué if it were not for you.' She in return addressed him for the first time as 'Dear Ron'.[51] Nine months later the Falklands crisis caused a temporary hiccup; but after some initial hesitation Reagan gave Britain the full support Mrs Thatcher felt entitled to expect. Arrangements had already been made for Reagan to visit London after the Versailles summit in June 1982. The trip had been planned at the nadir of Mrs Thatcher's domestic unpopularity to lend support to an embattled ally; in the event it took place a few days before the Argentine surrender, at the climax of her military triumph. As well as meeting the Prime Minister in Downing Street, the President went riding with the Queen in Windsor Great Park and addressed members of both Houses of Parliament in the Royal Gallery, where he overcame a sceptical audience by praising Britain's principled stand in the Falklands and borrowing freely from Churchill in asserting the moral superiority of the West. Freedom and democracy, he predicted, would 'leave Marxism–Leninism on the ash-heap of history'.* While the rest of his visit to Europe was disrupted by anti-nuclear demonstrations, the warmth of his reception in London moved the 'special relationship' visibly onto a new level.[52]

At subsequent summits Reagan treated Mrs Thatcher explicitly as his prime ally. He was particularly pleased that she found time to attend the Williamsburg summit in the middle of the June 1983 election. White

---

*This was the first time anyone in Britain had seen an autocue – Reagan's 'sincerity machine' – which enabled him to speak with unnatural fluency without looking down at his notes. Mrs Thatcher quickly adopted it for her own major speeches.

House files show how his staff co-ordinated with hers to advance their joint agenda. 'Mrs Thatcher's attendance is good news for us,' one aide wrote to another in mid-May. 'She will support the President on the key issues.'

> As you know, we have been having trouble with her personal representative [Robert Armstrong] in the preparatory process. Instead of supporting us in beating down unhelpful French initiatives, Armstrong has been attempting to mediate between us and the French.

To put a stop to this, they drafted a letter for the President to write to the Prime Minister. 'I may need your support Sunday afternoon when we instruct our personal representatives to draw up the first draft of the joint statement.'

> Although we will try to accommodate legitimate French concerns, and we do not wish to embarrass François Mitterand, we must insist on a joint statement which has a tone of realistic optimism, and we must resist a call for a new Bretton Woods conference.
>   I hope I can count on your support on these issues, and that my sherpa, Allen Wallis, can count on Robert Armstrong's support during the drafting sessions.[53]

Afterwards Reagan thanked her for her help, not only on the economic issue, but on defence as well. 'Thanks to your contribution during Saturday's dinner discussion of INF [Intermediate-range Nuclear Forces],' he told her, 'we were able to send to the Soviets a clear signal of allied determination and unity.'[54] And before the London meeting the following year he wrote to her that he planned to provide her with 'the same stalwart support' that she had given him at Williamsburg.[55] They made a powerful and well-rehearsed double act.

From now on Mrs Thatcher invited herself to Washington at the drop of a hat. As soon as she had secured her re-election in June 1983 she asked to come over in September 'to continue bilateral discussions with the President'.[56] 'This will be a major substantive visit addressing a wide range of meaty issues,' Assistant Secretary of State William Clark minuted, 'designed to "kick-off" her second term. In a sense the visit itself is the message; but Mrs Thatcher will have much on her mind,' including East-West relations, the Middle East and a number of bilateral economic concerns.[57] 'She will speak plainly about British interests,' the US Embassy in London warned, 'and will appreciate plain speaking from us.'[58] Henceforth this was the basis of the relationship, as Lady Thatcher explicitly acknowledged in her memoirs: 'I regarded the *quid pro quo* for my strong public support of the President as being the right to be direct with him and members of his Administration in private.'[59] 'She not only had her say,' Richard Perle remembered, 'but was frequently the dominant influence in decision-making.'[60]

If, as an outsider, she was able to have this degree of influence, it was because, compared with Whitehall, Washington is highly decentralised. American government is a continuous struggle between different agencies – the State Department, the Pentagon, the National Security Adviser, the CIA and others – all competing for the President's ear. Well briefed by the British Embassy, Mrs Thatcher knew the balance of views on every issue and where her intervention, judiciously applied, might be decisive. It was well known that Reagan did not like quarrelling with her, so those Presidential advisers on her side of a particular argument had every incentive to deploy her to clinch their case. George Shultz, who replaced Al Haig as Secretary of State in the summer of 1982, recalled that he always found her influence with Reagan 'very constructive', and was 'shameless' in calling on her aid when required.[61] Others, however, found her interventions maddening.

When she could not come to Washington in person, she would write or telephone. She regularly reported to Reagan her views on other leaders she had met on her travels, and pressed her ideas of the action he should take in the Middle East or other troublespots. The files now open in the Reagan Library show White House staff having to cope with this tide of advice, sometimes with some irritation. 'Please move this reply before she has time to send yet another message!!!!,' one aide minuted another in November 1981 after she had sent three letters in five days. On this occasion the draft reply thanked her tactfully for 'the candid insights you have shared with me from your talks with crown Prince Fahd and your visits to Bahrein and Kuwait'.[62] In January 1984 the State Department proposed that a planned letter about nuclear proliferation should be sent from Weinberger to Heseltine, 'given the already heavy use of the Reagan/Thatcher channel for issues of major bilateral importance and urgency'.[63]

Sometimes their letters were purely personal, as when they remembered each other's birthdays, congratulated one another on being reelected, or expressed horror and relief when the other narrowly escaped assassination. At least once, at the height of the miners' strike in 1984, Reagan simply sent his friend a note of encouragement. 'Dear Margaret,' he wrote:

In recent weeks I have thought often of you with considerable empathy as I follow the activities of the miners and dockworkers' unions. I know they present a difficult set of issues for your government. I just wanted you to know that my thoughts are with you as you address these important issues; I'm confident as ever that you and your government will come out of this well.
Warm regards, Ron.[64]

Two years later, when Reagan in turn was in trouble over damaging revelations about his administration's involvement in the exchange of arms for the release of Iranian hostages, in defiance of its declared policy, Mrs Thatcher rushed publicly to his defence: 'I believe implicitly in the President's total integrity on that subject,' she told a press conference in Washington.[65] As the Iran–Contra scandal deepened the following year and America was seized by a mood of gloomy introspection, she visited Washington again – fresh from her own second re-election – and toured the television studios, vigorously denying that Reagan was politically weakened and defending his honour. 'I have dealt with the President for many, many years,' she told a CBS interviewer, 'and I have absolute trust in him.' Moreover, she insisted, 'America is a strong country, with a great President, a great people and a great future. Cheer up! Be more upbeat! . . . You should have as much faith in America as I have.'[66]

Such fulsome encomiums, repeated every time she went to Washington and lapped up by the American media, were regularly condemned by her opponents at home for showing an excessive degree of grovelling subordination. Yet the truth is that in her private dealings with Washington she never grovelled. On a whole range of issues, from the Falklands to nuclear disarmament, on which she had differences with the Americans, she fought her corner vigorously. As Richard Perle remembered: 'She never approached the conversations she had . . . with American officials and with the President from a position of supplication or inferiority. Quite the contrary.'[67]

Her first battle was over the consequences for British firms of American sanctions on the Soviet Union following the imposition of martial law in Poland in December 1981. She passionately supported the Polish Solidarity movement and was all in favour of concerted western action to deter the Russians from crushing the flicker of freedom in Poland as they had done in Czechoslovakia and Hungary. But the Americans' chosen sanction was to halt the construction of an oil pipeline from Siberia to Western Europe, which they proposed to enforce by applying sanctions to European firms, including the British company John Brown Engineering, which had legitimate existing contracts to build the pipeline. This, Mrs Thatcher objected, would hurt the Europeans more than the Russians, while it was not matched by comparable American sacrifices: the Americans had actually ended an embargo on grain exports to Russia which was hitting American farmers in the Midwest. She also objected to the Americans trying to impose American laws on British firms operating outside the USA.

When Alexander Haig called on her in London on 29 January 1982 she raised these concerns 'with unusual vehemence':

> She pointed out that whatever the perception in America, the cost of the sanctions imposed thus far are far greater to Europe than to the US, and went on to describe the impact on Western Europe's economy of further financial and trading sanctions in the strongest terms and predicted dire consequences for the Western Alliance should we proceed in that direction.[68]

For once she was speaking for Europe against America. In truth she was fighting for British interests, but with her usual ability to clothe national interest in a cloak of principle, she was also standing up for sovereignty and the rule of law against American extra-territorial arrogance. She visited Washington after speaking at the UN just after the end of the Falklands war and lectured the Americans without restraint. 'Her eyes blazed,' Nicholas Henderson wrote, 'and she launched into a fierce attack on the President's decision, pointing out that American exports to the USSR would grow this year because of the lifting of the grain embargo.'[69] 'The question is whether one very powerful nation can prevent existing contracts being fulfilled,' she told the House of Commons on 1 July. 'I think it is wrong to do so.'[70] The British Government instructed John Brown not to comply with the US embargo.

Reagan was distressed by his ally's intransigence, and tried to suggest that the effect on John Brown would not be so serious as she believed:

> I know, Margaret, that you feel as strongly as I that the Soviet and Polish authorities must be brought to realise that the reform process in Poland must be renewed . . . Surely, given our common view, you and I can – indeed we must – continue to work together to bring the Soviet and Polish authorities to their senses.[71]

But she would have none of his soft soap. 'I hear what you say about John Brown Engineering,' she replied. 'I can only reiterate my very serious concern for this British company if it is prevented from exporting the equipment which it is under contract to supply . . . I believe, as a matter of principle, that existing commercial contracts should be honoured.' She had no option but to take action to protect British companies; but at the same time, she promised, she would take only the minimum action, since she was 'very anxious that this matter should not be allowed to escalate and thus become a serious irritant in our relations'.[72]

Reagan in turn thanked her for 'the constructive framework in which you have placed our differences', adding that her letter 'exemplifies the tone and spirit which ought to guide US–UK relations'.[73] But Mrs Thatcher stuck to her guns. Meeting Caspar Weinberger in London in September, she still insisted that Britain 'was faced with the possibility that the US pipeline decision would result in four or five UK firms going bankrupt'. Moreover, she 'didn't believe that the sanctions would help ease the repression in Poland'. Yet her main concern was still to prevent damage to the Alliance. 'The only fly in the ointment,' she told Weinberger, 'is the John Brown thing.' 'She fervently hoped,' he cabled Reagan, 'that what the US did would be so minimal that she could ignore it. She desperately needed some face-saving solution.' Characteristically she was worried about fuelling anti-Americanism. 'Mrs Thatcher said she had a serious problem with unemployment and bankruptcies, and she didn't want her closest friend, the United States, to be blamed by her people.'[74]

As so often, she knew that she had allies in Washington. In this instance her pressure helped the new Secretary of State, George Shultz, to get the pipeline ban lifted in return for a package of joint measures limiting Soviet imports and the export of technology to Russia. Telling her of his decision on 12 November, Reagan thanked her – and Pym and the British Ambassador in Washington, Sir Oliver Wright – for helping achieve this consensus. 'I think we have succeeded in moving our friends closer to the US/UK point of view on East–West economic relations than many would have thought possible a year ago.'[75] This was the special relationship in action.

But the Polish pipeline question was just one of a number of 'chronic economic irritants' which Mrs Thatcher felt she had to raise with the Americans every time she visited Washington in the mid-1980s.[76] First there was the fallout of British Airways' price war with Freddie Laker's independent airline, Laker Airways, which succeeded in forcing the price-cutting upstart out of business in 1982. Much as she admired Laker as a model entrepreneur, Mrs Thatcher was worried that an American Justice Department investigation into BA's unscrupulous methods was holding up plans to privatise the national carrier. In March 1983 she appealed 'personally and urgently' to Reagan to suspend the investigation, once again threatening that it 'could have the most serious consequences for British airlines' and warning that if it was not stopped, 'our aviation relationship will be damaged and the harm could go wider'.[77] Advised by his staff that he could not interfere in the judicial process, Reagan replied regretfully that 'in this case I feel that I do not have the latitude to respond to your concerns'.[78] But seven months later he did stop the investigation – an 'almost unprecedented' intervention which left the Justice Department 'stunned'. Mrs Thatcher voiced 'her immense gratitude for the President's courageous decision'; but the Americans were 'deeply disappointed' that she still wanted further legislation to prevent private anti-trust actions, contrary to what they understood to be her belief in increased competition, and more American concessions to BA on routes, which was quite unrealistic. 'The British have been singularly unhelpful,' Reagan's National Security Adviser 'Bud' Macfarlane briefed him in December 1984.[79] At Camp David later that month – a meeting arranged primarily to discuss the President's Strategic Defense Initiative – Mrs Thatcher insisted before, during and after lunch that a series of lawsuits still hanging over the company was making it very difficult for her to privatise it. The White House was clearly exasperated by the way she kept on at this issue; but once again her 'sheer persistence' prevailed: in March 1985 Reagan intervened again to persuade BA's biggest creditors to settle out of court, thus clearing the way for privatisation to begin in 1986.[80]

Another running sore was the attempt of some American states to tax multinational companies on the proportion of their profits deemed to have been earned in that state. British objections to this 'unitary taxation' – at a time when British companies were investing heavily in America – bedevilled several of Mrs Thatcher's meetings with Reagan and his colleagues, before this too was eventually settled to her satisfaction. In this case, however, the resolution probably owed more to American multinationals making the same complaint than it did to Mrs Thatcher's protests.

Above all, she worried about the impact on Europe of the Americans' huge budget deficit, caused by the Reagan administration's policy of tax cuts combined with increased defence spending. After five years the deficit was running at $220 billion a year and the US was the world's largest debtor nation – especially heavily indebted to Japan. This was Mrs Thatcher's one serious criticism of her ally's economic policy. When she had been unable to bring spending under control in 1981 she had felt bound to raise taxes and she could not understand

Reagan's insouciance. 'The American double-deficit – both budgetary and trade,' wrote Bernard Ingham, 'was a constant source of worry to her prudent soul.'[81] At successive G7 summits (at Versailles in 1982, Williamsburg in 1983 and London in 1984) she warned that the unchecked deficit would raise interest rates and 'choke off world recovery'.[82] In fact US interest rates fell in the second half of 1984 and the booming US economy led the world out of recession. But still Mrs Thatcher worried, though she was reluctant to criticise in public. When she did, she couched her concern in tactfully flattering terms: 'No other country in the world can be immune from its effects,' she told the US Congress in February 1985, 'such is the influence of the American economy on us all.'[83] But having had 'useful talks' the next day with Reagan's economic team – she did not only talk to the President when she came to Washington, but to all the senior American policymakers she could get to – she wrote to him that she remained 'very concerned by . . . the continuing surge of the dollar':

> A firm programme for the reduction of the budget deficit is the most important safeguard against financial instability and I wish you every success with your Budget proposals to Congress.[84]

Reagan tried, in his fashion; but in practice the conflicting priorities of the Republican White House and a Democrat-dominated Congress ensured that the deficit persisted for the rest of the decade. A State Department briefing before her next visit to Washington later that year warned that 'Mrs Thatcher may use the occasion to lecture on US budgetary deficits and the resultant high dollar'.[85] No doubt she did; but this was one area in which her influence counted for little.

An even more sensitive issue on which Mrs Thatcher's intransigence exasperated Washington was the future of the Falklands. The Americans had, with some misgivings, eventually backed what the *Washington Post* called her 'seemingly senseless, small but bloody war' in the South Atlantic.[86] But as soon as the fighting was over, Washington's priority was to resume normal relations with Argentina (and South America as a whole) as quickly as possible, and renew the search for a lasting peace settlement. Even in his message of congratulation on her victory, Reagan stated firmly that 'A just war requires a just peace. We look forward to consulting with you and to assisting in the building of such a peace.'[87] An invitation to her to visit Washington a few days later was couched explicitly as an opportunity to consider how to achieve this goal.[88]

But Mrs Thatcher was not interested in a just peace. So far as she was concerned, she had defeated the aggressor, at great risk and considerable sacrifice, and she was not now willing to negotiate away what her forces had won. As she defiantly put it: 'We have not sent British troops and treasure 8000 miles to establish a UN trusteeship.'[89] Even in June 1982, however, Reagan's staff were keen that he should 'lay down a marker' for eventual negotiations and help point her towards 'necessary reasonableness and reconciliation'; as the euphoria wore off and she entered a more difficult phase, they anticipated, she would probably begin to 'unbend'.[90]

The first test of her flexibility came that autumn, when several Latin American countries sponsored a UN resolution calling for renewed negotiations to end what they called 'the colonial situation' in the Falklands. Mrs Thatcher immediately cabled Reagan asking that the US should oppose the resolution. But George Shultz and others in the administration – not least Jeane Kirkpatrick, still the American Ambassador at the UN – believed that the US should support it, since the whole purpose of the UN was to promote the peaceful resolution of disputes. Shultz initially feared that Reagan would take Mrs Thatcher's side. 'But I found that he too was getting a little fed up with her imperious attitude in the matter.'[91] The President ticked his agreement to Mrs Kirkpatrick backing the resolution, and wrote a delicate letter – in reply to what his staff called 'Mrs Thatcher's latest blast' – to explain why. 'We understand your reluctance to enter into negotiations when loss of life remains fresh in everyone's mind,' he wrote:

We can appreciate your desire for a cooling-off period and more concrete evidence from Argentina that it will not resort again to further use of force. Nevertheless we believe it is important that the options of negotiations or other means of peaceful settlement not be foreclosed, particularly in light of the fact that the Government of Argentina now suggesting negotiations is a different one from the one which launched the aggression.

'Margaret,' he ended, 'I know how you have anguished over this conflict from the beginning. Your courage and leadership throughout have been a source of deep personal inspiration to me. I count it a privilege to have been able to support you and Britain at this critical moment. You may be absolutely confident that I would do it all again the same way.'[92] Nevertheless the sting was that he was still going to support the UN resolution, which was duly carried by a large majority, with only a dozen Commonwealth countries joining Britain in opposing it.

Mrs Thatcher continued adamantly to reject any possibility of negotiations on the question of sovereignty. A year later, however, with a democratically elected government now installed in Buenos Aires, the State Department took a further step towards normalising relations by 'certifying' Argentina as eligible for a resumption of American arms sales. This, Reagan assured Mrs Thatcher, merely ended the embargo imposed in 1982. 'Certification does not mean arms sales.'[93] The announcement was tactfully postponed for a day to spare her embarrassment in the House of Commons; Vice-President George Bush thanked her for her understanding response.[94] For the next three years Reagan deferred to her sensitivity, and no arms were sold; but by 1986 the pressure from the Pentagon was becoming irresistible. Once again Mrs Thatcher went straight to the top. 'You should expect a typical Thatcher barrage,' John Poindexter briefed Reagan before their meeting at Camp David following the Reagan-Gorbachev summit at Reykjavik. 'You will want to tell Mrs Thatcher that we cannot continually put off how best to nurture Argentina's democracy.'[95] But this time she was more subtle, waiting until almost the last minute before dropping a final item almost casually into the conversation, as Geoffrey Smith described. '"Oh, arms to Argentina," she said, for all the world like a housewife checking that she had not forgotten some last piece of shopping. "You won't, will you?"' To the horror of his officials, Reagan fell for it. '"No," he replied. "We won't." So in one short sentence he killed weeks of careful preparation within his administration.'[96]

The most serious public disagreement of their whole eight-year partnership came in October 1983, when the Americans sent troops to the tiny Caribbean island of Grenada to put down a coup by a gang of left-wing thugs against the elected – but already Marxist – government led by Maurice Bishop. The Americans were always concerned about any left-wing takeover on their Caribbean doorstep and, fearful of another Cuba, had already been doing their best to destabilise Bishop's regime ever since 1979. But Grenada was a member of the Commonwealth, whose head of state was the Queen. The Foreign Office was alarmed at events on the island, but believed there was nothing to be done, since Grenada was a sovereign country. Several neighbouring Caribbean states, however, concerned for their own security, did want something done, and appealed to Washington for help. The Americans responded by diverting ships to the island, ostensibly to evacuate several hundred American students, but in fact to mount a counter-coup. They did so without consulting or even informing Mrs Thatcher until it was too late to halt the action. As a result she was humiliated by the revelation that her vaunted relationship with Washington was rather less close than she pretended.

The story of her reaction to the news of the American invasion has been vividly told from both sides of the Atlantic. According to Carol's life of Denis, Reagan telephoned while her mother was attending a dinner – ironically at the US Embassy. As soon as she got back to Downing Street she phoned Reagan back and railed at him for several minutes: some versions say a quarter of an hour. 'She didn't half tick him off,' Denis told Carol. '"You have invaded the Queen's territory and you didn't even say a word to me," she said to him, very upset. I think that Reagan was a bit shocked. There was nothing gentle about her tone, and not much diplomacy either.'[97] In Washington, Reagan was briefing Congressional leaders when she rang: he went into the next room to take her call. 'As soon as I heard her voice,' his memoirs relate in his usual folksy style, 'I knew she was very angry . . . Grenada, she reminded me, was part of the British Commonwealth and the United States had no business interfering in its affairs.'

> She was very adamant and continued to insist that we cancel our landings . . . I couldn't tell her that it had already begun. This tumbled me because of our close relationship.[98]

At the end of 'what was obviously a very vigorous discussion', Caspar Weinberger recalled, during which 'the unhappiness being expressed from London came through clearly . . . the President returned with a rather rueful look on his face which made it clear that even his persuasive powers . . . had not convinced the Prime Minister'.[99] More graphic still, 'Bud' Macfarlane describes Reagan listening patiently to her outburst, 'occasionally holding the receiver a couple of inches from his ear. When she had finished, he said he hoped that we could still look to her for understanding and support and that we would keep her informed, and hung up.'[100]

In fact these published accounts are all highly coloured, though they accurately convey Mrs Thatcher's fury. The diplomatic exchanges tell a slightly different story. Washington received the call for help from the Organisation of Eastern Caribbean States (OECS), led by the formidable Mrs Eugenia Charles, Prime Minister of Dominica, on Sunday 23 October. The same day a suicide attack in Beirut killed some 300 American soldiers serving in the multinational peace-keeping force in Lebanon. There was no logical connection, but there was no doubt in British minds that the American resolve to act quickly in Grenada was fuelled by the outrage in Beirut: it was easier to hit back in Grenada than in Lebanon. Reagan and his military advisers decided almost immediately to accede to the OECS request and began planning the operation in the greatest secrecy. At 4 p.m. on Monday afternoon, in reply to a question from Denis Healey about the possibility of American intervention in Grenada, Howe told the Commons in good faith that he knew of no such intention: American ships were in the area solely to take off US citizens if it should become necessary, just as Britain had HMS *Antrim* in the area for the same purpose. Pressed further by a Labour MP, he assured the House that 'we are keeping in the closest possible touch with the United States Government . . . I have no reason to think that American military intervention is likely.'[101]

Less than three hours later, however, at 6.47 p.m., while Mrs Thatcher was still in Downing Street hosting a reception, there came a cable from Reagan telling her that he was giving 'serious consideration' to the OECS request. He assured her that if an invasion did go ahead, the British Governor-General would be the key figure in appointing a provisional government as soon as the troops had landed. He also promised categorically: 'I will . . . undertake to inform you in advance should our forces take part in the proposed collective security force, or of whatever political or diplomatic efforts we plan to pursue. It is of some assurance to know I can count on your support and advice on this important issue.'[102]

Mrs Thatcher received this message before she went out to dinner but, in view of the promise of further consultation, did not think it required an immediate reply. Only three hours later, however, at ten o'clock, there came a second, much shorter cable, in which the President informed her curtly: 'I have decided to respond positively to this request.'

> Our forces will establish themselves in Grenada. The collective Caribbean security force will disembark on Grenada shortly there-after . . . We will inform you of further developments as they occur. Other allies will be apprised of our actions after they are begun.
>
> I expect that a new provisional government will be formed in Grenada shortly after the collective security force arrives. We hope that Her Majesty's government will join us by extending support to Grenada's new leaders.[103]

What these two cables clearly show is that the Americans were perfectly well aware of Britain's primary responsibility in Grenada, but had decided that Mrs Thatcher's support for unilateral US action could be taken for granted. As a robust Cold Warrior, they assumed, the Iron Lady would applaud the suppression of a Communist coup anywhere in the world. But if they thought she would be gratified to be informed a few hours before the other allies, they were badly mistaken. She was outraged, first that the Americans should think of invading the Queen's territory, which touched in her the same patriotic trigger as the Argentine invasion of the Falklands; worse still that they should do it without telling her. There is no doubt that she felt personally let down. But she did not get on the telephone immediately. First she held a midnight meeting with Howe and Michael Heseltine. They agreed a reply setting out Britain's objections to military action and urging the Americans to hold their hand. They argued, first, that intervention was more likely to endanger the British and US citizens on the island than protect them; second, that while the OECS had called for military action, much of the rest of the Caribbean was against it; and, third, that a US invasion would be seen by the rest of the world as America bullying a small neighbour, damaging public support for the deployment of cruise missiles in Europe.[104] In addition, Mrs Thatcher worried that America intervening militarily in the Caribbean would be used by the Russians to legitimise their invasion of Afghanistan. She told her staff that she remembered seeing newspaper placards in 1956 reading 'Britain Invades Egypt' and knew instantly that it was wrong.[105]

Only after sending Britain's reasoned objection did she telephone Reagan, at about two o'clock in the morning, London time. Unfortunately no transcript of her call was made. But both Howe, in his memoirs, and Mrs Thatcher at the time, contradict the story that she gave the President an earful. 'Slightly to my surprise,' Howe writes, 'Margaret was nervous of saying too much on the telephone for fear the call was being intercepted' – even though 'this particular speech channel was one of the most secure in the world.'[106] 'I would not speak very long even on the secret telephone,' she told Reagan a few days later, 'because even that can be broken. I'm very much aware of sensitivities.'[107] All she did was to ask him to consider carefully the advice in her cabled message. So much for her giving Reagan 'a prime ticking off'.

A few hours later – just before 7 a.m. in London, just before 2 a.m. in Washington and only three hours before the troops landed – came Reagan's reply, diplomatic but uncompromising. He thanked Mrs Thatcher for her 'thoughtful message', claimed to have 'weighed very carefully' the issues she had raised, but insisted that while he appreciated the dangers inherent in a military operation, 'on balance, I see this as the lesser of two risks'. He stressed the danger of Soviet influence in Grenada, felt that he had no choice but to intervene, and repeated his hope that 'as we proceed, in co-operation with the OECS countries, we would have the active co-operation of Her Majesty's Government' and the support of the Governor-General in establishing an interim government.[108]

That afternoon Howe had to explain to the Commons why he had inadvertently misled the House the day before. He still claimed to have kept 'closely in touch' with the American Government over the weekend, and confirmed that he and Mrs Thatcher had opposed military intervention; but he could not deny that their advice had not been asked until it was too late and had been ignored when given. He could not endorse the American action, but neither could he condemn it, leaving himself open to the mockery of Denis Healey, who savaged the Government's 'impression of pitiable impotence'. Not for the first time, he charged, Mrs Thatcher had allowed 'President Reagan to walk all over her'.[109]

Next day – during an uncomfortable Commons debate – Reagan rang to apologise for the embarrassment he had caused her. Mrs Thatcher's side of the conversation is uncharacteristically monosyllabic. Reagan began with a nervous joke, alluding to his cowboy past. 'If I were there, Margaret,' he suggested, 'I'd throw my hat in the door before I came in.' 'There's no need to do that,' she replied. He then explained why the operation had had to be planned in such haste and secrecy:

When word came of your concerns – by the time I got it – the zero hour had passed and our forces were on their way . . . But I want you to know it was no feeling on our part of lack of confidence at your end. It's at our end. I guess it's the first thing we have done since I've been President in which the secret was actually kept until it happened . . .

'I know about sensitivity, because of the Falklands,' she replied. That was why she would not talk freely on the phone. But the action was under way now and she hoped it would be successful. It was 'going beautifully', he assured her; but as he talked on optimistically, she sounded sceptical. The end of the conversation was polite but distinctly chilly:

'There is a lot to do yet, Ron.'
'Oh, yes.'
'And it will be very tricky.'
'We think that the military part is going to end very shortly.'

'That will be very, very good news. And then if we return to
democracy that will be marvellous.'
'As I say, I'm sorry for any embarrassment that we caused you,
but please understand that it was just our fear of our own
weakness over here with regard to secrecy.'
'It was very kind of you to have rung, Ron.'
'Well, my pleasure.'
'I appreciate it. How is Nancy?'
'Just fine.'
'Good. Give her my love.'
'I shall.'
'I must return to this debate in the House. It's a bit tricky.'
'All right. Go get 'em. Eat 'em alive.'
'Goodbye.'[110]

When her turn came to face questions in the Commons, Mrs
Thatcher was obliged to put the best face possible on her humiliation. Needled by Labour glee at the breach of her special relationship,
she made the best case she could for the American action, recalling
that they had intervened to restore democracy in Dominica in exactly
the same way in 1965.[111] Nevertheless she was still seething. 'That man!'
she railed to the writer Brian Crozier, one of her unofficial security
advisers. 'After all I've done for him, he didn't even consult me.'[112] Two
weeks later, when the Irish Taoiseach, Garret Fitzgerald, came to
Chequers, she likened the American intervention to Soviet 'fraternal'
invasions of Czechoslovakia and Hungary. 'The Americans are worse
than the Soviets, Garret,' she fumed, 'persuading the Governor to issue
a retrospective invitation to invade after they had taken him aboard an
American warship.'[113] And on a late-night BBC World Service phone-
in, she vented her fury on an American caller who accused her of
failing to stand alongside the Americans in fighting Communism:

We in the Western countries, the Western democracies, use our force
to defend our way of life. We do not use it to walk into other
people's countries, independent sovereign territories . . . If you are
pronouncing a new law that wherever Communism reigns against
the will of the people . . . there the United States shall enter, we
are going to have really terrible wars in the world.[114]

The Americans were bewildered by Mrs Thatcher's attitude. They
did not understand her sensitivity about the Commonwealth and could
not see that their action was any different from what she herself had

done in the Falklands. Senior members of the administration were angry that Britain did not give them the same support they had given Britain in the South Atlantic. 'When she needed us we were there,' a State Department official told David Dimbleby. 'We just didn't understand . . . this strong feeling that we shouldn't have done this.'[115] Reagan regretted the dispute, but was unrepentant because he thought she was 'just plain wrong'.[116] And in due course, as it became clear that the invasion – unlike some other American military interventions – had been wholly successful in its limited objectives, Mrs Thatcher herself came to feel that she had been wrong to oppose it. At any rate she quickly put the episode behind her and set herself to making sure that there was no lasting damage to her most important international relationship. In her speech at the Lord Mayor's banquet in November she made a point of emphasising the fundamental strength of the Alliance, despite occasional minor differences: a point duly noted in Washington.[117] Reagan was keen to reciprocate. Vice-President Bush wrote to her in December that he wished they could 'sit down and chat because I have been troubled by recent tensions and I know it hasn't been easy for you either'.[118]

The tension passed. Nevertheless Mrs Thatcher's initial reaction to Grenada was a telling glimpse of her ultimate priority. Disposed as she was to defer to American leadership, her instinct was to repel any infringement of what she saw as British – or in this case Commonwealth – sovereignty. Had she been consulted she might well have agreed to a joint operation to restore democracy. She wanted to be America's partner, not its poodle. She was deeply hurt by Reagan's failure to consult her. But the lesson she learned was that next time the Americans needed her she must not let them down.

The test came in April 1986, when Washington was provoked by a spate of terrorist attacks on American tourists and servicemen in Europe, presumed to be the work of Libyan agents. Libya's eccentric President, Colonel Gaddafi, had been a particular *bête noire* of Reagan's from the moment he entered the White House, and by 1986 Reagan was itching to punish him. When a TWA plane was sabotaged over Greece on 2 April, and five servicemen were killed by a bomb in a Berlin nightclub three days later, the President determined to bomb Tripoli in retaliation. The US plan involved using F-111s based in Britain, partly for accuracy, but also deliberately to involve the European allies in the action. But Reagan's request put Mrs Thatcher on the spot at a time when her authority was weakened by the Westland crisis. France and Spain refused the Americans permission to overfly their territory; and Mrs Thatcher knew she would invite a political storm if she agreed to let the American mission fly from British bases.

Britain too had suffered from Libyan terrorism – notably the shooting of a London policewoman in 1984. MI5 had no doubt of Libya's responsibility for the latest attacks. But again Mrs Thatcher worried about the legality of the proposed action. Just three months earlier, speaking to American journalists in London, she had explicitly condemned retaliatory action against terrorism. 'I must warn you that I do not believe in retaliatory strikes that are against international law,' she declared. 'Once you start going across borders then I do not see an end to it . . . I uphold international law very firmly.'[119] Some time earlier she had refused to endorse an Israeli attack on the headquarters of the Palestine Liberation Organisation (PLO) in Tunis, asking Garret Fitzgerald to imagine what the Americans would say if Britain 'bombed the Provos in Dundalk'.[120] She had also refused to follow a unilateral American embargo on Libyan oil.

But when Reagan asked her permission, late in the evening of 8 April, she felt that she had no choice but to agree. Particularly after Grenada, she could not afford to deny the Americans the payback to which they felt they were entitled after the Falklands. In her view – and theirs – this was what the Alliance was all about. 'The cost to Britain of not backing American action,' she wrote in her memoirs, 'was unthinkable.'[121] Her only escape was to try to convince the Americans that retaliation would be counterproductive. After hasty consultation with Geoffrey Howe, George Younger (who had recently replaced Heseltine at Defence) and Charles Powell, she sent back a holding reply asking for more detail about intended targets, warning of the risk of civilian casualties and spelling out the danger that the United States would be seen to be in breach of international law unless the action could plausibly be justified under Article 51 of the UN Charter as 'self-defence'.

The next day she held more *ad hoc* meetings with relevant ministers, including the Attorney-General, Michael Havers. All were unhappy, but their doubts only hardened Mrs Thatcher's resolve, as Charles Powell recalled:

> The Foreign Office were whole-heartedly against it, believing it would lead to all our embassies in the Middle East being burned, all our interests there ruined. But she knew it was the right thing to do and she just said, 'This is what allies are for . . . If one wants help, they get help.' It just seemed so simple to her.[122]

Howe, Younger, Havers and Whitelaw eventually backed her, but they all knew that the strike would spark enormous controversy. The raid was well flagged in the Sunday papers on 13 April, with the disclosure that Mrs Thatcher had met the American General Vernon Walters the day before and reports of KC-10 tankers – capable of refuelling F-111s in flight – arriving at RAF Mildenhall.[123] Yet the Cabinet's defence and overseas policy committee (with both Howe and Younger absent) was told only when the planes were already on their way back. Norman Tebbit – a hawk on most issues and normally a reliable ally of the Prime Minister – was particularly critical, both of the raid itself and of the failure to consult the Cabinet. The following day his concern was echoed by Nigel Lawson, Kenneth Baker and John Biffen. In fact only Quintin Hailsham was fully supportive, with an irrelevant discourse about his American mother. But Mrs Thatcher (in Baker's account) insisted: 'This is the right decision in the long-term interests of Britain. The US keeps hundreds of thousands of troops in Europe to defend Europe. She is entitled to ask to use our bases.'[124]

After the event, when the television news showed pictures of the dead and injured in the streets of Tripoli, the opposition parties once again condemned her slavish subservience to American wishes, asserting that British complicity in the bombing would expose British travellers to Arab retaliation. Opinion polls showed 70 per cent opposition to the American action – 'even worse than I had feared,' Mrs Thatcher wrote in her memoirs.[125] To Woodrow Wyatt she admitted to feeling 'very lonely'.[126] But in public she was defiant. 'It was inconceivable to me,' she told the House of Commons, 'that we should refuse United States aircraft and personnel the opportunity to defend their people.'[127]

One opponent who backed her was the SDP leader David Owen. 'Her refusal,' he wrote five years later, 'would have done immense damage to our relations with the Reagan administration.' In his view Mrs Thatcher not only displayed courage and loyalty, but demonstrated 'one of the distinguishing features of great leadership – the ability to turn a blind eye to . . . legal niceties'. In the event, he believed, 'the bombing did deter Libya . . . even though it was, by any legal standard, retaliation not self-defence and therefore outside the terms of the UN Charter'.[128] In her memoirs Lady Thatcher too defended the bombing as having been justified by results. 'It turned out to be a more decisive blow against Libyan-sponsored terrorism than I could ever have imagined . . . The much-vaunted Libyan counter-attack did not . . . take place . . . There was a marked decline in Libyan-sponsored terrorism in succeeding years.'[129] There is a problem, here, however. The Thatcher–Owen defence is contradicted by the verdict of the

Scottish court in the Netherlands which convicted a Libyan agent of the bombing of the US airliner over Lockerbie in 1989 which killed 289 people, the most serious terrorist outrage of the whole decade. Oddly, Mrs Thatcher fails to mention Lockerbie in her memoirs. This might be because it dents her justification of the American action in 1986. Alternatively it could be because she knew that the attribution of guilt to Libya – rather than Syria or the PLO – was false.*

But her principal reason at the time for backing the American raid was to show herself – by contrast with the feeble Europeans – a reliable ally; and in this she was triumphantly successful. Doubts raised in Washington by her reaction to Grenada were drowned in an outpouring of praise and gratitude. 'The fact that so few had stuck by America in her time of trial,' she wrote, 'strengthened the "special relationship".'[131] She got her payback later that summer when Congress – after years of Irish-American obstruction – approved a new extradition treaty, closing the loophole which had allowed IRA terrorists to evade extradition by claiming that their murders were 'political'. The Senate only ratified the new treaty after pressure from Reagan explicitly linking it to Britain's support for the US action in April. Here was one clear benefit from the special relationship.

Defusing the Cold War

But these were side shows. The central purpose of the Atlantic alliance was to combat the Soviet Union; and it was here that the eight years of the Reagan–Thatcher partnership saw the most dramatic movement. The sudden breach of the Berlin Wall in 1989, followed by the collapse of the Soviet Union itself a couple of years later, were totally unpredicted and, even as the events unfolded, unexpected. Yet both Reagan and Mrs Thatcher had been working for exactly that result; and with hindsight it can be seen that their dual-track strategy in the mid-1980s was staggeringly successful in bringing it about.

Though Mrs Thatcher had always been unrestrained in condemning the Soviet Union as a tyrannical force for evil in the world, she also believed – just because it was so repressive – that it must eventually collapse from lack of popular support and economic failure. She wanted to win the Cold War by helping it to do so: to encourage the Russian people and their subject populations in Eastern Europe to throw off the shackles by their own efforts and find freedom for themselves. She was very excited by the Solidarity movement in Poland, and disappointed

---

*In *Statecraft* (2002) she did assert that Libya was 'clearly behind' the Lockerbie bombing.[130]

when it seemed to peter out under the initial impact of General Jaruzelski's martial law. Beneath her hatred of Communism she even retained traces of a wartime schoolgirl's admiration for the heroic sacrifices of the Russian people in the struggle against Hitler. She never lost sight of the ordinary people behind the Iron Curtain.

Visiting Germany in October 1982 she inspected the Berlin Wall for the first time – and looked forward boldly to its collapse:

> Every decade since the war the Soviet leaders have been reminded that their pitiless ideology only survives because it is maintained by force. But the day comes when the anger and frustration of the people is so great that force cannot contain it. Then the edifice cracks: the mortar crumbles . . . one day liberty will dawn on the other side of the wall.

Reprinting this passage in her memoirs eleven years later, Lady Thatcher took legitimate pride in the fulfilment of her prophesy. But she frankly admitted that her confidence had been 'vindicated earlier than I could ever have anticipated'.[132]

At this time the Cold War appeared to be at its bleakest. NATO was in the process of stationing cruise missiles in Europe in response to Soviet deployment of SS-20s. Reagan – widely portrayed in Europe as a trigger-happy cowboy – had embarked on an expensive programme of modernising America's nuclear arsenal, and in March 1983 made his famous speech in Orlando, Florida, labelling the Soviet Union an 'evil empire . . . the focus of evil in the modern world'.[133] The Russians had a propaganda field-day denouncing his warmongering provocation; but just six months later they furnished graphic evidence of what he meant by shooting down a South Korean airliner which strayed accidentally into Soviet air space, with the loss of 269 lives. 'This incident has vividly illustrated the true nature of the Soviet regime,' Mrs Thatcher fumed:

> Its rigidity and ruthlessness, its neuroses about spying and security, its mendacity and its apparent inability to understand, let alone apply, the normal rules of civilised conduct between nations, have been an object lesson to those who believe that good will and reason alone will be sufficient to ensure our security and world peace.[134]*

---

*It is at first sight odd that she needed to rehearse these views so eloquently to Reagan. The reason was probably to emphasise that she was personally in favour of tough retaliatory sanctions against the Soviet airline Aeroflot, but was thwarted as usual by the Europeans – in this case the French and the Greeks.

Yet it was at this very moment that she started making overtures to the Soviet Union. Leonid Brezhnev had died in November 1982 and she was keen to establish early contact with the new General-Secretary, the younger but still stone-faced Yuri Andropov. Even before the 1983 election, Pym had sent Malcom Rifkind to Moscow to try to improve relations. Encouraged by Anthony Parsons and Sir Christopher Mallaby, former head of Chancery in the Moscow embassy and now head of planning in the FO, Mrs Thatcher began to look seriously for openings after June 1983. 'There was a hint earlier this summer that Thatcher might be considering a trip to Moscow,' the US Embassy in London reported in September. 'We now know that she has no such plan. But she worries about lack of contact with Andropov and might favor contacts with him outside the Soviet Union.'[135]

On 8 September she held an all-day seminar at Chequers with academic experts on the Soviet Union to look at the possibilities. With hindsight she claims that she was already actively looking for a new type of Soviet leader who would change the Soviet system from within.[136] But another more urgent consideration was the recognition that defence spending could not go on rising by 3 per cent a year indefinitely.[137] Britain (5.2 per cent) already spent a substantially higher proportion of GDP on defence than either France (4.2 per cent) or West Germany (3.4 per cent).[138] Reagan might reckon that the US could always outspend the Soviets, but Mrs Thatcher did not have the same resources. She needed a fresh approach. In Washington three weeks later, therefore, and in her party conference speech a fortnight after that, she surprised her hearers by sounding a new note of peaceful co-existence based on realism: 'We have to deal with the Soviet Union,' she asserted. 'We live on the same planet and we have to go on sharing it.'[139] 'Whatever we think of the Soviet Union, Soviet Communism cannot be disinvented,' she conceded in Blackpool. It was necessary to open a dialogue with the new Soviet leaders, since 'The Soviet Union is unlikely to change much or quickly.'

At the same time she insisted that 'such exchanges must be hard-headed. We do not want the word "dialogue" to become suspect that way the word *détente* now is.'[140] She was by no means softening her view of the Soviet leadership: 'They do not share our aspirations: they are not constrained by our ethics . . . Their creed is barren of conscience, immune to the promptings of good and evil.' But that was precisely the West's strength. Andropov had recently spoken of an 'ideological struggle' for the future of mankind. 'That is Mr Andropov's challenge,' Mrs Thatcher responded. 'I accept it and I do so with the confidence . . . that in this battle we in the West hold all the cards.'[141]

She genuinely welcomed argument with the Soviets. When Jeane Kirkpatrick condemned the Kremlin's 'ideological aggression' she disagreed. Ideological aggression was fine, she insisted. Military aggression was a different matter. 'But I can see nothing wrong with the Russians using every word in the dictionary to press upon the world their point of view . . . The problem is on our side. We must *answer back* and take the offensive.'[142]

Her next step was to make her first trip as Prime Minister behind the Iron Curtain. In February 1984 she visited Hungary, selected as one part of the Soviet empire that was marginally freer than the rest, and had a long talk with the veteran leader, Janos Kadar, who welcomed her new concern for East–West co-operation and filled her in on the personalities to watch in the Kremlin. As usual, she passed on her impressions to the White House. 'Hungary's economic experiment has been conducted within strict limits,' she reported, '– controlled press, single political party, state ownership of all but the smallest economic units – and this will not change.' Nevertheless, she concluded, the West needed 'to find a way of living side by side with the communist system, repugnant as it is'.[143] Despite – or perhaps because of – her strongly anti-Communist reputation she was warmly received by ordinary Hungarians, a welcome which made a big impression on her. 'I am becoming convinced,' she wrote to Reagan, 'that we are more likely to make progress on the detailed arms control negotiations if we can establish a broader basis of understanding between East and West . . . It will be a slow and gradual process, during which we must never lower our guard. However, I believe that the effort has to be made.'[144]

A few days after she returned from Hungary, Andropov died. Mrs Thatcher immediately decided to attend his funeral. There she met not only his successor, the elderly and ailing Konstantin Chernenko; but also Mikhail Gorbachev, who was clearly the coming man. 'I spotted him,' she claims in her memoirs, 'because I was looking for someone like him.'[145] In fact the Canadians had already spotted him – Trudeau had told her about Gorbachev the previous September; and nearer home Peter Walker had also met him and drawn attention to him before she went to Moscow.[146] Even so, she did well to seize the initiative by inviting Gorbachev – at that time the youngest member of the Soviet politburo – to visit Britain. 'Our record at picking winners had not been good,' Percy Cradock reflected. But in Gorbachev's case 'we drew the right card'.[147]

Gorbachev came to Britain the following December. In order to get to know him, Mrs Thatcher invited him not to Downing Street, but to Sunday lunch at Chequers for unusually wide-ranging and unstructured talks. Gorbachev was not yet Soviet leader, and Mrs Thatcher was initially accompanied by six of her colleagues; but the two champions quickly dropped their agendas and simply argued, so freely that their interpreters struggled to keep up. Gorbachev was 'an unusual Russian', Mrs Thatcher told Reagan at Camp David the following week, 'in that he was much less constrained, more charming, open to discussion and debate, and did not stick to prepared notes'.[148] For her part, Howe wrote, 'Margaret was at her best: fluent but measured, thoughtful but shiningly and convincingly sincere.'[149] She made a point of challenging Gorbachev directly about aspects of the Soviet system, specifically the refusal of the right to emigrate, telling him that 'it was a sign of weakness to feel the need to keep one's people in'. She contrasted Gorbachev with Gromyko, who 'would have sharply replied that emigration was an internal matter and not open for discussion'. Gorbachev, she said, 'was not willing to debate the point, but did allow her to discuss it without cutting her off'.

'I found myself liking him,' she wrote in her memoirs.[150] Even Denis – equally pleasantly surprised by Gorbachev's wife Raisa – was aware that 'something pretty special' was happening.[151] The fact was that Mrs Thatcher relished having an opponent who was prepared to argue with her. 'He was self-confident and though he larded his remarks with respectful references to Mr Chernenko . . . he did not seem in the least uneasy about entering into controversial areas of high politics.'[152] Gorbachev evidently enjoyed their exchange as much as she did, even though – on her home ground – he was necessarily on the defensive much of the time. Despite their fundamental differences, Gorbachev and Mrs Thatcher were temperamentally alike: each recognised the other as a domestic radical, battling the forces of inertia in their respective countries. Famously, therefore, when she spoke to the BBC next day, Mrs Thatcher declared that this was a man she could 'do business with'.[153]

Some months later she explained what she meant. She had no inkling that Gorbachev was going to be the last Soviet leader. 'When I say I can do business,' she told a Romanian questioner at the UN who wanted her to tear up the Yalta Treaty, 'I understand – and I believe he does too – that in spite of those differences which will in my view remain because I do not think the Communist bloc will change in my lifetime – that there are certain things which are in the interests of both blocs.'[154] In Gorbachev's relative approachability, compared with his predecessors, she sensed an historic opportunity which should not be missed.

They met again briefly at Chernenko's funeral in March 1985, soon after which Gorbachev finally stepped into the top job. But she still made a point of being wary and had no intention of lowering her guard. The reality, she warned in Washington that summer, was that 'the new brooms in the Soviet Union will not be used to sweep away Communism, only to make it more efficient – if that can be done.'[155] Two months later, as if to demonstrate to Moscow that the Cold War was not over, Britain expelled twenty-five Soviet diplomats exposed as spies by the defector Oleg Gordievsky. When Gorbachev retaliated in kind, Mrs Thatcher expelled six more Russians. Yet all the while Geoffrey Howe was following up her diplomatic initiative by quietly touring all the Warsaw Pact capitals during 1984–5.

With her impeccable track record of standing up to the Soviets, Mrs Thatcher's advice that Gorbachev was a different sort of Soviet leader undoubtedly impressed the Americans. James Baker – Reagan's chief of staff, later Treasury Secretary – testified that she had 'a profound influence' on US thinking about Russia.[156] Yet this almost certainly exaggerates her role. The truth is that the Americans were already reassessing their own approach, at least from the time Shultz became Secretary of State, and Reagan personally was as keen as she was to engage the Soviet leaders. From the moment he became President he wrote a series of handwritten letters to his opposite numbers in Moscow, trying to strike a human response. From Brezhnev and Andropov he received only formal replies, but he did not give up.[157] When Mrs Thatcher described her talks with Gorbachev, he was 'simply amazed' how closely she had followed the same line that he had taken when meeting Foreign Minister Gromyko the previous September.[158] What can be said is that her clear-sighted public praise of Gorbachev helped the White House assure American public opinion that the President was not going soft when he too started to do business with the Soviet leader. On the other side she helped convince Gorbachev of Reagan's sincerity, and encouraged him to go ahead with the November 1985 Geneva summit, despite his suspicion of the American 'Star Wars' programme. Once Reagan and Gorbachev had started meeting directly, however, her mediating role was inevitably reduced.

Reagan's dedication to 'Star Wars' – the Strategic Defense Initiative (SDI) – was a delicate problem for Mrs Thatcher which she handled with considerable sensitivity and skill. The idea was a futuristic scheme, at the very limits of American space technology, to develop a defensive shield against incoming ballistic missiles, ultimately, it was hoped, making strategic nuclear weapons redundant. Reagan announced the project – with no prior warning to Britain or the rest of NATO – in March 1983. The allies were immediately alarmed. First of all they were sceptical of the technology and doubted that SDI would ever work with the 100 per cent certainty needed to replace the existing deterrent. Second, they feared that such an American initiative would breach the 1972 ABM Treaty and wreck the chances of further arms-control agreements by triggering a new arms race in space. Third, they feared that SDI would detach the USA from NATO: if the Americans once felt secure behind their own shield they would withdraw their nuclear protection from Europe; while if the Russians successfully followed suit, the British and French deterrents would be rendered obsolete.

Mrs Thatcher shared these fears; but she did not want to criticise the American initiative publicly because she knew Reagan was deeply committed to it. Unlike most of his advisers, who saw SDI as just another high-tech toy in the military arsenal, Reagan genuinely believed in the dream of abolishing nuclear weapons. In addition, she was excited by the science, believing that she, with her chemistry degree from forty years before, 'had a firm grasp of the scientific concepts involved'. Unlike the 'laid back generalists from the Foreign Office', she boasted in her memoirs, 'let alone the ministerial muddlers in charge of them . . . I was in my element.' She was keen to support the research programme, since 'science is unstoppable'.[159] 'We must remember,' she told a BBC interviewer, 'that it was the Soviet Union who put up the first anti-satellite satellite . . . It seemed to be not merely natural but advisable that the United States should carry on with their own research in these very, very important spheres.'[160] But deployment was a different matter. More than anyone she worried about destabilising the Alliance, giving the Russians an excuse to walk out of arms-control negotiations, and possible American withdrawal into isolationism. She had invested too much political capital – and money – in buying Trident to be willing to see it scrapped. Above all she regarded the idea that nuclear weapons could ever be abolished as dangerous fantasy.

During 1984 her worries grew and she determined to take the lead in representing Europe's concerns positively to the Americans. On 8 November she wrote to ask if she could call on Reagan at his 'Western White House' in California on her way home from signing the Hong Kong Agreement in Beijing just before Christmas. When Reagan replied that he would not be there until after Christmas, she invited herself to Washington instead. This was the most punishing schedule she ever imposed on herself (and on her staff). She left for China on the Monday evening following her Sunday talks with Gorbachev at Chequers. She signed the agreement in Beijing on the Wednesday, went on to Hong

Kong to reassure the population there on Thursday, and then flew on across the Pacific and the US to Washington, from where she was helicoptered to meet the President at Camp David on Saturday morning, returning to London overnight. This involved flying right round the world – fifty-five hours of flying time – in five and a half days. Quite apart from the hours in the air, this must surely make her the only leader to have held substantial talks, on three continents, with Russian, American and Chinese leaders inside a single week.[161]

Yet she gave no sign of jetlag. First, as already described, she gave Reagan her favourable impression of Gorbachev; but she also passed on his defiant response to SDI. 'Tell your friend President Reagan,' Gorbachev had told her, 'not to go ahead with space weapons.' If he did, 'the Russians would either develop their own or, more probably, develop new offensive systems superior to SDI.' Reagan assured her that 'Star Wars was not his term and was clearly not what he had in mind'. If the research proved successful he had actually promised to share the technology. 'Our goal is to reduce and eventually eliminate nuclear weapons.' Mrs Thatcher repeated that she supported the American research programme; but when the President was joined by Shultz and Macfarlane she launched into her own worries about SDI.

She took seriously Gorbachev's threats to retaliate. 'We do not want our objective of increased security to result in increased Soviet nuclear weapons.' But her real fear was that SDI would undermine nuclear deterrence, which she passionately believed had kept the peace for forty years:

> It would be unwise . . . to abandon a deterrence system that has prevented both nuclear and conventional war . . . If we ever reach the stage of abolishing all nuclear weapons, this would make conventional, biological or chemical war more likely.

Moreover, in response to Reagan's optimism that SDI would turn out to be feasible, she admitted that 'personally she had some doubts':

> In the past, scientific genius has always developed a counter system. Even if an SDI system proved 95 per cent successful . . . over 60 million people will still die from those weapons that got through.

Macfarlane tried to convince her, but she remained sceptical. Finally she asked 'if someone could come to London to give her a top-level US technical briefing'. Reagan 'nodded agreement and said it was time to break for lunch'.

Before, during and after lunch Mrs Thatcher banged on about British Airways and the Laker anti-trust case, followed by discussion of the US economy and the Middle East. All this gave time for Charles Powell to work up a statement which she now circulated, embodying four assurances that she wanted to be able to give to the press at the end of the meeting. 'We agreed on four points,' the statement declared:

(1) The US, and Western, aim was not to achieve superiority, but to maintain balance, taking account of Soviet developments;

(2) SDI-related deployment would, in view of treaty obligations, have to be a matter for negotiations;

(3) The overall aim is to enhance, not undercut deterrence;

(4) East-West negotiations should aim to achieve security with reduced levels of offensive systems on both sides.[162]

This was a brilliant diplomatic coup. Reagan's staff were not pleased at being bounced in this way; but the President happily accepted her four points, saying 'he hoped they would quell reports of disagreement between us'.[163] Thus in exchange for publicly expressing her strong support for the research, she secured – and promptly went out and publicised – assurances that the Americans would not deploy SDI unilaterally and would not abandon deterrence. Of course she knew that Shultz and others in the American administration shared her doubts and welcomed her support: she could not have done it alone. But she knew exactly what she wanted and played her hand skilfully to obtain it. Her flying visit, Percy Cradock wrote, 'repaired a dangerous crack between Washington and European capitals and was a marked success for British diplomacy and the Prime Minister personally'.[164] When Reagan sent a long cable to allied leaders setting out the American negotiating position for the resumed arms-control talks in Geneva a few weeks later it specifically included Mrs Thatcher's four points – though he also reiterated his personal dream of eventually eliminating nuclear weapons entirely.[165]

She got her 'comprehensive briefing' in London two weeks later from the director of SDI, who thanked her for the 'great privilege' of being able to present his project to her. 'We all particularly appreciate that you were willing to devote so much time to the subject,' Lt Gen. James Abrahamson told her.[166] She in turn thanked Reagan for keeping her informed.[167] But she was not yet ready to relax. 'Bud' Macfarlane recalled that 'Margaret Thatcher . . . was on the rampage for a year or more about SDI . . . She wouldn't let us hear the end of it.' She flew over to Washington again in February, looking for another 'concentrated discussion of the substantive problems'.[168] 'She doesn't want to go over the ground on SDI that she covered at Camp David,' the US Embassy in London cabled Washington. 'But she may talk up her four points . . . as a rallying ground for European support.'[169] Accorded the rare honour of addressing both Houses of Congress – just before she met Reagan – she contrived a neat quotation from Churchill speaking to the same audience in 1952, in the very early days of nuclear weapons. 'Be careful above all things,' the old warrior had warned, 'not to let go of the atomic weapon until you are sure and more than sure that other means of preserving peace are in your hands.' Implicitly repudiating Reagan's vision of a world without nuclear weapons, she emphasised that the objective was 'not merely to prevent nuclear war, but to prevent conventional war as well' – and nuclear weapons were still the surest way of doing that.[170]

At her meeting with Reagan she raised a new worry, as she reminded him when she got home:

As regards the Strategic Defense Initiative, I hope that I was able to explain to you my preoccupation with the need not to weaken our efforts to consolidate support in Britain for the deployment of cruise and for the modernisation of Trident by giving the impression that a future without nuclear weapons is near at hand. We must continue to make the case for deterrence based on nuclear weapons for several years to come.[171]

'Bud, you know, she's really missing the point,' Reagan told Macfarlane. 'And she's doing us a lot of damage with all this sniping about it.'[172] In fact, Mrs Thatcher was very careful not to snipe in public; but the Americans were irritated by other British criticism, particularly a speech by Howe in March which sharply differed from his Prime Minister's loyal support. Mrs Thatcher was furious – the more so, possibly, since she was sent the text in advance but failed to read it because she uncharacteristically fell asleep on the flight home from Chernenko's funeral.[173] But in fact Howe's public expression of widely shared European concern served her private purpose. Next time she saw Macfarlane at the Bonn G7 in May she immediately buttonholed him:

'Now, Bud,' she began, from several feet away, without even saying hello, 'are you keeping SDI under appropriate restraint, adhering to the ABM Treaty and so forth?' 'Yes, Prime Minister,' I replied, 'things are on course.' She nodded with satisfaction and walked off.[174]

In July she was back in Washington, where she had persuaded the White House to set up a seminar on arms control attended by Reagan, Shultz, Weinberger and the whole American top brass. On this occasion she talked non-stop, letting none of them get a word in, insisting 'in many, many different ways . . . that all this talk of SDI was de-legitimising nuclear weapons. She went on and on in that vein' – so passionately that Kenneth Adelman, the director of the US Arms Control Agency, passed Donald Regan, the President's chief of staff, a note: 'Thatcher loves the Bomb.'[175] It may have been after this meeting that Shultz remarked ruefully to Reagan: 'Boy, she's not a very good listener, is she?' 'No,' Reagan replied. 'But she's a marvellous talker.'[176] She certainly made her point. Over lunch she confronted the President directly with the implications of his enthusiasm for getting rid of nuclear weapons altogether. 'If you follow that logic to its implied conclusion,' she told him, 'you expose a dramatic conventional imbalance, do you not? And would we not have to restore that balance at considerable expense?' In response, Macfarlane recalled, Reagan 'looked her square in the eye and said, "Yes, that's exactly what I imagined".'

It was a rather awkward silence there while both sides absorbed the weight of what had just been exchanged. I think the staffs of both sides agreed this had better never get out.[177]

In truth, no one else in the administration believed in Reagan's naive vision of a nuclear-free future. The Pentagon never saw SDI as a substitute for missiles. 'We get a brief respite from that rubbish when she comes,' Richard Perle told David Dimbleby.[178]. Though Reagan would never admit it, Macfarlane argues, the real point of SDI was that it was a massive bargaining chip, which raised the technological stakes higher than the struggling Soviet economy could match. Gorbachev recognised this, which was why he tried to rouse western public opinion against it. Mrs Thatcher initially did not: she was more concerned that the Russians would meet the American challenge, leaving Europe exposed. But she assuaged her anxiety by concentrating on the lucrative crumbs she hoped British firms might pick up from the research programme. 'You know, there may be something in this after all,' she responded when Macfarlane dangled the prospect of contracts worth $300 million a year.[179] In fact Britain gained nothing like the commercial benefits she hoped for from SDI – no more than £24 million by 1987 rather than the £1 billion the MoD optimistically predicted in 1985. But by the time she came to write her memoirs she realised that her fears had been misplaced. SDI, though never successfully tested, let alone deployed, achieved its unstated purpose by convincing the Russians that they could no longer compete in the nuclear arms race, so bringing them to the negotiating table to agree deep cuts in nuclear weapons, even before the fall of the Berlin Wall. And she gives the credit to Reagan for having, in his artless way, 'instinctively grasped the key to the whole question'. By initiating SDI he 'called the Soviets' bluff. They had lost the game and I have no doubt that they knew it.'[180]

But that revelation lay ahead. In October 1986 she was horrified when Reagan met Gorbachev at Reykjavik and offered off his own bat not only to cut strategic nuclear weapons by half in five years, but to eliminate them entirely in ten years. The moment passed: Gorbachev overplayed his hand by trying to get Reagan to scrap his beloved SDI as well. This Reagan would not do, since his dream of eliminating nuclear weapons was dependent on SDI being successful. But it was a bad moment for Mrs Thatcher when she heard how far Reagan had been willing to go. One Cabinet colleague who was with her at the time 'never saw her more incandescent'.[181] 'When I heard about it,' she herself recalled, 'I just felt as if there had been an earthquake underneath my feet . . . The whole thing was shaking. We hadn't a defence any more. I thought "My goodness me, I must get over."'[182] She marched off to telephone the President immediately.

What alarmed her on this occasion was not just that she regarded talk of abolishing nuclear weapons as a utopian fantasy. More immediately, in blithely proposing to eliminate a whole class of weapons in a bilateral deal with the Russians, Reagan was completely ignoring Britain's Trident and the French independent deterrent. Implicitly Trident would have to be scrapped too: there was no way Britain could have continued to buy a weapon that the Americans themselves had abandoned. But the merest suggestion of scrapping Trident would play straight into the hands of the British peace movement which she had spent so much energy combating over the past five years. In 1983 maintaining the British deterrent had been her trump card against Michael Foot's unilateralist rabble. Now with the next election looming and Labour posing a serious challenge, her best friend in the White House was casually threatening to tear it up. British press coverage of Reykjavik largely blamed Reagan for blocking a historic deal by refusing to give up 'Star Wars'. Mrs Thatcher was much more worried about what he had been willing to give up.

So she did get over to Washington as soon as she could, inviting herself to Camp David for another flying visit on 15 November. The US Embassy in London told Washington exactly what she was coming for, citing a source whose name is blacked out but was surely Charles Powell. 'Asked how he would describe Mrs Thatcher's central objective during the visit ***** replied "Reassurance"':

> Reassurance that strategic arms negotiations will not overlook conventional imbalances in Europe; reassurance that political delicacies in Britain will be taken into account; reassurance that negotiating positions do not undermine Britain's Trident program; reassurance that we know where we are heading.[183]

'You will recall that she spoke to you on the phone about her concerns the day after Reykjavik,' Poindexter briefed Reagan, who doubtless needed no reminding:

> Specifically she questions whether we can have effective deterrence without ballistic missiles. She does not believe it prudent to make major reductions without redressing conventional and chemical imbalances. Mrs Thatcher also fears that elimination of ballistic missiles will undercut her domestic political position.

The Americans were anxious to help her, recognising that she was 'in a pre-election phase', while Labour's unilateralism 'would deal a severe blow to NATO'.[184] 'Mrs Thatcher's overriding focus will be the British public's perception of her performance,' another memo noted. 'Our interest is in assuring that the results of the meeting support a staunch friend and ally of the US.' Nevertheless White House staff were determined not to be bounced again, as they believed they had been in 1984, by Mrs Thatcher arriving with a document already up her sleeve. 'We have found,' Poindexter noted, 'even with friends like Mrs Thatcher – that joint statements, which are usually a compromise, do not serve our policy interests.'[185] This time they took care to have their own text prepared in advance.

US objectives, Shultz explained to Reagan, were first, to 'strengthen Alliance cohesion . . . by reconciling your commitment to eliminate offensive ballistic missiles within ten years with Mrs Thatcher's commitment to deploy UK Tridents within the same time frame'; second, 'to find a mutually acceptable formula [five or six words are here blacked out] that drastic nuclear reductions . . . are inadvisable as long as conventional and chemical imbalances exist in Europe'; and third, to secure British endorsement of US policies.[186]★ It is clear that the Americans' real objective was the last. Just as she had done on SDI two years earlier, Mrs Thatcher secured the assurance she wanted that nuclear deterrence remained central to NATO policy and Trident would go ahead. This was spun to the British press as another triumph of Thatcherite diplomacy, comparable with the time Clement Attlee flew over to Washington in 1949 and supposedly dissuaded President Truman from using the atom bomb in Korea. 'She opened her handbag,' Geoffrey Smith wrote, 'and took out a paper . . . It was an occasion for everybody to say simply "Yes, Minister."'[187] The reality was rather different.

The Americans were happy to let her claim a triumph. But the truth is that the paper she came away waving was written in the White House. The assurances she secured were part of an 'agreed statement to the press' which explicitly endorsed Reagan's Reykjavik objectives and most of his specific proposals: a 50 per cent cut in strategic weapons over five years, deep cuts in intermediate nuclear forces – which Mrs Thatcher did not like at all – and a ban on chemical weapons, plus continuing SDI research. Only the aspiration to phase out strategic weapons altogether in ten years was tactfully omitted. The statement, Shultz recorded, 'represents a reiteration of US policy, i.e. no change. It reflects in a public presentation a stress on the priority of the first phase of the arms reduction discussed at Reykjavik.'[188]

Mrs Thatcher was still deeply worried about where American policy was heading. To her mind, even talking about abolishing nuclear weapons in the future dangerously undermined the West's defensive posture. It was only the balance of terror – 'mutually assured destruction' – which had kept the peace in Europe for forty years. Not only would it be foolish to abandon nuclear weapons: it was even more foolish to imagine it was possible to abandon them. 'You cannot act as if the nuclear weapon had not been invented,' she told the American interviewer Barbara Walters in January 1987. 'The knowledge of how to make these things exists.' New countries were acquiring that knowledge all the time. 'If you cannot be sure that no one has got them, then you have got to have a weapon of your own to deter other people.'[189] Her unapologetic enthusiasm invited the charge, both at home and in America, that she was a nuclear fanatic. On the contrary,

---

★The censored words are presumably something like 'to meet Mrs Thatcher's view'. But then why censor them? One can only guess that they are less complimentary than that – something like 'Mrs Thatcher's obsession'.

she insisted, she was simply a realist. 'You cannot disinvent the nuclear weapon,' she told the *Daily Express* in April, 'any more than you can disinvent dynamite.'[190] She was right; but she did seem to make the argument with a disturbing relish.

Reagan's *démarche* at Reykjavik briefly shook her confidence in the American alliance. 'After Reykjavik,' President Mitterand recalled, 'I saw Mrs Thatcher start to wonder. The European option seemed to come closer.'[191] But her wobble did not last long: she had even less faith in the Europeans. Having gained the reassurance she sought, at least for the moment, she redoubled her commitment to NATO. She was still alarmed by the speed with which the Americans were pressing on with INF cuts and then cuts in short-range battlefield weapons. She worried that the Russians were skilfully drawing the Americans into agreements which undermined the West's deterrent capability; while Reagan's willingness to do a private deal with Gorbachev still gave her nightmares. But she took comfort from the fact that, as she told a CBS interviewer in July 1987, 'they did not come to an agreement':

> They just did not, and if they even had outline arrangements, first they will have to come and consult with NATO; second, it would have to have been negotiated. So they did not get anywhere near to that. It did not happen.[192]

She was determined to see that it never happened; but she admits in her memoirs that the unshakeable importance of nuclear deterrence was 'the one issue on which I knew I could not take the Reagan Administration's soundness for granted'.[193]

At the same time, paradoxically, her other special relationship with Gorbachev flourished, highlighted by a triumphal visit to Moscow in March 1987. This was a shameless piece of pre-election theatre designed to play well on television screens at home, projecting the Prime Minister as a world leader as welcome in the Kremlin as she was in the White House. Harold Macmillan had pulled the same trick just before the 1959 election. But where he had famously sported a white fur hat, she invested in a whole new wardrobe of striking outfits (including a brown fur hat). In other respects her visit was like no other ever paid to the Soviet capital by a western leader.

First, she had another seven hours of formal talks with Gorbachev, plus several social meetings, including a visit to the Bolshoi Ballet. As before, their conversation ranged widely from the relative merits of Communism and capitalism to regional conflicts, arms control and the future of nuclear weapons. Once again Gorbachev gave as good as he got, rejecting Mrs Thatcher's criticism of Soviet subversion in Africa and Central America and meeting her lectures about human rights by pointing out the inequality of British society. But when she repeated her objection that eliminating strategic weapons would leave the Russians with conventional superiority in Europe, he admitted Moscow's opposite fear of being unable to match America's military spending. 'He was clearly extremely sensitive and worried about being humiliated by the West.'[194]

Just as important as her talks with Gorbachev, however, was the fact that she was also allowed to meet privately a number of prominent dissidents, most notably the nuclear physicist Andrei Sakharov and his wife Elena, who were now supporting Gorbachev's *perestroika*, and a number of Jewish *refuseniks* who exemplified its limits. She was permitted to attend a Russian Orthodox service at Zagorsk, forty-five miles outside Moscow, where she spoke to some of the worshippers and lit a candle symbolising freedom of conscience. Above all she was granted unprecedented access to the Soviet public. She was given fifty minutes unedited prime time on the main television channel, and she seized her chance brilliantly. Rather than talk straight to camera she insisted on being interviewed, so that she could be seen to *argue* with her three interviewers in the same way that she argued with Gorbachev. When they dutifully trotted out the party line and questioned how she could support nuclear weapons, she repeatedly interrupted them, contradicted them and tried to convince them from Russia's own experience of invasion and war. 'The Soviet Union suffered millions of losses in the Second World War,' she reminded them:

> The Soviet Union had a lot of conventional weapons. That did not stop Hitler attacking her. Conventional weapons have never been enough to stop wars. Since we have had the nuclear weapon, it is so horrific that no one dare risk going to war.

At the same time she told them bluntly that the Soviet Union had far more nuclear weapons than any other country; that it was the Soviet Union which had introduced intermediate-range weapons by deploying SS-20s, forcing the West to match them with Pershing and cruise; and the Soviet Union which had led the United States in developing anti-missile laser defences in the 1970s. The three stooges had no answer to this assault. The second half of the interview focused on personal matters: her work habits, her frugal meals and how she managed on so little sleep. The impact of her spontaneity was sensational. 'Her style, her appearance, her frankness about security matters made her appear like a creature from another planet,' wrote the *Guardian*'s Moscow correspondent, Martin Walker, '– and they found her terrific.'[195]

Finally she undertook an unprecedented walkabout in a Moscow housing estate, meeting and talking to ordinary Russians who flocked to meet and touch her, just as the Hungarians had done in Budapest three years before. 'Sometimes it almost appeared as if the Prime Minister was fighting a by-election in Moscow North,' one commentator remarked – except that nowadays she never drew such enthusiastic crowds at home.[196] 'The embodiment of the free world,' Ronald Millar wrote, 'she came on like a modern Tsarina, hailed in triumph by a Communist people.'[197] 'Journalists with no liking for her at all came back from Moscow saying that they had never witnessed anything like it.'[198] Many years later one of them reckoned that 'Margaret Thatcher, clad in her new Aquascutum wardrobe, careering around the outer Moscow tenement blocks' was still the most impressive exercise in political canvassing he had ever seen.[199] It was an astonishing performance which testified not only to the quasi-regal charisma she had acquired after eight years of representing Britain abroad, but also to her gift for symbolising in her own person the freedoms to which the 'captive nations' of Europe increasingly aspired. The experience confirmed her faith that the peoples of the Soviet empire would eventually throw off their yoke. 'I could sense,' she wrote in her memoirs, 'that the ground was shifting underneath the communist system.'[200] Her 1987 visit – for which Gorbachev also deserves credit – was almost certainly a factor in hastening the collapse of the Soviet system only three years later.

She still drew a clear distinction between the Russian people and their government. 'There is no mistaking the bracing air of change in the Soviet Union,' she told the Tory Party Conference that autumn. She congratulated Gorbachev for trying to reform the stagnant Soviet system; but warned that so far Moscow's external policy had not changed – only the style. 'We shall continue to judge the Soviet Union not by what they say but by what they do.'[201] 'It is in the nature of democracies to relax at the first sign of hope,' she told the same audience the following year. '*This we must not do.*'[202]

Yet she did not always heed her own warnings. In theory she knew that Gorbachev was at heart no democrat, but an unrepentant Communist: a moderniser who wanted to make Communism work better, not a western mole who had any intention of overthrowing it. But in practice many of her advisers felt that by her later years her 'extravagant admiration' for Gorbachev distorted her judgement. She prided herself on her discovery of the Soviet leader and took an almost proprietary interest in his success. At Chequers she would proudly show visitors exactly where he had stood in front of the fire in 1984.[203] While allowing that she had no illusions about Soviet foreign policy, Percy Cradock felt she was 'becoming dangerously attached to Gorbachev in his domestic role . . . Her formidable powers of self-identification and advocacy were enlisted on his behalf,' so that he became 'something of an icon' to her.[204]★

There is no doubt that Mrs Thatcher regarded her championing of Gorbachev as one of her greatest achievements. How much influence she really had in encouraging his reform programme is questionable: events inside the Soviet Union had a momentum of their own which Gorbachev was not able to control. It is striking that while she enthused about his warmth and intelligence, his memoirs are distinctly cooler about her. Whereas she frequently expressed confidence that he would never abuse his powers, he wrote that her achievement in reforming Britain was marred by her 'inherent authoritarianism'.[206] The impression is inescapable that this was another relationship which was rather more special on one side than on the other. Nevertheless Gorbachev paid her a somewhat grudging tribute:

> Mrs Thatcher was not an easy partner for us, and her fierce anti-Communism would often hinder her from taking a more realistic view on various issues. Still one must admit that in a number of cases she was able to substantiate her charges with facts, which eventually led us to review and criticise some of our own approaches.[207]

Certainly she played a role in helping to convince Gorbachev that the Soviet Union could never win the arms race, that Reagan would not give up Star Wars, but that he was nevertheless serious in wanting to engage in balanced arms reductions. 'I had no intention of allowing myself to become a kind of broker between the Americans and the Soviets,' she wrote, as if that would have been beneath her dignity;[208] but with her open line to Washington she could serve as a useful intermediary. Before she went to Camp David in 1986 Gorbachev sent his ambassador to her with a message he wanted to convey through her

---

★By the time she came to write *Statecraft* in 2002 her admiration had cooled. Gorbachev, she now wrote, 'failed spectacularly in his objective of saving communism and the Soviet Union', and altogether his role in ending the Cold War had been 'absurdly misunderstood'. His replacement by Boris Yeltsin was 'right for Russia'.[205]

to Reagan; when he himself visited Washington to sign the INF Treaty in December 1987 he made a two-hour refuelling stop en route to see Mrs Thatcher. She promptly telephoned Reagan to tell him what to expect. 'President Reagan said that he expected some tough sessions with Mr Gorbachev but that I had clearly softened him up.'[209]

For a heady time in the late 1980s she almost seemed to have re-created the wartime triumvirate of Roosevelt, Stalin and Churchill. Her relationship with Reagan and to a lesser extent with Gorbachev enabled her temporarily to punch – or at least be seen to punch – above Britain's real weight in the world. 'The others are as jealous as hell,' she told Woodrow Wyatt with satisfaction in December 1987 – meaning Kohl and Mitterrand.[210] Undoubtedly she played a role in the events which led to the sudden ending of the Cold War in 1989–91. She was visible, articulate and clear-sighted, and is entitled to share the credit for a consummation for which she had devoutly wished. But her role should not be exaggerated. Like Churchill in 1945, only more so, she was always the junior partner. It was always the Americans who called the shots; and the illusion of equality was swiftly exposed when Reagan was succeeded by George Bush.

Meanwhile her love affair with America pulled Britain away from developing her links with Europe.

8

Iron Lady II:
Europe and the World

Good European

During Mrs Thatcher's first term her relations with her European partners had been poisoned by the interminable wrangle over Britain's contribution to the Community budget. Later, her third term would be dominated by her increasingly bitter opposition to closer economic integration. Despite her strong bias towards the United States, however, her middle period (1983–7) was an interlude of improving relations with Europe. It was, as it turned out, only a temporary calm between two storms; but once the budget question had finally been resolved at Fontainebleau in June 1984, Britain actually took the lead for a time in Community affairs, with Mrs Thatcher the leading advocate of a rapid completion of the single European market.

'Her private attitude to Europe,' Percy Cradock has written, 'ranged from suspicion to undisguised hostility. She did not like the Europeans; she did not speak their languages; and she had little time for their traditions . . . What she saw as the continental penchant for grand generalisations offended her lawyer's mind.'[1] Whenever they were unhelpful, as she saw it, she would immediately hark back to the war and start railing about how disgraceful it was for Britain to be treated in this way: 'After all we saved all their skins collectively in the war etc, etc.'[2] She expected them still to be as grateful to Britain as she was to America, and was easily provoked to outbursts of contempt, for instance at their failure to support the bombing of Libya. Naturally she was more circumspect in public. She would never have gone as far as Enoch Powell, who bluntly described Germany and Italy in 1984 as 'our ex-enemies' and wondered 'how "ex" are they really?'[3] But that was exactly how she felt. The transcript of her talks at Camp David in December 1984 gives an authentic flavour of her view of the Continent:

> Praising US economic performance, Mrs Thatcher said that the strength of the dollar is a sign of weakness in Europe. She opined that the overall political situation in Europe is not especially encouraging. There is a socialist government in France; neither Holland nor Belgium seem to be able to get their act completely together; Germany is a question mark; and the Italians lack guts. There is a socialist government in Spain; Greece is a pain in the neck and certainly no friend of the US; but Portugal did have the guts to fight communism . . . None of this bodes especially well for Europe.[4]

Nevertheless she accepted the reality that Britain was in the Community and tried to be positive. 'We are not half-hearted members of the Community,' she told the 1983 party conference. 'We are in. And we are here to stay.'[5] So long as Labour was committed to withdrawal, she was bound to keep stressing that two million British jobs depended directly on continued membership.[6] Moreover, ten years after entry, the whole day-to-day functioning of the Government machine was geared to working within the EC, pulling powerfully against her occasional tugs in the opposite direction. Above all, from May 1979 until his retirement in 1985, she allowed her policy towards Europe to be largely guided by Britain's permanent representative in Brussels, Sir Michael Butler – a classic Foreign Office mandarin and convinced pro-European, but one who crucially supported her determination to hold out for a substantial budget rebate. She raged in private, but so long as Butler was there, he kept her more outrageous prejudices in check and her energy channelled into constructive engagement. After he had gone she was increasingly egged in the opposite direction by the ubiquitous and subtly Eurosceptic Charles Powell.

Even in her most positive period, however, Mrs Thatcher set in hand no long-term thinking about the future of Europe or Britain's place in it. She never held one of her Chequers seminars on Europe, as she did on relations with Eastern Europe, South Africa and several other subjects. She simply dismissed as fantasy the idea that there could ever be a 'United States of Europe in the same way that there is a United States of America'.[7] She assumed that her own idea of what the EC should be – a free-trade area and a forum for loose co-operation between sovereign nations – would naturally prevail.[8] As a result, from lack of imaginative empathy with other views and lack of her usual thorough homework, she failed to take seriously the fact that most other European governments had a quite different conception of how Europe should develop. They had given a good deal more thought to how to achieve their goal than she ever did to how she might prevent it.

Her relations with her Community partners were greatly improved in 1981 by the replacement of the haughty and supercilious Giscard d'Estaing as President of France by the veteran socialist, François Mitterrand. Though on the face of it Mitterrand and Mrs Thatcher might have been thought to be chalk and cheese, they actually got on unexpectedly well. First, he was a very sexy man with the confidence to treat her as a woman – and she responded, as she often did to a sexual challenge. Far more explicitly than with Reagan, there was an erotic undercurrent in her relations with Mitterrand which predisposed her to like him. It was he who famously – and to the bewilderment of her British critics – described her as having 'the eyes of Caligula and the mouth of Marilyn Monroe'.[9] The former were undisputed, but it took a Frenchman to appreciate the latter.★ John Major, in his brief time as Foreign Secretary, attended an Anglo-French summit at Chequers which he described as 'not so much a meeting as a flirtation, which they both clearly enjoyed'.[11]

Second, she quickly found that Mitterrand, though nominally a socialist, was a *patriotic* socialist – 'unlike ours', as she once tartly told Harold Evans.[12] Ten years older than Giscard (who was slightly younger than Mrs Thatcher), Mitterrand had fought in the resistance and was still grateful for British support in the war. When he visited London in September 1981 the Foreign Office cleverly managed to find the pilot who had flown him to England in 1940. He was as firmly committed to maintaining the French independent *force de frappe* as she was to the British nuclear deterrent, and thus shared her alarm at SDI and Reagan's bilateral negotiations at Reykjavik.

Third, quite early in their relationship Mitterrand won her undying gratitude by his prompt and unequivocal support for Britain's cause in the Falklands – decisively overruling his Foreign Minister Claude Cheysson and much of the Quai d'Orsay. Mrs Thatcher never forgot this timely assistance. For the rest of the decade there persisted a strong mutual respect between Mrs Thatcher and Mitterrand which transcended their political differences.

★According to Sir Reginald Hibbert, Britain's Ambassador to France at the time of the Giscard–Mitterrand transition, it was a positive help to their relationship that Mitterrand did not speak English, so that his conversations with Mrs Thatcher were conducted through an interpreter. Giscard – unusually for a French leader – had liked to show off his English, which often led to misunderstandings.[10]

By contrast, she never warmed to Helmut Kohl, who succeeded Helmut Schmidt as Chancellor of West Germany in 1982. She was as glad to see the back of Schmidt as she was of Giscard; but she thought Kohl boring, clumsy and provincial and persistently underestimated him. A huge man with a dominating physical presence and an enormous appetite, he perfectly embodied her resentment of Germany's postwar prosperity, which was never far below the surface. 'It's always been a misnomer to say that the Germans are the paymasters of Europe,' she told George Urban in 1984. 'The Germans have simply been paying reparations for all the things they did during the war.'[13] At first she patronised Kohl (as Schmidt and Giscard patronised her). But the longer he survived, as he grew in political stature and increasingly came to rival her as the dominant figure in Europe, the more her dislike grew. Kohl tried hard to woo her: but she would not be wooed. Once, quite early on, he proudly presented her with some wine from his own vineyard. Mrs Thatcher showed no interest whatever but merely asked about the agenda for their talks.[14] Several years later, in April 1989, he invited her to his home town in the Rhineland, plied her with his favourite dish, made from a pig's stomach with dumplings and sauerkraut, and took her to see the tombs of the Holy Roman Emperors in Speyer Cathedral – 'precursors', as Charles Powell noted, 'of earlier attempts at European Union'. While she inspected them 'without visible enthusiasm', Kohl took Powell behind a pillar. 'Now she's seen me here in my own home town,' he hoped, 'right at the heart of Europe and on the border with France, surely she will understand that I am not just German, I am European. You must convince her.' Powell promised to try. But the moment they boarded the plane to fly back to London, Mrs Thatcher 'threw herself into her seat, kicked off her shoes and announced with the finality which was her trademark: "My God, that man is so German." Powell, in his own words, 'aborted my mission to persuade her otherwise'.[15]

To her irritation, she could never break the Paris–Bonn axis which remained the central fact of European politics. But she made little effort to seek allies among the other European leaders who came and went during her time in Downing Street. She quite liked the Dutch premier, Ruud Lubbers whom she approved in her memoirs as 'a young practical businessman'.[16] But she was contemptuous of the Greeks and Italians whom she assumed to be more or less openly on the fiddle. Even her published memoirs are full of disparaging vignettes, some of which display a breathtaking failure of self-awareness. The Greek Prime Minister Andreas Papandreou, for instance, she describes as 'a charming and agreeable man in private [whose] whole persona changed when it was a question of getting more money for Greece'.[17] Most of her European partners would have said exactly the same of her. Giulio Andreotti of Italy 'seemed to have a positive aversion to principle';[18] while 'we never seemed to get by without a tear-jerking homily on the predicament of Ireland from . . . Dr Garret Fitzgerald'.[19] Her whole approach to Europe started from the assumption that the other countries were in the business of doing Britain down.

She regarded every European summit as another battle in a protracted war to defend British interests against the greedy and scheming foreigners. She was usually up till two or three in the morning strenuously rehearsing with her officials the arguments she was going to use next day. By contrast she was scornful of the other leaders' lack of a comparable grasp of detail and exasperated by their unbusinesslike and anecdotal style. As Bernard Ingham recalled: 'She had never told an anecdote in her life.' Listening to Kohl and Mitterand jawing away with no agenda was 'purgatory' to her.[20] More than this, she despised the whole ethos of compromise, deal-making and fudge, which was how the Community worked. 'She was quite simply too straight, too direct, too principled and altogether too serious for them.'[21] But by disdaining to play by the Community's prevailing rules she reduced her own effectiveness and damaged British interests. By contrast with their utopian fantasies, she liked to regard herself as strictly practical. 'Other countries have an enormous gap between their rhetoric about what they want to do and what they do in practice,' she told the Commons after the Luxembourg summit of 1985. 'The whole time, part of our task has been to diminish their expectations, and to bring them down from the clouds to practical matters.'[22] Yet the inconvenient fact was that the 'other countries' kept getting things done that she did not like; while behind the smokescreen of her defiant words she invariably ended up agreeing to what they had agreed.

After five years of wrangling, she finally achieved a budget settlement which satisfied her in June 1984. Up until then she continued to block all other progress in the EC – on VAT payments and reform of the Common Agricultural Policy – until she got her way. The three-year deal secured by Peter Carrington in 1981 was about to expire. Now she wanted a permanent settlement. There was deadlock at Athens in December 1983, when Mrs Thatcher felt that Mitterrand let her down by reneging on proposals for long-term structural changes which she thought the French had agreed; and deadlock again at Brussels in March 1984, when she refused an offer of £1.1 billion for the next two years, which would not have resolved the problem but left Britain still in the position of *demandeur* towards her partners. This time Kohl was adamant, and at one point actually walked out. Mrs Thatcher was isolated as usual, but refused to budge. There was renewed talk of expelling Britain from the Community, while Mrs Thatcher began seriously to examine the possibility of suspending payments, which hitherto she had always ruled out. Back home she portrayed herself shamelessly as poor little Britain being bullied by the others: 'There are nine of them being tiresome and only one of me,' she told Robin Day on *Panorama*. 'They could end the tiresomeness and stubbornness by giving me what I want.'[23]

In the end she settled for less than she wanted – a 66 per cent rebate, not the 'well over 70 per cent' which had been her goal.[24] In cash terms this was same figure (£1.1 billion) she had rejected at Brussels. But this time it was permanent. She also accepted an increase from 1 per cent to 1.4 per cent of each country's VAT returns that should be payable to the Community. At the time she represented Fontainebleau as a triumph for her firmness. 'Patient diplomacy and, I confess, a little impatient diplomacy, did the trick,' she boasted at the 1984 party conference.[25] But in reality Mitterand and Kohl settled only because they were so fed up with her and in their own time, infuriating her by leaving it right to the last minute. She kept trying to split them, but they would not be split: Kohl refused to see her alone. Eventually she did see Mitterand alone. He offered her 65 per cent, let her bargain it up to 66 per cent, then insisted that that was it. 'She almost broke into tears,' his aide Jacques Attali recalls – with perhaps some Gallic exaggeration. 'The first time I saw her realise that she was totally isolated and she broke, like glass, she couldn't even discuss it . . . then she accepted the deal.'[26] Even Bernard Ingham wondered how she would be able to sell her climb-down in the House of Commons. In fact she had no difficulty brushing off Neil Kinnock who had foolishly predicted that she would come back from Fontainebleau empty-handed. By soberly emphasising what she had brought back, 'she not merely got away with it, but . . . was actually recognised as something of a statesman in settling the way she did'.[27] In her memoirs she made a virtue of her realism: 'In every negotiation there comes the best possible point to settle: this was it.'[28]

The critical fact was that Mitterrand wanted a settlement under the French presidency. Mrs Thatcher knew that this was her best chance, and wisely took it. The other countries were just relieved that the 'Bloody British Question' was resolved at last. 'She got far more than she should have got,' the Danish Foreign Minister reflected ten years later. 'In the short run she won, but whether a political price had to be paid in the longer run is very difficult to say.'[29]

In the medium term it certainly appeared that Britain was now ready to play a more constructive role. Under the influence of George Urban, one of her unofficial foreign-policy advisers, who urged that if she would only learn to 'think European' she had a historic opportunity to become effectively the 'Queen of Europe',[30] Mrs Thatcher's language became noticeably warmer. 'The Community can now enter on a new chapter,' she told the Tory Party Conference that autumn.[31] Her speech to the US Congress in February 1985 included an astonishingly upbeat passage – probably written by Urban – in which she envisaged future generations looking back at 'these birth pangs of a new Europe'. Yet her language was deceptive. In context it was plain that she was thinking, as usual, of military co-operation and of Europe taking more responsibility for its own defence: 'the creation of a Europe able to share the load alongside you'.[32] As Roy Jenkins had noted back in 1977, she always tended to see the European Community as an arm of NATO. But this was not at all the way the other members saw it.

The rest of the Community was also ready to open a new chapter, marked by the appointment of an energetic new President of the Commission – Jacques Delors, formerly Mitterrand's Finance Minister. With hindsight, Mrs Thatcher dismissed Delors as a typical French socialist – 'highly-educated, entirely self-assured, a *dirigiste* by conviction from a political culture which is *dirigiste* by tradition' – and glossed his appointment as a bureaucratic stitch-up which had nothing to do with her.[33] In fact she was largely instrumental in the choice of Delors, since she vetoed the first French candidate, the former Foreign Minister Claude Cheysson, described by Lawson as 'a garrulous little bow-tied French socialist, full of do-gooding ideas and love of high-spending'.[34] Delors by contrast had impressed the British as tough and practical: he had been responsible for scrapping most of the left-wing policies on which Mitterrand had been elected and implementing instead what Howe called 'our policies'.[35] Delors was indeed tough and practical, but he was a European visionary, as she discovered. She would have been better off with Cheysson.

Taking office in January 1985, Delors quickly fixed on the completion of the single market as the next big advance in the evolution of the Community. He looked first at other areas – common defence policy, progress towards a single currency, the reform of Community institutions – but he could not get sufficient agreement on any of these. So he settled for what he called '*les quatre libertés*' – free movement of goods, services, capital and people. This Mrs Thatcher was happy to go along with. It seemed consistent with her idea of the Community as essentially a free-trade area – a true common market

– and an opportunity for advancing Thatcherite economic ideas of deregulation and free enterprise on a European scale. 'Why cannot we make it as cheap for our citizens to travel by air within their own continent as they can to other continents?' she asked in a speech to the Franco-British Council in late 1984. 'Why cannot it be as easy for German businessmen to take out insurance direct at Lloyds of London as it is for British businessmen to buy German cars?'[36]

Accordingly Britain took the lead in formulating this agenda in a document entitled *Europe – The Future*. Lady Thatcher still insists that she was never anti-European, but on the contrary, as she claims in her memoirs, 'a European idealist'.[37] 'I don't want to paper over the cracks,' she told Conservative MEPs in March 1984. 'I want to rebuild the foundations.'[38] What she overlooked was that others were quite happy with the foundations and only wanted to get on with building on them. Carried away with her vision of Thatcherising the Community, she did not realise that Delors – and Mitterand and Kohl and almost all the smaller countries – saw the single market as part of a wider process of European integration. Claude Cheysson recalls a telling vignette at the end of the Fontainebleau summit, when Mitterand, summing up, said quietly: 'Good meeting . . . but maybe we could also sometimes consider the problems of society, social affairs, unemployment.' Mrs Thatcher, collecting her papers, only half heard and asked him to repeat what he had said:

> And then she stood up, which no one ever does at a European Council table and, not finding her words, stuttering, she said, 'But, Mr President . . . Britain didn't join for that.'[39]

At first, however, all went swimmingly. She appointed Arthur Cockfield as one of Britain's two members of the new Commission (the other was the former Labour minister, Stanley Clinton-Davis) and managed to ensure that Cockfield got the crucial competition portfolio. A pedantic number-cruncher of formidable energy and cantankerous self-belief, whose Cabinet colleagues were thoroughly glad to see the back of him, he seemed the ideal man to chase up British policy in Brussels. He wasted no time in publishing a detailed programme entitled *Completing the Internal Market*, listing 292 specific measures of deregulation to be achieved by 1992. Mrs Thatcher was delighted. This, she thought, was Britain at last leading the Community, as pro-Europeans had aspired to do ever since Macmillan first applied for membership, and extending to the over-governed continent the benefits of British free enterprise. But it was not so simple as that. Mrs

Thatcher did not understand that creating a single market necessarily involved not just deregulation, but the harmonisation of regulations across the Community, which impinged on matters hitherto the prerogative of national governments. In her view Cockfield, in his missionary zeal for the project to which she had appointed him, betrayed her by straying too far into the forbidden area of integration. Like practically every British politician who has ever been appointed to Brussels, he 'went native' and adopted a quasi-federalist perspective. 'Alas,' she wrote in her memoirs, 'it was not long before my old friend and I were at odds.'[40] She finally quarrelled with him in 1987 over the projected harmonisation of VAT rates in member countries, which he not only insisted was essential but was able to prove to her was provided for in the Treaty of Rome:

> She said it wasn't. I said it was, she said it wasn't, and her private secretary was therefore sent to get a copy of the Treaty of Rome and I asked him to read out Article 99, which says quite specifically, 'The Commission shall' – not may – 'present proposals for the harmonisation of indirect taxation' . . .
>
> Realising that I was going to get no reply, I pressed a little further. I said it was in the Treaty of Rome and you ought to have read it before you signed it. She said 'I didn't sign it.' I said 'I know you didn't, but you were a member of the Cabinet that did,' and that also was greeted in total silence.[41]

Though the rest of the Community regarded him as a conspicuous success, Mrs Thatcher declined to reappoint Cockfield for a second term.

In the meantime, however, in order to make progress on the single market, she realised that she would have to acquiesce in other developments which she subsequently came to regret. The so-called Single European Act – Delors' major initiative to carry the process of European integration forward – extended the application of weighted majority voting into new areas and increased the powers of both the Commission and the Parliament. Mrs Thatcher was afraid that the completion of the single market would be held up by other countries exercising their national vetoes, and positively bullied her partners to accept majority voting in this area, as she explained in typically 'us' and 'them' style to the BBC's John Simpson in December 1985:

> We do need to get some of our trade and business into the Common Market which is stopped now because they will not agree to certain

standards, because one person can veto it . . . so we need to stop some of those abuses.[42]

She did what she could to block what she regarded as the most utopian proposals. She successfully opposed a much more ambitious 'Draft Treaty on European Union' which was approved by the Parliament in February 1984; and at Milan in June 1985 she tried to prevent the calling of a full-scale intergovernmental conference (IGC) to rewrite the Treaty of Rome, in favour of proceeding incrementally by limited agreements. But to her fury she was outmanoeuvred by the Italian Prime Minister, Bettino Craxi, who pulled what Charles Powell called 'a procedural trick' which the British 'rather remarkably' failed to foresee; and a full IGC was duly convened at Luxembourg in December 1985, with an agenda now going well beyond the single market.[43]

There, however, she was remarkably positive and constructive. She drove forward agreement on the practical measures required to implement the single market, believing that the wider implications of the new treaty were no more than woolly aspirations which would come to nothing. In particular she believed that she had qualified the 'irrevocable' commitment to economic and monetary union (EMU) originally signed up to by Heath, Brandt and Pompidou in 1972, substituting instead a reference to economic and monetary 'co-operation'; and also that she had preserved the right of national veto in such sensitive areas as border controls, customs and drugs policy, and indeed any matter which any member country regarded as vital, under the so-called Luxembourg Compromise. Nigel Lawson claims that he warned her that these safeguards would prove to be worthless, but the Foreign Office reassured her.[44] The Foreign Office congratulated itself that the Single Act was 'written on our agenda'[45] and the Government proclaimed a negotiating success. Commending it to the House of Commons, Mrs Thatcher insisted that the 'modest' reforms agreed could perfectly well have been agreed without an intergovernmental conference, and generally played down their significance.[46]★

As a result of these assurances, the Single European Act was whipped through Parliament with scarcely a murmur of dissent. The Labour

---

★Alan Sked and Chris Cook quote Mrs Thatcher declaring: 'It does not change anything. If it did I would not have signed it . . . There is no erosion of essential national sovereignty.'[47] But they cite no source, and the CD-Rom of her complete public statements has no record of her using these words in Parliament or anywhere else.

party was in the process of reversing its former opposition to all things European, while Tory Eurosceptics – as they were later called – believing that Mrs Thatcher shared their antipathy to any hint of federalism, trusted in her vigilance and accepted her assurances that they had nothing to worry about. In fact, whatever she and the Foreign Office believed, the Single European Act as interpreted in Brussels did very significantly extend the powers of both the Commission and the Strasbourg Parliament, and led on logically to the Treaty of Maastricht in 1992 and eventually to the single currency.

The fact is that Mrs Thatcher 'gave away' more sovereignty in 1985 than Heath in 1973 or Major in 1992. She subsequently claimed that she was deceived by the other leaders who broke assurances that they had given her. 'I trusted them,' she recalled bitterly in 1996. 'I believed in them. I believed this was good faith between nations co-operating together. So we got our fingers burned. Once you've got your fingers burned, you don't go and burn them again.'[48] 'Frankly,' Charles Powell agrees, 'we were diddled.'[49] Yet she admitted in her memoirs that there was a 'studied ambiguity' about the Act's reference to EMU which was bound to cause trouble in due course.[50] The idea that Mrs Thatcher, of all people, did not read the Act closely before signing it is incredible to anyone who knew her. 'I never remember an occasion in the six years I worked for her when she negotiated something without knowing what she was talking about,' Sir Michael Butler has stated.[51] David Williamson, Secretary-General of the Community from 1987, recalled her telling him specifically, 'I have read every word of the Single European Act.'[52] So why did she sign it? Lord Cockfield believes that she simply deluded herself, believing what she wanted to believe.[53] Bernard Ingham by contrast thought she knew what she was doing: 'I think she knew at the time that she was taking risks . . . She was taking a calculated risk with a very clear view in mind.'[54] In other words she believed that the substantial bird in the hand was worth a flock of shadows in the bush. Delors confirms this interpretation, recalling that she hesitated and asked for an extra few minutes to think about it before she signed.[55]

As usual, she blames others, but has only herself to blame. Blinded by the strength of her own conviction, she did not understand the equal strength of the other leaders' will to maintain the momentum of economic, political and social integration. She believed that she had preserved Britain's essential independence by steadfastly refusing to join the ERM, and trusted in her ability to continue to do so. Having got what she wanted – the single market – she believed she could send back the rest of the menu. The weakness of her approach, however, as soon became clear, was that she had no strategy to channel, divert or hold back the integrationist tide beyond the merely negative and counterproductive response of saying 'no'. The ultimate price of her long battle over the budget up to 1984 was that she found little sympathy, and no allies, among Britain's European partners, when she once again pitched herself against them after 1987.

Yet Mrs Thatcher did, ironically, sanction one powerfully symbolic act of European integration – the old dream of linking Britain physically to the Continent by building a Channel tunnel. This was a project she had strongly supported as a member of Ted Heath's Government in the early 1970s. When the incoming Labour Government scrapped it in 1974, she condemned their short-sighted penny-pinching, arguing – somewhat out of character – that the country could not live on bread and cheese alone but needed some 'visionary ideas' as well.[56] Now, as Prime Minister, she still liked the idea of a 'grand project', but insisted that it would have to be financed and built entirely by private enterprise. Initially it seemed that this condition would be enough to sink the project. Visiting Dover during the 1983 election she privately assured local politicians – who did not want a tunnel – that the likelihood was 'very remote':

> She is firmly of the opinion that there is no question of the British Government guaranteeing it or subsidising it in any way at all, and she can't see the economic return on one financed from purely private resources.[57]

At her first meeting with Mitterrand in 1981 they both spoke warm words about wanting a tunnel in principle; but it did not become a serious possibility until the economy improved. Then a number of her favourite businessmen began to show an interest – among them Nigel Broackes of the property developer Trafalgar House; Ian MacGregor, thinking of all the orders a tunnel would generate for British Steel; and (not yet in the Government) David Young. The National Westminster Bank took the lead in persuading the DTI that a tunnel could be financed without a Government guarantee. On this basis, Mrs Thatcher's enthusiasm cautiously increased. Ideologically she was keen to give the private sector a chance to show what it could do, while she could see a political dividend from a big project which would create a lot of jobs. British officials deny that her change of front was a *quid pro quo* for Mitterrand's help at Fontainebleau; but with the budget question settled she was certainly looking to make some gesture of goodwill towards the French President. Even so her *volte-face* took her colleagues by surprise. Visiting Paris for a bilateral summit in December 1984, she started talking all round the question during a whisky-fuelled late-night conversation in the British Embassy. She began by rehearsing the familiar arguments against a tunnel – 'that the traffic would be devastating to Kent, that it would destroy the ferries, that it would cost too much'; but as she went on she unexpectedly talked herself round to the opposite point of view and concluded: 'It's time we did something exciting' or (in another recollection) 'something that will stand in the memory of this administration'. Howe, Lawson and Ridley all fell obediently into line. 'She finished the evening,' according to the British Ambassador, 'declaring that, if accomplished, it would be the most exciting project of the century, which left everyone in the room more or less dumbfounded.'[58]

Next morning she was still of the same mind, and she and Mitterrand duly agreed to inject 'a new urgency' into studying the options. Both of them initially favoured a road, rather than a rail link: he wanted a bridge, she a drive-through tunnel. To Mrs Thatcher, railways were the archetypal nationalised industry – dirty, old-fashioned and at the mercy of the unions – whereas the private car was a symbol of individual freedom. 'Many people have a great dream,' she said in a television interview, 'that they would like to get in their car and drive all the way through to Calais. So we must consider that possibility too.'[59] In practice, however, it became clear that a rail link was cheaper and more practical. Over the next year several bidders competed for the contract, including Nigel Broackes' EuroRoute; but in the end it was the Channel Tunnel Group, headed by the former Ambassador to the US (and before that France), Nicholas Henderson, which gained the Prime Minister's ear and won the prize.

The decision was announced by the two leaders at Lille in northern France in January 1986. Mrs Thatcher made a humorous speech recalling previous attempts to build a tunnel, going back to Napoleon, and claimed that Churchill had supported a Channel bridge on condition that the last span was a drawbridge which could be raised in case of French attack. Times had now changed, she suggested.[60] As a rare gesture to Anglo-French fraternity she was persuaded to deliver the final part of her speech in French. Doubtless remembering Ted Heath's ghastly mangling of the language in 1972, she learned the words phonetically, going over them again and again until she had the pronunciation right – coached by the French wife of the deputy under-secretary of the Foreign Office, Robin Renwick. 'I have never met another adult who had such power of concentration, the absolute will of getting it as perfect as she could,' Lady Renwick recalled.[61] She delivered it 'impeccably', in Charles Powell's view, and he thought her effort made 'rather a good effect . . . President Mitterrand was quite visibly . . . rocked by this sudden display of fluency in French' – though the television pictures appear to show him looking more embarrassed than impressed.[62] Speaking in her constituency five days later she began by saying what a pleasure it was not to have to speak in French.[63]

This was the high point of Mrs Thatcher's enthusiasm for Europe. Briefly, as Nicholas Ridley wrote, 'she saw the tunnel as her contribution to free trade and open markets . . . a concrete monument to her view of Europe'.[64] Charles Powell agrees. 'She saw it as a practical expression of the European ideal. She was fed up with all the rhetoric about political institutions and European union, whatever that meant . . . It was practical, not guff as she would say.'[65] At the same time she was still excited by the grandeur of the project. 'Perhaps most important,' she declared at Lille, 'it will represent a monument to the imagination and enterprise of this generation – a beacon for future generations to remember us by.'[66] To Woodrow Wyatt in 1987 she referred to it proudly as 'my tunnel'.[67]

And yet it goes entirely unmentioned in her memoirs. Opened in 1994, the Channel tunnel does indeed stand today as one of the few concrete legacies of Mrs Thatcher's rule. For travellers to the Continent – both drivers taking their vehicles quickly and painlessly to Calais and rail passengers whisked from London to Paris in less than three hours by Eurostar – it is an established success. But as a demonstration of what private enterprise could do it was an ambiguous success. It was indeed financed (on the British side) by private capital, as Mrs Thatcher insisted it should be; but only at a loss to the shareholders who were persuaded to invest in it. It did not make money. Then private enterprise was not willing to fund the projected high-speed rail link from London to Folkestone, a necessary part of the service which is now years behind schedule and will, after all, have to be paid for by the taxpayer. The lesson, as of so much of the privatisation experience, is that big infrastructural projects of this sort cannot be built without public money.

Pragmatism in Hong Kong
Outside the major theatres of Europe and the Cold War, Britain still faced a troublesome legacy of post-imperial problems in other far-flung corners of the world. During her first term Mrs Thatcher had been confronted with two such hangovers of empire, in Africa and the South Atlantic, both of which she handled successfully, though in opposite ways. In Rhodesia she suppressed her initial instinct, allowed herself

to be guided by the Foreign Office and achieved a peaceful settlement. In the Falklands she followed her instinct, ignored the Foreign Office and brought off an improbable military triumph. Now in her second term she faced a more intractable problem than either: the approaching expiry of Britain's hundred-year lease on Hong Kong, which was due to revert to China in 1997. Britain had immense commercial interests at stake as well as political responsibility for this anomalous enclave of Far Eastern capitalism, which was threatened with extinction in a decade's time unless the Chinese Communists could be persuaded to permit its survival after the handover.

Once again all Mrs Thatcher's instincts were aroused. First, Hong Kong was, like the Falklands, a British colony threatened with takeover by a neighbouring state. Although undeniably most of the territory was legally due to be returned to China, Hong Kong island itself was British sovereign territory which could in theory be retained, or at least used as a bargaining counter. Second, Hong Kong was a haven of freedom, prosperity and economic enterprise – though little democracy – besieged by Communism. Third, she did not like the Chinese. In practice she was a good deal less hawkish towards China than towards the Soviet Union, partly because it was not European, so the suppression of freedom was less of an affront to European values than in Russia, but largely because it was not expansionist and posed no military threat to the West.[68] She accepted China as a fact of life and an ancient civilisation, culturally different and commanding respect on its own terms. But she had a 'visceral dislike' of the Chinese system and felt deeply that it should be possible to save Hong Kong from being swallowed by it. Coming straight after the Falklands, the problem of Hong Kong caused her 'a lot of mental difficulty'.[69]

The parallel was inescapable in the summer of 1982, since she was due to visit China in September, with the laurels of her Falklands victory still fresh on her brow. In defiance of the world she had gone to war to save 1,800 subsidy-dependent Falkanders from the brutal mercies of the Argentines. It was a difficult moment to be contemplating tamely handing over a far larger population of vastly more enterprising British citizens of Hong Kong to foreign tyranny. Yet the facts of the two situations were entirely different. On the one hand, China's legal claim on 90 per cent of the territory was irrefutable – and Mrs Thatcher believed profoundly in the sanctity of law – while no one suggested that Hong Kong island was economically viable on its own. On the other, China possessed overwhelming military superiority, and anyway the island was indefensible: the Chinese could simply have cut off the water supply. Defiance was not an option.

So Britain had no choice but to negotiate – from a weak position – and try to secure the best possible result by diplomacy. Unwelcome as it was, Mrs Thatcher recognised the reality; but she still hoped, at the outset, to be able to bargain the sovereignty of Hong Kong island for continued British administration of the whole colony under nominal Chinese rule: in other words a form of the 'leaseback' idea originally proposed for the Falklands. Her purpose, when she first put her mind to the problem, was to strike a hard bargain. Still fired up by the Falklands, she approached it, according to Percy Cradock, then British Ambassador in Beijing, in 'a combative and uncooperative spirit', with 'a predisposition to solutions based on legal or even military strength', and tested them all to destruction before reluctantly abandoning them.[70] 'She looked quite hard at the idea that we should simply stand pat, hold our own and tell the Chinese to take a running jump.'[71] More than once Michael Heseltine, as Defence Secretary, had to tell her that Hong Kong island really was indefensible.[72]

But when she met Deng Xiaoping in Beijing in September 1982 she found him unyielding. Believing that it was in China's interest to preserve the prosperity of Hong Kong, she held out the possibility of ceding sovereignty in return for continued British administration. But Deng knew that he held all the cards and called her bluff. Like Mrs Thatcher herself in regard to the Falklands, he regarded sovereignty as non-negotiable. If Britain made difficulties, he warned, China would simply reoccupy Hong Kong before 1997. She was impressed, despite herself, though physically repelled by his chainsmoking and his use of a large spitoon. On coming out she remarked to Percy Cradock 'how cruel he was'.[73]

It was Cradock who persuaded her – reluctantly – to shift her ground. In March 1983 she sent a letter to the Chinese Prime Minister Zhao Ziyang indicating a more positive approach. Specifically she undertook that she would not merely consider but 'recommend' ceding sovereignty in return for certain assurances about Hong Kong's future. That cleared the way for Geoffrey Howe to open negotiations with Beijing on the basis of Deng's characteristically paradoxical formula 'one country, two systems', which offered the possibility of preserving the essentials of Hong Kong's capitalist way of life under Chinese rule. What this might mean in practice was impossible to know. The people of Hong Kong were suspicious that they were being sold down the river; but Howe still had no cards to play. In principle the Chinese recognised no distinction between sovereignty and administration, so he had nothing to bargain with. But he persisted, with quiet skill, and eventually secured an agreement in September 1984, guaranteeing Hong Kong's 'special status' within China for fifty years after 1997, plus agreement on passports, air travel and land ownership. Under Cradock's guidance Mrs Thatcher was persuaded to accept it as the best deal that could be achieved. She hailed the settlement at the Tory Party Conference, emphasising that Hong Kong had not been betrayed. The government of Hong Kong had agreed to it 'in good conscience', she assured the representatives. 'That means a lot to us.'[74] At the end of the year she flew to China again to sign the agreement and reassure the people of Hong Kong in person.

The Americans gave their blessing, hoping that the settlement would help open China to the West. 'The initial State reaction to the Agreement is that it is a pretty good one,' a White House aide noted laconically, 'and that the British did a reasonably good job in negotiating it.'[75] Reagan's private congratulations, however, sounded a slightly more cautious note. 'I am heartened by your conviction that the agreement secures the major principles your government sought,' he wrote to Mrs Thatcher, 'and I hope that it will be accepted with similar confidence by the people of Hong Kong.'[76]

It was a realistic settlement and the best she could do. With no sanctions to employ, she had no option but to gamble on Peking's good faith. Less than five years later, however, the Chinese suppression of dissidents in Tiananmen Square in June 1989 severely shook her confidence. Mrs Thatcher was 'horrified' by the massacre of Tiananmen Square. 'We have got to do something,' she raged to Woodrow Wyatt. 'We cannot desert them like this and just say things are going to be all right.'[77] In public she strongly condemned the Chinese leadership; but at the same time she rejected calls that Britain should repudiate the 1984 agreement. Like it or not, Cradock argued, there was still no chance of putting anything better in its place. 'We had not concluded an agreement with Deng Xiaoping because we thought he was a liberal.'[78] Even before the massacre she had been keen to enable Hong Kong Chinese citizens to settle in Britain if they wanted.[79] Now, overruling the doubts of her Home and Foreign Secretaries (by then David Waddington and Douglas Hurd) and the objections of a sizeable number of Tory backbenchers, she insisted on legislation to grant British passports to 50,000 top Hong Kong administrators and business people so as to allow them to come to Britain if need be. This was intended to reassure them, so that they would not in fact come, but stay in Hong Kong.

After the events of 1989, there was pressure both in Britain and in Hong Kong itself to introduce more democracy in the colony before the handover. Mrs Thatcher claims that she had wanted to do this all along, but that 'no one else seemed much attracted by my ideas', so she did not pursue it.[80] There was just one sentence about democracy in the 1985 agreement, and this was a last-minute addition never accepted by the Chinese.[81] Before Mrs Thatcher left office, Cradock negotiated an increase from ten to eighteen elected seats on the Legislative Council. Subsequently Chris Patten, appointed the last British Governor in 1992, stepped up the pace. For a time, China became 'paranoid about security and obsessed with sovereignty',[82] and the prospect that it would honour the agreement after 1997 began to look bleak. Old China hands like Cradock – and Geoffrey Howe – criticised Patten for needlessly provoking Beijing. But Lady Thatcher declined to join them. In her memoirs she consoled herself that China's supposedly Communist economic policy 'amounts to a thorough-going embrace of capitalism'. It was not in China's interest to destroy Hong Kong's prosperity. 'At some point the increasing momentum of economic change in China itself will lead to political change'.[83] She remained optimistic that the handover would go all right, as indeed it did. Overall, the settlement of Hong Kong was another considerable success for her foreign policy. But like the evolution of Rhodesia into Zimbabwe, it was a success achieved by traditional diplomacy, not Thatcherite confrontation.

South Africa and the Commonwealth

The third of Harold Macmillan's interlocking circles of influence through which Britain related to the world was the Commonwealth. Compared with the Atlantic alliance and the European Community, this loose association of former British colonies and dominions was considerably diminished in importance since Macmillan's day. But it was still another set of relationships which Mrs Thatcher had to keep up, and a biennial forum of international diplomacy which gave her considerable trouble. At the beginning of her first term she earned considerable credit by the unexpectedly pragmatic way she resolved the Rhodesian problem, and by her willingness to recognise the new Zimbabwe. But that success only brought into greater salience the cause which really excited the Commonwealth in the 1980s to the exclusion of all others – the affront to the conscience of a multiracial organisation represented by the persistence of white minority rule in South Africa. Before long Mrs Thatcher had dissipated most of the credit she had won in Rhodesia by her determined refusal to support economic sanctions against the regime in Pretoria. As a result she was soon even more embattled within the Commonwealth than she was in Europe, portrayed by much of the rest of the world as a friend and protector of apartheid – whereas she saw herself as its most practical opponent.

There is no clearer example of Mrs Thatcher's refusal to acquiesce in a fashionable consensus than her stubborn resistance to sanctions against South Africa. She became the focus of all the frustration and hatred of the anti-apartheid movement not only in Britain but around the world. As with her perverse support for nuclear weapons, progressive opinion could not understand how anyone could be against such an obviously virtuous cause. Once again her insensitivity to others' passionately held beliefs, her certainty that she was right and her appearance of revelling in her isolation seemed wilfully provocative. Yet again there is a good case for maintaining that she was in fact proved right by the eventual outcome, and her critics wrong.

Mrs Thatcher had very little love for the Commonwealth. Like many ardent patriots, she took an intense but vicarious pride in the record of the British empire; she had no personal experience or family links with any part of it, and she felt none of the same enthusiasm for the 'family' of independent nations which made up its modern, more or less democratic successor. As she frankly admitted in the early 1960s, 'Many of us do not feel the same allegiance to Archbishop Makarios or Dr Nkrumah or to people like Jomo Kenyatta as we do towards Mr Menzies of Australia.'[84] She prized the Commonwealth in so far as it was an expression of Britain's continuing global responsibility and specialness among the nations; and she was furious when the Americans ignored it by invading Grenada. But most of the time she thought it merely provided a stage for post-colonial posturing by nationalist leaders happy to squeeze as much aid as possible from Britain while insulting and abusing the former imperial power at every opportunity. 'It required,' a Buckingham Palace aide delicately put it, 'considerable forbearance and Mrs Thatcher was not very good at forbearing.'[85]

'It is *their* club,' she was once heard to rage, '*their* Commonwealth.'[86] In fact she often seemed to regard the Commonwealth, like the European Community, as another conspiracy of the unscrupulous and the profligate, given to idealistic schemes which had to be tempered by a dose of British realism. Her impatience can be seen in some of her correspondence with President Reagan. 'We are now working towards the Commonwealth Conference in Australia at the end of September,' she wrote following the Ottawa G7 in 1981. 'Our Australian colleagues are rather keen to have a grand declaration about the rights of the Third World countries. We are trying to tone it down because it would be wrong to raise false hopes.'[87] On her return from the 1983 heads of government conference in New Delhi she evidently vented her frustration with an institution which blurred her polarised view of the world. Reagan's reply was sympathetic. 'Given the predominant "non-aligned" orientation of most Commonwealth countries,' he wrote, 'I understand the difficulties you faced.' He agreed that Britain and the US should work together to avert a proposed world economic conference 'which could weaken international monetary institutions', and specifically shared her reservations about 'some of . . . Prime Minister Trudeau's recent proposals. While we are uncomfortable with several passages in the communiqué, I personally appreciate your efforts to moderate and improve the language of the original drafts.'[88] This glimpse of Mrs Thatcher reporting back to Washington on discussions within the Commonwealth clearly demonstrates where her loyalties lay.

Denis Thatcher was once heard in a moment of embarrassing silence at a Downing Street reception asking loudly, 'Who do you think is worse, Sonny bloody Ramphal [Secretary-General of the Commonwealth] or Ma sodding Gandhi?'[89] His wife would not have expressed herself so colourfully; but she fully shared his exasperation with Commonwealth leaders who protested loudly at the denial of democracy in South Africa while presiding happily over one-party states themselves. Many of them had tribal or caste inequalities in their own countries; while almost all were socialists of one kind or another who ran corrupt command economies which had only impoverished their people. Yet when she got to know them as individuals she got on pretty well with several of them: Kenneth Kaunda at Lusaka in 1979; Kenya's Daniel Arap Moi; even Robert Mugabe.[90] The leaders she really disliked were the white liberals like Trudeau who made much of their support for the Third World and were always ready to make excuses for Soviet subversion. She much preferred his successor Brian Mulroney, and enjoyed a lively relationship with Bob Hawke, Prime Minister of Australia from 1983.

She believed she got on with Hawke because 'like me, he was blunt and direct'.[91] Hawke's view of her, however, was rather different. He was impressed by her application – she was 'the hardest working head of government I ever met . . . always extraordinarily well briefed for every meeting' – but he did not think she had 'a first-class mind':

> In argument she often seemed to be playing catch-up. She sought to buy time while exchanging views so that she could more easily absorb contrary positions and give herself room to marshal her thoughts and responses.

In particular he was irritated by her methods of derailing debate. First, she was 'an inveterate interrupter. I never dealt with a leader who interrupted other speakers so often.' Then she was always going off at irrelevant tangents; and she would deliberately persist in what she knew to be a misleading argument. In fact Hawke thought her 'less than straightforward' and 'a little slippery'. Nevertheless he confessed 'a certain admiration for Margaret Thatcher'.[92]

She forged an intriguing bond of mutual respect with Indira Gandhi, the only other woman – apart from the Queen – she ever had to deal with as an equal. When they had first met, in 1976, Mrs Thatcher literally sat at the older woman's feet and sought her advice on how she had succeeded in a male-dominated world. But by the early 1980s, a Foreign Office minister recalled, 'they could do business together with the utmost relaxation. It became a relationship between two rather regal figures, who simply instructed their officials to reach agreements.'[93] Their politics were poles apart – Mrs Thatcher thought her counterpart's 'weak spot was that she never grasped the importance of the free market' – but she was happy to assure Reagan in 1981 that Mrs Gandhi was 'not a Marxist';[94] and in her memoirs she recognised a leader after her own heart. Though her policies were 'more than high-handed' – a euphemism for Mrs Gandhi's 1975 State of Emergency – 'only a strong figure with a powerful personality could hope successfully to rule India.'[95] Mrs Thatcher felt it very personally when Mrs Gandhi was assassinated in October 1984, just two weeks after she herself had narrowly escaped the same fate in the Grand Hotel, Brighton.

She also admired Lee Kuan Yew, the long-serving Prime Minister of Singapore, who had contrived for a quarter of a century to combine a vigorous free-market economy with a distinctly authoritarian welfare state. 'He had his own kind of democracy to be sure,' she wrote in *The Path to Power*, but 'for me, the success of Singapore demonstrated how, given the right economic framework . . . living standards could be transformed.'[96] Though supposedly a socialist himself, Lee was robustly anti-Soviet and had long experience of dealing with China. Like every British Prime Minister since Harold Wilson, Mrs Thatcher found 'Harry' Lee a shrewd and sympathetic confidant on a wide range of world affairs.

Her lack of sympathy with the Commonwealth as an institution, however, was a constant source of conflict with the Queen, who was devoted to her far-flung family of young nations and was often worried that Mrs Thatcher's isolation over South Africa might provoke a serious crisis. In June 1986 there was talk that Zambia and India might walk out. Mrs Thatcher told Woodrow Wyatt that she would not mind if they did, but 'other people would mind' – clearly meaning the Queen.[97] Every time Mrs Thatcher took a contrary position at Commonwealth Conferences – at Nassau in 1985, at Vancouver in 1987, at Kuala Lumpur in 1989 – there were rumours that the other members might try to expel Britain. But these conferences – unlike G7 summits – were the one form of international gathering where Mrs Thatcher had to play second fiddle to the Queen. Since the Queen was the focus of unity, and Mrs Thatcher invariably the embodiment of division, the gulf between them was very obvious.

Her strenuous opposition to sanctions left Mrs Thatcher vulnerable to the charge that, if not a racist herself, she was at any rate the friend of racists; a supporter of apartheid in practice even as she claimed to condemn it. It was taken for granted that her view of South Africa was coloured by Denis, who had long-standing business connections with the country going back to his exporting days with Atlas Preservatives and still had friends in Natal; and also by the 'Twickenham tendency' within the Tory party, the right-wing rugby-supporting pro-white lobby represented by people like the Member for Luton, John Carlisle. In fact Mrs Thatcher was remarkably free of race prejudice. She was no more prejudiced against Africans than she was against Germans, Greeks, Italians and others who had the misfortune not to be British: her approach to South Africa was based far more on politics than on colour. She had always thought apartheid 'irrational and bad economics',[98] not only morally wrong but practically unsustainable. She believed it could not long survive the liberalising demands of a modern economy and would inevitably be undermined by increased trade and international contacts, not by sanctions and boycotts.

Mrs Thatcher understood South Africa, like every other regional problem, as just another battleground in the global struggle between Western freedom and Soviet Communism. She regarded white South Africa, despite apartheid, as part of the West – Christian, capitalist, subject to the rule of law and in principle democratic – threatened by a Soviet-backed black liberation movement which aimed to destabilise the economy, destroy those liberal traditions and move South Africa into the Soviet camp. She opposed the principal black party, the African National Congress (ANC) – led by Oliver Tambo and a largely exiled leadership from outside South Africa while Nelson Mandela and other leaders served indefinite jail sentences – first as socialists, the tools of Communists if not actually Communists themselves; and second as terrorists, devoted to victory through 'armed struggle'. Making no allowance for the fact that so long as they were denied the vote the ANC had no legal outlet for political struggle, she was adamant that a precondition of any settlement in South Africa must be the cessation of violence.

She was certainly influenced by the scale of British business interests in South Africa. The UK was the biggest outside investor in South Africa, which was Britain's fourth-biggest trading partner. British industry – and particularly the defence industry – was heavily dependent on South African minerals. Sanctions, she constantly reminded the left, would damage not just British profits but British jobs. Moreover around 800,000 white South Africans would be entitled to come to Britain if they were forced to flee South Africa, just as Portugal had been obliged to take an influx of ex-colonials from Angola and Mozambique. Other countries which jumped on the sanctions bandwagon did not have the same direct economic interest at stake.

Altogether she thought there was a lot of hypocrisy and easy moral outrage in the anti-apartheid movement. Her object – as she explained in an interview in *The Sowetan* in 1989 – was to end apartheid without destroying the South African economy in the process:

> We do not want to see a future South African Government which really does represent the majority of South Africans inheriting a wasteland . . . In far too many countries in Africa 'liberation' has been followed by economic disaster and has brought few practical benefits to ordinary people. This can and must be avoided in South Africa.

The way to avoid this outcome was not less trade, but more. 'What the country needs is opening up to the outside world. The last thing it needs is to close in on itself even more.'[99] 'It was South Africa's isolation,' she argued in her memoirs, 'which was an obstacle to reform.'[100] The whole policy of demonising South Africa as if it was uniquely wicked was not only unfair, but positively counterproductive. Sanctions actually hurt the blacks more than they did the whites, and would not achieve the objective of ending apartheid. 'Insofar as sanctions did work,' she declared on a visit to Norway in 1986, 'they would work by bringing about starvation and unemployment and greater misery amongst the immense black population . . . I find it morally repugnant to sit here or anywhere else and say that we decide that should be brought about.'[101] Some of the most prominent South African opponents of apartheid, like the veteran white liberal Helen Suzman, agreed with her; which only strengthened Mrs Thatcher's suspicion that the

ANC demanded sanctions precisely because its aim was to destroy South Africa's capitalist economy.

Convinced of the rightness of her analysis, Mrs Thatcher set herself to block the imposition of further Commonwealth and EC sanctions beyond those already in place, like the ban on sporting contacts with South Africa, while working behind the scenes to try to influence the Pretoria Government from within. Casting herself as President Botha's candid friend – 'probably', as she claimed in her memoirs, 'the only helpful contact he had with western governments'[102] – she invited him to Chequers in June 1984, provoking inevitable demonstrations, and treated him (in Bernard Ingham's words) to some 'very plain speaking'.[103] She urged him to release Mandela, to stop harassing black dissidents, stop bombing ANC camps in neighbouring states and grant Namibian independence. She kept up the pressure in a sustained correspondence over the next five years. But all this was in private: she refused publicly to join the clamour for the release of Mandela, so she earned no credit with the anti-apartheid movement. Botha was grateful for her friendship but ignored the candour. There was no significant movement in South Africa so long as he remained in power.

Mrs Thatcher's attitude to South Africa was much more principled and honourable than her critics recognised. At the same time she was less constructive than she could have been because she badly misjudged the internal opposition to apartheid. First, by insisting on classing the ANC as Communist terrorists, she completely failed to appreciate that Mandela, Tambo and the rest of the ANC leadership were as deeply rooted in Western democratic values, liberal humanism, the Bible and Shakespeare as she herself was. Mandela was brought up as a Methodist on the very same hymns and prayers and poems as she was – though after his enforced leisure on Robben Island he had a much deeper knowledge of English literature and history than she had. If only she had known that one of his best-loved and most frequently quoted poems was W. H. Henley's Victorian doggerel *Invictus*, which had been a favourite of her father back in Grantham:

> It matters not how strait the gate
> How charged with punishment the scroll,
> I am the master of my fate,
> I am the captain of my soul.[104]

Sadly Mrs Thatcher's rigid Cold War mindset prevented her realising how much she and the prisoner of Robben Island had in common.

Then she compounded her reluctance to recognise the ANC by seeking a more 'moderate' and pro-Western alternative which she could promote instead. Influenced by her mystical guru Laurens van der Post, and by other mavericks like James Goldsmith and the zoo owner John Aspinall, who persuaded her that the Zulus were 'a proud separate nation' with no wish to be dominated by the mainly Xhosa ANC, she pinned extravagant hopes on the Inkatha party led by the Zulu chief Mangosuthu Buthelezi. The more the world's attention focused on Mandela – the more the British left lionised him and Labour councils renamed streets for him – the more stubbornly she championed Buthelezi as 'the representative of the largest group of black South Africans'[105] and 'the head of the biggest nation in southern Africa'.[106] She praised him as a friend of free enterprise, a courageous opponent of sanctions and 'a stalwart opponent of violent uprising' – unaware that all the time Pretoria was secretly arming Inkatha to fight the ANC.[107] In taking sides in this way, in a struggle she did not really understand, Mrs Thatcher was playing with fire. As the Jamaican Prime Minister Edward Seaga warned in 1987: 'If she goes on calling them communists it will be self-fulfilling.'[108]

It was in 1985 that Mrs Thatcher first set herself in direct opposition to the conscience of the world. That summer, as violent uprisings in townships all over South Africa brought the country close to civil war, President Botha declared a state of emergency. Alarmed, American and Swiss banks called in their debts and refused to make further loans, causing a devastating run on the rand. Under pressure from American public opinion, Reagan felt reluctantly obliged to tighten US sanctions before Congress passed a tougher package; and France and other European countries began to press for concerted EC action. Mrs Thatcher's response was to hold one of her policy seminars at Chequers in September. But her mind was already fixed: among the selected academic and diplomatic experts she invited no one sympathetic to the ANC. When Oliver Tambo visited London the next month she forbade any member of the Government to meet him, reportedly declaring that anyone who thought the ANC could form a government was living in 'cloud cuckoo land'.[109] In September she successfully vetoed the proposed EC sanctions; so when the Commonwealth heads of government assembled at Nassau in the Bahamas in October it was already clear that Mrs Thatcher was going to be isolated.

The demand for sanctions was led by Hawke, Mulroney and Rajiv Gandhi (who had succeeded his mother the previous year). Mrs Thatcher resisted strongly, though less successfully than her own characteristically self-congratulatory account suggests.When they lectured her for 'preferring British jobs to black lives', she writes, she turned on them and 'to their palpable alarm . . . began to tell my African critics some home truths':

> I reminded them of their own less than impressive record on human rights. And when the representative from Uganda took me to task for racial discrimination . . . I reminded him of the Asians which [*sic*] Uganda had thrown out on racial grounds, many of whom had come to settle in my constituency in North London, where they were model citizens and doing very well.

She bitterly describes the hostility she felt directed at her. 'It was extraordinary how the pack instinct of politicians could change a group of normally courteous, in some cases even charming, people into a gang of bullies. I had never been treated like this and I was not going to stand for it.'[110] But she makes no allowance for the antagonism she aroused in them by her stubborn insistence that she knew best. The unfortunate Geoffrey Howe, sitting beside her, felt it all too deeply. She eventually accepted a limited extension of sanctions immediately – a ban on the import of krugerrands and no funding of trade missions to South Africa – but with the threat of further measures if 'adequate progress' was not made towards reform. By this suspended threat, the *Annual Register* commented, 'Britain had become, albeit reluctantly, part of a Commonwealth process on South Africa. To that extent Mrs Thatcher had been moved further than she had wished to go.'[111] Doubtless for this reason she came out, as Howe described, determined to deny that she had given any ground at all:

> Before the world's television cameras, Margaret set out to present not the successful achievement of a concerted Commonwealth policy . . . but only the triumphant insignificance of the concessions *she* had had to make to achieve it. With forefinger and thumb only a few millimetres apart . . . Margaret proclaimed that she had moved only 'a tiny little bit'.With four little words she . . . humiliated three dozen other heads of government, devalued the policy on which they had just agreed – and demeaned herself . . . Even I could scarcely believe my ears.[112]

The only way she had managed to delay further sanctions was by proposing to send a group of 'eminent persons' (EPG) to South Africa to assess the situation on the ground. Though they were to be away for weeks at a time, she proposed that Howe should be one of them, assuring him – in a manner that even she admits was 'less than tactful' – that she could take care of the Foreign Office perfectly well in his absence.[113] When he objected she nominated Ted Heath's former Chancellor, Tony Barber, as the British representative under the joint chairmanship of Malcolm Fraser, the former Prime Minister of Australia, and a former leader of Nigeria, General Olusegun Obasanjo. President Botha let the EPG into the country in the spring of 1986, and allowed them to meet ANC leaders, including Mandela – whose first question was to ask Fraser if Don Bradman (the great Australian cricketer) was still alive. They were impressed by Mandela and were close to negotiating a formula for his release when Botha wrecked their efforts by bombing ANC bases in Zambia, Zimbabwe and Botswana. They immediately abandoned their mission and soon afterwards submitted a gloomy report concluding that there was 'no genuine intention on the part of the South African government to dismantle apartheid' and advocating strengthened sanctions – including the banning of international flights – as the only way of bringing Pretoria to negotiate with the ANC. Mrs Thatcher was said to be 'disgusted' that Barber signed the report – though he did what he could to minimise the reference to sanctions – and in her memoirs briskly dismissed the 'eminent persons' initiative as an 'unmitigated disaster'.[114]

By now she had lost patience with Botha. Privately she warned him that by falling back on a policy of 'total crackdown' he was making it hard for her to hold the line against sanctions. Behind the scenes she was urging him to do all the things the opponents of apartheid around the world wanted him to do: release Mandela, un-ban the ANC and start negotiating before it was too late. Having committed herself so vehemently against sanctions, she needed him to repay her by showing some willingness to embrace reform voluntarily; and this he was refusing to do. She made another effort to buy time by sending Howe – this time representing the EC – to try again where the EPG had failed: but not for the last time she undermined him by reported comments – vigorously circulated by Bernard Ingham – that she had no intention of changing her mind on sanctions. As he trekked around southern Africa, Howe was accordingly rebuffed and insulted by Kaunda and Mugabe – Kaunda accused Mrs Thatcher of 'kissing apartheid' and said he was only receiving Howe out of 'love and respect' for the Queen – and snubbed by Botha. On his return he wrote a long dignified letter to Mrs Thatcher which came very close to a threat of resignation: but he got no reply.[115] 'By now,' she writes in her memoirs, 'I was firmly in charge of our approach to South Africa, making the main decisions directly from No. 10.'[116] But the fiasco of Howe's mission demonstrated very clearly that her approach was not working.

Publicly Mrs Thatcher revelled in her isolation. Charged by a television interviewer that she risked breaking up the Commonwealth by continuing to hold out against sanctions, she retorted: 'But if I were the odd one out and I were right, that wouldn't matter, would it?'[117] To Woodrow Wyatt she insisted that she had no intention of weakening. In the same breath, however, she was forced to concede that 'we may have to make a few gestures'.[118] She had one important ally in the White House. 'As you,' President Reagan wrote to her, 'I remain opposed to punitive sanctions which will only polarise the situation there and do the most harm to blacks.' But Reagan too found himself under pressure to give ground:

> You noted you may be forced to accept some modest steps within the European and Commonwealth contexts to signal your opposition to apartheid, and in all frankness we may be faced with the same situation if Congress, as expected, passes some sanctions Bill later this summer or fall.[119]

The Senate duly voted 84–16 to approve a comprehensive package of economic sanctions. The EC too went ahead with a further package, agreed in June but held back for three months to see if Howe's mission achieved anything. Mrs Thatcher now had no choice but to acquiesce. Yet at a special Commonwealth Conference held in London in August she was still defiant. 'My refusal to go along with the sanctions they wanted was attacked by Messrs Kaunda, Mugabe, Mulroney and Hawke,' she recalled. 'I found no support.' 'Her iciness . . . towards Mulroney and Fraser in particular,' Hawke wrote, 'descended into rude hostility.'[120] She scolded their 'irrational' posturing at the expense of black South Africans, claiming – despite the conclusion of the eminent persons' report – that in all sorts of minor ways apartheid, 'if not dead, was at least rapidly dying'.[121] For the first time in the history of the Commonwealth, the London conference overrode British dissent and agreed to implement the package of measures proposed at Nassau. 'The only redeeming aspect of the British participation,' Hawke wrote, 'was the surreptitious exchange of notes and a cartoon lampooning his Prime Minister between me and . . . Geoffrey Howe. Geoffrey . . . was in a hopeless position: he was appalled by Margaret's views and behaviour, but had to maintain the appearance of support.'[122]

The next row was at Vancouver in October 1987, where Mrs Thatcher – through Bernard Ingham – released figures purporting to show that behind Mulroney's loud enthusiasm for sanctions, Canada's trade with South Africa had actually increased in 1986. The Canadians protested that the figures were out of date, but Mrs Thatcher was delighted by their indignant reaction to this 'intrusion of fact upon rhetoric'; while Ingham's gleeful account of the episode – 'Vancouver 1987 was hilarious' – shows how confrontational these conferences had become.[123] This offence was nothing, however, compared to Mrs Thatcher's reply to a question at her final press conference, when she described the ANC as 'a typical terrorist organisation'.[124]

Admittedly she was provoked by a threat that British firms in South Africa might be targeted unless she accepted sanctions. But this was no slip of the tongue, since she deliberately went back to pick up a question she had been asked earlier. Subsequently she backtracked, differentiating between terrorism, which she unreservedly condemned, and the ANC in its political role, which she acknowledged 'does represent some of the black South Africans – not by any means all of them' and would therefore have to be part of any settlement.[125] Realising that all she had done by equating the ANC with the IRA was to dignify the IRA, she drew a distinction between the two bodies, admitting that the British Government had recently opened diplomatic contacts with the ANC. Just the previous month Howe had actually entertained Tambo – non-committally – at Chevening. In this respect, she eventually conceded, the ANC was 'on all fours with something like the PLO'.[126] But words have wings, and clarifications never catch up with the original gaffe. Her dismissive phrase betrayed her fundamental hostility to the ANC; and made her efforts to be seen as a peace-broker in South Africa less plausible than ever.

Yet just a few months earlier she had taken her most positive step in this direction with the appointment of a new ambassador to South Africa. Robin Renwick had caught her eye in 1979–80 as head of the Rhodesia desk in the Foreign Office; he had taken a leading part in devising the Zimbabwe settlement, and subsequently wrote a book demonstrating – in the light of the Rhodesian experience – that economic sanctions never worked. Here was a diplomat after her own heart. In July 1987 she sent him back to southern Africa to pursue what he called 'unconventional diplomacy' in Pretoria. Publicly he was still required to echo her exaggerated faith in Buthelezi. But at the same time he was implicitly authorised to build bridges to the ANC. Over the next three years, he wrote later, he received 'no instructions but full backing from her' for the important part he played in helping to negotiate the release of Mandela and eventually the peaceful transition to majority rule.[127]

The critical opening came in 1989 when President Botha suffered a stroke and was forced – unwillingly – to step down. His successor, F. W. de Klerk, was not at first sight a great improvement. When he came to Chequers in the summer of 1989 Mrs Thatcher, according to Charles Powell, 'thought he was just another bloody Boer'.[128] But Renwick had already identified him as a genuine reformer who had learned the lesson of Rhodesia and wanted to talk to the responsible black leaders before it was too late; Mrs Thatcher seized on him as a South African Gorbachev and was hopeful that there would now be some movement in Pretoria. 'They know they've got to,' she told Woodrow Wyatt.[129]

That spring she made a constructive venture into southern African affairs by helping to save the American-brokered UN settlement which secured South African withdrawal from Namibia in exchange for Cuban withdrawal from Angola. This was the second of two visits to black Africa designed to counteract the hostility aroused by her opposition to sanctions. In January 1988 she visited Kenya and Nigeria, two of the most pro-British and pro-western of the African states. The next year she made a bolder trip to Zimbabwe and Malawi, with an unannounced foray into Namibia. In Harare she took credit for the Lancaster House settlement and the £200 million in aid that Britain had poured into Zimbabwe since independence: she did not expect to shift Mugabe on sanctions, but she did inspect with him the camps on the Mozambique border where British troops were helping to train the Mozambique army to fight anti-Government rebels. By good luck – or Renwick's astute management – she was able to go on to Namibia the very day the UN plan was due to come into operation; instead, with South Africa threatening retaliation against renewed SWAPO incursions from Angola, it was on the brink of falling apart. Mrs Thatcher met the South African Foreign Minister Pik Botha at Windhoek airport and told him forcibly that if South Africa acted unilaterally 'the whole world will be against you – led by me'. She urged him to act only with UN authority, and herself persuaded the UN special representative to authorise South African action against SWAPO. Mrs Thatcher did not often have much use for the UN – certainly not where British interests were involved – but on this occasion her timely backing saved the settlement. The following year Namibia gained its independence and SWAPO won the first elections. No one else, in Renwick's view, could have achieved this outcome. 'Margaret Thatcher boarded her plane extremely reluctantly. She clearly was attracted by the prospect of continuing to conduct the affairs of Namibia.'[130]

She really wanted to visit South Africa, meet Mandela and broker herself the sort of deal her emissaries had failed to pull off; but Tambo, suspicious of her support for Inkatha, vetoed the idea. 'We don't see how she can be an honest broker when she is so closely allied to the regime,' an ANC spokesman explained.[131] She still refused to recognise the ANC until it categorically renounced violence. She had long accepted the principle of one-person, one-vote, but she was still interested in exploring alternatives – a federal constitution, Swiss-style cantons or a system of tribal devolution – designed to prevent the ANC gaining absolute power in a unitary South Africa, and she tacitly encouraged those who were egging Buthelezi to secede. Yet between them Renwick and the Foreign Office gradually weaned her off these fantasies. In October 1989 Renwick arranged for her to give an interview to the township newspaper *The Sowetan*, in which she dismissed the idea of dividing South Africa as impractical. 'Partition would be like trying to unscramble an omelette and I simply cannot see how it would work.'[132] As so often when head and heart pulled her in different ways, the head prevailed.

But then at the Commonwealth Conference in Kuala Lumpur the same month she sparked another row on the eternal sanctions issue. This was just a few weeks after she had sacked Geoffrey Howe from the Foreign Office and promoted the inexperienced John Major in his place. Major found his first exposure to the atmosphere at Commonwealth meetings 'fairly bloody. There was dispute on nearly every sentence and much of the discussion was emotional.'[133] But after sixteen hours he and his fellow Foreign Ministers managed to achieve an agreed text which minimised the differences. This was presented to the press as a successful outcome and Mrs Thatcher herself proposed its adoption by the heads of government – only to repudiate it the next day by publishing a statement (drafted by Charles Powell) spelling out her objections. In their memoirs, both she and Major deny that she humiliated him: he affirms that he was consulted about Powell's clarification and made no objection, though that was not at all the impression the press had at the time. But the other leaders – Hawke, Mulroney, even Lee Kuan Yew – objected furiously to her 'duplicity' in unilaterally repudiating a statement in which they thought they had already bent over backwards to accommodate her.[134]

On this occasion Mrs Thatcher had a case for arguing that things were at last moving in South Africa. Since de Klerk's accession, Walter Sisulu and seven other long-term prisoners had been released and the new Government was clearly committed to dialogue: in elections in September 70 per cent of the white electorate had voted for change. 'In this new situation,' the Powell text stated, 'Britain believes that the

Commonwealth should concentrate now on encouraging change rather than on further punishment.'[135] The fact that de Klerk made his historic speech foreshadowing the end of apartheid less than four months later suggests that Mrs Thatcher was right. But she had been making similar claims, over-optimistically, for the past four years: there was an equally good case for keeping up the pressure until the cause was finally won. Even if she was right, her fellow leaders were entitled to be angered by the high-handed way she breached the spirit of the Commonwealth by simply publishing her own unilateral statement telling the world they were all wrong. More and more clearly by this stage in her premiership Mrs Thatcher openly advertised her contempt for other views.

When de Klerk announced in February 1990 the immediate release of all remaining political prisoners, including Mandela, and the unbanning of all political organisations, including not only the ANC but the South African Communist Party, she regarded it as the vindication of her lonely struggle. 'People are very silly saying sanctions did it. It wasn't sanctions at all,' she told Woodrow Wyatt. 'It was due to you,' he faithfully assured her, 'putting the pressure on them but from a friendly angle.'[136] To the Commons the day after Mandela's release she insisted:'I do not think sanctions have achieved anything.'[137] She immediately lifted those measures which Britain could rescind unilaterally, as she had promised de Klerk she would, and pressed European and Commonwealth leaders to follow suit. She was correspondingly disappointed that Mandela's first speech before the massed cameras of the world's press rehashed all 'the old ritual phrases' about socialism and nationalisation. She had hoped that he would now distance himself from the party which had sustained him for the last twenty-seven years: she should have realised that this was the last thing he was likely to do.[138] When he came to London in April to attend a rock concert in his honour he declined an invitation to Downing Street, telling Renwick that 'he appreciated the role she had played in pressing for his release and wanted to meet her – but at a time when the rest of the movement had been reconciled to the idea'.[139]

A few weeks later Mandela stopped off again in England en route to the USA. This time – 'as a courtesy' – he telephoned Mrs Thatcher. He urged her to maintain sanctions until the transition to majority rule was complete. She was unmoved, but scolded him about his punishing schedule of international tours, warning that it would kill a man half his age. 'If you go on like this, you won't get out of America alive.'[140] He realised, he told his biographer Anthony Sampson, that she was 'a very powerful lady . . . one I would rather have as an ally than an enemy'.[141]

They finally met in July when he visited London again to address MPs in Westminster Hall and called on the Prime Minister in Number 10. Robin Renwick rehearsed both of them for the occasion, telling Mrs Thatcher that Mandela had been waiting twenty-seven years to tell his story, so she must allow him to tell it without interruption. She let him talk for nearly an hour. Tactfully he recognised that she had opposed apartheid in her own way, and thanked her for her efforts to get him released. He also thanked her for her role in Zimbabwe and in improving East–West relations, but urged her again to maintain the pressure on de Klerk for a negotiated settlement. Then she spoke for thirty minutes, urging him to give up the armed struggle, talk to Buthelezi and abandon the ANC's commitment to nationalisation. They continued over lunch with 'an intense discussion of economic policy' and what form of constitution the new South Africa should have.[142] 'I could not make the slightest bit of headway with her on the question of sanctions,' Mandela wrote. As before, 'she chided me like a schoolmarm for not taking her advice and cutting down on my schedule.'[143] She still knew best what was good both for South Africa and for him. But when a reporter in Downing Street asked Mandela, as he came out, how he could talk to someone who had denounced him as a terrorist, he replied that he was working with South Africans who had done much worse things than that. For her part, Mrs Thatcher found Mandela dignified and impressively unbitter, but still 'stuck in a kind of socialist time warp'; she still feared he might turn out a 'half-baked Marxist' like Mugabe.[144]

After her fall from power she continued to be supportive of de Klerk, critical of the ANC and sympathetic to Chief Buthelezi. In May 1991 she finally got to visit South Africa for herself. From President de Klerk she received the country's highest award, the Order of Good Hope, for her contribution to ending apartheid; she also went to KwaZulu and pointedly praised Buthelezi for his part in the struggle and 'the way you have refused to adopt that left-wing rhetoric which wins cheers and loses investment'.[145] She did not see Mandela. Eventually, however, she was obliged to recognise that the ANC was the only force capable of uniting the country, while Buthelezi's demand for Zulu autonomy only threatened to plunge it into civil war. In 1994 she joined other former allies in urging him privately to swallow his pride and take part in the first elections in the new South Africa, which at the last moment he agreed to do.

South Africa showed Mrs Thatcher at her best and worst. She was principled and courageous, but at the same time stubborn and self-righteous. She had a good case against sanctions but failed to win

support for her view, preferring to lecture and thereby alienate potential allies rather than try to persuade them. Rather she seemed to glory
in her isolation, as if the fact of being isolated made her right. At
successive Commonwealth Conferences, her policy adviser Percy
Cradock wrote, she was invariably assigned the villain's role – 'a part
she played, or overplayed, with relish'.[146] Of all the European and
Commonwealth leaders, Chancellor Kohl was most sympathetic to her
argument – Germany too had substantial commercial interests in South
Africa – but he was deterred by Mrs Thatcher's divisiveness from
wishing to be seen to be in her corner. She thought him cowardly,
letting her take all the flak, but he took a different view of international diplomacy. Her only powerful ally outside South Africa was
President Reagan: but while he personally shared her Cold War perspective, South Africa was not an issue on which he wished to upset black
America or pick a fight with Congress, so she got less help there than
she might have hoped.

Was she right? The outcome might suggest so. But most of those
who supported sanctions still believe that they were an essential part
of the pressure that eventually compelled white South Africa to change.
David Owen, for instance – on many issues an admirer of Mrs Thatcher's
style – believes that American financial sanctions in particular changed
the mind of the South African business community.[147] While Mrs
Thatcher was still denouncing the ANC as Communists and terrorists, more far-sighted business leaders like Harry Oppenheimer, David
Rockefeller and David Astor, and major companies like Shell – who
shared her desire to end apartheid while preserving the economy –
were already building bridges to them to prepare for a peaceful transition. Undoubtedly she played a part in persuading de Klerk to move
as far and as quickly as he did. The night before his historic speech in
February 1990 he passed a message via Renwick to tell Mrs Thatcher
that she would not be disappointed. But her role should not be exaggerated: there were bigger forces at play. As with Gorbachev in Russia,
she was lucky that a leader came along at the right moment whom
she could appear to influence; she had not previously had much effect
on Botha. De Klerk – again like Gorbachev – barely mentions Mrs
Thatcher in his memoirs.

The Middle East

By the 1980s Britain had no remaining direct responsibility in the
Middle East. But it was still a part of the world in which Mrs Thatcher
took a close interest, first because it was a major troublespot in which
the Americans had become deeply involved, at least since Jimmy Carter's

successful brokering of a peace treaty between Israel and Egypt in 1978; second because Britain had a history of involvement in the region going back to the Balfour Declaration, the Palestine mandate and the creation of the state of Israel, and still maintained close links, notably with King Hussein of Jordan and the rulers of several of the Gulf states; and third because the substantial Jewish community in her Finchley constituency, and her strong admiration for Jewish culture and values, had long predisposed her to support Israel.

She regarded Israel – like South Africa – as essentially part of the West: the only democracy in the region, with a prosperous and enterprising economy (though she was not so keen on the socialistic *kibbutzim*), ringed by hostile neighbours and threatened by Palestinian terrorism. Her instinct was to class the PLO – the perpetrators of a string of bombings and hijackings of American and European targets since the early 1970s – with the IRA and the ANC as terrorist organisations which should be treated as international pariahs until they abjured the use of violence. At the same time, however, she knew that the state of Israel had itself been founded in terrorism. She could not forget that the current Israeli Prime Minister, Menachem Begin, had been the leader of the Irgun gang which bombed the King David Hotel in Jerusalem, killing ninety-one British soldiers, in 1946, and swore never to shake his hand (though eventually she did). She also recognised that Israel had seized Palestinian territory by force in 1967 and had occupied it ever since in defiance of the UN. She was sympathetic to the fate of the displaced Palestinians – she had visited a Palestinian refugee camp in Syria when she was Leader of the Opposition in 1976 – and believed, as a friend of Israel, that the Israelis would only secure peace when they were prepared to give up some of the occupied territory to get it. Her hope, as in South Africa, was to encourage 'moderate' Palestinians to come forward with whom the Israelis could negotiate. Much as she disliked the PLO, however, she recognised the need to talk to it a good deal earlier than she did with the ANC. In July 1982 she authorised Douglas Hurd – then Minister of State at the Foreign Office – to meet the head of the PLO's political bureau, Farouk Kaddoumi: 'a shift in policy', Hurd noted in his diary, 'only dragged out of a reluctant Prime Minister'. Nine months later she went a step further and met Kaddoumi herself as part of a delegation led by King Hussein.[148]*

---

*She never knowingly met the PLO leader, Yasser Arafat; but according to David Steel she shook hands with him, without recognising him, at President Tito's funeral in 1980.[149]

Whenever she visited the region, or received Middle Eastern leaders in London, she made a point of reporting to President Reagan her conversations and impressions. She was very keen to be consulted in the making of American policy, and anxious to press the Americans to maintain the momentum of Carter's peace process. After visiting the Gulf on her way to the Commonwealth Conference in Melbourne in September 1981, for instance, she sent Reagan what his staff described as 'a rather somber assessment of views she picked up during her recent talks with a variety of senior Arab political figures'. Richard Allen told the President he should read the whole letter, but summarised its main points for him:

- A mood of disappointment and alienation now dominates moderate Arab thinking about the US. (Arabs hesitate to express the true strength of their feeling directly to us.)

- The view prevails that we are one-sidedly committed to Israel and ignore the Palestinians.[150]

This message, an aide noted, 'calls for a response'. But two more letters followed before the White House got round to drafting a reply in which the President thanked Mrs Thatcher for 'the candid insights that you have shared with me':

I understand the perceptions of the Arab leaders on the peace process alluded to in your letter. A comprehensive Middle East peace remains our objective, and I agree fully that one cannot be achieved unless it addresses the Palestinian problem.[151]

The next month Reagan was thanking her again for 'the information you passed on concerning your talks with King Hussein in London, which I made good use of during his visit here'. The American view, he assured her, was that Israeli withdrawal was 'the fundamental basis of a settlement on the West Bank and Gaza'.[152] This was the basis of proposals which he set out in September 1982. But Mrs Thatcher never felt the Americans put enough pressure on Israel, or gave strong enough support to King Hussein, whom she saw as the key mediator in the region. ('We absolutely have to support King Hussein'.)[153] In March 1983 she was again giving Washington 'her read-out on meetings with King Hussein in London . . . She makes a powerful case that the President weigh in with the Arabs to demonstrate again that we are committed to the September 1 proposals.' Reagan in return pressed her to stiffen Hussein.[154] She was very critical of Israel's bloody invasion of southern Lebanon in June 1982, but equally sceptical of the value of the multinational – predominantly American – UN peacekeeping force sent to Beirut, and restricted British participation to a token contribution of just 100 troops. The killing of 300 American and French troops by a suicide bomber in October 1983 only confirmed her view that they were a sitting target: she urged Reagan not to retaliate but rather to withdraw the multinational force.[155] The next year, reluctantly, he did so. In her memoirs she describes the American intervention in Lebanon as a lesson in the folly of military action without a clearly attainable objective.[156]

By February 1984, following the massacre of refugees in the Sabra and Shatila camps in southern Lebanon – encouraged if not actually committed by Ariel Sharon's occupying Israeli army – Mrs Thatcher's patience with Israel was wearing thin. 'Whenever there was a problem,' she told Caspar Weinberger, 'it seemed that Israel annexed what it wanted. She urged that there should be a reappraisal of Israeli policy.'[157] An opportunity arose later that year when Yitzhak Shamir's hard-line Likud Government was replaced by a Labour–Likud coalition to be headed by Shimon Peres and Shamir in turn. At Camp David before Christmas she told the Americans that 'she personally knew the new Israeli Prime Minister very well and favourably. Prime Minister Peres wanted to be constructive, and if we are to get anywhere in the Middle East we should attempt to do it while he is Prime Minister.' When George Shultz replied that though the outlook was certainly more hopeful, Peres still faced domestic problems with both the economy and Lebanon, Mrs Thatcher asked impatiently 'if we were waiting for progress on the economy and Lebanon before mounting a new initiative'.[158] She still sensed little urgency in Washington.

In September 1985 she visited Egypt and Jordan – 'the two key moderate Arab states' – to encourage President Mubarak and King Hussein to keep up the momentum for peace; and the following spring she paid her first visit as Prime Minister to Israel. 'I felt that President Mubarak and I understood one another,' she wrote in her memoirs. 'He was a large personality, persuasive and direct – the sort of man who could be one of the key players in a settlement.' She confessed to 'some sympathy' with his view that 'the Americans were not being sufficiently positive'. She thought King Hussein had been taking 'a real risk' in trying to promote a peace initiative, but was being let down by the Americans. 'I thought he deserved more support. I wanted to do what I could to help.'[159] Before leaving Jordan she and Denis made a point of visiting another refugee camp. In Israel she was again

impressed by Peres, but dismayed by Shamir – another former terrorist
– who rejected any question of giving up Jewish settlements on the
West Bank in exchange for peace.

In 1986 Shamir took over as Prime Minister. Visiting Washington
the following summer Mrs Thatcher again vented her frustration with
Israeli intransigence and, in a wide-ranging discussion with Secretary
Shultz, chided the Americans for acquiescing in it:

> She regretted that there had been no major Western initiative since
> the Camp David accords; noted that President Reagan's 1982 speech
> had been superb but had been rejected by Begin; characterised Peres
> and Hussein as two positive figures who are doing everything possible
> to advance the peace process and deserve our support; and . . . asked
> rhetorically whether it was not timely to move forward by promoting
> an international conference.

Shultz replied that it was no good promoting a new initiative without
Likud support: the American approach was 'to seek to find a way of
getting Shamir and Likud on board':

> Mrs Thatcher asked the Secretary whether he thought that Shamir
> ever intends to negotiate over the West Bank or Jerusalem or whether
> in fact it is Shamir's view that all of biblical Israel belongs to modern
> Israel. If the latter, Shamir is simply holding the entire world ransom
> and there will never be negotiations.
> The Secretary agreed that Shamir is not prepared to negotiate
> territory but is ready to negotiate about interim arrangements.
> Mrs Thatcher characterised this position by Shamir as hypocrit-
> ical because it denies basic rights to the Arabs and removes Israel's
> credibility as the only Middle East democracy.[160]

Mrs Thatcher got nowhere on the Middle East, but she deserves
credit for trying. Despite her admiration for Israel and substantial
dependence on her own Jewish voters in Finchley, she saw that there
would be no serious pressure on Israel to negotiate so long as successive US administrations were terrified of offending the powerful
American Jewish lobby. She told the Americans so, with her usual
frankness, but this was one area in which they did not listen to her.
Far from withdrawing from the occupied territories, the Israelis carried
on planting more Jewish settlements in the West Bank and Gaza.
President Clinton made more effort than any of his predecessors to
broker a real compromise. But more than a decade after Mrs Thatcher's

I. The new Prime Minister celebrates her election victory at Conservative Central Office in the early hours of 4 May 1979. (Mark Thatcher is on her right.)

2. 'Every Prime Minister should have a Willie'. Mrs Thatcher confers with her deputy William Whitelaw at the 1982 Conservative party conference. 3. Acknowledging the applause for her speech at the 1979 party conference, flanked by Defence Secretary Francis Pym (*left*) and Foreign Secretary Lord Carrington. (Lord Gowrie is at the back.)

4,5. Mrs Thatcher with her two long-serving Chancellors of the Exchequer, Geoffrey Howe (*above*) and Nigel Lawson (*below*).

6. The Prime Minister, with Ian Gow, leaves 10 Downing Street to face the House of Commons following the Argentine invasion of the Falklands, 3 April 1982.

7. Scenes of Edwardian enthusiasm welcome HMS *Invincible* on her return to Portsmouth following the recapture of the Falklands, July 1982.

8. Mrs Thatcher meets some of 'our boys' on her visit to the Falklands in January 1983. In the background, 'miles and miles of bugger all'.

9. Michael Foot leaves his Hampstead home, December 1981.

10. Labour's 'dream team'. Neil Kinnock (*right*) with deputy leader Roy Hattersley at the Labour party conference, October 1983.

11. GLC leader Ken Livingstone (*left*) shares a controversial press conference with Sinn Fein president Gerry Adams at County Hall, July 1983. 12. NUM president Arthur Scargill speaks at a miners' rally in London, 1984.

13. Mrs Thatcher launches the 1983 Conservative manifesto, flanked by Willie Whitelaw and Cecil Parkinson (*seated*) and Norman Tebbit, Geoffrey Howe, Francis Pym, Michael Heseltine and Tom King (*standing*).

14. Michael Heseltine walks out of 10 Downing Street after resigning from the Cabinet, January 1986.

15. Mrs Thatcher launches the 1987 Conservative manifesto, flanked this time by (*from left*) Lord Young, Nigel Lawson, Willie Whitelaw, Norman Tebbit and Geoffrey Howe.
16. Hitting the campaign trail with Denis and her battlebus, June 1987.

fall, hope of an Arab–Israeli settlement remains further away than ever. In her memoirs – published in 1993 – she eloquently restated her admiration for the Jewish people and the state of Israel ('one of the heroic sagas of our age') but reflected on the paradox of modern Jews denying others the rights they were so long and tragically denied themselves:

> I only wished that Israeli emphasis on the human rights of the Russian *refuseniks* was matched by proper appreciation of the plight of landless and stateless Palestinians.[161]

Aid and arms

Mrs Thatcher viewed the whole world through Cold War spectacles as a battleground for conflict with the Soviet Union, a struggle for geopolitical advantage to be waged by all means – political, cultural, economic and military. Whatever might be the particular local circumstances of different countries, she saw Britain's role in every corner of the globe as helping the Americans to combat those they classed as Communists and support those regimes – however undemocratic and repressive – approved by Washington as friends of the West. As well as taking a high-profile role as a global evangelist for the wealth-creating benefits of free enterprise, she had two practical means of exerting influence in the developing world: the provision of aid and the sale of military equipment. She was sceptical of the former, and Britain's aid budget declined sharply during her years in power. But she was a great enthusiast for the latter, and Britain's share of the world arms trade grew spectacularly.

Her attitude to aid mirrored on a global scale her suspicion of the welfare state at home. Soon after she took office the 'North–South Commission' – set up under the auspices of the World Bank, chaired by former West German socialist Chancellor, Willy Brandt, and including among its most active members Ted Heath and the Secretary-General of the Commonwealth, Sonny Ramphal – presented its report calling for a concerted international effort to raise the living standards of the world's poor. With Heath's energetic advocacy the report sold 68,000 copies in Britain; 10,000 people attended a mass lobby of Parliament; the opposition parties and the churches demanded a positive response. Mrs Thatcher, however, was unmoved. Reflecting the monetarist critique of Milton Friedman and Melvyn Krauss in America and, nearer home, of Peter Bauer – professor of economics at the London School of Economics, to whom she gave a peerage in 1983 – she believed that hand-outs from rich countries to poor countries merely propped up corrupt regimes and perpetuated dependency, instead of promoting free trade and enterprise, which would enable the under-developed to develop prosperous economies of their own. 'The whole concept of "North–South" dialogue, which the Brandt Commission had made the fashionable talk of the international community,' she wrote in her memoirs, 'was in my view wrong-headed.'

> Not only was it false to suggest that there was a homogeneous rich North which confronted a homogeneous poor South: underlying the rhetoric was the idea that distribution of world resources rather than the creation of wealth was the way to tackle poverty and hunger ... What the developing countries needed more than aid was trade: so our first responsibility was . . . to give them the freest possible access to our markets. Of course 'North–South' dialogue also appealed to those socialists who wanted to play down the fundamental contrast between the free capitalist West and the unfree communist East.[162]

Mrs Thatcher had only to sniff a progressive consensus to be against it. There in three words – 'fashionable', 'rhetoric', 'socialists' – her hostility to the aid lobby is encapsulated. Assailed in the House of Commons for her negative response to Brandt, she asserted that the Government's aid budget for 1981–2 was higher in real terms than for most of the 1970s.[163] But the figures over the whole decade tell a different story. Overseas aid suffered heavily in Howe's first round of spending cuts in 1979–80; it did recover briefly in 1981 but then remained static at around £1.1 billion for the rest of the decade, representing a fall in real terms of about 7 per cent. On coming into office Mrs Thatcher's Government inherited a target accepted by all the major industrialised countries except the United States and Switzerland that they should all try to raise their aid budgets to 0.7 per cent of GNP. But instead of rising towards this target, Britain's performance declined from 0.52 per cent in 1979 to 0.31 per cent in 1989. (By comparison France just met the target, the Scandinavian countries comfortably exceeded it, while Germany, Japan and Italy lagged around the British level; the US managed a meagre 0.2 per cent.)[164] When talking up Britain's contribution to overseas development Mrs Thatcher preferred to include private investment, which boosted the figure to 2.5 per cent of GNP. But this cannot properly be considered aid. Moreover she made no apology for the fact that most of the aid Britain did give came with strings attached:

I think about 80 per cent of our aid . . . is tied to purchasing goods from Britain, and that's right. We give aid overseas, it helps them, and we give it in a way that gives us jobs. It's very, very beneficial to us all.[165]

What she resolutely opposed was the sort of co-ordinated international action proposed by the Brandt commission. In October 1981 a global summit in Cancun, Mexico, co-chaired by the Mexican President and Pierre Trudeau, raised exactly the sort of hopes she was determined to dash. She only attended – and persuaded Reagan to attend – because she thought it important that they should be there to argue the free-market case; specifically she was anxious to block proposals to place the International Monetary Fund and the World Bank under direct UN control. She and Reagan deliberately set out to ensure that the conference imposed no new commitments, insisting that it had no power to do so, since several important countries were not present.[166] At her final press conference she claimed – contrary to most impressions – that the summit had been 'very successful'.[167] But her definition of success, she revealed in her memoirs, was that such a gathering was never repeated. 'The intractable problems of Third World poverty, hunger and debt would not be solved by misdirected international intervention, but rather by liberating enterprise, promoting trade – and defeating socialism in all its forms.'[168]*

A particularly effective way of killing two birds with one stone was by linking aid to the sale of arms. By this means she could boost an important British industry – protecting jobs at home – while simultaneously supporting regional allies and helping to counter Soviet influence. The arms trade was a perfect marriage of her two primary concerns. Particularly after the Falklands, Mrs Thatcher took a close interest in the products of the defence industry. She unashamedly loved modern high-tech weaponry, partly as the physical expression of military power but also for its technological wizardry: she seized every opportunity to show off her unfeminine knowledge of different calibres and specifications and, like Shaw's Andrew Undershaft in *Major Barbara*, relished shocking the *bien pensants* by insisting that bigger and better armaments did not cause war but actually promoted peace. Acting as a saleswoman for British arms manufacturers also gave her

---

*Out of office she argued frankly that aid generally did more harm than good. 'Britain too had a modest aid programme when I was Prime Minister,' she wrote in 2002, 'and we tried to target it as well as possible. Some aid has doubtless done some good.'[169]

a useful entrée to Third World kings and presidents: she had something to sell which they wanted, and she enjoyed dealing personally,
leader to leader, trading in the very symbols and sinews of national
power. Normally the Defence Secretary was the front man in negotiating these sales; but Mrs Thatcher's role, as Michael Heseltine recalled,
was 'not inconspicuous'. Her part in clinching sales to Saudi Arabia,
the Gulf States and Malaysia was widely reported, and he found her
always very supportive. 'I knew I had only to ask my office to contact
No. 10 to wheel in the heavy guns if they could in any way help to
achieve sales of British equipment.'[170]

If the arms trade is regarded as a business like any other, then Mrs
Thatcher's high-level salesmanship, if slightly undignified for a Prime
Minister, was admirable. Britain was a major arms manufacturer and
needed to sell its products, against stiff competition, in order to remain
so. Mrs Thatcher called her efforts 'batting for Britain' and made no
apology for beating the drum. A flavour of her enthusiasm can be
gained from a press conference she gave to Arab correspondents at
Downing Street in April 1981 when she waxed lyrical about what
Britain could offer:

> We are particularly good on aircraft. We have also been very good
> on tanks. We have been particularly good on armour. We are
> absolutely outstanding on radar, on avionics in aircraft, on some
> aero engines, on carbon fibre . . . The [development] of jet was
> ours, the swing wing was ours; radar was ours . . . Of course we
> are pleased when other people order our things: they are good,
> they are extremely good. The Harrier is perhaps the best plane in
> the world. The Tornado is very, very advanced. The Rapier is quite
> superb.[171]

In 1985 Michael Heseltine, with Mrs Thatcher's support, appointed
Peter Levene, the managing director of his own arms-trading company,
at an unprecedented salary to become head of defence procurement
at the MoD. As a poacher-turned-gamekeeper, Levene earned his salary
over the next six years by forcing down the prices the Government
paid for military equipment. One way of cutting the manufacturers'
costs was by helping them sell their products around the world. Partly
as a result of his efforts Britain climbed during the 1980s from being
the fifth- to the second-largest supplier of military equipment after the
United States. But Mrs Thatcher herself set up many of the biggest
and most contentious deals, including major contracts with King
Hussein of Jordan, General Suharto of Indonesia and General Augusto

Pinochet of Chile. She lubricated these deals by soft loans and vigorous use of the export credit system. The Treasury worried about this over-generous provision of credit for arms sales, one official told the Scott Inquiry, but 'the Prime Minister would not necessarily see that as definitive. She would see other arguments as being more powerful.'[172]* The result was a less good deal for the taxpayer than at first appeared. Many of the arms supposedly purchased – by Jordan, Iraq and probably others – were never paid for at all. Even before the Gulf War intervened, Nicholas Ridley admitted that Iraq owed £1 billion and the true figure may have been nearer £2.3 billion.[174] In practice Mrs Thatcher was subsidising British companies with public money – something she refused to do in other areas of industry.

Her greatest coup was the huge Al-Yamamah contract with Saudi Arabia, negotiated in two parts in 1985 and 1988, said to be the biggest arms deal in history, worth something like £40 billion to British Aerospace and other British companies, and partly paid for in oil. Mrs Thatcher met Prince Bandar, a nephew of King Fahd and son of the Saudi Defence Minister, at least twice in 1985, once in Riyadh in April, the second time in Salzburg in August when she was supposed to be on holiday. On the announcement of the first part of the deal – for forty-eight Tornado fighter/bombers, twenty-four Tornado air-defence aircraft, thirty Hawk advanced training aircraft and thirty basic training aircraft – Heseltine told the press that Mrs Thatcher's contribution 'cannot be overstated'.[175] She secured the second part – for another forty-eight Tornados, sixty Hawks, eighty-eight Black Hawk helicopters (to be built by Westland) and six minehunters, plus an air base and command system – at a stopover in Bermuda on her way to Australia in 1988. Given her usual readiness to boast of her achievements, however, it is curious that this goes unmentioned in her memoirs.

The obvious reason is embarrassment over reports which soon emerged of huge commissions, running into millions of pounds, paid to middlemen – among them her own son. Mark's business interests had already attracted attention in 1984, when questions were raised about a large contract for the building of a university in Oman, which Mrs Thatcher had personally secured on her visit – with Mark in

---

*Kenneth Baker recalls a meeting in 1982 when she impatiently brushed aside the objections of the Treasury and Department of Trade in her anxiety to subsidise the sale of two frigates to Pakistan. 'You must find a way,' she told Leon Brittan and Arthur Cockfield. 'You are accountants and accounting is all about taking a sum of money from one person and giving it to someone else. Sort it out.'[173]

attendance – in 1981. The company principally concerned was Cementation Ltd, for which Mark was then acting as a 'consultant'. With no relevant qualifications or experience, his only possible value was his contacts, and specifically his name. 'We did pay him,' the company admitted, 'and we used him because he is the Prime Minister's son.'[176] In the Commons and on television Mrs Thatcher indignantly denied any impropriety: she had been 'batting for Britain' not for any individual company, and Mark's activities were his own affair.[177] In fact, since Cementation was the only British company bidding for the university contract, this defence was disingenuous. Mrs Thatcher must have known that her son stood to profit if Cementation won the contract, though that is not necessarily to say that she should therefore not have lobbied for them. The allegation that Mark was enriching himself on the back of his mother's patriotic salesmanship, however, did not go away. Much bigger sums were involved five years later in the Al-Yamamah contract, from which Mark was alleged to have pocketed £12–20 million for his role as a 'facilitator'. There is no doubt that he became inexplicably wealthy around this time, nor that he and his business partner Steve Tipping were active in the arms trade and in the Middle East.[178] The evidence is circumstantial but can be neither proved nor disproved, since an investigation of the Al-Yamamah deal by the National Audit Office was never published.

A second criticism of Mrs Thatcher's enthusiasm for arms sales is that it distorted the allocation of the aid budget – a charge highlighted by the saga of the Pergau Dam project in Malaysia. Mrs Thatcher visited Malaysia in April 1985 specifically to try to repair relations, which had been damaged by the Government's decision to increase university fees for overseas students. Malaysia had retaliated with a 'Buy British Last' campaign, as a result of which, she wrote in her memoirs, 'Britain always seemed to be at the bottom of the list when bids for contracts in Malaysia were concerned.' On that occasion she 'got on rather well' with the Prime Minister, Dr Mahathir, whom she characterised as 'tough, shrewd and practical'.[179] Three years later she went back and negotiated – without reference to the Foreign Office – a deal whereby Britain financed the construction of an economically unviable and environmentally damaging hydroelectric power station in northern Malaysia in return for an agreement to buy British defence equipment (including Tornado aircraft, artillery, air-defence radar and Rapier anti-missile systems) worth £1.3 billion. Subsequently a pro-Third World pressure group, the World Development Movement, took the Government to court, alleging that this was an improper diversion of 'aid' for commercial purposes, and in 1994 won their case when the

High Court ruled the deal illegal. Douglas Hurd, then Foreign Secretary
in John Major's Government, was embarrassed, the more so since,
feeling himself bound by Mrs Thatcher's promise, he had overruled his
officials who advised him in 1991 to cancel the project. To the foreign-
affairs select committee investigating the affair Hurd claimed to have
been unaware of the 'irregular and incorrect' linkage of aid to arms
sales.[180] He was obliged to refund the aid budget £65 million from
Treasury reserves.

The Pergau affair threw a murky light on Mrs Thatcher's cavalier
way with aid. First, the dam itself was an expensive white elephant –
exactly the sort of project Mrs Thatcher would never have subsidised
at home. As Simon Jenkins pointed out in *The Times*, at the very time
she was throwing money at Pergau she was refusing Government
support for the Channel-tunnel rail link, 'in which many of the companies fighting for Malaysian contracts might have had a hand. Bluntly
the taxpayer built a dam in northern Malaysia rather than a railway in
southern England because railways do not sell arms.'[181] Second, it was
only the most blatant example of her willingness to abuse the already
modest aid budget for purposes she considered more important. In
December 1994 Hurd was forced to reveal that three more aid projects – in Turkey, Indonesia and Botswana – had been found to breach
the criteria of the 1980 Overseas Development and Co-operation
Act.[182] The money that was wasted on the Pergau project was more
than Britain gave over the same period to Somalia, Ethiopia and
Tanzania combined, while wealthy Oman received more British 'aid'
than Ethiopia.[183] Moreover it emerged that nearly half the money
expended under the Aid and Trade Provision (ATP) for projects in
Third World countries went to finance contracts won by a handful of
favoured companies – Balfour Beatty, GEC, BICC and Amec – all of
which were major contributors to the Conservative party.[184] In short,
British aid was recycled to the Prime Minister's friends and supporters
at home and abroad.

The third charge against Mrs Thatcher's pursuit of arms sales is that
much of it was carried on secretly, in contravention of the Government's
declared policy. The most glaring instance – or at least the one that
came to light – was the supply of military equipment to Saddam
Hussein's Iraq throughout the eight years of the Iran–Iraq war when
Britain was supposed to be restricting the flow of arms to both sides.
This turned into a major embarrassment in 1990 when Saddam invaded
Kuwait and Britain and her allies found themselves at war with a
country they had been busily arming just a few weeks earlier. But this
is an occupational hazard of the arms trade: much the same had

happened with Argentina in 1982. The real scandal was the secrecy – duplicity – with which the policy had been conducted for the previous ten years.

Officially the West was neutral in the bloody war of attrition which began in 1980 when Iraq launched its troops against Iran: up to 1985 Britain continued to train pilots and supply low-level equipment impartially to both sides. In practice, however, both Britain and the United States covertly supported Iraq. Saddam was a revolting tyrant, but he was a tyrant of a familiar sort whom they could get along with: Iran's fanatical Ayatollah Khomeini, on the other hand, seemed much more dangerous. With the trauma of the Teheran hostage crisis still fresh in American minds, Iran outranked even Gaddafi's Libya as Washington's 'public enemy number one'. As Mrs Thatcher told Caspar Weinberger in 1984, 'the West did not need another success by Moslem fundamentalists'.[185] Moreover, the war provided a tempting opportunity. So long as the Shah was on the Peacock Throne, Britain had been a major supplier of arms to Iran. But Khomeini's Islamic revolution had closed that market. British manufacturers were now keen to get into Iraq instead. Their American counterparts were hamstrung by Congress, which not only imposed an embargo on trade with both sides, but actually enforced it, so the Reagan administration was happy to see Britain secretly supply Baghdad. It was easier to deceive the House of Commons than it was to deceive Congress.

Officially Britain followed the American lead by banning the export of 'lethal' equipment to either side. But a meeting of the Cabinet's Overseas and Defence Committee (OD) on 29 January 1981, chaired by Mrs Thatcher, agreed to define the critical word 'as flexibly as possible'.[186] Before the end of the year the MoD's arms-trade subsidiary International Military Services (IMS) had won a contract to build an integrated weapons complex at Basra in southern Iraq; and this was just the beginning. Adam Butler – Minister for Defence Procurement in 1984–5 – told the Scott Inquiry that over the next four years 'something like ten times as much defence equipment [was] exported to Iraq than to Iran'.[187] A Foreign Office briefing acknowledged that 'UK support for Iraq is implicit in [the] quantity of defence equipment supplied to Iraq since war began in 1980'.[188] In December 1985 Mrs Thatcher approved a doubling of the 'defence allocation' to Iraq, which in Lord Justice Scott's view made nonsense of the pretence of even-handedness between the combatants.[189]

For a time in 1983–4 when an Iranian victory seemed likely, however, the Foreign Office worried that this 'tilt' to Iraq might be imprudent and began to hedge for a more balanced neutrality. In

November 1984 Richard Luce – restored as Minister of State after his Falklands resignation – proposed more detailed 'guidelines' to restrict the supply of arms to either side. But the DTI had no wish to see the lucrative Iraqi market abandoned to the French and Russians. The head of the Middle East section objected that it was 'difficult to see any real benefit in this self-denying ordinance',[190] while British diplomats in Washington, Baghdad and Riyadh warned that any action that seemed to assist Iran would be badly received in those capitals. At just the moment when she was trying to negotiate the Al-Yamamah deal, the fear of upsetting the Saudis resonated particularly loudly with Mrs Thatcher. Though she eventually approved the new guidelines – Powell minuted Howe: 'The PM is content with what is proposed' – she did so only on condition that they were not announced until after Al-Yamamah was concluded.[191] By the time Howe disclosed them to Parliament in October 1985 they had already been in operation for nearly a year.

Except that they never really operated at all. Giving evidence at the Matrix Churchill trial in 1990, Alan Clark – Minister of State at the DTI from 1986 to 1989, when he moved to the MoD – dismissed them with typical candour as 'tiresome and intrusive', mere 'Whitehall cosmetics'.[192] They were framed to be deliberately ambiguous, he told the Scott Inquiry: 'high-sounding . . . yet imprecise enough to allow real policy consideration to override them'.[193] Both at the DTI and later at the MoD, Clark was an enthusiast for selling arms as freely as possible, not only to the Iraqis but to the Iranians as well. Scott found ample evidence to confirm that the Defence Export Sales Secretariat (DESS) interpreted the guidelines as loosely as possible, so that only finished weapons were classed as 'lethal'. Every other sort of military equipment, from aircraft spares to laser range-finders, and above all lathes for manufacturing artillery shells, went through without difficulty. They were made by a number of firms, all of which enjoyed a close relationship with the MoD, with little effort to disguise either their purpose or their destination. One of those most heavily involved, Matrix Churchill in Coventry, was actually acquired in 1987 by a subsidiary of the Iraqi Government, presumably to get round the fact that Britain had just signed a pact banning the export of ballistic-missile technology to the Third World. Matrix Churchill was then developing the Condor 2 missile with a range of 1,000 kilometres and capable of carrying nuclear warheads, in which Baghdad was known to be interested.[194] When questions were asked in Parliament they were batted away by junior ministers – Francis Maude for the Treasury, John Redwood for the DTI.[195] Meanwhile Clark advised the companies how to get round the guidelines by framing the export applications not for military use but as 'general engineering'.[196]★

On 2 December 1986, when there was some question of changing the guidelines, Charles Powell wrote to the Foreign Office that Mrs Thatcher found them 'very useful' when answering questions in the House of Commons and had no wish to alter them.[198] Two days later she gave a perfect example of what he meant when she told the House that 'British policy on arms sales to Iran and Iraq is one of the strictest in Europe and is rigidly enforced, at substantial cost to British industry. That policy has been maintained scrupulously and consistently'.[199] Presumably this formula accorded with her reading of the guidelines. But the reality was very different from the impression given to Parliament.

Is it possible that she did not know what was really going on? There is no doubt that some individuals in all the relevant departments knew. In January 1988 a Foreign Office official warned the companies making lathes to ship them quickly, because 'if it becomes public knowledge that the tools are to be used to make munitions, deliveries would have to stop at once'.[200] When the story of the so-called Iraqi 'Supergun' being manufactured in Yorkshire broke in 1990, the Tory MP for Bromsgrove, Sir Hal Miller, told the Commons that he had been asked two years earlier by the managing director of Walter Somers (one of the private steel firms making the gun) to clear it with the Government, and had done so, meeting officials from the MoD and DTI, and a third whom he assumed to be from intelligence.[201] But did Mrs Thatcher know? Quite apart from the fact that no Prime Minister so prided herself on knowing what was going on in every corner of Whitehall, the involvement of the intelligence service is the clearest indication that she was fully informed. After the scandal broke, the Scott Inquiry set up by John Major concentrated – so far as Mrs Thatcher was concerned – on whether she knew that the 1985 guidelines were secretly relaxed in 1988, when the Iran–Iraq war ended. But this was a very minor issue. More important is the overwhelming evidence that she knew – she must have known – that the guidelines had been worthless ever since 1985.

For one thing she received a quarterly report listing arms sales,

---

★Four years earlier, in March 1985, five senior Republican senators had written to President Reagan to express dismay at British sales of military equipment to Iran. The reply from the White House assured them that British policy prohibited the supply of military equipment impartially to either side, but acknowledged that the British definition of 'military' was narrower than the American.[197]

country by country, all round the world, and she had given explicit approval to a substantial (and unannounced) level of exports to Iraq. Of course the undercover trade might have been omitted from this list. But she also received intelligence reports, and we know that she read them avidly. In 1991 a young official who had resigned from the Joint Intelligence Committee (JIC) because of its 'obsession' with arms sales, testified that she was 'fascinated by the intelligence world and the international arms trade'.[202] More specifically, Scott quotes an intelligence digest dated 29 March 1988 – before the guidelines were changed – summarising the British machine-tool industry's involvement in Iraqi weapons manufacture and singling out Matrix Churchill as 'heavily involved'. This was initialled by Mrs Thatcher.[203] Again, at the end of that year, an MoD minute noted that she had agreed that a particular export licence already granted could not be revoked without revealing the intelligence source: it would have to be submitted to her again 'as she was involved last time'.[204]

Then there was the fact that large amounts of British equipment reached Iraq indirectly via other countries – notably Jordan. In her evidence to the Scott Inquiry, Mrs Thatcher claimed to have been deeply shocked by the discovery of this 'glaring loophole' (as Scott called it).[205] She attached great importance to Britain's relationship with Jordan and took pride in the three big arms deals she had made with King Hussein since 1979 – suspiciously large for such a tiny country. Other ministers followed her lead in claiming to have no idea that much of this equipment was destined for Iraq. But as usual there was one exception. Alan Clark told Scott that it was common gossip in the MoD that 'more than half the material purchased by Iraq was actually consigned to Jordan'. Pressed, he agreed that he 'could not sustain this figure arithmetically' but said it was 'a kind of slang expression for "a lot" . . . There was a tendency for the trickier items to be consigned to Jordan.'[206] An instance came to light in 1983 when HM Customs intercepted a consignment of 200 sub-machine guns bound for Iraq via Jordan: three men were charged and fined, but their conviction was later set aside.[207] But Mrs Thatcher did not need customs to tell her that this was happening. In October 1985 the JIC circulated a confidential document entitled 'Use of Jordanian facilities for the transshipment of war material to Iraq'; and the Scott Inquiry was given details of twenty-five more intelligence reports on the same subject between 1986 and 1991.[208] Is it possible that the Prime Minister read none of them? She had certainly done so by July 1990 when she commissioned from the Cabinet Office a document known as the 'Iraqnote' tracing the history of defence exports to Iraq, which stated:

'Iraq systematically uses Jordan as a cover for her procurement activities almost certainly with the connivance of senior figures within the Jordanian administration.'[209] Her pretence that this came as a great shock to her the following month is demonstrably untrue.

The scandal of the arms trade to Iraq only began to unravel in the last months of Mrs Thatcher's premiership, and the Scott Inquiry concentrated largely on when she had known what after 1988. But the covert arming of Iraq had begun very much earlier, in 1981, and was well established during her second term, when British manufacturers were given every encouragement and assistance to export military equipment energetically to Iraq, both directly and (via Jordan) indirectly, in cynical contradiction of the Government's professed policy of scrupulous restriction. There is ample evidence that Mrs Thatcher both knew of and encouraged this policy: it would have been very remarkable if she had not. So why did she do it? She was not normally cynical, and she prided herself on her high ethical standards. The answer is twofold.

First, she genuinely believed that every country was entitled to purchase the means to defend itself, that a free trade in armaments promoted peace, not war, and that others would sell them if Britain did not. Second, however, her Manichean world view disposed her to the dangerous doctrine that 'my enemy's enemy is my friend'. If Iran was the enemy of the West, then it was in Britain's interest to help arm Iraq. In her own mind she knew that it was right, even though it might be difficult to defend the policy to Parliament. So she closed her mind to the impropriety of deceiving Parliament, and probably also deceived herself: she had a great capacity for not admitting what she did not want to know. She allowed the policy to be led by those with fewer scruples than herself, without associating herself too closely with the detail, and persuaded herself that the form of words developed for use in the Commons covered what was going on. But there can be no doubt that she both willed the end and winked at the means. The policy stemmed from the same robust world view that she applied to every area of her foreign policy, from the Falklands to nuclear disarmament, from the bombing of Libya to the ending of apartheid. But in all those theatres she stood up boldly for what she believed. In the case of Iraq the execution of her policy required that Parliament was systematically misled over a period of eight or nine years. This was a major stain on her record.

9

Enemies Within

A need for enemies

One of Margaret Thatcher's defining characteristics as a politician was a need for enemies. To fuel the aggression that drove her career she had to find new antagonists all the time to be successively demonised, confronted and defeated. This is unusual: the normal instinct of politicians the world over is to seek agreement, defuse opposition and find consensus. The taste for confrontation is particularly alien to the British Tory party, whose traditional preference, as exemplified in Mrs Thatcher's time by people like Francis Pym and Willie Whitelaw, has always been to emphasise national unity around common values. By contrast Mrs Thatcher actively despised consensus: she needed always to fight and to win. She viewed the world through Manichaean spectacles as a battleground of opposed forces – good and evil, freedom and tyranny, 'us' against 'them'. The overriding global struggle between capitalism and Communism was reflected at the domestic British level by the opposition of Conservative and Labour, and more generally in a fundamental distinction between, on one side, 'our people' – honest, hard-working, law-abiding, mainly middle-class or aspiring middle-class taxpayers, consumers and homeowners – and, on the other, a ragtag army of shirkers, scroungers, socialists, trade unionists, 'wets', liberals, fellow-travelling intellectuals and peace campaigners. All these anti-social elements had to be taken on and beaten to make a world safe for Thatcherism.

The Falklands war was Mrs Thatcher's apotheosis, because it gave her a real, unquestioned enemy whom she could fight literally and unambiguously, with preponderant – though not universal – public support: her evident relish for the fight offended many who thought her cause was right. The Cold War was nearly as good, because here too there was a clear opponent whom she could attack rhetorically –

though again many found her enthusiasm for nuclear weapons alarming. Nearer home she had to restrain her combative instinct. She had to remember that the European leaders with whom she tussled at EC summits were not enemies but her Community partners; that the wets who dared to criticise her policies were party colleagues; and that even striking miners were British citizens with a different experience of life from hers. But she explicitly jettisoned the traditional Tory ideal of 'one nation', which she considered a euphemism for social appeasement. She divided the country frankly into 'our people', who were to be encouraged, protected and rewarded with tax cuts, mortgage relief and all sorts of hidden subsidies to keep them voting Tory, and the rest whose votes she did not need, who were told to stand on their own feet and stop whingeing.

Although in theory she rejected the concept of class and saw herself as a pure meritocrat, demolishing the barriers to talent and equal competition, she was in truth an unabashed warrior on behalf of her own class, the lower and middling middle class – 'the sort of people I grew up with', as she acknowledged in a speech to a Conservative audience in 1990. 'These are the people I became leader of this party to defend.'[1] Though she occasionally betrayed a weakness for genuine aristocrats like Peter Carrington, she had no time for the public-school and Oxbridge-educated upper middle class whom she held responsible for Britain's postwar decline. Of course she made exceptions for individuals – otherwise she could not have functioned in the Tory party at all – but in general she thought them decadent, defeatist and ineffectual. 'You know, Tony,' she once told Anthony Parsons, 'I'm very proud that I don't belong to your class.'[2] Likewise she entertained no illusions, and above all no social guilt, about the working class. There is an ill-concealed note of satisfaction in her memoirs when she describes the violent intimidation directed at some working miners during the 1984–5 coal strike, which furnished 'a useful antidote to some of the more romantic talk about the spirit of the mining communities'.[3] So far as she was concerned, the only proper ambition for those born into the working class was to get out of it as quickly as possible, and her policies – most obviously the sale of council houses – were specifically designed to encourage those that could to do so.

Mrs Thatcher not only needed enemies, but she was extraordinarily lucky in her enemies. One after another, throughout her career, her opponents played into her hands: Ted Heath, the public-sector unions, the Labour party and the SDP, the Tory 'wets'. At the nadir of her popularity in her first term, General Galtieri saved her by invading the Falklands; while in her second term, the miners' leader Arthur Scargill led the critical domestic challenge to her premiership with crass ineptitude. She was not so lucky with Jacques Delors, whom she tried to set up as the Galtieri or Scargill of her third term, but who proved a more wily opponent than either. Right at the end, however, when her luck was finally running out, another foreign villain, Saddam Hussein, appeared – only just too late to save her again. For more than ten years the secret of her success was being seen to vanquish a succession of pantomime enemies.

The second term was the time to deal with her domestic opponents. For most of her first term she was on the back foot. But once the Falklands had helped her to survive the crises of her first three years, Mrs Thatcher returned to office with a clear intention to take the offensive. She had routed the Labour party at the polls. But socialism was a hydra-headed enemy which still held important citadels of power beyond Westminster, which must be reduced before the Thatcherite vision of Britain could be fully realised. Two above all threatened her authority. First, left-wing Labour councils still controlled local government in most of the country's major cities: most visibly, just over the river from Westminster, the leader of the Greater London Council, Ken Livingstone, was mounting a cheekily provocative challenge which she could not endure. She had already determined in the 1983 manifesto to deal with Livingstone by the simple expedient of abolishing the GLC (and with it the other metropolitan councils). That, however, would require legislation. Meanwhile she faced a still more dangerous challenge from the Tories' old nemesis, the National Union of Mineworkers, now headed by the militant class warrior and would-be revolutionary, Arthur Scargill, openly bent on destroying her government as he had previously destroyed Heath's. Having prudently backed off in 1981, Mrs Thatcher was now ready for this challenge too. But first she signalled a tough new attitude to trade unionism by picking a fight with the small but significant group of white-collar workers employed at the Government's top-secret satellite listening post, Government Communications Headquarters, based at Cheltenham.

The problem of trade unionists at GCHQ had caught her attention during the 1981 Civil Service strike. The fact that striking tax collectors cost the Government £350 million in lost revenue merely irritated her; but the idea that intelligence personnel could endanger national security by industrial action enraged her, confirming her suspicion that trade unionism was fundamentally anti-patriotic. Codebreakers, she believed, should no more be unionised than members of the armed forces. She wanted to ban unions from GCHQ there and then; but at that time she was talked out of it by Frank Cooper and

Douglas Wass. The Americans had been alarmed by the disruption of intelligence, however, and Mrs Thatcher placed the highest priority on Britain's intelligence relationship with the US. Particularly after the Falklands and Grenada crises she wanted to assure them that it would not be repeated. So in January 1984, with no prior consultation with the unions concerned, she persuaded Howe to announce an immediate ban on GCHQ employees belonging to unions.

The case was a reasonable one – MI5 and MI6 are not unionised, and it was something of an historical anomaly that GCHQ was different. But the abrupt way in which the Government proposed to end the anomaly seemed high-handed and unreasonable. Howe himself was plainly embarrassed and would have been happy to accept a compromise brokered by Robert Armstrong whereby staff could have retained their union membership ('the card in the pocket') but would have had to sign a no-strike agreement. But Mrs Thatcher – stiffened by Bernard Ingham – was adamant that there could be no dual loyalty. The right to union membership, she told the Commons, was a 'privilege' which did not extend to security personnel.[4] To the unions this was tantamount to accusing their members of treason. The left claimed that the Government was removing a basic civil right and won a temporary victory when the High Court declared the ban illegal on the ground that the lack of consultation was 'contrary to natural justice'. This judgement was later overturned in the Court of Appeal, but the case of the handful of GCHQ workers who chose to be sacked rather than give up their membership remained a live grievance for the rest of the Thatcher years: the first of a number of episodes which showed the Government acting in an increasingly illiberal and authoritarian manner. The Prime Minister had won 'a hollow victory', Alan Watkins suggested in the *Observer*. 'Conservative backbenchers and Ministers do not now feel specially proud either of themselves or of Mrs Thatcher.'[5] Howe thought the episode symptomatic of Mrs Thatcher's 'absolutist instinct'.

> It was probably the clearest example I had seen so far of one of Margaret's most tragic failings: an inability to appreciate, still less accommodate, somebody else's patriotism ... A citizen, she seemed to feel, could never safely be allowed to carry more than one card in his or her pocket, and at GCHQ that could only be Her Majesty's card.[6]

As an anglicised Welshman, Howe had no problem with the idea of dual identity. But it was a concept which – as became clear again in the Northern Ireland context – Mrs Thatcher's all-or-nothing mindset could not accommodate.

Scargill and the miners

The skirmish over GCHQ was no more than a curtain raiser to the real battle which overshadowed the whole of 1984: the Government's life-or-death showdown with the NUM. Ever since 1926 the miners had been recognised as the vanguard of the labour movement. Harold Macmillan once declared that the three institutions with which no Prime Minister should tangle were the Vatican, the Brigade of Guards and the miners. In her first term Mrs Thatcher had gone some way towards bringing the unions to heel. Prior's 1980 Employment Act had been followed by Tebbit's in 1982, and the effect of both was reinforced by mounting unemployment. The Government had successfully withstood a steel strike and a Civil Service strike. On succeeding Tebbit in 1983, Tom King introduced a third instalment of legislation designed to make union leaders more accountable to their members by means of secret ballots. The unions were battered and cowed, but they would not be thoroughly defeated until the miners had made their last-ditch stand.

Mrs Thatcher had always known that she would have to face a miners' strike sooner or later. John Hoskyns was convinced from the start that coal 'would provide the ultimate test of the Government's will and authority'.[7] In February 1981 – to Hoskyns' disgust – she accepted temporary humiliation by postponing a confrontation she was not yet ready to win. Since then, however, the Government had been quietly making its dispositions. An *ad hoc* committee, MISC 57, chaired by Sir Robert Wade-Gery from the Cabinet Office, met 'in conditions of extreme secrecy for most of 1981' to devise ways to ensure that the Government would be able to sit out a long strike whenever it came. Over the next two years cash limits on the Central Electricity Generating Board (CEGB) were relaxed to allow the unobtrusive build-up of large stocks of coal in the power stations, which had been lacking in 1981. At the same time power stations were converted where possible to burn oil instead of coal, and fleets of road hauliers were recruited to move coal if the railwaymen should come out in support of the miners.[8] This, as Hugo Young pointed out, was a very rare example of strategic foresight on Mrs Thatcher's part.[9]

Then in February 1983 Nigel Lawson signalled that the Government was ready by appointing Ian MacGregor from British Steel to become chairman of the National Coal Board (NCB). Fresh from turning round the steel industry, with the loss of almost half the workforce, MacGregor was plainly being sent to do the same for coal: his track record in the United States included the defeat of a two-year strike by the United Mineworkers. Scargill – delighted to have been given the sort of antagonist he wanted – showed that he had got the message by greeting the new chairman as a 'Yankee steel butcher, waiting in the wings to chop us to pieces'.[10] Finally, in her post-election reshuffle Mrs Thatcher persuaded Peter Walker to take on the Department of Energy with the explicit expectation that he would face a challenge from Scargill: she needed a good communicator, she told him, to put the Government's case.[11] What she meant was that she needed a 'wet' – not a hard-faced monetarist – to win the coming propaganda war.

The economic case for shrinking the coal industry was incontestable. The rundown had been going on under governments of both parties since the 1960s. The moderate President of the NUM from 1971 to 1982, Joe Gormley, had broadly accepted it: the strikes of 1972 and 1974 had been about pay, not pit closures. But the industry was still over-producing coal that could not be sold. When MacGregor took over, the NCB was heading for a loss of £250 million in 1983–4. If the Government's policy towards nationalised industries was to mean anything this had to be stopped. But to achieve economic viability the NCB would have to close loss-making pits in traditional mining areas in Yorkshire, Scotland and south Wales and concentrate production in profitable modern pits like Selby in North Yorkshire and the Vale of Belvoir in Leicestershire. Coal mines, however, cannot be closed as easily as factories; whole communities with a proud and deeply rooted way of life depend on them. The new NUM leaders, Arthur Scargill and his saturnine Vice-President Mick McGahey, were not only militant left-wingers looking to break another Tory Government: they also came from Yorkshire and Scotland respectively. They took their stand on the view that the union could not allow the closure of any pit at all except on grounds of safety or geological exhaustion: they did not accept the concept of an uneconomic pit. This was the economics of the madhouse.

But Scargill was not making an economic case at all. Behind the Luddite insistence that miners' jobs must be guaranteed for life, his purpose was to mount a political challenge to the Government. He openly boasted of leading a socialist – more accurately a syndicalist – revolution to overthrow capitalism, asserting that after Mrs Thatcher's 1983 landslide, extra-parliamentary action was 'the only course open to the working class and the labour movement'.[12] He had first come to prominence by leading the mass picketing of the Saltley Gate coke works, which was perceived – rightly or wrongly – as having forced the Heath Government to cave in to the miners in 1972, and from the moment he was elected to succeed Gormley in December 1981 he was thirsting to repeat that revolutionary moment. Three times in 1982–3 he called on the NUM membership in national ballots to vote for strikes: three times, by majorities rising from 55 to 61 per cent, they voted him down. After the successful strikes of the 1970s too many miners – those whose jobs were not threatened – had too much to lose by going on strike: they had good pay, cars, mortgages and an increasingly middle-class way of life. They were no longer the down-trodden proletariat of Scargill's imagination. Moreover the Coal Board, with Walker's encouragement, was offering generous redundancy terms to those who did lose their jobs when pits closed. By 1984 it was plain to Scargill that he would never get his strike if he relied on the membership voting for one – certainly not by the 55 per cent majority required by the NUM constitution. So when the NCB announced on 6 March 1984 that another twenty uneconomic pits would close over the next twelve months, with the loss of 20,000 jobs, he determined to engineer a national strike without the tiresome inconvenience of a national ballot.

He contrived it by encouraging a series of regional strikes, starting in the most directly affected and most militant areas, Yorkshire and Scotland, which would put moral pressure on the others to join in. As McGahey bluntly put it: 'We shall not be constitutionalised out of a strike . . . Area by area will decide and there will be a domino effect.'[13] Pickets were dispatched to less militant areas to help them to the right decision. But only Yorkshire, Scotland and the small Kent coalfield – where there were no ballots – were solid in support of the strike. Most other areas which did ballot, voted against striking: the crucial moderate coalfield, Nottinghamshire, recorded a majority of nearly four to one against and most pits in the county carried on working. In south Wales only ten out of twenty-eight pits supported the strike, but the local leaders called all their members out anyway. Thus Scargill's strategy split the union whose strength in the past had always been its unity. In fact there were indications that had he held a ballot in the early weeks of the strike, he might have won it – especially after he had pushed through a rule change requiring only a simple majority.[14] But by refusing to hold a ballot he not only set area against area but miner against miner within each area, pit and village. By mid-April, when the strategy was approved – by a majority of only 69–54 – by a special delegate conference, forty-three out of 174 pits were still working. To enforce and widen the strike Scargill revived on a much bigger scale his old weapon from 1972 – the mass picketing of working pits and also of ports and depots to prevent the movement of coal. Flying pickets were organised as a quasi-military operation, with men bused from all over the country to key sites: they were given strike pay only if they were prepared to picket. But this time the police were equally organised – the Government had made its preparations on this front too – and met them in equal numbers. Soon the television news every night led with what looked like pitched battles between medieval armies, one side armed with batons and riot shields, the other with bricks, spikes, darts, ball bearings and all manner of homemade weapons.

The public was appalled; but though there was widespread sympathy for the miners, faced with the loss of their livelihood, there was remarkably little public support for the strike, because of Scargill's methods. By waging the dispute with such blatant contempt for democracy – by defying the rules of his own union and openly challenging the elected Government – by strutting and ranting like a tinpot demagogue, refusing to condemn the violence of the pickets (which he blamed entirely on the police) and refusing to admit the possibility of closing any pits at all, Scargill alienated not only the public at large but also those who should have been his allies, the Labour party and the other unions. Neil Kinnock, less than a year into his leadership of the party, was cruelly exposed: emotionally disposed to support the miners but aware that it would be political suicide to do so, able neither to condemn the strike nor fully support it. He did criticise the failure to hold a ballot, condemned the violence – but also the police response – and did his best to express support for the miners without endorsing Scargill's more extreme objectives. But the more uncomfortably he wriggled, the more contemptuously Mrs Thatcher was able to pillory him as a weasely apologist for the enemies of democracy.

Likewise the rest of the union movement gave the miners verbal but little practical support. The steel unions above all were desperate to keep what was left of their industry working, and defied the NUM pickets designed to stop coal getting to the steel plants. But the electricians, the power workers and even the railwaymen also turned a deaf ear to Scargill's truculent demand for 'the total mobilisation of the trade union and labour movement'.[15] In July the dockers refused to unload imported coal intended for the steel industry. For a time the Government was seriously worried that this might mark a widening of the strike; but the dockers' muscle was not what it was. The ports of Liverpool and Southampton were closed, but two-thirds of cargoes now came in through non-registered ports like Felixstowe and Dover. The non-unionised lorry drivers were not prepared to be bullied, and the TGWU called the action off after just ten days. The longer the coal strike lasted, the clearer it became that the TUC had no wish to get involved. Passionately as Scargill appealed to working-class solidarity, he was asking others to risk their jobs when thousands of his own members were still working. By flouting the NUM's own rulebook Scargill had thrown away the public sympathy which was the miners' greatest asset.

So the Government held all the cards. And yet the year-long strike still represented a major crisis for Mrs Thatcher. The longer it dragged on the more it highlighted the division of the country which she seemed to symbolise. Its defeat was absolutely vital to her political survival, yet she could not afford to appear too directly involved and above all must not appear vindictive. It was no secret that she loathed the coal industry which, as she wrote in her memoirs, 'had come to symbolise everything that was wrong with Britain'.[16] Equalled only by the railways, coal was the epitome of the old-fashioned, inefficient, union-dominated, loss-making nationalised industry, so intrinsically uncommercial that it could not be privatised. It was physically dirty, too; the future, she believed, lay with clean modern nuclear energy. She shared none of the sentimental veneration with which older Conservatives like Macmillan viewed the miners. To her they were the stormtroops of that backward-looking socialism which she was in politics to destroy, and Scargill was their perfect representative. Yet she was bound to keep saying warm words about the industry and what a bright future it could have once production was concentrated on the profitable pits, in order to counter Scargill's repeated allegation that the Government was intent on destroying it.

'There is an excellent future for the coal industry,' she told the Commons in 1983, 'provided it can tackle its financial problems and produce coal at a competitive price. Our proven coal reserves will last 300 years at present rates of extraction.'[17] After the strike began she repeatedly insisted that the Government had invested more than £3 billion – nearly £2 million a day – in coal since 1979. 'That is faith in the future of the coal industry.'[18] No government in history, she claimed, had ever invested in coal as much as this one.[19] It was not the Government, but Scargill's insistence on burdening the industry with crippling costs, that threatened its viability.

At the same time she had to pretend to treat the strike as an ordinary industrial dispute and leave the handling of negotiations with the NUM to the Coal Board. 'I haven't intervened in nationalised industries for years,' she declared in June. 'It took us time to get it right,' she admitted when reminded that the Government had intervened to avert a strike in 1981; but she insisted that it would not do so again.[20]

From all sides – by the opposition parties, by the churches, by business leaders worried about the effect of a long strike on their own profits – she was condemned for not intervening in the traditional way with beer and sandwiches at Number Ten. In the Commons Kinnock continually accused her of abdicating the Government's responsibility to bring the two sides together. But Government interference to impose a solution, she insisted, would be tantamount to surrender.[21] 'The Government will leave the National Coal Board to deal with the matter as it thinks fit.'[22]

The Government's only role was to uphold the liberty of those miners – and others – who wanted to work. 'This is not a dispute between miners and the Government,' she told Robin Day on *Panorama*. 'This is a dispute between miners and miners . . . It is some of the miners who are trying to stop other miners going to work.'[23] In those circumstances it was the job of the police to protect the freedom to work, and the job of the Government to support the police. The most serious confrontation took place at the Orgreave coke depot near Sheffield, just down the road from Scargill's headquarters, where 5,000 pickets gathered on 29 May to try to stop the movement of coal to Scunthorpe steelworks. They were beaten back by even greater numbers of mounted and heavily armoured police, but the battle was renewed daily for three weeks, with incidents of appalling violence on both sides: on the first day alone 104 police officers and twenty-eight pickets were injured, and by the end several hundred – including Scargill himself – had been arrested. The issue here was no longer the future of the coal industry but the maintenance of law and order and on that subject Mrs Thatcher could not be neutral. 'What we have got,' she said on 30 May, 'is an attempt to substitute the rule of the mob for the rule of law, and it must not succeed . . . The rule of law must prevail over the rule of the mob.'[24] After three weeks it did. Scargill had designated Orgreave to be another Saltley; but this time the gates stayed open and the lorries kept rolling. The battle of Orgreave was a decisive defeat for Scargill's storm troops.

The critical difference between 1972 and 1984 was that this time the police operation too was centrally controlled. As soon as the strike began the Home Secretary, Leon Brittan, set up a National Reporting Centre in New Scotland Yard to co-ordinate intelligence between the forty-three independent police forces in England and Wales and ensure that adequate manpower and equipment was available to the chief constables wherever it was needed. The Home Office had learned a lot from the 1981 riots: as a result of that experience the police were far better equipped and trained to deal with mass violence than ever before. 'If we hadn't had the Toxteth riots,' Willie Whitelaw reflected, 'I doubt if we could have dealt with Arthur Scargill.'[25] Second, they adopted a strategy of stopping coachloads of miners before they even got to the sites they were intending to picket: groups of Kent miners found themselves turned back at the Dartford tunnel. This was widely condemned – not only by the far left – as an unwarrantable breach of civil liberty. Co-ordination between local forces, it was alleged, was a sinister step in the direction of a national police force under the control of the Government, and ultimately a police state. But Brittan, strongly supported by Mrs Thatcher, insisted that the police had always had the power to prevent a breach of the peace wherever they antic-ipated one and were quite right to do so.[26] In due course the High Court agreed. The number of pickets at Orgreave gave the police no option but to deploy even greater numbers. Undoubtedly there were disturbing implications in the level of policing needed to contain the strike. But at least it was contained by the police. When MacGregor told Mrs Thatcher that in America they would have brought in the National Guard with tanks and armoured cars, she was quite shocked. 'Oh my goodness,' she exclaimed, 'we can't do that. That would be political suicide in this country.'[27] Certainly the police were sometimes heavy-handed in the face of intolerable provocation. But the truth was that Labour attacked the policing of the strike because they could neither support nor condemn the strike itself. The party conference in October carried a motion that the police should stay out of indus-trial disputes altogether, which was plainly ridiculous. Most of the public recognised that centralised policing was needed to prevent centralised intimidation. If they did not like it they blamed Scargill more than the Government.

Thus Scargill's bully-boy tactics played into the Government's hands. No Prime Minister could have failed to denounce them, and Mrs Thatcher did not restrain her condemnation of his calculated assault on freedom, democracy and the rule of law. But once or twice she went too far with overtly military talk of 'victory' or 'surrender'. It was in an end-of-session speech to Conservative MPs on 19 July that she was reported to have described the striking miners as 'the enemy within', drawing an explicit comparison with the external enemy whom she had defeated two years earlier in the South Atlantic. There is no authorised text, but one newspaper reported her words: 'We had to fight the enemy without in the Falklands and now we have to fight the enemy within, which is much more difficult but just as dangerous to liberty.'[28]

Like most such phrases, this one was not original: the *Daily Express* had already applied it jointly to Scargill and Livingstone in a front-page headline the previous year.[29] But it sparked a furious reaction. Like the intelligence officers at GCHQ, miners resented the slur on their patriotism. 'Any Prime Minister of Britain,' Kinnock charged, 'who confuses a Fascist dictator who invades British sovereign territory with British trade unions and with miners is . . . not fit to govern this country.'[30] Mrs Thatcher was forced to explain that she had meant only the militant minority, not the miners in general; she even denied that she had intended any comparison with Argentina.[31] But she never retracted the expression. In October she repeated and explained it in an interview with the *Sunday Mirror*: 'The "Enemy Within" are those people who turn to violence and intimidation to *compel* people to do what they can't *persuade* them to do.'[32]

Fair enough. The phrase stuck, however, and was remembered, because it appeared to encapsulate her attitude to the coal strike, which seemed to many, who accepted that it had to be defeated, unhelpfully warlike. The Government, the opposition argued, should hold the ring, not be seen to take sides. Denis Healey exploited echoes of the Falklands by accusing her of 'glorying in confrontation'.[33] But ten days after the 'enemy within' speech she was at it again, telling Kinnock in a setpiece debate in the Commons that there was 'only one word to describe his policy when faced with a threat from home or abroad, and that word is appeasement'.[34] And then in her speech to the Tory Party Conference in Brighton – delivered a few hours after the IRA's bombing of the Grand Hotel – she did not scruple to draw a parallel between the NUM and the IRA. In truth, that morning in that hall she did not need to spell it out. But she devoted the last three pages of her speech to the coal strike, condemning 'an organised revolutionary minority who are prepared to exploit industrial disputes but whose real aim is the breakdown of law and order and the destruction of democratic parliamentary Government', and ended in her most Churchillian tones:

> The nation faces what is probably the most testing crisis of our time – the battle between the extremists and the rest. We are fighting, as we have always fought, for the weak as well as the strong. We are fighting for great and good causes. We are fighting to defend them against the power and might of those who rise up to challenge them. This Government will not weaken. This nation will meet that challenge. Democracy will prevail.[35]

Two weeks later the *Sunday Times* revealed that the NUM had sent a representative to Tripoli to seek money – successfully – from the

Libyan president Colonel Gaddafi, who also made no secret of funding
the IRA. Coming just a few weeks after Libyan agents had shot dead
a young policewoman from the diplomatic sanctuary of their London
embassy, this was Scargill's most spectacular blunder, condemned as
strongly by Kinnock and the TUC as it was by Mrs Thatcher. But it
allowed her to widen her attack still further. In a third speech, delivered at the Carlton Club in November, she equated the striking miners
– and the hard left in general – with Libyan and Palestinian terrorists.
'We must never give in,' she warned, 'to the oldest and least democratic trick of all – the coercion of the many by the ruthless and
manipulating few . . . The concept of fair play . . . must not be used
to allow the minority to overbear the tolerant majority.'

> Yet these are the very dangers which we face in Britain today. At
> one end of the spectrum are the terrorist gangs within our borders,
> and the terrorist states which finance and arm them. At the other
> are the hard left operating inside our system, conspiring to use union
> power and the apparatus of local government to break, defy and
> subvert the laws.[36]

By such speeches Mrs Thatcher deliberately raised the stakes. By
defining the coal strike as part of the global struggle against Communism
and terrorism she nailed her authority to the outcome of a contest which
the Government could not afford to lose and on which she repeatedly
declared there could be no compromise. 'You never compromise with
violence.'[37] 'You can never compromise on the right of management to
manage in any industry.'[38] It was therefore implausible to believe that she
would sit back in Number Ten and let the dispute take its course. As she
admitted in her memoirs, 'So much was at stake that no responsible
government could have taken a "hands-off" attitude.'[39] In truth she took
the closest interest in every aspect of the dispute. She not only chaired
a large ministerial committee, MISC 101, consisting of nearly half the
Cabinet, which met once a week throughout the strike, but more importantly she met both Peter Walker and Leon Brittan nearly every day to
keep an eye on developments, and constantly had to be restrained from
ringing chief constables with her views on detailed aspects of policing.[40]
In August she took her usual brief holiday in Switzerland. 'In my absence,'
she wrote, 'Peter Walker took effective charge of day-to-day policy in the
coal strike. But a prime minister is never really on holiday.' So even in
Switzerland she remained in constant touch.[41] In September she postponed a planned visit to Malaysia and Indonesia because she did not
want to be out of the country at a critical stage of the dispute.

At the beginning, it is true, she had been content to leave the conduct of negotiations to the NCB. But increasingly she became worried that MacGregor's grasp of public relations was as bad as Scargill's. The future American Ambassador, Raymond Seitz, then an attaché in the US Embassy, wrote that while on one side Scargill, 'the rabble-rousing leader of the NUM, strutted before the cameras with all the swagger and bile of a tinpot dictator', on the other 'Ian MacGregor . . . represented management with all the political and social sympathy of a bar-room bouncer . . . I recall cringing whenever he appeared on television.'[42] MacGregor's worst moment came when – supposedly as a joke – he held a bag over his face like a criminal as he hurried past the cameras without speaking. After this Mrs Thatcher sent Tim Bell to try to improve his image; but still he came across as old, insensitive and out of touch: the Bishop of Durham struck a chord by calling him 'an imported elderly American'.[43] While the NCB's case was supposed to be that the miners were being offered generous terms and a bright future, MacGregor seemed to be exactly the Yankee butcher Scargill had said he was. The longer the strike dragged on, the more grateful Mrs Thatcher was for Walker's smooth communication skills.

At the same time, however, she worried that MacGregor was not as tough as she had thought, but might be ready to offer a deal to get the industry back to work, ignoring the wider political issue. She wanted victory, not a settlement. 'I was always concerned that Ian MacGregor and the NCB team would unwittingly give away the basic principles for which the strike was being fought . . . Peter Walker and I felt throughout that Ian MacGregor did not fully comprehend the devious ruthlessness of the NUM leaders he was arguing with.'[44] Fortunately for her, Scargill was not really devious at all, but – like General Galtieri – too puffed up with his own rhetoric to grasp a compromise when it was offered. She confesses to being 'enormously relieved' when the most hopeful negotiations of the strike so far broke down in the middle of July because Scargill still refused to admit the concept of an uneconomic pit.[45]

Her other worry was that more groups of workers might be induced to join the strike. So long as the NUM remained isolated the Government was confident that Scargill's boasts that the strike was proving 'devastatingly successful' were mere bombast.[46] As early as May he was claiming that the Government had only eight weeks' coal supply left.[47] But Sir Walter Marshall of the CEGB assured the Prime Minister in July that coal stocks at the power stations and pitheads were sufficient for at least eighteen months with no need for power cuts; while the movement of coal by rail and lorry to the rest of industry continued with only minor disruption.[48] The only thing that could change the picture was sympathetic action by other unions, amounting cumulatively to something like a general strike: another Winter – or Summer – of Discontent. In order to avert this ever-present nightmare, Mrs Thatcher was ready to do whatever was necessary. Hence the Government took care not to be seen to import coal for use in the power stations, which were kept going entirely from the stocks already built up; imported coal was used only to supply the steelworks, which were not so sensitive. Likewise – contrary to the principle of not interfering in public-sector pay disputes – ministers were desperate to avert trouble on the railways. When the NUR rejected an offer of 4 per cent and called an overtime ban from the end of May, the threat was bought off with an offer worth nearer 7 per cent. A leaked letter from one of her private secretaries showed that Mrs Thatcher had been worried that either too low or too high an offer could have repercussions on the coal strike:

> She agrees that BR should increase its pay offer in order to keep the negotiations in play. She accepts that the offer can be increased along the lines suggested so long as the productivity conditions are insisted upon. She would be concerned if the offer were improved beyond this point as it would put the offer made to the miners in a poor light.[49]

The Government also discouraged the chairmen of other nationalised industries – British Rail, British Steel, the CEGB – from using the new industrial-relations legislation against secondary picketing. After all the political odium of putting them on the Statute Book, it seemed to many Tories craven to leave the new laws untested in just the sort of dispute they were designed to deal with. 'Instinctively I had a good deal of sympathy with this view,' Lady Thatcher later admitted.[50] But in the circumstances she accepted Walker's argument that using 'Tory laws' to defeat the strike would be seen as unnecessarily provocative: there was no need to risk giving the TUC a pretext to come off the fence, when the existing criminal law was perfectly sufficient to deal with intimidation. Though in public she insisted that it was entirely up to MacGregor and the rest whether or not they chose to use the civil law,[51] behind the scenes the Government leaned heavily on both British Steel and British Rail to dissuade them from doing so. It was far more effective – and in keeping with the spirit of the legislation – to encourage individual NUM members to take the union to court, as two Yorkshire miners successfully did. In September the High Court ruled that the union had indeed breached its own constitution by calling a strike without a ballot. Scargill was fined £1,000 (which was paid by an anonymous donor) and the union £200,000. When it refused to pay, its assets were ordered to be sequestrated. It turned out that they had already been transferred abroad, out of reach of the court. But the judgement further deterred other unions from any thought of risking their own funds. In this respect Tebbit's 1982 Act did have an effect.

Ministers were briefly worried by the short-lived dock strike in July – and again by another dispute over the unloading of coal for the Ravenscraig steel plant in Scotland, which threatened another stoppage in September. By far the most serious alarm of the whole strike, however, arose from the possibility that the pit deputies' union NACODS, representing the men responsible for the maintenance and safety of the pits, might join the strike, which would have closed all the mines immediately and caused irreparable damage. Up until the summer enough deputies had kept working to keep the pits in good repair: local managers had turned a blind eye to those who stayed away. But in August the NCB suddenly announced that it would stop paying those who refused to cross NUM pickets. NACODS promptly voted by a majority of 82 per cent to strike from the end of October – principally over their own grievance but also in support of the miners' campaign against pit closures. This was when Mrs Thatcher really thought MacGregor had blown it. 'We were in danger of losing everything because of a silly mistake,' she recalled on television in 1993. 'We had to make it clear that if that was not cured immediately then the . . . management of the NCB could indeed have brought the Government down. The future of the Government at that moment was in their hands and they had to remedy their terrible mistake.'[52] MacGregor was told in no uncertain terms that the deputies must be bought off; and after anxious talks under the auspices of the arbitration service ACAS, they were. In his self-justifying memoir MacGregor blames Walker for undermining him; but it was really Mrs Thatcher who insisted that NACODS must be given whatever was required to keep them working.[53] The price included a great deal of what Scargill had been demanding: reconsideration of the NCB's closure plans in the light of supposedly changed circumstances; an undertaking to keep five of the most contentious pits open pending further review; and an enhanced review procedure including an independent element. In the Commons Mrs Thatcher fulsomely endorsed this package as the basis of a possible settlement with the NUM.[54] Once again, as in the

Falklands, she knew her enemy. Had Scargill only had the flexibility to grasp this deal he could have claimed a substantial victory. As it was he still refused to contemplate anything less than the unconditional withdrawal of all pit-closure plans; and so, four months later, he went down (like Galtieri) to unconditional defeat.

For the Government the key to victory lay with the 50,000 miners in Nottinghamshire and other 'moderate' coalfields who had continued working in the face of verbal and physical pressure to join the strike. To Mrs Thatcher they were heroes of democracy. '"Scabs" their former workmates call them,' she told the Tory Party Conference. 'Scabs? They are lions.'[55] 'The courage and loyalty of working miners and their families will never be forgotten,' she promised the Lord Mayor's Banquet in November.[56] There is no question that it took courage to defy the bullies. Her praise, however, did them no favours in their own communities, where being lauded by the Prime Minister made them look like the stooges of a hated Tory Government – as to an extent they were. An Old Etonian businessman-turned-journalist called David Hart – disingenuously described by Lady Thatcher as 'a friend who was making great efforts to help the working miners'[57] – played a part in setting up a National Working Miners' Development Committee to stiffen and co-ordinate the working miners' movement. Dividing his time between a suite in Claridges and undercover visits to the coalfields, from where he sent well-informed articles to *The Times*, Hart had the ear of both MacGregor and Mrs Thatcher, though Peter Walker would have nothing to do with him. He also helped finance the legal action by the two Yorkshire miners which got the strike ruled illegal, and pulled off a dramatic public-relations coup by arranging for Scargill to be served a writ for contempt of court, live on television, during a debate at the Labour Party Conference. It seems that Mrs Thatcher gained a vicarious thrill from hearing of his dashing exploits behind enemy lines – Ronnie Millar calls him 'a kind of Blue Pimpernel'.[58] But Hart's was a dangerous game, which could easily have rebounded against the Government if his activities had been exposed.

Eventually the strikers started to go back. By the end of October the realisation that they were going to get no significant support from other unions, and the evident fact that the CEGB had enough coal to sit out the winter, led all but the most militant to conclude that the cause was hopeless. The NCB bribed them with deferred bonuses – puffed in newspaper advertisements as 'the best package ever offered to any group of workers'[59] – and in the middle fortnight of November some 11,000 took the bait. By the end of the year 70,000 out of 180,000 miners were working (Scargill of course disputed the figure) and MacGregor announced that as soon as the number reached 51 per cent the strike would be over. Yet still it lasted for another two months, partly because a new TUC initiative raised hopes of a face-saving compromise. Mrs Thatcher was alarmed. She wanted nothing short of outright victory but was afraid that MacGregor was weakening. Any pretence of non-intervention was now abandoned. Ever since the NACODS agreement she had been insisting that the NCB had no room for any further movement. In November she took it upon herself to warn the NUM that 'the NCB can not and will not yield'.[60] Now she intervened again to insist that the NCB should require not just an assurance but a written guarantee that it alone could decide when pits must be closed, and went on television on 25 January 1985 to make her involvement perfectly clear. 'Let's get it written down,' she told Alastair Burnet on *TV Eye*. 'I want it dead straight, honest and no fudging.'[61]

Immediately it was alleged that she was deliberately torpedoing the chance of a negotiated settlement. Kinnock charged that the new conditions had 'her dirty fingerprints all over [them]' and called her 'a stubborn Salome who wants the miners' head on a plate' – as indeed she did.[62] But her visible intervention threatened to stir up NACODS again, so she was quickly obliged to reaffirm that the October deal – including the independent review element – would be fully honoured, while still repeating that the Board would not give up the right to manage.[63] At this late stage she did not want to antagonise the TUC either, so on 19 February she agreed to meet a seven-man committee – a very rare event in her premiership – to assure them that she recognised their good faith. They claimed to detect signs of movement in the NUM's intransigence. But she did not believe it – she quoted Scargill still boasting that his objectives were the same as on the day the strike began – or if she did, she did not want to put it to the test. She still asserted that the strike would end only when enough miners realised that the cause was hopeless, and appealed to them directly not to pin their hopes on talks which were still doomed.[64] If she had kept clear of direct involvement at the beginning of the strike, her determination that there should be no fudging at the end was public and unmistakable.

She finally got her victory on 3 March – almost exactly a year after the strike had begun. With men now going back at the rate of 9,000 a week – accompanied by renewed scenes of violence, especially in Yorkshire – a delegate conference voted to preserve what remained of the union's authority by ordering an orderly return to work the following Monday, even though nothing at all had been achieved. There was no agreement over pit closures; no pay rise until the overtime ban was lifted; and no promise of an amnesty for convicted pickets. Scargill still wanted to fight on, while simultaneously claiming a famous victory. But the majority of his members, and almost the whole of the rest of the country, could see that in a battle of two stubborn wills, Mrs Thatcher's had proved the stronger.*

Yet it was not a popular victory. Mrs Thatcher expressed 'over-whelming relief' and tried not to crow. 'There would have been neither freedom nor order in Britain if we had given in to violence,' she declared, once again praising all those, both miners and others, who had kept on working to keep the economy and the country going, as well as the police who had protected their liberty to do so.[65] Most of the public accepted that the NUM's position had been untenable. But there was no public celebration. Despite Scargill's tactics there was real sympathy for the miners and particularly for their wives, seen as long-suffering heroines of their communities' doomed struggle. Collections for the miners' families raised at least £5 million, possibly £10 million, during the strike – conscience money, in large part, contributed by those in work to allay a sense of guilt about those who were losing their livelihood through no fault of their own. There was still a romance about redundant miners which did not extend in the same way to unemployed steel or construction workers. When the south Wales miners marched back to work with banners flying behind a brass band, their pride was widely shared. Mrs Thatcher reaped no political credit for having defeated them. On the contrary she was felt to have been as inflexible and divisive a class warrior as Scargill himself. At the turn of the year listeners to the *Today* programme voted Scargill and Mrs Thatcher respectively as Man and Woman of the Year: the pollster Peter Kellner invented a composite figure called Martha Scarthatch whom the public loved to hate.[66] Instead of getting a lift in the polls, as minis-ters expected, the Government soon found itself trailing in third place behind both Labour and the Alliance.

The economic costs of the dispute were high. In his 1985 budget Nigel Lawson reckoned the direct cost to the Government in public expenditure at £2.75 billion, while economic output over the year 1984–85 was down by 1 per cent, the balance of payments by £4 billion. Steel, the railways and other industries dependent on coal were

---

*After the strike ended, a backdated pay rise was concluded when a special confer-ence voted – once again against Scargill's recommendation – to end the over-time ban. Most of the outstanding charges against pickets collapsed for lack of witnesses willing to give evidence. But the rate of pit closures increased, as Scargill had always said it would.

left with heavy debts; the cost to the CEGB of burning oil instead of coal was reckoned at £2 billion, while the cost of policing was around £250 million.[67] The highest price, however, was paid by the coal industry itself. Scargill always claimed that the Government's purpose was to destroy the industry. Over the next ten years the rate of pit closures accelerated, so that by 1994 there were only nineteen left in operation, employing just 25,000 miners. The bright future repeatedly promised by MacGregor and the Government throughout 1984 never materialised, mainly because the privatisation of electricity supply ended the protected market for overpriced coal. When the strike ended the anti-Scargill working miners broke from the NUM to form their own Union of Democratic Miners amid renewed assurances of Government investment, but soon found themselves facing the same inexorable rundown. Thus Scargill could claim to have been vindicated. His critics would answer that it was the strike itself which set back the industry's prospects in the short term, and that anyway the reality was that coal had no long-term future. In truth, until Scargill's determination to stage a political confrontation, the Thatcher Government was no more ruthless than its Labour predecessors in trying to manage the inevitable rundown as generously as possible.

Nevertheless the strike left a lasting legacy of anger, bitterness and social division. At a time when unemployment in the whole economy was still rising ineluctably, heavily concentrated in the old industrial regions of the north and west, the strike dramatised the human suffering in those parts of the country which felt themselves thrown on the scrapheap while London and the south of England boomed. Challenged politically by what she called 'Mr Scargill's insurrection', Mrs Thatcher did not seem to care, but concentrated all her attention on defeating the 'enemy within', who in turn became a focus of admiration for all other deprived and alienated groups who loathed her Government. In the long run the defeat of the NUM marked her decisive victory not just over the miners but over the unions and the left as a whole: as she somewhat insensitively boasted in Malaysia a few weeks after the strike ended – this was the visit she had postponed in September – 'not one union gave support, because they were learning the facts of life'.[68] Short-term unpopularity notwithstanding, her victory helped to consolidate the Conservatives' ideological hegemony and underlined how much baggage Labour had to shed before it could hope to be re-elected. When all is said it was a necessary victory; but it was a flawed and bitterly contested one, which highlighted the negative side of Thatcherism as vividly as the positive.

Livingstone and the GLC

Scargill's counterpart in local government was Ken Livingstone – the provocatively left-wing thirty-six-year-old leader of the Greater London Council, who had replaced the moderate Andrew Mackintosh in a bloodless coup the day after Labour's victory in the May 1981 elections, and had since – as 'Red Ken' – become the Tory tabloids' latest bogeyman. Livingstone was the figurehead for a number of local council leaders around the country determined to defy the Tory government, most notably David Blunkett in the so-called 'People's Republic of Sheffield', Derek Hatton, the cocky spokesman of Militant-controlled Liverpool, and Ted Knight ('Red Ted') in the London borough of Lambeth. But the Government's protracted showdown with Livingstone was in some respects the mirror image of its confrontation with Scargill. 'Red Ken' too was defeated in the end. But whereas Scargill's blatant contempt for democracy dissipated public sympathy for the miners' cause, Livingstone by skilful public relations contrived to make corrupt and extravagant municipal socialism appear a great deal more popular than it really was and successfully cast Mrs Thatcher as the enemy of democracy for abolishing it. The GLC and six other metropolitan councils outside London were finally wound up in 1986, removing another focus of opposition to the Government's centralising hegemony. But the abolition of London-wide local government was another messy operation which left a sour taste in the mouth and an uneasy democratic void which was not made good for fifteen years. The fact that Lady Thatcher barely mentions this battle in her memoirs suggests that she felt in retrospect not very proud of it herself.

Scrapping the metropolitan councils, however, was just one part of a wider assault on local government which ran all through Mrs Thatcher's three administrations, starting with Michael Heseltine's efforts to control local spending in her first term and ending with the fiasco of the poll tax in her third. The second term began with the new Environment Secretary, Patrick Jenkin, introducing legislation – which Heseltine had previously rejected – to place a statutory ceiling on the amounts that local authorities could raise from the rates. This, though targeted at allegedly spendthrift Labour councils, seriously infringed what had hitherto been a hallowed Conservative principle, the autonomy of local government; it was vehemently opposed by a phalanx of senior party figures excluded or purged from Mrs Thatcher's Cabinet – Ted Heath, Geoffrey Rippon, Francis Pym and others. The same group, strongly supported in the Lords, led a powerful all-party and cross-bench opposition to the abolition of the GLC and later to the poll tax. Whatever the case for each of these measures – and there were respectable arguments for all of them – the determination with which Mrs Thatcher pursued them in defiance of long-standing Conservative principle and practice suggests a degree of hostility to local government that requires some explanation.

Margaret Thatcher grew up in local government. She always claimed that she 'owed everything' to her father; and Alfred Roberts' whole life was local politics. From her early childhood until long after she left home he was a Grantham town councillor and chairman of the finance committee, for one year mayor and latterly an alderman. Certainly he followed international affairs as well, and stimulated his daughter's interest in them; but his status in the town depended on his twenty-year stint as 'Grantham's Chancellor of the Exchequer', battling to hold down – but sometimes also defending his decision to put up – the rates, and he used to take Margaret with him to see his various committees at work. Thus she was steeped from an early age in the day-to-day re-alities of local government. It is therefore striking that from the moment she got away to Oxford, moved out of Alfred's orbit and embarked on her own political career, she showed not merely no interest in local government but a positive antipathy towards it. This is not just a retro-spective judgement. When as a newly elected backbencher in 1959 she won the chance to pilot her own private member's Bill through the Commons, the cause she chose to take up was a measure to force coun-cils to open their proceedings to the press. During discussions with the Ministry of Housing, one of the officials she had to deal with noted presciently that 'Mrs Thatcher is obsessed with the minority of coun-cils who might act irresponsibly', rather than with 'the great majority . . . whose relations with the press are basically satisfactory'.

> I could not help thinking that it was a pity that a Bill of such impor-
> tance to local authorities should be in the hands of a private member,
> whose knowledge of local government is limited, and who clearly
> holds a low opinion of local authorities, their members and officials.[69]

That low opinion was confirmed by her experience as Education Secretary in the early 1970s when she was obliged to work closely with local-education authorities, most of which – Conservative as much as Labour – were set on a policy of comprehensivisation of schools which she instinctively disliked but was largely powerless to prevent. That policy set her at odds with her own local councillors in Finchley. Ten years later her agent still found it inadvisable to schedule meet-ings with them:

Allowing her to sit round the same table would have ended with blood on the floor, and it would not have been hers. That they are Tory councillors matters little to her. She cannot see a councillor, let alone a bunch of them, without the conviction rising rapidly in her that they could be running their council under a much stricter financial regime.[70]

Whatever might have been the case in her father's day, she believed by the 1970s that local government had become inefficient, extravagant and unrepresentative. As successive governments piled more and more functions and responsibilities onto them, she thought that local authorities had become both too big and intrinsically socialistic, providing all sorts of previously undreamed-of services and bleeding the ratepayers − not usually the same people as the recipients − to pay for them. 'I suppose we need them,' she once acknowledged − 'with a resigned sigh' − to Kenneth Baker.[71] But increasingly, as Prime Minister, she saw local authorities (of whatever political colour) as obstacles blocking the implementation of Thatcherite policies of privatisation, deregulation and consumer choice. Hence the thrust of her Government's policies across the whole range of service provision was to take responsibility away from local authorities to give it instead to other agencies, private enterprise or central government. Not only did rate-capping deprive councils of the autonomy to set their own budgets, but in each individual area of policy their powers were progressively circumscribed. Housing departments were not only forced to sell their housing stock but forbidden to use the proceeds to replace it. Schools were encouraged to opt out of the control of education authorities. Bus services were privatised. Services like cleaning, refuse collection, school meals and swimming pools were required to be put out to competitive tendering. David Young's new youth-training schemes were no longer run by the Department of Education through local authorities, but by the Manpower Services Commission. Geoffrey Howe's Enterprise Zones, Michael Heseltine's regeneration of Liverpool and the redevelopment of London's docklands were promoted directly by Whitehall, through Urban Development Corporations, bypassing the local authorities. Elsewhere City Action schemes and remedial housing projects were promoted by the Department of the Environment through its own agencies, not local planning departments. It has been calculated that more than fifty separate Acts of Parliament between 1979 and 1989 directly reduced the powers of local government; and the process continued after 1990.[72]

In this way, by an accumulation of *ad hoc* policies over ten years,

Mrs Thatcher undermined the vitality and the very purpose of local government. The Government claimed that it was returning power to individuals and consumers, breaking the power of town-hall empires of self-serving local politicians and politicised council officers, particularly in housing and education. Undoubtedly there were abuses, particularly in London where Labour councillors in one borough were frequently employed as housing or race-relations officers in another. Mrs Thatcher was fond of quoting a tag from Dostoevsky, drawn to her attention by Robert Conquest, that 'Socialism is the feudalism of the future';[73] and it was unquestionably true that Labour councils in deprived inner cities fostered an anti-business ethos and a culture of benefit dependency which actually perpetuated poverty. That said, however, the practical effect of her policies was to use the abuse of local government as an excuse to diminish it still further, concentrating power ever more centrally on Whitehall. This contradicted a long Tory tradition, going back to Burke or further, of backing the local against the central power. With the rise of socialism in the twentieth century, fear of the overmighty state had become an even stronger article of Conservative faith. Tory councils in the 1960s and 1970s had seen themselves as bastions of liberty against the creeping interference of Whitehall. But the Tory Government of the 1980s, finding itself opposed by some high-profile socialist authorities in the cities, reversed this tradition. Behind her libertarian rhetoric, Mrs Thatcher's instinct to impose her views was authoritarian, interventionist and essentially centralising.

In diminishing the autonomy of local government she damaged many of the values which Conservatives – herself included – had always stood for: local pride, local responsibility, dispersed power, and a tradition of active local government going back to Joe and Neville Chamberlain in Birmingham. This was the complaint of someone like Francis Pym, with deep family roots in Cambridgeshire back to the seventeenth century, who warned in *The Politics of Consent* that while no Conservative worried about how Patrick Jenkin might use his new powers, 'many of us are most apprehensive about what a future Government might do with them'.[74] Mrs Thatcher often seemed to proceed on the assumption that there would never be another Labour Government. But it was not only shire Tories like Pym who were alarmed that their Government was destroying something precious: Tory radicals who were the strongest supporters of free-market economic policies were even more suspicious of the state gathering to itself ever greater power. If Mrs Thatcher thought she was serving democracy by weakening local government, she should have been reminded of Friedrich Hayek's warning in *The Road to Serfdom*: 'Nowhere has democracy worked well without a great measure of local self-government, providing a school of political training for the people at large as much as for their future leaders.'[75] Principle aside, this was a factor of direct practical relevance to the Conservative party, whose local organisation was largely based in local government. With so few significant powers left to local councils by the end of the 1980s, fewer able and public-spirited people came forward to serve on them, while activism at the grass roots of the party shrivelled. Thus when the triumphs of her General Election victories had passed away she left her successors a much weakened – and ageing – power base.

The question remains why she was so hostile to local government. Was it just a by-product of her overriding determination to control public spending? Did it reflect an authoritarian temperament – a compulsion to control coupled with a growing intolerance of opposition? Or does at least part of the explanation lie deeper, back in Grantham and her relationship with her father? One of those who witnessed at close hand her irrational, almost visceral dislike of local government was Janet Young, the long-time leader of Oxford City Council, elevated to the Lords by Heath in 1971 and the only other woman to sit (briefly) in Mrs Thatcher's Cabinet from 1981 to 1983. Lady Young ascribed what she calls Mrs Thatcher's 'absolute hang-up about local government' to the Grantham Labour group's ousting of Alfred Roberts from his position as alderman in 1952.[76] It is true that in a television interview with Miriam Stoppard in 1985 Mrs Thatcher famously wept as she recalled this episode. The Freudian Leo Abse, too, sees the abolition of the GLC as her revenge for the action of the Grantham Labour group thirty years before.[77] But this is narrow and unconvincing. It was all local government she hated, not just Labour councils. It makes more sense to see her determined assault on local government as a rejection – perhaps unconscious – of Alfred himself, in delayed revenge for her repressed and joyless childhood. For all her posthumous idealisation of Alfred, the truth is that as soon as she was able to leave home she put as much distance as she could between herself and her family, rarely returned to Grantham, abandoned her parents' Methodism and saw her father – though he lived until 1970 – remarkably infrequently. Undoubtedly Alfred taught her a lot (above all the habit of hard work) and she inherited many, though by no means all, of his beliefs. But it is hard to see the determination with which she set about dismantling the sphere of government to which her father devoted his life as an act of filial reverence. It was surely the reverse.

The pretext for the Government's determination to shackle local government was that its spending was out of control. At a time when the Treasury was trying to cut public spending by requiring painful economies from every department in Whitehall, local government was responsible for around a quarter of total national expenditure, which the Government could not directly control. In fact local-government extravagance was a myth. Local expenditure rose less rapidly in the early 1980s than central-government spending (though this can partly be explained by the high cost of unemployment to the Treasury, as well as by the Government's electoral commitments to the NHS and to defence). Indeed in real terms and as a proportion of total public spending, local-authority spending actually fell slightly between 1980 and 1983.[78] Heseltine's controls − cutting the rate-support grant and penalising authorities which exceeded set targets − were very effective: the great majority of councils kept within them and cut their budgets substantially, only to find that their grants were cut again the following year. The impression that local spending was out of control was almost entirely derived from a few highly publicised Labour councils − including the GLC, Merseyside and West Midlands − in areas with serious social problems which believed they had a mandate to defend services by resisting 'Tory cuts'. It was more than balanced by restraint elsewhere. The truth is that the Government was considerably more successful in squeezing local spending than it was in cutting its own.★

London was actually a special case, where most of the overspend was due to subsidising a 32 per cent cut in fares on London Transport. Cleverly marketed as 'Fares Fair', this was a popular and not particularly left-wing policy which had figured prominently in Labour's 1981 manifesto. It was not unmanageably extravagant until it fell foul of Heseltine's penalties on councils which exceeded Whitehall spending limits, which deprived Livingstone's GLC of £111 million on which the previous Tory administration had budgeted. There was no thought that it would be declared illegal until Lord Denning and two other judges in the Court of Appeal unexpectedly ruled in favour of Bromley borough council − a Tory-controlled suburb whose residents derived little benefit from London Transport − that the subsidy was 'unbusinesslike' and breached the GLC's duty to balance its budget. The House

---

★The effects of relentless economies were evident in the closure of baths and lavatories, reduced opening hours of libraries and poor maintenance of all sorts of local amenities. An inquiry into the rundown state of public parks in 2001 specifically blamed the lack of investment since 1980:[79] and the same pattern was visible across the whole range of public provision.

of Lords agreed, forcing the GLC reluctantly to double fares again – that is, to raise them 36 per cent above their original level.

'Fares Fair' aside, there is no question that Livingstone was provocatively left-wing. From the moment Labour won the May 1981 elections he declared his intention of using the GLC as a platform to oppose the Government more effectively than the party was able to do in Parliament. As well as displaying the ever-rising London unemployment figure on the roof of County Hall, he also provided beds in County Hall for participants in the so-called 'People's March for Jobs' when they reached London from the north of England. Unlike other councils, the GLC had little responsibility for housing (most of its large estates having been already devolved to the boroughs) or for social services; but Livingstone and his allies made up for this by making grants to all sorts of social groups – single mothers, battered wives, gays and lesbians, ethnic minorities, anti-racist and anti-nuclear protesters – which attracted huge derision in the Tory press. In fact these grants never amounted to more than about 2 per cent of the GLC's budget; but they soon came to epitomise the impression of reckless spending for frivolous or subversive purposes which the Government had a duty to stop. More offensive still, Livingstone also breached the party consensus on Northern Ireland by defending Sinn Fein and implicitly the IRA, accusing Britain of pursuing a policy of murder and intimidation against Catholics – a charge which Mrs Thatcher described as 'the most disgraceful statement I have ever read'[80] – and advocating British withdrawal from the province as the only way to stop the bombs in London. In July 1981 he entertained the mother of one of the republican hunger strikers at County Hall, and in 1983 he shared a press conference with Gerry Adams, insisting that Sinn Fein/IRA were not 'criminals or lunatics', but politicians with a legitimate agenda to rid their country of a colonial regime. By comparing Britain's oppression of Ireland with Hitler's treatment of the Jews, however, he merely confirmed his reputation as a posturing extremist. The *Sun* dubbed him 'the most odious man in Britain'.[81]

More seriously, the GLC was politically corrupt. No one ever suggested that Livingstone and his colleagues lined their own pockets. But they made a policy of providing well-paid jobs on the GLC payroll for an army of sympathetic activists and left-wing councillors in Lambeth, Islington and other boroughs; they used the award of grants to all sorts of pressure groups and social-support groups as a blatant means of buying votes; and they spent public money freely on political advertising campaigns, many of them nothing to do with London, characterised by the Tories as 'propaganda on the rates'. If they did not overstep the boundary of what was legal they certainly blurred it. As Livingstone's biographer John Carvel put it, 'The problem had more to do with political morality than so-called overspending.'[82]

Mrs Thatcher's real objective all along was the abolition of the rates. But that was repeatedly denied by the inability of the Department of the Environment to come up with a satisfactory alternative. Instead, at the Prime Minister's personal insistence, the 1983 manifesto promised two major initiatives to curb the excesses of local government. The first, giving the Government statutory power to cap the level of rates that any council might raise, was introduced by a reluctant Patrick Jenkin in December. His officials were no more enthusiastic. 'What would you do if your minister had just ordered you to abolish local democracy?' Terry Heiser, then a deputy secretary in the DoE, asked Simon Jenkins.[83] Of course he swallowed his doubts and got on with it – so effectively that he became Permanent Secretary the following year. The Bill was denounced by Heath and Rippon in the Commons and encountered serious opposition in the Lords, but nevertheless became law in July 1984 when Jenkin immediately invoked its provisions to impose a cap on eighteen authorities: sixteen Labour but also – to deflect charges of partisanship – two Conservative. There followed a great battle of brinkmanship as a dozen of the rate-capped councils, including the GLC, Lambeth and Liverpool, defied the Government and threatened not to set a budget for 1985–6. Liverpool held out longest, until dramatically denounced by Neil Kinnock at the Labour Party conference as a prelude to purging Militant from the Labour party. But the posturing of the far left played into the Government's hands. At the 1984 party conference, Mrs Thatcher claimed that the Government was merely 'reasserting Parliament's ultimate responsibility for controlling the total burden of taxation on our citizens, whether levied by central or local government'.[84] Thus the independence of local government was quietly extinguished.

Much more contentious was the proposed abolition of the GLC and the six other metropolitan counties of Greater Manchester, Merseyside, South Yorkshire, Tyne and Wear, West Midlands and West Yorkshire. The inclusion of the latter in a *putsch* really aimed at the GLC aroused surprisingly little protest. The metropolitan counties were much less extravagant than the GLC, but they had also had less time to put down roots, having only been created by Peter Walker's reorganisation of local government under Heath in 1973, and were widely perceived as a wasteful and unnecessary tier of bureaucracy. Moreover their abolition merely handed their functions back to the old city corporations – Manchester, Liverpool, Leeds, Newcastle, Birmingham and Sheffield –

which had discharged them before. The GLC by contrast was to be replaced by nothing above the level of the thirty-two London boroughs.

The case for abolishing the GLC was that it had very few substantial powers. Housing had already been devolved to the boroughs, as was responsibility for most roads (except major trunk roads) and education in the outer boroughs. Education in the inner boroughs was run by the Inner London Education Authority (ILEA) – a separate body, though composed of many of the same people. The Metropolitan Police came directly under the Home Secretary, the docks under the Port of London Authority and water supply under the Thames Water Authority. After the 'Fares Fair' controversy the Government was already in the process of taking London Transport out of the GLC's remit, too. Nevertheless it still retained responsibility for refuse disposal, the London ambulance service and the fire brigade, main roads and traffic management, and above all strategic planning for the capital, involving long-term questions of population, employment and transport. These functions were not enough, perhaps, to occupy an authority of the size and ambition of Livingstone's regime in County Hall. But they had to be discharged – particularly transport – on a London-wide basis and the proposal to abolish London-wide government altogether struck most Londoners as crude and vindictive. Both Michael Heseltine and his successor Tom King had opposed the suggestion before June 1983; and both Patrick Jenkin, who was now put in charge of it, and Kenneth Baker, who was appointed to assist him in September 1984 and replaced him a year later, were on record as having previously advocated a stronger GLC. Abolition was seen, correctly, as the Prime Minister's personal *fiat*.

It is clear that she thought the GLC would be an easy target. There was every reason to believe that not just 'loony left' councils, pilloried daily in the Tory press, but local government itself was far from popular. In 1983 an opinion poll carried out for NALGO, the main local-government trade union, found that local government was generally seen as 'wasteful and politically motivated', social workers were 'poorly regarded' and the privatisation of council services was widely welcomed.[85] Such polls gave some sort of cover to the Government's action. Yet in the event the GLC turned out to have a surprising hold on public affection, for a number of reasons. First, the policy of subsidising bus and tube fares – as happened in practically every other capital city in the world – was generally recognised to be a sensible way of tackling London's transport problem at a time when public transport was underused and traffic congestion was becoming chronic. Second, despite his demonisation by the Tory press, Ken Livingstone was a skilful media performer who came across as a disarmingly engaging character – quite unlike the strutting Scargill. Third, the clumsy way the Government set about the task of abolition was exposed by the GLC's unexpected deployment of a brilliant advertising campaign devised by the firm of Boase Massimi Pollitt at a cost of £14 million (plus another £11 million for other campaigns advertising GLC services, which served the same function). At least until rate-capping took effect, the GLC had money to spend on these campaigns because, ironically, it had evaded Heseltine's spending controls. By reluctantly accepting the legal judgement against 'Fares Fair', agreeing to double fares and repaying the £125 million deficit incurred in 1982–3 from the heavy rate increase imposed in 1982, Livingstone gained himself money to burn in 1983–4 and 1984–5, with only a modest rate increase in 1983 and an actual *cut* (of 7.5 per cent) in 1984. In this way, exploiting the tortuous arithmetic of local-government support, Livingstone's GLC 'escaped the trap in which almost every other Labour authority was caught'.[86] It was over-spending way above Heseltine's target – contributing £301 million (and the ILEA another £97 million) to the total overspend of £770 million by all English local authorities – but until rate-capping came into force there was nothing the Government could do.

The Government's major blunder was to try to cancel the GLC elections due in May 1985. The difficulty ministers faced was that they could not put the complex legislation to abolish the seven councils through all its parliamentary stages before 1986. With the Government likely to be suffering a mid-term dip in popularity, elections in 1985 would be liable to produce – as in 1981 – Labour gains, which would be interpreted as a vote against abolition just as the Bill was going through Parliament. The obvious course would have been to extend the term of the existing GLC for a few more months; in fact this was Mrs Thatcher's initial instinct. But Jenkin thought it would look ridiculous to start the process of terminating the GLC by prolonging its life. Instead he proposed to scrap the elections and replace the elected councillors for the transitional period with temporary stand-ins nominated by the boroughs, who would have been predominantly Tory. Unwisely Mrs Thatcher allowed herself to be persuaded, arguing in the House that 'it would clearly be wrong to prolong a mandate after it had been exhausted'.[87] 'If the Iron Lady had stuck to her gut instincts,' John Carvel commented, 'she would have avoided what was probably the worst humiliation of her administration.'[88] As it was, the decision to introduce what was known as the Paving Bill – to pave the way for abolition by scrapping the 1985 elections – provoked a storm of criticism that the Government was suspending democracy.

It was this denial of democracy which gave the GLC the opening for its highly effective advertising campaign urging Londoners to 'Say No to No Say'. One poster showed a picture of the Houses of Parliament with the question 'What kind of place is it that takes away your right to vote and leaves you with no say?' Another featured a ballot box in the shape of a dustbin. The agency not only covered London with these posters, but evaded restrictions on political advertising on television by placing adverts behind the goals at an England–Romania football match televised from Bucharest. The campaign struck a chord with people who had no liking for Livingstone's politics. Ted Heath once again led the protests in the Commons with a powerful speech charging that the Bill, by proposing to change the complexion of London government without elections, 'lays the Conservative party open to the charge of the greatest gerrymandering in the last 150 years'.[89] Nineteen mainly senior Tories joined him in voting against the Bill on Second Reading on 11 April and several more abstained; but this was only enough to cut the Government's majority to ninety-three. The Lords, however, proved less tractable: their lordships objected to being asked to vote hypothetically for a measure that assumed the passage of another Bill which had not yet been presented. By means of a three-line whip bringing in the largest attendance since the 1971 vote on joining the EEC, the Government just squeaked through Second Reading, on 11 June, by 237 votes to 217. On this occasion Bertie Denham, the Government Chief Whip in the Lords, was able to mobilise the hereditary peers, who voted 178–53 for the Government. But he could not demand the same turn-out twice. Two weeks later, when his appeals faced impossible competition from Wimbledon, Henley and the Lords Test Match, a wrecking amendment was carried by 191 to 143, with forty Tory peers present but abstaining. The Government was forced to back down and agree to extend the life of the existing GLC for another eleven months after all, saving what face it could by placing additional restrictions on what it could do in its final phase.[90]

Jenkin's folly, the *Daily Express* marvelled, had let Red Ken pose as 'the champion of the British Constitution – courtesy of the Peerage – and the friend of democracy'.[91] Whereas in January already half of Londoners had opposed the abolition of the GLC, by September that figure had risen to 74 per cent.[92] Mrs Thatcher let Jenkin take the blame, distancing herself from the defeat by declaring that the Lords had actually improved the Bill, as though the proposed scrapping of the elections had been nothing to do with her.[93] Afraid that Jenkin was losing the propaganda war – she writes scathingly in her memoirs of his 'inability to put over a case'[94] – she moved Kenneth Baker, a much smoother communicator, into the DoE to be his number two, and eventually to replace him. 'I put him in to defeat Ken Livingstone,' she told Woodrow Wyatt in 1986, 'and I believe he did.'[95] But in fact the only thing that defeated Livingstone was the passage of Jenkin's second Bill.

Meanwhile the deferral of the GLC's demise posed a potential embarrassment in her own constituency. The local GLC councillor for Finchley, Neville Beale, had intended to retire in 1985. But the last thing Mrs Thatcher wanted at that moment was a by-election in Finchley which would have turned into a media circus and a mid-term referendum on herself. So she summoned Beale to a private lunch in the flat at Number Ten where, *tête-à-tête* until joined by their agent, she alternately charmed and bullied him into promising to stay on.[96]

The Government then faced further battles on the substantive abolition Bill, an unwieldy monster of ninety-eight clauses and seventeen supplementary schedules which took up much of the 1984–5 session. Once again attention focused on London. Critics seized on the fact that abolition would leave the capital the only major city in the world without its own elected government and charged that the Government had completely failed to make the case for it. Far from saving £100 million a year as ministers asserted, abolition would result in so much duplication of services that it would actually cost something like £225 million over the first five years.[97] The provision of strategic services would still need to be co-ordinated across the metropolis, while none of the GLC's functions was actually being abolished: they were merely reassigned between the thirty-one boroughs, the City of London, five Government departments and a bewildering array of unelected quangos and committees.

Heath led the usual small, heavyweight but ineffectual vote against the Bill on Second Reading on 4 December. But a much more serious rebellion formed around an amendment, taken on the floor of the House, to replace the GLC with some form of new elected authority with powers yet to be decided. More than a hundred Tories either supported this amendment or abstained; the Government's majority fell to just twenty-three. Mrs Thatcher was unmoved, rejecting any sort of replacement GLC as merely creating a 'son of Frankenstein'.[98] But her arguments were becoming a little strained. In an interview with the *Evening Standard* she maintained that London 'is not and never has been an entity as such'; and a moment later that 'London does not belong just to Londoners . . . London belongs to the United Kingdom, so there is nothing illogical about abolishing the GLC.'[99] Off the record she frankly acknowledged her true motivation. 'Rebel Labour authorities,' she told Tory councillors in March, 'had to be defeated and put down', and she was reported to have 'compared their actions with those of some miners'.[100] The Bill's opponents in the Lords inflicted several more defeats on detailed amendments relating to the disposal of functions after abolition, forcing Jenkin to make a number of concessions, including a joint committee of boroughs to provide some co-ordination. On the main point, however, the Government got its way and the Act received the Royal Assent on 16 July. The GLC spent its last eight months defiantly spending yet more money to preserve as many favoured schemes as possible, but was finally abolished on 31 March 1986 with a great street party outside County Hall and fireworks on the river costing £250,000.

The claims and counterclaims about whether abolishing the GLC saved or cost money have never been authoritatively resolved. The Government eventually suggested that abolition saved £50 million a year (rather than the £100 million predicted).[101] But that figure ignores generous rate-support settlements and increased subsidies to London Transport in the first few years to cover the transition. All the same functions still had to be administered and, after all the tabloid ridicule, all but ninety-three of the 2,500 voluntary groups that the GLC had subsidised continued to be supported.[102] The immediate impact was cushioned by the Lawson boom and the 'Big Bang', when London seemed to be thriving. The recession of the early 1990s, however, told a different story. Increasingly the lack of strategic planning and investment in the capital became obvious as the infrastructure, particularly of transport, visibly decayed while traffic congestion and pollution worsened. While the French Government was spending £400 million a year on the Paris metro, the London Underground had to make do with just £60–70 million.[103] No new tube lines were commissioned, no fast Heathrow link, no link to the new Channel tunnel. 'The Thatcher government abolished London's governing body,' the historian Roy Porter wrote in 1994, 'and looked to market forces as the fairy godmother.'[104] But they did not deliver. In 1997 a report by the Rowntree Foundation explicitly blamed London's inability to tackle its problems on the lack of co-ordination between the boroughs, central government and fifty unelected quangos.[105]

After the abolition of the GLC, London possessed neither a forum for the discussion of its problems, nor a single voice to speak for it. A huge amount of shared expertise built up over decades, inherited by the GLC from the old LCC, was thrown away; while mayors, fire officers, educationists and environmentalists from other world cities had no counterpart in London to speak to. Some people, like Simon

Jenkins, argue that the removal of the upper tier stimulated healthy diversity and a burst of local innovation in the boroughs. 'Westminster and Wandsworth became leaders in municipal privatisation. Camden and Islington took more trouble over their appearance. Pedestrian and traffic management schemes mushroomed over the capital.'[106] The opposite view, maintained by Roy Porter, is that 'the balkanisation of the metropolis encouraged rotten boroughs, political localism and extremism of all stripes', the Labour lunacies of Lambeth and Hackney fully matched by Lady Porter's high-handed rule in Westminster.[107] Both agree, however, that the lack of a central planning authority was a gap which the boroughs could not fill.

The GLC was not perfect: everyone – even Ken Livingstone – is agreed about that. Its already diminished powers were out of scale with its size, and it had become corrupt and overblown. Though many of its controversial policies no longer look so 'loony' twenty years later, Livingstone and his allies unquestionably abused the opportunity it offered for political posturing. But a major capital like London needs both a strategic planning body and accountable leadership. The GLC as constituted in 1983 was not functioning well in either role; but simply abolishing it because it was – as Norman Tebbit frankly put it – 'Labour-dominated, high-spending and at odds with the Government's view of the world'[108] was a short-sighted act of political spite which left behind worse problems than it solved. Fifteen years later the vacuum had to be filled. The incoming Labour Government decided to fill it with a slimmed-down assembly and a directly elected mayor. Nothing shows more clearly what the people of London thought about the destruction of the GLC than the fact that they immediately took great pleasure in electing as the first occupant of that office an older and more moderate Ken Livingstone. At the time this was generally seen as a slap in the face for Tony Blair, whose own candidate was overwhelmingly rejected. But it was really a delayed retort to Mrs Thatcher. The whirligig of time on this occasion brought in a very appropriate revenge.

Spies, moles and 'wimmin'

Behind the open political challenges of Scargill and Livingstone, Mrs Thatcher believed that her Government – and the country – also faced a persistent threat from a variegated coalition of left-wing dissidents, subversives and fellow-travellers, all more or less knowingly serving the interests of the Soviet Union, which must be countered by all means necessary in the cause of Freedom. Believing that she was engaged in a life-or-death struggle with the forces of evil both at home and abroad, she took very seriously anything which could be seen as a threat to national defence or the armed forces. 'Most Prime Ministers,' Nigel Lawson wrote in his memoirs, 'have a soft spot for the security services, for which they have a special responsibility. But Margaret, an avid reader of the works of Frederick Forsyth, was positively besotted by them.'[109] In fact some Prime Ministers – Heath and Callaghan, for instance – have taken a fairly relaxed view of the alarming intelligence that the security services continually churn out. Of Mrs Thatcher's recent predecessors, Harold Wilson was the one whose obsession with security most nearly matched her own; but he was worried much of the time that the security services were spying on him. Mrs Thatcher by contrast – guided at first by Airey Neave, later by Maurice Oldfield of MI6 and a number of unofficial 'voices' from the intelligence world, like Brian Crozier – had no doubt that she and they were fighting the same global enemy, and she welcomed enthusiastically all the help MI5 and MI6 could give her. She read all the intelligence reports with close attention, and after the Falklands became the first Prime Minister to attend meetings of the Joint Intelligence Committee, now located in the Cabinet Office.

It cannot really be said that the women's 'peace camp' at Greenham Common posed a serious threat to national security. The 1983 election had delivered a resounding defeat to nuclear unilateralism, which was quite clearly a massive vote-loser for the Labour party. Nevertheless CND continued to march and campaign vigorously against nuclear weapons, while a few hundred heroically determined women kept up their stubborn vigil outside the US base in Oxfordshire where the first cruise missiles arrived at the end of the year, making occasional attempts to breach the perimeter before they were ejected. Their protest was ramshackle, eccentric, idealistic and very British, but essentially futile. In the Commons Mrs Thatcher worried that 'such protests tend to give the impression to the Soviet Union that this country has neither the capacity nor the resolve to defend itself or to keep defence expenditure at a sufficient level to deter';[110] and in a television interview with Brian Walden she sighed: 'I do wish people . . . would understand there's no public opinion in the Soviet Union.'[111] Fighting for Freedom with a capital F, she was not so keen to see that freedom exercised. But in fact nothing burnished her Iron Lady image more effectively than the contrast between herself, with her immaculate hair and powerful suits, and the woolly hatted feminists and mystical tree-huggers of the peace camp. She gloried in the contrast, confident that on this issue at least Middle England identified overwhelmingly with her.

Yet the women of the peace camp and other CND supporters were subjected to continual surveillance and harassment by the police and MI5. Not only was the camp itself frequently raided and broken up, but activists' phones were tapped, their mail was opened and several suffered mysterious break-ins at their homes – leaving aside the still-unsolved murder of an elderly rose-grower of strong unilateralist convictions named Hilda Murrell. 'The use made of civil servants and the security services to monitor and harass nuclear dissidents,' one respected journalist wrote in 1995, 'would have been excessive had Thatcherite Britain been in a state of virtual war; in a peaceful country it was unforgivable.'[112] Nor was it only nuclear dissidents who were targeted. MI5 infiltrated NUM headquarters during the miners' strike and made unprecedented use of bugging and phone-tapping to track the deployment of pickets. In 1985 it emerged that MI5 had also been asked to vet senior figures in the BBC; in January 1987 the police actually raided the Glasgow offices of the BBC and confiscated material relating to a series of programmes the Government did not like. The centralisation of policing during the miners' strike; persistent allegations that the RUC and the security forces were operating a shoot-to-kill policy in Northern Ireland; the removal of union rights from workers at GCHQ; and a new readiness to use the Official Secrets Act to pursue civil servants who leaked embarrassing documents – all created a disturbing sense of an authoritarian government using unprecedentedly heavy-handed methods to suppress what it regarded as dangerous dissent.

The first prosecution was of a junior MoD clerk named Sarah Tisdall, who was given a six-month sentence in March 1984 for passing to the *Guardian* an unclassified document relating to the arrival of cruise missiles at Greenham Common. The second, more serious case was that of a middle-ranking MoD official, Clive Ponting, who leaked to Tam Dalyell evidence that Michael Heseltine had misled the House to cover Mrs Thatcher's inaccuracies about the sinking of the *General Belgrano*. Prosecuted under the Official Secrets Act, Ponting claimed that he had acted in the public interest; and to the Government's fury he was acquitted in February 1985 by a jury which rejected the judge's direction that the national interest was whatever the Government said it was and found that no breach of national security had been committed. In the House Mrs Thatcher curtly accepted the verdict – 'of course I do, I always have' – but still insisted that confidentiality between ministers and their officials must be absolute.[113]

Though Tory spokesmen had regularly criticised the 1911 Act in opposition – particularly the catch-all Section 2 under which any information down to the colour of the toilet paper in the Welsh Office could be classified as secret – Mrs Thatcher in office showed no disposition to reform it. Willie Whitelaw made a half-hearted attempt in 1979 which was overtaken by the Blunt affair. Thereafter Mrs Thatcher rejected any thought of liberalisation: much as she admired most things American, she specifically opposed anything like the American Freedom of Information Act.[114] 'I don't know why you're always banging on about open government,' one Cabinet minister told Peter Hennessy. 'She doesn't believe in open government for the Cabinet, let alone people like you.'[115] The failure of the Ponting prosecution convinced her rather that the existing legislation should be tightened up. But she was still in no hurry until a libertarian Tory MP, Richard Shepherd, forced the issue by introducing a private member's Bill in 1988. The Government imposed a three-line whip to defeat Shepherd's Bill, then introduced its own. Douglas Hurd's 1989 Act scrapped the discredited Section 2, only to replace it with tighter restrictions on information relating to defence, international relations, the security services and the police. It expressly denied Ponting's 'public interest' defence. Though many areas of government – social services, Treasury matters, even the nuclear-power industry – were in theory opened up, the effect in practice was to tighten secrecy where it mattered. Critics pointed out that under the new provisions the Thames Television programme *Death on the Rock* – which the Government tried to suppress in 1988 – could not have been made.

The Government also appeared needlessly authoritarian by its efforts to block publication of the memoirs of a retired MI5 officer, Peter Wright. There is no question that the book, *Spycatcher*, was a serious breach of the confidentiality expected of secret-service personnel; the Government was thoroughly entitled to ban it, as it had done many less sensational books before. The problem was that Wright was now living in Australia and he published his book there, as well as in Ireland and America, whence its contents quickly became available in Britain; extracts even appeared in the British press. Trying to stop its publication now was a classic case of shutting the stable door after the horse had bolted. The Government case was also weakened by the fact that it had earlier – in a brief burst of openness following the Blunt affair – given the green light to a book by Chapman Pincher alleging that Sir Roger Hollis, the head of MI5 from 1956 to 1965, had been a Soviet agent. Wright had been Pincher's principal source. Nevertheless Mrs Thatcher was determined to pursue *Spycatcher* – 'irrespective of the outcome' – in order to assert the principle that former spies could not with impunity write about their experiences.[116] She even sent Robert Armstrong, in a questionable extension of the normal function of the Cabinet Secretary, to plead the case in the Australian courts. In vain.

Both the Supreme Court of New South Wales and eventually the House of Lords ruled that it was too late to keep secret what everyone who was interested had already read. The Government's persistence long after the cause was lost merely made it appear stubborn and vindictive.

Faith in the City

Mrs Thatcher did not see enemies only in the shadows. She believed that the very pillars of the establishment were against her. She considered that the whole professional class – the upper middle-class liberal intelligentsia and the distinguished generation of public servants collectively anatomised by Noël Annan as 'Our Age' – was riddled with a sort of pale-pink socialism which was scarcely less corrosive than outright Trotskyism. Of course she made exceptions of individuals: but her instinctive preconception was that the whole traditional governing elite was made up predominantly of quislings and appeasers.

This liberal Establishment had several centres, only one of which – the Civil Service – was under her direct control. Over her decade in office she made a systematic effort, by a mixture of patronage and example, to mould the Whitehall village to her view of the world, and to a considerable extent succeeded. Four other centres of influence, however, remained more or less independent and overwhelmingly resistant to the Thatcherite gospel: the churches (particularly the Church of England); the universities; the broadcasters (particularly the BBC); and the arts community. Together these overlapping elites comprised what used to be called the political nation; nowadays sociologists classify them as 'opinion formers', while the tabloids call them the 'chattering classes'. All felt themselves under attack by a Conservative Government which was out of sympathy with all their values and assumptions. Seen from Downing Street, conversely, they were all faces of the same hydra-headed enemy which Mrs Thatcher believed she had been called to office to defeat.

More publicly than any other recent Prime Minister before Tony Blair, Mrs Thatcher was a practising Christian. Alec Home, Harold Wilson and Ted Heath had all in their different styles professed to be believers; but Mrs Thatcher advertised the religious basis of her politics more than any of them. She not only attended the parish church near Chequers most Sundays when she was there, but she never shied from asserting what she believed should be the central place of Christianity in national life. It is impossible to know the exact nature of her personal faith. She once told an interviewer that she prayed 'when she had need of it';[117] and on another occasion told John Humphrys that 'the fundamental reason of being put on earth is so to improve your character that you are fit for the next world'.[118] But she was steeped in the language and practice of Christianity from childhood and believed in it implicitly as a force for good. 'I doubt if she was a very religious person in terms of strong beliefs,' one of her closest colleagues wrote, 'but she believed passionately in the Christian morality.'[119]* She still enjoyed reading theological books – she told David Frost in 1988 that her recent reading had included works by Cardinal Hume, C. S. Lewis, Stuart Blanch (the former Archbishop of York) and the Chief Rabbi – and in 1987 she started rereading the Old Testament from the beginning, telling her staff each day where she had got to. She even regarded herself as something of an expert in biblical exegesis, telling Frost that 'parts of the Old Testament should not be in untutored hands'.[121]

She blamed the Church, however – all the churches – for their abdication of moral leadership in the face of permissiveness and for a general loss of moral values in society. Whereas the Church of England had once been known as 'the Conservative Party at prayer', and her father's brand of Methodism had been identified with self-reliance, individual responsibility and thrift, she thought the churches had become politically wet if not actually left-wing, infected by a sort of soggy collectivism which looked to the state, instead of the individual, to solve all social ills. No one personified this sort of hand-wringing churchmanship better than the Archbishop of Canterbury, Robert Runcie, whom she appointed – in preference to the still more liberal Hugh Montefiore – soon after she became Prime Minister and who was therefore in office for almost her entire premiership. From the start Runcie did not shrink from criticising the harsh social consequences of the Government's economic policies. In his Christmas sermon in Canterbury Cathedral at the end of 1981 he condemned what he saw as a lack of compassion for the unemployed: 'hearts that have been hardened in . . . unimaginative complacency . . . contempt for working people, neglect of the hungry'.[122] Seven months later he outraged the Prime Minister in her hour of victory by his evenhandedly compassionate sermon at the Falklands thanksgiving service

---

*A story told recently by Matthew Parris suggests that she would have liked to believe, but could not quite bring herself to claim a faith she did not honestly hold. When working for her in opposition, Parris had to answer a letter from a woman who had lost her husband, wanting to know if Mrs Thatcher believed in an afterlife. He referred it to her. She responded with a letter in her own hand, carefully phrased to say precisely what she meant and no more: 'Christians believe in an afterlife, and I am a Christian.'[120]

at St Paul's, in which he prayed for all those who had fought and died on both sides, called war itself 'detestable' and condemned the arms trade into the bargain. The *Sun* called this an 'Insult to the Heroes' and reported that Mrs Thatcher was 'spitting blood'.[123] She was constrained from responding in public, partly because Runcie was a good friend of Peter Carrington and Willie Whitelaw but also because – improbably in the light of his donnish manner – he had a distinguished war record, winning the Military Cross as a tank commander, and therefore could not easily be dismissed as a pacifist wimp. Years later she was still reluctant to criticise Runcie to his biographer ('He's a very nice man'), but she admitted that she thought there should have been more thanks for the defeat of aggression in his Falklands sermon.[124]

The same year she was infuriated by the report of a Church working party, entitled *The Church and the Bomb*, which supported what she called 'one-sided disarmament' (though in fact the synod subsequently voted narrowly in favour of deterrence); and later by the Church's strenuous campaign for sanctions against South Africa. Above all, however, she faced continual criticism of the human damage wreaked by the Government's economic policies, encapsulated in a report on inner-city poverty, *Faith in the City*, published in December 1985, which an unnamed Government minister foolishly described – before it was even published – as 'pure Marxist theology'.[125] Other Tory MPs rushed to add their pennyworth: one asserted that it proved that the Church of England was run by 'a load of Communist clerics'.[126] Mrs Thatcher herself refrained from public comment, but her dim view of the report was widely leaked. What she objected to, she told Woodrow Wyatt, was the assumption that the solution to poverty lay in higher benefits. 'There is nothing about self-help or doing anything for yourself in the report.'[127] When the Bishop of Durham – and only slightly less strongly, Runcie himself – condemned the Government's confrontational handling of the miners' strike, however, she felt able to respond. It was not that she believed the Church should keep out of politics, but that she believed its politics were wrong.* 'You may have noticed,' she told

---

*Christian supporters of the Government made a concerted effort to combat this leftish Christian critique. Digby Anderson edited *The Kindness that Kills: The Churches' Simplistic Response to Complex Social Issues*, published by the IEA in 1984; Brian Griffiths (head of the Downing Street Policy Unit from 1986) defended Christian monetarism in *Monetarism and Morality: A Response to the Bishops* in 1985; and Mrs Thatcher's former PPS, Michael Alison, co-edited a collection called *Christianity and Conservatism* in 1990. In *The Path to Power* Lady Thatcher wrote that 'Near the end of my time as Prime Minister, I became increasingly . . . interested in the relationship between Christianity and economic and social policy.'[128]

the Conservative Central Council in March 1985, 'that these clerical voices have been ranging fairly confidently into the sphere of economic management with their quite detailed advice.' If they trespassed onto her territory, she was happy to pursue them onto theirs:

> Well, perhaps I may venture to refer to the parable of the talents. Those who traded with their talents, and multiplied them, were those who won approval. And the essence of their performance was their willingness to take risks to make a gain.[129]

Biblical point-scoring aside, however, she was hurt by the allegation that her policies showed a lack of compassion, and worried by the widespread impression that Christians could no longer be Conservatives. She believed absolutely the contrary. Her politics and her religion were based alike on the primacy of individual choice and individual responsibility. 'The heart of the Christian message,' she told Laurens van der Post in her 1983 television interview with her favourite mystic, 'is that each person has the right to choose.'[130] She always cited a line from one of her favourite patriotic hymns, 'I Vow to Thee, My Country', emphasising individual salvation: 'Soul by soul and silently, Her shining bounds increase.' 'Not block vote by block vote,' she spelled it out in an American interview, 'but soul by soul.'[131] She did not believe in collective morality or collective compassion, via taxation, but in individual charity – which depended on a degree of individual wealth. 'No one would remember the Good Samaritan if he'd only had good intentions,' she told Brian Walden. The important point was that 'he had money as well'.[132] At the same time it was noticeable that the hymns she liked all seemed to be the most martial ones. For instance, when asked to select one for BBC television's *Songs of Praise* in 1982 – admittedly it was for Remembrance Sunday – she chose this:

> O Valiant Hearts, who to your glory came
> Through dust of conflict and through battle flame,
> Tranquil you lie, your knightly virtue proved,
> Your memory hallowed in the land you loved.[133]

She believed passionately that in politics she was fighting for Good against Evil; and she expected the churches to be on her side, not carping from the wings and giving comfort to the enemy. She could not resist berating a CND-supporting vicar in her constituency by pointing out that his church was empty on Sundays.[134] Unless provoked, she was generally careful not to bring religion into her political speeches.[135] She recognised that many sincere Christians – like the Labour left-winger Eric Heffer – were not Tories, and knew that it would cause an outcry if she suggested that they should be. But at the same time she was keen to demonstrate that good Christians could be – and in her view, should be – Conservatives; so she was not afraid to preach her own distinctive political theology whenever she was given the chance in an appropriate setting. In March 1981 she revisited the City church of St Lawrence, Jewry, where she had preached once before when she was Leader of the Opposition, to expound her favourite parable of the talents: 'Creating wealth,' she told her lunchtime audience of bankers and stockbrokers, 'must be seen as a Christian obligation if we are to fulfil our role as stewards of the resources and talents the Creator has provided for us.'[136] Not content with reinterpreting well-loved stories, she seemed to be adding a new category to the Sermon on the Mount: 'Blessed are the wealth creators.'

Seven years later, in May 1988, she invited herself to address the General Assembly of the Church of Scotland, where she delivered a seriously misjudged political speech which was promptly dubbed 'The Sermon on the Mound'.★ The novelist Jonathan Raban devoted a whole pamphlet to exposing the ignorance, perversity and sheer banality of this embarrassing effusion; while Ludovic Kennedy has described the fury of the Scottish divines at her 'effrontery, not so say insensitivity' in treating them to 'a weird amalgam of fundamental Conservatism and simplistic Sunday school homilies'.[137] Her speech was for the most part another paean to the importance of wealth creation – '"If a man will not work he shall not eat," wrote St Paul to the Thessalonians' – and individual choice as the core of Christianity: 'No one took away the life of Jesus; he *chose* to lay it down.' Most revealing, however, was a passage in which she confessed that she 'always had difficulty with the Biblical precept to love our neighbour "as ourselves" until I read some of the words of C. S. Lewis':

> He pointed out that we don't exactly love *ourselves* when we fall below the standards and beliefs we have accepted. Indeed we might even *hate* ourselves for some unworthy deed.[138]

This, as Raban pointed out, was a wonderfully self-serving piece of casuistry, providing an ingenious argument for hating – or at least

---

★The Mound is the Edinburgh street on which the Assembly Hall of the Church of Scotland is situated.

condemning – others when they fail to live up to the standards 'we' have set for them.[139] Nowhere is the essentially judgemental character of Mrs Thatcher's political faith – her belief in sheep and goats, them and us, 'true believers' and the rest – more clearly expressed than here, in the guise of theology.

Though the Prime Minister's initiative in the appointment of bishops had been greatly curtailed by a new system introduced in 1976 whereby she was given only two names to choose from, Mrs Thatcher took her diminished responsibility very seriously and made a point of trying to appoint the more conservative of the options put up to her. 'They only give me two choices,' she once complained to Woodrow Wyatt, 'both from the left.' Another time when he asked her why she had appointed so-and-so she said, 'You should have seen the other one.'[140] In fact, she could ask for more names and at least once did so, when she went determinedly against the wishes of Runcie, the Church establishment and, it was said, the Queen by insisting on the nomination of the Anglo-Catholic Graham Leonard, a leading opponent of the ordination of women and most of the other modernising trends in the Church, to the important see of London, rather than the favourite, John Habgood, then Bishop of Durham. (She compensated Habgood with the Archbishopric of York in 1983.)

Though she did once suggest to Wyatt that it might be better if the Church was disestablished,[141] there was no doubt of Mrs Thatcher's personal involvement in these appointments. When she appointed Philip Goodrich, the brother of her old schoolfriend Margaret Goodrich, to be Bishop of Worcester in 1982, she wrote to Margaret, 'I have moved your brother.'[142] Throughout the 1980s it was a standing joke within the Church that the Crown Appointments Commissioners could get whomever they wanted chosen for any see by putting his name up along with that of the Bishop of Stepney, Jim Thompson, one of the Prime Minister's *bêtes noires*, mainly because he was a regular contributor to the *Today* programme's 'Thought for the Day'. In 1987 she chose Mark Santer, then Bishop of Kensington, rather than Thompson, to be the new Bishop of Birmingham without realising that Santer was a CND supporter. In fact her options were limited: throughout the 1980s only one bishop, Bill Westwood of Peterborough, was a declared supporter of the Government.

Right at the end of her time she had the chance to replace Runcie at Canterbury. With no obvious front-runner, she made a bold choice by picking a complete outsider, the very non-Establishment, state-school-educated evangelical George Carey – a moral and theological conservative who nevertheless supported the ordination of women –

in preference to any of the Establishment candidates headed once again by the Old Etonian Habgood. 'In choosing him,' *The Times*'s religious correspondent Clifford Longley commented, 'Mrs Thatcher's known impatience with theological and moral woolliness . . . will have been a factor.'[143] There was never a chance that she would choose the Bishop of Liverpool, David Sheppard, who had been a member of the team that produced *Faith in the City* and campaigned energetically against poverty on Merseyside and beyond. But Carey's elevation left a vacancy at Bath and Wells which her successor promptly filled, in one of his first ecclesiastical appointments, by finally promoting Jim Thompson.

She did try to bend the bishops to her way of thinking by inviting eight of them to Chequers in November 1987. 'She wants to bring about a moral revolution,' the Bishop of Oxford, Richard Harries, told the press, 'and she wants the Church to play its part.'[144] But she found a much more effective champion of her religious views in the person of the Chief Rabbi, Immanuel Jakobovits, whose robust preaching of clear Old Testament values reminded her of her father. She frequently stated her admiration of the way the Jews in her constituency looked after their own community, without relying on the state. 'In the thirty-three years that I represented it,' she wrote in her memoirs, 'I never had a Jew come in poverty and desperation to one of my constituency surgeries . . . I often wished that . . . Christians . . . would take closer note of the Jewish emphasis on self-help and acceptance of personal responsibility.'[145] Jakobovits issued exactly the sort of rejoinder to *Faith in the City* that she would have liked to make herself.[146] The number of ministers of Jewish extraction in her Cabinets – Keith Joseph, Nigel Lawson, Leon Brittan, David Young, Malcolm Rifkind and later Michael Howard – and also among her private advisers – Alfred Sherman, Norman Strauss, David Wolfson, Stephen Sherbourne – attracted some notice and even suggestions of favouritism; but it was largely accidental. She certainly liked clever, classless outsiders, which many of these people were; but the description also covered plenty of others like Alan Walters, Tim Bell and Brian Griffiths who were not Jewish. There is no suggestion that she showed undue favour towards Jews, only that she was, as Nigel Lawson wrote, unusually free of 'the faintest trace of anti-Semitism'.[147] She was very far from being uncritically supportive of the state of Israel. But she did find it politically useful to hold up Jakobovits as a model by which implicitly to criticise Runcie. She knighted him – rather incongruously – in 1981; and wanted to send him to the House of Lords to balance the Anglican bishops there, but with curious deference to protocol was not sure she could, until she finally took the plunge – to general applause – in 1988.

'Academic poison'

The Prime Minister might grumble about the bishops, but she could not do very much about them: and perhaps they did not greatly matter anyway. The case of the universities was different. If the nation's institutions of higher education were obstructing the realisation of the Government's vision, it was within the Government's power to bring them to heel. And that was precisely what she set out to do.

Mrs Thatcher's relations with the academic community were paradoxical. Though not herself an intellectual, she used intellectuals to advise her more systematically and effectively than any previous Prime Minister. She used the deliberately homely language of housewife economics to lead the most ideologically driven government of the century, giving her name to a distinctive political philosophy in a way that none of her predecessors had done. And Thatcherism prevailed: she won the ideological argument and shifted the political agenda decisively in her direction for a generation. Ideas that had been derided when she and Keith Joseph first began to argue them in 1975 were taken for granted by a Labour Government twenty-five years later. Yet the intellectuals never forgave her. Of course she had her academic supporters – not only monetarist economists from unfashionable redbrick universities like Alan Walters and Patrick Minford, but leading lights of the ancient universities too: people like Maurice Cowling and Edward Norman at Peterhouse, Cambridge; Michael Howard (whom she appointed Regius Professor of History in 1980 and knighted in 1986) and the philosopher Anthony Quinton (given a peerage in 1982) at Oxford; not forgetting John Vincent, professor of history at Bristol, who contributed robustly Thatcherite columns to both *The Times* and the *Sun*. But Thatcherite academics were always a minority – if, by the end of the decade, a highly visible and vocal one. The fact remains that the great majority of university teachers loathed her, and she candidly despised them.★

The roots of Mrs Thatcher's antipathy to universities go back to her experience at Oxford during and just after the war. As a hard-working and serious-minded chemistry student she felt excluded from the more glamorous arts and politics circles where her real interests lay; even

---

★A poll just before the 1987 election found that only 18 per cent of university lecturers intended to vote Conservative, compared with 39 per cent each for Labour and the Alliance.

when she became President of the Conservative Association in her final year she was patronised by the more self-confident young men who had come back from the war to polish their repartee at the Union. She writes of Oxford in her memoirs with a striking lack of warmth, and much of the intellectual excitement she does describe was clearly imaginary.[148] Oxford gave her an unpleasant foretaste of the sort of cultural snobbery she encountered again when she became Tory leader and then Prime Minister; she resented it then, and never forgave it.

Moreover the cast of her mind was intrinsically anti-academic. She had a temperamental preference for hard knowledge over what she regarded as woolly speculation. Ideas for their own sake did not interest her at all. Told in 1968 that the leader of the French *événements,* Daniel Cohn-Bendit, had been awarded a degree for 'posing a series of very intelligent questions', she replied briskly that she would have been 'happier had he also found a series of intelligent answers'.[149] Later, as Education Secretary, she quoted with approval a critic who complained that 'we are feeding doubts into our children, not beliefs'.[150] She had very little time for academics unless they came up with solutions to problems.

Her experience as Education Secretary in the early 1970s, visiting universities at the height of student radicalism and being shouted down by left-wing demonstrators who mindlessly denounced all Tory ministers as 'Fascists', further confirmed both her dim view of the quality of education being taught and her contempt for the trendy professors and craven vice-chancellors who permitted this sort of intolerance to go on. Remembering her own student days of hard work and plain living, she regarded modern students and most of their lecturers as idle parasites who lived off the taxpayer while abusing the hand that fed them. But she blamed the students less than their tutors. 'Revolutionary doctrines like communism,' she told Brian Walden in 1988, 'usually came from intellectuals and academics . . . Some academics and intellectuals . . . are putting out what I call poison. Some young people, who were thrilled to bits to get to university, had every decent value pounded out of them.'[151] She complained to Woodrow Wyatt in 1986 that even a High Tory like Hugh Trevor-Roper, the Master of Peterhouse whom she had ennobled in 1979, was not immune: 'Like all these academics they think they have to genuflect to the *Guardian* way of thinking.'[152]

She resented the universities' claims to intellectual autonomy while expecting to be funded by the state, and complained of their anti-capitalist culture. She was deeply unimpressed by the 364 economists who wrote to condemn the 1981 budget. The wealth creators she most admired had not been to university at all. 'The universities have failed

Britain,' she told Ralf Dahrendorf – the former West German minister and European Commissioner who had been director of the LSE since 1974. 'You,' she repeated, more personally, in case he failed to get the point, 'have failed us.'[153] Only two institutions were exempt from this blanket condemnation. The Open University, which she had saved from being strangled at birth by Iain Macleod in 1970, gave good value for the Government's money by turning out graduates more cheaply than conventional residential universities; she worried about left-wing bias in some of its correspondence material, but at least its students were highly motivated adults who did not waste their time on drink, sex and campus politics. Better still, the independent University College of Buckingham, founded in 1974, was a private university on the American model which got no funding from the Government at all.

Joseph had tried to convert the universities to the beauty of the free market by his brave campaign around the campuses between 1975 and 1979, during which he was regularly abused, spat at and shouted down. Once in power Mrs Thatcher adopted more direct methods, first by simply cutting their budgets, later by taking them under direct political control, forcing them on the one hand to seek alternative sources of income and on the other to process more students with fewer staff and resources. In 1981 Mark Carlisle cut the funds allocated by the University Grants Committee by 18 per cent over three years; Joseph tightened the squeeze still further with an additional 2 per cent cut in 1983. Two years later he published a Green Paper which spelled out the Government's unprecedentedly utilitarian view of universities' function: they would henceforth be required to be both more commercial and more vocational, paying their own way and serving the needs of the national economy 'more effectively' on a share of resources that was to continue to fall by 2 per cent a year.[154] Subjects the Government disapproved of like sociology, criminology, industrial relations and peace studies came under the severest pressure. Having already cut its budget twice, Joseph wanted to abolish the Social Science Research Council altogether – like Mrs Thatcher he believed 'social science' to be a contradiction in terms – but in the end he was persuaded to reprieve it under a more acceptable name – the Economic and Social Research Council – which reflected a shift of emphasis.

Curiously some of the heaviest cuts fell on pure science. This appears to have been an unintended consequence of the cutting of the UGC grant, which destroyed a delicate and complex mechanism of science funding built up over many years. In an interview for the magazine *Nature* in 1985 Mrs Thatcher was unsympathetic, criticising the way the Science Research Council spent the funds at its disposal, alleging too much duplication, timidity and red tape.[155] Part of the problem was that the increasing emphasis on profitable development diverted money away from pure research. But the result was that over the five years 1981–6 the proportion of national GDP devoted to research and development together fell from 0.72 per cent – which already compared poorly with other European countries – to 0.62 per cent.[156] A pressure group called Save British Science was formed in January 1986 to highlight the decline. Back in 1982 Mrs Thatcher had rejected the recommendation of a House of Lords committee that she should appoint a Minister for Science, on the ground that her own scientific background made it unnecessary. Now she realised that if she was going to be her own Minister of Science she must be seen to do something. So she set up a Cabinet committee, with herself in the chair, to try to redirect resources to pure science. But the damage was done. The squeeze on the universities in general and science in particular had already led many of the country's best scientists to move to the United States.★

It was this more than anything else which provoked Oxford to the unprecedented snub of refusing the Prime Minister an honorary degree. All her recent Oxford-educated predecessors, from Attlee to Heath, had received this honour within a year of taking office. But the university had missed the moment in 1979 because it was already embroiled in controversy over an honorary degree to President Bhutto of Pakistan. It funked it again in 1983 and by the time the proposal came up for a third time in 1985 the opposition had grown formidable. Supporters of the award argued that the university would look petty in the eyes of the world if it denied the customary honour to a Prime Minister who – like her or loathe her – was not only the first woman but already one of the longest-serving holders of the office. Opponents, however – with scientists to the fore – argued that it would be monstrous to award such an honour to the head of a government which had inflicted 'deep and systematic damage to the whole public education system in Britain, from the provision for the youngest child up to the most advanced research programme'. Professor Denis Noble, FRS, urged Convocation that it was being offered 'the last chance for any serious academic institution to stop the catastrophe that we face as a scientific and educational nation'.[158] By a majority of more than

---

★As Leader of the Opposition, Mrs Thatcher used to boast about the number of Nobel prizes won by British scientists – seventy-two by 1975, proportionately more than any other country and nearly twice as many as the United States. But under her Government the figure nosedived. Britain won thirteen prizes in the 1970s, but only four in the 1980s and two in the 1990s.[157]

two to one – 738 to 319 – the dons voted to withhold the degree. While Tory MPs and columnists spluttered loyally on her behalf, Mrs Thatcher responded icily, with a touch of sour grapes. 'If they do not wish to confer the honour, I am the last person who would wish to receive it.'[159] 'Perceptive observers,' wrote Hugo Young, 'noted an under-tone of contempt rather than bitterness.'[160] 'No, it did not wound me,' she told an interviewer on American television, 'because I know Oxford . . . I was not surprised . . . It is a political vote . . . That is the way the socialists work. We Conservatives . . . would never have dreamed of opposing Harold Wilson as a Labour Prime Minister for an honorary degree.'[161] Her family was wonderful, she told the *Evening Standard*. Mark sent her a big bunch of flowers from America saying 'Never mind, Mum, we still love you'.[162] The inevitable effect was to extin-guish any lingering affection for her *alma mater*. 'I went to Oxford University,' she only half joked at the 1989 party conference, 'but I've never let it hold me back.'[163] A decade later, when she had finished her memoirs, she pointedly donated her papers to Cambridge.

Not till her third term did she get round to restructuring the univer-sity system. Up to 1987, under Keith Joseph, university block grants were still administered by the autonomous and academic-dominated University Grants Committee. Budgets were cut, but universities could still decide their own priorities. Kenneth Baker's 1988 Act, however, replaced the UGC with a new Universities Funding Council on which academics were outnumbered by businessmen, and subjected the universities to an unprecedented degree of detailed central direction by Whitehall. Henceforth the Government would fund universities on a contract basis: as the monopoly purchaser of university services, the Department of Education could decide what should be taught, direct how many staff were required in each department and set specified research outputs for each institution, like so many plants in a nation-alised industry. This clumsy combination of market forces and state control pleased no one. 'They are privatising everyone else and nation-alising us,' John Ashworth – now Vice-Chancellor of heavily squeezed Salford – complained.[164] John Griffith, Professor of Public Law at the London School of Economics, compared the destruction of the univer-sity system to the dissolution of the monasteries.[165]

Initially the polytechnics had fared relatively well. Funded by local authorities, they escaped the squeeze on the universities and continued to expand: in 1987 they actually overtook the universities, at least in terms of student numbers. The theory was that they worked closely with local industry in just the way the Government approved. Baker, however, removed them from local control and merged them with the rest of the university system: in due course the Major Government allowed them to rebrand themselves as universities. Thus the binary system – the brainchild of Toby Weaver, Mrs Thatcher's mentor in her time at the DES – was abolished and with it, ironically, the notion of diversity and choice in higher education.

Baker did in fact find more money to ease the implementation of his reforms, making up in some measure for the shortfall of earlier years. But the effect of ten years of Thatcherism, in Nicholas Timmins' words, was to leave higher education 'operating as a leaner, meaner, more crowded and more impersonal machine'.[166] With reduced resources, the system was required to produce 30 per cent more graduates than at the start of the decade. Inevitably the quality of the education provided – and certainly the quality of the experience – declined. Academic salaries had been allowed to fall relative to every other group in the public sector: by 1985 a junior lecturer earned less than a policeman or a nurse, and professors far less than their peers in once-comparable professions. In addition Baker abolished the security of tenure which had hitherto been seen as the guarantee of academic freedom. If university lecturer had been a privileged and enviable occupation in the 1960s and 1970s – the decade of Malcolm Bradbury's ultra-trendy sociologist Howard Kirk – that was very far from the case by 1990. No group in society, with the possible exception of trade-union leaders, suffered a steeper fall in status.

The result was a brain-drain of talent and a demoralisation of the whole academic community which alarmed many who counted themselves in other respects among Mrs Thatcher's strongest admirers. Brian Cox, who had some claim to having started the whole education debate as editor of the Black Papers in the late 1960s; Max Beloff, founding principal of Buckingham; the historians Robert Skidelsky and Elie Kedourie; and the novelist Kingsley Amis – all warned that the Government's clumsy combination of market forces and state control was destroying the very nature and purpose of universities, to the extent that even the Prime Minister herself began to feel that she had got it wrong. 'I have to concede that these critics had a stronger case than I would have liked,' she wrote in her memoirs. 'A philistine subordination of scholarship to the immediate requirements of vocational training,' she protested, 'was certainly no part of my kind of Thatcherism.' In 860 pages, this is an almost unique admission of error. She claims to have been at work, before she left office, on 'a radical decentralisation of the whole system'.[167] There were few in the beleaguered universities, however, who did not believe that the policy sprang directly from her personal animus against everything they stood for.

'Trotskyists' in the BBC

All Prime Ministers become paranoid about the BBC. As problems mount and their popularity slides, they invariably accuse the media of turning against them, unfairly criticising the Government while giving the opposition a soft ride. Margaret Thatcher was no exception. It is in the nature of governments to resent criticism, particularly at the hands of a state-owned broadcaster. But Mrs Thatcher disliked the BBC on principle, long before she became Prime Minister, just because it was state-owned and publicly financed. She saw it as a nationalised industry, subsidised, anti-commercial and self-righteous: like the universities, she believed, it poisoned the national debate with woolly liberalism and moral permissiveness at the taxpayers' expense. Visiting Broadcasting House as Leader of the Opposition in 1978 she 'arrived with all guns firing . . . showed scant interest in, let alone tolerance of, the editors' problems, and berated them on their failings over a wide area, particularly their coverage of Northern Ireland'.[168] As a shadow minister back in 1969 she had advocated financing the BBC by advertising instead of the licence fee. 'Why not?' she demanded on *Any Questions?* 'You don't need to have advertising on every single wavelength. You could have your Third Programme, there's no earthly reason why you should not have commercial advertising on one wavelength, to finance the rest of the operation.'[169] These two themes – Northern Ireland and finance – dominated her relations with the BBC throughout her premiership.

Of course her knowledge of the Corporation's output was largely second-hand. She had never watched much television and she heard the radio only in the early morning, when she listened religiously to *Farming Today* as she got up and also let it be known that she kept a critical ear cocked to *Today,* the programme which boasted that it set the day's political agenda and in consequence formed the basis of most Tory complaints of bias.★ Those around her – not least Denis – took it for granted that *Today* was, as Woodrow Wyatt described it, 'run for Socialist propaganda by Brian Redhead' – the admitted Labour sympathiser who had been its chief presenter since 1975.[171] Denis once cheerfully told the BBC's political editor John Cole, as though it was common knowledge: 'Of course, everybody at the BBC's a Trotskyist,' and was surprised when Cole was startled. 'Oh, nothing personal, old boy,' he assured him.[172]

★Charles Powell called *Farming Today* 'the bane of my life', since every morning he had to chase up some obscure item that had caught her interest.[170]

Mrs Thatcher was always particularly concerned about the reporting of terrorism. Her first public criticism of the BBC as Prime Minister was provoked by a contentious edition of *Panorama* in November 1979 which showed masked IRA men enforcing roadblocks in Northern Ireland: the allegation was that the programme makers had set up the incident in order to film it. In the Commons she warned that 'my Right Hon. Friend the Home Secretary and I think that it is time that the BBC put its house in order.'[173] In fact Willie Whitelaw, though critical of individual programmes like this one, was always a robust defender of the BBC's independence. As a former opposition Chief Whip he remembered Harold Wilson's attempts to browbeat the BBC in the 1960s, when he felt the Corporation had treated the Tories 'most fairly'.[174] For as long as he was Home Secretary he was able to shield the BBC quite effectively from Mrs Thatcher's wrath. But the 1981 riots exposed another difference between the Prime Minister and her deputy. She was horrified by the television pictures which seemed to her to encourage the spread of 'copy-cat' rioting from one city to another. In July that year she used a speech to the Parliamentary Press Gallery to warn the broadcasters that in the television age they bore a heavy responsibility for 'setting the tone and standards of society'. Characteristically she judged domestic reporting in a Cold War context as a weapon in the global battle of ideas:

> If the television of the Western world uses its freedom continually to show all that is worst in our society, while the centrally controlled television of the Communist world and the dictatorships show only what is judged as advantageous to them and suppress everything else – how are the uncommitted to judge between us?[175]

She was still more outraged by the reporting – particularly the BBC's reporting – of the Falklands war. She thought that in this crisis the Corporation was not just anti-Government and anti-Conservative as usual, but anti-British, as exemplified by programmes examining in great detail alternative possible landing places on the islands and above all by the broadcasters' punctilious insistence on referring objectively to 'British forces' instead of 'our forces' as she expected. (She preferred the ITN coverage in this respect.) Many people felt very strongly, she told the Commons, that 'the case for our country is not being put with sufficient vigour on certain . . . BBC programmes'; and she reminded the broadcasters of their responsibility to stand up for 'our task force, our boys, our people and the cause of democracy'.[176] Later, when Diana Gould embarrassed her during the June 1983 election by questioning her about the *Belgrano*, she blamed the BBC: 'Only the BBC,' she railed, 'could ask a British Prime Minister why she took action to protect our ships against an enemy ship that was a danger to our boys.'[177] When she got back to Downing Street she got her PPS, Michael Spicer, to ring Cecil Parkinson to propose abolishing the BBC. 'It was a good joke,' Spicer recalls.[178] But if so it was a bit near the bone.

The truth was that she did not really understand the idea of journalistic freedom. At a Chequers seminar with some of her favourite academics in January 1981, she worried about the penetration of the media by subversives. The historian Professor Michael Howard tried to assure her that the people she objected to were not Communists, just healthily opposition-minded sceptics exercising a hallowed British tradition of dissent; but she was not convinced.[179] She believed not only that in time of war the broadcasters should form part of the nation's war effort, but that in the context of terrorism and the Cold War the BBC had a duty to be on 'our' side. Instead she believed it gave 'covert support' to unilateralism and was 'ambivalent' in its coverage of the IRA.[180]

She had two means to discipline the BBC: first by exercising the Government's power to appoint the chairman and governors, who in turn appointed the Director-General; second by keeping it on a tight financial rein. Her first chance to appoint a chairman was in 1980, when the front runner to succeed Sir Michael Swann was Mark Bonham-Carter, vice-chairman since 1975. Asquith's grandson, a former Liberal MP and the former chairman of the Race Relations Board, appointed by Roy Jenkins, Bonham-Carter was just the sort of chairman she did not want, so to keep him out she accepted Willie Whitelaw's suggestion: George Howard, the owner of Castle Howard in Yorkshire. Outwardly a bluff county squire in Whitelaw's own mould, Howard was in fact by no means a conventional Tory but 'a truly eighteenth-century figure', given to wearing kaftans and beads.[181] Nevertheless he was a great deal more acceptable to Mrs Thatcher than Bonham-Carter. The following year, defying the expectation that a Tory chairman should be balanced by a non-Conservative deputy, she appointed the former editor of *The Times* – and monetarist convert – William Rees-Mogg to be vice-chairman. Over the next five years she was also able to appoint nine new governors who between them, under Howard and Rees-Mogg's more interventionist leadership, gave the board 'a more hostile and opinionated composition'.[182] Her nominees included David Young's brother Stuart, a millionaire accountant from Finchley; Daphne Park, a former diplomat, now Principal of Somerville; Sir John Boyd, a former trade-union leader of resolutely right-wing views; and Malcolm McAlpine, a director of the family building firm. By contrast when a vacancy arose in 1984 for a governor with some specialist knowledge of the arts, she rejected both the writer John Mortimer – a known Labour supporter – and the former dancer Moira Shearer (wife of the Liberal journalist Ludovic Kennedy) in favour of the former director of the Edinburgh Festival and English National Opera, the Earl of Harewood. The convention that the governors should represent the full political spectrum was frankly abandoned.

When Howard stepped down in 1983 she raised Stuart Young to the chairmanship, with the expectation that he would move the Corporation towards becoming more commercial. He had been a governor only since 1981, and his sole previous interest in broadcasting had been as part of a consortium which had bid for the TV-am franchise. To her disappointment, however, once appointed he 'went native', combined with the Director-General, Alasdair Milne, to oppose the introduction of advertising and lobbied successfully for renewal of the licence fee. Mrs Thatcher made no secret of her dislike of the licence fee – 'a compulsory levy on those who have television sets', whether they watched the BBC or not – but in March 1985 she was constrained to renew it for another five years, pegged for the first two years but rising in line with inflation after that, while making clear in the Commons that 'we do not rule out the possibility of changes' – specifically not excluding advertising – in the future.[183] The same month Leon Brittan set up a departmental committee chaired by Professor Alan Peacock, its members supposedly handpicked to come up with the right answer, to inquire into the future funding of the BBC. In the event Peacock and his colleagues came down against advertising, mainly because studies showed that there was not enough to go round and the competition would cripple ITV.[184] Whitelaw too, though no longer Home Secretary, weighed in heavily and actually threatened to resign rather than remain in a government that forced advertising on the BBC. Mrs Thatcher was 'greatly disappointed'[185] but was obliged to back down, though she still hoped to look again at the alternatives in five years' time.

Meanwhile Stuart Young died, aged only fifty-two, giving her a third chance to appoint a chairman who would do her bidding. Her first choice this time was Lord King, the dynamic chairman who had turned round British Airways. But King could not yet be spared from privatising BA, so she turned – on Rupert Murdoch's recommendation – to Marmaduke Hussey, the former managing director of Times Newspapers, who had gained a tough reputation by standing up to the print unions during the year-long stoppage at *The Times* and *Sunday Times*. He had no experience of either broadcasting or public service: on his appointment to the BBC he confessed that he had 'not set foot inside the place'.[186] But in the Prime Minister's eyes this was a recommendation. He insists in his memoirs that he barely knew Mrs Thatcher and received no instructions from her.[187] Nevertheless his brief, spoken or unspoken, was reported to be to 'get in there and sort it out – in days and not months'.[188] Hussey certainly wasted no time. Almost his first act – on the advice, he says, of Victor Rothschild – was to sack the Director-General.

Alasdair Milne was a lifelong BBC insider who had succeeded Ian Trethowan in the top job just after the Falklands war. He had long been a *bête noire* of the Prime Minister, who identified him with everything she thought wrong with the Corporation and thought him incapable of restoring order to an institution she regarded as out of control. In 1985 he incurred another black mark for a programme called *Real Lives* which profiled two men recently elected to the Northern Ireland assembly, the former IRA commander Martin McGuinness, now wearing the colours of Sinn Fein, and a member of Ian Paisley's Democratic Unionist Party, Gregory Campbell. Brittan, with Mrs Thatcher in the background, asked for the programme to be pulled. Milne and the BBC controllers defended it, but Rees-Mogg persuaded the governors to 'withdraw' it before it was shown. In an interview with the BBC's *Newsnight* Mrs Thatcher denied censorship, defending the need to deny terrorists what she had called in a speech a fortnight earlier 'the oxygen of publicity'.[189] But even *The Times* considered that Brittan's 'quasi-diktat' was 'scarcely distinguishable' from censorship.[190]

After this Mrs Thatcher decided it would be more dignified to keep out of spats about individual programmes. She carefully distanced herself from Norman Tebbit's heavy-handed criticism of the BBC's reporting of the American bombing of Libya in April 1986, which soon widened into an allegation of anti-Conservative bias across the Corporation's whole output. She made no comment on the BBC's decision not to broadcast a play about the Falklands which it had commissioned, from the distinguished playwright Ian Curteis, allegedly on the ground that it was too favourable to the Government, at exactly the same time that it was showing a highly tendentious series called *The Monocled Mutineer* about First World War deserters. But another major storm blew up in early 1987 when the Government learned that as part of a series called *Secret Society*, presented by Duncan Campbell of the *New Statesman*, the BBC was about to show a programme about a spy-satellite project known as Zircon. This time, under pressure from the

MoD, Milne agreed at the last minute to scrap the programme. But Mrs Thatcher was outraged that the Corporation could have made such a programme at all. In the Commons she condemned 'left-wing organs like the *New Statesman* and people anxious to ferret out the secrets of national security to sell them . . . for personal gain'.[191] The *New Statesman* pointed out that this was an excellent definition of what journalists do in a free society.[192] Two days later the police raided the BBC's Glasgow offices and took away three vanloads of material relating not just to the Zircon programme but to the whole *Secret Society* series. Mrs Thatcher denied all knowledge of the raid, insisting that it was purely a matter for the police and the court which issued the warrant under the Official Secrets Act.[193] But if she did not order the police action she certainly created the climate in which such a thing could be contemplated. Douglas Hurd – the Home Secretary – was 'alarmed at the unreality of her zest for secrecy and the party's growing obsession against the BBC'.[194] And she certainly had advance knowledge of Hussey's response to the affair.

The abrupt dismissal of a well-regarded Director-General – aged fifty-six and less than five years in the post – was a shocking event which seemed to indicate a cruder degree of pressure on the BBC than any previous government had dreamed of. Even the *Sunday Telegraph* was moved to warn that 'the Tory vendetta against the BBC is real and dangerous'.[195] Though Mrs Thatcher once again protested that the governors were entirely independent, by 1987 every one of them had been appointed by her Government. Milne's removal was 'nothing to do with us', she 'primly' told Wyatt; but it was evident that even Wyatt did not believe her.[196] She had appointed Hussey to 'sort out' the BBC and he lost no time in starting at the top. She seems genuinely to have had nothing to do with the elevation of Michael Checkland – an accountant with no experience of making programmes – as Milne's replacement; but she certainly approved the appointment of John Birt from London Weekend Television as his deputy and eventual successor. 'They were a curious pair,' John Drummond, then Controller of Radio 3, recalled, 'blustery, harrumphing old Hussey and the chilly, Armani-suited Birt. They seemed to me to have only one thing in common: a fundamental contempt for the BBC and what it stood for.'[197] But this was exactly the point. Lady Thatcher wrote in her memoirs that the new Hussey–Birt regime – she did not mention Checkland – was 'an improvement in every respect'.[198]

But she had to leave real action on broadcasting to her third term.

Friends in Fleet Street

During one of Mrs Thatcher's rows with the BBC the broadcaster Aubrey Singer recalled General de Gaulle's justification for the Government controlling French television: 'They have the newspapers: I have television.' 'Why,' Singer asked, 'should Mrs Thatcher have both?'[199] The constantly simmering conflict between her Government and the BBC certainly contrasted with – and arguably balanced – the generally reliable support she enjoyed from most of the printed media. Of course there were exceptions. Among the broadsheets, the *Guardian* was the house magazine of the progressive establishment, read by all those Labour and Alliance-voting teachers, lecturers, social workers and local-government officers who most hated her: in her view the printed equivalent of the BBC, but without the BBC's obligation to at least appear impartial. Among the tabloids, the *Daily Mirror* remained solidly Labour, in opposition to its deadly rival the *Sun*. But the bulk of Fleet Street* from the relatively highbrow *Times* and *Telegraph* through the crucial mid-market *Mail* and *Express* – all with their Sunday sisters – to the soaraway Thatcherite *Sun* and the even more populist *Daily Star*, was firmly, if not always uncritically, in the Tory camp. Measured by total circulation, the press supported the Government in the 1987 election by a margin of roughly three to one.[200]

Mrs Thatcher was naturally very happy with this situation. She was not worried by the *Guardian*'s hostility, but rather welcomed its opposition as confirmation that she was doing all right. She expected her enemies to oppose her, just as she expected her allies to support her. But she took it for granted that anyone not for her was against her. When a new broadsheet, the *Independent*, was founded in 1986 she quickly classed it as an enemy. 'It is not independent at all,' she told Wyatt in 1989. 'It is dedicated to trying to destroy me.'[201] The corollary was that she took great care to keep her supporters loyal.

Unlike many Prime Ministers – Harold Wilson and John Major, for instance, who were both obsessed by them – she did not actually read the papers very much. She received a daily digest from Bernard Ingham first thing every morning, which gave her the flavour and told her what he thought she ought to know. But Ingham kept from her personal criticism that would hurt or anger her; and some at least of the spinning which he did on her behalf was done without her knowledge.

---

*'Fleet Street', of course, ceased to be located in Fleet Street during the 1980s, largely as a result of Rupert Murdoch's removal of News International to Wapping in 1985, which was followed by practically all the rest of the national press. But the name is still useful, and it was still correct at the start of the decade.

When Norman Tebbit confronted her with cuttings of some of the poison that was being written about him in the summer of 1986 she was horrified. She was well aware of the importance of the press – particularly the *Sun* and the *Daily Mail* – in maintaining a swell of support for her personality and policies. She liked to have her attention drawn to helpful or supportive articles; she always made a point of reading Woodrow Wyatt's weekly column in the *News of the World* – and thanking him effusively for it. But she did not often give interviews to favoured editors. She left all that sort of thing to Ingham and Wyatt. If she did meet editors, it was not to learn what was on their mind but to tell them what was on hers. When Simon Jenkins became editor of *The Times* in 1990 'she lectured him for about twenty minutes and then said, "Have you got anything you would like to say yourself?"'[202]

On the other hand she was shameless in rewarding supportive editors with honours. She wrote a personal letter thanking Larry Lamb for the *Sun*'s support in 1979 and gave him a knighthood – the first tabloid editor to be so honoured – the following year. Over the next decade she also knighted John Junor of the *Sunday Express*, David English of the *Daily Mail*, Nick Lloyd of the *Daily Express* and Geoffrey Owen of the *Financial Times*; and gave a peerage to Denis's old chum Bill Deedes on his retirement from editing the *Daily Telegraph* in 1986. (On the other hand she very pointedly did not give a knighthood or any other recognition to Deedes' successor, Max Hastings, who was never forgiven for sacking Carol Thatcher soon after his arrival.) She also both knighted and then ennobled Woodrow Wyatt. The proprietors – Lord Rothermere, Lord Hartwell, Lord Thomson – mostly had peerages already, but she lost no time in raising Victor Matthews of Trafalgar House (owners of the two *Express* titles and the *Daily Star*) to the same rank in 1980, and did the same for David Stevens when United Newspapers acquired them in 1985. The great exception to this plethora of inky nobility was Rupert Murdoch, who could not be offered a peerage because he was an American citizen and would probably not have accepted one anyway.

But Mrs Thatcher did everything else she could to show her appreciation of Murdoch's support. In November 1979 she marked the tenth anniversary of News International's acquisition of the *Sun* with a glowing message of congratulation, making clear that she saw the paper as an ally, or even a partner: 'May you long continue to set out in plain, basic English the issues which confront Britain as we try to arrest and reverse our decline.'[203] 'The *Sun* is the paper that is very good to us,' she told Wyatt – Murdoch's oldest British friend and the principal intermediary between them – in 1988.[204] Throughout Wyatt's diary runs the refrain 'The *Sun* is marvellous . . . Rupert is marvellous . . . We depend on him to fight for us.'[205] In return she would do all she could to advance his ever-expanding media interests.

First she helped him to snap up *The Times* and *Sunday Times* when Lord Thomson relinquished them in 1981. It was actually John Biffen, newly appointed Trade Secretary, who failed to refer Murdoch's bid to the Monopolies Commission, despite his already extensive share of both the daily and Sunday market through the *Sun* and the *News of the World*, on the pretext that the two titles were not at that time profitable, following the 1978–90 stoppage. That might have been true of *The Times*, but the underlying position of the *Sunday Times* was immensely strong. Biffen has always claimed that he acted entirely independently of Downing Street. But many years later Wyatt boasted of his role in brokering the deal. 'I had all the rules bent for him . . . Through Margaret I got it arranged that the deal didn't go to the Monopolies Commission which almost certainly would have blocked it.'[206]

The rest of Fleet Street was dismayed and the Establishment horrified at seeing the former 'top people's paper', known around the world as 'The Times of London', sold to a brash Australian who already owned the *Sun*, the *New York Post* and a whole stable full of other titles in Australia and the US. Though Murdoch gave assurances of editorial independence, and elaborate safeguards were erected to try to ensure that he observed them, in practice they quickly turned out to be worthless when Harold Evans – switched from the *Sunday Times* to become the new editor of *The Times* – showed an unacceptable sympathy for the infant SDP. Murdoch is said to have promised Mrs Thatcher that he would have the paper back on side by Easter.[207] She tried to help by offering Evans a third-rate quango – the chairmanship of the Sports Council. He was not tempted, but was sacked anyway in March 1982, safeguards notwithstanding, to be replaced by the more reliably Conservative Charles Douglas-Home.[208]

Mrs Thatcher's view of editorial independence was encapsulated by a revealing remark she made to John Cole at a Buckingham Palace garden party at the time of 'Tiny' Rowland's purchase of the *Observer* in 1980 – a bid that was referred to the Monopolies Commission, on much less ground for concern than existed in the Murdoch case. 'I do find it odd,' she remarked, 'that journalists at the *Observer* who feel free themselves to write what they think, become so agitated when a man who has a bit of money, and believes he has something to say through the media, takes over their paper'.[209] She seemed to see no difference between an individual journalist writing as one voice among many and a proprietor imposing his views on a whole paper. She saw nothing wrong in a rich man using his 'bit of money' to buy himself a platform of disproportionate influence.

Second, the Government was very helpful towards Murdoch's battle with the print unions over the move of his entire operation to Wapping in 1985. Like the miners' strike, this was another symbolic struggle between old-style trade unionism, defending jobs – and in the printers' case grotesque overmanning and the systematic blackmail of a peculiarly vulnerable industry – and management's right to manage. As in the coalfields, angry pickets tried to prevent Murdoch's new workforce (mainly recruited from the Electricians' Union) getting to work, turning the streets around 'Fortress Wapping' into a nightly battleground. The Government was fully entitled to treat it as a law-and-order issue which had to be won; but at the same time it was an intensely political confrontation and another vital test of Thatcherism on the ground. According to Andrew Neil – editor of the *Sunday Times* from 1983 to 1994 – Murdoch obtained Mrs Thatcher's personal assurance before the dispute began that 'enough police would be available to allow us to go about our lawful business. She assured him that there would be . . . and she kept her word'.[210] Behind the scenes Wyatt was once again closely involved in secret negotiations with Eric Hammond of the AEU. Conversely when Douglas Hurd proposed having talks with Brenda Dean of the print union SOGAT, Mrs Thatcher stopped him.[211] As with the NUM, she wanted victory, not compromise.

The curiosity of Mrs Thatcher's gushing support for Murdoch is how she squared it with her dislike of pornography. Had she ever turned the pages of the *Sun*, she would have been appalled; but Ingham's daily digest spared her this embarrassment. Of course she knew about the topless Page Three girls; but she frankly closed her eyes to the rest of the paper's daily diet of sleazy sex in exchange for the paper's robust support, rationalising it as the price of freedom. In a speech to the Press Association in 1988 she vowed that she would 'strain everything [to] protect our young people from some of the violence and pornography they would otherwise see'.[212] The key word here was 'some'. She did support legislation to ban so-called 'video nasties'; and she appointed William Rees-Mogg in 1988 to head a Broadcasting Standards Council to try to stem the tide of sex and violence on TV. Yet she did not seem to mind what Murdoch purveyed either in his newspapers or later on satellite television. Though it was plainly Murdoch's *Sun* that was continually driving the whole of the press to

ever-lower depths of taste and decency, she never uttered a public word
of criticism. Privately she complained at the *News of the World* drag-
ging up the Parkinson affair again in 1988, telling Wyatt that Murdoch
'sells newspapers on this fearful stuff which is giving a very bad idea
to the young that everybody behaves in a scandalous manner'.[213] She
was still more enraged when the same paper ran a story about the
businessman Ralph Halpern claiming to have pinched her bottom:

> I don't know how Rupert can do this. He says he supports us but
> he doesn't. This is a most hurtful and wounding thing to go into
> his newspapers. It means I can't see either of those editors again.

Murdoch was unabashed. 'It was tasteless, I agree,' he told Wyatt, 'but
she shouldn't consort with such people.'[214]

Such incidents did nothing to shake her general view that Murdoch's
political support outweighed his cultural consequences. She showed
no interest at all in controlling the intrusive excesses of the tabloid
press, even when photographers took pictures of her Health Secretary,
John Moore, in hospital; or the *News of the World* set a trap to catch
the deputy chairman of the Tory party, Jeffrey Archer, paying off a
prostitute. In 1990 she once again showed Murdoch outrageous
favouritism by allowing him to hijack satellite television in its infancy
by buying out the competition, without reference to the Monopolies
Commission. Her anxiety to keep Murdoch's newspapers on side, and
her willingness to bend the regulations to buy their continuing support
– cynically documented by Woodrow Wyatt – was the grubbiest face
of Thatcherism. Murdoch enjoyed a special place in the Prime Minister's
circle of the elect – not a courtier but a powerful independent ally
and family friend, rather like Ronald Reagan – who had direct access
to her whenever he sought it. He was the only newspaper proprietor
invited to the Downing Street lunch to mark her tenth anniversary in
1989, and was several times invited to spend Christmas with the family
at Chequers. Yet she never once mentions Murdoch in her memoirs.

The arts in the market place

Mrs Thatcher had an educated person's proper respect for the arts, but
she had little feel for them. Like Christianity, the great books, paintings and music of the past provided a cultural heritage to be praised
and raided for validation of the present. From her diligent childhood
she retained a superficial familiarity with the major English classics;
she could still quote from memory large chunks of poetry she had
learned at school; and having both played the piano as a girl and sung

in the Oxford Bach Choir at university she had a better-than-average knowledge of music. Within the fairly narrow limits of what she liked, she was by no means a philistine. As Prime Minister she still occasionally went to the opera – though with how much real pleasure remains uncertain: she once told Ronnie Millar that her favourite was *Die Fledermaus*.[215] She collected porcelain and (with advice from experts) Chinese scrolls. And if she did not have much time or taste for reading fiction – beyond the occasional Freddie Forsyth or John le Carré thriller, or Solzhenitsyn read as homework on the Soviet Union – she did read an astonishing amount of serious non-fiction (philosophy, theology, science and history) not directly related to the business of government.* With the exception of Ted Heath – whose near-professional musicianship was balanced by a considerable art collection – she was the most culturally literate Prime Minister since Anthony Eden: probably more so than Macmillan, for all his vaunted reading of Trollope and Jane Austen, and certainly more than either of her immediate predecessors, Wilson and Callaghan, or her successors, John Major and Tony Blair.

Yet her taste in the arts was characteristically simple and relentlessly functional. She had no patience with complexity or ambiguity, no time for imagination. She thought art should be beautiful, positive and improving, not disturbing or subversive. (In the course of her sermon to the General Assembly of the Church of Scotland she made the extraordinarily medieval suggestion that part of the national wealth should be used 'to support the wonderful artists and craftsmen whose work also glorifies God'.)[217] She liked books which told her things she needed to know. She had a retentive memory and liked to be able to quote things that she had read long ago. But she could not talk about the arts. When Hugh Thomas arranged a dinner for her to meet a number of sympathetic writers and artists, the novelist Anthony Powell found that 'she only likes talking of public affairs'.[218] She did once surprise Philip Larkin by quoting to him almost correctly a line from one of his poems, which suggests that she had read some poetry more modern than Kipling. 'You know,' she said, '"Her mind was full of knives."' The line she half-remembered was 'Your mind lay open like a drawer of knives'. Larkin was flattered that she remembered it

---

*Among other things she read biographies of Einstein and Lord Liverpool (her longest-serving predecessor, whose fifteen years (1812–27) evidently set her a target to beat); a history of the Jews; Allan Bloom's *The Closing of the American Mind*; and Archbishop John Habgood's *The Ten Commandments*. 'I am always trying to read a fundamental book,' she told Hugo Young in 1983.[216]

at all – 'I thought if it wasn't spontaneous she'd have got it right' – but reflected that 'she might think a mind full of knives rather along her own lines – not that I don't kiss the ground she treads'.[219] Still the impression is of a view of poetry as a treasury of good nuggets rather than of compressed emotion.

Likewise, showing off her collection of Chinese scrolls to George Walden, she discussed their merits 'in wonderfully Thatcherite phrases, praising the "vigorous strokes" and "sense of purpose," of the artists'. Visiting Venice in 1980, she admired Carpaccio's *Life of Saint Ursula* in the Accademia for its 'strong narrative and detailed style'. 'In painting as in politics,' Walden commented, 'Thatcher liked to know what was going on.'[220] The paintings she really liked were the portraits of national heroes – Nelson, Wellington, Churchill – and great British scientists – Newton, Faraday – with which she filled the walls of Number Ten; and she always took visitors on a tour of the pictures, pointing the political moral of each one. Her idea of art was essentially didactic.

What she disapproved of was the view of the arts as yet another nationalised industry, a playground of spoiled children – gifted maybe, but self-indulgent – who expected to be supported by the taxpayer for the gratification of an elite who should be made to pay for their own pleasures. It was for political as much as musical reasons that she went several times to Glyndebourne, to demonstrate her approval of unsubsidised opera. Her particular *bête noire* in the arts establishment was Peter Hall, constantly demanding better funding for the union-dominated and strike-hit National Theatre while claiming the right to mount scandalous affronts to public decency like Howard Brenton's *The Romans in Britain* (1980) with its famous scene of a Roman soldier buggering an ancient Briton, or *Pravda*, Brenton and David Hare's thinly disguised satire on Rupert Murdoch (1985). She only once attended a performance at the National, when Ronnie Millar took her to see *Amadeus* in 1980. She was horrified by Peter Shaffer's depiction of Mozart as a foul-mouthed brat and insisted, against all the evidence, that he was not, *could not have been*, like that. She did not go to the theatre to have her certainties upset.[221]

Roy Strong found her equally unsympathetic to the needs of the Victoria and Albert Museum. Despite collecting in a small way herself, she seemed to him to have 'an *idée fixe* about museums, that they were dead things, piled-up lumber from Britain's past which was now holding the country back'; they were stuffy and above all uncommercial, and represented everything she was trying to lead the country to reject.[222] Visiting York – site of the national transport museum – during the miners' strike she warned explicitly that the archaic attitudes of the

NUM would turn Britain into a '"museum society" of outdated, in-efficient and uneconomic industry'.[223] Her praise of 'Victorian values' did not extend to valuing their physical heritage.

As a result, Government policy towards the arts was a matter of containing public spending, requiring value for the money allocated and demanding that arts organisations should become more self-supporting – in other words, more commercial. Her model for arts patronage was the United States: companies and galleries, she believed, should not look to the state for funding but to private enterprise. In fact, the level of public subsidy – already pretty static since 1973 – was not cut in absolute terms. The Arts Council's budget actually increased from £63 million in 1979–80 to £176 million in 1990–1, which on paper more than kept ahead of inflation, allowing Lady Thatcher to claim in her memoirs that it 'rose sharply in real terms'.[224] It did not feel like that on the ground, however, where costs rose faster than general inflation and most institutions felt their income constantly reduced. In particular the Government no longer maintained the fabric of buildings like the V & A. 'Within five years,' Strong wrote, 'it had become axiomatic that up to 50% now had to be raised from the private sector.'[225] In reality the figures show that over the arts as a whole, business sponsorship – though it had risen from a base of almost nothing in the 1970s to £20 million by 1986 – still amounted to less than 10 per cent of total income by the end of the decade.[226] But the proportion was steadily increasing, while Arts Council support was increasingly given in the form of 'incentive funding', conditional on securing private backing. No doubt this made arts organisations leaner, more efficient and more anxious to get 'bums on seats'. But the need to attract sponsorship also dictated that artistic criteria were increas-ingly subordinated to commercial considerations, resulting in big, safe exhibitions, middle-brow plays with small casts and bankable TV stars, and frequent revivals of the most popular stalwarts of the operatic repertoire.

Of the four arts ministers who between them spanned the Thatcher decade, two – Norman St John Stevas (1979–81) and Grey Gowrie (1983–5) – were flamboyant personalities with a genuine interest in the arts and the confidence to fight their corner. The other two – Paul Channon (1981–3) and Richard Luce (1985–90) – were political placemen more concerned to please the Prime Minister. Stevas had been Arts Minister before, as Mrs Thatcher's junior at Education under Heath. But in the cost-cutting climate of 1979–80 his natural extravagance – not least in the way he redecorated his own office – was one reason she lost patience with him.[227] Channon, by contrast, seemed to Strong to be 'terrified of ever upsetting her'.[228] His principal contribution was to appoint the Prime Minister's favourite cultural commissar, William Rees-Mogg, to be chairman of the Arts Council in 1982 (he was already vice-chairman of the BBC) with a brief to apply Thatcherite prescriptions to the arts in much the same way that Ian MacGregor was appointed to British Steel and the National Coal Board.

In place of the cherished 'arms-length' principle stoutly defended by previous chairmen who had seen their job as championing the arts against the Government, Rees-Mogg was happy to be seen as the instrument of Government policy towards the arts. It was he, with his Director-General Luke Rittner, who drove the policy of requiring business sponsorship; they also tried to direct money away from the big national companies towards the regions, provoking a stand-up fight with Peter Hall, who claimed to be speaking for the theatre as a whole but could too easily be portrayed as fighting only for his own National Theatre. Lord Gowrie – who resigned in 1985 because he could not live on a ministerial salary – also seemed to Hall 'more concerned with pleasing Thatcher than with the creative potential of the arts'. He once suggested that the National could save money by moving out of Denys Lasdun's purpose-built temple on the South Bank – only opened in 1976 – to go back to squatting in a West End theatre.[229] His more diplomatic successor Richard Luce did succeed in negotiating with the Treasury a three-year settlement in 1987 which was supposed to give companies stability to plan ahead; but this was wrecked by the return of high inflation in 1988–9 which left them worse off than before.

Mrs Thatcher really only valued the arts as a source of national prestige. She had some regard for the Royal Opera House, partly because Robert Armstrong was secretary to the board, but also because she realised that opera – unlike the theatre – was an internationally competitive business in which Britain should be in the top league. When the GLC cut its grant to Covent Garden in 1981 she deplored its uncharacteristic parsimony:*

> Many of us believe that it is important that this country should continue to have one of the best opera houses in the world and some of the best ballet facilities in the world. They add to and enhance the reputation of this country as a great centre for the arts and opera.[230]

---

*By contrast, when Hall closed the smallest of the National Theatre's three auditoria in 1984 as a dramatic gesture to draw attention to the loss of funding, the GLC gave him the additional money needed to reopen it.

Six years later, when Covent Garden was going through one of its periodic crises, she attended a gala production of *Otello* with Placido Domingo – sponsored by the merchant banker Morgan Grenfell – on which the company's future funding was believed to depend. She seemed to enjoy it, and spoke enthusiastically to the cast on stage after the performance. 'The subsidy seems safe for the time being,' Frank Johnson noted wrily in the *Spectator*.[231]

In 1988 she suddenly decided that it would be a great coup to buy the Thyssen collection for the nation. This was a fabulous private hoard of paintings ranging from Old Masters to post-Impressionists, a selection of which had been shown at the Royal Academy to great enthusiasm. The cost would have been at least £200 million. But Mrs Thatcher – in rare alliance with the Prince of Wales – set her heart on bringing it to Britain: she sent the Cabinet Secretary to Switzerland to negotiate personally with Baron Thyssen. He failed – it turned out that the collection was effectively already promised to Spain; yet she still gave a full page of her memoirs – half of the entire space she devoted to the arts – to the attempt.[232] She indulged one or two other personal follies. She tried hard to get planning regulations relaxed to allow another of her favourite millionaries, Peter Palumbo, to realise a long-held ambition to build a Mies van der Rohe skyscraper on an important site in the City. (She failed, but eventually compensated Palumbo by making him chairman of the Arts Council in succession to Rees-Mogg.) She gave enthusiastic approval to another favoured developer's vandalism of Battersea Power Station to build a huge leisure complex which never materialised, leaving the historic building gutted and open to the weather. And she poured a vast amount of public money – as well as distorting the transport infrastructure of east London – into supporting the Reichmann brothers' megalomaniac development of Canary Wharf, for which there was in the short term no commercial demand at all. (It eventually justified itself, but the brothers had gone bankrupt in the meantime.) Generally, however, she had no interest in creating cultural monuments at public expense, like Pompidou or Mitterrand in Paris. The new British Library was constantly starved of funds and endlessly delayed, an unloved public-sector project which fell between several departments and suffered badly from the lack of Prime Ministerial impetus to keep it moving.

Towards the end of the 1980s, however, she did start to think that the country ought to do something memorable to mark the millennium. 'We are really going to be rather lucky if we live to that day,' she told an audience of magazine editors in July 1988. 'We must celebrate it with something special.'

I am very well aware that if we are going to do something great or do anything very special it will take about ten years to do it, but at the same time I think we should not only build something special or do something special – we should be able to do something which affects every town, city and every village.

All she could think of in 1988 was buying the Thyssen collection (which she recognised was not enough); pedestrianising Parliament Square (a project of interest only to the Westminster village); doing 'something rather special with young people'; or 'something which we can look back on and say "Yes, this is how we celebrated the Millennium."' 'I think,' she concluded, 'that come the 1990s we will have to set up a group to really take this in hand.'[233] Whatever the ultimate choice she clearly expected the decision to be hers. We may be sure she would have commissioned something more enduring than a vapid dome.

10

Irish Dimension

The IRA: a real enemy

Mrs Thatcher faced one real enemy within: Irish republican terrorism. When she came into office in 1979 the 'troubles' in Northern Ireland were already ten years old. Ever since Harold Wilson had sent in the army – originally to protect the Catholic minority from the Protestant backlash against their demand for civil rights – Britain had been caught up in a bloody security operation in Northern Ireland, attempting to keep peace between the communities while increasingly targeted as an occupying force by the Provisional IRA. In 1972 Ted Heath had suspended the devolved Parliament at Stormont – the 'Protestant Parliament for a Protestant people' whose abuse of its power over half a century since partition had provoked the nationalist revolt – since when successive Secretaries of State, starting with Willie Whitelaw, had striven to devise new initiatives to resolve the conflict, while the 'provos' kept up a vicious guerrilla campaign against military and Unionist targets alike. From a peak in 1971–3, when 200 British soldiers and around 600 civilians died in three years, the toll had settled down to about a dozen soldiers, a similar number of police and forty or fifty civilians killed each year; but there were also regular bombings and murders on the British mainland, mostly in London, though the worst single incident was the bombing of a Birmingham pub in 1976 which killed twenty-one people and injured a hundred more.

Over the next decade the terror continued, and several times it touched Mrs Thatcher herself very closely. At the outset of the election campaign which brought her to power, her mentor Airey Neave – the man who had masterminded her seizure of the Tory leadership in 1975, became her shadow Northern Ireland Secretary and acted as her guide in security matters for the next four years – was blown up in his car in the precincts of the Palace of Westminster, apparently by the INLA, a splinter faction from the IRA. At the very end of her time in office another of her closest confidants, Ian Gow – another staunch Unionist – was murdered at his house in Sussex. Exactly midway between these two horrors the IRA's most audacious coup, the bombing of the Grand Hotel in Brighton in October 1984, came close to killing the Prime Minister herself and did kill or seriously injure several of her ministerial colleagues or their wives. At a purely human level, Margaret Thatcher had more reason than most to loathe the IRA.

Her instinctive political response was resolutely Unionist. Northern Ireland was British; the majority of its people professed their loyalty to the British Crown and flag: they were therefore entitled to the same unquestioning support as the people of the Falklands, Gibraltar or Hong Kong. Up until 1972 the Unionist MPs at Westminster had sat on the Tory benches and most of her keenest supporters on the right wing of the party – like Neave and Gow – still made little distinction. 'Any Conservative,' she wrote in her memoirs, 'should in his bones be a Unionist too.'[1] Moreover she always set her face against any cause – anywhere in the world, let alone in her own country – which sought to advance itself by violence. In so far as she thought about it at all she saw the Northern Ireland situation primarily as a security matter. In one of her first big speeches as party leader – the 'Iron Lady' speech in January 1976 in which she warned of the military threat posed by the Soviet Union – she noted in passing, in calling for higher defence spending, 'we are fighting a major internal war against terrorism in Northern Ireland and need more troops in order to win it'.[2] This was politically incorrect: talk of war was to adopt the IRA's rhetoric. The proper line was to treat terrorism as a policing matter, with the troops there merely to support the civil power. She never made this mistake again. But the slip betrayed her instinct.

In opposition she left Northern Ireland very much to Airey Neave, whose hard-line Unionist agenda envisaged the restoration of devolved government to the majority without the sort of power-sharing which Heath and Whitelaw had attempted to broker in 1973. Whitelaw told Garret Fitzgerald – then Irish Foreign Minister – in 1975 that he would resign if Mrs Thatcher tried to abandon power-sharing.[3] She did not; but for the next four years Neave gave no encouragement to the idea of reviving it. Mrs Thatcher took no active interest in the subject – Fitzgerald continued to find her ill-informed and poorly briefed – and Neave was poised to become Secretary of State when he was killed. His death only redoubled her determination to defy his murderers.

'Some devils got him,' she told the press outside Flood Street, 'and they must never, never, never be allowed to triumph. They must never prevail.'[4] One of her first public engagements as Prime Minister was to give the address at his memorial service.

For the next ten years she regularly repeated the promise that Northern Ireland was British and would remain British so long as the majority of its population wished it. Every autumn her party conference speech included an emotionally worded tribute to the courage and endurance of the people of Ulster. Yet in truth she had no deep concern for the province or its people. Ministers and officials who worked with her on Northern Ireland agree that she regarded it as a place apart whose customs and grievances she did not begin to understand.[5] The BBC's political editor John Cole, a Protestant Ulsterman himself, wrote that she had 'a total lack of feeling for a province that was remote from her own background'.[6] On the occasion of the signing of the Anglo-Irish Agreement in 1985 Garret Fitzgerald was astonished by her reaction to the possibility of European Community money to help Northern Ireland. 'More money for those people,' she said. 'Why should they have more money? I need that money for my people in England.'[7] Mrs Thatcher was always most revealing when caught off guard. The people of Northern Ireland were not 'her' people.

The more she saw of Unionist politicians over the years the less she liked them. As Grey Gowrie, a junior minister in Northern Ireland in 1981–3, recalled, 'She couldn't easily understand how people who ... professed loyalty to the British Crown could be quite so unBritish in their behaviour.'[8] Douglas Hurd, Northern Ireland Secretary in 1984–5, described her frankly in his diary as 'an anti-Unionist Unionist'.[9] Increasingly she saw Ulster as a drain on British resources and a diversion of her hard-pressed defence budget. What really moved her was the steady toll of young British lives – 'our boys' – lost in the province. From thirty-eight in 1979 the figure dwindled over the next decade to an average of nine a year. But there was no year in which at least two soldiers were not killed. She made a point of writing a personal letter to the family of each one. She also made several unannounced visits to the troops to demonstrate her support for them. She was strongly in favour of the policy of 'Ulsterisation' by which the army was withdrawn as far as possible to a reserve role and replaced on the streets with the Royal Ulster Constabulary (RUC). In fact she was as keen as any nationalist to get the troops out of Northern Ireland if only it had been possible. Yet the irreducible fact, as she acknowledged in a lecture dedicated to the memory of Airey Neave in 1980, was that 'No democratic country can voluntarily abandon its responsibilities in a part of its territories against the will of the majority of the population there.'[10] Britain could not expel Ulster from the United Kingdom, much as many in the Foreign Office and other parts of the British Establishment might have wished to. Like every other Prime Minister since Gladstone, Mrs Thatcher found herself with an insoluble problem. But the longer she lived with it, the more she too eventually moved towards making an effort to resolve it.

Her first Secretary of State, replacing the assassinated Neave, was Humphrey Atkins. In appointing the third consecutive Tory Chief Whip to fill that office, Mrs Thatcher seemed consciously or unconsciously to be echoing Heath's assumption that what the unruly Irish needed was a touch of discipline. In fact Atkins – like Whitelaw and Pym before him – was a natural conciliator whose approach was to try to bring the two communities together. He immediately started talks about talks which, with no political impetus behind them, swiftly foundered. The Unionists and their allies on the Tory benches, cheated of the restored ascendancy which they believed Neave had promised them, considered Atkins 'a disastrous choice, a puppet in the hands of his civil servants'.[11] Enoch Powell – since 1974 reborn as the most articulate defender of the Union, fanatically convinced that the Foreign Office was a nest of traitors dedicated to ending it – subsequently alleged that Neave had secured his vote in the crucial division which brought down the Callaghan Government in March 1979 by promising restored local government on the UK model. After Neave's death, however, when he claimed his payback, Mrs Thatcher denied knowledge of any such promise, thus fuelling his suspicion that she too was already planning to sell Ulster's birthright at the first opportunity.[12]

Meanwhile the republicans greeted the new government with an upsurge of violence. On the August bank-holiday weekend the IRA killed eighteen soldiers at Warrenpoint in County Down and blew up Lord Mountbatten – the Queen's cousin and Prince Charles' godfather – with two other members of his family on holiday in the Republic. Mrs Thatcher responded with typical defiance by flying immediately to visit the troops at Crossmaglen near the border in South Armagh: ignoring official advice she insisted on being photographed wearing a combat jacket and beret of the Ulster Defence Regiment. She also went on a courageous forty-five-minute walkabout in central Belfast. This visible demonstration of her support made a powerful impact in Northern Ireland. She went again on Christmas Eve, when a member of the Parachute Regiment kissed her under the mistletoe. Thereafter she made a similar morale-boosting visit nearly every year.

She found no rapport with the Irish Taoiseach, Jack Lynch, when he came to Downing Street in September. But at the end of 1979 Lynch handed over to the flamboyant Charles Haughey, a different style of leader altogether, with whom she initially got on surprisingly well. Despite his reputation as an unreconstructed nationalist – he was best-known in Britain for his part in a gun-running episode in 1970 which caused his temporary dismissal from Lynch's Government – Haughey came to office determined to find a solution to what he provocatively termed the 'failure' of Northern Ireland. He bounced into Downing Street in May 1980 with a terrific charm offensive and came out claiming to have inaugurated an era of 'new and closer co-operation' between Dublin and London based on increasing security co-operation on both sides of the border and an apparent willingness on the Irish side to consider almost anything – short of joining the Commonwealth – to woo the north to throw in its lot with a united Ireland. He even hinted at ending Ireland's cherished neutrality by joining NATO.[13] Mrs Thatcher was tempted, but remained cautious.

In December 1980 they met again in Dublin, under the shadow of the first republican hunger strike. Mrs Thatcher took with her an unprecedentedly high-powered team, including Lord Carrington and Geoffrey Howe as well as Atkins. Again Haughey exerted all his charm to create a sense of momentum, and succeeded in slipping past her guard an optimistic communiqué which recognised that Britain, Northern Ireland and the Republic were 'inextricably linked' and called for joint studies of 'possible new institutional structures' giving 'special consideration of the totality of relationships within these islands'. At his press conference Haughey spoke of 'a very significant meeting, a constructive meeting, a meeting which in my view had brought a very considerable . . . forward political movement', and stated that the Northern Ireland problem was 'now firmly on a new plane'. Though he later denied the words, the spin was that the two leaders had achieved 'an historic breakthrough'.[14] Mrs Thatcher was plainly embarrassed. On her return to London she gave two television interviews repeating that Northern Ireland was an integral part of the UK and stating firmly that 'there is no possibility of confederation'. She wrote an appeasing letter to Ian Paisley; but uncharacteristically she declined to make a statement in the House. In her memoirs she claims that the phrase about 'the totality of relationships' – 'a red rag to the Unionist bull' – was slipped through without her approval.[15] Her former private secretary Ken Stowe – now Permanent Secretary at the Northern Ireland Office – has confessed that he did not point it out to her. When it appeared in the communiqué she was furious: 'Ian Gow will go spare,' she raged. 'You have destroyed my reputation with the Unionists.'[16] She subsequently blamed the Foreign Office for stitching her up; but her discomfort was due to the fact that she had let herself be carried along by Haughey's blarney.

In fact Haughey's boldness outraged his own hardliners in Fianna Fail as much as it did the Unionists. He quickly retreated back into old-style nationalism, and his relationship with Mrs Thatcher never recovered. But Unionist alarm was not so easily assuaged. Opinion polls in Britain showed a swell of public support for being rid of Northern Ireland altogether. Mrs Thatcher's strenuous denials that Ulster had anything to fear from the 'new institutional structures' discussed at Dublin did not reassure them that Carrington and the Foreign Office were not in the process of talking her round as they had done successfully in relation to Rhodesia.

At the same time tension and violence in the province were stretched to breaking point by republican prisoners in the Maze prison going on hunger strike. Back in 1973 Whitelaw had most unwisely – as he later recognised – conceded IRA prisoners 'political' status which allowed them to wear their own clothes and enjoy other privileges denied to ordinary criminals. Roy Mason's withdrawal of this status in 1976 prompted a carefully escalated series of protests, starting with a 'blanket protest' against wearing prison uniforms, followed in 1978 by the 'dirty protest', in which the prisoners smeared their cells with excrement. The first hunger strike began in October 1980 when seven men started a 'fast to death'; they were later joined by thirty more. It was called off in December, two weeks after the Dublin summit, when one of the strikers, said to be twenty-four hours from death, yielded to the appeal of the Catholic Primate, Cardinal O'Fiaich, to save his life. The IRA claimed that the Government had given way. Atkins insisted that the prisoners had merely accepted terms which had been available to all prisoners in Northern Ireland before the strike began. Both sides claimed a moral victory. But the real propaganda battle was joined at the beginning of March 1981 when Bobby Sands began a second fast, followed at staggered intervals over the spring and summer by several others.

Mrs Thatcher's attitude to the hunger strikes was predictably uncompromising. Just as she would not submit to terrorism, she vowed that she would never give in to moral blackmail by convicted murderers.

She repudiated absolutely the suggestion that the offences for which
the IRA prisoners were imprisoned were 'political'. 'There can be no
political justification for murder or any other crime,' she told the
Commons on 20 November 1980.[17] 'There is no such thing as political murder,' she repeated on the radio a few days later.[18] And in
December, at her press conference following the Dublin summit, she
spelled it out again:

> Murder is a crime. Carrying explosives is a crime. Maiming is a
> crime ... Murder is murder is murder. It is not now and never can
> be a political crime. So there is no question of political status.[19]

Conditions in the H–Blocks were actually far better than in prisons
on the mainland, with single cells, regularly cleaned when the prisoners messed them, and excellent facilities for exercise and study. The
Government had implemented all the recommendations of the
European Commission on Human Rights, and Mrs Thatcher was
entitled to claim that the Maze was now 'one of the most liberal and
humane regimes anywhere'.[20] Inmates were allowed to wear, not their
own clothes, but civilian-style prison-issue clothes, and enjoyed extraordinary freedom to associate and maintain their political morale. The
new demands made by Sands and his colleagues in the second hunger
strike would have given the prisoners almost complete internal control
of the prison – something no government could have conceded. All
this was widely recognised. Yet the hunger strikers won enormous
public sympathy in the nationalist community, both north and south,
and the prospect of a succession of young men starving themselves to
death disturbed liberal consciences in Britain too.

The strike gained a fortuitous boost just after it started with the
death of Frank McGuire, the independent republican MP for Fermanagh
and South Tyrone. Sinn Fein immediately nominated Sands as an
'anti-H-Block' candidate. The SDLP (Social Democratic and Labour
Party) felt compelled to give him a clear run and on 9 April 1981 he
was elected by a majority of 1,400 votes over the former Unionist
leader Harry West – a result which resounded powerfully in the United
States and around the world. Four weeks later Sands died: 'murdered'
– so the republicans charged – in a British 'death camp'.[21] In vain did
Mrs Thatcher insist that Sands had died by his own volition and was
himself – 'let us not mince our words' – a convicted murderer.[22] The
'true martyrs', she declared, were the victims, not the perpetrators of
terrorism.[23] On 21 May two more strikers died. Courageously visiting
Northern Ireland one week later, Mrs Thatcher was determined to stick

the responsibility where it belonged. Asked on television if she was prepared to see 'an endless stream of hunger strikers die', she replied:

> That is a matter for those who go on hunger strike and those who are encouraging them to do so. I am not urging them to go on hunger strike. I am urging them not to die . . . It is they [the IRA] who are sentencing their own people to death, not me.[24]

'It is a tragedy,' she declared in a speech at Stormont Castle, 'that young men should be persuaded, coerced or ordered to starve themselves to death in a futile cause. Neither I nor any of my colleagues want to see a single person die of violence in Northern Ireland – policeman, soldier, civilian or prisoner on hunger strike . . . The PIRA [provisional IRA] take a different view. It would seem that dead hunger strikers, who have extinguished their own lives, are of more use to PIRA than living members. Such is their calculated cynicism. This Government is not prepared to legitimise their cause by word or by deed.'[25]

She was brave and she was right. The IRA's claim to be treated as political prisoners or prisoners of war was entirely spurious. Had they confined their attacks to military targets they might have claimed to be an 'army' conducting a dirty but defensible guerrilla war against an occupying power, but by cold-bloodedly targeting random civilians, as they regularly did, in defiance of the accepted norms of warfare as formulated in the Geneva Convention, they forfeited any right to be treated as soldiers. To this day Sinn Fein accuses the British Government of 'criminalising the Irish struggle'.[26] But it was they themselves who did that by espousing methods that were purely criminal. No government could have conceded the legitimacy of terrorism.

Nevertheless her ruthlessness was breathtaking. Over that summer – this was the same summer when Brixton and Toxteth were torn by riots and her personal popularity touched its lowest level – seven more martyrs went, one by one, to their slow deaths inside the Maze, while outside another seventy-three civilians, RUC men and soldiers were killed in the accompanying violence, before the IRA finally bowed to pressure from the Church and some of the remaining strikers' families and called a halt at the beginning of October. In a sense Mrs Thatcher had won. She had stood firm in the face of all the allegations of heartlessness and inflexibility that could be thrown at her, and it was the IRA which eventually blinked. This was perhaps the first time the world realised what she was made of. Her resolution certainly impressed the Americans. When six months later General Galtieri tried to tell Alexander Haig's envoy that 'that woman wouldn't dare' try to retake the Falklands, General Vernon Walters told him: 'Mr President, "that woman" has let a number of hunger strikers of her own basic ethnic origin starve themselves to death without flickering an eyelash. I wouldn't count on that if I were you.'[27]

But in another sense the gunmen had won a huge propaganda victory. Not only did Jim Prior, newly appointed Secretary of State in September, immediately concede many of the strikers' demands as soon as they ended their action, but the undeniable courage of the strikers, the depth and selflessness of their devotion to their cause, however cruelly they had pursued it when at large, made a deep impression both in Ireland and around the world. Within Ireland, Bobby Sands' face displayed on posters made him as potent a recruiting sergeant for the IRA as Lord Kitchener for the British army seventy years before; while from America a fresh stream of dollars flowed into its coffers, giving it the funds to buy more sophisticated weaponry and sufficient Semtex to supply the bombers for the next ten years. For most of the world, knowing little of the detail of the situation, the deaths of the hunger strikers brutally dramatised the impression that Britain was indeed a colonial power occupying Northern Ireland against the will of its oppressed population. The IRA's manipulation of the hunger strikes was as cynical as Mrs Thatcher said; but it was highly successful. It even had an effect on Mrs Thatcher herself.

In the short term there was nothing to be achieved through further co-operation with Dublin. At a summit with Garret Fitzgerald – briefly Taoiseach in the second half of 1981 – some flesh was put on the 'new institutional structures' agreed with Haughey by the establishment of an Anglo-Irish Intergovernmental Council. But both governments were too bruised by the hunger strikes to want to do much with it – Fitzgerald accused the British of having deliberately sabotaged promising efforts to end the strikes – and within a few weeks Haughey returned to power and promptly soured relations further by taking Argentina's side over the Falklands. A summit planned for July 1982 was abandoned and there were no contacts even in the margins of European Council meetings. Instead, Prior pursued a new initiative designed to build a consensual framework within which local powers might once again be entrusted to a devolved executive. This step-by-step approach – modelled on Prior's earlier approach to trade-union reform – was known as 'rolling devolution'. The first stage was a seventy-eight-member assembly to be elected by proportional representation. Mrs Thatcher never believed in it – Prior says she was 'very much against the whole idea', fearing that it would set an unwelcome precedent for Scotland and Wales;[28] but she went along with it for lack of any alternative. By the time the legislation was going through Parliament her attention was in the South Atlantic; but she allowed Ian Gow – her PPS – to lobby openly against it. Inevitably the scheme pleased neither community: the Unionists still hoped for a return to straight majority rule, while the SDLP would accept nothing short of power-sharing. All the local parties contested the first elections in October 1982, but both Sinn Fein (who won five seats on the back of the hunger strikes) and the SDLP (who could not afford to get out of step with Sinn Fein) boycotted the assembly, so that it met as an almost purely Protestant body, which defeated its purpose. The next year the official Unionists boycotted it as well. Prior believed it could have worked if the Government had thrown its weight behind it; Fitzgerald believes it had no chance in the poisoned wake of the hunger strikes.[29] Either way, rolling devolution was a dead duck by June 1983.

Meanwhile continuing shootings and bombings in Northern Ireland were dramatically supplemented by several more spectacular atrocities in London. In October 1981 a nail bomb at Chelsea barracks killed two passers-by and horrifically injured another forty, mainly soldiers. The same month a bomb-disposal expert lost his life defusing a device in Oxford Street. In July 1982 bombs in Hyde Park and Regent's Park killed eight military bandsmen – the softest of military targets – along with a number of their horses; and in December 1983 a bomb outside Harrods killed five Christmas shoppers and wounded another ninety-one. Each time Mrs Thatcher dropped whatever she was doing to hurry to the scene and visit the survivors in hospital, solemnly renewing her pledge to defeat the bombers.

But in fact she did not attempt to confront the IRA head on. Military intelligence told her that it could not be done. There were allegations that the army operated an unofficial 'shoot to kill' policy in Northern Ireland, eliminating rather than attempting to arrest suspected terrorists; and continued nationalist protests against heavy-handed interrogation and the use of plastic bullets against demonstrators. But the number of troops deployed actually fell slightly over the decade, from 13,000 in 1979 to 11,500 in 1990. Rather, as she faced up to the prospect of unending carnage, Mrs Thatcher began to look seriously at the possibility of promoting a political solution.

The Anglo-Irish Agreement

Several factors pushed her in this direction. First was the return of Garret Fitzgerald as Taoiseach in December 1982, soon followed by her own re-election in June 1983. Just as she thought the chance for progress in the Middle East should be seized while Shimon Peres was Prime Minister of Israel, so she believed it might be possible to achieve something with the moderate and constructive Fitzgerald which she could not do with the posturing Haughey. Fitzgerald recognised that Ireland could only be united by consent. He had spoken in 1981 of a 'republican crusade' to reform those aspects of the Irish constitution which antagonised Protestants, and specifically of scrapping clauses 2 and 3 which laid territorial claim to the Six Counties.[30] But instead of grand gestures, he was anxious to proceed incrementally by rebuilding the confidence of northern nationalists in the SDLP and diminishing support for Sinn Fein and the IRA. Though she found him at times tiresomely verbose and academic, Mrs Thatcher 'trusted and liked and perhaps even admired Garret Fitzgerald', in the words of one of her junior ministers in the Northern Ireland Office. 'She thought he was straight and that he wasn't trying to pull a fast one on her.'[31] At least – unlike Haughey – he expressed a proper outrage at the bombs in London. Geoffrey Howe has spoken of 'an extraordinary chemistry' between the two leaders which he compares to her relationship with Mikhail Gorbachev.[32]

Second, despite her Unionist sympathies Mrs Thatcher did actually – as with the Palestinians – come to a partial appreciation of the nationalist case. Fitzgerald wrote in his memoirs that she always resisted his use of the term 'alienation' to describe the northern Catholics' sense of exclusion from the institutions of Northern Ireland, believing it to be a Marxist term. But she acknowledged the reality. When she was persuaded that the IRA and their Sinn Fein apologists were not Irish infiltrators but predominantly British citizens, an indigenous northern movement poorly supported in the Republic, and that the legitimate nationalist party, the SDLP, won a lot of impeccably democratic votes – 18 per cent in 1983, compared with 13 per cent for Sinn Fein – she became convinced that the law-abiding Catholic community had somehow to be reconciled to the British state. The journalist Edward Pearce recalls a dinner conversation in 1985 at which Charles Moore, then editor of the *Spectator*, asked her 'What about the Protestants?' 'She leaned into the table and in her best taut, intense . . . way [replied] "Yes, Charles, and what about the Catholics?" . . . All the fierceness which she would misuse in hating the Germans and despising the unemployed was turned towards getting a decent equity for the minority. It was wonderful.'[33] She could never accept the idea of dual allegiance – she resented the anomalous right of the Irish to vote in British elections, and thought like Enoch Powell that they should be treated logically as foreign – but she came to see that the legacy of history gave the Republic an interest in the equitable government of the north.[34] In other words she recognised that there was not just a security problem in Northern Ireland, which might be solved by stronger policing, but a real political problem which required a political solution.

Third, she was influenced – as on Rhodesia, Hong Kong and other comparable issues – by the Foreign Office. In 1998 Ted Heath revealed that back in 1972 Alec Douglas-Home, when Foreign Secretary, had advised that 'no sustainable framework for keeping Northern Ireland within the UK could ever be contrived' and urged him to work towards a united Ireland; and this undoubtedly remained the department's longterm objective.[35] To this extent Powell and the Ulster conspiracy theorists were right. Mrs Thatcher did not go so far, but she would not have given the mandarins a green light if she had not been persuaded that something must be attempted which the Unionists would not like. The Anglo-Irish Agreement which eventually emerged in 1985 was the fruit of painstaking spadework by the Foreign Office and the Irish foreign ministry, co-ordinated by the Cabinet Secretary, Robert Armstrong, and his opposite number in Dublin, Dermot Nally, with minimal involvement of the Northern Ireland Office and behind the backs of the Unionists.

Most important of all, she was significantly influenced by American pressure. The Irish lobby in Washington, led by the Speaker of the House of Representatives, Tip O'Neill, and Senators Edward Kennedy and Daniel Moynihan, was very powerful – second only to the Jewish lobby – and very partisan, continually issuing violent denunciations of British colonial oppression and the alleged denial of human rights in Northern Ireland. Ronald Reagan, with his own Irish background, was susceptible to this line; while Mrs Thatcher, faced with hostile demonstrators every time she visited America, was uncomfortably aware that Northern Ireland strained her special relationship with the US. At the time of the hunger strikes in 1981 the President refused to become involved in Britain's internal affairs, though the White House delicately warned London that it was in danger of 'losing the media campaign here in the United States'.[36] But following his sentimental visit to the land of his fathers in the summer of 1984 – at a time when Washington horsetrading additionally required him to buy O'Neill's acquiescence in American aid to the Nicaraguan Contras – Reagan became increasingly anxious to encourage his favourite ally to be more constructive.

For all these reasons, then, from the moment she was re-elected in June 1983, Mrs Thatcher began to look more favourably on the idea of recognising an 'Irish dimension' in tackling the Ulster problem. As early as December 1982 she had told Sir David Goodall, one of the Foreign Office officials most closely involved in the covert talks: 'If we get back next time I think I would like to do something about Ireland.'[37] The catalyst was provided by the New Ireland Forum, established in May 1983 by the new leader of the SDLP, John Hume, with the encouragement of Garret Fitzgerald, to bring together all the constitutional nationalist parties on both sides of the border to seek a peaceful way forward to undercut Sinn Fein and the IRA. Mrs Thatcher was slow to grasp the opportunity it offered. She admits in her memoirs that she was 'intensely wary' of it, fearing it would be just another platform for denouncing the British; but she did not reject it out of hand.[38] At the same time she and Fitzgerald – meeting in the margin of the European summit at Stuttgart in June 1983 – agreed to revive the Anglo-Irish Council, under whose aegis officials of both countries were able to meet without fanfare sixteen times between November 1983 and March 1985. Then in September 1984, when Prior left the Government (more or less at his own wish), she signalled a fresh start by appointing Douglas Hurd to the Northern Ireland Office, telling him she wanted 'someone of intellect and toughness' there.[39]

Four weeks later the process was derailed when the IRA exploded a massive bomb in the Grand Hotel in Brighton, where the Prime Minister and most of the Conservative hierarchy were staying during the party conference. She was very lucky to survive unscathed. The bomb ripped out the whole central section of the hotel and badly damaged her bathroom. When it went off, just before three in the morning, she had just been putting the finishing touches to her speech for the next day with Ronnie Millar and John Gummer. As they left, Robin Butler came in with a last letter for her to sign before she got ready for bed. But for that, she would have been in the bathroom at the critical moment and, though she might not have been killed, she would certainly have suffered serious injury from flying glass. Her sitting room, however, and the bedroom where Denis was asleep, were undamaged. Her first thought was that it was a car bomb outside; her next was to make sure that Denis was all right. 'It touched me,' Butler recalled, 'because it was one of those moments where there could be no play-acting.'[40] As Denis quickly pulled on some trousers over his pyjamas, she crossed the corridor to the room where the secretaries had been typing the speech. Only now did the scale of what had happened become clear.

Amazingly the lights had stayed on. Millar, who had been thrown against a wall by the explosion as he walked away from her room, described the scene. 'There were no cries for help, no sound at all, just dust, clouds of dust, followed by the occasional crunch of falling masonry from somewhere above. Otherwise silence. It was eerie.' Pausing only to gather up the scattered pages of the precious speech which had burst from his briefcase, he hobbled back the way he had come and found Mrs Thatcher in the secretaries' room 'sitting on an upright chair, very still. The girls were standing on chairs peering out of a side window, bubbling with excitement . . . At length she murmured, "I think that was an assassination attempt, don't you?" '⁴¹ Geoffrey and Elspeth Howe, the Gummers, David Wolfson and others who had been sleeping on the same corridor gathered in various states of undress, speculating about the possibility of a second device. They still did not know whether anyone had been hurt. It was a quarter of an hour before firemen arrived to escort them to safety down the main staircase and out through the kitchens, to be driven to Brighton police station. There they were gradually joined by other members of the Cabinet, among them Keith Joseph 'immaculate in a Noel Coward dressing gown over his silk pyjamas', carefully guarding his ministerial red box.⁴² Mrs Thatcher was still wearing the evening gown she had worn to the Conservative Agents' Ball a few hours earlier. Following a quick consultation with Willie Whitelaw, Leon Brittan and John Gummer, she insisted that the final day of the conference must go on as planned. She refused to return to Downing Street but – with her security men anxious to hustle her away – changed into a blue suit and gave a calmly determined interview on camera to the BBC's John Cole. 'Even under the most appalling personal strain,' he noted, 'Margaret Thatcher . . . was a supreme political professional.'⁴³ She was then driven to Lewes Police College, where – sharing a room with Crawfie while Denis shared with the detectives down the corridor – she snatched a couple of hours' sleep.

She woke to see the television pictures of Norman Tebbit being pulled agonisingly out of the rubble and hear the news that five people – among them John Wakeham's wife and the Tory MP Anthony Berry – had been killed and Margaret Tebbit badly injured. She was shocked but still determined that the conference should go ahead. Alistair McAlpine persuaded Marks & Spencer to open early so that those who had lost their belongings could be freshly kitted out; Harvey Thomas, who had himself been lucky to survive, redirected the proceedings, substituting a more solemn style for the usual waving flags and patriotic music; and at 9.30 a.m. precisely Mrs Thatcher walked into

the conference centre to emotional applause to give her speech, shorn
of the normal party point-scoring but prefaced by a defiant denunciation of the bombers. The bomb, she said, was not only 'an inhuman
and undiscriminating attempt to massacre innocent, unsuspecting men
and women'. It was also 'an attempt to cripple Her Majesty's democratically elected Government':

> That is the scale of the outrage in which we have all shared, and
> the fact that we are gathered here now, shocked but composed and
> determined, is a sign not only that this attack has failed but that all
> attempts to destroy democracy by terrorism will fail.[44]

Mrs Thatcher's coolness, in the immediate aftermath of the attack
and in the hours after it, won universal admiration. Her defiance was
another Churchillian moment in her premiership which seemed to
encapsulate both her own steely character and the British public's stoical
refusal to submit to terrorism. 'We suffered a tragedy not one of us
could have thought would happen in our country,' she told her
constituents in Finchley the following weekend. 'And we picked
ourselves up and sorted ourselves out as all good British people do,
and I thought, let us stand together, for we are British.'[45] Her popularity rating temporarily recovered to near-Falklands levels. In public
she appeared unruffled by the attack. But the psychological damage
may have been greater than she showed. Carol immediately flew back
from Korea and found her mother at Chequers on the Sunday morning
'calm but . . . still shaken'. 'This is the day I was not meant to see,' she
told Carol.[46] For ever afterwards she felt that Margaret Tebbit's fate –
confined to a wheelchair for life – had been intended for her.[47] Though
the lights had not gone out at Brighton, she always carried a torch in
her handbag thereafter; and in 1987 she told Woodrow Wyatt that she
no longer wore her best jewellery to party conferences 'so that there
will be something left behind for the family if there is a terrorist
attack'.[48] The assassination of Indira Gandhi two weeks after Brighton
underlined how vulnerable she was. Denis bought her a watch and
wrote her a rare note: 'Every minute is precious.'[49]

Brighton had a political effect as well. 'Though it killed only a few
unfortunate people,' McAlpine suggested some years later, 'it had a
profound effect on the Tory party.'[50] The annual conference, hitherto
remarkably open, was henceforth ringed by tight security. Many felt
that not only Norman Tebbit, but Mrs Thatcher too, was never the same
again. She seemed to lose some of her self-confidence and her political touch. Emma Nicholson, an admirer of the early Thatcher who

later defected to the Liberal Democrats, believes that she became harder, because more isolated, after 1984:

> She lost her way, I believe, because the Brighton bomb effectively locked her away in a Nixonian bunker, staffed by overzealous ideological activists and cut off from the voters she needed to see and hear and touch. The IRA won a more profound victory than was immediately apparent from her survival.[51]

In the short run Mrs Thatcher's enthusiasm for talks with Dublin was understandably dented. The next month Garret Fitzgerald came to Chequers to try to make progress on the lines explored by the New Ireland Forum, whose report had been published in May. This set out three possible solutions: a united Ireland, a federal or confederal Ireland, or some form of joint sovereignty. Fitzgerald recognised that the first two were out of the question; but following the patient groundwork of the Armstrong–Nally talks, he hoped to win Mrs Thatcher's support for some version of the third option. If she would agree to give Dublin a role in the government of Northern Ireland – he was happy to call it 'joint authority' rather than joint sovereignty if that helped – he thought he could win a referendum in the south to scrap clauses 2 and 3 of the Irish constitution. Mrs Thatcher, however, doubted whether he could deliver this, except in return for an unacceptable degree of southern interference in the north. She was not prepared to pay a high price to be rid of clauses which she did not think should have been in the Irish constitution in the first place. Three years after the Falklands she would not consider shared sovereignty – to which Geoffrey Howe, for instance, as an anglicised Welshman at ease with the problem of dual identity, was attracted. 'Mrs Thatcher really from the beginning,' Robert Armstrong recalled, 'was not prepared to consider anything which suggested any derogation of the sovereignty of the United Kingdom in Northern Ireland, anything at all.'[52] She only wanted to commit the Irish to closer security co-operation across the border, ideally by means of a security zone on the Irish side where British troops would be allowed to operate. Alternatively she was prepared to consider redrawing the border and repatriating nationalists to the Republic.[53] Fitzgerald was disappointed, but still unprepared for the devastating post-summit press conference in which Mrs Thatcher dismissed all three of the Forum's options out of hand. She started positively, describing the talks as 'the fullest, frankest and most realistic bilateral meeting I have ever had with the Taoiseach' – though 'full and frank' is an accepted diplomatic euphemism for disagreement, while 'realistic' was always Thatcher code for her brutal way with others' inflated expectations. But right at the end, when asked about the Forum's proposals, she slipped her leash:

> I have made it quite clear – and so did Mr Prior when he was Secretary of State for Northern Ireland – that a unified Ireland was one solution that is *out*. A second solution was confederation of two states. *That is out*. A third solution was joint authority. *That is out*. That is a derogation from sovereignty. We made that quite clear when the Report was published.[54]

It was not so much what she said but the withering tone in which she said it. Her uncompromising triple repetition 'out . . . out . . . out' was taken as a gratuitous slap in the face for Fitzgerald and seemed to slam the door on all the hopes that had been raised by their relationship. The Irish press next day was seething with fury, and London–Dublin relations seemed to be back to square one. But in fact this diplomatic disaster turned out to be the low point from which the 1985 Agreement emerged. Mrs Thatcher herself realised that she had gone too far and recognised that she would have to give some ground to repair the damage. Above all, her provocative language persuaded Reagan that it was time to get involved. Not only was the White House bombarded with the usual wild communications from Irish pressure groups like the Ancient Order of Hibernians;[55] but more constructively O'Neill, Kennedy, Moynihan and forty-two other Senators and Congressmen wrote to him that 'Mrs Thatcher's peremptory dismissal of the reasonable alternatives put forth by the Forum' had dashed the most hopeful opportunity for peace since the Sunningdale accord of 1973.[56] They urged Reagan to press her to reconsider when she came to Camp David in December; and he did exactly as they asked. A draft prepared for the President recommended what he should say:

> I must tell you frankly that the public perception in America of the outcome of the November summit was not favorable. I am concerned that unless there is the appearance of progress at the next Anglo-Irish summit, a radicalisation will occur in Irish-American opinion which would endanger the current bipartisan support that our Northern Ireland policy enjoys. I am therefore asking you, in the words used by Douglas Hurd on December 4, to apply 'talent and determination . . . to the central task of reconciliation' and that you

give the public – to the greatest extent possible – a basis for belief that some progress is being made. I will ask the same of Fitzgerald before your next meeting.[57]

Reagan may not have used quite these words, but the record confirms that Northern Ireland was discussed over lunch. Mrs Thatcher assured the President that 'despite reports to the contrary, she and Garret Fitzgerald were on good terms and we are working toward making progress on this difficult question'. He replied that 'making progress is important, and observed that there is great Congressional interest in the matter', specifically mentioning O'Neill's request that he appeal to her to be 'reasonable and forthcoming'.[58] To the Speaker himself Reagan wrote that he had 'made a special effort to bring your letter to her personal attention ... I also personally emphasised the need for progress in revolving the complex situation in Northern Ireland and the desirability for flexibility on the part of all the involved parties.'[59]

An appeal from this quarter was not one that Mrs Thatcher could ignore.* She was now convinced, Robert Armstrong told Fitzgerald in January 1985, that she could not 'stand pat' on the issue.[62] On 16 January she entertained John Hume at Chequers, which seems to have been something of a revelation to her. 'Towards the end of the meeting she told him that when they had first met she had not understood how people could have different loyalties, but she understood this a lot better now.'[63] In the negotiations that followed her first concern was still security; but she realised that in order to get this she must concede what were called 'confidence-building measures' on the ground – mainly addressing practical grievances over policing, prisons and the court system – to reconcile the northern Catholic population to the British state. She still ruled out the sort of comprehensive constitutional settlement Fitzgerald had originally wanted. Hurd wrote in his diary in March: 'The truth is we want a minimalist agreement.'[64] Yet she was now prepared to accept some sort of 'Irish dimension' in

---

*She was also susceptible to a mixture of flattery and gentle blackmail. When she visited Washington again in February, she was keen to emulate Churchill by speaking to both Houses of Congress. Reagan was all for it; but the invitation lay with Tip O'Neill. In Washington you seldom get anything for nothing. She used her speech to emphasise the importance of consent in the Northern Irish context, and to warn the Americans to 'be under no illusions about the Provisional IRA'.[60] But she knew what her audience expected of her. Likewise, in July, speaking to the American Bar Association in London, she thanked Congress for passing a new extradition treaty that would stop Irish terrorists finding immunity in the USA[61]. But here again she knew there was a *quid pro quo*.

exchange for assurances that Dublin accepted Ulster's right to remain British so long as the majority wished it, without formally amending the Irish constitution. It still took months of tortuous negotiation between officials, and a crucial meeting between Mrs Thatcher and Fitzgerald in the margin of the Milan EC summit in May, to overcome her doubts; she was still worried that they were going too far, too fast. But eventually she bit the bullet and agreed to accord Dublin not just consultation on Northern Irish matters, but guaranteed institutional input in the form of a commission to be jointly chaired by the Secretary of State for Northern Ireland and an Irish minister, with a permanent secretariat housed outside Belfast. This was the core of the Anglo-Irish Agreement finally signed by the two leaders at Hillsborough Castle on 15 November 1985.

It was a measure of how tightly the negotiations had been conducted within a narrow circle of insiders that Mrs Thatcher was unprepared for the fury of the Unionist response. From April a Cabinet committee comprising Willie Whitelaw, Lord Hailsham, Norman Tebbit and John Biffen had been kept informed; and the full Cabinet was told in late October. But the Northern Ireland Secretary – Hurd until September, then Tom King – was never centrally involved; and the Northern Ireland Office, widely seen as being too close to the Unionists, was kept well in the background. While Dublin had kept John Hume closely informed throughout, the Unionist leaders – James Molyneaux of the official Unionist party and Ian Paisley of the still more uncompromising Democratic Unionists – were deliberately excluded. They were excluded, obviously, because everyone knew there would be no agreement if they were included. But then no one should have been surprised that they objected. In fact they had inevitably picked up hints of what was in the wind – the Orange Order and other 'loyalist' organisations had been marching against rumours of a sell-out all summer – and had made their position very clear to the Prime Minister personally.

On 2 August Molyneaux and Paisley explicitly warned her that 'any attempt to involve the Government of the Irish Republic in the direction or control of our affairs will meet with united Unionist opposition. Even a consultative role for the Irish Republic would be a violation of the Government's assurance of Ulster's right to self-determination.'[65] Later that month they met Mrs Thatcher in Downing Street and told her that they were 'profoundly anxious about the secrecy of the talks' and resented not being consulted.[66] By mid-September they knew that she was determined to ignore their warnings. 'I am convinced,' she wrote to them, 'that our present dialogue with the Irish Republic represents our best hope of improving co-operation in a number of areas, including security . . . I repeat my unqualified assurance that sovereignty over Northern Ireland will be undiminished.' Their reply was blunt:

> We specifically sought an assurance that you interpreted undiminished United Kingdom sovereignty over Northern Ireland as precluding any British-Irish machinery dealing only with Northern Ireland . . . We take it that your omission to confirm this in your letter is deliberate . . . You have failed to make *de jure* recognition of the right of the people of Northern Ireland to self-determination a condition precedent to consideration of Irish demands.[67]

She could not say she had not been warned. But the truth was that she had closed her mind to the Unionist reaction in the interest of being seen to make an effort. Nevertheless she was shaken by the violence of the Unionist rejection of the Agreement and the storm of denunciation which they levelled at her, which was 'worse than anyone had predicted to me'.[68] In the Commons Enoch Powell enquired icily if she was aware that 'the penalty for treachery is to fall into public contempt'. She replied that she found his remarks 'deeply offensive'.[69] Ian Paisley told her that 'having failed to defeat the IRA you now have capitulated and are prepared to set in motion machinery that will achieve the IRA goal . . . a united Ireland';[70] and from his pulpit he thundered against 'Jezebel, who sought to destroy Israel in a day'. His deputy Peter Robinson called the Agreement 'an act of political prostitution'; and Molyneaux spoke of 'a universal cold fury' such as he had never known in forty years in public life.[71] But if these reactions were predictable she was most upset by the resignation of her former PPS, Ian Gow, from his junior job in the Treasury, to which she had only just appointed him. Gow was her Unionist conscience, as well as her most devoted supporter: if he could not bring himself to accept the Agreement, she feared that perhaps she had gone too far.

'How will it be possible to proceed without the consent of the majority?' the *Spectator* demanded. 'The supporters of the agreement are being profoundly impractical . . . if they think that reconciliation can be forced on Northern Ireland.'[72] It was true that there was a fundamental inequity in the way the Agreement was negotiated behind the back of one of the two communities that would have to make it work. Always hypersensitive to any hint of a sell-out, the Unionists were bound to try to wreck it, as they had wrecked Sunningdale and other promising initiatives in the past. 'British we are and British we shall remain,' Paisley roared at a mass demonstration in Belfast on 24

November. 'Now Mrs Thatcher says that the Republic must have a say in our province. We say never, never, never, never, never.'[73] But this time the Unionists' bluff was called. Claiming that the Agreement could not be implemented against the democratic will of the majority community, all fifteen Unionist MPs resigned their seats and stood again in by-elections, held simultaneously on 26 January. They made their point, slightly spoiled by the loss of one seat, Newry and Armagh, to the SDLP. But in the House of Commons they gained the support of only thirty Conservative MPs: the Government won an over-whelming all-party majority of 473–47. The fact that Fitzgerald faced a much closer vote in the Dail, where Haughey – following Sinn Fein – charged his rival with abandoning the goal of Irish unity, helped convince British opinion that Ulster was crying wolf as usual. Polls in both Britain and the Republic showed strong public support: most people felt that an agreement denounced by the diehards on both sides was probably on the right lines.

As time passed Mrs Thatcher came to regret the Anglo-Irish Agreement. She was bitterly disappointed that it failed to deliver the sort of cross-border co-operation against terrorism that she had hoped for. In 1987 Haughey returned to power in the Republic, and though he did not tear up the Agreement he remained truculent and unhelpful over such matters as shared intelligence and the extradition of a terrorist priest, Patrick Ryan, in 1988. Far from reducing violence, the Agreement provoked the paramilitaries on both sides to increased activity. One of the most horrific incidents was the IRA's bombing of the annual Remembrance Day ceremony at Enniskillen in County Fermanagh in November 1987, which killed eleven people and injured another sixty. 'At that moment,' Charles Powell believed, after all Mrs Thatcher thought she had done to try to reconcile the nationalists, 'the iron really entered her soul.'[74] Once again she demonstrated her solidarity by attending the delayed remembrance service in the town two weeks later. Over the next two years the IRA also stepped up attacks on British military personnel in Northern Ireland itself (where twenty-one soldiers were killed in 1988 and twelve in 1989), on the mainland (ten bandsmen were killed in an attack on the Royal Marines School of Music in September 1989) and on the Continent. In March 1988 the SAS thwarted a planned attack on bandsmen in Gibraltar by shooting dead three suspects before they could plant their bomb. Mrs Thatcher had no time whatever for critics who charged that the security services were operating an illegal 'shoot to kill' policy, and was outraged that Thames Television dared to make a programme questioning the official version of the event and alleging that the victims

had been unarmed. At the Tory Party Conference she made an unusually extended attack on the IRA and offered the policemen, prison
officers, soldiers, civil servants and judges of Northern Ireland 'our
deepest admiration and thanks for defending democracy and . . . facing
danger while keeping within the rule of law – unlike the terrorist
who skulks in the shadows and shoots to kill'. She would not admit
that the security forces themselves ever overstepped the limit, but promised once again that 'this Government will never surrender to the IRA.
Never.'[75]

The same month she prevailed upon Douglas Hurd, now Home
Secretary, to introduce a ban on the broadcasting of Sinn Fein and
IRA spokesmen, intended to deny them what she called – in a favourite
phrase borrowed from the Chief Rabbi – 'the oxygen of publicity'.[76]
In her memoirs she rejects the charge of censorship, insisting that the
ban was both justified and successful.[77] In fact the broadcasters quickly
circumvented it by using an actor to speak Gerry Adams' words better
than he could have spoken them himself, while the Irish lobby in the
United States was able to present the denial of free speech as one more
example of British oppression. Hurd noted in his diary at the time: 'It
is a poor decision . . . I'm not proud of it,' and later, as Foreign Secretary
under John Major, was instrumental in getting the ban lifted.[78]

By 1993 Lady Thatcher had concluded that the whole philosophy
behind the 1985 Agreement had been a mistake. 'In dealing with
Northern Ireland,' she wrote, 'successive governments have studiously
refrained from security policies that might alienate the Irish
Government and Irish nationalist opinion in Ulster, in the hope of
winning their support against the IRA. The Anglo-Irish Agreement
was squarely in this tradition.' The results of this approach, however,
had been meagre. 'Our concessions alienated the Unionists without
gaining the level of security co-operation we had a right to expect.
In the light of this experience it is surely time to consider an alternative approach.'[79]

She does not suggest what such an alternative approach might be:
the implication is tougher security, even a 'military' solution. But she
had not attempted that in office, nor were her successors tempted by
it. The same logic that impelled her, against her instincts, has driven
them; and the 1985 Agreement has in fact gradually borne fruit. It can
now be seen as the start of a process which eventually led to the Good
Friday Agreement of 1998. First, it served a warning to the Unionists
that their bluff could be called: London's repeated guarantee that
Northern Ireland would remain a part of the United Kingdom, so
long as the majority of its people wanted, did not give them a veto

on how Britain chose to implement its sovereignty. This had an enlightening effect on David Trimble, if not on the immovable Paisley. Second, it did help to reconcile the nationalists to British rule, shored up the position of the SDLP and, most significantly, began to convert Sinn Fein and the IRA itself to the idea that more might be achieved by negotiation than by endless violence. At the same time the machinery of co-operation established in 1985 provided mechanisms to defuse problems between the two governments; and the Agreement did – as was perhaps Mrs Thatcher's primary motivation – convince the United States that Britain was genuinely trying to resolve the problem, which led to better American understanding of the Unionist position and encouraged increased international, particularly American, investment in Northern Ireland.[80] All these beneficial developments flowed from the 1985 Agreement. It was understandable, as the murder of soldiers continued unabated, that Mrs Thatcher should have felt disappointed; understandable too, when Ian Gow was killed in the drive of his own house in 1990, that she should feel guilty that perhaps she had betrayed Ulster after all. But she was wrong to disparage the Agreement. She was brave and far-sighted to have concluded it, and it should stand among her diplomatic achievements alongside the Zimbabwe and Hong Kong settlements. If peace ever comes to Northern Ireland, she will have played her part in the process.

11

Elective Dictatorship

'She who must be obeyed'

The idea that the Prime Minister is merely the first among equals has long been a fiction. The power of the Prime Minister *vis-à-vis* his Cabinet colleagues has been increasing at least since the time of Lloyd George, for a number of reasons to do with the growth of the state, the increasing complexity of the government machine and the escalating demands of the media. Both Harold Wilson and Ted Heath in their day were criticised for being excessively 'presidential', though Wilson, unusually, became less so in his second administration. Unquestionably, however, the concentration of power in the person of the Prime Minister grew still more pronounced under Mrs Thatcher, as a result partly of her longevity in the job, partly of her personality.

During her first term she was to some extent constrained by her own relative inexperience, by the presence in the Cabinet of several heavyweight colleagues profoundly sceptical of her approach, and by the dire economic situation. Even so, by placing her few reliable allies in the key departments, she broadly got her way most of the time and managed to remove or neutralise most of her critics. By the middle of her second term she had achieved a Cabinet much more nearly of her own choice. Though the old wet/dry dichotomy had been resolved, there were still three identifiable groups around the table. Despite the loss of Parkinson, she now had a solid core of true believers: Lawson, Howe and (till 1986) Keith Joseph, reinforced by Norman Tebbit, Leon Brittan, Nicholas Ridley, David Young and (from 1986) John Moore. In the middle there was the ballast of steady loyalists who took their cue from Willie Whitelaw: Tom King, Norman Fowler, Nicholas Edwards, George Younger, Michael Jopling and (from 1986) Paul Channon, to whom may be added the senior, sometimes cantankerous but generally supportive figure of Lord Hailsham. Then, coming into the Cabinet between 1984 and 1986 was a new generation of ambitious former Heathites who were happy, after a period of probation, to turn their coats: Douglas Hurd, John MacGregor, Kenneth Baker, Kenneth Clarke and Malcolm Rifkind.

Mrs Thatcher's most ardent allies and supporters – people like Nicholas Ridley and, on the back benches, George Gardiner – worried that she was storing up trouble for the future by promoting too many of these fair-weather friends from the left of the party, rather than true believers from the right. But she scarcely seemed to worry any more about the left–right balance, because by 1983 she thought the economic argument had been won. She was uneasily aware that the ablest candidates tended to be of the left; but she appointed them as individuals to serve her, not as representatives of wings of the party. She promoted Kenneth Baker and Kenneth Clarke because they were good at presentation. 'What I needed was Ministers who could fight battles in the media as well as in Whitehall,' she wrote in her memoirs.[1] 'For every few Thatchers, Josephs and Ridleys you need at least one Ken Baker to concentrate on communicating the message.'[2]

In addition there remained three unclassifiables in the Cabinet. Peter Walker, the most enduring of the old wets, was fully occupied as Energy Secretary dealing with Arthur Scargill in 1984–5. His success in that crucial assignment gave him special licence to dissent on other questions, notably public spending. 'I never heard Margaret tangle with Peter Walker,' Kenneth Baker wrote. 'Margaret always treated Peter with great care and respect and I never heard her criticise him.' And again: 'The only Minister to whose disagreement Margaret listened, with her head bowed, was Peter Walker, who invariably spoke up for the other point of view.'[3] She may have listened, as the price of keeping him in the Cabinet, but she was rarely deflected. Walker in turn showed much less inclination after 1983 to make his reservations public: in 1987 he moved to the Welsh Office and continued to keep out of wider controversies in return for a relatively free hand in the principality.

John Biffen was an increasingly loose cannon as Leader of the House. He still reckoned himself to be 'bone dry' economically, but he worried about the social consequences of the Government's policies. He was a free-market monetarist who believed in balanced budgets, he told John Ranelagh, but 'I was not actually a low-taxation person, so therefore I was less convinced of supply-side economics than some people.'[4] His fastidiousness was offended by Mrs Thatcher's increasingly messianic style, and in May 1986 he dared to suggest on television that the Tory party should offer a more 'balanced ticket' at the next election. It was only his popularity in the House that prevented her sacking him immediately, but from that moment on Biffen's days were numbered.

Above all Michael Heseltine lurked in the Ministry of Defence, never a wet but not a Thatcherite either, defiantly his own man, unashamedly ambitious and identifiable long before December 1985 as the likeliest challenger if the Prime Minister's authority should slip.

This was the personnel: but the Cabinet as a body had a much diminished sense of corporate identity. It met only once a week, on Thursday, compared with twice a week under previous administrations, and rarely enjoyed anything approaching general discussion. Peter Hennessy's 1986 analysis found that the Thatcher Cabinet not only met less frequently (forty to forty-five times a year) but created much less paper for general circulation, so that its members were measurably less well informed. Moreover Mrs Thatcher created fewer Cabinet committees than her predecessors: 125 in her first six and a half years – that is less than twenty a year – compared with 160 in the previous three years under Callaghan.[5] Sometimes she would set up an *ad hoc* committee of three or four ministers, often chaired by herself, to deal with a subject that had arisen; more often than not she would simply get the relevant minister to prepare a paper for herself alone; she would then interrogate him on it personally with two or three of her advisers from the Cabinet Office or the Policy Unit, thus acting as 'judge and jury in her own cause' without reference to the Cabinet.[6] This might almost be a definition of presidential government. None of these practices originated with Mrs Thatcher: but she took them further than any of her predecessors. Cabinet was reduced to an occasion for reporting decisions, not the place for taking them. Lawson calls it a 'rubber stamp' and claims to have regarded Thursday mornings as his most restful two hours of the week, a chance to catch up on his correspondence.[7]

Just occasionally the Cabinet was allowed to act as a court of appeal, but only rarely did a minister who took his case to Cabinet get his way. In 1984 Patrick Jenkin successfully resisted a proposed cut in funds for council-house maintenance. 'Patrick won,' Baker wrote, 'but I do not think that Margaret ever really forgave him for it.'[8] More often Mrs Thatcher made sure in advance, with Willie Whitelaw's help, that the appealing minister would not find enough support. When Quintin Hailsham, for instance, refused to accept a Cabinet committee decision to break barristers' and solicitors' monopolies, he insisted on taking it to Cabinet but was outvoted. 'He banged his sticks on the table, stormed out and drove home,' Ridley recalled, 'where he promptly ran into a brick wall. He ran into a brick wall at Cabinet too, and the legal monopolies were duly broken.'[9] Alternatively – as with Michael Heseltine and the future of Westland helicopters – Mrs Thatcher made sure the issue did not go to the Cabinet at all. Peter Walker complains that many decisions made in *ad hoc* groups were not even reported to Cabinet: the first other ministers knew was when they read it in the newspapers.[10] In these instances the Cabinet was not even a rubber stamp.

Ridley maintains that Mrs Thatcher's enemies, like Walker and Heseltine, spread myths about her abuse of the Cabinet system only because they had lost the arguments.[11] Peter Hennessy agrees that her use of committees and bilateral meetings was not only perfectly constitutional but an efficient answer to the problem of overload which had threatened to swamp the Wilson and Callaghan Governments. He emphasises that she did use the Cabinet informally as a political sounding board and was quick to draw back when she sensed serious opposition – for example to the Think Tank's proposed cuts in NHS spending in 1982.[12] On the other hand Nigel Lawson has acutely described how her use of bilaterals served to fragment the Cabinet, allowing the Prime Minister to divide and rule. Each minister would do his individual deal with her, with no need to persuade his colleagues; but having done it he would feel not only no obligation, but a positive disincentive, to support an embattled colleague. Mrs Thatcher's practice of leading the argument herself against any minister who was putting a case, very much in the manner of a chief prosecutor interrogating a defendant, did not encourage others to contribute, unless they too wished to have their heads bitten off. 'Thus what began as a method for the most expedient conduct of business ended as a means of getting her own way irrespective of the merits or political costs.'[13] Those with the longest experience could best appreciate how things had changed. Hailsham, who had first sat in Cabinet under Macmillan in 1957 and subsequently under Home and Heath, acknowledges that the increased use of *ad hoc* committees was 'a considerable convenience', allowing ministers to get on with the work of their own departments. 'But for all its advantages the system has undoubtedly diminished the intimate sense of collegiality which animated us when I first belonged.'[14]

Several colleagues tried to persuade Mrs Thatcher to share the load by forming some sort of inner cabinet, as most previous Prime Ministers had done; but she refused to do so. Her most senior colleagues were precisely those whom she most distrusted. In the very early days of her government she did have a sort of economic inner cabinet composed of the Treasury ministers plus Keith Joseph and John Nott,

which met for Thursday breakfasts before the full Cabinet; but that
petered out in 1980. Thereafter, apart from the special case of the
Falklands War Cabinet, the only approach to an inner group she ever
allowed was the so-called 'A-Team' in the run-up to the 1987 election; but that she conceived less as a sharing of power than as a means
of clipping the wings of Norman Tebbit, then party chairman. In his
memoirs Geoffrey Howe recalled the camaraderie of the early days
when he and others would be invited for relaxed late-night conversations in the upstairs flat at Number Ten: that never happened after
the first term. She still had her favourites, of course, who for a time
could do no wrong in her eyes – notably in this middle period David
Young, who had the great advantage of not being an MP and so could
not conceivably be a rival. But none of them lasted long. By the second
term she had learned to keep everything firmly in her own hands,
with just her handful of trusted courtiers. Howe likened the Thatcher
Cabinet to the solar system, with the Prime Minister as the sun around
whom her ministers revolved as planets in their separate orbits, with
no encouragement to shine in their own right or opportunity to
combine as a team.[15]

Dealing with the Prime Minister one-to-one was a testing business,
too. She was still always formidably well-briefed from a variety of
different sources – the official departmental brief, another from the
Policy Unit and often a third in her handbag whose origin the unfortunate minister never quite knew, which she would produce
triumphantly to catch him out; she could always find a weak point
even when he thought he had everything covered. At her best she had
not only read everything but had, in Charles Powell's words, 'a phenomenal recall of detail'. She did not just absorb information but actively
digested what she read:

> She used to wade through these huge documents, underlining as
> she went, and one got to know the signs. A straight underlining just
> meant 'I'm committing that to memory'; a squiggly line meant 'this
> is rubbish'; a double underlining meant 'I agree'; and a triple under-
> lining meant 'bullseye'.[16]

She made it her business to give ministers a hard time. 'I think
sometimes a Prime Minister should be intimidating,' she once declared.
'There's not much point in being a weak floppy thing in the chair, is
there?'[17] Much of the time this approach was highly effective, so long
as she was dealing with a strong character who could handle her firmly,
argue his corner and bring her round to a sensible policy if necessary.

On this view her destructive style was simply a way of testing policies – and the minister who would have to defend them – against every possible line of attack before she agreed to them. When on one occasion Norman Fowler protested at her brutality she told him: 'Stop getting cross with me, I'm only doing my job.'[18] But the longer she stayed in the job, the more she tended to have formed her view in advance and the less prepared she was to listen to other arguments. After 1983 she became increasingly irrational and harder to deal with. Ministers would look forward to a vigorous discussion, one recalled, only to find themselves subjected to a one-sided tirade: they became afraid to mention this or that subject for fear of setting her off on some hobby horse.[19] Her briefing was now not always so well focused. Another bruised ex-minister reflected that her command of detail was often in conflict with her desire to dominate: she only really wanted to hear the detail which supported her view.[20] Nicholas Timmins quotes an unnamed participant at the two seminars on the NHS which she held at Chequers in April and May 1988:

> These were just awful. Margaret at her worst. We would have two- or three-hour meetings and she would end up screaming like a fishwife and complaining about the bloody consultants and the hospitals, and her doctor friends had told her this, or told her that, or we would end up with unbelievably rambling conversations in which we failed to get to grips with anything.[21]

'Margaret categorised her Ministers,' Kenneth Baker wrote, 'into those she could put down, those she could break down, and those she could wear down.'[22] This is a vividly revealing comment: one way or another they must all be kept 'down'. Mrs Thatcher prided herself on liking a good argument; but she argued to *win* – or as she told Nigel Lawson bluntly during their difference about the exchange rate in 1988: 'I must prevail.'[23] She never learned to concede even a small point with good grace. There was another revealing episode when John Major first caught her attention at a whips' dinner at Number Ten in July 1985, at a time when the Government was trailing in third place in the polls. Major took the chance to tell her frankly about backbench worries: she got angry and attacked him in unfairly personal terms. The story is that she was impressed by the way he stood up to her and promoted him soon afterwards. Denis actually congratulated him and told him, 'She enjoyed that.' But Major did not enjoy it at all: he thought she had behaved unforgivably when he was only doing his job, part of which was to tell her unpalatable truths.[24] Viewed positively, this was an example of Mrs Thatcher working constructively, testing subordinates through tough argument with no quarter given but no grudges taken. Alternatively it was an example of sheer bad manners which nearly provoked Major to resign: a bullying type of man management which was not productive. By the middle of her second term the latter view was gaining ground. One disillusioned colleague – not a wet – reflected after six years in the Cabinet that they had all started out wanting to be loyal to her in 1979, but that she lost all her best supporters by undermining them and never thanking them or congratulating them for anything they did. 'The fact is,' he concluded, 'she despised people.'[25]

If a Prime Minister – as Attlee asserted – needs to be a good butcher, Mrs Thatcher passed that test with flying colours. As well as those she got rid of for ideological reasons, several ministers who in her view failed to deliver were sacked (often with a withering valediction in her memoirs): David Howell, 'whose shortcomings as an administrator had been exposed when he was at Energy and nothing I saw of his performance at Transport suggested to me that my judgement was wrong';[26] Patrick Jenkin for being too slow to abolish the GLC; Peter Rees after only two years as Chief Secretary; John Moore – once the golden boy – for failing to make the case for NHS reform; Paul Channon, admittedly after a surprisingly good run as Trade and then Transport Secretary. The turnover of ministers was extraordinarily high. Over the whole eleven years from 1979 to 1990 no fewer than thirty-six Cabinet ministers departed. Eight resigned as a result of a policy failure (Carrington and Atkins over the Falklands), personal or political embarrassment (Parkinson, Brittan, Ridley) or disagreement with the Prime Minister (Heseltine, Lawson, Howe). Thirteen retired more or less voluntarily either through ill health (Whitelaw), to 'spend more time with the family' (Fowler, Walker) or to go into business (Nott, Younger). But fifteen were involuntarily removed – only six of them in immediate post-election reshuffles. Though Mrs Thatcher always claimed to hate sacking people, the casualty rate was designed to keep the survivors on their toes. By the time Howe resigned in October 1990 the Prime Minister herself was the only survivor from her first Cabinet.

Her colleagues' loyalty was particularly strained by the way she used Bernard Ingham to aggrandise her own position by undermining them. During the first term Norman St John Stevas, Jim Prior, Mark Carlisle and Francis Pym had all found themselves anonymously rubbished in the press even as she publicly defended them. During the second, Patrick Jenkin, Peter Rees, Norman Tebbit and John Biffen suffered similar insidious disparagement. As Nigel Lawson complained, 'Ingham . . . consistently briefed the press on the basis that everything that went right was Margaret's own personal achievement, while everything that went wrong was the fault of her Ministers.'[27] 'We need a new edition of Machiavelli's *The Prince*,' John Nott told *Panorama* in 1988, 'to explain the way the Lobby has been used by Number 10 to raise the cult of personality so far as the Prime Minister is concerned, at the expense of colleagues who have happened to disagree at the time.'[28] It was no accident that Ingham particularly undermined successive Leaders of the House – Stevas, Pym, Biffen – who believed they had responsibility for presenting Government policy. 'He made it very clear,' Biffen recalled, 'that it was his job to present Government policy, as seen through the Prime Minister's eyes, and that the rest of us were all partially sighted. I . . . made it clear that I was not prepared to put up with this.'[29] His reward was to be rubbished himself.

Admittedly he asked for it by his suggestion that the Government should fight the coming election with a 'balanced ticket', since 'no one seriously supposes that the Prime Minister would be Prime Minister throughout the entire period of the next Parliament'.[30] Calling for the Prime Minister's resignation, even at some time in the future, is not a good idea. But the next day Biffen found himself described all over the press as 'a semi-detached member of the Government' whose tenure of office was unlikely to be prolonged. Though John Wakeham persuaded her to keep him in place until the election, Ingham had already given him notice and Mrs Thatcher barely spoke to him again.

Ingham attracted criticism from constitutional watchdogs on two grounds: first that he briefed for the Prime Minister alone, not for the Government as a whole, so that differences within the Government invariably found their way into the press with a heavy slant to her advantage; and second that he acted as a party spokesman though he was officially a civil servant paid by the taxpayer. From around 1983 he ceased to be quoted anonymously as 'a source close to Downing Street' and became a political personality and an object of controversy in himself. As Robert Harris wrote, 'he no longer simply released the news: the manner in which he released it often *was* the news'.[31] In July 1983, for instance, he overstepped the mark by accusing the Shadow Chancellor, Peter Shore, of talking 'bunkum and balderdash'. But Mrs Thatcher defended her press secretary, as she always did, saying that he was 'fully within his instructions . . . in making these points [in] characteristically vivid and robust phrases'.[32] She would never hear a word against him, even when, as in January 1985, he caused a run on the pound by suggesting that the Government would not intervene to support it.

In his memoirs Ingham claims that he normally saw Mrs Thatcher only about twice a week. But this is nonsense. In fact her day began each morning with a meeting with her private office, at which Ingham would talk her through his daily press digest. What is true is that she did not need to tell him what to say. He had an extraordinary ability to read her mind and could represent her views pretty accurately by a sort of osmosis. He undoubtedly presented a crude caricature of 'battling Maggie', the angry housewife and sturdy British patriot, surrounded by fainthearts, scheming foreigners and 'moaning minnies', and underplayed both the more sophisticated and the more cautious sides of her personality: as Lawson said, 'He was really only at home with the tabloids.'[33] But in fact the sort of language Ingham used was not so different from the way that she – and Denis – talked in private. Speaking on *Any Questions?* as a young frontbencher way back in 1966, for instance, she had described Lord Montgomery's view on servicemen's wives as 'nonsense, poppycock and balderdash'.[34] Ingham was guilty only of expressing her real views more uninhibitedly than she could nowadays afford to do directly herself. The effect, however, was to suggest that she was not really responsible for the Government at all, but just as impatient as the ordinary voter with the inadequacies of her own ministers.

Ingham himself wanted to leave after the 1987 election, thinking that seven and a half years was long enough and possibly recognising that his increased visibility was reducing his usefulness. Willie Whitelaw, among others, urged her to let him go. But as with the Foreign Office's attempts to move Charles Powell, Mrs Thatcher would not hear of it, declaring her loyal bulldog 'indispensable'.[35] So Ingham stayed with her to the end, enlarging his empire in 1989 by becoming head of the entire Government Information Service. In the beginning he had served Mrs Thatcher well, helping her to project her personality and her message effectively in the media; but long before 1990 he had become a symptom of all that was wrong with her government and was blamed by many for helping to insulate her from reality so that she became ever more imperious and out of touch. Of course like other features of her government, Ingham's licence to speak for the Prime Minister off the record was not entirely new – Harold Wilson had sometimes used his press secretary Joe Haines in a similar way – but she extended and systematised the practice to an unprecedented degree. Where she had pushed out the boundaries, her successors inevitably went further still. John Major restored a system more like that which had prevailed under Heath and Callaghan. But Alastair Campbell's central role in Downing Street since 1997 and his tight control of the presentation of the Blair Government in the media have made Ingham's efforts in retrospect look amateurish. The word 'spin', which has come to define New Labour, was not in use in Ingham's day. Nevertheless it was he, in his much cruder way, who established the technique.

Just as she used Ingham to enforce her political control of the Government, Mrs Thatcher used her private office to assert her control over the government machine. As already described, she did not so much reform Whitehall as dominate it. But she went far towards changing the culture of the Civil Service by her close interest in appointments, by her tireless probing of the work of all departments, and by centralising the processes of government onto herself to an extent not seen since Churchill in the war. Hers was the first British Government since Attlee's to be driven by a clear ideological thrust: and she was a far more directive character than Attlee. As a result the emphasis of Whitehall was switched from the formulation of policy to the management and delivery of policies already determined. 'The present government,' an official in the Department of the Environment minuted – specifically in relation to the abolition of the GLC, but the point has wider application – 'does not proceed from analysis to conclusion, but from commitment to action.'[36] Likewise an economic adviser who went back into the Treasury in 1981 after a two-year absence found it already 'very noticeable . . . that morale had dropped quite significantly for the economists. They felt that the sort of work they were doing was much more in the nature of justification of politics rather than serious analysis of different policy options.'[37] Officials in other departments experienced the same narrowing of their function. In this sense the Civil Service *was* politicised.

The personnel of her private office through whom she exerted her will over Whitehall had largely changed since the first term. Clive Whitmore had gone, replaced successively as principal private secretary by Robin Butler (1982–5), Nigel Wicks (1985–8) and Andrew Turnbull (1988–90). All were highly efficient, but none had quite the same rapport with her. On the other hand she had acquired a new political secretary, Stephen Sherbourne, 'who understood politics as well as any Cabinet Minister and whose shrewdness never failed me'[38] – except, one might suggest, at the time of Westland. Sherbourne stayed for five years, from 1983 to 1988, and was badly missed when he left. He was an exceptionally sensitive operator in the margins between politics and government, who acted as confidant, speechwriter and all-purpose right-hand man, moving easily between the upstairs and downstairs parts of Number Ten; more than anyone else, he filled part of the gap left by Ian Gow, except that he was not an MP. His successor John Whittingdale did not have the same combination of experience and skill, so that she relied more than ever on the trusted duumvirate of Powell and Ingham.

David Wolfson left in 1985 and was not replaced; but that year she appointed a new head of the Policy Unit, Brian Griffiths, who assumed an increasingly important role. After two directors, Ferdinand Mount and John Redwood, who had focused primarily on family issues and privatisation respectively, Griffiths enlarged the membership of the Policy Unit – filling the gap left by the demise of the CPRS – and resumed the more wide-ranging remit Hoskyns had enjoyed in the early days. Griffiths was a monetarist economist, but also a devout Welsh Anglican – described by one critic as 'a salvationist nutter'[39] – who brought a fervent moralism into Number Ten which chimed with Mrs Thatcher's expanding ambition as she moved into the 'Social Thatcherism' of the third term. He was particularly influential in education and broadcasting policy, but also acted as surrogate for Alan Walters in economic policy – Lawson called him 'a pale echo of Walters'[40] – during the latter's absence in America. Griffiths stayed until November 1990, but his influence was reduced in 1989 when Walters returned.

As well as Walters, who continued to advise from a distance between 1984 and 1989, Mrs Thatcher employed two other special advisers inside Number Ten. Percy Cradock replaced Anthony Parsons as her foreign-affairs adviser, initially on Hong Kong but later more generally, though he never managed to exercise much influence over policy towards Europe; and Robin Ibbs replaced Derek Rayner as special adviser on efficiency in government. Outside the government machine she also had her 'voices' – the source of many of those informal briefs which ministers found so aggravating – her network of informal advisers ranging from Woodrow Wyatt and Laurens van der Post to David Hart and Jack Peel (the former General Secretary of the National Union of Dyers, Bleachers and Textile Workers who was her 'deep throat' in the trade-union world), supplemented by a secret army of moles all over the public service – doctors, generals, academics sympathetic to her purpose – who were encouraged to ring her privately with the view from their particular front line. By all these means she strove to neutralise the institutional influence of the Civil Service. She was the spider at the centre of the web, and nothing moved – or failed to move – without her knowing about it.

Above all, though, from 1984 onwards, she relied increasingly on Charles Powell, who assumed a more and more central role at the heart of government, extending well beyond his original remit in foreign affairs so that he became, by the end, not merely her real Foreign Secretary but the effective deputy Prime Minister. He elbowed out her principal private secretaries, Nigel Wicks and Andrew Turnbull, and trespassed on the territory of successive Cabinet Secretaries, Robert Armstrong and Robin Butler; he conceived it as his job to serve the Prime Minister in any way she wanted. In style and function he was the antithesis of Ingham – 'as polished as Ingham was blunt'[41] – yet they performed complementary roles. Where Ingham projected Mrs Thatcher vigorously to the world, Powell represented her invisibly but extremely effectively across Whitehall. Like Ingham, Lawson wrote, but in the opposite sense, 'he never saw it as his role to question her prejudices, merely to refine the language in which they were expressed . . . He wrote the best and wittiest minutes . . . of anyone in Whitehall.'[42] Moreover he was cool, organised, efficient and infinitely persuasive, when she was becoming increasingly wilful and tempestuous. Powell could translate her wishes into coherent form and, with a word in the right place, ensure that they were implemented. No Prime Minister ever had a more effective *alter ego*.

The decline of Parliament

Mrs Thatcher was never a great parliamentarian. Though she revered the institution of Parliament she never liked the place or had any feel for its ambience or traditions. Her sex was a factor here, partly because as a young female Member she could never be one of the boys – she had a young family to get back to, and she would never have been one for sitting around in bars anyway – but also because she found it difficult to make herself heard without shouting, particularly when she became leader and a target for Labour heckling. But even after she had established her command of the House, she never wooed or flattered it: her manner was always to hector and assert, and when she was interrupted or in difficulties she would simply shout louder. Roy Jenkins in typically magisterial manner compared her with other Prime Ministers he had observed from Attlee onwards: 'Her combative belief in her own rightness ensures that she is rarely discomfited and never overwhelmed. But she brings no special qualities of persuasiveness or debating skill which enable her to move minds.'[43]

Charles Powell believes that she was actually too respectful of Parliament. She knew she was not a good speaker, was nervous before she had to make a speech and consequently over-prepared. Her speeches tended to be loaded with statistics and came alive only when she was interrupted and had something to respond to. As a result she spoke as rarely as possible in debates – far less frequently than her predecessors. She did so only when she had to, that is in the debate on the Address at the beginning of each session, in confidence debates when she was obliged to answer Foot or Kinnock directly – Labour did not table many of those, knowing they would always lose – and on other exceptional occasions like the Falklands or the Westland crisis when she had to defend herself. More often she made statements (after every European summit, for instance) and then answered questions, which was what she was good at. Though she had not been so good in opposition, when she did not have all the resources of the Civil Service at her disposal, from the moment she became Prime Minister she dominated Question Time, regularly making mincemeat first of Michael Foot and then of Neil Kinnock. Whereas she felt respect for Foot as a parliamentarian and scholar – though no fear of him as an opponent – she had none at all for Kinnock, whom she thought shallow, posturing and hollow. Though some of his emotive allegations angered her, she frankly did not think him up to the job and took great pleasure in exposing his ignorance and incapacity in front of her baying supporters every Tuesday and Thursday afternoon. The twice-weekly circus of Prime Minister's Questions suited her down to the ground. But it did not add much to the dignity or usefulness of Parliament.

The abuse of Prime Minister's Questions had started with Harold Wilson, but it got more systematic under Mrs Thatcher. Two devices made a mockery of any serious questioning. First there was the 'open' question, by which MPs one after another simply asked her to list her engagements for the day, after which they could ask her anything they liked as a supplementary. Then there was the stream of sycophantic 'questions' from Government backbenchers, usually planted by the whips, which simply invited her to congratulate the Government or bash the opposition. Bernard Weatherill, who succeeded George Thomas as Speaker in 1983, tried to put a stop to these abuses, but Mrs Thatcher would not hear of it. She did not see Question Time as an opportunity for accountability to the House, but as her chance to project her message to the nation – via radio, which had started broadcasting the proceedings in 1978. Weatherill wanted to restore the former practice whereby questions of detail were deflected to the departmental minister concerned, leaving the Prime Minister to answer for broad strategy.[44] But Mrs Thatcher liked open questions precisely because they enabled her to display her command of detail: the fact that she might be asked about anything gave her the excuse she needed to keep tabs on every department. She regarded Prime Minister's Questions as 'the real test of your authority in the House' and prepared for them with obsessive thoroughness: she prided herself that 'no head of government anywhere in the world has to face this sort of regular pressure and many go to great lengths to avoid it'.[45] This shallow gladiatorial bunfight, she thought, was what Parliament was all about.

With the security of huge majorities after 1983 she had no need, most of the time, to bother about the House of Commons. Francis Pym believed that the experience of the second term fully vindicated his warning that big majorities do not make for good government.[46] She certainly did not bother about the Opposition. Having little experience of how Parliament worked, she had no patience with the 'usual channels' approach by which skilled manipulators like Willie Whitelaw and John Wakeham ensured the smooth dispatch of business. She saw no need to cut any deals with the Labour party, and was suspicious of Leaders of the House like Pym and Biffen who were too accommodating to them. Whenever any difficulty arose, her bible was Erskine May, the parliamentary rule-book.[47] She was more sensitive to her own back benches, however. Landslide majorities actually give rebels greater leeway to vote against the Government with little risk of defeating it, and Tory dissidents made use of this freedom on a number of issues – rate-capping, the abolition of the GLC, the freezing of family allowance, charges for dental and eye tests and not least the poll tax – on some at least of which the Government moved some way to meet them. On other issues, like Keith Joseph's plan to charge university fees in 1984 or the proposed sale of Land-Rover to General Motors in 1986, ministers backed down completely in the face of a threatened revolt, though this was not something Mrs Thatcher was prepared to tolerate too often. The latter episode in particular, which caught her at a weak moment after Westland, infuriated her and she was determined to put it right as soon as possible. After 1987 she was much less ready to compromise with backbench worries about the poll tax.

Inevitably, as all Prime Ministers do, she became increasingly remote from her backbench supporters. During her first term, when her position in the Cabinet was precarious and she still remembered who it was that had made her leader, she was careful to keep her lines of communication open; as a result, in Jock Bruce-Gardyne's judgement, 'she preserved a natural rapport with her backbenchers which I cannot recall with any of her predecessors'.[48] Edward du Cann, as chairman of the 1922 Committee up to 1984, had ready access to her at all times. His successor, Cranley Onslow, never enjoyed the same privilege. Like Ted Heath before her, she came to see the 1922 Executive as a bunch of self-important has-beens disappointed at having never won promotion. As early as May 1984 Alan Clark recorded that 'even so loyal and devoted a person as Peter Hordern [MP for Horsham since 1964] had been upset by the Lady's behaviour in snapping and sneering at him when the '22 Executive went to see her and gave her their views on the problems of the day.' This, Clark commented, was 'silly of her. She's stirring up trouble' – though it did not seriously damage her for another six years.[49]

What she really lacked after 1983 was a good PPS to keep her in touch with the back benches as Ian Gow had done so brilliantly in her first term. Gow's first successor, Michael Alison, who stayed in the job until 1987, was charming and honourable but more interested in church politics than in Westminster. He was followed in rapid succession by Archie Hamilton, Mark Lennox-Boyd and Peter Morrison, 'all of whom', as one Tory MP wrote, 'adored her and carried her bag with distinction. She loved a toff, and was enormously susceptible to their flattery and foppery. The first three were genuinely popular with their colleagues, but none could match Ian's subtlety and political insight.'[50] 'At last,' Jeremy Hanley joked when Morrison was appointed in 1989, 'Margaret's got herself an aide who knows how to carry a handbag.'[51] Unfortunately it became apparent at the crisis of her leadership in November 1990 that Morrison did not know how to do much else. All four of Gow's successors, bizarrely, were Old Etonians. The reason was that Mrs Thatcher felt it was unfair to take someone good off the ministerial ladder for an unpaid job, however important, but thought it a suitable position for wealthy men who did not need a salary. As she grew more confident she failed to realise how vital a good PPS was to her own position.

Julian Critchley – who, after his unmasking in 1980 as the author of an article in the *Observer* describing Mrs Thatcher unflatteringly as 'the Great She-Elephant', made a living as the Tory party's licensed satirist – wrote more than once of the Prime Minister's rare visits to the House of Commons tearoom to meet her supporters. 'The most self-effacing MP,' he warned in 1984, 'is in danger of being run down by . . . the Prime Ministerial convoy.'

> He may gingerly emerge from his room only to be trampled under foot by a posse led by the determined figure of Mrs Thatcher who passes down the corridor in a cloud of powder blue. In step behind her are two apparatchiks bearing files, and bringing up the rear the tall figure of Mr Michael Alison, her PPS. Faced by this juggernaut, some fall on their knees, others take refuge within the nearest doorway.

Most alarming for hapless backbenchers was if she chose to join their table and question them intently about the money supply. If they were unwise enough to sign the bill, they would get a stern lecture on the iniquity of credit.[52] Five years later little had changed except the identity of the PPS:

> Sometimes the Prime Minister herself has been known to take tea. Mrs Thatcher never moves beyond the Chamber without Mr Mark Lennox Boyd in tow ... He will get the tea; a chorus of the newly-elected will provide the sympathy. Older hands will mumble their apologies and slide away, for Mrs Thatcher's temper is as uncertain as her views are fixed.[53]

Critchley exaggerated for comic effect; but not very much.

To compensate for the lack of serious opposition in the Commons, the House of Lords became increasingly assertive, to the extent that the Government suffered regular defeats in the Upper House – more than 200 between 1979 and 1987. Though the Tories always had a large nominal majority in the Lords, there was a substantial component of crossbenchers – in addition to Labour and Alliance peers – who did not take a party whip but considered issues on their merits. Mostly these defeats were reversed when the legislation came back to the Commons, but on some major issues, like the so-called 'paving' Bill to abolish the 1985 elections to the GLC, the Lords' will prevailed. Mrs Thatcher was not amused by this show of independence by the peers, particularly since she had appointed so many of them. 'I sent them there to support me,' she told Nicholas Ridley. 'They ought to know better.' She considered reducing their powers, but concluded that it was not worth the effort.[54] It was Willie Whitelaw's job after 1983 to get the Government's business through the Lords. He steered a delicate path with typical bluff skill. As Leader of the House, he stood up for the Lords' right not to be taken for granted, to revise and to be listened to on points of detail. But at the same time, as he told the parliamentary press gallery in March 1984, 'I will do my best to ensure that the Government will not be defeated on major issues of principle.' To be effective as a revising chamber, he insisted, the Lords must accept the Government's objectives and oppose it only in detail.[55]

So long as he was there, Whitelaw was usually able to get the Government's business through. But after his retirement in 1988 his successor, Lord Belstead, did not command the same authority and the Lords inflicted a rising tally of defeats on the admittedly shoddy legislation of the third term – Kenneth Baker's Education Bill, Douglas

Hurd's Broadcasting Bill, the poll tax, the aborted football supporters' scheme among others. When they threatened to defeat the Government over a matter of academic freedom in Baker's Bill, Mrs Thatcher told Belstead – in words which Baker 'could never imagine her saying to Willie' – 'Be robust . . . they have no business to change this. Be robust.'[56] On another occasion she demanded indignantly: 'What are all the Tory peers whom I have created doing?' The answer was that many of them were sacked Cabinet ministers who owed her no favours, while the rest were captains of industry who were happy to accept their titles but never went near the House.

The House of Lords, despite its indefensible composition, was a useful counterweight to the Government's unchecked hegemony in the Commons; but it could not redress the increasing irrelevance of Parliament in the political process. The 'elective dictatorship' of which Lord Hailsham had warned in 1975 – when he objected to a Labour Government elected by 39 per cent of the votes cast (and only 29 per cent of the electorate) ruling as though it commanded a majority mandate – was a far more pressing reality in the mid-1980s when Mrs Thatcher used her huge parliamentary majorities to push through her revolution on the basis of no more than 43 per cent support (or 31 per cent of the whole electorate). The size of her majorities, Labour's impotence and her own functional view of Parliament as a legislative sausage-factory meant that opposition to her policies found expression elsewhere: in local government, in parts of the press, occasionally on the streets, but above all on television and radio. Again, this shift of the political debate from Westminster to the airwaves had been under way for some time, but it was markedly accelerated in the Thatcher years, measured by the steep decline in serious press reporting of Parliament: in so far as debates were reported at all, it was in the form of satirical columns by the likes of Frank Johnson, Matthew Parris and Edward Pearce. The journalists would say that the debates were no longer worth reporting, and they might be right; the process was self-fulfilling. But all that most of the public ever heard of Parliament was the crude knockabout of Prime Minister's Questions.*

As well as trying to clean up Question Time, Bernard Weatherill tried to combat the growing practice of ministers making policy announcements on television and radio rather than in the House. He

---

*Another symptom of this decline was the increased cost of Hansard, from forty pence per day in 1979 to £7.50 per day in 1995, vastly more than the rate of inflation. What had hitherto been seen as a fundamental public service was now just another commercial operation which, like everything else, had to pay its way.

once scored a minor victory by obliging Mrs Thatcher to come to the House to make a statement after she had announced something on the *Today* programme, though she protested that she was busy preparing to entertain a visiting head of government.[57] But this – if it happened at all, and it has not been possible to identify the occasion – was an isolated and unimportant check to an irresistible trend, which like so many other developments of the Thatcher years has gone on developing ever since. Ministers now spend far more of their time making statements on the air and being questioned by television and radio interviewers than they do speaking or answering questions in the House. The only important exception to this process was Norman St John Stevas' introduction of departmental select committees in the Government's very first year, which he managed to slip past Mrs Thatcher when she was preoccupied with other matters. They were a useful innovation, though their critics complained that they were another factor taking away from the primacy of the chamber. But their members were chosen by the whips, and the chairmen could usually be leaned on when the Government had something to hide.

The obvious response to the usurpation of Parliament by television was to televise Parliament. This had been widely canvassed, both by the broadcasters and by those concerned for the centrality of Parliament, for the past twenty years or more – Nye Bevan had supported it in 1959 – and the pressure kept mounting during the 1980s after the successful introduction of radio broadcasting in 1978. But Mrs Thatcher strongly opposed letting television cameras into the chamber, partly because she believed that they would damage the reputation of the House by showing in full colour the rowdiness which was already offending radio listeners, and change its character by encouraging publicity seekers to play to the gallery; but partly also because she thought it would do her personally no good. Gordon Reece and Bernard Ingham both tried to persuade her that she would only gain from being seen trouncing Kinnock at the dispatch box twice a week; but she was afraid she would come over as strident (as well as being seen wearing glasses to read her brief) and feared that the BBC would edit the exchanges to her disadvantage. When the issue came to a vote in late 1985 – at the height of her vendetta with the BBC – she did not speak publicly against it, but Tory MPs were seen to wait to see which way she was voting before following her into the 'No' lobby. The proposal was defeated by twelve votes. Two years later in February 1988 she spoke and lobbied openly against the cameras: a majority of Tories still followed her line, but this time a six-month experiment was agreed by a majority of fifty-four.[58] The televising finally started in November 1989. Most observers thought the effect was, as Reece had anticipated, to underline the Prime Minister's dominance. But the cameras caught their first moment of real parliamentary drama when they were able to broadcast Geoffrey Howe's devastating resignation speech in November 1990. After that there was no going back – though here again very little is ever shown on terrestrial channels apart from Question Time.

The power of patronage

For most of its life the Thatcher Government was not popular. Between General Elections it usually trailed in the polls – often in third place – and even its two landslide election victories were gained with well under half the votes cast. Yet except for a brief period in the spring of 1986, after Westland and the bombing of Libya, few commentators anticipated anything other than a third Tory victory in 1987 and probably a fourth after that. Labour under Neil Kinnock was slowly rowing back from the extremism of the early 1980s, becoming a better organised and credible opposition; yet such was Mrs Thatcher's dominance that it took an extraordinary leap of faith to imagine anyone else forming the next government. There was a despairing fatalism on the left, and a corresponding complacency on the right, that the political pendulum had been halted and the Tories would be in power for ever. The restraints traditionally imposed by the expectation of a periodic alternation of power between the main parties consequently exerted a diminishing force. As a result, from the mid-1980s, the Government began to give off an unmistakable odour of corruption arising from over-confidence, constitutional corner-cutting and mounting hubris.

The Tories had held power for an unbroken decade before, from 1951 to 1964. But that span comprised four different Prime Ministers: each renewal of the mandate, in 1955 and 1959, was achieved under a different leader. Prior to Mrs Thatcher, six years had been considered a good innings for a twentieth-century Prime Minister: Asquith served eight (1908–16), but Lloyd George (1916–22), Attlee (1945–51), Macmillan (1957–63) and Wilson (1964–70) had established six as the benchmark. (Baldwin, Churchill and Wilson racked up more by coming back for a second or third bite.) By the time of her second re-election in June 1987, however, Mrs Thatcher had already surpassed most of these and was only a few months from overhauling Asquith and Churchill, with the nineteenth-century records of Lord Salisbury (thirteen), Gladstone (fourteen in four administrations) and even Lord Liverpool (fifteen years) coming into view. She showed as yet no sign of slowing down. But the impact on political life of such unbroken continuity was already being felt, not only in her personal dominance of the government machine but in the unbalancing of the party system.

First, Mrs Thatcher had no scruples about using the Prime Minister's power of patronage in a frankly partisan manner to reward her supporters. She revived the award of honours for political services – abandoned by Harold Wilson – and gave them in abundance: peerages to discarded ministers, an average of four or five knighthoods a year to long-serving MPs, MBEs and OBEs to constituency workers. In this respect as in others she was explicitly reversing the practice of Ted Heath, whose parsimony in the handing out of baubles was deeply resented within the parliamentary party. Even such a loyal supporter as Nicholas Ridley felt that Mrs Thatcher's generosity erred too far the other way.[59] But rewards were clearly tied to good behaviour. Julian Critchley, an MP since 1959, was punished for his irreverence by being made to wait for his knighthood until John Major's time; by contrast George Gardiner, elected only in 1974, got his in 1990 in compensation for her refusal to give him office.*

She was even more blatant in honouring the proprietors and editors of loyal newspapers and other friendly journalists. And then there was the steady flow of honours to businessmen and industrialists in recognition of donations to Tory party funds. There may not have been a fixed tariff of payments as in the days of Lloyd George and his notorious honours-broker, Maundy Gregory; but it was well understood that the chairmen and directors of companies which gave generously would not be forgotten. The only difference between Lloyd George and Mrs Thatcher, the author of one inquiry concluded, was that she 'dispensed with the middle man'.[60] Analysis by the Labour party revealed that twenty-eight out of forty-one businessmen honoured between 1979 and 1983 had contributed a total of £2.7 million to the Tory party in that period. There were peerages for many of the Prime Minister's favourite supporters: Sir Robert McAlpine, Victor Matthews of Trafalgar House, Sir Charles Forte, Sir James Hanson, Sir Marcus Sieff of Marks & Spencer, Sir Arnold Weinstock of GEC, Sir Nicholas Cayzer of British and Commonwealth Shipping. Looked at the other way, directors of fourteen out of eighteen companies which had contributed more than £90,000 were honoured.[61] The practice went on throughout the decade, culminating in a final list in December 1990 which included

---

*Both, ironically, ended up by being expelled from the party as a result of their opposite attitudes to Europe: Gardiner for supporting Sir James Goldsmith's Referendum Party in 1997, Critchley for refusing to recant his long-standing convictions when the party line changed under William Hague.

peerages for Sir Jeffery Sterling (P&O), Sir Hector Laing (United Biscuits), Sir Gordon White (Hanson) and Peter Palumbo, all of whom had been generous contributors over the years. There was little fuss about any of these awards, partly because Mrs Thatcher was only carrying on a practice which had long been winked at, so long as it was not abused too obviously, but mainly because she was wise enough – unlike Wilson – not to put forward any really scandalous names. Contributing to the funds of the governing party was just something that major British companies were expected to do – as it still is, though the governing party has changed. In 1984 she agreed to strengthen the system of scrutiny by establishing a committee composed of Lords Shackleton, Grimond and Pym. Not until 1990 did she present them with two names they deemed unsuitable: they drew the line at an honorary knighthood for Rupert Murdoch and a peerage for Jeffrey Archer.

Overall Mrs Thatcher actually gave considerably fewer peerages than Wilson – 193 over her eleven years, compared with Wilson's 152 in 1964–70 and another eighty-one in 1974–6. But she certainly appeared to give them in a more partisan way, and her longevity meant that the cumulative effect was increasingly unbalanced. The casualty rate from the Cabinet ensured a steady traffic to the House of Lords. After the 1987 election no fewer than nine former Cabinet ministers went to the Upper House: only John Nott was punished for having had the temerity to resign before she was ready to lose him. Conversely in June 1983 she refused two-thirds of a list of twenty-seven names – some of them admittedly undistinguished – proposed by Michael Foot in an effort to reduce Labour's deficit in the Lords. She pointedly denied peerages in a number of cases where they would normally have been expected: as well as Nott, neither Sir Douglas Wass, retiring head of the Treasury, nor Sir Michael Palliser, Permanent Secretary of the Foreign Office, received the customary gongs. She also withheld lesser honours from officials who joined the Civil Service strike in 1981; and from athletes who competed in the 1980 Moscow Olympics in defiance of her attempted boycott.[62] On this basis she could scarcely complain that Oxford University denied her a customary honour.

One of Mrs Thatcher's most provocative announcements on taking office was to declare her intention of reviving hereditary honours, which had been in abeyance since Macmillan's invention of life peerages in 1960. Having asserted the principle, however, she did nothing about it for four years, and then undercut the point by awarding them only to those – Willie Whitelaw and George Thomas – with no heir to inherit. She also wanted to give a hereditary title – the only sort he would accept – to Enoch Powell (who also had only daughters), but was dissuaded by Whitelaw. The following year Macmillan, at the age of ninety, belatedly accepted the earldom traditionally due to former Prime Ministers. But that was the extent of the revival until 1991 when John Major was persuaded, allegedly at Mrs Thatcher's personal request, to award a baronetcy to Denis. Though she herself took only a life peerage in 1992, this bizarre resurrection ensured that Mark on Denis's death in June 2003 would inherit his title.

A second area where Mrs Thatcher was blatantly partisan was in making appointments to public bodies. From the chairmanship of nationalised industries to the dozens of obscure quangos, boards and advisory bodies of which British public life is made up, she took a close interest in getting into place men (and occasionally women) who were, in the phrase indelibly associated with her premiership, 'one of us' – that is, if not actually paid-up Conservatives, at least sympathetic to her purpose. She had equally little compunction about getting rid of people she found unhelpful, like the Governor of the Bank of England, Gordon Richardson, whose tenure was not renewed in 1982 following differences over monetary policy in 1980–1. His replacement, Robin Leigh-Pemberton, was a former Tory leader of Kent County Council and chairman of the National Westminster Bank, with no central banking experience at all, but a sound monetarist.

Perhaps the Governor of the Bank needed to be a supporter of the Government's central policy. But Mrs Thatcher's interest in public appointments extended far beyond economic matters into the area of culture and the arts. The then Secretary-General of the Arts Council, Roy Shaw, was so affronted by the appointment of Alistair McAlpine to the Council in 1980 that he likened it to 'putting an atheist on the bench of bishops'. This was unfair – McAlpine is a considerable collector – but the minister responsible, Norman St John Stevas, was sufficiently embarrassed to explain that the suggestion came 'from a very high source'.[63] Two years later the writer Richard Hoggart – author of *The Uses of Literacy* – was dropped from the vice-chairmanship; seeking an explanation, Shaw was told bluntly: 'I'm afraid Number 10 doesn't like him.'[64] Potential bishops, like candidates to become Governor of the BBC, were blackballed on frankly political grounds, and even nominations for trustees of national galleries were closely scrutinised and sometimes rejected: the former director of the British Council who had dared to criticise cuts in his funding was gratuitously blocked from becoming a trustee of the Tate.[65]

Already during the 1983 election Neil Kinnock charged that Mrs Thatcher was engaged in a deliberate process of 'removing all opposition in the great institutions of Britain, from the Bank of England to British Rail, from Church to BBC, from Arts Council to the Commission for Racial Equality, from the Manpower Services Commission to regional health authorities', appointing 'fellow-travellers to positions of social and civic power [in] a clear effort to create a state in the image of Margaret Thatcher, a genteel junta of yes-men'.[66] Where previously the convention had been that Whitehall kept a list of 'the great and the good', broadly balanced to reflect political sympathy and party background, industrialists carefully balanced with trade unionists, it became 'a standing joke' in the 1980s that the euphemism for finding the right sort of people to serve on bodies was persons 'with business experience'.[67] Very often, of course, this too meant contributors to party funds. The Deregulation Task Force, a quango set up by the DTI to push through the removal of controls which industry found tiresome, was headed by the chairman of a company which had donated £221,000 the previous year, and included the operations director of another which had donated £413,000.[68] These people were being engaged by the Government to implement policies of direct benefit to themselves. When it came to the universities, by contrast, academics were deliberately kept in a minority on the reconstituted University Funding Council. 'Such was the paranoia of Thatcherism at this time,' Simon Jenkins wrote, 'that "the enemy" must never be in a majority on any quango.'[69]

Of course Prime Ministers have always used patronage to reward their own supporters. The difference in the 1980s, as Noël Annan suggested, was that Mrs Thatcher did not merely reward her supporters, but appointed them to positions where they were expected to pursue an active policy of changing the dominant culture.[70] And change it they did. Towards the end of Mrs Thatcher's hegemony the television presenter Jeremy Paxman set out to answer the question 'Who runs Britain?' At the end of his book *Friends in High Places* he concluded that 'the only plausible answer is the Prime Minister'. But he anticipated that 'when the Thatcher era is over, the balance of power will shift again, and the collegiate spirit in both major parties remains strong enough for the dominant role of Downing Street to be reduced'.[71] Seven years later a similar inquiry by Andrew Marr concluded that this had not happened. Despite John Major's much less dominating personality and his lack after 1992 of the sort of overwhelming parliamentary majority that had sustained his predecessor, Marr described Mrs Thatcher's enduring legacy as a new 'patronage state' where favoured industrialists could buy influence and merchant banks made a fat living from government fees:

For the first five or six years of her rule, she and her supporters really did seem to be outsiders who had seized control of the system. But as the eighties progressed, the outsiders and mavericks hardened into a new establishment clique . . .

What started as a guerrilla raiding party against the corporate state eventually aged and spread into an auxiliary state, an influence-network run exclusively through Downing Street and barely connected to the official civil service or the Commons.[72]

A change of government in 1997 made very little difference. Tony Blair inherited the new conventions of Mrs Thatcher's patronage state and simply exploited them more ruthlessly than even she had dared, for the benefit of New Labour. Thatcherite hubris in the 1980s met the nemesis it deserved in the late 1990s. But the civilised tradition of bipartisanship – hitherto one of the unsung decencies of British life – had been destroyed for ever.

Rival queens

One question that continued to fascinate the public about the phenomenon of a woman Prime Minister was how she got on with the Queen. The answer is that their relations were punctiliously correct, but there was little love lost on either side. As two women of very similar age – Mrs Thatcher was six months older – occupying parallel positions at the top of the social pyramid, one the head of government, the other head of state, they were bound to be in some sense rivals. Mrs Thatcher's attitude to the Queen was ambivalent. On the one hand she had an almost mystical reverence for the institution of the monarchy: she always made sure that Christmas dinner was finished in time for everyone to sit down solemnly to watch the Queen's broadcast. Yet at the same time she was trying to modernise the country and sweep away many of the values and practices which the monarchy perpetuated. She and Elizabeth had very little personally in common – though Denis and Prince Philip got on well. The Queen was said to dread her weekly audience with her Prime Minister because Mrs Thatcher was so stiff and formal – rather as Ted Heath had been: she much preferred the chumminess of her two Labour Prime Ministers, Harold Wilson and James Callaghan. It was not, as some suggested, that Mrs Thatcher was too grand, rather that she displayed an exaggerated reverence. 'Nobody would curtsey lower,' one courtier confided;[73] and the Queen wondered 'Why does she always sit on the edge of her seat?'[74]

If the Queen dreaded Mrs Thatcher coming to the Palace, however,

Mrs Thatcher loathed having to go once a year to Balmoral. She had
no interest in horses, dogs or country sports and regarded the outdoor
life – long walks and picnics in all weathers – which the Royal Family
enjoyed on holiday, as 'purgatory'.[75] Though she frequently told interviewers that she loved nothing better than a country walk, she never
had any suitable shoes and had to be forced into borrowed Hush
Puppies or green wellingtons.[76] She could not wait to get away and
on the last morning was up at six as usual, with her thank-you letter
written, anxious to be off as soon as Denis was ready. The Queen was
almost certainly equally glad to see her go.

More seriously, while Mrs Thatcher regarded having to attend the
Queen as a waste of time – by contrast with every other engagement
in her day, she would read the agenda only in the car on the way to
the Palace – the Queen had real grounds for resenting Mrs Thatcher.
First she feared that the Government's policies were wilfully exacerbating social divisions: she worried about high unemployment and was
alarmed by the 1981 riots and the violence of the miners' strike. Second,
she was upset by Mrs Thatcher's ill-concealed dislike of her beloved
Commonwealth: she was disturbed by the raising of university fees for
overseas students, which hit one of the most practical benefits of the
Commonwealth, and by the whole South African sanctions controversy which regularly pitted Britain against all the other members,
with embarrassing calls for Britain to be expelled. At the
Commonwealth heads of government conference every other year,
from Lusaka in 1979 onwards, the Queen worked hard to make herself
the focus of unity while Mrs Thatcher often seemed bent on splitting
the organisation apart.

The Queen also worried about defence cuts affecting the survival
of cherished regiments with which she or other members of her family
had connections: while Mrs Thatcher was concerned solely with military capability, Her Majesty was more interested in cap badges and
mascots. She worried about Mrs Thatcher's hostility to the Church of
England, of which she was the Temporal Head, and about the effect
of constant cost-cutting on other voluntary organisations of which she
was patron. Sometimes Mrs Thatcher was obliged to defer to her: she
had to abandon her petty attempt to deny the SDP's right to be represented at the Cenotaph on Remembrance Sunday, for instance; and it
was said that she ruled out privatisation of the Royal Mail from fear
of the Queen's objections – though that may equally have been an
example of her own conventional monarchism. But she refused to
allow the Queen to visit the European Parliament or – following her
own triumphant visit – the Soviet Union. More than by any of these

minor tussles, however, the Queen could not fail to be irritated by Mrs Thatcher's own increasingly regal style.

The impression that Mrs Thatcher was developing monarchical pretensions first gained currency when she took the salute at the forces' victory parade through the City of London at the end of the Falklands war, a role that many thought more properly the Queen's. Then the following January her visit to the islands was unmistakably a royal progress to accept the thanks and adoration of the population. The solemnity of the ceremonial, the hushed tones of the broadcasters and 'the constant references to "her" troops,' David Watt noted in *The Times*, 'proclaim that this is a royal visit';[77] while Peregrine Worsthorne wrote in the *Sunday Telegraph* that Mrs Thatcher's manner was 'more regal than the Queen's' and feared that her 'new and exalted status' would go to her head; he looked forward to an early election to bring her back to political reality.[78] Later that month when she visited the offices of the *Glasgow Herald* to mark its bicentenary, its editor thought her manner more 'regal' than that of the Queen a few weeks later: 'She talked to all the waitresses in the boardroom before departing.'[79] Following her overwhelming re-election in June 1983 more than one cartoonist pictured her Trooping the Colour on the Queen's horse; and Conor Cruise O'Brien wrote in the *Observer* that she was developing a parallel monarchy, becoming 'a new style elective executive monarch, as distinct from the recessive ceremonial one'.[80]

From now on the trend only increased. Her foreign tours were more and more like the Queen's, with all the trappings of crowds and walkabouts, little girls presenting bouquets, guards of honour and nineteen-gun salutes. As the Queen grew older and less glamorous – royal glamour being increasingly concentrated on the young Princess of Wales – Mrs Thatcher became more powerful and wreathed in myth, the very embodiment of Britannia. To the crowds who came out to see her, she far more than the Queen now embodied Britain. By 1988 Robert Harris was writing in the *Observer*: 'We have become a nation with two monarchs . . . On her housewife/superstar progress around the world, Margaret Thatcher has steadily become more like the Queen of England than the real thing.'[81] Increasingly the Queen appeared to be the housewife, Mrs Thatcher the superstar.

She was also quicker off the mark than the Palace in visiting the scene of disasters, where once again the journalist Christopher Monckton noted that 'she seems curiously indistinguishable from the Queen'.[82] Whenever there was an accident or terrorist attack Mrs Thatcher always dropped everything to go at once – as her schedule allowed her to do: when the IRA bombed Harrods at Christmas 1983, for instance, she and Denis were attending a carol service at the Festival Hall, but immediately left at the interval. By contrast, Downing Street briefed, 'the Royal Family couldn't be relied on to go' at all, and certainly not for several days.[83]

In July 1986 the *Sunday Times* splashed a front-page story claiming to reveal tensions between Downing Street and the Palace, specifically over South Africa but also more generally alleging that the Queen thought the Government's economic policies 'uncaring, confrontational and socially divisive'.[84] Mrs Thatcher was privately furious and blamed elements within the Palace for trying to undermine the Government; but she was determined not to blame the Queen or give any countenance to the idea of a constitutional crisis.[85] Though Rupert Murdoch told Woodrow Wyatt that a row with the Queen would do her good, Mrs Thatcher did not believe it: she feared that if the idea of a rift between the Government and the monarch took hold she would be the loser.[86] In fact the report was a piece of journalistic mischief-making which was swiftly repudiated: the Queen was as anxious to deny it as Mrs Thatcher. Nevertheless the picture of her political sympathies was substantially accurate as Mrs Thatcher – off the record – later admitted to Brian Walden. 'The problem is,' she lamented, 'the Queen is the kind of woman who could vote SDP.'[87]

The problem was a good deal more serious with Prince Charles, an archetypal Tory 'wet', whose position allowed him to voice his worries more publicly than his mother would ever do. In October 1985 – nine months before the *Sunday Times* story – he was reported to have spoken in New York about 'divided Britain' and specifically criticised Government policy, or lack of it, towards the inner cities. On this occasion Mrs Thatcher rang the Palace to complain.[88] Later that year he set up the Prince of Wales Community Venture, a community service scheme for young people, and tried without success to get the Government to back it. After the 1987 election, when she recognised that there was 'a big job to do' in the cities, Charles was briefly encouraged: he urged her to go into the cities herself and meet community leaders, and invited her to lunch at Kensington Palace to meet some of them. She declined. Later she agreed to host a lunch herself at Number Ten, but that was cancelled. Eventually he did persuade her to attend a Business in the Community reception, where she was said to have been impressed and to have learned a great deal. 'Hooray is all I can say,' Charles wrote, 'and I do *hope* this first encounter will bear fruit eventually.' But again he was disappointed. 'Absolutely nothing happened.'[89] The fact was that Mrs Thatcher was suspicious of Charles' dabbling in politics and had no wish to encourage him.

One of her last acts in the summer of 1990 was to push through a big increase in the Civil List with minimum debate before Parliament rose. The usual left-wingers – Tony Benn and Dennis Skinner – objected that the Queen was getting a large pay rise well above the level of inflation while her subjects struggled to pay the poll tax. Mrs Thatcher replied that 'an overwhelming number of people regard the royal family as the greatest asset the United Kingdom has . . . The royal family are a focus of patriotism, of loyalty, of affection and of esteem. That is a rare combination and we should value it highly.'[90] Strongly though she supported the monarchy, however, both with words and with public money, the indirect effect of Thatcherism during the 1980s was not kind to the Royal Family. On the one hand, the management of the royal finances – like those of other national institutions – came under closer scrutiny as the old deference waned: palaces, yachts, trains and retainers once taken for granted now had to be justified on a value-for-money basis. On the other, the media – led by the increasingly uninhibited Murdoch press – threw off all restraint in prying into the private lives and marriages of the younger members of the family. The 1990s was a difficult decade for the House of Windsor.

As Prime Minister, Mrs Thatcher drew skilfully on a range of feminine roles – housewife, mother, nurse, headmistress – to project her message; but the longer she went on, the more she grew into the role of queen, which she could play so much better than the frumpy occupant of Buckingham Palace. The Falklands transformed the Iron Lady almost overnight into Boadicea, the warrior queen who had fought the Romans. Much as Mrs Thatcher admired Victorian values, the Widow of Windsor was not an appealing role model. But increasingly she came to identify with Elizabeth I – Gloriana – who had presided over England's first great period of mercantile expansion and national assertion, surrounded by her court of flatterers and buccaneers, all eager to do her bidding and dependent on her favour. She encouraged the comparison by her susceptibility to handsome protégés like Cecil Parkinson and John Moore, flatterers like Woodrow Wyatt and Lord Young, favourite businessmen like Lord Hanson and Lord King; and even adopted the chilling phrase, when one of her ministers displeased her, 'Shall we withdraw our love?'[91] In her memoirs she echoed Elizabeth by writing that 'I did not believe I had to open windows into men's souls.'[92] And it was surely no accident that at the crisis of her premiership in November 1990 she appeared at the Lord Mayor's Banquet in the City wearing a defiantly regal, high-collared Elizabethan dress, looking like Judi Dench in *Shakespeare in Love*.

Above all she increasingly used the royal plural. In truth the widespread mockery she attracted for this habit is a bit unfair. In her early years she was criticised for the opposite habit of talking about the Government in the first person singular. 'Unemployment is the most difficult problem that I face,' she told Sue Lawley in 1981. 'I do feel deeply concerned when I have people who want jobs and can't get them. But I know that I can't conjure them out of thin air.'[93] Her nightmare, she told Brian Walden in 1988, was that 'when I had got the finances right, when I got the law right . . . the British sense of enterprise and initiative would have been killed by socialism.'[94] She even talked possessively about 'my coal mines'[95] and 'my housing estates'.[96] This language inevitably provoked allegations of personal rule. Nevertheless when she was later criticised for using the plural she protested that she did so because she was 'not an "I" person':

> I am not an 'I did this in my Government', 'I did that', 'I did the other' person. I have never been an 'I' person, so I talk about 'we' – the Government . . . It is not I who do things, it is we, the Government.[97]

Sometimes, when she wanted to stress collective responsibility, this was true. At other times, however, she distanced herself from the Government and used the first person singular to give the impression that its failings had nothing to do with her. In fact she veered wildly between singular and plural, sometimes in the same sentence, as in her assurance to Sue Lawley that she cared about unemployment: 'I wouldn't be human if we didn't.'[98] Her every waking thought was so taken up with the business of governing that she really made no distinction between herself as an individual and herself as leader of the Government, or more specifically the leader of the travelling circus which accompanied her, as in the account she gave to Donald MacIntyre of a busy few weeks in 1989:

> We went across to Japan for an official visit . . . We called in Moscow on the way back. We got back. We than had the whole run-up to the party conference. We went to Nottingham. We did several regional tours that week . . . and then we came back from the party conference and we unpacked and did the speeches and the briefing for the Commonwealth Conference and on the Monday we took off for Malaysia . . . We just got back at 4 a.m. on the Wednesday morning, came here and started work.[99]

Increasingly, however, she began to use the plural when she quite unambiguously meant herself alone. 'We are in the fortunate position in Britain,' she told an interviewer on her way to Moscow in 1987, 'of being, as it were, the senior person in power.'[100] 'When I first walked through that door,' she declared in January 1988, 'I little thought that we would become the longest serving Prime Minister of this century.'[101] And most famously, the following year, again on the steps of Downing Street: 'We have become a grandmother.'[102]

The cult of Maggie

By the middle of the decade Mrs Thatcher had become an institution, a seemingly permanent part of the national landscape, around whom there grew up a personality cult unlike anything seen in Britain before. For a start she gave her name to an '-ism' as no previous Prime Minister had done: a relatively clear, if sometimes contradictory body of ideas, attitudes and values to which her personality gave unusual coherence. There had been Bevanism in the 1950s, and Powellism in the late 1960s, but these were fringe phenomena of the left and right: neither was a political philosophy which defined an era as Thatcherism did. Mrs Thatcher dominated the politics of the 1980s as no other individual had done since Gladstone. 'She has towered over all her contemporaries,' Professor S. E. Finer wrote in 1987. 'I do not believe that in our lifetime we shall see her like again.'[103] She was as Brian Walden wrote, 'a unique politician . . . the master spirit of this age'.[104]★ She exerted a hold on the national imagination that went far beyond politics. Old and young alike could not imagine life without her. When elderly patients were asked by psychiatrists to name the Prime Minister, it was said that for the first time in forty years they always got it right. Meanwhile small boys were reported wistfully asking their fathers: 'Dad, can a man be Prime Minister?'

To her admirers she was 'Maggie', to her opponents simply 'Thatcher' – but both held her responsible for everything, good or bad, that happened in what a flood of books inevitably called the

---

★This domination was reflected in a fresh outpouring of books by journalists and academics, among them Hugo Young and Anne Sloman, *The Thatcher Phenomenon* (1986), based on a radio series broadcast in 1985; Peter Jenkins, *Mrs Thatcher's Revolution* (1987), Dennis Kavanagh, *Thatcherism and British Politics* (1987), Kenneth Minogue and Michael Biddiss, *Thatcherism: Personality and Politics* (1988) and Robert Skidelsky, *Thatcherism* (1988). Five years earlier political scientists had worried about the problems of three-party politics and 'governing without a majority'. Now they assumed Conservative hegemony for the foreseeable future and worried about a one-party state.

Thatcher decade: half the population believed that she was single-handedly saving the country, the other half that she was single-handedly wrecking it. 'In recent months,' Noel Malcolm wrote in the *Spectator* in 1989, 'the popular press has credited her with "moving" to outlaw the sale of human kidneys, "ordering" senior ministers to cooperate with Toyota in its search for a factory site . . . and "demanding" that the Foreign Office send aid to Afghanistan. ("Maggie's Aid for Afghan Children").'[105] 'I constantly saw on the poster of the *Evening Standard*,' Douglas Hurd recalled, '"Maggie Acts!" on something. Often in those cases she wasn't even aware of the situation. But the whole ethos of No. 10 was that it was "Maggie Acts!"'[106] 'The way these stories are presented,' Malcolm wrote, 'reflects not only the stylistic requirements of vivid journalism but also the methods of her press secretary . . . who is happy to attribute all decisive action to the Prime Minister herself, symbolically detaching her from the Government and then blaming members of the Government for being "semi-detached".'[107]★

Love her or hate her, she was inescapable, like a force of nature. Alternative nicknames proliferated, invented by Julian Critchley, Denis Healey and others: 'The Great She-Elephant', 'Attila the Hen', 'Catherine the Great of Finchley', 'the Maggietollah' (by analogy with Iran's Islamic revolutionary dictator, Ayatollah Khomeini), or just 'That Woman'. *Private Eye* called her 'the Supreme Ruler of the Universe'. But all were too contrived and none replaced the simple 'Maggie' which in itself contained all the different persona she had adopted. There is a wider range of resonant role models available to a woman politician than to a man, and Mrs Thatcher played them all, from house-wife and mother (even, to the troops in the Falklands, a pin-up), through a variety of female authority figures to domestic battleaxe. The satirical television programme *Spitting Image* portrayed her as a termagant in a man's suit, forever bullying her cowering ministers (encapsulated in a famous sketch of her ordering a meal in a restaurant. 'I'll have the steak.' 'And what about the vegetables?' 'They'll have the same as me'). The programme also produced latex models that could be bought as dog toys: Mrs Thatcher's wore a breastplate and helmet made of cooking utensils, thus combining the housewife and the

---

★No one except members of the public ever called her Maggie to her face. Wellwishers would call out, 'Good on you, Maggie' or 'You show 'em, Maggie'; and demonstrators chanted, 'Maggie out'. The tabloids called her Maggie. But her colleagues called her 'Margaret' or 'Prime Minister', and behind her back (with a touch of irony) 'The Lady'.

warrior in one. When her enemies tried to turn these images against her, they only enhanced her aura of power. The domestic battleaxe fitted into a well-loved British comic tradition represented by come-diennes like Peggy Mount and Hattie Jacques – not forgetting Wilde's Lady Bracknell and Ena Sharples in *Coronation Street*; while the image of the cruel queen – Rider Haggard's chilling *She* (the original 'She Who Must be Obeyed') or Kali ('the grim Indian goddess of destruction' invoked by Paul Johnson in 1987) – merely lent her a semi-mythical capacity to inspire fear that is not available to a male Prime Minister. Male tyrants are simply loathed, but a powerful woman attracts fasci-nated admiration from both sexes.*

Denis Healey tried hardest to find a description to evoke the paradox of her hard-faced femininity. 'Florence Nightingale with a blowtorch' he once called her; another time 'a mixture of a matron at a minor public school and a guard in a concentration camp'.[110] What all these images have in common is a powerful sexual ambivalence, as Wendy Webster noted in 1990.

> Like many female stars who have played with notions of gender, she has always painstakingly emphasised . . . the meticulous conven-tionality and respectability of her private life, but in her public performance she was increasingly seen as a phenomenon which tran-scended both genders, reconciling the dual nature of both mascu-line and feminine imagery in her person. She was both the glamorous female star . . . and also the hard masculine warrior and leader – an Iron Lady clothed in soft female flesh.[111]

Or, as François Mitterrand encapsulated it with classic French economy: '*les yeux de Caligula, la bouche de Marilyn Monroe*'.[112]

The media were fascinated by the feminine side of her personality: they were always on the look-out for tears or other signs of weakness which might reveal 'the woman within'. She famously wept twice on television, once when Mark was lost in the desert in 1981, and again in 1985 when telling Miriam Stoppard about her father's deposition from Grantham council. Yet paradoxically, Webster suggested, 'it is those aspects of her image which are associated with femininity that are seen

---

*The Freudian Leo Abse wrote of public-school-educated Tory MPs voting for the cane when they elected her in 1975, and devoted a whole chapter to Mrs Thatcher's 'sado-masochistic' relationship with the electors[108]; while the feminist Beatrix Campbell found plenty of women who loathed Mrs Thatcher's politics yet could not help admiring her 'because she's strong'.[109]

as constructed, while those associated with masculinity are often seen as innate'.[113]

'Femininity is what she wears,' Beatrix Campbell agreed, 'masculinity is what she admires. She wants to be a woman who does what men do.' To the despair of feminists, Britain's first female Prime Minister did nothing to feminise the male world of politics: on the contrary, with her language of conflict and confrontation, her belief in military power and her love of nuclear weapons, 'she offered feminine endorsement to patriarchal power and principles'.[114] Her use of language was always determinedly masculine, even when she implicitly included herself. 'This generation,' she gloried after the Falklands war, 'can match their fathers and grandfathers in ability, in courage and in resolution. We have not changed.'[115] Hymning her vision of freedom to the Tory conference in 1989, she spoke of 'Freedom that gives a man room to breathe . . . to make his own decisions and to chart his own course.'[116] She never had any truck with equal opportunities or political correctness. 'What has women's lib ever done for me?' she once demanded;[117] and one of the reasons she loathed Elspeth Howe was because she had been, until 1979, deputy chairman of the Equal Opportunities Commission. The virtue she admired above all others and claimed for herself was strength. 'If you want someone weak,' she once told Jimmy Young, 'you don't want me. There are plenty of others to choose from.'[118]

Yet at the same time she was very feminine, and derived much of her power from exploiting her femininity. 'I like being made a fuss of by a lot of chaps,' she once remarked.[119] Whether by calculation or instinct, she was skilful at wrongfooting men who did not know how to argue with a woman as bluntly as they would have with another man. They never knew whether she was going to mother them, flirt with them or hit them over the head − metaphorically − with her handbag. Her handbag (that most feminine appendage, carried by practically every woman from the Queen downwards) became an important component of her image. Other Prime Ministers have had their identifying props, like Churchill's cigar or Wilson's pipe. But Mrs Thatcher's handbag became much more than that. It was the physical symbol of her authority, like a royal mace or sceptre, which announced her presence. It was also a miraculous receptacle, like Mary Poppins' portmanteau, from which she could seemingly produce at will the killer quotation or statistic to win an argument. And above all it became an active verb, so that when she belaboured some offending minister she was said to 'handbag' him. Nothing more potently embodied a woman's dominance over a Cabinet of men.

Mrs Thatcher enjoyed denigrating men, while asserting the natural superiority of women. 'If you want a speech ask a man,' she once said. 'If you want something done, ask a woman.'[120] Women, she claimed, were used to juggling their time and doing several things at once, unlike poor one-dimensional men: in 1982 she specifically compared running the Falklands war with running a household, boasting that 'every woman is a manager twenty-four hours a day'.[121] 'Women have to cope, always cope,' she said in 1987.[122] 'You do just keep going. There is a difference between men and women in that way.'[123] Eight years in Downing Street had not worn her down, because 'mums take a lot of wearing down, thank goodness'.[124] She rejected the compliment that she was 'the best man in the Cabinet', boasting 'I am much better than that. I am the best woman in the Cabinet.'[125]

Yet all this was essentially self-praise. She found very few others of her sex worthy of promotion either within government or the wider public service. Janet Young, the only other woman to sit briefly in her Cabinet, is sharply disparaged in her memoirs as not up to the job.[126] Lady Young in turn commented that Mrs Thatcher simply did not like women.[127] She claimed special virtue for women, but liked being the only one. Increasingly as she got older she did not encourage other women to follow the example of her own career, but told them that their special role was as home-makers and mothers, bringing up the family. She supported the right of women to be lawyers, doctors, engineers, scientists or politicians, she told the Conservative Women's Conference in 1988. How could she not? But, she went on, 'many women wish to devote themselves mainly to raising a family and running a home':

> And we should have that choice too. For the family is the building block of society. It is a nursery, a school, a hospital, a leisure place, a place of refuge and a place of rest. It encompasses the whole of society. It fashions our beliefs. It is the preparation for the rest of our life. And women run it.[128]

In the beginning she used her clothes to point the contrast between her outward femininity and her inner toughness, starting with her delighted response when the Russians christened her the 'Iron Lady' in 1976:

> Ladies and gentlemen, I stand before you tonight in my green chiffon evening gown, my face softly made up, my fair hair gently waved

. . . The Iron Lady of the Western World? Me? A cold warrior? . . .
Well, yes, if that is how they wish to interpret my defence of values
and freedoms fundamental to our way of life.[129]

As Leader of the Opposition she allowed Gordon Reece to advise
her on what to wear, what looked well on television and what did
not, what jewellery to avoid, and generally to mould and – at that
period – soften her image. Thereafter, as Prime Minister, she always
paid careful attention to her wardrobe and the particular impression
she wanted to convey on each occasion. She loved dressing up and
felt strongly the resonance of certain outfits, which she would wear
again if they reminded her of a good occasion, or not if they held bad
associations. She writes in her memoirs that she did not wear a new
suit to the 1979 Dublin summit because she knew it was going to be
a bruising occasion, and 'I didn't want to risk tainting it with unhappy
memories.'[130] On the television programme *The English Woman's
Wardrobe* in 1986 she delighted in telling viewers exactly what she had
worn in different crises.[131] On party occasions she nearly always wore
blue; she very rarely wore red; but on her visit to Poland in 1988 she
wore green, because she was told that in Poland green was the colour
of hope.[132]

Like Barbara Castle – but unlike the famously untidy Shirley Williams
– she recognised that clothes were of huge importance to a woman
politician, an asset if chosen with care, a liability if worn badly. 'She
was convinced,' Nigel Lawson wrote, 'that her authority . . . would be
diminished if she were not impeccably turned out at all times. She
was probably right.'[133] From about 1985, however, as her power grew,
so her style of dressing became more commanding. Charles Powell's
wife Carla was credited with getting her into what was called 'power-
dressing', following the styles set by the matriarchs of the American
TV series *Dynasty* and *Dallas*: stronger, simpler cuts, darker colours and
big shoulders. It was before her 1987 visit to Moscow that she discovered Aquascutum: thereafter she got most of her clothes from there,
though she was still said to use a 'little lady' in Battersea who had been
making clothes for her since the 1970s.[134]

The way she used clothes to express her personality was well
described by the fashion journalist Brenda Polan in 1988:

Margaret Thatcher, when we first became aware of her, was middle
class mimsy . . . She looked like a middle class mum would do on
special days, like a lady magistrate, like the vicar's wife. Very unthreat-
ening. The fabrics were not expensive, there was nothing sexy about

them. It was very tailored . . . and all it told you was that here was a very respectable lady.

What she's done over the years progressively is in fact get sexier, and much more powerful. The fabrics are richer, there's more bulk. She's adopted what most Englishwomen find very frightening, which is a sort of hard-edged French chic . . . there's a certain sort of unforgivingness to it, a certain arrogance.

She has discovered for herself a sort of power dressing, and that's what an awful lot of fashion in the last decade has been about.

Her great achievement was in managing to look powerful and feminine at the same time, transcending the tendency of women politicians in the past to wear severely mannish suits which made them look like 1930s lesbians. This was how she was able to appear more royal than the Queen, who – having no power to express – still looked 'mimsy' and middle-class. Visiting Poland in 1988, she wore – when she was not wearing green – a cashmere coat in deep caramel with a big fur collar and matching hat. 'Rather like a Holbein painting of Henry VIII, here was a figure which was saying: "I am powerful."'

What Margaret Thatcher is doing . . . is expressing power in dress . . . I think Margaret Thatcher is a ruler, who thinks of herself as a ruler. . . . This is now expressed with . . . a complete confidence that this powerful person with an enormous presence is ME.[135]

Her regal manner gave rise to the fantasy among some of her more besotted admirers that she was not a Grantham grocer's daughter at all, but actually came of aristocratic stock, her grandmother having supposedly been seduced by one of the Cust family while working as a housemaid at Belton House. There is no evidence for this at all: it is pure snobbery, a version of the Cinderella fairy-tale embraced by romantics who thought her real origins too mundane for their princess.[136] Ronnie Millar, to his credit, was too sensible to believe this story. Yet at the same time he noted that she had somehow transcended her origins. By conviction she was meritocratic and opposed to class distinction. By her policies she strove to create a more classless Britain and to a considerable extent succeeded, with barrow boys making fortunes in the City and the Tory party increasingly taken over by spivs and estate agents who made the likes of Julian Critchley shudder.

And yet, as she progressed from lower middle class Grantham girl to a world figure whose every word commanded attention . . . she seemed to acquire an air of – I can't avoid the word – breeding . . . as though somewhere in her family tree the genes had skipped a couple of generations and were now reborn in her.

Thus, paradoxically and despite herself, in Millar's view, the more she tried to abolish class, 'the more she seemed to embody class distinction'.[137]

Yet the knowledge that this woman who now gave herself such airs was just a grocer's daughter aroused the most furious antipathy among those – particularly in the arts world – who felt that her whole personality was phoney. 'Of all the elements combined in the complex of signs labelled Margaret Thatcher,' wrote the novelist Angela Carter in 1983, 'it is her voice that sums up the ambiguity of the entire construct. She coos like a dove, hisses like a serpent, bays like a hound', all in a contrived upper-class accent 'reminiscent not of real toffs but of Wodehouse aunts'.[138] Some of this line of criticism was even more personal. The theatre director Jonathan Miller deplored her 'odious suburban gentility and sentimental, saccharine patriotism, catering to the worst elements in commuter idiocy' and told the *Sunday Telegraph* in 1988 that he found the Prime Minister 'loathsome, repulsive in almost every way'.[139] The Oxford philosopher Lady Warnock also disliked Mrs Thatcher's 'patronising, elocution voice' and claimed to find the spectacle of her showing off her clothes on television 'not exactly vulgar, just *low*'.[140] The snobbery of these comments says more about the speakers than it does about Mrs Thatcher; except that their violence exemplifies the visceral response that her multiple personality aroused in her worshippers and detractors alike.

By now she was extraordinarily dominant on television. An academic study of her television technique showed that she intimidated even the most experienced interviewers by turning the tables and attacking them, refusing to be interrupted, while accusing them of interrupting her. She put them on the defensive by using their Christian names. 'She tends to personalise issues and take questions as accusations,' Donald McCormick commented. For instance, he once dared to suggest that she was inflexible. 'Inflexible?' she retorted. 'I am inflexible in defence of democracy, in defence of freedom, in defence of law and order and so should you be, so should the BBC be and so should everyone else be.'[141]

'She has an instant appraisal of what you are trying to suggest to her,' Peter Sissons admitted, 'and if you haven't done your homework she'll kill you stone dead – not with words but with a look.' 'I've not seen one interview in recent years where she hasn't wiped the floor with the interviewer with contemptuous ease,' wrote the novelist

William Boyd. It was only partly, as Mark Lawson suggested in the *Independent* in 1989, that she favoured sycophantic interviewers like David Frost who would give her a respectful ride:

> The tugging of the forelock would have been the appropriate gesture for the majority of Frost's questions; he was operating in the approved style of interview as courtship, for which we can blame Brian Walden.[142]

Interviewers generally, in the view of the *Observer*'s John Naughton, lacked 'the guts or the resourcefulness to stand up to a politician who combines the *hauteur* of Trollope's Mrs Proudie with the jugular instincts of a fishwife'.[143] The psychologist Anthony Clare called her 'the most outrageous female performer since Edna Everage' – Barry Humphries' grotesque Australian drag-queen, the original 'housewife/superstar':

> She positively exults in getting whatever Buggins is unfortunate enough to have his turn in the ring and clouting him round the head and kneeing him in the groin, and all the time she smiles that damnable smile.[144]

The pioneer of modern television interviewing, Robin Day, once famous for his bullying of defenceless politicians, was so ashamed of his inability to stand up to Mrs Thatcher that he actually apologised for failing the public. He felt that she had so changed the rules of the game by coming to the studio already primed to say what she was determined to say, irrespective of the interviewer, that his well-honed barristerial techniques were useless. He once joked that he planned to start his next interview by asking: 'Prime Minister, what is your answer to my first question?' In his memoirs he accused Mrs Thatcher of deliberately 'devaluing the television interview as an instrument of democratic dialogue'.[145] This was true; but it was also true that the doyen of searching interviewers had been reduced to a pussycat.

And yet she hated television. She rehearsed intensively for these major interviews, with Bernard Ingham playing Robin Day or whoever, and when she got to the studio she had to be handled very carefully. 'She needs settling like a horse, highly spirited,' Gordon Reece told Woodrow Wyatt. 'She gets nervous if people surround and crowd her. She must be kept calm.'[146] As she once told Ronnie Millar, 'I'm not a performer, dear.'[147] Like everything else in her life, she only taught herself to dominate by determination and hard work.

Above all she still needed fantastically little sleep. Four hours a night was perhaps an exaggeration, but she could certainly go for several days on that little, and never slept for more than five or six. She sometimes caught up a bit at Chequers at weekends, but during the week she rarely went to bed before two o'clock, and was up again at six. She dominated the Government by sheer physical stamina, as Charles Powell – who matched her pretty well – told Penny Junor:

> She was tensed up all the time, highly strung, very active. She would be up at 5 a.m., telephoning all hours of the day and night, meeting this person and that, get this done, that done, never stopping for a moment . . . She for some reason I never understood – an extra gland or something – could cope with three hours a night for weeks at a time and it didn't affect her performance.[148]★

Her health was generally robust, though she did suffer from colds and a number of minor ailments which never laid her low for long. She never put on weight, although she took no exercise; but she took a number of vitamin pills and was widely believed to have some form of hormone replacement therapy to keep her young. She had three minor operations while she was Prime Minister: one for varicose veins in 1982, the second for a detached retina in 1983; and the third to correct a contraction of the fingers of her right hand, Dupuytren's contracture (also known as 'coachman's grip'), in 1986. She had a painful tooth abscess during the June 1987 election, and generally her teeth gave her increasing trouble. She also – inevitably in her sixties – needed reading glasses, but did not like to be seen wearing them in public, so her briefs for Prime Minister's Questions and speech scripts had to be printed in large type. She would never admit to any hint of weakness. She was particularly annoyed, therefore, when she nearly fainted from the heat during a diplomatic reception at Buckingham Palace in November 1987, giving rise to speculation that she was finally cracking up and a spate of articles offering pseudo-medical advice that she should slow down.[149] She was sensitive to any suggestion that she was beginning to show her age, and tried to stop the party conference in 1989 serenading her sixty-fourth birthday by singing 'Happy Birthday to You'.

It was part of her legend that she never relaxed but was – as she told a television audience – 'always on the job'.[150] But it was true. She

---

★Not the least of John Major's difficulties in following her, inheriting a machine that had got used to servicing a Prime Minister who never slept, was that he needed his eight hours a night.

hated holidays and, if persuaded to take one, always jumped at an excuse to cut it short. She was often asked how she relaxed, and her answers were always unconvincing. In an interview with Chris Moncrieff for the Press Association in May 1989, for instance, she first brushed off the idea of relaxing at all; then considered it for a moment as if it was a wholly strange idea before reaching wildly for an answer that was quite untrue:

> We do not have very much time to relax. How would I relax? To me it is sheer joy to go out for a walk in the countryside, in the fresh air, sheer joy.

Then her natural honesty reasserted itself and she confessed to her only real relaxation:

> For a woman perhaps . . . it is easier . . . because there is always something in the house to turn your hand to. There is always something to tidy up, something to think about, something to organise so you have always got a lot of practical things to do – always – so if you really find yourself sitting and brooding, there is always a lot you can go and do and that, too, is therapeutic.[151]

She could not be idle for a moment, so she did not really regard running the country as work at all. It was her life.

She had no real friends, because she had never left time in her life for friendship. Those whom she refers to in her memoirs as old friends – Janet Young, for instance – did not recognise the description in the way that they would use the word. In a sense Denis was her best friend. They were much closer in Downing Street than they had been in the earlier part of their marriage. He had friends, certainly, but they had few as a couple, because they had never operated as a couple. They never entertained privately in Downing Street. They did very occasionally go out to dinner quietly with other couples – to Ian and Jane Gow, or Charles and Carla Powell – where she could briefly and genuinely relax. Nicholas Edwards and his wife once asked Margaret and Denis to supper on a Sunday evening. She was tense at first – Denis only came later – but relaxed after a couple of whiskies. Edwards was pretty sure that none of her other colleagues had ever dared to ask them.[152]

Nor, despite all her paeans to the centrality of family life, was the family really very close. It never had been when the children were young, when she was making her career and Denis was away travelling for long periods for his work. Carol's account of their childhood in her biography of Denis portrays her mother as a very remote and preoccupied parent: the twins were largely brought up by nannies. 'It was very much drilled into me that the best thing I could do for my mother was not to make any demands on her,' she told interviewers in 1996 when her book came out. 'Her attitude was "Please hurry, so I can take you to school and then I can get to work".'[153] By the time Mrs Thatcher was Prime Minister, Mark and Carol were in their late twenties and early thirties. They both dropped in and out of Downing Street from time to time, but Carol had the good sense to take herself out of the way and made her own career in Australia for much of the time, working as a journalist, though she came back in 1983 to cover her mother's re-election for the *Daily Mail*. Mark's unsuccessful motor racing, his mishap in the Sahara and controversy about his involvement in arms dealing in the Middle East, using his mother's name to enrich himself, made him an increasing embarrassment and a potential danger. Bernard Ingham was not alone in fearing that he would involve Mrs Thatcher in a serious scandal if he stayed in the country – Denis had the same worry – so in 1984 he was packed off to Texas with a number of introductions to make his living there.

In Dallas Mark soon married an oil heiress and produced the son who allowed his mother to proclaim herself a grandmother. 'I really was absolutely delighted,' Mrs Thatcher told a women's magazine. 'Mark is coming up to thirty-three and I really was getting worried that they were not going to get married.'[154] It was reported that Mark used to ring his mother every Sunday evening from wherever he was – and wherever she was – in the world. 'A different note comes into her voice when she speaks about Mark,' Wyatt noted in 1987. 'She obviously dotes on him. I think he is a pretty good washout. He gives a lot of trouble to his mother. She puts up with it as mothers do with their favourite son or child.'[155] In a curious reflection of her essentially masculine outlook, she was uncritically devoted to Mark while continuing to undervalue Carol, as Carol herself – now living with a ski instructor in Switzerland and still unmarried – rather pathetically confirmed in 1996:

> Mark is married to a beautiful girl, has two fabulous children and various mansions scattered around the world. I'm an ancient spinster of no fixed abode living in a rented holiday flat in a ski resort. I still don't measure up awfully well on the Richter Scale.[156]

Janet Young once wished Mrs Thatcher a good Christmas and was appalled when she replied that she was having a whole lot of political associates to Chequers – people like Keith Joseph (whose marriage had just ended) and the unmarried Gordon Reece and Ronnie Millar – whom she referred to as 'my lame ducks'. Of course she had the family too (Mark and Carol if they were around, and at least once her sister Muriel and her husband) but they were always outnumbered by political friends. Christmas Day was rigidly structured around church in the morning, a traditional lunch which ended punctually in time for the Queen's broadcast at 3 p.m., then a short walk (described by one jaundiced guest as 'a route march down to the police post at the side entrance'), followed later by a cold buffet supper, often joined by other political guests who lived nearby.[157] On Boxing Day there would be another lunch for favoured friends and allies – people like Rupert Murdoch, the American Ambassador, Lord King and Marmaduke Hussey. On these occasions Mrs Thatcher was the perfect hostess, not overtly political but tirelessly devoted to ensuring that everyone had everything they wanted. Yet at the same time, though the atmosphere was carefully relaxed, these lunches like everything else in her life were unmistakably political gatherings – a symbolic summoning of key supporters at the turn of the year.

The sad truth is that Mrs Thatcher, behind the hugely successful front which enabled her to dominate her generation, was a driven, insecure and rather lonely woman who lived for her work and would be lost when her astonishing career ended, as one day it eventually must. In her early days her phenomenal energy, her single-mindedness, her inability to relax, to admit any weakness or trust anyone to do anything better than she could do it herself, were all strengths and part of the reason for her success; but the longer she went on, the more these strengths turned to weaknesses – a loss of perspective, growing self-righteousness, a tendency to believe her own myth, an inability to delegate or trust her colleagues at all, so that instead of leading a team and preparing for an eventual handover to a successor, the Government became ever more centred on herself. There were bound to be tears in the end, and there were.

12

Stumble and Recovery

Helicopters, leaks and lies

The episode that threw the sharpest light on Mrs Thatcher's conduct of government was the crisis over the future of Westland helicopters which erupted at the beginning of 1986. More than any other incident in her whole premiership, Westland exposed to public gaze the reality of her relationship with her colleagues and the far greater trust she placed in unelected officials in her private office. The issue was relatively trivial in itself; but the questions raised went to the heart of constitutional government. As a result, the Westland affair came closer than anything else – before the combination of Europe and the poll tax arose in 1990 – to bringing her rule to an untimely end.

It arose from the refusal of one ambitious and independent-minded minister to be bullied. Michael Heseltine had always been the cuckoo in Mrs Thatcher's nest. Neither a monetarist nor a wet, he was an energetic and unapologetic corporatist very much in the manner of Ted Heath: his political hero was Lloyd George. Mrs Thatcher was forced to recognise him as an effective minister, both at the Department of the Environment, where he pioneered the sort of management practices which Derek Rayner later applied to the whole of Whitehall, and at Defence, where he deployed the case against unilateral nuclear disarmament with conviction and flair. But she distrusted both his interventionist instincts and his ambition, and doubted his grasp of detail. She had firmly suppressed his vision of urban regeneration on Merseyside and elsewhere through private/public partnership, and was frankly jealous of his ability to rouse the adulation of the party conference: she always found a reason to miss his speeches. Likewise she resented his exploitation of the sort of photo-opportunity – looking over the Berlin Wall or wearing a flak jacket to visit Greenham

Common – that she regarded as her own preserve. In the MoD he was dealing with matters in which she took a particularly close interest. It was inevitable that the two biggest egos in the Cabinet would clash on this territory.

First of all Mrs Thatcher was not amused when Heseltine, in response to continued controversy about the sinking of the *General Belgrano* in 1982, set up an internal MoD inquiry to assure himself that there was 'not a Watergate in there somewhere'.[1] In fact Clive Ponting's review satisfied him that Mrs Thatcher had been fully justified in ordering the action.[2] But when he proposed to correct some of the false statements that had initially been put out about the sinking she overruled him. It was this refusal to come clean – rather than the action itself – which so outraged Ponting that he leaked the details to Tam Dalyell, leading to his prosecution under the Official Secrets Act – which Heseltine strongly supported – and the embarrassment to the Government of his unexpected acquittal.

Second, Mrs Thatcher suspected Heseltine of deliberately using the MoD budget as a tool of economic policy, enabling him to run the sort of interventionist industrial strategy she disapproved of. In particular he fought – to the point of threatening resignation – for one of the two new frigates commissioned to replace those lost in the Falklands to be built by Cammel Laird on Merseyside, instead of both going to Swan Hunter on the Tyne, which was the cheaper option. Heseltine believed that Norman Tebbit at the DTI had tried, with the Prime Minister's backing, to rig the decision unfairly in favour of Swan Hunter, and in retrospect regarded this episode as a dry run of what happened over Westland. On this occasion Heseltine got his way, but so much personal capital had been invested on both sides that Mrs Thatcher could not afford to lose the next such battle. 'From then on,' Nigel Lawson believed, 'she was as determined to do him down as he was to run his department in his own way.'[3]

Yet a third source of conflict, therefore, arose over nuclear policy, and specifically the British response to President Reagan's Strategic Defense Initiative. In her memoirs Lady Thatcher makes no apology for keeping this question under 'tight personal control' since in her view 'neither the Foreign Office nor the Ministry of Defence took SDI sufficiently seriously'.[4] Though she had her own doubts about the programme, she was adamant that Britain must be seen to back it. Heseltine was much less enthusiastic and resented her taking this sort of major defence decision unilaterally without reference to himself as the responsible minister.

These tensions were the background to the Westland crisis. Heseltine was already fretting at Mrs Thatcher's interference in his department. He was also critical of her indifference to the state of the inner cities and 'sickened by the poison which poured from the Prime Minister's lips concerning Europe'.[5] As early as October 1985 Peter Jenkins predicted in the *Sunday Times* that he might be 'brewing up towards a spectacular resignation'.[6] Sympathetic colleagues like Peter Walker were well aware of the risk of an explosion and were anxious to prevent it. In truth it was probably unavoidable, since both Heseltine and Mrs Thatcher were flexing their muscles for a showdown.

Lady Thatcher blames the whole Westland crisis on one man's over-weening ambition and egotistical refusal to accept the discipline of collective responsibility.[7] Certainly Heseltine was riding for a fall. Unquestionably he did get the relatively minor issue of the future of a small helicopter manufacturer out of perspective. He elevated the question of whether Westland should join up with the American firm Sikorsky or a somewhat shadowy consortium of European arms manu-facturers (including British Aerospace and GEC) into a major issue of principle reflecting an American or European orientation in foreign policy, and by extension a trial of strength between himself and the Prime Minister. When she threw the Government's weight behind the American option – which was also the Westland board's preference – he blatantly flouted her authority by continuing to lobby energetically for the European alternative. First he induced the European national armaments directors to declare that in future they would buy only European-made helicopters. Then he planted correspondence in the press still pushing the European case after Leon Brittan, the new Trade and Industry Secretary, had announced the Government's support for Westland's decision in favour of Sikorsky.

This was outrageous behaviour by a Cabinet minister, defying the decision of his own government. Heseltine's justification was that he had been systematically denied the opportunity to press the European option within the Government, so was forced to take the fight outside. In particular he accused the Prime Minister – after his resignation – of having unilaterally cancelled a meeting of the Cabinet's Economic Affairs Committee arranged for 13 December 1985 because at a previous meeting four days earlier he had won too much support. On the contrary, Mrs Thatcher insisted, there was no need for a second meeting since the majority view was quite clear at the first: the Government had made its decision and Heseltine alone refused to accept it.

Most testimony suggests that by this time she was right. Initially Heseltine had gained a good deal of support. Of those ministers allowed to discuss the issue, not only the Europhile Geoffrey Howe but more surprisingly Brittan's predecessor at the DTI, Norman Tebbit, had wanted to give Heseltine more time to try to make the European consortium stand up. Both of these were alienated, however, by the Defence Secretary's 'obsessive' (Howe) and 'myopic' (Tebbit) pursuit of his objective.[8] Always a cat who walked by himself, Heseltine played his hand extremely badly. When it came to a stand-up fight with the Prime Minister, the relative merits of rival helicopter manufacturers were forgotten: his potential allies slipped back to the Prime Minister. Nevertheless he did have grounds for grievance. Mrs Thatcher was by no means as neutral as she pretended. Not only did she clearly favour the American option, but she was just as determined to defeat Heseltine as he was to defeat her.★ Colleagues like Willie Whitelaw and John Biffen believed as a matter of principle that a senior minister with a strongly held conviction in his own area of responsibility was entitled to take his case to Cabinet.[11] But Westland never went to Cabinet. The one time Heseltine tried to force it onto the agenda, on 12 December, he was peremptorily ruled out of order.

The trouble was that Mrs Thatcher was prepared neither to accommodate Heseltine by giving him the chance to put his case in full Cabinet, nor to confront him directly and force him to back down. By mid-December it was plain that he did not accept the Government's decision. With hindsight, she should have sacked him, or required his resignation, then. But he was too powerful: she did not dare. He would not have gone quietly, like the despised wets: on the back benches he would have become a much more dangerous rallying point for her critics than Pym. She chose instead to try to undermine him by the familiar method of press manipulation and inspired leaking deployed by Bernard Ingham over the past six years against several less formidable colleagues from Norman St John Stevas to Peter Rees. This time she – or someone on her behalf – carelessly laid a charge which blew up in her own face, and came closer than anything between the Falklands invasion and the poll tax to bringing her down.

★In his memoirs Heseltine alleges that she backed Sikorsky as a payback to Al Haig for providing Britain with American airborne radar cover in the Falklands war.[9] But this is nonsense: Mrs Thatcher never had any time for Haig, besides which the whole problem in the Falklands was that British forces did *not* have an airborne early-warning system. Far more plausible, though difficult to substantiate, is the network of secret Anglo-American co-operation in the arms export field, in which Sir John Cuckney, the chairman of Westland, was heavily involved, and a Sikorsky connection with the huge Al-Yamamah arms deal with Saudi Arabia and the whole murky arms-to-Iraq saga (see chapter 15).[10]

The mistake was to leak a Law Officer's letter. There is a strict convention, jealously guarded by the Law Officers themselves, that legal advice is confidential. Yet Mrs Thatcher, who had once been a lawyer and was generally a stickler for correct procedure – however she might bend the spirit of it – and Brittan, a QC who should certainly have known his brother-lawyers' sensitivity, chose to use a letter commissioned from the Solicitor-General, Sir Patrick Mayhew, without his permission, to discredit Heseltine. They had ample provocation. Over Christmas and the New Year Heseltine continued his efforts to keep the European option in play. On 3 January 1986 he gave *The Times* an exchange of letters with the merchant bankers acting for the European consortium in which he warned that Westland risked losing future European orders if it accepted the American rescue – explicitly contradicting assurances which Mrs Thatcher had given Sir John Cuckney a few days earlier. Mrs Thatcher understandably determined that this must be repudiated. Instead of doing so directly, however, she persuaded Mayhew to write to Heseltine querying the basis for his warning, and then arranged for a damaging simplification of his letter to be made public.

Mrs Thatcher subsequently admitted that it was she who initiated Mayhew's letter. 'I therefore, through my office, asked him to consider writing to the Defence Secretary to draw that opinion to his attention.'[12] In fact she thought Mayhew's effort pretty feeble. He did no more than suggest, tentatively, that on the evidence he cited, Heseltine might be overstating his case.[13] He asked for clarification, – which Heseltine promptly provided (and Mayhew accepted).[14] But Mayhew's letter did contain the words 'material inaccuracies'; and it was these two words, torn out of context, which were leaked to the Press Association with a crude spin which was reflected in the next day's headlines. 'YOU LIAR' screamed the *Sun*; while *The Times* paraphrased the same message more sedately as 'Heseltine Told by Law Chief: Stick to the Facts'.[15] Mrs Thatcher afterwards maintained that while she regretted the way that it was done, 'it was vital to have accurate information in the public domain'.[16] 'It was a matter of duty that it should be known publicly that there were thought to be material inaccuracies' in Heseltine's letter.[17] But there was no contrary information in Mayhew's letter. The only possible purpose of leaking it was to discredit Heseltine and maybe provoke him to resign. The difference between this and earlier operations to discredit failing or dissenting ministers was that Mayhew – and his senior, the Attorney-General, Sir Michael Havers – were outraged by the use made of his letter and demanded an inquiry to discover the culprit.

The leaked letter by itself did not provoke Heseltine to resign. Of course when he dramatically walked out of the Cabinet two days later there was speculation that his action was premeditated, especially since he was able within a few hours to publish a 2,500-word statement detailing his complaints about Mrs Thatcher's style of government. But it was no secret at Westminster that he had been close to resignation for months; so it is not surprising that he should already have roughed out his grievances, to be polished up when the moment arose. His closest associates in the Cabinet were convinced that he did not mean to resign that day. John Wakeham had talked to him the evening before and thought he had dissuaded him.[18] Heseltine told his wife that morning that the moment to go was not yet.[19] The more interesting question is whether Mrs Thatcher deliberately forced his hand. She certainly laid down the law very firmly in Cabinet, insisting that the public wrangling between ministers must stop and that all future statements about Westland must be cleared though the Cabinet Office. But Heseltine accepted this without demur, until Nicholas Ridley intervened to spell out that this requirement should apply to the repetition of past statements as well. It was this that seemed to be gratuitously aimed at humiliating Heseltine. His response was to gather up his papers and leave the room. No one was sure whether he had resigned or merely gone to the bathroom. Peter Walker thinks he could still have been stopped if someone had got to the door before him.[20] But Lady Thatcher wrote with undisguised satisfaction in her memoirs that while some of the Cabinet were 'stunned' by his *démarche*, 'I was not. Michael had made his decision and that was that. I already knew who I wanted to succeed him.'[21] The suspicion is that Ridley had been primed to push Heseltine over the brink.

Obviously Mrs Thatcher was not sorry to see her most dangerous colleague self-destruct. She adjourned the Cabinet for coffee, conferred briefly with Whitelaw and Wakeham, then called George Younger back and offered him the Ministry of Defence. Younger insists that he had not been tipped off; but the MoD was the job he had always wanted and he accepted on the spot. She then asked him who should take over Scotland. He proposed Malcolm Rifkind, and was surprised when she made no objection but instantly agreed. She had already worked out that there was no serious alternative. Cabinet then resumed. By chance the next item on the agenda was Younger introducing a paper on the Scottish poll tax; throughout the following discussion he was confusingly referred to as Secretary of State for Defence. Never was a resigning minister so quickly replaced.[22]

A few hours later Heseltine published his statement giving his side of the argument and alleging 'the complete breakdown of Cabinet government'.[23] Whatever the truth of the cancelled meeting on 13 December, and making every allowance for Heseltine's own cavalier way with collective responsibility, the charge struck home. The picture of a Prime Minister bypassing the Cabinet to get her way by manipulating smaller meetings of selected colleagues was convincing and gave ready ammunition to her critics. But she had always made a virtue of being a strong Prime Minister. The public brawling over Westland had actually shown her to be surprisingly weak. Arguably she should have sacked Heseltine, or called him to order, much earlier. But as she explained, almost plaintively, on television: 'Had I done that, I know exactly what the press would have said: there you are, old bossyboots at it again.'[24] In fact the embarrassment of the Defence Secretary pursuing his own policy in opposition to the Prime Minister and the Trade Secretary for several weeks before spectacularly resigning was a direct result of her antagonistic way of running the Government as a series of bilateral trials of strength between herself and those of her colleagues who were prepared to stand up to her in an atmosphere of personal distrust and rivalry. Michael Heseltine was not the first or the last of Mrs Thatcher's ministers to conclude that this was no way to run a government. But the argument over helicopters, and the departure of Heseltine, was only the beginning of the Westland affair. Far more serious was the unravelling of the apparently trivial matter of the leak of Mayhew's letter, which called into question not the Prime Minister's strength but her honesty.

Leaks were a particularly sensitive matter in 1985, following the Government's prosecution of Sarah Tisdall and Clive Ponting for passing classified information. Sir Michael Havers had been responsible for those prosecutions: he was not inclined to take a less serious view of the leaking of the Solicitor-General's advice to a colleague. The morning that Mayhew's letter was splashed all over the papers he went straight to Number Ten threatening to go to the police unless an inquiry was set up immediately to find the source. Mrs Thatcher had no choice but to agree. The difficulty was that she was being asked to investigate a process which she herself had set in motion and in which her own private office was, at the least, involved. If she did not know already how the letter had reached the Press Association, she had only to ask her own staff to be told in five minutes. So inviting Robert Armstrong to undertake a ten-day inquiry was a charade from the start. It could only be a cover-up, and it was.

After all the inquiries and the testimony of most of the protagonists there remains only a narrow area of disagreement about what happened. It is admitted that Mrs Thatcher asked Mayhew to write a letter over the weekend. He took his time, but did so on the Monday morning, sending copies to the Treasury, the Foreign Office and the DTI. Mrs Thatcher made it clear to the DTI that she considered it 'urgent that it should become public knowledge before 4 p.m.', when Westland was due to hold a press conference to announce its decision.[25] She has never explained why it would not have been sufficient to give the Westland board privately the gist of Mayhew's opinion, or by what means she believed his letter could properly have been made public. Brittan's head of information at the DTI, Colette Bowe – a Civil Service high-flier only temporarily serving a spell as an information officer – was well aware that she was being asked to do something irregular. She tried to consult her Permanent Secretary, but unluckily he was out of the office and out of contact. (One result of Westland was that Permanent Secretaries were in future equipped with car phones.) So she contacted her superior in the Government Information Service, Bernard Ingham, hoping that he would handle the matter through the Number Ten press office. One way or another he declined. The *Observer* later alleged that he told Miss Bowe in the clearest possible terms to do it herself. 'You will★★★★★★★ well do what you are ★★★★★★★ well told.'[26] Ingham calls this 'a plain straightforward lie'. He writes in his memoirs: 'I told Colette Bowe I had to keep the Prime Minister above that sort of thing.'[27] He only regrets that he did not tell her more forcefully to have nothing to do with it herself. He does not explain why, as the Government's chief press officer dealing with an inexperienced junior, he did not instruct her firmly not to leak the letter but simply washed his hands and looked the other way. In fact Miss Bowe clearly understood that in leaking the letter she was acting on her minister's behalf, with Number Ten's knowledge, if not directly on instructions.★

In view of the subsequent controversy, it is important to note that Mrs Thatcher, in reporting to the Commons the result of Armstrong's inquiry, plainly acknowledged Number Ten's complicity in the leak. '*It was accepted that the DTI should disclose the fact* [that Mayhew considered Heseltine's letter inaccurate] *and that, in view of the urgency of the matter, the disclosure should be made by way of a telephone call to the Press Association.*' That admission unambiguously implicates her office, which is usually taken to mean Ingham and Charles Powell. She insisted that

---

★Colette Bowe is the one leading participant in the Westland drama who has not yet published her account of these events; but she has placed it in a bank for ultimate disclosure.

she herself was not consulted, but only because she did not need to be:

> They considered – and they were right – that I should agree that [Mayhew's opinion] should become public knowledge as soon as possible . . . In so far as what my office said to the DTI was based on the belief that I should have taken that view, had I been consulted, it was right.

She repeated, however, that 'had I been consulted, I should have said that a different method must be found of making the relevant facts known'.[28]

Under questioning she several times repeated that she wished the disclosure had been made by 'a more correct method' – even though there is no correct method of making public a Law Officer's advice. But in answer to a friendly question from Cranley Onslow she let slip an admission that she *had* given her approval. '*It was vital to have accurate information in the public domain . . . It was to get that accurate information to the public domain that I gave my consent.*'[29] Only Tam Dalyell seems to have picked this up. When he quoted it back to her in the main Westland debate four days later she explained that she had meant her consent to an inquiry, not her consent to the leak. But the context makes it plain that this was not so. Later, before the select committee which investigated the affair, Robert Armstrong glossed her words as 'a slip of the tongue'.[30] But slips of the tongue not infrequently betray the truth. It is extraordinary that the persistent Dalyell let this critical admission go.

Instead she was allowed to continue to maintain that she had not known about the leak, or at least the method of it, until 'some hours later'.[31] She then went through the charade of setting Armstrong to inquire into the actions of her own office. For ten days, while Armstrong pretended to pursue his bogus inquiry, Mrs Thatcher pretended still to know nothing. Then when he presented his report, concluding that the DTI had leaked the letter on Brittan's instruction, she made a pantomime of shocked amazement. 'Leon, why didn't you *tell* me?'[32] Michael Havers, promised his scapegoat, was impressed. 'Unless the PM is the most marvellous actress I've ever seen in my life she was as shocked as anybody that in fact it was on Leon Brittan's instructions.'[33] With a famous actor for a son, perhaps Havers should have been able to recognise good acting when he saw it.

It was the Prime Minister's veracity that was at stake in the House of Commons on 23 and 27 January. More strictly it was her ability to avoid being caught in a demonstrable untruth, since most MPs of all parties found it impossible to believe that she had not checked up, either in advance or very soon afterwards, on how her closest aides had implemented her instructions. Alan Clark has described both occasions with his usual appalling frankness. John Wakeham showed him a copy of Mrs Thatcher's 23 January statement before she made it. 'How *can* she say these things without faltering?' he wondered:

> But she did. Kept her nerve beautifully. I was sitting close by, and could see her riffling her notes and turning the pages of the speech. Her hand did not shake *at all*. It was almost as if the House, half-horrified, half-dumb with admiration, was cowed.[34]

She was momentarily embarrassed by one recently sacked minister who asked if she was 'satisfied' that her statement had 'enhanced the integrity of her Government?' She replied deadpan that she had tried, by setting up the inquiry, to give the House 'as full a report as I possibly can'.[35] But most Conservatives were desperate to believe her, so she was able to get through. Someone had to pay the political price, however, and the fall guy was Leon Brittan.

Her statement was carefully framed to protect all parties: Brittan and his officials, the Prime Minister and her officials, all had 'acted in good faith'. The Attorney-General, in agreement with the Director of Public Prosecutions, had accordingly decided that no one should be prosecuted. Most significantly Mrs Thatcher acknowledged that the DTI had not only 'the authority of its Secretary of State [but] cover from my office for proceeding'.[36] That word 'cover' was included at Brittan's insistence; yet it was not enough to save him. He was forced to resign next day – not because he took responsibility for the leak, but because he 'no longer commanded the full confidence of his colleagues'.[37]

The ugly truth was that Brittan had never been popular. He was too brainy, supercilious, soft – and Jewish. He had made a poor showing in the House, most glaringly when Heseltine tricked him into denying that he had received a letter from the Chief Executive of British Aerospace. He had to come back to the House a few hours later to admit that he had in fact received it. In the matter of Mayhew's letter he had been at worst naive. He was not a willing scapegoat. But the Tory party's famous 'men in grey suits' – in this case Whitelaw, Wakeham and the chairman of the 1922 Committee, Cranley Onslow – told him firmly that the backbenchers wanted his head. Like Lord Carrington after the Falklands invasion, someone had to be sacrificed to save the Prime Minister. Brittan's price was a fulsome exchange of letters in which she put on record that she had tried to persuade him to stay – thereby implicitly acknowledging that he had done no wrong – and all but promised to bring him back into high office very soon. In her memoirs she betrayed a touch of guilt. 'It was a meeting of the '22 Committee, not any decision of mine, which sealed his fate . . . I hated to see the better man lose . . . But I was by now thinking hard about my own position.'[38]

Brittan's sacrifice did not get her off the hook. Labour had set down an adjournment motion for Monday 27 January. There were still unanswered questions, above all about the role of Bernard Ingham and Charles Powell. If Mrs Thatcher had not personally authorised the leak, then one or both of them must have done so, in which case they had abused their position as civil servants. Likewise the Cabinet Secretary Robert Armstrong appeared to have lent himself to a sham inquiry designed not to discover the truth but to obscure it. The trivial matter of the leaked letter seemed to have exposed a culture of manipulation and deceit at the heart of the Government which the Prime Minister had still to clear up. Her speech, like her statement four days earlier, had to be carefully drafted to cover every angle. A form of words had to be agreed with Brittan to ensure his silence, and Heseltine might yet torpedo her. She and her staff, including Armstrong, spent the whole weekend – except for Saturday evening when she had to attend her annual dinner dance in Finchley – working on it, unusually in the Cabinet Room, the Cabinet table piled high with files. 'They all claim,' Douglas Hurd noted in his diary, 'there are answers on all the points outstanding to close this fiasco. But I fear these are complicated.'[39] Hurd was one of several senior ministers, including Whitelaw, Howe, Biffen and Wakeham, who met at Number Twelve Downing Street on Monday morning to go through the Prime Minister's draft speech 'rewriting important passages to give fuller information'. 'We have paid the price as a Government for the temporary collapse of collective responsibility,' Hurd told Wakeham, 'so we need to ensure that it does not happen again.'[40] Never again before November 1990 was Mrs Thatcher's dependence on colleagues so painfully exposed.

Simultaneously in Number Ten Ronnie Millar was summoned to lend his final polish to the text. He found Mrs Thatcher exceptionally tense and indecisive. It was then that she remarked – at least half-seriously in Millar's view – that she might not be Prime Minister by six o'clock that evening.[41] Ingham maintains that this was a joke;[42] and she herself later claimed on television that it was 'just one of those things you say'.[43] But she unquestionably believed it at the time; and it could have come true, if Neil Kinnock had taken his opportunity.

But Kinnock blew it. He had two possible lines of attack. He might have taken the constitutional high ground and tried to mobilise the disquiet felt on both sides of the House at the blurring of the conventions of good government and the politicisation of the Civil Service. Or he might have conducted a forensic examination of the gaps, evasions and admissions in her previous testimony. Instead he plunged straight into a vague rhetorical denunciation of the Government's 'dishonesty, duplicity, conniving and manoeuvring' which instantly created a partisan atmosphere and united the Tories in the Prime Minister's defence. Within a minute he was punctured when the Speaker obliged him to withdraw the word 'dishonesty'.[44] 'For a few seconds,' Alan Clark wrote, 'Kinnock had her cornered, and you could see fear in those blue eyes. But then he had an attack of wind, gave her time to recover.'[45]

The result of Kinnock's blustering was that she was able to get away with adding almost nothing to her previous story, beyond admitting that it was she who had initiated Mayhew's letter, that it was leaked without his permission and that it was Havers who had demanded an inquiry. These details apart, she held to her line that the leak arose from 'a genuine difference of understanding between officials as to exactly what was being sought and what was being given'. She apologised after a fashion, but repeated that she knew nothing about the disclosure 'until some hours after it had occurred'. When she was told 'in general terms, that there had been contacts' between her office and the DTI, 'I did not know about the Secretary of State for Trade and Industry's own role in the matter of the disclosure until the inquiry had reported.' She said nothing at all about Powell or Ingham. As she gained in confidence she turned the attack back on Kinnock for 'playing politics with people's jobs', and ended with a defiant promise to carry on with 'renewed strength to extend freedom and ownership . . . and to keep our country strong and secure'.[46] Clark thought it 'a brilliant performance, shameless and brave. We are out of the wood.'[47]*

It was left to David Owen to make the speech that Kinnock should have made. But by then it was too late. Mrs Thatcher did not have to answer Owen. He focused precisely on the role of Powell and Ingham, and by implication the Prime Minister's role in authorising them. 'I do not believe it will be understandable to those who have worked

---

*Clark's cynicism was equally shameless. He recorded Ian Gow telephoning him very gloomily the previous day. 'Ian's trouble . . . is that he is, *au fond*, a man of honour. Personally I don't give a blow. Lie if necessary.'[48] Presumably he had no doubt that she did.

in the Government machine,' he charged (a dig at Kinnock's lack of government experience), 'that those two senior officials could have given the cover when asked by [Brittan].'

I find it very hard to believe that Mr Powell, who was a diplomat . . . a person of outstanding integrity, would have agreed . . . unless he had a pretty clear view of how the Prime Minister wanted the matter to be dealt with . . .
Frankly, no one who has seen the way that Mr Ingham has operated over the past few years . . . can possibly believe that this mild, insignificant, modest, quiet and unassuming Yorkshireman did not give his authority to that lady in the Department of Trade and Industry . . .

'By not admitting that she . . . gave a steer and guidance to Mr Ingham and Mr Powell,' Owen concluded, 'she has left those two with no alternative other than to resign.'[49]

But of course Powell and Ingham did not resign. Mrs Thatcher had thrown her protection over them. The Defence Select Committee which tried to disentangle the whole affair found it 'extraordinary' that they were not disciplined in any way; nor was Colette Bowe. Of course Miss Bowe could not be disciplined since she was admittedly acting on her minister's instructions; it was Brittan who carried the can for the DTI. By the same token, if Powell and Ingham were not disciplined or even reprimanded for providing 'cover' from Number Ten, it could only be because they too were acting on their mistress's instruction: in which case she should have accepted the responsibility. In fact Mrs Thatcher managed to hide behind her officials, with the repeated insistence that she was not consulted, while at the same time denying that they had exceeded their powers. She blocked the select committee by refusing to allow Powell and Ingham to give evidence; instead Robert Armstrong appeared for the Civil Service as a whole and performed a masterly whitewash on the whole business. But by then it did not matter. The crisis passed the moment Neil Kinnock failed to put Mrs Thatcher on the spot on 27 January. No one recognised this more clearly than the man who had started it all, Michael Heseltine. Speaking in the debate immediately after Owen, Heseltine characterised Kinnock's speech as the worst parliamentary performance for a decade. 'It is the constitutional duty of the Opposition to exploit the Government's difficulties,' he reflected with a touch of frustration, 'but they cannot even make a decent job of that.' Realising that there was no more mileage to be got out of pursuing the Prime Minister, he congratulated her instead on her 'difficult and very brave' statement and pronounced himself satisfied with the words she had used. 'What the Prime Minister said today brings the politics of the matter to an end.' He would be supporting the Government in the lobby that evening.[50]

In that moment of prudent political calculation Heseltine set his course for the next five years. Resigning from the Government in January 1986 did his career no harm at all. He would have received no further promotion from Mrs Thatcher – certainly not the department he most coveted, the DTI. By walking out, instead of waiting to be sacked, he was able to carve out a distinctive position as a dissenting but loyal alternative Prime Minister, touring the Tory constituency associations as the challenger-in-waiting if and when she stumbled. When the moment came in November 1990 he wielded the knife yet failed to claim the crown. But by keeping clear of the wreckage of her final years he gained another seven years of office under John Major – five of them at the DTI – ending as a more than usually powerful deputy Prime Minister.

By contrast Brittan's career in domestic politics was finished. The promises Mrs Thatcher made to buy his silence were not kept. She could not face bringing him back into the Cabinet after June 1987: his presence would have been a constant rebuke to her and a reminder of her rockiest moment. Instead she sent him to Brussels as an EC Commissioner in place of Arthur Cockfield, overlooking – in her anxiety to be rid of him – his record as a convinced pro-European. Released from his debt of silence, Brittan lost no time in stating explicitly on television (in April 1989) what he had declined to spell out in 1986, that Powell and Ingham had expressly authorised the Westland leak.[51]

Mrs Thatcher herself was the biggest loser from the Westland imbroglio; for she lost what had hitherto been her most priceless asset, her reputation for integrity. It was already a little tarnished by the *Belgrano* episode. But if she was economical with the truth of that affair she had the excuse of national security: there was a war on. The Westland cover-up concerned nothing more serious than a leaked letter: yet she left the inescapable impression that she had misled the House of Commons to save her own embarrassment and protect her entourage, letting a hapless colleague take the rap for a piece of skulduggery she had initiated. For one who prided herself on her honesty and preached a moralistic politics based on a clear sense of right and wrong, it was a painful and humiliating shock, the lowest point of her career. She recovered, but never fully regained the moral high ground.

Henceforth she was just another slippery politician who would lie when cornered.

Moreover she was shown to be politically vulnerable. Up to this point she had led a charmed life. She had come though the dark days of recession and riots in 1980–1; she had triumphed in the Falklands and at the polls, survived the Brighton bomb and defeated the miners. There had been banana skins in the first years of her second term, but Westland was her first serious stumble. As a result she lost political authority, at least for some months. She made a singularly weak appointment by promoting Paul Channon to replace Brittan at the DTI – the fourth occupant of that job since the election and the seventh in less than seven years. More important, she was obliged temporarily to accept a more collegiate style of government: in particular she was unable to get her way over the proposed sale of Land-Rover to the American company General Motors in February. She was obliged to take the issue to Cabinet in a way she would not normally have done, where among others Norman Fowler – with a West Midlands constituency – reflected a wave of patriotic opposition to the sale. 'When the Norman Fowlers of this world believe that they can afford to rebel,' she wrote witheringly in her memoirs, 'you know that things are bad.'[52]

For the first time since 1982 there was serious muttering that she should go. The bookies were offering odds on various successors: Howe, Tebbit, Walker, Hurd, Heseltine.[53] In the *Spectator* Ferdinand Mount wrote that 'many Tory MPs, weary of the hectic ride . . . longing for the quiet life', saw the restoration of collective responsibility as a means to end 'all this radical dynamic stuff . . . Either she mends her ways and opts for consensus and collective responsibility, or she goes, and we get a consensus minded leader. Either way, we can't lose.'[54]

In fact Mrs Thatcher recovered pretty quickly. If for a time she paid a bit more deference to Cabinet – and some members detected no difference – the effect did not last. She gave a strong performance on *Panorama* in February, trying to put Westland behind her, and made a confident speech to the Conservative Central Council in March. Her resolute support for the American bombing of Libya in April caused another row, both in the country and within the Cabinet; but she rode the storm and thereby demonstrated her recovered strength. By the time of the party conference in October she was firmly back in the saddle. In truth Westland turned out to be only a hiccup. In the long run its effect was to confirm her distrust of colleagues, reinforce her devotion to her small band of trusted aides in Number Ten and increase her determination in future to allow ambitious ministers less rope than she had given Heseltine. Cabinet government was what it had been all about; but Cabinet government was not the winner.

'That Bloody Woman'

The early months of 1986 were the lowest period of Mrs Thatcher's premiership. She had been unpopular in 1980–1, but then she was sustained by her own burning belief that what she was doing was right and by the support of a small band of like-minded believers. There was something epic, Churchillian, in her defiance of the odds. In 1986, by contrast, the revelations and evasions of Westland had left her morally damaged, her reputation for straight-talking integrity in tatters. Having lost two ministers and only narrowly survived herself, her authority was palpably weakened: she could not afford any more resignations, so was temporarily obliged to pay more deference to her colleagues than had become her habit since the Falklands war. Just as the attention of Westminister was beginning to turn towards the next election there were suggestions that she was becoming a liability, no longer an asset to the Government's chances of re-election, and increasing talk that after seven years she was running out of steam, had been in office long enough and would have to step down some time in the next Parliament. Commentators began to speculate that the succession would lie between Michael Heseltine and Norman Tebbit.

This was not Mrs Thatcher's intention at all. She was uneasily aware that her second term, despite economic recovery and the success of privatisation, had not been the unqualified triumph it should have been. Too much of the Government's energy had been diverted into defeating the miners and other distractions, at the expense of more positive objectives. In retrospect, she attributed the loss of momentum to the lack of detailed preparation before the 1983 election, for which she unfairly blamed Geoffrey Howe. But it was not in her nature to think of giving up. On the contrary, she was determined to demonstrate that both her energy and her radicalism were undiminished. With the economy apparently sorted out, unemployment falling at last and Lawson proclaiming an economic miracle, she was eager to turn to what had always been her real purpose, the remoralisation of British society. ('Economics is the method. The object is to change the soul'.)[55] In her first two terms she had cut inflation by busting the taboo of full employment and begun a radical rebalancing of the mixed economy, but she had barely touched the third pillar of the postwar settlement, the welfare state. Belatedly, as many of her supporters believed, she now resolved to regain the political initiative by fighting the next election on this social agenda, with 'a set of policies . . . which my advisers, over my objections, wanted to call Social Thatcherism'.[56] In practice she was much less certain of exactly what these reforms should be than her missionary language implied; but she was absolutely determined to regain the sense of forward movement.

'There has been the odd report that Thatcherism has run its course, and is on its way out,' she told the Conservative Central Council in March in the speech that marked the beginning of her fightback from Westland. 'As an informed source close to Downing Street,' she riposted – a sly dig at recent criticism of Bernard Ingham – 'I have to report that these reports are eyewash. We're only just beginning. We've barely got past the stage of excavation, let alone of topping out!'

> You may feel that the first seven years of Conservative Government have produced some benefits for Britain. And so they have. But the next seven are going to produce more – many more. And the next seven after that, more still.[57]

This was not a prospect which gladdened the hearts of her more ambitious colleagues. The problem was that if she was not exhausted, there was plenty of evidence that the public was growing tired of her. The Conservatives lagged consistently third in the polls behind both Labour and the Alliance, and in April her personal popularity rating fell to its lowest point – 28 per cent – since the inner-city riots of 1981. The same month the Government lost a by-election (only the second it had lost to Labour since 1979) in the London borough of Fulham. And that was before the outcry over the American bombing of Libya. On 13 April Tebbit and his chief of staff Michael Dobbs (seconded from Saatchi and Saatchi) paid an uncomfortable visit to Chequers to present the Prime Minister with the results of polling carried out by Saatchis, which showed not only that the Government was seen to have 'lost its way' and 'run out of steam' but that she herself had ceased to be an asset on the doorsteps. She was given credit for having defeated General Galtieri, conquered inflation and tamed the unions, but now seemed to have run out of worthwhile enemies:

> With the lack of new battles to fight the Prime Minister's combative virtues were being received as vices: her determination was perceived as stubbornness, her single-mindedness as inflexibility and her strong will as an inability to listen.[58]

Collectively, Tebbit and Dobbs had to tell her, these attributes were becoming known as the 'TBW factor' – standing for 'That Bloody

Woman'. Saatchis' recommended strategy for the next election involved the Prime Minister taking a lower profile.

Of course she vehemently disagreed. She had no intention of being pushed into the background. She was already suspicious that Tebbit was pursuing his own agenda, and her suspicions can only have been confirmed when he went public a few weeks later with a singularly lukewarm endorsement of her leadership, echoing precisely the criticism that Saatchis' findings had revealed:

> It's a question of her leadership when our aims aren't clearly defined. When people understand what she's doing there's a good deal of admiration for her energy and resolution and persistence, even from those people who don't agree with her. Now there's a perception that we don't know where we're going so those same qualities don't seem so attractive.[59]

She believed on the contrary that people *did* know what she stood for, and that being known as a strong leader was her greatest selling point. 'If they don't want a strong leader they do not want me,' she said on American television in May. 'There are plenty of other parties to choose from if they want a weak one.'

> But if they want a strong one who believes in what she does and does it because she believes it is right for Britain . . . then I think they might think that I still have a role to play.[60]

The next month she boasted on British television that this reputation was appreciated right round the world:

> Wherever one goes one is recognised, and that happens abroad. You can go to the most lonely . . . far-away places and they will recognise you. 'Mrs Thatcher, Mrs Thatcher, strong leader. Mrs Thatcher strong.' This is most extraordinary, almost in any language.[61]

Rejecting Saatchis' polling, therefore, she commissioned alternative research from the American firm of Young and Rubicam which was already pitching to displace Saatchis and duly came up with more acceptable results. Their finding suggested not that Mrs Thatcher herself was the problem, but that too much of the Tories' appeal had been directed at the ambitious and successful ('succeeders' in advertising jargon), and not enough at ordinary people ('mainstreamers'). On this reading her strength of purpose was still an asset so long as she did not appear doctrinaire but committed to delivering real improvements in people's lives.[62] This was much more what she wanted to hear. She always believed that she had a special rapport with the long-suffering, hard-working, law-abiding middle class whom she regarded above all as 'her' people, and specifically wanted to do more for them now that she had got the economy right and sorted out the unions. That was to be her mission for the third term. From now on she received two parallel sets of polling advice, the official line from Saatchis via Tebbit and Central Office, and unofficial material from Young and Rubicam behind Tebbit's back, which she shared only with a small group of trusted ministers – Whitelaw, Wakeham, Lawson and Hurd – and her private office. This damaging duplication continued right though 1986 and into the election the following year.

Professional politician that she was, however, she did not ignore the evidence of the polls: she was prepared to make some effort to present a softer image and at least the appearance of a more collegiate style of government. In her speech at the Scottish party conference in May 1986, she tried to tackle the widespread perception that she was 'uncaring' with a substantial passage insisting that 'Caring is what you do, not just what you say':

> It is because we care about the old that we have increased the old-age pension to record levels . . . It is because we care about the disabled that we have far and away the best record of help and support of any Government . . . It is because we care about finding jobs that we set up the Youth Training Scheme . . .

But then she spoiled the effect by stretching the definition of 'care' rather wider than what most people meant by it, to cover the things she really cared about:

> It is because we care about Britain's reputation in the world that we are a staunch ally, a courageous partner, playing our full part in the world community . . . We care enough about our country to be determined to defend it. It is because we care that we don't care for Socialism . . . It is because we care that we are Conservatives.[63]

'If she didn't care,' she once asked Bernard Ingham, 'why did they think she committed every atom of her being to the job of turning Britain round?'[64]

In June she gave an interview to *Woman* magazine evidently arranged to reinforce the same message. The interviewer's first question was: 'I want to ask you, Mrs Thatcher, whether you are a caring person.' 'Yes, I think and hope and believe so,' she replied, 'but I do not necessarily believe that people are most caring who talk about themselves being caring most.' She went on to talk about inviting deaf children and disabled people to Number Ten, then about Mark and Carol and her hope some day for grandchildren.[65] In July she took the chance to display her femininity on television – and counteract the *Spitting Image* caricature – by taking part in *The English Woman's Wardrobe* (not in fact shown until November) in which she talked enthusiastically about her clothes, showing off which outfits she had worn on different occasions and even confiding where she bought her underwear ('From Marks & Spencer, of course, doesn't everyone?').[66] Then in August she took her brief summer holiday in Cornwall instead of Switzerland and was pictured in a headscarf supposedly walking David Wolfson's dog along a beach, but looking more as if she was being pulled along by the dog. All these were clear attempts to present the commanding Prime Minister as a normal human being – just as before the 1983 election – though actually the headscarf made her look more like the Queen.

More seriously she tried to counter the image of bossiness by presenting a more collective style of leadership. Following two more disastrous by-elections in formerly safe seats – Ryedale (in Yorkshire) lost to the Alliance, West Derbyshire held by a whisker – and bad local election results, she accepted John Wakeham's advice that she should set up (and most importantly be seen to set up) a Strategy Group to take a grip on policy and presentation in the run-up to the election. In appearance this was a sort of inner cabinet of a sort she had never previously admitted since the 'Thursday breakfasts' attended by the inner core of monetarist economic ministers in 1979. Its members – immediately dubbed the 'A-Team', from a current television programme – were Willie Whitelaw, the holders of the three senior offices of state (Howe, Lawson and Hurd), Tebbit as party chairman and Wakeham as Chief Whip. There was no place for the semi-detached Biffen, or any of the spending ministers. In reality the A-Team was more for show than substance: it had less to do with sharing power than with shackling Tebbit, a means of retaining election planning in her own hands. Nine policy groups were set up, composed of a mixture of MPs, academics and businessmen, to produce ideas for the third term; but they had very little input into the 1987 manifesto. 'Several ministers who today enjoy a reputation for radicalism,' she sneered in her memoirs, 'arrived at our meetings with proposals that would not . . . pull the skin off a rice pudding.'[67] In fact much of this caution stemmed from Mrs Thatcher herself, who was always bolder in her rhetoric than when faced with specific proposals. Nevertheless it is true that most of the groundwork for the reforms of the third term was done under her eye in the Downing Street Policy Unit, under the direction of its latest head, Brian Griffiths, rather than in the departments.

There was one very important exception. The policy initiative which turned out to be the most contentious after 1987 was agreed as far back as 1985, and originated not in the Policy Unit but in the Department of the Environment. After it blew up in her face, the poll tax was regularly cited as the epitome of Mrs Thatcher's domineering style, the result of her personal obsession with abolishing the rates, pushed through a tame Cabinet purely by her insistence. In fact no reform of the Thatcher years was more exhaustively debated through all the proper committees. As usual, the Prime Minister was one of the last to be persuaded that it was practicable. Once convinced, she was unswerving in her refusal to abandon it and in her memoirs she still defended it as right in principle. But it was successive Secretaries of State for the Environment and Scotland (and their juniors) who made all the running at the beginning.

Of course Mrs Thatcher's desire to honour her 1974 commitment to abolish domestic rates was undiminished. She had always disliked the rates on principle as a tax on property which acted as a disincentive against making improvements; and she was keen to find a way to stop Labour councils piling heavy rate demands on Tory householders in order to spend the money on their own voters who were largely exempt from payment. But since Michael Heseltine's abortive search for a workable alternative in 1979–83, her attention had been diverted into other ways of controlling local extravagance. It was Patrick Jenkin, seeking to regain favour after the debacle of his attempt to scrap the GLC elections, who unwisely revived the question by setting up yet another departmental inquiry in late 1984, delegating his juniors, Kenneth Baker and William Waldegrave, to find the holy grail. Waldegrave in turn consulted his old boss in Ted Heath's Think Tank, Victor Rothschild. Mrs Thatcher later credited Rothschild with 'much of the radical thinking' which produced the community charge;[68] but many other bright sparks on the cerebral fringe of the Tory party, including the Adam Smith Institute, also had a hand in it.

The event which overcame her initial scepticism was the furious outcry against the revaluation of Scottish rates in February 1985, which threatened a steep hike in rateable values particularly in middle-class areas. Willie Whitelaw came back 'severely shaken' by the anger he encountered on a visit to the affluent Glasgow suburb of Bearsden in March; the same week the Tories lost a safe regional council seat which comprised a quarter of George Younger's highly marginal Ayr constituency.[69] Whitelaw and Younger convinced the Prime Minister that something must be done urgently: their alarm coincided neatly with Waldegrave's review team coming up with an alternative which they believed would work. So she convened a conference at Chequers on 31 March at which Baker, Waldegrave and Rothschild gave a glossy presentation of their proposal, complete with colour slides and flip charts. Waldegrave ended his pitch with words allegedly suggested by Patrick Jenkin: 'And so, Prime Minister, you will have fulfilled your promise to abolish the rates.'[70] She was persuaded.

Five weeks later she paid her annual visit to the Scottish party conference and was able to tell the representatives that the Government had listened to their anger. 'We have reached the stage where no amount of patching up of the existing system can overcome its inherent unfairness,' she announced. The Government was now looking at a fundamental reform of local government finance. 'The burden should fall, not heavily on the few, but fairly on the many.'[71] The idea that everyone who used council services should pay equally towards the cost of them was on paper not a bad one. It was wrong in principle, and corrupting in practice, that only one-third of households paid full rates, yet everyone could vote for expenditure to which they did not contribute. 'My father always said that everyone ought to pay something,' she told Woodrow Wyatt, 'even if it is only sixpence.'[72] It was not envisaged that the charge would be more than £50–100 per head.

Nigel Lawson had missed the Chequers seminar: in his absence Peter Rees for the Treasury opposed the plan, but he carried insufficient clout to stop it. Lawson later submitted a paper warning the Cabinet committee which considered it that the proposed flat-rate charge would prove 'completely unworkable and politically catastrophic'.[73] He correctly predicted that it would be hard to collect, while Labour councils would simply hike up their spending and blame the Government for the new tax. He proposed instead a banded tax on capital values (very similar to that with which Heseltine eventually replaced the poll tax in 1991). Having voiced his dissent, however, Lawson subsequently lay low: he neither exerted his authority as Chancellor, nor attempted to combine with Heseltine and Walker (both former Environment Secretaries) to co-ordinate opposition to the charge. When Rees's successor, John MacGregor, tried to reopen the Treasury case against the charge in September 1985 he 'got his head

bitten off' by the Prime Minister and did not try again.[74] In his memoirs
Lawson seeks to distance himself from the disaster that followed. But
no new tax can be introduced against the opposition of the Treasury.
Having identified the flaws in the poll tax so accurately, Lawson bears
substantial responsibility for having failed to stop it.

It was Kenneth Baker (having succeeded Jenkin the previous
autumn) who published in January 1986 a Green Paper, *Paying for
Local Government*, setting out the detail of what was officially called
the community charge. His presentation to the Commons was given
a mixed welcome by Tory MPs. Some indeed, as Baker recalled, 'roared
their approval';[75] but several raised prescient questions which he would
have done well to heed. The press too mostly damned the new charge
– which *The Times* insisted was properly a tax, not a charge – as crude,
centralising and likely to create more losers than winners.[76] 'Losers
howl, while winners give little thanks,' *The Economist* pointed out. 'And
the big losers, young singles and couples, are floating voters.'[77] Four
months later Baker departed to Education, leaving Nicholas Ridley
holding his baby.* Nevertheless at that year's Scottish conference Mrs
Thatcher basked in the applause of the representatives for her promise
of immediate legislation in Scotland, ahead of England and Wales.[79]
Contrary to subsequent claims, the Government did not use Scotland
cynically as a testbed for an unpopular policy, but introduced it there
first because the existing grievance was most urgent there. The following
year, opening her General Election campaign in Perth as usual, Mrs
Thatcher boasted that the Scottish legislation had passed its final stage
the previous week. 'They said we couldn't do it. They said we wouldn't
do it. We did it.'[80] She had no doubt that the change would be popular,
at least with her own party.

The other new policies developed in 1986–7 followed the same
central theme of curbing the power of local government, specifically
over housing and education. Those parts of the welfare state which
were provided nationally, like health and social security, were a good
deal more difficult to reform. But Mrs Thatcher had become very
taken with the notion, supposedly derived from Dostoevsky, that local-
authority council estates and local-authority schools with a near-
monopoly of education in their areas exemplified a new feudalism.
Her objective for the third term was to free tenants and parents from
the stranglehold of what she termed – forgetting all those authorities
still controlled by her own party – 'municipal socialism'. The idea was

---

*Lady Thatcher called Baker 'the foster-father of the community charge'[78], but
actually he was the midwife. He delivered it, but left others to bring it up.

to find ways of offering the users of these services an element of 'choice'.

Education was the area where she was most determined to get a grip. She remembered very well from her own experience in 1970–4 that the Secretary of State had virtually no power over local education authorities (LEAs). She believed passionately in the importance of improving state education, but was inhibited by consciousness of her own failure to halt the onward march of comprehensivisation, which she now believed had 'ruined education'.[81] In 1981 she had been happy to send Keith Joseph to raise the profile of what had always been a Cinderella department, but she was disappointed that in five years he made little practical difference, beyond replacing O-Levels with a new GCSE exam. He was reluctantly persuaded that the right's cherished scheme for introducing choice into education by giving parents vouchers to shop around between competing schools was impracticable; and he maintained the department's traditional view – which had been coming under increasing challenge ever since James Callaghan's Ruskin College speech in 1976 – that politicians had no business dictating the content of the curriculum. He also got bogged down in a long-running teachers' pay dispute which he was too honourably non-interventionist to resolve. The first sign that Mrs Thatcher was beginning to lose patience came in her speech to the 1985 party conference. When Joseph finally retired seven months later she signalled her wish for a fresh start by appointing Kenneth Baker in his place with a clear brief to get things moving.

'The things she wanted were very inchoate in her own mind,' Baker recalled, 'but she felt that something had to be done.'[82] In her speech to the party conference that autumn she set out three objectives and three ways to achieve them. The objectives were to 'bring back the three Rs into our schools; bring back relevance into the curriculum; and bring back discipline into our classrooms . . . The fact is that education at all levels . . . has been infiltrated by a permissive philosophy of self-expression.' The proposed ways forward were: 'by giving parents greater freedom to choose; by allowing head teachers greater control in their school; by laying down national standards of syllabus and attainment'.[83] Here in embryo were the main provisions of Baker's 1988 Education Act.

Baker immediately took up the invitation to devise a national curriculum with an enthusiasm which led to some differences with Mrs Thatcher in the next Parliament. But finding ways to inject parental choice into the schools system was much more difficult. Nigel Lawson wanted to take all schools out of LEA control and centralise the whole system under the Treasury. It was Nicholas Ridley who picked up from Joseph's special adviser Stuart Sexton the idea of letting individual schools 'opt out' of LEA control to be funded directly by the DES: in effect, as he describes it, 'a plan to give vouchers to the schools as opposed to the parents'.[84] As so often, Mrs Thatcher's first reaction was hostile: Michael Portillo recalls her giving the members of the No Turning Back group 'a verbal drubbing' when they proposed it to her.[85] Baker too was initially opposed. By the time of the 1986 conference the only new initiative he was ready to announce was the establishment of around twenty City Technology Colleges – specialist state schools funded directly by the Government – an important symbolic departure from the comprehensive principle but too few in number to make a major impact. Only over the next six months was Mrs Thatcher persuaded by Brian Griffiths to make 'opting out' the centrepiece of education policy; she then virtually forced it on a reluctant Baker in time for inclusion in the 1987 manifesto.

Meanwhile Baker confirmed his reputation as an effective minister by resolving the teachers' pay dispute which had tormented Joseph. He won enough money from the Treasury to fund a substantial salary increase; but used that sweetener to abolish the existing pay structure and the unions' bargaining rights, exercised for decades by the Burnham Committee. Henceforth teachers were still employed locally, but paid centrally, like civil servants. Contradicting all the talk of rolling back the state, the Teachers' Pay and Conditions Act (1987) was another centralising measure which vested unprecedented powers in the Secretary of State, foreshadowing more of the same after the election.

'Housing,' according to Nicholas Ridley, 'was the area where Margaret Thatcher thought it was easiest to start to dismantle the dependency culture.'[86] The sale of council houses had been a huge political success, but the Government was vulnerable to the charge that selling off the best houses had only made worse the lot of those trapped in high-rise flats in the less desirable estates where no one wanted to buy their property even if they could have afforded to. The free-market solution advocated by Ridley was to try to break the 'almost incestuous relationship' between council housing departments and their tenants by increasing the supply of private housing available for rent: abolishing rent controls while raising council rents to comparable commercial levels would theoretically give tenants a choice of possible landlords – private landlords, housing associations or tenants' co-operatives – as alternatives to councils.[87] This, he succeeded in persuading the Prime Minister, could be presented as a way of extending the benefits of Thatcherism to those who had not hitherto enjoyed its fruits. Tenant's Choice, as it was called, was duly given a prominent place in the radical prospectus for the third term, second only to educational reform. In fact its relevance to the real problems of housing and the growing blight of homelessness was never likely to be more than marginal, and so it proved.

It was even harder to find radical initiatives in social security that were politically practicable. Social security was far the biggest single element of public spending, but serious economy was problematic so long as unemployment remained so high. It was another area characterised in the first two terms by incessant tinkering rather than major reform. Norman Fowler had announced in 1984 what was supposed to be the biggest review of the welfare system since the Beveridge Report; but the results, in Nicholas Timmins' words, were 'relative molehills'.[88] The complexity of Supplementary Benefit was replaced by a simpler but cruder system of Income Support; Housing Benefit was also simplified and targeted more closely; Family Income Supplement was replaced by Family Credit and a new discretionary Social Fund which provided loans for emergency expenditure for the most needy. In accordance with Mrs Thatcher's frequent insistence that the level of benefits should not be so generous as to discourage claimants from looking for work, these changes generally benefited families with children and the elderly at the expense of single people. But with three million unemployed the last were not all work-shy drifters. Overall, however, Fowler was remarkably successful in protecting his total budget – to the dismay of true Thatcherites who had hoped to see it substantially cut. The one area where he did achieve a significant saving was in relation to the State Earnings Related Pension Scheme (SERPS) introduced by Barbara Castle in 1975, which had become unsustainably expensive. Fowler would have liked to scrap it altogether, on the argument that it was no business of the state to provide more than a basic subsistence pension; but the outcry forced him merely to cut it back, while giving incentives to SERPS holders to take out private schemes instead. This turned out in the next decade to be an expensive disaster.

Mrs Thatcher was frustrated – she once called the social-security budget 'a time bomb' which would have to be defused before it was too late.[89] But the welfare system – if not so rooted in public affection as the NHS – contained too many sacred cows to be easily reformed. In principle there were a lot of benefits Mrs Thatcher would have liked to cut if she had thought it politically possible. She would have liked to phase out child benefit altogether, instead of reducing its value stealthily by freezing it year after year, going back to a more targeted system of child tax allowances instead. Even freezing it, however, provoked a significant backbench rebellion every year. As a woman now past sixty with no thought of retiring, she would have liked to equalise old-age pensions for men and women alike at the age of sixty-five; but here again the outcry from many of her own most ardent supporters would have been prohibitive. As a general principle she would have liked to target assistance more sharply at those she was happy to call – in the Victorian terminology – the 'deserving' as opposed to the 'undeserving poor'.[90] But as she resignedly told John Moore (DHSS Secretary from June 1987) when he suggested some of these things: 'You're right, John, you're right. But we can't. We can't.'[91] The 1987 manifesto was entirely devoid of radical proposals on social security.

Nowhere was Mrs Thatcher more cautious than towards the National Health Service. She was still scarred by the reaction to the leak of the CPRS report in 1982. Though the financing of the NHS was even more of a time bomb than social security – because the demand was infinite and ever-expanding – she was not ready to look at radical solutions before 1987 and it was not clear that she ever would be. 'There is no constituency for change,' she told Ken Stowe, her former principal private secretary, now Permanent Secretary at the DHSS, whenever he proposed it. 'We can't do it.'[92] 'The NHS was still seen as the touchstone of our commitment to the welfare state,' she wrote in her memoirs.[93] Ever since 1982 Labour's most potent cry had been the constantly repeated allegation that she was planning to 'privatise' the NHS. Much as she would have liked to shift the emphasis of healthcare towards a more American-style, insurance-based system, she accepted the political reality that it was impossible. In 1987, as in 1983, she recognised the need 'to soothe the voters' anxieties', not alarm them.[94] Accordingly she missed no opportunity, at Prime Minister's Questions, in interviews and later on the hustings, to boast of how much the Government was spending on health – £15 billion in 1986 compared with £8 billion in 1979 – how many more doctors and nurses were employed, how many more patients were treated every year, how many hip replacements, how many cataract operations, in a veritable deluge of statistics designed to drown the difficult questions. Repeatedly contrasting her record with Labour's spending in the 1970s and insisting that it required a growing economy to pay for the sort of health service the country demanded, she improved her 1983 mantra that the NHS was 'safe in our hands' to the still more tendentious claim that 'the NHS is safe *only* with us'.[95] Almost the only mention of health in the 1987 manifesto was a list of 125 hospital building programmes in construction or planned.

This list was first unveiled by Norman Fowler at the party conference the previous October, trailing a long computer printout down from the podium for the benefit of the cameras. More than ever, the whole 1986 conference was a brilliant public-relations exercise, choreographed by Saatchi and Saatchi under the slogan 'The Next Moves Forward' and designed to convey the message that the Government was not a one-woman band but a young and vigorous team full of energy and new practical ideas for improving public services. Each day a succession of ministers trooped to the platform to set out their wares. On Tuesday Norman Lamont offered further privatisation, including water supply, the British Airports Authority and the return of Rolls-Royce to the private sector; John Patten claimed that rent deregulation would create a million more homeowners in five years; Baker announced his City Technology Colleges and promised new powers for parents and school governors over sex education; Ridley trailed compulsory competitive tendering for council services; while John Major paraded an old chestnut by promising a new crackdown on benefit fraud. On Wednesday Douglas Hurd announced longer sentences and new powers to seize criminals' assets; Fowler trumpeted his £3 billion hospital building programme and action to reduce waiting lists; and John Moore chipped in with a £15 million plan to tackle crime on the London underground. Thursday brought Nigel Lawson holding out the prospect of zero inflation and income tax down to twenty-five pence; David Young with more help for the young unemployed; and Malcolm Rifkind taking credit for replacing the rates. The coverage was everything Tebbit and Central Office could have hoped for. 'This has been a good week for the Conservatives,' Geoffrey Smith reported in *The Times*, 'because more than ever before there has been the impression of a ministerial team', taking the spotlight off the Prime Minister's closing speech. This was just as well, since the party 'can no longer afford to rely on her electoral appeal'.[96]

But nothing could stop her grabbing the spotlight back on Friday morning. Defiantly sporting a red rose – 'the rose of England' – in rejection of Labour's adoption of the emblem as its own new-look motif, she spoke for only thirty minutes but won her usual rapturous ten-minute ovation. It was a combative, almost an electioneering speech, making only the vaguest commitments for the future, but celebrating her government's achievements hitherto and warning repeatedly of the undiminished danger posed by Labour. Three themes stood out. Once again she denied that the Tories were not a 'caring' party, reciting her usual litany of spending on the health service and pensions, and damning Labour by contrast for supporting striking NHS workers, striking teachers and striking miners who tried to 'deprive industry, homes and pensioners of power, heat and light', while constantly undermining the police in the fight against crime and drugs. 'Mr President, we're not going to take any lessons in caring from people with that sort of record.' Second, she picked up – for the first time – the phrase 'popular capitalism' and made it her own:

So popular is our policy that it's being taken up all over the world. From France to the Philippines, from Jamaica to Japan, from Malaysia to Mexico, from Sri Lanka to Singapore, privatisation is on the move . . . The policies we have pioneered are catching on in country after country. We Conservatives believe in popular capitalism, believe in a property-owning democracy. And it works!

But above all she devoted the final section of her speech to denouncing Labour's reaffirmed commitment to a non-nuclear defence policy and the closure of American bases in Britain. To her this was always the overriding question of politics, as well as the one on which Labour was most vulnerable. 'Let there be no mistake about the gravity of that decision,' she warned:

You cannot be a loyal member of NATO while disavowing its funda-mental strategy. A Labour Britain would be a neutralist Britain. It would be the greatest gain for the Soviet Union in forty years. And they would have got it without firing a shot.[97]

The Government's poll ratings picked up immediately, so that by December the Tories were back in a clear lead for the first time for nearly two years: 41 per cent against 32 per cent for Labour and 22 per cent for the Alliance, which had come badly unstuck over defence. Whereas in the early summer there had been growing belief in the likelihood of a Labour victory, by the end of the year the betting had swung overwhelmingly back towards the Tories, by 65 per cent to 18 per cent.[98] Over the spring that lead was maintained and even extended. Though she had no need to go to the country again before 1988, Mrs Thatcher had much less hesitation than in 1983 about seizing this advantage while the going was good. Having won twice previously in May and June she had become convinced that the early summer was a lucky time for her, and she was keen to get the ordeal over as soon as possible so that she could get back to work. She regarded elections,

Ronnie Millar commented, as 'a massive interruption'. Yet at the same time 'she never took anything for granted'.[99] She was deeply superstitious about any appearance of counting chickens, and amid all the rush and hassle of the campaign, she would be found neurotically packing and tidying up for a quick exit in case she should lose.

Accordingly she was anxious to be seen to consult widely on the date. Kenneth Baker describes a general discussion after Cabinet in March 1987 at which ministers were evenly divided between June and October. At that stage Mrs Thatcher was anxious to keep both options open. When Ken Clarke proposed announcing immediately that the election would be in the autumn, she objected; 'No, no. The only weapon I have is surprise.'[100]

In fact she held almost all the cards. On the one hand the economy was booming and unemployment falling at last, producing in a majority of the population the famous 'feelgood factor' which almost always wins elections. On the other, left-wing Labour councils defying the Government by refusing to set legal budgets and promoting all sorts of immorality and political correctness in schools were continuing to provide the tabloids with good headlines about the 'loony left' and Kinnock's inability to control his party; while the Alliance was damagingly split between the SDP leader David Owen, whose enthusiasm for nuclear weapons was scarcely less than Mrs Thatcher's own, and rank-and-file Liberals who managed to pass a unilateralist resolution at their September conference, with the Liberal leader David Steel caught uncomfortably in the middle. In February the two opposition parties clashed in a by-election in Greenwich. An unappealing far-left Labour candidate was trounced by the SDP's fresh-faced and much more photogenic Rosie Barnes. The Tories nearly lost their deposit, yet the Government was the real winner, since the result revived the flagging fortunes of the Alliance. So long as Labour and the Alliance cancelled each other out, the Tories could not lose.

Then on 17 March Nigel Lawson introduced the perfect pre-election budget in which he was able to cut the standard rate of income tax by another two pence while simultaneously finding money for increased spending on health and other services, without even raising duties on petrol, drink or cigarettes. Two weeks later the Tories' resurgence was crowned by Mrs Thatcher's triumphant visit to Moscow. She was indignant when reporters dared to suggest that her visit was designed with an eye on the upcoming election. 'Enlarge your view,' she told them scornfully. 'I'm here for Britain.'[101] But of course it was, just like Macmillan's visit in 1959. As David Owen wrote, 'The television coverage . . . was . . . virtually a daily party political broadcast beaming back from Moscow, fantastic for the Conservatives.'[102] The impact was doubled by the contrast with Kinnock's disastrous trip to Washington a few days earlier when he and Denis Healey were received by President Reagan with a barely disguised snub. They were accorded just a quarter of an hour of the President's time, and the White House put out an uncompromising statement to the effect that Labour's non-nuclear defence policy would be damaging to NATO.

Before making her final decision Mrs Thatcher waited for the local elections on 7 May, then spent the weekend at Chequers with the A-Team plus David Young, analysing the results. Having been prepared for some losses, the Conservatives actually made modest gains. The big winners were the Alliance, with a gain of 453 seats, while Labour lost 227. But the overall distribution of votes gave the Tories around 40 per cent, Labour 30 per cent and the Alliance 27 per cent, which was roughly in line with the latest polls. The omens could scarcely have been better, and it was no surprise that, having slept on it, Mrs Thatcher announced next day that the election would be on 11 June.

Hat-trick: June 1987

Yet June 1987 was by no means such a walkover as June 1983 had been. Despite the polls there was a nervousness in the Tory camp that perhaps the Government had been in office too long, that Mrs Thatcher's style of leadership had become a liability and that the oldest cry in democratic politics – 'Time for a Change' – might exert a potent effect. By contrast with the shambles of 1983, Labour mounted a very slick and professional campaign, expertly run by Peter Mandelson and Bryan Gould, which seized the initiative in the first week, while there was always the possibility of a late surge by the Alliance. These jitters were compounded by personal rivalry within Central Office and a lack of trust between Smith Square and Downing Street. As a result the Tories, from a strong position, fought a poor election and almost talked themselves into believing they were going to lose. In fact the outcome almost exactly mirrored the polls at the beginning and victory was almost certainly in the bag all along. But it was, as Lady Thatcher wrote with some understatement in her memoirs, 'not . . . a happy campaign'.[103]

The rivalry in Central Office was due to Mrs Thatcher's decision, since she could not sack Tebbit, to supplement him. She would really have liked to bring back Cecil Parkinson, who had so skilfully handled the 1983 election for her. More than anything else at critical moments she liked to have familiar faces around her. The suavely handsome Parkinson could always calm her nerves, where the saturnine and edgy Tebbit only jangled them. She was also officially without the services of her two 'laughing boys' who had done so much to promote her in 1979 and 1983, Tim Bell and Gordon Reece. Bell had left Saatchis to set up his own agency – the main reason for her loss of confidence in Saatchis – and Tebbit refused to use him as an independent consultant; while Reece had gone to work for Guinness – now mired in a City scandal – and was therefore for the moment politically untouchable. Michael Dobbs, whom she never liked, was no substitute. But she was persuaded by Whitelaw and Wakeham that Parkinson must remain in purdah until he had purged his sin by fresh contact with the electorate. So she turned to her all-purpose favourite of the moment, David Young, and put him into Central Office as a sort of rival chairman with specific responsibility for her tours, the manifesto and the party's television broadcasts: all the most visible parts of the campaign. This was not just a recipe for divided leadership: Young had no credentials for the job. A businessman parachuted into the Cabinet via a seat in the Lords, he had never fought an election in his life; he knew nothing about party management or party machinery. His elevation to the Cabinet had already aroused the jealousy of colleagues who had come up the hard way through the Commons; his irregular appointment to Central Office was equally resented by Tebbit and the party professionals, especially when he backed Tim Bell and Young and Rubicam – known as 'the exiles' – in the battle for the Prime Minister's ear. 'Too many cooks,' Tebbit complained, 'spoil the broth, especially when the chef does not know who is putting in what behind his back.'[104]

The idea that Mrs Thatcher might consent to take a back seat stood little chance in the leader-centred media circus of a modern election; in fact she was determined as always to lead from the front. She wanted the Tory campaign to look simultaneously to the past and the future, both trumpeting the achievements of her first two terms and setting out a positive programme for the third. It was she who proposed splitting the manifesto into two separate pamphlets in a single slipcase, one (dark blue) entitled *The First Eight Years*, the other (pale blue) *The Next Moves Forward*, written under her personal supervision with minimal input from any of her colleagues. It was drafted by Robin Harris (director of the Research Department), Brian Griffiths (head of the Downing Street Policy Unit) and Stephen Sherbourne (her principal private secretary), and largely written by John O'Sullivan, with the usual polishing by Ronnie Millar. When this group told her that they really needed a senior minister to resolve disputes she prevaricated for some time before asking John MacGregor – a safe pair of hands but not a member of the A-Team – to take the chair. The commitments on education and housing were hammered out at the last minute between Mrs Thatcher and her advisers and the two responsible ministers, Baker and Ridley. Baker was still unenthusiastic about 'opting out' and had to be bullied every step of the way; but eventually the section on education filled eight pages. Sherbourne testified that Mrs Thatcher was 'personally responsible for the document's detail and radicalism'.[105] Largely excluded from these deliberations, however, Nigel Lawson considered the manifesto poorly written and full of policies that had not been properly thought through. 'Had it not been for the strength of the economy,' he wrote in his memoirs, 'the 1987 manifesto would have been a disaster: as it was it was merely an embarrassment.'[106]

It was also her idea to start the campaign slowly, so as not to peak too soon. ('Three weeks is long enough.')[107] This allowed Labour to seize the initiative, putting the Government on the defensive on health, unemployment and the collapse of manufacturing before the Tories were out of the starting blocks. In particular Labour made an unprecedented impact with their first television broadcast, a glossy film (made by Hugh Hudson, director of the recent hit *Chariots of Fire*) shamelessly devoted to promoting Kinnock as a glamorous, idealistic young leader with his attractive wife, filmed walking hand-in-hand along a rocky coastline with seagulls overhead. It was shallow, totally devoid of content but highly effective: Kinnock's popularity jumped sixteen points overnight.[108] By contrast the first Tory broadcast (made by Saatchis) was entirely backward-looking, a crude amalgam of red scares and tub-thumping patriotism. Film of Scargill and Livingstone was juxtaposed with old newsreels of the Battle of Britain, Nazi rallies (subtly equated with miners' pickets), Churchill's voice announcing the end of the war and Mrs Thatcher's favourite hymn 'I Vow to Thee, My Country', ending with the slogan 'It's Great to be Great Again'. Even the *Annual Register* thought this 'must surely have struck home like a sick joke in many parts of the country north of a line drawn from the Severn to the Wash'.[109] David Owen quite fairly accused the Tories of hijacking patriotism for party purposes, as if it were a Tory monopoly. 'You do begin to wonder whether Mrs Thatcher is now claiming the credit for winning the Second World War.'[110]

Carol returned from a visit to Jordan towards the end of the first week of the campaign and was horrified by what she saw of the Tory campaign. It probably did not greatly matter that John Wakeham gave a floundering performance on a radio phone-in on the Wednesday. Much more serious was that Mrs Thatcher herself, at her first morning press conference on the Friday, plunged the newly minted education policy into confusion by suggesting that schools which opted out would be able to charge fees.[111] Baker quickly contradicted her, and she withdrew the suggestion; but the slip dogged her for the rest of the campaign. She had to keep denying any intention of charging fees, yet could never resist hinting that opted-out schools would nevertheless be free to raise additional resources by other means, thus allowing Labour to keep alleging that she had a hidden agenda of back-door privatisation in education as in health. This was a clear result of last-minute policy-making, and there were other confusions in relation to housing as well.

Carol rang her mother that night to tell her she had 'better get her act together or start packing'. The next day she attended a small meeting in the flat at Number Ten attended by Young, Sherbourne and Tim Bell – just the sort of unofficial gathering Tebbit objected to. According to both Young and Carol, Mrs Thatcher was not just worried by the poor start to the campaign but close to despair. 'It's not been a good week for us,' she admitted. 'Kinnock had a marvellous programme – it's hardly worth bothering, let's give up, it's the end.' Bell calmed her down and cheered her up, told her what was wrong and how to put it right, and generally restored her confidence. Carol and Denis helped convince her that to get the campaign back on track she should concentrate less on the future and more on the achievements of the last eight years, coupled with good old-fashioned attacks on Labour.[112] This was broadly what she did.

Her personal campaign, once it got going, consisted as usual of four elements. She began each day by chairing the morning press conference at Central Office, flanked by four or five of her colleagues – often a couple of the younger faces, John Moore, John Major or Chris Patten – plus either Tebbit or Young, and sometimes both. The proceedings opened with a presentation by the minister responsible for that day's lead topic, but once questions started she answered most of them herself in her most headmistresslike manner, setting the media agenda for the rest of the day. Then she would set out on a whistlestop visit to some part of the country, usually flying from Gatwick to pick up her armoured battlebus, emblazoned with the slogan 'Moving Forward with Maggie', from which she would descend on unsuspecting schools, factories or old people's homes with minimal advance warning, where she would pose for the cameras in a hard hat or a white coat, hanging wallpaper or driving a forklift truck, with children, animals or centenarians.

The contrivance of these photo-opportunities was manifestly phoney. In Leicester she visited a private school on bank-holiday Monday which had to be specially opened for her; later that day she was driven three times at high speed round the Austin Rover test track at Nuneaton. Visiting another school – a state school this time – in north Kent, she was criticised for handing out 'I love Maggie' hats to the children (she who was always condemning political propaganda in the classroom), then took the helm of a vintage paddle steamer on the Medway. Once, in Suffolk, she alarmed her minders by plunging into a crowd of shoppers for an impromptu walkabout. But in general the real needs of security, and an invariable straggle of demonstrators chanting 'Maggie out' wherever word of her presence got about, meant that she was kept well away from any contact with real voters. It was easier to do walkabouts in Moscow than at home. Reporters complained that she only visited 'islands of success in otherwise depressed areas'. But the obvious political point was to associate her with prosperity and economic growth. On Tyneside she visited the massive Metro shopping centre in Gateshead and announced that 'entrepreneurship is back'.[113] In Wales she toured the Cardiff Bay redevelopment project.* In Scotland – her only overnight stop away from London – she visited the Marconi electronics factory in Fife and the Scottish and Newcastle brewery in Edinburgh, where Denis downed a pint and she modestly sipped at a half. 'I was testing for clarity,' she explained. 'He was testing for taste.'[115]

Five of these tours concluded with a speech at an evening rally of supporters bused from all over the area. These events – in Newport, Solihull, Edinburgh, Chester and Harrogate – were patriotic spectaculars staged by Harvey Thomas with dry ice and laser effects, Union Jacks, 'Jerusalem' and an Elgar-like 'coronation anthem' specially composed by Andrew Lloyd Webber. Her speeches consisted mainly of well-worn material rehashed by Sherbourne, O'Sullivan and Millar celebrating – for a Tory audience – the march of Thatcherism since 1979. She no longer fought shy of the word but gloried in it. 'That's what I call Thatcherism,' she crowed in Solihull, describing the success of the West Midlands.[116] The principal soundbite on the television news was usually a blood-curdling attack on Labour, designed to demolish

---

*Nicholas Edwards accompanied her on her visit to Wales, where she was upset by the hostile crowds, penned back by tight security. 'Oh what dreadful people,' she exclaimed. 'We are really wasting our time – what is the point of all your efforts if they appreciate them so little?' 'This was alien territory,' Edwards reflected, 'far from the England she knew and understood.'[114]

the reassuring image presented by Kinnock's glossy broadcast. 'We've had Labour Governments before,' she warned in Newport, 'but today Labour is more extreme, more left-wing, more socialist than ever.'

> Labour's manifesto is the tip of the socialist iceberg: one-tenth visible, nine-tenths below the surface . . . What people are being asked to buy is smoke-screen socialism, a make-believe message carefully packaged and presented. But no amount of slick presentation can disguise the policy beneath the gloss or the true political intent below the almost invisible manifesto.[117]

Or again in Edinburgh on 2 June:

> Behind the mask of moderation, the Labour party is in the grip of the hard left. And they won't let go. Within days of the election of a Labour Government, the unions would be back in the driver's seat and their leaders would once again be the nation's masters. We must not let it happen.[118]

Labour had already played into Mrs Thatcher's hands before the election started by confirming the non-nuclear defence policy which had served it so badly in 1983. Now Kinnock provided the gift-wrapping with a disastrous interview with David Frost on 24 May in which, pressed on his alternative strategy in the event of a Soviet attack, he talked of 'using all the resources you have to make any occupation totally untenable'. The Tories could hardly contain their delight. Kinnock then invited further ridicule by citing the heroic resistance of the Afghan mujahedin as a model. At Newport two days later Mrs Thatcher pounced. 'So now we know,' she intoned. 'Labour's non-nuclear defence policy is a policy for defeat, surrender, occupation and . . . prolonged guerrilla fighting.'

> The Labour leader has abandoned all his claims that conventional forces can provide an effective defence against nuclear weapons. He has conceded that once this country has renounced its independent deterrent, it has no alternative but to surrender to a nuclear threat. He has left himself no policy but to yield to invasion and to trust in the forlorn hope that a guerrilla struggle would eventually persuade the army of occupation to withdraw.
>   Mr Chairman, I do not understand how anyone who aspires to Government can treat the defence of our country so lightly.[119]

Labour never recovered, and Mrs Thatcher made sure – despite David Owen's protests – that she tarred the Alliance with the same brush. Only the Tories, she insisted in her every speech, would give Britain the strong defence without which nothing else mattered.*

Finally there was television. Here the strategy of limiting her exposure initially had some effect. She was only scheduled to give two major national interviews compared with seven in 1983, though she usually gave a regional one wherever she was each day and also did radio interviews for *Today*, *The World This Weekend* and her favourite *Jimmy Young Programme*. This was partly the broadcasters' initiative, but it suited Central Office, who also used her very sparingly in the party's election broadcasts, until the final one. When she was interviewed – by Jonathan Dimbleby for *This Week* and Robin Day for *Panorama* – she was hectoring and aggressive, 'determined to tax her questioners with personally holding any viewpoint she disliked before slipping into her standard responses'.[120] 'Can I ask another question, Prime Minister?' Day was forced to beg. 'We are not having a party political broadcast, we are having an interview which depends on me asking some questions occasionally.'[121] Every time she appeared she vindicated those in Central Office who wanted to keep her under wraps; but Mrs Thatcher bitterly resented the suggestion that she was a liability. 'I did venture to say that I had won two elections,' she recalled later.[122] Convinced that the campaign was going horribly wrong, she insisted on a higher profile in the final week: she actually volunteered to go on David Frost's Sunday morning programme on TV-am, which had to scrap a planned discussion to accommodate her.

The next day she stole the headlines again by paying a flying visit to the European summit in Venice, repeating the trick she had played by attending the Williamsburg G7 in 1983. She was not there long enough to do much more than be photographed with the other leaders; but it was an act Kinnock could not follow. Labour could only mock her royal pretensions with a feeble satire involving Willie Rushton and others singing 'A Regular Royal Queen' from *The Gondoliers* which only underlined the fact that, whether Central Office liked it or not, she was inescapably the central issue of the campaign. The idea of presenting the Government as a team had gone by the board. Analysis for the Nuffield election study showed that, after the Prime Minister,

---

*Saatchis created one of their most memorable posters to dramatise the issue showing a British soldier with his arms raised in surrender, captioned 'Labour's Policy on Arms'.

the most reported figures on the Tory side were Michael Heseltine, Ted Heath – both studiously loyal, though Heath could still not bring himself to mention her by name – and Jeffrey Archer.[123]

The big question was how long she intended to go on. The day she called the election she incautiously told the BBC's John Cole that she hoped it would not be her last as Tory leader. 'I hope to go on and on, because I believe passionately in our policies.'[124] Four days later she was greeted at the Scottish party conference in Perth with adoring chants of 'Ten more years'.[125] But for the rest of the campaign, in phone-ins and interviews, she had to keep denying the phrase. 'It's not for me to say I would go on and on,' she told the *Daily Telegraph*. 'I have to submit myself to the judgement of the people at elections and the judgement of my party every year.' At the same time she was anxious not to be seen as a lame duck. The electorate had a right to know whom they were electing:

> So I suggest you do know whom you are going to get. It's me! But you never know. You don't know what's going to happen in the future. Until, it happens you go on.[126]

At her final morning press conference she repeated that it was up to the party, but added: 'I am very fit, and would wish to see through a third term.'[127]

A second question that blew up in the last week of the campaign arose from her use of private medicine for her various minor operations. The issue was first raised on a radio phone-in by a male nurse who suggested that it showed her lack of confidence in the NHS. When the press picked this up the next morning she responded defiantly:

> I, along with something like five million other people, insure to enable me to go into hospital on the day I want, at the time I want and with the doctor I want . . . I exercise my right as a free citizen to spend my own money in my own way, so that I can go in on the day, at the time and with the doctor I choose, and get out fast.

She paid her taxes, like anyone else, she insisted; but if she used the NHS the press would accuse her of queue-jumping.[128]

For this she was heavily attacked by Labour and pressed hard on television by both David Frost and Robin Day, in some of the most interesting exchanges of the election. Frost, while admitting that he used private medicine himself, questioned whether wealthy people like them should have the right to buy better service if by doing so they drained resources from the NHS. She denied that private medicine had this effect and retorted that he was talking about compelling people to use the state system. 'They run that system in the Soviet Union. It does not result in a better Health Service.' No Government had ever spent more on the NHS than hers. Frost – belying his reputation for subservient interviewing – argued back that Cabinet ministers might still take more interest in the NHS if they used it themselves. She threw him momentarily (a good example of her argumentative technique) by responding that Norman Tebbit and John Wakeham had used the NHS to treat their Brighton injuries; so Frost switched to the stronger ground of education. Again she denied that the existence of private schools lowered standards in the state sector ('Because you have a different system from the state system it does show what standards of excellence can be achieved') and insisted that she was in the business of levelling up, not levelling down – at which point they were interrupted by a commercial break. But Frost had briefly succeeded in raising the stale electoral point-scoring to a higher level of philosophical debate.[129]

The tension between Downing Street and Central Office finally snapped a week before polling day on Thursday 4 June, when the *Daily Telegraph* published the latest Gallup poll which appeared to show Labour closing the gap on the Tories to just 4 per cent: Tories down to 40.5 per cent, Labour up to 36.5 per cent, the Alliance still struggling on 21 per cent. It was a rogue poll, but Mrs Thatcher's nerves were already close to breaking point – not helped by a painful tooth abscess – and some of those around her had their own reasons for talking up the crisis. At the regular early-morning meeting at Central Office she tore into Tebbit and Dobbs, as Dobbs recalled:

> Her demeanour at that meeting was unreasoning and unreasonable and close to hysteria. It was impossible to put a point or even to be listened to. It was quite clear that there was no point in saying anything. . . .[130]
>
> In more than a decade of working for her I had seen her in pain, in tears, in triumph but never had I seen her in such a condition.[131]

Coming away from the meeting, Willie Whitelaw commented prophetically: 'There is a woman who will never fight another election.'[132]

She was irritable at the following press conference, which included her defiant refusal to apologise for using private healthcare when and where she wanted. It was not what she said so much as the belligerent way she said it that gave offence. The press conference, she wrote in her memoirs, 'was widely considered to be a disaster, and I was held to blame'.[133] That day's programme was a visit to the Alton Towers entertainment park in Shropshire, which should have been a fun day out, providing good pictures of the Prime Minister confidently enjoying herself. Instead the mood was grim, as they all waited apprehensively for the next Marplan poll which was rumoured to be going to cut the Tory lead to 2 per cent. Labour seemed to have found momentum at just the right moment. 'It really did appear that we were on the run,' David Young wrote later.[134] Even Enoch Powell – fighting what turned out to be his last election in Northern Ireland – claimed to detect 'a whiff of 1945'.[135] Whether or not Mrs Thatcher really believed she could lose the election, she was certainly worried. She wanted not just to win but to win well: she would have regarded anything less than another three-figure majority as a serious setback to her international authority. Her response was to order Saatchis' poster campaign – featuring a British bulldog wearing a Union Jack – to be scrapped in favour of a more aggressively anti-Labour message advocated by both Young and Rubicam and Tim Bell. This was when Young and Tebbit came close to a stand-up fight: Young is said to have gripped Tebbit by the lapels and shaken him, shouting that they would lose the election if Mrs Thatcher was not happy. The Prime Minister must have whatever she wanted. Tebbit was forced to give way. Saatchis were obliged to adapt their rivals' ideas.

The new posters, backed by an unprecedented blitz of newspaper advertising, were in fact staggeringly unoriginal, yet another rerun of the old slogan 'Life's Better Under the Conservatives: Don't Let Labour Ruin It.' Tim Bell's new version was 'Britain's Great Again: Don't Let Labour Wreck It.' Over this repeated caption the new ads spelled out the Thatcher Government's achievements in big black capitals:

WE HAVE OUTLAWED SECONDARY PICKETING AND THE VIOLENCE THAT GOES WITH IT

THE BASIC RATE OF INCOME TAX IS THE LOWEST FOR NEARLY FIFTY YEARS

1 MILLION COUNCIL HOMES HAVE BEEN SOLD TO THEIR TENANTS

WE HAVE MAINTAINED BRITAIN'S DEFENCES AND BROUGHT RUSSIA TO THE NEGOTIATING TABLE

DON'T UNDO 8 YEARS' WORK IN 3 SECONDS[136]

These full-page ads filled a total of 154 newspaper pages in the final week of the campaign, at a cost of £3 million. Alistair McAlpine sanctioned the additional expenditure, on the principle that it was 'better to be the party in power with an overdraft than a rich opposition'.[137] But the contrast with 1983 – when Mrs Thatcher vetoed the adverts planned for the last week, believing them to be unnecessary – could not have been clearer.

The truth of 'Wobbly Thursday' has been contested in the rival memoirs and televised recollections. Tebbit insists that despite Young's interference he remained in full control throughout the campaign: 'We finished the campaign exactly as planned on the ground where Labour was weak and we were strong – defence, taxation and the economy.'[138] He claims to have been perfectly confident throughout, asserting that Young got needlessly agitated 'principally because he had never fought an election before'.[139] Young retorts that it was not just he who was concerned that the campaign was going wrong: 'The Prime Minister was concerned, all senior colleagues in the party were concerned,' concern was coming in from all over the country. Something drastic had to be done to keep the Lady happy.[140] Rodney Tyler's instant paperback, *Campaign!*, which leaned heavily on the 'exiles' camp, claimed that Young and Bell had plucked triumph from impending disaster.[141] David Butler and Dennis Kavanagh's verdict is more even-handed but broadly supports Tebbit. 'Apart from a more positive thrust to the advertisements, there was little change in the planned strategy.'[142] In any event 'Wobbly Thursday' was a storm in a teacup, since the Marplan poll when it came put the Conservatives back into a ten-point lead.

Mrs Thatcher quickly recovered her confidence. On Sunday afternoon she held a so-called 'family rally' at Wembley conference centre with the usual flag-waving, a galaxy of soap stars and comedians, including the impersonator Janet Brown (who never quite made the career she should have done from impersonating Mrs Thatcher), and a singalong to the *Dad's Army* signature tune adapted by Ronnie Millar, 'Who Do You Think You Are Kidding, Mr Kinnock?' Mrs Thatcher's speech rather archly picked up the theme by christening her supporters 'Mum's Army':

Next Thursday when the people go to the polls I believe Mum's Army will include thousands of traditional Labour supporters – Mums and Dads and sons and daughters from all over this beloved land of ours – who just can't stomach the defence policy – or rather the no-defence policy – of today's Labour party and its present leader.[143]

The *Guardian's* Terry Coleman thought the whole event desperately tacky: 'Two hours of smutty jokes, baying, braying and then a fair old rant. Nothing I have ever seen in the grubbiest of American elections touched its depths.' Bewildered, he contrasted this 'degraded circus' with hearing Mrs Thatcher talking with simple conviction in her constituency the previous day. She only arrived at Wembley in time for her own speech; yet she sanctioned and gloried in what went before. Coleman concluded that there were two Margaret Thatchers. 'You buy one, you buy the other.'[144]

That evening she recorded the party's final broadcast which was devoted entirely to herself – another victory over those who would have sidelined her. The first half was a compilation of moments from her conference speeches, notably celebrating the Falklands victory (1982) and her defiance of the Brighton bomb (1984), over the usual patriotic background music. The second half was a five-minute talk direct to camera, all about peace, prosperity and freedom, carefully delivered 'in her softest and most persuasive tones' after exhaustive coaching by Tim Bell, Ronnie Millar and Antony Jay (one of the writers of *Yes, Minister*).[145] Those five minutes were said to have taken fourteen hours to film, as though the whole election depended on getting it right. She hated speaking straight to camera. The next morning, by contrast, before flying off to Venice, she recorded her *Panorama* interview with Robin Day and bullied him in her most commanding style. Here again, in the two broadcasts, she showed two very different faces; but there was no doubt which was the real Margaret Thatcher.

She returned from Venice for her final rally in Harrogate on Tuesday evening. Why Harrogate of all places, a rock-solid Tory seat? Nothing could have better embodied the criticism that she wilfully averted her eyes from the problems of less prosperous parts of the country. 'What better place could there be,' she asked, 'than a northern city like Harrogate to dispel the myth that the North is poor, neglected and benighted while perpetual sunshine bathes the South?'[146] The right answer would have been 'Almost anywhere'. But there were no hecklers in the Royal Hall to provide it.

Back in the television studio, however, she 'came within an ace of disaster' in an eve-of-poll interview with David Dimbleby for BBC News. The lesson of the past three weeks was that so long as she kept to the high ground of the past she was fine, but whenever she left the familiar script to speak of the future she was liable to commit a gaffe. Now, attempting to contrast her practical compassion with others' warm words, she dropped her guard. 'But please,' she insisted, 'if people just drool and drivel that they care, I turn round and say: "Right, I also look to see what you actually do".''Drool and drivel?' Dimbleby repeated. 'Is that what you think saying that you care about people's plight amounts to?' She realised immediately that she had blundered, drew back and apologised repeatedly for using those words. Thinking he had a major story, Dimbleby was astonished that the interview, recorded in the morning, was not shown till the very end of the nine o'clock news, too late to draw an effective Labour reply. Was there, he wondered, Central Office pressure on the BBC? Or simply prudent self-censorship by a cowed Corporation apprehensive of offending the Prime Minister? Either way Mrs Thatcher was relieved that her unfortunate words were not more prominently exposed.[147]

In the end, beneath the superficial excitements of gaffes and rows, June 1987 was another hollow, negative campaign almost entirely lacking in serious content, as the *Spectator* – then edited by Charles Moore – justly complained:

> On the rare occasions when political questions have been discussed it has been with the same impoverished vocabulary and the same cowardice and evasion that were apparent in 1983. Although the Conservatives produced a thoroughly workmanlike manifesto with several brave proposals, they soon gave up trying to discuss it. A couple of confusions about policies for schools and nothing more was heard of the entire document for the rest of the campaign.

Labour were no better; but they were fighting an essentially conservative campaign to undo what they saw as the damage inflicted by eight years of Thatcherism. It was the Conservatives who were supposed to be transforming the country; but they did not dare to fight on that prospectus. Mrs Thatcher liked to see herself as a straight-talking conviction politician. She was proud of leading one of the most radical, mould-breaking governments of the century. Yet at none of her three general elections did she place clearly before the electorate what she intended to do if elected, or re-elected. In 1987 she was happy to boast of the success of policies that were never put before the electorate in 1979 or 1983. The message was that a third Thatcher Government would deliver more of the same. ('You know whom you're going to get. It's me!') The election was fought on the Tory record of the past eight years, but the future was contested on Labour's terms as an old-fashioned spending auction. The newspaper adverts in the final days were all about the level of spending on the 'caring' services:

The competition between the two parties was simply about who was likely to spend more and how much had been spent already – the Tories boasted of their profligacy: Labour accused them of meanness.[148]

Thus at the very height of her electoral success, in securing her unprecedented third election victory, Mrs Thatcher did not dare to seek and certainly did not secure any sort of mandate for 'Social Thatcherism'. She won easily again, essentially because the voters did not trust Labour on the economy or defence, while the Alliance remained popular enough to split the opposition, but too divided to make its dreamed-of breakthrough. 'Mr Kinnock had in his favour,' *The Times* commented, 'eight years of the most vilified Prime Minister of modern times; three million unemployed and a country apparently enraged by the condition of its health service. Yet he could not win.'[149] By keeping the Government on the defensive on health, employment and the state of the inner cities, Labour was widely judged to have 'won' the campaign. Yet Kinnock managed to recover only about half of the three million votes Foot had lost in 1983, and that ground was almost all regained from the Alliance. On a slightly increased turn-out (75 per cent), Labour's share of the vote increased from 27.6 per cent to 31.7 per cent, but the Tory share also rose slightly to 43.4 per cent, while the Alliance declined to 23 per cent. This gave Mrs Thatcher 376 seats (a loss of twenty-three), Labour 229 (up just twenty) and the Alliance a mere twenty-two, with the Scottish and Welsh nationalists at three each, trimming the Government's overall majority from the swollen 144 it had won in 1983 to a still-more-than-comfortable 102. In raw parliamentary terms it was another landslide.*

Analysed more closely, the figures confirmed a widening gulf between the prosperous and booming south and the depressed and still-declining north. The small national swing of 1.6 per cent to Labour hid wide regional variations: no movement at all in the south, 3.6 per cent in northern England and 5.8 per cent in Scotland, where the Tories – despite all Mrs Thatcher's hopeful rhetoric about the spirit

---

*Mrs Thatcher's personal result in Finchley was very little changed from 1983:

Mrs M. Thatcher (C)	21,603
J. Davies (Lab)	12,690
D. Howarth (Lib/All)	5,580
(Two others)	190
Majority	8,913[150]

of Adam Smith – lost ten of their twenty-one seats. They won none at all in several northern cities. It was becoming increasingly hard for the Tories to claim to be a national party. The result vindicated a cartoon published in *The Times* before the campaign started showing Mrs Thatcher mounted on a white charger shouting, 'Cry God for Maggie, South-East England and St George.'[151] It also bore out precisely what One Nation Tories like Ian Gilmour had predicted when she first became leader in 1975. Yet the Conservatives still fared better in the north than Labour in the south. They won sixty-three seats in the north of England and sixty-seven in the Midlands; Labour only won twenty-six seats south of a line between the Severn and the Wash, twenty-three of those in London. Moreover the Alliance was still runner-up in 60 per cent of Tory seats, mainly in the south. It was also clear that Mrs Thatcher had permanently broken the old class-based pattern of voting: she still held the allegiance of that class of newly affluent skilled workers, traditional Labour supporters whose votes she had first attracted in 1979 and retained by breaking the power of the unions and helping them buy their council houses. Driven back onto its dwindling bedrock of the poor, unskilled and unemployed, Labour was even less of a national party than the Tories. In a three-party system, under an electoral system which under-represented minorities, the new expanded middle class concentrated in southern England was enough to deliver an impregnable majority.

In the hour of victory it seemed that Mrs Thatcher could be Prime Minister for life if she wanted. Speaking to the crowds in Downing Street on Friday morning she was openly delighted with her achievement. 'I think the real thing now is we have done it three times . . . With a universal franchise the third time is terrific, is it not?'[152] 'We have just had the most fantastic triumph,' she told ITN's Michael Brunson. 'The third time with the same Prime Minister with a full franchise and a majority of about a hundred. It would have been a triumph the first time, the third time it is remarkable.'[153] Pressed again about how long she intended to go on, she made no bones about her intention to complete the third term, dismissed the idea of grooming a successor ('Good heavens, no') and did not demur when Robin Day suggested that she might still be Prime Minister in the year 2000, when she would be only seventy-five. 'You never know,' she replied, 'I might be here, I might be twanging a harp. Let us just see how things go.'[154] She had no doubt that she had won a huge personal mandate.

Denis was more realistic. Watching with Carol from an upstairs window as Margaret acknowledged the cheering crowd below, he 'turned to get himself a refill and said, "In a year she'll be so unpopular you won't believe it"'.[155] In fact it took a bit longer than that. But it was prescient all the same.

13

No Such Thing as Society

'Society – that's no one'

In June 1987 Thatcherism moved into a new phase. Having sorted out the economy, as she believed, Mrs Thatcher now wanted to take on British society and specifically the culture of dependency which had grown out of forty years of socialised welfare. But this ambition quickly brought the contradictions of her philosophy into sharp focus. With the exception of curbing the unions, which had required legislation, and privatisation (which only involved undoing what had been done in the past), most of what she had achieved so far had been achieved by *not* doing things – *not* intervening as previous governments had done to settle strikes or to save jobs. So far she, Howe and Lawson, with their advisers, had been following a clear programme which had worked more or less as intended. The hands-off, free-market approach had undoubtedly had a stimulating effect on those parts of the economy that survived its rigours. Now she proposed to tackle something much more difficult and amorphous, where there were not the same clear doctrinal guidelines. According to the pure milk of free-market economics, the state should not be in the business of providing education, housing or medical care at all. But in practice abolishing public provision was not an option: too many voters were indeed dependent on it. She could trim a little at the margins; but fundamentally she could only try to improve the delivery and quality of services. And she could only do this by intervening directly to reform the way they were run. Partly from this inexorable logic, therefore, partly from her own restlessly interfering temperament, she was driven into an activist, centralising frenzy at odds with the professed philosophy of rolling back the state. This was to cause all sorts of trouble in the next three years.

Usually Mrs Thatcher denied any conflict, insisting that all her reforms were simply aimed at giving power back to schools, parents, tenants and patients. But an article she wrote for the *Sunday Express* a week after the election reveals a rare awareness of this contradiction. (No doubt it was largely written for her; but nothing was ever published in Mrs Thatcher's name without her correcting every word.) Conscious of the criticism that her government since 1979 had served only the interests of the better-off, she set four goals for 'a Government which seeks to serve *all* the people *all* the time'. The first three were quite conventional: to ensure liberty and security, to preserve the value of the currency and (more vaguely) to ensure 'fairness' for all. But the fourth recognised the tension between the philosophy of minimum government and her instinct to tell people what to do:

> Fourth, in full recognition of human frailty, and together with all the other great institutions, it must seek to set standards by which people lead their lives. A society which knows what is expected of it has a sure base for progress.

Immediately she entered all sorts of disclaimers:

> We do not seek to lead people's lives for them, nor to boss them around, nor to regulate them into apathy . . . A government for *all* the people must have the humility to recognise its limitations and the strength to resist the temptation to meddle in the citizens' lives.[1]

Nevertheless the ambition had been declared in the first sentence: the Government 'must seek to set standards by which people live their lives'. That is unmistakably the voice of nanny.

It was during an interview for the magazine *Woman's Own* that autumn that Mrs Thatcher delivered the statement which seemed to define her philosophy more perfectly than anything else she ever said. Arguing that people should not look to 'society' to solve their problems, she asserted:

> There is no such thing as society. There are individual men and women, and there are families. And no Government can do anything except through people, and people must look to themselves. It's our duty to look after ourselves and then to look after our neighbour.[2]

As is usually the case with famous sayings, she had made the same point several times before, for instance in her 1985 television interview with Miriam Stoppard, when she explained that she and her sister were brought up to be responsible for their own actions. 'You do not blame society. Society is not anyone. You are personally responsible.'[3] And she said it again to Jimmy Young in 1988: 'Don't blame society – that's no one', going on to explain that the streets would not be dirty if only people did not drop litter.[4] So her words were not a misquotation or taken out of context. But this time they created enormous outrage.

In her memoirs Lady Thatcher protested that she had been deliberately misunderstood. All she had meant was that society was not an abstraction, 'but a living structure of individuals, families, neighbours and voluntary associations . . . Society for me is not an excuse, but an obligation.'[5] In a purely literal sense it is obviously true that society is made up of individuals, grouped into families and other associations. But because it is composed of small platoons does not mean that society, as an aggregate of those components, does not exist. On the contrary, society has a collective existence on at least two levels. First there is the emotional sense of a national community, a concept traditionally important to Conservatives of all stripes, whether One Nation paternalists or gung-ho imperialists. Mrs Thatcher more than most professed a semi-mystical view of Britain as a family united by common values, an ideal to which she frequently appealed when it suited her. But more concrete than that, modern society has also a statutory existence as a network of legal and financial arrangements built up to discharge collective responsibilities beyond the capacity of the immediate neighbourhood. It was a perfectly legitimate Conservative position to argue that society in this sense had taken on too many responsibilities, which should be reduced. It was not meaningful for the head of a government charged with administering those responsibilities to maintain that it did not exist.

She clearly did not intend to deny the first meaning. But she did seek to deny the second, equating it – as she did to Jimmy Young – with 'socialism':

I think for years we got into the wrong track. It was partly socialism. Everything, you know, 'It's the Government's fault' . . .

Well, who is society? You say society is to blame. It is you and me and our next door neighbour and everyone we know in our town, in our school, in our business.[6]

This was absurdly reductive. In trying to reduce responsibility to the individual's immediate neighbourhood she was denying much of

the Conservative past. The 1968 party document *Make Life Better*, for
example, which embodied the 'One Nation' view of Ted Heath and
Iain Macleod, had explicitly sought to balance individual opportunity
with collective responsibility. On the one hand it envisaged a 'free
society in which men and women are free to make the most of their
individual talents . . . free to achieve and excel, free to sustain variety
and choice in their lives':

> *But it is a society – not a collection of individuals,* a society in which
> the young are cared for as well as the old, the backward as well as
> the pacesetters, the deprived as well as the high fliers.[7]

At the time Mrs Thatcher went along with that orthodoxy. 'None
of us can opt out of the society of which we are a part,' she asserted
conventionally in her first party conference speech as Education
Secretary in October 1970.[8] But by the time she was Leader of the
Opposition she was beginning to air a more limited view of social
responsibility, for instance in her Iain Macleod Memorial Lecture in
1977:

> Man is a social creature, born into family, clan, community, nation,
> brought up in mutual dependence . . . Our fellow feeling develops
> from self-regard . . . Adam Smith . . . showed how the market
> economy obliges and enables each producer to serve the consumer's
> interest by serving his own.[9]

From this she went on to develop her view that Christian morality
consists in individual choice, leading on to her praise of Victorian self-
help and philanthropy and the idea that individual charity was both
more virtuous and socially more beneficial than collective provision
via taxation. This was a theme she continued to sound as Prime
Minister. She rejected the charge that her policies promoted selfishness by insisting that the richer the wealthy became, the better they
were able to fulfil their social responsibility by giving more to charity.
'Those who care, and they are the great majority of us, now have the
means to give,' she told the 1988 party conference. 'And they are giving
in full measure.'

Over £1,500 million a year to boost charities, rebuild churches, help
medical research and feed the hungry. That's a marvellous record.
And it doesn't stop at individuals. Many businesses are now giving
a percentage of their profits to help the community in which they

are situated ... The fact is that prosperity has created not the selfish society but the generous society.[10]*

In practice, of course, this was a drop in the ocean of government spending. She could never abolish the welfare state and knew perfectly well that she could not; but she made no secret of the fact that in her ideal world it would not exist, beyond what she referred to in 1983 as 'basic social services' for the old and incapable.[12] Like the Jews in her constituency whom she held up to admiration for never troubling the social services, she believed that self-respecting families should look after their own without looking to the state for support. Though bound to keep on supporting state education and state medicine, she believed that responsible individuals – like herself and Denis – should make their own arrangements.

Her statement that there was 'no such thing as society' gave offence mainly because it seemed to legitimise selfishness and reduced public provision for the poor to the bounty of the rich. It denied that sense of social solidarity which Conservatives as much as socialists had in their different ways always tried to inculcate, replacing it with an atomised society bound together only by contractual obligations. It offended Tory philosophers like Roger Scruton, editor of the *Salisbury Review*, as well as thoughtful ex-ministers as different as Francis Pym and John Biffen. But it also had implications for other public amenities beyond the social services: transport, art and leisure facilities, sewers and prisons. The doctrine that citizens should be allowed to keep as much as possible of their own money to spend on personal consumption, while essential public facilities like roads and railways, museums and libraries, swimming pools and playing fields were financed wherever possible by private enterprise – or private benefaction – rather than by the state, as in most other European countries, derived from the same belief that Adam Smith's multiplicity of individual decisions would somehow work their magic and the market would provide. By the end of the decade – still more by the end of the century – it was becoming apparent that this was not the case. There was necessary collective investment in public facilities which only the state could provide. There was such a thing as society after all.

The consequence of the Prime Minister's denial of society at the

---

*Her own favourite charity, she told Robin Day during the 1987 election, was the NSPCC. 'I sometimes wish that instead of giving up 20 per cent of my salary, I could just let them have it. And Denis for Sports Aid Foundation, the Lord's Taverners. Yes, we all work for these causes.'[11]

very moment when she was promising, at the party conference, to devote her third term to 'social affairs' was that she found herself embarked on a hotchpotch of incoherent reforms, in some respects more ambitious than originally intended and generally ill-thought out. It was not only that reform of the National Health Service forced itself onto the agenda, in addition to the plans already announced in the manifesto for education, housing and the poll tax. The Government soon became embroiled in a swathe of other legislation involving broadcasting, football supporters, firearms, the legal profession, official secrets, pubs, homosexuality, child support and war criminals. Mrs Thatcher's promise to 'resist the temptation to meddle in the citizens' lives' was soon forgotten. As she boasted in her speech at the 1987 conference: '"Can't be done" has given way to "What's to stop us?"'[13] 1988 was in the words of one commentator, 'the high water mark of Thatcherite triumphalism and swagger . . . The Year of Hubris'.[14] The drive to reform every corner of British society was taken up by a new generation of ambitious younger ministers – many of them originally protégés of Ted Heath, now keen to make up for lost time by jumping on the Thatcher bandwagon, believing they could get away with anything, with no cautionary elders like Whitelaw and Hailsham left in the Cabinet to restrain them. Meanwhile the economic miracle which was supposed to make all things possible was turning sour.

Thus Mrs Thatcher's third term was a saga of boastful talk and much-proclaimed radicalism, but also a lot of misdirected energy due to a fundamental contradiction at the heart of the Government's purpose and a crippling lack of trust and sympathy between an increasingly irrational Prime Minister and her closest colleagues, which eventually resulted in her brutal deposition.

The new Cabinet

The first thing she had to do on returning to Downing Street was to reshape the Cabinet. She had little room for manoeuvre in the senior positions: Lawson and Howe were bound to stay where they were: the former was the economic hero of the hour and the latter, much as he exasperated her, was her perfect foil in the Foreign Office. She might have thought of kicking him upstairs to be Lord Chancellor, but the time was not yet. Whitelaw was irreplaceable as Lord President and deputy Prime Minister. Hurd was proving an effective Home Secretary; Baker and Ridley were billed to play leading roles in her education, housing and local-government reforms; it made sense to leave Younger, Rifkind and King at Defence, Scotland and Northern Ireland. On the other hand Norman Fowler had earned a move from the DHSS after six years; Peter Walker was already lucky to have survived four years at Energy; Paul Channon, promoted hastily on Leon Brittan's resignation, had made no impact at the DTI; John Wakeham was due a Cabinet post after four years as Chief Whip; and she was keen to bring back Cecil Parkinson and promote some younger favourites like John Moore and John Major. To make room there was one obvious candidate for the chop – John Biffen; while Norman Tebbit had told her just before polling day that he wished to leave the Government.

Biffen's departure was inevitable and widely predicted. One of the original monetarists, he had become disenchanted with Mrs Thatcher's hard-nosed approach to government and did not care who knew it: his letter accepting his dismissal was curt and pointed, stressing the need for a successful economy to be balanced by a high level of social spending, particularly on health and education.[15] Tebbit's withdrawal, on the other hand, was a surprise. Its ostensible reason was his need to care for his wife, permanently paralysed by her injuries in the Brighton bombing. But unquestionably the tensions of the election, and the gulf of mistrust that had opened between himself and Mrs Thatcher from the moment he became party chairman, played a part. 'I didn't want him to go,' she told Woodrow Wyatt[16]; but she was probably not too sorry. She did not believe that his ambition was dead, but suspected that he thought he would be better placed to succeed her from outside the Cabinet. Two weeks later Wyatt noted that he was assiduously courting the new intake of MPs.[17] The loss of both Tebbit and Biffen, however, should have sounded a warning that she was alienating colleagues who had once been among her key supporters.

Mrs Thatcher had intended to complete what she had begun before the election by appointing her favourite miracle-worker, David Young, to be the new chairman. Young had been openly angling for the job; but the suggestion provoked such hostility that she was forced to abandon it. Whitelaw told her firmly that the party would not wear it. It was announced that Tebbit would retain the post for the time being: then, after some speculation that she could find no one to take it, she appointed a solid junior minister, Peter Brooke, to fill the role in the post-election period (as Gummer had done after 1983). Meanwhile she moved Young (with his energetic Commons sidekick, Kenneth Clarke) from the Department of Employment, where they were credited with having got unemployment at last starting to come down, to the DTI, where another miracle was needed to honour her election-night pledge to tackle the inner cities. Clarke was disappointed not to get his own department, but swapped the title of Paymaster-General for the Chancellorship of the Duchy of Lancaster. Channon moved to Transport, which allowed John Moore – young, blond and telegenic, currently seen as the Prime Minister's chosen heir – to take on the DHSS, while Fowler completed the circle by going to Employment.

Biffen's removal left an obvious vacancy for Wakeham as Leader of the House. John Major also entered the Cabinet for the first time as Chief Secretary to the Treasury, replacing John MacGregor who moved to Agriculture, at the expense of Michael Jopling, the second involuntary departure. Finally Mrs Thatcher created a vacancy for Parkinson – her previous, now tarnished golden boy – by moving Walker from the Department of Energy. That might have been assumed to be the end of Walker's ministerial career. But she had a problem replacing Nicholas Edwards, who had decided to stand down after eight years as Welsh Secretary. The party had been reduced to only eight MPs in Wales, none of them Cabinet material. So she offered the job to Walker, whose Worcester constituency was at least in the right direction. This was at first sight, as Julian Critchley wrote, 'a demotion, even a humiliation'.[18] But Walker accepted on condition that he was given a free hand to run the principality in his own way. Mrs Thatcher agreed, with the result that for the next three years he was able to pursue a remarkably successful regional policy, using Government money to attract a higher level of inward investment than any other part of the UK, so that Wales supposedly became known as 'little Japan beyond England'.[19] John Major found Walker 'the toughest negotiator of them all' when it came to fixing departmental budgets. He positively believed in public spending, and conducted himself as 'a man who did not care whether he remained in the Cabinet or not, and was not remotely interested in being a team player if that meant making concessions to an economic policy he distrusted'.[20] In fact Walker was as 'semi-detached' as Biffen ever was, and continued to make barely coded speeches criticising Government policy. Yet Mrs Thatcher valued him enough to keep him in place until he left the Cabinet of his own accord in May 1990.

There was one more enforced retirement. Lord Hailsham was now nearly eighty. Mrs Thatcher had left him on the Woolsack for eight years as an act of human kindness to a lonely old widower, but in 1986 he had married for the third time, and she now felt that Michael Havers deserved his turn at the highest legal office after eight years as Attorney-General. Hailsham reluctantly agreed to 'lay aside my wig and put my father's gold robe back in its tin box'.[21] 'I think the crux was Michael's pension,' he wrote sadly to Wyatt. 'At all events I went quietly.'[22] In fact Havers served for just four months – long enough to secure his pension – before he too resigned, under cover of ill-health but really because Willie Whitelaw was incensed by his mishandling of the Criminal Justice Bill in the House of Lords.[23] Mrs Thatcher then made one of her boldest and most surprising appointments, plucking the former Lord Advocate, Lord Mackay of Clashfern, from the Scottish bench to head the English legal system. Mackay was not even a Conservative, but an independent-minded and austere presbyterian – a member of the strictly teetotal and sabbatarian 'Wee Frees' – who turned out to be a radical reformer, immune to the sentimental reverence for legal tradition which had so crippled Hailsham. Unfortunately Lady Thatcher barely mentions Mackay in her memoirs, so there is still a mystery about how she came to appoint him.

The old division of the Cabinet into 'wets' and 'dries' had long since been superseded. Of the original wets, only Whitelaw and Walker now survived. From 1981, with the accession of Lawson, Tebbit, Parkinson and Ridley to senior positions, Mrs Thatcher had begun to forge a Cabinet much more in her own mould than the one she had been obliged to form in 1979. By 1987, however, the balance was tilting against her again. Besides Lawson and Howe – who could no longer be counted as unquestioning loyalists – only Ridley, Parkinson, Moore and perhaps David Young were instinctively of her way of thinking. The critical mass of the new Cabinet was made up of up-and-coming pragmatists from the centre-left of the party – Hurd, Baker, Clarke, MacGregor, Fowler, King, Rifkind and Major – who had come into politics under Heath. They had absorbed the lessons Keith Joseph and Mrs Thatcher had taught, but they were by no means natural Thatcherites. Of course the Cabinet as a body counted for very little in the determination of policy. Most of its members would continue to support her so long as she was riding high. But its changing composition should have been another warning that it would not automatically back her when the going got rough.

In addition, after only seven months she lost Willie Whitelaw, who was taken ill at a carol service in December and resigned in January 1988. Many see this as a critical turning point. It was during a late-night speechwriting session with her wordsmiths at Blackpool that Mrs Thatcher famously remarked that 'Every Prime Minister should have a Willie.' When she realised what she had said she swore them all to secrecy; but the story inevitably got out.[24] The unconscious *double entendre* drew a lot of ribaldry, but her point was absolutely true: every Prime Minister does need a Willie, though few are lucky enough to have one. Whitelaw was not only rigidly loyal himself, but he had the authority to impose loyalty on others. For eight and a half years his reassuring and defusing presence was hugely important to the survival and success of Mrs Thatcher's governments. His departure left the Government without its sheet-anchor in the increasingly heavy seas of the next three years.

'What's to stop us?'

The Government made a much more purposeful start to its third term than it had done to its second. When the new Parliament met on 25 June Mrs Thatcher hailed the Queen's Speech as 'one of the most substantial and radical in years', and in a bullish speech to the 1922 Committee three weeks later she sent her troops away for the summer with the fate-tempting admonition that a majority of 101 was pretty good but 'we have to do better next time'.[25] She stamped on the first stirrings of discontent about the community charge, describing it for the first time as the 'flagship' of the Government's programme, and ruled out any question of a free vote, since it was 'a foremost part of our manifesto'.[26] Over the summer, however, she gave priority to another commitment which had not featured prominently in the manifesto. Addressing jubilant party workers in Central Office on election night, she had surprised the commentators by declaring: 'We have a really big job to do in the inner cities. Politically we must get right back in there, because we want them too, next time.'[27] This was immediately glossed to mean, not so much that she wanted to tackle urban dereliction in itself, as that she wanted to win more urban seats: but the two were obviously connected. Responding to criticism that responsibility for the inner cities was divided between seven departments, she announced on 24 July that she herself would chair a committee to co-ordinate strategy.

Following her usual very brief holiday in Cornwall – interrupted on 19 August by a horrific incident in the quiet Wiltshire town of Hungerford when a single gunman ran amok, killing sixteen people – she used the latter part of the recess to demonstrate that she did care about the forgotten parts of Britain which she had seemed wilfully to ignore in the election. She visited several run-down inner cities – Glasgow, Cleveland and Wolverhampton – touring carefully selected scenes of urban decay to preach her message that enterprise, not Government subsidy, would create the jobs to bring regeneration. A photo-call in Cleveland resulted in a famous picture of the Prime Minister, with her handbag, marching determinedly into a wasteland which had once been a steelworks. When a journalist asked where the money would come from to revive such areas, she demanded that *he* tell *her*.[28] She saw the solution less in terms of money than in the antici-pated impact of the three Bills already announced – Ridley's new forms of tenancy, Baker's education reforms and the community charge, all designed to weaken the grip of Labour councils which she saw as the cause, not a reflection, of urban deprivation. 'Where one finds poverty in the inner cities,' she had declared back in 1979, 'there one finds that Socialist government has operated for many years.'[29] She found timely support for her view in the memoirs of the Labour defector Robert Kilroy-Silk – he defected not to another party but to television – who wrote that the greatest obstacle to the creation of jobs in Liverpool was the anti-business culture promoted by the Militant-led council.[30]

So far as physical regeneration was concerned her model was the redevelopment of London's docklands, which she praised during the election as 'a classic example of Toryism at work. Take the dereliction, improve it, make progress, do it by putting in a little bit of taxpayer's money to prime the pump and along comes industry.'[31] There was actually nothing specifically Tory about it – the proposal for a Docklands Development Corporation had first been put forward by the Labour MP Bob Mellish in the 1960s – but it fitted well with Mrs Thatcher's desire to bypass obstructive councils. The idea was to create a body which could override the local authorities, cut through the jungle of local planning regulations, buy up and redevelop derelict land and offer incentives to attract business to the area. The London Docklands Development Corporation was eventually established in 1981 by Michael Heseltine, with a similar body for Merseyside (planned before that summer's riots). Their success encouraged Ridley to announce another four Urban Development Corporations in 1986 (on Teesside, Tyne and Wear, the West Midlands and Trafford Park, Manchester). Now Mrs Thatcher resolved to set up four more (in Sheffield, Leeds, Bristol and Central Manchester) and more than double the amount of money put into them. In December Ken Clarke – rather than Ridley – was put in charge of the inner-city programme, initially with a budget of £2 billion.* By the time Mrs Thatcher herself chaired a multi-departmental press conference – attended by Ridley, Channon, Hurd, Baker, Fowler and Clarke – in March 1988 to launch a White Paper, *Action for Cities*, that figure had been raised to £3 billion.

The programme, with a multiplicity of subordinate schemes – Enterprise Zones, Business in the Community, City Action Teams, Derelict Land Grants – achieved considerable success over the next

---

*Ridley fought to keep responsibility for the cities within the DoE. It was David Young who persuaded Mrs Thatcher that Clarke was a more suitable candidate for the job '"because he looks like he lives in one" . . .'[32] But turf wars between departments persisted.

decade, at least in physically redeveloping derelict areas. Much of the benefit, however, certainly in London, accrued to 'yuppies' and other middle-class incomers, rather than to the original inhabitants who could not afford the new housing and found themselves either displaced or servicing the new population. Mrs Thatcher, when she visited these gleaming new developments, tended to enthuse about the physical trans-formation rather than ask where the former inhabitants had gone. Indeed she often seemed more worried by litter than more fundamental prob-lems. 'Every time I came back from some spotlessly maintained foreign city,' she wrote in her memoirs, 'my staff and the Secretary of State for the Environment knew they could expect a stiff lecture on the litter-strewn streets of parts of London.'[33] It was after visiting Tel Aviv in 1986 that she persuaded Richard Branson to head a so-called litter task force. Then in March 1988 – just two weeks after launching *Action for Cities* – she appeared in St James's Park, with Ridley in embarrassed atten-dance holding a bin bag, picking up specially scattered litter with a pointed stick to launch a Tidy Britain campaign. Likewise she seemed to be more worried about the bad impression that beggars and rough sleepers gave foreign visitors to London than she was about the beggars themselves. Clarke told his biographer that Mrs Thatcher 'didn't have a clue about the inner cities'.[34] Resolutely suburban herself, she regarded them as hostile territory – 'resentful colonies' in Simon Jenkins' phrase – to be contained.[35] She did not seriously expect to win them back for the Tories, unless perhaps by the deliberate gerrymandering employed by Dame Shirley Porter (one of her favourite council leaders) in Westminster. She does not mention *Action for Cities* or even Urban Development Corporations in her memoirs, except to remark with evident satisfaction that Heseltine's efforts on Merseyside 'had only ephemeral results'.[36] The cities were not part of her England.

The party conference at Blackpool was an unabashed victory rally not spoiled as the 1983 equivalent had been by revelations about Cecil Parkinson and Sara Keays. 'That makes three wins in a row,' Mrs Thatcher told the adoring faithful with no pretence of modesty. 'Just like Lord Liverpool. And he was Prime Minister for fifteen years. It's rather encouraging.' She scorned calls for 'consolidation' voiced by Quintin Hailsham, among others, who had warned that the Tories were supposed to be a conservative party. Describing the past eight years as 'a great political adventure', she went on defiantly:

> Is this where we pitch our tents? Is this where we dig in? Absolutely
> not. Our third election victory was only a staging post on a much
> longer journey. I know with every fibre of my being that it would

be fatal for us just to stand where we are now. What would be our slogan for the 1990s if we did that? . . . Whose blood would run faster at the prospect of five years of consolidation?

At the end she tried to deflect Peregrine Worsthorne's criticism that the Government was showing signs of 'bourgeois triumphalism' by quoting Kipling's warning (in *Recessional*) to keep 'An humble and a contrite heart'. But even her attempted humility sounded boastful. Two sentences later she was crowing, 'What's to stop us?'[37]★

One week later the mood was abruptly punctured by the collapse of the New York stock market. The same weekend southern England was hit by a great storm – popularly designated a hurricane – which wreaked a band of destruction from Cornwall to Kent, claiming eighteen lives and uprooting fifteen million trees. The coincidence of the two events seemed eerily symbolic. When the stock market reopened on Monday morning, London duly followed New York and Tokyo down the tube: 23 per cent was wiped off share values in one day. 'Black Monday' delivered a devastating blow to Mrs Thatcher's view of Britain's restored 'greatness'. Though in principle she believed in the global market, she was shocked by the reminder of the British economy's vulnerability to a crash on Wall Street, and the helplessness of her government to act independently.

The most embarrassing effect in the short run was the wreck of the privatisation of British Petroleum, whose shares went on sale at the worst possible moment. After a string of successes over the spring and summer with British Airways, the British Airports Authority and Rolls-Royce, the Government was suddenly left with millions of shares on its hands in what *The Times* called 'the biggest flotation flop in history'.[39] Lawson refused to 'pull' the sale, but the Treasury was obliged to underwrite the issue itself at just seventy pence a share – instead of 120 pence – giving rise to gleeful Labour jeers of re-nationalisation. In fact the losers were neither the Government nor the public, but the bankers. The episode proved to be only a blip in the sequence of successful privatisations. The second instalment of BP shares the following summer netted the taxpayer the biggest yield yet.

★'Dear Peregrine,' she scoffed in an interview for Worsthorne's own paper, the *Sunday Telegraph*. 'Why does he talk about "*boo-jhwha*"? Why can't he find a plain English word for the plain people of England, Scotland, and Wales? The *boo-jhwha* live in France . . . The danger is that all this talk about bourgeois triumphalism will be used to cast discredit on the common sense, the voluntary spirit, and the generosity of the British character. *British*, not bourgeois.'[38]

Far more serious in the long run were the measures Lawson took to try to mitigate the impact of the stock-market crash on the British economy. Amid widespread – but as it turned out erroneous – fears of an American-led recession, he cut interest rates by half of 1 per cent on 20 October, then by another half per cent on 4 November, to boost demand. In his memoirs he defends these cuts as very much less than the Labour party and much of Fleet Street and the City were demanding. Both he and Mrs Thatcher claim to have been unmoved by the general panic over a perfectly normal 'correction' of overvalued stocks.[40] Nevertheless with the economy in fact already beginning to overheat, cutting interest rates at all turned out to be exactly the wrong medicine at the wrong time.

Social Thatcherism: education, housing and health

In November all the key planks of the Government's programme were unveiled, starting with Baker's Education Bill, known as the Great Education Reform Bill, or 'Gerbil' for short. It was really five Bills in one, each one of which – setting up a National Curriculum, giving schools the right to opt out of local-authority control, establishing City Technology Colleges, reforming the universities, and (as an after-thought) abolishing the Inner London Education Authority – could have been a substantial measure on its own. But the perils of introducing major legislation with inadequate prior consultation were illustrated as Baker and his colleagues, battered by conflicting pressures from various parts of the educational establishment on the one hand and the Prime Minister on the other, were forced to improvise policy as they went along. By the time the Bill finally concluded its passage through Parliament in July 1988 it had swollen from 137 clauses to 238 and taken up 370 hours of parliamentary time – a postwar record.

The content of the curriculum was the subject of a major battle between Baker and Mrs Thatcher. She wanted what she called a 'basic' curriculum of just three subjects, English, maths and science, occupying no more than 70 per cent of classroom time. Baker thought this much too limited. 'It was a sort of Gradgrind curriculum, in my view, not a rounded one.'[41] He wanted a comprehensive curriculum on the model of the French *baccalauréat* with three 'core' subjects and another seven 'foundation' subjects – history, geography, technology, art, music and a foreign language, plus religious education – with detailed testing at age seven, eleven, fourteen and sixteen, and he threatened resignation to get his way. Mrs Thatcher let herself be overruled by his combination of enthusiasm and blackmail, but on this occasion her instincts were right. 'All I wanted was the three Rs,' she complained.[42]

'I never imagined that we would end up with the bureaucracy and the thicket of prescriptive measures which eventually emerged,' she wrote in her memoirs.[43] Baker's successors, John MacGregor and Ken Clarke, subsequently pruned the thicket to something rather nearer her original preference.

Yet she could be highly prescriptive herself. Once she had agreed that history should be included, she became passionately involved in trying to impose her view on the working group charged with drawing up the detail of what should be taught. 'Though not a historian myself,' she wrote, 'I had a very clear – and as I naively imagined uncontroversial – idea of what history was.'[44] She wanted a Churchillian emphasis on British history as a chronology of great men and battles, Magna Carta, Parliament and Empire, sharply at odds with the more sceptical and source-based fashion of modern history teaching. 'Ken Baker,' she believed, 'paid too much attention to the DES, the HMI and progressive educational theorists' both in appointing the curriculum working group and in his guidance to it. She was 'appalled' by its interim report, which she considered 'comprehensively flawed' – 'insufficient weight given to British history ... not enough emphasis on history as chronological study' – and demanded 'major, not just minor, changes'. In July 1989 she replaced Baker with John MacGregor, whom she expected to be more amenable, and maintained 'constant pressure' on him to deliver them. He did cut the number of subjects and the amount of testing, but was still in her view too ready to listen to the teachers. By the time she left office she was frustrated that 'the whole system' – not just the history part of it – 'was very different from that which I originally envisaged'.[45] Simplified further by Kenneth Clarke and then John Patten, however, reinforced by a new inspectorate (OFSTED) and published tables of performance, the national curriculum eventually settled down as one element in a real lifting of standards over the next decade.

Giving schools the freedom to opt out of local-authority control proved equally contentious. Conservative authorities had no more wish than Labour ones to lose their best schools, while Baker and Mrs Thatcher were still at odds over how rapidly to drive the policy forward. She 'rather strayed from the script' in Baker's view, by asserting in September 1987 that 'I think ... most schools will opt out.' A moment later she qualified this to: 'Really I think that most schools should be able to escape.'[46] The latter represented her hope; the former was over-optimistic. Baker, doubtful that the DES had the manpower to run the whole system, envisaged only a few schools in some of the worst left-wing authorities opting out as a warning to the others. Even then backbench pressure in the Commons and a number of defeats in the Lords forced him to raise the proportion of parents required to vote before a school could opt out. In November 1988 schools in Skegness and Tameside became the first to vote for 'grant-maintained' status. But only about fifty had followed by the time Mrs Thatcher fell. The pace quickened somewhat after 1992, but still only 1,100 (out of 24,000) had opted out by 1997, when New Labour put a stop to it. By contrast local management of schools (LMS) – the less ambitious policy which gave heads and governors (including more parent governors) power to manage their own budgets and appointments – was a considerable success. But opting out – setting individual schools in competition with one another – was deliberately designed to make the planning or even co-ordination of the education system in each local-authority area impossible. Under the guise of devolution it actually increased central control, while doing nothing to increase parental choice, as Lady Thatcher herself subsequently acknowledged.[47] With the DES holding the purse strings, grant-maintained schools were not genuinely independent at all; rather, as Simon Jenkins has argued, they represented another instance of Tory nationalisation in defiance of the party's professed belief in diversity and choice.[48]

As already seen, the same criticism was levelled at the Government's reform of the universities. The ending of the binary system facilitated a huge increase in student numbers – from 700,000 in 1988 to one million in 1993 – but here too Mrs Thatcher was forced to acknowledge that the results were not what she had intended. City Technology Colleges were not a great success either: only fifteen were ever established at four times the anticipated cost.[49] Meanwhile the abolition of the ILEA was the clearest case of policymaking on the hoof. It was admittedly an anomaly that the ILEA had not only survived the abolition of the GLC but had actually gained legitimacy from its parent body's demise. Baker's Bill originally proposed to allow individual boroughs to opt out, in the hope that the ILEA would gradually wither away: it was an unlikely alliance of Norman Tebbit and Michael Heseltine who backed an amendment to scrap it altogether. Like the GLC, the ILEA had its faults – extravagance and political posturing – but its abolition also dissipated a lot of expertise and useful co-ordination across the capital and led to a good deal of wasteful duplication.

By comparison with Baker's monster, Ridley's Housing Bill was modest and attracted relatively little controversy. Here too council tenants were empowered to opt out of local-authority control. Housing Action Trusts (HATs) were supposed to improve rundown estates by converting them to private ownership. At the same time new forms of rented tenure ('assured' and 'shorthold' tenancies) were designed to bring more private rented property onto the market. In fact little of this came to pass. Despite large sums of public money on offer as an inducement, tenants proved unwilling to exchange the public-sector landlord they knew for the uncertainty of the private sector: as a result no HATs at all were set up before November 1990 and only four by 1996, while the amount of private renting increased only marginally. In her memoirs Lady Thatcher blamed 'the deep-rooted hostility of the Left to the improvement and enfranchisement of those who lived in the ghettoes of dependency which they controlled'.[50] But in fact her policies over the past decade had done as much to demoralise council tenants, first by stigmatising them as second-class citizens if they could not afford to buy their houses, then by steadily cutting subsidies and raising rents, which had the perverse effect of forcing more people onto housing benefit, creating so-called 'welfare ghettoes' where only those on benefit could afford to live.[51] It was naive to expect such people to vote for private landlords.

The real story of housing in the late 1980s was a shocking increase in the number of people without homes at all, who resorted to sleeping on the streets, under flyovers and in shop doorways of London and other big cities. This sudden phenomenon of visible homelessness was due to a combination of reasons, at least three of them the direct result of Government policy: the reduction in the public housing stock due to the non-replacement of the million former council houses sold to their tenants; higher rents in both council and private rented housing; and the withdrawal of benefits from several categories of claimant, specifically the young and single unemployed. In addition an increasing rate of family break-up was creating more demand for homes, while more young people, for a variety of reasons, good and bad, were leaving home. The situation was further exacerbated towards the end of the decade by the number of homes repossessed when their proud purchasers – who had been encouraged to buy their houses in the heyday of council-house sales a few years earlier – were unable to keep up the mortgage payments when interest rates soared after 1988. All these factors together made homelessness a disturbingly visible – and for the Government politically embarrassing – problem by 1990.

Mrs Thatcher was extraordinarily unsympathetic towards the home-less. In the Commons she regularly listed all the measures the Government was taking to provide alternatives: hostels, bed-and-breakfast accommodation and the like. But she revealed her true feelings in her memoirs. 'Unfortunately there was a persistent tendency in polite circles to consider all the "roofless" as victims of middle class society,' she wrote, 'rather than middle class society as victim of the "roofless".'[52] From her cosy suburban perspective she regarded the young homeless on the streets as social misfits who should go back to their families – ignoring the fact that many had not got families, had been thrown out, abused by their families, or simply (in approved Thatcherite manner) had left homes in areas of high unemployment and moved to London or other big cities looking for work. She lumped them all together as suffering from 'behavioural problems':

> Nor are behavioural problems solved by bricks and mortar. I was not prepared to endorse changes in social security benefits relating to the under-25s which were suggested by Tony Newton and the Social Security Department: I thought it vital that we should not add to the already too evident lure of the big city for young people. We wanted them back with their families, not in London living on benefits.[53]

In 1989, in accordance with this philosophy, John Moore cut the entitlement of sixteen- and seventeen-year-olds to unemployment benefit.

Mrs Thatcher refused to see homelessness as simply a reflection of poverty. Despite evidence from a variety of authoritative reports, she strenuously denied that as the rich got richer the poor were getting poorer. 'Everyone in the nation has benefited from the increased prosperity – everyone,' she insisted in May 1988, invoking the theory popularised by the Reagan administration in the United States that the benefit of tax cuts and other incentives for the rich would 'trickle down' to benefit the entire economy.[54] 'Because the top goes up,' she told Brian Walden the same month, 'we are able to distribute much, much more.'[55] In fact Government figures showed conclusively that 'trickle-down' did not work. While average household incomes rose by 36 per cent in real terms between 1979 and 1992, the income of the top 10 per cent increased by 62 per cent while that of the bottom 10 per cent actually *fell* by 17 per cent. In the same period the proportion of the population living on less than half the national average more than doubled, from 10 to 25 per cent.[56] Other surveys found that the proportion of households officially defined as 'poor' increased between 1983 and 1990 – the Lawson boom years – from 4 to 21 per cent (and that included a quarter of the nation's children).[57]

Nor was poverty merely a matter of income. The 1987 edition of *Social Trends*, published by the Central Statistical Office, reported not only a widening gap between rich and poor but specifically a widening health gap, with the poor showing much greater liability to illness and shorter life expectancy, while a number of poverty-related illnesses like rickets and even consumption, previously eradicated, were making a comeback.[58] The Government's Chief Medical Officer, Sir Donald Acheson, blamed the effect of poor diet and poor housing.[59] Back in 1980 a report on inequalities in health commissioned by the Labour Government from Professor Sir Douglas Black had sounded the same warning: the DHSS, on Mrs Thatcher's instructions, had buried it. Seven years later the position was very much worse. And that was before Norman Fowler's social-security reforms came into effect in April 1988.

Fowler's changes in eligibility for housing benefit, Income Support, Family Credit and the new discretionary Social Fund were designed to help families with young children, the elderly, disabled and other 'deserving' groups at the expense of the 'undeserving' – the young and unemployed. In the Commons Mrs Thatcher asserted that there would be 'five million gainers compared with fewer than one million losers', with another two million unaffected.[60] This was not how it felt on the ground. After some highly publicised cases of pensioners whose housing benefit was cut because they had a bit of money put away, John Moore appeased Tory backbench concern by raising the savings limit at which benefit was lost so as not to penalise thrift. Some poor families unques-tionably did gain. But the reality was that between 60 and 80 per cent of recipients were worse off as a result of the changes: Social Fund payments in particular were not getting through to those who needed them.[61] Moreover, to rub salt in the wound, Lawson's budget the same month took another two pence off the basic rate of income tax and cut the top rate from 60 to 40 per cent; and John Moore froze Child Benefit into the bargain. Never was the Government's double standard so sharply demonstrated.

Mrs Thatcher insisted that social-security spending had grown by 40 per cent since 1979 and now amounted to one-third of total govern-ment spending, £46 billion a year. 'I repeat, £46 billion. Had the right hon. Gentleman's Government paid anything like that, he would have shouted it from the housetops with acclaim.'[62] (The reason, of course, was the high unemployment of the past nine years.) In theory she would have liked to find ways to reduce this burden radically, rather than boast about it. In June 1987 she appointed John Moore, a free-market ideologue with a serious interest in American ideas of welfare reform, to take over the DHSS and encouraged him to believe that she wanted him to think the unthinkable. In practice, however, she did not back him. For example he would have liked to scrap Child Benefit altogether. She agreed – she thought universal benefits, paid to millions of middle-class parents who did not need them, 'absurd' – but she knew the public outcry would be too great; she would agree only to freeze it year by year, thus letting it wither gradually, like the state pension.[63] Even this provoked a substantial rebellion by Tory MPs which cut the Government's majority to forty-seven. Sacred cows could be starved, but they could not be slaughtered.

In fact most of Moore's attention was focused on the health side of his giant department as the Government was drawn – very much against Mrs Thatcher's will – into major reform of the National Health Service. It was already clear during the election that the state of the NHS was at the top of the public's concerns. However strenuously the Prime Minister insisted that the NHS was not merely 'safe' in her hands but was being funded with unprecedented generosity, the public saw only underfunding, deteriorating services and mounting crisis. That autumn the situation deteriorated further, with seemingly daily stories of staff shortages, long waiting lists, bed closures, postponed operations and deaths – all attributed to a deliberate policy of 'Tory cuts'. At first Mrs Thatcher kept on reeling off her statistics, claiming that real spending on the NHS had risen by 30 per cent since 1979, and the share of GNP devoted to health from 4.8 to 5.5 per cent. But increasingly, as the *Annual Register* commented, 'this tactic began to seem arid and repetitious'.[64] Her figures were also misleading: health spending had indeed increased between 1979 and 1983 – reaching 6.7 per cent of GNP that year – but it had fallen over the past four years, while the British Medical Association (BMA) reckoned that the NHS needed to grow by 2 per cent a year just to keep up with the demands of an ageing population and new medical developments. International comparisons showed that Britain's *per capita* spending on health was now the lowest in northern Europe. In December the combined Royal Colleges published a report entitled *Crisis in the NHS*; the *British Medical Journal* declared the service to be 'in terminal decline'; while in the Commons Neil Kinnock told Mrs Thatcher that she was 'making a fool of herself' by continuing to deny what every shade of expert opinion was telling her. 'It is useless,' he quoted the former Chief Medical Officer, Sir George Godber, 'for Ministers to repeat barely relevant multiples of past expenditure, staff employed, or numbers going in and out of hospital . . . What matters is the volume of services not provided or too long delayed.'[65] In the end she had to be seen to respond.

In the short term there was nothing for it but to inject more money.

In the autumn spending round Moore had not merely failed to get more out of the Treasury: he had not even tried, as John Major, the new Chief Secretary, recalled:

> John was a former Treasury minister convinced of the virtues of low spending, and rather quixotically he tried to match his policies to his philosophy. In pursuit of this admirable consistency he bid for too little money in the public expenditure settlement, rather than too much . . . a rare and honest approach that earned him opprobrium.[66]

On top of his quixotic principles, Moore was also seriously ill in the autumn of 1987. In his absence his deputy Tony Newton came to the Commons just before Christmas to admit a shortfall in funding in 1987–8 and announced an extra £100 million to meet the emergency, plus an additional £700 million (soon raised to £1.1 billion) on the estimates for 1988–9.

But more money alone could not be the whole answer – and it was certainly not one that Mrs Thatcher or her Chancellor were prepared to contemplate. Opinion polls indicated public willingness to pay higher taxes to fund the health service, and some – though by no means all – Tory MPs were urging Lawson to put higher NHS spending before further tax cuts in his next budget. But this was contrary to everything she believed in. In her heart she was perfectly clear what she would have liked to do: she would have liked to move away from tax-funded healthcare altogether, as she told Woodrow Wyatt (with wild exaggeration) in November 1987. 'Every family pays £60 a week towards the NHS. If they put that into private health care schemes they would get better service and attention. No waiting for hip operations or all the rest of it.'[67] Back from his sickbed in January 1988, Moore pointed out that France and Germany spent more of their national wealth on private medicine; and suggested that hospitals should do more to generate income for themselves by marketing their services.[68] But in practice she knew that privatisation on any significant scale was out of the question. Public opinion demanded that the NHS must remain essentially taxation-based and free to patients at the point of service. That being so, and the tax base being finite, the only alternative was to look at ways of improving delivery of the service.

For the past three years the free-market boffins in her Policy Unit, led by John Redwood and David Willetts, had been exploring the idea – originally developed by Professor Alain Enthoven of Stanford – of creating an 'internal market' within the NHS: doctors, hospitals and health authorities would buy and sell services to and from each other, thereby introducing an element of commercial discipline within a publicly funded service. The concept had already gathered a degree of cross-party support, ranging from the economist John Vaizey – a former social democrat turned Thatcherite convert who had written a book on healthcare in 1984 – to the SDP leader David Owen – a doctor before he went into politics – who had embraced it in 1985. Up to the end of 1987, however, Mrs Thatcher was not impressed. She did not initially grasp the idea of a purchaser/provider split, and was very reluctant to take on any radical reform at all. How long would it take to introduce such a system, she asked Moore? 'Ten years,' he told her. 'But John,' she replied, 'we have to fight elections!'[69]

When she finally recognised that she must do something her first thought was to ask the CPS (now headed by Willetts) to conduct an inquiry. At the other extreme she considered setting up a Royal Commission. But the first would have seemed too ideological to carry public support, the second too consensual to reach any useful conclusions, besides taking too long. She knew she had to grasp the nettle quickly. So in the end she decided to do the job herself inside Number Ten, with the minimum of outside consultation. Interviewed by David Dimbleby on *Panorama* on 25 January she took her colleagues – and possibly even herself – completely by surprise by announcing, out of the blue, that she was setting up a small internal review to be chaired by herself. She did not dispute Dimbleby's suggestion that the Government had seemed to be 'dithering and uncertain about what to do', but rejected a Royal Commission – 'first, because it would take far too long' and second, because the last Royal Commission on the NHS, appointed by Callaghan in 1976, had come to no useful conclusions at all. 'We shall . . . make our own enquiries, our own consultations,' she declared, 'and then when we are ready we shall come out with our own proposals, just exactly as we have done for other things . . . it will be far quicker than any Royal Commission.'[70] This was a very characteristic piece of late-Thatcher decision-making: cautious, then suddenly impulsive, but keeping control firmly in her own hands.

The membership of the review – it was not a Cabinet committee – comprised the Prime Minister in the chair, with Moore and Newton from the DHSS (later replaced by Kenneth Clarke and David Mellor), Lawson and Major from the Treasury and her health-service adviser Roy Griffiths (seconded from the supermarket Sainsbury's), backed by three civil servants and members of the Policy Unit. Its deliberations reflected the *ad hoc* nature of its birth. Mrs Thatcher wanted to do something but was nervous of everything that was proposed. Seeking to stem the bottomless cost to the Exchequer, Lawson wanted more charges for services within the NHS. Mrs Thatcher was afraid they would be too unpopular, but eventually agreed to charges for eye and dental tests which she had previously ruled out.* Moore proposed to encourage private provision by allowing patients with private insurance to opt out of the system altogether, but that proved impractical – since private hospitals do not provide a comprehensive service – as well as politically perilous. For her part Mrs Thatcher was keen to encourage the growth of private medicine by giving tax relief on private health insurance; but Lawson and later Clarke resisted this, Lawson because he disliked rigging the tax system to influence behaviour by special favours and exemptions, Clarke because he believed in preserving the fundamental principle of the NHS. Both wanted the service to continue to be largely funded by general taxation, though Lawson eventually conceded a measure of tax relief for private insurance for the over-sixties – what Clarke called 'the last vestigial remains of Margaret's original idea'.[72]

At some of these sessions, held at Chequers over the spring and summer, Mrs Thatcher was seen in her worst 'fishwife' mode: demanding, impatient and volatile. Archie Hamilton, her PPS at the time, told Alan Clark that Moore made the mistake of trying to please her:

> During the high months of his status as her chosen successor he framed the Health Service reforms exactly on the basis of what he thought she wanted. But she kept changing her mind. One minute she wanted to go further, the next she got an attack of the doubts, wanted to trim a bit. Each time the unfortunate John agreed, made the adjustments, came back for approval. The result was a total hotchpotch and 'she ended up thinking he was a wanker and got rid of him'.[73]

---

*Once persuaded, she was characteristically adamant. In April she visited the tearoom – now a rare event – to quell an incipient backbench revolt and flatly rejected a compromise proposed by Wakeham and the Chief Whip David Waddington (which many felt Willie Whitelaw would have persuaded her to accept). 'The party was taken right to the brink,' Baker recalled, 'and Margaret was quite prepared to risk humiliation.'[71] When the measure came to a vote at the beginning of November the Government's majority fell to just eight (for opticians) and sixteen (for dentistry), despite heavy whipping and the promise of an extra £2 billion for the NHS in 1989–90 as a sweetener.

In fact Moore had never fully recovered from his pneumonia of the previous autumn: when he returned to work he was visibly struggling to keep on top of the job, and had difficulty making himself heard in the House of Commons. In July 1988, therefore, Mrs Thatcher split the DHSS in two, leaving Moore in charge of Social Security while giving Health to Kenneth Clarke, who already knew the department from his three-year stint as Minister of State under Norman Fowler. On paper at least, this was a serious setback for Thatcherism: in a key area of welfare reform a free-market 'true believer' was replaced by an unreconstructed Heathite with a robust attachment to the NHS. 'John Moore was pursuing a line which Margaret was very keen on, which made everything compulsory private medical insurance,' Clarke told his biographer. 'I was bitterly opposed to that ... The American system is ... the world's worst health service – expensive, inadequate and with a lot of rich doctors.'[74] As so often, Mrs Thatcher had found that right-wingers did not make the most effective ministers. She persuaded herself instead that Clarke, as 'a firm believer in state provision', was therefore 'the best possible advocate of reform'.[75] There was something in this. Clarke's appointment was certainly the best possible answer to the charge that she was bent on privatising the NHS. At the same time, as Simon Jenkins somewhat cynically suggests, the change suited her temperament: 'From being a drag on radicalism, she could now switch roles to one of complaining about the caution of others. For her, this was far happier.'[76]

In fact she had no need to complain of Clarke's caution. He was determined to introduce real reform within the tax-based system and did not shrink from language that rang alarm bells among defenders of the status quo. Soon after taking office he criticised the quality of management in the NHS and promised that the ministerial review would recommend 'fairly drastic steps' to transform a 'ramshackle bureaucracy into a well-run business' – though he hastened to add that it would be 'a business not of a commercial kind but a business delivering patient care and treatment'.[77] Paradoxically Clarke was more radical than Mrs Thatcher. It was Clarke, with useful support from John Major, who persuaded a still-doubtful Prime Minister that the internal market was the only way to go. At the same time Virginia Bottomley – one of his Ministers of State and later Health Secretary herself – believed that 'Ken Clarke deserves the credit for saving the NHS.'[78]

The policy as it finally emerged in Clarke's White Paper, *Working for Patients*, published in January 1989, had two main features. On the one hand, hospitals were given the power to choose to become self-governing 'NHS Trusts' within the health service, funded by the taxpayer but in control of their own budgets, independent of the Regional Health Authority. On the other, doctors were encouraged to become 'GP fundholders', managing their own budgets to buy the most appropriate services for their patients: instead of sending them automatically to the local hospital, they should be able to shop around to find the best – or best-value – provider. Money would thus follow the patient, and the most efficient hospitals (those that actually knew what operations cost, for a start) would secure the biggest funding. Like all reforms of the NHS since its inception, Clarke's plans aroused furious opposition from the doctors. The BMA launched an aggressive poster campaign in defence of the status quo, asserting that the NHS was 'underfunded, undermined and under threat'. 'They are the most unscrupulous trade union I have ever dealt with,' Clarke recalled, 'and I've dealt with every trade union across the board.'[79] At the same time they rejected Clarke's proposed new GP contracts, claiming they were 'Stalinist'.[80] Clarke imposed them anyway, beginning in April 1990, and the opposition eventually crumbled.

Clarke's determination contrasted with Mrs Thatcher's persisting nervousness. She still felt bound to keep on denying Labour allegations that the service, if not being privatised immediately, was being softened up for privatisation. 'How can something be privatised if there is nothing being charged?' she asked Woodrow Wyatt in exasperation.[81] But the public did not believe her. A poll commissioned by the BMA in March 1990 found that 73 per cent still thought that the NHS was not 'safe' in Tory hands. She had an 'enormous wobble' (David Willetts' description) at the last minute when she actually tried to stop the reforms in their tracks, advised by some of her private 'voices' like David Wolfson (no longer in Number Ten), Derek Rayner (her former efficiency adviser) and Robin Ibbs (his successor) that they would not work. It was even said that Charles Haughey, of all people, had warned her never to tangle with the doctors before an election.[82] Clarke stood firm, insisting with the support of his new NHS Chief Executive, Duncan Nichol, that the reforms must be enacted before the next election precisely to demonstrate the Government's commitment to the NHS. In the presence of several witnesses she told him petulantly 'It is *you* I'm holding responsible if *my* NHS reforms don't work.'[83]

He did agree to slow down the introduction of hospital trusts, backtracking to allow a number of trials first. But in fact most hospitals did opt to become trusts – fifty-seven came into operation in April 1991 and almost all had followed suit by 1994. The spread of GP fundholding, by contrast, was slow, patchy and unpopular. The more idealistic doctors objected to being asked to run their practices as businesses, while it was widely alleged that preference was given to the patients of fundholders over non-fundholders, creating a two-tier system with more resources going to wealthier practices than to the poorer. In fact the system gradually settled down and was working quite well when it was abolished by Labour after 1997 and replaced by a not-so-very-different system of Primary Care Groups.

The NHS reforms, ironically, were one of Mrs Thatcher's most successful achievements, securing, in Simon Jenkins' words, 'a real change in the management of the NHS without undermining its principle'.[84] Treatment was still delivered free to all patients at the point of service and was overwhelmingly funded out of general taxation. By the mid-1990s the NHS was treating more patients, more efficiently than in the 1980s, and the creaking old service was enabled to stagger on for another decade. Of course the new NHS trusts were not really self-governing, but firmly under Treasury control – in this sense Clarke could be said to have completed the nationalisation of the hospitals which Bevan in 1948 had only begun – but the system was arguably better managed and more accountable than before. Critics maintain, on the contrary, that the requirements of the internal market – with doctors, hospitals and regional health authorities competing to buy and sell services to one another – choked the service with a lot of wasteful duplication and additional bureaucracy. David Owen, one of the original champions of the internal market, blames Mrs Thatcher for spoiling a good idea by her obsession with private medicine, which drained public confidence and resources from the NHS.[85] Over her decade in office private health insurance doubled to 11 per cent of health spending, and it went on growing after she left, reaching 19 per cent in 1993. Around the end of the century the service hit another spending crisis and the same old arguments returned with renewed urgency; by 2002 it was becoming more and more difficult for Gordon Brown – inheriting the mantle of Lawson and Clarke – to maintain that the nation's healthcare could be funded for much longer on general taxation. The alternative of compulsory private insurance, which Mrs Thatcher had not dared or been strong enough to push through in 1989, was now firmly back on the agenda.

One other major headache for successive Health ministers was the proposed reform of the care of mental illness embodied in Roy Griffiths' 1988 report *Community Care*. The laudable idea was finally to close down the old Victorian insane asylums and treat mental patients wherever possible in their own homes. This was a rare instance in the Thatcher years of giving more responsibility to local authorities; but it was going to be very expensive, requiring comprehensive co-operation between doctors, social workers, district nurses, housing officers and the like if patients were not to fall through the net and end up on the streets – which is what actually happened in the 1990s. Both Moore and Clarke were reluctant to go ahead, but Nicholas Ridley at the Department of the Environment was surprisingly in favour and Mrs Thatcher, to the amazement of her staff, agreed. She knew all about the old asylums, since she had one of the worst at Friern Barnet in her constituency. In July 1990, however, at the height of the poll-tax controversy, Clarke postponed implementation of the project in order to save piling additional costs onto local government which would result in even higher poll-tax bills. Care in the Community, as the policy was called, was eventually implemented in 1993, but without the necessary resources to allow it to work properly – with shameful and tragic results.

The final verdict on Social Thatcherism is a mixed one. Nicholas Timmins, the 'biographer' of the welfare state, concludes that despite her instincts Mrs Thatcher actually strengthened the welfare state – at least the NHS, education and those parts of the social services used by the middle class, making them more efficient in order to keep her key constituency happy. She might have wished that 'her' voters did not look to the state for their health and education – and mortgage tax relief – but the fact was that they did: opinion surveys consistently showed that the public remained as firmly wedded to the basic principles of the welfare state as ever.[86] As a result services were trimmed at the edges by charging for things like eye tests and school meals which had previously been free, and greatly increasing the cost of prescriptions, but the central pillars remained untouched. The main exceptions were those services principally relied on by the poor: public-sector housing and the basic state pension, whose value was allowed to wither away, and other forms of income support. Poverty visibly increased as a substantial 'underclass' was cut off from the rising prosperity of the majority. But in the big picture the scale of social provision was undiminished over the Thatcher years: it still took around 25 per cent of GDP at the end as it had at the beginning. 'The welfare state remained remarkably un-rolled back thirteen years after Margaret Thatcher took power . . . The stark change . . . was the growth in economic inequality.'[87]

The poll tax

Meanwhile the poll tax, launched with great *éclat* as the 'flagship' of the Government's programme for the third term, was facing an increasingly difficult passage through Parliament and was building into a major political disaster. Back in 1985 Mrs Thatcher had been slow to be convinced that it was practicable. Once sold on it, however, she set her face against the swelling chorus of opposition and determined to stake her own position and the electoral prospects of the Tory party on forcing it through. Although by 1989 only Nicholas Ridley among her Cabinet colleagues still fully shared her commitment to it – others who had been involved at its inception, like Kenneth Baker and George Younger, increasingly distanced themselves from the way Ridley had bungled its introduction – she elevated support of it into a test of loyalty to herself, with ultimately fatal results. In particular she insisted on calling it the 'community charge'. 'Like every other minister,' John Major recalled, 'I had to make a conscious effort to avoid infuriating Margaret by referring to it as the "Poll Tax". I didn't always succeed.'[88]

Already within weeks of the election the first whispers of revolt were stirring within the party. Sir George Young – a somewhat eccentric Old Etonian known to the press as 'the bicycling baronet', but more to the point a junior Environment minister for five years from 1981 with some right to feel aggrieved at being dropped from the Government in 1986 – emerged as a leading dissenter on grounds of equity, pointing out that his personal liability would fall from £2,000 to around £300 a year while others, much poorer, would pay more. In the Commons Mrs Thatcher agreed that some people would gain under the new system, but insisted that the losers would be those unlucky or foolish enough to live in high-spending boroughs:

> If people pay a high community charge it will be because they have grossly extravagant local authorities which are frequently taking time to get expenditure down.[89]

It was up to the electors in those authorities to vote for lower spending. Was it not unfair, she was asked on television, that the charge would be higher in deprived Greenwich than in affluent Buckinghamshire? No, she replied, because the rates were unfair already, 'and there are going to be fewer unfairnesses in the community charge':

> The whole thing is being geared so that if you get the same level of services at the same level of efficiency in different places you will get the same level of community charge. If you are not getting the same level, either you are getting more services or extravagant services or inefficient services, so you will have a much better monitor.

Moreover, she claimed, the principle that every local resident should pay the same community charge, regardless of income, was *not* regressive, since the charge still covered only 25 per cent of local-authority expenditure (less in Scotland): the rest was met by central government out of general taxation, so higher-level taxpayers would still pay more.[90]

At this stage, however, she still envisaged phasing the charge in gradually. 'Where you are making a major change it is best to do it in easy stages by a transition period, and that is what we are doing.'[91] Baker had planned to run the new system in gradually over several years. But then for the second time on this issue the Government let itself be bounced by the unrepresentative enthusiasm of the party faithful. Just as Whitelaw and Younger had overreacted to Scottish fury about rates revaluation in 1985, so Ridley and Mrs Thatcher were impressed by speaker after speaker at the Blackpool conference in October 1987 calling for the hated rates to be scrapped without delay. 'We shall have to look at this again, Nick,' she whispered to him on the platform.[92] A few weeks later Ridley announced that 'dual running' would be abandoned and the community charge introduced all at once in April 1990. In her memoirs Lady Thatcher confessed that this 'may have been a mistake'.[93]

When the Bill came up for its Second Reading in December, Tory apprehension was most powerfully voiced by Michael Heseltine, who recalled his search for a workable alternative to the rates between 1979 and 1982 and predicted that the poll tax – he did not bother to call it the community charge – would be massively unpopular. 'Responsibility for the rates,' he warned, 'is confused in the legacy of history. Responsibility for the poll tax will be targeted precisely and unavoidably at the Government who introduced that tax. That tax will be known as the Tory tax.'[94] Seventeen Tories, including George Young, Ted Heath and Ian Gilmour, voted against and another fifteen, including Heseltine, abstained; but the Government still had a comfortable majority of seventy-two. The whips packed the standing committee to ensure that the Bill faced no serious challenge there. But by the time it returned to the floor of the House for the Report Stage in April, dissent had solidified around a proposal, moved by Michael Mates – a close associate of Heseltine – to grade the charge into three bands according to income. This was actually in line with Mrs Thatcher's 1974 promise to replace the rates by 'taxes more broadly-based and related to people's ability to pay'.[95] Now, however, she declared that 'a banded community charge would just be income tax by another name. It would be yet another burden on income tax payers and . . . it would be immensely complicated, with marginal relief of all kinds.'[96] Mates' amendment, she wrote in her memoirs, 'would have defeated the whole purpose of the flat-rate charge'.[97] On this at least Lawson supported her since, as David Butler and his co-authors wrote in their history of the whole debacle: 'However much the Treasury hated the poll tax, it hated a surrogate income tax far more.'[98]

In fact the poll tax was not really a flat-rate charge: it did allow means-testing at the bottom of the scale. The Government was never given credit for the fact that around seven million poorer people – later increased to nine million, or one in four of the total number of charge payers – were eligible for rebates of up to 80 per cent of their liability; while those on Income Support had even the remaining 20 per cent taken into account in calculating their benefit. So the very poorest were not greatly affected, though households on low wages certainly were. But these substantial rebates compromised the initial simplicity of the idea, while increasing the burden on those who were liable for the full whack, who still numbered twenty-five million compared with just nineteen million who paid rates. These were the real losers – like the lollipop lady in Leyton faced with an additional bill of £1,138. When this case was quoted at her in the Commons, however, Mrs Thatcher merely replied that she must have 'a very extravagant local authority'.[99] 'What you vote for, you pay for,' she told her restless backbenchers the following year.[100] 'The community charge is a way of asking people to pay for what they vote for, and when they do they will vote against Labour authorities.'[101] The problem was how they were to pay the bill in the meantime.

She had no thought of buying off the rebels. 'If you look through the list,' she told Wyatt, 'they are all the embittered, the discontented or disappointed people.' (She was right. Twelve were ex-ministers whom she had dropped and seventeen backbenchers of more than ten years' standing whom she had never promoted.) What was worrying, she conceded, was that 'they seem to be getting almost into a group now . . . They are now a gang.'[102] For some days before the crucial vote there was speculation that the Government might actually be defeated. But Ridley agreed to widen the net of those eligible for rebates; and strong whipping did the rest. Thirty-eight malcontents voted against the Government (including Heseltine, John Biffen and Jonathan Aitken); but it still gained a majority of twenty-five. 'Rather good in the circumstances,' she thought.[103] On Third Reading a month later the number of outright rebels had fallen back to seventeen with ten abstainers, giving a comfortable majority of sixty-three.

Defeat was more likely in the Lords, where an amendment similar to Mates' was moved by Lord Chelwood, formerly Sir Tufton Beamish, a caricature old buffer who had given his name to *Private Eye*'s archetypal knight of the shire, Sir Tufton Bufton. He was an unlikely rebel whose emergence at the head of the anti-poll-tax peers epitomised the clash between new Thatcherite and old paternalist Toryism. Constitutional theorists debated whether the Lords were entitled to reject the Bill altogether, on the pretext that it was not a 'money bill' but a local-government measure (an argument lent some credence by the fact that Lawson had declined to sponsor it). Lord Hailsham helpfully weighed in to refute this argument, and Willie Whitelaw also reappeared to beg their Lordships not to provoke a crisis which might threaten their own existence. The Government Chief Whip, Bertie Denham, exerted unprecedented pressure to bring in hereditary peers not normally seen in the House. ('Never seen so many people,' Wyatt noted. 'When I saw Henry Bath [the eighty-three-year-old Marquess] I realised how intense the whipping had been.'[104] Sheer numbers duly carried the day and the Second Reading was carried by 317 to 183 – the biggest turn-out since the days of Lloyd George's 'People's Budget' and the 1913 Home Rule Bill. Mrs Thatcher later claimed to have won the argument in the Lords, since a majority of cross-bench peers – forty-three out of seventy-five – had supported the Government.[105] If so, the whipping in of backwoodsmen was unnecessary overkill which only contributed to the impression that the poll tax was being forced through in defiance of democracy and common sense.

The Lords did pass a number of amendments extending relief to the disabled, student nurses and other groups, but backed down when Ridley rejected them. The Bill finally received the Royal Assent in July 1988. The average charge was now expected to be about £200 per head. A year later that estimate had risen to £278; by January 1990 it was £340, with many councils anticipating even higher levels. In her memoirs Lady Thatcher blamed 'the perversity, incompetence and often straightforward malice of many local councils' for seizing the chance to push up spending and let the Government take the blame. But this was precisely what Lawson and Heseltine had predicted they would do. Lawson argues that they should have capped spending first; and in retrospect she agreed.[106] But that would have contradicted accountability, which was supposed to be the whole point. Mrs Thatcher still saw the charge as a stick with which to beat Labour. 'We understand why Labour does not like it,' she charged in July 1989:

> It will show up the extravagance of Labour councils with their ratepayers' money, and the economy of Conservative councils which look after the money raised from community charge payers.[107]

Instead, opposition continued to build right across the political spectrum. In April 1989 the charge came into force in Scotland, a year ahead of England and Wales, amid widespread refusal to pay, orchestrated by the Scottish National Party and supported by some left-wing Labour MPs. The Labour leadership, while opposing the tax, was careful to avoid the illegality of being seen to advocate non-payment. But by September between 15 and 20 per cent of those registered had not paid; while a significant number simply did not register. This Scottish resistance fuelled alarm among Tory MPs in England, prompting a series of ever more desperate efforts to cushion the impact by offering transitional relief over the first few years – in effect a return to dual running. But Ridley's first proposal by which low-charging councils would have subsidised high-charging ones only infuriated Tory councillors who felt they were being penalised for their thrift.

In July 1989, realising that Ridley was a public-relations disaster in this area, Mrs Thatcher replaced him with the much more voter-friendly Chris Patten, who warned her that the flagship was threatening to sink the whole fleet but nevertheless took on the job of trying to save a policy he did not believe in. At first she was 'quite adamant that she was not going to have the Treasury dish out all this money' to ease the transition.[108] But in October Patten did squeeze substantial additional funding out of Lawson to head off the latest revolt led by Rhodes Boyson – another ex-minister – who had warned that the poll tax as it stood was electoral suicide. In theory, Patten now claimed, no one should be more than £3 a week worse off. But that calculation was based on an average bill of £278, which was already out of date. When Labour members pointed out that even Mrs Thatcher's own Barnet council was preparing to set a charge well above the Government's guideline, she was reduced to retorting that the charge in neighbouring Labour boroughs was even higher.[109]

In February 1990 Tory councillors in Oxfordshire and Yorkshire resigned from the party rather than be responsible for introducing the tax. In March there were disturbances in Manchester, Bristol, Birmingham, Hackney, Lambeth, Swindon and even true-blue Maidenhead. The Government's popularity, which had held up well for two years, went into free fall and on 22 March it suffered a crushing defeat in a by-election in Mid-Staffordshire, where a majority of nearly 14,000 was overthrown on a 22 per cent swing. The next day *The Times* bluntly called the charge 'inane';[110] the *Sunday Times* dubbed it 'iniquitous'.[111] The climax came a week later with a huge demonstration in Trafalgar Square which turned into the worst riot seen in the capital for decades. Cars were overturned and set on fire, shop windows smashed, arson and looting were rife and some 450 people were injured, mainly police. Mrs Thatcher expressed her 'absolute horror' at the violence and tried unsuccessfully to pin the blame on Labour:

> Where the hard left campaigns of lawbreaking are organised by Labour Party members, and publicly defended by Labour MPs, no weasel words from the Leader of the Opposition can alter the plain fact that they are inescapably Labour's responsibility.[112]

When she came to write her memoirs Lady Thatcher was still angry at the rioters' ingratitude:

> I was appalled at such wickedness . . . A whole class of people – an 'underclass' if you will – had been dragged back into the ranks of responsible society and asked to become not just dependants but citizens; their response was to riot.[113]

She really believed that she was doing community-charge payers a favour. By focusing on the violent minority, however, she missed the point: though the far left as usual hijacked a peaceful demonstration to their own pseudo-revolutionary ends, the poll-tax disturbances up and down the country were predominantly a middle-class revolt. A few pages earlier, in fact, she recognised this truth. 'I was deeply worried,' she wrote apropos the Mid-Staffordshire result. 'What hurt me was that the very people who had always looked to me for protection from exploitation by the socialist state were those who were suffering most.'[114] Alan Clark nailed the essential flaw in his diary for 25 March. 'No one will pay,' he wrote:

> By no one I mean all the slobs, yobs, drifters, junkies, freeloaders, claimants, and criminals on day-release who make their living by exploitation of the benefit system and overload local authority expenditure. As usual the burden will fall on the thrifty, the prudent, the responsible, those of 'fixed address' who patiently support society and the follies of the chattering class.[115]

In other words the charge missed those it was intended to hit and punished those it was designed to protect: in Chris Patten's words, it was 'targeted like an Exocet missile' on the middle class in marginal constituencies.[116] Butler, Adonis and Travers reckon that something like twenty-seven million people were worse off – some households by as much as £1,500 – compared with perhaps eight million who gained.* It was not surprising that Tory MPs began to fear for their seats.

The poll tax was finally introduced in England and Wales on 1 April 1990 at an average of £363 per head. Some councils were soon reporting levels of non-payment as high as 50 per cent. Mrs Thatcher set up a Cabinet committee, chaired by herself, to consider further measures of relief, but she still refused to consider any serious retreat from the basic principle. 'We're not changing it,' she told Woodrow Wyatt. 'We're adjusting it.'[118] She still blamed irresponsible councils which set their charge too high: she now wanted much more widespread capping, to keep the average below £400. But Patten refused to go down this road: he announced the capping of no more than twenty high-spending councils (eighteen of them Labour-controlled) and even this was challenged in the courts. The only alternative was to keep on dishing out money from the Treasury to try to reduce the impact in the second year, which was likely to be election year. In July Patten secured from John Major – the new Chancellor, following Lawson's resignation the previous October – a further £3.2 billion to extend transitional relief to another four million people (making eleven million in all). This was a grotesque inversion of Thatcherite economics. By now the charge had become a fiasco from which the only escape seemed to be through ditching the Prime Minister herself.

Nothing did more than the poll tax to precipitate Mrs Thatcher's downfall. It seemed to epitomise the least attractive aspects of her political personality – a hard-faced inegalitarianism combined with a pig-headed authoritarianism – and at the same time demonstrated a fatal loss of political judgement. The last was the most surprising. Despite her cultivated image of bold radicalism and unbending resolution, she had actually shown herself, in office and before that in opposition, a very shrewd and cautious politician who had always taken care not to get too far ahead of public opinion. The poll tax was the one issue on which her normally sensitive political antennae really let her down. It was not that the warning signs were not there from the beginning; but she failed to read them, perversely and uncharacteristically nailing her authority to a scheme that had few friends, even among her keenest supporters, and invited huge unpopularity for no commensurate gain.

---

*Andrew Neil, then editor of the *Sunday Times*, claims that his opposition to the poll tax crystallised when he learned that his cleaner would be paying more poll tax than he himself, at a time when his top rate of income tax had just been cut from 60 to 40 per cent.[117]

'THE WOMAN AT NO. 10'

17. Mrs Thatcher curtseys to the Queen as she arrives for a dinner to celebrate the 250th anniversary of the Prime Minister's office, December 1985.

18. Pausing on the main staircase in front of photographs of her predecessors.

19. Working on her boxes in the upstairs flat.

THE PRIME MINISTER ABROAD
20. Dancing with Zambian President Kenneth Kaunda at the Commonwealth Conference, Lusaka, August 1979. 21. Attending a Russian Orthodox service at Zagorsk, near Moscow, March 1987. 22. Visiting Saudi Arabia, with Crown Prince Fahd, September 1981. (Douglas Hurd and Denis walk behind.)

SPECIAL RELATIONSHIPS
23. Mrs Thatcher's farewell visit to Washington near the end of Ronald Reagan's presidency, November 1988.

24. With Mikhail Gorbachev in Moscow, March 1987.

ANTAGONISTS IN EUROPE
25. Jacques Delors addresses the TUC
Conference, September 1988.
26. Mrs Thatcher with Helmut Kohl
(*centre*) and François Mitterrand at the
Fontainebleau European Council,
June 1984.

THE ROUGH AND THE SMOOTH
27. Bernard Ingham beside Mrs Thatcher at a
press conference, March 1986.
28. Charles Powell two paces behind at the
Toronto G7 summit, June 1988.

29. 'We are a grandmother': Mrs Thatcher displays her two-month-old grandson
outside 10 Downing Street, May 1989.
30. Celebrating becoming the longest-serving Prime Minister of the century on 3 January 1988.
31. Walking with Denis in the grounds of Chequers.

32, 33. 'The sheep that turned'. Television pictures of Geoffrey Howe making his resignation speech in the House of Commons (*above*) and Mrs Thatcher listening to it (*below*), flanked by John Major (*left*) and Kenneth Baker, 13 November 1990.

34. Mrs Thatcher's farewell speech on leaving Downing Street, with Denis and Mark looking on, 28 November 1990.

35. Baroness Thatcher in the House of Lords before the State Opening of Parliament, June 2001.

In her memoirs she still insists that the community charge was right in principle and would have been accepted in time, had it not been sabotaged by the very left-wing councils it was intended to curb. Maybe the principle of a small fixed charge for council services, payable equally by all, was defensible, on the analogy of the BBC licence fee – though Mrs Thatcher bitterly disliked the licence fee – but it would only be tolerable if it really was small. Since the starting point was that rates were too high, as well as unfairly apportioned, it was always likely that the community charge would be high too. Moreover it was always going to be highest in the poorest areas with the most expensive social problems. As a simple matter of arithmetic, there were bound to be more losers than gainers, which made it bad politics, even if it had been good economics; and the losers were precisely the lower- and middle-income middle class who were her natural constituency. Above all it was simply impractical. As a young frontbencher attacking the Wilson Government's abortive Land Commission back in 1965, Margaret Thatcher had enunciated the admirable principle that 'a tax should be certain in its incidence, cheap to collect and simple'.[119] She should have recalled her own advice twenty years later; for the poll tax was neither certain nor simple, and least of all cheap. It was more expensive to collect, and with all the cost of rebates and transitional subsidies it cost the taxpayer in the end something over £20 billion to set it up and then abolish it.[120] Not for nothing did Butler and his co-chroniclers of the saga call their book *Failure in British Government*. The poll tax was the most spectacular failure of Mrs Thatcher's premiership and it cost her her job.

Permanent revolution

As if it had not already got enough on its plate with the reform of education, the health service and the poll tax, the third Thatcher Government was also hyperactive on practically every other front of domestic politics. As is the way with Governments when things start to go wrong, however, practically all of these restless interventions ran into difficulties of one sort or another until, as Noël Annan wrote, 'Suddenly the shore appeared littered with broken-backed Conservative reforms.'[121]

Privatisation had been the unexpected triumph of the second term. But the attempt to maintain momentum after 1987 led the Government into more problematic territory. British Steel, sold back to the private sector in December 1988, was the last relatively straightforward operation. At least Mrs Thatcher had the political sense not to rush into privatising the railways: she left that poisoned chalice to her successor.

But she was committed to privatising water and electricity, both of which raised sensitivities which had not applied to telephones or gas.

Water was a particularly emotive issue – rather as she had found milk to be when she was Education Secretary. The public had a strong instinctive feeling that water, unlike gas and electricity, was a precious natural resource, a God-given necessity of life like air itself, which should not be owned or even distributed for profit but held by the Government in trust for everyone. Most of this was irrational: water supply was a customer service like any other, and one crying out for new investment to replace antiquated pipework, sewage treatment plants and the like: it made sense to seek this from the private sector. It was not widely realised that a quarter of the industry was privately owned already; or that, as Mrs Thatcher never tired of pointing out, water was privately run in many other countries: 'Even Socialist France knows that privatised water is a better deal than nationalised water.'[122] Nevertheless there persisted a deeply held belief that private companies were not to be trusted with public health. There were also concerns about continued access to rivers and reservoirs for leisure use: millions of anglers feared being barred from private property.

The solution, as Ridley realised as soon as he took over the Environment job from Kenneth Baker in 1986, was not simply to sell off the nine existing Water Authorities as Baker had been planning, but to separate the commercial business of supplying water from the environmental responsibility for monitoring purity and pollution. It was not until November 1988, however, that Ridley was ready to bring forward his Bill to sell shares in ten new regional water companies while creating a National Rivers Authority to act as environmental watchdog. Mrs Thatcher was enthusiastic. 'It's going to be a great thing,' she told Wyatt. 'It's going to do a great deal of good for the environment, improving the quality of it.'[123] But once again Ridley's disdainful manner was a liability when it came to selling an unpopular policy (and Michael Howard, his Minister of State, was not much better). Public opinion remained resolutely hostile, and in March 1989 Mrs Thatcher admitted that 'the subject of privatisation of water has not . . . been handled well or accurately'.[124] Privately she was 'very worried about the bad presentation' which was rapidly turning water into another poll tax.[125] One of the first acts of Ridley's successor, Chris Patten, on taking over as Environment Secretary in July was to write off the industry's debts to the tune of £4.4 billion and promise another £1.1 billion of public money – described as a 'green dowry' – to tempt investors to risk their money. With this inducement the sale went ahead successfully in December 1989, with a second instalment the following

July. Over the next ten years, when steeply increased charges failed to prevent hosepipe bans in summer and flooding in winter, the water companies were regularly criticised for putting profits before investment. But the fact was that much higher investment went into the water industry after privatisation than before; while fears about public health largely melted away.

Electricity posed different problems. The minister responsible in this case was the newly rehabilitated Cecil Parkinson, who was keen to demonstrate that his Thatcherite credentials were unimpaired, even if he was no longer a contender for the succession.* As with gas, the privatisation of electricity was strongly opposed from within the industry by the powerful chairman of the Central Electricity Generating Board, Lord Marshall, who was determined both to prevent the break-up of the CEGB and to keep nuclear energy under its control. Mrs Thatcher was torn between her desire (strongly supported by Lawson) to inject some real competition into this privatisation – as Peter Walker had failed to do with gas – and her 'undying gratitude' to Marshall for keeping the power stations running during the 1984–5 coal strike. 'She had made him a peer,' Parkinson recalled, 'and always referred to him, almost reverentially, as "dear Walter".'[127] Lawson wanted to split the CEGB into four or five competing companies. But Parkinson devised a compromise involving just two new companies, PowerGen and National Power, the larger of which (the latter) would keep control of nuclear power. Marshall reluctantly accepted this.

The problem was that when subjected for the first time to proper commercial analysis, the cost of nuclear power turned out to be prohibitive: the private sector would not take it on without open-ended guarantees which the Government could not give. First Parkinson had to remove the cost of decommissioning the nine oldest Magnox power stations from the package; then John Wakeham, who succeeded him in July 1989, was forced to exclude nuclear power from the scheme altogether and postpone the planned flotation of the twelve new distribution boards from the spring to the autumn of 1990. This was a huge embarrassment, particularly in view of Mrs Thatcher's personal commitment to nuclear power. Ever since her brief stint as shadow Energy Minister in 1967 she had always seen nuclear power as the

---

*Parkinson also won rapturous applause at the 1988 Tory Party Conference by promising that coal – 'the ultimate privatisation' – would be next.[126] But Mrs Thatcher was constrained by her sense of obligation to the breakaway Union of Democratic Miners which had helped beat the 1984–5 strike by defying Scargill's pickets; and coal was not privatised in her time.

clean, modern energy source of the future. Now concern over global warming caused by the burning of fossil fuels reinforced her view. She still maintained that nuclear power would be cheaper in the long run; but in the short run the Government could only argue that at least privatisation had revealed the true cost of nuclear power which public ownership had kept hidden. The sale of the two new generating companies, twelve regional distribution companies and the National Grid eventually went ahead in 1991. The nuclear industry was finally privatised in 1996.

If privatisation was one Thatcherite policy which was running into rougher water the longer it went on, the reverse was true of trade-union legislation. The incremental approach initiated by Jim Prior in 1980 and followed up by Norman Tebbit in 1982 and Tom King in 1984 had already eroded the unions' will to resist, even before the defeat of the miners and the Wapping printers signalled the final humbling of old-style union power. Now Norman Fowler, in 1988, followed by Mrs Thatcher's sixth and last Employment Secretary, Michael Howard, in 1990, tied up some loose ends. Fowler's Act reinforced the requirement to hold strike ballots, strengthened the rights of individual members against their union, and banned the misuse of union funds; Howard's finally outlawed the closed shop and ended the unions' legal immunity from civil damages. The fact that these Bills were passed with scarcely a murmur of protest was a measure of how thoroughly the union behemoth had been cowed since 1979. The unions were actually beginning to recover some sparks of renewed confidence in the summer of 1989 with successful strikes by local-government workers and the railwaymen. The brute fact remained that trade-union membership had fallen from twelve million in 1979 to just 8.7 million ten years later.

The unions' loss of muscle was further dramatised in 1989 by the inability of the dockers to prevent Fowler's abolition of the infamous dock labour scheme, conceded at its moment of greatest weakness by the Heath Government in 1972, which effectively guaranteed registered dockers a job for life. During the 1980s employers had successfully bypassed the scheme by switching their traffic to the new container ports like Felixstowe, where it did not operate. Long before 1989 it was an anachronism waiting to be abolished. Nicholas Ridley had wanted to abolish it in 1985, but in the wake of the miners' strike Mrs Thatcher did not wish to invite another long industrial struggle. She was still cautious when Fowler, strongly supported by Lawson, wanted to take it up again after June 1987. 'It's all right for you to write articles about it,' she told Woodrow Wyatt in December 1988. 'But we can't do it in this session, with electricity and water.' Wyatt suspected that she was 'running away' from the issue.[128] She finally agreed in April 1989, as a means of regaining the initiative when the Government seemed to be losing its way, but only after seeking assurances from Lawson that sterling could stand a long strike, and even then insisted on more generous compensation than either Fowler or Lawson thought necessary. As late as this she was still anxious to avoid giving the unions a platform to mount what might prove a popular stand.

One important area of national life which Mrs Thatcher was still determined to sort out was television. She had already gone some way towards bringing the BBC to heel by her appointment of more inter-ventionist chairmen and governors; but she had been thwarted in her wish to replace the licence fee with advertising. Now she wanted to put the whole television industry onto a more commercial basis by breaking up what free marketeers regarded as the cosy BBC/ITV duopoly. Soon after the 1987 election she summoned senior figures in both the BBC and the ITV companies to a seminar in Downing Street. Though the occasion was officially described as a 'consultation', the Prime Minister did all the talking, warning them that their industry was 'the last bastion of restrictive practices'. She was determined to intro-duce more competition – 'I don't want the big boys threatening the little boys' – but at the same time intended to clean up the content. 'I am a regulator,' she told them. 'It is the Government's duty to restrict too much violence and pornography. We must get the framework right.'[129]

Her resolve was stiffened by more spats with the broadcasters over their handling of what she regarded as security issues. In March 1988 she was outraged when the BBC and ITN refused to hand over to the police news film of the brutal killing of two British soldiers in Belfast, arguing that to do so would put their own crews at risk and make the coverage of events in Northern Ireland impossible in future. In the Commons Mrs Thatcher dismissed such pleas out of hand. 'Either one is on the side of justice in these matters or one is on the side of terrorism.'[130] The next day RUC officers visited BBC and ITN offices and threatened senior executives with arrest unless they surren-dered the film. They reluctantly complied.

Much more serious was the row over Thames Television's investi-gation of the shooting dead of three IRA terrorists by the SAS in Gibraltar the same month. If hitherto her anger had been largely directed at the BBC, this episode thrust the independent companies too into the firing line. The issue was the broadcasters' right to inves-tigate security matters that the Government did not want investigated. There is no dispute that the three terrorists – two men and a woman

– had been planning to plant a bomb intended to kill British soldiers at a military ceremony. In a highly successful operation the security services had been tracking their movements across France and Spain for some weeks. But Geoffrey Howe told the Commons that the three were shot, rather than arrested, because they had appeared to be reaching for weapons. It turned out, however, that they were unarmed, lending support to the suspicion already current in Northern Ireland that the security forces were operating an unacknowledged 'shoot to kill' policy – or as Enoch Powell (no friend of terrorists) alleged, a policy of 'deliberate, cold-blooded pre-meditated murder'.[131] The Thames programme, *Death on the Rock*, found eye-witnesses to challenge the Government's account, asserting that two of the suspects had been shot with their hands up and the third finished off at point-blank range on the ground. Howe put heavy pressure on the chairman of the Independent Broadcasting Authority, the former Labour Cabinet minister George Thomson, to drop the programme, on the ground that it would prejudice the inquest still to be held in Gibraltar. But Thomson and his colleagues refused to be browbeaten and the programme was broadcast on 28 April.

Mrs Thatcher – loudly backed by many of her backbenchers – was once again apoplectic at the broadcasters daring to criticise the security forces, who should rather be congratulated on a job well done. 'It's not a question of being furious,' she said the next day. 'It's much deeper than that. The freedom of people depends on the rule of law ... If you ever get trial by television ... that day freedom dies.'[132] But here she was on weak ground. There was no pending trial to be prejudiced; the events were not *sub judice* and the programme, as Lord Thomson insisted, was merely 'normal current affairs journalism'.[133] 'So far as the Gibraltar episode is concerned,' Auberon Waugh pointed out in the *Spectator*, 'it would appear that the offending media are far more concerned to uphold the rule of law than is the Government.'[134] In the end an inquiry headed by the former Northern Ireland minister, Lord Windlesham, gave some comfort to the Government by concluding that *Death on the Rock* was in some respects inaccurate. Nevertheless he cleared the programme of deliberate bias and ruled that the company was perfectly entitled both to make it and to show it. There were legitimate questions to be asked about the truth of the Government's account and the legality of the whole operation, and it was the job of a free media to ask them. By contrast, as Peregrine Worsthorne wrote in the *Sunday Telegraph*, 'Mrs Thatcher's Government certainly did mount a patently false campaign of disinformation aimed at stifling criticism.'[135]

Later that year Douglas Hurd took censorship a stage further by announcing that Sinn Fein – a legal political party, with elected councillors in Northern Ireland and one Westminster MP (Gerry Adams, though he refused to take his seat) – would be banned from broadcasting. This, as Michael Cockerell has written, was a 'logical extension' of what Mrs Thatcher had been arguing for years.[136] Back in 1985 she had warned the broadcasters against giving terrorists 'the oxygen of publicity'.[137] Now she was moving to cut off the supply, not merely from avowed terrorists but from their political apologists. The BBC and ITN were again unhappy at this curtailing of their ability to report events in Northern Ireland: but by now they were too cowed by the imminent White Paper on the future of broadcasting to dare to challenge it. Hurd himself was uncomfortable with the ban and instantly regretted it. 'Did it to help Tom King' (then Northern Ireland Secretary), he wrote weakly in his diary. 'It is a poor decision.'[138] The ban was a propaganda gift to the IRA, particularly in the United States, and ineffective, since the broadcasters simply used actors to read the Sinn Fein leaders' words better than they could have spoken them themselves. It was ultimately lifted as part of John Major's hesitant peace process in 1993.

Hurd showed himself weak in relation to the White Paper, too. Broadcasting, as Nigel Lawson wrote, 'was a subject on which Margaret held a great many firm views and prejudices':

> In general [she] was excited by the prospect of breaking the duopoly and encouraging diversity . . . But at the same time [she] was deeply concerned at actual and potential bias on television, especially in news programmes, and with the prospect of moral degradation.[139]

She was torn, in other words, between Adam Smith – or more specifically in this context, Rupert Murdoch – and Mary Whitehouse. In practice she let the former prevail.

She set out her free-market philosophy in a speech to the Press Association in June 1988, and at the same time tried to meet the objection that where television was concerned, more would mean worse:

> I shall welcome more television channels, because I think that the free movement of expression and ideas is guaranteed far better by numbers and variety than it can ever be by charters and specific statutes . . .
> There are some people who say that it will drive television downmarket. Now, I have always believed that there is a market for the

best ... I do not like the argument and I do not believe it is necessarily true that television goes downmarket. I think British people can be a lot more discriminating than that, and I think that the opportunity of more channels or subscriber channels – will perhaps enable us also to have some very upmarket television, which I am very certain that many people would welcome.[140]

This is at best wishful thinking ('I do not like the argument') and, as it turned out, disastrously wrong. The passage is full of such uncharacteristically woolly qualifications – 'not *necessarily* true', 'people *can* be more discriminating', 'will *perhaps* enable us' – that it does not sound as if she herself really believed what she was saying. The truth is that she rarely saw television (except for a few iconic programmes like *Yes, Minister*) and did not really care about its quality.

In a Cabinet committee stacked to support her views, Hurd found himself outgunned:

Fortified by two radical ministers [Lawson and David Young], by a slightly bizarre range of advisers [notably Brian Griffiths] and by her own dislike of most of the broadcasting establishment, she struck out boldly into a thicket which proved impenetrable. We in the Home Office ... tried to produce some ... cautionary advice, but the expedition struggled on regardless.[141]

Unkinder critics have suggested that Hurd let himself be bullied from fear of jeopardising his hopes of the Foreign Office. His flaccid performance certainly counted against him in the contest to succeed Mrs Thatcher in November 1990.[142] But in fact he did succeed in blocking two of the Prime Minister's pet projects. She would have liked to privatise Channel 4 (which had only been set up by Willie Whitelaw in 1980, with a specific remit to produce minority programmes); and she had still not given up hope of scrapping the BBC licence fee. 'Of course they ought to be on a subscription basis,' she told Wyatt in December 1988.[143] But to her annoyance Duke Hussey had 'gone native like all the others' and successfully fought the proposal.[144] The Bill as it eventually emerged was directed almost entirely at reforming and extending commercial television.*

---

*Mrs Thatcher was very reluctant to renew the BBC Charter for another six years in 1990. 'I have fought three elections against the BBC,' she railed, 'and I don't want to fight another against it.'[145] As it turned out she did not get the chance.

The most contentious proposal of the White Paper which Hurd published in November 1988 was to hold an open auction for the next round of ITV franchises, which would simply be sold to the highest bidder. The undiluted commercialism of this suggestion caused such an outcry, however, that before the White Paper reappeared as a Bill a year later, the Government was forced to write in a quality threshold which successful bidders would be required to meet. The value of this safeguard, however, remained to be seen. Other provisions which would change the face of British television were the establishment of Channel 5, new arrangements for the licensing of cable and satellite channels and a requirement that the BBC and ITV should be obliged to buy 25 per cent of their programmes from independent producers. The Bill abolished the Independent Broadcasting Authority (IBA) – punishment for its defiance of the Government over *Death on the Rock* – and gave statutory authority to the Broadcasting Standards Council already established under the chairmanship of William Rees-Mogg. 'Together,' Mrs Thatcher told the Commons, 'these reforms will mean much more choice and higher standards. British television will remain among the best in the world.'[146]

But the contradiction between choice and regulation was glaring. The IBA was replaced by a new Independent Television Commission, headed by an industrialist, George Russell (former chairman of Alcan Aluminium), with Lord Chalfont – a former Labour minister who now made no secret of seeing subversives under every bed – as his deputy. Russell's job was to bring a 'lighter touch' to the commercial regulation of the industry. But at the same time Chalfont announced that 'One of my main concerns will be objectivity in television journalism';[147] while Rees-Mogg's brief was 'to safeguard decency and keep off our screens the violence that is unacceptable'.[148] Mrs Thatcher wanted to deregulate commercially, while regulating content more closely, but she failed to see that the former made the latter virtually impossible. As Lawson wrote: 'She suffered from the delusion that tends to affect all politicians, even professedly free-market ones, that they can regulate anything if they really wish to.'[149]

The auction of ITV franchises did not take place until 1991, some months after Mrs Thatcher had left office. It was, as many predicted, a fiasco: a lottery with no consistent pattern. Some of the existing companies (Central, Scottish) had their franchises renewed for a mere £2,000, while Yorkshire paid £37 million. In the London region Thames – a company with an excellent record – lost out to Carlton, a newly formed consortium with no record at all and an unconvincing prospectus. But the most sensational loser was the breakfast channel

TV-am, whose £14 million bid was easily topped by GMTV's £34 million. Its chairman, Bruce Gyngell, was one of Mrs Thatcher's favourite businessmen. His defeat drew from her a very rare apology, which he read out to a stunned Claridges ballroom:

> Dear Bruce,
>   When I see how some of the other licences have been awarded, I am mystified that you did not receive yours, and heartbroken . . . I am only too painfully aware that I was responsible for the legislation.
>   Yours, Margaret.[150]

The franchise auction, as Hurd later wrote, 'satisfied no one'. Reviewing Lady Thatcher's memoirs in 1993, he frankly acknowledged that the Broadcasting Bill for which he was responsible was 'one of the least successful reforms of these years'.[151]

Meanwhile Mrs Thatcher did everything she could to help Rupert Murdoch dominate the new medium of satellite television. Just as John Biffen had allowed him to buy *The Times* and *Sunday Times* without reference to the Monopolies Commission back in 1981, so now Hurd's successor at the Home Office, David Waddington, bent the Government's own rules governing satellite broadcasting to allow Murdoch's Sky TV to swallow its only rival, BSB, again without reference to the Monopolies Commission. Whereas other newspaper proprietors were allowed to own no more than 20 per cent of terrestrial television channels, Murdoch's News International was permitted to own nearly 50 per cent of BSkyB by the device – which Waddington admitted was technically illegal – of classifying it as 'non-domestic'.[152] Also in the name of 'choice' existing restrictions were relaxed to allow television companies to buy exclusive rights to major sporting events – the plums with which Murdoch hoped to woo audiences to his satellite channels.

Mrs Thatcher 'loves the whole idea' of Sky, Wyatt recorded, 'because it whittles down the influence of the BBC. It makes the area of choice more open and it is more difficult for people of left-wing persuasion to mount steady drip-drip campaigns against her.'[153] She signalled her favour by giving an interview to Sky News on its opening day – though it was seen by very few viewers. Meanwhile she was convinced that the American CNN was 'the best news programme there is',[154] and made a point of telling a press conference in November 1988 that she had watched the American presidential election result on CNN via cable at Number Ten.[155] In the same way she told Wyatt that she now listened to LBC in the mornings instead of the BBC's *Today* programme, claiming to find it 'less irritating with less bias'.[156]

The charge against Mrs Thatcher's broadcasting policy is that she deliberately wrecked British television, hitherto widely regarded as the best in the world, by commercialising it, from a mixture of crude free-market dogma spiked with political malice. By 1989 she had success-fully cowed both BBC and ITN to the point where they were reluctant to make programmes which might upset the Government; while the effect of increased 'choice' since the 1990 Act has been in practice less diversity and ever lower quality. Ironically – but quite predictably – her policies actually increased the 'moral degradation' of television which the Mary Whitehouse side of her make-up found so offensive. Just as Murdoch's purchase of the *Sun* and then *The Times* forced the whole of Fleet Street to follow his titles relentlessly downmarket, so the shamelessly commercial ethos of Sky TV has had the same trivi-alising effect on British television. Companies whose only interest is in making money will stoop deeper and deeper into the gutter to gratify public taste for easy entertainment, leaving less and less room for investigative reporting, serious documentaries, the arts or even quality drama. The auction of franchises was a bonanza for the Government but left the winners less to spend on programmes. Of course the tide of commercialism was running strongly already; but a government concerned with quality and moral standards would have tried to hold it back, not let it rip. 'Like the Thatcherite attack on the universities,' Ian Gilmour has written, the 1990 Broadcasting Act was 'sheer vandalism . . . the outcome of the politics of revenge and reward'.[157] Or as the future Director-General of the BBC, Greg Dyke, wrote in 1994: 'Never has government done so much damage to one industry in such a short period of time as the Conservatives have done to broadcasting over the past 6–7 years.'[158] Given the amount of time most of the population – and particularly children – spend watching television, nothing the Thatcher Government did had a more direct effect on the daily life of British people in the following decade. It is a dire legacy.

Football was another subject of passionate concern to millions, about which Mrs Thatcher was eager to legislate on a basis of very little knowl-edge. Crowd trouble at football matches had become a serious blight on the game in recent years. Football clubs had tried to deal with it by better stewarding, separating home and visiting fans and banning alcohol from grounds. But its persistence reflected a wider social problem of disaffected young men for whom football violence provided an outlet: football was the victim of their behaviour, not its cause. To Mrs Thatcher, however – as one of her colleagues who was interested in football noted – football fans, even when not rioting, were an alien breed, little better than striking miners, another face of the 'enemy within'.[159] She was particularly concerned at the travelling fans who damaged Britain's reputation abroad. The last straw was serious trouble involving England fans at the European championships in Germany in the summer of 1988. Mrs Thatcher summoned football officials to Downing Street to vent her anger and threw her weight behind a national membership scheme by which only registered supporters would be admitted to matches. Something similar had been proposed by the Popplewell inquiry into safety at football grounds in 1986; but it had been enacted only at Luton FC, whose populist chairman, David Evans, was one of Mrs Thatcher's most strident backbench supporters. Now she leaned on the current sports minister, Colin Moynihan – a thirty-three-year-old former British Olympic cox and a lightweight in every sense – to come up with a national identity-card scheme to be compulsory if the clubs would not introduce it voluntarily.

Moynihan's scheme was condemned by practically everyone in football and also by the police, who said that it would prove unworkable. It would break down on big match days precisely when it was needed: most trouble occurred outside the grounds not inside. In the Commons Kinnock begged Mrs Thatcher to listen 'just for once . . . to their voices of experience and knowledge, and scrap the idea'.[160] But she was unmoved. The Bill was introduced initially in the Lords, but was halted in April by the Hillsborough disaster, when ninety-four Liverpool fans were crushed to death and another 174 injured before an FA Cup semi-final with Sheffield Wednesday. Though the tragedy had nothing to do with crowd violence, Mrs Thatcher, backed by Ridley and Moynihan, thought Hillsborough an additional reason for implementing identity cards without delay. After visiting the scene she told Wyatt: 'It must be the end of terraces. We must have seats and tickets only.'[161] Hurd, supported by most of the rest of the Cabinet, tried to buy time by setting up another inquiry, chaired by Lord Justice Taylor. The Prime Minister reacted 'stormily', determined to press ahead without waiting for Taylor.[162] Three days later Hurd recorded in his diary:

> More ministerial meetings. M.T. all over the place. Constantly interrupting. Not a full storm, but exasperating. Ingham and Moynihan egg her towards intransigence. Gradually we wear her down from an Act in July to an Act in November, which might give time for Taylor's interim report, which is the crucial point.[163]

In fact, Taylor was not ready in time, so Ridley pushed the Bill through both Houses before the summer recess. But when Taylor did report, the following January, he expressed 'grave doubts' about the impact of the scheme on public safety and it was quietly abandoned. Kinnock gleefully invited Mrs Thatcher to 'make a little history' by admitting that she had been wrong.[164] That was too much to expect. In her memoirs she does not even mention the Football Spectators Act (though it remains on the Statute Book). The Taylor report did lead to the adoption of all-seater stadiums which have certainly made the game safer, though at the expense of some of its character. But the real impact of Thatcherism on football was the huge influx of money derived from the brave new world of commercial television.

Another highly conservative corner of national life which the Government tried to reform was the legal profession. Mrs Thatcher was anxious not to be seen to be concerned only with trade-union restrictive practices: in her free-market mode she was keen to attack professional vested interests too. Though she had an almost mystical reverence for the rule of the law, she had no great regard for lawyers – as bumptious barristers like Kenneth Clarke and David Mellor were on occasion firmly reminded. Her brief experience as a young woman trying to make her way at the bar in the 1950s had armed her against the claims of legal protectionism. The 1985 Administration of Justice Act had allowed banks and building societies to undertake conveyancing, breaking the solicitors' monopoly of that lucrative but normally straightforward business and making the buying and selling of houses both cheaper and easier. But so long as the ancestor-worshipping Lord Hailsham occupied the Woolsack, there was no possibility of tackling the bar's hallowed prerogatives. In 1987, however, her inspired appointment of James Mackay brought a fresh Scottish broom to bear.

In January 1989 Mackay published three Green Papers, proposing to break the barristers' monopoly by allowing solicitors to plead in court and to become High Court judges, while a new Legal Affairs Commission, appointed by the Government and dominated by non-lawyers, was to be established to oversee the profession. These heresies were predictably denounced by the barristers and judges as spelling 'the virtual abolition of the independent Bar'.[165] Lord Lane, the Lord Chief Justice, described Mackay's paper with typical hyperbole as 'one of the most sinister documents ever to emanate from government'.[166] Hailsham and two of his predecessors used similarly apocalyptic language, while Lord Devlin charged the Government with 'treating judges like civil servants'.[167] Faced with this barrage, Mrs Thatcher initially backed her Lord Chancellor. 'There are still some dissentient voices,' she acknowledged, 'but I think broadly speaking what he proposes is right.'[168] By the time the Green Papers had hardened into a White Paper in July, however, the lay commission had been abandoned and a number of modifications introduced, such as increasing the training requirement for solicitors, which in practice confirmed the obstacles that prevented solicitors overcoming the division of the profession to any significant extent. With those concessions the Bill became law in 1990; but the impact was disappointing. A decade later the barristers' grip on the higher courts was as strong as ever (though administrative reforms which Mackay put through under John Major did make the system somewhat more cost-effective). Mrs Thatcher had once again shown herself readier to take on some vested interests than others. 'The lawyers, unlike the miners,' Simon Jenkins reflected, 'had too many friends in high places for a frontal assault.'[169]

There were other ill-considered or abortive measures in this last hyperactive year, forced on unwilling ministers by an impatient Prime Minister. The Child Support Agency was her response to the fact that by 1989 more than a quarter of babies were born out of wedlock: 2.4 million children were being brought up in single-parent families and 800,000 of those single parents – usually mothers – were living on Income Support. Mrs Thatcher had always claimed to be a great supporter of the family. But tax changes brought in by both Howe and Lawson, and an easing of the divorce law in 1987 which made it possible to divorce after one year instead of three, actually militated against the institution of marriage and what she called 'family values'. Outraged by the number of absent fathers evading their responsibilities Mrs Thatcher badgered Tony Newton – who succeeded Moore at the Department of Social Security in July 1989 – to bring in a Bill to compel them to pay their proper share towards the support of their children. The idea was well-intentioned but bungled in its implementation: a bad case of hasty legislation which had to be redrawn very soon after its introduction.

There was also a botched plan for student loans, which the banks declined to implement; and finally in the summer of 1990 a Bill to allow suspected war criminals to be charged in Britain with offences committed in other countries half a century before. This was something Mrs Thatcher strongly supported – in deference perhaps to her Finchley constituents and other Jewish friends – against the doubts of Geoffrey Howe and a phalanx of senior figures in the House of Lords. When the peers – swayed by powerful speeches from Hailsham, Willie Whitelaw, Alec Home, Roy Jenkins and the eighty-eight-year-old former

Nuremberg prosecutor Lord Shawcross – rejected the Bill by 207 votes to forty-seven (after the Commons, on a free vote, had approved it by a similar margin), she was determined to use the Parliament Act to drive it through. John Major eventually did so in 1991. But the great age of the few accused and the difficulty of collecting evidence after such a lapse of time meant that no one was ever successfully prosecuted under the Act.

All these, on top of the poll tax, contributed to a mounting impression of a government which had lost its way. Alan Clark complained in his diary of 'all this rotten, irrelevant, unnecessary legislation which clogs our time';[170] while Noël Annan blamed this sudden spate of 'broken-backed' reforms on the Government's arrogant propensity to make policy on the hoof and specifically on Mrs Thatcher's reliance on special advisers and one-eyed party think-tanks. 'Some thought that those old-style committees of inquiry gave better answers . . . because they canvassed a variety of opinions.'[171] For seven or eight years Mrs Thatcher had been portrayed by her opponents as a fanatical dogmatist driven by ideology, when in fact she had been extraordinarily cautious: now she did seem to have lost her judgement in a flurry of doctrinaire quick fixes which did not work. Hitherto she had been seen as hard-faced but competent. Now after ten years in office she suddenly appeared as alarmingly incompetent. For overshadowing everything else, the economic achievement on which her authority was founded was suddenly going wrong.

Inflation again

If the Thatcher Government had one overriding objective in May 1979 it was the conquest of inflation. Conquer inflation, the Prime Minister and her economic advisers believed, by means of sound monetary policy, and everything else would follow. By June 1983 they were able to boast that inflation was conquered – if not in quite the way they had projected – and over the next four years steady growth and rising living standards for the majority duly followed. Unemployment was falling at last, public spending was under control, the balance of payments was in surplus, interest rates were at their lowest for years. By June 1987 Lawson was hailed as the 'miracle' Chancellor who had found the holy grail which had eluded all his postwar predecessors. But the control of inflation always remained, as he had once rashly described it, 'judge and jury'.[172] Not content with getting it down to 3 per cent by 1987, he announced that his next ambition was to bring it down to zero.[173]

Yet within a year the miracle started to go badly wrong. Hubris met its poetic nemesis. A combination of overconfidence, poor forecasting and consequent policy errors fuelled a credit boom which sucked in massive quantities of imports, leading to a runaway trade deficit and an upturn in inflation. Far from the zero Lawson had targeted, by the end of 1989 the figure was pushing 10 per cent, practically back to where it had been in 1979. After ten years of Mrs Thatcher, in other words, inflation was actually higher than it ever was under Harold Macmillan – the supposed father of inflation – while unemployment, though down, was still around two million and likely to rise again as a new recession threatened. This was where the Conservatives had come in. More than the poll tax or divisions over Europe, this central failure of economic management called in question the success of the whole Thatcherite project since 1979. As the huge bonus of North Sea oil began to run out, all the old problems seemed to be returning. As unemployment fell from its 1986 peak, the trade unions were beginning to recover their confidence. Pay was growing faster than productivity which – though much improved – still lagged behind most comparable economies. Manufacturing had never recovered from the previous recession; investment had been low and the national infrastructure was visibly crumbling. The Lawson boom was after all just another rerun of the Barber boom of 1973 which had ended in tears and the defeat of the Heath Government. Moreover, of particular concern to Mrs Thatcher, the combination of renewed inflation and high interest rates hit particularly hard the new middle class of self-employed small businesspeople, entrepreneurs and new homeowners, whose aspirations she had specifically set out to advance and protect. 'Good housekeeping' suddenly seemed a sour joke.

Several factors contributed to this mortifying reversal. Always more cautious than her expansive Chancellor, Mrs Thatcher was already worried that the boom was getting out of hand in the autumn of 1986. Lawson was confident that he could rein it back after the election if necessary. But the 'Big Bang' and the deregulation of the City had removed from his armoury many of the controls which previous Chancellors had been able to use to cool an overheating economy. Moreover in the autumn of 1987 Treasury forecasts underestimated how rapidly the economy was already growing. Lawson raised interest rates a point, to 10 per cent, in August. But when the stock market crashed in October, his concern – shared by almost all the City pundits – was to prevent a downturn such as had followed the Wall Street crash of 1929, leading to a world recession. To forestall this threat he cut interest rates again, in three steps between October and December, down to 8.5 per cent. In his defence, Lawson points out that the pundits and the opposition parties were all urging him to do more. Cutting interest rates, however, turned out to be the wrong medicine at the wrong time. The economy was already growing faster than the Treasury realised, and the cuts gave it an additional stimulus which was not needed. Mrs Thatcher was in America at the time of the crash, where the Federal Reserve took the opposite course and tightened credit. Nevertheless she approved Lawson's strategy, as she wrote in her memoirs, 'to make assurance double sure'.[174]

Then Lawson's first budget of the new Parliament threw further fuel on the fire. Undeterred by warnings that it might be the wrong moment, he was determined to crown his reputation as a great reforming Chancellor with another spectacular tax-cutting package. With revenues buoyant, he was able to balance the books with a surplus for 1988–9 and plan for zero public borrowing in 1989–90, while leaving himself £4.2 billion to give away. Not only was he able to trim the standard rate of income tax by another two pence to twenty-five pence in the pound, while announcing his ambition to cut it eventually to twenty pence; but he simultaneously slashed the top rate – which Howe had cut to 60 per cent back in 1979 – down to 40 per cent: one of the lowest rates in the world. All intermediate tax bands were abolished. At the same time Capital Gains Tax was reformed and simplified; and married women were at last assessed separately from their husbands – an equalisation which Mrs Thatcher strenuously opposed.

This was Lawson's apogee. The opposition parties – and some One Nation Tories – denounced the budget for blatantly favouring the rich, at the very moment when Fowler's social-security reforms were withdrawing many benefits from the poor. 'It's tax cuts galore but not if you're poor,' was the *Daily Mirror*'s headline. Executives earning £70,000 a year gained an extra £150 a week, while families struggling on that much a week had their income cut.[175] Labour's shadow Chancellor, John Smith, called it 'immoral . . . wrong . . . foolish . . . divisive . . . corrupting'; while even the *Financial Times* worried that the rewards were 'one-sided'.[176] Mrs Thatcher privately had her doubts: she would have settled for a top rate of 50 per cent, and she thought announcing a 20 per cent target an unnecessary hostage to fortune.[177] But most Tory MPs were ecstatic, and she could not fail to join in the general enthusiasm. 'Nigel's budget,' she told the Conservative Central Council four days later, was 'a humdinger' which wrote 'the obituary for the doctrine of high taxation . . . It was the epitaph for Socialism.'[178]

But 1988 was a classic instance of the maxim that the morning-after verdict on budgets is usually wrong.* Lawson's tax cuts, whether or not they were equitable, were fatally mistimed.† They were followed the next day by yet another cut in interest rates. But over the next few months, as consumers rushed to spend their gains, the deficit soared and inflation turned up, the Chancellor was forced into an embarrassing reversal: he was obliged to raise interest rates again repeatedly but without effect, so that by September the base rate was back to 12 per cent, and a year later reached 15 per cent, thus clawing back from homeowners all the benefit given away in March. Yet Lady Thatcher, in her memoirs, did not criticise the tax cuts. 'The overall tax changes . . . were of the right size and direction. If they had not been accompanied by loose monetary policy, all would have been well.'[180]

Here was her quarrel with Lawson. His real error, for which she could not forgive him, was not the budget but his monetary policy. In her memoirs she bitterly blamed Lawson for throwing away all that they had achieved together over the previous nine years by pursuing a mistaken monetary policy against her will and behind her back. The rot set in, she believed, when Lawson lost faith in the Medium Term Financial Strategy, which he himself had devised, stopped targeting £M3 or any other measure of money supply because of the difficulty of measuring it, and started to pay more attention to the sterling exchange rate as a more reliable indicator, until during 1986 he had begun to target a particular rate – between 2.80 and 3.00 Deutschmarks – not as a rough guide, but as a fixed goal. 'We actually picked up our inflationary tendency during a time when we were trying to hold our pound level with . . . three marks,' she told the BBC World Service in May 1989 – when Lawson was still Chancellor. 'We picked up inflation by trying to shadow the Deutschmark.'[181] In her memoirs she explained that this was a fundamental error of economic principle. 'It

---

*Michael Brown, MP for Brigg and Cleethorpes, later recalled just one dissenter. 'The late Nicholas Budgen [he died in 1998] spoilt our tea room celebrations and pooped our party by saying it was the most irresponsible Budget he had heard and predicted that it would be downhill ever after. In one fell swoop, Mr Budgen said, Mr Lawson had squandered the previous five years of responsible economic management.'[179]

†Inflation was accidentally fuelled by another error. Thwarted by Mrs Thatcher's refusal to allow him to cut tax relief on mortgage interest, Lawson made a gesture in that direction by withdrawing it from houses bought jointly – but with a four-month time delay. This led to a mad rush as people clubbed together to buy properties before the deadline, which caused house prices in the south-east to rocket by 15 per cent in four months, and 30 per cent in the whole year.

is . . . quite impossible to control both the exchange rate *and* monetary policy . . . You can either target the money supply or the exchange
rate, but not both.'

> The only effective way to control inflation is by using interest rates
> to control the money supply. If, on the contrary, you set interest
> rates in order to stick at a particular exchange rate . . . you steer
> straight on to the reefs.[182]

The value of a currency, to a monetarist, is no different from that
of any other commodity: it must be allowed to find its level in a free
market. All attempts to peg it are futile. By targeting a particular value
Lawson unaccountably forgot all the hard-learned lessons of the past
decade and went back to the bad old days of Harold Wilson trying to
defend the fixed parity of sterling in 1964–7. By using monetary policy
to target a desired exchange rate, he was obliged first to *cut* interest
rates when he should have raised them, fuelling inflation, and then
when the pound began to fall to *raise* them when the economy (and
homeowners) were crying out for them to fall. On this analysis Lawson's
policy – which Mrs Thatcher claimed to have known nothing about
in its initial stages – was simply wrong.

But in reality it was not so simple. Her own attitude at the time
was not so clear as she later pretended. On the contrary she was, in
Lawson's word, 'schizoid' about sterling. Though in theory a good
monetarist who was happy to see its value determined by the market,
in practice she saw the national currency – 'our pound' – as a symbol
of national pride and national strength. She liked to see it going up,
as an expression of the world's confidence in Britain, and hated to see
it fall: she had felt Wilson's 1967 devaluation and the Heath Government
being forced out of the European 'snake' in 1972 as national humili-
ations, and was terrified in 1985 when sterling fell to near-parity with
the dollar. At that time she was tempted by the idea of joining the
ERM 'to protect us from all this'.[183]

In fact between a low exchange rate on the one hand and low interest
rates on the other she was ambivalent. She could see the benefit of the
low pound between 1983 and 1987, which helped Britain recover from
the 1980–1 recession. She liked the lower interest rates which that involuntary devaluation made possible and did not want to tie sterling into
the ERM for fear of having to raise interest rates to protect a fixed
parity. She was not initially against the ERM on principle – she had
criticised the Callaghan Government for failing to join in 1978 – but
increasingly became so from a contradictory mixture of patriotism and

free-market economics. She both feared having to defend an unrealistic parity and resented the loss of national independence in being tied, officially or unofficially, to the Deutschmark. Where chauvinism and economics pulled her different ways, the former generally prevailed; but both chauvinism and economics led her to distrust Lawson's hankering to manage the markets by international agreement. 'Something always goes wrong,' she complained, 'when Nigel goes abroad.'[184]

But she was – on her own admission – isolated. Most of the Cabinet would have happily gone along with the judgement of the Chancellor and the Foreign Secretary, supported by the overwhelming consensus of Fleet Street and the City, in favour of joining the ERM as soon as possible. She had imposed a personal veto in 1985, and maintained it until 1990; but she could not stop Lawson working to achieve the same result by informal means. Part of her problem was that currency management was the jealously guarded preserve of the Treasury and the Bank; but that had never worried previous Prime Ministers with more amenable Chancellors. Her real difficulty was that Lawson was intellectually and politically too strong for her. After five years in the job – and two more as Financial Secretary before that – he had, as she acknowledged, 'complete intellectual mastery of his brief' and complete confidence in his own ability.[185] 'Nigel Lawson listened to others only as a prelude to what he had intended to do anyway,' John Major – his Chief Secretary in these crucial years – wrote later. 'No trace of self-doubt ever crossed his mind.'[186] Mrs Thatcher was not often at a disadvantage, but she lacked the technical expertise to argue successfully with Lawson, even when all her instincts told her he was wrong. She could not bully him, as she did most of her other ministers. Moreover his reputation gave him an unusual independence. He was widely believed to have no further political ambition, but to be only waiting for his moment to step down for a lucrative job in the City. ('He has these two children about nine and he has got to educate them,' she told Wyatt. 'And he's got no money.')[187] But so long as the party and the press believed that he could do no wrong she could not afford to lose him, let alone sack him. She had no choice but to go along publicly with his policy while doing her best to undermine it from within – rather as she had done with Heseltine, and ultimately with the same result.

Up to June 1987 she stuck to the line that she had first enunciated back in 1980, that Britain would join the ERM 'when the time is ripe'.[188] 'One day we will go in,' she assured the *Financial Times* in November 1986. 'But when we go in . . . I want to go in from strength.'[189] In fact she was increasingly opposed in principle and determined that the time would never be right. But so long as the policy was to join eventually, Lawson felt entitled to prepare the ground by starting to align sterling with the Deutschmark immediately, maintaining downward pressure on the pound by instructing the Bank of England to buy other currencies. He claims that Mrs Thatcher knew perfectly well what he was doing. 'It was always an implausible insult to her formidable intelligence,' he wrote in his memoirs, 'to suggest that she could possibly have been unaware of it, even if I had wished to keep her in the dark, which of course I did not.'[190] He insists that he was quite open with journalists: she had only to read the newspapers. Maybe Bernard Ingham kept her in the dark. But she also saw the figures every day and could see the foreign currency reserves growing: Lawson writes that 'she positively loved the steady accumulation of reserves'.[191] He strenuously denies that he deceived her.★

The truth is that she semi-deliberately deceived herself. It was quite typical of her mode of operation to turn a blind eye to policies she disliked in the hope that either they would turn out all right or, if not, she could evade the blame. She liked the accumulating reserves, and she liked the low interest rates even more. So long as Lawson did not tie himself to a fixed parity, and the cost of keeping within his target range was not too high, she was content to avoid a showdown with her brilliant Chancellor. It was Alan Walters in America who alerted her to the implications of what Lawson was doing. She then claimed to have just discovered, in the course of giving another interview to the *Financial Times* in November 1987, what everyone in the City had known for months:

They asked me why we were shadowing the deutschmark at three to the pound. I vigorously denied it. But there was no getting away from the fact that the chart they brought with them bore out what they said.

The embarrassing implication was that they were better informed than she was. 'How could I possibly trust him again?'[193] But she used the *Financial Times* interview to repudiate any suggestion of shadowing the Deutschmark:

★As further evidence he cites her admission in an interview with Simon Jenkins after she left office that letting Lawson shadow the Deutschmark had been her 'great mistake'.[192]

Mrs Thatcher denied categorically and repeatedly that there was any exchange rate target for the pound, whether against the D-Mark or any other currency or basket of currencies . . . 'There is no specific range,' she said. 'We are always free . . . We are not confined to any particular limits and I do not like us to be, because to do that is to tempt people to have a go and you cannot beat a speculator except over a short period.'[194]

Yet she was still powerless. Lawson had the power to act, while she could only make pronouncements. At a tense meeting on 8 December he managed to persuade her that the Treasury's intervention in the money market was fully funded – 'sterilised', in the jargon – so would not lead to inflation. She agreed (willingly, he insists) that they should buy Deutschmarks and francs rather than dollars, and on that basis he carried on.[195] For another three months, she wrote in her memoirs, 'I sought to discourage too much exchange rate intervention, but without much success . . . Nigel . . . had boxed himself into a position where his own standing as Chancellor would be weakened if the pound went above DM3.'[196] But by the beginning of March 1988 the line was becoming impossible to hold. In forty-eight hours on 2–3 March, £1 billion of reserves were expended. Even Lawson's officials were now advising that he would have to uncap sterling when Mrs Thatcher – 'in a highly agitated state' – called him in to tell him the same thing in no uncertain terms. It was 'an unpleasant meeting', Lawson recalled. He resented her tone and considered resigning. Likewise she felt that she would have been 'fully justified' in sacking him. But it was only ten days before his great tax-cutting budget. He could not resign, and she could not sack him.[197]

Sterling duly rose through the DM3 ceiling; but Lawson was still anxious to stop it rising any further. At Prime Minister's Questions Kinnock for once managed to exploit his opportunity. The first time she deflected his question, sticking to the formula that she and Lawson were absolutely agreed on the importance of keeping inflation down; but the second time she rose to the bait and declared bluntly: 'There is no way in which one can buck the market.'[198] She thought this was just a simple truth; but Lawson saw it as a deliberate attempt to undermine his policy. 'There may indeed be circumstances in which one cannot buck the market,' he wrote. 'But in the context Margaret's remark was inevitably taken to mean that any policy for sterling was being thrown out of the window.'[199] The whole political world could now see that the Prime Minister and her Chancellor were at loggerheads.

In this context the budget was a triumph for the Chancellor not only in terms of his headline-grabbing tax cuts. 'At the same time,' *The Times* noted, 'he celebrated a victory over the Prime Minister, making it clear that he will continue to run economic policy and that he will, if necessary, intervene in the foreign exchange markets to prevent the pound rising too far.'[200] Though he did accept the deletion – by Brian Griffiths on Mrs Thatcher's instruction – of any direct reference to shadowing the Deutschmark, Lawson's budget speech explicitly reasserted his goal of exchange-rate stability; and the next day he underlined his independence by cutting interest rates again. Even to a close confidant like Wyatt, Mrs Thatcher did her best to play down the dispute at the heart of the Government: she did not want him writing about it in the *News of the World.* A week earlier she had categorically denied it – 'Not at all. It simply isn't true' – a denial Wyatt duly repeated to his readers.[201] Now she admitted: 'Well there was a difference to some extent . . . He can't expect to make all the economic policy. He's part of the Government and I'm the First Lord of the Treasury.' While acknowledging that Lawson had 'done brilliantly', she pointed out that he was only building on Geoffrey Howe's foundations. 'Thus,' Wyatt noted, 'she indicated that she is not so pleased with Nigel as she has sometimes been.'[202]

Easter brought some breathing space, but relations were now permanently strained. At Prime Minister's Questions on 12 May Mrs Thatcher again conspicuously failed to endorse Lawson's policy when invited to do so: three times she declined to approve his statement that letting sterling rise any higher would be 'unsustainable'. This, in Lawson's view, was 'an astonishing and immensely damaging performance' which instantly gave sterling's upward spiral another twist:

All she had to do was to reply 'The Chancellor and I are in full agreement about everything' . . . and she would have defused the situation without in any way compromising herself . . . But she simply could not bring herself to defuse the situation in the conventional way – and, as a result made it infinitely worse.[203]

It did not need the opposition to exploit this chasm. The next day at the Scottish party conference Geoffrey Howe put his oar in – 'quite gratuitously', in Mrs Thatcher's view – by backing Lawson's wish to join the ERM sooner rather than later: the Government could not go on for ever hiding behind the formula that they would enter when the time was ripe. She refused to see the two of them together to settle the matter and reiterated that 'we were not going to join the ERM at present and that was that'.[204] Yet three days later she was forced to make another truce with Lawson, on the basis that she forbade any further intervention but allowed him to continue to use interest rates to influence the exchange rate. In this way they agreed a further cut – to 7.5 per cent – which neither of them really wanted and which had to be reversed a fortnight later. Lady Thatcher says that she agreed as 'the price of tolerable relations with my Chancellor'.[205] Lawson contends that on the contrary she pressed it on him to demonstrate their unity.[206] Asked by a Tory stooge in the Commons if this latest cut did not demonstrate 'complete and utter unanimity in the management of our economy under the capable management of the Chancellor?', she answered simply 'Yes', and went on to affirm her approval of his 'most excellent policy'.[207] Again *The Times* reported that Mrs Thatcher had 'conceded victory to the Chancellor of the Exchequer yesterday in the battle over sterling's exchange rate [and] enthusiastically endorsed Mr Nigel Lawson's economic strategy'.[208] Tory MPs were delighted and the pound steadied below Lawson's new ceiling of DM3.20. But this was no way to run an economy.

That summer growth touched 5 per cent, the fastest since 1973, pulling in imports and piling up a deficit of £2.1 billion in July alone – more than half the Treasury's projected deficit for the entire year. Still supremely confident, Lawson shrugged it off as 'a very second-order matter' which would be self-correcting, thanks to the large budget surplus. Cheekily, given that he himself had been a financial journalist in his twenties, he mocked the 'teenage scribblers in the City' as 'prisoners of the past' who failed to realise that the economy was now strong enough to bear a temporary deficit without an old-style sterling crisis; and dismissed the doubling of inflation – to 6 per cent – as a temporary blip.[209] From June, however, he was forced to change tack and started to raise interest rates by a series of rapid small steps from 7.5 to 13 per cent by the end of the year. He acted too slowly, however, to have the necessary impact. From the other side of the Atlantic Alan Walters was telling Mrs Thatcher that he should go to 12 per cent immediately. Much as she disliked high interest rates, she was now prepared to be the tougher of the two.

In July she announced that she had persuaded Walters to return to Britain as her private economic adviser. He had never been out of touch while he had been away, but the news that he was to be officially re-installed in Downing Street was an unmistakable slap in the face for Lawson. Once again he considered resigning under cover of the coming reshuffle; but he had missed his moment. The time to go would have been after the budget. Now that his big giveaway was beginning to look rather less clever than it had seemed in March he had no choice but to stay and deal with the consequences. Likewise Mrs Thatcher had no option but to keep both Lawson and Geoffrey Howe in place (which was precisely why she wanted Walters as a counterweight). The party's faith in the Chancellor was still undimmed, as *The Times* reported on 22 July:

> There has been deep dismay among Conservative MPs at the criticism of Mr Lawson from Sir Alan Walters, Mrs Thatcher's former economic adviser who is on his way back to 10 Downing Street next year. Some MPs fear that such criticism . . . could provoke Mr Lawson into leaving the Government and pursuing a lucrative career in the City.

As a result, the report continued, 'Mrs Thatcher last night was clearly straining every sinew to keep him within the Government.' Addressing the end-of-session meeting of the 1922 Committee, she was left in no doubt of the prevailing view: when the chairman, Cranley Onslow, 'pointedly referred to how they all admired the Chancellor', he was met with 'a desk-banging chorus of approval'. She responded by heaping extravagant – but carefully selective – praise on Lawson's head, describing the budget as 'quite the most brilliant we have seen . . . brilliant in concept, brilliant in drafting and brilliant in delivery' and saying that he had handled the stock-market crash in October 'marvellously'. She did not mention their disagreement over sterling.[210]

Mrs Thatcher never seems to have realised how intolerable the threat of Walters' return was bound to be for Lawson. She imagined that because he had been her adviser previously, from 1981 to 1983, he could resume the same position as if he had never been away. But the situation now was different. Then he had been an obscure professor, bound by Civil Service conventions; now he was 'a minor celebrity', as Lawson put it, identified by the press as Mrs Thatcher's economic guru and an uninhibited critic of Lawson's policies. Lawson warned her that such a candid critic inside Number Ten could only make trouble for the Government. 'I begged her to think again. But she had clearly made up her mind.'[211] They were such different personalities that she professed not to believe that the self-confident Lawson could be seriously upset by Walters' remarks. 'Alan Walters is a very sweet man,' she explained to Wyatt, 'but very naive politically. If a journalist rings him up and asks him a question he innocently answers it saying what he thinks.'[212] Walters, she told Robin Oakley of *The Times*, 'is that remarkable person, a very modest economist, and a very effective one.'[213] Modest or not – and Wyatt for one thought him a good deal less modest than he pretended – she plainly preferred Walters' advice to Lawson's.

For another year, therefore, the Government was hobbled by this damaging rift at its heart. Nicholas Ridley – now almost Mrs Thatcher's last uncritical ally in the Cabinet – describes the 'deep and mutual hostility' that now existed between the Prime Minister and the Chancellor and their 'considerable feat of acting' in broadly concealing it from the rest of their colleagues.[214] John Major writes that she was careful never to argue with Lawson openly in Cabinet: indeed she still rather deferred to him. 'She certainly never treated him in the cavalier, intolerant and often discourteous style she displayed towards Geoffrey Howe.'[215] Publicly she continued to endorse him in lavish terms – 'I fully, gladly, joyfully, unequivocally, generously support the Chancellor,' she declared in June 1989 – though the extravagance of her language only confirmed that the Lady did protest too much.[216]

In terms of immediate policy, in fact, they were no longer so far apart during 1989 as they had been the previous year. Bitterly as she blamed Lawson's misguided exchange-rate policy for having let inflation take hold again, she had no doubt that, since it had taken hold, bringing it back under control must be the Government's paramount priority. 'Our overriding – I repeat overriding – objective,' she quoted Lawson approvingly on 13 June, 'is to bring inflation back down.'[217] Since she continued to rule out joining the ERM so long as inflation was high, she had no alternative to Lawson's only other anti-inflationary instrument, the use of interest rates. 'Increases in interest rates,' she insisted, 'are far less damaging than a perpetual increase in inflation.'[218] There are hints that she might have preferred to raise taxes instead, repeating the formula of Howe's 1981 budget, which she increasingly looked back on as her Finest Hour. But Lawson had no intention of reversing what he regarded as the crowning achievement of his Chancellorship. His reliance on interest rates was widely condemned, most memorably by Ted Heath, who in November 1988 likened him to 'a one-club golfer'. ('If one wishes to take on Sandy Lyle and the rest of the world one needs a complete bag of clubs.'[219]) From within the Cabinet Peter Walker warned of the damage being done to industry by the application of 'one simplistic economic dogma'.[220] Criticism from Heath, Walker and the CBI, however, was usually enough to convince Mrs Thatcher that she was on the right track. She was clear that inflation, misguidedly unleashed, must be wrestled down again whatever the pain involved. 'I don't want Nigel to go,' she told Wyatt. 'He has got to finish what he started first.'[221]

In retrospect she realised that she should have let him go, or sacked him. It was clearly an intolerable position to have the two dominant personalities of the Government locked in fundamental disagreement, neither trusting the other, each determined to prevail. Mrs Thatcher's partisans, like Ridley, have no doubt that Lawson was in the wrong. 'The constitutional position is that the Prime Minister is First Lord of the Treasury and as such has ultimate authority over the Chancellor. If a Treasury Minister . . . differs from her in the ultimate, he either has to give way or resign.'[222] Lawson, on this view, was overweening and arrogant in setting his will against the Prime Minister, pursuing his own policy covertly behind her back. She not only had a perfect right to sack him but she should have done so.

Lawson, however, maintains that in managing the exchange rate in preparation for entering the ERM he was following the Government's declared policy: it was Mrs Thatcher who was covertly undermining it. If she had wanted to change the policy she should have done so openly, by agreement with the Cabinet or at least – as in 1980–1 – with an inner group of economic ministers. Instead she continued to pay lip service to joining the ERM 'when the time is ripe' and winked at his policy which, he insists, she was perfectly aware of. After December 1987 she continued to run with the hare and hunt with the hounds, fulsomely endorsing his economic management in public while repeatedly semaphoring her dissent from it and vetoing the consummation of his strategy. Whenever her ambivalence drove him to the brink of resignation, as in July 1988 (when she announced the return of Walters) or again in May 1989 (when she blamed him for the return of inflation), she bent over backwards to persuade him to stay.

Like the dispute with Heseltine over Westland, the issue in the end was not the rights or wrongs of policy but the way she ran the Government. In her central dispute with Lawson she may well have been right: her instincts were sometimes sounder than his intellectual *chutzpah*. He unquestionably let the economy run out of control in 1987–8. Faced with a strong minister whom she could not dominate, however, she once again worked to undermine him instead of confronting him. In 1986 Heseltine kicked over the traces and walked out. Lawson stuck to his post, probably longer than he should have done; but in the end she made his position untenable by openly preferring the advice of her private adviser. By this time she was doing much the same in foreign policy, listening to Charles Powell rather than Geoffrey Howe and the Foreign Office. Fundamentally the problem was that she did not trust her colleagues. Heseltine, Tebbit, Lawson, Howe – she saw them all in turn as challenges to her authority; and she could not tolerate rivals. It was this inability to lead a team which ultimately brought her down. Lawson unquestionably made mistakes and overplayed his hand. But the responsibility for resolving the dispute within the Government was hers: instead she let it fester. It was no way to run a Government and it eventually destroyed her.

Disasters

Inflation, high interest rates, the poll tax and water privatisation – all contributed to the impression of an increasingly accident-prone Government that had lost its way. Up to the end of 1988 the Government's support still held up surprisingly well – better than in the first two years of either of the previous Parliaments. But the return of inflation and the persistent rumours of friction between the Prime Minister and her Chancellor, unconvincingly denied, destroyed public confidence that the Government knew what it was doing. Bernard Ingham dates the change of perception precisely to the moment in December 1988 when Edwina Currie had to resign as a junior Health Minister after claiming with unwise candour that 'most' of the country's egg production was infected with salmonella. Mrs Currie did not matter in herself. But from that point, in Ingham's view, 'nothing went right for the Government'.[223] Salmonella was followed by other health scares: listeria, botulism, legionnaire's disease. Mrs Thatcher responded by setting up a Cabinet committee on food safety chaired, as usual, by herself. But the sense of political decay was aggravated by a sequence of accidents and disasters which cumulatively reinforced the view that the country, after ten years of Thatcherism, was in a mess.

The sequence had actually started before the 1987 election, with the sinking of a cross-Channel ferry, symbolically named the *Herald of Free Enterprise*, off the Dutch port of Zeebrugge, with the loss of 187 lives. Luckily the boat sank in shallow water, or the casualties might have been many times higher. But everything about the accident – from the fact that the *Herald* was part of the P&O fleet owned by one of Mrs Thatcher's favourite businessmen, Jeffrey Sterling (knighted in 1984), to Nicholas Ridley's characteristically crass joke a few days later about someone sailing, like the ferry, 'with his bow doors open' – associated it indelibly with the Tory Government.[224] The accident was due to the neglect of regulations in pursuit of a quick turnaround – putting profit before safety. Later the same year a horrific fire at King's Cross station on the London underground killed thirty people; and the following summer 166 workers died in an explosion on a North Sea oil rig. In December 1988 thirty passengers died in a rail crash at Clapham. Just before Christmas an American

airliner was brought down over the Scottish town of Lockerbie, with
the loss of 270 lives. This was a bomb, not an accident – the worst
single act of terrorism on British soil; but it was followed by more
accidents in the early months of 1989. Another plane crashed on the
M1 motorway in Leicestershire in January. There was another train
crash at Purley in south London in March, and a few days later yet
another on the edge of Glasgow. Then came the Hillsborough disaster
in April. Finally, in August, fifty-one young people were drowned
when a pleasure boat on the Thames, the *Marchioness*, was run down
by a dredger. Though of course the Government was not directly
responsible for any of these events, each one could be attributed to
deregulation, staffing cuts or lack of investment. They were the sort
of accidents the British public expected to see on their television
screens in Third World countries, not their own.

Mrs Thatcher made a point of visiting the scene of nearly every
incident. As she said when she cut short her holiday to visit the scene
of the Hungerford shootings in August 1987, 'I had to come. The only
thing you can do is to be with the people who have suffered.'[225]
Accompanying her to Sheffield in the aftermath of the Hillsborough
disaster, Douglas Hurd described her as 'shaken' by what she saw, but
'remorseless in her compassion'. He was afraid that the last thing the
survivors would want was the Prime Minister at their bedside, but
found that, on the contrary, she was welcomed:

> She took control of the situation, talked to them in a way I wouldn't
> have dreamt of doing. But she was right. They will remember that
> all their lives; not just a bossy Margaret Thatcher coming in and
> making a nuisance. She got the feel of it right. I was impressed.[226]

She was undoubtedly sincerely moved by the carnage and the
courage of the victims on these occasions; yet she was accused of
'ambulance chasing', exploiting tragedy for her own self-promotion
and usurping a role more suited to the Queen or members of the
Royal Family. She simply felt that it was her duty to go, just as in
her first Shadow Cabinet job in 1967 she had criticised Alf Robens
for not visiting the scene of the Aberfan disaster. 'When tragedy strikes,
the person in command should go to the scene as quickly as possible.'[227]
But Robens was chairman of the National Coal Board, not Prime
Minister. Mrs Thatcher's compulsion to rush immediately to
Zeebrugge, Aberdeen, Clapham and the rest reflects her conviction
that whatever happened, anywhere in the country, she was the person
in command and should be seen to be so. After visiting the survivors

of the Purley crash, where only four people died, she told Wyatt: 'I didn't want people to think I only went to the very biggest crashes and neglected these smaller ones.'[228] Cynics suggested that people should carry a card stating that if they were involved in an accident they did not want to be visited by the Prime Minister. But the local Labour MP – the future Speaker Michael Martin – complained when she did not visit the scene of the Glasgow rail crash. When he went on to accuse her of 'ambulance chasing' she told him he could not have it both ways.[229]

In October 1988 the Labour party published a policy paper, *Neglect into the Nineties*, highlighting widespread concern that a lack of public investment in the national infrastructure since 1979 had left the fabric of the nation's assets – roads, railways, bridges, sewers, schools, libraries and other public buildings – dangerously dilapidated and unmodernised. The effect of ten years of cuts and economies enforced by tight control on the budgets of local authorities, Whitehall departments and nationalised or soon-to-be privatised utilities was beginning to show. Between 1979 and 1990 public expenditure on transport fell in real terms by 5.8 per cent.[230] Moreover, far from growing in line with the booming economy in the second half of the decade, investment in transport actually fell faster, by 14 per cent between 1986 and 1989.[231] Failure to match continental levels of investment in the railways was perhaps not surprising, though the consequences became clear two decades later. Despite – or because of – growing up in a railway town, Mrs Thatcher had always disliked the railways, regarding them as old-fashioned, dirty, union-ridden and essentially socialist. She placed her faith in the private car – or what she called in 1990 'the great car economy'[232] – the very embodiment of individual freedom and convenience. Yet despite the fact that Britain's roads were already the second most crowded in Europe (after Italy), that the number of vehicles on the roads increased by nearly one-third between 1980 and 1990, while the amount of freight carried on the railways continued to decline, 1988 was the first year since the motorway programme started in the 1950s that not a single mile of new motorway was under construction in England and Wales. In 1989 Cecil Parkinson promised to double spending on roads over the next ten years. His plans included adding a fourth lane to the outer London ring road, the M25, which Mrs Thatcher had only opened, amid great fanfares, in 1986; it had then become instantly congested, the Government in its first assault on public spending in the early 1980s having cut the original plan from four lanes to three.

Successive Transport Ministers – Ridley, Moore, Channon and

Parkinson (at least three of them keen privatisers) – eventually got round Treasury limits by inviting private financing of major infrastructural projects, beginning with the Channel tunnel and a new Thames bridge at Dartford, financed by Trafalgar House.* Once, as a high-spending Education Secretary in Ted Heath's government, Mrs Thatcher had been keen on prestige projects like Concorde, the Channel tunnel and the third London airport, and highly critical of Labour for cancelling the last two. As Prime Minister, however, she had developed the view that such things should be built by private enterprise, without support from the taxpayer. She therefore refused to give public money to the high-speed rail link without which the trains from London to Paris would spend longer crawling fifty miles through Kent than they did on the other four-fifths of the journey. After her fall the Major Government devised the Private Finance Initiative under which such projects as the long-overdue Heathrow rail link, the Docklands Light Railway and the extension of the Jubilee line were developed with a mixture of private and public money. But for the previous ten years the dogma that major public projects must be built exclusively by private enterprise delayed these and other desperately needed improvements to the crumbling national transport system.

In March 1989 a piquant article by the thirty-two-year-old deputy editor of the *Spectator*, Dominic Lawson, implicitly blamed his father for the failure of infrastructural investment over the past five years. Lawson *fils* quoted from a Treasury Green Paper published in 1984, *The Next Ten Years: Public Expenditure and Taxation into the Nineties*:

> It would of course . . . be open to the Government to decide, once the virtuous circle of lower taxes and higher growth had been established, to devote some of these resources to improved public services rather than reduced taxation.[233]

By 1988 this virtuous circle had been achieved; yet in his budget that year the Chancellor, with the Prime Minister's approval, had chosen to press ahead with yet more tax cuts. On this at least Nigel Lawson and Margaret Thatcher were agreed – reduced taxation was a higher priority than public services. Fifteen years on, the legacy is plain to see.

---

*The Department of Transport, with seven Secretaries of State between 1979 and 1990, suffered a greater turnover of ministers than any other except Trade, which got through ten.

Even at the time there were plenty of warning voices, not only from the left. The same month as Dominic Lawson's article, the novelist A. N. Wilson, also in the *Spectator*, concluded reluctantly that Thatcherism – like the rhythm method of birth control – 'doesn't bloody work':

> Wherever you choose to examine it, the Thatcherite idea has failed to work. It is not in a position to withdraw public spending altogether . . . Instead it opts for the worst possible alternative where bits of money are offered and everyone is in the red.

Writing from an unashamedly middle-class perspective, Wilson asserted that decent public services were important not, as Thatcherites seemed to believe, only for the poor, but to everyone. Hence the middle-class backlash:

> Trains, museums, operas, hospitals, universities cannot exist without public funding and those of us who pay high rates of tax have a right to expect something better than the present government offers . . .
> We need to return to the simple idea that public services require public spending and it is the responsibility of governments to administer this spending . . . Mrs Thatcher with her famous Gladstonian dictum that Governments have no money . . . has subtly evaded her fiscal and social responsibilities in almost every area until a crisis forces her to throw in money too late.

It was time, Wilson concluded, to vote for a party which at least believed in public spending:

> Unless we all decide to vote Labour . . . we may face a dud future with dud trains, dud libraries, dud museums, dud hospitals and the poor getting poorer – sans eyes, sans teeth, sans everything.[234]

Large numbers of the public suddenly agreed. The spring of 1989 saw a decisive change in the public's attitude to the Thatcher Government. In February the young William Hague, defending one of the safest Tory seats in the country in Richmond, Yorkshire, suffered the biggest drop in the Tory vote at any by-election since 1979: from 35,000 to less than 20,000. Had the two splinters of the old Alliance – the recently merged Liberal Democrats and David Owen's rump SDP – not shared 27,000 votes between them, he would have lost by several thousand. Then in June the elections to the European Parliament inflicted the Tories' first national defeat under Mrs Thatcher's leadership. On an admittedly low poll the Government won only 33.5 per cent to Labour's 38.7 per cent, and only thirty-two seats to Labour's forty-five – precisely reversing the 1984 result. That month Labour moved into a lead in the polls which it never relinquished while Mrs Thatcher remained Prime Minister. Her personal popularity rating slumped sharply, and never recovered.

The miracle was over.

14

A Diet of Brussels

The declaration of Bruges

Margaret Thatcher's aggressive style of politics was founded on the identification of enemies. Her success was measured by the trophies stuffed and mounted on her walls: Ted Heath in 1975; the 'wets' and General Galtieri in her first term; Arthur Scargill and Ken Livingstone in her second. For the third term she lit on a new antagonist worthy of her mettle: the President of the European Commission, Jacques Delors.

In most respects Delors was perfectly cast for the role: he was both a foreigner and a socialist, so that by fighting him she united in one crusade her two great causes, British patriotism and the defeat of socialism – a combination with maximum populist appeal to her supporters. But Delors turned out to be a more difficult opponent than Scargill or Galtieri, partly because she had been instrumental in appointing him in the first place, preferring him to his French rival Claude Cheysson in 1985; still more because she had taken a leading role in driving forward the first tranche of his reform of the Community, the Single European Act, in 1986; but above all because in anathematising Delors she was taking on a powerful section of her own party and the wider political establishment which was committed to Britain's role in Europe. Hitherto the Tory grandees, though sceptical of her policies and wary of her moral fervour, had been willing to let her fight their battles for them: they had no convincing alternative to her economic policies, but were agreeably amazed when they proved successful without provoking revolution. Now that she was directly challenging a central tenet of their faith, however, they stirred themselves to more active resistance which ultimately brought her down.

In her memoirs Lady Thatcher claims that the European Community changed fundamentally in the later 1980s, and that Delors was 'a new kind of European Commission President' with grander ambitions than his predecessors – determined, now that the single market was agreed if not yet fully functioning, to press on to the next objectives enshrined in the founding treaties: economic and monetary union (EMU) and the harmonisation of social policy and labour law. The Treaty of Rome had set the nebulous objective of 'ever-closer union', building into European institutions the belief that there must always be movement – sometimes rapid, sometimes stalled, now in one area, now in another, but always in the direction of closer integration. Mrs Thatcher tried to portray Jacques Delors as a power-hungry bureaucrat determined to expand his empire. 'The French socialist,' she reflected grimly, 'is an extremely formidable animal.'[1] Certainly Delors was ambitious to maintain momentum: he had no intention of letting the single market settle down before seeking fresh areas of advance. But he could have done nothing without the active encouragement of the leaders of the major countries of the Community, any more than Roy Jenkins could have launched the EMS without the political will of Giscard d'Estaing and Helmut Schmidt. Mrs Thatcher blamed the unelected bureaucrat Delors for exceeding his powers; but Delors was only pursuing a course set by François Mitterrand and Helmut Kohl and supported by all the other elected leaders.

She made a point of treating Delors as just an official. After the London summit in 1986 she chaired the concluding press conference with Bernard Ingham as usual on one side of her and Delors on the other. 'She quite simply forgot that he was there,' Charles Powell recalled.[2] When finally she asked him to say a word about the CAP, Delors was so fed up that he declined. Mrs Thatcher then mocked him as a 'strong silent man' and carried on answering all the questions herself, assuming that he agreed with what she was saying. He was not amused. By 1988, however, she believed that Delors had 'slipped his leash as a *fonctionnaire* and become a fully fledged political spokesman for federalism'. This might be acceptable to foreigners, she believed, with their shallower democratic tradition and well-founded distrust of their domestic politicians. 'If I were an Italian I might prefer rule from Brussels too. But the mood in Britain was different.'[3]

She had to believe that Delors was behaving improperly in order to argue that he was taking the Community into new areas of integration which Britain had not signed up for when it joined the Common Market. But the goal of economic and monetary union had been set in 1972. Indeed the original target – as Ted Heath never ceased to remind her – had been to achieve it by 1980; and it had been explicitly reaffirmed in the Single European Act which she had signed in 1986. She tried to maintain that what she signed up to was only 'the progressive realisation of economic and monetary union', which was a different matter from agreeing to economic and monetary union *per se*. But this was just semantics. She also argued that no one had yet decided what the term actually meant. Mrs Thatcher insisted that it did not necessarily entail a single currency or a single central bank, institutions which would involve an unacceptable pooling of national sovereignty. Her difficulty was that this was exactly what all the other members did think it meant. Her need to demonise Delors derived partly from her knowledge that she had been slow to grasp what she now perceived as a mortal threat to Britain's interest: on the contrary she had actually welcomed and promoted the Act from which the mandate to press on to economic union was derived. She now insisted that she had been tricked. She could not see, because she did not want to see, that movement towards economic and monetary union was, as John Major wrote in his memoirs, 'the logical extension of the changes she had set in train'.[4]

In resisting what she conceived as a mortal threat to Britain's historic identity – symbolised by the sanctity of sterling – Mrs Thatcher found the great cause of her last years in office, and of her retirement. Here was an external enemy, more threatening by far than a distant South American dictator, whose defeat required the Iron Lady once again to don the armour of Churchillian defiance. In opposing the insidious spectre of rule by Belgian bureaucrats and German bankers, while insisting that Britain's true interest lay with the United States – 'the new Europe across the Atlantic'[5] – she believed that she was indeed emulating her hero, not only the defiant British bulldog of 1940 but the half-American chronicler of 'the English speaking peoples'. But her identification with 'Winston' was self-deluding: Churchill was not the simple cartoon patriot that she imagined. Not only did he issue a number of resounding (if vague) statements in support of European unity between 1945 and 1951, which were regularly quoted by Ted Heath and other Tory pro-Marketeers in the 1960s and 1970s (these can easily be matched by other quotations which point the opposite way), but in private letters, even before the end of the war, he voiced an emotional identity with Europe which was quite alien to Mrs Thatcher's overriding deference to the United States. In October 1942, for instance – on the very eve of Alamein – Churchill wrote to Anthony Eden: 'I must admit that my thoughts rest primarily . . . in the revival of the glory of Europe.'

Hard as it is to say now, I trust the European family may act unitedly as one, under a Council of Europe in which the barriers between nations will be greatly minimised and unrestricted travel will be possible. I hope to see the economy of Europe studied as a whole. Of course we shall have to work with the Americans in many ways and in the greatest ways, but Europe must be our prime care.[6]

Of course, calling for the economy of Europe to be 'studied as a whole' is not the same as merging currencies – though the one might well lead to the other over fifty years. The point is, however, that Mrs Thatcher rarely thought of Europe in terms of 'glory' and would never have regarded the Continent as Britain's 'prime care'. On the contrary, Europe was her greatest blind spot. She knew and reluctantly accepted that Britain was irreversibly a member of the Community: but in her heart she wished it was not so. She had no respect for European politicians of any stripe. Her deep-rooted disdain for what she called in her memoirs 'that un-British combination of high-flown rhetoric and pork-barrel politics which passed for European statesmanship' blinded her to the political reality of what was inexorably growing on the other side of the Channel.[7] She veered between denouncing federalist ambitions as a mortal threat to Britain's sovereignty and dismissing them as fantasy that would never happen. As a result she never engaged seriously with what Britain's role in the evolving Community should be. On other subjects, from Russia to global warming, she set out to inform herself, listened to advice and devised a coherent diplomatic strategy which she then adhered to. Her policy towards South Africa was based on partial information and a good deal of prejudice; but it was a rational strategy which she stuck to with courage and determination – and it worked. On the subject of Europe, however – the central problem of British foreign policy – there were, as her policy adviser Percy Cradock wrote, 'no large strategic discussions; no seminars'.[8] She knew what she thought, and she knew what the rest of the Community ought to think, too, if they knew what was good for them. Consequently she was always two steps behind events, unable to lead or even to participate fully, but only to react angrily to what others proposed.

Of course she had a case. She regularly cited the Governor of the Bundesbank, Karl Otto Pohl, in support of her view that the single market did not necessarily require a single currency. Pohl, however, as Nigel Lawson wrote, 'proved a broken reed' when it came to resisting the momentum of most of his fellow central bankers.[9] She was entitled to point out – as she did repeatedly – that Britain was 'way ahead' of other countries in implementing the provisions necessary to allow a single market – let alone a single currency – to function properly: the abolition of exchange controls (which Britain had ended in 1979), free capital movements and the dismantling of a host of protectionist barriers. She was constantly complaining that the French were still blocking the import of Nissan cars manufactured in Britain, or imposing unfair duties on Scotch whisky;[10] and she believed they should honour what was already agreed before they went on to grander schemes. 'Some of them,' she complained in her usual 'us' and 'them' manner after the Hanover council in 1988, 'seem to put forward some of these grandiose ideas long before they have been willing to do the things which they can do . . . They are not really at liberty to lecture us when we in fact have done more practically than they have.'[11] 'So you see,' she said on *The Jimmy Young Programme* a few weeks later, 'we are the practical ones. We were the ones who first sorted out the budget. We are the ones who have now sorted out agriculture. We are the ones who are now sorting out the free movement of goods, investment.'[12] She believed in small practical steps, an incremental approach, rather than grand schemes. This she thought was the British way, and there-fore by definition the better way. But the truculent manner in which she told them so only irritated her partners and alienated potential allies. She was so scornful of 'grandiose' and 'airy-fairy' schemes that she argued her alternative case very badly. The merits of her argument for a Europe of independent nations were smothered by the self-righteousness of her performance.

Moreover she saw divisions over Europe as a threat to her authority at home. With only two reliable allies in the Cabinet – Ridley and Parkinson – and flanked by a Chancellor and Foreign Secretary who both, for different reasons, wanted to join the ERM as soon as possible, she became obsessed with the idea that Lawson and Howe were 'in cahoots' against her and must be kept from ganging up on her if her will was to prevail. In fact both Howe and Lawson insist that they had scarcely any contact with each other. Their attitudes to the ERM were entirely distinct. Since going to the Foreign Office, Howe had become a convert to the full EMU package, including the single currency, and wanted to join the ERM as soon as possible in order to maintain Britain's standing as a leading member of the Community. Lawson by contrast was as strongly opposed to the single currency as Mrs Thatcher herself. He wanted to join the ERM primarily as a monetary discipline; but he also thought that being inside the ERM would give Britain greater leverage to *prevent* a single currency than it could exercise outside it. This difference in objectives should have allowed Mrs Thatcher to play them off against each other while maintaining her own authority: instead she dealt with each of them separately, while demonstrating no confidence in either, which eventually, just before the Madrid summit in June 1989, did drive them to make common cause.

'Of the two,' she believed, 'Geoffrey was the more ill-disposed to me personally,' though Lawson posed politically the greater threat.[13] Despite their disagreement over the exchange rate, she still had a soft spot for her brilliant if sadly wayward Chancellor; but she had long ago decided that Howe was hopelessly woolly. It is doubtful if she really believed that Lawson was after her job – though she managed to give him that impression – but she certainly thought Howe was. At any rate she felt that both of them, after five years in their respective jobs, were becoming too big for their boots: the longer she lasted in office herself, the less she could tolerate rivals in her universe. The result was that the conduct of government became less and less collective: instead of dealing with an inner group of senior ministers, or even bilaterally with her leading colleagues, she hugged the two principal areas of policy more and more closely to her own chest, guided only by her private circle of trusted advisers.

Above all she relied increasingly on Charles Powell. Still officially no more than her foreign-affairs private secretary, Powell was by now effectively her real Foreign Secretary, while Howe held only the title. Her official foreign-affairs adviser, Percy Cradock, had far less access to her than Powell. He retained some influence on policy towards China and Russia; but where Europe was concerned he had none. By 1988, he wrote, 'there was no room for persuasion. The lines were drawn and it was a matter of executing rather than debating policy, and executing her policy at that . . . At this time and on this issue, dissenting advice was wasted.'[14] Sir Michael Butler – no longer British representative in Brussels since 1985, but still closely involved in trying to frame a positive alternative to EMU – agrees. 'She really stopped listening to people.'[15]

At Hanover in June 1988 Mrs Thatcher set out to block the establishment of a European Central Bank; but as so often she was outmanoeuvred. Chancellor Kohl persuaded her to agree to a committee mainly composed of central bankers – including her own appointee, the Governor of the Bank of England, Robin Leigh-Pemberton – to study the question; then they slipped in Delors to chair it. Still she convinced herself that the creation of a central bank was not within the committee's terms of reference. 'I see no reason why they should even discuss it,' she declared on television.[16] Lawson was amazed at her naivety. 'Prime Minister,' he claims to have told her, 'there is no way that a committee with those terms of reference can possibly do anything else than recommend the setting up of a European Central Bank.' She 'abruptly changed the subject, no doubt feeling that I was being awkward again'.[17] Charles Powell confirms that the committee, once set up, 'put on an unexpected turn of speed' and within nine months came up with the three-stage timetable for EMU which was to be the next great bone of contention between Mrs Thatcher and the rest of the Community.[18] If she had been seriously engaged with the issue, she should have fought it from within. On the contrary, either she still thought it would never happen or she believed that she could veto it later. 'Long before there was any question of a formal opt-out,' Michael Butler recalled, 'she in effect opted out . . . She really did opt out of the discussion completely. She gave Robin Leigh-Pemberton no instructions.'[19]

Another example of her deafness to what she did not want to hear was her choice of Leon Brittan to replace Arthur Cockfield as Britain's senior commissioner in Brussels. She refused to reappoint Cockfield because she thought he had 'gone native', and persuaded herself that Brittan, because he had been dry on economic policy at the Treasury and tough on policing as Home Secretary, would naturally be sound on Europe as well. He was very reluctant to leave the House of Commons, and it took three meetings to persuade him. At none of these meetings, however, did she ask his views: she simply told him hers. She should have known that Brittan was strongly pro-European. He had argued in favour of joining the ERM at the famous November 1985 meeting when she imposed her personal veto by one vote against seven. He had also argued for early entry in his first speech from the back benches after Westland. But she was so anxious to push him out of domestic politics into a suitably prestigious job, to get out of her promise to bring him back into the Cabinet, that she overlooked his record – and then felt betrayed when he too went native.[20] 'They go native as soon as they get there,' she complained to Woodrow Wyatt. 'It's too extraordinary.'[21]

Brittan's appointment was widely condemned as a 'disgraceful pay-off' for his silence over Westland.[22] Ted Heath charged, unfairly, that by appointing 'a discredited minister' she was degrading the idea that commissioners were servants of the whole Community, not just tools of their national governments.[23] Mrs Thatcher responded by insisting that Brittan was 'extremely able', which no one doubted, but made clear her expectations of him. 'He will fight our corner, and he will fight Europe's corner.'[24] She was sure he would be 'an excellent Commissioner, both for Europe and . . . maintaining the British identity'.[25]

The turning point in Mrs Thatcher's public attitude to the

Community was her speech to the College of Europe in Bruges in September 1988. She had been booked to speak there, ironically, by the Foreign Office, which hoped it would provide a suitable occasion for a 'positive' speech on Europe. By the time she came to deliver it, however, two more developments had determined her to use it as an opportunity to slap down Jacques Delors. First, in a speech to the European Parliament in July, Delors had deliberately trailed his coat by suggesting that 'an embryo European government' should be established within six years and that in ten years '80 per cent of laws affecting the economy and social policy would be passed at a European and not a national level'.[26] Speaking on *The Jimmy Young Programme* Mrs Thatcher dismissed this angrily as, on the one hand, 'extreme' and 'over the top' and, on the other, an unreal pipedream. The goal of monetary union, she scoffed, was 'some airy-fairy concept which in my view will never come in my lifetime and I hope never at all!'[27]

Then Delors compounded his offence by bringing his federalist pretensions into the British political arena. Again it was the Foreign Office which thought it might be helpful to have him address the TUC Congress at Bournemouth. Delors gave what he regarded as a fairly standard speech, expounding the vision of harmonised laws on hours of work, working conditions and collective bargaining which the following year became the European Social Charter. But he succeeded in converting the traditionally anti-European British trade unionists almost overnight to the realisation that Europe could offer a way of regaining some of the ground they had lost during ten years of Thatcherism – which of course was exactly what Mrs Thatcher objected to. Delors was surprised at the warmth of his reception. In truth the delegates were simply grateful to a visiting dignitary who spoke to them as if they mattered. But Mrs Thatcher's reaction, as Charles Powell recalled, was 'volcanic, or Vesuvian, though that was not unusual as far as Europe was concerned. What really bugged her was seeing the President of the Commission trying to play a political role.'[28] If the Foreign Office had hoped to soften Labour hostility to the Community, they succeeded, as Lawson put it, 'beyond their wildest dreams'.[29] But for twenty years Labour's hostility had been a major factor in keeping Mrs Thatcher positive towards Europe: the moment Labour began to reverse itself, she immediately felt free to do the same.

Unusually the first draft of the Bruges speech was written in Number Ten, by Charles Powell in close collaboration with Mrs Thatcher: the summer recess gave her more time than usual to devote to speechwriting. The Foreign Office was horrified with Powell's draft and set about trying to tone it down. Several revised drafts went back and forth, with phrases they thought they had removed reappearing – 'if anything in stronger form'.[30] Alan Clark somehow saw one of the FCO drafts in his capacity as Trade Minister and claimed to have helped rewrite it. 'The Eurocreeps have written for her a really loathsome text,' he wrote in his diary, '*wallowing* in rejection of our own national identity.'[31] In fact the speech as eventually delivered contained a good deal that was positive, including the assertion that 'Our destiny is in Europe, as part of the Community.' But from her opening remarks, when she congratulated the chairman on his courage in inviting her to speak and joked that it 'must seem rather like inviting Genghis Khan to speak on the virtues of peaceful coexistence', Mrs Thatcher insisted that Britain was committed to the Community on her own terms:

> We British are as much heirs to the legacy of European culture as any other nation . . . For three hundred years, we were part of the Roman Empire . . . Our ancestors – Celts, Saxons, Danes – came from the continent . . . We in Britain are rightly proud of the way in which, since Magna Carta in 1215, we have pioneered and developed representative institutions to stand as bastions of freedom . . .
>
> But we in Britain have in a very special way contributed to Europe. . . . Over the centuries we have fought to prevent Europe falling under the dominance of a single power . . . Only miles from here . . . lie the bodies of 120,000 British soldiers who died in the First World War . . . Nearly 70,000 British servicemen are stationed on the mainland of Europe. All these things . . . are proof of our commitment to Europe's future.

But Britain had its own view of that future. 'Europe,' she insisted, 'is not the creation of the Treaty of Rome . . . The European Community is one manifestation of that European identity, but it is not the only one.' She went on to set out five 'guiding principles', of which the most important was the first: the best way to build a successful Community was not through closer integration but through 'willing and active co-operation between independent sovereign states':

> To try to suppress nationhood and concentrate power at the centre of a European conglomerate would be highly damaging . . . Europe will be Europe precisely because it has France as France, Spain as Spain, Britain as Britain, each with its own customs, traditions and identity. It would be folly to try to fit them into some identikit European personality.

Of course, she conceded, Europe should 'try to speak with a single voice' and 'work more closely on the things we can do better together than alone'. But then came the two killer sentences:

But working closely together does not require power to be centralised in Brussels or decisions to be taken by an appointed bureaucracy . . . We have not successfully rolled back the frontiers of the State in Britain, only to see them re-imposed at a European level with a European superstate exercising a new dominance from Brussels.

This was the key passage. She went on to set four more guiding principles: that solutions should be practical, not utopian; that Europe should be committed to enterprise and open markets; that it should not be protectionist; and that it should maintain its commitment to NATO. Along the way she denied any need for a European Central Bank; insisted on the maintenance of frontiers to control the movement of drugs, terrorists and illegal immigrants; asserted that there was no necessity for any new documents or treaties; and finished provocatively by appealing for a Europe 'which preserves that Atlantic community – that Europe on both sides of the Atlantic – which is our noblest inheritance and our greatest strength'.[32] But most of the controversy the speech aroused centred on her first principle.

It was not so much the content, but the highly charged language which ruffled feathers – rather like Enoch Powell's 'River Tiber' speech on race in 1968. It seems commonplace today, but in 1988 talk of a 'European conglomerate' with bureaucrats exercising 'dominance from Brussels' was – in Michael Butler's words – 'very dangerous stuff indeed'.[33] No one had ever spoken of a European 'superstate' before.* It was also in his view simply wrong. The dichotomy between a free-trade area (good) and a superstate (bad) was false, since the Community had already developed far beyond the one, and no one wanted the other. By signing the Single European Act Mrs Thatcher herself had already agreed to everything that was now on the table.[35] Geoffrey Howe likewise believed that her description of the present reality and

---

*In fact Mrs Thatcher herself had used the phrase once, soon after she became Prime Minister, in a syndicated article during the 1979 European elections. Dismissing the call for a 'fully-fledged federal union', she declared: 'We, in our party, believe that such a new super-state would be in the interest of neither ourselves nor our partners'.[34] But she never used the word again until the Bruges speech.

future ambitions of the Community 'veered between caricature and misunderstanding':

> The picture of a 'European identikit' being imposed, 'ossified by endless regulation' (when very often a single Community regulation replaces twelve national ones) through 'decisions taken by an appointed bureaucracy' (when decisions are in fact taken by the Council of Ministers), was sheer fantasy.[36]

Rather than a rational statement of policy, Howe saw the speech as a psychological liberation which represented 'subconsciously at least, her escape from the collective responsibility of her days in the Heath Cabinet'. But for the need to make her career in an overwhelmingly pro-European party, he reflected, she should really have been an anti-Marketeer – like Powell, John Biffen or Teddy Taylor – all along. At Bruges she finally came out in her true colours. But from the point of view of her devoutly pro-European Foreign Secretary it was 'a little like being married to a clergyman who had suddenly proclaimed his disbelief in God'.[37]

The Bruges speech was not entirely negative. In one prescient passage she sought to widen the concept of Europe beyond the twelve members of the existing Community:

> We must never forget that east of the Iron Curtain, people who once enjoyed a full share of European culture, freedom and identity have been cut off from their roots. We shall always look on Warsaw, Prague and Budapest as great European cities.

She had no inkling that in scarcely more than a year the Iron Curtain would be torn down; but it is greatly to her credit that she never accepted that the Cold War division of Europe should be permanent. Of course she was invoking the captive nations of the east to bolster her argument against deepening the Community in the west. Nevertheless her vision was in this respect more generous and inclusive than the orthodoxy of Brussels. Yet there is still a revealing difference of emphasis in her memoirs, where she writes of 'a wider Europe stretching *perhaps* to the Urals and *certainly* to include that New Europe across the Atlantic'.[38] America, not Europe, remained her touchstone of democracy and freedom.

It was not primarily what she said at Bruges but the way the speech was 'spun' by Bernard Ingham which ensured that it haunted the Tory party for years to come. 'There were some very pro-European passages in it,' Anthony Parsons reflected. 'But the net effect was negative,' because of the way it was packaged for 'patriotic' home consumption.[39] 'In fact,' Lawson agreed, 'it said a number of things that needed to be said, in a perfectly reasonable manner . . . But the newspaper reports, which reflected the gloss Bernard Ingham had given when briefing the press . . . were very different in tone and truer to her own feelings: intensely chauvinistic and . . . hostile to the Community.'[40]

Mrs Thatcher herself was delighted with the effect of the speech, as she told the Tory Party Conference that October with typical immodesty:

It caused a bit of a stir. Indeed, from some of the reactions you would have thought I had re-opened the Hundred Years War. And from the avalanche of support, you'd have thought I'd won it single-handed.

Thinking she had hit the button, she took the chance to reinforce before the domestic audience in Brighton the message she had delivered at Bruges, making still more explicit her distinction between British enterprise and 'those who see European unity as a vehicle for spreading Socialism', and elaborated even more colourfully her central soundbite:

We haven't worked all these years to free Britain from the paralysis of Socialism only to see it creeping in through the back door of central control and bureaucracy from Brussels.

'Ours,' she concluded, 'is the true European ideal. It is that ideal which will fire our campaign in the European elections. That is why we must win every possible seat in the European Parliament for the Conservative cause.'[41]

She was convinced she would win, she told *The Times*, because federalism was 'against the grain of our people':

We have brought it out into the open. People who wanted to tie it up in more regulations, people who wanted a federal Europe, are very cross. Everybody else is cheering like mad.[42]

Some certainly were. The consistently anti-European *Spectator* was delighted that she had 'noticed the political implications' of the single market and started asking questions 'just in time', when the Foreign Office had begun to think she was going to 'come quietly'. But still the paper wondered if she would actually do anything different. 'The story up till now has been stirring declarations, followed by actual results distressingly satisfactory to Brussels.'[43]

To try to keep her up to the mark a group of prominent Tory 'Eurosceptics', as they came to be called, formed the Bruges Group to campaign against ceding any further powers to the Community. Founded by a precocious Oxford undergraduate called Patrick Robertson and chaired by Ralph Harris of the Institute of Economic Affairs, the group was mainly composed of leading Thatcherite academics like Norman Stone, Patrick Minford, Roger Scruton and Alan Sked, who later founded the UK Independence Party – the sort of people who had provided much of the intellectual excitement of early Thatcherism but now merely purveyed an increasingly strident nationalism. The former head of the Downing Street Policy Unit, Ferdinand Mount, warned that they would be unwise to build too many hopes on the speech. 'What the Bruges speech actually says,' he pointed out in the *Spectator* five months later, 'is that "our destiny is in Europe, as part of the Community", and this seems to be the direction in which public opinion . . . seems to be moving in a sluggish sort of way.'

> The Bruges speech was, I think, counterproductive, not because it annoyed Mr Heath and the federalists, but because its more caustic passages . . . encouraged unrealistic expectations among the hyper-nats, while the reality is that Mrs Thatcher is not about to engineer the break-up of the Community or the withdrawal of Britain from it.[44]

This was the crunch. The problem with the Bruges speech was that it did not represent a policy. It was rather, as Nye Bevan described unilateral disarmament in 1957, 'an emotional spasm'. Its impact on the development of the Community was minimal; while its effect on the Conservative party over the next decade was almost wholly disastrous. In the short term, it split the party, releasing in the grass roots a vein of suppressed hostility to the Community which had been building up for years and now burst out unchecked with the leader's undisguised approval, while at the same time infuriating most of the Cabinet and the party hierarchy whose lifelong commitment to Britain's role in Europe as pursued by Macmillan and Heath was undiminished. The Prime Minister's abrupt reversal of the party's established attitude to Europe led inexorably to Geoffrey Howe's resignation from the Government just over two years later and to the parliamentary party's withdrawal of support which forced her own downfall in November 1990. In the medium term, paradoxically, she seemed to win the argument. In the bitter aftermath of her fall, the Bruges speech was seen to have shifted the centre of gravity of the party dramatically away from its previous support for Europe, forming the basis of the Major Government's ambivalent attitude to the Maastricht Treaty in 1992, when Britain formally 'opted out' of the second and third stages of the Delors reforms. Douglas Hurd, Major's Foreign Secretary, wrote in 1993 that the Bruges speech had worn well over the previous five years and was now uncontroversial.[45] Yet in the longer term, as Michael Heseltine wrote, the speech 'unleashed the hounds that were to eat away at the vitals of party unity from then on – to no discernible political benefit'.[46] Not only was Major's Government crippled by his inability to command or reconcile the warring factions; but after his defeat in 1997 the party went on, under his successor William Hague, to adopt an even more rigid posture of hostility to the single currency which failed to impress more than a small minority of the electorate, leading Mrs Thatcher's once all-conquering party to a second comprehensive defeat in 2001. This was the legacy of the Bruges speech.

The 'ambush' before Madrid

Delors unveiled his programme in April 1989, in two parts: one his three-stage timetable for economic and monetary union, the other the so-called 'Social Charter'. Mrs Thatcher immediately rejected both documents out of hand. The first, she told the Commons, 'is aimed at a federal Europe, a common currency and a common economic policy which would take economic policies, including fiscal policy, out of the hands of the House, and that is completely unacceptable'.[47] The second was 'more like a Socialist charter of unnecessary controls and regulations which would . . . make industry uncompetitive and . . . increase unemployment and mean that we could not compete with the rest of the world for the trade that we so sorely need'.[48] Outright opposition to both initiatives formed the basis of her platform for the elections to the European Parliament on 15 June.

Since the introduction of direct elections in 1979 the Tories had always won these five-yearly polls quite easily. They were, after all, the pro-European party. In June 1979, on a low turn-out, they won sixty seats to Labour's seventeen, with nearly 50 per cent of the vote. Even in 1984, at a low point in the Government's fortunes, they still confounded the opinion polls by winning forty-two Euro-seats to Labour's thirty-five, with nearly 40 per cent of the vote to Labour's 36 per cent. June 1989, however, found the Conservatives not only beset by rising inflation and the poll tax, but in disarray over Europe too. Mrs Thatcher authorised a manifesto, and a campaign, at odds with the views of most of her candidates, who were almost by definition Europhiles. The tone was set by a disastrously negative poster, displayed on hoardings all round the country, showing a pile of vegetables with the slogan: 'Stay at home on 15 June and you'll live on a diet of Brussels.' In campaign speeches and television interviews she cast herself as Battling Maggie fighting off the foreign foe. 'We fought and won the Battle for Britain,' she told the Conservative Women's Conference (she did not quite say the Battle *of* Britain). 'Now we must win the battle to create our sort of Europe.'[49]

Much of her language was lifted direct from the Bruges speech. 'We didn't join Europe to be swallowed up in some bureaucratic conglomerate,' she reiterated in her major rally of the campaign, at Nottingham on 12 June, 'where it's Euro-this and Euro-that and forget about being British, or French or Italian or Spanish.' She never mentioned the ERM or EMU, but concentrated her fire almost exclusively on the bureaucratic menace posed by the Social Charter, summed up once again in the refrain: 'We haven't rolled back the frontiers of socialism in this country to see them re-imposed from Brussels.'[50] Meanwhile Ted Heath, still the party's second most visible campaigner, stumped the country, ridiculing her scaremongering and insisting that there was 'little in the [Delors] Report with which an intelligent Conservative cannot agree'.[51] Amazingly, Mrs Thatcher felt it prudent to pay tribute in the Commons to Heath's 'vision' in taking Britain into the Community in the first place.[52] (He was seen to nod slowly in acknowledgement.) But the party's final broadcast – which she claimed to have written herself as an improvement on 'the frivolous and obscure advertisements we had used earlier'[53] – ended with another stark negative: 'Don't let Labour in through the back door. Vote Conservative on Thursday.'[54]

The result was the Tories' first defeat in a national election under Mrs Thatcher's leadership. On a significantly increased poll, up from 32 to 37 per cent, the party gained only 33 per cent of the vote – its lowest-ever share – and lost thirteen seats to Labour, precisely reversing the 1984 result so that Labour now held forty-two to the Tories' thirty-five. Of course the outcome owed less to enthusiasm for a federal Europe than to the Government's growing unpopularity for other reasons nearer home, plus the sense that Mrs Thatcher, after ten years as Prime Minister, was getting seriously out of touch. The European context also gave voters an outlet for concern about the environment: the Green party took an unprecedented – but never to be repeated –

15 per cent of the vote (largely at the expense of the newly merged Liberal Democrats), though needless to say they won no seats. Whatever the mix of reasons, the result delivered a sharp warning to Tory MPs that Neil Kinnock's Labour party had finally become electable again, while the Prime Minister was becoming a liability whom they might need to jettison before the next election if they wanted to save their seats.

Kinnock had claimed that the elections would be a referendum on ten years of Thatcherism, and naturally hailed the result as heralding that her time was up. Mrs Thatcher equally strenuously denied it – though she had been happy to portray the contest as a choice between freedom and socialism – but she was said to be 'shaken' by the result, which she officially described as 'disappointing', and was reported to have told ministers to 'calm it' – that is to slow down plans for controversial legislation like privatisation of the railways.[55] In her memoirs Lady Thatcher argued that the 1989 result was not really a vote against herself, since most of the Tory candidates were Euro-federalists, 'a residue of Heathism'.[56] Labour's victory was really a vote against her federalist opponents and hence a victory for her! This is ingenious, but unconvincing. The great truth about elections, which Labour had been learning throughout the 1980s and the Tories would learn in the 1990s, is that the electorate will not vote for a divided party. In 1989 the public was bewildered by the spectacle of a party leader standing against the established policies of her own side. As Geoffrey Howe put it: 'The discordant populism which . . . confused and undermined our candidates, our workers and our voters was the new note that had been struck in the Bruges speech. The party was effectively being split by the defection of its own leader.'[57] As a result her aura of electoral invincibility had been badly dented.

The next week the simmering tension between Mrs Thatcher and her senior colleagues came to a head in the run-up to the European Council in Madrid, when she persisted in trying to exclude her Chancellor and Foreign Secretary from any consultation about the decisions that might be taken at the summit. In public she continued to insist that there was no disagreement between them about the ERM. 'I don't know of anyone who seriously suggests at the moment that we should join the ERM,' she had blithely declared, with Howe sitting beside her, at her press conference to launch the European election campaign.[58] That might have been strictly true insofar as neither Howe nor Lawson thought it practical to join immediately; but they were both convinced that it would strengthen Britain's hand in forthcoming negotiations about EMU if she would come off the fence at Madrid and give a commitment to join within a set timescale. She was more determined than ever to do no such thing. She prepared for the summit by convening a conference of her private advisers – Charles Powell, Brian Griffiths, Alan Walters and Bernard Ingham – with no elected politicians present at all. 'This,' Hugo Young comments, 'was the kitchen cabinet which had now replaced the formal Cabinet as the forum of influence.'[59]

On Wednesday 14 June Howe and Lawson sent her a joint minute setting out their advice that she should give a 'non-legally binding' undertaking at Madrid to join the ERM by the end of 1992, and asked her for a meeting. 'Could we discuss this with you?'[60] She was furious – she describes their request in her memoirs as an attempt to 'ambush' her – but grudgingly agreed to see them the following Tuesday, 20 June, when she bluntly rejected their arguments and refused to tie her hands. A few hours later she sent Howe a paper adding further conditions before Britain could contemplate joining, including the final completion of the single market, which might take years. 'The hand of Walters,' Lawson wrote, 'was all too visible.'[61] Their response was to ask for another meeting. She was angrier than ever, tried to talk to the two of them separately by telephone but eventually agreed to see them together at Chequers early on Sunday morning, just before she left for Madrid. There is not much disagreement between the three of them about what happened at this 'nasty little meeting', as she called it. In her view they tried to 'blackmail' her by threatening to resign if she would not agree to state her 'firm intention' to join the ERM not later than a specified date. 'They said that if I did this I would stop the whole Delors process from going on to Stages 2 and 3. And if I did not agree to their terms and their formulation they would both resign.'[62] 'The atmosphere was unbelievably tense,' Lawson confirms:

> Margaret was immovable. Geoffrey said that if she had no time whatever for his advice . . . he would have no alternative but to resign. I then chipped in, briefly, to say, 'You know, Prime Minister, that if Geoffrey goes I must go too.' There was an icy silence, and the meeting came to an abrupt end, with nothing resolved.[63]

'I knew that Geoffrey had put Nigel up to this,' Lady Thatcher wrote. 'They had clearly worked out precisely what they were going to say.'[64] Lawson does not deny it, but insists that this was 'the only instance in eight years as Cabinet colleagues when we combined to promote a particular course of action'.[65] All they were doing, in the first instance, was asking – as Chancellor and Foreign Secretary – to be consulted. Yet she bitterly resented what she called 'this way of proceeding – by joint minutes, pressure and cabals'.[66] It is difficult to argue with Percy Cradock's verdict that the fact that 'a ministerial request for consultation could be construed as a conspiracy . . . illustrated an alarming breakdown of communication and trust within government'.[67]

Prime Minister and Foreign Secretary flew together to Madrid, but Mrs Thatcher did not speak to her colleague on the plane – 'the buff curtain across the gangway remained drawn' – and when they got to the British Embassy she closeted herself all evening with Powell and Ingham, while Howe enjoyed a relaxed supper downstairs with the Ambassador and his staff. When she spoke in the Council the next morning, 'her Foreign Secretary still had not the least idea what she intended to say'.[68]

In fact she was unwontedly conciliatory and constructive. It was widely suggested that following her rebuff in the European elections she came to Madrid with 'diminished clout' and conducted herself less stridently as a result – though she of course denied it.[69] She insisted afterwards that she had defied Howe and Lawson's 'blackmail' by still refusing to set a date for joining the ERM. But in reality she did move most of the way to meet them, by advancing from the vague formula that Britain would join 'when the time is right' to a much more specific set of conditions – not, as she had threatened on 20 June, the final completion of the single market, but merely further progress towards completion, plus British inflation falling to the European average, progress by other countries towards the abolition of exchange controls, and further liberalisation of financial services. These new tests were much more flexible and open to interpretation than her stance hitherto, as was demonstrated just over a year later when John Major was able to persuade her that sufficient progress had been made to declare that the conditions had been met.

On the wider issues at Madrid, EMU and the Social Charter, Mrs Thatcher congratulated herself that she had stood firm. She claimed to have prevented President Mitterrand fixing a timetable for the second and third stages of the Delors Report before the first stage had been completed and happily described the report at her post-summit press conference as 'a good basis for future work, but not the only basis . . . Let me stress that there is absolutely nothing automatic about going beyond Stage 1. All that is for future decision.' She still insisted that there were other – unspecified – ways of realising EMU without either a single currency or a central bank, and was cross with Mitterrand for calling her 'a brake on Europe'. That was 'a bit rich', she retorted, when France had not yet abolished exchange controls. 'I am the accelerator,' she boasted. 'He has scarcely got into the car yet.'[70]

So far as the Social Charter was concerned, however, she described in her memoirs how she tried unsuccessfully to win over the 'rather sound' Portuguese Prime Minister, Cavaco Silva, to her viewpoint. 'Don't you see,' I said, 'that the Social Charter is intended to stop Portugal attracting investment from Germany because of your lower wage costs? This is German protectionism.' But Sr Silva was unconvinced. He 'would doubtless have been sounder still', she reflected wrily, 'if his country was not so poor and the Germans quite so rich . . . So I was alone in opposing the charter.'[71]

The faithful Wyatt thought that Mrs Thatcher had done 'brilliantly' at Madrid. 'She is very pleased that she has got it stated that the Delors report was only one approach to greater economic union.'[72] She got an unusually good press for her more constructive tone. 'Our leader,' wrote Hugo Young in the *Guardian*, 'has made her compact with the real world . . . It can only do her quite a lot of good.'[73] But she had not really achieved anything at all, as the following year showed. Whether, as Lawson and Howe believed, she would have gained herself more leverage at future meetings by agreeing to set a clear timetable to join the ERM cannot be proved. The fact is that Britain was now isolated, however she conducted herself. She did not significantly hold up progress towards EMU by being marginally more constructive; but neither would she have achieved any more by being intransigent. It was too late.

Her fury was reserved for Howe and Lawson, who had backed her into a corner and demonstrated that they had the power to bring her down. At the time she pretended that she had called their bluff. 'My Foreign Secretary said that if I didn't commit myself to a date he'd resign,' she reportedly told an 'intimate'. 'I didn't commit myself and he hasn't resigned. What sort of Foreign Secretary have I got?'[74] In her memoirs she describes how they backed down. As the members of the Cabinet arrived for the first Thursday meeting after Madrid, instead of sitting at the table as she usually did, 'I stood in the doorway – waiting. But there were no resignations.'[75] Howe comments that neither he nor Lawson was aware of 'this piece of retrospective theatre . . . Neither of us . . . noticed or have since been able to recall any change in Margaret's routine.'[76] In fact there was no need for resignations since the threat had achieved most of what they wanted. Years later she admitted to Wyatt: 'They overpowered me.'[77] She knew she could not have survived either or both of them resigning. But she vowed that 'I would never, never allow this to happen again.'[78] Four weeks later she employed the Prime Minister's ultimate power to break the Howe–Lawson axis. She resolved to punish Howe – and warn Lawson – by removing him from the Foreign Office. But it was a messy operation.

She was due for a reshuffle anyway – she normally held one before the summer holidays, and a shake-up of personnel is every Prime Minister's response to plummeting poll ratings – but this one was exceptionally sweeping. Just as Harold Macmillan in July 1962 started out wanting to change his Chancellor, Selwyn Lloyd, and ended up sacking one-third of the Cabinet, so now Mrs Thatcher tried to camouflage Howe's removal as part of a general redeployment. Only eight out of twenty-one Cabinet ministers (Lawson, Hurd, Fowler, Clarke, Walker, Rifkind, Mackay and Belstead) stayed where they were. Two (Paul Channon and John Moore) she removed; and two more (George Younger and David Young) left voluntarily. (Young, having failed to become party chairman, settled for deputy chairman instead; Younger left to become chairman of the Royal Bank of Scotland.) The other nine were switched around. Among the middle ranks John Wakeham moved to Energy, Cecil Parkinson from Energy to Transport, John MacGregor from Agriculture to Education, Tom King from Northern Ireland to Defence, Nicholas Ridley from Environment to the DTI, Tony Newton from Chancellor of the Duchy of Lancaster to Social Security, while Kenneth Baker – whom Mrs Thatcher thought of as the great communicator – became party chairman (and Chancellor of the Duchy of Lancaster). Into the Cabinet for the first time came Peter Brooke (Northern Ireland), Chris Patten (Environment), John Gummer (Agriculture) and Norman Lamont (Chief Secretary). Of these only the last could be called a Thatcherite; though below the Cabinet Peter Lilley became Financial Secretary. The overall effect of the changes, Lady Thatcher noted in her memoirs, was that the balance of the Cabinet 'slipped slightly further to the left'. But 'none of this mattered,' she assured herself, 'as long as crises which threatened my authority could be avoided'.[79]

But all this minor juggling was overshadowed by the removal of Geoffrey Howe from the job he had held for the past six years. Howe had no warning of what was coming: a few days earlier he was specifically assured by the Chief Whip, David Waddington, that he had nothing to fear. It was a brutal way to treat one of her most loyal colleagues, her shadow Chancellor in opposition and the architect of the 1981 budget, who in his quiet way had borne the heat of the early economic reforms. The debt she owed Howe's dogged persistence for her survival and success was incalculable; yet Mrs Thatcher had come to despise but simultaneously fear him, believing that he was positioning himself to replace her. 'He wants to do the job,' she told Wyatt, 'but I don't think he is capable of it.'[80] In her memoirs there is a hint of apology for the way she treated him, but she suggests that Howe brought it on himself:

> This quiet, gentle but deeply ambitious man – with whom my relations had become progressively worse as my exasperation at his insatiable appetite for compromise led me sometimes to lash out at him in front of others – was now out to make trouble for me if he possibly could . . . He thought he had become indispensable.[81]

Having decided to remove Howe from the Foreign Office she offered him the choice of becoming Leader of the House or Home Secretary. He accepted the former, but held out for the consolation title of deputy Prime Minister to salve his pride. With hindsight she thought she should have sacked him altogether, rather than leave him bruised but still in a position from which he could wound her fatally the following year. Howe, too, quickly realised that he would have done better to make a clean break. He prints in his memoirs the letter of resignation he wrote but did not send.[82] By becoming deputy Prime Minister he hoped to inherit the sort of position within the Government that Willie Whitelaw had occupied before his illness. If Mrs Thatcher had not by this time lost all sense of Cabinet management she would have invited him to fill that crucial vacancy: Howe would have made a very good Willie, had she been prepared to trust him. But 'because Geoffrey bargained for the job,' she sneered, 'it never conferred the status which he hoped. In practical terms it just meant that [he] sat on my immediate left at Cabinet meetings – a position he may well have come to regret.'[83] Bernard Ingham made a point of telling the press that there was no such job as deputy Prime Minister anyway, so the title did not amount to a row of beans. She exacted one more petty revenge by depriving Howe of Chevening, the country house in Kent which he and Elspeth had made their second home for the past six years. She apparently believed that he was using it as a sort of alternative Chequers, a rival power base from which to challenge her; but Kenneth Baker was not alone in thinking this 'an unnecessarily spiteful act which Margaret was to regret'.[84] Moreover since the Howes had no other home, she then had to ask Lawson to give up the other grace-and-favour residence at her disposal – Dorneywood in Buckinghamshire – so that they could move there. The whole business was deeply undignified.

And that was not the end of it. Someone – possibly Ingham, possibly

Howe himself – leaked the fact that she had also offered him the Home Office, which naturally upset Douglas Hurd (though Hurd consoled himself with the reflection that her gaffe gave him 'credit in the bank' which he was able to cash in three months later.[85] Then if she was really determined to have a new Foreign Secretary, Hurd – with his diplomatic background and four years as Minister of State, followed by four years at the Home Office – was obviously the best-qualified candidate. Probably for that very reason, however, she was determined to look elsewhere. After Peter Carrington and Francis Pym, both Old Etonians, and the Wykehamist Howe, she did not want another pro-European toff at the Foreign Office; and at this point she was still strong enough to appoint whom she wanted. She wanted a Foreign Secretary with no 'form', who would uncomplainingly do her bidding. So she appointed John Major.

She had already identified Major as a possible long-term successor. As Chief Secretary at the Treasury since 1987 he had impressed her with his quiet mastery of detail and calm judgement, notably on the NHS inquiry. Always on the look-out for competent right-wingers, she had persuaded herself that he was more of a Thatcherite than he really was. 'He is another one of us,' she assured a sceptical Nicholas Ridley.[86] In fact, though dry on economic issues, Major was by no means Thatcherite on social policy; he was also unenthusiastic about the poll tax. Even if she had been right, however, thrusting him into the Foreign Office at the age of forty-five, with no relevant experience or aptitude, was bad for him and also bad for her: he could not help looking like her poodle.* When offered the job he very sensibly demurred – 'Are you sure this is a good idea?' – but she insisted. Major was apprehensive and embarrassed, knowing well that Hurd would have been a better choice.[88]

Altogether the 1989 reshuffle was a political shambles which antagonised practically all her colleagues and delighted only the opposition. When Mrs Thatcher told the House that her engagements for the day included her weekly audience with the Queen, the Labour wit Tony Banks asked: 'Is the right hon. Lady intending to reshuffle her as well?'[89] Comparison was freely made with Macmillan's 'Night of the Long Knives', which was widely felt to have signalled his loss of grip. 'After the messy Cabinet reshuffle in which she booted Sir Geoffrey Howe

---

*She was typically tart in defending the appointment, telling David Owen – whom Callaghan had parachuted into the same job at an even younger age – that at least Major had two years' Cabinet experience before becoming Foreign Secretary.[87]

out of the Foreign Office,' Robin Day predicted in his memoirs published that year, 'the Thatchocracy may well end sooner than expected.'[90] Tory MPs showed where their sympathy lay by cheering and waving their order papers when Howe came into the House. No one but Margaret Thatcher, Lawson wrote, could have failed to get the message.[91] Loyal supporters like Ian Gow foresaw trouble ahead;[92] while even Wyatt worried that 'she has made a bitter enemy of Geoffrey Howe'.[93] For her part Mrs Thatcher blamed Howe for making such a fuss, and was deeply hurt by the battering she received in the press. Wyatt wrote that he had 'never known Margaret so upset as she was this morning. She was railing at the unfairness of it all.'[94] She quickly recognised that by leaving Howe in office she had got the worst of all worlds. The novelist Anthony Powell met her soon afterwards at a private dinner when she scarcely addressed a word to her hostess but 'talked all the time of getting rid of Geoffrey Howe, for whom she seems to feel some animus'.[95] Meanwhile the rest of the Cabinet felt that if she could treat Howe like that, none of them was safe. Kenneth Baker persuaded her to declare formally that this was the team with which she intended to fight the next election (probably two years away). In fact there were to be three more resignations and two more voluntary withdrawals before the survivors finally called time on her.

From now on Mrs Thatcher took a positive delight in flaunting her hostility to all things European. That summer France hosted a G7 summit to coincide with the bicentenary of the French revolution. Mrs Thatcher could not resist trailing her coat with some undiplomatic references to the Bastille and the guillotine. In an interview for *Le Monde* – followed up with a string of domestic interviews – she contrasted the violent utopianism of 1789 with the legality and moderation of the English revolution of 1688, pointing out that 'Human rights did not begin with the French revolution':[96]

Human rights did not start two hundred years ago. They may have started two hundred years ago in France and that is a cause for celebration for France . . . but . . . there were many many things before that, including . . . the whole foundation of human rights in the Jewish and Christian religions, including the great Magna Carta where the barons seized power from the king, including in 1688–89 when we had a Bill of Rights and a quiet revolution.[97]

In fact she did not think the French revolution was something to be celebrated at all, as she made clear after Madrid, when a Labour MP asked her why she was standing aloof from 'the next European revolution'. 'It took us a long time to get rid of the effects of the French revolution 200 years ago,' she replied, 'and we don't want another.'[98] Before attending the celebrations she told Wyatt, 'I am thinking of getting some scarlet pimpernels to wear round my neck';[99] and in Paris she presented President Mitterrand with a first edition of *A Tale of Two Cities* – one of the formative books of her adolescence – which she explains in her memoirs 'made somewhat more elegantly the same point as my interview'.[100] She denied that her comments caused any friction with the French or spoiled Mitterrand's party; but she clearly relished the fracas.[101]

At Strasbourg in December she unilaterally vetoed the adoption of the Social Charter. 'It has no operational significance,' she gloated at her press conference afterwards.[102] Specific proposals would have to be considered on their merits, not adopted *en bloc*. She was happy to accept common rules in some areas, like health and safety and freedom of movement; but she rejected the harmonisation of working hours, compulsory schemes of worker participation and the like. More importantly, however, she was unable to block the next stage of progress towards EMU. It needed only a majority of member countries to call an Intergovernmental Conference (IGC) to set a definite timetable. But she still insisted that it would require unanimity for the conference to decide anything, and so long as she was there this was out of the question:

> I made very clear that Britain cannot accept the Delors Stage 2 and 3 proposals and this is not just the Government's view, but that of all the main Parties in Parliament. We are not prepared to see Parliament's powers in the crucial areas of economic and financial matters diminished.[103]

She still made a show of offering a constructive alternative to the Delors blueprint by embracing an ingenious scheme developed by 'the irrepressible Michael Butler', as Lawson calls him.[104] Instead of merging the existing currencies into a single new currency, Butler proposed that the existing notional European currency, the *ecu*, should be built up as an additional currency alongside the franc, Deutschmark, lira, pound and the rest. John Major took up the 'hard *ecu*' enthusiastically when he became Chancellor following Lawson's resignation in October 1989 and did his best to sell it around Europe throughout 1990. At the Dublin summit in June Mrs Thatcher commended it with faint praise as 'a reasonable next stage which in my view is quite a big next stage and really takes us as far as the eye can see at the moment'.[105]

She was prepared to envisage it functioning like the Deutschmark as a sort of substitute gold standard. But Nicholas Ridley doubts that she ever believed it except as a way of buying time.[106] Even Major says she supported it only as 'a diversion or a wrecking tactic'.[107]

Some years later Butler still maintained that if only Mrs Thatcher had argued strongly for it from the beginning, in the same way that she pushed for the Single European Act, the hard *ecu* might have carried the day:

> She was perfectly favourable to the plan as presented. The only trouble was that she wanted it to be an alternative to monetary union and not presented as an evolutionary market-driven approach to it.[108]

Though it would start as a common currency, the official Government line, as Major put it, was that 'in the very long term, if people and governments so choose, it could develop into a single currency'. Howe, Hurd and Leigh-Pemberton all dutifully backed this cautious formulation. But once again Mrs Thatcher sabotaged the policy of her own government, declaring roundly in the House of Commons on 28 June: 'I do not believe that that formula could develop into a single currency.'[109] With that she demolished any possibility that the other eleven would buy the British idea.

Mixing regularly with his fellow Finance Ministers in the Community, Major could see that she was living in a world of her own:

> The Prime Minister was flatly hostile to the single currency and appeared to me to have no idea of how committed our partners were to it. She was confident it wouldn't work, and seemed to believe that if she asserted that it would fail, then fail it would.[110]

Blinkered by her own self-righteousness, she liked to imagine that she was not so isolated as she seemed but was actually speaking up for the smaller nations against the domination of Paris and Bonn, as she told Wyatt after Dublin:

> Always the Chancellor of West Germany and the President of France cook something up together without consulting anybody else and drop it on the Summit meeting and try to force it through. If it was not for me all kinds of things would happen which would never be acceptable to anybody.[111]

'I do not think we are out of step,' she declared at her post-summit press conference. 'I think steadily others are coming in step with us.'[112] Alternatively she persuaded herself that it was actually good to be isolated, that in being isolated she was actually leading Europe. 'Sometimes you have to be isolated to give a lead.'[113] But this was self-delusion.

The truth was that, right or wrong, she was the worst possible advocate for her vision. Her ceaselessly confrontational style became – in the view of her long-suffering colleagues who had to try to pick up the pieces after her bravura performances – 'counterproductive'.[114] 'It wears out a bit,' Douglas Hurd recalled. 'I think that quite a lot of her colleagues began to regard it as theatre.'[115] Nigel Lawson – who shared her opposition to EMU and her belief in a deregulated free-market Europe – sums up the impact of her anti-diplomacy:

> For her unanimity meant she had a veto; and if you had a veto you used it. It was as simple as that. For everyone else, unanimity gave them a card that could from time to time be played to secure a national objective. Once the others realised that Margaret was playing by quite different rules, there ceased to be any reason . . . to make any concessions to the UK, since nothing could be secured in return . . .
>
> This, along with other aspects of her style and tone of voice, came to irk the others so much that they instinctively sank their differences and joined forces against her. Ironically, by 1989 she had become the Community's great unifying force – and the unity she had forged was against the UK. Partly as a result of her undoubted triumph in the Community Budget negotiations of her early years as Prime Minister, she believed that only head-on confrontation yielded results in Europe; and she revelled in being one against eleven. But on most issues this approach was foolish and threw away many opportunities to build alliances and exploit differences among the others . . .
>
> Had she proposed withdrawal from the Community altogether, at least there would have been some intellectual coherence. But she knew that was not possible . . . so she pursued a policy which ensured that, while remaining in the Community, the UK's objectives were least likely to be secured.[116]

Eventually at the Rome IGC in October 1990 she was ambushed by the other leaders into setting a fixed timetable for Delors Stage 2. This was the last straw, which precipitated the clash with Howe that brought about her fall. The repeated 'No, no, no' with which she dismissed in the House of Commons Jacques Delors' aspirations for the further integration of the Community was 'so manifestly a declaration of defiance or, if you like, of UDI on her part, or on Britain's part' that Howe finally decided he could no longer stay in the Government.[117] Her own resignation followed three weeks later. Out of office she railed furiously against the Maastricht Treaty, from which John Major – following her lead – succeeded in negotiating a series of British opt-outs, from the single currency and most of the provisions of the Social Chapter. Yet almost all her former colleagues and advisers – even Charles Powell – agree that she would have accepted Maastricht in the end, as Major did, because at the end of the day she always accepted the best available deal.[118] More subtly Hurd suggested that she would have vetoed Maastricht, but then signed up at Lisbon six months later;[119] while another senior minister thought she would have been 'shouting it from the rooftops' if she could have secured the same deal that Major secured at Maastricht.[120]

The truth is that Mrs Thatcher's European policy was no policy at all. It reflected, but also greatly exacerbated, instinctive British suspicion of the Continent. It pointed up real difficulties – of sovereignty, of democratic accountability, of economic divergence – in the way of 'ever-closer union' of the Community. There was a case for proceeding one step at a time, just as there was – and still is – a case for preferring a community of independent nations to a superstate. But by continually saying 'no' Britain only lost influence on a process from which it was in the end unable to stand aside, thus repeating the dismal game of catch-up which Britain had been playing at every stage of Europe's development since 1950. Europe was the greatest challenge facing Mrs Thatcher's premiership. It was also the greatest failure of her premiership. And it was a failure directly attributable to her own confrontational, xenophobic and narrow-minded personality.

15

Tomorrow the World

The export of Thatcherism

By the mid-1980s Thatcherism had become an international phenomenon. Partly just because she was a woman, which meant that in all the photographs of international gatherings she stood out, in blue or red or green, from the grey-suited men around her (and was always placed chivalrously in the middle); partly on account of the strident clarity of her personality, her tireless travelling and her evangelical compulsion to trumpet her beliefs wherever she went; partly as a result of Britain's unlikely victory in the Falklands war; partly in recognition of her close relationship with Ronald Reagan and her intermediary role between the Americans and Mikhail Gorbachev – for all these reasons Margaret Thatcher had become by about 1985 one of the best-known leaders on the planet, a superstar on the world stage, an object of curiosity and admiration wherever she went and far more popular around the world than she ever was at home.

Above all she was the most articulate and charismatic champion of a wave of economic liberalisation which was sweeping the world, turning back the dominant collectivism of the past half-century. She did not, of course, originate it. The anti-socialist and anti-corporatist counter-revolution was a global phenomenon observable literally from China to Peru. It originated, if anywhere, in Chicago, where both Friedrich Hayek and Milton Friedman had been at different times professors. The turning of the intellectual tide was reflected before Mrs Thatcher even became Tory leader by both of them being awarded the Nobel prize for economics – Hayek in 1974, Friedman in 1976. It was in Chile that their heretical ideas were first determinedly put into practice when General Augusto Pinochet, having overthrown (with American help) the democratically elected Marxist government of Salvador Allende in 1973, brought in the so-called 'Chicago boys'

to instigate an extreme experiment in free-market reform enforced
by the methods of a police state. The politics were detestable, but the
economics set a model for the rest of South America and beyond.

In Britain the Institute of Economic Affairs had been preaching
free-market solutions for years, attracting negligible interest from senior
politicians with the exception of the half-crazed Enoch Powell, until
Keith Joseph underwent his damascene conversion in 1974, drawing
Mrs Thatcher in his wake. But her election to the Tory leadership the
following year was a reflection, not the cause, of an ideological shift
that was already under way. In 1976 the Oxford historian Robert
Blake drew attention to 'one of those rare and profound changes in
the intellectual climate which occur only once or twice in a hundred
years . . . There is a wind of change in Britain, and much of the
democratic world – and it comes from the right, not the left.'[1] Blake
was correct, but the international perspective is important.

In those early days of her leadership Mrs Thatcher knew that she
was riding, or hoped to ride, a global wave. In one of her first major
speeches in January 1976 she congratulated the people of Australia
and New Zealand for electing governments dedicated to reversing
socialism, and hoped to learn from them. 'What has happened in
Australasia is part of a wider reawakening to the need to provide a
more positive defence of the values and traditions on which Western
civilisation, and prosperity, are based.'[2] 'Across the Western world the
tide is turning,' she declared in March 1979, just before the General
Election which brought her to power, 'and soon the same thing will
happen here.'[3]

The idea that she was the pathfinder only seized her some years
later. 'In 1981,' she recalled, 'a finance minister came to see me. "We're
all very interested in what you're doing," he said, "because if you
succeed, others will follow." That had never occurred to me.'[4] By 1986,
however, she had begun to glory in the claim that Britain had led the
world. 'The policies the Government has pioneered are catching on
in country after country,' she told that year's Tory Party Conference;[5]
and from now on this boast became steadily more inflated. 'Other
countries' socialists know a good thing when they see one,' she told
the Conservative Central Council in March 1988:

> They are cutting taxes and privatising industries in socialist Australia,
> in socialist New Zealand and in socialist Spain. And if *perestroika*
> keeps on rolling along, we might be able to point to even more
> surprising converts.[6]

Two months later she told the Conservative Women's Conference:

> Other governments – and other socialist governments – are now
> coming here to see how it is done . . . Foreign countries may take
> their cuisine from Paris, but they take their economics from London.[7]

And in October 1989, when cracks were already appearing in the
Berlin Wall, she explicitly claimed the credit for the earthquake that
was shaking Eastern Europe:

> The messages on our banners in 1979 – freedom, opportunity, family,
> enterprise, ownership – are now inscribed on the banners in Leipzig,
> Warsaw, Budapest and even Moscow . . . We did not know it at the
> time, but the torch we lit in Britain, which transformed our country
> . . . became a beacon that has shed its light across the Iron Curtain
> into the East . . . We knew that we were starting a British revolu-
> tion – in fact we were the pioneers of a world revolution.[8]

Incontestably the British example – particularly privatisation – played
a part. But equally obviously the counter-revolution had its own
momentum, in both East and West, as one social democratic country
after another ran into the same sort of problems that Britain had
encountered in the 1970s and responded in more or less the same way.
In France, François Mitterrand was elected in 1981 on a wave of left-
wing enthusiasm with a socialist programme of nationalisation and
high welfare spending which quickly resulted in inflation, unemployment and threatened national bankruptcy. It was Jacques Delors, his
Finance Minister, who initiated a historic reversal, starting with drastic
spending cuts and a refusal to bail out failing companies and moving
on to privatisation. 'I did not appoint you in order to pursue Mrs
Thatcher's policies,' Mitterrand allegedly objected. But within a year
or two the great survivor of French politics had adapted to the new
orthodoxy with the characteristically Gallic formulation that 'The State
must know how to efface itself.'[9] Over the next decade the same necessity imposed itself right across Europe. In the fifteen years from 1985
over 100 billion dollars worth of state assets were sold off, including
such flagship national companies as Renault, Volkswagen, Lufthansa,
Elf and the Italian oil company ENI, adding up to 'the greatest sale
in the history of the world'.[10]

Above all the free-market contagion spread to the citadels of
Communism itself – to China as early as 1981 (where the experiment
of economic liberalisation remained under strict political control) and

then to the Soviet Union in the form of Mikhail Gorbachev's *pere-stroika* programme, whose inherent contradictions rapidly precipitated the collapse of the whole Communist system. Mrs Thatcher was entitled to celebrate the triumph of ideas which she had not only followed but proselytised with missionary fervour. Because she was such a visible and effective champion of resurgent capitalism, so that in much of the world her name became synonymous with privatisation, she was not the only one to exaggerate the influence of Britain's example. The American historians Daniel Yergan and Joseph Stanislaw, for instance, wrote in 1998 that 'By the 1990s it would turn out that Margaret Thatcher had established the new economic agenda around the world.'[11] Historians do like to put a name to movements. But the British historian Peter Clarke was surely more accurate when he observed in 1991 that 'Other countries have adapted to the harsher economic climate of the 1980s with moves towards the free market; but that does not justify labelling them as examples of Thatcherism.'[12] The very fact that the phenomenon has been virtually universal – so that, as Mrs Thatcher herself noted, not just conservative but even nominally socialist governments were equally forced to conform to the global *Zeitgeist* – is the proof that it had its own irresistible momentum, irrespective of her contribution, significant though that was.

The collapse of Communism and the 'problem' of Germany

Nevertheless the sudden – and, until it happened, quite unexpected – collapse of Communism in the autumn of 1989 was a triumphant vindication of all that Mrs Thatcher had stood for and striven to bring about since 1975. Whether you call it Thatcherism or some other name, the fall of the Berlin Wall, the liberation of the Soviet empire and the disintegration within two years of the Soviet Union itself represented the ultimate victory for her philosophy and her – and Ronald Reagan's – military strategy. The overriding context of all her politics for forty years had been the Cold War; and now suddenly the West had won it.

In her memoirs she gave the principal credit to Reagan 'whose policies of military and economic competition with the Soviet Union forced the Soviet leaders . . . to abandon their ambitions of hegemony and to embark on the process of reform which in the end brought the entire Communist system crashing down'. But since the actual collapse had occurred after Reagan's time she felt obliged to extend the credit to his successor, George Bush, who 'managed the dangerous and volatile transformation with great diplomatic skill'; and even, through gritted teeth, to some of the other European allies, 'who resisted both Soviet pressure and Soviet blandishments to maintain a strong western defence – in particular Helmut Schmidt, Helmut Kohl, François Mitterrand and . . . but modesty forbids'.[13] This was false modesty, however. As the President's staunchest ally she had no doubt who deserved most credit, after Reagan himself, for the success of their joint strategy. In all the speeches she made at international conferences and self-congratulatory ceremonies after her fall from power, the same phrase recurs like a refrain. In Korea in September 1992: 'President Reagan and I got our message through to the Soviet people by every means possible.'[14] At the Fraser Institute in Toronto in November 1993: 'Ronald Reagan and I started by saying, let's make it quite clear to the Soviet Union that they will never win militarily.'[15] And at the National Press Club in Washington in June 1995 a wider view of their complementary partnership:

> Both Ronald Reagan and I deliberately set out to reverse state control, liberate individual initiative and stand up to a Soviet Empire which was every bit as evil as he described it . . . *His* main task lay in foreign and defence policy – which was only natural for a super-power. My main task was in economic affairs – to roll back collectivism in all its forms. This included, of course, a campaign against communism everywhere – the most total tyranny in the world.[16]

In retirement she had no doubt that this was her greatest achievement.

Of course the Soviet empire collapsed for both external and internal reasons. NATO's refusal to lower the nuclear threshold, challenging Moscow instead to an arms race which it could not win, exerted critical pressure from the outside; while Gorbachev's belated attempts to liberalise the sclerotic Soviet economy (*perestroika*) and open up the hidebound secrecy of Soviet society (*glasnost*) released pent-up dissent within. Clearly the first was primarily the policy of the Reagan administration, and specifically the President's personal determination to develop the 'Star Wars' missile-defence shield. But even before Reagan came into office Mrs Thatcher was an outspoken advocate of increased defence spending and nuclear modernisation, and she played a major part (despite her doubts about SDI) in helping to keep the Alliance united behind it. She also encouraged Gorbachev in his domestic reform programme, though it would be foolish to exaggerate her influence in this respect. More important, probably, was the impact of her several excursions behind the Iron Curtain, starting with Hungary in 1984, which certainly helped stimulate the pressure for democracy wherever she went.

Following her spectacular conquest of Moscow in 1987 she visited

Poland in November 1988. This was a controversial trip, since she could be said to be succouring General Jaruzelski, the Soviet puppet who had suppressed Solidarity, on Moscow's orders, in 1981; but Jaruzelski was treading a skilful path and she could equally claim to be backing him against the hardliners in Moscow. She insisted on holding talks with Lech Walesa and other leaders of Solidarity – then still illegal – as well as members of the Government, toured the Gdansk shipyard and laid a wreath at the grave of Father Jerzy Popielusko, the dissident priest murdered by the security services in 1984, where she received a heroine's welcome from a crowd of several thousand waving Solidarity banners and chanting 'Vivat Thatcher'. Critics carped that she supported trade unions abroad while oppressing them at home; but she insisted that there was no comparison. 'Let me point out that Solidarity is a great deal more than a trade union,' she told the Commons on her return. 'Solidarity is the only expression of opposition to Communism and Socialism in Poland. Solidarity wishes to have a plural society of the kind that we have, and is very much against the kind of Communism expressed by some people in this country.'[17] A few months later Solidarity was the government of Poland.

She paid a second visit to the crumbling Soviet Union in June 1990 where, after a day of serious talks with Gorbachev in Moscow about the implications of German reunification, she flew on to the Ukraine and then to Armenia, where she was once again greeted by enthusiastic crowds. Then in September she went back to Hungary and to Czechoslovakia, both now free democracies, where she was rapturously received as the living embodiment of anti-Communism, the Western leader who had kept faith with the freedom movements in Central and Eastern Europe and helped them to throw off their oppressor. In Prague she apologised for Munich, which she had always felt personally as a stain on Britain's honour, and renamed a square in honour of Churchill. Naturally she revelled in the crowds' adulation: at home she met only hostile demonstrations. These scenes in Prague, Budapest, Warsaw and Kiev were her apotheosis as the heroine of freedom, a title she was to carry proudly into her retirement. She ends the second volume of her memoirs with an account of her reception at the church of the Holy Cross in Warsaw in 1993, when she was invited to stand in front of the altar while children presented her with flowers and their parents applauded. This was her life's vindication. 'All the general propositions favouring freedom I had either imbibed at my father's knee or acquired by candle-end reading of Burke and Hayek were suddenly embodied in the worshippers and their children and illuminated by their smiles.'[18] This was how she wanted to be remembered.

Nevertheless the sudden collapse of Communism did not bring her unmixed joy. On the contrary, her last year in office was one of her most difficult on the international front. For the immediate consequence of the opening of the Berlin Wall was an irresistible momentum to reunite the two parts of Germany, a prospect which exacerbated her fear and loathing of the wartime enemy. At the same time she was having to come to terms with a new administration in Washington in which she had much less confidence than she had in Ronald Reagan. At her moment of ideological victory, therefore, she found herself more isolated on the world stage than ever before.

She was relieved when Vice-President George Bush trounced the Democrat Michael Dukakis in November 1988 to ensure continuity of Republican rule. But she would never have the same rapport with Bush that she had with Reagan. The new President, she wrote patronisingly in her memoirs, was 'one of the most decent, honest and patriotic Americans I have met . . . But he had never had to think through his beliefs and fight for them when they were hopelessly unfashionable as Ronald Reagan and I had had to do.'[19] Bush, unsurprisingly, had no wish to be patronised. Guided by a new team of advisers – James Baker as Secretary of State, Dick Cheney as Secretary of Defense, Brent Scowcroft as National Security Adviser – he determined to make his own alliances. In particular, even before the fall of the Berlin Wall, Bush had identified Helmut Kohl as the European leader with whom he should forge a special relationship. With Mrs Thatcher it was necessary for him to show that he was his own man. 'I kept in mind the importance of the US-British relationship and was determined to work closely with Margaret,' he wrote, 'but I had to speak for myself . . . I was determined that the President of the United States must lead the alliance.'[20]

Bush's relations with his European allies are fully documented in *A World Transformed*, his remarkably candid joint memoir written with Brent Scowcroft, which reprints a lot of documents, transcripts of telephone conversations and diary accounts of the intense diplomacy accompanying the end of the Cold War – far more than has yet received security clearance at the Bush Library in Texas.* From this there emerges a vivid picture of the tensions between the leading players and the extent of Mrs Thatcher's isolation as Bush and Kohl, with much less objection than she hoped for from Mitterand and Gorbachev,

---

*Much of the material relating to Bush's dealings with Chancellor Kohl has been declassified, however, confirming the accuracy of what appears in *A World Transformed*. Only a few disparaging remarks by Kohl about Mrs Thatcher are omitted.

rushed to consummate the reunion of the two Germanies far faster than she thought wise or desirable.

Even before the heady events of November, however, from the very beginning of Bush's presidency, she was afraid that Washington was going soft on nuclear disarmament. Gorbachev was trying to split NATO by offering cuts to prevent the alliance modernising its short-range nuclear forces (SNF). Kohl, under domestic pressure from the Social Democrats and Greens, wanted to delay modernisation and reduce the number of missiles immediately. By contrast, Scowcroft wrote, 'Thatcher was unyielding on any changes that might weaken NATO defences.'[21] She wanted the Americans to let her handle Kohl, which they were unwilling to do – partly because 'Margaret . . . was even more unyielding than we, and far more emotional about the dangers of compromise', but also because Bush was not willing to play second fiddle to her.

She was very annoyed when Kohl's Foreign Minister, Hans-Dietrich Genscher, tried to 'bounce' the alliance into SNF cuts by announcing them in the Bundestag before they had been agreed.* She gave Bush her views in a telephone conversation he described as 'vintage Thatcher':

> NATO was not Germany, she said, and we could not have Bonn dictating to the alliance . . . It was up to Washington and London to 'rescue' the alliance . . . We must be firm with Germany . . . There could be no question, no question, she repeated, of negotiations on SNF. 'The Germans know full well that flexible response depends on SNF and that therefore these forces have to be kept up to date' . . . 'What is important is agreement between the US and Britain . . . because without those two countries there would be no NATO.'[23]

But the Americans did change their position on SNF negotiations. Mrs Thatcher, Scowcroft recalled, was 'not happy . . . particularly since we had not consulted with her beforehand':

> The truth of the matter was that we knew what Thatcher's reaction would be . . . We believed we had to make this gesture to the

---

*Genscher, leader of the small German centre party, was one of Mrs Thatcher's particular *bêtes noires*. By virtue of holding the balance under a proportional voting system, the Free Democrats had managed by astutely changing partners to remain continuously in power, giving Genscher wholly disproportionate influence both as kingmaker and as Foreign Minister since 1974, in which position, she wrote, 'he normally favoured a softer, more accommodating approach to the Soviets'.[22]

Germans . . . and, had we consulted the British, it would have been very awkward to proceed over their strong objections.[24]

In her memoirs Mrs Thatcher regretted that 'the new American approach was to subordinate clear statements of intention . . . to the political sensibilities of the Germans. I did not think that this boded well.'[25] Before the May 1989 NATO summit in Brussels she was still 'unhappy and apprehensive' about the American proposal for immediate cuts in conventional forces, linked to SNF negotiations; but at the end of the day she knew the limits of her influence. She told the envoys who came to brief her in London, 'If the President wants it, of course we will do it.'[26] Yet even as they sat down to dinner in Brussels she buttonholed Bush. 'We must not give in on this,' she told him. 'You're not going to give in, are you?' In the end James Baker and the Foreign Ministers − still Howe for Britain − found a form of words she could accept. 'Our strategy of using our conventional forces proposal to encourage a deal over the nuclear forces problem worked,' Bush wrote. The next morning, to his relief, 'Margaret waxed enthusiastic. I suspect she did not want to be separated from the United States.'[27] But while the Americans congratulated themselves on 'a resounding success', the press had no doubt that Mrs Thatcher had suffered a humiliating defeat.[28]

The next day Bush went on to Germany and delivered a speech at Mainz in which he referred to West Germany and the United States as 'partners in leadership'. Mrs Thatcher took this as a snub to her special relationship with Washington. 'In truth she need not have worried,' Scowcroft wrote. 'The expression had no exclusionary intent and was meant only for flourish and encouragement.'[29] Nevertheless it was widely interpreted as reflecting a real and important shift in transatlantic relationships. Bush tried to make up by describing Britain as America's 'anchor to windward'. 'This was kindly meant, but not exactly reassuring,' Percy Cradock commented. 'The anchor to windward is a lonely position and not the one we had imagined we occupied.'[30]

At least one special relationship did persist, however, between Scowcroft and Charles Powell, whom Scowcroft regarded as 'my opposite in the British Government'. Secure lines were installed so that the National Security Adviser could speak directly to his counterparts in London, Paris and Bonn. 'All either one of us had to do was to push a button and lift the receiver to have the phone ring on the other's desk . . . We soon learned how to explore in a comfortable, offhand manner the limits of the flexibility we felt our principals would have on various issues.' Scowcroft felt that by this time Powell was 'the only serious influence on Thatcher's views on foreign policy':

He was close to her, had uncanny insights into her thinking and even, given her powerful personality, could be very persuasive. To me, the association with Powell and the way it facilitated US–British co-operation were the embodiment of the famous special relationship.[31]

Mrs Thatcher naturally watched the dominoes come down across Eastern Europe with unrestrained delight, as first Poland and Hungary moved towards democracy without provoking Soviet intervention; then the Hungarians allowed refugees from East Germany to cross into Austria; and finally the East German authorities themselves opened the Berlin Wall on 9 November and the population emerged like the prisoners in *Fidelio* to tear it down with pickaxes, crowbars and their bare hands and dance exultantly on the ruins. Bulgaria, Czechoslovakia and Romania followed before the end of the year as the so-called 'velvet revolution' brought the dissident playwright Vaclav Havel to power in Prague, while President Ceausescu and his monstrous wife were summarily executed in Bucharest on Christmas Day. Bliss was it in that dawn to be alive. But Mrs Thatcher, mindful of the excesses of 200 years before, was already wary of things getting out of hand. Back in 1982 she had predicted that the Wall would fall one day:

The day comes when the anger and frustration of the people is so great that force cannot contain it. Then the edifice cracks: the mortar crumbles . . . One day, liberty will dawn on the other side of the wall.

But she admitted she had not expected it so soon. When it happened, she told reporters in Downing Street that she had watched the television pictures with the same enthusiasm as everyone else and celebrated 'a great day for liberty'. But even at that moment she was quick to stamp on questions about German reunification. 'I think you are going much too fast, much too fast,' she warned. 'You have to take these things step by step and handle them very wisely.'[32] But she quickly found that the impetus of events was too strong for her.

She had three admissible reasons for resisting the prospect of a united Germany. First, she was afraid that its sheer economic strength would upset the balance of the European Community. Second, she was afraid that a neutral or demilitarised Germany would leave a gaping hole in

NATO's defences against a still-nuclear Soviet Union. Third, she feared that the loss of East Germany (and the disintegration of the Warsaw Pact generally) might destroy Gorbachev and thus jeopardise the biggest prize of all, democracy in the USSR. All these were rational arguments for caution. But they were underpinned in Mrs Thatcher's mind by another, inadmissible reason – her virulent and unappeased loathing of the wartime enemy.

'This was an ugly thing,' the historian George Urban wrote, 'known but to a few, and unmentionable in decent company.'[33] 'I never believed that German nationalism was dead,' she told him back in 1984 when the prospect of reunification was still remote:

> I always believed that when the next German generation was old enough to think and lead the country the drive to reunite Germany would be there again. But we don't want that, because there is no question that if the Germans were reunited they would, once again, dominate the whole of Europe.[34]

Now the danger was suddenly real and she was alarmed. Urban was present at a CPS lunch in December 1989 when the Prime Minister 'felt she was among friends and could let her hair down. I was amazed to hear her uttering views about people and countries . . . which were not all that different from the Alf Garnett version of history.'

> You know, George, there are things that your generation and mine ought never to forget. We've been through the war and we know perfectly well what the Germans are like, and what dictators can do, and how national character doesn't basically change.[35]

Those present who had not heard her in this vein before were said to be 'appalled', and she was 'bombarded with counter-arguments'.[36] But when Hugh Thomas suggested that reunification should be welcomed as a victory over Communism, she turned on him: 'Don't you realise what's happening? I've read my history, but you as an academic don't seem to understand.'[37] The key word was that she had read *her* history; she had no need for anyone else's. She had time for historians only when they agreed with her. 'I'm beginning to wonder whether any of you are still sound,' she rebuked them as she left.[38]

There is no easy explanation of why Margaret Thatcher found it so much harder than others of her generation to forget the war. Certainly it dominated her adolescence from the age of fourteen to twenty – her last four years at school, her first two at university – but she was not alone in that. Grantham suffered fairly heavy German bombing – probably heavier than anywhere outside London except for Coventry and Plymouth; also from 1941 Lincolnshire was full of US airbases and US airmen, which sharpened her awareness of the Americans' role in saving Europe from itself. She had heard first-hand testimony of the nature of the Nazi regime from the young Jewish refugee whom her parents briefly had to stay before the war; later she had a large Jewish community in her Finchley constituency. But all this pales in comparison with the experience of her male contemporaries who actually fought in France, Belgium, North Africa and Italy, let alone those who liberated the concentration camps, almost all of whom – certainly the future politicians among them – seem to have come back determined to rebuild the Continent, ready to forget the war and move on. She had suffered no personal loss of family or close friends to explain her enduring bitterness. Yet forty years later she was still consumed by an 'atavistic fear of Germany and [a] suspicion of the German people *qua* people'.[39]

Equally curious is the fact that her animus was reinforced by Charles Powell. Sixteen years younger, a sophisticated former diplomat with an Italian wife, Powell should not have been prey to the same prejudice, but he was – as was embarrassingly revealed when Mrs Thatcher held one of her Chequers seminars on the subject of Germany in March 1990, attended by a clutch of her favourite British historians – Lord Dacre (Hugh Trevor-Roper), Norman Stone, George Urban and Timothy Garton-Ash – plus two distinguished Americans, Gordon Craig and Fritz Stern. Powell wrote an introductory paper which was subsequently leaked to the *Independent on Sunday*. Maybe he was just trying to please his mistress; but it was a shocking compendium of what Urban called 'saloon bar clichés' about the German character, including 'angst, aggressiveness, assertivenesss, bullying, egotism, inferiority complex [and] sentimentality'. The historians were appalled to find Mrs Thatcher apparently unaware of the Germans' crippling sense of guilt or the efforts that the postwar generation had been making for thirty years to expunge the shame of their fathers. In her view they had not changed and could not change. 'I do not believe in collective guilt,' she wrote in her memoirs. 'But I do believe in national character.'[40] When Dacre reminded her that NATO had always supported German reunification – 'We should rejoice, because we've won' – she vehemently disagreed.[41] When Urban argued that a united Germany would help restore the whole of Central Europe, she retorted angrily: 'What you're saying is "suck up to rich uncle, so that he is nice to you". No, no.'[42] Finding herself isolated, she was still defiant:

Very well, I am outnumbered round this table. I promise you that I will be sweet to the Germans, sweet to Helmut when he comes next week, but I shall not be defeated. I shall be sweet to him, but I shall uphold my principles.[43]

Douglas Hurd, who was present – playing the part of 'the demure understudy . . . sitting there like a well-disciplined prefect, too nice and too much of a gentleman to make waves, but obviously pained and unhappy'[44] – tried to limit the diplomatic damage caused by the leak by stressing that the conclusions of the seminar were 'overwhelmingly reassuring'.[45] And Norman Stone wrote a piece in *The Times* describing the occasion as 'a pragmatic British prime minister, at a time of great change, endeavouring to understand what was going on . . . She asks the right questions. She gets the best from her experts.'[46] This was loyal but unconvincing. 'Throughout the day,' Urban concluded, 'she let it be known that she was speaking for the robust no-nonsense instincts of the great British public, and no continental politician was going to tell her what to think or do.'[47]

The story of the Chequers seminar did not leak until July – by coincidence or design the same week that Nicholas Ridley expressed similarly anti-German sentiments in an interview with Dominic Lawson, now editor of the *Spectator*. Apparently unaware that his words would be reported, he spoke unguardedly of monetary union as 'a German racket to take over the whole of Europe . . . I'm not against giving up sovereignty in principle, but not to this lot. You might just as well give it to Adolf Hitler, frankly.' The magazine sharpened the message with a Nicholas Garland cartoon on the front cover showing Ridley drawing a Hitler moustache on a picture of Chancellor Kohl; while inside Lawson commented that 'Mr Ridley's confidence in expressing his views . . . must owe a little something to the knowledge that they are not significantly different from those of the Prime Minister.'[48] Though she promptly denied it, all her ministers knew that this was true. Ridley apologised and 'withdrew' his remarks. But after three days trying to save him, Mrs Thatcher was finally compelled by the executive of the 1922 Committee, reportedly reflecting the outrage of two-thirds of Tory backbenchers, to accept his reluctant resignation. In her memoirs Lady Thatcher still saw no reason for Ridley – her last remaining soulmate in the Cabinet – to resign for what she called 'an excess of honesty'. A 'gaffe', she wrote, was simply 'telling an inconvenient truth'.[49]

As soon as the Wall came down in November 1989 she knew that Kohl would lose no time in pressing for reunification of the two

Germanies; but she believed that the four wartime allies, if they were resolute, could still prevent it, or at least delay it for ten or fifteen years. Unification was not a matter for the Germans alone, she insisted, but affected NATO, the EC, the Russians and the whole balance of power in Europe. There was 'too much euphoria', she told President Bush by telephone on 17 November, 'too many efforts to see into the crystal ball'. She hoped the special EC summit called by President Mitterrand the next day would 'pull in the reins'. 'Gorbachev should be our main concern, for none of this could have happened without him. "Destabilise him and we lose the possibility of democracy in the Soviet Union," she warned.'[50] Ironically, as the Cold War ended, the Iron Lady's over-riding concern was to reassure the old enemy. She even tried to argue that the Helsinki Agreement precluded any alteration of borders. In Paris she hoped to form an Anglo-French axis to contain Germany, but found Mitterrand unhelpful. A week later she flew to Camp David to share her fears with the President directly. 'She particularly worried that talk of reunification or changing borders would only frighten the Soviets,' Bush recorded:

> 'The overriding objective is to get democracy throughout Eastern Europe,' she told me. 'We have won the battle of ideas after tough times as we kept NATO strong' . . . She added that such change could take place only in an environment of stability. 'That means NATO and the Warsaw Pact stay. NATO should stay anyway . . . Focus on democracy now.'
>
> Margaret argued that Germany's fate was much larger than a matter of self-determination . . . She pulled a map out of the large handbag she always carried with her. She traced the old 1937 borders and the territories now in Poland which were marked upon it. 'Look at Germany,' she said. 'Reunification means Gorbachev is lost. He loses the integrity of the Warsaw Pact . . . We can't stop it from eventually happening if they want it. But for now, concentrate on democracy.'[51]

'The atmosphere,' Mrs Thatcher acknowledged, 'did not improve as a result of our discussions.'[52] In fact Brent Scowcroft felt 'some lingering sympathy for Thatcher's position', believing that she 'had her eyes on some very important priorities'.[53] But from the moment Kohl had telephoned him to describe the 'festival atmosphere [like] an enormous fair' as the Wall came down, the President was firmly on Kohl's side.[54] 'We don't fear the ghosts of the past,' he assured the Chancellor. 'Margaret does.'[55] For his part Kohl was exasperated by Mrs Thatcher's obstruction. 'I think it is a great mistake on Maggie's part to think this is a time for caution,' he complained.[56] Her ideas were 'simply pre-Churchill. She thinks the postwar era has not come to an end. She thinks history is not just. Germany is so rich and Great Britain is struggling. They won a war but lost an empire, and their economy. She does the wrong thing. She should try to bind the Germans into the EC.'

Kohl still professed to see reunification as a long process over several years, with West Germany meanwhile remaining in NATO and the GDR in the Warsaw Pact – as Mrs Thatcher wanted. 'I will not do anything reckless,' he promised. 'I have not set up a timetable. We are part of Europe and will continue as part of the EC . . . The integration of Europe is a precondition for change in East Europe to be effective.' 'Newspapers write such nonsense,' he added. 'Even Henry Kissinger mentions two years. It's not possible: the economic imbalance is too great.'[57] Bush suspected that Kohl really hoped for unification much sooner than this, but did not want to prejudice it by seeming to press too fast. Nevertheless he was happy to give Kohl 'a green light. I don't think I ever cautioned him about going too fast.' In his relaxed view 'self-determination was the key, and no one could object to it'.[58]

Brent Scowcroft still shared Mrs Thatcher's worry about Gorbachev's response. 'It was still possible that the Soviets would conclude that a united Germany was intolerable and oppose it, by force if necessary. Or they would successfully impose conditions on it taking place which would render it unacceptable to us.'[59] The difference was that while the Americans, determined that the new Germany should be a member of NATO, were working to overcome Soviet opposition, Mrs Thatcher was trying to deploy Gorbachev's objections as a brake. From their private conversations she believed that Mitterrand also shared her alarm and hoped that he would join with her to slow the process down; but whatever he may have said in private, Mitterrand was realistic. He had no intention of opposing the cherished project of his friend Helmut Kohl, but still put the preservation of the Franco-German axis before her idea of a Franco–British one. 'He made the wrong decision for France,' she asserted in her memoirs.[60]

The diplomatic method eventually agreed was the 'Two-plus-Four' process, whereby the two Germanies negotiated the domestic details of unification in an international context approved by the United States, the Soviet Union, Britain and France. This met Mrs Thatcher's wish to involve the Russians, despite American fear that it would give them a chance to be obstructive. But Bush gambled that Gorbachev could be won over, and he was right.

Mrs Thatcher's other concern was that premature euphoria about the end of the Cold War would lead to reductions in defence spending. When she met Bush at Camp David – just before he was due to meet Gorbachev in Malta for the latest round of arms-limitation talks – she was adamant that he should give nothing away. 'We had a good visit,' Bush wrote, 'but she did not want to see any defense cuts at all of any kind.'

> I explained that the pressures are on, budget-wise; but the thing that got me was that I couldn't . . . convince her that we've got to do less in the way of defence spending . . . She is as rigid as can be on this . . .

Once again, however, she recognised the limits of her influence. 'In the end . . . Margaret sent me a nice telegram pledging her full support in very comforting words.'[61]

At the NATO summit in Brussels in December she was very unhappy about American proposals for cutting conventional forces in Europe, fearing that the Russians would simply pull their forces back beyond the Urals, from where they could easily sweep west again at a moment's notice. Despite Kohl's repeated assurances that neutralisation was out of the question, he was under strong domestic pressure to reduce the number of allied troops and NATO missiles on German soil; she was afraid that Gorbachev might exploit this weakness to make neutralisation his condition for accepting unification. In the end, however, Scowcroft noted, 'it became apparent that, while not happy, she would acquiesce in what we wished to do'.[62]

By February 1990 she accepted that she was losing the battle, but was still anxious to save Gorbachev's face. 'I fear that Gorbachev will feel isolated if all the reunification process goes the West's way,' she told Bush by telephone. 'He's lost the Warsaw Pact to democratic governments.' Then Bush's account went on:

> Margaret's fears of a united Germany, however, came ringing through. She darkly perceived that Germany would be 'the Japan of Europe, but worse than Japan. Japan is an offshore power with enormous trade surpluses. Germany is in the heart of a continent of countries most of which she has attacked and occupied. Germany has colossal wealth and trade surpluses. So we must include a bigger country, the Soviet Union [or] you, in the political area.'

'It was not enough to anchor Germany in the EC,' she believed. 'That might become Germany's new empire: the future empires will be economic empires.'[63] On this occasion Scowcroft found her arguments becoming more sophisticated and her tone 'much improved', but still found her fears 'worrying'.[64] He was 'dismayed' that her anxiety not to upset Gorbachev led her to back a 'demilitarised East Germany', outside NATO, instead of a united Germany in NATO as the Americans wanted. Meeting Bush in Bermuda in April, she still argued that 'we should allow Soviet troops to remain for a transitional period – it would help Gorbachev with his military'. 'I don't agree,' Bush replied, 'I want the Soviets to go home.'[65]

In fact she had already accepted the inevitable at the end of March when Kohl came to Britain for the Anglo-German Konigswinter conference, held that year in Cambridge. This was the occasion on which she had promised to be 'sweet to Helmut'. Seated a few places away from each other over dinner, however, it was observed that the two leaders 'exchanged barely a social word throughout the meal'.[66] Heaping insincere encomiums on the Chancellor, Mrs Thatcher formally gave her blessing to the new Germany, so long as it was in NATO and retained 'sizeable' British, French and American forces, including short-range nuclear weapons, on its soil; but much of her speech dwelt on Britain's role in securing West Germany's freedom since 1945 by means of the Berlin airlift and the British army on the Rhine. She never missed an opportunity to remind the Europeans how much they owed to Britain. In his reply Kohl dutifully praised her in return – with a double-edged joke about her driving a tank while visiting British troops – welcomed her agreement, but simply ignored her concerns about NATO forces and nuclear weapons.[67] Paddy Ashdown noticed that 'whenever Kohl used the word "Margaret" he looked in the opposite direction and injected a certain steely tone into his voice'.[68] It was clear that he had not forgiven her obstruction of his grand project.

Her acceptance was made easier by the results of the first free elections held in the old GDR. One of her arguments for delay had been that the East had lived under authoritarian rule for so long – first under the Nazis, then under Communism – that it could not be expected to adapt quickly to democracy. In fact the voters confounded her by voting heavily for Kohl's CDU, giving a clear endorsement both to his policy of rapid unification and to broadly free-market economic policies (the former Communists won only 16 per cent) and allaying her fears of neutralism. Visiting Moscow in June, Mrs Thatcher played her part in helping to secure Gorbachev's acquiescence that the reunited Germany could join NATO – in return for badly needed Western credits to shore up the Soviet economy. In July Gorbachev survived a last-ditch challenge from his own hardliners; and

Kohl flew to Moscow to receive the Soviet blessing in person. The new Germany came into being on 3 October, less than eleven months after the opening of the Wall.

It can be argued that in resisting German reunification Mrs Thatcher was only asking some pertinent questions which needed to be asked, without actually delaying its consummation at all. But that ignores diplomatic reality. In Percy Cradock's view her effort to prevent the inevitable was 'the single most spectacular miscalculation' of her whole foreign policy, which damaged Britain's relations with the new Germany for no diplomatic gain.[69] Douglas Hurd thought the idea that Mitterrand and Gorbachev would help her block reunification 'unreal'.[70] With Bush in favour, she only advertised her own irrelevance in the new international order. The better course, as Alan Clark tried to persuade her in January, would have been to go with the grain of events:

> I argued cogently for accepting, and exploiting, German reunification while they still needed our support. No good. She is determined not to . . . During the coffee break I cornered her. 'These are just a re-run of the old Appeasement arguments of 1938.' 'Yes,' she said, eyes flashing (she's in incredible form at the moment), and I'm not an appeaser.'[71]*

Once again she was still fighting the war. As the tabloid press delights in demonstrating every time England plays Germany at football there is still plenty of domestic mileage in this sort of crude Hun-bashing. But it was a culpable failure of leadership in a Prime Minister, and another indication that she was losing her judgement. One of the first things John Major (born in 1943) set out to do on entering Number Ten was to rebuild Anglo-German relations on the basis of a warm personal relationship with Helmut Kohl.

Yet in her memoirs Lady Thatcher was unrepentant. She acknowledged that her policy had 'met with unambiguous failure'. But she still maintained that the dark shadow on the glorious revolution of 1989

---

*Among her inner circle Woodrow Wyatt also tried to convince her that reunification was irresistible.[72] Ironically this was a reversal of their positions thirty years earlier when Wyatt was a fellow panellist on Mrs Thatcher's very first appearance as a young backbencher on *Any Questions?* Wyatt – then a Labour MP who had fought in the war – was at this time strongly in favour of keeping Germany divided. It was Mrs Thatcher who warned that the desire for unification was so strong that if NATO stopped supporting it democratically, the Federal Republic might choose to reunite with the Communist East.[73] It is remarkable that she understood the German drive for unity better in 1960 than she did in 1990.

was the re-emergence of a 'familiar bogey from the past – the German Question'. She still feared that reunification had created 'a German state so large and dominant that it cannot be easily fitted into the new architecture of Europe'. She thought that 'premature' unification had led the French to place more importance than ever on the Franco-German axis, while hastening the 'rush to Eurofederalism', as different ways of 'tying down Gulliver'; and also encouraged dangerous talk of American withdrawal from Europe. She still – in 1993 – thought the right policy for Britain was to build a British-French entente to counterbalance the dominance of Germany.[74] What she failed to foresee was that the task of absorbing the relatively backward GDR would actually *weaken* the Federal Republic over the next fifteen years, so that by the time she came to write her final testament, *Statecraft*, in 2002, the new Germany was much less powerful than she had anticipated.

Even with Germany locked into NATO she still worried that facile talk of a 'peace dividend' from the ending of the Cold War would lead to a short-sighted lowering of the West's nuclear guard. Washington was pressing for an early NATO summit, eventually held in London in July, to bring forward cuts in both nuclear and conventional forces in Europe. To her dismay Mrs Thatcher found herself once again 'at odds with the Americans'. As Bush relates, she still objected to weakening nuclear deterrence by diluting the doctrine of flexible response:

> She argued that we were abandoning the fundamentals of solid military strategy for the sake of 'eye-catching propositions' . . . She saw the move to declare nuclear weapons 'weapons of last resort' as undermining our short-range forces and as slipping us to a position of 'no first use of nuclear weapons', leaving our conventional forces vulnerable . . . She demanded an entirely new draft.[75]

On this issue Mitterrand did share her concern. But France was not part of NATO's military structure, and all the other leaders were enthusiastic, so once again Mrs Thatcher had to swallow her objections and accept 'a compromise text close to the original draft'. Flexible response was modified and the Alliance declared that it was 'moving away' from forward defence. At her insistence the words 'weapons of last resort' were stiffened with an assertion that there were 'no circumstances in which nuclear retaliation in response to military action might be discounted'. Mrs Thatcher was still not happy with 'this unwieldy compromise'.[76] But she had no veto in NATO as she had in Europe, so she had to accept it. 'It was a landmark shift,' Bush wrote. 'It offered the Soviets firm evidence of the West's genuine desire to change NATO. Our offer was on the table.'[77]

The final act of the Cold War was also, suitably enough, the final act of Mrs Thatcher's premiership. As the votes were being cast in the first ballot for the Conservative leadership in November 1990, she was in Paris attending a meeting of the Conference on Security and Co-operation in Europe (CSCE), at which she committed Britain to substantial cuts in the stationing of conventional forces in Germany. It was a largely ceremonial occasion, with congratulatory speeches celebrating the victory of freedom over tyranny and resolution over co-existence. It was, in its way, the triumph of everything Mrs Thatcher had been fighting for all her political life. Yet it came about not only at the moment of her political demise, but in a manner and on terms with which she was far from happy. At some psychological level she could not handle victory. As one enemy capitulated, she needed to find new ones to warn against. In her enforced retirement, as the Soviet Union finally crumbled into its constituent republics, leaving a power vacuum awash with insecure nuclear weapons, nationalist tensions and unstable 'rogue states', she surveyed the aftermath with the grim satisfaction of a born Cassandra. 'The world of the "new world order" was turning out to be a dangerous and uncertain place in which the conservative virtues of hardened Cold Warriors were again in demand.'[78] Nothing gave her more pleasure than seeing naivety disillusioned. The fools, she implied, should never have got rid of her.

The environment and global warming

A major new issue appeared on the political agenda in the late 1980s – and Margaret Thatcher, with all her other domestic and international concerns, deserves much of the credit for putting it there. The 'environment' had been the fashionable word for a complex of interconnected social problems – town planning, traffic growth, the disappearing countryside, pollution – since the 1960s, officially recognised by Ted Heath's creation of a new Department of the Environment, bringing together the old ministries of Housing and Local Government and Transport, in 1970. Jim Callaghan split Transport off again in 1976, but the DoE survived at least in name, though the main preoccupation of successive Secretaries of State from Heseltine to Ridley was local government and the poll tax. Around 1988, however, environmental concerns suddenly acquired a new dimension with the discovery of global warming, caused – probably – by the build up in the earth's atmosphere of so-called 'greenhouse gases': carbon-dioxide, methane and chlorofluorocarbons. From parochial questions of road building and waste disposal which were normally beneath a Prime Minister's notice, the environment assumed, almost overnight, the status of an international challenge which transcended even the Cold War.

Mrs Thatcher denied that she was a late convert to the importance of protecting the environment. As early as June 1984 she used her chairmanship of the London G7 summit to push through a commitment to increased research to tackle pollution, specifically the headline phenomenon of the moment, 'acid rain'. Up until then, however, she had not appeared to take environmental problems very seriously, being always inclined to equate them with litter, graffiti and crime. During the Falklands war she was reported to have told the Scottish Conservative conference that 'when you have spent half your political life dealing with humdrum issues like the environment, it is exciting to have a real crisis on your hands'.[79] These words were not actually in her published script; but there is no doubt that they accurately reflected her feelings. When John Ashworth, her first chief scientific adviser, presciently commissioned the CPRS to look at climate change in 1980, she asked incredulously, 'Are you telling me I should worry about the weather?'[80] And Kenneth Baker recalls her being 'very cool' about 'green' policies in May 1984, at that stage still resisting measures to reduce acid rain by adding desulphurisation plants to power stations, by insisting they were too expensive and seeking other reasons to explain the blight of trees in Scandinavia.[81] Confronted by demonstrations in Norway in 1986, her instinct was still to deny that Britain was the principal polluter.[82] When she did suddenly take up the 'green' agenda in September 1988, *The Times* commented that she had hitherto been 'widely regarded as a sceptic on the issue'[83] and William Waldegrave whispered cynically to Baker: 'I never thought I'd live to hear it.'[84]

As a combative Tory politician her gut reflex was to see environmental campaigners, particularly Greenpeace, as just another branch of CND, a mix of sincere but naive sentimentalists – 'You know some of them want us all to go back to a village life,' she told the *Financial Times* in 1989[85] – and much more sinister 'green socialists' who exploited public anxiety about pollution as an argument against capitalism, free enterprise and even economic growth.* She insisted on the contrary

---

*In 1985 the small and hitherto obscure Ecology party renamed itself the Green party and fielded 133 candidates at the 1987 election (though none gained more than a few hundred votes). Meanwhile Friends of the Earth had emerged as a highly effective pressure group under its articulate director, Jonathon Porritt, who was also one of the leaders of the Greens. 'He is very good actually,' Mrs Thatcher acknowledged in 1989. 'He is not unreasonable.'[86] But she thought most of the Greens' egalitarian and anti-business policies were 'quite crazy'.[87]

that socialism, inherently inefficient and unaccountable, was the great polluter, whereas free enterprise was both more efficient and better able to spend resources on environmental protection. Indeed, she suggested in 1998, cleaning up pollution was 'almost a function of prosperity, because it is the East European block, their chemical factories, that have been pouring stuff into the Rhine'.[88] The following year she made this identification still more explicit:

> As we peel back the moral squalor of the socialist regimes in Eastern Europe we discover the natural and physical squalor underneath. They exploited nature every bit as ruthlessly as they exploited the people. In their departure, they have left her choking amidst effluent, acid rain and industrial waste.[89]

She also believed that coal and other fossil fuels beloved of the left were intrinsically dirty, whereas nuclear energy was clean and safe. 'The answer to the greenhouse effect is of course to have more nuclear,' she declared in 1988.[90] 'Had we gone the way of France and got 60 per cent of our electricity from nuclear power we would not have our environmental problems.'[91] Those who campaigned against nuclear power on environmental grounds were simply wrong, like those who imagined they were promoting peace by opposing nuclear weapons. She saw it as her business to cut through this sort of emotive nonsense to deal with the facts. Proud of her credentials as a scientist in a world of arts-educated generalists, she believed that she understood the scientific arguments. 'She told me . . . that she remembered the importance of the carbon cycle from her school chemistry lessons,' Ridley wrote. 'I had to confess that I did not.'[92] She believed that scientific problems would be solved by the further development of science, not by regulation. 'When a problem is identified – when it has a scientific cause and effect – then we deal with it on the basis that we know what to do,' she told *The Times* in 1988. 'We've done that on the smaller things. We'll do it on the bigger things.'[93]

Her faith in science caused some cynicism in the universities, which complained that government support for pure science had actually been cut since 1979, with too much of what was left going into defence and applied commercial research. In 1987 Mrs Thatcher belatedly acknowledged this concern and set up a new Cabinet committee, chaired by herself, to try to meet it. One project she had always backed, however – even before the Falklands gave her a special interest in the area – was the British Antarctic Survey (BAS). It therefore gave her great patriotic satisfaction that it was the scientists of the BAS who in

1985 discovered a large hole in the earth's ozone layer, nearly as large as the United States and growing. International efforts had already been under way for some time to limit the emission of halogen gases, principally chlorofluorocarbons (CFCs) used in refrigerators and aerosol sprays: a UN-sponsored conference in Montreal in 1987 set a target of halving the use of CFCs in ten years. But the fact that the hole in the ozone layer was a British discovery undoubtedly helped persuade Mrs Thatcher to throw her weight into efforts to remedy it. She was also greatly influenced by the right adviser in the right place at the right time, Britain's Ambassador to the United Nations from 1987 to 1990, Sir Crispin Tickell, a career diplomat who happened to be a serious amateur meteorologist. It was Tickell who brought the urgency of the problem to Mrs Thatcher's attention and persuaded her to make it the subject of a major speech, which he then helped her to write.

A decade later her speech to the Royal Society in September 1988 was remembered as 'a true epiphany, the blinding discovery of a conviction politician, which overnight turned the environment from being a minority to a mainstream concern in Britain'.[94] At the time it made rather less impact. Bernard Ingham recalls that she 'put an enormous amount' of work into it, but was disappointed with the coverage it received.[95] She had been counting on the television lights to enable her to read her script, but the cameras did not show up. In fact the importance of the speech was more that she made it at all than what she said. Most of it was a standard affirmation of the Government's commitment to science: she did not fail to mention her own scientific background ('my work on glyceride monolayers in the early 1950s') and the prominence she had given to the portraits of Faraday, Newton, Boyle and Dorothy Hodgkin in Number Ten. Only towards the end did she turn to the three recently observed phenomena of greenhouse gases ('we are creating a global heat trap which could lead to climatic instability'); the hole in the ozone layer ('which protects life from ultra-violet radiation'), and acid rain ('which has affected soils, lakes and trees downwind from industrial centres'). She stressed the need for more research, as well as immediate steps to cut emissions, and emphasised how much money the Government was already spending on cleaning Britain's rivers. ('The Thames now has the cleanest metropolitan estuary in the world.') But the soundbite extracted for the BBC radio news was markedly downbeat. 'Stable prosperity,' she concluded, 'can be achieved throughout the world provided the environment is nurtured and safeguarded. Protecting this balance of nature is therefore one of the great challenges of the late twentieth century.'[96] This was scarcely a ringing call to arms.

She followed it up, however, just over two weeks later, with a considerably sharper statement of the same commitment in her speech to the Tory Party Conference. Much of this was aimed squarely at combating the Greens:

> We are far too sensible to think that in 1988 we can turn the clock back to a pre-industrial world where Adam delved and Eve span. The Garden of Eden had a population of two. Our world has a population of five billion going on six. It has more than doubled in my own lifetime. Those people need to cook meals, heat homes, clothe themselves, find work. They need factories, roads, power stations. All these things are part of our lives today and the ambition of the third world tomorrow.

'So the choice facing us,' she insisted, 'is not industrial development or a clean environment. To survive we need both.' She recalled the London fogs, still a feature of the capital when she went to live there in the early 1950s, but banished by the Clean Air Act of 1956 ('passed by a Conservative Government'). 'In the past, science has solved many problems which at the time seemed insuperable. It can do so again.' She promised to take a lead with other countries in efforts to halt the shrinking of the Brazilian rainforest and cut the use of fossil fuels, and finished with a characteristically bold attempt to annex the green agenda for the Tories. Just as, in defending nuclear weapons, she claimed to be 'the true peace movement' so now she boasted that 'we Conservatives . . . are not merely friends of the earth – we are its guardians and trustees for generations to come':

> The core of Tory philosophy and of the case for protecting the environment are the same. No generation has a freehold on this earth. All we have is a life tenancy – with a full repairing lease. This Government intends to meet the terms of that lease in full.[97]

If this was meant to take the wind out of the Greens' sails it probably did the opposite, by acknowledging that global warming was a real problem. Over the next few months their showing in the opinion polls climbed to around 10 per cent, and in June 1989 they appeared to make a breakthrough as a serious political force by winning 15 per cent of the vote in the European elections. Mrs Thatcher dismissed this as just the usual midterm protest vote that had previously gone to the Liberals or the Alliance. (She was right: in 1992 the Greens fell back to a mere 1.3 per cent.) 'No party in Britain,' she insisted, 'is greener in terms of what we do.'[98] Of course opposition parties cannot do anything. But she was entitled to claim that her Government was making the international running on environmental protection.

In March 1989 she chaired a three-day conference in London on Saving the Ozone Layer, attended by 123 nations, which strengthened the Montreal protocol by setting a new target of ending CFC emissions entirely by the end of the century: she spoke at both the beginning and the end. Within Whitehall and the EC she chased progress vigorously on the tightening of anti-pollution regulations, backing the DoE against the Treasury and other departments which raised the sort of objections on grounds of cost that she herself had made a few years earlier.[99] In August she told President Bush of 'her intention to overhaul Britain's environmental legislation' – clearly trying to encourage him to do the same.[100] And in November she made a major speech to the UN General Assembly in which she announced the establishment of a new climate research centre in Britain and called for 'a vast international co-operative effort' to save the global environment.[101]

All this was before the final report of the Intergovernmental Panel on Climate Change was published in June 1990. This – the unanimous conclusion of 300 international scientists – warned that if no action were taken to curb the emission of greenhouse gases, average global temperatures would rise by anything between 1.4 and 2.8 per cent by 2030, causing sea levels to rise with disastrous consequences for low-lying areas such as Bangladesh, Holland and East Anglia. (Mrs Thatcher was particularly fond of pointing out that one Commonwealth country, the Maldive Islands, with a population of 177,000, would disappear entirely.)[102] This was the first authoritative international confirmation that global warming was really happening, though the evidence was already visible in severe drought leading to famine in Sudan, Ethiopia and much of central Africa. But Mrs Thatcher, encouraged by Crispin Tickell, had already anticipated its recommendations. Opening the promised new research centre – the Hadley Centre for Climate Prediction and Research – near Bracknell in Berkshire in May 1990, she committed Britain to stabilising carbon-dioxide emissions by 2005, which actually meant a 30 per cent cut over fifteen years, back to the 1990 figure. 'This,' she told George Bush pointedly, 'is a demanding target.'[103]

But the Americans dragged their feet. At the London conference the previous year they had combined with the Soviet Union and Japan to reject an earlier target date for the elimination of CFCs. Now Bush told a conference in Washington that more research was needed before action on carbon dioxide would be justified. Mrs Thatcher pressed him to take it seriously:

> When we met in Bermuda [in April] I told you of my belief that we would soon need an international effort to stabilise emissions of carbon dioxide as a first response to the problem of global warming.

She set out the need for further progress on both carbon dioxide and CFCs at upcoming conferences in London and Geneva, and was careful to flatter the important role played by the US at Montreal. It was in the Americans' interest, she urged, to tackle the problem since the effect of ozone-layer depletion was greatest in temperate latitudes. 'I need hardly say how important it is that we work together to make the attempt a success and I very much hope that you will look at this question again.'[104]

Her words fell on deaf ears. At the second World Climate Conference in Geneva in November, 137 countries agreed that global warming was a reality and pledged themselves to take action. But while the EC, Japan and Australia advocated freezing CO_2 emissions at 1990 levels by the year 2000 (five years sooner than Mrs Thatcher had proposed), the Americans, this time supported by the USSR and Saudi Arabia, opposed the setting of firm targets. In her speech at the conference – one of her last appearances on the world stage before her fall – Mrs Thatcher tactfully made no direct criticism of American or Russian reluctance. But she pointed out that North America produced 26 per cent of total CO_2 emissions, the Soviet bloc the same and the rest of the developed world only 22 per cent; and repeated the importance of international action. 'There is little point in action to reduce the amounts being put into the atmosphere in one part of the world, if they are promptly increased in another.' For once she had to admit that Europe was showing the way. 'I hope that Europe's example will help the task of securing world-wide agreement.'[105]

Global warming apart, the Thatcher Government's record on environmental matters was rather less impressive than she liked to make out. Her vision was selective, distorted by political partisanship and her insistence that market forces were the answer, not part of the problem. During her first two terms environmental protection was not a priority. Most of what was done to clean up water supplies, rivers and beaches was driven from Brussels, not London – fortuitously helped by the decline of dirty manufacturing industry – while the prevailing climate of cost-cutting and deregulation led to a steady lowering of standards. Enforcement was primarily a responsibility of local government, but environmental protection was exactly the sort of service that suffered most from cuts enforced by rate-capping. Not until 1987 did the Government act on the recommendation of a 1976 Royal Commission to create a national Inspectorate of Pollution within the DoE, and then it employed only 130 inspectors.[106] Nor did the privatisation of gas, electricity and water help. For all her conference talk of conservation and trusteeship, the essential ethos of Thatcherism was commercial: short-term profit-taking was the rule, and environmental costs that did not show up in the balance sheet tended to be ignored. Despite the 1973 oil crisis, measures to improve energy conservation were neglected, and the adoption of recycling was slow by European standards. Nigel Lawson had an aversion to using the tax system to encourage 'green' behaviour and consistently rejected the idea of carbon taxes and other fiscal incentives. Above all too little support was given to the development of renewable sources of energy – solar, tidal, wind and wave power, in all but the first of which Britain had world-beating potential.

Mrs Thatcher's blind spot about markets is illustrated by one of the problems she felt most strongly about: litter. It was part of her belief in individual responsibility. 'Everyone has a responsibility for the environment,' she told *The Times* in 1988. 'It's no use throwing . . . cigarette packets and Smith's crisp packets out of car windows and then complaining that the banks on the motorways are in a filthy state.'[107] In another newspaper interview she blamed much of the problem on modern packaging:

> In my young day there was not such a thing as a Coca-Cola tin, we had bottles and we saved them and we took them back and got one penny return on bottles so it was very convenient for your pocket money if you collected them and took them back.[108]

Quite right; but she failed to relate the problem of superfluous packaging to the nature of the modern market place. It was the consumer society itself which created so much litter; and, strenuously as she disapproved, it was not a problem that Coca-Cola, McDonald's or any of the other guilty companies showed much inclination to tackle.

A second blind spot was her love affair with the motor car, or what she called in March 1990 'the great car economy'.[109] It was not that the Government actually built a lot of roads; on the contrary, the building of new motorways failed to keep pace with the inexorable growth of traffic using them. But between 1980 and 1990 the number of private cars rose from 16.5 million to 22.8 million – nearly 40 per cent. At the same time the number of goods vehicles fell, though the amount of road freight increased (it was carried in ever-larger lorries) while the tonnage carried by rail fell. Mrs Thatcher's dislike of the railways was well known. Trains were collectivist, crowded and dirty; whereas the private car – even stuck in a traffic jam – was the very symbol of individuality and personal freedom. When she hymned the legacy of the Victorians it was not of the railways that she was thinking. In fact, of course, rail was an environmentally far cleaner, less polluting way of moving both goods and people than roads. But while France and other continental countries developed fast, modern rail systems in the 1980s. Britain preferred to follow the American model: lack of investment left British Rail more antiquated and rundown than ever. Progress was made, with the help of differential duties, in converting most cars to run on lead-free petrol by the end of the decade – the one green tax Lawson accepted. But the primacy of the car in transport policy was unchallenged. Mrs Thatcher certainly never gave any support to bicycling.

Third, her evangelical faith in nuclear power blinded her to its environmental drawbacks – both the long-term danger of storing nuclear waste with an afterlife of millions of years and the immediate risk of accidents, highlighted by the catastrophic blow-out at Chernobyl in the Soviet Ukraine in 1986. In the Commons and in interviews Mrs Thatcher bullishly played down the dangers of 'nuclear' (as she called it), deflecting reports of leaks at Windscale (renamed Sellafield in 1984) by praising the industry's unequalled safety record,[110] maintaining the cover-up imposed by previous governments on past accidents and insisting that a Chernobyl disaster could never happen in Britain, since 'the Chernobyl design would never have got through our Nuclear Inspectorate'. In her enthusiasm she never missed an opportunity to score a debating point at the expense of coal:

> In fact we have lost far more lives from coal mining and from oil than we have lost from nuclear. That I am afraid is one of those facts, so just remember that. The coal and the coal-mining are quite dangerous.[111]

In an interview for the BBC programme *Nature* in 1989 she denied embracing the environmental agenda simply to promote nuclear power, but admitted that the discovery of global warming reinforced her commitment. 'Yes, I would prefer more nuclear power because it is not fundamentally interfering with the world's eco-systems.'[112] What other damage it might be doing did not concern her. At the third international North Sea Conference in March 1990 Britain infuriated neighbouring countries by refusing to outlaw the dumping of radioactive waste under the seabed.[113] Mrs Thatcher believed that in fifty years or so science would solve what she called the 'interim problem' of nuclear waste.[114] 'The problems science has created science in fact can solve and we are setting about it.'[115]

Science, she believed, worked through industry and the market, as she told the UN General Assembly in 1989:

It is industry which will develop safe alternative chemicals for refrigerators and air-conditioning. It is industry which will devise biodegradable plastics. It is industry which will find the means to treat pollutants and make nuclear waste safe . . .

'The multinationals,' she urged, 'have to take the long view. There will be no profit or satisfaction for anyone if pollution continues to destroy our planet.' But the power to halt it lay with consumers:

As people's consciousness of environmental needs rises, they are turning increasingly to ozone-friendly and other environmentally safe products. The market itself acts as a corrective. The new products sell and those which caused environmental damage are disappearing from the shelves.[116]

Undoubtedly Mrs Thatcher claimed too much for the Tory approach to the environment. Her repeated refrain in 1989–90 that the Conservatives were somehow especially concerned with saving the planet – 'I belong to a conservative party, conserving';[117] or again 'It is prosperity which creates the technology that can keep the earth healthy. We are called Conservatives with good reason'[118] – was one that others found hard to swallow, like her implication that Toryism was synonymous with true Christianity. Quite apart from the gaps in her environmental awareness, some critics found her view of the problem offensively utilitarian. The Labour MP Leo Abse objected that she spoke of protecting the planet purely in terms of a legal obligation – 'A life tenancy with a full repairing lease' – and of money spent on cleaning rivers simply as good housekeeping – 'money well and necessarily spent'.[119] She was certainly unnecessarily contemptuous of those who took a more mystical or holistic view of mother earth.

But no politician is perfect. On the biggest issue of all Mrs Thatcher listened to the warnings of Tickell and others, grasped the seriousness of the crisis and devoted a lot of energy – at a time when she was beset with other problems – to persuading others, not least President Bush, of the urgency of doing something about it. In Tickell's view the 1992 Earth Summit in Rio de Janeiro, at which 170 countries including the Americans finally agreed to cut CO_2 emissions by 2000, would never have happened without her effort. Five years later the 1997 Kyoto agreement set a new target of cutting emissions back to the 1990 level by 2010 – only for the US, now led by Bush's resolutely isolationist and oil-oriented son, to refuse to ratify it.

But by then Lady Thatcher had changed her mind. As part of her increasingly slavish subservience to American leadership in the late 1990s, she concluded in her last book, *Statecraft*, that 'President Bush was quite right to reject the Kyoto protocol'. Half-baked scaremongering about climate change, she now believed, had been seized on by the left to furnish 'a marvellous excuse for worldwide, supranational socialism'. The environmental movement was just the latest manifestation of fashionable anti-capitalism, containing 'an ugly streak of anti-Americanism'. Just as she turned violently against European integration as soon as the Labour party began to support it, so she reversed her support for environmentalism when she found herself in bed with her political opponents. She now questioned the evidence that the climate was actually warming at all; denied that CO_2 emissions or any other human activity were responsible even if it was; and doubted that global warming could be checked 'at an acceptable price'. All past predictions of global disaster had been disproved, and she expected this one to be no different. Climate change, if it was occurring, did not 'mean the end of the world; and it must not either mean the end of free-enterprise capitalism'.[120] This U-turn, made for frankly political reasons, marks a sad retreat from her brave pioneering in the late 1980s, when she had in her own way been a good friend of the earth.

Arms and the Gulf

Meanwhile, in her last months in office, the scandal of the covert arming of Iraq began to break. When the Iran–Iraq war finally ended in stalemate in July 1988, Alan Clark (then still in the DTI) and the latest Minister for Defence Procurement in the MoD, Lord Trefgarne, immediately began lobbying the Foreign Office to lift the 1985 guidelines restricting arms sales to both combatants.* Geoffrey Howe was sympathetic and in August minuted Mrs Thatcher, spelling out the commercial benefits of 'a phased approach to borderline cases'. Charles

---

*Clark and Trefgarne initially hoped that restrictions on supplying Iran could now be eased as well; but this became politically impossible in February 1989 when Ayatollah Khomeini declared a *fatwa* on the British writer Salman Rushdie to avenge alleged blasphemy in his latest novel, *The Satanic Verses*.

Powell replied that she was 'in general content with the strategy', but it would need careful watching: 'The PM will wish to be kept very closely in touch at every stage and consulted on all relevant decisions.'[121] One of the questions that Lord Justice Scott's subsequent inquiry had to answer was whether this instruction was obeyed. Having studied the exchanges between Clark, Trefgarne and the new Foreign Office minister William Waldegrave, Scott concluded that after December 1988 the relevant correspondence was not copied to the Prime Minister; she was therefore unaware of the subtle semantic revision which allowed the three ministers henceforth to interpret the guidelines more generously.[122] In truth, however, whether or not she knew of the new wording, she cannot have failed to notice that exports to Iraq increased rapidly as soon as the war ended. In October she specifically approved new export credits worth £340 million.[123]

The following month Saddam Hussein turned his violence against his own population and started murdering and gassing the Iraqi Kurds. Yet the flow of British machine tools to his munitions factories continued unabated. The only effect on British policy was to make those in the know more anxious to keep it secret: ministers, including Mrs Thatcher, continued to hide behind Howe's 1985 guidelines, insisting to Parliament that nothing had changed. On the ground the British sales effort could scarcely have been more blatant. In April 1989 no fewer than seventeen major British companies, including Rolls-Royce, British Aerospace, Thorn EMI and GEC, attended the Baghdad arms fair, where a model of the supposedly secret 'Supergun' was openly displayed: 25 per cent of their expenses were met by the DTI, and one of BAe's representatives was officially on secondment to the MoD at the time.[124] At last some alarm bells began to ring in Downing Street. In May Mrs Thatcher was sufficiently disturbed by the intelligence she was receiving to set up a Cabinet Office working group on Iraqi procurement (WGIP). But what was it that had disturbed her? According to Scott – based on the evidence she gave to his inquiry in December 1993 – she 'had become concerned about the extent of the Iraqi network for the procurement of materials and equipment for proliferation purposes, as well as of conventional defence-related goods and equipment, from the UK'.[125] In other words she only became concerned when she thought the Iraqis were obtaining nuclear materials, not just conventional equipment, which she had been happy to supply for years.★

★The Americans were not even worried about helping Saddam acquire a nuclear capacity. In April 1989 Iraqi scientists attended an advanced thermonuclear seminar in Portland, Oregon.[126]

Within the Ministry of Defence at least one officer was becoming alarmed at 'the scale on which the Iraqis are building up an arms manufacturing capability'. In June Lt-Col Richard Glazebrook circulated a paper drawing attention to 'the way in which UK Ltd is helping Iraq often unwittingly to set up a major indigenous arms industry'.[127] He managed to block the export of an infra-red surveillance system but still the build-up went on: he failed to stop a consignment of helicopter spares and a Marconi communications system which would enhance the Iraqi forces' effectiveness in the field. In July his Secretary of State, George Younger, put up to the Cabinet's OD committee a proposal to grant export licences for a £3 billion sale by BAe of 'the "know-how", equipment and components necessary to enable Iraq to assemble 63 Hawk aircraft'. This, according to Scott, was the first admission to senior ministers, including Mrs Thatcher, that the interpretation of the 1985 guidelines had been changed.[128] In their evidence Clark, Trefgarne and Waldegrave argued that the order fell within the revised guidelines, since the Hawk, though capable of being adapted for chemical weapons, was not strictly designed to be lethal. Sharp as ever, Mrs Thatcher wrote in the margin 'Doubtful'; but she failed to pick up the crucial word 'revised'.[129]

A note by the deputy Cabinet Secretary, Leonard Appleyard, set out the humanitarian case against this latest sale and warned of a hostile press if it was approved. Mrs Thatcher underlined several passages, indicating that she shared these concerns. Charles Powell had initially favoured the sale, since 'the pot of gold is enticingly large'; and Percy Cradock agreed. But after reading Appleyard's note Powell changed his mind. 'Iraq is run by a despicable and violent government,' he now wrote, 'which has gloried in the use of CW [chemical weapons] and a substantial defence sale to them would be seen as highly cynical and opportunistic . . . All for a pot of gold which looks pretty uncertain anyway: it is far from clear that the Iraqis can pay.' Both Nigel Lawson and the new Foreign Secretary, John Major, he believed, would be against the sale.[130]

Mrs Thatcher told the Scott Inquiry that she agreed – on moral grounds:

> The issue, she said, 'seemed to me very, very clear cut . . . it was such a straightforward decision'. 'Even though this is a big order,' she said, 'you cannot let [that] influence your judgement against your deep instinct and knowledge that it would be wrong to sell this kind of aircraft, that could be used for ground attack, to a regime that had in fact used chemical weapons on the Kurds.'[131]

On this occasion the committee refused an export licence.

Yet even now – despite her fine words – the Prime Minister was no more ready than her junior colleagues to stop supplying Iraq with the ability to build sophisticated weapons. If Scott is right, she may not have seen a paper which Waldegrave wrote for Major in October emphasising the importance of the Iraqi market:

> I doubt if there is any future market on such a scale anywhere where the UK is potentially so well placed if we play our diplomatic hand correctly . . . We must not allow it to go to the French, Germans, Japanese, Koreans, etc.

Maybe she would not have echoed quite so bluntly Waldegrave's cynical readiness to overlook the execution of a British journalist, Farzad Bazoft, and the continuing persecution of the Kurds. ('A few more Bazofts or another bout of internal repression would make this more difficult'.)[132] But she certainly approved the general thrust of Waldegrave's paper, and remained keen to keep the trade flowing as freely as possible. In the spring of 1990 the seizure of the Supergun parts being manufactured in Sheffield, HM Customs' investigation of Matrix Churchill and the arrest of three directors of another British company, Euromac, for exporting nuclear triggers suddenly shone a glare of publicity on the whole subject of arms to Iraq. Yet right up to the end of July Mrs Thatcher was seeking to ease rather than tighten the restrictions. She still rejected Nicholas Ridley's recommendation to neutralise the Supergun embarrassment by scrapping restrictions altogether: a meeting chaired by Major's successor, Douglas Hurd, on 19 July confirmed the embargo on 'lethal' material. But the same meeting recommended relaxing controls on the export of lathes for the manufacture of weapons – and Powell minuted on 26 July that 'the Prime Minister found the Foreign Secretary's presentation convincing'.[133] In the event the new policy was never implemented: it was wrecked by Saddam's invasion of Kuwait a few days later and hastily buried. But by approving it Mrs Thatcher retrospectively endorsed the earlier shift of practice on which the whole Scott Inquiry centred. The fact is that right up to the last moment she had been eager to arm Britain's new enemy.

As the details of this murky episode continued to leak out over the next two years her successor sought to limit the political damage by appointing the Scott Inquiry. While this achieved its immediate purpose by kicking the subject into touch, Scott and his assiduous assistant Presiley Baxendale, QC embarked on a thorough trawl through all the relevant departmental records, supplemented by eighty-seven days of oral hearings, which ultimately – after more than three years – shed an unprecedented amount of light on processes of government normally kept closely hidden. Mrs Thatcher herself – by now Lady Thatcher – was obliged to give evidence on 8 December 1993. She did so reluctantly, with a lofty pose of amnesia, maintaining that she had known nothing about an area of her government in which she was well known to take a close interest. Her manner was characterised by Matthew Engel in the *Guardian* as 'part Nixon, who took the responsibility but not the blame, part Reagan, who remembered nothing, and part Ceausescu, who regretted nothing and how dare they'.[134] Woodrow Wyatt loyally raged that it was 'quite intolerable that one of the greatest Prime Ministers of all time should be pilloried and cross-questioned by some girl QC and the idiot man, Justice Scott, who thinks there should be no secrets in government dealings with other countries', but he thought that she had seen them off quite well. 'Obviously Margaret did know much more about the sale of arms to Iraq than she was letting on. But she was quite justified . . . because we needed the exports.'[135]

In his report, eventually published in February 1996, Scott treated her protestations with tactful credulity; but he nevertheless printed a good deal of evidence which allowed readers to draw different conclusions. Where there was a direct conflict of evidence he accepted that the MoD official who stated that the Prime Minister had been involved in granting a particular export licence in 1988 must have been 'mistaken'.[136] He found 'inherently credible' her claim that she had missed Younger's reference to the revised guidelines in 1989 because she had been 'concerned with the big picture'.[137] Finding 'no documentary indication' that she was kept informed of the junior ministers' relaxation of the guidelines, he dismissed Clark's assertion to the contrary as 'based on assumptions and not on any direct knowledge'.[138]

At the same time Scott's report fully confirmed that the Government had from the beginning of the Iran–Iraq war actively assisted Iraq while maintaining a public posture of even-handedness, and that this was not insubordination by juniors acting on their own but was 'known to the Prime Minister'.[139] He unequivocally condemned the repeated and deliberate deception of Parliament, which he concluded was undertaken not for reasons of commercial confidentiality but for administrative convenience and fear of public outcry.[140] There was not much comfort here for Lady Thatcher, though she still protested her innocence. 'If there was no change in the guidelines – and there was not –', she told the House of Lords, 'then the question of deliberately misleading the House falls to the ground.'[141] But because the report concentrated so much on who knew what when, and whether or not she saw a particular memo, and because Scott chose to publish his findings in five fat volumes without a summary, the major fact of Britain's systematic arming of a particularly brutal dictator over a period of ten years was lost in the mass of detail.* For all his thoroughness in investigating the minutiae of Whitehall, Scott entirely failed to investigate the network of informal connections between government, business and the security services which was the real motor of the secret arms trade in the 1980s.

Scott's lack of curiosity is strange since it was a rare glimpse into this shady world which had forced Major to set up his inquiry in the first place. In November 1992 HM Customs' case against three directors of Matrix Churchill for illegal exports to Iraq collapsed with the revelation – let slip with characteristic nonchalance by Alan Clark – that they had been acting with the full knowledge and approval of MI6. There followed the still more damaging discovery that half a dozen senior ministers – including Kenneth Baker, Ken Clarke, Malcolm Rifkind, Peter Lilley and (under protest) Michael Heseltine – had been persuaded to sign Public Interest Immunity Certificates to prevent this information being revealed to the court, thereby letting innocent men go to prison to protect the fiction of the Government's non-involvement.† This scandal only lifted a corner of the blanket of disinformation which covered the Government's activity in this area. The full extent of its covert involvement has subsequently been

---

*When the report was debated, the Major Government claimed that Scott had disposed of the allegation that Britain had armed Iraq because it had followed the policy of not exporting 'lethal' material – that is, finished weapons. But even if true – and the Supergun, the flow of weapons via Jordan and other countries and Britain's narrow interpretation of the world 'lethal' all refute it – this is a technicality. The plain fact is that British firms, with the active encouragement of the Government, did export to Iraq the means to manufacture lethal weapons, as well as a range of other equipment which clearly served to build up Saddam's military machine. It is a legalistic quibble to maintain – as Lady Thatcher asserted in the Lords and as John Major still claimed in his memoirs[142] – that Britain did not help to arm Iraq.

†Heseltine, to his credit, initially refused to sign and did so only on the assurance that his reservations would be conveyed to the trial judge. The others tamely accepted the word of the Attorney-General, Sir Nicholas Lyell, that it was their duty to sign. In fact Lyell failed to pass on Heseltine's reservations; but the defendants' counsel, Geoffrey Robertson, QC, successfully contested the withholding of the documents. It was Mr Justice Smedley's ruling that they should be released which extracted Clark's admission that he had been 'economical with the *actualité*'.

suggested by a number of journalistic exposés, including a *Private Eye* special entitled *Not the Scott Report*, published three months before the real thing, but perhaps most damningly by the former chairman of one of the companies most closely involved.

Gerald James was a merchant banker, a member of the right-wing Monday Club and initially a keen admirer of Mrs Thatcher. He was drawn into the arms business through connections in intelligence and went on to build up a multinational explosives business at the MoD's bidding, but was swiftly removed when things began to go wrong. Bitter at the way he felt he had been used and then – like the Matrix Churchill directors – made a scapegoat for the Government's own inadmissible activities, James tried unsuccessfully to persuade Scott to widen his inquiries; then, when Scott declined, published his own indictment, *In the Public Interest*, subtitled by his publishers 'A devastating account of the Thatcher Government's involvement in the covert arms trade – by the man who turned Astra Fireworks into a £100 million arms manufacturer'. Inevitably it is an angry and unfocused tirade. Some of his allegations are unsupported and unsubsantiable, but others are very specific. Though not privy to the whole picture, James saw enough to realise that he was only a pawn in a very complex game. 'The government,' he asserted, 'through the civil service and its Intelligence agents in the City and elsewhere, is wholly involved in every aspect of the defence industry.'[143] 'Nothing goes on – no deals, no contracts – in which the government is not principally involved.'[144]

At one level the MoD operated through its own wholly-owned subsidiaries, Royal Ordnance (RO) and International Military Services (IMS), until they were sold to the newly privatised British Aerospace in 1987 and 1991 respectively. But they also used a large number of private companies, including Astra and Matrix Churchill, Ordtech, Euromac, Sheffield Forgemasters (who built the Supergun) and Walter Somers. All these firms worked closely with the MoD and the DTI. Gerald James' company, Astra, was put together by the MoD specifically to compete with RO, and it was the MoD which encouraged it to buy the Grantham-based munitions company BMARC (later charged with illegally making components for Iran) in 1987 and the Dutch explosives manufacturer PRB (which made the propellant for the Supergun) in 1989. The acquisition of PRB, with greater liabilities than were realised, proved the ruin of Astra, and the company went into receivership in 1992; a damning DTI report criticised the directors, accountants, auditors and the Stock Exchange, and disqualified James and five other directors from running public companies in future.

In response James accused the inspectors of ignoring the systematic evasion of the rules that were supposed to guide arms exports. Among other things he claimed that he warned the DTI in 1990 that the UK had granted export licences to Portugal – an obvious blind – 'sufficient to enable that country to participate in all-out global warfare', but no action was taken on his information.[145] In his book James alleged that the DTI knew that Astra was deceiving its own shareholders but did nothing to enlighten them:

> The decision by the DTI inspectors to ignore completely the government's responsibility to Astra shareholders lies at the very root of what was wrong in Thatcher's Britain . . . The inspectors were employed by the government through the DTI, up to its neck in illegal export of arms . . . There was never any danger of their investigating the government's role in Astra, and they swept aside the very idea of it on the third page of their report.[146]*

The covert trade was facilitated by middlemen in the City. Two were particularly ubiquitous – Stephan Adolph Kock, a former Rhodesian soldier, now defence consultant to the Midland Bank, who was a director of both Astra and BMARC and was also involved in negotiating Mrs Thatcher's Pergau Dam deal; and Sir John Cuckney, who had a finger in every part of the defence pie. A former MI5 man, Cuckney was chairman of IMS from 1974 to 1985 as well as a director of two private armaments companies – TI Group (the parent company of Matrix Churchill, whose sale to the Iraqis he organised) and Astra Holdings. He was also a director of the Midland Bank and the man responsible for ensuring that the failure of client countries like Jordan and Iraq to pay for the goods they had supposedly bought was quietly made good by the taxpayer under the Export Credit Guarantee Scheme. In addition, of course, he was chairman of Westland at the time of the 1986 embarrassment. James asserts that the Westland crisis was a by-product of Mrs Thatcher's huge Al-Yamamah deal with Saudi Arabia. The reason Mrs Thatcher was so keen for the American firm Sikorsky to buy Westland was so that Astra could 'weaponise' Black Hawk helicopters for Saudi Arabia with Sikorsky technology, built by its subsidiary

---

*It was not only Astra that was not investigated. The director of a haulage firm employed to move explosives – with extraordinary police security – between RO factories in Scotland told the *Guardian* in 1993 that he had written to the Prime Minister in 1988 to warn her that they were shipping to Iraq three times the quantity of fuses specified in the contract. But again nothing was done.[147]

BMARC in Grantham.[148] The whole Westland saga, on this reading, was 'just another example of the way the US and UK worked together to beat Congressional limitations on arms supplies to the Middle East':

> The Americans were not allowed to supply helicopters direct, so Thatcher, who had moved Sir John Cuckney into position as chairman of Westland, arranged for the US company United Technologies/Sikorsky to take a financial interest in the company, nominate two directors and license the British helicopter company to build them.[149]

James subsequently learned that the helicopters were not destined for Saudi Arabia at all, but for Iraq.

He asserts that the flow of defence equipment from British firms not just to Iraq, but to Iran, Saudi Arabia, Jordan, Suharto's Indonesia, Pinochet's Chile and other dubious allies throughout the 1980s, was co-ordinated and directed by MI6 in close alliance with American intelligence. For instance, the Oman hospital deal from which Mark Thatcher's company Monteagle was alleged to have pocketed £50,000 commission in 1981 was not what it seemed. 'They dressed up all the expenditure to make it seem that Margaret Thatcher's part in it had to do with building a hospital and a university.' But in fact it was all about building silos for US precision-guided missiles intended to stop the Soviet Union using Afghanistan to thrust into the Gulf.[150] Thus the habit of deception which was later applied to arming Iraq grew out of the routine suspension of ethical constraints during the Cold War.

But Scott did not explore any of this. He explicitly excluded Al-Yamamah and other Middle Eastern arms deals from his remit.[151] He did not take evidence from James, or from Cuckney, Kock or any of the other middlemen whose activities were by then attracting press scrutiny – in addition to *Private Eye*, the *Guardian's* Richard Norton-Taylor was particularly persistent – or even from any of the MoD's official arms salesmen, as the Labour frontbencher Michael Meacher pointed out in a letter to the *Guardian* in June 1994:

> Only cross-examination at public hearings of . . . Sir John Cuckney, Sir James Blyth [Head of Defence Sales from 1981], Mr Stephan Adolph Kock, Sir Colin Chandler [Head of Defence Export Services, 1985–9], Sir Peter Levene [Chief of Defence Procurement, 1985–91] and representatives of the Midland Bank International Trading Finance Department will reveal the truth of what arms were traded

and when, how the deals were set up, what was the role of the intelligence services, what commissions were paid and to whom, and which politicians and civil servants authorised this trading.[152]

Nor did parliamentary inquiries do any better. The DTI select committee, chaired by the Tory MP for Hastings, Kenneth Warren, a businessman with defence interests who was himself a director of at least one Iraqi-owned firm, accepted at face value the Government's claim that ministers knew nothing about the Supergun before 1990. It was unable to question Sir Hal Miller, who revealed that he had told the Government about the gun in 1988, but had subsequently been persuaded to keep quiet since charges against his constituents had been dropped. ('I do not see what good it will do,' he excused himself. 'I have no wish to embarrass the Government'.)[153] It was likewise prevented from interviewing the two DTI officials most closely involved in the affair, on the grounds that they had retired. Gerald James additionally alleged that Warren colluded with one of the principal witnesses – the British director of the Supergun project in Iraq – in suppressing evidence about Mark Thatcher's role in the affair.[154] Certainly his committee's report, published just before the 1992 election, was an unrevealing whitewash, described by one of its own members as 'anodyne'.[155] Warren was duly knighted in 1994. Sir Nicholas Bonsor's Defence select committee followed his example by declining to investigate the Government's dealings with Astra;[156] the Foreign Affairs select committee failed to interview several key witnesses in its probing of the Pergau Dam affair; while the Public Accounts Committee's investigation of the huge commissions paid to middlemen in the Al-Yamamah deal was suppressed by the Auditor-General, Sir John Bourn, who had himself been Under-Secretary for Defence Procurement in the MoD at the time. Making every allowance for James' personal agenda, it is hard to quarrel with a letter he wrote to the chairman of the Public Accounts Committee – the Labour MP Robert Sheldon – in November 1994 setting out what a proper inquiry into the arms trade would have to involve:

It would have to include . . . all the records of IMS, Royal Ordnance . . . and other companies involved with the Propellant and Arms cartels . . . the secret and detailed records of ECGD [the Exports Credit Guarantee Department] and the records of government intelligence agencies like MI5, MI6, GCHQ as well as those of the MoD, DTI, FCO and the various arms export control committees and bodies. In addition the detailed and secret records of Midland Bank and its arms department MITS, Morgan Grenfell and other bankers involved.[157]

Neither Scott, however, in an inquiry lasting more than three years, nor any other public inquiry, looked into any of these ramifications of the secret state.

The arms-for-Iraq saga and the cover-up which surrounded it formed the basis of the perception of sleaze which eventually engulfed the Major Government in 1997. In his memoirs John Major indignantly denies any personal wrongdoing, and he can probably be believed, though the same indulgence cannot be applied to all his ministers. The corruption began with Mrs Thatcher, who actively encouraged a huge growth in British arms exports and winked at the methods used to promote them in breach of her government's professed policy. The fact is that she loved the arms trade and was fascinated by the intelligence world. Her normally high ethical standards were suspended in this grey area where the claims of free trade and national security overlapped. The suggestion that she did not have a very shrewd knowledge of what was going on is incredible. There was no area of government which she supervised more closely.

'No time to go wobbly'

Mrs Thatcher had just arrived in the United States on Thursday 2 August 1990 to attend the fortieth anniversary conference of the Aspen Institute in Colorado when the news came in that Saddam Hussein had invaded Kuwait. She was accompanied, as was now her habit, only by Charles Powell and Bernard Ingham (plus a duty clerk, two technicians and a Special Branch officer) and was the guest of the US Ambassador to London, Henry Catto, who owned a ranch in Aspen. Western intelligence was caught unawares by the invasion. Back in London, Douglas Hurd learned of it only from the radio. But Mrs Thatcher had no need of colleagues to determine her reaction. Her condemnation of aggression was always unhesitating, even if the aggressor had until very recently been a favoured customer. She immediately took a clear view that the Iraqi action – like Argentina's in 1982 – must be reversed, by force if necessary. Little as she liked telephone diplomacy, she lost no time in making a series of calls: to European heads of government, starting with François Mitterrand, whose prompt support over the Falklands she had never forgotten; to Commonwealth leaders; friendly Arab leaders; and the current members of the Security Council. Most promised support for some form of collective action. The exception, to her disappointment, was King

Hussein of Jordan who – as she later told President Bush – was 'not helpful. He told me the Kuwaitis had it coming.'[158]

Bush had of course been making many of the same calls himself, so by the time he joined Mrs Thatcher in Aspen the next morning they had already assembled the nucleus of an international coalition against Iraq. They talked for two hours, discussing economic sanctions but not at this stage military options, then went outside to speak to the press. 'Prime Minister Thatcher and I are looking at it on exactly the same wavelength,' Bush told them. But Mrs Thatcher sounded much the more forceful of the two. While Bush hoped for a peaceful settlement and called for the Iraqis to withdraw in accordance with UN Resolution 660 (carried 14–0 by the Security Council overnight), it was she – as he later recognised – who 'put her finger on the most important point by insisting that Iraq's aggression was a test of the international community's willingness to give the Resolution teeth:

Iraq has violated and taken over the territory of a country which is a full member of the United Nations. That is totally unacceptable and if it were allowed to endure then there would be many other small countries that could never feel safe.

The fundamental question is this: whether the nations of the world have the collective will effectively to see that the Security Council Resolution is upheld, whether they have the collective will effectively to do anything which the Security Council further agrees to see that Iraq withdraws and that the government of Kuwait is restored to Kuwait.

'What has happened,' she added, 'is a total violation of international law. You cannot have a situation where one country marches in and takes over another country which is a member of the United Nations.'[159]

But of course it was not quite as altruistic as that. Though neither leader acknowledged it, their real concern was that – having annexed the Kuwaiti oil fields – Saddam might, if not prevented, go on to seize the even more important Saudi reserves. 'They won't stop here,' Mrs Thatcher told Bush. 'They see a chance to take a major share of oil. It's got to be stopped.' 'We must win this,' she insisted. 'Losing Saudi oil is a blow we couldn't take. We cannot give in to dictators. [And] we can't make an oil embargo work without a blockade.'[160]

'Had Saddam's invasion of Kuwait that summer been allowed to stand,' Lady Thatcher wrote twelve years later, 'he would have gained control of a quarter of the Gulf's oil reserves. Had he been permitted to go further and advance right down the Gulf he would have gained

control of over 60 per cent of the world's oil reserves.'[161] In fact this
was a danger she had already foreseen two months before the invasion of Kuwait. In a speech to the NATO Council meeting in Scotland
in June Mrs Thatcher had argued that following the end of the Cold
War, NATO should be prepared to extend its sphere of operations
beyond Europe. 'It is not long,' she recalled, 'since some of us had to
go to the Arabian Gulf to keep oil supplies flowing' during the Iran–Iraq
war. (She made it sound as if she had commanded the Armilla Patrol
personally.)

> We shall become very heavily dependent on Middle-Eastern oil
> once again in the next century. With the spread of sophisticated
> weapons and military technology to areas like the Middle East,
> potential threats to NATO territory may originate more from outside
> Europe.[162]

In the event Kuwait was liberated under the aegis of the UN, not
by NATO. But it is significant that two months before Saddam's aggression Mrs Thatcher had already declared the protection of oil supplies
a legitimate NATO interest. Her outrage about Iraq's violation of
Kuwaiti sovereignty, though perfectly sincere as far as it went, was at
the same time a convenient cover for deeper national and western
interests.

It is still disputed whether or not Mrs Thatcher's presence in Aspen
at the critical moment helped determine Bush's response to the Iraqi
invasion. Douglas Hurd (who was not there) believes she did so 'quite
substantially'.[163] But the Americans insist that the President needed no
stiffening; and Bernard Ingham (who was there) agrees. 'George Bush
had a backbone before he arrived in Aspen and did not acquire it from
Mrs Thatcher . . . Her familiar distinctive contribution [was] a clear
and simply expressed analysis of the situation.'[164] Doubt arose from the
fact that in his first public response the President had stated that he
was 'not contemplating' military action. This choice of words, Scowcroft
admitted, was 'not felicitous', but he insists that it was not meant to
rule out the use of force, but to keep all options open.[165] Nevertheless
the belief took hold in Britain that Bush was a bit of a wimp who
was impelled to strong action only by Mrs Thatcher's robust example
– an impression which she was happy to perpetuate. Actually it was
not until some weeks later that she told Bush that this was 'no time
to go wobbly'. There was certainly a difference of emphasis between
them: Bush was more concerned than Mrs Thatcher to assemble the
widest possible coalition of western and Moslem nations, and to take

no military action without the specific authority of the United Nations, while she wanted to invoke Article 51 of the Charter to justify action in self-defence without further ado. But there is no doubt of Bush's personal resolve. When he did eventually send American troops into action he did so despite having only narrow congressional support: the vote in the Senate was 52–47.

Mrs Thatcher stayed in Aspen for four days, making more telephone calls between scheduled visits to the SDI research centre and an atmospheric research centre. Her speech to the conference on Sunday 5 August had been planned as a wide-ranging survey of the world after the end of the Cold War; but she took the chance to repeat her uncompromising stand on the challenge of the moment:

> Iraq's invasion of Kuwait defies every principle for which the United Nations stands. If we let it succeed, no small country can ever feel safe again. The law of the jungle would take over from the rule of law.[166]

On her way home she stopped off in Washington to see the President again. While she was with him Defense Secretary Dick Cheney called with the news that King Fahd had agreed to allow American forces to be stationed on Saudi soil: this was the key decision which made it possible to mount a military operation to expel Iraq from Kuwait.* The same day the Security Council voted 13–0 to impose sanctions on Iraq. Mrs Thatcher immediately argued that this gave all the authority needed to impose a blockade to enforce them. But Bush shied away from the world 'blockade' which in international law constituted an act of war. He preferred the more diplomatic 'quarantine', which was the term President Kennedy had used to bar Soviet ships from Cuba in 1962.

The Gulf crisis came at an opportune moment for Mrs Thatcher, both internationally and domestically. So far as her relations with Bush were concerned, she was delighted to have the chance to demonstrate once again that Britain was still America's best friend in a crisis. She had been disturbed by the new administration's 'tilt' towards Germany, while the Bush White House had found her attitude to German reunification incomprehensible. In the 'new world order' they saw emerging

---

*It was also a fateful decision, since it was the stationing of infidel troops on Moslem soil which triggered Osama bin Laden's hostility to the United States and led eventually to the terrorist attack on New York and Washington on 11 September 2001.

after 1989 her preoccupation with World War Two and her simple Cold War moralism seemed embarrassingly anachronistic. But Saddam's challenge immediately exposed a familiar ambivalence in Europe, while restoring Britain's credit as the one ally ready to stand shoulder-to-shoulder with Washington when there was fighting to be done. When Mrs Thatcher scoffed that only France among the Europeans had 'the stomach for a fight', Spain's socialist Prime Minister, Felipe Gonzalez, retorted that 'We don't have the same warmongering ardour that she is capable of at times.'[167] Whether or not her presence in Aspen significantly influenced Bush's reaction, their identity of view instantly recreated the sort of Anglo-American special relationship she had enjoyed with Reagan.

A major international crisis also seemed just the thing to rebuild her position at home, taking the voters' minds off the poll tax and inflation. The possibility of military action to repel another aggressive dictator could only revive memories of the Falklands. As in 1982 Mrs Thatcher relished the chance to show that she was not afraid of war. 'There is never any lack of people anxious to avoid the use of force,' she wrote in her memoirs.[168] Woodrow Wyatt found her on 10 August 'very bullish about the possibility of squashing Iraq'.[169] Eight days later there occurred the incident that put a new phrase into the vocabulary of politics. The question was what to do about two Iraqi oil tankers which were trying to beat the allied blockade. 'We had lengthy discussions with the British about it,' Scowcroft recalled, 'and of course Margaret Thatcher said go after the ships.' But this risked upsetting the Soviets, who still retained some influence with Iraq, so James Baker persuaded Bush to hold off for three days. 'Margaret went along with this delay only reluctantly,' Bush wrote:

> I called her at about three in the morning her time – although I wasn't looking forward to it . . . We knew how strongly she wanted to stop those ships. She insisted that if we let one go by it would set a precedent. I told her I had decided to delay and why. It was here, not earlier, as many have suggested, that she said, 'Well, all right, George, but this is no time to go wobbly.'[170]

'George always loved that,' Barbara Bush wrote, 'and wobbly he did not go.'[171] Thereafter, Scowcroft recalls, 'we used the phrase almost daily'.[172] Unquestionably Bush was irritated by the impression that Mrs Thatcher had had to stiffen him at Aspen, and made a joke of this story to counter it. For her part Mrs Thatcher was happy to use 'No Time to Go Wobbly' as the title of the penultimate chapter of her memoirs.

Meanwhile she devoted her diplomatic efforts to berating anyone else she thought insufficiently robust – notably King Hussein who came to Downing Street in early September seeking support for a deal to save Saddam's face. 'He walked into a firestorm,' Charles Powell recalled. 'She flew at him. She said she thought he had calculated entirely wrongly, he'd made the wrong decision by encouraging Iraq, by appearing to support Iraq. She gave him the toughest time I should think he's ever had in his life.' 'I was not discourteous,' she insisted later. 'I was firm – very firm indeed.'[173] The Soviet Foreign Minister, Yevgeny Primakov, also came to Chequers trying to broker a peace settlement, but was treated by Mrs Thatcher to 'a diatribe on the inevitability of war'.[174] Above all she was contemptuous of those – most prominently Ted Heath – who muddied the waters by flying to Baghdad to try to negotiate the release of a number of British hostages whom Saddam was holding as pawns in a cruel game of diplomatic poker. In the Commons she was curtly dismissive of Heath's freelance efforts: she was bound to welcome the return of thirty-three whom he had managed to bring out, but pointed out that there were still another 1,400 British nationals in the country.[175] She resolutely refused to negotiate with such barbarism.

In fact her bellicosity, in a situation where British territory was not at stake, probably did her less good than she expected. The polls registered no significant recovery of her popularity over the next three months and the fact that British troops were committed did not save her when her leadership was on the line. Nevertheless she enjoyed having a 'real' crisis on her hands again: she welcomed the diversion from the poll tax, even if the voters did not. But this time – remembering the trouble she had had with the Foreign Office in 1982 – she was determined to keep control firmly in her own hands. Once again she formed a small war cabinet – but it was not a properly constituted Cabinet committee, just an *ad hoc* ministerial group chaired by herself with Hurd and Tom King as Foreign and Defence Secretaries, Patrick Mayhew the Attorney-General (necessary for questions of international law) and John Wakeham, as a former Chief Whip taking the role Cecil Parkinson had filled in 1982, plus the Chief of Defence Staff, Sir David Craig, and Percy Cradock in his capacity as chairman of the Joint Intelligence Committee. Sir Patrick Wright of the Foreign Office was excluded, as was the Cabinet Secretary, Robin Butler. In his place Powell took the minutes, which were not circulated to the full Cabinet, as they were during the Falklands war. Peter Hennessy quotes the view of an unnamed 'insider' that Mrs Thatcher was cutting procedural corners ever more blatantly. 'She became even odder over the Gulf and it was getting pretty chaotic. Bureaucratically it was getting into a tangle. It was constitutionally pretty dangerous.' There was relief in Whitehall when John Major, on taking over in November, 'swiftly regularised the position'.[176]

Her first military commitment, as early as 7 August, was to send two squadrons of Tornados and one of Jaguars to Saudi Arabia, Bahrain and Oman, and a destroyer and three minesweepers to join the destroyer and two frigates already in the Gulf. In view of Tom King's latest defence review, *Options for Change*, published in July – which following the end of the Cold War had proposed to halve the British army on the Rhine within an overall manpower cut of 18 per cent – she initially hoped to limit Britain's ground contribution to an infantry or parachute battalion. But the Americans were pressing for tanks, so in September the Chief of the General Staff, Sir John Chapple, persuaded her to send the 7th Armoured Brigade (the 'Desert Rats') from Germany, plus two armoured regiments and an infantry regiment, led by Sir Peter de la Billière but ultimately under the command of US General Norman Schwarzkopf. (The French by contrast retained operational independence.)[177] The army chiefs hoped that war in the Gulf would win them the same sort of reprieve that the Falklands had secured the Royal Navy.

Mrs Thatcher personally insisted on Peter de la Billière, who had impressed her as the SAS commander in charge of the Iranian Embassy siege back in 1980. He was what she called 'a fighting general' who had served in Korea, Malaya, Aden and Oman and even spoke passable Arabic. He was supposed to be on the point of retirement, but he was the obvious man for the job and she let it be known that if he was not appointed she would make him her adviser in Downing Street.[178] 'Cynics later remarked that this was the factor which clinched my nomination,' de la Billière wrote.[179] The MoD gave way and sent him to the Gulf, where he fully justified Mrs Thatcher's instinct.

Almost as if she sensed that her own time might be short, she was impatient to act quickly, without waiting to see if sanctions might do the job without recourse to war and without seeking further authority from the UN. When Parliament was recalled on 6 September dissenting voices in all parties called for caution and delay. She argued on the contrary that ruling out early military action only played into Saddam's hands:

> To undertake now to use no military force without further authority of the Security Council would be to deprive ourselves of a right in international law expressly affirmed by Resolution 661 . . . It would be to hand an advantage to Saddam Hussein and it could put our own forces in greater peril . . .

Let us not forget that in Saddam Hussein we are dealing with a person who, without warning, has gone into the territory of another state with tanks, guns and aircraft, has fought and taken that state against international law and against the will of its people. A person who will take such action against one state will take it against another if he is not stopped and his invasion reversed.[180]

'I told them we already *have* the authority and don't need to go back to the UN,' she reported to Bush. 'We should not go back to the UN and risk a split vote, which would weaken our position. It took five days to get Resolution 665, and even then we couldn't get the word "force" into the text.'[181] Despite their build-up of troops, she feared that the Americans were too willing to 'go the extra mile' to secure a peaceful settlement and might in the end fail to act at all. She worried that trying but failing to get a UN resolution, due to a Russian or Chinese veto, would be worse than not trying at all, and saw no need to take the risk. But her position, in the view of Lawrence Freedman and Efraim Karsh, was 'wholly unrealistic if there was to be any hope of sustaining a broad coalition'.[182] By contrast with the approach of the younger President Bush and Donald Rumsfeld in 2003, Bush and Baker judged it essential to secure another UN resolution; and by patient diplomacy they eventually succeeded. Resolution 678, authorising the use of force unless Iraq withdrew from Kuwait by 15 January 1991, was carried on 29 November by twelve votes to two (Cuba and Yemen voting against, China abstaining). But by that time Britain had a new Prime Minister.

On 30 September Mrs Thatcher was back in New York to speak about family values to a UN Children's Summit and had dinner with Bush and Scowcroft. 'Margaret Thatcher was impatient to plan an early military action based on the existing resolutions,' Bush wrote. 'She remained leery of going back to the UN. "We risk amendments . . ." she said. "I don't think we need an extra reason to go."' At the same time she wanted the allies to plan military action in their own time, neither letting Saddam provoke them into going earlier nor allowing the timetable to be delayed. 'We had to move during the cool months – November to March,' she argued. 'If we waited for sanctions to work it would take us to the following November.' 'Unless we can show we have tried to stay within the international consensus,' Bush and Baker countered, 'we risk losing public support for what we have to do.' But 'Margaret was not persuaded, and insisted that if we went for a resolution we would raise doubts as to whether we could go forward without one.'[183] She believed that in order to hold the coalition together they had to move by mid-February.

'Once we have the necessary forces in place,' she cabled on 18 October, 'we should go sooner rather than later. Otherwise we risk losing the support of Arab governments who will not understand delay and come to question our resolve.' 'Saddam Hussein,' she added characteristically, 'has got to lose and be seen to lose.'[184]

Colin Powell, then chairman of the American Chiefs of Staff, wanted to give sanctions longer to work. General Schwarzkopf did not think he yet had enough troops. But Bush shared Mrs Thatcher's fear that hanging about in the desert for months would put too much strain on the coalition. At the CSCE (Conference on Security and Cooperation in Europe) in Paris on 19 November she argued that Saddam's use of hostages alone was reason enough to use force and promised 'another brigade and some minesweepers'.[185] She still worried that giving the military everything they wanted would mean further delay. But at her very last Cabinet three days later, after she had tearfully announced her resignation, she was better than her word and pushed through the commitment of another armoured brigade and an artillery brigade, all from the British army on the Rhine, making a total British contribution of 45,000 personnel.

Her removal from office just as these preparations were gathering pace left her feeling cheated of another war. 'One of my few abiding regrets,' she maintained in her memoirs, 'is that I was not there to see the issue through.'[186] Her fall, according to Peter de la Billière, 'caused consternation' among the troops in the Gulf and dismayed the allies, particularly the Saudis, who could not understand how a democracy could replace a leader without an election.[187] In fact 'Desert Storm' was so overwhelmingly an American operation that her absence made little difference. After two weeks of overwhelming bombardment, the vaunted Iraqi army offered little resistance and Kuwait was liberated in a matter of days. As time passed, however, Lady Thatcher persuaded herself that she would not have acquiesced in the American decision to halt the pursuit of Saddam's fleeing forces and leave the dictator still in power – free to oppress and terrorise his people, free to bomb and gas the Kurds, free to rebuild his military and possibly nuclear potential. 'The opinion of the UN counted for far too much and the military objective . . . far too little,' she wrote in her memoirs. 'In war there is much to be said for magnanimity in victory. But not before victory.'[188] 'They should have surrendered, their equipment, the lot,' she declared on television three years later:

When you're dealing with a dictator he has got not only to be defeated, well and truly, but he's got to be seen to be defeated, by his own people, so that they identify the privations they've had to go through with his actions; and we didn't do that.

She felt it a bitter irony that five years after his invasion of Kuwait, Saddam – alone of the principal players of August 1990 – was still in place:

> There is the aggressor, Saddam Hussein, still in power; there is the President of the United States, no longer in power; there is the Prime Minister of Britain, who did quite a lot to get things there, no longer in power. I wonder who won.[189]

She was entitled to wonder. Yet the fact is that, as the former Chief of the Defence Staff, Field-Marshal Sir Michael Carver, wrote in 1992, 'the decision to call a halt was a rare example of voluntarily ceasing hostilities at the right moment'.[190] Having achieved the limited objective of getting Iraq out of Kuwait, the coalition had no authority to go on to topple Saddam, while the Americans quite rightly wanted neither to be seen to inflict unnecessary slaughter on a defeated enemy nor to get sucked into a long-term occupation of Iraq. 'When she was in office,' Percy Cradock recalled, 'there was no serious talk of that kind, for good reasons.'[191] Charles Powell likewise told Woodrow Wyatt that, whatever her belligerent instinct, 'she was very much piping down on that because we had to keep within United Nations resolutions and it was absolutely clear that intervention by force . . . was limited to getting Saddam out of Kuwait.'[192] In retirement Mrs Thatcher forgot that when in office she was very punctilious about respecting international law. From the start of the crisis she was always careful to limit the coalition's objective to reversing the occupation of Kuwait: she repeatedly denied any intention of removing Saddam which, she told a press conference in Paris on 19 November, was 'a matter for the people of Iraq'.[193] Though she believed strongly in the proper application of military force, she was also passionately legalistic.

Three weeks after leaving office Mrs Thatcher allowed herself to admit a tinge of guilt for having helped to build up Iraq's military machine for ten years before 1990. 'Would Saddam Hussein have committed his flagrant aggression against Kuwait,' she wondered in a speech reflecting on the lessons of history, 'had he not imagined that the Western stance of mildly benevolent neutrality, shown in his war against Iran, would be repeated? We cannot know.'[194] But she never referred to the subject again.

16

On and On

Ten more years?

On 3 May 1989 Margaret Thatcher chalked up ten years as Prime Minister. Sixteen months earlier, on 3 January 1988, she had already become the longest-serving Prime Minister of the twentieth century, beating Asquith's record of eight years and 251 days between 1908 and 1916. (Asquith in turn surpassed Churchill by only twelve days.) Mrs Thatcher was well aware of such milestones. She scrupulously corrected Woodrow Wyatt when he congratulated her a day early on overtaking Asquith. 'Not yet,' she told him. 'It's tomorrow.'[1] Nevertheless she was reluctant to draw too much attention to the anniversary, partly from superstition, partly for fear that people would say ten years was enough. She could not prevent a number of celebrations being staged to mark the event. On 3 May the 1922 Committee gave her lunch at the Savoy; the next day she entertained the Cabinet and their wives to dinner at Number Ten, and on Sunday she held a lunch at Chequers for a select gathering of special friends and supporters, with a bias towards friends in the media, including Rupert Murdoch. All these were essentially private occasions, however. At the Savoy she made a strongly upbeat speech reliving some of the high points of the past decade but containing, as Kenneth Baker noted, 'no element of valediction'.[2] But the text was not released to the press. To satisfy the media's love of anniversaries she gave interviews to all the main television and radio channels – BBC, ITN, Sky, TV-am, IRN – in which she made it clear that she had no intention of resting on her laurels.*

---

*She also attended a party for the launch of one of two books celebrating the anniversary. Thanking the publishers, she tempted fate by looking forward to 'putting a bit more business their way in 1999. I am getting a taste for anniversaries and I hope we shall meet again.'[3]

'Naturally we feel quite a sense of achievement that we have completed ten years,' she declared – with characteristic use of the plural – on the pavement outside Number Ten, 'but it is not so much the ten years, it is that during this time Britain has been transformed.' 'There is no thought of slowing down,' she told Michael Brunson of ITN, 'because we have built a marvellous basis and we want to go on.'

> It is just going to be very exciting in the next ten years, coming up to the millennium, and I think that we want to make a real special effort to see that everything is even better than now.[4]

She dismissed all suggestions that there had been losers as well as winners over the past ten years ('The standard of living for almost everyone is higher and that is a good thing'), but insisted there was much more still to do. When John Cole suggested that she might like to see more of her new grandson she replied: 'Oh, I shall be tempted by babysitting, of course, isn't any grandma? . . . But I think not just yet.'[5]

Several of her senior colleagues, even as they applauded her achievement, felt she should have chosen this moment to announce that she would step down soon, when she could still have gone in triumph. 'Probably her greatest mistake,' Willie Whitelaw reflected later, 'was not to make up her mind to give up before the 1992 election.'[6] Peter Carrington actually invited her to his house in Oxfordshire to urge her to retire 'rather sooner than had been in my mind'.[7] Some of her most ardent admirers privately took the same view, but dared not tell her. Kenneth Baker witnessed an exchange around this time between Tim Bell and Gordon Reece. 'You must tell her,' Bell urged. 'I can't,' Reece replied. 'I love her': at which Denis, overhearing, interjected, 'Steady on. She's my wife.'[8]

According to Carol, Denis had made up his mind as early as June 1987 that she should not fight another election as leader. He told her so around December 1988 and briefly thought he had convinced her. 'She'd made up her mind to go. She got as far as looking for convenient times to go and see the Queen.' But at this stage Willie Whitelaw told her it would split the party. Denis knew she did not really want to give up and accepted defeat gracefully.[9] But from now on he made no secret of his longing to name the day. He made a joke of it, knowing that she would never agree. 'Let's go on Tuesday,' he would say. 'Why does it always have to be a Tuesday?' she would reply.[10] He did not force the issue: it was her decision, but he had seen enough of politics to suspect that she would be hurt in the end if she stayed too long.

As long ago as 1969 Mrs Thatcher had been fearful of retirement. 'Sometimes I wonder how I will react to a life without a future,' she told the *Observer*, 'because it's something you have to realise; sooner or later you are cast aside politically. I look at some of my colleagues who have done top jobs and are now on the back bench. Perhaps' – she tried to persuade herself – 'the satisfaction of having done a job is enough.'[11] But already she knew it was not. And this was before she had even reached the Cabinet. Twenty years later, as the prospect of the end of the road became a reality, Ronnie Millar found her sitting alone in the garden at Chequers: 'Oh well,' she sighed, 'there is always the mashed potato circuit.' A year later he found her again alone and sad. When he asked her what was the matter, she said: 'Sometimes I think that all that really matters is one's friends.'[12]

If only that had been true. But she had no real friends, or interests outside politics. 'Yes, I have a fascinating life,' she told Woodrow Wyatt in 1988. 'But I sometimes wish I could go out into business and make some money. And have a nice house to retire into.'[13] She was more honest on Soviet television in 1987, when she told her interviewer frankly that being Prime Minister was 'the most fascinating thing I have ever done. I have been doing it for eight years, experience is cumulative and I do not wish to do anything else.'[14] Yet she knew that she would be rejected eventually. Wyatt found her in March 1990 depressed and not expecting to be able to go on much beyond the next election. 'It's me they don't like. It always has been. I don't expect any gratitude in politics. I am sure I will be able to win it for one last time. I'll have one great effort at it.' Why the last time? Wyatt asked. 'Because after that I wouldn't be able to go on . . . because the press wouldn't let me. They won't take me any more.'[15]

In truth she had always felt she was living on borrowed time – especially since the Brighton bomb. The reason she and Denis bought a house in Dulwich in 1986 was to ensure that they would not suddenly find themselves homeless, like Heath when he was unexpectedly turned out of Downing Street and had to squat in the flat of a Tory MP. She knew that much of her own party, let alone the opposition and the media, were just waiting for her to slip. Peter Hennessy quotes an unnamed senior official who vividly imagined her state of mental siege:

She needs very little sleep and sits up in that study of hers on the first floor of No. 10 till the small hours. It's as if she's looking out the window and sees the camp fires of her enemies who are

surrounding her, just waiting for her to go. And she knows that so
many of the old ways and policies she despises will begin to re-
appear the moment she does.[16]

That was the real reason she was determined to go on. It was not
just that she loved the job and felt no loss of ability to do it. It was
more that as she got into her stride she saw herself as having only just
begun. Sometimes she felt that the transformation she had wrought was
indeed historic and already irreversible; more often she felt that it could
all be undone very quickly if she was not there to maintain the forward
momentum. She therefore had no intention of stepping down with the
job, as she saw it, uncompleted. 'She is absolutely convinced,' Wyatt
recorded, 'that she has by no means finished putting England straight.'[17]
In her memoirs she wrote that she still had three objectives: 'the restoration of our economic strength' – an admission that the Government
had lost ground since 1987; 'the fulfilment of our radical social reforms'
(which she now believed she had started too late, and accepted would
be a long process: she talked in 1988, for instance, of cutting Child
Benefit after the *next* election, that is around 1993;[18] and 'the remod-
elling of Europe on which I had embarked with the Bruges speech'.[19]
In addition she undoubtedly felt that the fall of Communism had opened
up a new era in international politics, and that with Reagan gone she
was now the senior leader of the West with the opportunity to shape
the new order. Hailing the events of that momentous autumn at the
Tory Party Conference, her implication was unmistakable:

> Only those who have shown the resolve to defend the freedom of
> the West can be trusted to safeguard it in the challenging, turbulent
> and unpredictable times that lie ahead.
>
> Mr President, the decade and the century which open up before
> us must see the lasting triumph of liberty, our common cause. The
> world needs Britain – and Britain needs us – to make that happen.[20]

Like Churchill after the death of Stalin she felt a duty to mankind to
stay at her post. The conference responded by chanting deliriously 'Ten
more years' – interspersed with 'Happy birthday to you' – for several
minutes despite Willie Whitelaw's attempts to quiet them.

Enoch Powell, interviewed that year for a television programme
about her, believed that Mrs Thatcher was getting less cautious, more
ambitious to tackle deep-seated problems as her perspective length-
ened. 'Up to 1989,' he suggested, 'she went along':

But in 1989 she has upset it all, and quite deliberately, because she reckons that [Europe] can be sorted out before she loses the opportunity to play her hand in sorting it out. This lengthening of vision . . . I think, is very perceptible in the Prime Minister right now, and . . . it's something that I welcome.[21]

Powell here put his finger on the strange mixture of recklessness and caution, over-confidence and insecurity, which characterised her last two years.

Finally, she could not think of going until she was sure that she could hand over to a worthy successor who would protect her legacy and carry on her work with the same zeal that she had brought to it. And like most dominant leaders she saw no one who fitted the bill. As long ago as 1986, after the Cabinet's hesitation over the bombing of Libya, she had told Wyatt: 'As I go on in this job I think I can't go because who on earth is there to succeed me?'[22] She was determined to deny any candidate of her own generation – that is Howe, Heseltine, Lawson or Tebbit ('I saw no reason to hand over to anyone of roughly my age when I was fit and active')[23] – but did not believe that anyone in the next generation was yet ready. In her memoirs she named Hurd, Baker, Clarke, Major, Chris Patten 'and perhaps Norman Lamont and Michael Howard' as possible candidates in this category. The first three already had more Cabinet experience than she had had in 1975. In fact in two of her television interviews she cited her own unpredicted emergence 'right from the back' of the party[24] as a reason why she had to bring on a wide range of possible younger contenders to give the party a choice when the time came. But this disguised her real problem: that none of the leading contenders from the next two political generations were Thatcherites.

According to Cecil Parkinson, one of her aims was 'to stay as leader until the balance of the Cabinet could be restored or, even better, tilted back in favour of the conviction group'.[25] Not only were Hurd, Clarke and Baker more or less unrepentant old Heathites. The ablest of the next cohort were no better: these were the 'Blue Chips' of the 1979 intake (Chris Patten, William Waldegrave, David Mellor), to whom can be added Malcolm Rifkind, though he had been in Parliament since 1974. The younger generation of true believers (Michael Portillo, Peter Lilley, Francis Maude, Michael Forsyth and Michael Howard) were all at least one Parliament behind, elected for the first time only in 1983. This is a perennial problem of party leaders: each in turn inherits a generation of MPs elected under the aegis of his or her predecessor and likely to bear the imprint of that political background. But for

Mrs Thatcher this provided a good excuse for staying on. As she told Wyatt in 1988: 'I've got to wait for a younger generation who are going to do the things that I believe in.'[26]

If she had wanted to groom a truly Thatcherite successor in the short term, the obvious candidate – since Parkinson's disgrace – was Norman Tebbit. But Tebbit's Essex style represented the unacceptable face of Thatcherism. 'I couldn't get him elected as leader of the Tory party even if I wanted to – nor would the country elect him if he was,' she once told Rupert Murdoch.[27] This tended to be the problem with right-wingers of her own generation: people like Nicholas Ridley, Rhodes Boyson, George Gardiner; Parkinson excepted, the left were so much smoother. In any case – apart from the question of his injuries in the Brighton bomb – Tebbit had already fallen from favour before the 1987 election, when she suspected him of using his control of Central Office to further his own ambition. The one presentable right-winger of the Clarke–Baker generation whom she had tried to bring on was John Moore, briefly puffed by the media as her chosen heir; but he had muffed his big chance at the Department of Health and disappeared from view in 1989. All this explains her identification, quite early on, of John Major.

Major had the advantage of fitting neither category. Elected in 1979 with little ideological baggage, he was not obviously either wet or dry but made his mark first as a whip, then as an able, industrious, self-effacing junior minister at Social Security until appointed Chief Secretary to the Treasury in 1987. Quietly ambitious, he allowed the Prime Minister to think he was more of a Thatcherite than he really was: in fact, having known poverty as a boy and unemployment as a young man, he had a strong sympathy for the underdogs in society. But Mrs Thatcher tended to assume that only public schoolboys could be wet. She liked his classlessness and his efficiency. John Junor records her in April 1988 assessing her colleagues 'with her usual candour' – this to a journalist – dismissing Howe contemptuously as 'more and more like a blancmange' and Baker as 'an able enough administrator but fundamentally . . . wet' and naming Major, even then, as 'the best of the younger bunch and the man most likely to succeed her'.[28] As early as June 1987 she might have been thinking of Major when she suggested to Rodney Tyler that 'perhaps the one who keeps it going will not have to be quite so combative as me, because by then the ship will have its own momentum'.[29] But of course she did not see that happening for a long time yet. In May 1989 Mark Thatcher drew Wyatt's attention to the fact that Major was the only current minister invited to her anniversary lunch at Chequers. Wyatt had never met him before but was impressed. 'I am glad you like him,' she told him later, 'because I think he's splendid.'[30]

Given that she had no intention of stepping down in the foreseeable future, it was difficult to strike the right note in public. As she had already learned in 1987, talk of going 'on and on' was counterproductive. She must not sound as if she intended to stay for ever. In an interview with Robin Oakley for *The Times* in October 1988 she admitted that 'obviously one isn't indestructible . . . quite':

> Some time there will come along a person who can do it better than I can. And I'm always on the lookout. But I expect myself to do it for the fourth term. I hope to do it for the fourth term and I hope we would be returned for a fourth term.[31]

A year later, however, feeling tired and battered after Nigel Lawson's resignation, she qualified this by telling the short-lived *Sunday Correspondent* that she would stand down some time after the next election.[32] 'I had to say it, Kenneth,' she told Baker. 'When I said before the last election I would "go on and on and on", I was accused of being arrogant.'[33] But when the reporting of this interview made her appear to be a lame duck, she moved quickly to correct the impression. 'I have had so many protests,' she announced in a series of interviews on a visit to Washington three weeks later, 'that by popular acclaim I am quite prepared to carry on.'[34] 'They were calling me a lame duck,' she said on IRN. 'I have never been a lame duck in my life and I do not intend to start being one now.' Did that mean she would go 'on and on and on and on'? the interviewer asked. 'No, that's not what I said. I said that if I stand for the fourth election and win I am quite prepared to go on to the fifth election.' 'And the sixth?' 'Well, let us take two more first.'[35]

This was really throwing caution to the wind. Back in England three days later she told David Dimbleby on *Panorama*: 'I am very fit. I love the work . . . I would like to continue as long as possible.' When he asked if that meant on and on and on, she replied:

> I stay on as long as the electorate and my party wishes me to and I hope that will be quite a long time . . . I would not be averse to breaking another record for the length of Prime Ministership.[36]

Since the only modern record still ahead of her was Lord Salisbury's thirteen years and nine months, that would have taken her to the spring of 1993. But maybe she was not joking when she told Laurens van der Post back in 1983 that it was 'a great comfort to us' that Walpole had stayed in office for twenty-one years.[37]

But if the party conference loved the idea of 'ten more years', most of her parliamentary colleagues were much less enthusiastic. In politics, any long-serving leader represents a block on the prospects of others. After ten years a very high proportion of Tory MPs not in the Government had either had their chance or knew that it was never going to come; while those in office were uncomfortably aware that the only way she could freshen the Government, since she had no intention of retiring herself, was to keep shuffling the faces around her. One way and another, her support base at Westminster was growing dangerously thin.

First, there had always been a substantial group of now quite senior MPs on the left of the party whose careers had been blighted by her election as leader in 1975, who had never had any advancement from her and long ago given up expecting it, who had lain low during the years of her pomp but were now beginning to emerge from the shadows in the belief that their time might be coming at last. Among these were not only long-term malcontents, like Julian Critchley (MP for Aldershot since 1959), and those like Michael Mates (MP for Petersfield since 1974), and Keith Hampson (MP for Ripon and later Leeds North-West since 1974) who had openly pinned their hopes on the pretender Michael Heseltine, but others more recently elected like Richard Shepherd (MP for Aldridge-Brownhills since 1979), Robert Rhodes James (MP for Cambridge since 1982) and Andrew Rowe (MP for Mid-Kent since 1983), who were no less disappointed that their talents had been passed over. At the same time the numbers of aggrieved rejects grew steadily: people like Ray Whitney, a former Foreign Office minister, dropped after two years at the Department of Health in 1986; Sir George Young, a junior minister of unquestioned ability at Health and then the Environment from 1979 to 1986, now sidelined though still under fifty; and Neil Macfarlane, Sports Minister for four years from 1981, now put out to grass and 'dead against everything that Margaret is doing'.[38] These two groups – plus another fifty or so who sat for the most marginal seats – formed a potentially lethal army whose personal prospects could only benefit from a change of leader.

Moreover Mrs Thatcher was becoming increasingly remote from her troops. This happens to all Prime Ministers. If anything Mrs Thatcher was unusual in that it did not happen until her second or third term. In her first term she was still very aware that it was the backbenchers who had made her leader and was careful, with the help of Ian Gow, to keep in touch with them. Also at the beginning she knew most of them. By 1987 not only was she becoming ever more isolated by her office, but there were two new intakes of younger MPs, some of them no older than her children, most of them elected for precarious seats, whom she often failed to recognise and treated with scant respect. No longer did she tour the tearoom with her PPS picking up the mood, as she had in Gow's time: now her rare visits were alarming royal events. Faced with a revolt against NHS charges the day before she was due to fly to Poland in January 1988, she raged to Baker that it was 'intolerable that I have to face the party and Jaruzelski in the same week'.[39] Backbenchers increasingly complained of lack of access to her. Ann Winterton (elected in 1983) told Wyatt that 'she won't listen to anybody and when you go to see her in a little group or separately she just gives you a lecture and you're never allowed to say what you want'.[40] Steven Norris wanted to raise a worry about the privatisation of electricity but was treated to a twenty-seven-minute monologue which took up almost the whole of his half-hour interview.[41] Rupert Allason – known to her by reputation as the author of numerous books about spies and the security services – attended a dinner for her to meet some of her new backbenchers in the autumn of 1987; he asked what he thought was a perfectly innocuous question about the Official Secrets Act, and was slapped down for being 'typically unhelpful'. He was an admirer, but she treated him as an enemy.[42] By 1990 too many of her MPs had had similar experiences. Alan Clark thought her troubles stemmed partly from the unpopularity of the poll tax and the bad opinion polls. 'But I am inclined to think that the party in the House has just got sick of her.'[43]

Within the Cabinet it was the same story. Only Nicholas Ridley and Cecil Parkinson could still be counted unqualified supporters. For the rest Robin Butler, the Cabinet Secretary, judged that 'a serious number . . . seriously wanted to get rid of her' for two or three years before November 1990.[44] Parkinson remembers looking round the table and calculating that if Mrs Thatcher had ever needed to win an important vote in this Cabinet she would not have won it.[45] Since January 1988 she had lacked the stabilising presence of Willie Whitelaw to defuse tensions and hold the Cabinet together: Lord Belstead and John Wakeham were no substitute for Willie's mollifying authority. As a result the Cabinet increasingly lacked any sense of loyalty or common purpose. 'As far as I can make out,' Clark grumbled in March 1990, 'practically every member of the Cabinet is quietly and unattributably briefing different editors or members of the Lobby about how awful she is.'[46]

The impression of a disintegrating government was enhanced by a steady drip of voluntary as well as involuntary departures. When the new Cabinet met for the first time after the clumsy July 1989 reshuffle, Mrs Thatcher tried to allay their insecurity by announcing that this was the team she wanted to fight the next election. In fact over the next fifteen months five more senior ministers peeled off – two (Lawson and eventually Howe) over personal and policy disagreements, one (Ridley) stitched up by the press and two (Fowler and Walker) because they had simply had enough and – in Fowler's euphemism – wished to spend more time with their families. By now the boot was on the other foot. 'As reshuffle time came round,' Cecil Parkinson noted, 'while in previous years ministers had been sitting on the edge of their seats in case they should be dropped, now she . . . was waiting anxiously to see if anyone else would want to go, when she wanted them to stay.'[47] By the summer of 1990 Howe was the last survivor from her original 1979 Cabinet, and her inability to retain her colleagues had begun to raise serious doubts about her man management.

As a team leader she was increasingly autocratic and unpredictable. The brutal removal of Howe from the Foreign Office sent a chilling signal that she felt no gratitude even to her most faithful servant. Senior ministers like Lawson and Hurd resented her interference in their departments while others like Ken Clarke, engaged in controversial reforms, did not feel they always had her full support. She publicly humiliated Malcolm Rifkind – always her least favourite minister – in 1989 by appointing one of his juniors, Michael Forsyth, to be Scottish party chairman against his known opposition. She still often gave the impression that she was not responsible for the Government at all but somewhere above and beyond it in a sphere of her own, surrounded by a private coterie of advisers who wielded far more influence than her nominal colleagues. Bernard Ingham in particular drew renewed criticism in 1989 when he expanded his role to become head of the Government Information Service, with the rank of deputy secretary. Robin Butler tried to suggest that he should give up being chief press secretary as well, but Mrs Thatcher would not hear of it.[48] Ingham's rubbishing of Howe's elevation to deputy Prime Minister drew sharp criticism from former ministers like Quintin Hailsham and David Howell; while at least one MP called for both Ingham and Powell to be moved.[49] Nigel Lawson blames Ingham for encouraging Mrs Thatcher to think she could take the party and the Cabinet for granted.[50]

In her televised memoirs in 1993 Lady Thatcher came close to conceding her critics' charge that Cabinet government had all but ceased to exist towards the end:

It may be that I was getting a little bit irritated that so many of my real, initial . . . six strong men and true that I always knew that I had to have were getting fewer and fewer and therefore I was having to bear a much bigger burden of seeing that the ship went forward in the direction in which we had always wanted it to go. So maybe I was getting a little bit testy because it was putting really much more and more on me to fulfil the purpose for which we were elected.[51]

This was the opposite of what should have happened if she had taken the trouble to build a real team over the past ten years and carried her colleagues with her. But what had happened to her initial 'six strong men' by 1989? It is unclear precisely whom she meant, but of the original economic team appointed in May 1979, Keith Joseph had retired, she had long ago alienated Nott and Biffen, and both Howe and Lawson were being driven inexorably towards resignation. This was what Howe in his memoirs called the 'Catherine wheel effect' by which Mrs Thatcher threw off her colleagues one by one like sparks into the night while she went spinning on brilliantly alone.

The truth is that she was becoming impossible to work with. The *Observer* columnist Alan Watkins wrote in 1991 that 'her mental stability was giving increasing cause for concern'.[52] This may be going too far. The only instances he cites are a couple of intemperate retorts to Kinnock in the House of Commons, when she accused him first of taking his instructions from the African National Congress, and then of being a 'crypto-Communist'.[53] But the question was certainly being asked. In March 1989 Wyatt wrote that he was constantly being asked if he belonged to 'the "Has Margaret gone mad?" group'.[54] Over the next few weeks he records Robin Day, Peregrine Worsthorne and Arnold Weinstock all telling him she was losing her grip.[55] A year earlier he himself had been concerned to find her 'prickly and a trifle shirty', resenting any criticism. 'It was the first time for a long time I got a hint that she seemed to think nothing she does is wrong or open to doubt.'[56]

Contrary to her own denials, there is also testimony from several quarters that she was getting tired. Kenneth Baker 'noticed that even Margaret towards the end was slowing up. There were days when her red boxes were not completed, and her meetings were sustained more by instinct that anything else.'[57] 'Notwithstanding her reputation for hard work,' her last PPS Mark Lennox-Boyd, remembered, 'Margaret used to get extremely tired', so that one of his responsibilities was 'to protect her from unnecessary demands on her energy'.[58] She herself confirmed this to Wyatt in November 1990:

She says she doesn't work so late into the night now. She finds herself much fresher and able to get on with her boxes and so forth around six or six-thirty in the morning than after a hard day's work.[59]

Moreover as she came up to sixty-five she was finally beginning to look her age. For years the adrenaline of power had seemed to keep her permanently blooming, her fresh complexion and immaculate hair a constant source of wonder to those obliged to meet her again at breakfast the morning after a late night. In May 1989 it seemed that her secret had been revealed when the papers seized gleefully on something she had let slip in an anniversary interview with the American magazine *Vanity Fair* – that she had regular sessions with an Indian therapist who gave her electric-shock treatment in the bath. She was very cross at the publicity this attracted, since she disliked admitting any physical weakness.* Her ministers were mostly too polite to comment on her physical deterioration. But in November 1989 the new leader of the merged Liberal Democrats, Paddy Ashdown, found himself standing beside the Prime Minister at the prorogation of Parliament and took the chance to study her at close quarters – somewhat ungallantly:

> She really is a poor old thing. She looks lined, with her hair swept up but getting very thin. She kept on staring at the ground and muttering to herself . . . She looked just like any old grandmother who ought to be at home playing with her grandchildren . . . For the first time I felt some affection for her.[62]

Even as Mrs Thatcher insisted on her determination and fitness to carry on, there was a growing sense that her time was inexorably running out. It was not just that the opinion polls, from almost exactly the moment of her tenth anniversary, turned steadily against the Government (and got worse in 1990); nor the loss of the European Parliament elections in June – the Tories' first defeat in a national election under her leadership, an event which John Biffen unhelpfully described as 'a political watershed'.[63] She had come through dreadful

---

*She was irritated when Wyatt asked her if it was true, which clearly indicated to him that it was.[60] A few days later, in an interview with the *Sunday Mirror*, she again tried to brush it off ('Oh, I should forget about that'), but did not deny it. Did she use Royal Jelly too? she was asked. She had tried it, she replied – it was actually made in her constituency – but the only thing she admitted to taking every morning was vitamin C.[61]

by-elections and dire opinion polls before, in 1981 and again in 1986, and recorded landslide victories less than two years later. She saw no reason why she could not do it again. But this time round two things had changed. First, whereas in those previous pits of unpopularity her personal approval rating had always kept ahead of the Government's, now her own figure fell commensurately. By the spring of 1990 it had settled at a lower level – around 25 per cent – than she had ever touched previously. At the same time Labour had begun to look (as Biffen again put it) 'distinctly electable'.[64] Partly as a result of Neil Kinnock's efforts to shed unpopular policies (nationalisation, unilateralism, withdrawal from Europe), partly also at the expense of the Alliance – which had split after the 1987 election and then messily re-formed, taking it out of serious contention for the best part of two years – by late 1989 Labour was pushing towards 50 per cent in the polls and in February 1990 (for the first time since a brief moment in 1986) registered as the party thought most likely to win the next election.[65] Rather as Jim Callaghan had sensed a 'sea-change' in the political atmosphere in 1979, there were signs of another in 1989.

Mrs Thatcher was determined to recognise no such thing. 'Kenneth,' she told Baker, 'we must stop that impression. It's totally false.'[66] In her party conference speeches she scorned the idea that Labour had changed. 'The Labour leopard can't change its spots,' she jeered at Brighton in 1988, 'even if it sometimes thinks wistfully of a blue rinse.'[67] At Blackpool the following year she mobilised the full resources of her speechwriters to excoriate Labour's easy jettisoning of its most cherished beliefs. 'Not for us, disposable ideals,' she sneered. 'Not for us, throwaway convictions . . . If you believe the reports, Brighton last week was the scene of an unprecedented mass conversion. Nothing like it since the Chinese General who baptised his entire army with a hosepipe.'

> Isn't it amazing? The party which fought to stop council tenants having the right to buy their homes now tells us it is the party of home ownership. The party which called for one-sided nuclear disarmament now says it stands for strong defence. The party which took us to the IMF, like some third world country, now primly poses as a model of financial rectitude. And it's all happened, as dear old Tommy Cooper used to say: 'Just like that'. Would you believe it? Well no; actually I wouldn't.
>
> You see one can't help wondering: if it's that easy for the Labour leader to give up the principles in which he does believe, won't it be even easier for him to give up the principles in which he does not believe? The truth is: nothing has really changed. Labour just

wants power at any price and they'll say anything to get it. Labour's real prescription for Britain is the disease half the world is struggling to cure.[68]

She was worried by the polls, but she half-believed that everything would come right as it always had before, as soon as they got the economy back under control. 'Our first priority must be to get inflation down,' she told Baker on appointing him party chairman in July. 'Mortgage and interest rates will follow, and then we'll be all right.'[69] But she was hurt by the personal polls. 'They say I am arrogant,' she complained to Wyatt. 'I am the least arrogant person there is.' He assured her that this was just the way the newspapers portrayed her. 'Everybody respects you and even if they don't like you, they know that you are the best person to run the country.'[70] If that had once been true it was becoming rapidly less so. The point was shrewdly made by 'one of her closest media advisers' – could it have been Tim Bell? – who told John Ranelagh in 1990 that she was the victim of her own success:

In 1979, 1983, 1987, they needed Mrs Thatcher to slay dragons . . . Now in 1990 many of the dragons are perceived to be slain, i.e. trade unions, communism, socialism, unemployment. The economic dragon was slain. It re-emerged only because of the Government's perceived errors. The new dragons are perceived to be of the Government's own making, i.e. the Community Charge, the trade gap, interest rates, the mortgage rate, Tory splits, Europe. The result of this is that people no longer know what they needed Mrs Thatcher for . . . Telling them they need the Prime Minister to sort out the economy may be believed, but there are no votes in it because people believe it's the Government's fault it has gone wrong.[71]

Even her closest media advisers could not do much about this.

'The Chancellor's position was unassailable'

When Mrs Thatcher determined, after the Madrid summit, that she must break what she saw as the Lawson–Howe axis, she made the wrong choice by demoting Geoffrey Howe. Her real problem was with Nigel Lawson. There is a good case that she should have sacked Lawson the year before, when it became clear that they were pursuing irreconcilable financial policies. The trouble was that she admired and was slightly afraid of Lawson, despite her loss of trust in him, whereas she increasingly despised Howe; so Howe was the easy scapegoat, while she went on protesting her 'full and unequivocal and generous backing' for Lawson.[72] But the fundamental difference between the Chancellor and the Prime Minister remained, and within three more months it came to a head.

Ministerial resignations often occur for what appear to be inadequate reasons. The last straw which precipitates the decision frequently seems no more than a pretext. Many observers – including Mrs Thatcher herself – felt that Nigel Lawson's departure fell into this category. There was a widespread impression that by October 1989 he was looking for a way out – he had already discussed resignation with a sympathetic Willie Whitelaw in June, and his friend Sam Brittan had been urging him to go for even longer[73] – and eventually took what David Owen called 'a semi-valid opportunity' by inflating a grievance that he was 'thick-skinned enough to have shrugged off', had he really wanted to stay.[74] Lawson insists that on the contrary he did not want to resign while the economy was still undergoing serious problems which he did not want to be accused of running away from; but that he was left with no choice because Mrs Thatcher made his position untenable.

The 'semi-valid opportunity' was the return of Alan Walters as her personal economic adviser. Lawson had warned her when she first mooted it that this was a bad idea, and John Biffen, interviewed earlier in the year, anticipated that it was bound to cause trouble:

> I don't think the Chancellor is too keen to have anyone marking his homework. And I don't think that Alan Walters has come all the way back across the Atlantic just to have a ripe old age. So I think it's a fascinating prospect.[75]

Lawson's difficulty was not simply that Walters reinforced Mrs Thatcher's refusal to join the ERM. He had been living with that difference of opinion since 1986 and could have gone on living with it. His more serious problem was that Walters made no secret of his view that the Chancellor's determination to hold the value of sterling above DM3 was misguided and unsustainable. First in America and now back in London he told anyone who would listen that the policy was doomed. Thus what Lawson calls the 'countdown to resignation' was triggered at the beginning of October by the Bundesbank's decision to raise German interest rates, forcing Britain to follow suit with yet another increase at the worst possible political moment, just before the Tory Party Conference. Despite Walters' warning that high interest rates were already threatening to drive Britain into recession, Mrs Thatcher reluctantly agreed to go to 15 per cent, provoking further howls of protest from the CBI and TUC. But that weekend the story of Walters' advice and her reluctance found its way into the *Sunday Times*. Walters denied responsibility for the leak, but to Lawson's fury Number Ten declined to issue a refutation. As Lady Thatcher tartly wrote in her memoirs, Walters was not only 'doing precisely what a prime minister's adviser should' – that is giving an alternative opinion. 'He also had the merit of being right . . . Nigel . . . was becoming hypersensitive.'[76] She maintained that the fact that she 'backed Nigel against Alan's advice and against my own instincts' showed that Lawson's complaint was groundless.[77] But the next day, despite the interest-rate hike, sterling fell below DM3.

The *Daily Mail*, representing the hard-pressed mortgage payers of Middle England, ran a front-page splash denouncing 'This Bankrupt Chancellor', and Fleet Street seethed with rumours of his imminent resignation.[78] Yet two days later Lawson still managed to win a standing ovation at Blackpool for a fighting speech defending high interest rates in the short term as the only way to beat inflation; and the next day Mrs Thatcher backed him with only an imperceptible difference of emphasis. Then she flew off for ten days to the Commonwealth Conference in Kuala Lumpur, with her new Foreign Secretary John Major, to defy the world over South African sanctions. When Harold Macmillan left for an extended Commonwealth tour in 1958 he took care to resolve his 'little local difficulty' with his Chancellor first.

In her absence the *Financial Times* stirred the pot by printing extracts from an article by Alan Walters congratulating himself that 'so far Mrs Thatcher has concurred' with his advice to keep out of the 'half-baked' ERM.[79] The *Independent* published the whole article a few days later.[80] It had actually been written for an American magazine the previous year, some months before Walters returned to England. Mrs Thatcher maintained that this made it unobjectionable. Since it was still due to be published in America, and since Walters himself had given it to the *Financial Times*, Lawson was entitled to feel differently. But Walters' article, he subsequently told the House of Commons, 'was of significance only inasmuch as it represented the tip of a singularly ill-concealed iceberg, with all the destructive potential that icebergs possess'.[81] He spelled out his deeper objection in his memoirs:

What made my job impossible was Number 10 constantly giving the impression that it was indifferent to the depreciation of sterling. I cannot recall any precedent for a Chancellor being systematically undermined in this way.[82]

It was not so much the fact of his difference with the Prime Minister which mattered. 'It was her persistent public exposure of that difference, of which Walters was the most obvious outward and visible symbol.'[83]

In the Commons on Tuesday 24 October Labour's shadow Chancellor, John Smith, had an easy target mocking 'the confusion and disarray in the formulation and explanation of Government economic policy'. Lawson could only reply, weakly, that Walters was 'a part-time adviser and his views . . . are not the views of the Government'. In a television interview he recalled the convention that 'advisers do not talk or write in public. I think it is a good convention that should be adhered to.'[84] A few hours earlier, in Kuala Lumpur, Mrs Thatcher was asked about Walters' article and used for the first time the formula that was to become her mantra over the next two weeks: 'Advisers advise, ministers decide. That's the difference.'[85] But Lawson had already told Howe that he was on the brink of resignation.

The two protagonists have given their own accounts of the series of meetings – four in all – that took place before his decision was announced. Thursday 26 October was an exceptionally fraught day for Mrs Thatcher. She had only got back from Malaysia at four o'clock on Wednesday morning, after an eighteen-hour flight, and was obviously 'absolutely exhausted'.* In the circumstances Lawson felt it would be unfair to tackle her at their regular bilateral meeting that afternoon, but warned her that they needed to talk about the Walters problem. 'She replied that she saw no problem' – but she agreed to see him first thing on Thursday morning, with no secretaries present.

She claims to have been 'quite unprepared for what he had to say' – for which the only possible excuse is that she had been out of the country for ten days. She listened quietly while Lawson told her that either Walters or he would have to go: he did not want to resign but unless she agreed that Walters should leave by the end of the year, he would have no choice. 'I told him not to be ridiculous . . . Alan . . . was a good and devoted member of my staff who had . . . always acted within the proprieties . . . There was no question of my sacking him.' According to Lawson, 'she then said something which I found more revealing than everything else taken together: "If Alan were to go, that would destroy *my* authority."'

---

*In an interview with Jean Rook two days later she said that she had got straight down to work on her boxes as soon as she had unpacked, and then got only about an hour and half's sleep the next night, because her 'human clock' was all wrong. So she was still exhausted on Thursday.[86]

She begged him to reconsider and arranged to see him again at two o'clock. Again she claims she thought that would be the end of the matter: she expected Lawson to be on his way to Germany by then for a meeting with the German Finance Minister. Later that morning he attended Cabinet as normal, betraying no hint of what was in his mind. But at two o'clock he was back, bringing with him his letter of resignation. 'At first she refused to take it; but then she took it and popped it in her handbag, unopened, saying she did not wish to read it.' This time she tried to flatter him into changing his mind, heaping 'extravagant praise' on his record and even holding out – 'without of course committing herself' – the prospect of the Governorship of the Bank of England, in which he had once expressed an interest. 'In fact, she said everything except the one thing that would have persuaded me to stay.' But now she had to rush off to answer Prime Minister's Questions, so the issue was still left unresolved.

In the House, Kinnock made hay with the spectacle of a Prime Minister with two Chancellors and invited her to 'get rid of the part-time one'. She doggedly repeated that 'Advisers advise and ministers decide.'[87] Then she had to make her statement on the Commonwealth Conference and field further questions about South Africa for half an hour – a demanding session during which she had to put Lawson out of her mind. Leaving the chamber, however, she called John Major to her room and told him 'I have a problem.' When Lawson met her for the last time at around five o'clock, he says that she asked his advice about his successor; she says that she told Lawson she had already chosen Major. Either way, they parted in what Lawson called 'an atmosphere of suppressed emotion'.[88] When she called Major in again he found her close to tears and felt the need to hold her hand for a moment.[89]

Their exchange of letters was released at six o'clock. Besides the usual courtesies, Lawson's was brief and pointed. 'The successful conduct of economic policy,' he wrote, 'is possible only if there is, *and is seen to be*, full agreement between the Prime Minister and the Chancellor of the Exchequer.'

Recent events have confirmed that this essential requirement cannot be satisfied so long as Alan Walters remains your personal economic adviser. I have therefore concluded that it is in the best interests of the Government for me to resign my office without further ado.[90]

Hers was longer, paying tribute to his important contribution over the past ten years, with just one mildly barbed sentence: 'It is a matter of particular regret that you should decide to leave before your task is complete.' But she made no mention whatever of his reason for leaving.[91]

In her memoirs Lady Thatcher admitted that by 1989 she and Lawson 'no longer had that broad identity of views or mutual trust which a Prime Minister and Chancellor should'.[92] So why was she so anxious for him to stay? Why did she press him so assiduously to reconsider? In truth, apart from the short-term political damage to herself, she must have been thoroughly relieved to see him go, so that she could start again with a more amenable Chancellor. She wasted no time in carrying out a swift, limited and unusually well-received reshuffle, announced that same evening, which rectified some of the mistakes of July. Yet neither of the key appointments was her first preference.

'Ideally,' she recalled, 'I should have liked to make Nick Ridley Chancellor.' But she recognised that 'under these difficult circumstances, Nick's scorn for presentational niceties might well have compounded the problem'.[93] So she turned once again to Major, who was beginning to look like her answer to every vacancy. Major was clearly much better suited to the Treasury than to the Foreign Office, and it was the job he had always wanted.[94] Yet he was initially reluctant to move again when he was just getting used to the Foreign Office. 'I told him that we all had to accept second best occasionally. That applied to me just as much as to him.'[95]

Equally Douglas Hurd was still the obvious choice for the Foreign Office, as he had been in July – yet she still looked at every possible way to avoid appointing him. She first thought about trying to get George Younger back; then considered Tom King, but she had only just moved him to Defence; she even toyed with going back to her 1983 intention and appointing Parkinson – but he too had only just gone to Transport. Kenneth Baker claims the credit for persuading her that this time it really had to be Hurd, who had earned the promotion after four years at the Home Office.[96] When she rang at about six to make the offer she was clearly 'still in shock' at Lawson's resignation – Hurd himself was 'flabbergasted' – and did not disguise her doubts. 'You won't let those Europeans get on top of you, will you, Douglas?'[97]

The one move she was really pleased with was the choice of David Waddington, Chief Whip since 1987, to go to the Home Office – the first time in four attempts, she congratulated herself, that she had managed to send a right-winger there.[98] The drawback, however, was Waddington's replacement. It had to be an outsider, because his deputy, Tristan Garel-Jones, was unacceptable to the right. But Tim Renton had not only never been a whip; he had been Howe's PPS at the

Treasury, then his Minister of State for three years at the Foreign Office, followed by two years at the Home Office under Hurd. He was an Old Etonian, still a close friend of Howe and definitely not 'one of us'. She did not want to make him Home Secretary yet wanted to complete the reshuffle that night, so she simply switched him into Waddington's old place instead. From the point of view of managing her increasingly restless backbenchers over the next twelve months it was a singularly ill-judged appointment.

She was able to put a positive gloss on the whole reshuffle by emphasising that all three principal appointments – Major, Hurd and Waddington – had achieved their lifetime's dream. 'It has worked out very strangely,' she told Jean Rook. 'We are very sad to be without Nigel, but we have an excellent Chancellor of the Exchequer, an excellent Foreign Secretary, an excellent Home Secretary for each of whom it was their ambition.'[99] The press for the most part agreed. The most ironic fallout of Lawson's resignation, however, was that Walters went too. He was in America when the news broke but immediately realised that his position would be impossible and, despite Mrs Thatcher's efforts to dissuade him, insisted on stepping down as well. Thus by sacrificing Lawson to try to keep Walters, Mrs Thatcher had ended by losing both of them. Lawson reflected wrily that, 'however painful it was to me personally, I had performed a signal service to my successor and to the Government in general'.[100]*

Despite the swift reshuffle, which arguably improved the Government, Lawson's resignation, following so soon after Howe's demotion, unquestionably damaged Mrs Thatcher by throwing a fresh spotlight on her inability to retain her closest colleagues. Her former adviser and Central Office chief of staff, now turned racy political novelist, Michael Dobbs, described her in the *Evening Standard* as 'a political Chernobyl'.[102] Another of the departed, Norman Tebbit, warned that it was 'dangerous for a captain to appear semi-detached from the team', adding pointedly that she had abused the loyalty of 'her best political friends' and could not afford 'many more mishaps'.[103] The Executive of the 1922 Committee solemnly warned her to get her act together. Some private comments were even more ominous. Among many letters of sympathy, Lawson received two from influential party bigwigs. 'She could so easily have got rid of Walters,' Willie

---

*According to Wyatt, Mrs Thatcher still hoped that a City firm might give Walters a job so that he could still advise Major – 'or even me' – informally; and a later entry suggests that Rupert Murdoch might have been willing to oblige. But nothing seems to have come of this proposal.[101]

Whitelaw wrote, 'but increasingly I fear that she simply cannot bring herself to be on the losing side in any argument. That failing may ditch us all.'[104] Peter Thorneycroft suggested that the party faced what he called 'a very large problem in strategy' – he could only have meant the leadership – 'and in some ways your resignation has brought it to a head'.[105] The 'men in grey suits' were stirring.

The damage was compounded when Mrs Thatcher appeared on Brian Walden's Sunday-morning interview programme on 29 October – the date had been arranged months earlier – followed in the same slot by Lawson the next week. Walden told Wyatt beforehand that he wanted to question the Prime Minister as helpfully as possible.[106] In fact his journalistic instinct and her lack of candour made for a devastating exposé, watched by three million people with their Sunday lunch. Instead of telling the truth – that there had developed between herself and her Chancellor a difference of view which regrettably made it impossible for him to carry on – she gushingly repeated her claim that she had 'fully backed and supported' him. ('To me the Chancellor's position was *unassailable*,' she insisted – and repeated the word with rising emphasis another six times during the interview. 'I couldn't believe that he would go when he's been such a strong Chancellor and his position was unassailable.' Reiterating that 'advisers advise, ministers decide', she dismissed Lawson's objection to Walters as inexplicable – 'It's just not possible that this small particular thing could result in this particular resignation' – but floundered when Walden asked the killer question:

– Do you deny that Nigel would have stayed if you had sacked Professor Alan Walters?
– I don't know. I don't know.
– You never even thought to ask him that?
– I . . . that is not . . . I don't know. Nigel had determined that he was going to put in his resignation. I did everything possible to stop him.
– But . . .
– I was not successful. No, you're going on asking the same question.
– Of course, but that's a terrible admission, Prime Minister.
– I have nothing further to . . . I don't know . . . of course I just don't know . . . I'm not going on with this.[107]

Wyatt thought Walden's questioning not at all helpful, but 'outrageously impertinent to a Prime Minister'. For her part Mrs Thatcher tried to maintain that Walden had wasted the interview by banging on at the same question.[108] But the second instalment of this two-part trial by television the following Sunday gave Lawson the opportunity flatly to contradict her. He told Walden that he had made perfectly clear to the Prime Minister in their three conversations on the Thursday why he was resigning – 'quite clearly and categorically' because she refused to part with Walters. But having no wish to brand Mrs Thatcher publicly as a liar, he had prepared the best answer he could when Walden asked him why he thought she had said she did not know why he resigned:

> I've been puzzling about that . . . I was surprised when she said that and I've been racking my brains, and the only conclusion that I can come to is that she found it impossible to believe that I meant it.

'So she didn't do everything in her power to keep you, did she?' Walden pressed him.

> No, she didn't, but she did implore me very strongly to stay . . . and she was extremely kind about my job as Chancellor of the Exchequer. But no, the issue on which I had originally seen her, that she was not disposed to change her mind about.[109]

No one who watched these two programmes could have had any doubt which witness was telling the truth. Not for the first time, but more publicly than over Westland three years earlier, Mrs Thatcher's reputation for straight speaking had taken a severe knock. It was no longer a question about which of them was right about the economics of the ERM and the exchange rate. Most economists would now say Lawson was wrong. But if she really did not understand why Lawson had resigned – in the Commons on 7 November she was still saying that she found it 'totally incomprehensible'[110] – she was too insensitive to continue long in office. If she did understand, but chose to keep Walters anyway, that only confirmed that she valued her advisers more than her elected colleagues.* Either way she was increasingly living in a world of her own.

The start of a new parliamentary session gave the Prime Minister's critics the chance to test their level of support. The rules devised by

---

*Major thought she understood all right when he comforted her on 26 October. '"It's unnecessary. He's being silly" was the view she expressed,' he wrote, 'but I don't think she really believed it.'[111]

Alec Home under which Mrs Thatcher had successfully challenged Ted Heath in 1975 allowed for a leadership contest to be held every year. No one had yet invoked this provision, and Home certainly never intended that it should be used to challenge an incumbent Prime Minister, though there was some talk of Geoffrey Rippon standing in 1981. But the rule was there, and after fourteen years there was an irresistible temptation to try it out. Michael Heseltine had worked hard since 1986 to establish himself as the alternative leader in waiting; but he was not going to throw it all away by a premature challenge. To all enquiries he replied with the careful formula that he could 'envisage no circumstances' in which he would stand against the Prime Minister. What was needed was a so-called 'stalking horse' – such as many people had assumed Mrs Thatcher to be in 1975 – who would give the party the chance to register dissatisfaction with the leader, with no expectation of winning but with the possibility of giving way to a serious candidate if he attracted enough support. Various names were canvassed, including discarded ministers like Ian Gilmour and David Howell, before in November 1989 an unlikely candidate finally came forward in the person of Sir Anthony Meyer.

Meyer was already a somewhat anachronistic Member of Parliament, a sixty-nine-year-old third baronet whose father had been an MP before him, a former diplomat, first elected for Eton and Slough in 1964 but safely returned for West Flint (now known as Clwyd North West) since 1970. He had served as PPS to Maurice Macmillan in 1970–4, but was one of those who had received no advancement from Mrs Thatcher. His main political passion was Europe: he was one of the very few open supporters of a federal community, which was already causing him problems in his constituency. He was clearly someone with nothing to lose by putting his head above the parapet and plainly relished his brief celebrity. He declared his candidacy on 28 November. In doing so he had no direct contact with Heseltine, though he did check with one of his lieutenants, Keith Hampson, that his candidacy would not be unhelpful. He stood on the tactful platform that Mrs Thatcher was no longer the best person 'to safeguard her own splendid achievements', but did not stint his criticism of her attitude to Europe.[112]

Kenneth Baker calls Meyer's quixotic mission 'a serious challenge by a frivolous candidate, standing as the representative of those who had been dismissed, disappointed or disenchanted by Thatcher',[113] which is a fair description but underestimates the number of Tory MPs who were not terminally disenchanted but merely wanted to send the Prime Minister a warning message. She was only mildly irritated, telling Baker that it was 'not good for the party',[114] but took the challenge seriously enough to ask George Younger to manage her campaign, though she did not campaign herself – 'and no one seriously thought that I should'.[115] As a member of the Cabinet for the past ten years, Younger was somewhat remote from the backbenchers, but he was assisted by an energetic team headed by Ian Gow, Tristan Garel-Jones, Richard Ryder, William Shelton (who had been part of her team in 1975) and Mark Lennox-Boyd. For once in the short history of Tory leadership contests, the incumbent ran a good campaign; the contrast with the rerun twelve months later could not be more striking.

Nevertheless the result was less than overwhelming. Younger and Baker predicted that between forty and fifty colleagues might vote against Mrs Thatcher. In the event only thirty-three actually did so, but another twenty-seven abstained – twenty-four of them by spoiling their ballot papers.* One of the other three was Heseltine, who turned up to walk conspicuously along the corridor without entering the committee room where the vote was being held. Mrs Thatcher won by 314–33 – by any normal standard a convincing endorsement, yet sixty MPs had deliberately withheld their support. She celebrated with champagne and told the press it was a 'splendid' result; Baker announced that the contest had cleared the air and 'the leadership question is now settled'.[118] But behind the scenes Younger and Garel-Jones warned her that another fifty – perhaps another hundred – had given their support only conditionally. Garel-Jones told her that she needed to sort out the poll tax; Younger that the problem was less the poll tax than her increasing hostility to Europe, which a still predominantly pro-European party disliked. He also advised her to get rid of Powell and Ingham, and to spend more time listening to her supporters in the tearoom.[119] She refused to consider the former, but did try to spend more time in the tearoom. 'I may not have complied,' she wrote in her memoirs, 'but I did listen.'[120]

'She was, I think, a little more disconcerted by the . . . result than was generally realised,' Nicholas Ridley wrote. 'She always wanted to feel that she had a really strong and solid base of support in the parliamentary party.'[121] But the more serious implication lay not in the figures, which were good enough, but in the fact that the contest had

---

*Meyer told the press that he was 'quite surprised to get so many votes. I thought I'd be beaten by the abstentions.' The overall result, he thought, was 'rather better than I'd expected and not quite as good as some of my friends were hoping for'.[116] Robin Oakley reckoned that since fifty-eight of the voters were ex-ministers and another ninety-seven backbenchers to whom she had given no preferment, Mrs Thatcher had done quite well to have only sixty votes denied her.[117]

taken place at all. Meyer had set a precedent which other more serious candidates could follow. When Carol said cheerfully to her mother, 'That's over, then', she replied, 'Oh no, that's just the beginning.'[122] She knew that leadership contests were now very likely to become an annual event; and others – allies and opponents – had the same anticipation. Ian Gow told Alan Clark that he was worried by the prospect of another challenge in 1990. He had had a hard time getting the votes this time, and it would be harder still next time.[123] Tragically, Gow was no longer alive a year later to see how right he was.

The Major–Hurd axis

Lawson's departure opened a new phase in the Thatcher Government. Though routinely portrayed by the media as a dictator, the Prime Minister was in fact profoundly weakened from November 1989. In place of Howe and Lawson, the twin pillars of her middle period, Mrs Thatcher now had a new pair of senior colleagues who, if they combined as their predecessors had done before Madrid, had her in an armlock. Neither John Major nor Douglas Hurd was 'one of us'; but she absolutely could not afford to lose another Chancellor or sack another Foreign Secretary. Though less senior and less assertive personalities than Lawson and Howe, Major and Hurd were thus, if they chose, in a position to dictate to the Prime Minister. And in the gentlest possible way they did.

Below the major offices, too, the rising stars were Kenneth Clarke and Kenneth Baker. Clarke made no pretence of being a Thatcherite, but he was forceful, energetic and in some ways more radical than Mrs Thatcher: carrying responsibility for the Government's most contentious legislation, he was in a strong position. As party chairman Baker had bound his fortune irrevocably to hers. 'Unlike Chris Patten,' she wrote in her memoirs, 'Ken had genuinely moved to the centre.' His talent was presentation, not ideas. But 'I never forgot that for every few Thatchers, Josephs and Ridleys you need at least one Ken Baker to concentrate on communicating the message.'[124] She was grateful for his loyalty. But he was not a true believer either.

Further down again, with new faces like Chris Patten, Norman Lamont and John Gummer in the Cabinet since July 1989, joined during 1990 by Michael Howard (who replaced Fowler in January), David Hunt (who replaced Walker in May) and Peter Lilley (who replaced Ridley in July), this was an altogether different and much younger Cabinet. Seven of them were under fifty, and the average age, excluding Mrs Thatcher herself, was just fifty-three. Excepting Howe, who was sidelined, these were not those who had accompanied her on the long march from 1975, but a new generation she had picked up along the way. She treated them more like children than as equals; and they increasingly treated her with the affectionate tolerance extended to a wayward mother.

Unlike their predecessors, Major and Hurd met regularly for breakfast at the Foreign Secretary's official residence in Carlton Gardens to co-ordinate their approach.[125] 'We both believed the Prime Minister needed to be coaxed, and not browbeaten,' Major recalled;[126] and his Permanent Secretary, Peter Middleton – used to six years of Lawson's very different method – observed how skilfully he did it. 'Major went out of his way to be sensitive to what the PM wanted to do, and the fact that he was sensitive meant they got on pretty well. It also meant he got his way on most issues.'[127] For his part Hurd followed Howe's tactic of not attempting to argue with Mrs Thatcher but simply waiting till she had finished before going on patiently with what he had been saying.[128] But he told Wyatt in March that he had no serious disagreements with her over foreign policy: he just had to 'nudge' her tactfully in the right direction – for instance over German reunification – and she eventually came round, without ever admitting that she had changed her mind.[129] At the same time he made a point of protecting his back by ensuring that no one in the Foreign Office had contact with Number Ten except through the Permanent Secretary.[130]

She still had doubts about Hurd's capacity to stand up to the wily Europeans. 'The trouble is Douglas is a gentleman and they're not,' she once expostulated.[131] But Major, she believed, was 'perfect'.[132] Several times over the next few months she told Wyatt that Major was her chosen successor. 'Yes, he is the one I have in mind.'[133] 'That has always been my intention, as you know.'[134] As a result she indulged him like a favourite son, averting her mind from the fact that he too lost no time in signalling his wish to join the ERM – the subject was never even mentioned when she appointed him – while he in turn suppressed his doubts about the poll tax.

Meanwhile he had a difficult economic inheritance. The economy was slowing down. Unemployment, which had been falling steadily since 1986, turned up again over the winter; while inflation carried on rising, from 7.7 per cent in November to 9.4 per cent in April and 10.9 per cent in October 1990 – 'a figure,' Lady Thatcher wrote, 'I had never believed would be reached again while I was Prime Minister.'[135] Pay rises were booming to keep pace, while following Lawson's resignation the pound had fallen to around DM2.70. Major came under considerable pressure to raise interest rates still higher; but he felt – with Mrs Thatcher – that they were already high enough. In January he announced that they would remain at 15 per cent for as long as necessary to halt the price spiral. 'If it is not hurting,' he warned, 'it is not working.'[136]

His budget, on 20 March, was cautiously neutral. Predicting that inflation would begin to fall soon, he was afraid of doing anything that might tip the economy into recession. Excise duties were raised by 10 per cent, but at the same time tax allowances were also raised in line with inflation. His room for manoeuvre was further constrained by the need to cushion the impact of the poll tax. The one innovation was the introduction of a new tax-free scheme, known as TESSA, to encourage saving. He predicted that recovery would begin in 1991: the first of many such hopeful forecasts made by Major himself and his successor over the next few years.

Two days later the public gave its verdict when Labour won the Mid-Staffordshire by-election with a swing of 21 per cent, turning a 'safe' Tory majority of 14,000 into a Labour majority of over 9,000. Huge swings at by-elections were nothing new, and had more often than not been reversed at the subsequent General Election; but this was one of the biggest, on a General Election-size turn-out, and the first time that Labour rather than the Alliance was the beneficiary. Actually the poll tax rather than the budget was the main issue in Mid-Staffordshire. With Wyatt, Mrs Thatcher put on a brave face, agreeing that it 'could have been worse'[137] but Major's political secretary, Judith Chaplin, recorded that she was 'in an absolute tizz over the poll tax, demanding fundamental changes and extra money – she rightly sees it as one of the things that could bring her down'.[138] The following weekend nationwide protests against the tax culminated in serious rioting in Trafalgar Square. In April Labour's lead in the polls widened to twenty-four points – 52 per cent to the Government's 28 per cent – while Mrs Thatcher's personal approval rating fell to 23 per cent, two points lower than her previous nadir in 1981.

On these figures the Government faced complete wipe-out in the English local election results in May. In fact with Labour winning 40 per cent overall to the Tories' 32 per cent, the Liberal Democrats' 18 per cent and the Greens' 8 per cent, the Tories' performance was still among their worst ever and they lost control of another twelve councils. Such was the anticipation of a massacre, however, that Kenneth Baker contrived a PR triumph from the Government's success in losing fewer seats than expected and above all in holding on to the two defiantly Thatcherite London boroughs of Westminster and Wandsworth, plus a number of other victories against the trend in places like Hastings, Trafford and Southend. Taking her cue from Baker, Mrs Thatcher made the most of the first good news she had had for months. 'Overall,' she claimed, 'the opinion polls have been confounded . . . because the community charge is beginning to work. It will increasingly bring the profligate and the inefficient to book.'[139] In her memoirs she argued that where Tory councillors had campaigned aggressively in support of the poll tax and set their local rate below that of neighbouring Labour-controlled boroughs, they had done well.[140] There is some evidence that she was right. But it was too late. Even in the majority of Tory areas, the bills were still intolerably high, and the fundamental principle of equal payment by all was not accepted. Major and Patten still had to spend millions of pounds trying to soften the impact with transitional relief, while taking new powers to cap overspending. It is just possible, as Lady Thatcher maintains, that the poll tax would have been accepted in the end if everything else had been going well for the Government. But it was not. And the more defiantly she identified herself with the poll tax, the more unpopular both it and she became.

In an interview with Jimmy Young in June, and in a number of speeches around the same time, she insisted that she was not 'running out of steam'. In one speech to the Conservative Women's Conference she mentioned a number of possible new policy initiatives: private roads, rent-into-mortgage schemes, increased rights for schools to opt out, longer sentences for drug dealers, even legislation to control dangerous dogs.[141] Labour promptly claimed that she had 'let slip plans for an extremist fourth term manifesto born out of the far-right, far-fetched and far-out dogma of fringe research institutes'.[142] She was indeed thinking about the next manifesto, and she had been holding brainstorming meetings with the CPS, the IEA and the Adam Smith Institute. In her end-of-session speech to Tory backbenchers she announced that she was setting up a series of committees, one for each department, to bring forward new ideas. This did not, she cautioned, imply a spring election: on the contrary, she explicitly accepted the possibility that this time the Government might have to go all the way to 1992. But she insisted that current difficulties over water and electricity privatisation, NHS reform and the poll tax were only short-term. 'When interest rates come down there can be nothing that will stop us.'[143]

But even Jimmy Young could not fail to put to her the criticism that her confrontational style was 'out of date' and she herself was increasingly perceived as 'out of touch', so that 'although you were once the Tory party's greatest asset, you are in fact now its greatest liability'. She replied indignantly that she could not change her style,

and that others – not least television interviewers – were pretty aggressive in confronting *her*. She refused to apologise for fighting 'like a
tiger' for what she believed in: liberty and justice were never out of
date. 'I think Britain has done very well indeed from the fighting which
I have done on her behalf.' But she confirmed that she increasingly
saw herself as a world-historical figure: 'My goodness me, it has been
worth it to pull this country out of the slough of socialism and to see
that Eastern Europe is now following.'[144] For a moment she almost
seemed to be speaking of herself in the past tense.

At the end of June the Government suffered an embarrassment
when the EC ruled that British Aerospace should repay £44 million
of Government 'sweeteners' provided by Lord Young, the then Trade
and Industry Secretary, to enable it to buy Rover in 1988. Pressed by
Kinnock to say whether she had known about this deal, Mrs Thatcher
stuck to the line she had taken the previous December that she was
'kept aware' of the negotiations, but refused to admit to any deception, insisting merely that the belated privatisation of Rover – after
the proposed sale to General Motors in 1986 was blocked by what she
called 'anti-American hysteria' – was a thoroughly good thing which
saved the British taxpayer billions in subsidy.[145] She had always admitted
that it was necessary to pay a 'dowry' to get the company off the
Government's hands.[146] In her memoirs she brushed off the row,
claiming that the fact 'that the terms had to be revised reflected the
new interest of the European Commission in probing the details of
state aid to industry, rather than . . . a reflection on the basic soundness of the deal itself'.[147] But at the time it was another example of
apparent high-handedness and lack of candour.

In the middle of July she suffered yet another blow with the forced
resignation of Nicholas Ridley after his unguarded comments about
the Germans, followed by the leaking of the Chequers seminar. She
fought hard to keep Ridley, telling Wyatt, 'Of course, what they are
really doing is trying to get at me', and was 'greatly distressed' when
he had to go.[148] As Wyatt realised, losing Ridley left her more than
ever the prisoner of Major, Hurd and Howe.[149]

Then on 30 July Ian Gow was murdered by the IRA. Though he
had not been part of her private office since 1983, he and his wife
Jane were still among her closest friends, one of the few couples with
whom she and Denis would sometimes dine informally *à quatre*.
'Margaret is quite shattered,' Wyatt wrote. 'She spoke with more
emotion than I have heard for a long time and for considerable length
. . . She missed him and misses him.'[150] She immediately went down
to Sussex to comfort his widow and read the lesson at his funeral on

10 August, still very upset.[151] But she forced herself to keep on with her normal programme, telling her staff to cancel no engagements but to give her plenty of work to keep her busy.[152] Work was always her best therapy, and on this occasion she had no time to grieve. On 1 August she flew off to Colorado, and a few hours later Saddam Hussein invaded Kuwait.

All the time Major, with Hurd in the background, was working at trying to bring the Prime Minister round to joining the ERM. Since Madrid, she had been publicly committed to joining as soon as the conditions she had laid down there were fulfilled: free movement of capital between all the major countries in the system; completion (or near-completion) of the internal market; and British inflation coming down to somewhere near the European average. She repeatedly denied that she had no serious intention of joining at all, though she could still project the date far into the future. On 27 March, with one of those incautious flourishes she sometimes could not resist, she told Kinnock: 'I stand by the statement that we made in Madrid. I was not able to join the EMS during my first decade – I hope to do so during my second.'[153] Since France and Italy were due to free capital movements on 1 July and the single market was already virtually complete, the critical condition was inflation – which was still rising.

It was no surprise that Major, on moving back to the Treasury, was quickly convinced of the case for joining. He had only left for the Foreign Office four months earlier and, as *The Times* pointed out, there was practically no one of influence in the Treasury, industry or the City who was not in favour of early entry.[154] In his memoirs Major argued that by 1989 joining the ERM was 'the only coherent policy on offer. Despite carping at Nigel for wanting to join . . . Margaret had no alternative policy of her own to put in place.' The Government had no monetary targets, no possibility of shadowing the DM – which anyway 'gave us all the disadvantages of ERM membership without the advantages' – and no alternative to high interest rates. Foreign confidence had been undermined by the Government's unpopularity and the poll-tax riots. 'Economic policy was falling apart and we needed a new anchor . . . The ERM offered the lodestar we needed.'[155]

Major started trying to talk her round at the end of March. 'I felt from the outset that she could be persuaded to enter if the decision to do so did not humiliate her.' He tried to convince her that she could not stop the single currency just by saying 'No', and that the attempt to do so only damaged her. At first 'she simply did not take the point. It was magnificent, but it was not politics.'[156] The next stage of EMU was due to be discussed at the Intergovernmental Conference in Rome in December 1990. 'Our exclusion from the EMU was making us bystanders in this debate. The Prime Minister did not like this argument, not least because it was true. Yet it did register with her.'[157] But he still felt she shied away from the topic.

Judith Chaplin believed that Mrs Thatcher agreed in principle as early as April.[158] Lady Thatcher says that she held out longer than that. She claims to have been alarmed that Major was 'going wobbly' on her. 'I was extremely disturbed to find that the Chancellor had swallowed so quickly the slogans of the European lobby,' she wrote in 1993. 'Intellectually he was drifting with the tide.'[159] At the end of May he sent her a paper warning of the danger of a 'two-tier Europe'. 'What's wrong with that,' she wrote on it, 'if the other tier is going in the wrong direction?' She was not worried by the spectre of the other eleven countries going ahead with EMU without Britain. 'So be it. Germany and France would have to pay all the regional subventions – OR there would be NONE in which case the poorer nations could NOT agree.' On 31 May, at one of their regular evening bilaterals, 'I tried to stiffen John's resolve and widen his vision.' Her vision – the vision of the Bruges speech made suddenly realistic by the fall of the Berlin Wall – was enlargement of the European Union to the east, to embrace the former countries of the Warsaw Pact. She thought the idea of a 'variable geometry' Europe, with different countries opting in or out for different purposes, was a model to be positively pursued, not one to be frightened of. She feared that Major's argument for joining the ERM to avoid becoming 'isolated' would equally lead him, a few years down the road, to accept the whole package of EMU and the single currency.[160] She wanted to resist EMU totally, not compromise with it. In June she brought Ridley into the argument to give herself an ally against Major and Hurd.[161]

It was quite normal for Mrs Thatcher to reopen an argument her colleagues thought she had accepted. But in the end she did give way. Even Charles Powell was telling her it would be a useful discipline, and she could not hold out for ever against the overwhelming consensus. On 14 June she conceded the principle but still insisted on delaying till the autumn. On 4 July she started to consider possible dates, but now she wanted to tie sterling to a *narrower* band than the Treasury proposed – which Major found 'a bewildering change of front'.[162] To his surprise neither the Gulf crisis nor the appearance of a new book by Alan Walters caused her to backtrack. By 4 September she was ready to agree – on one condition: she wanted a simultaneous cut in interest rates. The Bank and the Treasury had convinced her that only membership of the ERM would make that possible; but they equally opposed doing the two things simultaneously. The Governor of the Bank, Robin Leigh-Pemberton, wrote to her: 'I implore you not to try and take your dividend before it's been earned. If we join the ERM you'll see that the exchange rate will rise and you will have a glorious moment in which to lower interest rates.'[163] But she was adamant. An interest-rate cut on the eve of the Tory Party Conference was, in Kenneth Baker's phrase, her 'fig leaf'.[164] 'No cut, no entry,' she told Major. 'We had no choice but to defer to her.' At the last moment she had a fresh attack of doubt and had to be re-convinced by Peter Middleton.[165] But finally she gave the go-ahead on 4 October. 'Do it,' she now agreed. 'Do it tomorrow.'[166]

She made the announcement herself on the pavement outside Number Ten, with Major beside her but saying nothing: it was important that it should be seen as her decision. Accordingly she emphasised the interest-rate cut – back to 14 per cent – as much as ERM entry, asserting that 'the fact that our policies are working and are seen to be working have [sic] made both these decisions possible'. She admitted that inflation was not yet coming down, but argued that since other countries' inflation was rising faster, 'we are coming nearer to the European average', so the Madrid conditions 'have now been fulfilled'. She affirmed that ERM entry 'will underpin our anti-inflationary stance . . . We have done it because the policy is right.'[167]

The instant reaction was ecstatic. Share prices soared, and the prospective Tory candidate for Chester, Gyles Brandreth, wrote excitedly in his diary:

> Hot news! . . . Everyone agrees it's a brilliant move: Major, Hurd, Kinnock, the Bank of England, the TUC. Nigel Lawson is euphoric. . . . Mrs T. is giving a press conference outside Number 10. 'Rejoice! Rejoice!' Naturally there's heated speculation about 'a dash to the polls'.[168]

Actually press comment was more mixed than this suggests. In his memoirs Major took understandable pleasure in quoting the enthusiasm of some of the papers which were most critical, with the benefit of hindsight, when Britain was forced out of the mechanism less than two years later. 'Both politically and economically,' the *Financial Times* wrote, 'entry is shrewdly timed.'[169] But others were not so sure. *The Times* acknowledged that the timing 'could hardly be less propitious for much of British industry', and called the decision 'a triumph of politics over economics'.[170] The simultaneous interest-rate cut gave the impression, as Leigh-Pemberton had warned, that the Government was just trying to stimulate a mini-boom to carry it through the next election: it did not impress the markets, but actually made further cuts more difficult. By abandoning her veto at this moment, one writer charged, Mrs Thatcher had 'performed a double somersault to grab a political lifebelt'.[171] After years of saying that she would join 'when the time is right', Peter Jenkins noted, 'it may be that Mrs Thatcher has joined when the time is wrong'.[172]

The timing was certainly unfortunate, since sterling finally joined the system just at the moment when, after ten successful years, it was entering a difficult period following German reunification and Chancellor Kohl's quixotic decision – another triumph of politics over economics – to absorb the East German currency at parity with the Deutschmark. But the real argument that has raged ever since is whether sterling joined at the wrong rate: DM2.95, with a 6 per cent margin. William Keegan of the *Observer* was one journalist who argued at the time that the rate was unsustainably high; and it quickly became the conventional wisdom among economists and politicians – both opponents and supporters of entry – that DM2.60 would have been more realistic. But Major in his memoirs insists that 'Any suggestion that we could have entered at a significantly lower rate is utterly unrealistic.'[173] He admits that the Bundesbank proposed a marginally lower rate of DM2.90; but on the other hand the Banque de France wanted DM3. There was little room for manoeuvre either way. Sterling had been rising over the summer, on rumours that entry was on the cards, and DM2.95 was the current rate, as well as the average over the past year. In fact Mrs Thatcher decided that there should be no negotiation with Britain's partners at all. Having bitten the bullet, she insisted on the existing parity, partly because she always liked a strong pound and partly because she did not want entry to be accompanied by devaluation. Major was obliged to present his fellow Finance Ministers with a *fait accompli*. This failure of consultation was not responsible for fixing the parity too high, but it threw away much of the goodwill that sterling's entry should otherwise have generated.[174]

When the Commons reassembled two weeks later Kinnock did not query the parity but focused on the easy political target, taunting Mrs Thatcher for having abandoned the conditions she had reiterated only a fortnight earlier and asking what had happened 'to make her completely cave in?' In her reply she was clearly uncomfortable, and flannelled unconvincingly:

Yes, we could have gone on further and waited until inflation had visibly come down, but so many of the conditions had been met and there was so much speculation about when we were going to go in . . . that we took advantage of the excellent opportunity . . . of monetary conditions coming within their limits to end all the speculation.

Kinnock invited her to clarify her personal position by speaking in the debate the following week, jeering that she was 'just plain frit'. This was all the thanks she got for finally doing what everyone had been urging her to do for years. 'I am amazed that Opposition Members are being so small-minded about it,' she complained. 'Did they not want to go in?'[175]

Afterwards she made a virtue of the fact that she had never wanted to join at all. She had been pushed into it by the cumulative pressure of Lawson and Howe before Madrid, then of Major and Hurd, to the point where she could no longer resist. When sterling was forced out of the mechanism again in September 1992 she felt that she had been vindicated. Even at the time Ridley was assuring friends and opponents alike that she had only agreed with the intention of leaving again at the first opportunity;[176] while Major recalled that she talked privately of realigning if it began to hurt, and reflected that such remarks 'showed a startling lack of commitment (or understanding) of the system she had just agreed we should enter'.[177] He denies that he pushed her into it unwillingly. 'The suggestion that this formidable woman was a pushover in the hands of her new Chancellor was unreal.' She agreed 'because she was a political realist and knew that . . . there was no alternative'.[178] But essentially it was true. The fact was that by October 1990 she was no longer in control of economic or European policy. In the second volume of her memoirs she defended her decision by painting the ERM as a sort of substitute for the MTFS, 'intended to demonstrate to the financial markets that our commitment to low inflation was unshakeable'. She hoped that by giving ground on the ERM she would strengthen her hand in continuing to resist EMU – Lawson's old argument:

But the maintenance of a parity within the ERM became an end in itself . . . This led to a monetary overkill which certainly brought inflation down very rapidly, but at the price of inflicting an unduly severe recession on the British economy.[179]

The irony of the ERM saga is that after years of opposition she finally agreed to join at an unsustainable rate at the worst possible moment. If she was thus proved right from one point of view, she was equally wrong from another. She was not only formally responsible, as

Prime Minister, for the ultimate decision to go in; she was also, by imposing her personal veto from as far back as 1985, directly responsible for the fact that Britain did not join five years earlier, in more settled conditions, at a rate which sterling would have been able to sustain and at a time when membership would have helped contain inflation. Lawson's attempt to shadow the Deutschmark as a substitute for membership contributed to – though it did not wholly cause – the resurgence of inflation after 1987. After 1992 Lady Thatcher and her increasingly Europhobe supporters were able to cite the disaster of 'Black Wednesday' as proof that she had been right all along. But it might have been a different story if she had listened to Lawson in 1985.

If the timing of the decision was a piece of short-term opportunism to please the party conference, it was almost too successful. On arriving in Bournemouth Mrs Thatcher had to spend the first few days fending off speculation about an early election. 'It's full steam ahead for the fourth term,' she announced confidently – but added 'whenever that may be'.[180] 'Everyone's talking about dates except me,' she told reporters. 'I'm not even thinking about it yet.'[181] In fact she explicitly told the party agents not to expect an early poll. There would have to be 'a good strong period of favourable opinion polls' first – and though the gap had narrowed over the summer it was much too soon to talk of that.[182] While the message hammered out by successive ministers from the platform was that the Government was still full of energy to carry the Thatcher revolution into the fourth term, Baker carefully discouraged the sort of pre-election mood that Norman Tebbit had created at the 1986 conference.

Ronnie Millar found Mrs Thatcher more relaxed than he had expected, 'in excellent humour throughout the week'.[183] No one could have guessed from her closing speech that it would be her last as leader. She was on fighting form from the start. Beginning with a tribute to Ian Gow and a pledge to defeat terrorism, she plunged immediately into global affairs with the reflection that 1990 had been 'the best of times . . . the worst of times':

> The worst of times as a tyrant struck down a small country that stands at the gateway to the Gulf; the best of times as tyranny crumbled and freedom triumphed across the continent of Europe.

The common theme, she spelled out, was the need to resist dictators. The Berlin Wall had been toppled because 'this Government stood firm against all those voices raised . . . in favour of appeasement'. She did not need to mention that that very morning in Bournemouth

Ted Heath had announced that he was flying to Baghdad to negotiate for the release of British hostages. 'Mr President,' she intoned,
'dictators can be deterred, they can be crushed – they can never be
appeased.'

Then she was back home, singling out practically every member of
the Cabinet – excluding Geoffrey Howe – for special praise before
inviting the audience to applaud 'What a fabulous team we've got!'
She chose not to dwell on the decision to join the ERM, citing it
only as proof that 'our policies of firm financial discipline were seen
to be working', but reiterated that 'this Government has no intention
of agreeing to the imposition of a single currency' and brought the
house down with one of Millar's cheekiest soundbites: 'That would be
entering a federal Europe through the back-Delors.' She professed to
hope that the Community would accept Major's 'important proposals
for a common currency' instead.

Next she had some fun mocking Neil Kinnock, the so-called 'Prime
Minister in waiting'. 'It occurs to me, Mr President, that he may have
quite a wait.'

> I can see him now, like the people queuing up for the winter sales.
> All got up with his camp bed, hot thermos, woolly balaclava, CND
> badge . . . Waiting, waiting, waiting . . . And then when the doors
> open, he rushes in – only to find that, as always, there's 'that woman'
> ahead of him again. I gather there may be an adjective between
> 'that' and 'woman', only no one will tell me what it is.

There followed a more serious, extended attack on Labour as a party
which had 'ditched its principles, disguised its policies and denied its
past', then some less successful knockabout at the expense of the Liberal
Democrats' new logo, the yellow 'bird of freedom' which her speechwriters had wittily thought of comparing to the dead parrot in the
famous *Monty Python* sketch. 'This is an ex-parrot. It is not merely
stunned, it has ceased to be, expired . . .'* It raised a laugh, but the
Lib Dems had the last laugh when they won the Eastbourne by-
election six days later. Meanwhile she pressed on – via a little-noticed
reference to 'the kind of open, classless Britain I want to see', which

---

*'Unfortunately,' her political secretary John Whittingdale recalls, 'the Prime
Minister had not even heard of *Monty Python*.' 'Are you sure this is funny?' she
asked anxiously. She had to be shown the video, at which she set herself very
professionally to master John Cleese's intonation. But she was still doubtful. 'Monty
Python?' she asked 'Are you sure he's one of us?'[184]

was echoed by John Major six weeks later as if he was saying something new – to list some of the new policies she hoped to get on to in her fourth term.

She intended to cut income tax further 'as soon as it's safe to do so'. She wanted to create more new shareholders by means of further privatisation – 'We'll privatise the major ports, then tackle British Rail' – and more new homeowners by a rent-into-mortgage scheme. The Government was going to enable more schools to opt out of local-authority control, and she hinted at having another try at education vouchers. 'Much has been done,' she boasted. 'But more remains to be done.'

Finally she came back to foreign policy, with a firm statement of the West's resolve to get Saddam Hussein out of Kuwait by military force if necessary; another celebration of the triumph of freedom in Eastern Europe – linked to her favourite theme that the countries of Western Europe should not surrender their sovereignty at the very moment when those in the east were reasserting theirs; and a last gleeful obituary of socialism, which she mocked 'must now return for ever to its proper place – the Reading Room of the British Library where Karl Marx found it. Section: History of Ideas; Subsection: Nineteenth century; Status: Archaic.'[185]

It was as good a conference speech as she had ever made: confident, wide-ranging, by turns scornful and visionary. Its reception, Ronnie Millar wrote, was 'if anything, even more delirious than usual':

> On the platform, surrounded by her applauding and apparently adoring Cabinet, the star acknowledges the rapturous acclaim of her public, both arms held aloft as they have been every year since 1975. In the body of the hall 'TEN MORE YEARS!' roar the faithful five thousand, stamping their feet in time with the words. 'TEN MORE YEARS! TEN MORE YEARS!! TEN MORE YEARS!!!' they cry fortissimo. The floor trembles. The rafters shake. It is as though by the sheer force of their utterance and its constant repetition they feel they can compel the future. Even by the Leader's standards it is a salute to end all salutes. As it turns out to be . . .[186]

Just over a month later she resigned.

17

The Defenestration of
Downing Street

The sheep that turned

Mrs Thatcher's downfall was a drama which unfolded with shocking suddenness. For political journalists those three weeks in November 1990 were a once-in-a-lifetime story of rumour and intrigue, calculation and backstabbing, all conducted in the bars and tearooms, clubs and private houses of the Westminster village. For the general public – angry, exultant or simply bewildered by the speed of events – it was a Shakespearean soap opera played out nightly in their living rooms. Though all the elements of a climatic bust-up had been coming together over a long period, with persistent talk of another leadership challenge, speculation about Michael Heseltine's intentions and questions about how long she could go on, few at Westminster or in the media really believed that she could be toppled as swiftly or abruptly as she was. The conventional wisdom of political scientists held that a Prime Minister in good health and in possession of a secure majority was invulnerable between elections. She might be given a warning shot but she could not be defeated. When suddenly she was gone, Tory MPs were amazed at what they had done. Chris Cook and Alan Sked call it 'the most ruthless act of political ingratitude in the history of modern Britain'.[1] Nicholas Ridley wrote of 'mediaeval savagery',[2] others of treachery, betrayal, assassination, defenestration, even ritual sacrifice. Matthew Parris wrote in anthropological terms of the Tory 'tribe' having to kill and eat its mother figure.[3] For the next decade the party was riven by the consequences of its act of regicide, and well into the new century the trauma shows little sign of healing. Yet like most great events, the drama of November 1990 was a sequence of accidents with only in retrospect an underlying inevitability. John Biffen came up with the best metaphor for what happened. 'You know those maps on the Paris Metro that light up when you press a button to go from A to B?' he told Alan Watkins. 'Well, it was like that. Someone pressed a button and all the connections lit up.'[4]

Of all her colleagues Geoffrey Howe was perhaps the least likely political assassin. Yet there was poetic justice in the fact that it was he who pressed the button. Several of those closest to the Prime Minister – Ronnie Millar for instance – had feared that the contemptuous way she treated Howe might in the end rebound on her. Ian Gow, an ardent admirer of Mrs Thatcher but also an old friend of Howe, was deeply critical of the way she had moved him from the Foreign Office in 1989. If she had to shift him, he told John Ranelagh just a few weeks later, she should have presented it to him and to the media as a promotion to a more senior position chairing committees, co-ordinating Government business and leading the newly televised House of Commons: a real deputy Prime Minister. Instead she went out of her way to present it as a kick in the teeth:

> That's why Geoffrey was wounded. That was very, very bad. And I'm afraid that the omens for Geoffrey and Mrs Thatcher working happily together are not good. As I look ahead, I am filled with foreboding.[5]

Howe would in fact have chaired the 'Star Chamber' if it had been needed; but Major and Lamont managed to resolve the 1990 spending round without serious difficulty. It was also reported in July that he would not be excluded from the group drawing up the next manifesto.[6] But this was in the context that he was being excluded from practically everything else. He was upset when John Wakeham was given responsibility for the co-ordination of Government publicity. Like most lawyers he was strongly opposed to the Government's retrospective War Crimes Bill and shocked by Mrs Thatcher's determination to use the 1911 Parliament Act to override its rejection by the House of Lords. Above all he was so comprehensively frozen out of policy towards Europe that he only learned that Britain was finally joining the ERM when the Queen asked him what he thought of the news.[7] As a result he felt he could contribute only by speaking publicly. First in a speech to the Bow Group on the conference fringe – the deputy Prime Minister did not get to speak in the conference proper – he stressed the importance of Britain being 'in the driver's seat [not] the rear carriage' of the European train. This was one of the tiredest metaphors in the political phrasebook: Mrs Thatcher quite sensibly retorted that it was 'very silly to get on a train if you don't know its destination';[8] and on another occasion that 'people who get on a train like that deserve to be taken for a ride'[9] – but it was nevertheless a serious argument with which Hurd and Major agreed as much as Lawson had. Then in a television interview with Brian Walden during the Rome summit Howe hinted that the Government as a whole was not so implacably opposed to the eventual emergence of a single currency as the Prime Minister. 'This,' Lady Thatcher wrote in her memoirs, was either disloyal or remarkably stupid.'[10]

She was convinced of Howe's disloyalty, as Woodrow Wyatt's diary repeatedly records. 'You know what he's like and what he's up to now' was a typical complaint in February.[11] She believed that he was still deeply ambitious and scheming to replace her. Yet at the same time she did not really believe he would ever strike at her: she did not think he had the guts. With hindsight she thought it 'surprising that he remained so long in a position which he clearly disliked and resented'. By the end, she wrote, 'we found each other's company almost intolerable'.[12] But whose fault was that? In December 1989 Peter Carrington told Wyatt – fishing for just such information – that Howe was not as loyal as Wyatt pretended to believe. 'What he is saying to me every time I see him . . . is that he hates her and that she has been horrible and he wishes she would go.'[13] But wishing she would go is not the same as plotting to displace her. Most observers thought Howe's tolerance was inexhaustible. George Walden most vividly describes what many others had also witnessed when he attended a lunch at Number Ten while Howe was still Foreign Secretary:

> I do not know what shocked me most – the way she treated him or Howe's docile reaction. We were talking round Europe and different economic models. The slightest deviation from the hard Thatcher line and poor Geoffrey was slapped down. He lowered his head, got on with his lunch, then came doggedly back and was slapped down again. These were not abrasive arguments or barbed comments. They were personal insults. When he hazarded a view about the workings of industry he was told that if he knew so much about industry, why didn't he go and work there?
>
> To speak to your Foreign Secretary in the way she did in private would have been bad enough. To do so in front of myself and another outsider was extraordinary. Clearly she had reached the stage where no one dared tell her that she simply couldn't treat people like that.

When Howe finally cracked, Walden wrote, it was 'like seeing a battered wife finally turning on a violent husband'.[14]

What caused him to crack was her intemperate reaction to the European Council held in Rome the last weekend in October 1990. In truth even Howe admitted that she had some ground to be upset. The next stage of EMU was due to be discussed at the Intergovernmental Conference fixed − over her objections − for December. But then the Italians called an extra Council in October and used it to try to pre-empt the wider discussions at the IGC by setting a timetable for the second and third stages of the Delors plan immediately. Contrary to prior assurances, Kohl and Mitterrand went along with this, and Mrs Thatcher found herself at Rome suddenly confronted by the other eleven ready to commit themselves to start stage 2 in 1994 and complete the single currency in 2000. Hurd was as shocked as Mrs Thatcher by the Italian ambush; once again Britain was cast as the lone obstructive voice. She objected that it was absurd to set a timetable before it was even agreed what form stages 2 and 3 should take. 'My objections were heard in stony silence,' she wrote in her memoirs.[15] At her end-of-summit press conference and then in a series of television and radio interviews she was 'assertive and angry',[16] claiming that her partners were living in 'cloud-cuckoo land'. She repeated her refusal to be steamrollered into a single currency and threatened to veto the whole process, insisting that Britain would *never* consent to abolish the pound.

What made her most angry was that the Italians were trying to put the cart before the horse on EMU at the expense of what she considered far more urgent matters: the Gulf, Eastern Europe, South Africa and above all the agreement of a common Community posi-tion on the Uruguay round of GATT, which had already been in tortured negotiation for four years and now had to be completed by the end of the year. 'That shows you the sort of priority of this Council,' she expostulated. 'Run away from the urgent decisions and take refuge in the vague ones.' Agreement on GATT was blocked by Mitterrand and Kohl − the leaders of the two richest farming coun-tries in the Community acting from motives of blatant 'nationalist selfishness'; yet they had the gall to criticise *her* for being non-*communautaire*.[17] 'I think it was disgraceful,' she told ITN. 'The urgent things they go nationalist and say no; the things which are vague and in the distance they can take refuge in vague phrases and then blame us . . . We are not prepared to commit ourselves until we have got the detail worked out.'[18]

Back in Britain she reported to the House of Commons on Tuesday

30 October. At Prime Minister's Questions Kinnock seized on Howe's rather different tone with Brian Walden and tried to get her to endorse her deputy: this she pointedly declined to do, merely asserting that Howe was 'too big a man to need a little man like the right hon. Gentleman to stand up for him'. What Howe had actually said was that Britain's proposal for a common currency – the hard ecu – might in time grow into a single currency. This was no more than Major had also said, and was in fact the Government's policy. In her written statement Mrs Thatcher duly toed this line – the first time, Howe believed, that she had done so:

> The hard ecu would be a parallel currency, not a single currency. If, as time went by, peoples and Governments chose to use it widely, it could evolve towards a single currency. But our national currency would remain unless a decision to abolish it were freely taken by future generations of Parliament and people. A single currency is not the policy of this Government.

She went on to insist that Britain was not isolated or obstructive:

> Britain intends to be part of the further political, economic and monetary development of the European Community . . . When we come to negotiate on particular points, rather than concepts or generalities, I believe that solutions will be found which will enable the Community to go forward as Twelve. That will be our objective.

So far, so moderate. But then Kinnock riled her with the usual charge that her performance in Rome had damaged Britain's interest, quoting the view of 'her fellow-Conservative . . . Commissioner Brittan' that it would still be possible to retain the pound within a single currency. Mention of the Commission seemed to release her safety catch. Leon Brittan, she said, was 'a loyal member of the Commission', an unelected body whose object was to increase its powers at the expense of national parliaments. She went on, with mounting emphasis:

> The President of the Commission, M. Delors, said at a press conference the other day that he wanted the European Parliament to be the democratic body of the Community, he wanted the Commission to be the Executive and he wanted the Council of Ministers to be the Senate. *No. No. No.*[19]

Once again it was her tone – defiant, intransigent and glorying in her intransigence – more than her actual words which horrified her colleagues. Suddenly she was Horatius holding the bridge, Drake scattering the Armada, Churchill fighting on the beaches, all in one. For another twenty minutes she continued in this vein, egged on by delighted Eurosceptics and buoyed up by a wave of backbench enthusiasm. 'It was already clear,' David Owen wrote, 'that she was on an emotional high and the adrenalin was pumping round her system as she handbagged every federalist proposal.'[20] 'In a sustained rant,' Matthew Parris wrote, 'scarcely pausing for breath as her voice rose with her temper, she let fly with a mixed salvo of reason, unreason, scorn, argument and vulgar abuse.'[21] 'This was real conviction politics,' marvelled Kenneth Baker, 'boldly enunciated with little thought of the immediate consequences'.[22] In particular – answering a question from the Labour Eurosceptic Nigel Spearing – she departed from her carefully phrased backing of the hard ecu:

> The hard ecu . . . could be used if people chose to do so. In my view, it would not become widely used throughout the Community . . . I am pretty sure that most people in this country would prefer to continue to use sterling.

'I nearly fell off the bench,' Major wrote. 'With this single sentence she wrecked months of work and preparation. Europe had been suspicious that the hard ecu was simply a tactic to head off a single currency, and now the Prime Minister, in a matter of a few words, convinced them it was.' It was only after this, he believes, that she 'reached for her gun' and blasted Delors with her famous triple negative. In fact he is wrong about the order, but he had no doubt about the likely effect of her 'unscripted outburst'. 'I heard our colleagues cheer, but knew there was trouble ahead.'[23] From the SDP bench below the gangway, Owen kept his eye on Geoffrey Howe. 'He looked miserable and unhappy, truly, I thought, a dead sheep. How wrong I proved to be.'[24]

If Howe needed any further prompting the next day's press – led by the *Sun* with the gleeful headline 'Up Yours, Delors' – pushed him over the edge.[25] He had already drafted his resignation letter before he attended Cabinet on Thursday morning. With now-characteristic insensitivity Mrs Thatcher lectured him in front of his colleagues over the fact that two or three Bills to be included in the Queen's Speech were not quite ready. Some of them felt later that this was the final provocation.[26] But Howe denies it. 'Far from being the last straw, this final tantrum was the first confirmation that I had taken the right decision.'[27]

His resignation letter – running to over 1,000 words – repeated his concern that Britain should remain on the 'inside track' in Europe. 'Now that we are finally inside the ERM we have a great opportunity at last to shape Europe's monetary arrangements in the years ahead.' Conversely, he believed, 'the risks of being left behind on EMU are severe.' He insisted that he was '*not* a Euro-idealist or federalist'; his vision of Europe was 'practical and hard-headed'. Nevertheless he was 'deeply anxious' that the mood Mrs Thatcher had struck, both at Rome and in the House, 'will make it more difficult for Britain to hold and retain a position of influence in this vital debate'. He did not want a single currency *imposed* any more than she did, but 'more than one form of EMU is possible. The important thing is not to rule in or out any one particular solution absolutely.' 'In all honesty,' he concluded, 'I now find myself unable to share your view of the right approach to this question.'[28]★

Mrs Thatcher regarded this as typically feeble stuff and tried to brush off Howe's complaints, as she had done Lawson's, as differences of style only, not of policy. 'I do not believe these are nearly as great as you suggest,' she replied.[30] They parted with mutual relief and a formal handshake – the first time, Howe thought, they had ever shaken hands in fifteen years – leaving Mrs Thatcher to carry out her fourth reshuffle of the year, the sixth in fifteen months.

Desperately needing allies, she tried to persuade Norman Tebbit to come back to shake up education, where she thought John MacGregor had gone soft. Tebbit considered it overnight but declined, still pleading his duty to his wife. But she was now determined to move MacGregor anyway and thought his mild manner made him the ideal replacement for Howe as Leader of the House. Ken Clarke had already thoroughly antagonised the doctors, nurses and ambulance drivers, so she decided to switch him to tackle the teachers' unions instead. Clarke did not want to leave the Department of Health and resisted, emphasising his opposition to education vouchers. But she had not forgiven him for having stood up to her when she had cold feet about his NHS reforms earlier in the year, so she insisted. To the despair of the right she then promoted an equally reluctant William Waldegrave to take over Health, which he confessed was 'completely new territory' to him.[31] Altogether

---

★A few days later, speaking in Glasgow, Hurd took a similar line, insisting that 'there is no dread conspiracy against us, there is simply an argument'. Britain just had to fight its corner, 'without frightening ourselves with ogres'.[29]

this reshuffle was an assertion of authority which was not calculated to improve the Government.

The day after Howe's resignation *The Times* printed what Gyles Brandreth called 'a wonderful picture of the Thatcher Cabinet of 1979. Eleven years later and there's not one of them left. She's eaten every single one.'[32] Wyatt was jubilant at Howe's departure; but even he acknowledged that 'it makes the Government look a bit untidy'.[33] This was an understatement. Nevertheless for nearly two weeks, Mrs Thatcher seemed to have ridden out this latest crisis, helped by Bernard Ingham's bullish briefings. 'She will survive it,' *The Times* asserted confidently. 'If Sir Geoffrey believes he can precipitate a leadership election this month . . . he must surely be mistaken.'[34] Nicholas Ridley later claimed to have spoken to no one who realised that the fuse under the Prime Minister's position had been lit.[35] Parliament was not sitting – her report on the Rome summit had been the fag-end of the previous session – so Howe had no early opportunity to make a resignation statement. Michael Heseltine congratulated him on his 'courageous decision' but told him it did not materially affect his own position. Just to post a reminder that he was still in the wings, however, he reworked an article intended for the *Sunday Times* and published it as an open letter to his Henley constituents before leaving on a visit to the Middle East. This was a mistake which allowed Ingham to charge him with cowardice: 'Whenever we're in difficulty he lights the blue touch paper and retires to a safe distance – in this case to Amman.'[36]

But why should Ingham have wished to provoke Heseltine? The answer would seem to be that Mrs Thatcher wanted to flush him into the open. On 2 November she did not share Wyatt's confidence that she would not face another leadership challenge, and over the next few days that apprehension seems to have hardened into a conviction that she would be challenged again.[37] The same machinery that had allowed Meyer to challenge the year before was still in place, and not a day passed without another Tory MP calling for a contest to 'lance the boil'.[38] That being so, she resolved to get it over quickly. On Tuesday 6 November she arranged with Cranley Onslow, the chairman of the 1922 Committee, to bring forward the date of any contest by two weeks, with the closing date for nominations on Thursday 15 November and the first round of voting the following Tuesday. Alan Watkins calls this 'a shameless piece of gerrymandering designed by her and Mr Onslow to safeguard her position'.[39] In fact Onslow was 'completely flabbergasted' by her decision and tried to dissuade her.[40] What was extraordinary about it was not the haste but the fact that she was due to be out of the country on 20 November attending the CSCE conference in Paris. She knew this, but thought either that it did not matter, since she did not intend to canvass personally any more than she had against Meyer, or that it would be of positive benefit to her by reminding Tory MPs of her standing as an international stateswoman – rather as she had gone to Williamsburg in the middle of the 1983 election and to Venice in 1987. The idea that she did not expect a serious contest when she changed the date does not stand up. On the contrary, she expected Heseltine to stand but thought the best way of beating him was to beat him quickly. 'It'll be a fort-night's agony,' she told Ronnie Millar. 'Oh well. Never mind.'[41] It was a fateful miscalculation.

Normal political business resumed on 7 November, with the opening of the new session of Parliament. Despite a concerted effort by Labour MPs to throw her off her stride, Mrs Thatcher opened the debate on the Queen's Speech in characteristically combative style, outlining new Bills ranging from longer sentences for criminals, through the setting up of the Child Support Agency, to privately financed roads and priva-tised ports. She wiped the floor as usual with Kinnock and played down the differences with Howe, squaring her own scepticism about the hard ecu with the possibility that it nevertheless *could* evolve into a single currency with the clever formula that 'We have no bureau-cratic timetable: ours is a market approach, based on what people and governments choose to do.' When John Reid asked why in that case Howe had resigned, she replied – with a dangerous echo of the Lawson resignation – that only Howe could answer that.[42] Howe let it be known that he would make a statement the following Tuesday. Meanwhile Major, in his autumn economic statement, was forced to admit that the economy was now officially in recession; and the next day the Conservatives were hammered in two more by-elections in Bootle and Bradford North – the latter a Labour marginal where they not only failed to compete but slumped to third place behind the Liberal Democrat.

The weekend papers were full of speculation about Heseltine's next move. Most of them thought this was the moment he had been posi-tioning himself for ever since 1986. Heseltine himself still hesitated. 'I have only one bullet in my gun,' he had told Andrew Neil back in July. 'I can't afford to miss.'[43] On the other hand he did not want to delay so long that he gained the leadership only after Mrs Thatcher had led the party to defeat. As he told the former Chief Whip Michael Jopling, who urged him to hold on, he wanted to be Prime Minister, not Leader of the Opposition.[44] In fact the press – egged on by Ingham

– left him little choice. Monday's headlines were variations on the Downing Street-inspired theme: 'Put up or shut up.' *The Times*, which only a week before had scouted the likelihood of a contest, now pointedly contrasted Heseltine's dithering with Mrs Thatcher's decisiveness in 1975. 'If Mr Heseltine fails to throw his cap into the ring, he will thoroughly deserve to have it stuffed down his throat.'[45] Mrs Thatcher told Baker after the Cenotaph ceremony on Sunday morning that she thought Heseltine would stand. Yet Ingham still expected him to back off.[46] His intention was presumably to call Heseltine's bluff. If so, it was another miscalculation. 'Of all the nails that Ingham inadvertently hammered into his mistress's coffin,' Nigel Lawson wrote, 'this was the most decisive.'[47] When Howe delivered his *coup de grâce* the next day, Ingham had left Heseltine no option but to seize the moment.

Meanwhile on Monday evening Mrs Thatcher was due to speak at the Lord Mayor's banquet in the Guildhall. Three days before nominations closed, she used the occasion to declare that she was ready for all comers. With the television cameras in attendance, she turned up dressed like Queen Elizabeth I at Tilbury in a black velvet gown with a high collar, cloak and pearls. Never in all her years of power dressing had she worn anything so ostentatiously regal: at the very moment when she needed to show some humility her dress positively screamed hubris. Then when she came to speak, she plunged – after just a few words of thanks to the Lord Mayor – straight into a declaration of defiance framed in a clumsy cricketing metaphor:

> Since I first went into bat eleven years ago, the score at your end has ticked over nicely. You are now the 663rd Lord Mayor. At the Prime Minister's end, we are stuck on 49. I am still at the crease, though the bowling has been pretty hostile of late. And in case anyone doubted it, can I assure you that there will be no ducking the bouncers, no stonewalling, no playing for time? The bowling's going to get hit all round the ground. That is my style.[48]

Millar, who was there, and Wyatt, who watched on television, thought the speech went well: 'a rollicking fighting speech' was Wyatt's loyal view.[49] Conversely Alan Clark was told that it was 'greeted with virtually complete silence. She started punchily, then got flatter and flatter.'[50] In truth most of it, devoted to the economy, was unremarkable; but her opening words were badly misjudged, as Baker, more in tune with feeling in the country, realised. 'Margaret's supporters loved this sort of bravura performance where the melodrama was enhanced by her extraordinary get-up. But it reinforced the antipathy of all those who couldn't stand her or her style.'[51] It was just the wrong image to have projected on the eve of the battle of her life.★

Howe made his statement on Tuesday afternoon, shortly after Prime Minister's Questions, to a packed House which nevertheless had no expectation that it was about to witness one of the parliamentary occasions of the century. Its impact was greatly enhanced by being one of the first major occasions to be televised. Years earlier Denis Healey had likened the experience of being attacked by Howe to being 'savaged by a dead sheep'. Others called him 'Mogadon Man'. But there was nothing soporific about this speech. He still never raised his voice above its habitual courteous monotone. But almost from his first words he gripped the House with a hitherto unsuspected passion. He started lightly by dismissing the idea that he had resigned purely over differences of style, noting that after sharing 'something like 700 meetings of Cabinet or Shadow Cabinet during the past eighteen years, and some 400 hours alongside each other at more than 30 international summit meetings . . . something more than simple matters of style would be necessary to rupture such a well-tried relationship'. He recalled the privilege of serving as Chancellor for four years, paying tribute to Mrs Thatcher's essential contribution to their economic achievements, but also suggesting that 'they possibly derived some little benefit from the presence of a Chancellor who was not exactly a wet himself'.

The core of his speech then spelt out their real differences over Europe. First, he recalled that he and Lawson had wanted to join the ERM since at least 1985 and revealed for the first time – with Lawson sitting beside him nodding his assent – that they had both threatened to resign if she did not make a definite commitment to join at the time of Madrid. He gently corrected Mrs Thatcher's increasingly public placing of all the blame for the renewal of inflation on Lawson by insisting that it could have been avoided if Britain had joined the ERM much earlier. Next, he mocked her 'nightmare image' of a Europe

---

★In her memoirs Lady Thatcher admits that the cricketing metaphor was a mistake, writing mysteriously that 'words now began to fail me'.[52] But the speech was written in her private office as usual by Charles Powell and Andrew Turnbull, then 'polished' on the Sunday evening by Ronnie Millar.[53] On this occasion Millar – not a cricketer – got it wrong. But as Alan Watkins remarked, 'Bernard Ingham, a Yorkshireman, should at least have been able to tell her that ducking was precisely what one did with bouncers.'[54] A reader from Wakefield wrote pertinently to *The Times* that what the country needed was not a single batsman staying at the crease all day slogging the bowling all round the ground, but a good captain utilising all the team's talents in order to win matches. 'That's cricket.'[55]

'teeming with ill-intentioned people scheming, in her words, to "extinguish democracy" and "dissolve our national identities"', preferring to quote against it both Macmillan's 1962 warning against retreating into 'a ghetto of sentimentality about our past' and Churchill's vision of a 'larger sovereignty' which alone, he had declared in 1950, could protect Europe's diverse national traditions. Again he warned against getting left out of the forging of new institutions. Of course Britain could opt out of the single currency, but she could not prevent the others going ahead. 'The risk is not imposition but isolation . . . We have paid heavily in the past for late starts and squandered opportunities in Europe. We dare not let that happen again.' Finally he specifically condemned Mrs Thatcher's 'personalised incredulity' about the hard ecu which her own Government was supposed to be promoting. 'How on earth,' he asked, 'are the Chancellor and the Governor of the Bank of England . . . to be taken as serious participants in the debate against that kind of background noise?' Turning Mrs Thatcher's cricketing metaphor neatly against her, he suggested that it was 'like sending your opening batsmen to the crease only for them to find, the moment the first balls are bowled, that their bats have been broken before the game by the team captain'.

Personally, Howe concluded, he had tried to reconcile the differences from within the Government, but he now realised that 'the task has become futile: trying to stretch the meaning of words beyond what was credible, and trying to pretend that there was a common policy when every step forward risked being subverted by some casual comment or impulsive answer'. The conflict between the 'instinct of loyalty' to the Prime Minister, which was 'still very real', and 'loyalty towards what I perceive to be the true interests of the nation' had become intolerable. 'That is why I have resigned.' In the very last sentence came the killer punch. 'The time has come for others to consider their own response to the tragic conflict of loyalties with which I have myself wrestled for perhaps too long.'[56]

Lawson called it 'the most devastating speech I, or I suspect anyone else in the House that afternoon, had heard uttered in the House of Commons . . . It was all the more powerful because it was Geoffrey, that most moderate, long-suffering and patient of men, that was uttering it.'[57] 'It was the measured way in which Howe gave the speech which made it so deadly,' Paddy Ashdown wrote:

> The knife went in coolly at the beginning and never stopped turning. He made the House laugh at her expense; he made her look ridiculous . . . Here on full display was all the venom and invective pent

up after years of humiliation suffered at the hands of Mrs Thatcher
. . . I fear Geoffrey stepped over the line between candour and
vengeance, but the result is that she appears terminally damaged.[58]

Even Ronnie Millar could not withhold his professional admiration. 'Never in my lengthening experience of the political scene,' he
wrote, 'was a demolition job done with such meticulous artistry.' It
was crafted with 'surgical precision, each word honed with Aesculapian
skill for maximum effect', delivered in a 'velvet monotone':

> In content, timing and delivery, it was a killer of the highest class,
> in turn witty, factual, regretful and lethal . . . He had come not to
> praise Margaret, but to bury her, and in eighteen minutes he had
> dug her political grave, filled it in beyond possibility of exhumation
> and conducted an autopsy while the victim was still alive and
> listening.[59]★

The victim herself was shocked and angry. Forced to listen impas-
sively, she was 'tense from top to toe', Major, sitting beside her, noted.[61]
'She kept her composure,' Baker wrote, but 'her face remained tight
as she muttered to me on the bench, "I didn't think he would do
something like that."'[62] In her memoirs she called Howe's performance 'poisonous' and professed herself 'hurt' that after all the battles
they had shared, 'he had deliberately set out to bring down a colleague
in this brutal and public way'. She called it 'this final act of bile and
treachery' as though Howe had not been loyal to a fault for all these
years – but consoled herself with the conclusion that 'the very bril-
liance with which he wielded the dagger ensured that the character
he assassinated was in the end his own'.[63]

Howe denies that his final sentence was a pre-arranged invitation to
Heseltine to end his hesitation.[64] But it is hard to see what else it could
have meant. Heseltine too denies collusion; yet his lieutenant Michael
Mates was canvassing possible allies, before Howe spoke, on whether it
would be helpful for him to mention Heseltine by name.[65] In such a
highly charged situation, a hint was more than enough. In fact Heseltine's
mind was already made up; but Howe's speech gave him a more
favourable wind than he would have had the previous week. An hour
after Howe sat down, Cecil Parkinson made a last attempt to dissuade

---

★Calman's pocket cartoon on the front page of *The Times* next day showed a
sheep swallowing Mrs Thatcher whole, with just her heels protruding, and the
caption 'Howe's That?'[60]

him. 'Cecil, she is finished,' Heseltine told him. 'After Geoffrey's speech, she is finished.'[66] The next day he announced his candidacy.

Tarzan's moment

He gave three reasons – a shrewd amalgam of real policy differences with an appeal to the survival instinct of Tory backbenchers. First, he agreed with Howe that Mrs Thatcher held 'views on Europe behind which she has not been able to maintain a united Cabinet. This damages the proper pursuit of British self-interest in Europe.' Second, and perhaps most important, polls showed that he was the alternative leader best placed to rebuild Tory support and win the next election. Third, he promised an immediate review of the poll tax. At this stage he did not promise to abolish it: the undertaking merely to look at it again was designed to attract both those who still believed in the principle and those who thought the only possible result of a review would be to scrap it entirely.[67] But he was careful not to repudiate Mrs Thatcher's record entirely. He said nothing about economic, industrial or social policy. On the contrary he claimed to have been 'at the leading edge of Thatcherism' over the past ten years. 'I am nothing if not radical. Every department I have ever had will testify to that.'[68] His record at least at the Department of the Environment – selling council houses, abolishing quangos and cutting the rate-support grant to over-spending local authorities – bore him out. Mrs Thatcher had more ground for doubting his performance at the MoD, but there too he had played a major part in the defeat of CND. His resignation from the Cabinet in 1986 had seemed to be a storm in a teacup at the time – but his criticism of her handling of Cabinet had subsequently been corroborated by Lawson and Howe. Finally he was a charismatic politician of undoubted Prime Ministerial calibre who had scrupulously refrained from open disloyalty over the past four years, while assiduously cultivating the constituencies and anxious MPs. Thus he was in every way a serious candidate and difficult for her to disparage.

In her memoirs she confessed that she resented Heseltine's challenge, first because (unlike Ted Heath in 1975) she was a proven election winner who deserved the chance to win again in 1991 or 1992; second because she was a world stateswoman on the verge of committing British troops to war in the Gulf; and third because she was not just party leader but Prime Minister, elected by the whole country and therefore not to be dismissed except – like Churchill in 1945 – by the British people.[69] At the time, however, she made no complaint but made a point of accepting the rules and treating the challenge philosophically as just one more hurdle of political life that she must overcome. 'I do not run away,' she told Charles Moore in an interview for the *Sunday Telegraph*:

> When someone says you have a contest you do not run away. We will fight it. Get it out of the way and then we will be free to get on with our work . . . It does obviously have some effect which I could well do without at the moment. Someone else decides to have one. The rules permit it, so we just get on with it.[70]

In common with most political commentators, she did not really think it conceivable that a Prime Minister in possession of a good majority could be thrown out between elections by her own party. Though she had always known that she had enemies who would be glad to see the back of her, she took it for granted that her senior colleagues and her appointees in the party organisation would rally round to ensure that the challenge was seen off, as it had been in 1989. She did not propose to canvass for herself, not just because to do so would have been undignified but because after fifteen years as leader she believed it should have been unnecessary. 'Tory MPs knew me, my record and my beliefs. If they were not already persuaded, there was not much left for me to persuade them with.'[71] She thought she could count on the Cabinet to back her unquestioningly against a challenger for whom most of them had little time; she expected Conservative Central Office and the whips to support her as the incumbent leader ('It's my office,' she told Wyatt);[72] and she assumed that she would have a committed and professional campaign team to maximise her vote. In fact none of these assumptions was borne out. She had herself formally nominated by Hurd and Major, but neither they nor the rest of the Cabinet subsequently did much more than that minimum to endorse her.* As party chairman Kenneth Baker made clear his own support for her, but ruled that Central Office should remain officially impartial: at least one of his vice-chairmen openly supported Heseltine. Tim Renton likewise chose to reflect the division in the party rather than the leader's will by keeping the whips' office scrupulously neutral.

---

*'She's wounded,' Hurd wrote in his diary. 'She's hard to work with, but most of us want to try, even though she finds it difficult to argue without causing offence.'[73] Major claims to have had no hesitation about seconding her nomination – 'I thought it bad politics to attempt to remove a sitting prime minister' – and says that he would have done more to support her campaign if anyone had thought to ask him.[74]

Above all the Prime Minister's supporters failed to put together a competent campaign team.

George Younger was again nominally her campaign manager, as he had been in 1989, largely because Peter Morrison persuaded him that otherwise it would have looked as if he was deserting her.[75] But Younger, though still MP for Ayr, was very fully occupied as chairman of the Royal Bank of Scotland. Even if he had been able to spend more time in the Commons, 'Gentleman George' was not the right man for the job: he was a grandee of the Scottish party who had been in the Cabinet from 1979 and scarcely knew most English MPs. The former Chief Whip, Michael Jopling, would have been a better choice: but he significantly refused to help. Tristan Garel-Jones had played an important role in 1989 but this time was not asked to help. ('I'd have got the old bat in,' he told Alan Watkins, who comments that he was 'probably right'.)[76] In practice the direction of the Thatcher campaign fell by default on Peter Morrison, her amiable but lazy PPS, helped by Michael Neubert (MP for Romford, a former whip and briefly a defence minister) and Gerry Neale (MP for North Cornwall). Beyond these it was not clear who was on the team and who was not. John Moore was said to be a member but was actually in America for most of the week; Norman Fowler says he was active on radio and television, though Lady Thatcher thinks he 'dropped out immediately'.[77] In fact her most visible cheerleader was Norman Tebbit, who characteristically took the fight to Heseltine by holding a cheeky press conference on his Belgravia doorstep.

Other supporters were frustrated not to be asked to do more. Rhodes Boyson – one ex-minister who had not defected – recalls bluntly that 'the pro-Thatcher campaign did not exist':

> On numerous radio and television programmes I spoke in favour of the retention of Mrs Thatcher as Prime Minister, but no contact was made with me by the official team that was supposed to be running her campaign. On the other hand I was regularly approached by the Heseltine campaign team, despite the fact that they knew I was committed to Mrs Thatcher.[78]

There is a well-established technique for Tory leadership elections – first developed by Peter Walker on behalf of Ted Heath in 1965 and refined by Airey Neave in support of Mrs Thatcher herself in 1975 – by which each MP is spoken to by at least two members of the campaign team, carefully chosen to elicit their true intentions: it is axiomatic that no promise of support is believed without being checked and double-checked. Such thoroughness is particularly important in the case of the incumbent leader, as Heath's team learned in 1975. But Morrison and his helpers failed either to conduct a thorough canvass or to treat what they were told with proper scepticism – as Tim Bell discovered:

> Ken Baker and I went through his list of who was going to vote for Margaret and found forty-six Heseltinies there the first time we glanced through it. He just rang people up and said 'Are you going to vote for Margaret?' and they said 'Yes', so he wrote them down. We knew we'd done our homework. He didn't have a clue.[79]

Morrison's willingness to believe what he was told is confirmed by many others. Steven Norris (MP for Oxford East 1983–7 and Epping Forest since 1988) had been part of her campaign team in 1989, but was another who was not asked to help a year later. In fact he would not have agreed again, since he was now intending to vote for Heseltine; but Morrison did not know this. He simply assumed Norris's continued support and failed to probe his evasive assurances.[80] Morrison was quite open about not running much of a campaign. The day before the ballot he told Alan Clark – who found him asleep in his room – that arm-twisting was counterproductive. He reckoned that Heseltine had 124 votes at most and predicted that 'some people may abstain on the first ballot in order to give Margaret a fright, then rally to her on the second'. Clark thought this was 'balls'. 'There is absolutely no oomph in her campaign *whatsoever*,' he lamented. 'Peter is useless . . . There isn't a single person working for her who cuts any ice at all.' He sensed 'the smell of decay . . . Something nasty is going to happen.'[81]

With hindsight Mrs Thatcher herself recognised that her insistence on going to Paris, which took her out of the country for the last two days of the campaign and the day of the ballot, might have been a mistake. It was not as if the CSCE was actually an important event. There was one symbolic treaty to be signed, cutting the levels of conventional forces; but it was more in the nature of an international celebration of the ending of the Cold War. President Bush, President Gorbachev, Chancellor Kohl and President Mitterrand were all going to be there, so Mrs Thatcher naturally wanted to be there too, to take her share of the credit. In truth it set the seal most appropriately on her premiership: but that was not her intention. By going to Paris she sent a signal that she was more interested in strutting the world stage than in meeting the worries of her troops at Westminster. She thought

it was more important for her to be seen doing her job than grub-
bing for votes; for the same reason she spent the Friday before the
poll in Northern Ireland. But this was not the message the party wanted
to hear. 'The plaudits are abroad,' Baker warned her, 'but the votes are
back home.'[82] He tried to persuade her to postpone the Ulster trip
and let Hurd represent her in Paris.[83] 'It's absolute madness,' Alan Clark
raged. 'There is no party mileage whatever in being at the Paris summit.
It just makes her seem snooty and remote.'[84] By contrast, he wrote,
Heseltine 'stands in the centre of the Members' Lobby, virtually challenging people to wish him good luck', while his team brought suppli-
ants to him for an audience.[85]*

It comes back to whether she should have stooped to canvass. Steven
Norris maintains that she could have turned round fifty votes if she
had made the effort, but that by choosing to go to Paris she deserved
to lose:

> The very miscalculation which led Margaret to squander her massive
> powers during the campaign were precisely the reason why so many
> of us saw the need to remove her. She had simply lost touch with
> her colleagues and . . . with the country . . . She showed by her
> indifference and incompetence that she deserved to be beaten.[87]

This assumes that she would have toured the tearooms if she had
not been in Paris. But that was not her strategy, while people like
Norris were going to vote against her anyway. There is an equally good
argument that she could quite safely have been out of the country,
getting on with the business of being Prime Minister, if only her
managers had been running an efficient campaign in her absence.
Maybe this underestimates the difficulty of running a campaign without
a candidate – especially since in this case her two principal supporters
were absent too (Hurd with her in Paris, Major in Huntingdon recovering from the removal of an infected wisdom tooth.) But one way
or another it came to the same thing. Tory MPs felt that she was taking
them for granted. It was not just that the Prime Minister herself did
not stoop to flatter and cajole them: her campaign team barely did so
either. As Major's biographer Penny Junor put it: 'She was seen to
assume their support, when they would have liked to have been asked
for it.'[88]

Fundamentally, the very fact that Mrs Thatcher could not put

---

*Norman Lamont told Wyatt that Heseltine had been canvassing 'like a child
molester hanging around the lavatories and waiting to pounce on people'.[86]

together a decent campaign showed that she had lost the support of the central core of the parliamentary party. The necessary level of enthusiasm simply was not there. Those MPs who were neither passionately for her nor passionately against were listening to their constituencies. Edwina Currie – once a prominent Thatcher supporter – let it be known that she would be voting against her, 'knowing full well that had she continued as party leader we would have lost my marginal seat and many others with it. By then voters other than committed Tories had had enough.'[89] When George Walden consulted his local party in Buckingham, the show of hands was for loyalty. But in private three-quarters of those who said they supported her told him it was time for her to go, and he suspects this was typical.[90] Ironically Mrs Thatcher herself had articulated the clinching argument. Replying to Kinnock and Ashdown at Prime Minister's Questions the previous autumn, she had asserted that 'the country's best long-term interests consist of keeping those who are in opposition there in perpetuity'.[91] It was precisely to ensure this that a large minority of Tory MPs thought that she should be replaced. Moreover they were right: with a new Prime Minister, Labour was kept in opposition, if not in perpetuity, at least for another seven years.

The one form of campaigning Mrs Thatcher did was to give three newspaper interviews – to the *Sunday Times*, *Sunday Telegraph* and *The Times*. But at least two of them were counterproductive. The first, with Michael Jones, was quite restrained: she repeated her views on Europe but quite moderately, claiming that she *was* a Euro-idealist, but the Europe she believed in was a Europe of freedom and diversity.[92] In the second, with Charles Moore, she was much more aggressive. First, she annoyed Douglas Hurd by floating the possibility of a referendum on the single currency.[93] Even Cecil Parkinson demurred, saying that this was 'precisely the sort of issue' that MPs were elected to decide,[94] while Heseltine pointed out that this was a good example of the type of unilateral policy announcement, ignoring the Cabinet, that he objected to. In the same interview she ridiculed the notion of Hurd as a unity candidate and set some alarm bells ringing by vowing to fight on whatever the size of vote against her. 'If we win according to the rules, we win.'[95]

But it was her third interview, with the new editor of *The Times*, Simon Jenkins, which was most controversial. It was notable, first, for the apocalyptic way Jenkins introduced it:

Under lowering rainclouds, Margaret Thatcher rested at Chequers before what could just be her last trip abroad as prime minister. She poured out a truly Wagnerian fury at the timing and content of Michael Heseltine's challenge to her leadership. Of that leadership she repeated as the thunder crashed outside, 'It's not finished yet . . . And it will be finished.'

More importantly, however, she used the interview to launch a powerful counterattack on Heseltine, charging that he would 'jeopardise all I have struggled to achieve'. Her staff had got hold of a copy of Heseltine's book *Where There's a Will*, and during the interview she stabbed at marked passages to make her point:

> If you read Michael Heseltine's book, you will find it more akin to some of the Labour party policies: intervention, corporatism, everything that pulled us down. There is a fundamental difference on economics and there's no point trying to hide it. Those of us who sat with Michael on economic discussions remember full well.

'It is one of my great accomplishments,' she claimed, 'that we have restructured our industry, got rid of so much over-manning, got the framework of law pretty well right.' But Heseltine, she alleged, would 'stop up the wellhead of enterprise' and take the country back to the bad old days:

> He says he would reduce the community charge, he would reduce taxation. That sounds just like the Labour party . . . We would end up with more community charge and more tax. We cannot go that way.

Jenkins concluded his article – published the day before the vote – with a shrewd assessment of the Prime Minister's situation:

> Mrs Thatcher this past weekend cuts the same solitary figure she cut in her first bid for the leadership. She came to the job as an outsider, the candidate of the 'peasants' revolt', of the dispossessed right wing. She studied the rules to which she is now vulnerable . . . She used these rules to combat the grandees . . . the party establishment, and crushed them. Now another generation is pushing forward. But she sees the battle not in generational but in ideological terms. The enemy is the same old guard, demanding the three Cs of consensus, compromise and corporatism, bound up in the person of Michael Heseltine.
>
> She has given the Conservative party three election victories in

a row, seeing it through good times and bad. To her, now is merely another bad time from which recovery is certain. Yet she must put up with tomorrow. Her resolution does not crack, but she does start forward in her chair and permit a rare glimpse of human vulnerability. 'After three election victories, it really would be the cruellest thing.'[96]

Her attack on Heseltine, who had been a member of her Cabinet for nearly seven years, may have cheered her committed supporters but it was badly received by middle-of-the-road MPs whose votes she needed. To characterise Heseltine – a successful businessman and self-made millionaire – as a virtual socialist seemed further evidence of failing judgement. In her memoirs she defended her strategy, insisting that the election *was* a contest of fundamentally opposed philosophies. 'It was a sign of the funk and frivolity of the whole exercise,' she wrote angrily, 'that they [Tory MPs] did not want to think anything was at stake apart from their seats.'[97] But their seats were just what they were thinking of; and six opinion polls published over the weekend indicated that the Tories would regain an instant lead over Labour – by margins ranging from 1 to 10 per cent – if Heseltine were leader.

The press reflected growing doubt that she would – or should – survive. The two *Telegraph* titles, the *Express* titles and the *Daily Mail* all stayed loyal. But *The Times* ran a series of editorials markedly sympathetic to Heseltine all week, before concluding on Tuesday morning that she should be supported after all. ('Don't worry,' Rupert Murdoch had assured Wyatt, 'it will be quite all right on the day, you'll see.)'[98] Murdoch's tabloids, the *Sun* and *Today*, stayed true, as did the *News of the World*.* But the *Sunday Times* broke ranks. Holding her responsible for renewed inflation, 'misplaced chauvinism' and the poll tax, Andrew Neil concluded that Mrs Thatcher was an 'electoral liability' and came out for Heseltine; as did the *Mail on Sunday*.[100] The *Financial Times* did not go that far, but argued that the Thatcher era needed to end soon. For a Prime Minister who had been sustained for years by an overwhelmingly supportive press, this was a very mixed verdict.

Altogether there was an unmistakable whiff of defeat in the air even before the vote. Douglas Hurd contributed to it by failing to deny categorically that he might stand himself. 'Against her, no,' he told an

---

*Mrs Thatcher showed her gratitude to the *Sun* by sending a defiantly upbeat message of congratulation for its twenty-first birthday: 'If it can come up fresh and bubbling for 21 years then so can I, and I shall do so.'[99]

interviewer, thus betraying that he recognised at least the possibility of a second ballot.[101] Willie Whitelaw issued a statement of support but told Wyatt that the whole thing was 'absolutely ghastly'. He believed that Mrs Thatcher should win, but he was afraid she would not win by enough. If it came to a second ballot he might have to advise her to stand down. 'Whatever happens, we can't have her humbled. But then she is wise enough to know that.'[102] John Major, nursing his wisdom tooth away from the snakepit of Westminster, thought that she would probably scrape through; but Jeffrey Archer, who came on Monday to tell him the gossip, told him that her chances were 'bleak'. Major's phone kept ringing with colleagues wanting him to be ready to stand if she did not win well enough.[103]

On Saturday night Mrs Thatcher held a dinner at Chequers for a few close friends plus her campaign team – Gordon Reece, Tim Bell and Alastair McAlpine; Ken Baker and her political secretary John Whittingdale; Morrison, Neubert and Neale; plus Mark and Carol, and of course Denis. Over dinner Carol sensed 'no particular feeling of unease' about the ballot. Morrison was still confident, predicting that she would get 220 votes to Heseltine's 110, with about forty abstentions. It was Mrs Thatcher herself who was now less sure, remembering the over-confidence of the Heath camp in 1975.[104] She never liked to count her chickens. But when Reece and Baker tried again to persuade her not to go to Paris, she refused to be diverted from her duty by mere party matters, saying that if she cancelled now she would seem to be 'running scared . . . That would be even worse. No, the decision is made.'[105] Next morning, as she left, she told Carol: 'I might lose, but I don't think I will.' But by this time Carol was beginning to feel forebodings, while Denis was 'positively pessimistic'. 'Crawfie,' he told his wife's faithful dresser, 'she's done for.'[106]

In Paris on Monday morning Mrs Thatcher had breakfast with George Bush at the American Embassy, followed by a joint press conference, mainly about the Gulf. She attended the first plenary session of the conference and emerged to give another press conference at the British Embassy, hailing the signing of what she called 'the biggest international disarmament agreement since the end of the last World War' and brushing off questions about the leadership.[107] After lunch with the other leaders at the Elysée Palace – at which her old adversary Helmut Kohl was particularly supportive – she made her own speech at the conference, confessing that she had initially been sceptical about the Helsinki process, but admitting that with the arrival of Gorbachev in the Kremlin it had worked in the end and hoping that the CSCE would provide a forum for continuing progress on establishing human rights in the old Soviet empire.[108] On Tuesday, while Tory MPs were voting in the House of Commons, she had talks with Gorbachev, Mitterrand and the President of Turkey and lunch with her favourite European leader, the Dutch Prime Minister Ruud Lubbers. The conference finished for the day around 4.30 p.m., and she returned to the British Embassy to await the result.

Back in London a meeting rather oddly composed of her campaign team (Younger, Tebbit, Morrison, Moore, Wakeham and Neale) plus party officials (Baker, Onslow and Renton) had drawn up alternative forms of words for her to use whatever the figures. Obviously if she won handsomely, or lost absolutely, there was no problem: discussion centred on what she should say if – as seemed increasingly likely – she led, but without the necessary margin to win on the first ballot. According to the rules (the same rules under which she had won in 1975) she had to gain not only a simple majority (187) but a margin of 15 per cent of all those entitled to vote – that is fifty-six votes. In the event of her falling short, Tebbit wanted her to make a clear commitment to fight on. Baker thought she should say she must consult her colleagues. It was Wakeham who proposed the compromise formula that she should declare her 'intention' to contest a second ballot. Mrs Thatcher accepted this advice, so that when the result came through she had her response ready.

Waiting in Peter Morrison's room at the embassy – Morrison had flown over to be with her for the result – she sat at the dressing table with her back to the company, displaying 'an inordinate calm'.[109] Charles Powell sat on the bed. Morrison, Ingham, Crawfie, Alastair Goodlad (deputy Chief Whip) and the Ambassador, Sir Ewen Fergusson, were also present. Around 6.20 p.m. Renton rang from London. (Powell, typically, had his own line and got the news half a minute earlier: behind Mrs Thatcher's back he gave a thumbs down.) Morrison answered, wrote down the figures and gave them to Mrs Thatcher. 'Not, I am afraid, as good as we had hoped.' She had only 204 votes to Heseltine's 152, with sixteen void or spoiled ballots: four votes short of the margin needed. She received the news calmly and after checking with Hurd that he and Major would still support her, immediately marched downstairs and out into the courtyard to give her pre-determined response to the waiting press. Dramatically interrupting John Sergeant's report for the BBC's *Six O'Clock News*, she seized his microphone and announced, live to the cameras:

I am naturally very pleased that I got more than half of the Parliamentary party and disappointed that it's not *quite* enough to win on the first ballot, so I confirm that it is my intention to let my name go forward for the second ballot.[110]★

It was meant to sound resolute and determined, but came out, in Alan Watkins' words, 'boastful and vainglorious . . . reminiscent of Mr Toad'.[112] Instead of saying she must consult her colleagues, as Baker had wanted, it sounded like another unilateral decision which brooked no advice from anyone. Nothing, in Watkins' view, did her more harm back home than this instant declaration on the steps of the Paris Embassy.[113]

Despite her reflex defiance, both Powell and Ingham believe that those around her, and probably Mrs Thatcher herself, knew in their hearts that she was finished.[114] So certainly did Denis. The first thing she did on coming back into the embassy was to ring him. 'Denis was fabulous: "Congratulations, Sweetie-Pie, you've won; it's just the rules," he said, as tears trickled down his face. He was crying for her, not for himself.' But when he put down the phone he turned to the friend who was with him and said: 'We've had it. We're out.'[115]

Meanwhile, as the political world scrambled to come to terms with the implications of the vote, Mrs Thatcher still had to attend a grand dinner at Versailles, laid on in the most lavish French style, complete with a ballet. She sent a message to Mitterrand that she would be late; but he, with typical gallantry, would not start without her. Her fellow leaders, united in appalled solidarity at the bizarre functioning of a parliamentary democracy which could depose a Prime Minister like an African dictator while she was out of the country, treated her with extravagant solicitude. 'She is a gutsy woman,' Barbara Bush recalled:

I gave her a big hug and told her that we had been waiting all day for the news. She said 'Not to worry' and went on to say she'd get it on the second ballot. George and I took Margaret by the arm and ran the gamut of the press.[116]

★That was not quite all. Asked by Peter Allen of ITN if the result did not mean that she had lost the confidence of the party, she repeated in almost the same words that she had got more than half the votes, if not quite the necessary margin – 'I think it was about 14.6 per cent' – and confirmed that 'I shall let my name go forward', this time omitting the word 'intention'. Then she turned her back on the hubbub, saying, 'I must go and do some telephone calls', and went back inside. A little later she sent Hurd out to make a brief, flat statement. 'The Prime Minister continues to have my full support and I am sorry that this destructive, unnecessary contest should be prolonged in this way.'[111]

Douglas Hurd was with her too:

> She carried herself magnificently at Versailles that evening. All eyes were upon her as dinner followed banquet, and course followed course at the immense table in the Galerie des Glaces. They looked upon her as some wounded eagle, who had herself wounded many in the past, but whom no one wished to see brought down, unable to soar again. Thanks to her own style and courage she was not humiliated . . . I never felt so admiring as on that last night in Paris in November 1990.[117]

But that evening, back in the Embassy with the faithful Crawfie, she was 'worn out'.

> She wasn't all right, she wasn't going to sleep, and we decided to have a drink, and then we just stayed up all night and talked about every aspect of her life – her childhood, her father, her mother, getting married to Denis, having the twins and her political career – and we just never went to bed, and then about half-past six we sort of got ready for the day.[118]

'Treachery with a smile on its face'

Mrs Thatcher returned to London next morning having had no sleep, still determined to fight on. She had after all comfortably defeated her challenger and fallen only four votes short of outright victory. At least one devoted commentator, William Rees-Mogg in the *Independent*, managed to persuade himself that her majority, though not quite enough to avert a second ballot, was nevertheless 'decisive'.[119] Woodrow Wyatt toyed with the notion that she could ask the Queen to grant her a General Election.[120] Mrs Thatcher herself still believed she could win the second ballot: 'if the campaign were to go into high gear and every potential supporter pressed to fight for my cause'.[121] She knew now that this had not been the case so far. But most observers shared the view bluntly expressed in his memoirs by Michael Heseltine. 'To anyone with the faintest knowledge of how Westminster politics work, her position was manifestly untenable. It says much for Mrs Thatcher's capacity for self-delusion that at first she stubbornly refused to recognise the fact.'[122]

The BBC's political editor John Cole felt the mood as soon as he got to the House of Commons on Wednesday morning. 'Conservative MPs began stopping me in the corridors and in the Members' Lobby to tell me that if she persisted in her declared intention to enter the second ballot, they would switch their votes to Michael Heseltine.'The Heseltine camp was now confident of winning if she stayed in the contest.[123] But by the same token, urgent discussions had already been going on all over London to prevent that eventuality. The younger members of the Cabinet had no wish to see Mrs Thatcher deposed to put Heseltine in her place. Whenever she went, they wanted her to be replaced by one of themselves. If it really looked as if she could not beat Heseltine, it followed that she should be persuaded to withdraw in favour of another candidate who could. The supposedly crucial meeting took place on Tuesday evening at the home of Tristan Garel-Jones in Catherine Place (near Buckingham Gate). Those present included four Cabinet ministers from the left of the party – Chris Patten, William Waldegrave, Malcolm Rifkind and Tony Newton – plus Norman Lamont from the right; two or three ministers from outside the Cabinet – John Patten, Douglas Hogg and (rather incongruously) Alan Clark. Douglas Hurd's PPS, Tim Yeo, was also invited; and Richard Ryder came later.*

It was not really much of a conspiracy. 'The really sickening thing,' Clark wrote, 'was the urgent and unanimous abandonment of the Lady. Except for William's little opening tribute, she was never mentioned again.'[125] But with thirty to forty of her supporters on the first ballot said to have deserted, the conclusion that she was finished was pretty obvious. Even Clark did not speak up for her but made a bizarre pitch for Tom King instead, possibly as a diversionary tactic. But the consensus of the group at this stage was to back Hurd. The importance of the Catherine Place meeting was not that it decided anything, but simply that it showed the way several of the younger ministers were thinking. Ken Clarke, John Wakeham and John Gummer had reached the same conclusion without being present; and others were holding countless similar conversations by telephone.

Before Mrs Thatcher returned to London three more formal consultations had taken place. John Wakeham was asked to canvass the Cabinet, but he had an inescapable engagement as Energy Secretary to launch the prospectus for electricity privatisation – the business of government was still just about being carried on – so he delegated the task

---

*They were not, as Clark suggests, all former 'Blue Chips'. Garel-Jones, the two Pattens and Waldegrave were; but Rifkind (whom Clark thought the dominant speaker) and Newton were not, and Lamont and Clark himself were supposed to be Thatcherites. Cecil Parkinson subsequently blamed 'the Catherine Place gang' for hijacking the next day's Cabinet consultation; but they were not so much a 'gang' as a representative group of younger ministers.[124]

to John MacGregor. Tim Renton collected the impressions of the whips; and the Executive of the 1922 Committee met at eleven o'clock to consider its advice to the Prime Minister. All told the same story of crumbling support. The question was who would tell Mrs Thatcher. Denis was the first to try when she returned to Downing Street at lunchtime. 'Don't go on, love,' he begged her. But she felt – 'in my bones' – that she owed it to her supporters not to give up so long as there was still a chance.[126] Wakeham warned that she would face the argument that she should step down voluntarily to avoid humiliation, but professed that this was not his own view. All the others ducked it. These were the famous 'men in suits' who were supposed to tell her when it was time to go. But over a working lunch at Number Ten 'the greybeards', as Hurd called them, 'failed to deliver the message'.[127] Renton did pass on Whitelaw's fear that she might be humiliated; but MacGregor failed to spell out the extent of the Cabinet's defection, and Cranley Onslow likewise hid behind the 1922's neutrality and offered no clear opinion. Against these muffled messages, Kenneth Baker assured her that the party workers were still strongly behind her; and Norman Tebbit argued that she was still the best candidate to beat Heseltine. 'The message of the meeting, even from those urging me to fight on, was implicitly demoralising,' Lady Thatcher wrote in retrospect.[128] But for the moment she formed the impression that she should still fight on.

The first requirement was to get Hurd and Major to re-nominate her. Hurd agreed at once, 'with a good grace'; but when she phoned Major in Huntingdon his hesitation was 'palpable'.[129] It was not that he was unwilling, he explained in his memoirs, but he would have liked some show of consultation before she committed herself. Instead, 'she simply assumed that she had my support . . . Taken aback, I paused before replying, "If that is what you want, I will" . . . Once again I despaired at her style even as I pledged my support.'[130]

She had still more difficulty in recruiting a new campaign team. Younger had stipulated before agreeing for the first ballot that he would not do it for a second. He believed that victory even by a single vote on the first ballot would have sufficed; but that failing to win at the first attempt made her position impossible.[131] John Wakeham found himself pitchforked into the vacancy by Tebbit simply announcing on television that he was the Prime Minister's new campaign manager. Wakeham was a wily fox; but he was not the man to inspire a last-ditch fightback since, as Alan Watkins wrote, 'he did not believe in the cause he was meant to be promoting . . . Inevitably he was more of an undertaker than a campaign manager.'[132] Not that anyone could have made much difference now. Garel-Jones declined to help, and so did Richard Ryder. She was not surprised at the former, but was hurt by the latter's defection. Ryder had been her first political secretary, and married her former secretary Caroline Stephens; together they had been at the heart of her private office in the heroic days of 1979–82, and she had promoted him rapidly after he entered Parliament in 1983. Another protégé whose desertion hit her hard was Peter Lilley, whom she had promoted to the Cabinet on Ridley's resignation in July but who had sent a message while she was still in Paris declining to help write her speech in the confidence debate which Labour had tabled for Thursday. Like Macbeth before his final battle, she was beset every hour by news of further haemorrhaging of support.

But still she had a statement to make in the Commons on the Paris summit. As she left Downing Street she called out to reporters: 'I fight on. I fight to win', managing, as she later wrote, to sound more confident than by now she felt. 'I watched it live,' Gyles Brandreth wrote in his diary, 'and the way she swept towards the camera was wonderful to behold. But the feeling seems to be it's all over.'[133] In the House she gave another characteristically brave performance, hailing 'the end of the Cold War in Europe and the triumph of freedom, democracy and the rule of law', spiritedly rebutting opposition taunts and thanking the one Tory loyalist who hoped that she would 'continue to bat for Britain with all the vigour, determination and energy at her command'. Only once, uncharacteristically, did she forget the second half of a question and have to be reminded what it was.[134] Then Tebbit took her round the tearoom in a belated effort to shore up her support. 'I had never experienced such an atmosphere before,' she wrote in her memoirs. 'Repeatedly I heard: "Michael has asked me two or three times for my vote already. This is the first time we have seen you."'[135]

Around five o'clock she saw the Queen and assured her that she still intended to contest the second ballot. What finally convinced her that her cause was hopeless was a series of individual interviews with the members of the Cabinet between six and eight that evening. This procedure has been widely regarded as another misjudgement. Lady Thatcher herself admitted that if John MacGregor had given her the full picture earlier she might have done it differently.[136] 'In asking for their support, I was also putting myself at their mercy.'[137] Others have suggested that her colleagues might have found it harder to tell her their view collectively round the Cabinet table in Downing Street, with the Chancellor and Foreign Secretary presumably supporting her, than they did in the more informal setting of her room at the House of Commons. The summons to see her individually also meant that they all congregated along the ministerial corridor – in Wakeham's, Patten's and Gummer's rooms – like schoolboys outside the headmaster's study, to concert what they were going to say before they went in. This explains why, when they saw her, so many of them said the same thing. Mrs Thatcher sat tense and upright at the end of one sofa next to the fireplace, the ministers on the opposite sofa. 'Almost to a man,' she wrote bitterly, 'they used the same formula. This was that they themselves would back me, of course, but that regretfully they did not believe I could win . . . I felt I could almost join in the chorus.'[138]

There were some variations. Clarke, Patten and Rifkind were the only three to tell her frankly that they would not support her if she stood again. Clarke – 'in the brutalist style he has cultivated' – warned her that Heseltine would become Prime Minister unless she made way for either Hurd or Major. She was 'visibly stunned' by this estimate.[139] Rifkind – 'probably my sharpest personal critic in the Cabinet' – and Patten – 'a man of the Left' – gave the same message. Only Baker and Parkinson told her that she could still win. The rest, with varying degrees of embarrassment (some with tears in their eyes) advised her to give up. Lilley, Howard, Gummer and Lamont (and also Francis Maude, who somehow slipped in, though not a member of the Cabinet) she regarded as traitors. Waldegrave, MacGregor and Newton had never been her supporters anyway. Only Peter Brooke ('charming, thoughtful and loyal'), David Waddington ('a steadfast friend . . . in deepest distress') and Tom King (who suggested that she might offer to go at the end of the Gulf war) managed to give the same advice without arousing her contempt.

The one interview she describes as light relief was that with Alan Clark ('a gallant friend'), who also somehow managed to get in to see her. He too told her she would lose, but encouraged her to go down fighting gloriously to the end. Earlier he had written in his diary that 'the immediate priority is to find a way, tactfully and skilfully, to talk her out of standing a second time'. Presumably this was his way of doing so. After a pause while she contemplated this Wagnerian scenario she said: 'It'd be so terrible if Michael won. He would undo everything I have fought for.'[140] So maybe Clark, while convincing her that he was still on her side, had more effect than the fainthearts whom she accused of deserting her.

By the end of this dismal procession Mrs Thatcher had accepted that the game was up. 'I had lost the Cabinet's support. I could not even muster a credible campaign team. It was the end.'[141] 'She was pale, subdued and shaking her head, saying "I am not a quitter, I am not a quitter,"' Baker recalled. 'But the tone was one of resignation, not defiance.'[142] She was upset not so much by her poor vote in the ballot, which could be attributed to electoral nerves, nor by the frank opposition of those who had never supported her, but by what she saw as the treachery of those from whom she felt entitled to expect loyalty. 'What grieved me,' she wrote, 'was the desertion of those I had always considered friends and allies and the weasel words whereby they had transmuted their betrayal into frank advice and concern for my fate.'[143] It was treachery, she charged later on television. 'Treachery with a smile on its face.'[144]

The best answer to this allegation comes from Kenneth Clarke. 'There was no treachery,' he told one of his biographers. The Cabinet gave her 'wholly sensible advice' that, having failed to win by a sufficient margin on the first ballot, she would not win the second and should now withdraw. 'That was nothing to do with the Cabinet. It was the parliamentary party where she'd suffered the defeat.'[145] There is no reason to think that the continued support of Howard, Lilley and Lamont would have reversed the tide and allowed her to beat Heseltine squarely at the second attempt. The damage was already done. 'It's no good, Woodrow,' Lamont told Wyatt. 'She is going to be terribly badly beaten by Heseltine. We can't possibly have Heseltine as Prime Minister. I would support her to the end . . . but it's no good.'[146] The fact was that not just her long-time enemies but many of her strongest supporters thought it was time for her to go, in order to protect her legacy. On this analysis it was not merely the party but Thatcherism itself which needed a new leader if it was to survive. It was cruel, but Margaret Thatcher had never been one to let personal feelings stand in the way of what she thought was right. Though she talked of loyalty, she had never shown much mercy herself to colleagues who threatened or disappointed her, from Stevas, Soames and Gilmour in the first term, through Pym, Rees and Biffen in the second, to Moore and Howe in the last phase – to say nothing of those like Prior, Heseltine, Tebbit and Lawson, driven to resign by the impossibility of working with her. As Prime Ministers go, she was a good butcher: that was part of her strength. But she could not complain when she was butchered in turn. She had only gained the leadership in the first place by boldly challenging Ted Heath when all his other colleagues were restrained by loyalty. She had lived by the sword and was always likely to perish by the sword. Really she would have wanted it no other way. As she said, she was not a quitter. What perhaps galled her most in retrospect about the Cabinet's advice was that it forced her to quit voluntarily when temperamentally she would rather have gone down to defeat, as Clark suggested. But her first priority was to defend her legacy, and she was reluctantly persuaded that self-immolation was the only way to do it.★

Before she went back to Number Ten to work on her speech for the confidence debate next day – an ironic task in the circumstances – a number of diehards came to urge that she could still win through if she got on the telephone and canvassed every Member personally. First Michael Portillo, with Norman Tebbit; then a deputation of backbenchers and junior ministers from the 92 Group – George Gardiner, John Townend, David Maclean, Chris Chope and Edward Leigh. She was grateful – 'With even a drop of this spirit in higher places,' she wrote later, 'it might indeed have been possible'[148] – but knew it was too late. Later in the evening another delegation from the No Turning Back group – Michael Forsyth, Michael Fallon, Neil Hamilton and Portillo again – came to Downing Street with the same purpose: their arguments were demolished, rather bravely, by John Gummer who was there helping with the speech. Earlier Gummer had been one of those in tears as he urged her to stand down; now it was Mrs Thatcher who 'had to wipe away a tear as the enormity of what had happened crowded in'.[149] The fight had finally gone out of her. Hamilton thought she 'presented the most pathetic spectacle he had seen in his life'.[150]

At 11.15 p.m. she rang Tim Bell and told him: 'I've decided to go. Can you come and see me?' He went, collecting Gordon Reece on the way, and 'blubbed hopelessly' in the car on the way.[151] Her two 'laughing boys', as she had called them in happier times, with Fallon and Portillo, sat up with her till two o'clock helping to write her resignation statement, while Andrew Turnbull rang round the Governor of the Bank and others to give them advance warning of her decision. Around 1.30 a.m. Jeffrey Archer arrived with her nomination papers for the second ballot, signed by Hurd and Major: he had driven to Huntingdon to get Major's signature – a wasted journey, as it turned out. On Horse Guards' Parade, after dining with Mark, Carol and Alistair McAlpine at Mark's club, Denis hugged Carol and cried: 'Oh, it's just the *disloyalty* of it all.'[152] But he had been giving the same advice as the Cabinet all along. Ronnie Millar recorded his 'intense relief' at the outcome. 'The last thing Denis Thatcher wants is to see his wife humiliated.'[153]

★Ronnie Millar, always ready with an apt quotation, cites Antony's farewell to Cleopatra: 'Finish, good lady, the bright day is done, and we are for the dark' – but with the crucial substitution of 'or' for 'and'. With a new leader, they believed, the party could recover; with her, it would not.[147]

As she always did before a big decision, she slept on it – briefly – before committing herself. When Portillo, Forsyth, Leigh and Michael Brown turned up again at 6.30 next morning Powell refused them admission. At 7.30 she asked Turnbull to arrange another audience with the Queen. Then at 9.00 she chaired her final Cabinet, brought forward to allow members to attend the memorial service for Lady Home. It was an intensely awkward occasion. She began by reading out her prepared statement, which was a model of dignified euphemism:

> Having consulted widely among colleagues, I have concluded that the unity of the party and the prospects of victory in a General Election would be better served if I stood down to enable Cabinet colleagues to enter the ballot for the leadership. I should like to thank all those in Cabinet and outside who have given me such dedicated support.[154]

Twice she almost broke down, but she rejected Parkinson's suggestion that James Mackay should read it for her. Mackay then read a statement of appreciation on behalf of the Cabinet – drafted by Robin Butler – and Hurd and Baker added personal tributes of their own. She then expanded on her statement by emphasising the importance of the Cabinet now uniting to defeat Heseltine – that was why she had resigned – and to protect all the things she had stood for over the past eleven years. Insisting that she could handle business but not sympathy, she recovered her composure to conduct the rest of the meeting in her usual brisk manner. After a short coffee break she reported on her latest talks with Bush and Gorbachev in Paris, and it was agreed to send another armoured brigade to the Gulf. 'She was clearly getting back into her stride,' Baker wrote. 'But towards the end of the meeting I could see that she was close to tears again.'[155]

The announcement of Mrs Thatcher's withdrawal from the contest was made at 9.25 a.m. (during the Cabinet's coffee break), though of course she remained Prime Minister until the party had elected her successor. The news, though not unexpected at Westminster, evoked extraordinary scenes of jubilation and disbelief among the public: she had been there so long that her departure was hard to comprehend. People reported spontaneous clapping and cheering on trains and planes, in pubs and in the street. Ten years later the *Guardian* printed a heavily slanted selection of people's memories of how they heard the news, making it almost equivalent to the news of President Kennedy's assassination exactly twenty-seven years before. The young artist Tracey Emin was walking through the Elephant and Castle:

I looked up at the buses, and people were banging on the windows and going 'Yeah!' And I noticed people were jumping up and down in the street . . . People looked so happy. I felt absolute jubilation.

The film director Ken Loach was reminded of how people had felt at the end of the war. But a secretary in Didsbury, near Manchester, recalled being in a pub when the news came through on the television:

Everyone shouted 'Hurrah!' and I stood up and said 'How dare you? She's the best thing that ever happened to this country' . . . I felt very sad, like we were losing a national figure whose importance we wouldn't fully appreciate until she'd gone.[156]

Last rites

Even in defeat Mrs Thatcher still had a last bravura performance up her sleeve. Another leader might have chosen to let someone else answer Labour's 'no confidence' motion – Hurd perhaps, or John MacGregor, since she no longer had a deputy. On the contrary, she saw it as a last opportunity to vindicate her record. Even as her position crumbled the previous evening, she had not stopped working on her speech for the next day: never had her dedication been more impressive or her power of concentration more extraordinary. She was up before dawn to carry on crafting it. 'Each sentence,' she wrote in her memoirs, 'was my testimony at the Bar of History.'[157] Crawfie got her doctor to give her an extra shot of vitamin C to keep her going.

Before the debate she had Prime Minister's Questions to answer. She was given a fairly gentle ride – even Kinnock managed a half-hearted tribute – and in two of her replies suggested that she had already started looking to the future. 'The same person, in a slightly different capacity, will be still be available to serve Britain in whatsoever way it happens,' she assured Tony Marlow; and when Jonathan Aitken hoped that she would continue to call for a referendum on the single currency, she confessed: 'What my hon. Friend says had in fact secretly occurred to me – that one's voice might be listened to after.'[158] But all this soft soap was just what she could not handle. She was afraid that if Kinnock, opening the debate, had shown the wit to smother her in sympathy she might have broken down. But as she wrote: 'Mr Kinnock, in all his years as Opposition leader, never let me down. Right to the end he struck every wrong note.' He made the same speech he would have made the previous week, or the previous year. His 'standard partisan rant' made it easy for her, when 'one

concession to the generosity that the House feels on such occasions
. . . might have disarmed me and eroded the control that was barely
keeping my emotions in check'.[159] As soon as she rose to speak she
replied in kind, mocking the Labour leader's 'windy rhetoric' and even
managing to contrast the Tories' relatively simple leadership ballot
favourably with Labour's byzantine electoral college.

She started her speech proper by reminding the House of Nicholas
Henderson's gloomy 1979 dispatch describing Britain's economic failure
and loss of influence in the world since 1945. 'Conservative government has changed all that,' she boasted. 'Once again, Britain stands tall
in the councils of Europe and of the world, and our policies have
brought unparalleled prosperity to our citizens at home.' She went on
to claim that her Government had 'given power back to the people
on an unprecedented scale': she cited the curbing of trade-union power,
wider home and share ownership, the extension of choice in health
and education, privatisation, lower taxes, two million more jobs, more
new businesses, an enterprise economy and higher living standards for
all. When the Liberal Democrat Simon Hughes intervened to ask about
increased poverty she simply denied it, repeating her insistence that
'people on all levels of income are better off than they were in 1979'
and asserted that the Liberals wanted everyone to be poor equally.
'One does not create wealth and opportunity that way.' Once the interventions started she really got into her stride; and by the time she
came on to defending her record in Europe she was ready to demolish
Kinnock one last time. He did not know whether he was in favour
of the single currency or not, she jeered, because 'he does not even
know what it means'. 'It is a hypothetical question,' he weakly interjected. 'Absolute nonsense,' she retorted:

> It is appalling. He says that it is a hypothetical question. It will not
> be a hypothetical question. Someone must go to Europe and argue,
> knowing what it means.

It was at this point that Alan Beith, the Liberal Democrats' deputy
leader, asked if she intended to 'continue her personal fight against a
single currency and an independent central bank when she leaves
office'. Before she could reply Denis Skinner interjected from below
the gangway: 'No. She's going to be the governor.' 'What a good idea!'
she shot back. 'I had not thought of that.'*

---

*Actually Skinner had made the same suggestion two days earlier, but no one
had picked it up then.[160]

But if I were, there would be no European central bank accountable to no one, least of all national Parliaments. The point of that kind of Europe with a central bank is no democracy, taking powers away from every single Parliament, and having a single currency, a monetary policy and interest rates which take all political power away from us . . . A single currency is about . . . a federal Europe by the back door. So I shall consider the proposal of the hon. Member for Bolsover. Now where were we? I am enjoying this.

From this moment, she had the House in the palm of her hand. The Eurosceptic Tory Michael Cartiss called out, 'Cancel it. You can wipe the floor with these people.' She went on to expound her vision of 'a free and open Britain in a free and open Europe . . . in tune with the deepest instincts of the British people', took credit for winning the Cold War, and ended with the Gulf, comparing it with the Falklands. Her last words were the apotheosis of the Iron Lady:

> There is something else which one feels. That is a sense of this country's destiny: the centuries of history and experience which ensure that, when principles have to be defended, when good has to be upheld and when evil has to be overcome, Britain will take up arms. It is because we on this side have never flinched from difficult decisions that this House and this country can have confidence in this Government today.[161]

It was an astonishing performance, a parliamentary occasion to equal – or rather trump – Howe's speech, which had precipitated the whole landslide just nine days earlier, never to be forgotten by anyone who was present in the House or watched on television. As Ronnie Millar commented, she really did seem to be enjoying herself:

> It was not so much what she said as the spectacle of an irrepressible human spirit . . . that gripped and moved the House. She had never shown to such superb effect in all the years of her supremacy. It was great theatre, gallant, without a trace of self-pity and was seen as such by the House which is at its best when, irrespective of Party, it recognises and salutes courage . . . By the time she sat down her domination of the House was so complete that her downfall seemed to some to have been a madness of the moment. Others who, in the ballot, had voted for her opponent, began to wonder what they had done.[162]

Woodrow Wyatt, still unable to comprehend why she had given in to the cowards, was disgusted by the hypocritical reception of her speech:

The Tory benches were cheering her, the foulest of the assassins were cheering her. There was a sense sweeping over the Tory benches of deep shame over what they had done to this marvellous woman . . . and the knowledge that they would live to rue the day.[163]

At the end of the debate Baker had a drink with her in her room. 'She was still resilient and looked as if she had freshly stepped off the boat after a great tour.'[164] She was still angry about what her own party had done to her. 'They've done what the Labour party didn't manage to do in three elections,' she told Carol. But for the moment she was still on a high. 'Carol, I think my place in history is assured.'[165] The next day her sense of betrayal increased. 'They sold me down the river,' she told Wyatt bitterly; she blamed 'anonymous secret balloting' and explained her poor campaign by saying that her managers had not wanted to boost Heseltine by treating him as an equal.[166] She was particularly hurt that younger ministers like Waldegrave, whom she had promoted, came out against her. 'It seemed as though I could really trust practically nobody.'[167] Two weeks later she was still bitter at the Cabinet advising her to stand down, and complained that only one member – Parkinson, presumably – would have gone out campaigning for her. 'They had no courage at all . . . I have been wronged.'[168] Parkinson himself recorded a sharp riposte when someone suggested that in the second ballot they would 'pin regicide on Heseltine'. 'Oh no,' Mrs Thatcher responded. 'It wasn't Heseltine, it was the Cabinet.' 'It was said without rancour. It was, to her, a simple statement of fact.'[169]

Nominations for the second ballot had already closed. To maximise the anti-Heseltine vote, and avoid the appearance of a Cabinet stitch-up, it was decided that both Hurd and Major should stand, thus giving Tory MPs what many had been demanding: a wider choice. Hurd, the older and much more experienced man – nominated by Tom King and seconded by Chris Patten – was the safe pair of hands. Major – nominated by Lamont and seconded by Gummer – was thirteen years younger and an unknown quantity. He had risen with astonishing speed (he had been Chancellor for only a year, and Foreign Secretary for three months before that) and seemed to owe his career entirely to Mrs Thatcher's patronage. But the fact that he was her protégé made it natural for those who felt guilty at ditching her to make amends by supporting him, though anyone who knew Major at all well knew he was not a Thatcherite. 'Many will vote for him thinking he is on the right wing,' Willie Whitelaw correctly predicted. 'They'll be disappointed and soon find out that he isn't.'[170] Mrs Thatcher already had doubts herself, and initially declared that she would not endorse any candidate; but this was quickly forgotten, and over the weekend she did more canvassing for Major – mainly by telephone – than she had ever done for herself. Ironically she had to counter an impulse among some of her diehard admirers to switch to Heseltine, from disgust at the way Major's most prominent backers had abandoned her. She told them – and tried to believe it herself – that the best way of preserving her legacy was to support Major. Though she recognised that Hurd had been loyal, she had never really trusted him; more than Heseltine in some ways, he represented everything in the party that she had striven to reject, as she explained to Wyatt:

It may be inverted snobbishness but I don't want old style, Old Etonian Tories of the old school to succeed me and go back to the old complacent, consensus ways. John Major is someone who has fought his way up from the bottom and is far more in tune with the skilled and ambitious and worthwhile working classes than Douglas Hurd is.[171]

The short campaign was very gentlemanly – Heseltine wrote that it was 'as though the poison had been let out of the system'[172] – and once the momentum had swung behind Major, the result was never in doubt. Heseltine had always known that his chance would have gone the moment Mrs Thatcher withdrew, and so it was. The result of the voting on 27 November gave Major 185 votes to Heseltine's 131 and Hurd's fifty-six. Though strictly speaking Major was still two votes short of an absolute majority, both Heseltine and Hurd immediately withdrew, leaving Major the clear winner – with, as Mrs Thatcher reflected wryly, nineteen votes fewer than she had won seven days earlier. Nevertheless it was the result she had campaigned for, so as soon as Hurd and Heseltine had made their statements she burst through the connecting door to Number Eleven to congratulate her successor. 'It's everything I've dreamt of for such a long time,' she gushed, hugging Norma. 'The future is assured.'[173] She wanted to go outside with Major while he spoke to the media, but was persuaded that she must let him have his moment of glory alone. She was photographed peeping sadly from an upstairs window while Major made his statement and answered questions. This was the moment when the reality of her loss of office must have hit her.

She had spent the previous few days packing up and holding farewell parties for her staff and supporters. It was for just this eventuality that she and Denis had bought the house in Dulwich, so at least she had somewhere to go; and the housewife in her was good at the business of packing and clearing up. So long as she was busy she had no time to grieve.★ While the journalists outside filed stories about history being made, Carol wrote, inside Number Ten all was strenuous activity:

> Margaret was standing in her stockinged feet surrounded by mobile wardrobes and tea chests, deciding whether to wrap the knick-knacks in two layers of paper to prevent breakage or whether one would do . . . All day Saturday Denis's battered Ford Cortina ferried stuff up and down to Dulwich. I was doing the same in my Mini Metro, taking my gear from Downing Street to Fulham.[175]

Margaret and Denis went to Chequers for the last time for the weekend, attended church on Sunday morning and were heartbroken to leave the country home they had made good use of for the past eleven years. On Monday she paid a short visit to thank the workers at Central Office, during which she unwisely suggested that she would be 'a very good back seat driver'. This was widely taken as a warning that she intended to manipulate Major even after she had left office. In fact she was referring to George Bush, not to Major at all. She had been 'very, very thrilled', she said, that Bush had telephoned after her resignation was announced. They had discussed the Gulf and it was in that context that she had declared: 'He won't falter, and I won't falter. It's just that I won't be pulling the levers there. But I shall be a very good back seat driver.'[176] Nevertheless she would have more temptation, and more opportunity, to interfere at home, so the phrase rang true, with a disturbing implication for Major.

She held a lunch at Number Ten for old friends and allies of the past decade, including Keith Joseph, Peter Thorneycroft and Nicholas Ridley, but magnanimously not excluding some of those, like Lilley, who had deserted her. Then in the evening there was a farewell party

---

★It was different when there was nothing more to do. Peregrine Worsthorne – who had not been an unwavering supporter – found himself summoned to Number Ten to say goodbye. After half an hour he made to go, but Bernard Ingham begged him not to leave her. When he finally left he passed Carol coming in with a cold chicken in a string bag for supper. 'Seldom have I witnessed a sadder scene.'[174]

for the staff at Number Ten, including all the drivers, cleaners, detectives and telephone girls as well as the members of her private office. Mrs Thatcher stood on a chair and told them: 'Life begins at sixty-five.' Various presentations were made. Her staff gave her a first edition of Kipling's poems and also a small high-frequency radio so that, as Andrew Turnbull told her, 'wherever you are in the world, you can continue to be cross with the BBC'.[177]

On Tuesday, while Tory MPs were still voting on her successor, she made her last appearance answering Prime Minister's Questions (though had the result not been decisive, she might have had to do it again on Thursday). Again it was an occasion more for tributes than for recrimination. Kinnock asked if her successor would scrap the poll tax and almost for the first time she slipped and referred to it by that name herself before correcting herself, professing to believe that the next government would not abandon it. When a Liberal Democrat asked if she would now consider the use of the single transferable vote for national elections she replied ironically: 'I am sure the hon. Lady will appreciate that I am all for first past the post.' Finally she told a Tory member that his was the 7,498th question she had answered in 698 sessions at the dispatch box. By the time she answered her last question a few minutes later the final tally was 7,501.[178]

Finally, on Wednesday morning, she left the stage, only with difficulty holding back the tears as she made her final statement:

> Ladies and Gentlemen. We're leaving Downing Street for the last time after eleven and a half wonderful years and we're very happy that we leave the United Kingdom in a very, very much better state than when we came eleven and a half years ago.

It had been 'a tremendous privilege', they had been 'wonderfully happy years' and she was 'immensely grateful' to all her staff and the people who had sent her flowers and letters:

> Now it's time for a new chapter to open and I wish John Major all the luck in the world. He'll be splendidly served, and he has the makings of a great Prime Minister, which I'm sure he'll be in a very short time.
> Thank you very much. Goodbye.[179]

When the car arrived in Dulwich, a journalist asked her what she would do now. 'Work. That is all we have ever known.'[180] Her trouble would be finding enough to do.

18

Afterlife

Unemployed workaholic

Bhe familiar spectacle of the removal vans in Downing Street the
morning after a General Election is an undignified one. Mrs Thatcher
had witnessed at first hand Ted Heath's abrupt and unanticipated ejec-
tion from office in February 1974. It was very largely the example of
his predicament, with no alternative home to retreat to, so that he was
forced to squat for several months in a small flat lent him by a Tory
MP, that had prompted her to buy an unsuitable house in Dulwich as
some sort of insurance policy against a similar fate. Her dismissal was
actually less abrupt than most: she had almost a week between her decision to resign and the moment of departure – six days to pack up and
say her farewells. Yet her defeat was also more brutal, since it was inflicted
not by the electorate but by her own MPs. In June 1983 and June 1987
she had been packed and psychologically prepared: in November 1990
she was not. The natural shock felt by any discarded leader was exacerbated by a bitter sense of grievance. 'I have never been defeated in
an election,' she told an American magazine five months after the event,
and she repeated the phrase five times during the same interview. 'I
have never been defeated in a vote of confidence in Parliament, so I
don't know what it would be like . . . I was never defeated by the
people.'¹ Though she knew she had been lucky to have lasted so long,
and never seriously contemplated trying to reverse the verdict, she never
got over the feeling that she had been cruelly wronged.

There is no established role in British life for former Prime Ministers.
In recent times Anthony Eden, Harold Macmillan and Harold Wilson
all resigned between elections from a mixture of declining health and
tarnished reputation. Apart from writing a dozen volumes of memoirs
between them, they largely took themselves off the political stage,

748

though Macmillan reappeared much later with the licence of extreme old age to excoriate Mrs Thatcher from the House of Lords. Her two more recent Conservative predecessors, Alec Douglas-Home and Ted Heath, were both defeated at General Elections; both stayed on in politics, but offered contrasting models of conduct. Home gracefully resigned the party leadership, joined his successor's Shadow Cabinet and then served loyally as Foreign Secretary from 1970 to 1974 before going back to the Lords. Heath by contrast bitterly resented being forced out of the leadership and stayed stubbornly in the Commons as a lone, angry but largely ineffectual critic of Mrs Thatcher and all her works. Where Home was hailed as a paragon of gentlemanly self-abnegation, Heath was correspondingly condemned for his unappeasable disloyalty. Though she was often angered by Heath's sniping against her, when her turn came, it was his example rather than Sir Alec's that Mrs Thatcher chose to follow.

Jim Callaghan found the best balance between retirement and elder statesmanship. Though only two years older than Mrs Thatcher when he left office, he had always cultivated an air of benign seniority. He did not wholly abandon politics, but he had a happy family life, a farm in Sussex and a quiverful of grandchildren to solace his defeat; above all he was able to bask in the satisfaction of a career unexpectedly fulfilled, without the need to keep refighting old battles. Mrs Thatcher enjoyed none of these blessings. She was a compulsive workaholic, still full of energy, with no interests outside politics. The loss of office deprived her almost overnight of her main reason for living. She had always dreaded the prospect of retirement. 'I think my definition of Hell is having a lot of time and not having any idea of what to do with it,' she told *She* magazine in 1987.[2] 'Happiness is not doing nothing,' she reiterated to *Woman's Own*. 'Happiness in an adult consists of having a very full day, being absolutely exhausted at the end of it but knowing that you have had a very full day.'[3] In interviews designed to make her seem like a normal person, she always insisted that she would have plenty to do when she left politics. Way back in 1970, for instance, she had claimed that she would love to have more time to go to the theatre, listen to music, go for long walks and do things with her hands. She would do sewing, take a carpentry course or read cookery books and try out all the recipes. In this way she said she could easily fill twenty or thirty years.[4] She made similar suggestions when Prime Minister. But in truth none of these things would have kept her happy for a moment. When she talked of having a full day she meant a full day's *work*; and what she meant by work was politics. She could no more walk away from politics than she could stop breathing.

'There will always be work for me to do and I shall just have to find it,' she had said in 1989.[5] But she was quite unsuited for any of the big international jobs – NATO, the World Bank, even the United Nations – with which her name was sometimes linked: she was never cut out to be a diplomat. John Major would have liked nothing better than to keep her fully occupied, preferably out of the country: but as he wrote in his memoirs, there was 'no credible job to offer her'.[6] She had no experience of business; and though she had once talked vaguely of finding 'something to do with some of the voluntary associations . . . I shall always be one of those people who is out doing things',[7] it was difficult to imagine her fundraising for the Lifeboats or running the National Trust. She was simply too commanding a personality to work with anyone in a subordinate or co-operative capacity. Former Prime Ministers of Luxembourg and Belgium, and former British Foreign and Defence Secretaries like Peter Carrington, David Owen and George Robertson, or party leaders who never held office like Neil Kinnock and Paddy Ashdown, have moved successfully into jobs with NATO or the EC; John Major, exceptionally, has managed to make a quiet niche for himself in the City. But the fact is that British ex-Prime Ministers are practically unemployable in any high-profile capacity.

In truth, Mrs Thatcher's situation was unprecedented. It was not just that she had dominated national life for eleven years, but that her record was the ideological touchstone against which her successor was measured. Most premierships end more or less in disappointment, or at least with a generally recognised need for a new leader – whether of the same party or the Opposition – to make a fresh beginning. Despite Mrs Thatcher's aberrations towards the end, however, most Tories still regarded her premiership overall as an historic success. A sizeable section of the party – comprising among others the Eurosceptic Bruges Group, the No Turning Back group and a new grouping, Conservative Way Forward, chaired by Cecil Parkinson and including Norman Tebbit among its leading members – remained angry that she had been deposed, and alert to ensure that there should be no betrayal of her legacy; while even those who had voted for a change mostly wanted only a softer tone and style, not a fundamental change of policies. Meanwhile Labour mocked Major for living in her shadow, while in reality they were just as much so themselves. The fact was that after eleven years *everything*, good or bad, was inescapably her legacy. 'Thatcherism' would have continued to set the political agenda for the rest of the decade even if Mrs Thatcher herself had gone into a nunnery on the day she left office.

It only made it worse that John Major was her protégé whom she had promoted rapidly over the heads of his contemporaries and finally endorsed as her successor. While colleagues and commentators saw the importance of Major quickly proving himself his own man, free of nanny's apron-strings, Mrs Thatcher continued to treat him as her unfledged deputy whose job it was to carry on the work which she had regrettably been prevented from finishing herself. Just as she had wanted to join him on the pavement outside Number Ten for his first press conference, so she had to be dissuaded from sitting immediately behind him at his first Prime Minister's Questions.[8] She thought she was still entitled to be informed and consulted, and the fact that Major's first big challenge was the Gulf War, which was in origin *her* war, helped cement that expectation: Charles Powell – who stayed with Major until the conclusion of the war in March 1991 – continued to give her weekly briefings far fuller than those given by convention to the leaders of the Opposition. Yet still she felt cut off from the information flow which had been her lifeblood for eleven years, and as a result she became increasingly critical.

As she became disillusioned with Major and voiced her criticism of the Government more and more publicly, she was increasingly accused of behaving as badly towards Major as Heath had done towards her. In some respects, indeed, she behaved worse. Much of her carping at Major was personal, mean-spirited and unfair, though she owed a clearer duty of loyalty to him than Heath had ever owed to her. Yet her situation was very different. Heath was widely seen as an embittered failure pursuing a lonely sulk. By contrast she still had a huge following in the party, the country and indeed the world. This undoubtedly gave her an authority to criticise, advise and warn her successor, if she chose to exercise it; but it also meant that her criticism was far more damaging to Major than Heath's could ever be to her. Though she continued to feel aggrieved at the circumstances of her removal, and believed passionately that she still had valuable experience and a right to contribute it, she also had a responsibility to deploy her influence and her huge celebrity discreetly and judiciously. This she manifestly failed – or refused – to do. The result was that for the Tories' remaining seven years in office she made Major's position vis-à-vis his own backbenchers almost impossible. By helping to exacerbate divisions in the party she contributed substantially to its heavy defeat in 1997, after which she continued to undermine the efforts first of William Hague and then – until her health began to fail – of Iain Duncan Smith to reunite the party around a new agenda. The wounds inflicted on the Tory party by her traumatic overthrow have not yet healed and never will until her still-unquiet ghost is exorcised.

Back-seat driver

Woodrow Wyatt rang Mrs Thatcher in Dulwich the day after she and
Denis arrived there and found her 'coming down to earth with a
bump'. She had no one to type letters for her or to acknowledge the
thousands of letters of sympathy and bouquets of flowers she was
receiving from members of the public. She did not even know how
to operate the telephone or the washing machine. The one reassuring
element of continuity was the police protection which still guarded
her at all times; so finding herself unable to dial a number, she sought
help from the Special Branch officers established in the garage. Thus
the first call Crawfie received from her began plaintively: 'This is
Margaret. From the garage.'[9] She still had a room in the House of
Commons and John Whittingdale as her political secretary, but her
first practical need was for a proper office. Alistair McAlpine came to
the rescue by lending her a house in Great College Street, and she
soon recruited a staff of eight, headed by Andrew Bearpark, who had
worked in her private office between 1986 and 1989. This arrangement served for the first few months, until the newly established
Thatcher Foundation acquired an appropriate headquarters in
Chesham Place.

Meanwhile she quickly realised that Dulwich was not a sensible
place for her to live. She and Denis had bought the mock-Georgian
house on a Barratt estate beside the South Circular in 1986 partly as
an insurance, partly as an investment; its attraction – for Denis – was
that it overlooked Dulwich and Sydenham Golf Club. But it was hopelessly impractical for an ex-Prime Minister who intended to remain
fully involved in public life, and whose schedule required her to be
able to get home quickly to change between engagements. She needed
to remain symbolically as well as literally in the thick of things. She
would have done better to have kept their old house in Chelsea, which
they had only sold in 1985. But now she wanted something still more
central. After just three weeks of commuting from Dulwich, she and
Denis were lent a luxurious ground-floor-and-basement duplex apart-
ment in Eaton Square, Belgravia, owned by Henry Ford's widow, while
they looked for something more permanent.* They eventually bought
(from the mysterious and reclusive Barclay brothers) a ten-year lease
– later extended to a life interest – on a five-storey, five-bedroom house

---

*93 Eaton Square had once been the home of another Conservative Prime
Minister, Stanley Baldwin, who lived there during World War One. A potential
embarrassment in 1990, however, was that it was just a few doors from Michael
Heseltine's town house. It would not have done to have stayed there too long.

a couple of streets away in Chester Square, just off Victoria, which was made ready for them to move into in the summer of 1991.

There were some consolations to salve her sense of rejection in the first few weeks. She received a warm – perhaps guilt-fuelled – reception in the Commons when she attended Major's first appearance at Prime Minister's Questions; and everywhere she appeared she was met with sympathy, tributes to her historic stature and admiration for her dignified bearing in adversity. On 9 December it was announced that the Queen had awarded her the Order of Merit – the highest honour in her gift, limited to just twenty-four individuals: Mrs Thatcher filled the vacancy left by the death of Laurence Olivier. More controversially, Denis was created a baronet. A few days earlier she and Denis had paid a well-publicised call on Ron and Nancy Reagan, who were passing through London, and took tea with them at Claridge's, reliving past glories; and on 12 December she received the Freedom of the City of Westminster – the first politician to be so honoured since Churchill. She used the occasion to make her first public utterance since leaving office: a short but pointed résumé of her core beliefs dressed up as the 'lessons of history'.[10] At the end of the year she was voted Woman of the Year for the fifth year running by listeners to the *Today* programme; she and Denis then flew off to spend the New Year for what turned out to be the last time at Lady Glover's *Schloss* in Switzerland.

While she was away her resignation honours list was published, which by tradition enabled her to recognise – in conventionally graded order – those who had served her in various capacities. First there were peerages for several more big donors to the Tory party – Sir Hector Laing, Sir Jeffrey Sterling, Sir Gordon White and Peter Palumbo – plus two pillars of her private office, David Wolfson from the early years and Brian Griffiths from the latter period. Next came knighthoods for Charles Powell, Bernard Ingham and Tim Bell; for George Gardiner and the editor of the *Daily Express*, Nick Lloyd; and also – generously – for the three hapless loyalists who had headed her doomed campaign to retain the leadership: Peter Morrison, Gerry Neale and Michael Neubert. Ian Gow's widow Jane became a Dame, as did Sue Tinson of ITN, one of Mrs Thatcher's few allies in the world of television. Then there were CBEs for her doctor, her appointments secretary, Harvey Thomas (who staged her conference appearances and pre-election rallies), and Olga Polizzi (who had supervised the redecoration of Number Ten); an OBE for John Whittingdale; MBEs for her personal detective, her invitations secretary, the housekeeper at Chequers and the fashion director of Aquascutum, among others; and at the bottom of the pile, the British Empire Medal for a clutch of cleaners, telephonists, messengers and security staff. All were honoured, in the pernicious British way, according to their rank.

Early in January 1991 she returned to Number Ten for the first time for a dinner to mark the retirement of Robert Runcie. It was as if she had never been away. Paddy Ashdown thought her 'very regal and generally dominating the performance', effortlessly eclipsing her unpretentious successor who was meant to be the host.[11] But this was her public face: privately she was much less composed. Wyatt repeatedly found her in low spirits. 'I am at times up and at times down,' she admitted two days after Christmas, 'and this is one of the down times.'[12] Cecil Parkinson, another loyal friend, thought her 'distracted and unhappy, but in total control of herself . . . She was clearly finding great difficulty in coming to terms with what had happened to her.'[13] 'The pattern of my life was fractured,' she told the American magazine *Vanity Fair* in March. 'It's like throwing a pane of glass with a complicated map upon it on the floor, and all habits and thoughts and actions that went with it and the staff that went with it . . . You threw it on the floor and it shattered.'

> Questions at the House were on Tuesday and Thursday, so on Monday and Wednesday we saw foreign statesmen. There were a certain number of overseas events – the economic summit, two European councils. All of this structure happened; you geared your clothes buying to external visits and your conferences. You geared your hair to when you were in the House etc., and then you had a certain amount of entertaining . . . a whole range of engagements throughout the year which became the pattern of my life . . . Sometimes I say 'Which day is it?' I never said that at No. 10.[14]*

One response to this disorientation was a tendency to drink more than she had ever done when her time was fully occupied. 'Margaret drank pretty heftily before dinner [at Michael Howard's],' Wyatt noted on 19 March, 'as did Denis. She was getting a bit tight.'[16] Or again when Wyatt called on her at Eaton Square on 5 April: 'She had some strong whiskies. I began to get a little drunk and she was getting a trifle high.'[17] She also ate more than she had ever done before – for instance, at a dinner with the Queen Mother at Clarence House:

---

*When the interview was published in May, *The Times*' pocket cartoonist Calman commented wrily: 'I know – it's called being unemployed.'[15]

Margaret ate everything. She had two enormous helpings of the first thing which was a kind of salmon mousse topped with lots of shrimps and then more shrimps in a sauce to go with it. She had an enormous helping of the second course and two large helpings of the pudding. Then she started eating cheese which I didn't have. She drank quite a lot too.[18]

Food was one pleasure she now had time to indulge. But it is quite wrong to suggest that she sought consolation in alcohol. She had always liked whisky, usually late at night; but she had a very light head and a little went a long way. The only difference after 1990 was that she drank earlier in the day and sometimes accepted one more glass than she would have done when in office; and, being unused to it, the difference showed. But she never approached Denis's level of intake.

She was still resilient, determined to look forward and keep herself busy. 'I have got to do a positive job, and do positive things,' she told Wyatt. 'I intend to go on having influence.'[19] She knew she had to step back from daily domestic politics, but in the very first days she set herself three tasks. First, she intended to travel widely and lecture, particularly in America, partly to keep on spreading her gospel, but also to make money. Denis was still earning a comfortable income from non-executive directorships, but having taken a reduced salary for eleven years she was determined to earn some money of her own. She had a pension of £25,000 and an MP's salary of £21,000, plus £27,000 office allowance and another £10,500 cost-of-living allowance for London Members. But the need to maintain a substantial office to answer all those letters was going to be expensive. In the short term a number of anonymous supporters paid the bills. Then, after some discreet lobbying, John Major awarded all former Prime Ministers a new annual allowance of £29,800, which helped. (It helped Ted Heath too.) Eventually she and Denis also cleared a useful profit on the sale of the house in Dulwich; but it was abroad that she could make real money. She soon signed on with the Washington Speakers' Bureau for a reported fee of $50,000 a lecture – second only to Reagan – and she commanded similar fees in Japan and all over the Far East. She made it a clear rule, however, that she would accept no payment for speeches in Britain, or for speaking in Russia, China, Hong Kong or South Africa – anywhere, in fact, where she was speaking *politically* as opposed to just exploiting her name. She was determined not to compromise her independence where she felt she could still have influence.

Within two years she was placed 134th in the *Sunday Times'* list of the country's richest people, with personal wealth estimated at £9.5 million.[20] Much the biggest part of this income, however, derived from her second task – the writing of her memoirs. These clearly had huge commercial potential. Rupert Murdoch was keen to acquire them for HarperCollins, and Woodrow Wyatt was equally keen to help win them for him; but negotiations were derailed when Mark Thatcher took charge of them with characteristic insensitivity. He talked loudly of getting eight, ten or even twenty million pounds for them, far more than Murdoch was willing to pay, and concentrated his effort on Murdoch's rival Robert Maxwell – with allegedly a £1 million fee for himself.[21] So Murdoch used the front page of the *Sunday Times* to denounce Mark's interference. Mrs Thatcher was upset, as she always was by any criticism of her son. 'How can Rupert do this to me?' she demanded of Wyatt. 'It is true,' Murdoch countered. 'None of her friends dare tell her what a dreadful mess Mark is making of her affairs.' 'I certainly don't,' Wyatt admitted. 'She would just get angry . . . She dotes on him.'[22] But in June the Maxwell deal fell through. A week later Mrs Thatcher signed up with an American agent, Marvin Josephson, who swiftly accepted an offer of £3.5 million from HarperCollins for two volumes to be published in 1993 and 1995. The word in the trade was that Mark had got the worst of both worlds by asking too much in the beginning and then losing the optimum moment by letting the negotiations drag on while their value fell.[23]

It was still a substantial deal. But the timetable was demanding, requiring her to write the first volume, covering her entire premiership, in not much more than eighteen months. It was announced that she would write every word herself; but no one seriously believed this. She had never claimed to be a writer. Her method of composing speeches had always been to edit, criticise and exhaustively rewrite the drafts of others; and it was the same with her memoirs. She hired Robin Harris, formerly director of the Conservative Research Department and later a member of her Policy Unit, to do most of the writing, with a young Oxford academic, Christopher Collins, to do the research and John O'Sullivan to add polish. They tackled the task as an almost military operation during 1992, sometimes abroad in Switzerland or the Caribbean, sometimes over intensive weekends at country hotels in southern England. Like her valedictory speech to the House of Commons on the day she resigned, but on a vastly bigger scale, Mrs Thatcher took the project immensely seriously, treating every word as her vindication before the bar of history. She did not intend to pull her punches – nor did she. But directing the writing of the book gave her something serious and all-consuming to do with her time; and completing it on schedule was a formidable achievement.

Her third project was to set up some sort of institution to preserve her legacy and propagate her ideas around the world. Her original model was the Konrad Adenauer Foundation – still a multi-million-Deutschmark business thirty years after its founder's death – but this fell foul of British charity law. In July 1991 the Charity Commission refused to grant the Thatcher Foundation charitable status since it was not politically neutral: this seriously affected its ability to raise funds, since companies could not claim tax relief. Here again Mark's abrasive fundraising manner was counterproductive: he allegedly told leading businessmen who had done well out of the Thatcher revolution that it was 'time to pay up for Mumsie' and scoffed when they offered too little.[24] Some of his mother's closest associates refused to have anything to do with it specifically because of Mark, and companies which had for years contributed generously to the Tory party conspicuously declined to support the Foundation – to the relief of Central Office, which did not look kindly on a rival organisation bidding for the same sources of funding. Nor was Mrs Thatcher herself much more successful in America. Money was short, she told Wyatt after a disappointing visit early in 1992, 'partly due to the recession and partly because people were giving money to President Bush'.[25] By 1993 no more than £5 million had been raised. The Foundation was nevertheless established in 1991 with its headquarters in Chesham Place (near Hyde Park Corner), which provided a suitably imposing office where Mrs Thatcher could receive foreign visitors: several remarked that its fine staircase and chandeliers, mementoes of the Falklands and a large globe were curiously reminiscent of Downing Street – though of course far grander.

Branches were also opened in Washington and Warsaw, with the objective of trying to encourage the spread of free-market ideas and western business practice in the new democracies of Central and Eastern Europe. The specific initiatives announced, however, were small beer. In 1993 the Foundation paid for ten young people to spend a month in Britain learning business skills; more recently it has enabled five Russians a year to spend three terms at the Cambridge Business School.[26] Though the Thatcher name still commanded huge prestige in Eastern Europe, the Foundation never had the funds to make much real difference. Even Lady Thatcher's own account of the development of capitalism in Russia in her last book, *Statecraft*, makes no mention of any role played by her Foundation. What the Foundation did instead was to evolve into an educational trust. In 1998 it gave £2 million to endow a new chair of enterprise studies at Cambridge.

The previous year Lady Thatcher had donated her papers to Churchill College, together with funds to catalogue them and build a new wing of the Archives Centre to house them. (The choice of Churchill was partly a calculated snub to Oxford, to repay its snub to her in 1985; but also a neat way of linking herself in perpetuity with her hero. 'They'll be with Winston,' she told Wyatt.)[27] The Foundation also paid for the distribution to libraries all round the world of a CD-Rom of her complete public statements produced (at its own expense) by Oxford University Press,★ and it funds a Margaret Thatcher website. All this has helped to make the record of her life available to historians; but it was not the crusading vehicle for global Thatcherism that was originally envisaged.

In the short term the main thing she could do was to travel extensively, which both got her out of Major's hair and enabled her to enjoy the adulation of her admirers around the world. As a global superstar she was far more recognisable than her unknown successor, and she met with rapturous receptions wherever she went. During 1991 she made five visits to the United States – in February to attend Ronald Reagan's eightieth-birthday celebrations in California and inspect the still-unfinished Reagan Library in Simi Valley, north of Los Angeles; in March to receive the congressional Medal of Freedom from President Bush at a lavish ceremony in the White House, followed by her first paid lectures in Republican strongholds like Dallas, Texas and Orange County, Los Angeles; in June to give two major speeches about world affairs in New York and Chicago; in September and again in November for further lecture tours. America was more than ever her spiritual home, and during and after the Gulf War she still had some standing in Washington, even if more often than not she had to be content with seeing Vice-President Dan Quayle – usually for breakfast – rather than the President. But she also went in May to South Africa for what was essentially the state visit she had never managed to make as Prime Minister, where she was fêted by President de Klerk but boycotted by the ANC; and then to Russia where she met both Gorbachev and Boris Yeltsin and was mobbed in the streets of Moscow and Leningrad. In September she aroused extraordinary enthusiasm in Japan and was given the red-carpet treatment in China (overshadowing a visit by Major a few days later). In October she was hailed as a heroine by crowds in

---

★At a party at the National Portrait Gallery to launch the CD-Rom in May 1999 Lady Thatcher held up the compact disc, containing some fourteen million words, between her finger and thumb and exclaimed in wonder: 'My whole life reduced to three and a half inches of plastic!'[28]

Poland; and in November she was welcomed as the liberator of Kuwait, whence she returned 'reverberating with vitality'.[29]

Wherever she travelled she felt no inhibitions about plunging into local politics. In South Africa she urged Mandela and Chief Buthelezi to talk and it was even suggested that she might act as a mediator to bring them together.[30] In Russia she gave strong backing to her now embattled friend Gorbachev, urging students at Moscow University to keep faith with *perestroika*; at the same time, however, she firmly supported the right of the Baltic republics to independence (which was not then the view of the British Government).[31] Three months later, when Gorbachev was briefly deposed by a hardline Communist coup, and western capitals held back to see the outcome before committing themselves, Mrs Thatcher took the lead in urging the Soviet people to take to the streets in protest. She openly supported the defiance of Boris Yeltsin, holed up in the Russian parliament building, and even managed to hold a twenty-five-minute telephone conversation with him to express her encouragement.[32] Likewise, arriving in Warsaw, where the post-Communist government had been making deep cuts in subsidies and public services, she was 'not at all shy about wading into the Polish election campaign, praising the embattled finance minister and dismissing left-wing parties'.[33] The whole world was now her constituency: or, as she herself put it with her habitual royal plural, 'We operate now on a global scale.'[34]

But she could not confine herself entirely to the world stage. The issues she felt most strongly about inevitably impacted on domestic politics. Any criticism she made of the Government's stance towards Iraq, the disintegration of Yugoslavia or – above all – Europe was inescapably a comment on her successor's lack of judgement, experience or resolution. At least she could have no complaint about the conduct of the war to liberate Kuwait. In her first intervention in the Commons on 28 February she simply congratulated Major on the war's successful conclusion and accepted his tribute to her staunchness the previous August. She did not yet criticise the coalition's failure to overthrow Saddam, though she did point out that the problem of Iraq was not resolved and warned darkly that 'the victories of peace will take longer than the battles of war'.[35] Within a few weeks, however, she was demanding that the Government should send troops to protect the Kurdish population fleeing from Saddam's forces in northern Iraq. In fact Major was already working on a plan to create 'safe havens' for the Kurds, for which he was able to secure French, German and eventually American backing; so on this occasion he was able to neutralise her intervention. It would not always be so easy.

In the autumn of 1991 Mrs Thatcher took an early, clear and courageous view on the break-up of Yugoslavia, which put her bitterly at odds with the Government over the following years as the complex inter-ethnic conflict escalated. As the Serbs sought to maintain by force their domination of the former federation, she boldly championed the right of the constituent republics – first Croatia and Slovenia, later Bosnia-Hercegovina – to break away. She saw the issue partly as one of nationalist self-determination, with echoes of her resistance to the federal pretensions of Brussels; but also as the latest front in the continuing battle of democracy against Communism. She first declared her view in a speech in Japan at the beginning of September, then followed up with two speeches in Washington and New York two weeks later. In the second – to the UN ambassadors' annual dinner – she laid down an explicit challenge to the international community:

> We cannot continue to stand back and allow the Yugoslav army, the Communist Serbian government and Serbian terrorists to crush the people of Croatia. Croatian civilians are being murdered and mutilated. Refugees are pouring across the borders. Croatia's beautiful cities and ancient churches are being destroyed. Unless we give them hope – and help to defend themselves – they are lost.

'The international community should remember three things,' she declared:

> First, the inherent right of self-defence cannot be removed from those who are facing death and destruction. But they cannot exercise it without the means to do so. Second, this is not just a struggle between national groups. It is one between Communists and those – the Croatians – who seek democracy. Third, it cannot just be considered as an internal matter for Yugoslavia. It goes far wider . . . It is not for us to say that Croatia and Slovenia should remain in Yugoslavia against the democratically expressed wishes of their people. These two nations have exercised their right of secession under the Yugoslav Constitution. Rather, we should be prepared to apply the strictest possible economic sanctions against any republic which tries to change borders by force – and provide military assistance to the victims of aggression.[36]

Major and Hurd, however, were determined to avoid either Britain or NATO getting sucked into a Balkan civil war and asserted a policy of non-intervention, with an embargo on the supply of arms to all sides, to which they stubbornly adhered in the face of mounting evidence of Serb atrocities. For the next few years Mrs Thatcher's militant anti-Communism was unusually allied with the humanitarian conscience of the world in demanding action against the Serbs, beating in vain against the cautious pragmatism of the British Government, which took the lead in blocking direct NATO, EC or UN intervention.

But the issue on which Mrs Thatcher set herself most uncompromisingly against her successor was, inevitably, Europe. From the time of her Bruges speech her attitude towards the Community had been hardening, but so long as she was in office her growing antipathy was restrained by the need to negotiate the best deal for Britain that she could achieve. From the moment she left office that restraint was off. Now she was free to follow her instinct, to criticise the deals which Major and Hurd secured, and she did so without inhibition or consideration of the pressures that would have weighed with her if she had still been in government. On the contrary, she felt no compunction about putting herself at the head of the hitherto quite small section of the Tory party which was bitterly opposed to any further European integration, thereby helping to tip the party's centre of gravity over the next seven years from a broadly pro-European to a strongly Eurosceptic, even Europhobic, stance. By leading the opposition on this issue she not only thwarted Major's vague ambition to put Britain 'at the heart of Europe', but also undermined his authority more generally, fuelling a civil war in the party which not only destroyed his government in the short term, but wrecked the credibility of the Tories as a governing party for years to come. This was her revenge for November 1990.

She never really intended to confine herself to foreign affairs anyway. She used a constituency function in Finchley at the beginning of March to declare plainly that she had not gone away. On the contrary, she announced, in terms that must have sent a chill down Major's spine, 'I am still around. I hope to continue to exert an influence, because I think it would be a jolly good thing for the Conservative party to have an elder statesman, especially a matriarch, to stand behind our present Prime Minister and see him carried forward to victory at the next election.'[37] Already she was critical of the small ways in which Major was trying to stamp his own style on the new government by gestures like paying compensation to haemophiliacs infected with HIV through blood transfusions, unfreezing child benefit and a new initiative to help rough sleepers. On the day he took office Major had spoken of wanting to create a 'classless society . . . at ease with itself'; he wrote later that he was trying to 'nudge Conservatism towards its compassionate roots'.[38] But Mrs Thatcher immediately detected a betrayal of her legacy. 'I see a tendency to try to undermine what I have achieved and to go back to giving more powers to government,' she declared on American television; her words were of course instantly reported back home.[39] In April she was said to have described the new government as 'the B-Team' – though of course almost all Major's ministers had been her own team just a few months earlier.[40] She was privately 'incandescent' about the Government's decision to replace the poll tax with a banded council tax, which she considered too compli-cated and 'much less fair';[41] and 'indignant' at the ending of mortgage tax relief above the basic rate, something she had always fiercely resisted. Both measures she believed would hit 'our own people'.[42]

On 2 June the *Sunday Telegraph* led its front page with the headline "'I'm disappointed in Major," says bitter Thatcher.'[43] Her office denied it, but could not prevent other papers taking up the story. *The Times* reported next day that 'in her table talk she is alleged to have said that he is grey, stands for nothing and has no ideas'.[44] A meeting was quickly arranged to try to refute such rumours. In fact Major saw her quite regularly to try to keep her onside; but their conversations, he told Wyatt, were 'stilted . . . We fence around, not really getting on to the points about which we disagree.'[45] Behind the polite smiles, both were seething with frustration. Mrs Thatcher complained that she was 'the only person in the country who has not got freedom of speech, except for privately among friends. They all complain if I make any comment at all';[46] while Major – according to the diary of his political secre-tary – was 'obsessed' with his predecessor, calling her 'mad, loopy, emotional' and telling his staff, 'I want her isolated, I want her destroyed.'[47] His problem was that he lacked the self-confidence to slap her down himself.

In mid-June Mrs Thatcher took the opportunity of two speeches to prestigious audiences in America to renew her war on the pretensions of the European Union. 'It is time to recognise, even in Brussels,' she told the Foreign Relations Council of Chicago, 'that the age of empire is past.' She warned that the dream of a single European foreign policy risked undermining NATO; condemned the Community's protectionist trade policies; and claimed that by selfishly delaying the admission of the former Soviet satellites, the Community was perpetuating the divi-sion of the Continent, replacing the Iron Curtain with a 'wealth wall'.[48] The next day, speaking to the Economic Club of New York, she warned against dividing the world into competing trade blocs and urged instead what was to become a favourite theme over the next ten years: the extension of the newly formed North American Free Trade Area (the

USA, Canada and Mexico) to include Europe (both Western and Eastern) to form a single Atlantic Economic Community.[49]

Having thus stolen the headlines for two days – provoking a furious outburst from Ted Heath, who accused her of peddling 'ignorant lies' about the Community – she came home and declared her full support for the line that Major and Hurd were taking towards Europe. In a television interview she insisted that she had no intention of trying to make a comeback; but then upstaged the Government again by intervening dramatically – after some well-trailed speculation about whether she would speak or not – in the Commons debate about the forthcoming Luxembourg Council:

> In a Commons performance of primal force that had Tory MPs applauding even as they squirmed, Margaret Thatcher yesterday backed John Major as a 'leader of vision' while simultaneously shredding his negotiating position on Europe.[50]

In sweeping style, which recalled her fateful triple negative of the previous year, she rejected any extension of majority voting, rejected a common European defence and foreign policy, rejected the suggestion that Britain should consolidate its membership of the ERM by joining the 'narrow band' of the mechanism and denounced any possibility of Britain joining the single currency, which would be 'the greatest abdication of parliamentary and national sovereignty in our history'. 'Our sovereignty,' she reminded the House solemnly, 'does not come from Brussels. It is ours by right and by heritage.'[51]

None of this exactly contradicted Major and Hurd, but her vehemence strongly suggested that she did not trust them to defend British sovereignty as resolutely as she would have done. So long as she remained in the Commons it was plain that she would dominate the House whenever she chose to speak. It therefore came as a huge relief to Major when she announced two days later that she would stand down at the next election.

She had been in two minds whether to stay in the Commons or go to the Lords. Though no great parliamentarian, she was clear that she must retain a platform in one or other House. Some of her supporters urged her to stay in the Commons, mainly to keep the Government up to the mark, but also to keep open the possibility of a comeback in the event of some future crisis. At the end of March she was still wavering, if only because she did not want to leave the Commons to Heath.[52] But she was too conscientious to have stayed in the Commons on a part-time basis: unlike Heath, who attended only when he felt like it, she would have felt obliged to turn up for every division, which would have interfered with her travelling, and she would still have felt committed to her Finchley constituents. Finally she decided that she would be freer to speak her mind if she made it clear that she had ruled out the possibility of a comeback. She marked her announcement with a long interview with Simon Jenkins in *The Times* headlined 'My Dash for Freedom'. 'Margaret Thatcher sat back in the chair, banged her hands on its arms and cried "Freedom!"'

> Now it's clear that I am not challenging John Major in any way. Some people have been thinking I was waiting in the wings. I never was. I wanted to give John a chance to find his own style, his own way and get into his own rhythm . . .
>
> A difficult period is now over. When I speak now it's because of one thing: I want to get across a viewpoint that I believe is right. I shall feel freer to answer direct questions. I am not going to change my views and I shall go on propagating them.
>
> I will still be around. I am not going. I have a house in central London which will act as a focus not only for people who believe in what I did but also for people in the academic world. We are out to influence thought, by argument.

Her bitterness was still raw. 'They chose to do *that thing* to me at a time when I was actually abroad negotiating and signing a treaty for my country,' she complained (forgetting that it was she who had chosen to hold the ballot on a day when she knew she was going to be abroad). She insisted that she had done her 'level best' for Major and was 'desperately anxious for him to be successful'. Yet she still could not resist pointing out that Major had not had to fight his way to the top as she had done. He had entered Parliament only in 1979: he had no experience of opposition. 'You can't expect a person who's not been in the heart of the fire and the teeth of the wind to have the same viewpoint as someone who has been through it all.' When Jenkins suggested that Major might wish to introduce a new political map, she retorted: 'I most earnestly hope not.'[53]

That October saw Major's first party conference as leader; but it was also Mrs Thatcher's first opportunity to receive the adoration of the faithful since her removal from office. She made her entrance on the Wednesday to a standing ovation – led, as it had to be, by Major – which brought the conference to a halt. 'She did not say anything,' Gyles Brandreth wrote, 'she just *was* and for five minutes we stood and clapped and stamped our feet and roared . . . You couldn't not be moved. It was wonderful.'[54] She made a pretence of trying not to steal the show, telling reporters: 'It's the Prime Minister's conference, not mine. We must all rally round and support him.'[55] Yet in practice her mere presence did dominate. Her reported disparagement of the Government over lunch was all round Blackpool within hours. Willie Whitelaw went on television to regret that she had not yet learned to let go; and there was general agreement that Major needed to remind her who was now the boss.[56]

But she had no intention of piping down. When the Commons reassembled in November she hijacked the latest European debate with another storming speech denouncing what she called the 'conveyor belt to federalism'; and for the first time she lent her support to those – ranging from Norman Tebbit on one side of the argument to Paddy Ashdown on the other – who were demanding a referendum before the forthcoming Maastricht Treaty was approved.[57] In fact Major was tempted by the idea of a referendum, but her advocacy made it impossible: he could not be seen to be pushed around by her. Two days later she condemned his refusal to hold a referendum as 'arrogant' – an epithet which, applied by her to John Major, struck most people as breathtaking. In the same interview she opened a second front by condemning the Government's failure to support Croatia and Slovenia against the Serbs. With unconcealed irritation she blamed ministers' failure to listen to her and insisted that things would have been different had she still been in charge.[58]

The storm provoked by this outburst convinced her that she had gone too far – she regretted the word 'arrogant' – and she did keep quiet for the next few months, while Major achieved a diplomatic triumph in December by negotiating Britain's right to 'opt out' of the most objectionable features of the Maastricht Treaty: the single currency and the Social Chapter. Mrs Thatcher remained sceptical, but she was inhibited from attacking an outcome which most of those who had served her in government – including both Douglas Hurd and Charles Powell – were convinced she would have been very happy to sign herself, had she still been in power. Wyatt noted that 'poor darling Margaret' was 'sad, if not bitter, at not still being in charge at Maastricht. But I think she is too shrewd politically to get herself out on a limb in not supporting the government on this.'[59] For all her disillusion with Major, she did want the Tories to win the coming election. On 12 December outward cordiality was restored when the Majors and most of the Cabinet attended the Thatchers' fortieth wedding-anniversary celebration at Claridge's. During the early months of 1992 she concentrated on her memoirs, paying just two visits to the United States where she managed to say nothing controversial. In the Commons she lent tacit support to Richard Shepherd's Private Member's Bill for a referendum on Maastricht, but tactfully refrained from either speaking or voting. She also swallowed her criticism of Norman Lamont's pre-election budget on 10 March.

Major called the election – for 9 April – the day after the budget. In appreciation of her restraint and doubtless in the hope that she would keep it up till polling day, he sent Mrs Thatcher a bunch of twenty-four pink roses. She was unimpressed. 'A bunch of flowers won't make up for a £28 billion deficit, Woodrow,' she complained.[60] Privately she thought Lamont's introduction of a lower tax band – cleverly designed to wrongfoot Labour – 'another swingeing blow at the top tax payers . . . That's hitting our own supporters again.'[61] But for the moment she bit her lip, so much so that Andrew Turnbull (previously her principal private secretary, and now Major's) told Wyatt on 17 March that 'her behaviour has been absolutely first-class . . . We couldn't have asked for more. She's been wonderful.'[62]

She played a fairly discreet part in the campaign, appearing just once with Major at a rally for Tory candidates where she raised morale with a strong endorsement of his leadership, and doing walkabouts in selected marginal seats from Southampton to Greater Manchester. (Two of those where she appeared were narrowly held, two lost.) She also supported Mark Lennox-Boyd in Morecambe and John Whittingdale in Colchester, and made a farewell appearance in Finchley to bless the adoption of her successor, Hartley Booth (who defended her majority without serious erosion). In his memoirs Major alleged that 'allies of my predecessor' did their best to undermine his campaign;[63] but Mrs Thatcher herself was in America for the last week, returning only on the evening of polling day in time to attend a round of election-night parties. She watched the results with Wyatt in a small room at the top of Alistair McAlpine's house in a mood of mellow magnanimity. She ticked off Wyatt and Alexander Hesketh for rejoicing at Chris Patten's defeat in Bath ('You shouldn't talk like that, either of you') and generally behaved 'with great dignity throughout the night, with no carping criticisms'. She emerged to tell the press: 'It is a great night. It is the end of Socialism.'[64] The next day she hailed Major's 'famous victory' and urged him now to press 'full steam ahead'.[65]

Yet within days she published a devastating interview article in the American magazine *Newsweek*, which expressed her real feelings. The article had been commissioned and largely written in London before the election in the expectation of a Conservative defeat and had to be hastily amended in the light of Major's unexpected victory. But still she did not pull her punches: she had been so determined to get it off her chest that she kept it secret from her staff who would, she knew, have tried to tone it down. The thrust of the piece, headlined 'Do Not Undo My Work', was contained in the withering judgement that there was 'no such thing as Majorism':

> I don't accept the idea that all of a sudden Major is his own man. He has been Prime Minister for 17 months and he inherited all these great achievements of the past eleven and a half years which have fundamentally changed Britain.

If Major was not his own man, whose was he? Hers, naturally. He was free to chart his own course 'within the constraints of the principles set out in the Conservative manifesto. Don't forget, I set out our principles before we came into power, so that people knew exactly what we stood for.' Specifically she warned against increased government spending and industrial intervention. 'There are one or two straws in the wind which we must watch.' (By this she almost certainly meant the hated Heseltine's move to the Board of Trade.) 'They've got to be jolly careful they don't give government too many extra powers and undo what I've done.' It was vital to keep public spending below 40 per cent of GDP. 'I shall try to keep them to this.'[66]

This was an astonishingly insensitive – indeed 'arrogant' – denigration of the elected Prime Minister on the morrow of his 'famous victory'. She could hardly have expressed herself more insultingly. The pity was, *The Times* commented, that much of what she said was right. 'If only she could find a way of saying so which did not sound so peevish . . . The status of British elder statesman requires equal parts of dignity, good humour and a sense of timing. Mrs Thatcher shows none of them.' Moreover, the paper added sharply, the proper forum for her views would have been her maiden speech in the House of Lords. 'By using foreign platforms . . . she makes it easier . . . to dismiss her as a has-been, parading personal bitterness . . . wherever fame offers a high enough fee.'[67]

Wyatt, Bernard Ingham and other friends warned her that she would dissipate her influence if she appeared to be pursuing a personal vendetta. But she was unrepentant. 'I only said I would keep quiet during the election time.'[68] She was determined not to be silenced. Within weeks she was back on the warpath with a speech in The Hague which ostensibly praised Major's Maastricht opt-outs but raised her anti-federalist rhetoric another couple of notches, first by comparing Brussels unfavourably with the Soviet Union ('A half-Europe imposed by Soviet tyranny is one thing: a half-Europe imposed by Brussels would be a moral catastrophe') and then by proposing a coalition to contain Germany. 'Germany's preponderance within the Community is such that no major decision can really be taken against German wishes.' In these circumstances, where once American forces had been needed to defend Europe from the Soviet Union, they should now remain 'to provide similar comfort against the rise of Germany today'.[69] 'The tea room talk is of Thatcher's speech in The Hague,' the newly elected Gyles Brandreth noted a few days later. 'It seems somewhat over-alarmist to me, but Bill Cash & Co. evidently agree with every word. "The lady across the water," sighed Nick Budgen, "we miss her so."'[70]

Six months earlier Maastricht had been seen as a success for Major's quiet diplomacy; only seven Tories voted against it. But no sooner was the election out of the way than the Eurosceptics – Cash, Budgen and a couple of dozen more – set out openly to try to prevent the treaty's ratification. On 21 May twenty-two of them voted against the Second Reading; and on 28 June Lady Thatcher (as she had now become) backed them. 'Maastricht,' she told David Frost, was 'a treaty too far'. She rejoiced that the Danes had voted narrowly in a referendum to reject it, and renewed her call for British voters to be given the same opportunity. 'If the people have their say it will be dead, and we are answerable to the people. It should be dead.' Meanwhile she put herself in direct confrontation with Major by vowing to vote against it in the House of Lords.[71]

There had been some speculation about what type of peerage she would take. Male Prime Ministers are traditionally entitled to an earldom – Macmillan belatedly accepted his in 1984 – so there was a possibility that she might become a countess. Having resurrected hereditary titles for others, it would have been consistent to take one herself. Rather quaintly, however, she felt that she and Denis lacked the means to support a hereditary title.[72] Wyatt thought she might have become a life countess, but that was a hybrid which Downing Street would not accept. Mark already had Denis's baronetcy to look forward to; so in the end she concluded: 'I thought it was enough to be a life peer.'[73] On 6 June she was gazetted as Baroness Thatcher of Kesteven in the County of Lincolnshire. Cynics noted that she had never cared for Grantham; Kesteven sounded so much more distinguished.*

---

*They had more scope for mockery when her coat of arms was unveiled two years later. They comprised a heraldic lozenge flanked by two supporters: on one side a Captain Birdseye-like admiral, with binoculars and more gold braid on his uniform than any admiral ever sported, representing the reconquest of the Falklands; and on the other no less a figure than Grantham's other famous son, Sir Isaac Newton, representing science. For her motto she took 'Cherish Freedom'.[74]

Introduced by Keith Joseph and John Boyd-Carpenter (her first ministerial boss at the Ministry of Pensions back in 1961), she took her seat in the Upper House on 30 June – 'like a lioness entering into what she must realise is something of a cage'[75] – just in time to speak in a debate on Maastricht on 3 July. 'Your maiden speech is supposed to be non-controversial,' Wyatt reminded her. 'But I shall only be following precedent,' she protested. 'Macmillan in his maiden speech attacked me.'[76] In fact she made a fairly gracious and even witty speech, written for her by Charles Powell, dissenting from Maastricht but expressing confidence in Major's ability to use the forthcoming British chairmanship of the Council of Ministers to influence the development of the Community in the right direction.

Her restraint was short-lived. She was working on her memoirs in Switzerland in August when the Vice-President of Bosnia came to beg her to make a fresh appeal on behalf of his country. She responded with a flurry of articles and TV interviews on both sides of the Atlantic, calling for military action to halt the continuing Serb assault on Gorazde and Sarajevo, end the brutal policy of 'ethnic cleansing' and save the Bosnian state. What was happening in Bosnia, she declared, was 'reminiscent of the worst excesses of the Nazis'.[77] Despairing of the 'paralysis' of the EC, she called on the Americans to take a lead. NATO, she wrote in the *New York Times*, was 'the most practical instrument to hand'. The Balkans were not 'out of area', but part of Europe.[78] In reply to those – specifically Conor Cruise O'Brien in *The Times* – who argued that western intervention would only exacerbate the conflict, she insisted that she was not calling for a full-scale military invasion, just the bombing of Serbian supply routes and the lifting of the arms embargo which prevented the Bosnians buying the means to defend themselves.[79] But her call fell on deaf ears. With a few exceptions – notably Paddy Ashdown and a number of Labour left-wingers like Ken Livingstone – most MPs of both parties, most of the Establishment, elder statesmen like Ted Heath and Denis Healey, and most commentators backed the Foreign Office line that Britain had no interest in getting drawn into the conflict: many frankly took the view that the best outcome to be hoped for was a quick Serb victory. The most that Major and Hurd would do was to contribute British troops to a UN force protecting convoys of humanitarian aid; but this only strengthened the argument against military intervention, since these troops would have become vulnerable to retaliation if NATO had bombed the Serbs. Douglas Hurd still believes that active western intervention would only have increased the bloodshed and made a bad situation worse.[80]

Nevertheless Lady Thatcher kept up her demand, with mounting contempt for the Government's inertia, for the next three years, until eventually the Americans stepped in with enough force to bring the Serbs to the negotiating table. In December 1992 she warned of a 'holocaust' in Bosnia and insisted: 'We could have stopped this. We could still do so.' By treating the conflict as a purely internal matter, the West had 'actually given comfort to the aggressor'.[81] In April 1993, following the first massacre at Srebrenica – the second, even worse one was in July 1995 – she rejected Hurd's plea that lifting the arms embargo would merely create 'a level killing field', as 'a terrible and disgraceful phrase'. Bosnia was 'already a killing field the like of which I thought we would never see in Europe again'. The horrors being perpetrated were 'not worthy of Europe, not worthy of the West and not worthy of the United States . . . It is in Europe's sphere of influence. It should be in Europe's sphere of conscience . . . We are little more than accomplices to a massacre.'[82] Privately she was said to have told Hurd: 'Douglas, Douglas, you would make Neville Chamberlain look like a warmonger.'[83]

In retrospect she was probably right. One can respect the reluctance of Major, Hurd, Malcolm Rifkind (who succeeded Hurd as Foreign Secretary in 1995) and initially Bill Clinton (who succeeded George Bush as US President in 1993) to escalate the war by taking sides. Their instinct all along was to try to secure a ceasefire and a negotiated settlement via a succession of intermediaries: they could not believe that the Serbs could be so ruthless and unreasonable. But the fact was that the deployment of American force was in the end the only thing that brought the Serbs to conclude the Dayton Agreement in 1995. As so often, Lady Thatcher's bleak view of human nature and the necessity of military strength to defeat aggressors was more realistic than the pragmatism of those who thought themselves the 'realists'. The slaughter could have been stopped earlier if Europe had found the will to act firmly in its own back yard. It was ironic that she who so opposed Europe's ambition to develop a single foreign policy should have been the one calling for it to act unitedly in Bosnia. Sadly events justified her scepticism and vindicated her view that no trouble anywhere in the world would ever be tackled without American leadership.

It was relatively easy for the Government to dismiss the former Prime Minister's lectures about Bosnia as – in Rifkind's phrase – 'emotional nonsense'.[84] She caused them more serious difficulty nearer home in the autumn of 1992 when the Maastricht Treaty finally came before Parliament. The Government suffered the worst possible curtain raiser to this debate on 16 September – 'Black Wednesday' – when Norman

Lamont was humiliatingly forced to abandon Britain's membership of the ERM. After all the wrangles with Lawson and Howe about joining, culminating in Mrs Thatcher's reluctant acquiescence in October 1990, sterling crashed out of the system after just two years, at the cost of some £15 billion of the country's gold reserves and dealing a blow to the Government's reputation for financial competence from which it never recovered. Securing Mrs Thatcher's agreement to Britain's belated entry had been Major's personal triumph as Chancellor: now premature exit wrecked his premiership. Lady Thatcher – in Washington at the time – could not help but be delighted. 'If you try to buck the market, the market will buck you.'[85] She could not gloat too openly in public, but nothing would stop her trumpeting her vindication in private. Lamont told Wyatt that she was 'ringing all her friends saying, "Isn't it marvellous, I told you so etc"'.[86] She warned against any thought of rejoining the ERM, but urged the Government to capitalise on its escape by cutting interest rates to beat the recession.

Two weeks later, just as the bruised party was gathering in Brighton for the annual conference, Lady Thatcher launched a direct attack on Maastricht in *The European* (a short-lived newspaper owned by the Barclay brothers) linking the ERM debacle explicitly to the treaty and wanting out of both. 'The first is a prerequisite to the fulfilment of the second,' she wrote. 'We found the confines of the first unbearable: the straitjacket of the second would be ruinous.' At least under the ERM there was an escape hatch; but Maastricht put Europe 'on a conveyor belt to a single currency' to which – despite Major's opt-out – Britain would quickly find itself committed. Once again she contrasted her vision of a confederal Europe of nation states with the federal nightmare of a United States of Europe, and repeated her intention to oppose ratification of the treaty.

'The Conservative Party needs to be united, not torn apart,' she wrote.[87] But nothing could have been more divisive than a former Prime Minister repudiating a treaty that her successor had signed, on which he had been re-elected just six months earlier and on which he had now staked his authority. The Major camp regarded the timing of her article as a breach of an agreement with the party chairman, Norman Fowler, that she would not speak at the conference. The *Sun* stirred the pot with a phone-in campaign to bring her back; while Norman Tebbit won rapturous applause for a violent attack on the whole concept of European union. Yet Hurd answered him effectively with one of the best speeches of his career; and the next day Lady Thatcher received a noticeably less enthusiastic welcome than the previous year. Major greeted her with a statutory kiss, but the ritual standing ovation lasted only two minutes and around a quarter of the hall remained seated; there were even some boos.

Back at Westminster on 4 November the Government faced two crucial Commons divisions on a so-called 'paving' vote, called by Major to reassure his European partners before the committee stage of the Maastricht Bill. With an overall Tory majority of just twenty-one, and two or three dozen Europhobes threatening to vote against the Government, Major's survival was on the line. The whips pulled out all the stops; but the rebels' mentors in the Lords did not hold back either. Tebbit – also now a peer – was busy buttonholing Members in the central lobby, while Lady Thatcher summoned wavering back-benchers to her room to tell them firmly what she expected of them. John Whittingdale – one of five new Members (Iain Duncan Smith was another) who opposed the treaty – was widely reported to have emerged in tears. 'The trouble with you, John,' she was said to have told him, 'is that your spine does not reach your brain.'[88] His version is that the wigging he received was no worse than he had been used to while working as her private secretary; at any rate he resisted her pressure and abstained.[89] At the last moment Major personally cajoled another leading Eurosceptic, Michael Cartiss, into the Government lobby with a promise that the Government would not finally ratify the treaty until after a second Danish referendum. By such means the Government won the first division by six votes, the second by three. Thus Major survived by the skin of his teeth. But he could not forget that at this crisis of his premiership his predecessor had done her best to destroy him.

For most of the first half of 1993 Lady Thatcher concentrated on her memoirs, while the Maastricht Bill ground through the Commons, suffering just two minor defeats in committee. But when it went up to the Lords in June she re-emerged to lead the attack in the Upper House. First, on 7 June she confronted the contention of those who claimed that she would have accepted the treaty had she still been in office, and denied that it followed inevitably from the Single European Act (SEA) which she had signed. She insisted that the Commission had broken assurances given at the time that the extension of majority voting would be applied only to the single market and not to other matters. 'Yes, we got our fingers burned under the SEA,' she conceded, but quoted Kipling's warning that 'the burnt Fool's bandaged finger goes wabbling back to the Fire'. The Maastricht Treaty was 'much, much wider' than the SEA. 'I could never have signed this treaty.'[90]

Then on 14 July she renewed her demand for a referendum with an emotional speech calling for no further surrender of sovereignty to

Brussels unless the people sanctioned it.[91] Forgetting that as a young backbencher in 1961 she had voted in favour of bringing back corporal punishment, she claimed that this was the first time in thirty-four years in Parliament that she had voted against the party line. Ninety Tories – led by Robert Blake and William Rees-Mogg – joined her. But with Willie Whitelaw, Geoffrey Howe and John Wakeham all speaking for the Government and the whips rounding up one of the biggest turn-outs in the Upper House since she had used the same methods to defeat the poll-tax rebels, the motion was overwhelmingly defeated by 445 votes to 176. Maastricht was duly ratified; but the schism that its passage caused in the Tory party has never healed.

The Mummy's curse

There was just one issue on which Lady Thatcher steadily supported the Government after 1992. She had felt deeply the agreement to hand over Hong Kong to China in 1997, and she felt a continuing respon-sibility – particularly after the Tiananmen Square massacre in 1989 – to ensure that China did not renege on its promise to preserve Hong Kong's capitalist system even after its re-absorption. She visited Hong Kong soon after Chris Patten had taken up his post as the last Governor charged with steering the colony through the final five years to the handover. Patten, with Major's support, had set out to create – rather belatedly – democratic institutions which it was hoped China would respect when it took over. Old China hands like her former adviser Percy Cradock shook their heads gloomily at the folly of provoking Beijing. But Lady Thatcher, after talks with Patten in London and Hong Kong and then after arguing the matter through privately with Charles Powell and Robin Harris, determined to back him. She had always had a soft spot for Patten (he was one of those, like Ken Clarke, whose robustness she respected, even though his views were inexpli-cably wet) and now she endorsed him as 'a new, imaginative and competent governor' and urged the Government to stand by him.[92] Other senior figures like Ted Heath, Geoffrey Howe and a clutch of former governors, Patten later wrote, were initially supportive. 'Only Margaret Thatcher was to remain so in public and in private, stalwartly and vigorously insisting that the joint declaration signed in her name should mean what it said.' When the whole foreign-policy establish-ment seemed to turn against him over the next few years, 'she was a better and stouter friend to me than she will ever know'.[93]

Between 1992 and 1997 Lady Thatcher probably devoted more time to Hong Kong and the Far East generally than to any other subject. Maastricht and Bosnia made the headlines; but Hong Kong was the issue on which she felt she still had a responsibility and could exert an influence. The Chinese leadership still treated her with enormous respect and she handled them – particularly the charmless Prime Minister Li Peng – with a skilful mixture of outspokenness and tact. There was a particularly sharp diplomatic crisis in March 1995 when the Chinese were making difficulties about a number of thorny issues concerning the handover: among other things, they had got it into their heads that the British were planning to remove Hong Kong's entire gold reserves with them when they left. Lady Thatcher flew out, with the approval of Patten and Major, and broke the log jam by announcing sweetly but decisively in the hearing of journalists at the red-carpet ceremony at the airport exactly what she had come to get straight. No more was heard about the gold reserves or any of the other stumbling blocks.[94] In public and in private she boldly proclaimed her confidence that economic development in China would inevitably bring political freedom in its wake; and she protested firmly about Beijing's treatment of dissidents. On every visit she made a point of enquiring after the now-disgraced Zhao Ziyang, with whom she had negotiated in 1984, and once even tried to send him a present.[95] When she wanted, she still had a matchless way of cutting through diplomatic formalities. In 1994 she announced that she had already booked rooms in Hong Kong so as to be present in person for the handover; and indeed when the day came, on 1 July 1997, she was there – with Tony Blair and Robin Cook, Prince Charles, Ted Heath and Geoffrey Howe – to witness the interminable ceremony in pouring rain. So far, she acknowledged in 2002, the Chinese had 'generally honoured their commitments'.[96]

During this period she travelled extensively all over the Far East, which was increasingly her favourite region of the world. The 'Pacific Tiger' economies of Japan, Taiwan, South Korea, Singapore, Thailand and Malaysia were the trailblazers of international capitalism in the 1990s, and she became fascinated – from the perspective of a privileged visitor jetting in and out to address business and political leaders – by their success in grafting western business practice onto traditional societies, which contrasted with her increasingly dim view of developments in Britain and Europe. In 1992 she was invited by the American corporation Citibank to join their so-called 'leadership series' of major conventions all over the Far East. George Bush, George Shultz and other former heavyweights were also on the payroll, but 'Madame Thatcher' was the star attraction. She insisted, however, that wherever she went she would spend half her time promoting British interests, putting herself (between engagements for Citibank) at the disposal of the local British Embassy to beat the drum for Britain, at Citibank's expense. This was a brilliant arrangement which allowed her to earn money – both for her Foundation and for herself – while at the same time feeling that she was still doing useful and patriotic public work. British ambassadors all over Asia valued her visits highly, while she in turn formed a glowing opinion of most of them, which somewhat revised her formerly poor view of diplomats.

She accepted only two other business invitations. First, in 1992 she attracted a storm of hostile publicity by becoming a consultant to the American tobacco giant Philip Morris, reportedly for £1 million a year (though actually nearer half that amount). No one had objected to Ted Heath sitting on the international review board of the account-ants Arthur Andersen, but the anti-smoking lobby was furious at Lady Thatcher selling out to the tobacco industry, especially since she had never been a smoker herself (though Denis was a lifelong forty-a-day man). She protested that tobacco was only a small part of the company's business and anyway she was only giving 'geo-political advice', not selling cigarettes. But it was an odd association for her to choose. Later in the decade she joined the advisory board of a big New York hedge-fund business, Tiger Asset Management. But again her role was purely consultative. She was adamant that she would not join the legal board of any company.

What she did do was a good deal of unofficial lobbying on behalf of British firms bidding for contracts around the world. She inter-vened, for example, to stop Kuwait backing down on an agreement to buy armoured cars from GKN, by ringing the Crown Prince and telling him firmly that he should stick to his word; another time she flew secretly from Hong Kong to Azerbaijan to help BP secure a major oil contract under the noses of the French and American ambassa-dors.[97] As Prime Minister she had always believed in 'batting for Britain' – particularly in the arms trade – by direct face-to-face diplomacy with her opposite numbers, and after leaving office she did not cease to exert her personal influence wherever it could still be effective. Though it could never compensate for the loss of real power, this more than anything else did make her feel that she was still serving her country.

The first volume of her memoirs, *The Downing Street Years*, was published in October 1993 – timed, as such books always are, to co-incide with the party conference. Over the summer, even as she lobbied and voted against Maastricht, Lady Thatcher had tried to present a face of unity by urging that 'We must all get behind John';[98] and now she sought to limit the damage by insisting that serialisation in the *Sunday*

Times should not begin until the weekend after the conference closed. But all the indications were that her book was not going to be helpful. 'Humility and loyalty are not words which come to mind when she is talking about the book,' one guest confided after a promotional dinner for booksellers at the Dorchester.[99] Although the real scores she had to settle were with those of her former colleagues who had ganged up on her, let her down or ultimately betrayed her, the media were sure to focus on what she had to say about the current Prime Minister. Rumours abounded even before the *Daily Mirror* leaked her unflattering view that Major, as Chancellor in 1990, had 'swallowed . . . the slogans of the European lobby' and 'intellectually . . . was drifting with the tide'. 'Perhaps because he had made his name as a whip,' she wrote, 'or perhaps because he is unexcited by the sort of concepts which people like Nigel and I saw as central to politics', his 'one great objective' was to keep the party together.[100] Bravely for a Murdoch editor, Simon Jenkins in *The Times* deplored the commercial imperatives that drove this sort of backbiting:

> I find it incredible that a leader so discomfited by her own predecessor could now savage her successor. But hype is hype. A cabinet is but a cabinet, but a book is the precious lifeblood of a master spirit. It must be sold, at whatever cost to the conduct of Her Majesty's Government.[101]

At Blackpool she made a big effort to be 'fulsomely loyal'; she was even seen to greet Michael Heseltine in the hotel restaurant.[102] But the mood of the conference was strongly to the right, with the three leading Eurosceptic ministers – Michael Portillo, Michael Howard and Peter Lilley, famously described by Major in an unguarded aside as 'the bastards' – all making what were seen as coded bids for the succession. Major temporarily silenced his critics with an enthusiastically received speech (which rapidly boomeranged on him) calling for the party to get 'back to basics'. In a television interview with David Frost, Lady Thatcher seized on this to claim that he was now back on 'the true path of Conservatism'.[103] This was the start of an intensive blitz of book-promotion – more radio and television interviews, signing sessions, a question-and-answer forum at the Barbican chaired by Jeffrey Archer – accompanied by a four-part BBC television series.

Both the book and the series showed that the Iron Lady had lost none of her passionate intensity. The book has its *longueurs*, but it is still by far the most comprehensive and readable of modern prime ministerial memoirs: partisan of course, but generally a clear and vivid account of her side of the arguments. Of course it aggrandises her role, exaggerates the degree to which she knew where she was going from the beginning, slides over her moments of doubt and hesitation and diminishes the role of most of her colleagues, aides and advisers. It is a shockingly ungenerous book, shot through with gratuitously withering comments not only about people like Michael Heseltine and Geoffrey Howe whom she had some cause to feel bitter about, but also about other inoffensive colleagues who had served her well. Only Willie Whitelaw, Keith Joseph and Denis are beyond criticism, plus of course Bernard Ingham and Charles Powell. Other officials are barely mentioned. Nevertheless *The Downing Street Years* is a good record. But the television series is in some ways an even better one, partly because it includes the testimony of colleagues and critics as well as Lady Thatcher herself, but mainly because it directly captures the unrelenting force of her personality. Dressed in bright blue, fixing the camera with staring eyes, leaning forward to emphasise her points, she is intent on restating her beliefs and demolishing her enemies with no hint of passion spent or recollection in tranquillity. When she comes to recalling her removal from office, the wounds are still raw: she is bitter, contemptuous, unforgiving and more than slightly mad – to the extent that many watching must have understood for the first time what her colleagues had to put up with. Her anger scorches the screen.[104]

Literary editors gave most of her senior colleagues – Howe, Lawson, Hurd and others – the chance to answer back by reviewing the book.[105] Lawson had already published his own thousand-page apologia, *The View from No. 11*, the previous year; Howe's *Conflict of Loyalty* followed in 1994, giving the public an unprecedented choice of accounts of the same events by the three senior members of a government, all of whom had left office in contentious circumstances within the space of thirteen months. That is in addition to a dozen other ministerial memoirs which had already appeared from Peter Carrington, Jim Prior, Norman Tebbit, David Young, Nicholas Ridley, Kenneth Baker and several more. The market was becoming glutted; but still *The Downing Street Years* sold well. Lady Thatcher spent two weeks signing copies in bookshops all around Britain, then flew off in November to do the same in America and Japan. The paperback edition appeared in Britain in March 1995 and did even better. Meanwhile her contract with HarperCollins obliged her to lose no time in getting on with the second volume covering her early years.

This, though autobiographically more interesting, had less commercial potential. Lady Thatcher was therefore persuaded to supplement the 450-odd pages describing her childhood and rise to power with another 150 pages giving her view of current events in the four and a half years since her fall. If *The Downing Street Years* had been unhelpful to her successor, *The Path to Power*, which appeared in May 1995 accompanied by another media circus, was much worse. This time she avoided personal criticism, but made it clear that she thought the Major Government had squandered her legacy and pursued the wrong policies in most areas – not only towards Europe and Yugoslavia, but also by losing control of public spending, which had risen steadily since she left office, and by introducing tax changes which penalised middle-class families. What was lacking since 1990, she concluded pointedly, was 'a sense of purpose'.[106] The *Sunday Times* trailed extracts under the headline 'Thatcher launches savage attack on Major's misguided policies'.[107] 'The ghost of Margaret Thatcher is once again howling along the corridors of Westminster,' Simon Jenkins wrote in *The Times*. 'Another book is rising from the graveyard.' He went on to mount a strong defence of Major, maintaining that, in his own style and more difficult circumstances than she had faced, he had not only done many things that she too would have done had she continued in office – switching from the poll tax to the council tax, increasing VAT, increasing NHS spending and compromising on Maastricht – but had carried her revolution into areas she had not dared touch, like the privatisation of coal and British Rail. Indeed, Jenkins concluded, Major had actually been a better Thatcherite than Lady Thatcher herself.[108]

Such rebukes cut no ice with Lady Thatcher. In another round of interviews to promote the book she broadened her attack, asserting that the Tories had lost their way because they were 'not being Conservative enough'.[109] She denied that she was undermining Major – though it was scarcely helpful to call Tony Blair 'the most formidable Labour leader since Hugh Gaitskell' when Central Office had been trying to rubbish him as an insubstantial soundbite politician[110] – but insisted that he could still recover. 'We must get back to Conservative policies.'[111] She condemned the admittedly clumsy withdrawal of the whip from a dozen persistent Maastricht rebels (having withdrawn it, all Major could do after a time was weakly give it back again) and even blamed the Government for a decline in the rule of law and parliamentary traditions. ('I didn't think we'd ever let those go to the extent that we are.')[112] At another packed public forum in Westminster Hall she called on the Government to 'cut some money from welfare dependency' and put it into 'strengthening the forces of law and order so that more criminals are caught', and went on to question the whole basis of the welfare state:

Some of them are artificially bringing themselves into poverty . . .
People who are old-fashioned like me are saying you are not entitled to take a penny piece if you can work to keep yourself. You
are not entitled to live out of your neighbour's pocket if you can
live by keeping yourself.[113]

By now she was simply ranting. Prejudice had finally taken over from
politics, unmediated by the memory of responsibility. Hearing her speak
without a text at this time was reminiscent of the clockwork singing
doll in Offenbach's *The Tales of Hoffmann*, which runs down every few
minutes unless wound up. She was suddenly an opinionated and easily
provoked old lady: press a button and she would respond with a tirade
until she ran out of steam and had to be prompted with another question, which set her off again. Unfortunately for Major, she still made
headlines and her words, as she set off on another whistle-stop signing
tour around the country, gave encouragement to those in the party
who were looking for a change of leader. Though she denied it, one
pregnant line in *The Path to Power* gave credence to this interpretation
of her purpose. 'I offer some thoughts about putting these things right,'
she wrote. 'It is now, however, for others to take the action required.'[114]
No one at Westminster could fail to hear the echo of Geoffrey Howe's
words which had precipitated the drama of November 1990.

Major accepted the challenge and got his response in first. On 22
June he startled the political world by resigning as party leader – though
not as Prime Minister – and inviting his critics to 'put up or shut up':
either put up a candidate to defeat him or else stop sniping. The
obvious candidate, long regarded as Lady Thatcher's favourite – though
she had never said anything publicly to encourage that idea – was
Michael Portillo. (The closest she had come to endorsing him was
some off-the-cuff flattery at his fortieth birthday party in May 1993.)
But Portillo decided, after some contrary signals, not to stand, and the
much less charismatic John Redwood came forward instead. In this
crisis of his premiership one might have expected Lady Thatcher, who
had been so affronted by the constitutional impropriety of a serving
Prime Minister being driven from office by a party revolt, to have
rallied to her successor's support, whatever her reservations about him.
In fact she remained studiedly neutral. She was promoting her book
in America at the time of the ballot on 4 July, but issued a curt statement saying merely that Major and Redwood were 'both good
Conservatives'.[115] This was scarcely an endorsement. She did bring
herself to congratulate Major, however, when he won just enough
votes to secure his position – 218 to Redwood's 89 – and told Wyatt

that she would henceforth support Major 'because the alternative is even worse'. Her nightmare was that a Blair Government dependent on the Liberal Democrats would introduce proportional representation and keep the Tories out for twenty years.[116] Blair might be a new sort of Labour leader, but his party was as socialist as ever – though now pursuing its goal through European federalism – so it was vital for the Tories to win again.

She saw a hopeful model for a Tory recovery in the Republicans' sweeping gains in the mid-term congressional elections in America, under the born-again leadership of Newt Gingrich. 'After an unhappy period when the momentum stalled,' she declared in Washington, the Republicans 'have now decided to regard the 1980s as a springboard, not an embarrassment. And the political dividend has been huge. I hope that British Conservatives will raise their sights and learn lessons from America.'[117] By the same token she saw the Democratic President Bill Clinton as 'nothing but a draft dodger and a coward',[118] as well as hopelessly woolly. 'He's a great communicator,' she acknowledged. 'The trouble is he has absolutely nothing to communicate.'[119]

The party conference that autumn coincided with her seventieth birthday, which provided the opportunity for another show of hatchet-burying. First, Major hosted a party for her at Number Ten. Then she was given the warmest ovation she had received for several years when she appeared on the platform at Blackpool – though her appearance was brought forward by a day so as not to overshadow Major's closing speech. Back in London she herself held a big party at Claridge's, attended by the Queen – a rare honour. Typically, however, the occasion was most spectacularly marked in Washington, where a lavish dinner was held in Union Station with the guests paying $1,000 per head to the Thatcher Foundation. Ronald Reagan, now incapacitated by Alzheimer's disease, was unable to attend, but Nancy read a tribute from him, and most of the Republican hierarchy from ex-President Bush to Charlton Heston was present to see her solemnly presented with the American flag.[120]

During 1995, as well as three trips to America, she also visited Singapore, Rome, Madrid, Peking, Hong Kong, Bahrain, Japan, France, India, Venice, Indonesia and Australia, mostly delivering variations of a standard speech on 'The Challenges of the 21st Century'. But in January 1996 she came back home to make what was billed as her first setpiece speech on domestic politics since 1990, in the form of a Keith Joseph Memorial Lecture. (Joseph had died in December 1994.) Much of it was a tribute to Joseph and a reminder – not free of self-congratulation – of the rediscovery of true Conservatism, which he and she had launched together in the 1970s. But she could not resist drawing lessons for the present which made nonsense of her supposed reconciliation with Major. Dutifully she asserted that 'in the present Prime Minister, the party has a leader who shares the broad analysis that Keith Joseph and I put forward'. But immediately she repeated her view that the party was trailing in the polls because it had abandoned that analysis. 'We are unpopular, above all, because the middle classes – and all those who aspire to join the middle classes – feel that they no longer have the incentives and opportunities they expect from a Conservative Government.' And then she took a swipe at those – she did not name them, but she clearly meant Major's closest colleagues Kenneth Clarke (now Chancellor), Michael Heseltine (now deputy Prime Minister) and Malcolm Rifkind (who had recently succeeded Hurd as Foreign Secretary) – who called themselves 'One Nation' Conservatives:

> As far as I can tell by their views on European federalism, such people's creed would be better described as '*No Nation* Conservatism'. And certainly anyone who believes that salvation is to be found further away from the basic Conservative principles which prevailed in the 1980s . . . is profoundly mistaken.

By contrast she pointedly picked out for commendation four right-wingers: Lilley, Howard, Portillo and Redwood.[121]

Just a few days earlier Major had warned that the party's only chance of recovery lay in unity, since the British electorate did not like parties that squabbled among themselves.[122] Moreover at Blackpool in October he had affirmed his personal commitment to 'One Nation' Conservatism and invoked the legacy of Iain Macleod.[123] To have Lady Thatcher so bluntly contradict him in a carefully scripted speech with the television cameras present was the last straw. 'We have been a One Nation party since the beginning of time,' he retorted, 'and we are now . . . I will not be pushed off what I believe to be right.'[124] Once again Simon Jenkins rode to his defence, insisting that Major had been in practice at least as good a Thatcherite as she was. (He had just published his sharply revisionist analysis of the Thatcher years, *Accountable to None*, provocatively subtitled 'The Tory Nationalisation of Britain'.) Her lecture, Jenkins wrote, was not only an act of 'calculated disloyalty', plainly aimed at trying to ensure the succession of one of her supporters after Major's defeat, but also 'grotesquely unfair to John Major and a travesty of Thatcherism in government. Lady Thatcher has become the Arthur Scargill of the right, peddling myths of the party's ideological history.'[125]

She was on much more solid ground when she kept to the world stage. In March 1996 she made one of her most prescient speeches when invited to speak at Fulton, Missouri, where fifty years earlier Churchill had coined his great image of an 'iron curtain' descending across Europe. With the help of the now indispensable Robin Harris, she rose to the occasion with a Churchillian survey of the world after the end of the Cold War, highlighting the rise of 'rogue states' – was she the first to use the phrase? – 'like Syria, Iraq and Gadaffi's Libya' and the danger from 'the proliferation of weapons of mass destruction'. The world, she warned, 'remains a very dangerous place . . . menaced by more unstable and complex threats than a decade ago'. But she feared that with the risk of imminent nuclear annihilation apparently removed, 'we in the West have lapsed into alarming complacency about the risks that remain'. Her preference was explicitly for pre-emptive military action to remove the threat – a policy that would have to wait for the presidency of the younger George Bush, acting under the provocation of the attack on the World Trade Center in September 2001. In the meantime she merely urged the West to press on with the development of 'effective ballistic missile defence which would protect us and our armed forces, reduce or even nullify the rogue state's arsenal and enable us to retaliate'. She called for a reinvigoration of NATO both by extending its membership to include Poland, Hungary and the Czech Republic and by allowing it to operate 'out of area' to defend the West's security. But as always she saw all progress and safety in terms of American leadership, with Britain as America's first ally. 'It is the West – above all perhaps the English-speaking peoples of the West . . . which we all know offers the best hope of global peace and prosperity. In order to uphold these things, the Atlantic political relationship must be constantly nurtured and renewed.'[126]

Three days later, back in London, she made another speech (at a conference about Kuwaiti prisoners still being held in Iraq) warning against the rundown in defence spending since 1989 (which had actually begun when she was still Prime Minister), and the folly of relying on the United Nations to deter aggressors like Saddam Hussein.[127] Then in May, in Prague, she widened her analysis still further by bringing together her belief in American leadership with her most frontal attack yet on the European Union. 'Some of the lesser dreams which went into Europeanism are by no means ignoble,' she conceded. 'But the overall European federalist project . . . is . . . a nightmare.'

For the drive towards a European superstate – with its own Government, its own laws, its own currency and its own citizenship – would achieve none of the goals which enthusiasts on either side of the Atlantic claim for it.

Were it to come about, another great power would have been born – equal or nearly equal in economic strength to the United States. Does anyone suppose that such a power would not soon become a rival to America? That it would not gradually discover different interests from those of the United States? That it would not by degrees move towards a different public philosophy – one less liberal, more statist? And that it would not eventually seek to establish its own military forces separate from those of the United States? . . .

Europe separated from the United States would in my view be unequivocally a bad thing – bad for America, bad for Europe, and bad for the world at large.

Her alternative was first to strengthen NATO; second, to promote her idea of an Atlantic economic union by merging the North American Free Trade Area with the European Community, 'including the countries of central and perhaps in time Eastern Europe'; and third, vaguely and least convincingly, the development of 'a real Atlantic political consciousness and public opinion', possibly based on 'new institutions'.[128] Whatever she meant by that was not spelled out. She denied that she was talking about an even bigger Atlantic superstate, but that is very much what it sounds like – an ironic terminus to her flight from a European superstate. The vision may be skewed, some of her apprehensions alarmist, but these speeches of 1996 are remarkable testimony to her determination to keep thinking about the global picture and to her ability, with the help of her wordsmiths, to articulate a powerful case for her bleak vision of a dangerous world which could only be saved by American leadership and military vigilance.

Back home that summer she sparked yet another furious spat with Major by making a donation – from her own pocket – to Bill Cash's anti-federalist European Foundation, when Central Office ruled that he could not accept funding from James Goldsmith (who had recently formed his own Referendum Party to run candidates against pro-European Tories). Lady Thatcher promptly invited Cash to lunch in Chesham Place and gave him a large cheque. 'This is treachery,' Major told his aides, before issuing his sharpest public rebuke yet to his predecessor, all the stronger for its outward mildness. 'Everyone must choose what to do with their own money. Lady Thatcher must answer for her own actions. Personally I would have given the money to the Conservative Party.'[129] In his weekly 'Nature Notes', *The Times* cartoonist Peter Brookes added to his taxonomy of political species by drawing Lady Thatcher as Rabid Old Bat (*Federalis anathema*), whose 'bite can prove gravely injurious to grey-haired bespectacled gentlemen'.[130]

But then she made it up yet again with another cloyingly insincere endorsement of Major at Brighton in October ('You and I, John, have put our principles, our Conservative principles, into practice year after year, not just when they were popular but when they were unpopular . . .'),[131] followed by another lecture in honour of a departed colleague, this time Nicholas Ridley, in which she was persuaded to concentrate her fire on Labour instead of the Government. It was only at the last minute that Tim Bell and Cecil Parkinson dissuaded her from wading into the latest Euro-row; but with the General Election only months away and a Labour victory seemingly almost certain, she did not want to be seen to rock the boat. Privately she had been telling friends that the country had 'nothing to fear' from Tony Blair, a patriot who, she said, 'will not let Britain down'.[132]* But now an unnamed 'ally' told *The Times*: 'She will not be blamed, or allow the blame to be heaped on her friends, for losing the Tories the election . . . Whatever misgivings she may have, she fears a Blair Government even more. That is why she stayed on side.'[133] The old tunes still came easily. 'Socialism is not dead,' she warned. 'It is not even asleep; it is visibly stirring . . . Some slogans run and run, so let me repeat: Don't Let Labour Ruin It.'[134]

Once again she was determined not to be sidelined when the election came. No sooner had Major announced the date than she was on the pavement outside Chesham Place giving an impromptu press conference, as she had so often done in Downing Street, to try to quash reports that she was secretly supporting Blair and might be about to 'do an Enoch' by urging Tories to vote Labour. 'The phrase "New Labour" is cunningly designed to conceal a lot of old socialism. Don't be taken in . . . Stay with us and with John Major until we cross the finishing line.'[135] Since she would not be ignored, Major had no option but to try to harness her. First, she paid a well-publicised visit to Central Office to enthuse the party workers; then she appeared with Major at a candidates' rally at which she praised his 'magnificent stewardship'

---

*If her definition of 'not letting Britain down' was backing America in every eventuality, Blair did her proud in 2003 by aligning Britain unswervingly behind George W. Bush's invasion of Iraq, in defiance of most of his party, public opinion and the United Nations. She herself at the height of her relationship with Ronald Reagan was never more obedient to American leadership.

and warned of the return of Labour's trade-union 'bully boys', affirming that Labour had undergone 'a conversion of convenience' only and was 'still interventionist in its psyche';[136] and on 16 April they spent a day together campaigning on Teesside, revisiting the now redeveloped site of the famous photograph of Mrs Thatcher striding off into a post-industrial wilderness in 1987. 'I do want be helpful,' she assured Major. 'But behind the bonhomie,' Major's biographer has written, 'the atmosphere remained tense and awkward.' He and Norma were relieved when she left them.[137]

On her own she was more uninhibited, responding to the old lure of the hustings. Barnstorming through Aldershot and Christchurch on 9 April, she ridiculed the increasingly common idea that Tony Blair was 'the new Thatcher':

> They have got the sex wrong, they have got the willpower, the reasoning wrong, the strength wrong. He is trying to take over our policies in part. It is a kind of conversion of convenience. I had to make the revolution happen by changing everything I found in Britain, because I had a conviction.[138]

For the most part she avoided getting drawn into controversy about Europe, which was still tearing the Tory party apart. Major – trying to hold the balance between Clarke and Heseltine on one side and the increasingly dominant Europhobes on the other – was seeking desperately to avoid a binding commitment for or against joining the Euro, sticking to the formula that Britain should negotiate and then decide. Lady Thatcher's sympathy lay with James Goldsmith's Referendum Party. Unlike several of her known friends, like Alistair McAlpine and Carla Powell, she could not be seen openly to back it, but she gave covert encouragement to some of its candidates, notably George Gardiner (who had been deselected by his constituency party in Reigate).[139] Meanwhile nearly 300 Tory candidates, facing Referendum Party opponents in their constituencies, explictly committed themselves in their election addresses against joining; and on 18 April, while touring a supermarket in Maldon with John Whittingdale, Lady Thatcher gave a straight answer when asked if she was in favour of the single currency. 'Good heavens, no. I was the one who invented the answer. No. No. No.'[140]

Eighteen years of Tory Government ended on 1 May 1997 in an even bigger Labour landslide than the polls had predicted. Labour won 419 seats and the Liberal Democrats – benefiting from widespread tactical voting – forty-six, reducing the Tories to a rump of 165 (their worst result since 1906) and giving Blair a majority of 179, which dwarfed even Mrs Thatcher's two big wins in 1983 and 1987. Seven years after her departure, the Thatcher era had finally imploded in a welter of division, recrimination and sleaze. During the 1980s it had seemed that the Tories might hold power for ever: Mrs Thatcher had boasted hubristically that Jim Callaghan would be 'the *last* Labour Prime Minister'. Now it was the Tories who were down and out, while Labour – 'New' Labour – seemed certain to be in power for at least two Parliaments. Lady Thatcher viewed this debacle with mixed feelings. On the one hand, she was a lifelong party warrior and believed enough of her dire warnings about resurgent socialism to deplore the state to which her old party had been reduced. On the other hand, she could not disguise a certain satisfaction in contemplating the shipwreck which she believed her successors had brought upon themselves by discarding her in 1990. 'The people who brought about that incident,' she charged the following year, 'are responsible for the biggest defeat the Conservative Party has ever had . . . They have let the Labour party in and big. You won't turn that round in one election.' The 1997 result was 'catastrophic for me, because I got things right and that defeat stemmed from that incident'.[141] She did not consider the alternative view that she had left Major a poisoned legacy – an economy running into recession, declining public services and a party already deeply split over Europe – and had done everything in her power over the past seven years to undermine his authority and widen the rift. Many commentators saw 1997 as the electorate's delayed verdict on Thatcherism, which Major had managed to stave off once in 1992 – with a little help from Neil Kinnock – but could not do a second time when faced with the greater electoral appeal of Tony Blair. All but the most committed partisans thought a change of government overdue and healthy.

At a deeper level, however, 1997 can be seen as Mrs Thatcher's greatest victory, which set the seal on her transformation of British politics. She had set out, on becoming leader in 1975, to abolish socialism and twenty years later she had succeeded beyond her wildest dreams. By her repeated electoral success, by her neutering of the trade unions, by the privatisation of most of the public sector and the introduction of market forces into almost every area of national life, she – and her successor – had not only reversed the tide of increasing collectivism which had flowed from 1945 to 1979, but had rewritten the whole agenda of politics, forcing the Labour party gradually and reluctantly to accept practically the entire Thatcherite programme – at least the means, if not in its heart the ends – in order to make itself electable. Neil Kinnock and after him John Smith took the party a long way down this road, without altogether abandoning traditional Labour values. The election of Tony Blair to succeed Smith in 1994 completed the process. Blair was a perfectly post-Thatcherite politician: an ambitious pragmatist with a smile of dazzling sincerity, but no convictions beyond a desire to rid Labour of its outdated ideological baggage. The rebranding of the party as 'New Labour' was the final acknowledgement of Mrs Thatcher's victory. 'We are all Thatcherites now,' Peter Mandelson acknowledged.[142] She had not only banished socialism, in any serious meaning of the word, from political debate; but she had effectively abolished the old Labour party. 'New' Labour was as dedicated as the Tories to wealth creation and market forces, even if it hoped – as Major too had done – to pursue them with more humanity than Mrs Thatcher had often shown. Back in the polarised 1970s the dream of most pundits had been that Britain should become more like America, with two capitalist parties differing in style and tone but agreed on essentials, like the Republicans and Democrats. The rise of New Labour had now brought this to pass. But instead of an alternation of parties, the consequence has been almost fatal to the Tory party. While Labour has seized the centre ground – Keith Joseph's 'common ground' – the Tories have been deprived of their principal *raison d'être*. Lady Thatcher's dated warnings cut no ice, because Blair was plainly no sort of socialist, and even Gordon Brown and the rest of his senior colleagues, who had all been student lefties in the 1970s, could now speak the language of competition as fluently as any Tory. It was, as she had reflected on leaving office, 'a funny old world'. Yet she could not be expected to shed many tears for her old party.

Three weeks after the election, just before attending his first European summit, Blair outraged old Labour stalwarts by inviting Lady Thatcher to Downing Street. 'She has a mind well worth picking,' his spokesman explained, 'and he wants to see her again.'[143] She was happy to give him the benefit of her advice. Blair, with his huge majority, his personal self-confidence and vaguely messianic leanings, was – as William Rees-Mogg wrote in *The Times* – her 'natural successor' in a way that poor insecure John Major had never been. Though he was Prime Minister longer than Attlee or Lloyd George and nearly as long as Macmillan, Baldwin and Wilson, Major's seven-year tenure in Number Ten quickly shrivelled to a mere fractious coda to the Thatcher years. Meanwhile the shattered Tory party had to elect a new leader. The front-runner, Michael Portillo, who would probably have won easily had he been able to stand, had lost his seat. Lady Thatcher initially indicated that she would not back any candidate, though she was anxious that her three remaining protégés, Lilley, Howard and Redwood, should not stand against each other but should unite to defeat Ken Clarke. 'Don't touch Ken,' she urged Tory MPs, 'remember his record.'[144] But when the thirty-six-year-old William Hague emerged as the fresh white hope – and still more when Redwood cynically teamed up with Clarke – she came off the fence to lobby for him. Hague had first come to prominence as a precocious schoolboy at the 1976 party conference, speaking from the podium under the benign maternal gaze of the leader, then had won a by-election in 1988. He was Mrs Thatcher's political child if ever there was one; and she now appeared with him for an excruciating photo-call outside the House of Commons, at which she wagged her finger and lectured the camera like a backward child:

I am supporting William Hague. Now, have you got the name? William Hague. For principled government, following the same kind of government which I led, vote for William Hague on Thursday. Have you got the message?[145]

Hague was duly elected – by ninety-two votes against seventy for Clarke – but over the next four years failed dismally to dent Blair's popularity or restore the public's faith in the Tories. Apart from the odd embarrassing eruption, Lady Thatcher finally began to fade from public view. She still maintained a 'coven' of her acolytes among the younger Europhobes – Francis Maude, Bernard Jenkin, David Heathcoat-Amory and 'indisputably her current favourite', Iain Duncan Smith – but Hague was careful to keep his distance from her.[146] While he would only rule out joining the Euro in the next Parliament, she maintained her total opposition to Britain ever joining it. ('I say we should not go in – period'.)[147] She was strongly opposed to Scottish devolution, as she always had been; but when she appeared in Glasgow shortly before the Scottish referendum and gave an interview to the *Scotsman* denouncing it, she succeeded only in upstaging Hague and boosting the hitherto faltering 'Yes' campaign. The leader of the SNP, Alex Salmond, hailed 'Mrs Poll Tax' as 'the living memorial as to why the Scots want their own Parliament'.[148] She was also very unhappy about the Good Friday Agreement in Northern Ireland, signed in April 1998; she was 'horrified' by the release of IRA prisoners, thought it 'horrible' to see Sinn Fein leaders welcomed in Downing Street and was 'pessimistic' about the agreement's chances of success.[149] After what she had suffered at the hands of Irish terrorists, her revulsion was understandable; but it reinforced the impression that she was stuck in the past.

Altogether she was increasingly seen as a batty old eccentric, a caricature of her former self, who won most headlines when she played up to her image – as when she descended on the British Airways stand at the 1997 party conference and excoriated the company for its unpatriotic new tail designs, making an elaborate pantomime of covering with her handkerchief the abstract patterns that had replaced the Union Jack. 'We fly the British flag,' she insisted, 'not these awful things.'[150] There was great amusement in January 1999 when she was said to be worried that Tony Blair was 'getting awfully bossy'.[151]

That year she caused fresh embarrassment by going out on a limb in support of the former Chilean dictator General Pinochet, who was arrested while visiting London for medical treatment, at the instance of a Spanish judge in connection with the disappearance of a number of Spanish citizens during the 1980s. Just a few days earlier she had entertained the general to tea, so his arrest was an affront to her – and by extension Britain's – hospitality, as well as a rude shock to the fraternity of former world leaders, raising the nightmare that she herself might be detained somewhere on her travels in connection with the sinking of the *Belgrano*. She wrote to *The Times* that Pinochet had not only been 'a good friend to this country' during the Falklands war, providing intelligence assistance which she claimed had saved British lives (though she had not mentioned this precious assistance in her memoirs), but had also put Chile back on the road to democracy.[152] It was true that Pinochet was a rare dictator who had voluntarily stepped down in return for assurances that he would not be prosecuted for crimes committed while he was in power: there was some force in Lady Thatcher's argument that it was not for Spain or Britain to interfere in Chile's delicate settlement with its recent past. Nevertheless the sight of the former Prime Minister championing an elderly dictator – visiting him more than once in his year-long detention on a Surrey executive housing estate and losing no opportunity to berate the Government for not releasing him – was a gift to her detractors and a further trial to a Tory leadership desperate to exorcise her image.*

In May 1999 the party held a dinner at the London Hilton to mark

---

*She also embarrassed her friends in 2001 by giving her outspoken support to the newly-elected Italian Prime Minister, the ring-wing media magnate Silvio Berlusconi, and his coalition partners the neo-fascist Alleanze Nationale, with whom Hague had promised that the Tories would have no links.

the twentieth anniversary of her coming to power. But instead of using the occasion to rededicate itself to her principles, as she expected, both Hague at the dinner and Peter Lilley, his deputy, at another meeting the same evening struck out in the opposite direction in a concerted effort to show that the party had learned the lesson of its 1997 defeat. Hague announced that it was time to move on from the 1980s and called it 'a great mistake to think that all Conservatives have to offer is solutions based on free markets'; while Lilley stated still more explicitly that 'belief in the free market has only ever been part of Conservatism'. The party needed to restore public confidence in its commitment to the welfare state; but it would only do so 'if we openly and emphatically accept that the free market has only a limited role in improving public services like health, education and welfare'.[153]

Coming from Ken Clarke, such sentiments would have surprised no one; but from one who had made his name as a Thatcherite Social Security Secretary under Major, and was still supposed to be one of the party's thinkers, this was extraordinary heresy. Lady Thatcher was reported to be 'livid. Simply livid . . . She went ballistic [and] she doesn't mind who knows it.'[154] This time she was not alone. Most of the party, and the press, whatever their view on the precise issue of private versus public funding, saw Lilley's speech as a disastrously inept attempt at repositioning, which made the party look utterly unprincipled. Instead of enabling Hague to move out of Lady Thatcher's shadow, the resulting outcry forced him to repudiate any such intention: within months Lilley was relieved of the deputy leadership and Hague reset his course up to the 2001 election back towards the right – appeasing the party faithful with no beneficial impact on the opinion polls. A full decade after her fall, the party was still obsessed – 'hag-ridden' was one often-used expression – by Margaret Thatcher. In October 1999 John Major got his own back for her unhelpful memoirs with his own autobiography, accompanied by the usual interviews, in which he revealed his exasperation with her behaviour over Maastricht, attacked her increasingly 'crazy' views on Europe and sought to correct her rosy view of his inheritance:

If you actually look at the situation in 1990 when I became Prime Minister, the party was very split, the poll tax had been a complete social and economic disaster, we had a recession that had been building up as a result of the boom in the late Eighties, we had interest rates in double figures at about 14 per cent. We had very high inflation, we had unemployment rising dramatically, we had growth going into the ground. There was a full-scale recession with negative equity.[155]

The following year Blair too decided it was time to draw a line under Thatcherism. 'There were things that were done in the Eighties that were good and we have kept,' he declared on the tenth anniversary of her resignation, 'but there were four fundamental failings':

Britain had a boom-and-bust economy where people's mortgage rates were all over the place. We had huge social division, three million unemployed and chronic under-investment in our public services. I take nothing away from the things that were done in the 1980s. But it really is time, in my view, that we move British politics beyond the time of Margaret Thatcher.[156]

And so it went on right up to the election. Ardently as the ageing Tory membership still adored her, the memory of Mrs Thatcher was a millstone around Hague's neck, as it had been around Major's. Asked in January 2000 who they blamed for the state of the NHS, for instance, 17 per cent of those questioned named Tony Blair, 13 per cent Frank Dobson (Labour's first Health Secretary) and 42 per cent Margaret Thatcher.[157] Shortly before Blair went to the country again in May 2001, Lady Thatcher descended on the party's spring conference in Plymouth and made one of her characteristically cloth-eared jokes. On her way to the hall, she said, she had passed a cinema showing a film entitled *The Mummy Returns*. She did not seem to realise that this was a horror film – nothing to do with a cuddly mother-figure. By applying it to herself she unwittingly evoked all the headlines and cartoons that had been portraying her for years as a ghost, a vampire, the undead or Frankenstein's monster still haunting the Tory party.[158] During the campaign Labour once again exploited her unpopularity with a poster combining Hague's face with her hair – a neat inversion of all those Tory posters down the years showing the left-wing bogey of the day lurking behind the Labour leader's moderate mask – and her every appearance in the campaign served only to remind the voters why they did not want the Tories back. Labour was returned with its huge majority virtually undented, and once again the Tories were looking for a new leader.

Again the obviously best-qualified candidate, Ken Clarke, was ruled out by his unacceptability to the now dominant Europhobes. Lady Thatcher weighed in with a long letter to the *Daily Telegraph* warning that Clarke's support for the euro was so fundamentally at odds with the majority of the party that he could only lead it to disaster.[159] Next day she was answered by the *Daily Mail* in a front-page editorial affirming that while it would 'always revere Margaret Thatcher's historic achievements' and remained 'implacably opposed to losing the pound', it nevertheless thought her latest intervention 'ill-advised':

> We have, after all, been here before. Let it not be forgotten that she intimated that Mr Major was her favoured successor. Look what happened. The Lady anointed William Hague. The result speaks for itself.
>
> Today the ineluctable fact is that the Tory party – which once stood for economic competence and political realism – is so obsessed with Europe that if it risks choosing the wrong leader again it risks the very real possibility of political extinction.[160]

Still the party went ahead and elected the totally inexperienced Iain Duncan Smith, whose only qualifications were that he had been one of the Maastricht rebels whom Major had temporarily deprived of the whip in 1994 and who was now Lady Thatcher's favourite son.* *The Week* summed up the press consensus with a cover cartoon of her embracing the new leader under the headline 'The Kiss of Death?'[161] Three months later a BBC documentary entitled '*The Curse of the Mummy*' revived her Plymouth joke to lay on her much of the blame for the party's dire state.[162] Her refusal to go quietly into the political night had left the former Prime Minister now virtually friendless.

Silenced

Not only did she have few friends, but her family provided little consolation for her old age. 'We are a grandmother,' she had proudly announced in 1989, when Mark's first child was born. Four years later Diane Thatcher gave birth to a second. But Margaret saw her grandchildren only rarely – and not much more of her own children. In 1994 Mark and Diane moved from Texas to South Africa, since when they have seldom returned to Britain. Carol still lives in Switzerland in a long-term relationship with a ski instructor, but she has never married. Neither of the twins, who turned fifty in 2003, has exemplified the ideal of a close-knit family which their mother always strove to project.

---

*A quarter of a century earlier, when she became Tory leader, Mrs Thatcher too was seen as inexperienced. Yet she had three years as a junior minister and nearly four years as a Cabinet minister under her belt, plus another seven years in various shadow posts. Iain Duncan Smith had no experience of government at all and had only been in Parliament – for Norman Tebbit's old seat – since 1992.

Mark's business dealings have continued to attract controversy. As well as renewed questions about his alleged kickbacks from the Al-Yamamah contract with Saudi Arabia and other arms deals, which surfaced again with much new circumstantial detail in 1994, his American affairs came under investigation by the Texas courts in 1995. He was sued by his partner, Jay Laughlin, for alleged conspiracy involving 'mail fraud, wire fraud, tax fraud, bankruptcy fraud, money laundering, usury, common law fraud, deceptive trade practices, perjury, theft and assault'.[163] It was also widely reported that his marriage was in trouble. Lady Thatcher was said to be 'heartbroken' by the Al-Yamamah allegations, which filled the Sunday papers the weekend before the 1994 party conference. She attended only briefly that year, looking unusually frail and haggard, and strenuously denied that Mark had done anything wrong, before flying on to Dallas to receive an honorary degree and incidentally see her eighteen-month-old grand-daughter for the first time.[164] Eventually Mark settled out of court with Laughlin for $500,000, but he still faced another $4 million case being brought against his Grantham Company (which traded in avia-tion fuel) by the Ameristar Fuel Corporation, as well as charges of tax evasion. After a family summit in April his mother was reported to have cleared his debts to the tune of £700,000.[165] Later that year he moved, with Diane and the children, to Cape Town; but his reputa-tion followed him and he has continued to attract the attention of both the police and the South African tax authorities.[166]

In 1995 a biography entitled *Thatcher's Gold* by two investigative journalists, Paul Halloran and Mark Hollingsworth, attempted to get to the bottom of Mark's unexplained wealth. The authors uncovered a lot of suggestive testimony without quite solving the problem.[167] But there is no doubt that Mark has done exceedingly well out of his mother's name, while she has steadfastly refused to hear any criticism of him. Then, in 1996, Carol broke cover with an affectionate biog-raphy of Denis, which incidentally drew a devastating picture of Margaret's remoteness as a mother. She was even more explicit in some of the interviews that accompanied publication. 'As a child I was fright-ened of her,' she revealed. Mark had always been their mother's favourite. 'I always felt I came second of the two. Unloved is not the right word, but I never felt I made the grade.' Though as an adult she had plainly grown fond of her father, she described her parents' marriage as a union of two ambitious and primarily work-directed people, rather than a happy family unit. 'Their priorities were not to each other or to us.'[168] 'It was very much drilled into me that the best thing I could ever do for my mother was not to make any demands on her.'[169] In a curiously artless way, almost as if she did not know what she was doing, Carol thus comprehensively torpedoed her mother's pretence that family had always been the most important thing in her life.

In August 1998 Lady Thatcher gave an unusually revealing interview to the retirement magazine *Saga*. Part of it was concerned with politics – her bitter analysis of the 1997 defeat and her absolute opposition to joining the euro, now or ever. But much more striking was her candid admission that she regretted not seeing more of her grandchildren:

> All one's thoughts were to have a nice house for the family . . . We see them at Christmas . . . Sometimes when we're in America we visit. And there is always the telephone of course . . . But, no, we don't see very much of them. My son and his wife regularly go from South Africa to America, but they haven't been here since they went to live in South Africa . . . My greatest delight is when my daughter-in-law sends me photographs of the grandchildren. Apart from seeing them in the flesh that is the greatest pleasure I have in the whole year, far exceeding anything else.

But when her interviewer, Douglas Keay, suggested that she had saved the country at the cost of losing her children, she refused to say that she would make a different choice if she could have her life again:

> Look, you can't have everything. It has been the greatest privilege being Prime Minister of my country, and having many friends all interested in the same subjects. Yes, I wish I saw more of my children. We don't have Sunday lunch together. We don't go on holiday skiing any more. But I can't regret. And I haven't lost my children. They have their lives. I took a different life.[170]

For seventy years her health had been extraordinarily good. She had suffered from colds, from one or two specific conditions like varicose veins and Dupuytren's contracture which had required minor operations, and increasingly from problems with her teeth. But considering the demands she had made on her constitution for the past forty years, it had held up astonishingly well. In so-called retirement she still got up early and kept herself busy all day, still exhausted her staff by her relentless schedule on foreign trips. Yet eventually the Iron Lady did begin to show signs of metal fatigue. While speaking in Chile in 1994 she suddenly lost consciousness and slumped forward onto the lectern. She quickly recovered, and apologised profusely to her hosts for her uncharacteristic moment of weakness; but this was probably her first very minor stroke.[171]

The most visible sign of frailty over the next few years was a loss of short-term memory. She began to repeat herself and seemed not to take in what was said to her. So long as she had a script, she remained a true professional who could still turn in a faultless performance. But off-script she could be a liability, either too predictable – simply repeating lines she had used a thousand times before, sometimes just a minute earlier – or else alarmingly unpredictable. Denis or whoever was with her at the time had to be skilled at nudging the needle on at the right moment. It was in Madeira, where she and Denis had gone to celebrate their golden wedding anniversary at the end of 2001, that she suffered a second minor stroke. Sometime early in 2002 she had a third, as a result of which it was announced on 22 March that she would do no more public speaking. But not before she had exploded one last bombshell with the serialisation of her latest book.

Statecraft: Strategies for a Changing World was neither a third volume of memoirs, though it had autobiographical elements, nor – as its title might suggest – an instruction manual in the art of government. Rather it was a survey of the international scene at the start of the new millennium, with Lady Thatcher's view of how things had been allowed to slide since 1990 and what should now be done to put them right. Every few pages her prescription was summarised in four or five bullet points printed in bold type, as in a school primer. The book – written once again with the help of Robin Harris – was dedicated to Ronald Reagan 'to whom the world owes so much': its central message was contempt for the woolly internationalism of the 'new world order' and the importance of American global leadership. She seemed almost to welcome the terrorist attack on the World Trade Center on 11 September 2001 as a vindication of her previous warnings, and positively looked forward to the Americans hitting back decisively and unilaterally:

So far . . . I am heartened by the fact that President Bush seems to have concluded that this is an American operation and that America alone will decide how it is to be conducted . . . That means taking out the terrorists and their protectors, and not just in Afghanistan but elsewhere too.[172]*

---

*On the specific question of Iraq she wrote that 'There will be no peace and security in the region until Saddam is toppled.' She was hesitant about attacking him unless he could be shown to have been involved in the atrocities of 11 September. 'But if he was, he must be made to pay the price.'[173]

Did she recall that she had once been a strong upholder of international law who had criticised unilateral American action in Grenada, warned Reagan against retaliation against Libya and opposed carrying the Gulf War all the way to Baghdad without UN authority? Or that she had long argued that nuclear weapons helped preserve the peace and practically defined a country's sovereignty? Now, faced with the prospect of nuclear weapons falling into the wrong hands, she wrote that she 'certainly would not rule out pre-emptive strikes to destroy a rogue state's capabilities'[174] – while at the same time she dismissed 'pointless protests about India's or Pakistan's nuclear capabilities'.[175] Now it all depended on whether it was America's friends or enemies who had the weapons.

Other chapters dealt with Europe's feeble response to the disintegration of Yugoslavia; her high hopes of China, Hong Kong, India and Asia generally; rather more cautious optimism about Russia; a somewhat muted restatement of her belief that Israel must eventually be persuaded to trade 'land for peace' to secure a just settlement in the Middle East; and a deeply sceptical discussion of the whole notion of 'human rights' which in the light of the Pinochet affair she now regarded as a hypocritical left-wing scam. Most controversial, however, was her latest and definitive blast against the European Union. In this she finally revealed the gut conviction which had underlain her attitude to the Continent all her life. 'During my lifetime,' she declared in a grand generalisation which had recently become one of her favourite lines, 'most of the problems the world has faced have come, in one fashion or another, from mainland Europe, and the solutions from outside it.' Of course she was thinking primarily, as always, of World War Two. Victory over Nazism had been won by Britain, the Commonwealth and America. 'The mainland Europeans benefited from an outcome which, by and large, they had not themselves secured: some have resented it ever since.'[176] But the same was also true of the Cold War: Communism was the problem, America the solution.

'At a personal level,' she reflected, 'I am conscious that much of my energy as Prime Minister was . . . taken up with Europe – and, if I had my time again, still more would have been so.' The next few sentences were practically a declaration of war:

Of course, Britain was not in those days fighting a war against a European power. But there was an increasingly intense struggle all the same . . . And, looking forward into the century that has just begun, there is every reason to imagine that this clash of aims and ideas is likely to continue.[177]

Europe, she had concluded after years of trying, was 'fundamentally unreformable'. It was 'an empire in the making . . . the ultimate bureaucracy', founded on 'humbug'; inherently protectionist, intrinsically corrupt, essentially undemocratic and dedicated to the destruction of nation states. 'It is in fact a classic utopian project, a monument to the vanity of intellectuals, a programme whose inevitable destiny is failure.'[178] That being so, she now called, as she had never done so explicitly before, for a fundamental renegotiation of Britain's membership and, if that failed – as it was bound to do – for Britain to be ready to leave the union and join the North American Free Trade Area instead, turning its back on the whole disastrous folly into which Ted Heath (with, she admitted, her support at the time) had taken the country in 1973.

This sensational *démarche* was serialised in *The Times*, starting on Monday 18 March. In fact the two European chapters were featured on the Monday; subsequent extracts were drawn from other parts of the book. But it was the first day's clarion call which made the news. This time the consensus was clear, right across the political spectrum, that she had finally lost touch with reality. Her reading of history was denounced as blinkered nonsense; the option of renegotiation was dismissed as fantasy; the idea of withdrawal from Europe as simply impractical. In the Commons, Tony Blair challenged Iain Duncan Smith to disown her views. 'To talk about withdrawal and rule out the single currency whatever the circumstances is not an act of patriotism. It is an act of folly.'[179] Duncan Smith refused to condemn his mentor; but several of his colleagues, including paid-up Eurosceptics like Michael Howard, were quick to do so. The 'negative caricature' promoted by 'small-minded, xenophobic and bickering Little Englanders', Francis Maude rebuked her, made it 'much more difficult for Conservatives to engage in the great debate about the future of the European Union . . . We do not believe it was wrong for Britain to join the EU. We do not believe that mainland Europe has been the source of all evil.'[180] A poll of constituency party chairmen found 71 per cent rejecting Lady Thatcher's view. 'I love her to death,' the chairman of North East Hampshire Conservatives told *The Times*, 'but she's gone too far. We do not tolerate extremists and she has gone into the extremist bracket.' 'She has a special place in Conservative Party history,' echoed another. 'What she did for this country was something we should be proud of. But times have moved on . . . She should gracefully take a step back and let those in charge get on with it.'[181]

The very next day she caught the press off guard by doing exactly that. Having dominated the media all week with her views on Europe, she announced on Friday that she had been advised by her doctors to cancel all her scheduled speaking engagements and accept no more. 'SILENCED' ran the headlines from the *Daily Mail* to the *Sun*. 'The voice that dominated world politics for a quarter of a century was stilled last night as Baroness Thatcher announced she had made her last public speech.'[182] 'Exit right,' the *Independent* noted: 'a great talker whose voice still echoed round the world stage'.[183] The weekend papers were filled with retrospectives of her career, picture spreads, memorable sayings and virtual obituaries which proclaimed that this was the end of the story. Some commentators doubted if she would really be able to contain herself, since 'the sound of silence and Lady Thatcher are not natural allies'.[184] No one pointed out that she had only forsworn public speaking, and that she had sparked the latest uproar without uttering a word. Nevertheless there was universal agreement that it was the end of an era. Iain Duncan Smith paid appropriate tribute, but was assumed to be heaving a deep sigh of relief.

Her three strokes, rather than memory loss, were given as the reason, though clearly the two were connected. She did in fact continue to make public appearances. Just three weeks after the announcement, she honoured an engagement to be guest of honour at a dinner to mark the fifth anniversary of Politico's bookshop. After speeches by Bernard Ingham, John Nott (promoting his belated memoirs) and Gyles Brandreth, she teased the audience by rising as though to speak; but she uttered only six words – 'Thank you for a lovely evening' – before sitting down again to a din of 'cheering, foot-stamping and banging of cutlery'.[185] For some other occasions she recorded a video message which would be played in place of a live speech. In October 2002 she attended the opening of the new Archives Centre, built to house her papers at Churchill College, Cambridge, to which the Thatcher Foundation had contributed £5 million. And she continued to issue brief statements on current events – praising Blair's 'bold and effective' leadership in the war on Iraq, for instance, but at the same time accusing New Labour of 'reverting to Old Labour with its irresponsible policies of tax and spend'.[186] She could not quite give up the habit of a lifetime. But essentially she had now finally retired.

Statesmen usually have to wait till they are dead before they are immortalised in bronze or marble. But the House of Commons made an exception for Margaret Thatcher by commissioning a white marble statue, nearly eight feet high, intended to stand in the Members' Lobby opposite those of Churchill and Lloyd George, as soon as the rule could be changed to allow it to be installed. In the meantime it was displayed in the Guildhall. It was an impressive likeness, though as the

Independent's Simon Carr wrote, it was 'not entirely representational – the mouth, for instance, is shut. However, the statue is 40 per cent larger than life, and analysts agree that's almost exactly right.' Much comment focused on the trademark handbag – an unusual feature in statuary – but as Carr further noted, the image was 'unfamiliarly serene':

> The magnificent monster we remember is nowhere to be seen. There is nothing of the wars – against Argentina, Ireland, the miners. The ferocity, the exuberant slaughter, belong to another life. She looks out impassively but with recognition over her life and works.[187]

But five months after its unveiling the statue was brutally decapitated by an unemployed man armed with an eight-foot scaffolding pole – an event that provoked extraordinary glee among her detractors, who relished the symbolism of the attack. It was only a statue that had been damaged, yet it acted as a harmless surrogate for the suppressed violence which much of the population had been dying to visit on the original for years. The image of the headless woman was powerfully redolent of the execution of Mary, Queen of Scots, or Anne Boleyn. People in the street interviewed for the television news, and others who wrote letters to the papers, were quite indecently delighted. *Private Eye* ran a clever parody of Shelley's 'Ozymandias':

> I met a traveller from, er, England
> Who said: – A great big lump of stone
> Stands in the Guildhall. Near to it, on the carpet,
> Half sunk, a shattered visage lies, whose frown
> And wrinkled lip and sneer of cold command
> Tell that its sculptor well those passions read
> Which yet survive, stamped on these lifeless things,
> The hand that mocked them and the heart that fed.
> And on the pedestal these words appear:
> 'My name is Ozymaggias, queen of queens.
> Look on my works, ye mighty, and despair.'[188]

Public reaction to the vandalism of her statue gave a tiny foretaste of what can be expected when Lady Thatcher eventually joins the pantheon of departed leaders. The BBC will find it even more difficult to strike the right tone than it did at the time of the Queen Mother's death. Margaret Thatcher has been not merely the first woman and the longest-serving Prime Minister of modern times, but the most admired, most hated, most idolised, most vilified public figure of the second half of the twentieth century. To some she was the saviour of her country who 'put the Great back into Great Britain' after decades of decline;[189] the dauntless warrior who curbed the unions, routed the wets, reconquered the Falklands, rolled back the state and created a vigorous enterprise economy which twenty years later still out-performs the more regulated economies of the Continent. To others, she was a narrow ideologue whose hard-faced policies legitimised greed, deliberately increased inequality by favouring the middle class at the expense of a large excluded underclass, starved the public serv-ices, wrecked the universities, prostituted public broadcasting and destroyed the nation's sense of solidarity and civic pride. There is no reconciling these views: yet both are true.

A third view would argue that she achieved much less than she and her admirers claim: that for all her boasts on one side, and the howls of 'Tory cuts' on the other, she actually failed to curb public spending significantly, failed to prune or privatise the welfare state, failed to change most of the British people's fundamental attitudes, but rather extended Whitehall's detailed control of many areas of national life, shrank freedom where she claimed to be enhancing it, downgraded Parliament and pioneered a style of presidential government which has been developed still further by Tony Blair. Nor did she raise Britain's influence in the world. On the contrary, by binding the country more firmly than ever to the United States and refusing to engage constructively with Britain's opportunity in Europe, she repeated the historic error which kept Britain outside the European community in its formative phase, perpetuating its ambivalent semi-isolation. This may prove in the long run her most damaging legacy.

There remains the question of how far Margaret Thatcher, as an individual, inspired and drove the policies that bore her name, or to what extent she simply rode a global wave of anti-collectivism and technological revolution which would have changed British society in most of the same ways, whoever had been in power. What she unde-niably did was to articulate the new materialistic individualism with a clarity and moral fervour which appeared to win the argument by sheer force of personality, even when the reality was less radical than the rhetoric. She was not a creative or consistent thinker. There were huge contradictions between her belief in free markets and liberal economics, on the one hand, and her flagrant partiality to her own class and her increasingly strident English nationalism on the other. But that was not the point. She was a brilliantly combative, oppor-tunist politician who, by a mixture of hard work, stamina, self-belief and uncanny instinct, bullied an awestruck country into doing things her way for more than a decade. Above all she was a tremendous performer, who raised genuine passions – on both sides of the political divide – which have been sadly absent in the bland, spin-doctored days since her departure. She may have achieved less than she claimed, but she still accomplished much that was necessary and overdue. Today the whole culture of incomes policies, subsidies and social contracts – and the double-digit inflation that made them seem inescapable – seems so remote that it is easy to forget how much courage was required in 1979–81 to set about dismantling it. The courage was not hers alone; but she was the leader. Ultimately the balance sheet demands a judgement as to whether the economic benefits of that cultural revolution outweighed the social cost. That will require a longer perspective than is yet attainable. But for better or worse the Britain we live in today – and which our children will live in for some decades to come – was forged in the 1980s, just as the Britain of the previous generation was forged in the 1940s. We are still living in a post-Thatcherite world, a Margaret Thatcher theme park. *Si monumentum requiris, circumspice.*

Notes and References

1 The Blessed Margaret

1 *Guardian*, 5 May 1979.
2 Ibid.
3 Remarks on the steps of Downing Street, 4 May 1979.
4 *Thatcher: The Downing Street Years*, BBC, 1993.
5 *Sun*, 5 May 1979.
6 *Sunday Telegraph*, 6 May 1979.
7 Conservative Party Conference, 10 October 1970.
8 Labour Party Conference, 1 October 1963.
9 *Sunday Telegraph*, 6 May 1979.
10 Ibid.
11 BBC interview with Michael Cockerell, 27 April 1979.
12 Speech to the CPS Summer School, Cambridge, 6 July 1979.
13 Margaret Thatcher, *The Downing Street Years*, p.10.
14 Interview, Sir Kenneth Stowe.
15 Sir Ian Gilmour in *Thatcher: The Downing Street Years*.
16 Lord Carrington reported in Nicholas Henderson, *Mandarin*, p.269.
17 *The Times*, 5 May 1980.
18 Ibid., 9 February 1984.
19 e.g. House of Commons, 12 June 1979 [Vol. 968, col. 229].
20 *Observer*, 6 May 1979.
21 Ronald Millar, *A View from the Wings*, p.272.
22 *Sunday Times*, 3 May 1981.
23 Nicholas Ridley, '*My Style of Government*', p.83.
24 *Daily Mail*, 5 May 1979.
25 *Observer*, 25 January 1979.
26 e.g. Simon Hoggart in the *Guardian*, 7 May 1979, Anthony Sampson in the *Observer*, 13 May 1979.
27 Millar, p.268.
28 *Guardian*, 5 May 1979.
29 Penny Junor, *Margaret Thatcher: Wife, Mother, Politician*, p.231.
30 Edward Heath, *The Course of My Life*, p.574.
31 *Guardian*, 7 May 1979.
32 *The Journals of Woodrow Wyatt*, Vol. 2, p.64 (9 April 1989).
33 e.g. *The Economist*, 12 May 1979.

34 Interview, Sir John Nott.

35 *Guardian*, 7 May 1979.

36 Thatcher, p.28.

37 Wyatt, Vol. 2, p.71 (16 April 1989).

38 Ridley, pp.25–7.

39 James Prior, *A Balance of Power*, p.114.

40 Interviews, Lord Carlisle, Lady Young.

41 Prior, p.122.

42 Ibid., pp.114, 118.

43 *Daily Mail*, 7 May 1979.

44 Interview, Sir John Nott; Prior, p.172.

45 Millar, p.319.

46 House of Commons, 9 February 1970 [Vol. 795, col. 1019].

47 Thatcher, p.561.

48 Sir Kenneth Berrill, quoted in John Hoskyns, *Just in Time: Inside the Thatcher Revolution*, p.172.

49 Sir John Nott, interviewed for *The Thatcher Factor*.

50 Patrick Cosgrave, *Thatcher: The First Term*, p.105; Noël Annan, *Our Age*, p.433.

51 Prior, p.66.

52 Robert Harris, *A Good and Faithful Servant: The Unauthorised Biography of Bernard Ingham*, p.122.

53 Cosgrave, p.105.

54 Patricia Murray, *Margaret Thatcher*, p.125.

55 Cecil Parkinson, *Right at the Centre*, p.217.

56 Michael Butler, *Europe: More Than a Continent*, p.116.

57 George Walden, *Lucky George*, p.191.

58 Interview, Sir Kenneth Berrill.

59 Woodrow Wyatt, *Confessions of an Optimist*, p.345.

60 Sir John Hoskyns interviewed for *The Thatcher Factor*.

61 Interview, Sir Charles Powell.

62 Nigel Lawson, *The View from No. 11*, p.128.

63 Parkinson, p.217.

64 Roy Jenkins, *European Diary, 1977–1981*, p.511 (22 October 1979).

65 Ibid., p.593 (28 April 1980).

66 Alan Clark, *Diaries*, p.215 (14 June 1988).

67 Percy Cradock, *In Pursuit of British Interests*, pp.176–7.

68 Interview, Sir Charles Powell; Wyatt, *Confessions of an Optimist* pp.345–6.

69 Interview, Paul Channon; John Peyton, *Without Benefit of Laundry*, p.58.

70 Geoffrey Howe, *Conflict of Loyalty*, p.233.

71 Lord Carrington, interviewed for *Thatcher: The Downing Street Years*,

72 Sir John Hoskyns, interviewed for *The Thatcher Factor*.

73 Murray, p.170.

74 Peter Hennessy, *Cabinet*, p.96.

75 Ibid., pp.97–8.
76 Interview, Lord Jenkin of Roding.
77 Lawson, p.127.
78 Interviews, Sir Michael Partridge, Sir Douglas Wass.
79 Murray, p.200.
80 Thatcher, p.20.
81 Walden, p.191; interview, Professor John Ashworth.
82 Jock Bruce-Gardyne, *Ministers and Mandarins*, p.46.
83 Walden, p.191.
84 Peter Hennessy, Gresham Lecture, 20 February 1996.
85 Parkinson, p.220.
86 Michael Edwardes, *Back From the Brink*, p.231.
87 Hoskyns, p.257.
88 Interviews, Sir John Nott, Sir Peter Middleton.
89 Hoskyns, p.164.
90 Thatcher, p.128.
91 Prior, p.134.
92 Norman St John Stevas, *The Two Cities*, p.83.
93 Reference missing.
94 Anthony King, *The British Prime Minister*, p.124.
95 Interview, Sir Kenneth Stowe.
96 Hoskyns, p.108.
97 Interview, Lord Hunt of Tanworth.
98 Hennessy, *Whitehall*, p.658.
99 Interview, Sir Robert Wade-Gery.
100 Interview, Sir Kenneth Stowe.
101 Thatcher, p.25.
102 John Ranelagh, *Thatcher's People*, p.239.
103 Hoskyns, p.86.
104 *Aspel and Company*, LWT, 19 July 1984.
105 Diana Farr, *Five at 10: Prime Ministers' Consorts since 1957*, p.200.
106 Millar, p.287.
107 Interview, Lord Wakeham; Carol Thatcher, *Below the Parapet*, pp. 100–1; Rodney Tyler, *Campaign!*, p.16.
108 Carol Thatcher, p.186.
109 Penny Junor, *John Major: From Brixton to Downing Street*, p.213.
110 Interview, Sir Kenneth Stowe.
111 King, p.129.
112 Junor, *Margaret Thatcher*, p.264; Millar, p.338.
113 Bernard Ingham, *Kill the Messenger*, p.293.
114 Ibid., p.221.
115 Millar, p.327; John Junor, *Listening for a Midnight Tram*, p.264.
116 Ranelagh, p.222.

117 Sir John Hoskyns at an ICBH witness seminar, 13 July 1995.

118 Speech to the Institute of Directors, 24 February 1987.

119 Sir John Hoskyns at an ICBH witness seminar, 13 July 1995.

120 Speech to the Institute of Directors, 24 February 1987.

121 Nigel Vinson, quoted in Ranelagh, p.241.

122 Speech to the Institute of Directors, 24 February 1987.

123 Nigel Vinson, quoted in Ranelagh, p.241.

124 Millar, p.290.

125 Hoskyns, p.127.

126 Ingham, p.9.

127 Harris, p.71.

128 Interview, Henry James.

129 Clark, p.319 (30 July 1990).

130 Millar, p.317.

131 Thatcher, p.302.

132 *The Times*, 4 October 1982.

133 Richard Cockett, *Thinking the Unthinkable*, pp.291–2.

134 Roy Jenkins, *European Diary*, p.480 (14 July 1979).

135 Wyatt, Vol. 1, p.258 (3 December 1986).

136 Howe, p.201.

137 Interview, Professor John Ashworth.

138 David Prior in Iain Dale, (ed.), *Memories of Maggie*, p.42.

139 Interview, Professor John Ashworth.

140 Peter Hennessy, *Whitehall*, p.651.

141 Sir Peter Emery in Dale, p.70.

142 Ingham, p.248; Carol Thatcher, pp.140–3.

143 John Cole, *As It Seemed to Me*, p.346.

144 Jenkins, pp.480–1.

145 Farr, p.199.

146 Hoskyns, p.230.

147 Millar, p.330.

148 Interview, Henry James.

149 Ingham, p.248.

150 Conservative Party Conference, 15 October 1980.

151 Hennessy, *Whitehall*, p.598.

152 Ibid., p.640.

153 Ibid., p.598.

154 Tam Dalyell, obituary of Lord Bancroft, *Independent*, 22 November 1996.

155 LSE lecture, 1983, cited in Bruce-Gardyne, p.225.

156 Butler and Kavanagh, *The British General Election of 1979*, p.65.

157 Thatcher, p.30.

158 Interview, Sir Kenneth Berrill.

159 Thatcher, p.30.

160 Interviews, Sir Frank Cooper, David Tanner.

161 Prior, p.136.

162 Clark, p.22 (5 July 1983).

163 Parkinson, p.161.

164 Interview, David Tanner.

165 Thatcher, p.48.

166 *Thatcher: The Downing Street Years.*

167 Thatcher, p.303.

168 Hennessy, *Whitehall*, p.585

2 Signals of Intent

1 House of Commons, 9 May 1979 [Vol. 967, cols 10–11].

2 Tony Benn, *Conflicts of Interest: Diaries 1977–80*, p.505 (15 May 1979).

3 House of Commons, 15 May 1979 [Vol. 967, cols. 73–87].

4 Ibid., 22 May 1979 [Vol. 967, cols 867–72].

5 Geoffrey Howe, interviewed for *The Thatcher Factor*; Howe, *Conflict of Loyalty*, pp.114–15.

6 House of Commons, 24 May 1979 [Vol. 967, cols 1220–7].

7 Margaret Thatcher, *The Downing Street Years*, p.50.

8 Howe, p.130.

9 Nigel Lawson, *The View from No. 11*, p.35.

10 Thatcher, pp.42–3.

11 Ibid., p.44.

12 *The Journals of Woodrow Wyatt*, Vol. 1, p.393 (22 July 1987); Ranelagh, pp.231–2.

13 House of Commons, 10 July 1979 [Vol. 970, col. 262].

14 Howe, p.142.

15 House of Commons, 24 July 1979 [Vol. 971, cols 345–6].

16 *Daily Mirror*, 13 June 1979.

17 *Observer*, 17 June 1979.

18 Ibid.

19 House of Commons, 18 June 1979 [Vol. 968, col. 954]; Simon Heffer, *Like the Roman: The Life of Enoch Powell*, p.825.

20 Patricia Murray, *Margaret Thatcher*, p.225.

21 House of Commons, 13 November 1979 [Vol. 973, col. 1498].

22 Ian Gilmour, *Dancing with Dogma*, p.25n; Peter Walker, *Staying Power*, p.161.

23 James Prior, *A Balance of Power*, p.122.

24 John Hoskyns, *Just in Time: Inside the Thatcher Revolution*, p.156.

25 e.g. House of Commons, 19 July 1979, 26 July 1979, 19 February 1980.

26 Thatcher, p.26.

27 House of Commons, 19 November 1975 [Vol. 901, cols 19–28].

28 Alan Clark, *Diaries*, p.219 (28 June 1988); interview, Sir Douglas Wass.

29 Murray, p.219.

30 Hoskyns, p.114.

31 Lord Carrington, interviewed for *The Thatcher Factor*.

32 Nicholas Henderson, *Mandarin*, p.387.

33 Lord Carrington, *Reflect on Things Past*, p.285.

34 Lord Carrington, interviewed for *The Thatcher Factor*.

35 George Walden, *Lucky George*, p.207.

36 Lord Carrington, interviewed for *The Thatcher Factor*.

37 Lord Gowrie, interviewed for *The Thatcher Factor*.

38 Jimmy Carter, *Keeping Faith*, p.113.

39 Henderson, p.269 (24 May 1979).

40 Thatcher, p.68.

41 Carter papers, CO 167.

42 Speech on the White House lawn, Washington, 17 December 1979.

43 Henderson, p.316; Sir Frank Cooper, interviewed for *The Thatcher Factor*.

44 Speech to the American Foreign Policy Association, New York, 18 December 1979.

45 Thatcher, p.88.

46 Summary of President Carter's telephone conversation with Mrs Thatcher, 28 December 1979 [Carter papers: vertical file – Afghanistan].

47 *Sunday Express*, 14 March 1980, cited in Heffer, pp.834–5.

48 Mark Stuart, *Douglas Hurd: The Public Servant*, p.108.

49 Carter papers: Plains file, Box 2.

50 House of Commons, 26 June 1979, [Vol. 969, col. 289].

51 Gilmour, p.289.

52 Alan Sked and Chris Cook, *Post-War Britain*, p.376.

53 Speech at a dinner for Chancellor Schmidt, 10 May 1979.

54 House of Commons, 20 March 1980 [Vol 981, col. 636].

55 e.g. ibid., 13 March 1979 [Vol. 964, cols 455–6].

56 Roy Jenkins, *European Diary*, p.466.

57 Thatcher, p.64.

58 Walden, p.194.

59 Jenkins, p.479.

60 Ludovic Kennedy, *On my Way to the Club*, p.354.

61 Thatcher, p.81.

62 Christopher Tugendhat, *Making Sense of Europe*, pp.120–2.

63 Ibid, quoting another unnamed Commissioner cited in John Newhouse, 'The Diplomatic Round', in the *New Yorker*, 22 October 1984.

64 Lord Carrington, interviewed for *The Thatcher Factor*.

65 Henderson, p.287 (13 August 1979).

66 Winston Churchill Memorial Lecture, Luxembourg, 18 October 1979.

67 House of Commons, 25 October 1979, 20 November 1979 [Vol. 972, cols 619–20; vol. 974, col. 208].

68 Jenkins, p.529.

69 Roy Jenkins, *Life at the Centre*, p.498.

70 Jenkins, *European Diary*, pp.528–30.

71 Ibid., p.529.

72 Henderson, p.338 (9 May 1980).

73 Jenkins, *European Diary*, p.519.

74 Sir Crispin Tickell, on *The Last Europeans*, Channel 4, 1995.

75 Jenkins, *European Diary*, pp.530–1.

76 House of Commons, 3 December 1979, 31 January 1980 [Vol. 975, cols 29–47; vol 977, col. 1557].

77 Ibid., 23 October 1979 [Vol. 972, cols 191–2].

78 Ibid., 18 March 1980, 20 March 1980 [Vol. 981, cols 202, 636].

79 Thatcher, pp.79–80.

80 House of Commons, 31 January 1980, 19 February 1980 [Vol. 977, col. 1557; vol. 979, col. 234].

81 Jenkins, *European Diary*, p.450.

82 House of Commons, 11 March 1980 [Vol. 980, col. 1149].

83 Conservative Party Conference, 12 October 1979.

84 House of Commons, 12 June 1979 [Vol. 968, col. 229].

85 Ibid., 13 November 1979 [Vol. 973, cols 1149–50].

86 Jenkins, *European Diary*, p.511.

87 BBC interview, *Campaign '79*, 24 April 1979.

88 *Thatcher: The Downing Street* Years, BBC 1993.

89 Thatcher, pp.81–2, quoting Rudyard Kipling 'Norman and Saxon (A.D. 1100)'.

90 House of Commons, 3 December 1979 [Vol. 975, col. 45].

91 Hoskyns, p.121.

92 Jenkins, *European Diary*, pp.545–7.

93 Ibid., pp.592–3.

94 Claude Cheysson, interviewed on *The Last Europeans*.

95 Jenkins, *European Diary*, p.547.

96 Thatcher, p.86.

97 Gilmour, pp.292–4.

98 Thatcher, p.86.

99 Gilmour, pp.292–5.

100 House of Commons, 20 May 1982 [Vol. 24, cols 467–70].

101 Lawson, p.111.

102 Carrington, p.319.

103 Lord Carrington, interviewed for *The Thatcher Factor*.

104 Tugendhat, p.123.

105 Jenkins, *European Diary*, p.375.

106 Jenkins, *Life at the Centre*, p.500.

107 House of Commons, 15 May 1979 [Vol. 967, cols 73–87].

108 Thatcher, p.73.

109 Sir Anthony Parsons, interviewed on 22 March 1996 for the British Diplomatic Oral History Project, Churchill College, Cambridge.

110 House of Commons, 25 July 1979 [Vol. 971, cols 620–30].

111 Gilmour, pp.281–2.

112 Anthony Sampson, *The Changing Anatomy of Britain*, p.7; Ben Pimlott, *The Queen*, p.467.

113 Interview, Henry James.

114 Carrington, p.277.

115 Interview, Henry James.

116 Anthony Verrier, *The Road to Zimbabwe*, p.244.

117 John Simpson, *Strange Places, Questionable People*, p.243.

118 Lord Carrington, interviewed for *The Thatcher Factor*.

119 Carrington, p.295; Patrick Cosgrave, *Thatcher: The First Term*, p.81.

120 Ronald Millar, *A View from the Wings*, p.320.

121 Pimlott, pp.467–8.

122 Interview, Sir Robin Renwick.

123 Carrington, p.286.

124 John Junor, *Listening for a Midnight Tram*, p.141.

125 Sir Anthony Parsons, interviewed in *Thatcher: The Downing Street Years*, BBC, 1993.

126 Carter papers, CO 167.

127 David Anderson, 'Mugabe is Right about Land', *Independent*, 4 May 2000.

128 Andrew Thomson, *Margaret Thatcher: The Woman Within*, p.33.

129 House of Commons, 21 November 1979 [Vol. 974, col. 410].

130 *Guardian*, 30 August 1979.

131 *The Times*, 14 November 1979.

132 Conservative Party Conference, 12 October 1979.

133 Speech to Parliamentary Press Gallery, 5 December 1979.

134 Norman Shrapnel, *The Seventies*, p.248.

135 *The Times*, 14 November 1979.

3 Heading for the Rocks

1 *The Times*, 12 November 1980.

2 Martin Holmes, *The First Thatcher Government, 1979–83*, p.155.

3 Interview, Sir Douglas Wass.

4 Phillip Whitehead, *The Writing on the Wall*, p.376.

5 House of Commons, 5 July 1979 [Vol. 969, col. 1553].

6 Ibid., 24 June 1980 [Vol. 987, col. 226].

7 William Keegan, *Mrs Thatcher's Economic Experiment*, p.148.

8 Ian Gilmour, *Dancing with Dogma*, p.24.

9 House of Commons, 26 June 1979 [Vol. 969, col. 296].

10 Margaret Thatcher, *The Downing Street Years*, p.97.

11 Nigel Lawson, *The View from No. 11*, p.67; Geoffrey Howe, *Conflict of Loyalty*, p.155.

12 Howe, p.163.

13 Ibid; Lawson, p.71; interview, Sir Peter Middleton.

14 Thatcher, p.97.

15 Denis Healey, *The Time of My Life*, p.491.

16 House of Commons, 27 July 1981 [Vol. 9, col. 828].

17 Howe, p.162.

18 Conservative Party Conference, 15 October 1980.

19 House of Commons, 9 March 1982 [Vol. 19, col. 719].

20 Lawson, p.77.

21 Jock Bruce-Gardyne, *Mrs Thatcher's First Administration*, p.93.

22 *The Times*, 20 September 1980.

23 John Ranelagh, *Thatcher's People*, p.227.

24 Whitehead, p.380.

25 John Hoskyns, *Just in Time: Inside the Thatcher Revolution*, p.267.

26 Ibid., p.122.

27 Samuel Brittan, interviewed for *The Thatcher Factor*.

28 House of Commons, 18 December 1980 [Vol. 996, col. 546].

29 *The Times*. 3 November 1981.

30 Lawson, p.72.

31 Patrick Minford, 'Mrs Thatcher's Economic Reform Programme', in Robert Skidelsky (ed.), *Thatcherism*, pp.96–8.

32 Healey, pp.491–2.

33 Peter Clarke, *A Question of Leadership*, pp.302–4.

34 *Guardian*, 26 March 1980.

35 *Observer*, 30 March 1980.

36 Thatcher, p.53.

37 House of Commons, 23 October 1979 [Vol. 972, col. 192].

38 Ibid., 30 October 1980 [Vol. 991, col. 692].

39 Hoskyns, p.187.

40 Lawson, pp.55, 57.

41 *News of the World*, 4 May 1980.

42 Conservative Party Conference, 15 October 1980.

43 Ibid, 16 October 1981.

44 *Nationwide (On the Spot)*, BBC, 14 May 1981.

45 House of Commons, 19 July 1979 [Vol. 970, col. 1990].

46 Ibid., 22 January 1981 [Vol. 997, col. 422].

47 Ibid., 4 March 1980 [Vol. 980, col. 241].

48 Ibid., 2 June 1981 [Vol. 5, cols 773–4].

49 Ibid., 5 February 1981 [Vol. 998, cols 415–23].

50 Labour Party Conference, 28 September 1976.

51 House of Commons, 2 February 1981 [Vol. 998, cols 415–23].

52 Ibid., 12 June 1979 [Vol. 968, col. 230].

53 Ibid., 5 February 1981 [Vol. 998, cols 415–23].

54 Norman Tebbit at the Conservative Party Conference, 15 October 1981.

55 *The Times*, 5 May 1980.

56 Michael Cockerell, *Live from Number 10*, p.262.

57 IRN interview, 28 November 1980.

58 Lawson, p.100.

59 House of Commons, 29 July 1980 [Vol. 989, cols 1301–14].

60 Conservative Party Conference, 15 October 1980.

61 *The Times*, date mislaid.

62 Ronald Millar, *A View from the Wings*, pp.287–8.

63 Hoskyns, p.231.

64 John Hoskyns, interviewed for *The Thatcher Factor*; Ranelagh, p.236.

65 *Nationwide (On The Spot)*, BBC, 14 May 1981.

66 Thatcher, p.104.

67 House of Commons, 26 June 1979 [Vol. 969, col. 285].

68 Whitehead, p.371.

69 Ibid.

70 Thatcher, p.100.

71 House of Commons, 15 May 1979 [Vol. 967, cols 73–87].

72 Ibid., 19 July 1979 [Vol. 970, col. 1989].

73 *Guardian*, 23 August 1979.

74 House of Commons, 15 May 1980 [Vol. 984, col. 1748].

75 Ibid, 6 December, 1979 [Vol. 975, col. 609].

76 *Weekend World*, LWT, 6 January 1980; House of Commons, 22 January 1980 [Vol. 977, col. 197].

77 Cockerell, p.260.

78 *The Times*, 11 February 1980.

79 Hoskyns, p.158.

80 House of Commons, 14 February 1980 [Vol. 978, col. 1741].

81 Lord Prior, interviewed for *The Thatcher Factor*.

82 *Panorama*, BBC, 25 February 1980.

83 James Prior, *A Balance of Power*, pp.166–7.

84 Hugh Stephenson, *Mrs Thatcher's First Year*, p.75.

85 House of Commons, 3 July 1980 [Vol. 987, col. 1759].

86 Gilmour, p.100.

87 Robert Taylor, *The Trade Union Question in British Politics*, p.273.

88 Thatcher, p.105.

89 Sir John Hoskyns, interviewed for *The Thatcher Factor*.

90 *The Economist*, 27 May 1978; Nicholas Ridley, '*My Style of Government*', p.16.

91 Lawson. p.199.

92 Sir Geoffrey Howe, interviewed for *The Thatcher Factor*.

93 Howe, p.252.

94 Thatcher, pp.676–7.

95 Speech to the US Congress, 20 February 1985.

96 House of Commons, 15 May 1979 [Vol. 967, cols 73–87].

97 Ibid., 12 June 1979 [Vol. 968, col. 229].

98 Ibid., 19 June 1979 [Vol. 968, col. 1114].

99 Ibid., 4 November 1981 [Vol. 12, col. 23].

100 Ibid., 28 February 1980, 5 February 1981 [Vol. 998, col. 481]; 18 June 1981 [Vol. 6, col. 1175]; 30 July 1981 [Vol. 9, col. 980]; 4 February 1982 [Vol. 17, col. 539].

101 House of Commons, 5 November 1981. [Vol. 12, cols 440–1].

102 Morrison Halcrow, *Keith Joseph: A Single Mind*, pp.135–7.

103 Lord Joseph, interviewed for *The Thatcher Factor*; Hugo Young, *One of Us*, p.144.

104 Prior, p.125.

105 House of Commons, 24 January 1980 [Vol. 977, cols 622–4]; 19 February 1980 [Vol. 979, col. 237].

106 Ibid., 5 February 1980 [Vol. 978, cols 231–2].

107 Lord Joseph, interviewed on *Thatcher: The Downing Street Years*.

108 Margaret Thatcher to Lord Boyle of Handsworth, 1 May 1980 [Boyle papers, EB 660/42820].

109 Thatcher, pp.114–15.

110 Ibid., p.121.

111 Halcrow, p.149.

112 *Weekend World*, LWT, 1 February 1981.

113 Interview, Sir Robert Wade-Gery.

114 House of Commons, 12 February 1981 [Vol. 998, col. 979].

115 Ibid., 10 February 1981 [Vol. 998, col. 737].

116 Thatcher, p.141.

117 Ibid., p.686.

118 Bernard Ingham, *Kill the Messenger*, p.233.

119 Joe Gormley, *Battered Cherub*, p.179.

120 House of Commons, 19 February 1981 [Vol. 999, cols 447–9].

121 Howe, p.221.

122 Lawson, p.107; Howe, p.221.

123 Thatcher, p.139n.

124 Ranelagh, p.241.

125 Alfred Sherman to Margaret Thatcher, 14 September 1980, in Halcrow, p.157.

126 *The Times*, 13 October 1981.

127 Thatcher, p.129.

128 Prior, p.134.

129 Roy Strong, *Diaries, 1967–1987*, p.277 (1 April 1981).

130 *The Times*, 8 January 1981.

131 Howe, p.198.

132 Thatcher, p.132.

133 Hoskyns, pp.282–5, 395.
134 Thatcher, pp.137–8.
135 Ibid., pp.133–6.
136 Howe, pp.202–4.
137 Thatcher, p.136.
138 Ranelagh, p.230.
139 Philip Stephens, *Politics and the Pound*, p.21.
140 *The Times*, 30 March 1981.
141 Lawson, p.103.
142 House of Commons, 12 March 1981 [Vol. 1000, cols 1001–4].
143 Speech at the Mansion House, 11 March 1981.
144 Gilmour, p.35.
145 Howe, p.209; Gilmour, p.35.
146 Patrick Minford, in Skidelsky, pp.96–8.
147 Lawson, p.98.
148 Prior, p.118.
149 Lord Gilmour, interviewed on *Thatcher: The Downing Street Years*, BBC, 1993; Gilmour, p.43.
150 Sir John Nott, interviewed for *The Thatcher Factor*.
151 *Financial Times*, 12 March 1981.
152 *Guardian*, 16 March 1981.
153 *The Times*, 13 July 1981.
154 *Daily Telegraph*, 11 March 1981; *The Times*, 11 March 1981.
155 Whitehead, p.383.
156 Ranelagh, p.235.
157 Conservative Central Council, Cardiff, 28 March 1981.
158 John Cole, *As It Seemed to Me*, p.254.
159 *TV Eye*, Thames TV, 18 February 1982.
160 Thatcher, p.574.
161 Young, p.239.
162 ITN interview, 13 April 1981.
163 *Nationwide (On the Spot)*, BBC, 14 May 1981.
164 Whitehead, p.387.
165 *The Times*, 9 July 1981.
166 Party Political Broadcast, 8 July 1981.
167 Hoskyns, pp.315–17.
168 Lord Whitelaw, interviewed for *The Thatcher Factor*.
169 House of Commons, 7 July 1981 [Vol. 8, cols 258–61].
170 Ibid.
171 Ibid., 9 July 1981 [Vol. 8, cols 575–8].
172 Thatcher, p.145.
173 House of Commons, 14 July 1981 [Vol. 8, cols 973–6].
174 Ibid., 16 July 1981 [Vol. 8 col. 1383].

175 Lord Whitelaw, interviewed for *The Thatcher Factor*.
176 Thatcher, p.424.
177 Ibid.
178 Hoskyns, p.301.
179 *The Times*, 17 July 1981.
180 Kenneth Baker, *The Turbulent Years*, pp.58–9.
181 Nicholas Henderson, *Mandarin*, pp.404–6.
182 *The Times*, 3 August 1981.
183 Ibid.
184 Howe, p.169.
185 Ibid., pp.222–3.
186 John Biffen, interviewed for *The Thatcher Factor*.
187 Thatcher, pp.26–7.
188 Howe, p.223.
189 Thatcher, p.149.
190. Hoskyns, pp.326–8.
191 *The Times*, 15 September 1981.
192 Thatcher, p.151.
193 Interview, Lord Carlisle.
194 Prior, p.173.
195 Hoskyns, p.323.
196 Cecil Parkinson, *Right at the Centre*, p.175.
197 Lawson, p.123.
198 Ibid.
199 John Junor, *Listening for a Midnight Tram*, p.261.
200 Ibid., pp.262–3.
201 Interview, Lord Crickhowell.
202 *The Times*, 7 October 1981.
203 Sir Robert Menzies Lecture at Monash University, Melbourne, 6 October 1981.
204 *The Times*, 9 October 1981.
205 Ibid., 7 October 1981.
206 Ibid., 8 October 1981.
207 Ibid., 9 October 1981.
208 Conservative Party Conference, 14 October 1981.
209 *The Times*, 4 October 1982.
210 Millar, pp.289–90.
211 Conservative Party Conference, 16 October 1981.
212 House of Commons, 28 October 1981 [Vol. 10, cols 881–7].
213 *The Times*, 13 October 1981.
214 IRN interview, 31 December 1981.

4 Salvation in the South Atlantic

1 House of Commons, 2 December 1980 [Vol. 995, cols 128–34].

2 Speech in Finchley, 22 October 1982.

3 House of Commons, 9 February 1982 [Vol. 17, cols 856–7].

4 *The Franks Report: Falkland Islands Review*, para. 152 (1992, Pimlico edition, p.45).

5 Interview, William Waldegrave.

6 Lord Whitelaw, interviewed for *The Thatcher Factor*.

7 David Owen, *Time to Declare*, p.547.

8 House of Commons, 3 April 1982 [Vol. 21, cols 633–8].

9 Julian Critchley, *Westminster Blues*, pp.124–5.

10 John Major: *The Autobiography*, pp.76–7.

11 Alan Clark, *Diaries*, p.64 (15 January 1984).

12 Ibid, p.97 (20 September 1984); Margaret Thatcher, *The Downing Street Years*, p.306.

13 Peter Hennessy, *The Prime Minister*, p.104.

14 House of Commons, 8 April 1982 (Vol. 21, col. 1084).

15 Thatcher, pp.188–9.

16 Interview, Sir Michael Palliser.

17 *The Journals of Woodrow Wyatt*, Vol. 2, p.245, citing Norman Tebbit (22 February 1990).

18 Hennessy, p.414.

19 Peter de la Billière, *Looking for Trouble*; BBC2, 25 July 2002.

20 Max Hastings and Simon Jenkins, *The Battle for the Falklands*, p.129.

21 Speech at the Conservative Party Conference, Brighton, 11 October 1978; *Panorama* (BBC, 26 April 1982); House of Commons, 4 May 1982, 11 May 1982, 13 May 1982 [Vol. 23, cols 15, 598, 944].

22 Hastings and Jenkins, p.271.

23 *Sunday Times*, 7 June 1987.

24 Antonia Fraser, *Boadicea's Chariot*, p.317.

25 Lord Lewin, interviewed for *The Thatcher Factor*.

26 Remarks outside 10 Downing Street, 25 April 1982.

27 Patrick Cosgrave, reported in *The Times*, 26 May 1995.

28 ITN interview, 5 April 1982.

29 Lord Lewin, interviewed on *Thatcher: The Downing Street Years*, BBC, 1993.

30 Interviews, Sir John Nott, Sir Frank Cooper, Sir Michael Palliser.

31 Nicholas Henderson, *Mandarin*, p.468.

32 Woodrow Wyatt, *Confessions of an Optimist*, p.345.

33 Ronald Millar, *A View from the Wings*, p.298.

34 Hennessy, p.416.

35 Lord Havers, interviewed for *The Thatcher Factor*.

36 Interview with Miriam Stoppard, *Woman to Woman*, Yorkshire TV, 19 November 1985.

37 Lord Lewin, interviewed for *The Thatcher Factor*.

38 Sara Keays, *A Question of Judgement*, p.29.

39 Hastings and Jenkins, p.381.

40 Nigel West, *The Secret War for the Falklands*, p.230.

41 Hastings and Jenkins, p.167; Geoffrey Smith, *Reagan and Thatcher*, p.86.

42 Caspar Weinberger, *Fighting for Peace*, p.149.

43 Cecil Parkinson, *Right at the Centre*, p.201.

44 Henderson, p.468.

45 Thatcher, p.215.

46 Ibid., p.208.

47 Carol Thatcher, *Below the Parapet*, p.194.

48 Thatcher, p.205.

49 Ibid., p.219.

50 House of Commons, 29 April 1982 [Vol. 22, col. 981].

51 Ibid., 6 May 1982 [Vol. 23, col. 282].

52 Sir Anthony Parsons, interviewed for the British Diplomatic Oral History Project, Churchill College, Cambridge.

53 Lord Lewin, interviewed for *The Thatcher Factor*.

54 Admiral 'Sandy' Woodward, *One Hundred Days*, pp.148–63.

55 House of Commons, 4 May 1982 [Vol. 23, col. 16].

56 Thatcher, p.215.

57 e.g. Paul Hirst, *After Thatcher*, p.106.

58 Lord Havers, interviewed for *The Thatcher Factor*.

59 William Whitelaw, *The Whitelaw Memoirs*, p.208.

60 Hastings and Jenkins, p.196.

61 Thatcher, p.217.

62 House of Commons, 6 May 1982 [Vol. 23, col. 279].

63 Interview, Lord Crickhowell; see also Nigel Lawson, *The View from No. 11*, pp.126–7; and Hennessy, p.420.

64 Interview, Sir John Nott.

65 House of Commons, 13 May 1982 [Vol. 23, col. 942].

66 Smith, p.93.

67 *The Times*, 15 May 1982.

68 Henderson, pp.460–3.

69 House of Commons, 20 May 1982 [Vol. 24, cols 477–83].

70 Interview, Sir Frank Cooper.

71 Carol Thatcher, p.197.

72 *The Times*, 22 May 1982.

73 Andrew Thomson, *Margaret Thatcher: The Woman Within*, pp.174–8.

74 *The Times*, 22 May 1982.

75 Carol Thatcher, p.198.

76 Private information.

77 Thatcher, p.230.

78 Henderson, pp.465–8.

79 Ibid., pp.468–70.

80 House of Commons, 14 June 1982 [Vol. 25, col. 700].

81 Ibid., 22 June 1982 [Vol. 26, cols 430–2].

82 Ibid., 17 June 1982 [Vol. 25, col. 1082].

83 *The Times*, 5 July 1982.

84 Conservative Party Conference, Brighton, 8 October 1982.

85 Leo Abse, *Margaret, Daughter of Beatrice*, p.127.

86 Speech to the Scottish Conservative Conference, Perth, 14 May 1982.

87 *The Times*, 23 July 1982.

88 Simon Jenkins, interviewed for *The Thatcher Factor*.

89 e.g. House of Commons, 6 May 1982, 11 May 1982. [Vol. 23, cols 279, 597–602].

90 Matthew Parris, *Chance Witness*, p.294.

91 Alan Sked and Chris Cook, *Post-War Britain*, p.418.

92 e.g. House of Commons, 23 November 1982, 18 January 1983 [Vol. 32, col. 705; vol. 35, col. 178].

93 Interview, Lord Crickhowell.

94 Rex Hunt, *My Falkland Days*, pp.370–5.

95 Carol Thatcher, p.201.

96 William Shakespeare, *Hamlet,* IV.4.18–20, 53–6; Noël Annan, *Our Age*, p.430.

5 Falklands Effect

1 *Daily Express*, 23 July 1982.

2 Speech to a Conservative rally at Cheltenham racecourse, 3 July 1982.

3 BBC Radio News, 22 July 1982.

4 *Daily Express*, 23 July 1982.

5 *The Times*, 16 August 1982.

6 *Daily Express*, 23 July 1982.

7 House of Commons, 3 November 1982 [Vol. 31, col. 20].

8 Ibid., 19 October 1982, 21 October 1982 [Vol. 29, cols 226, 502].

9 Ibid., 3 November 1982 [Vol. 31, col. 18].

10 Ibid., 1 March 1983 [Vol. 38, col. 128].

11 Ibid., 10 March 1983 [Vol. 38, col. 949].

12 Ibid., 9 November 1982 [Vol. 31, col. 424].

13 Ibid., 12 May 1983 [Vol. 42, col. 917].

14 Norman Tebbit, *Upwardly Mobile*, p.186.

15 Margaret Thatcher, *The Downing Street Years*, p.274.

16 *The Times*, 7 September 1982.

17 Conservative Party Conference, 8 October 1982.

18 House of Commons, 21 January 1982, 6 July 1982, 13 July 1982 [Vol. 16, cols 410–11; vol. 27, col. 144; vol. 27, cols 851–3].

19 Speech in Finchley, 22 October 1982.

20 Interview, Lord Jenkin of Roding.

21 Nigel Lawson, *The View from No. 11*, p.217.
22 Conservative Party Conference. 8 October 1982.
23 Thatcher, p.284.
24 Lawson, p.198.
25 Hugo Young, *One of Us*, p.83.
26 Conservative Party Conference, 8 October 1982.
27 *The Times*, 19 January 1983.
28 Nicholas Timmins, *The Five Giants*, p.372.
29 Ibid.
30 e.g. House of Commons, 12 May 1983 [Vol. 42, col. 917].
31 Ibid., 22 January 1980 [Vol. 977, col. 195].
32 Ibid., 15 May 1979 [Vol. 967, col. 81].
33 Chris Ham, *The Politics of NHS Reform*, p.9.
34 Lawson, p.303.
35 *The Economist*, 18 September 1982.
36 Thatcher, p.277.
37 Young, p.301; Michael Cockerell, Peter Hennessy and David Walker, *Sources Close to the Prime Minister*, pp.130–4.
38 Conservative Party Conference, 8 October 1982.
39 House of Commons, 1 December 1981 [Vol. 14, col. 133].
40 Ibid., 15 February 1983 [Vol. 37, col. 157].
41 Ibid., 11 March 1980 [Vol. 980, col. 1152].
42 Ibid., 28 July 1981 [Vol. 9, col. 980].
43 Timmins, p.373.
44 House of Commons, 28 February 1980 [Vol. 979, col. 1601].
45 Ibid., 29 April 1980 [Vol. 983, col. 1150].
46 Ibid., 12 April 1983, 2 December 1982 [Vol. 40, col. 666; Vol. 33, col. 392].
47 Michael Heseltine, *Life in the Jungle*, p.196.
48 House of Commons, 19 November 1981, [Vol.13, col. 418].
49 Lawson, pp.341, 821.
50 House of Commons, 24 July 1979 [Vol. 971, col. 342].
51 Ibid., 18 November 1982 [Vol. 32, col. 414].
52 Geoffrey Howe, *Conflict of Loyalty*, pp.280–1.
53 House of Commons, 24 March 1983 [Vol. 39, col. 1013].
54 Ibid., 22 December 1981 [Vol. 15, col. 867].
55 Interview, Professor John Ashworth.
56 Timmins, pp.374, 420–1.
57 House of Commons, 4 November 1981 [Vol. 12, col. 20].
58 David Butler, Andrew Adonis and Tony Travers, *Failure in British Government: The Politics of the Poll Tax*, p.35.
59 House of Commons, 4 November 1981 [Vol. 12, col. 20].
60 Butler, Adonis and Travers, p.27.
61 Thatcher, p.644.

62 Simon Jenkins, *Accountable to None: The Tory Nationalisation of Britain*, p.44; Heseltine, p.197.

63 Thatcher, pp.281, 284.

64 John Hoskyns, *Just in Time*, p.352; and interviewed for *The Thatcher Factor*.

65 *The Times*, 4 October 1982.

66 Ibid., 4 May 1982.

67 Ronald Millar, *A View from the Wings*, p.291.

68 House of Commons, 27 July 1982 [Vol. 28, col. 1226].

69 *The Times*, 24 August 1982.

70 Thatcher, p.281.

71 Conservative Party Conference, 8 October 1982.

72 *Sun*, 28 February 1983.

73 *News of the World*, 14 February 1983.

74 *Sunday Telegraph*, 14 November 1982.

75 *Weekend World*, LWT, 16 January 1983.

76 Speech to the Glasgow Chamber of Commerce, 28 January 1983.

77 General Election press conference, 31 May 1983.

78 IRN interview, 15 April 1983.

79 *The Times*, 14 January 1983.

80 Michael Cockerell, *Live from Number 10*, p.278.

81 Margaret Thatcher, interviewed by Sir Laurens van der Post, for *The Woman at Number Ten* (De Wolfe Productions, 1983).

82 Cockerell, p.278.

83 David Butler and Dennis Kavanagh, *The British General Election of 1983*, p.40.

84 Sir John Hoskyns, interviewed for *The Thatcher Factor*.

85 Butler and Kavanagh, p.40.

86 Lawson, p.246.

87 Kaufman is usually credited with the remark, but Butler and Kavanagh, p.62, attribute it to Shore.

88 *The Times*, 5 May 1980.

89 House of Commons, 5 June 1980 [Vol. 985, col. 1671].

90 Peter Hennessy, *Cabinet*, pp.154–5.

91 House of Commons, 24 July 1980 [Vol. 989, col. 761].

92 Conservative Party Conference, Brighton, 10 October 1980.

93 House of Commons, 19 May 1981 [Vol. 5, cols 151–2].

94 Ibid.

95 Ibid., 21 January 1982 [Vol. 16, col. 412].

96 Ibid., 5 June 1980 [Vol. 985, col. 1671].

97 Geoffrey Smith, *Reagan and Thatcher*, p.113.

98 House of Commons, 26 June 1980 [Vol. 987, col. 742].

99 Ibid., 15 July 1980 [Vol. 988, col. 1229].

100 Ibid., 24 February 1981 [Vol. 999, cols 739–41].

101 Ibid., 18 January 1983 [Vol. 35, col. 167].

102 Ibid., 25 November 1982 [Vol. 32, col. 1010].

103 Ibid., 14 December 1982 [Vol. 34, col. 121].

104 Conservative Party Conference, 10 October 1982.

105 Press conference with Chancellor Kohl, London, 4 February 1983.

106 House of Commons, 28 April 1983 [Vol. 41, col. 994].

107 Tebbit, p.200.

108 Lawson. p.246.

109 House of Commons, 19 April 1983 [Vol. 41, col. 159].

110 Cecil Parkinson, *Right at the Centre*, p.224.

111 Carol Thatcher, *Below the Parapet*, p.204.

112 Carol Thatcher, *Diary of an Election*, p.11.

113 Butler and Kavanagh, p.160.

114 Rodney Tyler, *Campaign!*, p.52.

115 Carol Thatcher, *Diary*, pp.34–5.

116 Ibid., p.57.

117 Ibid., pp.58–9.

118 *The Times*, 7 June 1983.

119 Ibid.

120 Ibid.

121 Thatcher, p.297.

122 Speech at the Metropole Hotel, Birmingham, 3 June 1983.

123 Butler and Kavanagh, p.104.

124 Speech at the City Hall, Cardiff, 23 May 1983.

125 Speech at the Royal Hotel, Harrogate, 26 May 1983.

126 IRN interview, 23 May 1983.

127 *The Jimmy Young Programme*, BBC Radio 2, 11 May 1983.

128 e.g. speech at Fleetwood, 7 June 1983.

129 Speech at George Watson's College, Edinburgh, 31 May 1983.

130 *Panorama*, BBC, 1 June 1983.

131 *World in Action*, Granada TV, 6 June 1983.

132 John Cole, *As It Seemed to Me*, p.270.

133 Speech at Birmingham, 3 June 1983.

134 David Owen, *Time to Declare*, p.574.

135 Election press conference, 18 May 1983.

136 Election press conference, 20 May 1983.

137 Remarks electioneering in Norfolk, 25 May 1983; Carol Thatcher, *Diary*, p.52.

138 Carol Thatcher, *Diary*, p.73.

139 Ibid., p.104.

140 Remarks electioneering in Norfolk, 25 May 1983; Carol Thatcher, *Diary*, p.53.

141 Michael Spicer in Iain Dale, (ed.), *Memories of Maggie*, p.61.

142 Robin Day, *Grand Inquisitor*, p.232.

143 Cockerell, p.282.

144 Butler and Kavanagh, p.167.

145 Carol Thatcher, *Diary*, p.48.

146 Michael Spicer in Dale, pp.60–1.

147 Cockerell, p.283.

148 Carol Thatcher, *Diary*, p.100.

149 Butler and Kavanagh, pp.112–13.

150 Ibid., p.125.

151 Speech at Newbury racecourse, 27 May 1983.

152 Carol Thatcher, *Diary*, p.88.

153 Thatcher, p.295.

154 Ibid., p.303.

155 Speech at a Wembley youth rally, 5 June 1983.

156 Millar, pp.292–3.

157 Andrew Thomson, *The Woman Within*, p.90.

158 Ibid., p.97.

159 Margaret Thatcher's election address, Finchley, June 1983.

160 Thomson, p.80.

161 *The Times*, 11 June 1983.

162 Butler and Kavanagh, p.160.

163 Ibid., p.296.

164 Francis Pym, *The Politics of Consent*, p.ix.

165 Thatcher, p.309.

166 Ibid., p.308.

167 Interview, Lord Jenkin of Roding.

6 Popular Capitalism

1 Nicholas Ridley, *'My Style of Government'*, p.86.

2 Interviewed on *Thatcher: The Downing Street Years*.

3 *The Times*, 16 June 1983.

4 Ibid., 23 June 1983.

5 Tessa Blackstone and William Plowden, *Inside the Think Tank*, p.180.

6 Ibid., 17 June 1983.

7 *Guardian*, 18 June 1983.

8 James Prior, *A Balance of Power*, p.229.

9 IRN interview, 28 July 1983.

10 ITN interview, 28 July 1983.

11 BBC radio interview, 6 August 1983.

12 *The Times*, 11 August 1983.

13 Statement, 6 October 1983.

14 *The Journals of Woodrow Wyatt*, Vol. 2, pp.110–11 (21 June 1989).

15 Alan Clark, *Diaries*, pp.45–6 (13 October 1983); p.57 (14 December 1983).

16 *The Times*, 14 October 1983.

17 Sara Keays, *A Question of Judgement*, p.306.

18 *Sunday Express*, 16 October 1983, cited in Keays, p.219.

19 John Junor, *Listening for a Midnight Tram*, p.305.

20 Rodney Tyler, *Campaign!*, p.16.

21 Speech to the Conservative Party Conference, 14 October 1983.

22 Clark, pp.37–8 (1 September 1983).

23 John Major, *The Autobiography*, p.108.

24 Margaret Thatcher, *The Downing Street Years*, p.312.

25 *The Times*, 10 October 1983 (Biffen), 14 October 1983 (Prior), 1 December 1983 (Pym); *Annual Register 1983*, p.32 (Walker).

26 David Butler, *The Times*, 9 December 1983.

27 Interview with John Cole, BBC, 27 May 1983.

28 Ronald Butt, *The Times*, 19 January 1984.

29 House of Commons, 31 January 1984 [Vol. 53, col. 138].

30 Speech to the Small Business Bureau Conference, 8 February 1984.

31 Interview on *Panorama*, BBC, 9 April 1984.

32 Lord Crickhowell in Iain Dale, ed., *Memories of Maggie*, pp.137–8.

33 *Daily Express*, 14 June 1983.

34 Interviews, Lord Wakeham and others.

35 *The Journals of Woodrow Wyatt*, Vol. 1, pp.242–3 (9 December 1986).

36 Thatcher, p.672.

37 *Thatcher: The Downing Street Years*, BBC, 1993.

38 Thatcher, p.673.

39 Alan Sked and Chris Cook, *Post-War Britain 1945–1992*, p.474.

40 *The Times*, 15 March 1984.

41 Francis Pym, *The Politics of Consent*.

42 House of Commons, 31 July 1984 [Vol. 65, col. 248].

43 Clark, p.109 (24 April 1985).

44 e.g. *Observer*, 1 July 1990, cited in Tyler, p.53n., though Tyler thinks she never actually said it.

45 Thatcher, p.421.

46 House of Commons, 23 October 1984 [Vol. 65, col. 552].

47 Conservative Party Conference, Brighton, 12 October 1984.

48 *Annual Register 1984*, p.30.

49 Nigel Lawson, *The View from Number 11*, p.470.

50 *The Times*, 18 January 1985.

51 William Keegan, *Mr Lawson's Gamble*, p.140.

52 Ibid., p.158.

53 *The Times*, 11 May 1985.

54 Ibid., 15 May 1985.

55 IRN interview, 24 May 1985.

56 *Sun*, 8 July 1985.

823

57 e.g. Alan Clark, p.285 (4 March 1990), citing Carol Thatcher.

58 Visit to Wallsend, 9 September 1985.

59 Thatcher, p.418.

60 Ibid., p.421n.

61 Ibid., p.422.

62 William Keegan, *Mrs Thatcher's Economic Experiment*, p.139.

63 Speech at the Conservative Party Conference, 11 October 1985.

64 Ibid.

65 Speech to the British Radio and Electronic Equipment Manufacturers' Association, Savoy Hotel, London, 11 December 1985.

66 *The Times*, 19 October 1985.

67 Keegan, p.178.

68 Lady Thatcher interviewed on *Thatcher: The Downing Street Years*.

69 Thatcher, p.697.

70 Lawson, p.499.

71 Ibid.

72 Nigel Lawson, interviewed on *Thatcher: The Downing Street Years*, BBC, 1993.

73 Lawson, p.500.

74 Interviewed on *The Jimmy Young Programme*, BBC Radio 2, 26 February 1986.

75 Lawson, p.374.

76 Sked and Cook, p.476.

77 Keegan, p.119.

78 Keegan, pp.182–3; Christopher Johnson, *The Economy Under Mrs Thatcher*, pp.11–14.

79 Keegan, pp.136–40.

80 Wyatt, Vol. 1, p.242 (9 December 1986).

81 Lawson, p.661.

82 Edmund Dell, *The Chancellors*, p.532.

83 Richard N. Kelly, *Conservative Party Conferences: The Hidden System*, pp.158, 184; *The Times*, 9 February 1986.

84 Lawson, p.224.

85 Interviewed on *The Jimmy Young Programme*, BBC Radio 2, 26 February 1986.

86 Interview for Italian television, RAI, 10 March 1986.

87 Speech to the Conservative Central Council, Felixstowe, 15 March 1986.

88 See Lawson, p.323, Geoffrey Howe, *Conflict of Loyalty*, pp.280–1, Ridley, p.79, Norman Tebbit, *Unfinished Business*, p.79; John Biffen and Jock Bruce-Gardyne, interviewed for *The Thatcher Factor*.

89 *The Times*, 26 July 1985.

90 Simon Jenkins, *Accountable to None: the Tory Nationalisation of Britain*, p.181.

91 Jenkins, pp.175–88; Nicholas Timmins, *The Five Giants*, pp.381, 434–7; David Butler and Gareth Butler, *British Political Facts, 1900–1994*, pp.332–4.

92 Jenkins, p.175.

93 Thatcher, p.600.

94 Kenneth Baker, *The Turbulent Years*, p.262.

95 Speech at the Conservative Party Conference, 10 October 1986.

96 Jenkins, p.179.

97 Lawson, p.211.

98 John Redwood in Iain Dale (ed.), *Memories of Maggie*, p.102.

99 Lawson, p.222.

100 John Redwood, loc. cit.

101 Speech at the Guildhall, 10 November 1986.

102 *Annual Register 1985*, p.28; *Annual Register 1984*, p.21.

103 George Grimstone, a Treasury official, interviewed on *The Great Sell-Off*, BBC, 26 January 1997.

104 *Annual Register 1986*, p.22.

105 Ibid.

106 Lawson, pp.215–16; Lord Tebbit, David Willetts, interviewed in *The Great Sell-Off*; Samuel Brittan, interviewed for *The Thatcher Factor*.

107 Lord Walker, interviewed for *The Thatcher Factor*; see also Peter Walker, *Staying Power*, pp.189–93.

108 Thatcher, pp.681–2.

109 Jenkins, p.203.

110 *The Times*, 9 November 1985.

111 Ibid., 15 November 1985.

112 Lord Joseph, interviewed for *The Thatcher Factor*.

113 Speech at the Conservative Party Conference, 13 October 1989.

114 Butler and Butler, pp.402–4.

115 *The Great Sell-Off*, BBC, 26 January 1997.

116 Jenkins, pp.35–6.

117 Thatcher, p.677.

118 Jenkins, p.40.

119 Speech to the Conservative Central Council, 15 March 1986.

120 David Lodge, *Nice Work*, p.326.

121 Anna McCurley, interviewed for *The Thatcher Factor*.

122 Peter York, *Peter York's Eighties*, p.88.

123 Ibid, pp.411–12.

124 Ibid., p.8.

125 Nicholas Timmins, *The Five Giants*, pp.508–9.

126 Speech to the Conservative Party Conference, 14 October 1977.

127 Thatcher, p.482.

128 *Punch*, 22 February 1984.

129 Arnold Kemp, *The Hollow Drum*, p.211.

130 Speech in Newport, 26 May 1987.

131 Wyatt, Vol. 1, p.275 (25 January 1987); Vol. 2, p.355 (25 September 1990).

132 Ibid., Vol. 1, p.306 (8 March 1987); p.521 (20 March 1988).

133 Ibid., p.629 (25 September 1988).

134 Ibid., p.33 (15 December 1985).
135 *The Times*, 19 April 1997.
136 Jock Bruce-Gardyne, interviewed for *The Thatcher Factor*.
137 *A Week in Politics*, Channel 4, 1 February 1985.
138 TV-am, 7 June 1987.
139 Conservative Party Conference, 14 October 1988.
140 Conservative Party Conference, 13 October 1989.
141 Tyler, p.251.
142 Speech to Mid-Bedfordshire Conservatives, 30 April 1982.
143 Conservative Party Conference, 12 October 1984.
144 Conservative Party Conference, 14 October 1988.

7 Iron Lady I: Special Relationships

1 Speech in Finchley, 22 October 1982.
2 Margaret Thatcher, *The Downing Street Years*, p.487.
3 Speech to Mid-Bedfordshire Conservatives, 30 April 1982.
4 Julia Langdon in Iain Dale (ed.), *Memories of Maggie*, p.307.
5 Adam Boulton, ibid., p.9.
6 David Reynolds, *Britannia Overruled*, p.256.
7 John Coles, *Making Foreign Policy: A Certain Idea of Britain*, p.176; interview, Tom King.
8 Raymond Seitz, *Over Here*, p.278.
9 Thatcher, p.518.
10 Charles Powell in Dale, pp.39–40.
11 Charles Powell, interviewed on *The Last Europeans*.
12 Richard Perle, interviewed for *The Thatcher Factor*.
13 Kenneth Baker, *The Turbulent Years*, p.256.
14 John Ranelagh, *Thatcher's People*, p.284.
15 Interview, Sir Michael Partridge.
16 *The Journals of Woodrow Wyatt*, Vol. 1, p.87 (9 February 1986).
17 Thatcher, p.492.
18 Ibid., p.309.
19 Sir Anthony Parsons, interviewed for the British Diplomatic Oral History Project, Churchill College, Cambridge.
20 Sir Percy Cradock, *In Pursuit of British Interests*, p.10.
21 Peter Hennessy, *Whitehall*, p.645.
22 Sir Roderick Braithwaite, interviewed for the British Diplomatic Oral History Project, Churchill College, Cambridge.
23 Alan Clark, *Diaries*, p.149 (19 November 1986).
24 John Cole, *As It Seemed to Me*, p.348.
25 Cradock, p.14.
26 Ibid., p.15.

27 See ibid.; George Urban, *Diplomacy and Disillusion at the Court of Margaret Thatcher*; interview, Sir Michael Palliser.

28 Cradock, p.24.

29 Sir Anthony Parsons, interviewed for *The Thatcher Factor*.

30 Charles Powell in Dale, p.40.

31 Alan Sked and Chris Cook, *Post-War Britain, 1945–1992*, p.504.

32 Ibid.

33 Speech at the Conservative Party Conference, 16 October 1981.

34 Interview, Raymond Seitz.

35 Ronald Millar, *A View from the Wings*, p.335.

36 Speech to the Conservative Party Conference, 12 October 1984.

37 Thatcher, p.251.

38 Ibid., p.171.

39 Geoffrey Smith, *Reagan and Thatcher*, p.26.

40 Cradock, p.58.

41 Tony Benn, *Free At Last: Diaries 1991–2001*, p.211 (4 November 1993).

42 Chris Ogden, *Maggie*, p.236.

43 Interview, Sir Michael Palliser.

44 Jacques Attali, *Verbatim*, p.271.

45 David Gergan, *Eyewitness to Power*.

46 Ronald Reagan, *An American Life*, p.354.

47 Speech at the Pilgrims' dinner, Savoy Hotel, London, 29 January 1981.

48 Speeches at the White House, Washington, 26 February 1981.

49 Reagan papers, Box 35, 8100164–8102258.

50 Robin Renwick, *Fighting with Allies: America and Britain in Peace and War*, p.50.

51 Ronald Reagan to Margaret Thatcher, 4 August 1981 (Box 35, 8100164–8102258).

52 *Newsweek*, 21 June 1982.

53 Reagan to Mrs Thatcher, 17 May 1983 (Box 35, 8301952–8303361).

54 Reagan to Mrs Thatcher, 17 June 1983 (Head of State file, Box 34, 152/04/4).

55 Reagan to Mrs Thatcher, 30 May 1984 (CO 167, 237000–245999).

56 John Poindexter memo, 29 July 1983 (CO 167, 160000–169999).

57 William Clark memo, 29 September 1983 (European and Soviet Affairs Directorate, NSC, Box 90902).

58 US Embassy briefing, September 1983 (*loc.cit.*).

59 Thatcher, p.469.

60 Richard Perle, interviewed for *The Thatcher Factor*.

61 George Shultz, interviewed on *Thatcher: The Downing Street Years*.

62 James M. Rentschler to Richard Allen, 23 November 1981 (Box 35, 8106458).

63 State Department memo, 18 January 1984 (Box 35, 8400187–8404387).

64 Reagan to Mrs Thatcher, 18 July 1984 (Box 35, 88404781–8407224).

65 Press conference in Washington, 15 November 1986.

66 *Face the Nation*, CBS, 17 July 1987.

67 Richard Perle, interviewed for *The Thatcher Factor*.

68 Alexander Haig to Reagan, 29 January 1982 (Box 35, 81060581–8200891).

69 Nicholas Henderson, *Mandarin*, p.479.

70 House of Commons, 1 July 1982 [Vol. 26, col. 1044].

71 Reagan to Mrs Thatcher, 2 July 1982 (Box 35, 8202120–8205267).

72 Mrs Thatcher to Reagan, 30 July 1982 *(loc.cit.)*.

73 Reagan to Mrs Thatcher, 9 August 1982 *(loc.cit.)*.

74 Minute of meeting between Mrs Thatcher and Caspar Weinberger, 8 September 1982 (NSC, Box 91330).

75 Reagan to Mrs Thatcher, 12 November 1982 (Head of State file, Box 34, 152/04/4).

76 Robert Macfarlane/George Shultz memo, 22 December 1984 (NSC, Box 90902).

77 Mrs Thatcher to Reagan, 29 March 1983 (Box 35, 8301952–8303361).

78 Reagan to Mrs Thatcher, 6 April 1983 *(loc cit.)*.

79 Smith, p.144.

80 Ibid., p.165.

81 Bernard Ingham, *Kill the Messenger*, p.257.

82 Briefing paper, June 1984 (CO 1167, 270790–289999).

83 Speech to US Congress, Washington, 20 February 1985.

84 Mrs Thatcher to Reagan, 22 February 1985 (Box 35, 8590152–8590923).

85 European and Soviet Affairs Directorate, NSC, Box 90902.

86 *Washington Post*, 17 June 1983.

87 Reagan to Mrs Thatcher, 18 June 1982 (NSC, Box 90902).

88 Reagan to Mrs Thatcher, 24 June 1982 (Head of State file, Box 34, 152/04/4).

89 William Clark memo to Reagan, 22 June 1982 (NSC, Box 91327).

90 Ibid.

91 George Shultz, *Turmoil and Triumph: My Years as Secretary of State*, p.152.

92 Reagan to Mrs Thatcher, 1 November 1982 (Box 35, 8205310–8207568).

93 Reagan to Mrs Thatcher, 7 December 1983 (Box 35, 8307330–83308843).

94 George Bush to Mrs Thatcher, 8 December 1983 (CO 167, 207000–215999).

95 John Poindexter memo to Reagan, 15 November 1986 (CO 167, 440030).

96 Smith, p.224.

97 Carol Thatcher, *Below the Parapet*, p.210.

98 Reagan, pp.454–5.

99 Caspar Weinberger, *Fighting for Peace: Seven Critical Years at the Pentagon*, p.82.

100 Robert Macfarlane, *Special Trust*, p.265.

101 House of Commons, 24 October 1983 [Vol. 47, cols 27–30].

102 Reagan to Mrs Thatcher, 24 October 1983 (Executive Secretariat, NSC, Box 91331).

103 Reagan to Mrs Thatcher, 24 October 1983 *(loc.cit.)*.

104 Geoffrey Howe, *Conflict of Loyalty*, p.330.

105 Interview, Sir John Coles.

106 Howe, p.330.

107 Memorandum of telephone conversation, 26 October 1983 (Executive Secretariat, NSC, Box 91330).

108 Reagan to Mrs Thatcher, 25 October 1983 (Ibid., Box 91330).

109 House of Commons, 25 October 1983 [Vol. 47, cols 143–6].

110 Transcript of a telephone conversation, 26 October 1983 (Executive Secretariat, NSC, Box 91330).

111 House of Commons, 27 October 1983 [Vol. 47, col. 422].

112 Brian Crozier, *Free Agent*, p.264.

113 *Irish Times*, 20 May 2000.

114 BBC World Service, 30 October 1983.

115 David Dimbleby and David Reynolds, *An Ocean Apart*, pp.316–17.

116 Renwick, p.244.

117 Speech at the Guildhall, London, 14 November 1985.

118 George Bush to Mrs Thatcher, 8 December 1983 (CO 167, 207000–215–999).

119 *New York Times*, 11 January 1986.

120 *Irish Times*, 20 May 2000.

121 Thatcher, p.445.

122 Renwick, pp.250–1.

123 *Sunday Times*, 13 April 1986.

124 Baker, p.121.

125 Thatcher, p.447.

126 Wyatt, Vol. 1, p.124 (20 April 1986).

127 House of Commons, 15 April 1986 [Vol. 95, col. 726].

128 David Owen, *Time to Declare*, pp.641–2.

129 Thatcher, p.449.

130 Margaret Thatcher, *Statecraft: Strategies for a Changing World*, p.232.

131 Thatcher, *The Downing Street Years*, p.449.

132 Ibid., p.263.

133 Reagan speech at Orlando, Florida, 8 March 1983.

134 Mrs Thatcher to Reagan, 15 September 1983 (Head of State file, Box 34, 152/04/4).

135 US Embassy briefing, September 1983 (NSC, Box 90902).

136 Thatcher, p.452.

137 Baker, p.262.

138 Reynolds, p.277.

139 Speech in Washington, 29 September 1983.

140 Speech at the Conservative Party Conference, 14 October 1983.

141 Speech in Washington, 29 September 1983.

142 Urban, p.38.

143 Mrs Thatcher to Reagan, 8 February 1984 (Box 35, 8400187–8704387).

144 Thatcher, 457.

145 Ibid., p.452.

146 Peter Walker, *Staying Power*, p.193.

147 Cradock, p.144.

148 Memorandum of conversation at Camp David, 22 December 1984 (NSC, Box 90902).

149 Howe, p.358.

150 Thatcher, p.461.

151 Carol Thatcher, p.222.

152 Thatcher, p.461.

153 BBC TV interview, 17 December 1984.

154 Press conference at the UN, New York, 24 October 1985.

155 Speech in Washington, 25 July 1985.

156 James Baker, interviewed on *Thatcher: The Downing Street Years*.

157 Letters displayed in the Reagan Library.

158 Memorandum of conversation at Camp David, 22 December 1984 (NSC, Box 90902).

159 Thatcher, p.463, p.466.

160 BBC radio interview, 21 December 1984.

161 Robin Butler in Dale, pp.108–9.

162 Memorandum of conversation at Camp David, 22 December 1984 (NSC, Box 90902).

163 Ibid.

164 Cradock, p.65.

165 Reagan to NATO leaders, January 1985 (Box 35, 8590010–8590047).

166 Lt Gen. James Abrahamson to Mrs Thatcher, 3 January 1985 (Box 35, 8500392–8500484).

167 Mrs Thatcher to Reagan, 14 January 1985 (*loc.cit.*).

168 Macfarlane, p.284.

169 US Embassy briefing, 20 February 1985 (NSC, Box 90902).

170 Speech to the US Congress, Washington, 20 February 1985.

171 Mrs Thatcher to Reagan, 22 February 1985 (Box 35, 8590152–8590923).

172 Macfarlane, pp.305–7.

173 Howe, p.396.

174 Macfarlane, p.307.

175 Smith, pp.166–7.

176 George Shultz, interviewed on *Thatcher: The Downing Street Years*.

177 Smith, p.167.

178 Dimbleby and Reynolds, p.328.

179 Macfarlane, p.306.

180 Thatcher, p.467, p.471.

181 Michael Jopling in Dale, p.144.

182 Margaret Thatcher in *Thatcher: The Downing Street Years*.

183 US Embassy briefing, 5 November 1986 (NSC, Box 90902).

184 John Poindexter memo to Reagan, 15 November 1986 (*loc.cit*).

185 Ibid.

186 George Shultz memo to Reagan, November 1986 (*loc.cit.*).

187 Smith, p.223.

188 George Shultz memo to Reagan, November 1986 (NSC, Box 90902).

189 Interview for ABC, 21 January 1987.

190 *Daily Express*, 22 April 1987.

191 Reynolds, p.282.

192 *Face the Nation*, CBS, 1 July 1987.

193 Thatcher, p.772.

194 Ibid., p.482.

195 Michael Cockerell, *Live from Number 10: The Inside Story of Prime Ministers and Television*, p.318.

196 Ibid.

197 Millar, p.311.

198 Rodney Tyler, *Campaign!*, p.95.

199 Adam Boulton in Dale, p.9.

200 Thatcher, p.485.

201 Speech to the Conservative Party Conference, 9 October 1987.

202 Speech to the Conservative Party Conference, 14 October 1988.

203 Urban, p.132.

204 Cradock, pp.100–1.

205 Thatcher, *Statecraft*, pp.7, 76.

206 Mikhail Gorbachev, *Memoirs*, p.547.

207 Ibid., p.548.

208 Reference missing.

209 Margaret Thatcher, *The Downing Street Years*, p.774.

210 Wyatt, Vol. 1, p.454 (6 December 1987)

8 Iron Lady II: Europe and the World

1 Percy Cradock, *In Pursuit of British Interests*, p.125.

2 Sir Robin Renwick, interviewed on *The Last Europeans*, Channel 4, 1995.

3 Simon Heffer, *Like the Roman: The Life of Enoch Powell*, p.885.

4 Memorandum of a conversation at Camp David, 22 December 1984 [NSC, Box 90902].

5 Speech to the Conservative Party Conference, 14 October 1983.

6 Speech to the Conservative Party Conference, 16 October 1981.

7 Speech to the Franco-British Council, Avignon, 30 November 1984.

8 Margaret Thatcher, *The Downing Street Years*, p.536.

9 Hugo Young, *One of Us*, p.383.

10 Sir Reginald Hibbert, interviewed for the British Diplomatic Oral History Project, Churchill College, Cambridge.

11 John Major, *The Autobiography*, p.122.

12 Harold Evans, *Good Times, Bad Times*, p.284.
13 George Urban, *Diplomacy and Disillusion at the Court of Margaret Thatcher*, p.82.
14 Interview, Sir John Coles.
15 Charles Powell, in Iain Dale (ed.), *Memories of Maggie*, pp.40–1.
16 Thatcher, p.318.
17 Ibid., p.545.
18 Ibid., p.70.
19 Ibid., p.337.
20 Bernard Ingham, interviewed on *The Poisoned Chalice*, BBC, 1996.
21 Bernard Ingham, *Kill the Messenger*, p.265.
22 House of Commons, 5 December 1985 [Vol. 88, col. 434].
23 *Panorama*, BBC, 9 April 1984.
24 Thatcher, p.543.
25 Speech to the Conservative Party Conference, 12 October 1984.
26 Jacques Attali, interviewed on *The Poisoned Chalice*.
27 Bernard Ingham, interviewed on *The Poisoned Chalice*.
28 Thatcher, p.545.
29 Danish Foreign Minister, interviewed on *The Poisoned Chalice*.
30 Urban, p.79.
31 Speech to the Conservative Party Conference, 12 October 1984.
32 Speech to US Congress, Washington, 20 February 1985.
33 Thatcher, p.547.
34 Nigel Lawson, interviewed on *The Poisoned Chalice*.
35 Geoffrey Howe, interviewed on *The Last Europeans*.
36 Speech to the Franco-British Council, Avignon, 30 November 1984.
37 Thatcher, p.536.
38 Speech to Conservative MEPs, 8 March 1984.
39 Claude Cheysson, interviewed on *The Last Europeans*.
40 Thatcher, p.547.
41 Lord Cockfield, interviewed on *The Poisoned Chalice*.
42 BBC interview, 4 December 1985.
43 Charles Powell, interviewed on *The Poisoned Chalice*.
44 Nigel Lawson, interviewed on *The Poisoned Chalice*.
45 Sir Robin Renwick, BBC interview, 18 January 1998.
46 House of Commons, 5 December 1985 [Vol. 88, col. 433].
47 Alan Sked and Chris Cook, *Post-War Britain, 1945–1992*, p.498.
48 Margaret Thatcher, interviewed on *The Poisoned Chalice*, BBC, 1996.
49 Charles Powell, interviewed on *The Poisoned Chalice*, BBC, 1996.
50 Thatcher, p.741.
51 Sir Michael Butler, interviewed on *The Last Europeans*.
52 David Williamson, interviewed on *The Last Europeans*.
53 Interview, Lord Cockfield.
54 Bernard Ingham, interviewed on *The Poisoned Chalice*.

55 Jacques Delors, interviewed on *The Poisoned Chalice*.
56 House of Commons, 30 April 1974 [Vol. 872, col. 967].
57 Remarks visiting Dover, 24 May 1983.
58 BBC, 18 January 1998.
59 BBC interview, 30 November 1984.
60 Speech at Lille, 20 January 1986.
61 Lady Renwick, interviewed on the BBC, 18 January 1998.
62 Charles Powell, ibid.
63 Speech at Finchley, 25 January 1986.
64 Nicholas Ridley, '*My Style of Government*', p.158.
65 Charles Powell, interviewed on *Consequences*, BBC Radio 4, 2 January 1996.
66 Speech at Lille, 20 January 1986.
67 *The Journals of Woodrow Wyatt*, Vol. 1, p.344 (12 May 1989).
68 Speech at Brussels, 23 June 1978.
69 Interview, Sir John Coles.
70 Cradock, pp.174–5.
71 Jonathan Dimbleby, *The Last Governor*, p.43.
72 Ibid., p.44.
73 Cradock, p.179.
74 Speech at the Conservative Party Conference, 12 October 1984.
75 Internal memo, 24 September 1984 (NSC, Box 91333).
76 Reagan to Mrs Thatcher, 17 October 1984 (Box 35, 8404781–80407224).
77 Wyatt, Vol. 2, p.99 (4 June 1989).
78 Cradock, p.224.
79 Wyatt, Vol. 2, p.10 (15 January 1989).
80 Thatcher, p.488.
81 Dimbleby, p.52.
82 *Independent*, 19 January 1995.
83 Thatcher, pp.494–5.
84 *Finchley Press*, 18 June 1962.
85 Sarah Bradford, *Elizabeth*, p.386.
86 *Sunday Telegraph*, 27 July 1986.
87 Reagan papers, 20 August 1981 (Box 35, 8102478–8106456).
88 Ibid., Box 35, 8307330–8308843.
89 Carol Thatcher, *Below the Parapet*, p.211.
90 Interviews, Sir John Coles, Chris Patten.
91 Thatcher, p.504.
92 Bob Hawke, *The Hawke Memoirs*, pp.320–2.
93 Hugo Young, *One of Us*, p.120.
94 Reagan papers, 27 May 1981 (Box 35, 8102478–8106456).
95 Thatcher, pp.161–2.
96 Margaret Thatcher, *The Path to Power*, p.386.
97 Wyatt, Vol. 1, p.155 (20 June 1985).

98 *This Week*, 22 December 1987.

99 *The Sowetan*, 2 October 1989.

100 Thatcher, *The Downing Street Years*, p.514.

101 Press conference in Oslo, 12 September 1986.

102 Thatcher, p.515.

103 Ingham, p.278.

104 Anthony Sampson, *Nelson Mandela*, p.215.

105 BBC, 27 June 1986.

106 Interview on Channel 10, Sydney, 4 August 1988.

107 Sampson, pp.321, 356.

108 Ibid., p.361.

109 Ibid., p.342.

110 Thatcher, pp.517–18.

111 *Annual Register 1985*, p.329.

112 Geoffrey Howe, *Conflict of Loyalty*, p.483.

113 Thatcher, p.518; Howe, p.484.

114 Anthony Barber, *Taking the Tide*, pp.165–72; Thatcher, p.519.

115 Howe, pp.493–6.

116 Thatcher, p.116.

117 Interview for Channel 4 News, 13 June 1986.

118 Wyatt, Vol. 1, p.155 (20 June 1986).

119 Reagan to Mrs Thatcher, 23 June 1986, (Box 35, 8690401–8690687).

120 Hawke, p.327.

121 Thatcher, pp.521–2.

122 Hawke, p.327.

123 Thatcher, pp.523–4; Ingham, p.280.

124 Press conference at Vancouver, 17 October 1987.

125 Interview for TV-am, 27 June 1986.

126 Press conference at Nairobi, 6 January 1988.

127 Robin Renwick, *Unconventional Diplomacy in Southern Africa*, p.152.

128 Sampson, p.387.

129 Wyatt, Vol. 2, p.60 (2 April 1989).

130 Renwick, p.133.

131 Sampson, p.390.

132 *The Sowetan*, 2 October 1989.

133 John Major, *The Autobiography*, p.125.

134 Hawke, p.333.

135 *Annual Register 1989*, pp.543–4.

136 Wyatt, Vol. 2, p.232 (4 February 1990).

137 House of Commons, 13 February 1990 [Vol. 167, col. 140].

138 Sampson, p.409.

139 Renwick, p.145.

140 Nelson Mandela, *Long Walk to Freedom*, p.574.

141 Sampson, p.415.

142 Sampson, p.418; Renwick, p.147.

143 Mandela, p.576.

144 Thatcher, p.533; Sampson, p.418.

145 Speech in KwaZulu, 21 May 1991.

146 Cradock, p.153.

147 David Owen, *Time to Declare*, p.297.

148 Mark Stuart, *Douglas Hurd: The Public Servant*, p.119.

149 David Steel, *Against Goliath: David Steel's Story*, pp.190–1.

150 Richard Allen memo to Reagan (Box 35, 8106458).

151 Reagan to Mrs Thatcher, November 1981 (*loc. cit*).

152 Reagan to Mrs Thatcher, 1 December 1981 (*loc. cit*).

153 Note of meeting between Mrs Thatcher and Caspar Weinberger, 29 February 1984 (Executive Secretariat NSC, Box 91331).

154 Mrs Thatcher to Reagan, 22 March 1983 (Box 35, 8301952–8300964).

155 Mrs Thatcher to Reagan, 5 November 1983 (Box 35, 8391259–8391521).

156 Thatcher, p.334.

157 Note of meeting between Mrs Thatcher and Caspar Weinberger, 29 February 1984 (Executive Secretariat NSC, Box 91331).

158 Memorandum of a conversation at Camp David, 22 January 1984 (NSC, Box 90902).

159 Thatcher, p.508.

160 Memorandum of a meeting between Mrs Thatcher and George Shultz, 17 January 1987.

161 Thatcher, p.510.

162 Ibid., p.168.

163 House of Commons, 26 October 1981 [Vol. 10, col. 560].

164 Oliver Morrissey, Brian Smith and Edward Horesh, *British Aid and International Trade: Aid Policy Making, 1979–89*, pp.90–6.

165 Interview for BBC Radio, 23 October 1981.

166 Ibid.

167 Press conference at Cancun, Mexico, 23 October 1981.

168 Thatcher, p.170.

169 Margaret Thatcher, *Statecraft: Strategies for a Changing World*, p.442.

170 Michael Heseltine, interviewed for *The Thatcher Factor*.

171 Press conference for Arab correspondents, 6 April 1981.

172 *Not the Scott Report (Private Eye*, November 1994), p.30.

173 Kenneth Baker, *The Turbulent Years*, p.261.

174 Gerald James, *In the Public Interest*, p.67.

175 *The Times*, 27 September 1985.

176 *Observer*, 12 January 1986.

177 House of Commons, 17 January 1984, 24 January 1984 [Vol. 52, cols 159, 766]; *Weekend World*, 15 January 1984; *Panorama*, 9 April 1984.

178 Paul Halloran and Mark Hollingsworth, *Thatcher's Gold*, pp.179–86.
179 Thatcher, *The Downing Street Years*, p.502.
180 Stuart, p.405.
181 *The Times*, 2 March 1994.
182 House of Commons, 13 December 1994 [Vol. 251, col. 777]; Stuart, p.407.
183 Andrew Marr, *Ruling Britannia*, pp.248–9.
184 Ibid., p.249.
185 Note of meeting between Mrs Thatcher and Caspar Weinberger, 29 February 1984 (Executive Secretariat, NSC, Box 91331).
186 *Not the Scott Report*, p.13.
187 Ibid., p.14.
188 Scott Report, D2 3–8.
189 Ibid., D2 120.
190 *Not the Scott Report*, p.14.
191 Scott Report, D1 75.
192 Alan Friedman, *Spider's Web: Bush, Saddam, Thatcher and the Decade of Deceit*, p.251.
193 *Not the Scott Report*, p.15.
194 *The Times*, 9 November 1989.
195 Ibid.
196 Friedman, p.251; K. R. Timmerman, *The Death Lobby*, p.282.
197 Reagan papers, CO167, 270790–289999.
198 Scott Report, D2 19.
199 House of Commons, 4 December 1986 [Vol. 106, col. 1078].
200 *Not the Scott Report*, p.18.
201 House of Commons, 18 April 1990 [Vol. 170, col. 1428].
202 *Not the Scott Report*, p.28.
203 Scott Report, G12 30.
204 Ibid., D2 328–30.
205 Ibid.
206 *Not the Scott Report*, p.28.
207 Ibid., p.9.
208 Ibid., p.24.
209 Ibid.

9 Enemies Within

1 Speech to the Conservative Central Council, Cheltenham, 31 March 1990.
2 *Thatcher: The Downing Street Years*, BBC, 1993.
3 Margaret Thatcher, *The Downing Street Years*, p.353.
4 House of Commons, 26 January 1984 [Vol. 52, col. 1047].
5 *Observer*, 4 March 1984.
6 Geoffrey Howe, *Conflict of Loyalty*, pp.345–8.

7 John Hoskyns, *Just in Time: Inside the Thatcher Revolution*, p.139.

8 Peter Hennessy, *Cabinet*, pp.32–3.

9 Hugo Young, *One of Us*, p.367.

10 *The Miner*, March 1983, quoted in Michael Crick, *Scargill and the Miners*, p.96.

11 Peter Walker, *Staying Power*, p.166.

12 Speech at the NUM conference, 4 July 1983, quoted in Young, p.367.

13 *Annual Register 1984*, p.8.

14 Crick, p.108.

15 *The Times*, 28 March 1984.

16 Thatcher, p.340.

17 House of Commons, 24 March 1983 [Vol. 39, col. 1011].

18 Ibid., 13 March 1984 [Vol. 56, col. 278].

19 *Panorama*, BBC, 9 April 1984.

20 *The Times*, 1 June 1984.

21 Ibid., 14 June 1984.

22 House of Commons, 13 March 1984 [Vol. 56, col. 279].

23 *Panorama*, BBC, 9 April 1984.

24 Speech to farmers at Banbury, Oxfordshire, 30 May 1984.

25 Young, p.368.

26 House of Commons, 15 March 1984 [Vol. 56, cols 512–13], *Panorama*, BBC, 9 April 1984.

27 Sir Ian MacGregor on *The Downing Street Years*, BBC, 1993.

28 *Yorkshire Post*, 20 July 1984.

29 Wendy Webster, *Not a Man to Match Her: The Marketing of the Prime Minister*, p.159.

30 *The Times*, 20 July 1984.

31 *Newsnight*, BBC, 27 July 1984.

32 *Sunday Mirror*, 3 October 1984.

33 *The Times*, 20 September 1984.

34 House of Commons, 31 July 1984 [Vol. 65, col. 252].

35 Speech at the Conservative Party Conference, 12 October 1984.

36 Lecture at the Carlton Club, 26 November 1984.

37 *A Week in Politics*, Channel 4, 1 February 1985.

38 Speech at York, 26 September 1984.

39 Thatcher, p.347.

40 Interview, Sir Michael Partridge.

41 Thatcher, p.362.

42 Raymond Seitz, *Over Here*, p.130.

43 *The Times*, 21 September 1984.

44 Thatcher, p.364.

45 Ibid., p.358.

46 *Annual Register 1984*, p.8.

47 *The Times*, 7 May 1984.

48 Thatcher, p.358.

49 Andrew Turnbull to Henry Derwent, Department of Transport, 16 April 1984, in the *Daily Mirror*, 6 June 1984.

50 Thatcher, p.353.

51 *Panorama*, BBC, 9 April 1984; House of Commons, 22 May 1984 [Vol. 60, col. 823].

52 *Thatcher: The Downing Street Years*, BBC, 1993.

53 Ian MacGregor, *The Enemies Within*, pp.280–2.

54 House of Commons, 30 October 1984, 6 November 1984 [Vol. 65, col. 1157; Vol. 67, col. 22].

55 Speech at the Conservative Party Conference, 12 October 1984.

56 Speech at the Guildhall, 12 November 1984.

57 Thatcher, p.365.

58 Ronald Millar, *A View from the Wings*, p.299.

59 *Daily Express*, 31 December 1984.

60 House of Commons, 6 November 1984 [Vol. 67, col. 23].

61 *TV Eye*, Thames TV, 25 January 1985.

62 *The Times*, 25 and 26 January 1985.

63 House of Commons 7 February 1985 [Vol. 72, col. 1098].

64 *A Week in Politics*, Channel 4, 1 February 1985.

65 *The Times*, 4 March 1985.

66 Ibid., 8 January 1985.

67 *Annual Register 1985*, p.18.

68 Press conference in Kuala Lumpur, 6 April 1985.

69 *Independent*, 23 November 1994; see *The Grocer's Daughter*, pp.126–34.

70 Andrew Thomson, *Margaret Thatcher: The Woman Within*, p.100.

71 Kenneth Baker, *The Turbulent Years*, p.111.

72 Simon Jenkins, *Accountable to None*, p.156; Andrew Marr, *Ruling Britannia*, p.104.

73 Interview with US correspondents, 3 July 1987.

74 Francis Pym, *The Politics of Consent*, p.19.

75 Friedrich Hayek, *The Road to Serfdom*.

76 Interview, Lady Young.

77 Leo Abse, *Margaret, Daughter of Beatrice*, p.110.

78 Jenkins, p.44, quoting CIPFA figures.

79 *Today*, BBC Radio 4, August 2001.

80 House of Commons, 23 July 1981 [Vol. 9, col. 492].

81 John Carvel, *Turn Again, Livingstone*, pp.94–5, 137.

82 Ibid., p.166.

83 Jenkins, p.48.

84 Speech at the Conservative Party Conference, 12 October 1984.

85 Alan Sked and Chris Cook, *Post-War Britain, 1945–1992*, p.437.

86 Carvel, p.160.

87 House of Commons, 12 June 1984 [Vol. 61, col. 769].

88 Carvel, p.182.

89 House of Commons, 11 April 1984 [Vol. 58, cols. 423–8].

90 Ibid., 5 July 1984 [Vol. 63, col. 457].

91 Carvel, p.186.

92 Ibid., p.174.

93 Interview, Lord Jenkin.

94 Thatcher, p.420.

95 *The Journals of Woodrow Wyatt*, Vol. 1, p.102 (16 March 1986).

96 Interview, Neville Beale.

97 Carvel, pp.192–3.

98 Ibid., p.183.

99 *Evening Standard*, 4 April 1985.

100 Remarks visiting a Conservative local-government conference, 9 March 1985.

101 *Annual Register 1986*, p.36.

102 Carvel, p.249, citing the *London Government Handbook, 1988*.

103 Roy Porter, *London: A Social History*, p.369.

104 Ibid., p.373.

105 Carvel, p.252.

106 Jenkins, p.171.

107 Porter, p.369.

108 Ibid., p.367.

109 Nigel Lawson, *The View from No. 11*, p.314.

110 House of Commons, 16 December 1982 [Vol. 34, col. 476].

111 Interview on *Weekend World*, LWT, 16 January 1983.

112 Marr, p.178.

113 House of Commons, 12 February 1985 [Vol. 73, col. 162].

114 Press conference for American correspondents in London, 7 December 1984.

115 Peter Hennessy, *The Prime Minister*, p.433.

116 Wyatt, Vol. 1, p.229 (24 November 1986).

117 Interview with Terry Coleman, *Guardian*, 2 November 1971.

118 *Today*, BBC Radio 4, 6 June 1987.

119 Nicholas Ridley, '*My Style of Government*', p.18.

120 Matthew Parris, *Chance Witness*, p.193.

121 Interview for TV-am, 30 December 1988.

122 Humphrey Carpenter, *Robert Runcie: The Reluctant Archbishop*, pp.219–20.

123 Ibid., pp.255–61.

124 Ibid.

125 *Sunday Times*, 1 December 1985.

126 *The Times*, 2 December 1985.

127 Wyatt, Vol. 1, p.22 (1 December 1985).

128 Margaret Thatcher, *The Path to Power*, p.556.

129 Speech to the Conservative Central Council, 23 March 1985.

130 *The Woman at No. 10*, ITV, 29 March 1983.

131 *New Yorker*, 30 September 1985.

132 *Weekend World*, ITV, 6 January 1980.

133 *Songs of Praise*, BBC, 21 October 1982.

134 Thomson, p.65.

135 Millar, p.284.

136 Address at St Lawrence, Jewry, 4 March 1981.

137 Ludovic Kennedy, *In Bed with an Elephant*, p.302.

138 Address to the General Assembly of the Church of Scotland, 21 May 1988.

139 Jonathan Raban, *God, Man and Mrs Thatcher*, p.48.

140 Wyatt, Vol. 1, p.496 (7 February 1988).

141 Ibid., p.500 (14 February 1988).

142 Interview, Margaret Wickstead.

143 *The Times*, 26 July 1990.

144 Ibid., 15 February 1988.

145 Thatcher, pp.509–10.

146 Young, pp.423–4.

147 Lawson, p.256.

148 Margaret Thatcher, *The Path to Power*, pp.35–8; see *The Grocer's Daughter*, pp.45–65.

149 Lecture to the Conservative Political Centre, 11 October 1968.

150 *Spectator*, 15 July 1972.

151 *Sunday Times*, 8 May 1988.

152 Wyatt, Vol. 1, p.246 (15 December 1986).

153 Jeremy Paxman, *Friends in High Places*, p.184.

154 Nicholas Timmins, *The Five Giants*, p.425.

155 *Nature*, 9 July 1985.

156 Tom Wilkie in Denis Kavanagh and Anthony Seldon, (eds), *The Thatcher Effect*, pp.316–29.

157 Speech to the National Press Club, Washington, 19 September 1975; *The Week*, 23 November 2002.

158 *The Times*, 30 January 1985.

159 *Mail on Sunday*, 3 February 1985.

160 Young, p.402.

161 Interview for CBS, 15 February 1985.

162 *Evening Standard*, 4 September 1985.

163 Speech to the Conservative Party Conference, 13 October 1989.

164 Peter Hennessy, *Whitehall*, p.428.

165 Jenkins, p.147.

166 Timmins, p.485.

167 Thatcher, *The Downing Street Years*, p.599.

168 Ian Trethowan, *Split Screen*, p.181.

169 *Any Questions?*, BBC Radio, 30 May 1969.

170 Interview, Sir Charles Powell.

171 Wyatt, Vol. 2, p.94 (17 May 1989).

172 John Cole, *As it Seemed to Me*, p.346.

173 House of Commons, 8 November 1979 [Vol. 973, col. 607].

174 William Whitelaw, *The Whitelaw Memoirs*, pp.263–4.

175 Speech to the Parliamentary Press Gallery, 10 July 1981.

176 House of Commons, 11 May 1982 [Vol. 23, col. 598].

177 Michael Cockerell, *Live from Number 10*, p.283.

178 Michael Spicer in Iain Dale (ed.), *Memories of Maggie*, p.61.

179 George Urban, *Diplomacy and Disillusion at the Court of Margaret Thatcher*, p.23.

180 Thatcher, *The Downing Street Years*, p.267.

181 John Drummond, *Tainted by Experience*, p.344.

182 Michael Leapman, *The Last Days of the Beeb*, p.32.

183 House of Commons, 14 March 1985 [Vol. 75, col. 429].

184 Alastair Hetherington in Denis Kavanagh and Anthony Seldon (eds), *The Thatcher Effect*, p.298.

185 Wyatt, Vol. 1, p.160 (29 June 1986).

186 *The Times*, 2 October 1986.

187 Marmaduke Hussey, *Chance Governs All*, p.197.

188 Cockerell, p.312.

189 *Newsnight*, BBC2, 30 July 1985; speech to the American Bar Association, 15 July 1985.

190 Cockerell, p.298.

191 House of Commons, 27 January 1987 [Vol. 109, col. 181].

192 Cockerell, p.315.

193 House of Commons, 3 February 1987 [Vol. 109, col. 806].

194 Stuart, p.168 (3 February 1987).

195 Cockerell, p.315.

196 Wyatt, Vol. 1, p.285 (2 February 1987).

197 Drummond, p.347.

198 Thatcher, *The Downing Street Years*, p.637.

199 Cockerell, p.298.

200 David Butler and Gareth Butler, *British Political Facts*, p.499.

201 Wyatt, Vol. 2, p.158 (15 November 1989).

202 Ibid., p.301.

203 William Shawcross, *Murdoch*, p.213.

204 Wyatt, Vol. 1, p.604 (17 July 1988).

205 Ibid., p.339, p.359 (3 May 1987, 4 June 1987).

206 Ibid., Vol. 3, p.582 (1 December 1995).

207 Michael Leapman, *Barefaced Cheek*, p.233.

208 Harold Evans, *Good Times, Bad Times*, pp.1–2.

209 Cole, p.221.

210 Andrew Neil, *Full Disclosure*, p.137.

211 Mark Stuart, *Douglas Hurd: The Public Servant*, p.224.

212 Speech to the Press Association, 8 June 1988.

213 Wyatt, Vol. 1, p.592 (3 July 1988).

214 Ibid., pp.609–10 (26 July 1988).

215 Interview, Sir Ronald Millar.

216 *Sunday Times*, 22 February 1983.

217 Address to the General Assembly of the Church of Scotland, 21 May 1988.

218 Anthony Powell, *Journals*, 27 March 1985.

219 Philip Larkin to Julian Barnes, 27 September 1985, in Philip Larkin, *Letters*, p.751.

220 George Walden, *Lucky George*, p.192.

221 Peter Hall, radio interview.

222 Roy Strong, *Diaries, 1967–1987*, p.231.

223 Press conference in York, 26 September 1984.

224 Thatcher, *The Downing Street Years*, p.633.

225 Strong, p.232.

226 Arts Council of Great Britain, *Annual Review 1988–9*.

227 Strong, p.277 (1 April 1981).

228 Ibid., p.289 (2 November 1981).

229 Peter Hall, *Making an Exhibition of Myself*, p.327.

230 House of Commons, 21 May 1981 [Vol 5, col. 418].

231 *Spectator*, 24 January 1987.

232 Thatcher, *The Downing Street Years*, p.633.

233 Speech to the British Society of Magazine Editors, 29 July 1988.

10 Irish Dimension

1 Margaret Thatcher, *The Downing Street Years*, p.385.

2 Speech at Kensington Town Hall, 19 January 1976.

3 Garret Fitzgerald, *All in a Life*, p.261.

4 BBC Radio News, 30 March 1979.

5 Interviews, Tom King, Sir Frank Cooper.

6 John Cole, *As It Seemed to Me*, p.291.

7 Fitzgerald, p.561.

8 Lord Gowrie, interviewed for *The Thatcher Factor*.

9 Mark Stuart, *Douglas Hurd: The Public Servant*, p.140.

10 Airey Neave Memorial Lecture, 2 March 1980.

11 Patrick Cosgrave, *The Lives of Enoch Powell*, p.429.

12 Private information.

13 Bruce Arnold, *Haughey: His Life and Unlucky Deeds*, pp.167–8.

14 Ibid, pp.173–4.

15 Thatcher, p.390.

16 Interview, Sir Kenneth Stowe.

17 House of Commons, 20 November 1980 [Vol. 994, col. 27].

18 *Analysis*, BBC Radio 4, 26 November 1980.

19 Press conference Dublin, 8 December 1980.

20 House of Commons, 14 May 1981 [Vol. 4, col. 881].

21 Sinn Fein poster commemorating the twentieth anniversary of the hunger strikes, 2001.

22 House of Commons, 14 May 1981 [Vol. 4, col. 881].

23 Speech to the Conservative Women's Conference, London, 20 May 1981.

24 BBC, 28 May 1981.

25 Speech at Stormont, 28 May 1981.

26 Sinn Fein poster, 2001.

27 Robin Renwick, *Fighting with Allies*, p.230.

28 James Prior, *A Balance of Power*, pp.194–7.

29 Institute of Contemporary British History witness seminar, 26 April 1995.

30 Fitzgerald, p.378.

31 Chris Patten, interviewed for *The Thatcher Factor*.

32 Institute of Contemporary British History witness seminar, 26 April 1995.

33 Edward Pearce in Iain Dale (ed.), *Memories of Maggie*, p.163.

34 Lord Gowrie, Chris Patten, interviewed for *The Thatcher Factor*.

35 Edward Heath, *The Course of My Life*, p.436.

36 Dennis C. Blair to Richard V. Allen, National Security Council memorandum, 10 June 1981 (Reagan Library).

37 Paul Bew, Henry Patterson and Paul Teague, *Between War and Peace: The Political Future of Northern Ireland*, p.55.

38 Thatcher, p.396.

39 Stuart, p.135.

40 Carol Thatcher, *Below the Parapet*, p.219.

41 Ronald Millar, *A View from the Wings*, p.301.

42 Ibid., p.302.

43 Cole, p.278.

44 Speech to the Conservative Party Conference, 12 October 1984.

45 Speech at Finchley, 20 October 1984.

46 Carol Thatcher, p.219.

47 Rodney Tyler, *Campaign!*, p.245; George Gardiner in Dale, p.46.

48 *The Journals of Woodrow Wyatt*, Vol. 1, p.415 (5 October 1987).

49 Carol Thatcher, p.219.

50 Alistair McAlpine in *Thatcher: The Downing Street Years*, BBC, 1993.

51 Emma Nicholson in Dale, p.289.

52 Sir Robert Armstrong, interviewed on *Endgame in Ireland*, BBC, 24 June 2001.

53 Fitzgerald, p.517; Stuart, p.140.

54 Press conference at 12 Downing Street, 19 November 1984.

55 Reagan papers, e.g. Co 167, 216000–226999.

56 Tip O'Neill, Edward Kennedy and others to Reagan, 20 December 1984 (NSC, Box 90902).

57 Reagan to Mrs Thatcher (draft) (NSC, Box 90902).

58 Record of meeting at Camp David, 22 December 1984 (NSC, Box 90902).

59 Reagan to O'Neill, 9 January 1985, in *Boston Globe*, 30 June 2002.

60 Speech to Congress, 20 February 1985.

61 Speech to the American Bar Association, Albert Hall, London, 15 July 1985.

62 Fitzgerald, p.531.

63 Ibid., p.529.

64 Stuart, p.145.

65 Arwel Ellis Owen, *The Anglo-Irish Agreement: The First Three Years*, pp.20–1.

66 Ibid., p.23.

67 Ibid., p.24.

68 Thatcher, p.403.

69 House of Commons, 14 November 1985 [Vol. 86, col. 681].

70 Owen, p.33.

71 Ibid., pp.38, 43.

72 *Spectator*, 30 November 1985.

73 Owen, p.41.

74 Charles Powell, interviewed on *Endgame in Ireland*, BBC, 24 June 2001.

75 Speech to the Conservative Party Conference, 14 October 1988.

76 She first used the phrase in her speech to the American Bar Association, Albert Hall, London, 15 July 1985.

77 Thatcher, p.412.

78 Stuart, pp.166–7.

79 Thatcher, p.415.

80 Institute of Contemporary British History witness seminar, 26 April 1995.

11 Elective Dictatorship

1 Margaret Thatcher, *The Downing Street Years*, p.562.

2 Ibid., p.758.

3 Kenneth Baker, *The Turbulent Years*, p.257, 260, 315.

4 John Ranelagh, *Thatcher's People*, p.105.

5 Peter Hennessy, *Cabinet*, pp.99–100.

6 Peter Hennessy, *Whitehall*, p.314.

7 Nigel Lawson, *The View from No. 11*, p.125.

8 Baker, p.262.

9 Nicholas Ridley, '*My Style of Government*', pp.28–9.

10 Peter Walker, *Staying Power*, pp.161–12.

11 Ridley, p.39.

12 Hennessy, *Whitehall*, p.316.

13 Lawson, pp.128–9.

14 Lord Hailsham, *A Sparrow's Flight*, p.300.

15 Lord Howe in the Tory Reform Group magazine, Winter 2001.

16 Charles Powell interviewed on *Thatcher: The Downing Street Years*.

17 Interviewed on *Thatcher: The Downing Street Years.*

18 Interview, Sir Kenneth Stowe.

19 Interview, Lord Crickhowell.

20 Interview, Lord Brittan.

21 Nicholas Timmins, *The Five Giants*, p.462.

22 Baker, p.256.

23 Lawson, p.918.

24 Penny Junor, *John Major: From Brixton to Downing Street*, pp.117–19.

25 Interview, Lord Jenkin.

26 Thatcher, p.307.

27 Lawson, p.850.

28 Sir John Nott, interviewed on *Panorama*, BBC, 5 January 1988.

29 Robert Harris, *A Good and Faithful Servant: The Unauthorised Biography of Bernard Ingham*, p.144.

30 *The Times*, 12 May 1986.

31 Harris, p.105.

32 *The Times*, 6 June 1983.

33 Lawson, p.467.

34 *Any Questions?*, BBC Radio, 10 June 1966.

35 Harris, p.157.

36 Simon Jenkins, *Accountable to None: The Tory Nationalisation of Britain*, p.165.

37 Hennessy, *Whitehall*, pp.677–8.

38 Thatcher, p.564.

39 Ranelagh, p.246.

40 Lawson, p.494.

41 Ibid., p.680.

42 Ibid.

43 Roy Jenkins, *20th Century Portraits*, p.215.

44 Lord Weatherill at an ICBH Witness Seminar, 25 February 2002.

45 Thatcher, p.41.

46 Francis Pym, *The Politics of Consent* pp.78, 87.

47 Interview, Lord Wakeham.

48 Jock Bruce-Gardyne, interviewed for *The Thatcher Factor*.

49 Alan Clark, *Diaries*, p.83 (23 May 1984).

50 Steven Norris, *Changing Trains*, pp.148–9.

51 Gyles Brandreth, *Breaking the Code*, p.53.

52 Julian Critchley, *Westminster Blues*, p.123.

53 Julian Critchley, *The Palace of Varieties*, p.41.

54 Ridley, p.33.

55 Willie Whitelaw, speech to the parliamentary press gallery, 28 March 1984, in Mark Garnett and Ian Aitken, *Splendid! Splendid! The Authorised Biography of Willie Whitelaw*, p.301.

56 Baker, p.259.

57 Lord Weatherill at an ICBH Witness Seminar, 25 February 2002.

58 Michael Cockerell, *Live from Number 10*, pp.300–2, 336–7.

59 Ridley, p.34.

60 Michael De-la-Noy, *The Honours System*, pp.134–5.

61 Ibid., p.133.

62 Ibid., p.130.

63 Jeremy Paxman, *Friends in High Places*, p.298.

64 Ibid.

65 Ibid., pp.298–9.

66 *Sunday Times*, 5 June 1983.

67 Simon Jenkins, p.102.

68 Andrew Marr, *Ruling Britannia*, p.245.

69 Simon Jenkins, p.144.

70 Noël Annan, *Our Age*, p.435.

71 Paxman, p.329.

72 Marr, p.243.

73 Sarah Bradford, *Elizabeth*, p.381.

74 Ben Pimlott, *The Queen*, p.460.

75 Lord Hunt in Pimlott, p.461.

76 Bradford, p.380.

77 Cockerell, p.277.

78 *Sunday Telegraph*, 16 January 1983.

79 Arnold Kemp, *The Hollow Drum: Scotland Since the War*, p.210.

80 *Observer*, 5 June 1983.

81 Ibid., 27 November 1988.

82 Cockerell, p.351.

83 Bradford, p.389.

84 *Sunday Times*, 20 July 1986.

85 Bradford, p.389; Pimlott, p.513.

86 *The Journals of Woodrow Wyatt*, Vol. 1, p. 179 (30 July 1986).

87 Andrew Neil, *Full Disclosure*, p.207; Wyatt, Vol. 2, p.372 (26 October 1990).

88 Jonathan Dimbleby, *The Prince of Wales*, p.323.

89 Ibid., pp.378–9.

90 House of Commons, 24 July 1990 [Vol. 299, col. 303].

91 Reference missing.

92 Thatcher, p.755.

93 *Nationwide*, BBC, 14 June 1981.

94 *Sunday Times*, 5 August 1988.

95 *Woman's Own*, 4 August 1981.

96 Speech to the WRVS, 19 January 1981.

97 *The Times*, 22 November 1989.

98 *Nationwide*, BBC, 14 June 1981.

99 *Sunday Correspondent*, 1 November 1989.

100 BBC Radio interview, 23 March 1987.

101 Remarks in Downing Street, 3 January 1988.

102 Remarks in Downing Street, 3 March 1989.

103 S. E. Finer in K. Minogue and M. Biddiss (ed.), *Thatcherism: Personality and Politics*, p.140.

104 *Sunday Times*, 8 May 1988.

105 *Spectator*, 25 February 1989.

106 Peter Hennessy, *The Prime Minister*, p.425.

107 *Spectator*, 25 February 1989.

108 Leo Abse, *Margaret, Daughter of Beatrice*, pp.13–17.

109 Beatrix Campbell, *The Iron Ladies*, pp.125–6.

110 Denis Healey, interviewed for *The Thatcher Factor*.

111 Wendy Webster, *Not a Man to Match Her: The Marketing of the Prime Minister*, p.73.

112 Hugo Young, *One of Us*, p.383.

113 Webster, p.80.

114 Campbell, pp.241, 246.

115 Speech at Cheltenham, 3 July 1982.

116 Speech at the Conservative Party Conference, 13 October 1989.

117 Patrick Cosgrave, *Margaret Thatcher: A Tory and her Party*, p.14.

118 Interview for *The Jimmy Young Programme*, BBC Radio 2, 26 February 1986.

119 Andrew Thomson, *Margaret Thatcher: The Woman Within*, p.50.

120 *Woman's Own*, 3 August 1982.

121 *Daily Express*, 26 July 1982.

122 *Illustrated London News*, June 1987.

123 Interviewed by Miriam Stoppard, *Woman to Woman*, Yorkshire TV, 19 November 1985.

124 *Woman's Own*, 31 October 1987.

125 *Sunday Correspondent*, 5 January 1989.

126 Thatcher, p.307.

127 Interview, Lady Young.

128 Speech to the Conservative Women's Conference, 25 May 1988.

129 Speech at Finchley, 31 January 1976.

130 Thatcher, p.80.

131 *The English Woman's Wardrobe*, BBC 2, 20 November 1986.

132 Thatcher, p.779.

133 Lawson, p.127.

134 Rodney Tyler, *Campaign!* p.191.

135 Brenda Polan, interviewed for *The Thatcher Factor*.

136 See *The Grocer's Daughter*, pp.4–5.

137 Ronald Millar, *A View from the Wings*, p.338.

138 *New Statesman*, 3 June 1983.

139 *Sunday Telegraph*, 10 January 1988.

140 Ibid.

141 Interviewed for *Newsnight*, BBC, 30 July 1985.

142 Cockerell, p.349.

143 Ibid., p.350.

144 Ibid., p.299.

145 Robin Day, *Grand Inquisitor*, pp.245–56.

146 Wyatt, Vol. 1, p.359 (4 June 1987).

147 Millar, p.275.

148 Junor, p.209.

149 *The Times*, 27 November 1987.

150 *Aspel and Company*, BBC, 21 August 1984.

151 Interview for the Press Association, 3 May 1989.

152 Interview, Lord Crickhowell.

153 *Evening Standard*, 1 April 1996.

154 *She*, 11 March 1987.

155 Wyatt, Vol. 1, p.225 (21 October 1987).

156 Interview for the Press Association, 30 March 1996.

157 Carol Thatcher, *Below The Parapet: The Biography of Denis Thatcher*, pp.240–2.

12 Stumble and Recovery

1 *Observer*, 17 February 1985, quoted in Michael Crick, *Michael Heseltine*, p.258.

2 Michael Heseltine, *Life in the Jungle*, p.281.

3 Nigel Lawson, *The View from No. 11*, p.674.

4 Margaret Thatcher, *The Downing Street Years*, p.463.

5 Peter Jenkins, *Mrs Thatcher's Revolution*, p.186.

6 *Sunday Times*, 13 October 1985.

7 Thatcher, p.433.

8 Geoffrey Howe, *Conflict of Loyalty*, p.467; Norman Tebbit, *Upwardly Mobile*, p.247.

9 Heseltine, p.299.

10 Gerald James, *In the Public Interest*, p.161 and *passim*.

11 Lord Whitelaw, John Biffen, interviewed for *The Thatcher Factor*.

12 House of Commons, 27 January 1986. [Vol. 90, col. 652].

13 The full text of Mayhew's letter is printed in Tam Dalyell, *Misrule*, pp.137–8.

14 House of Commons, 27 January 1986 [Vol. 90, col. 660].

15 *Sun*, 7 January 1986; *The Times*, 7 January 1986.

16 House of Commons, 23 January 1986 [Vol. 90, col. 455].

17 Ibid., [Vol. 90, col. 449–50].

18 Interviews, Lord Wakeham, Lord Crickhowell.

19 Crick, p.290.

20 Peter Walker, *Staying Power*, p.187.

21 Thatcher, p.432.

22 Interview, Lord Younger.

23 *The Times*, 10 January 1986.

24 *Face the Press*, Channel 4, 26 January 1986.

25 House of Commons, 23 January 1986 [Vol. 90, col. 450].

26 Robert Harris, *Good and Faithful Servant: The Unauthorised Biography of Bernard Ingham*, p.132.

27 Bernard Ingham, *Kill the Messenger*, p.336–7.

28 House of Commons, 23 January 1986 [Vol. 90, col. 450].

29 Ibid. [Vol. 90, col. 455].

30 Hugo Young, *One of Us*, p.443.

31 House of Commons, 27 January 1986 [Vol. 90, col. 657].

32 Jenkins, p.199.

33 Lord Havers, interviewed for *The Thatcher Factor*.

34 Alan Clark, *Diaries*, pp.133–4 (24 January 1986).

35 House of Commons, 23 January 1986 [Vol. 90, col. 453].

36 Ibid. [Vol. 90, col. 450].

37 *The Times*, 25 January 1986.

38 Thatcher, p.435.

39 Mark Stuart, *Douglas Hurd: The Public Servant*, p.174.

40 Ibid., p.175.

41 Ronald Millar, *A View from the Wings*, p.310.

42 Ingham, p.337.

43 TV-am, 7 June 1987.

44 House of Commons, 27 January 1986 [Vol. 90, cols 646–51].

45 Clark, p.135 (27 January 1986).

46 House of Commons, 27 January 1986 [Vol. 90, cols 651–8].

47 Clark, p.135 (27 January 1986).

48 Ibid., p.134 (26 January 1986).

49 House of Commons, 27 January 1986 [Vol. 90, cols 658–661].

50 Ibid. [Vol. 90, cols 661–2].

51 Leon Brittan, interviewed for *The Thatcher Factor*.

52 Thatcher, p.440.

53 Kenneth Baker, *The Turbulent Years*, p.157.

54 *Spectator*, 1 February 1986.

55 *Sunday Times*, 3 March 1981.

56 Thatcher, p.147.

57 Speech to the Conservative Central Council, Felixstowe, 15 March 1986.

58 Michael Cockerell, *Live from Number 10*, p.307.

59 *Spectator*, 24 May 1986.

60 Interview for CBS, 23 May 1986.

61 Interview for Central TV, 18 June 1986.

62 David Butler and Dennis Kavanagh, *The British General Election of 1987*, pp.32–4.

63 Speech to the Scottish Conservative conference, Perth, 16 May 1986.

64 Ingham, p.228.

65 *Woman*, 27 September 1986.

66 *The English Woman's Wardrobe*, BBC 2, 20 November 1986; Cockerell, p.310.

67 Thatcher, p.565.

68 Ibid., p.647.

69 David Butler, Andrew Adonis and Tony Travers, *Failure in British Government: The Politics of the Poll Tax*, p.64.

70 Ibid., p.74; Baker, p.122.

71 Speech to the Scottish Conservative conference, Perth, 10 May 1985.

72 *The Journals of Woodrow Wyatt*, Vol. 1, p.467 (20 December 1987).

73 Lawson, pp.573–4.

74 Interview, John MacGregor.

75 Baker, p.126.

76 *The Times*, 29 January 1986.

77 *The Economist*, 1 February 1986.

78 Thatcher, p.420.

79 Speech to the Scottish Conservative conference, Perth, 16 June 1986.

80 Speech to the Scottish Conservative conference, Perth, 15 May 1987.

81 Wyatt, Vol. 1, p.116 (5 April 1986).

82 *Times Literary Supplement*, 31 May 1996.

83 Speech to the Conservative Party Conference, 10 October 1986.

84 Nicholas Ridley, '*My Style of Government*', p.93.

85 *The Times*, 22 November 2000.

86 Ridley, pp.86–7.

87 Ibid., p.87.

88 Nicholas Timmins, *The Five Giants*, p.401.

89 *New York Times*, 20 January 1984.

90 Thatcher, p.627.

91 Interview, Lord Moore of Lower Marsh.

92 Interview, Sir Kenneth Stowe.

93 Thatcher, p.571.

94 Ibid., p.577.

95 Speech to the Scottish Conservative conference, Perth, 15 May 1987.

96 *The Times*, 10 October 1986.

97 Speech to the Conservative Party Conference, 10 October 1986.

98 David Butler and Gareth Butler, *British Political Facts, 1900–1994*, p.257.

99 Millar, p.312.

100 Baker, pp.259–60.

101 John Simpson, *Strange Places, Questionable People*, p.246.

102 David Owen, *Time to Declare*, p.678.

103 Thatcher, p.573.

104 Butler and Kavanagh, p.251.

105 Ibid., p.44.

106 Lawson, p.246.

107 Remarks visiting London docklands, 21 May 1987.

108 Butler and Kavanagh, p.154.

109 *Annual Register 1987*, p.15.

110 Cockerell, p.324.

111 Election press conference, 22 May 1987.

112 Rodney Tyler, *Campaign!*, pp.170, 174; Lord Young, *The Enterprise Years*, pp.209–10; Carol Thatcher, *Below the Parapet: The Biography of Denis Thatcher*, p.244.

113 Speech at Gateshead, 3 June 1987.

114 Nicholas Edwards in Iain Dale, *Memories of Maggie*, p.140.

115 *Glasgow Herald*, 3 June 1987.

116 Speech at Solihull, 28 May 1987.

117 Speech at Newport, 26 May 1987.

118 Speech at Edinburgh, 2 June 1987.

119 Speech at Newport, 26 May 1987.

120 Butler and Kavanagh, p.64.

121 Interview on *Panorama*, BBC, 8 June 1987.

122 Interviewed on *Thatcher: The Downing Street Years*, BBC, 1993.

123 Butler and Kavanagh, pp.94–5.

124 Interview for BBC TV, 11 May 1987.

125 Speech to the Scottish Conservative conference, Perth, 15 May 1987.

126 *Daily Telegraph*, 21 May 1987.

127 Election press conference, 10 June 1987.

128 Election press conference, 4 June 1987.

129 Interview for TV-am, 7 June 1987.

130 Michael Dobbs, interviewed on *Thatcher: The Downing Street Years*, BBC, 1993.

131 Michael Dobbs in Dale, pp.171–2.

132 Ibid.

133 Thatcher, p.585.

134 Lord Young, p.220.

135 Simon Heffer, *Like the Roman: The Life of Enoch Powell*, p.909.

136 Butler and Kavanagh, pp.109–11.

137 Lord Young, p.225.

138 Norman Tebbit, *Upwardly Mobile*, pp.257–65.

139 Norman Tebbit, interviewed for *The Thatcher Factor*.

140 Lord Young, interviewed for *The Thatcher Factor*.

141 Tyler, pp.213–51.

142 Butler and Kavanagh, p.251.

143 Conservative Family Rally at Wembley Stadium, 7 June 1987.

144 Terry Coleman, *Thatcher's Britain: A Journey through the Promised Lands*, p.140.

145 Butler and Kavanagh, p.157.

146 Speech at Harrogate, 9 June 1987.

147 Cockerell, p.230.

148 *Spectator*, 13 June 1987.

149 *The Times*, 13 June 1987.
150 Ibid.
151 Ibid., 13 May 1987.
152 Remarks in Downing Street, 12 June 1987.
153 Interview for ITN, 12 June 1987.
154 Interview for BBC, 12 June 1987.
155 Carol Thatcher, p.246.

13 No Such Thing as Society

1 *Sunday Express*, 21 June 1987.
2 *Woman's Own*, 31 October 1987.
3 Interview for Yorkshire Television, 2 October 1985.
4 Interview on *The Jimmy Young Programme*, BBC Radio 2, 27 July 1988.
5 Margaret Thatcher, *The Downing Street Years*, p.626.
6 Interview on *The Jimmy Young Programme*, BBC Radio 2, 27 July 1988.
7 Conservative Party, *Make Life Better* (1968).
8 Speech to the Conservative Party Conference, 7 October 1970.
9 Iain Macleod Memorial Lecture, 4 July 1977.
10 Speech to the Conservative Party Conference, 14 October 1988.
11 Interview for *Panorama*, BBC, 8 June 1987.
12 Interview for *Weekend World*, LWT, 16 January 1983.
13 Speech to the Conservative Party Conference, 9 October 1987.
14 Andrew Marr, *Ruling Britannia*, p.85.
15 John Biffen to Mrs Thatcher, 13 June 1987 (*The Times*, 15 June 1987).
16 *The Journals of Woodrow Wyatt*, Vol. 1, p.371 (14 June 1987).
17 Ibid. p.383 (30 June 1987).
18 Julian Critchley, *The Palace of Varieties*, p.106.
19 Ibid.
20 John Major, *The Autobiography*, p.102.
21 Lord Hailsham to Mrs Thatcher, 13 June 1987 (*The Times*, 15 June 1987).
22 Wyatt, Vol. 1, p.367n. (18 June 1987).
23 Mark Garnett and Ian Aitken, *Splendid! Splendid! The Authorised Biography of Willie Whitelaw*, p.320.
24 Ronald Millar, *A View from the Wings*, p.319.
25 *The Times*, 17 July 1987.
26 *The Times*, 17 July 1987; House of Commons, 21 July 1987 [Vol. 120, col. 204].
27 Remarks to party workers at Conservative Central Office, 12 June 1987.
28 Michael Cockerell, *Live from Number 10*, p.332.
29 House of Commons, 15 May 1979 [Vol. 967, cols 82–3].
30 Ibid, 25 June 1987 [Vol. 119, col. 53].
31 Remarks visiting London docklands, 21 May 1987.
32 Malcolm Balen, *Kenneth Clarke*, p.148.

33 Thatcher, p.152.

34 Balen, p.152.

35 Simon Jenkins, *Accountable to None: The Tory Nationalisation of Britain* p.156.

36 Thatcher, p.424.

37 Speech to the Conservative Party Conference, 9 October 1987.

38 *Sunday Telegraph*, 28 June 1987.

39 *Annual Register 1987*, p.31.

40 Nigel Lawson, *The View from No. 11*, p.747; Thatcher, p.700.

41 Kenneth Baker, interviewed in the *Times Educational Supplement*, May 1996.

42 Nicholas Timmins, *The Five Giants: A Biography of the Welfare State*, p.440.

43 Thatcher, p.593.

44 Ibid., p.595.

45 Ibid., pp.595–7.

46 Interview in the *Independent*, 10 September 1987.

47 Margaret Thatcher, *The Path to Power*, p.174.

48 Jenkins, p.134.

49 Timmins, p.445.

50 Thatcher, *The Downing Street Years*, p.601.

51 Timmins, pp.434–7.

52 Thatcher, *The Downing Street Years*, pp.603–4.

53 Ibid., p.603.

54 House of Commons, 17 May 1988 [Vol. 133, col. 801].

55 *Sunday Times*, 8 May 1988.

56 Timmins, pp.508–9.

57 *Breadline Britain*, reported in the *Independent*, 21 April 1998, 11 September 2000; John Rentoul, *The Rich Get Richer*, cited in *Annual Register 1988*, p.12.

58 *Social Trends*, 1987.

59 *Annual Register 1987*, p.25.

60 House of Commons, 12 April 1988 [Vol. 131, col. 14].

61 *Annual Register 1988*, p.10.

62 House of Commons, 12 April 1988 [Vol. 131, col. 16].

63 Wyatt, Vol. 1, p.655 (30 October 1988).

64 *Annual Register 1987*, p.9.

65 House of Commons, 15 December 1987. [Vol. 124, col. 918].

66 Major, pp.104–5.

67 Wyatt, Vol. 1, p.436 (8 November 1987).

68 House of Commons, 19 January 1988 [Vol. 125, cols 833–43].

69 Interview, Lord Moore of Lower Marsh.

70 Interview for *Panorama*, BBC, 25 January 1988.

71 Kenneth Baker, *The Turbulent Years*, p.254.

72 Chris Ham, *The Politics of NHS Reform: Metaphor or Reality?*, p.19.

73 Alan Clark, *Diaries*, pp.275–6 (26 February 1990).

74 Balen, p.166.

75 Thatcher, *The Downing Street Years*, pp.514, 616.

76 Jenkins, pp.65–88.

77 *Annual Register 1988*, p.13.

78 Ham, p.9.

79 Ibid., p.10.

80 *Annual Register 1989*, p.12.

81 Wyatt, Vol. 2, p.25 (5 February 1989).

82 Ham, p.11.

83 Timmins, p.472.

84 Jenkins, p.77.

85 David Owen, *Time to Declare*, pp.746–7

86 Eric Jacobs and Robert Worcester, *We British: Britain under the Moriscope*, cited in *Annual Register 1990*, pp.10–11.

87 Timmins, p.508.

88 Major, p.139.

89 House of Commons, 21 July 1987, 23 July 1987 [Vol. 120, cols 204, 481–2].

90 BBC TV, 24 July 1987.

91 Ibid.

92 Nicholas Ridley, '*My Style of Government*', p.125.

93 Thatcher, *The Downing Street Years*, p.654.

94 House of Commons, 16 December 1987 [Vol. 124, cols 1138–42].

95 Statement on housing policy, 27 September 1974.

96 House of Commons, 8 December 1987 [Vol. 124, col. 166].

97 Thatcher, *The Downing Street Years*, p.653.

98 David Butler, Andrew Adonis and Tony Travers, *Failure in British Government: The Politics of the Poll Tax*, p.119.

99 House of Commons, 26 April 1988 [Vol. 132, col. 200].

100 Speech to the 1922 Committee, 20 July 1989.

101 House of Commons, 20 July 1989 [Vol. 157, cols 516–17].

102 Wyatt, Vol. 1, p.536 (19 April 1988).

103 Ibid.

104 Ibid., p.561 (23 May 1988).

105 House of Commons, 24 May 1988 [Vol. 134, cols 193–4].

106 Thatcher, *The Downing Street Years*, p.654.

107 House of Commons, 27 July 1989 [Vol. 157, col. 1168].

108 Wyatt, Vol. 2, p.158 (17 September 1989).

109 House of Commons, 20 March 1990 [Vol. 169, col. 1008].

110 *The Times*, 23 March 1990.

111 *Sunday Times*, 25 March 1990.

112 Speech in Cheltenham, 31 October 1990.

113 Thatcher, *The Downing Street Years*, p.661.

114 Ibid., p.658.

115 Clark, p.287 (25 March 1990).

116 Chris Patten on *Desert Island Discs*, BBC Radio 4, 3 November 1996.

117 Andrew Neil, *Full Disclosure*, p.243.

118 Wyatt, Vol. 2, p.283 (1 May 1990).

119 House of Commons, 11 November 1965 [Vol. 720, col. 482].

120 Butler, Adonis and Travers, p.2.

121 Noël Annan, *Our Age*, p.446.

122 House of Commons, 28 November 1989 [Vol. 162, col. 576].

123 Wyatt, Vol. 1, p.673 (27 November 1988).

124 Speech to the Conservative local government conference, 8 March 1989.

125 Wyatt, Vol. 2, p.79 (4 May 1989).

126 Speech at the Conservative Party Conference, October 1988.

127 Cecil Parkinson, *Right at the Centre*, p.263.

128 Wyatt, Vol. 1, p.579 (4 December 1988).

129 Cockerell, pp.333–4.

130 House of Commons, 22 March 1988 [Vol. 130, col. 194].

131 Cockerell, p.340.

132 Interview on Japanese TV, 29 April 1988.

133 Cockerell, p.341.

134 *Spectator*, 14 May 1988.

135 Cockerell, p.344.

136 Ibid., p.347.

137 Speech to the American Bar Association, Albert Hall, London, 15 July 1985.

138 Mark Stuart, *Douglas Hurd: The Public Servant*, pp.166–7.

139 Lawson, p.722.

140 Speech to the Press Association, Savoy Hotel, London, 8 June 1988.

141 *Spectator*, 5 November 1993.

142 Baker, p.416; George Walden, *Lucky George*, p.300.

143 Wyatt, Vol. 1, p.681 (11 December 1988).

144 Ibid., Vol. 1, p.568 (30 May 1988).

145 Ibid., Vol. 2, p.308 (11 June 1990).

146 House of Commons, 21 November 1989 [Vol. 162, col. 31].

147 Cockerell, p.348.

148 House of Commons, 21 November 1989 [Vol. 162, col. 31].

149 Lawson, p.722.

150 *Independent*, 9 September 2000.

151 *Spectator*, 6 November 1993.

152 William Shawcross, *Murdoch*, p.511.

153 Wyatt, Vol. 2, p.31 (12 February 1989).

154 Wyatt, Vol. 2, p.25 (5 February 1989).

155 Press conference in Downing Street, 9 November 1988.

156 Wyatt, Vol. 2, p.383 (9 November 1990).

157 Ian Gilmour, *Dancing with Dogma*, pp.256, 259.

158 *Guardian*, 14 March 1994, cited in A.J. Davies, *We, The Nation*, p.339.

159 *Independent*, 20 October 2000.
160 House of Commons, 17 January 1989 [Vol. 145, col. 150].
161 Wyatt, Vol. 2, p.71 (16 April 1989).
162 Stuart, p.217; Baker, p.258.
163 Stuart, p.218.
164 House of Commons, 25 January 1990 [Vol. 165, col. 1046].
165 Ibid., 16 February 1989 [Vol. 147, col. 482].
166 *The Times*, 2 February 1989.
167 Ibid., 10 March 1989.
168 House of Commons, 14 March 1989 [Vol. 149, col. 286].
169 Jenkins, p.195.
170 Clark, p.296 (1 May 1990).
171 Annan, p.446.
172 Speech at Mansion House, 17 October 1985.
173 *The Times*, 31 March 1987.
174 Thatcher, *The Downing Street Years*, p.701.
175 Timmins, p.450.
176 *Annual Register 1988*, p.11.
177 Lawson, pp.815, 824.
178 Speech to the Conservative Central Council, Buxton, 19 March 1988.
179 *Independent*, 20 March 2000.
180 Thatcher, *The Downing Street Years*, p.674.
181 Interview for BBC World Service, 19 May 1989.
182 Thatcher, *The Downing Street Years*, pp.689–90.
183 Lawson, p.487.
184 William Keegan, *Mr Lawson's Gamble*, p.188.
185 Thatcher, *The Downing Street Years*, p.703.
186 Major, p.101.
187 Wyatt, Vol. 1, p.326 (27 March 1988).
188 Joint press conference with Chancellor Kohl, 28 March 1980.
189 *Financial Times*, 17 November 1986.
190 Lawson, p.788.
191 Ibid., p.784.
192 *The Times*, 29 June 1991.
193 Thatcher, *The Downing Street Years*, p.701.
194 *Financial Times*, 23 November 1987.
195 Lawson, p.788.
196 Thatcher, *The Downing Street Years*, p.702.
197 Lawson, p.795; Thatcher, *The Downing Street Years*, p.703.
198 House of Commons, 10 March 1988 [Vol. 129, col. 517].
199 Lawson, p.798.
200 *The Times*, 16 March 1988.
201 Wyatt, Vol. 1, p.516 (13 March 1988).

202 Ibid., p.520 (20 March 1988).

203 Lawson, p.834.

204 Thatcher, *The Downing Street Years*, p.704.

205 Ibid., p.705.

206 Lawson, p.836.

207 House of Commons, 17 May 1988 [Vol. 133, cols 800–1].

208 *The Times*, 18 May 1988.

209 *Annual Register 1988*, p.17.

210 *The Times*, 22 July 1988.

211 Lawson, p.842.

212 Wyatt, Vol. 1, pp.607–8 (24 July 1988).

213 *The Times*, 25 October 1988.

214 Ridley, p.211.

215 Major, p.130.

216 Press conference, 14 June 1989.

217 House of Commons, 13 June 1989 [Vol. 154, col. 698].

218 Ibid., 8 June 1989 [Vol. 154, col. 366].

219 Ibid., 29 November 1988 [Vol. 142, cols 598–604].

220 *Annual Register 1989*, p.7.

221 Wyatt, Vol. 2, p.99 (4 June 1989).

222 Ridley, p.205.

223 Bernard Ingham, *Kill the Messenger*, p.211.

224 *The Times*, 11 March 1987.

225 Remarks visiting Hungerford, 20 August 1987.

226 Stuart, p.154.

227 House of Commons, 26 October 1967 [Vol. 751, col. 1989].

228 Wyatt, Vol. 2, p.43 (5 March 1989).

229 House of Commons, 7 March 1989 [Vol. 148, col. 754].

230 Lawson, p.301.

231 *Annual Register 1990*, p.17.

232 Speech presenting environmental awards, London, 16 March 1990.

233 *Spectator*, 3 September 1988.

234 Ibid., 11 March 1989.

14 A Diet of Brussels

1 Margaret Thatcher, *The Downing Street Years*, p.558.

2 Sir Charles Powell, interviewed on *The Poisoned Chalice*, BBC, 30 May 1996.

3 Thatcher, p.742.

4 John Major, *An Autobiography*, p.345.

5 Thatcher, p.744.

6 Churchill to Eden, 21 October 1942, quoted in Michael Charlton, *The Last Colony in Africa*, p.156n.

7 Thatcher, p.727.

8 Percy Cradock, *In Pursuit of British Interests*, p.124.

9 Nigel Lawson, *The View from No. 11*, p.908.

10 e.g. *Daily Mail*, 17 May 1988.

11 Interview for BBC, 28 June 1988.

12 Interview for *The Jimmy Young Programme*, BBC Radio 2, 27 July 1988.

13 Thatcher, p.704.

14 Cradock, pp.124, 130.

15 Sir Michael Butler, interviewed for the British Diplomatic Oral History Project, Churchill College, Cambridge.

16 Interview for ITN, 28 June 1988.

17 Lawson, p.903.

18 Sir Charles Powell interviewed on *The Poisoned Chalice*.

19 Sir Michael Butler, interviewed for the British Diplomatic Oral History Project, Churchill College, Cambridge.

20 Interview, Sir Leon Brittan.

21 *The Journals of Woodrow Wyatt*, Vol. 2, p.30 (12 February 1989).

22 House of Commons, 28 July 1988 [Vol. 138, col. 542].

23 *The Times*, 23 July 1988.

24 *The Jimmy Young Programme*, BBC Radio 2, 27 July 1988.

25 House of Commons, 28 July 1988 [Vol. 138, col. 542].

26 Hugo Young, *This Blessed Plot*, p.548.

27 *The Jimmy Young Programme*, BBC Radio 2, 27 July 1988.

28 Sir Charles Powell, interviewed on *The Poisoned Chalice*.

29 Lawson, p.907.

30 *The Poisoned Chalice*.

31 Alan Clark, *Diaries*, pp.225–6.

32 Speech to the College of Europe, Bruges, 20 September 1988.

33 Sir Michael Butler, interviewed on *The Poisoned Chalice*.

34 Article for regional newspapers, 6 June 1979.

35 Sir Michael Butler, interviewed for the British Diplomatic Oral History Project, Churchill College, Cambridge.

36 Geoffrey Howe, *Conflict of Loyalty*, p.537.

37 Ibid., p.538.

38 Thatcher, p.744.

39 Sir Anthony Parsons, interviewed for *The Thatcher Factor*.

40 Lawson, p.907.

41 Speech to the Conservative Party Conference, 14 October 1988.

42 *The Times*, 25 October 1988.

43 *Spectator*, 1 October 1988.

44 Ibid., 18 February 1989.

45 Ibid., 6 November 1993.

46 Michael Heseltine, *Life in the Jungle*, p.348.

47 House of Commons, 27 April 1989 [Vol. 151, col. 1089].
48 Ibid., 18 May 1989 [Vol. 153, col. 470].
49 Speech to the Conservative Women's Conference, 24 May 1989.
50 Speech at Nottingham, 12 June 1989.
51 *The Times*, 30 May 1989.
52 House of Commons, 8 June 1989 [Vol. 154, col. 366].
53 Thatcher, p.749.
54 Conservative party election broadcast, 13 June 1989.
55 John Cole, *As It Seemed to Me*, p.338.
56 Thatcher, p.749.
57 Howe, p.572.
58 *The Times*, 23 May 1989.
59 Young, p.353.
60 Howe, p.578.
61 Lawson, p.932.
62 Thatcher, pp.712–13.
63 Lawson, p.933.
64 Thatcher, pp.711–12.
65 Lawson, p.932.
66 Thatcher, p.711.
67 Cradock, p.132.
68 Howe, p.582.
69 Interview for ITN, 27 June 1989.
70 Press conference, 27 June 1989; interview for Sky TV, 27 June 1989.
71 Thatcher, p.752.
72 Wyatt, Vol. 2, p.117 (26 June 1989).
73 *Guardian*, 29 June 1989.
74 Cole, p.327.
75 Thatcher, p.713.
76 Howe, p.583.
77 Wyatt, reference missing.
78 Thatcher, p.712.
79 Ibid., p.758.
80 Wyatt, Vol. 2, p.182 (29 October 1989).
81 Thatcher, p.712.
82 Howe, p.588.
83 Thatcher, p.757.
84 Kenneth Baker, *The Turbulent Years*, p.287.
85 Mark Stuart, *Douglas Hurd: The Public Servant*, p.234.
86 Nicholas Ridley, *'My Style of Government'*, p.40.
87 House of Commons, 25 July 1989 [Vol. 157, col. 850].
88 Penny Junor, *John Major: From Brixton to Downing Street*, p.158.
89 House of Commons, 25 July 1989 [Vol. 157, col. 848].

90 Robin Day, *Grand Inquisitor*, p.256.

91 Lawson, p.936.

92 John Ranelagh *Thatcher's People*, p.285.

93 Wyatt, Vol. 2, p.139 (26 July 1989).

94 Ibid., p.141 (28 July 1989).

95 Anthony Powell, *Journals*, p.204.

96 *Le Monde*, 11 July 1989.

97 Interview for BBC, 16 July 1989.

98 House of Commons, 29 June 1989 [Vol. 155, col. 1119].

99 Wyatt, Vol. 2, p.128 (9 July 1989).

100 Thatcher, p.753.

101 Interview for BBC, 16 July 1989.

102 Press conference, Strasbourg, 9 December 1989.

103 Ibid.

104 Lawson, p.943.

105 Press conference, Dublin, 26 June 1990.

106 Ridley, p.151.

107 Major, p.152.

108 Sir Michael Butler, interviewed for the British Diplomatic Oral History Project, Churchill College, Cambridge.

109 House of Commons, 28 June 1990 [Vol. 175, col. 493].

110 Major, p.151.

111 Wyatt, Vol. 2, p.318 (27 June 1990).

112 Press conference, Dublin, 26 June 1990.

113 Interview for BBC Radio, 14 June 1989.

114 Lawson, p.898.

115 Douglas Hurd, interviewed on *The Poisoned Chalice*.

116 Lawson, pp.898–9.

117 Geoffrey Howe, interviewed on *The Poisoned Chalice*.

118 Interview, Sir Charles Powell.

119 *Spectator*, 6 November 1993.

120 Interview, Lord Wakeham.

15 Tomorrow the World

1 Robert Blake, *The Conservative Opportunity*, p.3.

2 Speech at Kensington Town Hall, 19 January 1976.

3 House of Commons, 28 March 1979 [Vol. 965, col. 470].

4 Daniel Yergan and Joseph Stanislaw, *The Commanding Heights; The Battle Between Government and the Marketplace that is Remaking the Modern World*.

5 Speech to the Conservative Party Conference, 10 October 1986.

6 Speech to the Conservative Central Council, 19 March 1988.

7 Speech to the Conservative Women's Conference, 13 May 1988.

8 Speech to the Conservative Party Conference, 13 October 1989.

9 Yergan and Stanislaw, pp.308–10.

10 Ibid., p.13.

11 Ibid., p.123.

12 Peter Clarke, *A Question of Leadership*, p.316.

13 Margaret Thatcher, *The Downing Street Years*, p.813.

14 Speech in Korea, 3 September 1992.

15 Speech at the Fraser Institute, Toronto, 8 August 1993.

16 Speech at the National Press Club, Washington, DC, 26 June 1995.

17 House of Commons, 8 November 1998 [Vol. 140, col. 169].

18 Margaret Thatcher, *The Path to Power*, pp.603–4.

19 Thatcher, *The Downing Street Years*, pp.782–3.

20 George Bush and Brent Scowcroft, *A World Transformed*, pp.67, 69.

21 Ibid., p.60.

22 Thatcher, *The Downing Street Years*, p.785.

23 Bush and Scowcroft, pp.68–9.

24 Ibid., p.72.

25 Thatcher, *The Downing Street Years*, p.789.

26 Bush and Scowcroft, p.80.

27 Ibid., pp.82–3.

28 Ibid., p.83; *The Times*, 30 March 1990.

29 Bush and Scowcroft, p.84.

30 Percy Cradock, *In Pursuit of British Interests*, p.184.

31 Bush and Scowcroft, p.84.

32 Press conference in Downing Street, 10 November 1989.

33 George Urban, *Diplomacy and Disillusion at the Court of Margaret Thatcher*, p.99.

34 Ibid., p.83.

35 Ibid., pp.103–4.

36 *The Times*, 16 July 1990.

37 Urban, p.112.

38 *The Times*, 16 July 1990.

39 Urban, p.99.

40 Thatcher, *The Downing Street Years*, p.791.

41 Urban, p.141.

42 Ibid., p.138.

43 Ibid., p.128.

44 Ibid., p.139.

45 *The Times*, 16 July 1990.

46 Ibid.

47 Urban, p.136.

48 *Spectator*, 13 July 1990.

49 Thatcher, *The Downing Street Years*, p.312.

50 Bush and Scowcroft, p.190.

51 Ibid., p.192.
52 Thatcher, *The Downing Street Years*, p.794.
53 Bush and Scowcroft, p.193.
54 Transcript of telephone conversation, 9 November 1989, Bush papers, OA/1D CFO 1731.
55 Bush and Scowcroft, p.253.
56 Ibid., p.195.
57 Transcript of telephone conversation, 3 December 1989, Bush papers, OA/1D CFO 1729.
58 Bush and Scowcroft, pp.198–9.
59 Ibid., p.213.
60 Thatcher, *The Downing Street Years*, p.798.
61 Bush and Scowcroft, p.159.
62 Ibid., p.214.
63 Ibid., pp.248–9.
64 Ibid., p.249.
65 Ibid., p.265.
66 *The Times*, 30 March 1990.
67 Ibid.
68 Paddy Ashdown, *The Ashdown Diaries*, Vol. 1, pp.83–4 (29 March 1990).
69 Cradock, p.111.
70 Douglas Hurd, interviewed on *The Poisoned Chalice*, BBC, 1996.
71 Alan Clark, *Diaries*, p.276 (28 January 1990).
72 *The Journals of Woodrow Wyatt*, Vol. 1, p.196 (15 November 1989), p.198 (19 November 1989), p.206 (10 December 1989).
73 *Any Questions?* BBC Radio, 8 January 1960.
74 Thatcher, *The Downing Street Years*, pp.813–14.
75 Bush and Scowcroft, p.294.
76 Thatcher, *The Downing Street Years*, p.811.
77 Bush and Scowcroft, p.295.
78 Thatcher, *The Downing Street Years*, p.770.
79 Leo Abse, *Margaret, Daughter of Beatrice*, p.127.
80 Interview, Professor John Ashworth.
81 Kenneth Baker, *The Turbulent Years*, pp.148–9.
82 Press conference in Oslo, 12 September 1986.
83 *The Times*, 28 September 1988.
84 Baker, pp.148–9.
85 *Financial Times*, 11 December 1989.
86 Ibid.
87 Interview for *Le Monde*, 11 July 1989.
88 *Financial Times*, 11 December 1989.
89 Speech to the Conservative Central Council, 31 March 1990.
90 Interview for TV-am, 30 December 1988.

91 *The Times*, 20 October 1988.
92 Nicholas Ridley, '*My Style of Government*', p.105.
93 *The Times*, 26 October 1988.
94 *Independent*, 25 October 2000.
95 Bernard Ingham, *Kill the Messenger*, p.268.
96 Speech to the Royal Society, 27 September 1988.
97 Speech to the Conservative Party Conference, 14 October 1988.
98 Interview for *Le Monde*, 11 July 1989.
99 The Earl of Caithness, in Iain Dale, *Memories of Maggie*, p.37.
100 Bush papers, 140654.
101 Speech to the UN General Assembly, New York, 8 November 1989.
102 Speech to the Royal Society, 27 September 1988; interview for *She* magazine, February 1989.
103 Margaret Thatcher to George Bush, 7 June 1990 (Bush papers, John Sonunu files CA/1D CF 00151).
104 Bush papers, Sonunu files, CA/1D CF 00151.
105 Speech at the World Climate Conference, Geneva, 6 November 1990.
106 *Nature*, 1 March 1989.
107 *The Times*, 26 October 1988.
108 *Financial Times*, 11 December 1989.
109 Speech presenting environmental awards, Royal Society of Arts, 16 March 1990.
110 House of Commons, 8 December 1983 [Vol. 50, col. 459].
111 *Nature*, 1 March 1989.
112 Ibid.
113 *Annual Register 1990*, p.466.
114 Press conference in Oslo, 12 September 1986.
115 *Nature*, 1 March 1989.
116 Speech to the UN General Assembly, New York, 8 November 1989.
117 *Nature*, 1 March 1989.
118 Speech to the Conservative Party Conference, 13 October 1989.
119 Abse, p.126.
120 Margaret Thatcher, *Statecraft: Strategies for a Changing World*, pp.449–57.
121 Scott Report, D3 11–15.
122 Ibid., D3 102.
123 Ibid., D3 11–15.
124 Gerald James, *In the Public Interest*, p.214; *Not the Scott Report*, p.25.
125 Scott Report, C2 73.
126 James, p.285.
127 *Not the Scott Report*, p.22.
128 Scott Report, D3 105–6.
129 Ibid, D4 11–23.
130 Ibid, D6 15.
131 Ibid., D16.

132 Alan Friedman, *Spider's Web: Bush, Saddam, Thatcher and the Decade of Deceit*, p.167.

133 Scott Report, D3 164–5.

134 *Guardian*, 9 December 1993.

135 Wyatt, Vol. 3, pp.309–10 (8 December 1993, 9 December 1993).

136 Scott Report, D2 328–30.

137 Ibid., D6 13.

138 Ibid., D3 102.

139 Ibid., D2 120.

140 Ibid., D2 432–3.

141 House of Lords, 26 February 1996 [Vol. 569, col. 1259].

142 John Major, *The Autobiography*, p.557.

143 James, p.288.

144 Ibid., p.54.

145 Ibid., p.100.

146 Ibid., p.289.

147 Ibid., p.100.

148 Ibid., p.116.

149 Ibid., p.118.

150 Ibid., pp.61–2.

151 *The Times*, 12 February 1994.

152 James, pp.125–6.

153 *The Times*, 27 December 1990.

154 James, p.297.

155 *The Times*, 12 March 1992.

156 James, p.53.

157 Ibid., p.125.

158 Bush and Scowcroft, p.320.

159 Press conference at Aspen, Colorado, 2 August 1990.

160 Bush and Scowcroft, p.320.

161 Margaret Thatcher, *Statecraft: Strategies for a Changing World*, p.226.

162 Speech to the North Atlantic Council, Turnberry, 7 June 1990.

163 Mark Stuart, *Douglas Hurd: The Public Servant*, p.241.

164 Ingham, p.262.

165 Bush and Scowcroft, p.315.

166 Speech at Aspen Institute, Colorado, 5 August 1990.

167 *Financial Times*, 31 August 1990.

168 Thatcher, *The Downing Street Years*, p.826.

169 Wyatt, Vol. 2, p.342 (10 August 1990).

170 Bush and Scowcroft, p.352.

171 Barbara Bush, *A Memoir*, p.353.

172 Lawrence Freedman and Efraim Karsh, *The Gulf Conflict, 1990–91*, p.149.

173 BBC, 7 January 1996.

174 Freedman and Karsh, p.177.

175 House of Commons, 25 October 1990 [Vol. 178, col. 498].

176 Peter Hennessy, *Prime Minister*, p.442.

177 Michael Carver, *Tightrope Walking*, p.163.

178 Thatcher, *The Downing Street Years*, p.826.

179 Peter de la Billière, *Looking for Trouble*, p.18.

180 House of Commons, 6 September 1990 [Vol. 177, cols 734–43].

181 Bush and Scowcroft, p.363.

182 Freedman and Karsh, p.228.

183 Bush and Scowcroft, p.384.

184 Ibid., p.385.

185 Ibid., p.407.

186 Thatcher, *The Downing Street Years*, p.828.

187 De la Billière, pp.401–2.

188 Thatcher, *The Downing Street Years*, p.828.

189 BBC, 28 January 1996.

190 Carver, p.163.

191 Cradock, p.179.

192 Wyatt, Vol. 3, p.83 (11 August 1992).

193 Press conference in Paris, 19 November 1990.

194 Speech receiving the Freedom of the City of Westminster, 12 December 1990.

16 On and On

1 *The Journals of Woodrow Wyatt*, Vol. 1, p.479 (2 January 1988).

2 Kenneth Baker, *The Turbulent Years*, p.274.

3 Aurum Press reception at the House of Commons, 4 May 1989.

4 Press conference in Downing Street, 4 May 1989.

5 Ibid.

6 Lord Whitelaw, interviewed on *Thatcher: The Downing Street Years*, BBC, 1993.

7 Lady Thatcher, interviewed on *Thatcher: The Downing Street Years*.

8 Baker, p.274.

9 Carol Thatcher, *Below the Parapet: The Biography of Denis Thatcher*, pp.253–4.

10 Ronald Millar, *A View from the Wings*, p.330.

11 *Observer*, 16 March 1969.

12 Millar, p.346.

13 Wyatt, Vol. 1, p.549 (8 May 1988).

14 Interview on Soviet television, 31 March 1987.

15 Wyatt, Vol. 2, p.249 (4 March 1990).

16 Peter Hennessy, *The Prime Minister*, p.432.

17 Wyatt, Vol. 2, p.271 (8 April 1990).

18 Ibid., Vol. 1, p.655 (30 October 1988).

19 Margaret Thatcher, *The Downing Street Years*, p.755.

20 Speech to the Conservative Party Conference, 13 October 1989.

21 Enoch Powell, interviewed for *The Thatcher Factor*.

22 Wyatt, Vol. 1, p.124 (20 April 1986).

23 Thatcher, p.755.

24 Interview for TV-am, 4 May 1989.

25 Cecil Parkinson, *Right at the Centre*, p.12.

26 Wyatt, Vol. 1, p.548 (8 May 1988).

27 Andrew Neil, *Full Disclosure*, p.236.

28 John Junor, *Listening for a Midnight Tram*, p.301.

29 Rodney Tyler, *Campaign!* p.250.

30 Wyatt, Vol. 2, pp.82–6 (7 May 1989).

31 *The Times*, 26 October 1988.

32 *Sunday Correspondent*, 5 November 1989.

33 Baker, p.315.

34 *The Times*, 22 November 1989; Sky TV, TV-am, IRN, 24 November 1989.

35 Interview for IRN, 24 November 1989.

36 Interview on *Panorama*, BBC, 27 November 1989.

37 *The Woman at Number Ten*, ITV, 29 March 1983.

38 Wyatt, Vol. 2, p.377 (31 October 1990).

39 Baker, p.264.

40 Wyatt, Vol. 1, p.559 (19 May 1988).

41 Steven Norris, *Changing Trains*, p.150.

42 Private conversation, Rupert Allason, 30 March 1999.

43 Alan Clark, *Diaries*, p.289 (28 March 1990).

44 Hennessy, p.6.

45 *Cabinet Confidential*, BBC, 17 November 2001.

46 Clark, p.288 (28 March 1990).

47 John Cole, *As It Seemed to Me*, p.344.

48 Robert Harris, *A Good and Faithful Servant: The Unauthorised Biography of Bernard Ingham*, p.172.

49 Ibid., p.175; *Independent*, 28 October 1989.

50 Nigel Lawson, *The View from No. 11*, pp.467–8.

51 Interviewed on *Thatcher: The Downing Street Years*.

52 Alan Watkins, *A Conservative Coup*, p.128.

53 House of Commons, 13 February 1990; 18 October 1990 [Vol. 167, col. 137; Vol. 177, col. 1375].

54 Wyatt, Vol. 2, p.46 (14 March 1989).

55 Ibid., Vol. 2, pp.46, 78, 87 (14 March 1989, 1 May 1989, 8 May 1989).

56 Ibid., Vol. 1, p.531 (4 April 1988).

57 Baker, p.472.

58 Mark Lennox-Boyd, in Iain Dale, *Memories of Maggie*, p.168.

59 Wyatt, Vol. 2, p.383 (9 November 1990).

60 Ibid., pp.95–6 (21 May 1989).

61 Interview, *Sunday Mirror*, 5 June 1989.

62 Paddy Ashdown, *The Ashdown Diaries*, Vol. 1, pp.71–2 (18 November 1989).

63 *Annual Register 1989*, p.21.

64 Ibid.

65 David Butler and Gareth Butler, *British Political Facts, 1900–1994*, pp.256–7.

66 Baker, p.327.

67 Speech to the Conservative Party Conference, 14 October 1988.

68 Speech to the Conservative Party Conference, 13 October 1989.

69 Baker, p.281.

70 Wyatt, Vol. 2, p.169 (9 October 1989).

71 John Ranelagh, *Thatcher's People*, p.306.

72 House of Commons, 13 June 1989 [Vol. 154, col. 702].

73 Lawson, p.928.

74 David Owen, *Time to Declare*, p.763.

75 John Biffen, interviewed for *The Thatcher Factor*.

76 Thatcher, pp.713–14.

77 Ibid., p.707.

78 *Daily Mail*, 9 October 1989.

79 *Financial Times*, 18 October 1989.

80 *Independent*, 26 October 1989.

81 House of Commons, 31 October 1989 [Vol. 159, cols 208–10].

82 Lawson, p.957.

83 Ibid., p.959.

84 Ibid., p.958.

85 Interview for TV-am, 24 October 1989.

86 *Daily Express*, 28 October 1989.

87 House of Commons, 26 October 1989 [Vol. 158, col. 1044].

88 Thatcher, pp.715–18; Lawson, pp.960–4.

89 John Major, *The Autobiography*, p.134.

90 Lawson to Mrs Thatcher, 27 October 1989, in Lawson, p.964.

91 Mrs Thatcher to Lawson, 27 October 1989 (ibid. pp.964–5).

92 Thatcher, p.713.

93 Ibid., p.717.

94 Major, p.133.

95 Thatcher, p.717.

96 Baker, p.308.

97 Mark Stuart, *Douglas Hurd: The Public Servant*, p.234.

98 Baker, p.309.

99 *Daily Express*, 28 October 1989.

100 Lawson, p.967.

101 Wyatt, Vol. 2, p.181 (27 October 1989), p.190 (7 November 1989).

102 Quoted in Wendy Webster, *Not a Man to Match her: The Marketing of the Prime Minister* p.171.

103 *Annual Register 1989*, p.31.

104 Lawson, p.969.

105 Ibid.

106 Wyatt, Vol. 2, p.179 (26 October 1989).

107 Margaret Thatcher, interviewed on *The Walden Interview*, 29 October 1989; reprinted in *The Walden Interviews*, pp.30–52.

108 Wyatt, Vol. 2, pp.181–2 (29 October 1989).

109 Nigel Lawson, interviewed on *The Walden Interview*, LWT, 5 November 1989; reprinted in *The Walden Interviews*, pp.53–75.

110 House of Commons, 7 November 1989 [Vol. 159, col. 829].

111 Major, p.134.

112 *Annual Register 1989*, p.32.

113 Baker, pp.320–1.

114 Ibid., p.321.

115 Thatcher, p.830.

116 BBC, 5 December 1989.

117 Robin Oakley, *Inside Track*, p.134.

118 *The Times*, 6 December 1989.

119 Millar, p.345; Baker, pp.320–1; interviews, Lord Younger, Lord Wakeham.

120 Thatcher, p.830.

121 Nicholas Ridley, '*My Style of Government*', p.236.

122 Carol Thatcher, p.256.

123 Clark, pp.280–1 (20 Feburary 1990).

124 Thatcher, p.758.

125 Stuart, p.236.

126 Major, p.155.

127 Anthony Seldon, *Major: A Political Life*, p.112.

128 Cole, p.349.

129 Wyatt, Vol. 2, p.253 (11 March 1990).

130 Stuart, p.235.

131 Private conversation, William Waldegrave, 10 December 1997.

132 Wyatt, Vol. 2, p.189 (3 November 1989).

133 Ibid., p.260 (21 March 1990).

134 Ibid., p.288 (6 May 1990).

135 Thatcher, p.719.

136 Speech at Huntingdon, 27 October 1989.

137 Wyatt, Vol. 2, p.261 (23 March 1990).

138 Seldon, p.106.

139 *The Times*, 5 May 1990.

140 Thatcher, p.664.

141 Speech to the Conservative Women's Conference, 23 June 1990.

142 *Annual Register 1990*, p.14.

143 Speech to the 1922 Committee, 19 July 1990.

144 Interview for *The Jimmy Young Programme*, 18 June 1990.

145 House of Commons, 28 June 1990 [Vol. 175, cols 482–3].

146 *Daily Mail*, 17 May 1989.

147 Thatcher, p.680.

148 Wyatt, Vol. 2, pp.328–30 (13–14 July 1990).

149 Ibid., p.333 (17 July 1990).

150 Ibid., pp.339–40 (31 July 1990).

151 Ibid., p.343.

152 David Waddington, in Dale, p.217.

153 House of Commons, 27 March 1990 [Vol. 170, col. 203].

154 *The Times*, 30 March 1990.

155 Major, pp.134, 137–8.

156 Ibid., p.142.

157 Ibid., p.156.

158 Seldon, p.112.

159 Thatcher, p.721.

160 Ibid., pp.724–5.

161 Ibid., pp.724–6.

162 Major, p.159.

163 Seldon, p.114.

164 Major, p.164.

165 Seldon, p.104.

166 Major, p.161.

167 Press conference in Downing Street, 5 October 1990.

168 Gyles Brandreth, *Breaking the Code*, p.16.

169 *Financial Times*, 6 October 1990.

170 *The Times*, 6 October 1990.

171 *Annual Register 1990*, p.34.

172 Baker, p.370.

173 Major, p.163.

174 Sir Charles Powell on BBC, 16 September 1997.

175 House of Commons, 16 October 1990 [Vol. 177, col. 1053].

176 Cole, pp.351–2.

177 Major, p.164.

178 Ibid., pp.339–40.

179 Margaret Thatcher, *The Path to Power*, pp.570–1.

180 Remarks arriving at the Conservative Party Conference, 8 October 1990.

181 ITN, 9 October 1990.

182 BBC Radio News, 8 October 1990.

183 Millar, p.344.

184 John Whittingdale, in Dale, pp.279–80.

185 Speech to the Conservative Party Conference, 12 October 1990.

186 Millar, p.344.

17 The Defenestration of Downing Street

1 Alan Sked and Chris Cook, *Post-War Britain, 1945–1992*, p.551.
2 Nicholas Ridley, '*My Style of Government*', p.251.
3 *The Times*, 28 November 1990.
4 Alan Watkins, *A Conservative Coup*, p.213.
5 Ian Gow interviewed on 8 August 1989, in John Ranelagh, *Thatcher's People*, p.285.
6 *The Times*, 20 July 1990.
7 Geoffrey Howe, *Conflict of Loyalty*, p.639.
8 *Sunday Times*, 20 November 1990.
9 BBC Radio, 28 January 1990.
10 Margaret Thatcher, *The Downing Street Years*, p.833.
11 *The Journals of Woodrow Wyatt*, Vol. 2, p.246 (25 February 1990).
12 Thatcher, p.834.
13 Wyatt, Vol. 2, p.207 (11 December 1989).
14 George Walden, *Lucky George*, pp.301–2.
15 Thatcher, p.767.
16 Mark Stuart, *Douglas Hurd: The Public Servant*, p.47.
17 BBC, 28 October 1990.
18 ITN, 28 October 1990.
19 House of Commons, 30 October 1990 [Vol. 178, cols 869–92].
20 David Owen, *Time to Declare*, p.777.
21 *The Times*, 31 October 1990.
22 Kenneth Baker, *The Turbulent Years*, p.378.
23 John Major, *The Autobiography*, p.176.
24 Owen, p.777.
25 *Sun*, 31 October 1990.
26 Ranelagh, p.285; Cecil Parkinson, *Right at the Centre*, pp.118–19.
27 Howe, p.647.
28 Howe to Mrs Thatcher, *The Times*, 2 November 1990.
29 *The Times*, 6 November 1990.
30 Mrs Thatcher to Howe, *The Times*, 2 November 1990.
31 Chris Ham, *The Politics of NHS Reform*, p.13.
32 Gyles Brandreth, *Breaking the Code*, p.17 (2 November 1990).
33 Wyatt, Vol. 2, p.378 (1 November 1990).
34 *The Times*, 2 November 1990.
35 Ridley, p.232.
36 Michael Heseltine, *Life in the Jungle*, p.355; Bernard Ingham, *Kill the Messenger*, p.379.
37 Wyatt, Vol. 2, pp.378, 380, 384 (2, 4 and 12 November 1990).
38 *The Times*, 3 November 1990.
39 Watkins, p.149.

40 Baker, p.389.

41 Ronald Millar, *A View from the Wings*, p.348.

42 House of Commons, 7 November 1990 [Vol. 180, col. 32].

43 Andrew Neil, *Full Disclosure*, p.245.

44 Heseltine, p.361.

45 *The Times*, 12 November 1990.

46 Ingham, p.391.

47 Nigel Lawson, *The View from No. 11*, p.999.

48 Speech at the Guildhall, 12 November 1990.

49 Wyatt, Vol. 2, p.384 (12 November 1990).

50 Alan Clark, *Diaries*, p.347 (13 November 1990).

51 Baker, p.384.

52 Thatcher, p.838.

53 Millar, p.348.

54 Watkins, p.151.

55 *The Times*, 14 November 1990.

56 House of Commons, 13 November 1990 [Vol. 180, cols 461–5]; Howe, pp.697–703.

57 Lawson, p.1000.

58 Paddy Ashdown, *The Ashdown Diaries*, Vol. 1, p.96.

59 Millar, pp.349–51.

60 *The Times*, 14 November 1990.

61 Major, p.180.

62 Baker, pp.385–6.

63 Thatcher, p.840.

64 *Independent*, 22 November 2000.

65 Peter Walker, *Staying Power*, p.233.

66 Parkinson, p.25.

67 Heseltine, pp.362–3.

68 Sked and Cook, p.550.

69 Thatcher, pp.829–31.

70 *Sunday Telegraph*, 15 November 1990.

71 Thatcher, pp.836–7.

72 Wyatt, Vol. 2, p.388 (15 November 1990).

73 Stuart, p.252.

74 Major, p.181.

75 Interview, Lord Younger.

76 Watkins, p.179.

77 Thatcher, p.841.

78 Rhodes Boyson, *Speaking my Mind*, p.235.

79 Penny Junor, *John Major: From Brixton to Downing Street*, p.192.

80 Steven Norris, *Changing Trains*, p.156.

81 Clark, pp.354–7 (19 November 1990).

82 Baker, p.363.

83 Ibid., p.390.

84 Clark, p.349 (17 November 1990).

85 Ibid., p.352 (19 November 1990).

86 Wyatt, Vol. 2, p.394 (20 November 1990).

87 Norris, p.157.

88 Junor, p.193.

89 Edwina Currie, in Iain Dale, *Memories of Maggie*, p.246.

90 Walden, p.302.

91 House of Commons, 12 December 1989 [Vol. 163, col. 849].

92 *Sunday Times*, 18 November 1990.

93 Stuart, p.254.

94 Watkins, p.185.

95 *Sunday Telegraph*, 18 November 1990.

96 *The Times*, 19 November 1990.

97 Thatcher, p.841.

98 Wyatt, Vol. 2, p.388 (15 November 1990).

99 William Shawcross, *Murdoch*, p.512.

100 *Sunday Times*, 18 November 1990.

101 Stuart, p.251.

102 Wyatt, Vol. 2, pp.388–9 (15 November 1990).

103 Major, p.184.

104 Thatcher, p.841; Wyatt, Vol. 3, p.114 (11 October 1992).

105 Baker, p.392.

106 Carol Thatcher, *Below the Parapet: The Biography of Denis Thatcher*, pp.262–3.

107 Press conference in Paris, 19 November 1990.

108 Speech at the CSCE in Paris, 19 November 1990.

109 Ingham, p.395.

110 Statement to reporters, Paris, 20 November 1990.

111 Ibid.

112 Watkins, p.4.

113 Ibid., p.xvii.

114 Charles Powell, interviewed on LWT, 17 September 2000; Ingham, p.395.

115 Carol Thatcher, p.264.

116 Barbara Bush, *A Memoir*, pp.376–7.

117 *Spectator*, 6 November 1993.

118 *Maggie: The First Lady*, Part Four, ITV1, 27 March 2003.

119 *Independent*, 21 November 1990.

120 Wyatt, Vol. 2, p.395 (20 November 1990).

121 Thatcher, p.845.

122 Heseltine, p.368.

123 John Cole, *As It Seemed to Me*, p.376.

124 Parkinson, pp.33–34.

125 Clark, pp.359–61 (20 November 1990)

126 Thatcher, pp.846–7.

127 Watkins, p.17.

128 Thatcher, p.849.

129 Ibid., p.850.

130 Major, p.187.

131 Interview, Lord Younger.

132 Watkins, p.xviii.

133 Brandreth, p.22.

134 House of Commons, 21 November 1990 [Vol. 181, cols 291–310].

135 Thatcher, p.850.

136 Ibid., p.848.

137 Ibid., p.851.

138 Ibid.

139 Watkins, p.18.

140 Clark, pp.364–5 (21 November 1990).

141 Thatcher, p.855.

142 Baker, p.407.

143 Thatcher, p.855.

144 Interviewed on *Thatcher: The Downing Street Years*, BBC, 1993.

145 Malcolm Balen, *Kenneth Clarke*, p.208.

146 Wyatt, Vol. 2, p.397 (22 November 1990).

147 Millar, p.354.

148 Thatcher, p.855.

149 Ibid., p.856.

150 Watkins, p.23.

151 Junor, p.197.

152 Carol Thatcher, p.267.

153 Millar, p.355.

154 Resignation statement, 22 November 1990.

155 Baker, pp.409–11.

156 *Guardian*, 22 November 2000.

157 Thatcher, p.859.

158 House of Commons, 22 November 1990. [Vol. 181, cols 419–24].

159 Thatcher, p.859.

160 House of Commons, 20 November 1990 [Vol. 181, col. 306].

161 Ibid., 22 November 1990 [Vol. 181, cols 445–53].

162 Millar, pp.356–7.

163 Wyatt, Vol. 2, p.398 (22 November 1990).

164 Baker, p.414.

165 Carol Thatcher, p.269.

166 Wyatt, Vol. 2, p.400 (23 November 1990).

167 Ibid., p.405 (26 November 1990).

168 Ibid., p.420 (9 December 1990).

169 Parkinson, p.4.

170 Baker, p.396.

171 Wyatt, Vol. 2, pp.401–2 (23 November 1990).

172 Heseltine, p.371.

173 Junor, p.205.

174 Peregrine Worsthorne, *Tricks of Memory*, p.273.

175 Carol Thatcher, pp.270–1.

176 Remarks at Conservative Central Office, 26 November 1990.

177 Millar, p.362.

178 House of Commons, 27 November 1990 [Vol. 181, cols 737–42].

179 Statement on leaving Downing Street, 28 November 1990.

180 Carol Thatcher, p.274.

18 Afterlife

1 *Vanity Fair*, May 1991.

2 *She*, 11 March 1987.

3 *Woman's Own*, 23 September 1987.

4 *Any Questions?*, BBC radio, 30 September 1970.

5 TV-am, 4 May 1989.

6 John Major, *The Autobiography*, p.207.

7 *She*, 11 March 1987.

8 *The Journals of Woodrow Wyatt*, Vol. 2, p.411 (29 November 1990).

9 Brenda Maddox, *Maggie: The First Lady*, p.219.

10 Speech receiving the Freedom of Westminster, 12 December 1990.

11 Paddy Ashdown, *The Ashdown Diaries*, Vol. 1, p.106 (10 January 1991).

12 Wyatt, Vol. 2, p.428 (27 December 1990).

13 Cecil Parkinson, *Right at the Centre*, pp.47–8.

14 *Vanity Fair*, May 1991.

15 *The Times*, 9 May 1991.

16 Wyatt, Vol. 2, p.479 (19 March 1991).

17 Ibid., p.489 (5 April 1991).

18 Ibid., p.558 (25 July 1991).

19 Ibid., p.414 (2 December 1990).

20 *The Times*, 29 September 1992.

21 Paul Halloran and Mark Hollingsworth, *Thatcher's Gold: The Life and Times of Mark Thatcher*, p.268.

22 Wyatt, Vol. 2, p.501 (21 April 1991).

23 *Vanity Fair*, May 1991.

24 Halloran and Hollingsworth, p.280.

25 Wyatt, Vol. 2, pp.652–3 (4 February 1992).

26 *The Times*, 8 January 1993; interview, Julian Seymour.

27 Reference missing.

28 Personal knowledge.

29 Wyatt, Vol. 2, p.613 (29 November 1991).

30 *The Times*, 16 May 1991.

31 Ibid., 28 May 1991.

32 Ibid., 20, 21 August 1991.

33 Ibid., 2 October 1991.

34 Ibid.

35 House of Commons, 28 February 1991 [Vol. 186, col. 1120].

36 Speech in New York, 24 September 1991.

37 *The Times*, 4 March 1991.

38 Major, p.214.

39 *The Times*, 9 March 1991.

40 Ibid., 15 April 1991.

41 Wyatt, Vol. 2, pp.501–2 (24, 26 April 1991).

42 Ibid., p.479 (19 March 1991).

43 *Sunday Telegraph*, 2 June 1991.

44 *The Times*, 3 June 1991.

45 Wyatt, Vol. 2, p.581 (30 September 1991).

46 Ibid., p.498 (18 April 1991).

47 *Independent*, 20 September 1999.

48 Speech in Chicago, 17 June 1991.

49 Speech in New York, 18 June 1991.

50 *The Times*, 27 June 1991.

51 House of Commons, 26 June 1991 [Vol. 193, col. 1029].

52 Wyatt, Vol. 2, p.484 (27 March 1991).

53 *The Times*, 29 June 1991.

54 Gyles Brandreth, *Breaking the Code*, p.56.

55 *The Times*, 10 October 1991.

56 Ibid., 14 October 1991.

57 House of Commons, 20 November 1991 [Vol. 199, cols 290–8].

58 ITN interview, 22 November 1991.

59 Wyatt, Vol. 2, p.623 (12 December 1991).

60 Ibid., p.675 (15 March 1992).

61 Ibid., p.673 (11 March 1992).

62 Ibid., p.677 (17 March 1992).

63 Major, p.299.

64 Wyatt, Vol. 2, pp.690–1 (9 April 1992).

65 *The Times*, 11 April 1992.

66 *Newsweek*, 17 April 1992; *The Times*, 21 April 1992.

67 *The Times*, 21 April 1992.

68 Wyatt, Vol. 3, p.12 (22 April 1992).

69 Speech in The Hague, 15 May 1992.

70 Brandreth, pp.97–8 (18 May 1992).

71 *Frost on Sunday*, TV-am, 28 June 1992.

72 Wyatt, Vol. 2, p.405 (26 November 1990).

73 Ibid., Vol. 3, p.22 (6 May 1992).

74 *The Times*, 18 November 1994.

75 Wyatt, Vol. 3, p.64 (30 June 1992).

76 Ibid., p.64 (28 June 1992).

77 *The Times*, 6 August 1992.

78 *New York Times*, 6 August 1992.

79 *The Times*, 14 August 1992.

80 Douglas Hurd, *The Search for Peace*, pp.126, 141.

81 *Independent/The European*, 17 December 1992.

82 *The Times*, 14 April 1993.

83 Brendan Simms, *Unfinest Hour: Britain and the Destruction of Bosnia*, p.50.

84 Ibid., p.51.

85 *The Times*, 21 September 1992.

86 Wyatt, Vol. 3, p.100 (18 September 1992).

87 *The European*, 8 October 1992.

88 *The Times*, 26 November 1992.

89 Interview, John Whittingdale.

90 House of Lords, 7 June 1993 [Vol. 546, cols 560–6].

91 Ibid., 14 July 1993 [Vol. 548, cols 281–6].

92 *The Times*, 10 December 1992.

93 Chris Patten, *East and West*, pp.61–2.

94 Interview, Julian Seymour; Margaret Thatcher, *Statecraft: Strategies for a Changing World*, pp.191–2.

95 Patten, p.289.

96 Thatcher, p.193.

97 Interview, Julian Seymour.

98 *The Times*, 15 June 1993.

99 Ibid., 18 January 1993.

100 Margaret Thatcher, *The Downing Street Years*, pp.719, 721.

101 *The Times*, 2 October 1993.

102 Ibid., 8 October 1993.

103 *Breakfast with Frost*, TV-am, 17 October 1993.

104 *Thatcher: The Downing Street Years*, BBC TV, 20, 27 October and 3, 10 November 1993.

105 Howe in the *Financial Times*, Lawson in the *Evening Standard*, Hurd in the *Spectator*, 6 November 1993.

106 Margaret Thatcher, *The Path to Power*, p.469.

107 *Sunday Times*, 21 May 1995.

108 *The Times*, 24 May 1995.

109 *Breakfast with Frost*, TV-am, 11 June 1995.

110 *Sunday Times*, 28 May 1995.

111 *Today*, BBC Radio 4, 12 June 1995.

112 *Breakfast with Frost*, TV-am, 11 June 1995.

113 *The Times*, 13 June 1995.

114 Thatcher, *The Path to Power*, p.469.

115 Anthony Seldon, *Major: A Political Life*, p.579.

116 Wyatt, Vol. 3, p.535 (17 July 1995).

117 *The Times*, 14 July 1995.

118 Wyatt, Vol. 3, p.581 (29 November 1995).

119 Iain Dale, (ed.), *Memories of Maggie*, p.x.

120 *The Times*, 24 October 1995.

121 Keith Joseph Memorial Lecture, 11 January 1996.

122 Seldon, p.628.

123 Ibid., p.606.

124 *The Times*, 13 January 1996.

125 Ibid.

126 Speech in Fulton, Missouri, 9 March 1996.

127 *The Times*, 14 March 1996.

128 Speech in Prague, 1 May 1996.

129 *The Times*, 14 June 1996; Seldon, p.651.

130 *The Times*, 15 June 1996.

131 Ibid., 9 October 1996.

132 Paul Johnson in the *Sunday Telegraph*, 16 March 1997.

133 *The Times*, 23 November 1996.

134 Nicholas Ridley Memorial Lecture, 22 November 1996.

135 *The Times*, 18 March 1997.

136 Ibid., 7 April 1997.

137 Seldon, p.723.

138 *The Times*, 10 April 1997.

139 George Gardiner, *A Bastard's Tale*, p.256; Wyatt, Vol. 3, pp.674, 676 (15, 21 October 1996).

140 *The Times*, 19 April 1997.

141 Ibid., 28 August 1998.

142 *The Week*, 22 June 2002.

143 *The Times*, 26 May 1997.

144 *Independent*, 19 June 1997.

145 Ibid.; Maddox, p.225.

146 *Spectator*, 4 April 1998.

147 *The Times*, 28 August 1998.

148 *Independent*, 11 September 1997.

149 *The Times*, 23 April 1998.

150 Ibid., 10 October 1997.

151 *Sunday Times*, 31 January 1999.

152 *The Times*, 22 October 1998.

153 Ibid., 21 April 1999.

154 Ibid., 24 April 1999.

155 *Independent*, 11 October 1999.

156 Ibid., 23 November 2000.

157 *The Week*, 29 January 2000.

158 *Independent*, 23 May 2001.

159 *Daily Telegraph*, 21 August 2001.

160 *Daily Mail*, 22 August 2001.

161 *The Week*, 25 August 2001.

162 BBC 2, 3 November 2001.

163 *The Times*, 7 February 1995.

164 Ibid., 11, 12 October 1994.

165 *Sunday Times*, 8 December 1996.

166 *Independent*, 12 August 1998.

167 Halloran and Hollingsworth, *passim*.

168 *The Times*, 1 April 1996.

169 *Independent*, 4 April 1996.

170 *Saga* magazine, 28 August 1998.

171 Maddox, p.225.

172 Thatcher, *Statecraft*, pp.37–8.

173 Ibid., p.228.

174 Ibid., p.54.

175 Ibid., p.206.

176 Ibid., p.320.

177 Ibid., p.321.

178 Ibid., p.359.

179 *The Times*, 19 March 2002.

180 Ibid., 22 March 2002.

181 Ibid.

182 *Sun*, 23 March 2002.

183 *Independent*, 23 March 2002.

184 *Independent on Sunday*, 24 March 2002.

185 *Independent*, 10 April 2002.

186 Ibid., 1 May 2003.

187 Ibid., 2 February 2002.

188 *Private Eye*, 12 July 2002.

189 *Sun*, 23 March 2002.

Sources and Bibliography

Primary sources

Margaret Thatcher, *Complete Public Statements, 1945–1990* on CD-Rom (Oxford University Press, 1999)

Edward Boyle papers, held in the Brotherton Library, Leeds University
George Bush presidential papers, held in the George Bush Library, College Station, Texas
Jimmy Carter presidential papers, held in the Jimmy Carter Library, Atlanta, Georgia
Ronald Reagan presidential papers, held in the Reagan Library, Simi Valley, California
Interviews conducted for the British Diplomatic Oral History Programme, held in the Archives Centre, Churchill College, Cambridge
Interviews conducted for Brook Productions' TV series *The Thatcher Factor*, held at the London School of Economics

Conservative Party election manifestos, 1979, 1983, 1987, 1992
Parliamentary Debates, House of Commons, 1979–1992
——*House of Lords, 1992–2001*
Annual Register
The Economist
Independent
Spectator
The Times

Broadcast sources

The Woman at Number Ten (BBC, 1983)
Woman to Woman (Yorkshire TV, 1985)
The English Woman's Wardrobe (De Wolfe Productions, 1986)
Thatcher: The Downing Street Years (BBC, 1993)
The Last Europeans (Channel 4, 1995)
The Poisoned Chalice (BBC, 1996)

Consequences (BBC Radio 4, 1996)
The Great Sell-Off (BBC, 1997)
Endgame in Ireland (BBC, 2001)
The Curse of the Mummy (BBC, 2001)
Maggie: The First Lady (Brook Lapping, 2003)

Secondary sources

Leo Abse, *Margaret, Daughter of Beatrice: A Politician's Psycho-Biography of Margaret Thatcher* (Jonathan Cape, 1989)
Martin Adeney and John Lloyd, *The Miners' Strike, 1984–85: Loss Without Limit* (Routledge, 1986)
Kingsley Amis, *Memoirs* (Hutchinson, 1991)
Bruce Anderson, *John Major: The Making of the Prime Minister* (Fourth Estate, 1991)
Noël Annan, *Our Age: Portrait of a Generation* (Weidenfeld & Nicolson, 1990)
Bruce Arnold, *Margaret Thatcher: A Study in Power* (Hamish Hamilton, 1984)
——*Haughey: His Life and Unlucky Deeds* (HarperCollins, 1993)
Paul Arthur and Keith Jeffery, *Northern Ireland since 1968* (Blackwell, 1988)
Paddy Ashdown, *The Ashdown Diaries*, Vol. 1, 1988–1997 (Allen Lane, 2000)
Jacques Attali, *Verbatim* (Fayard, Paris, 1995)

Kenneth Baker, *The Turbulent Years: My Life in Politics* (Faber, 1993)
Malcolm Balen, *Kenneth Clarke* (Fourth Estate, 1994)
Anthony Barber, *Taking the Tide* (Michael Russell, 1996)
Julian Barnes, *Letters from London, 1990–1995* (Picador, 1995)
Anthony Barnett, *Iron Britannia: Why Parliament Waged its Falklands War* (Allison & Busby, 1982)
Andy Beckett, *Pinochet in Piccadilly: Britain and Chile's Hidden History* (Faber, 2002)
Tony Benn, *Conflicts of Interest: Diaries, 1977–80* (Hutchinson, 1990)
——*The End of an Era: Diaries, 1980–90* (Hutchinson, 1992)
——*Free at Last: Diaries, 1991–2001* (Hutchinson, 2002)
Paul Bew, Henry Patterson and Paul Teague, *Between War and Peace: The Political Future of Northern Ireland* (Lawrence & Wishart, 1997)
Patrick Bishop and Eamonn Mallie, *The Provisional IRA* (Heinemann, 1987)
Tessa Blackstone and William Plowden, *Inside the Think Tank: Advising the Cabinet, 1971–1983* (Heinemann, 1988)
Robert Blake and John Patten (eds), *The Conservative Opportunity* (Macmillan, 1976)
Andrew Boyle, *The Climate of Treason: Five Who Spied for Russia* (Hutchinson, 1979)
Rhodes Boyson, *Speaking My Mind* (Peter Owen, 1995)
Sarah Bradford, *Elizabeth: A Biography of Her Majesty the Queen* (Heinemann, 1996)
Gyles Brandreth, *Breaking the Code: The Westminster Diaries, May 1990–May 1997* (Weidenfeld & Nicolson, 1999)

Jock Bruce-Gardyne, *Mrs Thatcher's First Administration: The Prophets Confounded* (Macmillan, 1984)

——*Ministers and Mandarins: Inside the Whitehall Village* (Sidgwick & Jackson, 1986)

Barbara Bush, *A Memoir* (Scribner's, New York, 1994)

George Bush and Brent Scowcroft, *A World Transformed* (Alfred A. Knopf, New York, 1998)

David Butler, Andrew Adonis and Tony Travers, *Failure in British Government: The Politics of the Poll Tax* (OUP, 1994)

David Butler and Gareth Butler, *British Political Facts, 1900–1994* (Macmillan, 1994)

David Butler and Dennis Kavanagh, *The British General Election of 1979* (Macmillan, 1980)

——*The British General Election of 1983* (Macmillan, 1984)

——*The British General Election of 1987* (Macmillan, 1988)

Michael Butler, *Europe: More than a Continent* (Heinemann, 1986)

Beatrix Campbell, *The Iron Ladies: Why do Women Vote Tory?* (Virago, 1987)

John Campbell, *Edward Heath: A Biography* (Jonathan Cape, 1993)

——*Margaret Thatcher: The Grocer's Daughter* (Jonathan Cape, 2000)

Humphrey Carpenter, *Robert Runcie: The Reluctant Archbishop* (Hodder & Stoughton, 1996)

Lord Carrington, *Reflect on Things Past* (Collins, 1988)

Jimmy Carter, *Keeping Faith* (Collins, 1982)

John Carvel, *Turn Again, Livingstone* (Profile Books, 1999)

Michael Carver, *Tightrope Walking: British Defence Policy since 1945* (Hutchinson, 1992)

Michael Charlton, *The Last Colony in Africa: Diplomacy and the Independence of Rhodesia* (Blackwell, 1990)

Alan Clark, *Diaries* (Weidenfeld & Nicolson, 1993)

——*The Tories: Conservatives and the Nation State, 1922–1997* (Weidenfeld & Nicolson, 1998)

——*Diaries: Into Politics* (Weidenfeld & Nicolson, 2000)

Peter Clarke, *A Question of Leadership: Gladstone to Thatcher* (Hamish Hamilton, 1991)

——*Hope and Glory: Britain 1900–1990* (Allen Lane, 1996)

Michael Cockerell, *Live from Number 10: The Inside Story of Prime Ministers and Television* (Faber, 1988)

Michael Cockerell, Peter Hennessy and David Walker, *Sources Close to the Prime Minister: Inside the Hidden World of the News Manipulators* (Macmillan, 1984)

Richard Cockett, *Thinking the Unthinkable: Think-Tanks and the Economic Counter-Revolution, 1931–1983* (HarperCollins, 1994)

John Cole, *The Thatcher Years: A Decade of Revolution in British Politics* (BBC, 1987)

——*As It Seemed to Me* (Weidenfeld & Nicolson, 1995)

Terry Coleman, *Movers and Shakers* (Bantam, 1987)

——*Thatcher's Britain: A Journey through the Promised Lands* (Bantam, 1987)
John Coles, *Making Foreign Policy: A Certain Idea of Britain* (John Murray, 2000)
Patrick Cosgrave, *Margaret Thatcher: A Tory and Her Party* (Hutchinson, 1978)
——*Thatcher: The First Term* (Bodley Head, 1985)
——*Carrington: A Life and a Policy* (Dent, 1985)
——*The Lives of Enoch Powell* (Bodley Head, 1989)
Brian Cox, *The Great Betrayal* (Chapman, 1992)
David Cox (ed.), *The Walden Interviews* (Boxtree, 1990)
Percy Cradock, *Experiences in China* (John Murray, 1994)
——*In Pursuit of British Interests: Reflections on Foreign Policy under Margaret Thatcher and John Major* (John Murray, 1997)
Michael Crick, *Scargill and the Miners* (Penguin, 1985)
——*Michael Heseltine* (Hamish Hamilton, 1997)
Julian Critchley, *Westminster Blues* (Hamish Hamilton, 1985)
——*Heseltine: The Unauthorised Biography* (André Deutsch, 1987)
——*The Palace of Varieties: An Insider's View of Westminster* (John Murray, 1989)
——*Some of Us: People Who Did Well Under Thatcher* (John Murray, 1992)
Brian Crozier, *Free Agent: The Unseen War, 1941–1991* (HarperCollins, 1993)
Edwina Currie, *Life Lines: Politics and Health* (Sidgwick & Jackson, 1989)
——*The Edwina Currie Diaries, 1987–1992* (Little, Brown, 2002)
Ian Curteis, *The Falklands Play* (Hutchinson, 1987)

Iain Dale (ed.), *As I Said to Denis: The Margaret Thatcher Book of Quotations* (Robson Books, 1997)
——*Memories of Maggie* (Politico's, 2000)
Macdonald Daly and Alexander George, *Margaret Thatcher in Her Own Words* (Penguin, 1987)
Tam Dalyell, *Misrule: How Mrs Thatcher Misled Parliament from the Sinking of the Belgrano to the Wright Affair* (Hamish Hamilton, 1987)
A. J. Davies, *We, the Nation: The Conservative Party and the Pursuit of Power* (Little, Brown, 1995)
Robin Day, *Grand Inquisitor* (Weidenfeld & Nicolson, 1989)
Peter de la Billière, *Looking for Trouble* (HarperCollins, 1994)
Michael De-la-Noy, *The Honours System: Who Gets What and Why* (Virgin, 1992)
Edmund Dell, *The Chancellors: A History of the Chancellors of the Exchequer, 1945–1990* (HarperCollins, 1996)
Andrew Denham and Mark Garnett, *Keith Joseph* (Acumen, 2001)
David Dimbleby and David Reynolds, *An Ocean Apart* (BBC/Hodder, 1988)
Jonathan Dimbleby, *The Prince of Wales* (Little, Brown, 1994)
——*The Last Governor: Chris Patten and the Handover of Hong Kong* (Little, Brown, 1997)
Michael Dockrill, *British Defence since 1945* (Blackwell, 1988)
John Drummond, *Tainted by Experience: A Life in the Arts* (Faber, 2000)

· *Sources and Bibliography* ·

Edward du Cann, *Two Lives: The Political and Business Careers of Edward du Cann* (Images, Upton-upon-Severn, 1995)

Michael Edwardes, *Back from the Brink* (Collins, 1983)
Harold Evans, *Good Times, Bad Times* (Weidenfeld & Nicolson, 1983)

Ivan Fallon, *The Brothers: The Rise and Rise of Saatchi and Saatchi* (Hutchinson, 1988)
Diana Farr, *Five at 10: Prime Ministers' Consorts since 1957* (André Deutsch, 1985)
Garret Fitzgerald, *All in a Life* (Macmillan, 1991)
Norman Fowler, *Ministers Decide* (Chapman, 1991)
The Franks Report: Falkland Islands Review (Pimlico, 1992)
Antonia Fraser, *The Warrior Queens: Boadicea's Chariot* (Weidenfeld & Nicolson, 1988)
Lawrence Freedman and Virginia Gamba-Stonehouse, *Signals of War: The Falklands Conflict of 1982* (Faber, 1990)
Lawrence Freedman and Efraim Karsh, *The Gulf Conflict, 1990–91* (Faber, 1993)
Alan Friedman, *Spider's Web: Bush, Saddam, Thatcher and the Decade of Deceit* (Faber, 1993)

Andrew Gamble, *The Free Economy and the Strong State: The Politics of Thatcherism* (Macmillan, 1988)
George Gardiner, *A Bastard's Tale* (Aurum, 1999)
Mark Garnett and Ian Aitken, *Splendid! Splendid! The Authorised Biography of Willie Whitelaw* (Jonathan Cape, 2002)
David Gergan, *Eyewitness to Power: The Essence of Leadership: Nixon to Clinton* (Simon & Schuster, New York, 2000)
Ian Gilmour, *Britain Can Work* (Martin Robertson, 1983)
——*Dancing with Dogma: Britain under Thatcherism* (Simon & Schuster, 1992)
Ian Gilmour and Mark Garnett, *Whatever Happened to the Tories? The Conservative Party since 1945* (Fourth Estate, 1998)
Mikhail Gorbachev, *Memoirs* (Doubleday, 1996)
Joe Gormley, *Battered Cherub* (Hamish Hamilton, 1982)

Alexander Haig, *Caveat: Realism, Reagan and Foreign Policy* (Weidenfeld & Nicolson, 1984)
Lord Hailsham, *A Sparrow's Flight* (Collins, 1990)
Morison Halcrow, *Keith Joseph: A Single Mind* (Macmillan, 1989)
Peter Hall, *Making an Exhibition of Myself* (Sinclair-Stevenson, 1993)
Paul Halloran and Mark Hollingsworth, *Thatcher's Gold: The Life and Times of Mark Thatcher* (Simon & Schuster, 1995)
Chris Ham, *The Politics of NHS Reform: Metaphor or Reality?* (King's Fund, 2000)
Kenneth Harris, *Thatcher* (Weidenfeld & Nicolson, 1988)

Robert Harris, *Gotcha! The Media, the Government and the Falklands Crisis* (Faber, 1983)

——*The Making of Neil Kinnock* (Faber, 1984)

——*A Good and Faithful Servant: The Unauthorised Biography of Bernard Ingham* (Faber, 1990)

Brian Harrison, 'Mrs Thatcher and the Intellectuals' in *Twentieth Century British History*, 1994

Max Hastings, *Going to the Wars* (Macmillan, 2000)

——*Editor: An Inside Story of Newspapers* (Macmillan, 2002)

Max Hastings and Simon Jenkins, *The Battle for the Falklands* (Michael Joseph, 1983)

Bob Hawke, *The Hawke Memoirs* (Heinemann, 1994)

Denis Healey, *The Time of My Life* (Michael Joseph, 1989)

Edward Heath, *The Course of My Life* (Hodder & Stoughton, 1998)

Simon Heffer, *Like the Roman: The Life of Enoch Powell* (Weidenfeld & Nicolson, 1998)

Nicholas Henderson, *Channels and Tunnels* (Weidenfeld & Nicolson, 1987)

——*Mandarin: The Diary of an Ambassador* (Weidenfeld & Nicolson, 1994)

Peter Hennessy, *Cabinet* (Blackwell, 1986)

——*Whitehall* (Secker & Warburg, 1989)

——*The Prime Minister: The Office and its Holders since 1945* (Allen Lane, 2000)

Peter Hennessy and Anthony Seldon (eds), *Ruling Performance: British Governments from Attlee to Thatcher* (Blackwell, 1985)

Michael Heseltine, *Where There's a Will* (Hutchinson, 1987)

——*Life in the Jungle* (Hodder & Stoughton, 2000)

Judy Hillman and Peter Clarke, *Geoffrey Howe: A Quiet Revolutionary* (Weidenfeld & Nicolson, 1988)

Paul Hirst, *After Thatcher* (Collins, 1989)

Simon Hoggart and David Leigh, *Michael Foot: A Portrait* (Hodder & Stoughton, 1981)

Mark Hollingsworth, *The Ultimate Spin-Doctor: The Life and Fast Times of Tim Bell* (Hodder & Stoughton, 1997)

Martin Holmes, *The First Thatcher Government, 1979–1983* (Wheatsheaf, 1985)

Alistair Horne, *Macmillan, 1957–1986* (Macmillan, 1989)

——(ed.), *Telling Lives* (Macmillan, 2000)

John Hoskyns, *Just in Time: Inside the Thatcher Revolution* (Aurum, 2000)

Geoffrey Howe, *Conflict of Loyalty* (Macmillan, 1994)

Rex Hunt, *My Falkland Days* (David & Charles, 1992)

Douglas Hurd, *The Search for Peace* (Little, Brown, 1997)

Marmaduke Hussey, *Chance Governs All* (Macmillan, 2001)

Bernard Ingham, *Kill the Messenger* (HarperCollins, 1994)

Eric Jacobs and Robert Worcester, *We British: Britain under the Moriscope* (Weidenfeld & Nicolson, 1990)

· Sources and Bibliography ·

Gerald James, *In the Public Interest* (Little, Brown, 1995)

Kevin Jefferys, *Finest and Darkest Hours: The Decisive Events in British Politics from Churchill to Blair* (Atlantic Books, 2002)

Peter Jenkins, *Mrs Thatcher's Revolution: The Ending of the Socialist Era* (Jonathan Cape, 1987)

Roy Jenkins, *Gallery of 20th Century Portraits* (David & Charles, 1988)

——*European Diary, 1977–1981* (Collins, 1989)

——*A Life at the Centre* (Macmillan, 1991)

Simon Jenkins, *Accountable to None: The Tory Privatisation of Britain* (Hamish Hamilton, 1995)

Christopher Johnson, *The Economy under Mrs Thatcher, 1979–1990* (Penguin, 1991)

J. D. F. Jones, *Storyteller: The Many Lives of Laurens van der Post* (John Murray, 2001)

John Junor, *Listening for a Midnight Tram* (Chapman, 1990)

Penny Junor, *Margaret Thatcher: Wife, Mother, Politician* (Sidgwick & Jackson, 1983)

——*John Major: From Brixton to Downing Street* (Penguin, 1996)

Dennis Kavanagh, *Thatcherism and British Politics: The End of Consensus?* (OUP, 1987, 1990)

Dennis Kavanagh and Anthony Seldon, *The Thatcher Effect: A Decade of Change* (OUP, 1989)

——*The Major Effect* (Macmillan, 1994)

Sara Keays, *A Question of Judgement* (Quintessential Press, 1985)

William Keegan, *Mrs Thatcher's Economic Experiment* (Penguin, 1984, 1985)

——*Mr Lawson's Gamble* (Hodder & Stoughton, 1989)

Richard N. Kelly, *Conservative Party Conferences: The Hidden System* (Manchester University Press, 1989)

Arnold Kemp, *The Hollow Drum: Scotland since the War* (Mainstream, 1993)

Ludovic Kennedy, *On My Way to the Club* (Collins, 1989)

——*In Bed with an Elephant* (Bantam, 1995)

Robert Kilroy-Silk, *Hard Labour: The Political Diary of Robert Kilroy-Silk* (Chatto & Windus, 1986)

Anthony King, *The British Prime Minister* (Macmillan, 1985)

Norman Lamont, *In Office* (Little, Brown, 1999)

Philip Larkin, *Selected Letters, 1940–1985* (Faber, 1992)

Nigel Lawson, *The View from No. 11: Memoirs of a Tory Radical* (Bantam, 1992)

Michael Leapman, *Barefaced Cheek: The Apotheosis of Rupert Murdoch* (Hodder & Stoughton, 1983)

——*The Last Days of the Beeb* (Allen & Unwin, 1986)

J. J. Lee, *Ireland, 1912–85* (Cambridge University Press, 1989)

Oliver Letwin, *Privatising the World* (Cassell, 1988)

Shirley Robin Letwin, *The Anatomy of Thatcherism* (Fontana, 1992)

Geoffrey Lewis, *Lord Hailsham* (Jonathan Cape, 1997)

Magnus Linklater and David Leigh, *Not with Honour* (Sphere, 1986)

David Lodge, *Nice Work* (Secker & Warburg, 1988)

Alistair McAlpine, *Once a Jolly Bagman* (Weidenfeld & Nicolson, 1997)

Robert Macfarlane, *Special Trust* (Cadell & Davies, New York, 1994)

Ian MacGregor, *The Enemies Within: The Story of the Miners' Strike, 1984–85* (Collins, 1986)

Andy McSmith, *Kenneth Clarke: A Political Biography* (Verso, 1994)

Brenda Maddox, *Maggie: The First Lady* (Hodder & Stoughton, 2003)

Lady Olga Maitland, *Margaret Thatcher: The First Ten Years* (Sidgwick & Jackson 1989)

John Major, *The Autobiography* (HarperCollins, 1999)

Nelson Mandela, *Long Walk to Freedom* (Little, Brown, 1994)

David Marquand, *The Unprincipled Society: New Demands and Old Politics* (Jonathan Cape, 1987)

Andrew Marr, *Ruling Britannia* (Michael Joseph, 1995)

Arthur Marwick, *British Society since 1945* (Penguin, 1990)

Anthony Meyer, *Stand Up and Be Counted* (Heinemann, 1990)

Keith Middlemas, *Power, Competition and the State*, Vol. 3, *The End of the Post-War Era: Britain since 1974* (Macmillan, 1991)

Ronald Millar, *A View from the Wings* (Weidenfeld & Nicolson, 1993)

Alasdair Milne, *D-G: The Memoirs of a British Broadcaster* (Hodder & Stoughton, 1988)

Kenneth Minogue and Michael Biddiss (eds), *Thatcherism: Personality and Politics* (Macmillan, 1987)

Charles Moore and Simon Heffer, *A Tory Seer: The Selected Journalism of T. E. Utley* (Hamish Hamilton, 1989)

Kenneth O. Morgan, *The People's Peace: British History, 1945–1989* (OUP, 1990)

——*Callaghan: A Life* (OUP, 1997)

Oliver Morrissey, Brian Smith and Edward Horesh, *British Aid and International Trade: Aid Policy Making, 1979–89* (OUP, 1992)

Patricia Murray, *Margaret Thatcher* (W. H. Allen, 1980)

Andrew Neil, *Full Disclosure* (Macmillan, 1986)

Steven Norris, *Changing Trains* (Hutchinson, 1996)

Not the Scott Report (Private Eye, 1994)

John Nott, *Here Today and Gone Tomorrow* (Politico's, 2002)

Robin Oakley, *Inside Track* (Bantam, 2001)

Chris Ogden, *Maggie* (Simon & Schuster, New York, 1990)

Arwel Ellis Owen, *The Anglo-Irish Agreement: The First Three Years* (University of Wales, Cardiff, 1994)

David Owen, *Face the Future* (Jonathan Cape, 1981)

——*Time to Declare* (Michael Joseph, 1991)

Cecil Parkinson, *Right at the Centre* (Weidenfeld & Nicolson, 1992)

Matthew Parris, *Chance Witness: An Outsider's Life in Politics* (Viking, 2002)

Chris Patten, *East and West* (Macmillan, 1998)

Jeremy Paxman, *Friends in High Places: Who Runs Britain?* (Michael Joseph, 1990)

Edward Pearce, *Election Rides* (Faber, 1992)

——*Denis Healey: A Life in Our Times* (Little, Brown, 2002)

John Peyton, *Without Benefit of Laundry* (Bloomsbury, 1997)

Ben Pimlott, *The Queen* (HarperCollins, 1996)

Chapman Pincher, *Their Trade is Treachery* (Sidgwick & Jackson, 1981)

Clive Ponting, *Whitehall: Tragedy and Farce* (Hamish Hamilton, 1986)

Bernard Porter, 'Though not a Historian Myself: Mrs Thatcher and the Historians' in *Twentieth Century British History*, 1994

Roy Porter, *London: A Social History* (Hamish Hamilton, 1994)

Anthony Powell, *Journals, 1982–1992*, 3 volumes (Heinemann, 1995, 1996, 1998)

James Prior, *A Balance of Power* (Hamish Hamilton, 1986)

Peter Pugh and Carl Flint, *Thatcher for Beginners* (Icon Books, 1997)

Francis Pym, *The Politics of Consent* (Hamish Hamilton, 1984)

Jonathan Raban, *God, Man and Mrs Thatcher* (Chatto & Windus, 1989)

Timothy Raison, *Tories and the Welfare State: A History of Conservative Social Policy since the Second World War* (Macmillan, 1990)

John Ramsden, *An Appetite for Power: A History of the Conservative Party since 1830* (HarperCollins, 1998)

John Ranelagh, *Thatcher's People: An Insider's Account of the Politics, the Power and the Personalities* (HarperCollins, 1991)

Peter Rawlinson, *A Price Too High* (Weidenfeld & Nicolson, 1989)

Ronald Reagan, *An American Life* (Arrow, 1991)

John Rentoul, *The Rich get Richer: The Growth of Inequality in Britain in the 1980s* (Unwin, 1987)

Robin Renwick, *Fighting with Allies: America and Britain in Peace and War* (Macmillan, 1996)

——*Unconventional Diplomacy in Southern Africa* (Macmillan, 1997)

David Reynolds, *Britannia Overruled: British Policy and World Power in the Twentieth Century* (Longman, 1991)

Peter Riddell, *The Thatcher Decade* (Blackwell, 1989)

Nicholas Ridley, '*My Style of Government': The Thatcher Years* (Hutchinson, 1991)

Kenneth Rose, *Elusive Rothschild: The Life of Victor, Third Baron* (Weidenfeld & Nicolson, 2003)

Paul Routledge, *Scargill: The Unauthorised Biography* (HarperCollins, 1993)

Norman St John-Stevas, *The Two Cities* (Faber, 1984)

Anthony Sampson, *The Changing Anatomy of Britain* (Hodder & Stoughton, 1982)

——*The Essential Anatomy of Britain: Democracy in Crisis* (Hodder & Stoughton, 1992)

——*Nelson Mandela* (HarperCollins, 1999)

The Scott Report (HMSO, 1994)

Raymond Seitz, *Over Here* (Weidenfeld & Nicolson, 1998)

Anthony Seldon, *Major: A Political Life* (Weidenfeld & Nicolson, 1997)

Anthony Seldon and Stuart Ball, *The Conservative Century: The Conservative Party since 1900* (OUP, 1994)

William Shawcross, *Murdoch* (Chatto & Windus, 1992)

Robert Shepherd, *The Power Brokers: The Tory Party and Its Leaders* (Hutchinson, 1991)

——*Enoch Powell* (Hutchinson, 1996)

Norman Shrapnel, *The Seventies* (Constable, 1980)

George P. Shultz, *Turmoil and Triumph: My Years as Secretary of State* (Scribner's, New York, 1993)

Brendan Simms, *Unfinest Hour: Britain and the Destruction of Bosnia* (Allen Lane, 2001)

Brian Simon, *Bending the Rules: The Baker 'Reform' of Education* (Lawrence & Wishart, 1988)

John Simpson, *Strange Places, Questionable People* (Macmillan, 1998)

Alan Sked and Chris Cook, *Post-War Britain: A Political History, 1945–1992* (Penguin, 1993)

Robert Skidelsky (ed.), *Thatcherism* (Chatto & Windus, 1988)

Geoffrey Smith, *Reagan and Thatcher* (Bodley Head, 1990)

Ronald A. Smith, *The Premier Years of Margaret Thatcher* (Kevin Francis, 1991)

Jon Sopel, *Tony Blair: The Moderniser* (Michael Joseph, 1995)

David Steel, *Against Goliath: David Steel's Story* (Weidenfeld & Nicolson, 1989)

Philip Stephens, *Politics and the Pound: The Tories, the Economy and Europe* (Macmillan, 1996)

Hugh Stephenson, *Mrs Thatcher's First Year* (Jill Norman, 1980)

Roy Strong, *Diaries, 1967–1987* (Weidenfeld & Nicolson, 1997)

Mark Stuart, *Douglas Hurd: The Public Servant* (Mainstream, 1998)

Robert Taylor, *The Trade Union Question in British Politics: Government and Unions since 1945* (Blackwell, 1993)

Norman Tebbit, *Upwardly Mobile* (Weidenfeld & Nicolson, 1988)

——*Unfinished Business* (Weidenfeld & Nicolson, 1991)

Carol Thatcher, *Diary of an Election: With Margaret Thatcher on the Campaign Trail* (Sidgwick & Jackson, 1983)

——*Below the Parapet: The Biography of Denis Thatcher* (HarperCollins, 1996)

Margaret Thatcher, *In Defence of Freedom* (Prometheus Books, 1987)

——*The Downing Street Years* (HarperCollins, 1993)

——*The Path to Power* (HarperCollins, 1995)

——*The Collected Speeches*, edited by Robin Harris (HarperCollins, 1997)

——*Statecraft: Strategies for a Changing World* (HarperCollins, 2002)

George Thomas, *Mr Speaker* (Century, 1986)

· Sources and Bibliography ·

Andrew Thomson, *Margaret Thatcher: The Woman Within* (Allen Lane, 1989)
Kenneth R. Timmerman, *The Death Lobby* (Fourth Estate, 1992)
Nicholas Timmins, *The Five Giants: A Biography of the Welfare State* (HarperCollins, 1995)
Ian Trethowan, *Split Screen* (Hamish Hamilton, 1984)
Christopher Tugendhat, *Making Sense of Europe* (Viking, 1986)
Rodney Tyler, *Campaign! The Selling of the Prime Minister* (Grafton Books, 1987)

George Urban, *Diplomacy and Disillusion at the Court of Margaret Thatcher: An Insider's View* (Tauris, 1996)

Cento Veljanovski, *Selling the State: Privatisation in Britain* (Weidenfeld & Nicolson, 1987)
Anthony Verrier, *The Road to Zimbabwe* (Jonathan Cape, 1986)

George Walden, *Lucky George: Memoirs of an Anti-Politician* (Allen Lane, 1999)
Peter Walker, *Staying Power* (Bloomsbury, 1991)
Alan Walters, *Britain's Economic Renaissance: Mrs Thatcher's Reforms* (OUP, 1986)
——*Sterling in Danger: The Economic Consequences of Pegged Exchange Rates* (Fontana/IEA, 1990)
Dennis Walters, *Not Always With the Pack* (Constable, 1989)
Nicholas Wapshott and George Brock, *Thatcher* (Macdonald, 1983)
Marina Warner, *Monuments and Maidens: The Allegory of the Female Form* (Weidenfeld & Nicolson, 1985)
Alan Watkins, *Brief Lives* (Hamish Hamilton, 1982)
——*A Conservative Coup: The Fall of Margaret Thatcher* (Duckworth, 1991, 1992)
Charles Webster, *The National Health Service: A Political History* (OUP, 1998)
Wendy Webster, *Not a Man to Match Her: The Marketing of the Prime Minister* (Women's Press, 1990)
Caspar Weinberger, *Fighting for Peace: Seven Critical Years at the Pentagon* (Michael Joseph, 1990)
Nigel West, *The Secret War for the Falklands* (Warner Books, 1997)
Martin Westlake, *Kinnock: The Biography* (Little, Brown, 2001)
Phillip Whitehead, *The Writing on the Wall: Britain in the Seventies* (Michael Joseph/Channel 4, 1985)
William Whitelaw, *The Whitelaw Memoirs* (Aurum Press, 1989)
Sandy Woodward, *One Hundred Days: The Memoirs of the Falklands Battle Group Commander* (HarperCollins, 1992)
Peregrine Worsthorne, *Tricks of Memory* (Weidenfeld & Nicolson, 1993)
Peter Wright, *Spycatcher: The Candid Autobiography of a Senior Intelligence Officer* (Viking, 1987)
Woodrow Wyatt, *Confessions of an Optimist* (Collins, 1985)
——*The Journals of Woodrow Wyatt*, 3 vols (Macmillan, 1998, 1999, 2000)

Daniel Yergan and Joseph Stanislaw, *The Commanding Heights: The Battle Between Government and the Marketplace that is Remaking the Modern World* (Touchstone, New York, 1998)

Peter York, *Peter York's Eighties* (BBC, 1996)

Hugo Young, *One of Us: A Biography of Margaret Thatcher* (Macmillan, 1989, 1991)

——*This Blessed Plot: Britain and Europe from Churchill to Blair* (Macmillan, 1998)

Hugo Young and Anne Sloman, *The Thatcher Phenomenon* (BBC, 1986)

Lord Young, *The Enterprise Years: A Businessman in the Cabinet* (Headline, 1990)

Index

NB. The use of titles in this index is not consistent. Most individuals are referred to by the name or title under which they are first mentioned, but some by that under which they are best known.